Fodor's 99
Great Britain

W9-DES-214

The complete guide, thoroughly up-to-date

Packed with details that will make your trip

The must-see sights, off and on the beaten path

What to see, what to skip

Mix-and-match vacation itineraries

City strolls, countryside adventures

Smart lodging and dining options

Essential local dos and taboos

Transportation tips, distances and directions

Key contacts, savvy travel tips

When to go, what to pack

Clear, accurate, easy-to-use maps

Books to read, background essay

Fodor's Travel Publications, Inc.
New York • Toronto • London • Sydney • Auckland
www.fodors.com/

Fodor's Great Britain

EDITOR: Robert I. C. Fisher

Editorial Contributors: Robert Andrews, David Brown, Jacqueline Brown, Jules Brown, Lucy Hawking, Sue Gordon, Beth Ingpen, Helayne Schiff, Kate Sekules, Roger Thomas, Brandy Whittingham

Editorial Production: Stacey Kulig

Maps: David Lindroth Inc., Maryland Cartographics, *cartographers*; Robert Blake, *map editor*

Design: Fabrizio La Rocca, *creative director*; Guido Caroti, *associate art director*; Jolie Novak, *photo editor*

Production/Manufacturing: Robert B. Shields

Cover Photograph: Tom Ang/Tony Stone Images

Copyright

ISBN 0–679–00138–7

Special Sales

Fodor's Travel Publications are available at special discounts for bulk purchases for sales promotions or premiums. Special editions, including personalized covers, excerpts of existing guides, and corporate imprints, can be created in large quantities for special needs. For more information, contact your local bookseller or write to Special Markets, Fodor's Travel Publications, 201 East 50th Street, New York, NY 10022. Inquiries from Canada should be directed to your local Canadian bookseller or sent to Random House of Canada, Ltd., Marketing Department, 2775 Matheson Boulevard East, Mississauga, Ontario L4W 4P7. Inquiries from the United Kingdom should be sent to Fodor's Travel Publications, 20 Vauxhall Bridge Road, London SW1V 2SA, England.

PRINTED IN THE UNITED STATES OF AMERICA

10 9 8 7 6 5 4 3 2 1

CONTENTS

Maps

ON THE ROAD WITH FODOR'S

WHEN I PLAN A VACATION, the first thing I do is cast around among my friends and colleagues to find someone who's just been where I'm going. That's because there's no substitute for a recommendation from a good friend who knows your tastes, your budget, and your circumstances, someone who's just been there. Unfortunately, such friends are few and far between. So it's nice to know that there's *Fodor's Great Britain '99*.

In the first place, this book won't stay home when you hit the road. It will accompany you every step of the way, steering you away from wrong turns and wrong choices and never expecting a thing in return. It includes a wonderful, full-color map from Rand McNally, the world's largest commercial mapmaker. Most important of all, it's written and assiduously updated by the kind of people you *would* hit up for travel tips if you knew them. They're as choosy as your pickiest friend, except they've probably seen a lot more of Great Britain. In these pages, they don't send you chasing down every town and sight in Great Britain but have instead selected the best ones, the ones that are worthy of your time and money. To make it easy for you to put it all together in the time you have, they've created short, medium, and long itineraries and, in cities, neighborhood walks that you can mix and match in a snap. Just tear out the map at the perforation, and join us on the road in Great Britain. Will this be the vacation of your dreams? We hope so.

About Our Writers

Helping to make your trip the best of all possible vacations is an extraordinary band of hard-working writers.

Since **Kate Sekules** lives with a foot on either side of the Atlantic, her mission is getting the best of both worlds. Author of Fodor's guidebook to London, she has also updated most of the chapter on that metropolis for this edition. Thanks to her knack for coming up with the mots—both bon and juste—her wit is much in demand: *Vogue, W, The New Yorker, BBC Holidays, Harper's Bazaar,* and *Travel Holiday* are just some of the publications she writes for.

A New York native, **Brandy Whittingham** is working on a doctoral dissertation on London's Victorian architecture. Brandy wrote selected features in the London chapter, including the Close-Ups and Great Itineraries.

Robert Andrews loves warm beer, hairy dogs, and soggy moors, but hates shopping malls, sheep poop, and the sort of weather when you're not sure if it's raining—all of which he found in abundance while updating our chapters devoted to the Southeast, the South, the West Country, the Channel Islands, the Heart of England, and the Welsh Borders.

Based in Hampshire, **Sue Gordon** is the editor of a book on Britain's villages, has contributed to several walks books, and has also written guides to Boston and New England.

Lucy Hawking, a trilingual Oxford graduate, has flitted around the globe, writing for several London and New York publications. But now, thanks to the arrival of a handsome baby boy, she has settled in London where she works for the *Times*.

Always hoping to entertain—and surprise—his readers, **Roger Thomas** spends most every minute tracking down the latest and the best of Wales. He has to: He's editor of *A View of Wales* magazine. Roger has written many books on Wales and is an acknowledged Welsh expert.

Now based in Yorkshire, **Jules Brown** updated our chapters on the Lake District, Yorkshire, East Anglia, the Northeast, and Lancashire and the Peaks. For real kicks, this Oxford University graduate pulls on a pair of walking boots and strides across his home country, along Cornish, Yorkshire, and Northumberland coasts, and up and down the Lake District.

Beth Ingpen helped update the chapter on Scotland. A longtime editorial contributor to Fodor's Scotland, Beth works as a freelance editor and writer. She was previously publishing manager with the Royal Society of Edinburgh.

After 20 years of living in London, writer and editor **Jacqueline Brown** targets those culinary and cultural arenas that lie far beyond bully beef and Buckingham Palace. When she is not working as a freelance editor or helping to update the Gold Guide section of this book, Jacqueline can be found strolling rolling parklands in the countryside.

Though the sun may have set on the British Empire, there will always be an England—especially in the hearts of all Anglophiles, as **Robert I. C. Fisher,** the editor of *Fodor's Great Britain,* can attest. He often dreams of Vita Sackville-West's famous garden (in his heart, at least, he's part-owner) and of waking up one day with Jeremy Irons's accent.

Connections

We're pleased that the American Society of Travel Agents continues to endorse Fodor's as its guidebook of choice. ASTA is the world's largest and most influential travel trade association, operating in more than 170 countries, with 27,000 members pledged to adhere to a strict code of ethics reflecting the Society's motto, "Integrity in Travel." ASTA shares Fodor's devotion to providing smart, honest travel information and advice to travelers, and we've long recommended that our readers—even those who have guidebooks and traveling friends—consult ASTA member agents for the experience and professionalism they bring to your vacation planning.

On Fodor's Web site (www.fodors.com), check out the new Resource Center, an online companion to the Gold Guide section of this book, complete with useful hot links to related sites. In our forums, you can also get lively advice from other travelers and more great tips from Fodor's experts worldwide.

How to Use This Book

Organization

Up front is the **Gold Guide,** an easy-to-use section arranged alphabetically by topic. Under each listing you'll find tips and information that will help you accomplish what you need to in Great Britain. You'll also find addresses and telephone numbers of organizations and companies that offer destination-related services and detailed information and publications.

The first chapter in the guide, **Destination: Great Britain** helps get you in the mood for your trip. New and Noteworthy cues you in on trends and happenings, What's Where gets you oriented, Pleasures and Pastimes describes the activities and sights that make the United Kingdom unique, Fodor's Choice showcases our top picks, and Festivals and Seasonal Events alerts you to special events you'll want to seek out.

Chapters in this guide book are arranged geographically. *Fodor's Great Britain* begins with a chapter on London and proceeds to southern, central, and western England, pausing to stop in Wales. The book then moves up England's west coast to the Lake District, continues on to eastern England, and finally heads north to Scotland. Each chapter covers exploring the sights, then highlights regional topics such as dining and lodging, shopping, outdoor activities and sports, and arts and nightlife.

In the London chapter, we first let you in on the big picture, then follow with separate neighborhood sections that suggest—in A Good Walk—a wonderful way to discover each, then list all the neighborhood sights alphabetically. Each regional chapter is divided by geographical area; within each area, towns are covered in logical geographical order—with major cities, such as Stratford-upon-Avon, York, and Oxford handled like London, complete with Good Walks and Sights to See—and attractive stretches of road and minor points of interest between them are indicated by the designation *En Route*. And within town sections, all restaurants and lodgings are grouped.

To help you decide what to visit in the time you have, all chapters begin with our **recommended itineraries;** you can mix and match them to create a complete vacation. In addition, a section called When to Visit or Tour points out the optimal time for your journey. The **A to Z section** that ends all chapters covers getting there and getting around. It also provides helpful contacts and resources.

Tying each chapter together are Fodor's easy-to-use maps; each sight (city, town, or attraction) is marked by a circle with a number—simply connect the dots and you have the ideal city walk or country drive. Numbers in white and black circles—③ and ❸, for example—that appear on the maps, in the margins, and within the tours correspond to one another, for easy reference.

At the end of the book you'll find **Portraits,** with a historical chronology and recommended reading.

Icons and Symbols

★   Our special recommendations

✕   Restaurant

🏠   Lodging establishment

✕🏠   Lodging establishment whose restaurant warrants a special trip

☾   Good for kids (rubber duck)

☞   Sends you to another section of the guide for more information

✉   Address

☎   Telephone number

☾   Opening and closing times

💰   Admission prices (those we give apply to adults; substantially reduced fees are almost always available for children, students, and senior citizens)

Dining and Lodging

The restaurants and lodgings we list are the cream of the crop in each price range. Price charts appear in the Pleasures and Pastimes section that follows each chapter introduction.

Hotel Facilities

We always list the facilities that are available—but we don't specify whether you'll be charged extra to use them: When pricing accommodations, always ask what's included. In addition, assume that all rooms have private baths unless noted otherwise. However, there will be that odd hotel, usually at the lower end of the price scale, that still provides facilities that date back to the not-so-quaint days of yore—a "W. C." (Water Closet, or simple toilet) within the room, with bath or shower down the hall. Most of the hotels in this guide, however, have "en suite" facilities—that is, each guest room has a complete bath. When you book a room, it's best to confirm your request for a room with "en suite" facilities; In addition, be sure to mention if you have a disability or are traveling with children, if you prefer a certain type of bed, or if you have specific dietary needs or other concerns. Nearly all the hotels in this guide operate on one of two plans: the **European Plan** (with no meals), or the **Continental Plan** (Continental breakfast daily included

within room rate). Inquire as to which plan when booking.

Restaurant Reservations and Dress Codes

Reservations are always a good idea; we mention them only when they're essential or are not accepted. Book as far ahead as you can, and reconfirm as soon as you arrive. Unless otherwise noted, the restaurants listed are open daily for lunch and dinner. We mention dress only when men are required to wear a jacket or a jacket and tie. Look for an overview of local dining-out habits in the Gold Guide.

Credit Cards

The following abbreviations are used: **AE,** American Express; **DC,** Diners Club; **MC,** MasterCard; and **V,** Visa.

Don't Forget to Write

You can use this book in the confidence that all prices and opening times are based on information supplied to us at press time; Fodor's cannot accept responsibility for any errors. Time inevitably brings changes, so always confirm information when it matters—especially if you're making a detour to visit a specific place.

Were the restaurants we recommended as described? Did our hotel picks exceed your expectations? Did you find a museum we recommended a waste of time? Keeping a travel guide fresh and up-to-date is a big job, and we welcome your feedback, positive *and* negative. If you have complaints, we'll look into them and revise our entries when the facts warrant it. If you've discovered a special place that we haven't included, we'll pass the information along to our correspondents and have them check it out. So send us your thoughts via E-mail at editors@fodors.com (specifying the name of the book on the subject line) or on paper in care of the Great Britain editor at Fodor's, 201 East 50th Street, New York, NY 10022. In the meantime, have a wonderful trip!

Karen Cure

Karen Cure
Editorial Director

Great Britain

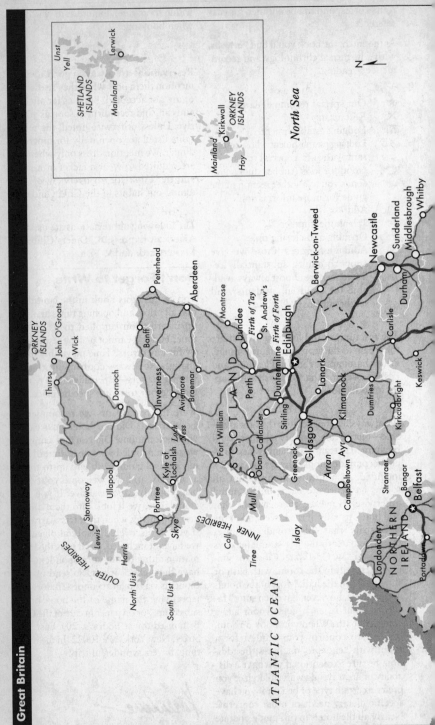

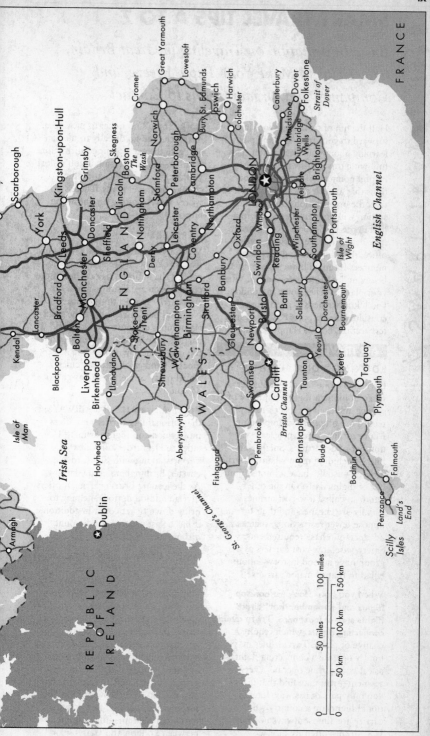

SMART TRAVEL TIPS A TO Z

*Basic Information on Traveling in Great Britain,
Savvy Tips to Make Your Trip a Breeze, and
Companies and Organizations to Contact*

Half the fun of traveling is looking forward to your trip—making plans, learning about your destination. The following travel tips will give you helpful pointers on many of the questions that arise at this stage. In addition, the organizations listed in this section will supplement the information in this guidebook. Your journey may begin at a Great Britain tourist office: the addresses and telephone numbers for main branches are listed below under **Visitor Information.** When your plane touches down in London, you'll know where to go, having consulted the Airports & City Transfers section, below. Happy landings!

AIR TRAVEL

BOOKING YOUR FLIGHT

Price is just one factor to consider when booking a flight: frequency of service and even a carrier's safety record are often just as important. Major airlines offer the greatest number of departures. Smaller airlines—including regional and no-frills airlines—usually have a limited number of flights daily. On the other hand, so-called low-cost airlines usually are cheaper, and their fares impose fewer restrictions, such as advance-purchase requirements. Safety-wise, low-cost carriers as a group have a good history—about equal to that of major carriers.

When you book, **look for nonstop flights** and **remember that "direct" flights stop at least once.** Try to **avoid connecting flights,** which require a change of plane. Two airlines may jointly operate a connecting flight, so ask if your airline operates every segment—you may find that it flies you only part of the way. International flights on a country's flag carrier are almost always nonstop; U.S. airlines often fly direct.

Ask your airline if it offers electronic ticketing, which eliminates all paperwork. There's no ticket to pick up or misplace. You go directly to the gate and give the agent your confirmation number—a real blessing if you've lost your ticket or made last-minute changes in travel plans. There's no worry about waiting on line at the airport.

CARRIERS

When flying internationally, you must usually choose between a domestic carrier, the national flag carrier of the country you are visiting, and a foreign carrier from a third country. National flag carriers have the greatest number of nonstops. Domestic carriers may have better connections to your home town and serve a greater number of gateway cities. Third-party carriers may have a price advantage.

British Airways (☎ 800/AIRWAYS) is the national flag carrier and offers mostly nonstop flights from 18 U.S. cities to Heathrow and Gatwick airports, along with flights to Manchester, Birmingham, and Glasgow. As the leading British carrier, it offers myriad add-on options, helping to bring down ticket costs. In addition, it has a vast program of discount airfare/hotel packages.

Because Britain is such a small country, internal air travel is much less important here than in the United States. Broadly speaking, for trips of less than 200 mi the train is quicker given the time required to get to and from city centers and airports, compared with the centrally based rail stations. Flying tends to cost more, and many internal U.K. flights exist primarily as feeders from provincial airports into Heathrow and Gatwick for international flights. For trips of more than 200 mi—for example, between London and Glasgow or Edinburgh—or where a sea crossing is involved, to places such as the Isle of Man, Belfast, the Channel Islands, or the Scottish islands, air travel has a considerable time advantage.

➤ MAJOR AIRLINES: **American Airlines** (☎ 800/433–7300; in London, ☎ 0181/572–5555) to Heathrow, Gatwick. **British Airways** (☎ 800/247–9297; in London, ☎ 0345/222111) to Heathrow, Gatwick. **Continental** (☎ 800/231–0856; in London, ☎ 0800/776464) to Gatwick. **Delta** (☎ 800/241–4141; in London, ☎ 0800/414767) to Heathrow, Gatwick. **Northwest Airlines** (☎ 800/447–4747; in London, ☎ 0990/561000) to Gatwick. **United** (☎ 800/241–6522; in London, ☎ 0845/844–4777) to Heathrow. **TWA** (☎ 800/892–4141; in London, ☎ 0181/814–0707 or at Gatwick Airport 01293/535353) to Gatwick. **Virgin Atlantic** (☎ 800/862–8621; in London, ☎ 01293/747747) to Heathrow, Gatwick.

➤ DOMESTIC AIRLINES: **British Airways** operates shuttle services between London Heathrow and Edinburgh, Glasgow, Belfast, and Manchester. Passengers can simply turn up and get a flight (usually hourly) without booking. There are also shuttle services from Gatwick. **British Midland** (☎ 0181/745–7321) operates from Heathrow to Belfast, Dublin, Glasgow, Leeds Manchester and Teesside. **Manx Airlines** (☎ 0345/256256) flies to the Isle of Man from Heathrow and London Luton. For services to the Channel Islands, *see* Chapter 6.

CHARTERS

Charters usually have the lowest fares but are the least dependable. Departures are infrequent and seldom on time, flights can be delayed for up to 48 hours or can be canceled for any reason up to 10 days before you're scheduled to leave. Itineraries and prices can change after you've booked.

In the U.S., the Department of Transportation's Aviation Consumer Protection Division has jurisdiction over charters and provides a certain degree of protection. The DOT requires that money paid to charter operators be held in escrow, so if you can't pay

with a credit card, **always make your check payable to a charter carrier's escrow account.** The name of the bank should be in the charter contract. If you have any problems with a charter operator, contact the DOT (☞ Airline Complaints, *below*). If you buy a charter package that includes both air and land arrangements, remember that the escrow requirement applies only to the air component.

CONSOLIDATORS

Consolidators buy tickets for scheduled international flights at reduced rates from the airlines, then sell them at prices that beat the best fare available directly from the airlines, usually without restrictions. Sometimes you can even get your money back if you need to return the ticket. Carefully read the fine print detailing penalties for changes and cancellations, and **confirm your consolidator reservation with the airline.**

➤ CONSOLIDATORS: **Cheap Tickets** (☎ 800/377–1000). **Up & Away Travel** (☎ 212/889–2345). **Discount Travel Network** (☎ 800/576–1600). **Unitravel** (☎ 800/325–2222). **World Travel Network** (☎ 800/409–6753).

COURIERS

When you fly as a courier, you trade your checked-luggage space for a ticket deeply subsidized by a courier service. It's all perfectly legitimate, but there are restrictions: You can usually book your flight only a week or two in advance, your length of stay may be set for a certain number of days, and you probably won't be able to book a companion on the same flight.

CUTTING COSTS

The least-expensive airfares to Great Britain are priced for round-trip travel and usually must be purchased in advance. It's smart to **call a number of airlines, and when you are quoted a good price, book it on the spot**—the same fare may not be available the next day. Airlines generally allow you to change your return date for a fee. If you don't use your ticket, you can apply the cost toward the purchase of a new ticket, again for a small charge. However, most low-fare tickets are nonrefundable. To get the lowest airfare, **check different routings.** Compare prices of flights to and from different airports if your destination or home city has more than one gateway. Also price off-peak flights, which may be significantly less expensive.

Travel agents, especially those who specialize in finding the lowest fares (☞ Discounts & Deals, *below*), can be especially helpful for booking a plane ticket. When you're quoted a price, **ask your agent if the price is likely to get any lower.** Good agents know the seasonal fluctuations of airfares and can usually anticipate a sale or fare war. However, waiting can be risky: the fare could go *up* as seats become scarce, and you may wait so long that your preferred flight sells out. A wait-and-see strategy works best if your plans are flexible. If you must arrive and depart on certain dates, don't delay.

CHECK IN & BOARDING

Airlines routinely overbook planes, assuming that not everyone with a ticket will show up, but sometimes everyone does. When that happens, airlines ask for volunteers to give up their seats. In return these volunteers usually get a certificate for a free flight and are rebooked on the next flight out. If there are not enough volunteers, the airline must choose who will be denied boarding. The first to get bumped are passengers who checked in late and those flying on discounted tickets, so **get to the gate and check in as early as possible,** especially during peak periods.

Although the trend on international flights is to drop reconfirmation requirements, many airlines still ask you to reconfirm each leg of your international itinerary. Failure to do so may result in your reservation being canceled.

Always **bring a government-issued photo ID to the airport.** You may be asked to show it before you are allowed to check in.

ENJOYING THE FLIGHT

For better service, **fly smaller or regional carriers,** which often have

higher passenger-satisfaction ratings. Sometimes you'll find leather seats, more legroom, and better food.

For more legroom, **request an emergency-aisle seat.** Don't sit in the row in front of the emergency aisle or in front of a bulkhead, where seats may not recline.

If you don't like airline food, **ask for special meals when booking.** These can be vegetarian, low-cholesterol, or kosher, for example.

When flying internationally, try to maintain a normal routine, to help fight jet lag. At night, **get some sleep.** By day, **eat light meals, drink water (not alcohol), and move around the cabin** to stretch your legs.

Many carriers have prohibited smoking on all of their international flights; others allow smoking only on certain routes or certain departures, so **contact your carrier regarding its smoking policy.**

FLYING TIMES

Flying time is about 6½ hours from New York, 7½ hours from Chicago, and 10 hours from Los Angeles.

HOW TO COMPLAIN

If your baggage goes astray or your flight goes awry, complain right away. Most carriers require that you **file a claim immediately.**

➤ AIRLINE COMPLAINTS: U.S. Department of Transportation **Aviation Consumer Protection Division** (✉ C-75, Room 4107, Washington, DC 20590, ☎ 202/366–2220). **Federal Aviation Administration Consumer Hotline** (☎ 800/322–7873).

AIRPORTS & CITY TRANSFERS

AIRPORTS

International flights to London arrive at either **Heathrow Airport,** 15 mi west of London, or at **Gatwick Airport,** 27 mi south of the capital. Most flights from the United States go to Heathrow, which is divided into four terminals, with Terminals 3 and 4 handling transatlantic flights (British Airways uses Terminal 4). Gatwick is London's second gateway. It has grown from a European airport into an airport that serves 21 scheduled

U.S. destinations. A third, new, state-of-the-art airport, **Stansted,** is to the east of the city. It handles mainly European and domestic traffic, although there is a scheduled service from New York. There are fast connections from all the London airports into the capital.

➤ AIRPORT INFORMATION: Heathrow Airport (☎ 011–44–181/759–4321). Gatwick Airport (☎ 011–44–1293/535353). Stansted Airport (☎ 01279/680500).

CITY TRANSFERS

Heathrow: The least expensive route into London is via the **Piccadilly line** of the **Underground** (London's subway system). Trains on the "Tube" run every four to eight minutes from all four terminals; the painless 40-minute trip costs £3.30 one-way and connects with London's extensive tube system. The quickest way into London is the new **Heathrow Express** (☎ 0845/600–1515), which ferries travelers in just 15 minutes to and from Paddington Station (in the city center and hub for many of London's Underground city lines). One-way tickets cost £10 for standard class and £20 for first class. Service is daily, from 5:10 AM to 10:40 PM, with departures every 15 minutes.

London Transport (☎ 0171/222–1234) runs two bus services from the airport; each costs £6 one-way and £10 round-trip and travel time each direction is about one hour. The **Airbus A1** leaves for Victoria Station, with stops along Cromwell Road, at Earls Court, and at Hyde Park Corner, every 30 minutes 5:40 AM–8:30 PM. The **Airbus A2** leaves for King's Cross and Euston, with stops at Marble Arch, and Russell Square every 30 minutes 6 AM–9:30 PM.

Gatwick: Fast, nonstop **Gatwick Express** trains leave for Victoria Station every 15 minutes 5:20 AM–12:50 AM; then hourly 1.35 AM–4.35 AM. The 30-minute trip costs £9.50 one-way. A frequent local train also runs all night. Hourly bus services (6:30 AM to 10 PM) are provided by **Flightline 777** to Victoria Coach Station. This takes about 90 minutes and costs £7.50 one-way.

Stansted: London's newest airport, opened in 1991, serves mainly European destinations. The **Stansted Skytrain** to Liverpool Street Station runs every half hour and costs £10 one-way although, at press time, fares were set to increase.

Cars and taxis drive into London on M4; the trip can take more than an hour, depending on traffic, from Heathrow. The taxi fare is about £40, plus tip. From Gatwick, the taxi fare is at least £80, plus tip; traffic can be very heavy.

BARGE TRAVEL

See the British Tourist Authority's booklet *Inland Waterway Holidays,* and contact the **Association of Pleasurecraft Operators** (✉ 35a High Street, Newport, Shropshire TF10 7AT, ☎ 01952/813572)or **U.K. Waterway Holidays** (✉ 1 Port Hill, Hertford SG14 1PJ, ☎ 01992/550616).

BIKE TRAVEL

Bikes are banned from motorways and most dual carriageways or main trunk roads, but on side roads and country lanes, the bike is one of the best ways to explore Britain. You will find the Ordnance Survey 1:50,000 maps invaluable. Some parts of Britain have bicycle routes in towns and through parts of the countryside; for example, in the Peak District National Parks, bikes can be hired by the day for use on traffic-free trails. Cyclists can use public bridleways—green, unsurfaced tracks reserved for horses, walkers, and cyclists.

BIKES IN FLIGHT

Most airlines will accommodate bikes as luggage, provided they are dismantled and put into a box. Call to see if your airline sells bike boxes (about $5; bike bags are at least $100) although you can often pick them up free at bike shops. International travelers can sometimes substitute a bike for a piece of checked luggage for free; otherwise, it will cost about $100. Domestic and Canadian airlines charge a $25–$50 fee.

BUS TRAVEL

Britain has a comprehensive bus (short-haul) and coach (long-distance) network. Coaches are much cheaper than trains, usually about half the price or even less, but are generally slower, although some motorway services with the modern Rapide coaches reduce the margin considerably. Seats on these supercoaches are comfortable, with meal and rest stops usually arranged on longer trips. (All coaches have washroom facilities on board.)

The British equivalent to Greyhound is **National Express,** which with its Scottish associate, **Scottish Citylink,** is by far the largest British operator. Victoria Coach Station in London is the hub of the National Express network, serving around 1,500 destinations. Information is available from any of the company's 2,500 agents nationwide, including those at London's Heathrow and Gatwick airport coach stations.

The classic British double-decker buses still operate on many of the routes of Britain's extensive network of local bus services. It's difficult to plan a journey by country bus, because privatization of lines has led to the development of many small companies and schedules are constantly changing. But the local bus station wherever you're staying, and maybe the local tourist information center, will have precise information. Most companies offer day or week "Explorer" or "Rover" unlimited-travel tickets, and those in popular tourist areas invariably operate special scenic tours in summer.

➤ BUS LINES: For details on National Express coach services throughout Britain, contact **Victoria Coach Station** (✉ Buckingham Palace Rd., London SW1W 9TP, ☎ 0990/808080) and **Scottish Citylink** (☎ 0990/505050) in Glasgow.

DISCOUNT PASSES

National Express's **Tourist Trail Pass** costs £49 for three consecutive days of travel, £79 for five days of travel out of 10 consecutive days, £119 for eight days out of 16, and £179 for 15 days out of 30. A **Discount Coach Card** for students and under-25s, which costs £7, qualifies you for 30% discounts on those prices. A Tourist Trail Pass can be bought with U.S.

dollars from **British Travel International** (✉ Box 299, Elkton, VA 22827, ☎ 703/298–2232 or 800/327–6097).

BUSINESS HOURS

BANKS

Most banks are open weekdays 9:30–4:30. Some have Thursday evening hours.

PUBS

Pubs are generally open Monday–Saturday 11–11, Sunday 11–10:30.

SHOPS

Usual business hours are Monday–Saturday 9–5:30; on Sunday, small shops stay open all day if they wish to, and larger stores now can too, since the Sunday trading laws were relaxed in late 1994. Outside the main centers, most shops close at 1 PM once a week, often Wednesday or Thursday. In small villages, many also close for lunch. In large cities—especially London—department stores stay open late (usually until 7:30 or 8) one day a week.

CAMERAS & COMPUTERS

EQUIPMENT PRECAUTIONS

Always **keep your film, tape, or computer disks out of the sun.** Carry an extra supply of batteries, and **be prepared to turn on your camera, camcorder, or laptop** to prove to security personnel that the device is real. Always **ask for hand inspection of film,** which becomes clouded after successive exposure to airport X-ray machines, and **keep videotapes and computer disks away from metal detectors.**

➤ PHOTO HELP: Kodak Information Center (☎ 800/242–2424). **Kodak Guide to Shooting Great Travel Pictures,** available in bookstores or from Fodor's Travel Publications (☎ 800/533–6478; $16.50 plus $4 shipping).

CAR RENTAL

Rates in London begin at $54 a day and $176 a week for an economy car, a manual transmission, and unlimited mileage. Air conditioning, often extra, is usually available with intermediate size cars. This does not include the 17.5% tax on car rentals.

➤ MAJOR AGENCIES: **Alamo** (☎ 800/ 522–9696, 0800/272–2000 in the U.K.). **Avis** (☎ 800/331–1084, 800/ 879–2847 in Canada, 008/225–533 in Australia). **Budget** (☎ 800/472– 3325, 0800/181181 in the U.K.). **Dollar** (☎ 800/800–4000; 0990/ 565656 in the U.K., where it is known as Eurodollar). **Hertz** (☎ 800/654– 3001, 800/263–0600 in Canada, 0345/555888 in the U.K., 03/9222– 2523 in Australia, 03/358–6777 in New Zealand). **National InterRent** (☎ 800/227–3876; 0345/222525 in the U.K., where it is known as Europ-car InterRent).

CUTTING COSTS

For the best deal, **book through a travel agent who is willing to shop around.**

Also **ask your travel agent about a company's customer-service record.** How has the company responded to late plane arrivals and vehicle mishaps? Are there often lines at the rental counter? During a holiday periods, does a confirmed reservation guarantee you a car?

Be sure to **look into wholesalers,** companies that do not own fleets but rent in bulk from those that do and often offer better rates than tradi-tional car-rental operations. Prices are best during off-peak periods. Rentals through wholesalers must be paid for before you leave the United States.

➤ RENTAL WHOLESALERS: **Auto Europe** (☎ 207/842–2000 or 800/ 223–5555, ☎ 800/235–6321). **Europe by Car** (☎ 212/581–3040 or 800/223–1516, ☎ 212/246–1458). **DER Travel Services** (✉ 9501 W. Devon Ave., Rosemont, IL 60018, ☎ 800/782–2424, ☎ 800/282–7474 for information or 800/860–9944 for brochures). **Kemwel Holiday Autos** (☎ 914/835–5555 or 800/ 678–0678, ☎ 914/835–5126).

INSURANCE

You are generally responsible for any damage to or loss of a rented car. Before you rent, **see what coverage you already have** under the terms of your personal auto-insurance policy and credit cards.

Collision policies that car-rental companies sell for European rentals typically do not cover stolen vehicles. Before you buy additional coverage for theft, check with your credit-card company and personal auto insur-ance—you may already be covered.

REQUIREMENTS

In Great Britain your own driver's license is acceptable. An International Driver's Permit is a good idea; it's available from the American or Cana-dian automobile association, and, in the United Kingdom, from the Auto-mobile Association or Royal Auto-mobile Club. International permits are universally recognized, and hav-ing one may save you a problem with the local authorities.

SURCHARGES

Before you pick up a car in one city and leave it in another, **ask about drop-off charges or one-way service fees,** which can be substantial. Note, too, that some rental agencies charge extra if you return the car before the time specified in your contract. To avoid a hefty refueling fee, **fill the tank just before you turn in the car,** but be aware that gas stations near the rental outlet may overcharge.

CAR TRAVEL

With well over 55 million inhabitants in a country about the size of Califor-nia, Britain has some of the most crowded roads in the world. But away from the towns and cities, you can find miles of little-used roads and lanes where driving can be a real pleasure—and adventure.

AUTO CLUBS

➤ IN AUSTRALIA: **Australian Auto-mobile Association** (☎ 06/247–7311).

➤ IN CANADA: **Canadian Automobile Association** (CAA, ☎ 613/247–0117).

➤ IN NEW ZEALAND: **New Zealand Automobile Association** (☎ 09/377–4660).

➤ IN THE U.K.: **Automobile Associa-tion** (AA, ☎ 0990/500600), **Royal Automobile Club** (RAC, ☎ 0990/ 722722 for membership, 0345/ 121345 for insurance).

THE GOLD GUIDE / SMART TRAVEL TIPS

➤ IN THE U.S.: **American Automobile Association** (☎ 800/564–6222).

EMERGENCY SERVICES

For aid if your car breaks down, contact the 24-hour rescue numbers of either the **Automobile Association** (☎ 01800/887766) or the **Royal Automobile Club** (☎ 01800/828282).

GASOLINE

Gasoline is commonly called "petrol" in the U.K. and is sold by the liter, with 4.2 liters to a gallon. Note that stations can be hard to find in rural areas, with many throughout the nation closed on Sundays.

MOTORAIL

One way to combine the convenience of the car with the speed of the train, useful for travel between Britain and the rest of Europe, is motorail. The car is put on a specially designed rail car while passengers relax in comfortable coaches or, in some cases, overnight sleeping compartments. Check for the latest services available through **Rail Europe's Rail Shop** (☎ 0990/300003).

ROADS

There's a very good network of superhighways (motorways) and divided highways (dual carriageways) throughout most of Britain, though in remoter parts, especially Wales and Scotland, where unclassified roads join village to village and are little more than glorified agricultural cart tracks, travel is noticeably slower. Motorways (with the prefix *M*), shown in blue on most maps and road signs, are mainly two or three lanes in each direction, without any right-hand turns. Other fast major roads are shown with the prefix *A*, shown on maps as green and red. Sections of fast dual carriageway have black-edged, thick outlines on maps; they have both traffic lights and traffic circles and some right turns. Turnoffs are often marked by highway numbers rather than place names.

The vast network of lesser roads, for the most part old coach and turnpike roads, might make your trip take twice the time and show you twice as much. Minor roads drawn in yellow or white, the former prefixed by *B*, the latter unlettered and unnumbered, are the ancient lanes and byways, a superb way of discovering the real Britain. Some of these (the white roads, in the main) are potholed switchbacks, littered with blind corners and cowpats, and barely wide enough for one car, let alone for two to pass. Be prepared to reverse into a passing place if you meet an oncoming car or truck.

Service stations on motorways are located at regular intervals and are usually open 24 hours a day; elsewhere they usually close overnight, and by 6 PM and all day Sunday in remote country areas.

ROAD MAPS

Good planning maps are available from the **AA** and the **RAC** (☞ Auto Clubs, *above*).

RULES OF THE ROAD

Drive on the left in Britain; this takes a bit of getting used to, and it's much easier if you're driving a British car where the steering and mirrors are designed for U.K. conditions. Study your map before leaving the airport, and be sure to give yourself plenty of time to adjust. The use of seat belts is obligatory in the front seat and in the back seat where they exist.

Speed limits are complicated, and traffic police can be hard on speeders, especially in urban areas. In those areas, the limit (shown on circular red signs) is generally 30 mph, but 40 mph on some main roads. In rural areas the limit is 60 mph on ordinary roads and 70 mph on motorways (☞ *below*). At traffic circles ("roundabouts"), circulation is clockwise, and entering motorists must give way to cars coming from their right.

THE CHANNEL TUNNEL

Short of flying, the "Chunnel" is the fastest way to cross the English Channel: 35 minutes from Folkestone to Calais, 60 minutes from motorway to motorway, or 3 hours from London's Waterloo Station to Paris's Gare du Nord.

➤ CAR TRANSPORT: **Le Shuttle** (☎ 0990/353535 in the U.K.).

➤ PASSENGER SERVICE: In the U.K.,
Eurostar (☎ 0345/881881), **InterCity
Europe** (✉:Victoria Station, London,
☎ 0171/834–2345, 0171/828–0892
for credit-card bookings). In the U.S.,
BritRail Travel (☎ 800/677–8585),
Rail Europe (☎ 800/942–4866).

CHILDREN & TRAVEL

CHILDREN IN GREAT BRITAIN

Be sure to plan ahead and **involve
your youngsters** as you outline your
trip. When packing, include things to
keep them busy en route. On sightseeing days try to schedule activities of
special interest to your children. If
you are renting a car don't forget to
arrange for a car seat when you
reserve. Most hotels in Great Britain
allow children under a certain age to
stay in their parents' room at no extra
charge, but others charge them as
extra adults; be sure to **ask about the
cutoff age for children's discounts.**

➤ LOCAL INFORMATION: For information on events for kids when in
London, call **Kidsline** (☎ 0171/222–
8070). Open 9 AM–4 PM during
holidays and 4 PM–6 PM during term
time. **Kids Out!** (£1.75) is a magazine
packed with ideas and events on
what to do. **Time Out**(£1.80) weekly
listings magazine has a section of
child-friendly activities and trips.
Kids' Britain covers a multitude
of places and things to do (Betty
Jerman, Macmillan, £4.99).

➤ BABY-SITTING: In London, try **The
Nanny Service** (✉ 6 Nottingham St.,
London W1M 3RB, ☎ 0171/935–
3515) and **Universal Aunts** (✉ Box
304, London SW4 0NN ☎ 0171/
738–8937).

FLYING

If your children are two or older, **ask
about children's airfares.** As a general
rule, infants under two not occupying
a seat fly at greatly reduced fares or
even for free.

In general the adult baggage
allowance applies to children paying
half or more of the adult fare. When
booking, **ask about carry-on
allowances for those traveling with
infants.** In general, for babies charged
10% of the adult fare you are allowed
one carry-on bag and a collapsible

stroller, which may have to be
checked; you may be limited to less if
the flight is full.

Experts agree that it's a good idea
to use safety seats aloft for children
weighing less than 40 pounds. Airlines,
however, can set their own policies:
U.S. carriers allow FAA-approved
models but usually require that you
buy a ticket, even if your child would
otherwise ride free, since the seats
must be strapped into regular seats.
Airline rules vary, so it's important to
**check your airline's policy about using
safety seats during takeoff and landing.** Safety seats cannot obstruct the
movement of other passengers in the
row, so get an appropriate seat assign-
ment as early as possible.

When making your reservation,
**request children's meals or a free-
standing bassinet** if you need them;
the latter are available only to those
seated at the bulkhead, where there's
enough legroom. Remember, however,
that bulkhead seats may not have
their own overhead bins, and there's
no storage space in front of you—a
major inconvenience.

GROUP TRAVEL

When planning to take your kids on a
tour, look for companies that specialize in family travel.

➤ FAMILY-FRIENDLY TOUR OPERATORS:
Grandtravel (✉ 6900 Wisconsin Ave.,
Suite 706, Chevy Chase, MD 20815,
☎ 301/986–0790 or 800/247–7651)
for people traveling with grandchil-
dren ages 7–17. **Families Welcome!**
(✉ 92 N. Main St., Ashland, OR
97520, ☎ 541/482–6121 or 800/
326–0724, FAX 541/482–0660).
Rascals in Paradise (✉ 650 5th St.,
Suite 505, San Francisco, CA 94107,
☎ 415/978–9800 or 800/872–7225,
FAX 415/442–0289).

CONSUMER PROTECTION

Whenever possible, **pay with a major
credit card** so you can cancel payment
or get reimbursed if there's a problem, provided that you can provide
documentation. This is the best way
to pay, whether you're buying travel
arrangements before your trip or
shopping at your destination.

THE GOLD GUIDE / SMART TRAVEL TIPS

If you're doing business with a particular company for the first time, **contact your local Better Business Bureau and the attorney general's offices** in your state and the company's home state, as well. Have any complaints been filed?

Finally, if you're buying a package or tour, always **consider travel insurance** that includes default coverage (☞ Insurance, *below*).

➤ LOCAL BBBs: **Council of Better Business Bureaus** (✉ 4200 Wilson Blvd., Suite 800, Arlington, VA 22203, ☎ 703/276–0100, ℻ 703/525–8277).

CRUISE TRAVEL

Cunard Line (✉ 555 5th Ave., New York, NY 10017, ☎ 800/221–4770) operates four ships that make transatlantic crossings. The *Queen Elizabeth 2* (*QE2*) makes regular crossings April–December, between Southampton, England, and Baltimore, Boston, and New York City. Arrangements for the *QE2* can include one-way airfare. Cunard Line also offers fly/cruise packages and pre- and post-land packages. Check the travel pages of your Sunday newspaper for other cruise ships that sail to Britain.

CUSTOMS & DUTIES

When shopping, **keep receipts** for all of your purchases. Upon reentering the country, **be ready to show customs officials what you've bought.** If you feel a duty is incorrect, appeal the assessment. If you object to the way your clearance was handled, get the inspector's badge number. In either case, first ask to see a supervisor, then write to the appropriate authorities, beginning with the port director at your point of entry.

IN GREAT BRITAIN

There are two levels of duty-free allowance for travelers entering Great Britain: one for goods bought outside the EU, the other for goods bought in the EU (Austria, Belgium, Denmark, France, Germany, Greece, the Irish Republic, Italy, Luxembourg, the Netherlands, Portugal, Spain, or Sweden, but not the Channel Islands).

Of goods purchased outside the EU, you may import duty-free: 200 cigarettes or 100 cigarillos or 50 cigars or 250 grams of tobacco; two liters of table wine and, in addition, (a) one liter of alcohol over 22% by volume (most spirits), (b) two liters of alcohol under 22% by volume (fortified or sparkling wine), or (c) two more liters of table wine; 60 milliliters of perfume; ¼ liter of toilet water; and other goods up to a value of £145, but not more than 50 liters of beer or 25 cigarette lighters.

If you are entering the United Kingdom from another EU country, you no longer need to pass through customs. If you plan to bring in large quantities of alcohol or tobacco for your own personal use (gifts included), check in advance on EU limits if you have not paid tax in the country of purchase with Customs and Excise (☎ 0181/910—3744). Although there is an allowance for goods bought tax free at duty free shops for intra-EU travel, by June 1999 it could be scrapped so the U.K. falls in line with the rest of the EU single market.

No animals or pets of any kind can be brought into the United Kingdom without a lengthy quarantine. The penalties are severe and strictly enforced. Similarly, fresh meats, plants and vegetables, illegal drugs, and firearms and ammunition may not be brought into Great Britain.

You will face no customs formalities if you enter Scotland or Wales from any other part of the United Kingdom, though anyone coming from Northern Ireland should expect a security check.

IN AUSTRALIA

Australia residents who are 18 or older may bring back $A400 worth of souvenirs and gifts (including jewelry), 250 cigarettes or 250 grams of tobacco, and 1,125 ml of alcohol (including wine, beer, and spirits). Residents under 18 may bring back $A200 worth of goods.

➤ INFORMATION: **Australian Customs Service** (Regional Director, ✉ Box 8, Sydney, NSW 2001, ☎ 02/9213–2000, ℻ 02/9213–4000).

IN CANADA

Canadian residents who have been out of Canada for at least 7 days may bring in C$500 worth of goods duty-free. If you've been away less than 7 days but more than 48 hours, the duty-free allowance drops to C$200; if your trip lasts 24–48 hours, the allowance is C$50. You may not pool allowances with family members. Goods claimed under the C$500 exemption may follow you by mail; those claimed under the lesser exemptions must accompany you. Alcohol and tobacco products may be included in the 7-day and 48-hour exemptions but not in the 24-hour exemption. If you meet the age requirements of the province or territory through which you reenter Canada, you may bring in, duty-free, 1.14 liters (40 imperial ounces) of wine or liquor *or* 24 12-ounce cans or bottles of beer or ale. If you are 16 or older you may bring in, duty-free, 200 cigarettes and 50 cigars.

You may send an unlimited number of gifts worth up to C$60 each duty-free to Canada. Label the package UNSOLICITED GIFT—VALUE UNDER $60. Alcohol and tobacco are excluded.

➤ INFORMATION: **Revenue Canada** (✉ 2265 St. Laurent Blvd. S, Ottawa, Ontario K1G 4K3, ☎ 613/993–0534, 800/461–9999 in Canada).

IN NEW ZEALAND

Although greeted with a "Haere Mai" ("Welcome to New Zealand"), homeward-bound residents with goods to declare must present themselves for inspection. If you're 17 or older, you may bring back $700 worth of souvenirs and gifts. Your duty-free allowance also includes 4.5 liters of wine or beer; one 1,125-ml bottle of spirits; and either 200 cigarettes, 250 grams of tobacco, 50 cigars, or a combo of all three up to 250 grams.

➤ INFORMATION: **New Zealand Customs** (✉ Custom House, ✉ 50 Anzac Ave., Box 29, Auckland, New Zealand, ☎ 09/359–6655, ☎ 09/309–2978).

IN THE U.S.

U.S. residents may bring home $400 worth of foreign goods duty-free if they've been out of the country for at least 48 hours (and if they haven't used the $400 allowance or any part of it in the past 30 days).

U.S. residents 21 and older may bring back 1 liter of alcohol duty-free. In addition, regardless of your age, you are allowed 200 cigarettes and 100 non-Cuban cigars. Antiques, which the U.S. Customs Service defines as objects more than 100 years old, enter duty-free, as do original works of art done entirely by hand.

You may also send packages home duty-free: up to $200 worth of goods for personal use, with a limit of one parcel per addressee per day (and no alcohol or tobacco products or perfume worth more than $5); label the package PERSONAL USE, and attach a list of its contents and their retail value. Do not label the package UNSOLICITED GIFT, or your duty-free exemption will drop to $100. Mailed items do not affect your duty-free allowance on your return.

➤ INFORMATION: **U.S. Customs Service** (Inquiries, ✉ Box 7407, Washington, DC 20044, ☎ 202/927–6724; complaints, Office of Regulations and Rulings, ✉ 1301 Constitution Ave. NW, Washington, DC 20229; registration of equipment, Resource Management, ✉ 1301 Constitution Ave. NW, Washington DC 20229, ☎ 202/927–0540).

DINING

Restaurants in Britain can be very expensive for what they offer. Be very sure to **check the menu posted outside** almost all establishments before venturing inside. As a general rule of thumb, wine bars and bistros offer reasonably priced meals in interesting surroundings, and you will find excellent budget food at lunchtime in good pubs and inns. When "pubbing," **remember that most pubs do not have any waitstaff and you are expected to go to the bar and order a beverage and your meal** (this can be particularly disconcerting when you are seated in a "restaurant" upstairs, but still expected to go downstairs and get your own drinks and food). **Be careful of the prices of drinks** in a restaurant. Many restaurants will charge you as much for a glass of mineral water as a whole 2-liter bottle would cost you in a supermarket.

MEALTIMES

Breakfast is generally served between 7:30 and 9 and lunch between noon and 2. Tea—often a meal in itself—is taken between 4 and 5:30, dinner or supper between 7:30 and 9:30, sometimes earlier, seldom later except in large cities. High tea, at about 6, replaces dinner in some areas like the north, where lunch is always called dinner.

DISABILITIES & ACCESSIBILITY

ACCESS IN GREAT BRITAIN

Compared to the U.S., Great Britain has a way to go in helping people with disabilities, but is moving toward making its major cities more accessible. In London, for instance, most underground (subway) stations have vast escalators and steps, but contact the London Transport system (☎ 0171/918–3312) for their booklet, "Access to the Underground," which gives facts about elevators and ramps at individual tube stations. The grand, regal London Black Cabs are perfectly accommodating in their spacious interiors for people using wheelchairs, and many London hotels have wheelchair ramps. Read the British Tourist Authority's booklets "London Made Easy" and "Access in London" for the final world on accessibility. Note that the BTA will provide lists of London hotels for people with disabilities; these hotels often post the sign "H" at their door to welcome such travelers.

➤ LOCAL RESOURCES: The biggest organization in Britain is **RADAR**, or the Royal Association for Disability and Rehabilitation, command central for travel information and advice on accommodations through the British Isles and Europe (✉ 12 City Forum, 250 City Rd., London, EC1, ☎ 0171/250–3222). Contact **London Transport's Unit for Disabled Passengers** (✉ 172 Buckingham Palace Rd., London SW1W 9TN, ☎ 0171/918–3312) for details on **Stationlink**, a wheelchair-accessible "midibus" service, as well as information on other access information. Another important organization is **Holiday Care Service** (✉ Imperial Building, Victoria Road, Horley, Surrey RH6 7PZ, ☎ 01293/774535). **Artsline**

(☎ 0171/388–2227) provides information on the accessibility of arts events.

MAKING RESERVATIONS

When discussing accessibility with an operator or reservations agent, **ask hard questions.** Are there any stairs, inside *or* out? Are there grab bars next to the toilet *and* in the shower/tub? How wide is the doorway to the room? To the bathroom? For the most extensive facilities meeting the latest legal specifications, **opt for newer accommodations,** which are more likely to have been designed with access in mind. Older buildings or ships may have more limited facilities. Be sure to **discuss your needs before booking.**

TRAVEL AGENCIES & TOUR OPERATORS

As a whole, the travel industry has become more aware of the needs of travelers with disabilities. In the U.S., the Americans with Disabilities Act requires that travel firms serve the needs of all travelers. Some agencies and operators specialize in making travel arrangements for individuals and groups with disabilities.

➤ IN THE U.K.: **Holiday Care Service** (✉ Imperial Buildings, 2nd floor, Victoria Rd., Horley, Surrey, RH6 7PZ, ☎ 01293/774535) is Britain's central source of travel information for people with disabilities.

➤ TRAVELERS WITH MOBILITY PROBLEMS: **Access Adventures** (✉ 206 Chestnut Ridge Rd., Rochester, NY 14624, ☎ 716/889–9096), run by a former physical-rehabilitation counselor. **Accessible Journeys** (✉ 35 W. Sellers Ave., Ridley Park, PA 19078, ☎ 610/521–0339 or 800/846–4537, FAX 610/521–6959), for escorted tours exclusively for travelers with mobility impairments. **CareVacations** (✉ 5019 49th Ave., Suite 102, Leduc, Alberta T9E 6T5, ☎ 403/986–6404, 800/648–1116 in Canada) has group tours and is especially helpful with cruise vacations. **Flying Wheels Travel** (✉ 143 W. Bridge St., Box 382, Owatonna, MN 55060, ☎ 507/451–5005 or 800/535–6790, FAX 507/451–1685), a travel agency specializing in customized tours and itineraries

worldwide. **Hinsdale Travel Service**
(✉ 201 E. Ogden Ave., Suite 100,
Hinsdale, IL 60521, ☎ 630/325–
1335), a travel agency that benefits
from the advice of wheelchair traveler
Janice Perkins.

➤ COMPLAINTS: **Disability Rights
Section** (✉ U.S. Department of Justice, Civil Rights Division, ✉ Box
66738, Washington, DC 20035–
6738, ☎ 202/514–0301 or 800/514–
0301, TTY 202/514–0383 or 800/
514–0383, FAX 202/307–1198) for
general complaints. **Aviation Consumer Protection Division** (☞ Air
Travel, *above*) for airline-related
problems.

DISCOUNTS & DEALS

Be a smart shopper and **compare all
your options** before making any
choice. A plane ticket bought with a
promotional coupon may not be
cheaper than the least expensive fare
from a discount ticket agency. For
high-price travel purchases, such as
packages or tours, keep in mind that
what you get is as important as what
you save. Just because something is
cheap doesn't mean it's a bargain.

CLUBS & COUPONS

Many companies sell discounts in
the form of travel clubs and coupon
books, but these cost money. You
must use participating advertisers to
get a deal, and only after you recoup
the initial membership cost or book
price do you begin to save. If you
plan to use the club or coupons
frequently, you may save considerably. Before signing up, find out what
discounts you get for free.

➤ DISCOUNT CLUBS: **Entertainment
Travel Editions** (✉ 2125 Butterfield
Rd., Troy, MI 48084, ☎ 800/445–
4137; $20–$51, depending on destination). **Great American Traveler**
(✉ Box 27965, Salt Lake City, UT
84127, ☎ 801/974–3033 or 800/
548–2812; $49.95 per year). **Mo-
ment's Notice Discount Travel Club**
(✉ 7301 New Utrecht Ave., Brook-
lyn, NY 11204, ☎ 718/234–6295;
$25 per year, single or family). **Privi-
lege Card International** (✉ 237 E.
Front St., Youngstown, OH 44503,
☎ 330/746–5211 or 800/236–9732;

$74.95 per year). **Sears' Mature
Outlook** (✉ Box 9390, Des Moines,
IA 50306, ☎ 800/336–6330; $19.95
per year). **Travelers Advantage**
(✉ CUC Travel Service, ✉ 3033 S.
Parker Rd., Suite 1000, Aurora, CO
80014, ☎ 800/548–1116 or 800/
648–4037; $59.95 per year, single or
family). **Worldwide Discount Travel
Club** (✉ 1674 Meridian Ave., Miami
Beach, FL 33139, ☎ 305/534–2082;
$50 per year family, $40 single).

CREDIT-CARD BENEFITS

When you use your credit card to
make travel purchases you may get
free travel-accident insurance, colli-
sion-damage insurance, and medical
or legal assistance, depending on the
card and the bank that issued it.
American Express, MasterCard, and
Visa provide one or more of these
services, so **get a copy of your credit
card's travel-benefits policy.** If you
are a member of an auto club, always
**ask hotel and car-rental reservations
agents about auto-club discounts.**
Some clubs offer additional discounts
on tours, cruises, and admission to
attractions.

DISCOUNT RESERVATIONS

To save money, **look into discount-
reservations services** with toll-free
numbers, which use their buying
power to get a better price on hotels,
airline tickets, even car rentals. When
booking a room, always **call the
hotel's local toll-free number** (if one
is available) rather than the central
reservations number—you'll often get
a better price. Always ask about
special packages or corporate rates.

When shopping for the best deal on
hotels and car rentals, **look for guaranteed exchange rates,** which protect
you against a falling dollar. Your rate
is locked in, even if the price goes up
in the local currency.

➤ AIRLINE TICKETS: ☎ **800/FLY–4–
LESS.**

➤ HOTEL ROOMS: **Hotels Plus** (☎
800/235–0909). **Hotel Reservations
Network** (☎ 800/964–6835).
Steigenberger Reservation Service
(☎ 800/223–5652). **Travel Interlink**
(☎ 800/888–5898).

THE GOLD GUIDE / SMART TRAVEL TIPS

PACKAGE DEALS

Packages and guided tours can save you money, but don't confuse the two. When you buy a package, your travel remains independent, just as though you had planned and booked the trip yourself. Fly/drive packages, which combine airfare and car rental, are often a good deal.

ELECTRICITY

To use your U.S.-purchased electric-powered equipment, **bring a converter and adapter.** The electrical current in Great Britain is 230 volts, 50 cycles alternating current (AC); wall outlets use three-pinned plugs, shaver sockets take two round oversize prongs.

If your appliances are dual-voltage, you'll need only an adapter. Don't use 110-volt outlets, marked FOR SHAVERS ONLY, for high-wattage appliances such as blow-dryers. Most laptops operate equally well on 110 and 220 volts and so require only an adapter.

EMBASSIES

➤ AUSTRALIA: **Australia House** (✉ Strand, WC2, ☎ 0171/379–4334).

➤ CANADA: **MacDonald House** (✉ 38 Grosvenor Sq., W1, ☎ 0171/258–6600).

➤ NEW ZEALAND: **New Zealand House** (✉ 80 Haymarket, SW1, ☎ 0171/930–8422).

➤ UNITED STATES: **U.S. Embassy** (✉ 24 Grosvenor Sq., W1, ☎ 0171/499–9000); for passports, go to the **U.S. Passport Unit** (✉ 55 Upper Brook St., W1, ☎ 0171/499–9000).

GAY & LESBIAN TRAVEL

➤ GAY- AND LESBIAN-FRIENDLY TOUR OPERATORS: **Hanns Ebensten Travel** (✉ 513 Fleming St., Key West, FL 33040, ☎ 305/294–8174, FAX 305/292–9665), one of the oldest operators in the gay market.

➤ GAY- AND LESBIAN-FRIENDLY TRAVEL AGENCIES: **Corniche Travel** (✉ 8721 Sunset Blvd., Suite 200, West Hollywood, CA 90069, ☎ 310/854–6000 or 800/429–8747, FAX 310/659–7441). **Islanders Kennedy Travel** (✉ 183 W. 10th St., New York, NY 10014, ☎ 212/242–3222 or 800/988–1181, FAX 212/929–8530). **Now**

Voyager (✉ 4406 18th St., San Francisco, CA 94114, ☎ 415/626–1169 or 800/255–6951, FAX 415/626–8626). **Yellowbrick Road** (✉ 1500 W. Balmoral Ave., Chicago, IL 60640, ☎ 773/561–1800 or 800/642–2488, FAX 773/561–4497). **Skylink Travel and Tour** (✉ 3577 Moorland Ave., Santa Rosa, CA 95407, ☎ 707/585–8355 or 800/225–5759, FAX 707/584–5637), serving lesbian travelers.

HEALTH

MEDICAL PLANS

No one plans to get sick while traveling, but it happens, so **consider signing up with a medical-assistance company.** Members get doctor referrals, emergency evacuation or repatriation, 24-hour telephone hot lines for medical consultation, cash for emergencies, and other personal and legal assistance. Coverage varies by plan, so **review the benefits of each.**

➤ MEDICAL-ASSISTANCE COMPANIES: **International SOS Assistance** (✉ 8 Neshaminy Interplex, Suite 207, Trevose, PA 19053, ☎ 215/245–4707 or 800/523–6586, FAX 215/244–9617; ✉ 7 Old Lodge Pl., St. Margaret's, Twickenham TW1 1RQ, England, ☎ 0181/744–0066); ✉ 12 Chemin Riantbosson, 1217 Meyrin 1, Geneva, Switzerland, ☎ 4122/785–6464, FAX 4122/785–6424; ✉ 10 Anson Rd., 14-07/08 International Plaza, Singapore, 079903, ☎ 65/226–3936, FAX 65/226–3937).

HOLIDAYS

ENGLAND AND WALES

January 1; April 2 (Good Friday); April 5 (Easter Monday); May 3 (Early May Bank Holiday); May 31, (Spring Bank Holiday); August 30 (Summer Bank Holiday); December 25–26.

SCOTLAND

January 1–2; April 2, May 3; May 31; August 30 (Summer Bank Holiday); December 25–26.

INSURANCE

Travel insurance is the best way to **protect yourself against financial loss.** The most useful plan is a comprehensive policy that includes coverage for trip cancellation and interruption, default, trip delay, and medical expenses (with a waiver for preexisting conditions).

Without insurance, you will lose all or most of your money if you cancel your trip, regardless of the reason. Default insurance covers you if your tour operator, airline, or cruise line goes out of business. Trip-delay covers unforeseen expenses incurred due to bad weather or mechanical delays. **Compare the fine print regarding trip-delay coverage** when comparing policies.

For overseas travel, one of the most important components of travel insurance is its medical coverage. Supplemental health insurance will pick up the cost of your medical bills should you get sick or injured while traveling. U.S. residents should note that Medicare generally does not cover health-care costs outside the United States, nor do many privately issued policies. Residents of the United Kingdom can buy an annual travel-insurance policy valid for most vacations taken during the year in which the coverage is purchased. If you are pregnant or have a preexisting condition, make sure you're covered. Australian travelers should buy travel insurance, including extra medical coverage, whenever they go abroad, according to the Insurance Council of Australia.

Always **buy travel insurance directly from the insurance company**; if you buy it from a cruise line, airline, or tour operator that goes out of business you probably will not be covered for the agency or operator's default, a major risk. Before you make any purchase, **review your existing health and home-owner's policies** to find out whether they cover expenses incurred while traveling.

➤ TRAVEL INSURERS: In the U.S., **Access America** (⊠ 6600 W. Broad St., Richmond, VA 23230, ☎ 804/285–3300 or 800/284–8300). **Travel Guard International** (⊠ 1145 Clark St., Stevens Point, WI 54481, ☎ 715/345–0505 or 800/826–1300). In Canada, **Mutual of Omaha** (⊠ Travel Division, ⊠ 500 University Ave., Toronto, Ontario M5G 1V8, ☎ 416/598–4083, 800/268–8825 in Canada).

➤ INSURANCE INFORMATION: In the U.K., **Association of British Insurers** (⊠ 51 Gresham St., London EC2V 7HQ, ☎ 0171/600–3333). In Australia, the **Insurance Council of Australia** (☎ 613/9614–1077, FAX 613/9614–7924).

LODGING

APARTMENT & HOUSE RENTALS

If you want a home base that's roomy enough for a family and comes with cooking facilities, **consider a furnished rental.** These can save you money, especially if you're traveling with a large group of people. Home-exchange directories list rentals (often second homes owned by prospective house swappers), and some services search for a house or apartment for you (even a castle if that's your fancy) and handle the paperwork. Some send an illustrated catalog; others send photographs only of specific properties, sometimes at a charge. Up-front registration fees may apply.

➤ RENTAL AGENTS: **At Home Abroad** (⊠ 405 E. 56th St., Suite 6H, New York, NY 10022, ☎ 212/421–9165, FAX 212/752–1591). **Drawbridge to Europe** (⊠ 5456 Adams Rd., Talent, OR 97540, ☎ 541/512–8927 or 888/268–1148, FAX 541/512–0978). **Europa-Let/Tropical Inn-Let** (⊠ 92 N. Main St., Ashland, OR 97520, ☎ 541/482–5806 or 800/462–4486, FAX 541/482–0660). **Hometours International** (⊠ Box 11503, Knoxville, TN 37939, ☎ 423/690–8484 or 800/367–4668). **Interhome** (⊠ 124 Little Falls Rd., Fairfield, NJ 07004, ☎ 973/882–6864 or 800/882–6864, FAX 973/808–1742). **Property Rentals International** (⊠ 1008 Mansfield Crossing Rd., Richmond, VA 23236, ☎ 804/378–6054 or 800/220–3332, FAX 804/379–2073). **Rental Directories International** (⊠ 2044 Rittenhouse Sq., Philadelphia, PA 19103, ☎ 215/985–4001, FAX 215/985–0323). **Rent-a-Home International** (⊠ 7200 34th Ave. NW, Seattle, WA 98117, ☎ 206/789–9377 or 800/488–7368, FAX 206/789–9379). **Vacation Home Rentals Worldwide** (⊠ 235 Kensington Ave., Norwood, NJ 07648, ☎ 201/767–9393 or 800/633–3284, FAX 201/767–5510). **Villas and Apart-**

ments Abroad (✉ 420 Madison Ave., Suite 1003, New York, NY 10017, ☎ 212/759–1025 or 800/433–3020, FAX 212/755–8316). **Villas International** (✉ 950 Northgate Dr., Suite 206, San Rafael, CA 94903, ☎ 415/499–9490 or 800/221–2260, FAX 415/499–9491). **Hideaways International** (✉ 767 Islington St., Portsmouth, NH 03801, ☎ 603/430–4433 or 800/843–4433, FAX 603/430–4444; membership $99; travelers arrange rentals among themselves).

B&BS

These are a special British tradition, and the backbone of budget travel. They are usually in a family home, few have private bathrooms, and most offer only breakfast. Guest houses are a slightly larger, more luxurious version. The first of a new breed of upscale B&Bs, more along the line of American B&Bs, have been spotted in the capital. All provide a glimpse of everyday British life.

Staying off the Beaten Track in England and Wales, by Elizabeth & Walter Gundrey (Arrow, £8.99), has given its author's name to the language, as in "Let's go Gundreying". The Automobile Association grades hotels and B&Bs and publishes guides (The **AA Bed and Breakfast Guide**, £8.99) and has information on inspected accommodations on the Web (www.theaa.co.uk/hotels). Sift through the **Which? Hotel Guide** (Which? Books, £14.99) for acclaimed B&Bs.

➤ RESERVATION SERVICES: Many of the most elegant, non-chain hotels in the U.K. belong to the **Small Luxury Hotels of the World** group (U.S., ☎ 800/525–4800; U.K., ☎ 800/964470), with access to easy reservations for many of the prestigious member inns and hostelries.

COTTAGES

Furnished apartments, houses, cottages, and trailers are available for weekly rental in all areas of the country. These vary from quaint, cleverly converted farmhouses to brand-new buildings set in scenic surroundings. For families and large groups, they offer the best values, but as they are often in isolated locations, a car is

vital. Lists of rental properties are available free of charge from the British Tourist Authority. Discounts of up to 50% apply during the off-season (October–March).

For cottages inspected to recognized standards, consult the British Tourist Authority and the *Good Holiday Cottage Guide* for personal recommendations on every aspect (**Swallow Press**, ☎ 800/430–8096; $11.25, in the U.K., 01438/869489; £5.75; or on the Web www.abeydes.co.uk/cottageguide).

FARMHOUSES

These have become increasingly popular in recent years; their special appeal is the rustic, rural experience. Consider this option only if you are touring by car. Prices are generally very reasonable.

Ask for the BTA booklet *Farmhouse Vacations.* Also contact the **Farm Holiday Bureau** and ask for their guide of cottages in the scheme: (✉ National Agricultural Centre, Stoneleigh Park, Kenilworth, Warwickshire CV8 2LZ, ☎ 01203/696909).

HISTORIC BUILDINGS

Want to spend your vacation in a Gothic banqueting house, an old lighthouse, a magical seaside castle, or maybe in an apartment at Hampton Court Palace? Several organizations, such as the Landmark Trust and the National Trust, have specially adapted historic buildings to rent. Most of them are self-catering.

➤ HISTORIC BUILDINGS: Try the **Landmark Trust** (✉ Shottesbrooke, Maidenhead, Berkshire SL6 3SW, ☎ 01628/825925), the **National Trust** (✉ Box 536, Melksham, Wiltshire SN12 8SX, ☎ 01225/705676), **Portmeirion Cottages** (✉ Hotel Portmeirion, Gwynedd, Wales LL48 6ET, ☎ 01766/770228), and the rather upscale **Rural Retreats** (✉ Retreat House, Station Rd., Blockley, Moreton-in-Marsh, Gloucestershire GL56 9DZ, ☎ 01386/701177).

HOME EXCHANGES

If you would like to exchange your home for someone else's, **join a home-exchange organization,** which will send you its updated listings of available exchanges for a year and will include your own listing in at least one of them. It's up to you to make specific arrangements.

➤ EXCHANGE CLUBS: **HomeLink International** (✉ Box 650, Key West, FL 33041, ☎ 305/294–7766 or 800/638–3841, FAX 305/294–1148; $83 per year).

HOSTELS

No matter what your age, you can **save on lodging costs by staying at hostels.** In some 5,000 locations in more than 70 countries around the world, Hostelling International (HI), the umbrella group for a number of national youth hostel associations, offers single-sex, dorm-style beds and, at many hostels, "couples" rooms and family accommodations. Membership in any HI national hostel association, open to travelers of all ages, allows you to stay in HI-affiliated hostels at member rates (one-year membership is about $25 for adults; hostels run about $10–$25 per night). Members also have priority if the hostel is full; they're eligible for discounts around the world, even on rail and bus travel in some countries.

➤ HOSTEL ORGANIZATIONS: **Hostelling International—American Youth Hostels** (✉ 733 15th St. NW, Suite 840, Washington, DC 20005, ☎ 202/783–6161, FAX 202/783–6171). **Hostelling International—Canada** (✉ 400-205 Catherine St., Ottawa, Ontario K2P 1C3, ☎ 613/237–7884, FAX 613/237–7868). **Youth Hostel Association of England and Wales** (✉ Trevelyan House, ✉ 8 St. Stephen's Hill, St. Albans, Hertfordshire AL1 2DY, ☎ 01727/855215 or 01727/845047, FAX 01727/844126); membership in the U.S. $25, in Canada C$26.75, in the U.K. £9.30).

HOTELS

Most hotels have rooms with private bathrooms, although some older ones may have only washbasins; in this case, showers and bathtubs (and toilets) are usually just down the hall. Generally, hotel prices include breakfast, but it's often only Continental. Prices in London are significantly higher than in the rest of the country;

they usually do *not* include breakfast, and often the quality and service are not as good. TICs will reserve rooms for you, usually for a small fee. Many hotels offer special weekend and off-season bargain packages.

UNIVERSITY HOUSING

In larger cities and in some towns, certain universities offer their residence halls to paying vacationers when school is out. The facilities available are usually compact single sleeping units, and they can be rented on a nightly basis.

➤ UNIVERSITIES: Contact the **British Universities Accommodation Consortium** (✉ Box 1450, University Park, Nottingham NG7 2RD, ☎ 01159/504571).

MAIL

POSTAL RATES

Airmail letters to the United States and Canada cost 43p for 10 grams; postcards 37p; aerogrammes 36p. Letters and postcards to Europe not over 20 grams, 31p (26p to EU member countries). Letters within the United Kingdom, first class 26p, second class and postcards 20p.

RECEIVING MAIL

If you're uncertain where you'll be staying, **arrange to have your mail sent to American Express.** The service is free to cardholders and traveler's-check holders; all others pay a small fee. You can also **collect letters at London's Main Post Office** in Trafalgar Square, Monday–Saturday 8:30–9, from 24–28 William IV Street, WC2N 4DL. Ask the sender to mark the envelope "Poste Restante" or "To Be Called For." The letter must be marked with the recipient's full name (as it appears on your passport) and you'll need your passport or another official form of identification for collection (☎ 0171/930–9580). This service can be arranged, free, for any main or sub post office throughout the U.K., so mail can reach you while you are traveling (☎ 0345/740740).

MONEY

The unit of currency in Britain is the pound sterling, divided into 100 pence (p). The bills are 50, 20, 10,

THE GOLD GUIDE / SMART TRAVEL TIPS

and 5 pounds (Scotland and the Channel Islands have their own £1 bills). Coins are £2 (issued in Spring 1998), £1, 50, 20, 10, 5, 2, and 1p. At press time, the exchange rate was about U.S. $1.65 and Canadian $2.01 to the pound sterling.

COSTS

A local paper will cost you about 35p and a national daily 35–50p (up to £1 on Sunday). A pint of beer is about £1.80, and a gin and tonic £2 (mixers are pricey in pubs, and re-member that British measures for spirits are on the mean side). A cup of coffee will run from 60p to £2, de-pending on where you buy it; a ham sandwich £1.75–£3.50; lunch in a pub, £5 and up (plus your drink).

A theater seat will cost from £7.50 to £40 or more in London, less else-where, while an evening of opera or ballet at Covent Garden could set you back around £120 each for the best seats, although you can get returns or "the gods" (seats high up) for a small fraction of that. Movie theater prices vary widely—from £2.50 in the daytime in the provinces (more in the evening) to anything up to £8 in central London. Nightclubs operate under no known system—even the membership fees are variable.

Gasoline costs about £2.25 a U.S. gallon (67p a liter), and up to 10p a gallon higher in remote locations for unleaded petrol, and roughly £2.42 a gallon (70p a liter) for normal leaded gasoline. But by the time you read this there may well have been more price increases following the new government party line in encouraging good ecological habits.

CREDIT & DEBIT CARDS

Should you use a credit card or a debit card when traveling? Both have benefits. A credit card allows you to delay payment and gives you certain rights as a consumer (☞ Consumer Protection, *above*). A debit card, also known as a check card, deducts funds directly from your checking account and helps you stay within your bud-get. When you want to rent a car, though, you may still need an old-fashioned credit card. Although you can always *pay* for your car with a debit card, some agencies will not allow you to *reserve* a car with a debit card.

Otherwise, the two types of plastic are virtually the same. Both will get you cash advances at ATMs worldwide if your card is properly programmed with your personal identification number (PIN). To increase your chances of happy encounters with cash machines in Great Britain, **make sure before leaving home that your card has been programmed for ATM use there—ATMs in Great Britain accept PINs of four or fewer digits only**; if your PIN is longer, ask about changing it. If you know your PIN as a word, learn the numerical equiva-lent, as most Great Britain keypads show numbers only, no letters. Both credit and debit cards offer excellent, wholesale exchange rates. And both protect you against unauthorized use if the card is lost or stolen. Your liability is limited to $50, as long as you report the card missing.

➤ ATM LOCATIONS: **Cirrus** (☎ 800/424–7787). **Plus** (☎ 800/843–7587) for locations in the U.S. and Canada, or visit your local bank.

EXCHANGING MONEY

For the most favorable rates, **change money through banks.** Although fees charged for ATM transactions may be higher abroad than at home, Cirrus and Plus exchange rates are excellent, because they are based on wholesale rates offered only by major banks. You won't do as well at exchange booths in airports or rail and bus stations, in hotels, in restaurants, or in stores, although their hours may be more convenient. To avoid lines at airport exchange booths, **get a bit of local currency before you leave home.**

➤ EXCHANGE SERVICES: **Chase Currency To Go** (☎ 800/935–9935; 935–9935 in NY, NJ, and CT). **International Currency Express** (☎ 888/842–0880 on the East Coast, 888/278–6628 on the West Coast). **Thomas Cook Currency Services** (☎ 800/287–7362 for telephone orders and retail locations).

TRAVELER'S CHECKS

Do you need traveler's checks? It depends on where you're headed. If you're going to rural areas and small towns, go with cash; traveler's checks are best used in cities. Lost or stolen checks can usually be replaced within 24 hours. To ensure a speedy refund, buy your own traveler's checks—don't let someone else pay for them: irregularities like this can cause delays. The person who bought the checks should make the call to request a refund.

OUTDOOR ACTIVITIES & SPORTS

➤ BICYCLING: The national body promoting cycle touring is the **Cyclists' Touring Club** (£25 a year, £12.50 for students and those under 18, £16.50 for those over 65, and £42 for a family of more than three; (✉ Cotterell House, 69 Meadrow, Godalming, Surrey GU7 3HS, ☎ 01483/417217). Members get free advice and route information, a bed-and-breakfast handbook, and a magazine.

➤ BOATING: For boat-rental operators along Britain's several hundred miles of historic canals and waterways, contact the **Association of Pleasure Craft Operators** (✉ 35A High St., Newport, Shropshire TF10 7AT, ☎ 01952/813572).

➤ CAMPING: Contact the British Tourist Authority in the U.S. or the **Camping and Caravanning Club** (✉ Greenfields House, Westwood Way, Coventry, West Midlands CV4 8JH, ☎ 01203/694995) for details on Britain's many and varied campsites.

➤ GOLF: If you plan to play often on the Britain's hundreds of fine courses, consult *The Golf Guide* (FHG Publications, ✉ Abbey Mill Business Centre, Seed Hill, Paisley, PA1 1TJ Scotland, ☎ 0141/887–0428; £9.95).

➤ WALKING: The **Ramblers Association** (✉ 1–5 Wandsworth Rd., London SW8 2XX, ☎ 0171/582–6878), publishes a quarterly magazine and a yearbook full of resources, and a list of B&Bs within 2 mi of selected long-distance footpaths.

Other organizations include the **Byways and Bridleways Trust** (✉ The Granary, Charlcutt, Calne, Wiltshire SN11 9HL); **Long Distance Walkers**

Association (✉ The Secretary, 21 Upcroft, Windsor, Berkshire, SL4 39H; ☎ 01753/866685); **Countryside Commission** (✉ John Dower House, Crescent Place, Cheltenham, Gloucestershire GL50 3RA ☎ 01242/521381) and the **Farm Holiday Bureau,** (✉ National Agricultural Centre, Stoneleigh Park, Kenilworth, Warwickshire CV8 2LZ, ☎ 01203/696909).

PACKING

LUGGAGE

How many carry-on bags you can bring with you is up to the airline. Most allow two, but the limit is often reduced to one on certain flights. Gate agents will take excess baggage—including bags they deem oversize—from you as you board and add it to checked luggage. To avoid this situation, make sure that everything you carry aboard will fit under your seat. Also, get to the gate early, and request a seat at the back of the plane; you'll probably board first, while the overhead bins are still empty. Since big, bulky baggage attracts the attention of gate agents and flight attendants on a busy flight, make sure your carry-on is really a carry-on. Finally, a carry-on that's long and narrow is more likely to remain unnoticed than one that's wide and squarish.

On international flights baggage allowances may be determined not by piece but by weight—generally 88 pounds (40 kilograms) in first class, 66 pounds (30 kilograms) in business class, and 44 pounds (20 kilograms) in economy.

Airline liability for baggage is limited to $1,250 per person on flights within the United States. On international flights it amounts to $9.07 per pound or $20 per kilogram for checked baggage (roughly $640 per 70-pound bag) and $400 per passenger for unchecked baggage. You can buy additional coverage at check-in for about $10 per $1,000 of coverage, but it excludes a rather extensive list of items, shown on your airline ticket.

Before departure, **itemize your bags' contents** and their worth, and label the bags with your name, address,

SMART TRAVEL TIPS / THE GOLD GUIDE

and phone number. (If you use your home address, cover it so that potential thieves can't see it readily.) Inside each bag, **pack a copy of your itinerary.** At check-in, **make sure that each bag is correctly tagged** with the destination airport's three-letter code. If your bags arrive damaged or fail to arrive at all, file a written report with the airline before leaving the airport.

PACKING LIST

Britain can be cool, damp, and overcast, even in summer. You'll want a heavy coat for winter and a lightweight coat or warm jacket for summer. There's no time of year when a raincoat or umbrella won't come in handy. For the cities, **pack as you would for an American city:** coats and ties for expensive restaurants and night spots, casual clothes elsewhere. Jeans are popular in Britain and are perfectly acceptable for sightseeing and informal dining. Casual blazers are popular here with men. For women, ordinary street dress is acceptable everywhere.

If you plan to stay in budget hotels, take your own soap. Many do not provide soap and some give guests only one tiny bar per room.

In your carry-on luggage **bring an extra pair of eyeglasses or contact lenses** and **enough of any medication you take** to last the entire trip. You may also want your doctor to write a spare prescription using the drug's generic name, since brand names may vary from country to country. **Never put prescription drugs or valuables in luggage to be checked.** To avoid customs delays, carry medications in their original packaging. And don't forget to copy down and carry addresses of offices that handle refunds of lost traveler's checks.

PASSPORTS & VISAS

For international travel, **carry a passport even if you don't need one** (it's always the best form of ID), and make **two photocopies of the data page** (one for someone at home and another for you, carried separately from your passport). If you lose your passport, promptly call the nearest embassy or consulate and the local police.

ENTERING GREAT BRITAIN

U.S. and Canadian citizens need only a valid passport to enter Great Britain for stays of up to 90 days.

PASSPORT OFFICES

The best time to apply for a passport or to renew is during the fall and winter. Before any trip, be sure to check your passport's expiration date and, if necessary, renew it as soon as possible. (Some countries won't allow you to enter on a passport that's due to expire in six months or less.)

➤ AUSTRALIAN CITIZENS: **Australian Passport Office** (☎ 13/1232).

➤ CANADIAN CITIZENS: **Passport Office** (☎ 819/994–3500 or 800/567–6868).

➤ NEW ZEALAND CITIZENS: **New Zealand Passport Office** (☎ 04/494–0700 for information on how to apply, 0800/727–776 for information on applications already submitted).

➤ U.S. CITIZENS: **National Passport Information Center** (☎ 900/225–5674; calls are charged at 35¢ per minute for automated service, $1.05 per minute for operator service).

SENIOR-CITIZEN TRAVEL

To qualify for age-related discounts, **mention your senior-citizen status up front** when booking hotel reservations (not when checking out) and before you're seated in restaurants (not when paying the bill). Note that discounts may be limited to certain menus, days, or hours. When renting a car, **ask about promotional car-rental discounts,** which can be cheaper than senior-citizen rates.

➤ ADVENTURES: **Overseas Adventure Travel** (✉ Grand Circle Corporation, ✉ 625 Mt. Auburn St., Cambridge, MA 02138, ☎ 617/876–0533 or 800/221–0814, FAX 617/876–0455).

➤ EDUCATIONAL PROGRAMS: **Elderhostel** (✉ 75 Federal St., 3rd floor, Boston, MA 02110, ☎ 617/426–8056). **Interhostel** (✉ University of New Hampshire, ✉ 6 Garrison Ave., Durham, NH 03824, ☎ 603/862–1147 or 800/733–9753, FAX 603/862–1113).

TRAVEL AGENCIES

To save money, **look into deals available through student-oriented travel agencies.** To qualify you'll need a bona fide student ID card. Members of international student groups are also eligible.

➤ STUDENT IDs & SERVICES: **Council on International Educational Exchange** (✉ CIEE, ✉ 205 E. 42nd St., 14th floor, New York, NY 10017, ☎ 212/822–2600 or 888/268–6245, FAX 212/822–2699), for mail orders only, in the United States. **Travel Cuts** (✉ 187 College St., Toronto, Ontario M5T 1P7, ☎ 416/979–2406 or 800/667–2887) in Canada.

➤ STUDENT TOURS: **Contiki Holidays** (✉ 300 Plaza Alicante, Suite 900, Garden Grove, CA 92840, ☎ 714/740–0808 or 800/266–8454, FAX 714/740–2034). **AESU Travel** (✉ 2 Hamill Rd., Suite 248, Baltimore, MD 21210-1807, ☎ 410/323–4416 or 800/638–7640, FAX 410/323–4498).

TAXES

AIRPORT

An airport departure tax of £20 (£10 for within U.K. and EU countries) per person is payable, and may be subject to more government increases, although it is included in the price of your ticket.

VALUE-ADDED TAX (VAT)

The British sales tax (VAT, Value Added Tax) is 17½%. The tax is almost always included in quoted prices in shops, hotels, and restaurants.

➤ VAT REFUNDS: You can get a **VAT refund** by The Direct Export method, where the shopkeeper arranges the export of the goods and does not charge VAT at the point of sale. It sounds easy, but purchases are sent on to your home separately, and you may prefer to take them with you. If so, try the more popular Retail Export scheme, run by most large stores. The special Form 407 (provided only by the retailer) is attached to your invoice. You must present the goods, form, and invoice to the customs officer at the last port of departure from the EC. Allow plenty of time to do this at the airport as there are often long lines. The form is then returned to the store and the refund forwarded to you, minus a small service charge. For inquiries, call the local Customs & Excise office listed in the telephone directory or helpline ☎ 01895/842226.

TELEPHONES

COUNTRY CODES

The country code for Great Britain is 44. When dialing a British number from abroad, drop the initial 0 from the local area code. To give one example: let's say you're calling Buckingham Palace—0171/839–1377—from the U.S. to inquire about tours and hours. First, dial 011 (the international access code), then 44 (Great Britain's country code), then 171 (London's center city code), then the remainder of the telephone number. There are two area codes in London: 0171 for inner London, 0181 for outer London. You do not need to dial either if calling from inside the same zone. Drop the zero from the prefix and dial only 171 or 181 when calling London from abroad.

DIRECTORY & OPERATOR INFORMATION

To call the operator, dial 100; directory inquiries (information) 192; international directory inquiries, 155.

INTERNATIONAL CALLS

AT&T, MCI, and Sprint international access codes make calling the United States relatively convenient, but you may find the local access number blocked in many hotel rooms. First ask the hotel operator to connect you. If the hotel operator balks, ask for an international operator, or dial the international operator yourself. One way to improve your odds of getting connected to your long-distance carrier is to travel with more than one company's calling card (a hotel may block Sprint, for example, but not MCI). If all else fails, call from a pay phone in the hotel lobby.

➤ ACCESS CODES: **AT&T Direct** (☎ In the U.K., there are AT&T access numbers to dial the U.S. using three different phone types—Mercury: 0500/890011; British Telecom: 0800/890011; and AT&T: 0800/0130011;

☎ 800/435–0812 for other areas).
MCI WorldPhone (☎ In the U.K.,
dial 0800/890222 to dial the U.S via
MCI; ☎ 800/444–4141 for other
areas). **Sprint International Access**
(☎ In the U.K., there are Sprint
access numbers to dial the U.S. using
two different phone types—Mercury:
0500/890877; and British Telecom:
0800/890877; ☎ 800/877–4646 for
other areas).

LONG-DISTANCE CALLS

For long-distance calls within Britain,
dial the area code (which usually
begins with a 01), followed by the
telephone number. The area code
prefix is only used when you are
dialing from outside the city. In
provincial areas, the dialing codes for
nearby towns are often posted in the
booth. For direct overseas dialing,
dial 010, then the country code, area
code, and number. For the international operator, credit card, or collect
calls, dial 155. Bear in mind that
hotels usually levy a hefty (up to
300%) surcharge on calls; it's better
to use the pay phones located in most
hotel foyers or a U.S. calling card.

PUBLIC PHONES

There are three types of public pay
phones: those that accept only coins,
those that accept only phone cards,
and those that take phone cards and
credit cards. For coin-only phones,
insert coins *before* dialing (minimum
charge is 10p). Sometimes phones
have a "press on answer" (POA)
button, which you press when the
caller answers.

For phone card telephones, buy BT
(British Telecom) cards from shops,
post offices, or newsstands. They are
ideal for longer calls, are composed of
units of 10p, and come in values of
£2, £5, £10 and more. An indicator
panel on the phone shows the number
of units you've used; at the end of
your call the card is returned.

TIPPING

Some restaurants and most hotels
add a service charge of 10%–15% to
the bill. In this case, you are not
obliged to tip extra. If no service
charge is indicated, add 10%–15%
to your total bill (but beware when

signing credit voucher slips that you
fill in the correct total in the box).
Taxi drivers should also get 10%–
15%. You are not expected to tip
theater or cinema ushers, elevator
operators, or bartenders in pubs.
Hairdressers and barbers should
receive 10%–15%.

TOUR OPERATORS

Buying a prepackaged tour or independent vacation can make your trip
to Great Britain less expensive and
more hassle-free. Operators that
handle several hundred thousand
travelers per year can use their purchasing power to give you a good
price. Their high volume may also
indicate financial stability. But some
small companies provide more personalized service; because they tend to
specialize, they may also be more
knowledgeable about a given area.

BOOKING WITH AN AGENT

Travel agents are excellent resources.
In fact, large operators accept bookings made only through travel agents.
But it's a good idea to **collect
brochures from several agencies,**
because some agents' suggestions may
be influenced by relationships with
tour and package firms that reward
them for volume sales. If you have a
special interest, **find an agent with
expertise in that area**; ASTA (☞
Travel Agencies, *below*) has a data-
base of specialists worldwide.

**Make sure your travel agent knows
the accommodations** and other services. Ask about the hotel's location,
room size, beds, and whether it has a
pool, room service, or programs for
children, if you care about these. Has
your agent been there in person or
sent others you can contact?

Do some homework on your own,
too: local tourism boards can provide
information about lesser-known and
small-niche operators, some of which
may sell only direct.

BUYER BEWARE

Each year consumers are stranded or
lose their money when tour operators—even very large ones with
excellent reputations—go out of
business. So **check out the operator.**
Find out how long the company has

been in business, and ask several travel agents about its reputation. If the package or tour you are considering is priced lower than in your wildest dreams, **be skeptical.** Try to **book with a company that has a consumer-protection program.** If the operator has such a program, you'll find information about it in the company's brochure. If the operator you are considering does not offer some consumer protection, ask for references from satisfied customers.

In the U.S., members of the National Tour Association and United States Tour Operators Association are required to set aside funds to cover your payments and travel arrangements in case the company defaults. It's also a good idea to choose a company that participates in the American Society of Travel Agent's Tour Operator Program (TOP). This gives you a forum if there are any disputes between you and your tour operator; ASTA will act as mediator.

➤ TOUR-OPERATOR RECOMMENDA-TIONS: **American Society of Travel Agents** (☞ Travel Agencies, *below*). **National Tour Association** (✉ NTA, ✉ 546 E. Main St., Lexington, KY 40508, ☎ 606/226–4444 or 800/755–8687). **United States Tour Operators Association** (✉ USTOA, ✉ 342 Madison Ave., Suite 1522, New York, NY 10173, ☎ 212/599–6599 or 800/468–7862, FAX 212/599–6744).

COSTS

The more your package or tour includes, the better you can predict the ultimate cost of your vacation. Make sure you know exactly what is covered, and **beware of hidden costs.** Are taxes, tips, and service charges included? Transfers and baggage handling? Entertainment and excursions? These can add up.

Prices for packages and tours are usually quoted per person, based on two sharing a room. If traveling solo, you may be required to pay the full double-occupancy rate. Some operators eliminate this surcharge if you agree to be matched with a roommate of the same sex, even if one is not found by departure time.

GROUP TOURS

Among companies that sell tours to Great Britain, the following are nationally known, have a proven reputation, and offer plenty of options. The classifications used below represent different price categories, and you'll probably encounter these terms when talking to a travel agent or tour operator. The key difference is usually in accommodations, which run from budget to better, and better-yet to best.

➤ SUPER-DELUXE: **Abercrombie & Kent** (✉ 1520 Kensington Rd., Oak Brook, IL 60521-2141, ☎ 630/954–2944 or 800/323–7308, FAX 630/954–3324). **Travcoa** (✉ 2350 S.E. Bristol St., Newport Beach, CA 92660, ☎ 714/476–2800 or 800/992–2003, FAX 714/476–2538).

➤ DELUXE: **Globus** (✉ 5301 S. Federal Circle, Littleton, CO 80123-2980, ☎ 303/797–2800 or 800/221–0090, FAX 303/347–2080). **Maupintour** (✉ 1515 St. Andrews Dr., Lawrence, KS 66047, ☎ 913/843–1211 or 800/255–4266, FAX 913/843–8351). **Tauck Tours** (✉ Box 5027, 276 Post Rd. W, Westport, CT 06881-5027, ☎ 203/226–6911 or 800/468–2825, FAX 203/221–6866).

➤ FIRST-CLASS: **Brendan Tours** (✉ 15137 Califa St., Van Nuys, CA 91411, ☎ 818/785–9696 or 800/421–8446, FAX 818/902–9876). **British Airways Holidays** (☎ 800/247–9297). **Caravan Tours** (✉ 401 N. Michigan Ave., Chicago, IL 60611, ☎ 312/321–9800 or 800/227–2826, FAX 312/321–9845). **CIE Tours** (✉ Box 501, 100 Hanover Ave., Cedar Knolls, NJ 07927-0501, ☎ 973/292–3899 or 800/243–8687, FAX 973/292–0463). **Collette Tours** (✉ 162 Middle St., Pawtucket, RI 02860, ☎ 401/728–3805 or 800/832–4656, FAX 401/728–1380). **DER Travel Services** (✉ 9501 W. Devon Ave., Rosemont, IL 60018, ☎ 800/782–2424, FAX 800/282–7474 for information or 800/860–9944 for brochures). **Gadabout Tours** (✉ 700 E. Tahquitz Canyon Way, Palm Springs, CA 92262-6767, ☎ 619/325–5556). **Insight International Tours** (✉ 745 Atlantic Ave., #720, Boston, MA 02111, ☎ 617/482–2000 or 800/582–8380, FAX 617/482–2884 or 800/622–5015). **Trafalgar Tours** (✉ 11 E. 26th St., New York, NY 10010, ☎ 212/689–8977 or 800/854–0103, ℻ 800/457–6644).

➤ BUDGET: **Cosmos** (☞ Globus, *above*). **Trafalgar** (☞ *above*).

PACKAGES

Like group tours, independent vacation packages are available from major tour operators and airlines. The companies listed below offer vacation packages in a broad price range.

➤ AIR/HOTEL: **British Airways Holidays** (☞ above). **Celtic International Tours** (✉ 1860 Western Ave., Albany, NY 12203, ☎ 518/463–5511 or 800/833–4373, ℻ 518/463–8461). **Continental Vacations** (☎ 800/634–5555). **Delta Vacations** (☎ 800/872–7786). **DER Travel Services** (☞ above). **TWA Getaway Vacations** (☎ 800/438–2929). **United Vacations** (☎ 800/328–6877). **US Airways Vacations** (☎ 800/455–0123).

Contact **Budget WorldClass Drive** (☎ 800/527–0700, 0800/181181 in the U.K.) for self-drive itineraries.

THEME TRIPS

➤ ADVENTURE: **Himalayan Travel** (✉ 110 Prospect St., Stamford, CT 06901, ☎ 203/359–3711 or 800/225–2380, ℻ 203/359–3669). **Mountain Travel-Sobek** (✉ 6420 Fairmount Ave., El Cerrito, CA 94530, ☎ 510/527–8100 or 888/687–6235, ℻ 510/525–7710). **Safaricentre** (✉ 3201 N. Sepulveda Blvd., Manhattan Beach, CA 90266, ☎ 310/546–4411 or 800/223–6046, ℻ 310/546–3188). **Wilderness Travel** (✉ 801 Allston Way, Berkeley, CA 94710, ☎ 510/548–0420 or 800/368–2794, ℻ 510/548–0347).

➤ ANTIQUES: **Travel Keys Tours** (✉ Box 162266, Sacramento, CA 95816, ☎ 916/452–5200).

➤ BICYCLING: **Butterfield & Robinson** (✉ 70 Bond St., Toronto, Ontario, Canada M5B 1X3, ☎ 416/864–1354 or 800/678–1147, ℻ 416/864–0541). **Country Lanes** (✉ 9 Shaftesbury St., Fordingbridge, Hampshire SP6 1JF, ☎ 01425/655022, ℻ 0425/655177). **Himalayan Travel** (✉ 110 Prospect St., Stamford, CT 06901, ☎ 203/359–3711 or 800/225–2380,

℻ 203/359–3669) **Vermont Bicycle Touring** (✉ Box 711, Bristol, VT, 05443-0711, ☎ 800/245–3868 or 802/453–4811, ℻ 802/453–4806).

➤ BARGE TRAVEL HOTELS: **H&H Narrowboat Hotels** (✉ 7 Bramshill Gardens, London NW5 1JJ, ☎ ℻ 0171/272–0033).

➤ COOKING SCHOOLS: **Le Cordon Bleu** (✉ 404 Airport Executive Pk., Nanuet, NY 10954, ☎ 800/457–2433).

➤ CUSTOMIZED TOURS: **Avanti Destinations** (✉ 851 SW 6th St., Ste. 1010, Portland, OR, 97204, ☎ 503/295–1100 or 800/422–5053, ℻ 503/295–2723). **4th Dimension Tours** (✉ 7101 S.W. 99th Ave., #106, Miami, FL 33173, ☎ 305/279–0014 or 800/343–0020, ℻ 305/273–9777). **Great British Vacations** (✉ 4800 S.W. Griffith Dr., #125, Beaverton, OR 97005, ☎ 503/643–8080 or 800/452–8434). **Travel Contacts** (✉ Box 173, Camberley, Surrey GU15 1YE, ☎ 0127667–7217, ℻ 012766–3477), which represents 150 tour operators, can satisfy just about any special interest in Great Britain.

➤ FISHING: **Rod and Reel Adventures** (✉ 566 Thomson Ln., Copperopolis, CA 95228, ☎ 209/785–0444, ℻ 209/785–0447).

➤ GOLF: **ITC Golf Tours** (✉ 4134 Atlantic Ave., #205, Long Beach, CA 90807, ☎ 310/595–6905 or 800/257–4981). **Stine's Golftrips** (✉ CHECK ADDRESS Box 2314, Winter Haven, FL 33883-2314, ☎ 407/933–0032 or 800/428–1940, ℻ 407/933–8857).

➤ HOMES AND GARDENS: **Coopersmith's England** (✉ Box 900, Inverness, CA 94937, ☎ 415/669–1914, ℻ 415/669–1942). **Expo Garden Tours** (✉ 70 Great Oak, Redding, CT 06896, ☎ 203/938–0410 or 800/448–2685, ℻ 203/938–0427).

➤ HORSEBACK RIDING: **Cross Country International Equestrian Vacations** (✉ Box 1170, Millbrook, NY 12545, ☎ 800/828–8768, ℻ 914/677–6077). **Equitour FITS Equestrian** (✉ Box 807, Dubois, WY 82513, ☎ 307/455–3363 or 800/545–0019, ℻ 307/455–2354).

➤ LEARNING: **IST Cultural Tours**
(✉ 225 W. 34th St., New York, NY
10122-0913, ☎ 212/563-1202 or
800/833-2111, FAX 212/594-6953).
Smithsonian Study Tours and Seminars (✉ 1100 Jefferson Dr. SW,
Room 3045, MRC 702, Washington,
DC 20560, ☎ 202/357-4700,
FAX 202/633-9250).

➤ LITERARY AND HISTORICAL TOURS:
Fresh Pond Travel Vacations (✉ 186
Alewife Brook Parkway, Cambridge,
MA 02138, ☎ 617/661-9200 or
800/645-0001, FAX 617/661-3354).
Specialty Travel (✉ Box 518, Wenham, MA 01984, ☎ 800/625-2553,
FAX 978/468-5023).

➤ NATURAL HISTORY: **Earthwatch**
(✉ Box 9104, 680 Mount Auburn
St., Watertown, MA 02272, ☎ 617/
926-8200 or 800/776-0188, FAX
617/926-8532) for research expeditions. **Victor Emanuel Nature Tours**
(✉ Box 33008, Austin, TX 78764,
☎ 512/328-5221 or 800/328-8368,
FAX 512/328-2919). **Wilderness
Travel** (✉ 801 Allston Way, Berkeley,
CA 94710, ☎ 510/548-0420 or 800/
368-2794, FAX 510/548-0347).

➤ PERFORMING ARTS: **Dailey-Thorp
Travel** (✉ 330 W. 58th St., #610,
New York, NY 10019-1817, ☎ 212/
307-1555 or 800/998-4677, FAX
212/974-1420). **Keith Prowse Tours**
(✉ 234 W. 44th St., #1000, New
York, NY 10036, ☎ 212/398-1430
or 800/669-7469, FAX 212/302-
4251).

➤ TENNIS: **Championship Tennis
Tours** (✉ 8040 E. Morgan Trail #12,
Scottsdale, AZ 85258, ☎ 602/443-
9499 or 800/468-3664, FAX 602/
443-9882). **Sportstours** (✉ 2301
Collins Ave., #A1540, Miami Beach,
FL 33139, ☎ 800/879-8647, FAX
305/535-0008). **Steve Furgal's International Tennis Tours** (✉ 11828
Rancho Bernardo Rd., #123-305, San
Diego, CA 92128, ☎ 619/675-3555
or 800/258-3664).

➤ WALKING: **Backroads** (✉ 801
Cedar St., Berkeley, CA 94710-1800,
☎ 510/527-1555 or 800/462-2848,
FAX 510-527-1444). **Butterfield &
Robinson** (☞ Bicycling, above).
Country Walkers (✉ Box 180, Waterbury, VT 05676-0180, ☎ 802/244-

1387 or 800/464-9255, FAX 802/
244-5661). **The Wayfarers: Footloose Through the Countryside of
Britain** (✉ Former Wesleyan Chapel,
Ireby, Carlisle CA5 1EQ, ☎ 0169/
732-2383, FAX 0169/732-2394; in
the U.S., ✉ Judy Allpress, The Wayfarers, 172 Bellevue Ave., Newport,
RI 02840, ☎ 401/849-5087 or 800/
249-4620, FAX 401/849-5878).

TRAIN TRAVEL

The long-awaited privatization of the
British rail system raises many questions about the future. Although
changes are happening far more
slowly than was originally projected,
by the time you read this, different
franchises will own various parts of
the rail network. The service should
not have been altered radically. The
main telephone number for **Britrail**
train information, prices, and schedules in Britain is ☎ 0345/484950.
Outside the U.K., dial ☎ 0161/236-
3522. The main administrative office
number is ☎ 0171/928-5151.

The monthly *OAG Rail Guide* (about
£6.95) covers all national rail services
and Eurostar, including private,
narrow-gauge, and steam lines, as
well as special services, buses, ferries,
and rail-based tourist facilities; it's
available at WH Smith branches and
most larger main line rail stations.
You can find detailed timetables of
most rail services in Britain and some
ferry services in the *Thomas Cook
European Timetable*, issued monthly
and available at travel agents and
some general bookstores in the U.S.

Note that travel by train to certain
cities during "peak business hours"
can be much more expensive than at
other hours of the day: A return trip
to London from Bath can cost £59
per person at peak, but only £36.50
at other times. An apex ticket bought
seven days in advance can save even
more, and cost only around £17.50.

DISCOUNT PASSES

If you plan to travel by train in Great
Britain, **consider purchasing a BritRail
Pass,** which gives unlimited travel
over the entire British Rail Network
and will save you money. You must
**buy your BritRail Pass before you
leave home.** They are available from

most travel agents or from BritRail Travel International (☞ Discount Passes, *below*). Note that EurailPasses are not honored in Britain and that the rates listed here are subject to change; year to year, slight increases are usually the order of the day.

The cost of a BritRail adult pass for 8 days is $249 standard and $355 first-class; for 15 days, $379 standard and $549 first-class; for 22 days, $485 and $700; and for a month, $565 and $800. The Youth Pass, for those ages 16–25, provides unlimited second-class travel and costs $199 for 8 days, $305 for 15 days, $389 for 22 days, and $450 for one month. The Senior Pass, for passengers over 60, is first-class only and costs $305 for 8 days, $469 for 15 days, $595 for 22 days, and $695 for one month. (These are U.S. dollar figures; Canadian prices will be a bit higher.) There are also Flexipasses, which allow 4, 8, or 15 days' travel in one month.

If you want the flexibility of a car combined with the speed and comfort of the train, try BritRail/Drive (from about $285 for one adult, with a $148 supplement for additional adults and $72.50 for children 5–15); this gives you a three-day BritRail Flexipass and three vouchers valid for Hertz car rental from more than 100 locations throughout Great Britain. A six-day rail pass with seven days of car rental is also available (from $490 car and driver, with $210 adult supplement, $105 children, with a current "free child per adult" deal for children under 5 traveling gratis). Larger cars, automatic transmission, and first-class rail seats will cost you more. If you call your travel agency or Hertz's international desk (☞ Car Rental *above*), the car of your choice will be waiting for you at the station as you alight from your train.

There is also a BritRail + Eurostar Flexipass that includes a round-trip rail journey through the Channel Tunnel to Paris; prices range from $383 (for a four-day round trip) to $445 (for an eight-day round trip).

If you want to explore a specific part of Britain in greater detail, the series of Regional Rail Rover unlimited

travel tickets offers excellent value; there are also All Line Rovers, covering the whole of Britain. Contact the Rail Travel Centres for details.

The Freedom of Scotland Travelpass allows unlimited standard-class travel: $159 for 8 days, $220 for 15 days, and $289 for 22 days. A Scotland Flexipass allows 8 days of travel over a 15-day period for $185.

Many travelers assume that rail passes guarantee them seats on the trains they wish to ride. Not so. You need to **book seats ahead even if you are using a rail pass**; seat reservations are required on some European trains, particularly high-speed trains, and are a good idea on trains that may be crowded—particularly in summer on popular routes. You will also need a reservation if you purchase sleeping accommodations.

➤ DISCOUNT PASSES: BritRail Passes are available from most travel agents or from **BritRail Travel International** (✉ 1500 Broadway, New York, NY 10036, ☎ 212/575–2667 or 800/677–8585; ✉ 94 Cumberland St., Toronto, Ontario M5R 1A3, ☎ 416/482–1777). For other discount rail passes, contact **Rail Travel Centres at the large mainline London or regional stations, such as Euston, King's Cross, Edinburgh, and so on.** (✉ Euston Station, London NW1 1DF, ☎ 0345/484950).

TRAVEL AGENCIES

A good travel agent puts your needs first. Look for an agency that has been in business at least five years, emphasizes customer service, and has someone on staff who specializes in your destination. In addition, **make sure the agency belongs to a professional trade organization,** such as ASTA in the United States. If your travel agency is also acting as your tour operator, *see* Buyer Beware in Tour Operators, *above*).

➤ LOCAL AGENT REFERRALS: **American Society of Travel Agents** (ASTA, ☎ 800/965–2782 24-hr hot line, FAX 703/684–8319). **Association of Canadian Travel Agents** (✉ Suite 201, 1729 Bank St., Ottawa, Ontario K1V 7Z5, ☎ 613/521–0474, FAX 613/521–0805). **Association of British**

Travel Agents (✉ 55–57 Newman St., London W1P 4AH, ☎ 0171/637–2444, FAX 0171/637–0713). **Australian Federation of Travel Agents** (☎ 02/9264–3299). **Travel Agents' Association of New Zealand** (☎ 04/499–0104).

TRAVEL GEAR

Travel catalogs specialize in useful items, such as compact alarm clocks and travel irons, that can **save space when packing.** They also offer dual-voltage appliances, currency converters, and foreign-language phrase books.

➤ CATALOGS: **Magellan's** (☎ 800/962–4943, FAX 805/568–5406). **Orvis Travel** (☎ 800/541–3541, FAX 540/343–7053). **TravelSmith** (☎ 800/950–1600, FAX 800/950–1656).

U.S. GOVERNMENT

Government agencies can be an excellent source of inexpensive travel information. When planning your trip, **find out what government materials are available.**

➤ ADVISORIES: **U.S. Department of State** (✉ Overseas Citizens Services Office, ✉ Room 4811 N.S., Washington, DC 20520; ☎ 202/647–5225 or FAX 202/647–3000 interactive hot line; ☎ 301/946–4400 computer bulletin board); enclose a self-addressed, stamped, business-size envelope.

➤ PAMPHLETS: **Consumer Information Center** (✉ Consumer Information Catalogue, Pueblo, CO 81009, ☎ 719/948–3334 or 888/878–3256) for a free catalog that lists travel titles.

VISITOR INFORMATION

➤ IN THE U.S.: **British Tourist Authority (BTA)** (✉ 551 5th Ave., 7th Floor, New York, NY 10176, ☎ 212/986–2200 or 800/462–2748; ✉ 625 N. Michigan Ave., Suite 1510, Chicago, IL 60611 (personal callers only); ✉ 620 Cranberry Place, Roswell, GA 30076 (no personal callers), ☎ 404/594–8818); ✉ Columbus Center, 1 Alhambra Plaza, Suite 1465, Coral Gables, FL 33134 (personal callers only).

➤ IN CANADA: (✉ 111 Avenue Rd., 4th floor, Toronto, Ontario M5R 3J8, ☎ 416/925–6326).

➤ IN THE U.K.: (✉ Thames Tower, Black's Rd., London W6 9EL, ☎ 0181/846–9000).

➤ IN LONDON: **London Tourist Information Centre** (Victoria Station Forecourt, summer, Mon.–Sat. 8–7 and Sun. 8–5; winter, Mon.–Sat. 8–6 and Sun. 8:30–4). **British Travel Centre** (✉ 12 Regent St., SW1Y 4PQ Oct.–Apr., weekdays 9–6:30, weekends 10–4; May–Sept., weekdays 9–6:30, Sat. 9–5, Sun. 10–4).

➤ BY PHONE: The London Tourist Board's **Visitorcall** (☎ 0839/123456) phone guide to London gives information about events, theater, museums, transport, shopping, and restaurants. A three-month events calendar (☎ 0839/401279) and an annual version (☎ 0839/401278) are available by fax (set fax machine to polling mode, or press start/receive after the tone). Visitorcall charges are 39p–49p per minute, depending on the time of the call. Note that this service is only accessible in the U.K.

➤ BY MAGAZINE AND NEWSPAPER: *Tatler, Harpers & Queen, British Vogue, World of Interiors, British House &Garden, The Face, London Times,* the *Evening Standard,* the *Independent,* and the *Manchester Guardian.*

WEB SITE

Do check out the World Wide Web when you're planning. You'll find everything from up-to-date weather forecasts to virtual tours of famous cities. Fodor's Web site, www.fodors.com, is a great place to start your on-line travels. For more information specifically on Great Britain, visit:

www.fodors.com,
www.visitbritain.com,
www.usagateway.vistibritain.com,
www.demon.co.uk/hotel-uk,
www.timeout.co.uk,
www.officiallondontheatre.co.uk,
www.ukcalling.co.uk.royal-albert.

WHEN TO GO

The British tourist season is year-round—with short lulls. It peaks from mid-April to mid-October, with another burst at Christmas (although most historic houses are closed from

SMART TRAVEL TIPS

THE GOLD GUIDE / SMART TRAVEL TIPS

October to Easter). Spring is the time to see the countryside at its freshest and greenest, while in fall the northern moorlands and Scottish Highlands are at their most colorful. June is a good month to visit Wales and the Lake District. During July and August, when most of the British take their vacations, accommodations in the most popular resorts and areas are in high demand and at their most expensive. The winter season in London is lively with the opera, ballet, and West End theater among the prime attractions.

CLIMATE

In the main, the climate is mild, although the weather has been extremely volatile in recent years. Summer temperatures can reach the 90s and the atmosphere can be humid. In winter there can be heavy frost, snow, thick fog, and, of course, rain.

The following list includes the average daily maximum and minimum temperatures for three major cities in Britain—but note that they are based on long-term averages and do not necessarily reflect the climatic swings of the last few years.

➤ FORECASTS: **Weather Channel Connection** (☎ 900/932–8437), 95¢ per minute from a Touch-Tone phone.

ABERYSTWYTH (WALES)

Jan.	44F	7C	May	58F	15C	Sept.	62F	16C
	36	2		45	7		51	11
Feb.	44F	7C	June	62F	16C	Oct.	56F	13C
	35	2		50	10		46	8
Mar.	49F	9C	July	64F	18C	Nov.	50F	10C
	38	4		54	12		41	5
Apr.	52F	11C	Aug.	65F	18C	Dec.	47F	8C
	41	5		54	12		38	4

EDINBURGH (SCOTLAND)

Jan.	42F	6C	May	56F	14C	Sept.	60F	16C
	34	1		43	6		49	9
Feb.	43F	6C	June	62F	17C	Oct.	54F	12C
	34	1		49	9		44	7
Mar.	46F	8C	July	65F	18C	Nov.	48F	9C
	36	2		52	11		39	4
Apr.	51F	11C	Aug.	64F	18C	Dec.	44F	7C
	39	4		52	11		36	2

LONDON

Jan.	43F	6C	May	62F	17C	Sept.	65F	19C
	36	2		47	8		52	11
Feb.	44F	7C	June	69F	20C	Oct.	58F	14C
	36	2		53	12		46	8
Mar.	50F	10C	July	71F	22C	Nov.	50F	10C
	38	3		56	14		42	5
Apr.	56F	13C	Aug.	71F	21C	Dec.	45F	7C
	42	6		56	13		38	4

1 Destination: Great Britain

TRUE BRIT

THE BRITISH ARE DIFFERENT, and proud of it. They still have odd customs, like driving on the left and playing cricket. Only reluctantly have they decimalized, turning their cherished pints into liters (except when ordering beer) and inches into centimeters. Until 1971 they still had a bizarre, three-tier, nondecimal coinage, whereby a meal check might add up, say, to four pounds six shillings and sevenpence halfpenny. And although the rest of Europe counts distances in kilometers, the British still cling to their miles—though they now buy fabric in meters, not yards. Logic is not always a prominent feature of the British character.

These are symptoms of a certain psychological gulf still existing between Britain and the rest of Europe, a gulf not greatly narrowed by its membership in the European Union since 1973. The English Channel, a relatively thin thread of water between Dover and Calais, has played a crucial role in British history, acting as a kind of moat to protect the "island fortress" from invaders (witness 1940), and preserving a separate mentality. Many Britons want to keep that moat, hence their wariness—more emotional than economic—of the Channel Tunnel. It is difficult to estimate just how deeply the opening of the tunnel will affect the British psyche. They have resisted integration into Europe for so many centuries that the reality of a link open for 24 hours a day, whatever the weather, may well be traumatic. Even today, that oft-quoted old newspaper headline, "Fog in Channel, Continent Isolated," retains some validity. But this proud and insular nation is not unwelcoming to visitors. On its own terms, it is glad to show them the delights and virtues of what it believes to be one of the most genuinely civilized societies in the world.

There is still some truth in the popular foreign perception that the British are reserved. They are given to understatement—"It's not bad" is the nearest Brits may get to showing enthusiasm—and may look a little solemn and stiff-upper-lipped, because they don't easily show their emotions. But they are not on the whole unhappy, even in today's anxious times. The British are easygoing, accepting of nonconformity and eccentricity, and their strong sense of humor and love of the absurd keeps them on an even keel. They have a strange habit of poking good-humored fun at what they love without meaning disrespect, not least at royalty and religion. This kind of humor often disconcerts foreigners.

It is a densely populated land. Scotland and Wales have wide open spaces but in England people are crammed 940 to the square mile, more thickly than in any European country save Holland. But it is also a green and fertile land, and because the countryside is a limited commodity, the English tend it with special loving care. Everywhere are trim hedgerows, tidy flower beds, and lawns mown smooth as billiard tables—one Oxford don, asked by an American visitor how the college lawn came to be so perfect, said casually, "Oh, it's been mown every Tuesday for the past 500 years." The English love gardens but are also at ease in untamed surroundings. They relish hiking over moors where the westerly gales blow, or splashing rubber-booted through streams, or bird-watching in a quiet copse. A few people, in their black or scarlet coats and riding caps, still go fox hunting with hounds—"the unspeakable in full pursuit of the uneatable," as Oscar Wilde put it. Others are violent in their condemnation of this blood sport.

This smallish island contains great scenic variety. The Midlands and much of eastern England tend to be flat and dull. But the watery fenlands, between Cambridge and the sea, the low horizons broken by rows of poplars or by a distant windmill or tall church spire have a misty, poetic quality, and the sunsets and swirling clouds evoke Turner skyscapes. Kent, southeast of London, with its cherry and apple orchards, is known as the garden of England; west of here are the wooded hills of Surrey, and to the southwest the bold, bare ridge of the South Downs, beloved of Kipling. Although the east coast of

Britain is mainly smooth, with long sandy beaches and an occasional chalky cliff, the west coast is far more rugged: Here the Atlantic gales set the seas lashing against the rocky headlands of Cornwall and south Wales.

The spine of northern England is a line of high hills, the Pennines, where sheep graze on lonely moors, and just to the west is the beautiful, mountainous Lake District, where Wordsworth lived. Scotland is even more lonely and mountainous. Beyond the urban belt of the lowlands around Edinburgh, you enter the romantic realm of the Highlands, a thinly populated region where heather and gorse cover the hillsides above silent fjordlike lochs and verdant glens. Roads here are few, but they all seem to lead westward to the Isles, blue-gray jewels in a silver Atlantic sea, with their strange Celtic names: Barra, Eigg, Benbecula, Skye.

Western Britain is washed by the warm waters of the Gulf Stream, and therefore its climate is mild and damp. Indeed, Britain's weather is something of a stock joke, and some foreigners imagine the whole country permanently shrouded in fog. This has not been true for years, since the use of smokeless fuel has cleared polluted mists from urban skies. Yet the weather *is* very changeable, by south European standards, with shower and shine often following each other in swift succession. At least it provides the thrill of the unexpected.

BRITAIN IS A LAND where the arts flourish. It is true that the artist, writer, or philosopher is not held in the same public esteem as, say, in France. The average Briton affects a certain philistinism, and "intellectual" and "arty" are common terms of reproach. Yet today's London is home to many of the most important, new and cutting-edge artists, designers, and writers in the world. Sales of books and of theater and concert tickets are amazingly high. Helped by the worldwide spread of the English language, the British publishing industry produces around 50,000 new titles a year—perhaps too many for profitability. A passion for classical music developed during the last war and has continued ever since, so that even the smallest town has its choral society performing Bach or Handel. London theater is regarded by many as the best around. In the provinces, hundreds of theaters, some of them small fringe groups in makeshift premises, attract ready audiences.

CULTURE THRIVES ALSO in a classical mode—for example, through the Royal Shakespeare Company with its base in the Bard's hometown of Stratford-upon-Avon. Like Shakespeare, many leading British writers and other creative artists are closely associated with some particular place, in a land where literature and the other arts have always been nourished by strong local roots, by some *genius loci*. A tour around Britain can thus become a series of cultural pilgrimages: to the Dorset that inspired the novels of Thomas Hardy, to the wild Yorkshire moors where the Brontë sisters lived and wrote, to Wordsworth's beloved Lake District, to the Scottish Border landscapes that pervade the novels of Sir Walter Scott, to Laugharne on the south Wales coast that Dylan Thomas's *Under Milk Wood* has immortalized, to Dickensian London, to the Constable country on the Suffolk/Essex border, or to nearby Aldeburgh where composer Benjamin Britten lived.

These personalities belong to British history—a long history that Britons tend to take for granted, though it lies deep in their psyche. Its memorials are on every side. It began in times long before Christ, when huge stone circles were raised at Stonehenge and Avebury, on the Wiltshire downs. Then came the Romans, who left their imprint across the land up to Hadrian's Wall in the north. Great feudal castles survive as reminders of the dark days when barons and kings were in constant conflict, and peaceful fields the length and breadth of the land became nightmarish landscapes of blood and death. Stately redbrick Elizabethan manors bear witness to the more settled and civilized age of Good Queen Bess.

Britain is rich in picturesque old towns and villages whose streets are lined with buildings dating from medieval or Elizabethan days, or later with old half-timber houses where black beams crisscross the white plasterwork, or with carefully proportioned facades that bring a measured classical elegance to the townscape. In many areas, buildings are of local stone—most strikingly in the mellow golden-brown Cotswold villages—and often a simple cottage is topped with a neat thatch roof. Above all, British architecture is famed for its cathedrals dating mostly from the Middle Ages, with Wells, Ely, and Durham among the finest. Local churches, too, are often of great beauty, especially in East Anglia where the wealth of the 15th-century wool trade led to the building of majestic churches on the edge of quite modest villages. Church builders of the past were profligate in their service to God, and modern Britain is deeply in their debt. Unfortunately, the Church is just as deeply in debt, because it has these mammoth edifices to maintain with dwindling congregations to help with its finances.

Despite constant social upheavals, the British maintain many of their special traditions. On a village green in summer, you may see a cricket match in progress between two white-clad teams. It is a slow and stately game that will seem boring to the uninitiated, yet is full of its own skills and subtleties. In village pubs people frequently play darts, or perhaps backgammon, checkers, or chess.

British society, although troubled by doubts and uncertainties, and constantly challenged to resolve key social problems, is certainly not in terminal decline, or even slowly fading away. But it is deeply troubled and seriously questioning many of its traditional, long-accepted institutions. As an American observer remarked during the Falklands War, "The British can be relied upon to fall at every hurdle—except the last." When the chips are down, the British come up trumps. This can't be explained rationally. What was it that sank the Spanish Armada or defeated Goering's Luftwaffe? It certainly wasn't superior economic resources or disciplined social organization. Maybe there is more in the souls of a free people united in a common purpose than generations of economists and sociologists could ever hope to understand. The British are such a people; and their quirkiness, their social "distance," and their habit of driving on the left are inseparable parts of a greater whole. Without Britain, even a changed Britain, the world would be a poorer place.

NEW AND NOTEWORTHY

It probably hasn't escaped your notice—especially since you're reading this and are planning a trip there—that London has undergone a huge resurgence and is now acclaimed as the center of Europe. It all started with Tony Blair, the dynamic, young(ish) Labour Prime Minister, and with the National Lottery, which continues to fund exciting projects. The New London is still booming, and the city's art, style, dining, and fashion scenes continue to sizzle. When your plane touches down at Heathrow, you will be assailed by one other realization: England is in the grip of millennium fever, which will only intensify as the numbers creep toward the big 2000. The nation is obsessed.

Among the several buildings due to open on or around the big day is the (rather infamous, some would say) **Millennium Dome,** at Greenwich. This multimillion-pound thing—actually a 320-meter structure designed by architect-provocateur Richard Rogers—is terribly controversial. The original plan was for it to house an extravaganza staged by that maestro of the musical, Cameron Mackintosh, but this scheme was axed early in 1998 because of the escalating costs and the impossible logistics. Now there is to be a cornucopia of architectural installations set up around the dome, including one by the avant-garde three woman outfit, Muff. Nothing about this project promises to be dull. However, what there is to see now—the Dome's shell—is not worth the long trip downstream, unless you're planning to revisit the wonders of the Royal Observatory, the Prime Meridien, or the Maritime Museum, et al.—which are, of course, highly recommended. If you do head out that way, you could drop in on the Millennium Experience Visitor Centre (Pepys House, Royal Naval College), with its graphic displays, models, videos, and interactive monitors—but don't expect much, since this is really designed for the locals, with employment information and the like on offer. May 2000 will see the 10-day **Millennium Maritime Festival** in the vicinity, with 2,000 vessels moored in and around Docklands, and races and such. Festivals of all sorts will be rife, but details are not yet available.

Docklands—the neighborhood in the southeast that contains Canary Wharf and the U.K.'s tallest building—has been picking up steam as a tourist destination in its own right, welcoming a third more visitors last year than the year before. Unfortunately, now the area has been left to fend for itself with the 1998 closing of the London Docklands Visitor Centre, though the Canary Wharf Tourist Information Centre (☎ 0171/512–9800) remains in place, as does the helpful TourEast London (☎ 0171/512–8512), which exists largely to promote the attractions of the charming East End. In January of the millennium, the Museum in Docklands will open to suck up all this disparate information and dispense it to you. Until then, why not view the Dome as part of the Tower of London's new package deal with Catamaran Cruisers; it includes a Yeoman Warder tour of the Crown Jewels in the morning, and a cruise to Greenwich in the afternoon, for a reasonable £12.50 (24-hr reservations line: ☎ 0345/023842).

Two new museums have hit the London scene recently: the **BBC Experience** is a guided tour of the Broadcasting House of the British Broadcasting Corporation—those fabulous folks who brought you Masterpiece Theater—including the Marconi Collection of early audiovisual equipment, and interactive bits where you can play at directing *EastEnders,* the popular cockney TV soap, or cast yourself in a role on *Desert Island Discs*. Modern art buffs will want to take in Islington's first major museum, the **Estorick Collection of Italian Art,** which features those naughty Futurists in a renovated Georgian building (Northhampton Lodge, 39A Cannonbury Sq., N1, ☎ 0171/704–9522). Don't forget to check out the new **British Library,** too, which already offers selected services to readers, although everything won't be completely operational until mid-1999. Note that you won't be able to browse the stacks without a special reader's ticket, any more than you ever could at the library's former haunt—the old, beautiful Reading Room at the British Museum, which is being redeveloped as part of the museum's Great Court Scheme, to be completed in, yes, the millennium.

As for the performing arts, the picture is a bit gloomy. Indeed, the Muses seem to be, for all intents and purposes, practically homeless in London these days. The world-renowned **Royal Opera House** is still shuttered, owing to an ongoing renovation. Its resident troupes are taking up temporary shelter, gypsylike, at other theaters in the interim. For the 1998–99 season, the **Royal Opera** will present full opera productions at the Barbican Theatre, the Shaftesbury Theater, and Royal Albert Hall, and concert versions at Royal Festival Hall, Barbican Hall, and Royal Albert Hall. The **Royal Ballet** has been performing in the Labatt's Apollo Theatre in Hammersmith and Royal Festival Hall; for the 1998–99 season, most productions should be concentrated in the newly refurbished Sadler's Wells Theatre. The English National Opera—or **ENO**, as it is called—has abandoned the Coliseum, its home since 1968. Possible sites for a new house, funded by the Lottery, include several places along the South Bank, King's Cross, or the sadly disused yet magisterial Battersea Power Station. Further clouds: late-breaking word has come that the **Royal Shakespeare Theatre** will no longer offer a summer season (which means that, yes, you may have to journey up to Stratford-upon-Avon to catch a summer performance of this legendary troupe—but better check with their London box office first, as all plans have not been finalized) and the Old Vic theater may close, with a resultant eviction of some of London's livelier theater troupes. Even with these trials and tribulations, the curtain has far from rung down on the arts scene in London. There are still a dazzling array of events to attend—as you'll see when you check out the weekly listings in *Time Out*.

Back in the former County Hall, above the Aquarium, are two new hotels, the **County Hall Marriott** and the **Travel Inn Capital.** Other hotels—opening too late for inclusion this go-round—were the luxurious One Aldwych, near the legendary Strand Hotel, the more modest Stakis Islington, and a slew of budget-level hotels outside the city center: a 224-room Holiday Inn Express in the City and a 50-room one in Victoria; the Park Plaza Hotel and a Travel Inn Capital in Euston; plus the swankier Chelsea Village (which is actually in Fulham); and a flagship 314-room Posthouse Forte hotel next to Canary Wharf that is expected to open in spring 1999. To get you there, the new Heathrow

Express is up and running—well, at least to Paddington, if not Docklands.

And so to restaurants. Ah, the restaurants. We are all wondering: how far can this thing go? How many new, trendy, talked-out, flavor-of-the-month gastrodomes can the city support? Of course, visitors seem to be doing their part by eating in a different place every meal. Even so, there will be at least 500 eateries even newer than the present listings, but never mind, just read up on them in the food supplements of the newspapers, especially the Saturday and Sunday editions, or log onto the London Tourist Board's restaurant Web site at **www.londondining.co.uk/london/dining/.** Our listings, now as ever, strike a balance between the new-and-trendy and the old-and-reliable, and include places where you can just get well fed without having to perform in some dining-as-theater routine. The new places are so numerous we can barely keep up with them, but we've reviewed some of the best and most talked about, including **Aubergine, Bluebird, Zafferano,** and the **Pharmacy** (a reasonable simulacrum of an actual pharmacy, down to the waitstaff garbed in hospital white. Of course, you won't want to miss some of the new luxe pubs that have heated up the scene, such as **The Enterprise** and **The Cow.** That is all we're going to tell you about newer-than-new London. Enjoy the city of cities, and congratulations for arriving before the millennium.

Meanwhile, in nearby Windsor, **renovations to Windsor Castle,** necessitated by the catastrophic fire of November 1992, have been completed. Heading over to Liverpool, the august National Trust (the overseers of such landmarks as Blenheim Palace and Knole) has recently opened **a new Beatles landmark**—the childhood Merseyside home of Paul McCartney, located at 20 Forthlin Road, in the Liverpool section of Allerton. Acquired by the National Trust in 1995, the mid-terraced 1950s council house is significant as the place where the Beatles were "born"—occupied by the McCartney family from 1955–63, it was here that Sir Paul lived from the age of 13 until the Beatles became established and where the group convened to compose songs and practice. Tours are only given by advance booking and via a special mini-bus service to the Liverpool neighborhood where the Beatle grew up.

Also in the city by the Mersey, the **dockside Tate Gallery** has re-opened after its long refit looking a lot better than before and sporting a café-restaurant that's added a bit of glamour to Albert Dock. More museum renovation, this time in Bradford, Yorkshire. The National Museum of Photography, Film, and Television has been revitalized, bringing together its high-tech collection and associated Pictureville movie house under one roof.

A restyled **Manchester city center** is slowly emerging from the debris of the IRA bombing of 1996. Most major renovations projects should be completed during 1999 and 2000, and massive new retail outlets—Marks & Spencer certainly, possibly Harvey Nichols, plus a host of other new names—are beginning to put down roots. In the meantime, new bars and restaurants are opening as fast as in London: Mash & Air has been only the first of a new-wave of mega-restaurants. The Gay Village has also gone from strength to strength, making it Britain's most active and enjoyable gay scene. Down in the West Country, the biggest event for 1999 is the **total eclipse of the sun,** due to take place August 11. The south coast of Cornwall is the best place to view this phenomenon and hotels are already taking bookings. Over in Wales, the top story is that work is proceeding with the construction of **Cardiff's** new national stadium, with completion expected in time for the 1999 Rugby World Cup, which the city is hosting. The new stadium will replace the famous Cardiff Arms Park, recognized worldwide as a shrine to the game of rugby.

Scotland's Glasgow is the **"U.K. City of Architecture and Design for 1999"** and will be the showcase for exhibitions in a comprehensive range of design disciplines, from product and graphic design to architecture and interiors. Venues will include Glasgow's galleries and museums, a new center for architecture and design called the Lighthouse (occupying a Charles Rennie Mackintosh–designed building), and other cutting-edge exhibition spaces citywide. Local community involvement will be a central focus, with new people-friendly housing, public plazas, and an access guide for disabled people among the extensive plans.

WHAT'S WHERE

London

If London contained only its famous landmarks—the Tower of London, St. Paul's, Big Ben, Parliament, Buckingham Palace—and its fabulous museums—the Victoria & Albert, the Tate and National galleries, and the British Museum—it would still rank as one of the world's top tourist destinations. But London is more—much, much more. It is a bevy of British bobbies, an ocean of black umbrellas, an unconquered continuance of more than 2,000 years of history. It's really a case of East End, West End, all around the town. The trick to taming Europe's largest city is to regard it as a number of villages. There is the heraldic splendor of Westminster, the chic of artistic Chelsea, the glamour of Kensington and Belgravia, the cosmopolitan charms of Soho, the ancient core of the City, and the East End, home of the irrepressible cockney. No matter which district you adopt as your home-away-from-home, London's contrasts can best be savored by strolling from one neighborhood to another, wandering thoroughfares of stately houses that lie next to a mélange of mean streets. With some of the best restaurants, hotels, shops, theater, dance, and opera around, London is simply the most interesting city in Europe.

The Southeast

Everyone wins in the Southeast. Here you'll find Kent—the "Garden of England"—major English icons, such as Canterbury Cathedral, the white cliffs of Dover, and Brighton's Royal Pavilion, and everywhere there are villages grown drowsy with age. Here, too, is that triumph of civilization, the stately country house in all its splendor. Knole, Ightham Mote, Penhurst Place, Sissinghurst—when viewed from afar, they seem to look like old master paintings set on easels. For a journey back to the Middle Ages, head first to the extraordinary castles of Bodiam, Leeds, and Hever. Because of the area's proximity to London, visitors with limited time can make easy excursions and round up a delightful choice of day trips options.

The South

The South is for time travelers. In just a few days (or even a long weekend) you can go from prehistoric Stonehenge to Victorian Salisbury. History has highlights by the hundreds here—Winchester Cathedral, Wilton House, and Beaulieu Abbey are just a few of the superlatives. And like a library, the South is tailor-made for browsing, thanks to its many literary landmarks. Make a pilgrimage to Jane Austen Country or travel to Dorset—immortalized by Thomas Hardy as his part-fact, part-fiction county of Wessex—to get away from the madding crowd. Central to England's history for more than four centuries, other destinations in the South remain highly popular: from the neoclassic beauty spot of Stourhead to the Isle of Wight's peaceful shores, from the New Forest's wild scenery to bustling ports such as Southampton and Portsmouth.

The West Country

Half the fun of exploring the three counties of Somerset, Devon, and Cornwall that make up the West Country is getting lost. Begin with Bristol—gateway to the West Country and fabled shipping port. You'll find on your way down to Land's End at the southernmost point of this long peninsula, every zig and zag of the road reveals rugged moorlands—this is where *The Hound of the Baskervilles* was set—lush river valleys, and festive coastal resorts. Explore the mist-wreathed sights of King Arthur Country, then head for Clovelly, jewel of the British Riviera. Beyond lie ancient market towns and romantic coves once frequented by Sir Francis Drake and other Elizabethan-era seafarers. Along the way, take in the region's beaches for that bracing wind-in-your-face feeling. Whatever your itinerary, be sure to stray from the main roads—it would be a great pity not to.

The Channel Islands

With more than 2,000 hours of sunshine ever year, the Channel Islands remains a favorite getaway for Britishers and tourists alike. This is England with a French accent; Jersey and Guernsey lie just off the coast of Brittany. These islands have excellent walking trails along majestic cliffs with fantastic ocean views. Pleasures await—pretty fishing harbors, princely villas (don't miss Victor Hugo's historic house in St. Peter Port), and sublime crab creole. But everyone winds up on the white-sand beaches; after all, the sun is yours for the basking.

The Thames Valley

The crack of a polo ball echoes across Windsor Great Park as Prince Charles scores another point. He loves to escape to his family abode here—Windsor, the largest inhabited castle in the world—and many Londoners follow, heading for tranquil Thames-side villages, each more charming than the last. Little wonder Kenneth Grahame was inspired to write *The Wind in the Willows* by the idyllic river scenes near Mapledurham (the great stately manor here was, in fact, the model for Toad Hall). In June and July all head for the Henley Royal Regatta to toast rowing's best with Pimm's "champers" and Kent strawberries. Year-round, the top magnet remains the great city of Oxford—seat of England's oldest university. Be sure to catch, nearby, the power, pomp, and solid magnificence of Blenheim Palace and the pretty-as-a-postcard village of Woodstock.

Shakespeare Country

Lovers of Shakespeare, and even those with only a passing acquaintance with the Bard, cannot resist the lure of the country in which he grew up, worked and—after a career in London—died. The center is, of course, Stratford-upon-Avon: The man dominates this town and magnificent Elizabethan-era sites bear witness to his days here—Shakespeare's Birthplace, Anne Hathaway's Cottage, and the Grammar School to name just three. Here, too, is the Royal Shakespeare Theatre, the greatest repertory theater in the world. If Stratford remains the focus for the visitor, Warwickshire—the ancient county of which Stratford is the southern nexus—also beckons. With its sleepy villages, thatched roofs, and quiet vistas, it is picture-postcard land—the birthplace of that image of "merrie olde Englande" which has been spread over the breadth of the world by the works of Shakespeare. Here, heaping doses of history await the traveler: the castles at Warwick Castle—"medieval England in stone"—and Kenilworth, the regal manor houses of Charlecote Park and Baddesley Clinton, and other time-hallowed stately piles.

The Heart of England

The "Heart of England" is a term we have borrowed from the tourist powers-that-be—and by which is meant the heart of *tourist* England, so immensely popular are its attractions. Begin with the city of Bath—nowhere else can one see, as the eminent writer Nigel Nicolson put it, "18th-century England in all its urban glory." After following in the footsteps of Beau Nash and Jane Austen through Bath's splendid terraces and crescents, head northwards to Regency-era Cheltenham to embark on a tour of the Cotswolds, a magical region which conjures up England at its most blissfully rural. More than ever, visitors come here to taste fully the glories of the old English village: its thatched roofs, low-ceiling rooms, and gardens meticulously built on a gentle slope. The finest Cotswold towns include Chipping Campden, Upper Slaughter, and Bourton-on-the-Water, but don't forget to explore such beauty spots as Hidcote Manor Gardens and Owlpen Manor. Near Gloucester is the sylvan Forest of Dean—a 25,000-acre paradise for hikers and nature lovers.

The Welsh Borders

Along England's border with the principality of Wales lies some of England's loveliest and most peaceful countryside. The border stretches from the town of Chepstow on the Severn estuary in the south to the city of Chester in the north. Herefordshire, in the south, has rich, rolling countryside and river valleys, gradually opening out to Shropshire's high hills and plateaus. In the north, the gentler Cheshire plain is dairy country, dotted with small villages and market towns, full of 13th- and 14th-century black-and-white, half-timber buildings typical of northwestern England. A highlight for some is the "Black Country" (named for its 19th-century coal pits); from Shrewsbury to Chester, you'll find several monuments of the industrial revolution, including the legendary Ironbridge Gorge. Gateway to the region from the British heartland is the bustling city of Birmingham, now undergoing an urban renaissance.

Wales

Many visitors still perceive Wales in terms of the *How Green Was My Valley* film of half a century ago—but today Wales is evergreen and unspoiled. On the western border of England, this is a country of outstanding natural beauty, with mountain scenery in its interior and long stretches of magnificent coastline. As conclusive proof of its scenic grandeur, Wales is home to three national parks, with Snowdonia the monarch of all it surveys. Both artistic *and* natural riches await: numerous medieval castles, the slate caverns at Blaenau Ffestiniog, charming seaside resorts, restored 19th-century mining villages, the glorious Bodnant Garden, the Victorian spa of Llandrindod Wells, steam train rides through the mountains of Snowdonia and central Wales, and the capital of Cardiff.

Lancashire and the Peaks

Birthplace of the boom and bravura of the industrial revolution, this northwest area still claims bustling cities like Manchester and Liverpool, renowned today for their championship soccer teams and rock legends. Fans of John, Paul, George, and Ringo will undoubtedly want to go on some of the special Liverpool tours tracing the Beatles' earliest days. As a respite, escape to the emerald tranquillity of the Peak District and Derbyshire's Wye Valley—home to two of the most regal houses in the land, Haddon Hall and Chatsworth. The district draws many hikers who delight in the area's rocky outcrops and meadowland. On the Lancashire coast, visitors can enjoy popular seaside resorts, the largest being Blackpool, with miles of beaches, a huge amusement park, and acres of gardens.

The Lake District

Bordered by Scotland and the waters of Solway Firth, Morecambe Bay, and the Irish Sea, this is a startlingly beautiful area of high and craggy hills, wild moorland, small stone-built villages, and, of course, glittering silvery lakes—more than 100 of them. The Lake District has been one of the most popular tourist destinations in Britain almost since the beginning of the 19th century, when poets and painters—Wordsworth, who was born and lived here, and Turner foremost among them—first extolled the region's allure. High points of any tour include Wordsworth's homes at Rydal Mount and Grasmere, John Ruskin's abode at Coniston, Beatrix Potter's tiny house at Hawkshead, and boating on the lakes of Derwentwater and Windermere. Follow in the footsteps of Coleridge, Ruskin, and De Quincey; everywhere you'll find specific locations that inspired great poems—including the very woods where Dorothy Wordsworth

once commented she had never seen "daffodils so beautiful."

East Anglia

The Vermont of Great Britain, East Anglia is a storied, quiet land—but one that has produced some of the country's greatest thinkers and poets. Milton, Bacon, Byron, and Thackeray received their education at Cambridge University—one of the world's top centers of learning and located in Cambridge, arguably the most gorgeous university town on earth. Beyond this magnificently medieval city, however, East Anglia is still the guardian of all that rural England holds dear. It enchants many visitors with its tulip fields, villages adorned with thatched-roof cottages, and around the valley of the River Stour, a Constable landscape to love with passion. More dramatic are the canals and fens of the reed-bordered Broads, which give travelers endless opportunities for peaceful boating. Not far away, however, you can find the bright lights: three of England's most splendiferous stately houses—Holkham, Blickling, and fit-for-a-Queen Sandringham. Beyond, two of England's greatest medieval cathedrals await in Norwich and Lincoln.

Yorkshire

A wilder, grander part of England in the north, the heather-covered Yorkshire Moors—full of open spaces, wide horizons, and hills that appear to rear violently out of the plain—were inspiration for the Brontë sisters, who, in the little hamlet of Haworth—heart of Brontë Country—wrote *Jane Eyre* and *Wuthering Heights*. The Moors are linked to the contrasting landscape of the Yorkshire Dales, with luxuriant green valleys, burgeoning rivers, waterfalls, and some of England's most tranquil villages (several of which figured in the tales of famed author and vet James Herriot). It would be almost unthinkable to journey to Yorkshire without paying a call on York—a must-see for those interested in impressive medieval monuments, including the largest Gothic church in the country, York Minster. Northwards lie the quaint seaside resort of Scarborough, the scenically splendid sights of the North York Moors, including picture-perfect Hutton-le-Hole, evocative Rievaulx Abbey, and Castle Howard, one of England's most famous treasure houses.

The Northeast

Embracing history, England's northeast corner refuses to be dwarfed by it. Windswept and wild, the Northeast is an area for the intrepid traveler, interested in ruined castles, holy islands, Roman walls, and the Northumberland Coast. Among the numberless monuments of a vigorous and often warlike past, Hadrian's Wall—the northernmost border of the ancient Roman Empire, is the most famous. Here, too, however, are some of England's most sumptuous castles, such as Alnwick and Raby. Other must-sees include Durham Cathedral—more fortress than church; Kielder Forest, which is Europe's largest planted forest; the Pennines, which comprise some of England's wildest and least populated countryside; and magical Lindisfarne Island, a landmark of early Christendom.

Scotland: Edinburgh to the Highlands

In southeast Scotland, Edinburgh is a thoroughly delightful city built, like Rome, on seven hills, with its own brooding castle affording spectacular views; the Old Town district, with all the evidence of its colorful medieval history; a large number of elegant, 18th-century classical buildings; and Arthur's Seat, a green and yellow-furze backdrop jutting up 800 ft behind the spires of the Old Town. Edinburgh also has some fine art museums, atmospheric pubs, a lovely botanical garden, and an annual theater festival. The Borders area—immortalized in the tales of Sir Walter Scott—takes in the rolling hills, moors, and farmland that stretch south from Lothian, the region crowned by Edinburgh, to England. An excursion to St. Andrews is a pilgrimage for golf aficionados; many a traveler hopes to return home with the tale of a Road Hole birdie on the Old Course of the Royal & Ancient. To the west lies exciting Glasgow, whose full-fledged urban renaissance began a decade ago.

Sooner or later, all feet march in the direction of mythical Brigadoon—toward those splendid heath-clad mountain slopes, shimmering lochs, and the great castles of baronial pride standing hard among the northern hills of Scotland. To enjoy the Highlands at their picture-postcard best, head for Royal Deeside, the burg that Queen Victoria made her own. Her Majesty's Balmoral—and numerous other castles—polka-dot this picturesque region of northeast Scotland. Northward lies Inverness and Loch Ness; perhaps you'll be the lucky person to sight Nessie—everyone's favorite monster and a founding member of the local chamber of commerce.

PLEASURES AND PASTIMES

"Doing the Statelies": The Treasure Houses of Britain

Curiosity as to how the other half lives is undoubtedly one of the most deep-seated traits of human nature, and it's extremely pleasing to know you can satisfy your healthy desire to snoop through Great Britain's stately homes for the payment of a very small amount of conscience money. The fact that you will see some of the greatest of the world's treasures at the same time is a happy bonus. But even the most highly developed sense of curiosity isn't enough to explain the fact that millions of people have surged on to the stately home trail. They have been urged to move by a great deal of exposure—the houses touched by the royal family upheavals, such as Althorp, the ancestral home of Princess Diana, and the Mountbatten home, Broadlands; the numerous television serials, which have brought new fame to such spectacular houses as Castle Howard and Blenheim Palace; the new spate of historical movies shot on location, including the numerous versions of Jane Austen's novels (Lyme Park played a starring role in *Pride and Prejudice*), *The Madness of King George* (the spectacular interiors of Wilton House dazzled here), *Sense and Sensibility* (partly shot at Saltram), or the over-the-top style of Charles II on view in *Restoration*. Today, thousands follow in the footsteps of Elizabeth Bennet and the Gardiners who paid a call on Mr. Darcy's regal Pemberely, one of the more fetching episodes penned by Miss Austen.

The reason for the pressing need for the owners of stately homes to throw them open is simply that they need the ready money. Spiritually rewarding as it must be to own vast tracts of countryside, paintings by Rembrandt and Gainsborough, a house designed by one of the Adam Brothers and furnished by Chippendale, tapestries by the mile and porcelain by the ton—it is all a dead loss as far as cash flow (and death duties) are concerned.

What you get for your entrance fee differs enormously from one house to another. In some houses you are left completely free to wander at will, soaking up the atmosphere. In some you are organized into groups that then process through the house like bands of prisoners behind enemy lines. Occasionally you may find that your mentor is a member of the family, who will gleefully relate stories of uncles, aunts, and cousins back to the Crusades. Those are often the best.

Three facts should be kept in mind. Many houses are unreachable except by car. Hours are always subject to change, so it's always best to call the day before and inquire: At times, people arrive standing on the doorstep staring at a bolted door. Also, most houses are open only in the warm-weather seasons, from April to October. However, some of these have celebrated parks—Blenheim Palace and Chatsworth come to mind—that are utter delights in themselves and are open through much of the year. Everyone has his or her own top-10 list—Knole, Longleat, Woburn, and so on—but don't forget lesser known neoclassic abodes and those wonderful mock-medieval Victorian piles, such as Castle Drogo in Devon, designed for Sir Julius Drewe, the founder of a chain of grocery stores. There is something keenly appropriate about the fact that the last great castle built in Britain was created for a shopkeeper. Napoléon would have approved.

The Performing Arts: From the Boards to the Bard

One of the main reasons so many people want to visit Britain is its enviable reputation in the performing arts. The country is exactly what Shakespeare described, an "isle full of noises, sounds and sweet airs that give delight and hurt not." In music and drama, opera and ballet, there are endless opportunities for visitors to enjoy themselves to the hilt. Although the political dogmas of Thatcherism and the restraints of the recession hit the bank accounts of arts organizations badly, thanks to the new Labour Party regime, the performing arts scene is still surprisingly healthy.

BALLET➤ Ballet is a surprising art to flourish in Britain, and it must be admitted that it only does so with a struggle. The Royal Ballet, the premier company, is going through a rather bad patch, suffering as it does from artistic arteriosclerosis. It is no longer adventuresome enough in its choice of repertoire, having to dance endless performances of favorite three-act classics just to make ends meet. Worse: its home base, the grand and glorious Royal Opera House at Covent Garden is now closed for several years for a massive renovation. Still, few other companies put on such a legendary *Giselle,* and the Royal Ballet is usually worth tracking down at whatever venue it is performing.

The sibling Birmingham Royal Ballet is just the reverse. With young, zesty director Peter Wright, it is yet another excellent reason for visiting Birmingham. The Festival Ballet, which renamed itself the English National Ballet with very little cause, is Britain's only major dance company without a permanent home. It regularly tours its repertoire of classics countrywide. There are several other smaller companies that tour the country, but that have suffered serious cutbacks from the financial restrictions of recent years.

FESTIVALS➤ Britain is a land of festivals, mostly, though not exclusively, in the summer. Whatever the size of the town, it will have a festival at some time. Some are of international scope, while others are small local wingdings. Leading the parade is the Edinburgh Festival, mid-August–early September, born in the dark days after World War II, when people needed cheering up. Today it is still going strong, with opera, drama, recitals, and ballet by artists from all over the world. The festival now has the added attraction of the Fringe, a concurrent event, with as many as 800 performances crammed into three weeks: small-scale productions from the classic to the bizarre, held in everything from telephone kiosks to church halls.

Smaller than Edinburgh's event, but still notable, are the dozens of festivals up and down the country. In Bath, the International Festival, late May–mid-June, is noted for its music especially. In Aldeburgh, a windswept East Anglian seaside town, the Festival of Music and the Arts, mid–late June, is dedicated to the memory of Benjamin Britten, and again is mainly a music festival. In Cheltenham there are two festivals, one musical in July, the other early–mid-October, dedicated to literature, with readings, seminars, and lectures. York has both an early-music festival in summer, and a Viking one in February. Llandrindod Wells, in Wales, goes Victorian and dresses up in late August. Worcester, Hereford, and Gloucester take turns mounting the annual Three Choirs Festival in mid-August, the oldest in the world, which has seen premieres of some notable music. Truro stages a Three Spires Festival in June in imitation. Wales has an annual feast of song and poetry late July–early August, called the Royal National Eisteddfod. At Chichester in Sussex there is a summer drama festival that has been so popular that the town has managed to build a theater specially for it. At Ludlow, Shakespeare is performed during the summer in the open air, with the dramatic castle as backdrop. All these festivals have the advantage of focusing a visit to a town and helping you to meet the locals, but be sure to book well in advance, as they are extremely popular.

MUSIC➤ Music performance, too, has seen a tremendous surge in popularity in the last 50 years. Recently, this popularity has been made concrete, as it were, with the opening of two major new concert halls, both with notable acoustics. Symphony Hall in Birmingham is the new home of the Birmingham Symphony. Apart from Birmingham, other cities have fine resident orchestras, including Liverpool, Manchester, and even the seaside town of Bournemouth.

In London, the three concert halls on the South Bank, together with the Barbican, the Albert Hall, and the Wigmore Hall, all provide the capital with venues for a rich and varied musical fare. For example, every night for six weeks in the summer, sponsored by the BBC, the Albert Hall hosts the "Proms"—the biggest series of concerts in the world, involving 10 or more orchestras and dozens of other artists.

OPERA➤ Apart from the two major companies in London, the English National Opera, and the Royal Opera at Covent Garden, there are two other national companies, the Welsh National at Cardiff, and the Scottish National in Glasgow.

They both have adventuresome artistic policies, attacking such blockbusters as Wagner's *Ring* and *The Trojans* of Berlioz. They also tour, the Welsh National especially, appearing in small towns around the principality, even performing in movie houses when no other stage is available. There is also a northern England company, originally a spin-off from the English National, called Opera North, which is based in Leeds, and is as venturesome as its begetter.

Opera has always been an extravagant art form, and the recession has hit it severely. But one company has managed to build itself a new home. Glyndebourne, in deepest Sussex, relies entirely on sponsors and its ticket sales, having no state subsidy. It opened a new theater in 1994, ending 50 years of its "let's-do-an-opera-in-the-barn" image. A visit there will cost you an arm and a leg, but you'll feel like a guest at a very superior house party.

The two London companies are poles apart. The Royal Opera at Covent Garden is socially the most prestigious. But it suffers from the problems that bedevil all companies that rely largely on international stars—not enough rehearsal time, a wobbly artistic policy, and stratospherically expensive seat prices. And again, like the Royal Ballet, it is performing at a wide array of venues for the next two years, as its famed, plush-and-gilt, 1812 theater at Covent Garden is getting a complete overhaul. The English National Opera (ENO) was originally a *Volksoper,* based at the small Sadler's Wells Theater in north London. It moved to the Coliseum, beside Trafalgar Square, some 30 years ago. It is still a peoples' opera, though now housed in a huge theater (this, too, is undergoing renovation and the ENO will be performing at another venue for the next two seasons). For the last decade it has had a brilliantly innovative directorial team that has settled its reputation as the leader of opera fashion. Seat prices for the ENO are half of those at the Royal Opera, and the productions are excitingly inventive. The company is a team, mostly of British singers, who act as well as they sing. The one drawback is that the auditorium sometimes dwarfs the voices.

THEATER➤ An evening taking in a play is a vital element of any visitor's trip to

Britain. Most visitors head first for London's West End—the city's fabled "Theatreland." Here, you might catch Maggie Smith and Vanessa Redgrave doing star turns, fabulous musical revivals, such as *Oliver,* more than one Andrew Lloyd Webber extravaganza, and, needless to say, Agatha Christie's *The Mousetrap.*

The pinnacle of the dramatic scene consists of two great national companies, the Royal National Theatre and the Royal Shakespeare Company (RSC). They do have separate identities, though it is not always easy to pin down the way in which they differ. The RSC (as it is always known) is the more prolific, performing in five auditoriums, including two at the Barbican in London—one a large house built to its own specifications, the other called The Pit, a small studio space. RSC has three stages at Stratford-upon-Avon—the large Memorial Theatre, the Swan, and The Other Place. Thanks to the financial help of an American philanthropist, the Swan was constructed inside the only part left of a Victorian theater, which burned down in 1936. Constructed on the lines of Shakespeare's Globe, it is one of the most exciting acting spaces anywhere in the country. The Other Place is a newer venue used for experimental staging.

The National Theatre plays in the three auditoriums in its concrete fortress on London's South Bank—the Olivier, the Lyttleton, and the Cottesloe, in descending order of size, the Olivier being huge and the Cottesloe studio-size. Of the two companies, the RSC is the more cohesive, with a very impressive volume of work and a steadily developing style, though it also suffers from serious lapses of taste and concentration in its productions. The great majority of its offerings are works of Shakespeare and the English classics, with occasional ventures into musicals. The National, on the other hand, ransacks world drama, and has had notable successes with Greek classics and French tragedy, as well as mounting some of the best stagings of American musicals anywhere outside Broadway. It also attracts star performers more than the RSC, which relies largely on teamwork, and creates stars from its own ranks. Both companies suffer from serious financial problems, even though some of their best productions are transferred to the commercial sector, and often develop into considerable hits.

As for the Bard of Bards, the astounding news is that his fabled "Wooden O"—the Globe Theatre, the most famous playhouse in the world, the first venue for many of Master Shakespeare's greatest plays—has risen once again on the banks of the Thames in London, not 200 yards from where the original stood. England has always held special temptations for Shakespeare fans—now the new Globe has added the thrill of seeing his plays performed in the actual neighborhood where he lived and in virtually the same stage set. It is almost as if one can experience *Hamlet* in its birthplace. Londoners, oddly, look on the whole project as less theater than Disneyfied theme park. Well, it took several years for them to warm up to the Stratford theater when it went up in the '30s, and it'll probably be a while before they get in step behind the rest of the world beating a path to the new Globe. But they will undoubtedly change their tune, considering the recent news that the Royal Shakespeare Company is seriously thinking of canceling its London summer season. For visitors and travelers alike, the Globe may wind up being the only summer Shakespeare show in town.

Beyond London, there are provincial theaters in most of the cities and large towns up and down the land, and many of them have developed their own national and international reputations. The Haymarket in Leicester is renowned for musicals, many of which have transferred to London. Theatre Clwyd in Mold, North Wales, is almost a national theater for Wales, with brilliantly cast revivals of the classics, which travel far afield. In Scarborough, a seaside town in Yorkshire, the dramatist-director Alan Ayckbourn has run for many years the Stephen Joseph Theatre, where he tries out his own plays, most of which are regularly transferred to London, appearing as often as not at the National Theatre.

But the delight of British regional theaters lies in their great diversity and local panache. In the little town of Richmond, in Yorkshire, is a charming little Georgian theater, seating about 200 in rows and balconies that still reflect the 18th-century class divisions. In Bagnor, near Newbury, Berkshire, a water mill has been converted into a lovely little theater overlooking a lake. Porthcurno, near Penzance, Cornwall, has the Minack Theatre, which is situated on a cliff top, overlooking the sea. The lovely 1819 Theatre Royal in Bury St. Edmunds is owned and run by the National Trust and is still fully functioning. There are woodland theaters, theaters in barns, and several in grand old country houses.

Food, Glorious Food

One important piece of advice—do not eat while in England. In the old days, this observation always got a laugh from a crowd. Today, comedians would have to eat their words, since London is spearheading a full-fledged restaurant boom, or rather, a restaurant atomic-bomb explosion. The city now ranks among the world's top dining scenes. A new generation of chefs has precipitated a fresh approach to food preparation, which you could call "London-style" though most refer to it as "Modern British." Everyone seems to have an opinion about it, and newspapers and magazines now devote columns if not pages to food and restaurant reviews.

This healthy scene rests on a solid foundation of ethnic cuisines. Thousands of (mostly northern) Indian restaurants have long ensured that Britishers view a tasty tandoori as a birthright. Chinese—Cantonese, primarily—outposts have been around a long time, as have Greek tavernas; now, Thai eateries are proliferating. Places serving Malaysian, Spanish, Russian, Korean, and a trace of Japanese (with more on the way?) are adding to the density of dining choices. After all this, traditional British food, lately revived from its deathbed, appears as one more exotic cuisine in the pantheon. More and more, new chefs are taking the starch—literally—out of old British favorites, giving a newer-than-new spin to traditional dishes. Roast suckling pig with strawberry papaya and chili noodles, however, may not be everyone's top pick. Undoubtedly, it won't be too long before one of-the-moment London spot features that favorite nursery-rhyme pie with 4-and-20 rock stars popping out of it in place of blackbirds.

As for cost, the democratization of restaurants means lighter checks than during the '80s, partly due to the popularity of fixed-price menus; still, England is not an inexpensive place for dining. Damage-control methods include having lunch as your main meal—many top places feature good-value lunch menus, halving the price of

evening à la carte—and ordering a pair of appetizers instead of an entrée, to which few places object. Seek out fixed-price menus, but watch for hidden extras added to the check, including a "cover," bread and vegetables charged separately, and a service tariff. Many restaurants exclude service charges from the printed menu (which the law obliges them to display outside), then add 10%–15% to the check, or else stamp SERVICE NOT INCLUDED along the bottom, in which case you should add the 10%–15% yourself.

A final caveat: Beware of Sunday. Many restaurants are closed on this day, especially for dinner; likewise, on public holidays. During the Christmas period, the London restaurant community all but shuts down—only hotels will be prepared to feed you. When in doubt, call ahead.

Cheers!: The Pub Experience

Britishers could no more live without their "local" than they could forgo dinner. The pub—or public house, to give it its full title—is ingrained in the British psyche as social center, bolt-hole, second home. Pub culture—revolving around pints, pool, darts, and sports—is still male-dominated; however, as a result of the gentrification trend that started in the late '80s by the major breweries (which own most pubs), transforming many ancient smoke- and spittle-stained dives into fantasy Edwardian drawing rooms, women have been entering their welcoming doors in increasing numbers. This decade, the trend has been toward the Bar, superficially identified by its cocktail list, creative paintwork, bare floorboards, and chrome fittings. The social function is the same: These are English pubs, but not as we formerly knew them.

In London, the best pubs are veritable Victorian-themed miniparks. Etched glass, chandeliers, fine wood paneling, art nouveau sculptures—all these elements make up some of the city's most distinctive interiors. Of course, there are many pubs in London (and throughout the country) that have been modernized in dubious taste, with too much chrome, plush, and plastic. But there are those that can be a real joy. They will often be called by the name of the local landed family—*The Bath Arms,* or *Lord Crewe's Arms,* "arms" meaning the family coat of heraldic arms on the inn sign—and very possibly they will have old beams and inglenooks, and a blazing log fire in winter. If you sit at a table in the corner, you can have privacy of a sort; but between those who prop up the bar, conversation is general, no introductions are needed, and new acquaintances are quickly made. Locals congregate in vast numbers at lunch and in the evening—either right after work, for a sundowner pint, or right after dinner. At these times, there's no easier way for a traveler to meet the locals. Keep in mind that what is referred to in America as beer, the Brits call lager. There are two types of lager: bitter and ale. If you like something with a mild hops taste, ask for Fullers London Pride or Youngs Special. If you want something with more of a bite, try Abbot Ale, Ruddles County, or Owd Roger. For real heft, there's always export lager, called pilsner. Whichever you order, just remember the locals drink their beer *warm!*

The Great Outdoors: Favorite Sport Activities

BOATING➤ Canals crisscross Britain, a legacy of pre-railway days that now enriches the weekend of many a Briton. In major tourist centers such as York, Bristol, Bath, and Stratford-upon-Avon you'll find many short river and canal cruises in season. The Broads in Norfolk and Suffolk, East Anglia, is one of the most popular areas in England for boating on canals and lakes. The Lake District has numerous opportunities for sailing, canoeing, rowing, and other boating excursions.

GOLF➤ There are hundreds of fine courses all over Great Britain, especially in Scotland, the birthplace of the sport, and visiting golfers are welcome at many private clubs.

TENNIS➤ Tennis is a favorite recreation in Britain, and most towns have municipal courts where you can play for a small fee. Country hotels, too, often have courts. The hotel service information in each chapter lists tennis availability. In addition, there's the Wimbledon Fortnight, held in late June and early July.

WALKING➤ The whole country is crisscrossed by meandering trails—there are more than 100,000 mi of footpaths in England and Wales. Some are tiny and local, some very long and of historic significance, such as Peddar's Way in East Anglia and the Pennine Way in Yorkshire.

WATER SPORTS➤ Britain brims with rivers and lakes, and it is possible to swim and fish on many of them. One drawback is that waters are often polluted; the other problem is that the water can be icy cold! Most local authorities operate indoor pools, and a few have outdoor ones; entrance fees are minimal. Nearly all large hotels now have pools, as indicated in the hotel entries.

In some areas, like Cornwall and the coast of Wales, there are excellent sandy beaches with good swimming, but generally, the sea around Britain is very cold most of the year and much of the coast is fringed with pebbled beaches. Many seaside towns have windsurfing boards available. Some beaches are awarded a European Blue Flag, granted to beaches with a high standard of water quality (they should be cleaned daily during high season), and good facilities. Britain wins very few each year, usually only a couple of dozen, mostly in Wales and the Southwest. To counter the disturbing picture created by winning so few European Blue Flags, Britain has instituted its own awards, the Seaside Awards—which, coincidentally, are also blue! Always ask if a beach has been given either a Flag or a Seaside Award before deciding to use it.

FODOR'S CHOICE

No two people agree on what makes a perfect vacation, but it's fun and helpful to know what others think. Here's a compendium drawn from the must-see lists of hundreds of Britain-based tourists. For detailed information about these memories-in-the-making, refer to the appropriate section in this book.

Quintessential London

★ **Changing of the Guard.** Adding a dash of color to the gloomiest of London days, this ceremony is mounted (daily, depending on the season) at both Whitehall and Buckingham Palace. The Life Guards—all scarlet tunics and silvergilt helmets—ride on horseback to Whitehall from Hyde Park, while, outside Buck House, the Guard of Color marches as the band plays (they have been known to cut loose to Billy Joel when Her Majesty is away).

★ **The Houses of Parliament at sunset.** Cross the Thames to Jubilee Gardens to see this view of London at its storybook best. The headliner is Big Ben, which looks almost as magical as when Walt Disney used it as a perch for Peter and the children in *Peter Pan*.

★ **Sunday Afternoon at Speakers' Corner, Hyde Park.** A space especially reserved for anyone with anything to say that they *must* say publicly makes for great entertainment. Speakers seem to be most oratorical on Sunday afternoons.

★ **St. Paul's Cathedral Thames-side.** The most thrilling vantage point to take in St. Paul's is at Cardinal Wharf on the southern embankment, right by Shakespeare's Globe. Here, you'll find Sir Christopher Wren's elegant little house (built so he could monitor progress on his masterpiece, directly across the river). From here, St. Paul's dome thrillingly soars above the city.

★ **Shakespeare's Globe.** As with a flick of a Wellsian time machine, this new, spectacular, open-to-the-skies reconstruction of Shakespeare's beloved "Wooden O" magically transports you back to Elizabethan London. In 16th-century fashion, audience participation is welcome: Jump in and hiss Iago—you'll have plenty of company.

★ **Tower Bridge at night.** A dramatically floodlighted Tower Bridge confronts you as you come out of the Design Museum on a winter's night. By day, have your camera ready to frame the nearby Tower of London between the splendid Victorian-style guard railings of the bridge.

Postcard-Perfect Villages

★ **Castle Combe, Bath Environs.** This village's magic is that it is so toylike, so delightfully all-of-a-piece: you can almost see the whole town at one glance from any one position. Ever since it was used as a stand-in for Puddleby-on-the-Marsh in the film of *Doctor Dolittle*, however, it may have become too famous for its own good.

★ **Cockington, Devon.** The "most Devonish hamlet in England," this old-world show village, located just outside Torbay in Devon, is a once-upon-a-time place, replete with magical thatched-roof cottages, springtime carpets of daffodils, and even a house that rests atop tree trunks.

★ **Hutton-le-Hole, Yorkshire.** It's almost too pastoral to be true: a tiny hamlet, based around a wide village green, and a stream babbling in the background. To accessorize this perfect picture, the loveliest village in North Yorkshire has sheep wandering around.

★ **Lower Slaughter, Cotswolds.** Postcard-pretty Lower Slaughter is one of the Cotswolds' "water villages," with Slaughter Brook running by the center road of the town. Little stone footbridges ford the brook, while the town's resident gaggle of geese can often be seen paddling their merry way through the sparkling water.

★ **Woodstock, Thames Valley.** The Thames Valley neighborhood is posh (just down the road is the Duke of Marlborough's Blenheim Palace), the coaching-inn hotels are alluring (Richard popped the question to Liz at The Bear), and the town square is a sublime chunk of the 18th century. What more do you want?

The Stateliest of Stately Homes

★ **Blenheim Palace, Thames Valley.** England's only rival to Versailles, this is Britain's largest stately home and the birthplace of Winston Churchill. Home to the Dukes of Marlborough, the early 18th-century Italianate mansion in Woodstock stands majestically in 2,000 acres of parkland and exquisite gardens landscaped by Capability Brown.

★ **Castle Howard, Yorkshire.** Built over 60 years (1699–1759), this famous home (the setting for TV's *Brideshead Revisited*) is without equal in northern England; a magnificent central hall spanned by a hand-painted ceiling leads to staterooms and galleries overflowing with precious furniture and works of fine art. Outside is a magnificent park, dotted with beautiful marble temples and follies.

★ **Haddon Hall, Lancashire and the Peaks.** Set within the Wye Valley—"the most beautiful vale in England"—Haddon Hall seems to be a medieval book illumination come to life: a 15th-century castellated manor bristling with slate roofs and towers, it appears like a miniature town from the surrounding hills (a fabulous photo op) and remains, in the words of historian Hugo Massingbird-Montgomery, "the beau ideal of an English country house."

⭐ **Holkham Hall, East Anglia.** Set amid a huge expanse of sandy beaches, dunes, and salt marsh backed by pine woods, this neoclassic Italian-style mansion in Holkham has the most spectacular room in Britain—a great hall modeled after ancient Rome's Baths of Diocletian, adorned with gold and alabaster—and 12 stately brocade-lined rooms filled with paintings by Gainsborough, Rubens, Raphael, Van Dyck, and other European old masters.

⭐ **Ightham Mote, Southeast.** Everyone's dream of a moated medieval manor house, this enchanting 14th-century abode has several additions reflecting different periods—a medieval Great Hall, a Tudor chapel, hand-painted Chinese wallpaper, and an 18th-century Palladian window.

Great Restaurants and Pubs

⭐ **Bibendum, London.** Once London's leading scene-arena, this chic see-and-be-seen spot is housed in the marvelous Michelin House, with its Art Deco decorations and brilliant stained glass. The kitchen serves simple dishes prepared perfectly—steak au poivre, boeuf bourguignon, tripe as it ought to be cooked, and Christmas pudding ice cream not to be missed. ££££

⭐ **La Tante Claire, London.** One of London's very best restaurants, cripplingly expensive (opt for the "bargain" set lunch), with a light and sophisticated decor, La Tante Claire is a showcase for chef Pierre Koffman's culinary delights, such as his roast spiced pigeon. ££££

⭐ **Le Caprice, London.** This may command the deepest loyalty of any London restaurant because it gets everything right: the glamorous, glossy black interior, the perfect pitch of the service, and the food, halfway between Euro-peasant and fashion plate. It also features some of the best people-watching in town. ££££

⭐ **Le Manoir aux Quat' Saisons, Great Milton, Thames Valley.** This 15th/16th-century manor house with sumptuous rooms has held its position as one of Britain's leading restaurants for years, where owner-chef Raymond Blanc exercises his award-winning French culinary skills. The set menus at lunchtime make it almost reasonable. ££££

⭐ **Miller Howe, Windermere, Lake District.** At this small, white Edwardian hotel with an international reputation for comfort and fine cuisine, every attention has been given to the interior decor, which includes fine antiques and paintings. It's beautifully situated, with views across Windermere to the Langdale Pikes. ££££

⭐ **Carved Angel, Dartmouth, Southwest.** Situated on the quay with views of the harbor, this eatery has long been considered one of Britain's best, serving Provençal cuisine and fresh local products, such as Dart River salmon and samphire, a seashore plant used in fish dishes. £££–££££

⭐ **Rules, London.** Come, escape from the 20th century. This historic landmark is London's answer to Maxim's in Paris, with an incomparably beautiful setting—one that has welcomed everyone from Dickens to the Duke of Windsor. The food may be good but the veddy-veddy English decor is absolutely delicious. £££

⭐ **People's Palace, London.** Thank goodness—thanks to this palace, you can finally have a civilized meal during your South Bank arts encounter. With menus by trendy chef Gary Rhodes, this has remarkably low prices considering it has one of the greatest river views in town. Here, the more British the dish, the more reliable it is. ££

⭐ **Landgate Bistro, Rye, Southeast.** All the fish from nearby waters is excellent at this lively, bustling establishment popular with locals. Be sure to sample the walnut and treacle tart. £–££

⭐ **The Black Friar, London.** You can't miss it—it's the only wedge-shape, ornate building with a statue of a friar on the front as you step out of Blackfriars tube station! Inside is one of London's most splendiferous pubs—all colored marbles, inlaid mother-of-pearl, and stained glass, with painted friars, devils, and fairies all about. The pints and the fetching locals are great. £

⭐ **Ye Olde Cheshire Cheese, London.** Yes, it is a tourist trap, but this most historic of all London pubs (it dates from 1667) deserves a visit because of its authentic heritage-rich decor—London at its Time Machine best. And this regular of Dr. Johnson and Dickens offers up the quintessential steak-and-kidney pie. £

Top Hotels

⭐ **Balmoral Hotel, Edinburgh, Scotland.** The attention to detail in the elegant rooms, the plush and stylish Grill Room restaurant, and the sheer élan that has re-created the Edwardian splendor of this former grand railroad hotel all make staying at the Balmoral very special. ££££

⭐ **Cliveden, Thames Valley.** William Waldorf Astor once called this palace home. Today it is the *ne plus ultra* of English hotels and it remains as stately as you can get, with palatial salons, elegant restaurants, 375 verdant acres, and a breathtaking parterre that overlooks the Thames. ££££

⭐ **Covent Garden Hotel, London.** Relentlessly chic, this is probably the most stylish hotel in London. Newly renovated, this former 1880's-vintage hospital now wallows in eye-knocking painted silks, *style anglais* ottomans, gleaming paneling, and 19th-century romantic oils—a sanctorum prized by off-duty celebrities. ££££

⭐ **Middlethorpe Hall, York, Yorkshire.** This handsome, superbly restored 18th-century mansion on the edge of the city has an award-winning French restaurant and rooms filled with antiques, paintings, and fresh flowers; the extensive grounds boast a lake, a 17th-century dovecote, and "ha-ha's"—drops in the garden level that create cunning views. ££££

⭐ **The Savoy, London.** This historic, grand, late-Victorian hotel, beloved by the international influential, has spacious, tasteful, bright, and comfortable rooms, furnished with antiques and serviced by valets. A room facing the Thames costs an arm and a leg, but there are few better views in London. ££££

⭐ **Old Parsonage, Oxford, Thames Valley.** It's rare to find an attractive, restored, 17th-century country-house hotel with stone gables and mullioned windows in the middle of a city. Open fires, fascinating pictures, comfortable rooms, and immaculate service make this a hotel to remember. ££££

⭐ **Ettington Park, Stratford-upon-Avon.** To avoid the crowds in Stratford, stay at this marvelously restored, huge Victorian house that stands in its own grounds (which contain a ruined church) and looks across tranquil river meadows haunted by herons. Some rooms have Victorian Gothic furnishings. £££–££££

⭐ **Hotel Portmeirion, Porthmadog, Wales.** This is one of the most elegant—and unusual—places to stay in Wales. Part of the Italianate toylike fantasy-village built by Clough Williams-Ellis, the hotel is built around an exotic garden enclave. £££–££££

⭐ **Thornbury Castle, Thornbury, Heart of England.** A baronial 16th-century manor house, this has huge fireplaces, mullioned windows, lovely antiques, and a superlative restaurant, to boot. £££–££££

⭐ **Owlpen Manor, Cotswolds, Heart of England.** Incomparably romantic, this hotel occupies a tiny, sequestered hamlet that is the quintessence of all things Cotswold. A Stuart-period estate, it's adorned with a handful of centuries-old stone manors and cottages, all exquisitely renovated. £££–££££

⭐ **Dukes, London.** This small, exclusive, Edwardian-style hotel is possibly London's quietest hotel, secreted in its cul-de-sac in the heart of St. James's. Decorated in patrician, antiques-splattered style, it's filled with squashy sofas and portraits of assorted dukes, and it offers the best in personal service. £££

⭐ **Hazlitt's, London.** Located in Soho, this hotel is in three connected early 18th-century houses, one the former home of famed essayist William Hazlitt. Disarmingly friendly, full of personality, devoid of room service, the hotel is loved for its Victorian charm. Book way ahead—this place is the London address of literary types and antiques dealers everywhere. £££

⭐ **Queensberry Hotel, Bath, Heart of England.** This intimate, elegant hotel on a quiet residential street near The Circus is in three 1772 town houses built for the marquis of Queensberry. Renovations have preserved the Regency stucco ceilings and cornices and original marble tiling on the fireplaces. £££

⭐ **Rising Sun, Lynmouth, Southwest.** A recent conversion from a 14th-century inn and a row of thatched cottages created this intriguing hotel with great views over Lynmouth fishing village, especially from the terraced garden out back. Legend has it that the poet Shelley spent his honeymoon on this site. ££

⭐ **Spread Eagle Inn, Stourton, the South.** Adjacent to Stourhead, this inn allows you the dreamy experience of living just steps away from England's most beautiful landscape park. It doesn't matter that the rooms have been heavily renovated—you'll be spending most of your time outdoors. ££

★ **Black Hostelry, Ely, East Anglia.** You'll have lots of privacy at this highly popular bed-and-breakfast with enormous rooms and old-fashioned English furnishings—it's right on the city's cathedral grounds, in one of the finest medieval domestic buildings still in use. £

★ **Blenheim Guest House and Tea Rooms, Woodstock, Thames Valley.** This small, inauspicious rooming house sits in one of the more magical corners of Britain—the quiet village cul-de-sac that leads to the imperial back gates of Blenheim Palace. £

Grand Cathedrals and Churches

★ **Canterbury Cathedral, Southeast.** The focal point of the city of Canterbury, this cathedral is a living textbook of medieval architecture, combining Gothic and Norman styles. The church is well known as the site of archbishop Thomas á Becket's murder in 1170, and a series of 13th-century stained-glass windows illustrates Becket's miracles.

★ **King's College Chapel, Cambridge, East Anglia.** One of the most beautiful buildings in England, this late-Gothic, English-style church has great fan-vaulting supported by soaring side columns. Its huge interior is filled with ever-changing light from the vast stained-glass windows. Every Christmas Eve, a festival of carols sung by the chapel's famous choir is broadcast around the world.

★ **Salisbury Cathedral, Salisbury, South.** Built in a short span of only 38 years (1220–1258), the towering cathedral has a spire that is a miraculous feat of medieval engineering, and an interior with remarkable lancet windows and sculpted tombs of crusaders and other medieval heroes.

★ **Westminster Abbey, London.** Britain's monarchs have been crowned at this most ancient of great churches since 1066. The present abbey, a largely 13th- and 14th-century rebuilding of an 11th-century church, has many memorials to royalty, writers, and statesmen, and the famous Tomb of the Unknown Warrior; its Henry VII Chapel is an exquisite example of the rich late-Gothic style.

Magnificent Museums

★ **British Museum, London.** In a monumental Greek edifice built in the first half of the 19th century, the vast collection of treasures here includes Egyptian, Greek, and Roman antiquities; Renaissance jewelry, pottery, coins, glass; and drawings from virtually every European school since the 15th century.

★ **Fitzwilliam Museum, Cambridge, East Anglia.** In a classical building with an opulent interior, you'll discover an outstanding collection of art (including paintings by John Constable, Gainsborough, and the French Impressionists) and antiquities, a large display of English Staffordshire, and a fascinating room full of armor and muskets.

★ **National Gallery, London.** Leonardos, Rubenses, and Rembrandts seem to wallpaper the enormous rooms here—an incomparably rich treasure trove of Old Masters. It's an awe-inspiring experience to see such beloved paintings as Jan Van Eyck's *Arnofini Marriage* in the flesh.

★ **National Gallery of Scotland, Edinburgh, Scotland.** The attractively decorated spacious rooms display a wide-ranging selection of paintings, from Renaissance times to Postimpressionism, as well as a fine collection of Scottish art.

★ **Tate Gallery, London.** The greatest glories of English painting are here, from Elizabethan portraits to the most avant avant-garde works. Most unforgettable image: Sir John Everett Millais' 19th-century oil of *Ophelia*.

★ **Wallace Collection, London.** The serene 18th-century mansion, Hertford House, which houses this sumptuous collection is as much a part of the appeal as its rich array of porcelain, paintings, sculptures, and furniture. Top treats here are Fragonard's *The Swing* and Thomas Sully's *Queen Victoria*, hung in a 19th-century rouge-pink salon that is the prettiest room in London.

FESTIVALS AND SEASONAL EVENTS

Tickets for popular sporting events must be obtained months in advance—check first to see if your travel agent can get them. There is a complete list of ticket agencies in *Britain Events,* free from the British Tourist Authority.

WINTER

1ST 2 WKS JAN.➤ **London International Boat Show** is the largest boat show in Europe. ✉ *Earls Court Exhibition Centre, Warwick Rd., London SW5 9TA,* ☎ *01784/473377.*

JAN. 31➤ **Charles I Commemoration** is held on the anniversary of the monarch's execution and brings out Londoners dressed in 17th-century garb for a march tracing his last walk from St. James's Palace to the Banqueting House in Whitehall. ✉ *London.*

MAR. 17–23➤ **British Antique Dealers' Association Fair,** the newest of the major fairs, is large and prestigious, with many affordable pieces. ✉ *Duke of York's Headquarters, King's Rd., Chelsea, London SW3,* ☎ *0171/589–6108.*

MAR. 18–28 AND SEPT. 16–26➤ **Chelsea Antiques Fair,** a twice-yearly fair with wide range of pre-1830 pieces for sale. ✉ *Old Town Hall, King's Rd., Chelsea , London SW3 4PW,* ☎ *01444/482514.*

MID-MAR.➤ **Open House** is a rare one-day chance to view historic London interiors of buildings usually closed to the public. ✉ *London,* ☎ *0181/341–1371*

MID-MAR.➤ **Crufts Dog Show** brings together more than 8,000 championship dogs for Britain's top canine event. ✉ *National Exhibition Centre, Birmingham B40 1NT,* ☎ *0121/780–4141.*

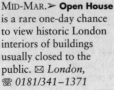

SPRING

EARLY APR.➤ **Chaucer Festival** allows Londoners to don medieval garb and parade from Southwark Cathedral to the Tower of London, where jugglers and strolling minstrels party the day away. ✉ *London,* ☎ *01227/470379.*

MID-APR.➤ **London Marathon.** *Information:* ✉ *Box 262, Richmond, Surrey TW10 5JB,* ☎ *0181/948–7935.*

MID-APR.➤ **Head of the River Boat Race, London** offers the spectacle of 420 eight-man crews from Oxford and Cambridge universities dipping their 6,720 oars in the Thames as they race from Mortlake to Putney. The best view is from Surrey Bank above Chiswick Bridge (tube to Chiswick); check out *Time Out* for the starting time, which depends on the tide.

APR. 21➤ **Queen's Birthday** earns a showy 41-gun salute at London's Hyde Park. In June (*see below*), Elizabeth II's ceremonial B-day is celebrated by Trooping the Colour.

MAY 25–28➤ **Chelsea Flower Show** is Britain's major flower show, covering 22 acres. ✉ *Royal Hospital, Chelsea, London SW3,* ☎ *0171/834–4333.*

LATE MAY–EARLY JUNE➤ **Glyndebourne Opera** opens its fourth season in its new, greatly enlarged auditorium. ✉ *Glyndebourne Festival Opera, Glyndebourne, Lewes, East Sussex BN8 5UU,* ☎ *01273/812321.*

SUMMER

LATE MAY–LATE AUG.➤ **Shakespeare Under the Stars** gives you the chance to see the Bard of Bard's plays performed at Regent's Park Open Air Theatre. Peformances are usually Monday–Saturday at 8, with matinees on Wednesday, Thursday, and Saturday. ✉ *Inner Circle, London NW1,* ☎ *0171/486–2431.*

EARLY JUNE➤ **Derby Day** is the world-renowned horse-racing event, at Epsom Racecourse, Epsom, Surrey. *Information:* ✉ *United Racecourses Ltd., Racecourse Paddock, Epsom, Surrey KT18 5NJ,* ☎ *01372/463072.*

EARLY JUNE➤ **Beating Retreat by the Guards Massed Bands,** when more than 500 musicians parade at Horse Guards,

Whitehall. ⊠ *Tickets from Household Division Fund, Block 8, Wellington Barracks, Birdcage Walk, London SW1E 6HQ,* ☎ *0171/414–3253.*

MID-JUNE➤ **Royal Ascot** is the most glamorous date in British horse racing. Usually held during the third week of June, the 4-day event is graced by the Queen and other celebrities. ⊠ *Ascot Racecourse, Ascot, Berkshire SL5 7JN,* ☎ *01344/22211.*

MID-JUNE➤ **Trooping the Colour** is Queen Elizabeth's colorful official birthday show at Horse Guards Parade, Whitehall, London. (Her actual birthday is in April.) Note that on the two previous Saturdays, there are two Queenless rehearsals—the Colonel's Review and the Major General's Review, with the former often under the supervision of Prince Charles. *Write for tickets early in the yr:* ⊠ *Ticket Office, H.Q. Household Division, Chelsea Barracks, London SW1 8RF,* ☎ *0171/414–2497.*

LATE JUNE–LATE JULY➤ **City of London Festival** fills the City with theater, poetry, classical music, and dance performed by international artists. ☎ *0171/377–0540.*

JUNE 21–JULY 4➤ The **Wimbledon Lawn Tennis Championships** are bigger every year. Applications for the ticket lottery are available October–December. ⊠ *All-England Lawn Tennis and Croquet Club, Church Rd.,*

Wimbledon, London SW19 5AE, ☎ *0181/946–2244.*

JUNE 30–JULY 4➤ **Royal Henley Regatta** attracts premier rowers from around the world. High society lines the banks of the Thames to cheer *both* the winners and losers during this 4-day event. ⊠ *Henley-on-Thames, Oxfordshire,* ☎ *01491/578034.*

EARLY–MID-JULY➤ **Llangollen International Musical Eisteddfod** sees the little Welsh town of Llangollen overflow with music, costumes, and color. ⊠ *Musical Eisteddfod Office, Llangollen, Clwyd LL20 8NG,* ☎ *01978/860236.*

MID-JULY➤ **Royal Tournament** features military displays and pageantry by the Royal Navy, Royal Marines, Army, and Royal Air Force. ⊠ *Earls Court Exhibition Centre, Warwick Rd., London SW5 9TA,* ☎ *0171/373–8141.*

MID-JULY–MID-SEPT.➤ **Henry Wood Promenade Concerts** is a celebrated series of concerts, founded in 1895. ⊠ *Royal Albert Hall, Kensington Gore, London SW7 2AP,* ☎ *0171/589–8212.*

EARLY AUG.➤ **Cowes Regatta** draws high flyers, top yachtsmen, and the occasional royal to this grand weeklong boating festival held off the Isle of Wight. ☎ *01983/291914.*

MID-AUG.–EARLY SEPT.➤ **Edinburgh International Festival,** the world's largest festival of the arts,

includes the nighttime Edinburgh Military Tattoo. ⊠ *Edinburgh Festival Society, 21 Market St., Edinburgh EH1 1BW,* ☎ *0131/226–4001.*

AUTUMN

EARLY OCT.➤ **Pearly Harvest Festival Service** n London draws a crowd of costermongers to the Church of St. Martin-in-the-Fields on the first Sunday in October. The Pearly Kings and Queens strut their famous costumes.⊠ *Trafalgar Square, London,* ☎ *0171/930–0089.*

MID-OCT.➤ **Cheltenham Festival of Literature** draws world-renowned authors, actors, and critics to the elegant, Regency-era town that calls itself the "gateway to the Cotswolds." ☎ *01242/522878.*

NOV. 5➤ **Guy Fawkes Day** celebrates a foiled 1605 attempt to blow up Parliament. Fireworks are held throughout London, but the place to be is the bonfire festivity on Primrose Hill near Camden Town, just outside the city.

EARLY NOV.➤ **Lord Mayor's Procession and Show** coincides with the Lord Mayor's inauguration, with a procession from the Guildhall to the Royal Courts of Justice. No tickets. ⊠ *The City of London,* ☎ *0171/606–3030.*

2 London

If London contained only its famous landmarks—the Tower of London, Big Ben, Parliament, Buckingham Palace— it would still rank as one of the world's top destinations. But London is so much more. It is a vast city of living history, whose story is still emerging in big events, like the death of Princess Diana in 1997, and small happenings, like the opening of what seems like the millionth new restaurant. A city that loves to be explored, London beckons with great museums, royal pageantry, and history-steeped houses. Visit the Duke of Wellington's house, track Jack the Ripper's shadow in Whitechapel, then get Beatle-ized at Abbey Road. In the end, you'll find London is a dickens of a place.

Updated by
Kate Sekules

LONDON IS AN ANCIENT CITY whose history greets you
at every turn. To gain a sense of its continuity, stand
on Waterloo Bridge at the hour of sunset. To the
east, the great globe of St. Paul's Cathedral glows golden in the fading sunlight as it has since the 17th century, still majestic amid the modern towers of glass and steel that hem it in. To the west stand the
mock-medieval ramparts of Westminster, home to the "Mother of Par-
liaments," which has met here or hereabouts since the 1250s. Past them
both snakes the swift, dark Thames, following the same course as when
it flowed past the first Roman settlement nearly 2,000 years ago.

For much of its history, innumerable epigrams and observations have
been coined about London by both her enthusiasts and detractors. The
great 18th-century author and wit, Samuel Johnson, said that a man
who is tired of London is tired of life. Oliver Wendell Holmes said,
"No person can be said to know London. The most that anyone can
claim is that he knows something of it." In short, the capital of Great
Britain is simply one of the most interesting cities on earth. There is
no other place like it in its agglomeration of architectural sins and sud-
den intervention of almost rural sights, in its medley of styles, in its
mixture of the green loveliness of parks and the modern gleam of
neon. Thankfully, the old London of Queen Anne and Georgian architecture can still be discovered, as in a palimpsest parchment, under
the hasty routine of later additions.

Discovering it takes a bit of work, however. Modern-day London still
largely reflects its medieval layout, a willfully difficult tangle of streets.
This swirl of spaghetti will be totally confusing to anyone brought up
on the rigidity of a grid system. Even Londoners, most of whom own
at least one dog-eared copy of the indispensable A–Z street finder (they
come under different names), get lost in their own city. But London's
bewildering street pattern will be a plus for the visitor who likes to get
lost in atmosphere. London is a walker's city and will repay every moment you spend exploring on foot. The visitor who wants to penetrate
beyond the crust of popular knowledge is well advised not only to visit
St. Paul's Cathedral and the Tower, but also to set aside some of his
or her time for random wandering. Walk in the city's backstreets and
mews, around Park Lane and Kensington. Pass up Buckingham Palace
for Kew, the smallest royal palace, beautifully situated in the botanical gardens. Take in the National Gallery, but don't forget London's
"time machine" museums, such as the 19th-century homes of Linley
Sambourne and Sir John Soane. Abandon the city's identikit chain stores
to discover the gentlemen's outfitters of St. James's. In such ways can
you best visualize the shape or, rather, the various shapes, of Old London, a curious city that engulfed its own past for the sake of modernity but still lives and breathes the air of history.

Today, that sense of modernity is stronger than ever. Everyone is talking about swinging-again London. *Vanity Fair* recently proclaimed it
"the coolest, hottest city in the world," and *Newsweek* announced that
the capital was the *only* place to be. Tony Blair's Labour Party has ush-
ered in a blast of youthful optimism and verve. A booming economy
has helped the city's art, style, fashion, and dining scenes to make head-
lines around the world. London's chefs have become superstars; its fashion designers have conquered Paris; its avant avant-garde artists have
stormed the august Royal Academy of Arts; the city's raging after-hours
scene is packed with music mavens ready to catch the Next Big Thing
after Oasis and the Spice Girls; and *enfants terribles* are turning up-
side down the National Theatre with radical stagings. Even Shakespeare

is ready for the millennium: the Bard's own Globe—the fabled "Wooden O"—has been reconstructed on the banks of the Thames just 200 yards from where it stood in the 16th century. Its 1996 preview season opened with *Two Gentlemen of Verona* and had cast members sporting Ray-Bans and sneakers. Just like Shakespeare, the city has cast off its stodgy, traditional image.

On the other hand, although the outward shapes may alter and the inner spirit may be warmer—Princess Diana's 1997 funeral was far removed from the conventional picture of a somewhat staid city of people who don't display their emotions—the baserocks of London's character and tradition remain the same. Deep down, Britons have a sense of the continuity of history. Even in the modern metropolis, some things rarely change. The British bobby is alive and well. The tall, red, double-decker buses still lumber from stop to stop, though their aesthetic match at street level, the glossy red telephone booths, are slowly disappearing. And, of course, teatime is still a hallowed part of the day, with, if you search hard enough, toasted crumpets still honeycombed with sweet butter. Then, of course, there is that greatest living link with the past—the Royal Family. Don't let the tag of "typical tourist" stop you from enjoying the pageantry of the Windsors, one of the greatest free shows in the world. Line up for the Changing of the Guard and poke into the Royal Mews for a look at the Coronation Coach.

The London you'll discover will surely include some of our enthusiastic recommendations, but be prepared to be taken by surprise as well. The best that a great city has to offer often comes in unexpected ways. Armed with energy and curiosity, and the practical information and helpful hints in the following pages, you can find, to quote Dr. Johnson again, "in London all that life can afford."

Pleasures and Pastimes

The Performing Arts

There isn't *a* single London "arts scene"—there is an infinite variety of them. As long as there are audiences for Feydeau revivals, drag queens, obscure teenage rock bands, hit musicals, body-painted Parisian dancers, and improvised stand-up comedy, someone will figure out how to stage them. Admission prices are not always bargain-basement, but when you consider the cost of a London hotel room, the city's arts and entertainment are easily affordable.

To find out what's showing during your stay, the weekly magazine *Time Out* (it comes out every Wednesday; Tuesday in central London) is an invaluable resource. The *Evening Standard*—especially the Thursday edition—also carries listings, as do the "quality" Sunday papers and the Saturday *Independent, Guardian,* and *Times.* You'll find racks overflowing with leaflets and flyers in most cinema and theater foyers, and you can pick up the free bimonthly "London Theatre Guide" leaflet from most hotels as well as from tourist information centers.

MUSIC

London is home to four world-class orchestras. The London Symphony Orchestra is in residence at the Barbican Centre, while the London Philharmonic lives at the Royal Festival Hall—one of the finest concert halls in Europe. Between the Barbican and South Bank, there are concert performances almost every night of the year. The Barbican also presents chamber-music concerts in partnership with such celebrated orchestras as the City of London Sinfonia. The Royal Albert Hall during the Promenade Concert season—July to September—is an unmissable pleasure. Also look for the lunchtime concerts held throughout the city in either smaller concert halls, arts-center foyers, or churches; they usually cost less than £5 or are free. St. John's, Smith Square, and St. Martin-in-the-Fields are the major venues and also present evening concerts.

THEATER

From Shakespeare to the umpteenth year of *Les Misérables* (or "The Glums," as it's affectionately known), London's West End has the cream of the city's theater offerings. But there's much more to see in London than the offerings of Theatreland and the national companies: of the 100 or so legitimate theaters operating in the capital, only about half are officially "West End," while the remainder fall under the blanket title of "Fringe," which encompasses everything from off-the-wall "physical theater" to premieres of new plays and revivals of old ones.

Shakespeare, of course, supplies the backbone to the theatrical life of the city. There can hardly have been a day since the one on which the Bard breathed his last, when one of his plays, in some shape or form, was not being performed. On the London stage, they have survived being turned into musicals (from Purcell to rock); they have made the reputations of generations of famous actors (and broken not a few); they have seen women playing Hamlet and men playing Rosalind. Every so often, the theatergoing public is sorely tempted to forbid the production of *Hamlet,* with so many versions being staged. But then something like the magnificent new reconstruction of Shakespeare's Globe Theatre comes about, and promises to show the play in a whole new light. If the Bard of Bards remains the headliner at Stratford-upon-Barbican, the London theater scene is amazingly varied. From a West End *Oliver* revival to an East End feminist staging of *Ben-Hur,* London remains a theatergoer's town.

OPERA AND BALLET

For decades, London's leading troupes, the Royal Opera and the Royal Ballet, have shared grandiose quarters at the Royal Opera House in Covent Garden—a fact that rather cut down on the number of opera and ballet performances which could be mounted in a season. Even with a backstage renovation done several years ago, there was still a great pressure on rehearsal and dressing room space. Now change is finally here: the grand Opera House has been closed for a major two-year renovation, and the resident companies are scurrying for other venues. When the red-and-gold curtain finally does go back up at "the Garden," however, only opera may been seen there: plans are in the offing for a completely new venue for the ballet.

The Delights of Dining

London now ranks among the world's top dining scenes. A new generation of chefs has precipitated a fresh approach to food preparation, which you could call "London-style" though most refer to it as "Modern British." Everyone seems to have an opinion about it, and newspapers and magazines devote pages to food and restaurant reviews. Everyone reads them and everyone dines out to the point where London has become the most significant foodies' town in Europe. The nouvelle push has taken the starch—literally—out of many of the city's menus, and this new energy is even finding a vogue for old standbys like angels-on-horseback (crisp bacon wrapped around oysters). The days are long gone when British cuisine was best known for shepherd's pie—ubiquitously available in pubs (though not made according to the song from *Sweeney Todd,* "with real shepherd in it")—and fish-and-chips. It probably won't be long before some of-the-moment hot spot unveils a trendy variation on the nursery-rhyme pie, with four-and-twenty rock stars popping out in place of blackbirds to sing for the king. This thriving dining scene rests on a solid foundation of ethnic cuisines. Thousands of (mostly northern) Indian restaurants have long ensured that Londoners view access to a tasty tandoori as a birthright. Chinese—Cantonese, primarily—outposts in London's tiny Chinatown have been around a long time, as have Greek tavernas. Now add Thai, Malaysian, Spanish, and Japanese cuisines to those easily found in England's capital. After all this, traditional British food, lately revived from a certain death, appears as one more exotic cuisine in the pantheon. If, in fact, you're out for traditional English food, but with a stylish twist, head to London's hot new "gastro-pubs."

As for cost, the democratization of restaurants means lighter checks than during the '80s, partly due to the popularity of prix-fixe menus; still, London is not an inexpensive city for dining. Damage-control methods include having lunch as your main meal—many top places feature good-value lunch menus, halving the price of evening à la carte—and ordering a pair of appetizers instead of an entrée, to which few places object. Seek out prix-fixe menus, but watch for hidden extras added to the check, including a "cover," bread and vegetables charged separately, and a service tariff. Many restaurants exclude service charges from the printed menu (which the law obliges them to display outside), then add 10%–15% to the check, or else stamp SERVICE NOT INCLUDED along the bottom, in which case you should add the 10%–15% yourself. Just don't pay twice for service—unscrupulous restaurateurs have been known to add service, but leave the total on the credit card slip blank. A final caveat: many restaurants are closed on Sunday, especially for dinner; the same is true on public holidays. Over the Christmas period, the London restaurant community all but shuts down—only hotels will be prepared to feed you. When in doubt, call ahead.

The Pub Experience

Londoners could no more live without their "local" than they could forgo dinner. The pub—or public house, to give it its full title—is ingrained in the British psyche as social center, refuge, second home. Pub culture—revolving around pints, pool, darts, and sports—is still male-dominated; however, as a result of the gentrification trend that was launched in the late '80s by the major breweries (which own most pubs), transforming many ancient smoke- and spittle-stained dives into fantasy Edwardian drawing rooms, women have been entering their welcoming doors in increasing numbers. This decade, the trend has been toward the Bar, identified by its cocktail list, creative paintwork, bare floorboards, and chrome fittings, and to the "gastro-pub," where a good kitchen fuels the relaxed ambience. These are English pubs, but not as we formerly knew them. When doing a London pub crawl, you must remember one thing: arcane licensing laws forbid the serving of alcohol after 11 PM (10:30 on Sunday; there are different rules for restaurants)—a circumstance you see in action at 10 minutes to 11, when the "last orders" bell triggers a stampede to the bar.

EXPLORING LONDON

London grew from a wooden bridge built over the Thames in the year AD 43 to its current 600 square mi and 7 million souls in haphazard fashion, meandering from its two official centers: Westminster, seat of government and royalty, and the City, site of finance and commerce. However, London's *un*official centers multiply and mutate year after year, and it would be a shame to stop only at the postcard views. Life is not lived in monuments, as the patrician patrons of the great Georgian architects understood when they commissioned the city's elegant squares and town houses. Close by, Westminster Abbey's original vegetable patch (or convent garden), which became the site of London's first square, Covent Garden, is now an unmissable stop on any agenda.

If the great, green parks are, as in Lord Chatham's phrase, "the lungs of London," then the River Thames is its backbone. The South Bank section absorbs the Southwark stews of Shakespeare's day and the current reconstruction of his original Globe Theatre, the concert hall from the '50s Festival of Britain, the arts complex from the '70s, and— farther downstream—the gorgeous 17th- and 18th-century symmetry of Greenwich, where the world's time is measured.

Numbers in the text correspond to numbers in the margin and on the London map.

Great Itineraries

In a city with as many richly stocked museums and marvels as London, visitors risk seeing half of everything and all of nothing. One could easily spend two solid weeks exploring the many layers of the city, but if time is limited you'll need to plan carefully. The following suggested itineraries will help your visit be exciting and efficient. See the neighborhood exploring sections below for complete information about individual sights.

IF YOU HAVE 1 DAY

Touring the largest city in England in the space of a single day sounds like an impossible goal, but it can actually—almost—be done in a single sunrise-to-sunset span. Think London 101. Begin at postcard London, the Houses of Parliament, best viewed from Westminster Bridge. If you're lucky, you'll hear Big Ben chiming, a sound likened to the heartbeat of the commonwealth. Move on to centuries-old Westminster Abbey—if and when Prince Charles becomes king, this is where his coronation will be staged—then tube it from the Westminster stop to Charing Cross (if you want to catch a glimpse of Her Majesty's two mounted sentries at Horse Guards Parade, bus it up Whitehall) to arrive at Trafalgar Square for your photo op with Nelson's Column and hundreds of pigeons. Take in the treasures of the National Gallery, which rank right up there with the collections of the Louvre and the Uffizi. History buffs might opt instead for a flip-book-fast tour of the adjacent National Portrait Gallery, heavy on the likes of England's heroes and litterateurs. Break for lunch in the Brasserie of the National Gallery, then take a short taxi trip over to a sight dear to your heart: for connoisseurs, this might be the Wallace or Tate Collection; for time travelers, the home of the Duke of Wellington or Sir John Soane's Museum; for kiddies, the London Dungeon or Madame Tussaud's. For a mid-afternoon session, choose between two royal monuments. First choice: heading west from Trafalgar Square, taxi through the impressive Admiralty Arch down the Mall to what there is reason to believe is the world's most photographed building, Buckingham Palace. During summer weeks, when the State Rooms are open to the public, their full pomp can be ogled. Theatreland awaits palace trekkers with a hit West End musical—a refreshing finale to the day. Second choice: eastward (take the tube to the Tower Hill stop) lies the Tower of London, home to the Beefeaters, the Crown Jewels, and the six resident ravens who nest on high. At dusk, after leaving the Tower, head across the way to the East End for a guaranteed spine chiller, a Jack the Ripper guided walking tour. Of course, if you have more than one day to spend, many of these sights would merit an extended visit—an entire afternoon, for example, could easily be spent at the National Gallery, the Tower, or Parliament.

A breakneck first day in London has been outlined above. On your second day you can slow down a bit, so you can afford to begin at the beginning of mankind's search for enlightenment and art: the legendary British Museum, resting place of such wonders as the Rosetta Stone, the Elgin Marbles, and the Lindow Man. If the idea of traipsing through "mankind's attic" doesn't grab you—the number of Londoners who have never been to the British Museum is vast—head for that amazing fun house, Sir John Soane's Museum, a time machine whose interiors will transport you to Regency-era England. Here in Bloomsbury other treats beckon: Pollock's Toy Museum, the Charles Dickens House, and, on Gordon Square, former address of Virginia Woolf and Lytton Strachey, the Percival David Foundation of Chinese Art. For an early lunch, tube it from Russell Square to Tottenham Court Road in Soho, for dim sum in Chinatown or nouvelle fare at a cute French bistro. Next, for a dose of magisterial grandeur, hop back on the tube to arrive at the St. Paul's stop and St. Paul's Cathedral. Walk off lunch by strolling south through Blackfriars—a quaint district full of crooked streets, historic courtyards, and minuscule cul-de-sacs—to the Thames River. After downing a refreshing pint at the Black Friar (possibly London's most ornately decorated 19th-century pub), cross Blackfriars bridge to Southwark's riverside embankment for a splendid view of St. Paul's dome. Keep an eye out for Cardinal's Wharf—here is the adorable house Sir Christopher Wren, architect of St. Paul's, built so he could easily check on the cathedral's construction. Take the time to drink in this scene (and photograph the cathedral framed by the alley's narrow walls), held to be one of the most enchanting views in all London. A stone's throw away is the rebuilt Shakespeare's Globe Theatre. If you're not catching a performance at the Globe (held only in warm-weather months), tour the adjoining museum. Keep heading eastward along the river, cross Southwark Bridge, then tube it from the Mansion House stop to Covent Garden. Dine at one of the area's chic restaurants, then watch the colorfully costumed street performers called buskers or attend a gala evening (book ahead) at the Royal Opera House.

Start your third day with Buckingham Palace's Changing of the Guard, held April–July at 11:30 daily, August–March at the same hour on alternate days. Warm up for this ceremony by viewing the superb treasures in the Queen's Gallery--Her Majesty's greatest paintings are here—and the nearby Royal Mews. If the state rooms of the palace are closed to viewing when you're in town, head through Green Park to Apsley House, the 18th-century mansion of the Duke of Wellington, and check out its memorably palatial interiors. Wander up Park Lane into Mayfair, one of London's ritziest neighborhoods, and stroll past Grosvenor Square and Oxford Street to Manchester Square and the Wallace Collection, whose gilded interiors are stuffed with 18th-century art. For a pub break, visit the Devonshire Arms, a Henry Higgins's-parlor look-alike on Duke Street, a few blocks south of the Wallace. (London fact: the Beatles used to chow down here.) For serious retail therapy, return south, then east to scout three great shopping destinations: Bond Street for world-class glitz, Regent Street for savvy sophistication, and Carnaby Street for some rocker-style street gear. For an evening highlight, why not book a performance of the Royal Shakespeare Company at the Barbican Centre?

Each section of London provides distinct clues to the city's past. In your first three days, you've made a start on piecing together the story of this great, crowded, endlessly fascinating city. Now you're ready to build on that foundation. Kick off day four at the South Kensington museums, a district planned by the Victorians to induce gallery gout and museum feet: the Victoria and Albert, the Natural History Museum, and the Science Museum. Art lovers will want to explore the first, while budding Einsteins will run for either of the latter. All three cultural palaces could easily consume an entire day, so you'll need to pick one to do it justice. Then head over to Knightsbridge to either mercantile-and-fashion giants Harrods or Harvey Nichols. Move on to Kensington Gardens, where almost everyone throws a kiss to the famous statue of Peter Pan, and to Kensington Palace, home to royals from Queen Anne to today's Windsors, where the state rooms are open to view year-round. For modern art buffs, the Serpentine Gallery should be the next stop. Along the way, let yourself venture into the many winding lanes and narrow courts in the area, and smell the roses in all those lovely well-kept squares.

Day five dawns at the City—London's ancient core. Built up around St. Paul's, the area has numerous attractions, including Dr. Johnson's House, the Old Bailey, the Museum of London, and several Christopher Wren churches. The nearby East End beckons with its Petticoat Lane sprawling market (open weekends), the Geffrye Museum—a must for decorative arts lovers—and the Spitalfields restoration. After lunch, serious folk will want to tube westward over to Holborn (✉ Chancery La., Temple stops) to visit the historic Inns of Court and the Temple, the historic foundations of Legal London. Farther along lies that storybook icon, Tower Bridge, which you must cross to reach the South Bank, where the London Dungeon awaits—this medieval waxworks show is devoted to the more gory aspects of British history (and there were plenty of them!).

On day six, leave the city behind for pleasures along the Thames, at Greenwich or the storied palace and gardens of Hampton Court—don't even *consider* attempting both—or, for another option, the less exalted but relentlessly picturesque village of Hampstead, located on the northern outskirts of London. Here you'll find Kenwood—a noble Robert Adam house—as well as Keats's and Freud's homes, and the bustling Camden Lock market. Just south of Hampstead is Regent's Park, surrounded by Nash's Terraces—a must for Regency-era buffs and admirers of splendid creations.

Begin your last day by taking the tube to the Knightsbridge stop and heading south for an early morning stroll through Belgravia; few tourists venture here, but it's London at its most *Upstairs, Downstairs*. Head over to the cavalcade of emporiums of Sloane Street and Sloane Square and enjoy some high-style shopping. Chelsea, along King's Road, is where much of London comes to shop and stroll. After viewing Wren's historic Royal Hospital, relax over lunch at a King's Road eatery, then stop by Cheyne Walk, where leading 19th-century artists lived, then bus over to Millbank to take in the Tate Gallery's incomparable collection of paintings by J. M. W. Turner, the romantic-period artist who painted the most beautiful sunsets of any century. As dusk settles, head over to the South Bank Arts Complex, where you might finish up your visit with a play in the Olivier Theatre or a concert in the Queen Elizabeth Hall. Don't fret if the performances are entirely booked: by now, you've learned that London itself is the most wonderful free show in all the world.

Westminster and Royal London

Westminster and Royal London might be called "London for Beginners." If you went no farther than these few acres, you would have seen many of the famous sights, from the Houses of Parliament, Big Ben, Westminster Abbey, and Buckingham Palace, to two of the world's greatest art collections, housed in the National and Tate galleries. You can truly call this area Royal London, since it is neatly bounded by the triangle of streets that make up the route that the Queen usually takes when journeying from Buckingham Palace to Westminster Abbey or to the Houses of Parliament on state occasions. The three points on this royal triangle are Trafalgar Square, Westminster, and Buckingham Palace. Naturally, in an area that regularly sees the pomp and pageantry of royal occasions, the streets are wide and the vistas long. With beautifully kept St. James's Park at the heart of the triangle, there is a feeling here of timeless dignity—flower beds bursting with color, long avenues of ancient trees framing classically proportioned buildings, constant glimpses of pinnacles and towers over the treetops, the distant *bong!* of Big Ben counting off the hours. This is concentrated sightseeing, so pace yourself. Remember that for a large part of the year, much of Royal London is floodlighted at night, adding to the theatricality of the experience.

A Good Walk

Trafalgar Square is the obvious place to start for several reasons. It is the geographical core of London, by dint of a plaque on the corner of the Strand and Charing Cross Road from which distances on U.K. signposts are measured. It is home to many political demonstrations, a raucous New Year's party, and the highest concentrations of bus stops and pigeons in the capital. After taking in the instantly identifiable **Nelson's Column** ① in the center (read about the area on a plaque marking its 150th anniversary), head for the **National Gallery** ② on the north side, Britain's greatest trove of masterpieces. Detour around the corner to see the **National Portrait Gallery** ③—a parade of the famous that can be very rewarding to anyone interested in what makes the British tick. East of the National Gallery, still on Trafalgar Square, see the muchloved church of **St. Martin-in-the-Fields** ④, then, stepping through grand Admiralty Arch down on the southwest corner, enter the royal pink road, the Mall, with St. James's Park running along the south side. On your right is the Institute of Contemporary Art, known as the ICA, housed in the great Regency architect John Nash's **Carlton House Terrace** ⑤. At the foot of the Mall is one of London's most famous sights, **Buckingham Palace** ⑥, home, of course, to the monarch of the land, with the nearby **Queen's Gallery** ⑦—with changing exhibitions from Her Majesty's vast art collection—and the **Royal Mews** ⑧ nearby. Turning left and left again, almost doubling back, follow the southern perimeter of St. James's Park around Birdcage Walk, passing the headquarters of the Queen's Guard, the **Wellington Barracks** ⑨, on your right. Cross Horse Guard's Road at the eastern edge of the park, walk down Great George Street, and across Parliament Square, and you come to another of the great sights of London, the **Houses of Parliament** ⑩— a mock-medieval extravaganza designed by two celebrated Victorianera architects, down to the last detail (Gothic umbrella stands)—built along the Thames and including the famous Clock Tower, usually known as Big Ben after the nickname of the bell that chimes the hour. For millions of citizens of the British empire, the sound of Big Ben's chimes is a link with the heart and soul of the commonwealth. A clockwise turn around the square brings you to yet another major landmark, breathtaking **Westminster Abbey** ⑪. Complete the circuit and head north up Whitehall, where you'll see a simple monolith in the middle of the street—the Cenotaph, designed by Edwin Lutyens in 1920 in commemoration of the 1918 Armistice. The gated alley there on your left leads to **Ten Downing Street** ⑫, where England's modest "White

House" stands. Soon after that you pass **Horse Guards Parade** ⑬, setting for the Queen's birthday celebration, Trooping the Colour, with the perfect classical Inigo Jones **Banqueting House** ⑭, scene of Charles I's execution, opposite. If it's art you're mad about, skip the last three sights and head directly down Millbank to the **Tate Gallery** ⑯—the most famous museum for British painting and sculpture.

TIMING

You could achieve this walk of roughly 3 mi in just over an hour, but you could just as easily spend a week's vacation on this route alone. Allow as much time as you can for the two great museums—the National Gallery requires *at least* two hours; the National Portrait Gallery can be whizzed round in less than one. Westminster Abbey can take half a day—especially in summer, when lines are long, both to get in and to get around. In summer, you can get inside Buckingham Palace, too, a half day's operation increased to a whole day if you see the Royal Mews, the Queen's Gallery, and/or the Guards' Museum. If the Changing of the Guard is a priority, make sure you time this walk correctly.

Sights to See

⑭ **Banqueting House.** Commissioned by James I, Inigo Jones (1573–1652), one of England's great architects, created this banqueting hall in 1619–1622 out of an old remnant of the Tudor Palace of Whitehall. Influenced by Andrea Palladio's work, which he saw during a sojourn in Tuscany, Jones remade the palace with Palladian sophistication and purity. James I's son, Charles I, enhanced the interior by employing the Flemish painter Peter Paul Rubens to glorify his father all over the ceiling. As it turned out, these allegorical paintings, depicting a wise monarch being received into heaven, were the last thing Charles saw before he was beheaded on a scaffold outside in 1649. ⊠ *Whitehall*, ☎ *0171/ 930–4179.* 🔳 *£3.25.* ⏱ *Mon.–Sat. 10–5.* Tube: Westminster.

⑥ **Buckingham Palace.** Supreme among the symbols of London, indeed of Britain generally, and of the Royal Family, Buckingham Palace tops the must-see lists—although the building itself is no masterpiece and has housed the monarch only since Victoria moved here from Kensington Palace on her accession in 1837. Its great gray bulk sums up the imperious splendor of so much of the city: stately, magnificent, and ponderous. In 1824 the palace was substantially rebuilt by John Nash, that tireless architect, for George IV, that tireless spendthrift. Compared to other great London residences, it is a Johnny-come-lately affair: the Portland stone facade dates from only 1913, and the interior was renovated and redecorated only after World War II bombs damaged it. It contains some 600 rooms, including the State Ballroom and, of course, the Throne Room. These State Rooms are where much of the business of royalty is played out—investitures, state banquets, receptions, lunch parties for the famous, and so on. The royal apartments are in the north wing; when the Queen is in, the royal standard flies at the masthead. The State Rooms are on show for eight weeks in August and September, when the royal family is away. Note that the finest artwork Her Majesty owns is on view at the **Queen's Gallery** (☞ *below*), at the south side of the palace. The **Changing of the Guard**, which, with all the pomp and ceremony monarchists and children adore remains one of London's best free shows, culminates in front of the palace. Marching to live music, the Queen's Guard proceeds up the Mall from St. James's Palace to Buckingham Palace. Shortly afterward, the new guard approaches from Wellington Barracks via Birdcage Walk. Once the old and new guards are in the forecourt, the gold guard symbolically hands over the keys to the palace. The ceremony takes place daily at 11:30 AM April– July, and on alternating days August–March, but the guards sometimes

London

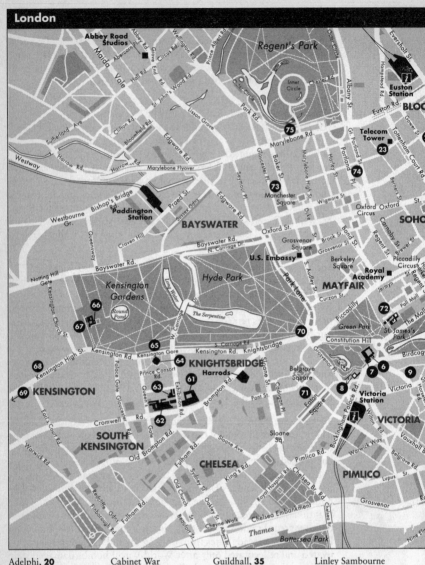

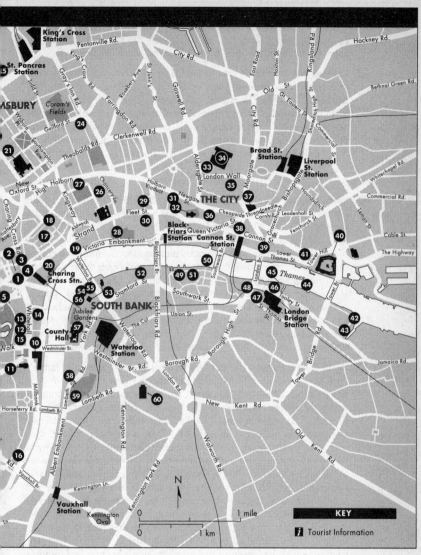

KEY

ℹ Tourist Information

cancel due to bad weather; check the signs in the forecourt or call 089/ 150–5452 . Arrive by 10:30 AM for a decent view of all the panoply. ✉ *Buckingham Palace Rd.,* ☎ *0171/839–1377.* 🎫 *£9.* ☉ *Aug. 8– Sept. 30, daily 9:30–4:30. Tube: St. James's Park, Victoria.*

⓯ Cabinet War Rooms. It was from this small maze of 17 bomb-proof underground rooms—in back of the hulking Foreign Office—that Britain's World War II fortunes were directed. During air raids, the Cabinet met here—the Cabinet Room is still arranged as if a meeting were about to convene; in the Map Room, the Allied campaign is charted; the Prime Minister's Room holds the desk from which Churchill made his morale-boosting broadcasts; and the Telephone Room has his hot line to FDR. ✉ *Clive Steps, King Charles St.,* ☎ *0171/930–6961.* 🎫 *£4.40.* ☉ *Daily 10–5:15. Tube: Westminster.*

❺ Carlton House Terrace. A glorious example of Regency architect John Nash's genius, Carlton House Terrace was built between 1812 and 1830, under the patronage of George IV (Prince Regent until George III's death in 1820). Nash was responsible for a series of West End developments, of which these white-stucco facades and massive Corinthian columns may be the most imposing. Today, the structure houses the ☞ **Institute of Contemporary Art,** better known as the ICA, one of Britain's leading modern-art centers. The ICAfé offers good hot dishes, salads, quiches, and desserts. The bar upstairs, which serves baguette sandwiches, has a picture window overlooking the Mall. ✉ *The Mall,* ☎ *0171/930– 3647.* 🎫 *1-day membership £1.50, additional charge for specific events.* ☉ *Daily noon–9:30, later for some events. Tube: Charing Cross.*

⓭ Horse Guards Parade. Facing Horse Guards Road—opposite St. James's Park at one end and Whitehall at the other—Horse Guards Parade is now notable mainly for the annual Trooping the Colour ceremony, in which the Queen takes the Royal Salute, her official birthday gift, on the second Saturday in June. (Like Paddington Bear, the Queen has two birthdays; her real one is on April 21.) There is pageantry galore, with marching bands and the occasional guardsman fainting clean away in his weighty busby (those curious, furry hats). Covering the vast expanse of the square that faces Horse Guards Road, opposite St. James's Park, at one end, and Whitehall at the other, the ceremony is televised and also broadcast on Radio 4. You can also see it from the Mall, but you have to get there very early in the morning for any kind of decent view. You can also attend the queenless rehearsals on the preceding two Saturdays. At the Whitehall facade of Horse Guards, two mounted sentries known as the Queen's Life Guard provide what may be London's most frequently exercised photo op. They change, quietly, at 11 AM Monday–Saturday, 10 on Sunday.

★ ❿ Houses of Parliament. Postcard London come to life, the Houses of Parliament are, arguably, the city's most famous and photogenic sight. Facing them you see, from left to right: Big Ben—keeping watch on the corner, the Houses of Parliament themselves, Westminster Hall (the oldest part of the complex), and the Victoria Tower. The most romantic view of the complex is from the opposite, south, side of the river, a vista especially dramatic at night when the spires, pinnacles, and towers of the great building are floodlighted green and gold. After a catastrophic fire in 1834, these buildings arose, designed in a delightful mock-medieval style by two Victorian-era architects: Sir Charles Barry and Augustus Pugin. The Palace of Westminster, as the complex is still properly called, was established by Edward the Confessor in the 11th century. It has served as the seat of English administrative power, on and off, ever since.

Now virtually the symbol of London, the 1858 **Clock Tower** designed by Pugin contains the bell known as Big Ben that chimes the hour (and the quarters); weighing a mighty 13 tons, the bell takes its name from Sir Benjamin Hall, the far-from-slim Westminster building works commissioner. At the other end of Parliament is the 336-ft-high **Victoria Tower,** newly agleam from its recent restoration and cleaning. The rest of the complex was scrubbed down some years ago; the revelation of the honey stone under the dowdy, smog-blackened facades, which seemed almost symbolic at the time, cheered London up no end. There are two Houses, the Lords and the Commons. The Visitors' Galleries of the House of Commons affords a view of the best free show in London, staged in the world's most renowned ego chamber (if you want to take it in during its liveliest hour, Prime Minister's Question Time, you'll need to book tickets in advance). ⊠ *St. Stephen's Entrance, St. Margaret St., SW1,* ☎ *0171/219–3000.* ☎ *Free.* ☉ *Commons Mon.–Thurs. 2:30–10, Fri. 9:30–3; Lords Mon.–Thurs. 2:30–10. Closed Easter wk, May bank holiday, July–Oct., 3 wks at Christmas. Tube: Westminster.*

★ ❷ **National Gallery.** Jan Van Eyck's *Arnolfini Marriage,* Leonardo da Vinci's *Virgin and Child,* Velázquez's *Rokeby Venus,* Constable's *Hay Wain* . . . you get the picture. There are approximately 2,200 other paintings in this museum—many of them instantly recognizable and among the most treasured works of art anywhere. The museum's low, gray, colonnaded, neoclassic facade fills the north side of Trafalgar Square. The collection ranges from painters of the Italian Renaissance and earlier—housed in the 1991 Sainsbury Wing, designed by the American architect Robert Venturi—through the Flemish and Dutch masters, the Spanish school, and of course the English tradition, including Hogarth, Gainsborough, Stubbs, and Constable.

The collection is really too overwhelming to absorb in a single viewing. The **Micro Gallery,** a computer information center in the Sainsbury Wing, might be the place to start. You can access in-depth information on any work here, choose your favorites, and print out a free personal tour map that marks the paintings you most want to see. Rounding out the top-10 list (the first four lead off above) are Uccello's *Battle of San Romano* (children love its knights on horseback), Bellini's *Doge Leonardo Loredan* (notice the snail-shell buttons), Botticelli's *Venus and Mars,* Caravaggio's *Supper at Emmaus* (almost cinematically lit), Turner's *Fighting Témééaire* (one of the artist's greatest sunsets), and Seurat's *Bathers at Asnières.* Note that free admission encourages repeat visits: although you may plan to see just the top of the top, the National Gallery, like so many first-rate collections, reveals more gems the more one explores. For a great time-out and fashionable lunch, head for the museum's Brasserie, in the Sainsbury Wing. ⊠ *Trafalgar Sq.,* ☎ *0171/839–3321; 0171/839–3526 recorded general information; 0171/389–1773 recorded exhibition information.* ☎ *Free; admission charge for special exhibitions.* ☉ *Mon.–Sat. 10–6, Sun. 2–6; June–Aug., also Wed. until 8; free 1-hr guided tours start at the Sainsbury Wing weekdays at 11:30 and 2:30, Sat. at 2 and 3:30. Tube: Charing Cross.*

❸ **National Portrait Gallery.** Just around the corner from the National Gallery, this is a much more idiosyncratic collection that presents a brief history of Britain through its people, past and present; it is an essential visit for all history and literature buffs. As an art collection it is eccentric, since the subject, not the artist, is the point. Highlights range from Holbein to Hockney. Many of the faces are obscure and will be just as unknown to English visitors, because the portraits outlasted their sitters' fame—not so surprising when the portraitists are such greats as Reynolds, Gainsborough, Lawrence, and Romney. But the annotation is comprehensive, the layout is easy to negotiate, being chronological, with the oldest at the top—and there is a new, separate research center for those who get hooked on particular personages. Don't miss the new Victorian and early 20th-century portrait galleries. ⊠ *St. Martin's Pl.,* ☎ *0171/306–0055.* ▨ *Free.* ☼ *Weekdays 10–5, Sat. 10–6, Sun. 2–6. Tube: Charing Cross, Leicester Sq.*

❶ Nelson's Column. Centerpiece of Trafalgar Square, this famed landmark is topped with E. H. Baily's 1843 statue of Admiral Lord Horatio Nelson, keeping watch from his 145-ft-high granite perch. The bas-reliefs depicting scenes of his life, installed around the base, were cast from cannons he captured. The four majestic lions, designed by the Victorian painter Sir Edwin Landseer, were added in 1867. The calling cards of generations of picturesque pigeons have been a corrosive problem for the statue; this may have been finally solved by the addition of a gel coating to the statue.

❼ Queen's Gallery. Housed in a former chapel at the south side of **Buckingham Palace**, this showcase offers a rotating sample of what is generally regarded as the finest private art collection in the world. The most famous pictures, including Vermeer's *The Music Lesson* and works by Rubens, Rembrandt, Canaletto are usually on view in Buckingham Palace. If you're lucky, you'll find some of the royal Leonardo da Vinci drawings on view—she owns them by the dozen. ⊠ *Buckingham Palace Rd.,* ☎ *0171/799–2331.* ▨ *£3.70, combined ticket for Queen's Gallery and Royal Mews £6.20.* ☼ *Tues.–Sat. 10–5, Sun. 2–5; closed Dec. 24–Mar. 4. Tube: St. James's Park, Victoria.*

☾ ❽ Royal Mews. Unmissable children's entertainment, this museum is the home of Her Majesty's Coronation Coach. Standing nearly next door to the Queen's Gallery, the Royal Mews were designed by famed Regency-era architect John Nash. Mewses were originally falcons' quarters (the name comes from their "mewing," or feather-shedding), but horses gradually eclipsed birds of prey. Now some of the magnificent royal beasts live here alongside the fabulous, bejeweled, glass and golden coaches they draw on state occasions. ⊠ *Buckingham Palace Rd.,* ☎ *0171/799–2331.* ▨ *£3.70, combined ticket for Queen's Gallery and Royal Mews £6.20.* ☼ *Oct.–Mar., Wed. noon–4; Apr.– Oct., Tues.–Thurs. noon–4; closed Mar. 25–29, Oct. 1–5, Dec. 23– Jan. 5. Tube: St. James's Park, Victoria.*

St. James's Park. London's smallest, most ornamental park and the oldest of its royal ones, St. James's Park makes a spectacular frame for the towers of Westminster and Victoria—especially at night, when the illuminated fountains play and the skyline beyond the trees looks like a floating fairyland. Its present shape more or less reflects what John Nash designed under George IV, turning the canal into a graceful lake (which was cemented in at a depth of 4 ft in 1855, so don't even think of swimming) and generally naturalizing the gardens. More than 30 species of birds—including swans that belong to the Queen—congregate on Duck Island at the east end of the lake. Along the northern side of the park, you'll find the grand thoroughfare known as **The Mall**—best seen on those days when the Queen is hosting her garden parties and it is thronged with hundreds of guests on their way to Buckingham Palace, most of whom have donned hat and frock to take afternoon tea with the monarch. At dusk on summer days, the deck chairs (which you must pay to use) are often crammed with office lunchers being serenaded by music from the bandstands. But the best time to stroll the leafy walkways is after dark, with Westminster Abbey and the Houses of Parliament rising above the floodlighted lake, and peace reigning.

❹ St. Martin-in-the-Fields. One of Britain's best-loved churches, St. Martin's was completed in 1726; James Gibbs's classical-temple-with-spire design became a familiar pattern followed for churches in early Colonial America. The church is also a haven for music lovers, since the internationally known Academy of St. Martin-in-the-Fields was founded here, and a popular program of free lunchtime and evening concerts continues today. The church's fusty interior has a wonderful atmosphere for music making—but the wooden benches can make it hard to give your undivided attention to the music. The **London Brass-Rubbing Centre,** where you can make your own souvenir knight from replica tomb brasses, with metallic waxes, paper, and instructions provided, is in the crypt. ⊠ *Trafalgar Sq.,* ☎ *0171/930–0089 or 0171/839–8362 credit-card bookings for evening concerts.* 🎫 *Brass rubbings from £1.* ☉ *Church daily 8–8, crypt Mon.–Sat. 10–8, Sun. noon–6. Tube: Charing Cross, Leicester Sq.*

⓰ Tate Gallery. The Tate—everyone drops the word "gallery"—overlooks the Thames, about a 20-minute walk from the Houses of Parliament, and is widely known as Britain's leading collection of modern art. "Modern" is slightly misleading, since one of the three collections here consists of British art from 1545 to the present, including works by Hogarth, Gainsborough, Reynolds, and Stubbs from the 18th century, and by Constable, Blake, and the Pre-Raphaelite painters from the 19th. Also from the 19th century is the J. W. M. Turner Bequest, now housed magnificently in the James Stirling–designed **Clore Gallery,** the largest collection of work by this leading British romantic artist. The Tate has an innovative policy of rehanging the whole gallery annually, which means that a favorite work may not be on view. Usually, however, your tour can deal you multiple pleasing shocks of recognition (Rodin's *The Kiss,* Lichtenstein's *Whaam!*). ⊠ *Millbank,* ☎ *0171/821–1313 or 0171/821–7128 recorded information.* 🎫 *Free; special exhibitions £3–£7.* ☉ *Mon.–Sat. 10–5:50, Sun. 2–5:50. Tube: Pimlico.*

⓬ Ten Downing Street. South of the Banqueting House (☞ *above*), you'll find the British version of the White House, occupying three unassuming 18th-century houses. No. 10 has been the official residence of the prime minister since 1732. The cabinet office, hub of the British system of government, is on the ground floor; the prime minister's private apartment is on the top floor. The chancellor of the exchequer occupies No. 11. Downing Street is cordoned off, but you should be able to catch a glimpse of it from Whitehall. *Tube: Westminster.*

Trafalgar Square. Permanently alive with people, Londoners and tourists alike, and roaring traffic, Trafalgar Square remains London's "living room"—great events, such as royal weddings, elections, sporting triumphs—will always see the crowds gathering in the city's most famous square. It is a commanding open space—originally built to reflect the width and breadth of an empire that once reached to the farthest corners of the globe—containing a bevy of must-see attractions, including **Nelson's Column** (☞ *above*) and the **National Gallery** (☞ *above*). Today, street performers enhance the square's intermittent atmosphere of celebration, which is strongest in December, first when the lights on the gigantic Christmas tree are turned on, and then—less festively—when thousands gather to see in the New Year.

❾ Wellington Barracks. This is the august headquarters of the Guards Division, the Queen's five regiments of elite foot guards who protect the sovereign and patrol her palace dressed in tunics of gold-purled scarlet and tall busbies of Canadian brown bearskin. If you want to learn more about the guards, you can visit the **Guards Museum;** the entrance is next to the Guards Chapel. ⊠ *Wellington Barracks, Birdcage Walk,*

☎ 0171/930–4466, ext. 3430. 🎫 £2. ☉ Sat.–Thurs. 10–4. Tube: St.
James's Park.

★ ⑪　**Westminster Abbey.** Nearly all of Britain's monarchs have been crowned
here since the coronation of William the Conqueror on Christmas Day
1066—and most are buried here, too. The main nave is packed with
atmosphere and memories, as it has witnessed many splendid coronation ceremonies, royal weddings, and more recently, the funeral of
Diana, Princess of Wales. It is also packed with crowds, so much so these
days, that in March 1998 an admission charge (a steep one, at that) was
set in place for entrance to the main nave. Other than the mysterious
gloom of the vast interior, the first thing that strikes most people is the
fantastic proliferation of statues, tombs, and commemorative tablets:
in parts, the building seems more like a stonemason's yard than a place
of worship. But it is in its latter capacity that this landmark truly comes
into its own. Although attending a service is not something to under-
take purely for sightseeing reasons, it provides a glimpse of the abbey
in its full majesty, accompanied by music from the Westminster choristers and the organ that Henry Purcell once played.

The present abbey is a largely 13th- and 14th-century rebuilding of the
11th-century church founded by Edward the Confessor, with one notable addition being the 18th-century twin towers over the west entrance, completed by Sir Christopher Wren. The nave is your first
sight on entering; you need to look up to gain a perspective on the truly
awe-inspiring scale of the church, since the eye-level view is obscured
by the choir screen, past which point admission is charged. Before paying, look at the poignant **Tomb of the Unknown Warrior,** an anonymous World War I martyr who lies buried here in memory of the
soldiers fallen in both world wars. Passing through the Choir, with its
mid-19th-century choir stalls, into the North Transept, look up to your
right to see the painted-glass Rose Window, the largest of its kind. You
can then proceed into one of the architectural glories of Britain, **Henry
VII Chapel,** passing the huge white marble tomb of Elizabeth I, buried
with her half-sister, "Bloody" Mary I. All around are magnificent
sculptures of saints, philosophers, and kings, with wild mermaids and
monsters carved on the choir-stall misericords (undersides), and exquisite
fan vaulting above (binoculars will help you spot the statues high on
the walls)—the last riot of medieval design in England and one of the
miracles of Western architecture.

Next you enter the **Chapel of Edward the Confessor,** where beside the
royal saint's shrine stands the **Coronation Chair,** which has been briefly
graced by nearly every royal posterior. In 1400 Geoffrey Chaucer became the first poet to be buried in **Poets' Corner,** which also has memorials devoted to William Shakespeare, William Blake, and Charles
Dickens. Exit the abbey by a door from the South Transept. Outside
the west front is an archway into the quiet, green **Dean's Yard** and the
entrance to the **Cloisters** and the **Brass-Rubbing Centre** (☎ 0171/
222–2085). ✉ Broad Sanctuary, ☎ 0171/222–5152 or 0171/222–
5152 for Undercroft, Pyx Chamber, Chapter House, and Treasury. 🎫
Nave £5. ☉ Mon.–Tues. and Thurs.–Fri. 9–4, Wed. 9–7:45, Sat. 9–
2:45 (last admission 1 hr before closing), Sun. all day for services only;
Undercroft, Pyx Chamber, Chapter House, and Treasury daily 10:30–
4. Henry VII Chapel closed Sun. Tube: Westminster.

Soho and Covent Garden

A quadrilateral bounded by Regent Street, Coventry/Cranbourn streets,
Charing Cross Road, and the eastern half of Oxford Street encloses
Soho, the most fun part of the West End. This appellation, unlike the

New York neighborhood's similar one, is not an abbreviation of anything, but a blast from the past—derived (as far as we know) from the shouts of "So-ho!" that royal huntsmen in Whitehall Palace's parklands were once heard to cry. One of Charles II's illegitimate sons, the Duke of Monmouth, was an early resident, his dubious pedigree setting the tone for the future: for many years Soho was London's strip show/peep show/clip joint/sex shop/brothel center. The mid-'80s brought legislation that granted expensive licenses to a few such establishments and closed down the rest. Today, Soho remains the address for many wonderful ethnic restaurants, including those of London's Chinatown.

Best known as Eliza Doolittle's stomping grounds in Shaw's *Pygmalion* and Lerner and Loewe's *My Fair Lady,* the former Covent Garden Market became the Piazza in 1980, and it still functions as the center of a neighborhood—one that has always been alluded to as "colorful." It was originally the "convent garden" belonging to the Abbey of St. Peter at Westminster (later Westminster Abbey). Centuries of magnificence and misery, vice and mayhem, and more recent periods of art-literary bohemia followed, until it became the vegetable supplier of London when its market building went up in the 1830s, followed by the Flower Market in 1870. When the produce moved out to the bigger, better Nine Elms Market in Vauxhall in 1974, the (now sadly defunct) Greater London Council stepped in with a rehabilitation scheme, and a new neighborhood was born.

A Good Walk

Soho, being small, is easy to explore, though it's also easy to mistake one narrow, crowded street for another, and even Londoners go astray here. Enter from the northwest corner, Oxford Circus, and head south for about 200 yards down Regent Street, turn left onto Great Marlborough Street, and head to the top of Carnaby Street. Turn right off Broadwick Street onto Berwick (pronounced berrick) Street, famed as central London's best fruit and vegetable market. Then step through tiny Walker's Court (ignoring, or not, the notorious hookers' bulletin board), cross Brewer Street, and you'll have arrived at Soho's hip hangout, Old Compton Street. From here, Wardour, Dean, Frith, and Greek streets lead north, all of them bursting with restaurants and clubs. Either of the latter two lead north to Soho Square—among the most charming of London's squares, it features a storybook Tudor cottage just made for a picnic setting—but for lunch, head one block south instead, to Shaftesbury Avenue, heart of Theatreland, across which you'll find Chinatown's main drag, Gerrard Street. Below Gerrard Street is Leicester Square, and running along its west side is Charing Cross Road, a bibliophile's dream. You'll find some of the best of the specialist bookshops in little Cecil Court, running east just before Trafalgar Square. During your Soho sojourn, take any excuse you can think of to visit either of the neighborhood's wonderful rival patisseries, **Maison Bertaux** (⊠ 8 Greek St.) or **Pâtisserie Valerie** (⊠ 44 Old Compton St.); both serve divine cakes, croissants, and éclairs and offer a perfect time-out.

The easiest way to find the **Covent Garden (The Piazza)** ⑰ market building and the Piazza is to walk down Cranbourn Street, next to Leicester Square tube, then down Long Acre, and turn right at James Street. Here, and around here, are St. Paul's—the actors' church—and the **Theatre Museum,** as well as plenty of shops and cafés. (If your aim is to shop, Neal Street, Floral Street, the streets around Seven Dials, and the Thomas Neale's mall all repay exploration.) From Seven Dials, veer 45 degrees south onto Mercer Street, turning right on Long Acre, then left onto Garrick Street, left onto Rose Street, and right onto Floral Street. At the other end you'll emerge onto Bow Street, right next to the **Royal Opera House** ⑱. Continuing on—passing the Manet-stocked **Courtauld Institute Galleries** ⑲—and turning left onto Russell Street, you reach Drury Lane, and the Theatre Royal. At the end of Drury Lane, turn right at the Aldwych, follow the ¾-mi-long Strand to the southern end, and take Villiers Street down to the Thames. See the York Watergate and Cleopatra's Needle by Victoria Embankment Gardens, cross the gardens northwest to the **Adelphi** ⑳, circumnavigating the Strand by sticking to the embankment walk, and you'll soon reach Waterloo Bridge, where (weather permitting) you can catch some of London's most glamorous views, toward both the City and Westminster around the Thames bend.

TIMING

The distance covered here is around 5 mi, if you include the lengthy walk down the Strand and riverside stroll back. Skip that, and it's barely a couple of miles, but you will almost certainly get lost, since the streets in both Covent Garden and Soho are winding and chaotic, and not logically disposed. Although getting lost is half the fun, it does make it hard to predict how long this walk will take. You can whiz round both neighborhoods in an hour, but if the area appeals at all, you'll want all day—for shopping, lunch, the Theatre and Transport museums, and the Courtauld Galleries. One way to do it is to start at Leicester Square at 2 PM, when the Half Price Theatre Booth opens, pick up tickets for later, and walk, shop, and eat in between.

Sights to See

⑳ **Adelphi.** Near the triangular-handkerchief Victoria Embankment Gardens, this regal riverfront row of houses was the work of all four of the brothers Adam (John, Robert, James, and William: hence the name, from the Greek *adelphoi*, meaning "brothers"), London's Scottish architects. The best mansion is 7 Adam Street.

Carnaby Street. The '60s synonym for swinging London fell into a postparty depression, reemerging sometime during the '80s as the main drag of a public-relations invention called West Soho. Blank stares would greet anyone asking directions to such a place, but it is geographically logical, and the tangle of streets—Foubert's Place, Broadwick Street, Marshall Street—do cohere, at least, in type of merchandise (youth accessories, mostly, with a smattering of designer boutiques).

⑲ **Courtauld Institute Galleries.** Several years ago, this collection was moved to a setting worthy of its fame: a grand 18th-century classical mansion, Somerset House. Founded in 1931 by the textile maven Samuel Courtauld, this is London's finest Impressionist and Postimpressionist collection (Manet's *Bar at the Follies-Bergère* is the star), with bonus Baroque works thrown in. Note that the galleries are closed through Fall 1998 for a major renovation; call to confirm opening hours. ⊠ *The Strand,* ☎ *0171/873–2526.* ⊡ *£4; White Card accepted.* ☉ *Mon.–Sat. 10–6, Sun. 2–6. Tube: Temple, Embankment.*

⑰ **Covent Garden (The Piazza).** The original "convent garden" produced fruits and vegetables for the 13th-century Abbey of St. Peter at Westminster. In 1630, the Duke of Bedford, having become owner, commissioned Inigo Jones to lay out a square, with St. Paul's Church at one end. The fruit, flower, and vegetable market established in the 1700s flourished until 1974, when its traffic grew to be too much for the narrow streets, and it was moved south of the Thames. Since then, the area has been transformed into the Piazza, a mostly higher-class shopping mall, which features a couple of cafés and some knickknack stores that are good for gifts. Open-air entertainers perform under the portico of St. Paul's Church, where George Bernard Shaw set the first scene of *Pygmalion* (reshaped as the musical *My Fair Lady*).

Leicester Square. This is the big magnet for nightlife lovers. Looking at the neon of the major movie houses, the fast-food outlets, and the disco entrances, you'd never guess the square—it's pronounced lester—was laid out around 1630. The Odeon, on the east side, is the venue for all the Royal Film Performances, and the movie theme is continued by a jaunty little statue of Charlie Chaplin in the opposite corner. Shakespeare sulks in the middle, chin on hand, clearly wishing he were somewhere else. One landmark certainly worth visiting is the **Society of London Theatre (SOLT) ticket kiosk**, on the southwest corner, which sells half-price tickets for many of that evening's performances (☞ Nightlife and the Arts, *below*).

⑱ **Royal Opera House.** The fabled home of the Royal Ballet and Britain's finest opera company is now closed until 2001—mammoth renovations will try to bring this 19th-century treasure into the 21st. Here, in days of yore, Joan Sutherland brought down the house as Lucia di Lammermoor, and Rudolf Nureyev and Margot Fonteyn became the greatest ballet duo of all time. For such delights, seats were top dollar—nearly £100—or just ½₀ of that lordly amount. Whatever the price, it was worth it if you loved red-and-gold Victorian decor, which always managed to give a very special feel to the hush that precedes the start of a performance. London's premier opera venue was designed in 1858 by E. M. Barry, son of Sir Charles, the House of Commons architect. Call for current updates on the performing schedule of the troupes; for further information, *see* The Arts, *below.* ✉ *Bow St.,* ☎ *0171/240–1066 or 0171/304–4000. Tube: Covent Garden.*

☾ The **Theatre Museum** aims to re-create the excitement of theater itself. There are usually programs in progress allowing children to get in a mess with makeup or have a giant dressing-up session. Permanent exhibits attempt a history of the English stage, with artifacts from the 16th century to Mick Jagger's jumpsuit, and tens of thousands of theater playbills and sections on such topics as Hamlet-through-the-ages and pantomime. ✉ *7 Russell St.,* ☎ *0171/836–7891.* 🎟 *£3.50.* ☉ *Tues.–Sun. 11–7. Tube: Covent Garden.*

Bloomsbury and Legal London

The character of an area of London can change visibly from one street to the next. Nowhere is this so clear as in the contrast between fun-loving Soho and intellectual Bloomsbury, a mere 100 yards to the northeast, or between arty, trendy Covent Garden and—on the other side of Kingsway—sober Holborn. Both Bloomsbury and Holborn are almost purely residential and should be seen by day. The first district is best known for its famous flowering of literary-arty bohemia, personified by the clique known as the Bloomsbury Group during this century's first three decades, and for the British Museum and the University of London, which dominate it now. The second sounds as exciting as, say, a center for accountants or dentists, but don't be put off—filled with magnificently ancient buildings, it's more interesting and beautiful than you might suppose.

Most travelers head here to find the ghosts of all those great Bloomsbury figures such as Virginia Woolf, E. M. Forster, Vanessa Bell, and Lytton Strachey. Ghosts of their literary salons soon lead into the time-warp territory of interlocking alleys, gardens and cobbled courts, town houses and halls where London's legal profession grew up. The Great Fire of 1666 razed most of the city but spared the buildings of legal

London, and the whole neighborhood—known as Holborn—oozes history. Leading landmarks here are the Inns of Court, where the country's top solicitors and barristers have had their chambers for centuries.

A Good Walk

From Russell Square tube station, walk south down Southampton Row, and west on Great Russell Street, passing Bloomsbury Square on the left, en route to London's biggest and most important collection of antiquities, the **British Museum** ㉑. Leaving this via the back exit leads you to Montague Place, which you should cross to Malet Street, straight ahead, to reach the **University of London** ㉒. On the left after you pass the university buildings is the back of the Royal Academy of Dramatic Art, or RADA (its entrance is on Gower Street), where at least half of the most stellar British thespians got their training. Circumvent University College at the top of Malet Place and head south down Gordon Street to reach Gordon Square, continuing south down busy Woburn Place and veering left down Guilford Street to reach Coram's Fields, then turn left south of there on Guilford Place, then right to Doughty Street and the **Dickens House** ㉔. Two streets west, parallel to Doughty Street, is charming Lamb's Conduit Street (whose pretty pub, the Lamb, Dickens inevitably frequented).

At the bottom of Lamb's Conduit Street you reach Theobald's Road, where you enter the first of the Inns of Court, Gray's Inn, emerging from here onto High Holborn (pronounced *hoe*-bun), heavy with traffic, since it (with the Strand) is the main route from the City to the West End and Westminster. Hatton Garden, running north from Holborn Circus and still the center of London's diamond and jewelry trade, is a reminder of when it *was* the west end. Pass another ghost of former trading, Staple Inn, and turn left down tiny Great Turnstile Row to reach **Lincoln's Inn** ㉖; pass its famous hall and continue around the west side of New Square to Carey Street, which leads you round into Portugal Street. Here you'll find the **Old Curiosity Shop,** probably one of the rare places in London Dickens did *not* frequent. Recross to the north side of Lincoln's Inn Fields to **Sir John Soane's Museum** ㉗. Cross the Strand to Temple Bar of the **Temple** ㉘, and pass through the elaborate stone arch to Middle Temple Lane, which you follow to the Thames.

TIMING

This is a substantial walk of 3 to 4 mi, and it has two distinct halves. The first half, around Bloomsbury, is not so interesting on the surface, but it features a major highlight of London, the British Museum, where you could easily add a mile to your total, and certainly at least two hours. The Dickens House is also worth a stop. The second half, Legal London, is a real walker's walk, with most of the highlights in the architecture and atmosphere of the buildings and streets. The exception is Sir John Soane's Museum, which will absorb an extra hour. The walk alone can be done comfortably in two hours and is best on a sunny day.

Sights to See

㉕ **British Library.** Since 1759, the British Library had always been housed in the British Museum on Gordon Square—but space ran out long ago, necessitating this grand new edifice, a few blocks north of the British Museum, between Euston and St. Pancras stations. Currently, the innumerable (somewhere around 18 million, actually) volumes are making their way north, an exodus that won't be completed until 1999. Happily, the library's treasures—the Magna Carta, Gutenberg Bibles, Captain Cook journals, and Charlotte Brontë letters—are already on view in the Rare Books Room. ⊠ *96 Euston Rd.,* ☎ *0171/412–7000.* ☜ *Free.* ☼ *Mon.–Sat. 10–5, Sun. 2:30–6 PM. Tube: Holborn or Tottenham Court Rd.*

㉑ British Museum. With a facade like a great temple, this celebrated treasure house—filled with plunder of incalculable value and beauty from around the globe—is housed in a ponderously dignified Greco-Victorian building that makes a suitably grand impression. This is only appropriate, for inside you'll find some of the greatest relics of humankind: the Elgin Marbles, the Rosetta Stone, the Magna Carta, the Ur Treasure—everything, it seems, but the Ark of the Covenant. The place is vast, so arm yourself with a free floor plan as soon as you go in or they'll have to send out search parties to rescue you.

The collection began in 1753 and grew quickly, thanks to enthusiastic kleptomaniacs during the Napoleonic Wars—most notoriously the seventh Earl of Elgin, who lifted marbles from the Parthenon and Erechtheum while on a Greek vacation between 1801 and 1804. Here follows a highly edited résumé (in order of encounter) of the BM's greatest hits: close to the entrance hall, in the south end of Room 25, is the **Rosetta Stone,** found in 1799, and carved in 196 BC with a decree of Ptolemy V in Egyptian hieroglyphics, demotic, and Greek. It was this multilingual inscription that provided the French Egyptologist Jean-François Champollion with the key to deciphering hieroglyphics. Maybe the **Elgin Marbles** ought to be back in Greece, but since they are here—and they are, after all, among the most graceful and heart-breakingly beautiful sculptures on earth—make a beeline for them in Room 8, west of the entrance. The best part is what remains of the Parthenon frieze that girdled the cella of Athena's temple on the Acropolis, carved around 440 BC. Also in the West Wing is one of the Seven Wonders of the Ancient World—in fragment form, unfortunately—in Room 12: the **Mausoleum of Halicarnassus.** Close to the main entrance are originals of King John's 1215 charter, the Magna Carta, as well as the spectacularly illuminated 7th-century Lindisfarne Gospels.

Upstairs are some of the most perennially popular galleries, especially beloved by children: Rooms 60 and 61, where the **Egyptian mummies** live. Nearby are the glittering 4th-century Mildenhall Treasure and the equally splendid Sutton Hoo Treasure. A more prosaic exhibit is that of Pete Marsh, sentimentally named by the archaeologists who unearthed the Lindow Man from a Cheshire peat marsh; poor Pete was ritually slain, probably as a human sacrifice. ✉ *Great Russell St.,* ☎ *0171/636–1555; 0171/580–1788 recorded information.* 🎟 *Free, 1½-hr guided tours £6.* ☼ *Mon.–Sat. 10–5, Sun. 2:30–6; tours twice a day in winter, 4 times daily in summer (phone for times). Tube: Tottenham Court Rd., Holborn, Russell Sq.*

㉔ Dickens House. This is the only one of the many London houses Dickens inhabited that's still standing, and it would have had a real claim to his fame in any case, since he wrote *Oliver Twist* and *Nicholas Nickleby* and finished *Pickwick Papers* here between 1837 and 1839. The house looks exactly as it would have in Dickens's day, complete with first editions, letters, and tall clerk's desk, plus a treat for Lionel Bart fans—his score of *Oliver!* ✉ *48 Doughty St.,* ☎ *0171/405–2127.* 🎟 *£3.50.* ☼ *Mon.–Sat. 10–5; closed Dec. 24–Jan. 1. Tube: Russell Sq.*

㉖ Lincoln's Inn. One of the oldest, best preserved, and most comely of the Inns of Court, Lincoln's Inn offers plenty to see—from the Chancery Lane Tudor brick gatehouse to the wide-open, tree-lined, atmospheric Lincoln's Inn Fields and the 15th-century Chapel remodeled by Inigo Jones in 1620. The wisteria-clad New Square is London's only complete 17th-century square. ✉ *Chancery La.,* ☎ *0171/405–1393.* ☼ *Gardens and chapel weekdays 12:30–2:30; guided tours available. Tube: Chancery Lane.*

☾ ㉓ **Pollock's Toy Museum.** Historians tell us that the Victorians invented the concept of childhood, and no better proof can be offered than this magical place, a treasure trove of a small museum in a 19th-century town house. Most of the objects are dolls, dolls' houses, teddy bears, folk toys—and those bedazzling mementos of Victorian childhood, Pollock's famed cardboard cutout miniature theaters, all red velvet and gold trim, with movable scenery and figurines. Happily, Pollock's still sells these toy theaters—a souvenir that will drive both children and connoisseurs mad with joy. ✉ *1 Scala St.,* ☎ *0171/636–3452.* 🎫 *£2.50.* ⊙ *Mon.–Sat. 10–5. Tube: Goodge St.*

㉗ **Sir John Soane's Museum.** Guaranteed to raise a smile from the most blasé and footsore tourist, this beloved collection hardly deserves the burden of its dry name. Sir John, architect of the Bank of England, who lived here from 1790 to 1831, created one of London's most idiosyncratic and fascinating houses. Everywhere mirrors and colors play tricks with light and space, and split-level floors worthy of a fairground fun house disorient you. In a basement chamber sits the vast 1300 BC sarcophagus of Seti I, lit by a domed skylight two stories above. ✉ *13 Lincoln's Inn Fields,* ☎ *0171/405–2107.* 🎫 *Free.* ⊙ *Tues.–Sat. 10–5. Tube: Holburn, Temple.*

㉘ **Temple.** This is the collective name for **Inner Temple** and **Middle Temple**, and its entrance—the exact point of entry into the City—is marked by a young (1880) bronze griffin, the **Temple Bar Memorial.** In the buildings opposite is an elaborate stone arch through which you pass into Middle Temple Lane, past a row of 17th-century timber-frame houses, and on into Fountain Court. If the Elizabethan **Middle Temple Hall** is open, don't miss its hammer-beam roof—among the finest in the land. There is no admission charge, but a tip should be given to the porter. ✉ *2 Plowden Buildings, Middle Temple,* ☎ *0171/427–4800.* ⊙ *Weekdays 10–noon and (when not in use) 3–4. Tube: Temple.*

㉒ **University of London.** A relatively youthful institution that grew out of the need for a nondenominational center for higher education, the University of London was founded by Dissenters in 1826, with its first examinations held 12 years later. Jews and Roman Catholics were not the only people admitted for the first time to an English university— women were, too, though they had to wait 50 years (until 1878) to sit for a degree.

The City

When an Englishman tells you that he works in the City, he isn't being vague. He's using the British equivalent of Wall Street. The City extends eastward from Temple Bar to the Tower of London, and north from the Thames to Chiswell Street. Despite its small size (it's known as the Square Mile), this area is the financial engine of Britain and one of the world's leading centers of trade. The City, however, is more than just London's Wall Street: it is also home to two of the city's most notable sights, the Tower of London and St. Paul's, one of the world's greatest cathedrals—truly, a case of the money changers encompassing the temple!

Twice, the City has nearly been wiped off the face of the earth. The Great Fire of 1666 necessitated a total reconstruction, in which Sir Christopher Wren had a big hand, contributing not only his masterpiece, St. Paul's Cathedral, but 49 additional parish churches. The second wave of destruction was dealt by the German bombers of World War II. The ruins were rebuilt, but slowly, and with no overall plan, leaving the City a patchwork of the old and the new, the interesting and the flagrantly awful. Since a mere 8,000 or so people call it home, the financial center of Britain is deserted outside the working week, with restaurants shuttered and streets forlorn and windswept.

A Good Walk

Begin at the gateway to the City, the Temple Bar of the **Temple** district, a bronze griffin on the Strand opposite the Royal Courts of Justice. Walk east to Fleet Street and turn left on Bolt Court to Gough Square, and **Dr. Johnson's House** ㉙, passing Ye Olde Cheshire Cheese on Wine Office Court en route back to Fleet Street and the journalists' church, **St. Bride's** ㉚. At the end of Fleet Street, cross Ludgate Circus to Ludgate Hill to reach **Old Bailey** ㉛ and the Central Criminal Courts. Continuing along Ludgate Hill, you reach **St. Paul's Cathedral** ㉜, Wren's masterpiece. The spirits of those who used to feed the pigeons on its steps—remember the old lady from *Mary Poppins*?—seem to hover nearby.

Retrace your steps to Newgate Street to reach London's meat market, Smithfield—where, for centuries, livestock was sold. Cross Aldersgate Street and take the right fork to London Wall, named for the Roman rampart that stood along it, with a remaining section of 2nd- to 4th-century wall at St. Alphege Garden. There's another bit outside the **Museum of London** ㉝, behind which is the important arts mecca of gray concrete, the **Barbican Centre** ㉞. Back on London Wall, turn south onto Coleman Street, then right onto Masons Avenue to reach Basinghall Street and the **Guildhall** ㉟, then follow Milk Street south to Cheapside. Here is another symbolic center of London, the church of **St. Mary-le-Bow** ㊱.

Walk to the east end of Cheapside, where seven roads meet, and you will be facing the **Bank of England** ㊲. Turn your back on the bank and there's the Lord Mayor's Palladian-style abode, the Mansion House, with Wren's St. Stephen Walbrook church—considered his finest effort by architectural historians—behind it, and the Royal Exchange in between Threadneedle Street and Cornhill. Now head down Queen Victoria Street, where you'll pass the remains of the Roman **Temple of Mithras** ㊳, then, after a sharp left turn onto Cannon Street, you'll come upon the **Monument** ㊴, Wren's memorial to the Great Fire of London. Just south of there is London Bridge. Turn left onto Lower Thames Street, for just under a mile's walk—passing Billingsgate, London's principal fish market for 900 years, until 1982, and the Custom House, built early in the last century—to the **Tower of London** ㊵, which may be the single most unmissable of London's sights. Children will want to head for the **Tower Hill Pageant** ㊶ and children of all ages will be enchanted by that Thames icon, the **Tower Bridge.**

TIMING

This is a marathon. Unless you want to be walking all day, without a chance to do justice to London's most famous sights, the Tower of London and St. Paul's Cathedral—not to mention the Museum of London, Tower Bridge, and the Barbican Centre—you should consider splitting the walk into segments. Conversely, if you're not planning to go inside, this walk makes for a great day out, with lots of surprising vistas, river views, and history. The City is a wasteland on weekends and after dark, so choose your time. There's a certain romantic charm to the streets when they're deserted, but it's hard to find lunch.

Sights to See

㊲ **Bank of England.** Known familiarly for the past couple of centuries as "The Old Lady of Threadneedle Street," the bank has been central to the British economy since 1694. Sir John Soane designed the Neoclassic hulk in 1788, wrapping it in windowless walls (which are all that survive of his building) to suggest a stability that the ailing economy of the post-Thatcher years tends to belie. ⊠ *Bartholomew La.,* ☎ *0171/601–5545.* 🖾 *Free.* ☉ *Easter–Sept., weekdays 10–5, Sun. and public holidays 11–5; Oct.–Easter, weekdays 10–6. Tube: Bank, Monument.*

㉞ Barbican Centre. An enormous concrete maze Londoners love to hate, the Barbican is home to the Royal Shakespeare Company and its two theaters, the London Symphony Orchestra and its auditorium, the Guildhall School of Music and Drama, a major gallery for touring exhibitions, two cinemas, and a convention center. Londoners have come to accept the place, if not exactly love it, because of its contents. ⊠ *Silk St.,* ☎ *0171/638–4141; 0171/628–3351 for RSC backstage tours; 0171/628–0183 guided tours.* 🖾 *Free; gallery £5, conservatory £1.* ☉ *Mon.–Sat. 9 AM–11 PM, Sun. noon–11; gallery Mon.–Sat. 10–7:30, Sun. and national holidays noon–7:30; conservatory weekends noon–5:30 when not in use for private functions (always call first). Tube: Moorgate, Barbican.*

㉙ Dr. Johnson's House. Samuel Johnson lived here between 1746 and 1759, while in the worst of health, compiling his famous dictionary in the attic. Like Dickens, he lived all over town, but, like Dickens's House, this is the only one of Johnson's abodes remaining today. It is an appropriately 17th-century house, exactly the kind of place you would expect the Great Bear, as Johnson was nicknamed, to live in. It is a shrine to the man possibly more attached to London than anyone else, ever, and it includes a first edition of his dictionary among the Johnson-and-Boswell mementos. After soaking up the atmosphere, repair around the corner in Wine Office Court to the famed Ye Olde Cheshire Cheese pub, once Johnson and Boswell's favorite watering hole.⊠ *17 Gough Sq.,* ☎ *0171/353–3745.* 🖾 *£3.* ☉ *May–Sept., Mon.–Sat. 11–5:30; Oct.–Apr., Mon.–Sat. 11–5. Tube: Chancery Lane, Temple.*

㉟ Guildhall. In the symbolic nerve center of the City, the Corporation of London ceremonially elects and installs its Lord Mayor as it has done for 800 years. The Guildhall was built in 1411, and though it failed to escape either the 1666 or 1940 flames, its core survived. The fabulous hall is a psychedelic patchwork of coats of arms and banners of the City Livery Companies. ⊠ *Gresham St.,* ☎ *0171/606–3030.* 🖾 *Free.* ☉ *Mon.–Sat. 10–5 (library closed Sat.). Tube: St. Paul's, Moorgate, Bank, Mansion House.*

Lloyd's of London. Architect Richard Rogers's (of Paris's Pompidou Centre fame) fantastical steel-and-glass medium-rise of six towers around a vast atrium, with his trademark inside-out ventilation shafts, stairwells, and gantries, may be the most exciting recent structure London can claim. The building housing the famous insurance agency is best seen at night, when cobalt and lime spotlights make it leap out of the deeply boring gray skyline, like Carmen Miranda dancing at a funeral. Since the firm nearly went bankrupt several years ago, the atrium gallery, once open to public view, has been closed. ⊠ *1 Lime St.,* ☎ *0171/623–7100. Tube: Eastcheap.*

㊴ Monument. Built to commemorate the "dreadful visitation" of the Great Fire of 1666, this is the world's tallest isolated stone column—the work of Wren. There is a viewing gallery (311 steps up—better for you than any StairMaster). ⊠ *Monument St.,* ☎ *0171/626–2717.* 🖾 *£1.* ☉ *Apr.–Sept., weekdays 9–5:30, weekends 2–5:30; Oct.–Mar., Mon.–Sat. 9–3:30. Tube: Monument.*

㉝ Museum of London. Anyone with the least interest in how this city evolved will adore this museum, especially its reconstructions and dioramas—of the Great Fire (flickering flames! sound effects!), a 1940s air-raid shelter, a Georgian prison cell, and a Victorian street complete with fully stocked shops. Come right up to date in the new "London Now" gallery. ⊠ *London Wall,* ☎ *0171/600–3699.* ⊡ *£4, free 4:30–5:50; White Card accepted.* ⊙ *Tues.–Sat. 10–6, Sun. noon–6. Tube: St. Paul's, Barbican.*

③① **Old Bailey.** The present-day Central Criminal Court is where legendary Newgate Prison stood from the 12th century right until the beginning of this one. Dickens visited Newgate several times (obviously in between pubs)—Fagin ended up in the Condemned Hold here in *Oliver Twist.* Ask the doorman which current trial is likely to prove juicy, if you're that kind of ghoul—you may catch the conviction of the next Crippen or Christie (England's most notorious wife murderers, both tried here). ⊠ *Newgate St.,* ☎ *0171/248–3277.* ⊡ *Free.* ⊙ *Public Gallery weekdays 10–1 and 2–4; queue at the Newgate St. entrance. No cameras allowed. Tube: Blackfriars.*

③⓪ **St. Bride's.** One of the first of Wren's city churches, St. Bride's was also one of the bomb-damaged ones, reconsecrated only in 1960 after a 17-year-long restoration. From afar, study its extraordinary steeple—its uniquely tiered shape gave rise, legend has it, to the traditional wedding cake! ⊠ *Fleet St.,* ☎ *0171/353–1301.* ⊡ *Free.* ⊙ *Mon.–Sat. 9–5, Sun. between services at 11 and 6:30. Tube: Chancery Lane.*

③⑥ **St. Mary-le-Bow.** This Wren church, dating from 1673, has one of the most famous sets of bells around—a Londoner must be born within the sound of Bow bells to claim to be a true cockney. The origin of that idea was probably the curfew rung on the bow Bells during the 14th century, even though "cockney" only came to mean Londoner three centuries later, and then it was an insult. In the crypt of the church you'll find The Place Below—a handy spot for great soups and quiches. Packed weekday lunchtimes, it's also open for breakfast, and Thursday and Friday evenings feature a posh vegetarian dinner. ⊠ *Cheapside,* ☎ *0171/248–5139.* ⊡ *Free.* ⊙ *Mon.–Thurs. 6:30–6, Fri. 6:30–4. Tube: St. Paul's.*

③② **St. Paul's Cathedral.** Often described as London's symbolic heart, St. Paul's is grand, stodgy, dirty, and enthralling. The dome—the world's third largest—will already be familiar, since you see it peeping through on the skyline from many an angle. The structure is, of course, Sir Christopher Wren's masterpiece, completed in 1710 after 35 years of building, then, much later, miraculously (mostly) spared by World War II bombs. Wren's first plan, known as the New Model, did not make it past the drawing board, while the second, known as the Great Model, got as far as the 20-ft oak rendering you can see here today before it also was rejected, whereupon Wren is said to have burst into tears. The third, however, was accepted, with the fortunate coda that the architect be allowed to make changes as he saw fit. Without that, there would be no dome, since the approved design had featured a steeple.

When you enter and see the dome from the inside, you may find that it seems smaller than you expected. You aren't imagining things; it *is* smaller, and 60 ft lower, than the lead-covered outer dome. Beneath the lantern is Wren's famous memorial, which his son composed and had set into the pavement, and which reads succinctly: *Lector, si monumentum requiris, circumspice*—"Reader, if you seek his monument, look around you." Up 259 spiral steps is the **Whispering Gallery,** an acoustic phenomenon; you whisper something to the wall on one side, and a second later it transmits clearly to the other side, 107 ft away. Ascend farther to the Stone Gallery, which encircles the outside of the dome and affords a spectacular panorama of London.

The poet John Donne, who had been dean of St. Paul's for his final 10 years (he died in 1631), lies in the south choir aisle. The vivacious choir-stall carvings nearby are the work of Grinling Gibbons, as are the organ's, which Wren designed and Handel played. Behind the high altar, you'll find the **American Memorial Chapel**, dedicated in 1958 to the 28,000 GIs stationed here who lost their lives in World War II. ⊠ *St. Paul's Churchyard,* ☎ *0171/236–4128.* ▦ *Cathedral, ambulatory (American Chapel), crypt, and treasury £3.50; galleries £3; combined ticket £6.* ☉ *Cathedral Mon.–Sat. 8:30–4:30 (closed occasionally for special services); ambulatory, crypt, and galleries Mon.–Sat. 9:30–4:15. Tube: St. Paul's.*

㊳ Temple of Mithras. Unearthed on a building site in 1954 and taken, at first, for an early Christian church, this was a minor place of pilgrimage in the Roman City. In fact, worshipers here favored Christ's chief rival, Mithras, the Persian god of light, during the 3rd and 4th centuries.

☾ Tower Bridge. Despite its venerable, nay, medieval, appearance, this is a Victorian youngster that celebrated its centenary in June 1994. Constructed of steel, then clothed in Portland stone, it was deliberately styled in the Gothic persuasion to complement the Tower of London next door and is famous for its enormous bascules—the "arms," which open to allow large ships through, which is a rare occurrence these days. The bridge's 100th-birthday gift was a new exhibition, one of London's most imaginative and fun. You are conducted in the company of "Harry Stoner," an animatronic bridge construction worker worthy of Disneyland, back in time to witness the birth of the Thames's last downstream bridge. Be sure to hang on to your ticket and follow the signs to the Engine Rooms for part two, where the original steam-driven hydraulic engines gleam, and a cute rococo theater is the setting for an Edwardian music-hall production of the bridge's story. ☎ *0171/403–3761.* ▦ *£5.70, combined ticket with Tower Hill Pageant £8.75.* ☉ *Apr.–Oct., daily 10–6:30; Nov.–Mar., daily 10–5:15 (last entry 1¼ hrs before closing). Tube: Tower Hill.*

☾ ㊶ Tower Hill Pageant. London's first "dark-ride" museum features automated cars that take you past mock-ups of scenes from most periods of London's past, complete with "people," sound effects, and even smells. There's also an archaeological museum with finds from the Thames, set up by the Museum of London. ⊠ *Tower Hill Terr.,* ☎ *0171/709–0081.* ▦ *£6.95, combined ticket with Tower Bridge £8.75.* ☉ *Apr.–Oct., daily 9:30–5:30; Nov.–Mar., daily 9:30–4:30. Tube: Tower Hill.*

☾ ㊵ Tower of London. This has top billing on many tourist itineraries for good reason. Nowhere else does London's history come to life so vividly as in this minicity of melodramatic towers stuffed to bursting with heraldry and treasure, the intimate details of lords and dukes and princes and sovereigns etched in the walls (literally in some places, as you'll see), and quite a few pints of royal, blue blood spilled on the stones. Be warned that visitor traffic at the sight of sights is copious, meaning not only lines for the best bits, but a certain dilution of atmosphere, which can be disappointing if you've been fantasizing scenes from *Elizabeth and Essex.* At least you need no longer spend all day in line for the prize exhibit, the Crown Jewels, since they have been transplanted to their current home, where moving walkways hasten progress at the busiest times. The reason the Tower holds the royal gems is that it is still one of the royal palaces, although no monarch since Henry VIII has called it home. Its most renowned and titillating function has been, of course, as a jail and site of torture and execution.

A person was mighty privileged to be beheaded in the peace and seclusion of **Tower Green** instead of before the mob at Tower Hill. In fact, only seven people were ever important enough—among them Anne Boleyn and Catherine Howard, wives two and five of Henry VIII's six; Elizabeth I's friend Robert Devereux, Earl of Essex; and the nine-days' queen, Lady Jane Grey, age 17. You can see the executioner's block, with its bathetic forehead-size dent, and his axe—along with the equally famous rack, plus other assorted thumbscrews, iron maidens, etc.—in the **Martin Tower,** which stands in the northeast corner.

Free tours depart every half hour or so from the Middle Tower. They are conducted by the 42 Yeoman Warders, better known as "Beefeaters"—ex-servicemen dressed in resplendent navy-and-red (scarlet-and-gold on special occasions) Tudor outfits. Beefeaters have been guarding the Tower since Henry VII appointed them in 1485. One of them, the Yeoman Ravenmaster, is responsible for making life comfortable for the Tower ravens—an important duty, since if Larry, Hardy, George, Hugin, Mumia, and Rhys were to desert the Tower (goes the legend), the kingdom would fall. Today, the Tower takes no chances: the ravens' wings are cut.

In prime position stands the oldest part of the Tower and the most conspicuous of its buildings, the **White Tower.** Henry III (1207–1272) had it whitewashed, which is where the name comes from. The spiral staircase is the only way up, and here you'll find the **Royal Armouries,** Britain's national museum of arms and armor, with about 40,000 pieces on display. Most of the interior of the White Tower has been much altered over the centuries, but the **Chapel of St. John,** downstairs from the armouries, is unadulterated 11th-century Norman—very rare, very simple, and very beautiful. Across the moat, **Traitors' Gate** lies to the right. Immediately opposite Traitors' Gate is the former Garden Tower, better known since about 1570 as the **Bloody Tower.** Its name comes from one of the most famous unsolved murders in history, the saga of the "little princes in the Tower." In 1483 the boy king, Edward V, and his brother Richard were left here by their uncle, Richard of Gloucester, after the death of their father, Edward I. They were never seen again, Gloucester was crowned Richard III, and in 1674 two little skeletons were found under the stairs to St. John's Chapel. The obvious conclusions have always been drawn—and were, in fact, even before the skeletons were discovered.

The shiniest, most expensive, and absolutely the most famous exhibits here are, of course, the **Crown Jewels,** now housed in the Duke of Wellington's Barracks. In their current setting you get so close that you could lick the gems (if it weren't for the wafers of bulletproof glass). Before you meet them in person, you are given a high-definition-film preview along with a few scenes from Elizabeth's 1953 coronation. Security is as fiendish as you'd expect, since the jewels—even though they would be literally impossible for thieves to sell—are *so* priceless that they're not insured. However, they are polished every February by Garrard, the crown jewelers. A brief résumé of the top jewels: finest of all is the Royal Sceptre, containing the earth's largest cut diamond, the 530-carat Star of Africa. This is also known as Cullinan I, having been cut from the South African Cullinan, which weighed 20 ounces when dug up from a De Beers mine at the beginning of the century. Another chip off the block, Cullinan II, lives on the Imperial Crown of State that Prince Charles is due to wear at his coronation—the same one that Elizabeth II wore in her coronation procession; it had been made for Victoria's in 1838. The other most famous gem is the Koh-i-noor, or "Mountain of Light," which adorns the Queen Mother's crown. When

Victoria was presented with this gift horse in 1850, she looked it in the mouth, found it lacking in glitter, and had it chopped down to almost half its weight.

The little chapel of **St. Peter ad Vincula** can be visited only as part of a Yeoman Warder tour. The third church on the site, it conceals the remains of some 2,000 people executed at the Tower, Anne Boleyn and Catherine Howard among them. Don't forget to stroll along the battlements before you leave; from them, you get a wonderful overview of the whole Tower of London.

✉ *H.M. Tower of London,* ☎ *0171/709–0765.* 💷 *£8.50, small additional charge for Fusiliers Museum.* ⊙ *Mar.–Oct., Mon.–Sat. 9:30–6:30, Sun. 2–6; Nov.–Feb., Mon.–Sat. 9:30–5. Yeoman Warder guided tours leave daily (subject to weather and availability) from Middle Tower, at no charge (but a tip is always appreciated), about every 30 mins until 3:30 in summer, 2:30 in winter. For tickets to Ceremony of the Keys (the locking of the main gates, nightly at 10), write well in advance;* ✉ *The Resident Governor and Keeper of the Jewel House, Queen's House, H.M. Tower of London, EC3. Give your name, the dates you wish to attend (including alternate dates), and number of people (up to 7), and enclose a SASE. Tube: Tower Hill.*

OFF THE
BEATEN PATH

JACK THE RIPPER'S LONDON – Cor Blimey Guv'nor, Jack the Ripper woz here! Several organizations offer tours of "Jack's London"—the (still) mean streets of the East End, the working-class neighborhood directly to the east of the City. Here, in 1888, the Whitechapel murders traumatized Victorian London. At the haunting hour, tour groups head out to Bucks Row and other notorious scenes-of-the-crime. **Original London Walks** (0171/624–3978) offers frequent tours leaving at 7 PM from the Tower Hill tube stop, while the **Jack the Ripper Mystery Walk** (0181/558–9446) departs at 8 PM from the Aldgate tube stop Wednesday and Sunday. Even with a large tour group, this can be a spooky and unforgettable experience.

The South Bank

That old and snide North London dig about needing a passport to cross the Thames is no longer heard now. For decades, natives never ventured beyond the watery curtain that divides the city in half; tourists, too, rarely troubled the area unless they were departing from Waterloo Station. Starting with the 1976 creation of the South Bank Centre, however, the South Bank—the riverside stretch between Waterloo Bridge and Hungerford Bridge—has been taken over by Culture with a capital and emphatically illuminated C. Today, developers and local authorities have expanded the South Bank's potential farther east with an explosion of attractions that is turning this once-neglected district into London's most happening new neighborhood. The Eighties brought renovations and innovations such as Gabriel's Wharf, London Bridge City, Hay's Galleria, and Butler's Wharf; the Nineties arrived, and so did such headline-making sights as the spectacular reconstruction of Shakespeare's Globe—the most famous theater in the world—the OXO Tower, and the London Aquarium. These will again be augmented in the lead-up to the millennium by the new Tate Gallery, a giant Ferris wheel, and a new look for the South Bank Centre itself. Clearly, the South Bank has become a dazzling perch for culture vultures.

Actually, it is fitting that so much of London's artistic life should once again be centered here on the South Bank—back in the days of Ye Olde London Towne, Southwark was the location for the theaters, taverns, and cock-fighting arenas that served as after-hours entertainment. The

Globe Theatre, in which Shakespeare acted and held shares, was one of several established here; in truth, the Globe was as likely to stage a few bouts of bearbaiting as the latest interpretations of Shakespeare. Today, at the reconstructed "wooden O," of course, you can just see the latter. Be sure to talk a walk along Bankside—the embankment along the Thames from Southwark to Blackfriars Bridge—for fabulous vistas of London's skyline.

A Good Walk

Start scenically at the south end of **Tower Bridge,** finding the steps on the east (left) side, which descend to the start of a pedestrians-only street, Shad Thames. Now turn your back on the bridge and follow this quaint path between cliffs of the good-as-new warehouses, which are now **Butler's Wharf** ㊷, but were once the seedy, dingy, dangerous shadowlands where Dickens killed off evil Bill Sikes in *Oliver Twist.* See the foodies' center, the Gastrodrome, and the **Design Museum** ㊸, then just before you get back to Tower Bridge, turn away from the river, along Horsleydown Lane, follow Tooley Street, and take the right turn at Morgan Lane to **HMS *Belfast*** ㊹, or continue to **Hay's Galleria** ㊺ with **London Bridge** and the **London Dungeon** ㊻ beyond. Next, turn left onto Joiner Street underneath the arches of London's first (1836) railway, then right onto St. Thomas Street, where you'll find the **Old St. Thomas's Operating Theatre** ㊼, with **Southwark Cathedral** ㊽ just across Borough High Street, and another of the South Bank's recent office developments, St. Mary Overie Dock, down Cathedral Street. See the west wall, with rose window outline, of Winchester House, palace of the Bishops of Winchester until 1626, built into it, and **the Clink** ㊾ next door. Continue to the end of Clink Street onto Bankside, detouring left up Rose Alley, where in 1989 the remains of a famous Jacobean theater, the Rose Theatre, were unearthed, though because of the office development surrounding the preserved foundations there's not much to see. The next little alley is New Globe Walk, where there is much to see: the reconstruction of that most famous of Jacobean theaters, **Shakespeare's Globe** (51). Next along Bankside is the 17th-century Cardinal's Wharf, where, as a plaque explains, Wren lived while St. Paul's Cathedral was being built, then Bankside Power Station, which is to become the new Tate Gallery by the year 2000.

Now you reach your fourth bridge on this walk, **Blackfriars Bridge,** which you pass beneath to join the street called Upper Ground, spending some time in the Coin Street Community Builders' embryo neighborhood, including Gabriel's Wharf, a small marketplace of designer workshops and wares, and its younger, much bigger sibling, the exciting **OXO Tower** (52). Farther along Upper Ground, you reach the **South Bank Centre** (53), with the **Royal National Theatre** (54) first, followed by the National Film Theatre, **Museum of the Moving Image (MOMI)** (55) and the **Royal Festival Hall** (56). You'll find distractions all over here, especially in summer—secondhand bookstalls, entertainers, and a series of plaques annotating the buildings opposite. Look to the opposite bank for the quintessential postcard vista of the Houses of Parliament—it's good from Jubilee Gardens, past the County Hall, which is now the **London Aquarium** (57), and Westminster Bridge to St. Thomas's Hospital and its **Florence Nightingale Museum** (58). Farther along the river **Lambeth Palace** (59)—for 800 years the London base of the Archbishop of Canterbury, top man in the Church of England—stands by Lambeth Bridge. If you take a detour to the right off Lambeth Road, you could be "doing the Lambeth Walk" down the street of the same name. A cockney tradition ever since the 17th century, when there was a spa here, the Sunday stroll was immortalized in a song from the 1937 musical *Me and My Gal.* A little farther east along Lambeth Road you reach the **Imperial War Museum** (60).

TIMING

On a fine day, this 2- to 3-mi walk makes a very scenic wander, since you're following the south bank of the great Thames nearly all the way. Fabulous views across to the north bank take you past St. Paul's and the Houses of Parliament, and you pass—under, over, or around—no fewer than seven bridges. It's bound to take far longer than a couple of hours, because the sightseeing is heavy. The Imperial War Museum, MOMI, Shakespeare's Globe, the Hayward Gallery, the Design Museum, and the Aquarium are major events, needing at least an hour apiece (depending on your interests), while the London Dungeon doesn't take long, unless you have kids in tow—which is why you'd go in at all. The other museums on this route—the Clink, Old Operating Theatre, Florence Nightingale, and the South Bank Centre foyers—are compact enough to squeeze together en route to your main event. And that's the nicest thing to do with this walk: have tickets waiting at the end. The National Theatres, the NFT, or Shakespeare's Globe can all oblige, but remember that the theaters stay dark on Sunday. Dinner or a riverside drink at the Gastrodrome restaurants, the OXO Tower, or the People's Palace is another idea for a big finish. Public transportation is thin on the ground around this way, so pick a day when you're feeling energetic, since there are no shortcuts once you're underway.

Sights to See

㊷ Butler's Wharf. An '80s development that is maturing gracefully, Butler's Wharf has many empty apartments in its deluxe loft-style warehouse conversions and swanky office blocks, but there *is* life here, thanks partly to London's saint of the stomach, Sir Terence Conran (also responsible for high-profile central London restaurants Bibendum, Mezzo, and Quaglino's). He gave it his "Gastrodrome" of four restaurants, a vintner's, a deli, a bakery, and who knows what else by now.

㊾ The Clink. The prison attached to Winchester House, palace of the Bishops of Winchester until 1626, its name still serves as a general term for jail. This was one of the first prisons to detain women, most of whom were "Winchester Geese"—a euphemism meaning prostitutes. The oldest profession was endemic in Southwark and now there is, of all things, a museum tracing the history of prostitution here, showing what the Clink was like during its 16th-century scandalous heyday. ⊠ *1 Clink St.,* ☎ *0171/403–6515.* ⚑ *£4.* ☉ *Daily 10–6. Tube: London Bridge.*

㊸ Design Museum. Opened in 1989, this was the first museum in the world to elevate the everyday design we take for granted to the status of art exhibit, slotting it into its social and cultural context. The top floor traces the evolution of mass-produced goods. Check out the very good Blueprint Café, with its own river terrace. ⊠ *Butler's Wharf,* ☎ *0171/403–6933.* ⚑ *£5.* ☉ *Daily 10:30–5:30. Tube: Tower Hill, then walk across river.*

㊽ Florence Nightingale Museum. Here you can learn all about that most famous of health care reformers, "The Lady with the Lamp." On view are fascinating reconstructions of the barracks ward at Scutari (Turkey), where she tended soldiers during the Crimean War (1854–1856) and earned her nickname, and a Victorian East End slum cottage, to show what she did to improve living conditions among the poor. The museum is in **St. Thomas's Hospital.** ⊠ *2 Lambeth Palace Rd.,* ☎ *0171/620–0374.* ⚑ *£2.50.* ☉ *Tues.–Sun. and public holidays 10–4. Tube: Waterloo, or Westminster and walk over the bridge.*

㊿ Golden Hinde. Sir Francis Drake circumnavigated the globe in this little galleon, or one just like it anyway. This exact replica has now finished *its* 23-year, round-the-world voyage—much of it spent along

American coasts both Pacific and Atlantic—and has settled here to continue its educational purposes. ⊠ *St. Mary Overie Dock,* ☎ *0171/403–0123.* ☞ *£2.30.* ☉ *Daily, 10–5. Tube: Blackfriars.*

45 **Hay's Galleria.** Once known as "London's larder" because of the edibles sold here, it was reborn in 1987 as a Covent Gardenesque parade of bars and restaurants, offices, and shops, all weatherproofed by an arched glass atrium roof supported by tall iron columns. Inevitably, jugglers, string quartets, and crafts stalls abound.

44 **HMS***Belfast.* At 656 ft, this is one of the largest and most powerful cruisers the Royal Navy has ever had. It played a role in the D-Day landings off Normandy. There's an outpost of the Imperial War Museum on board. ⊠ *Morgan's La., Tooley St.,* ☎ *0171/407–6434.* ☞ *£4.40.* ☉ *Mid-Mar.–Oct., daily 10–5:30; Nov.–mid-Mar., daily 10–4. Tube: London Bridge.*

60 **Imperial War Museum.** Housed in an elegantly colonnaded 19th-century building that was once the home of the infamous insane asylum called Bedlam, this museum of 20th-century warfare does not glorify bloodshed but attempts to evoke what it was like to live through the two world wars. Of course, there is hardware—a Battle of Britain Spitfire, a German V2 rocket—but there is an equal amount of war art (John Singer Sargent to Henry Moore). One very affecting exhibit is the *Blitz Experience,* which is what it sounds like—a 10-minute taste of an air raid in a street of acrid smoke with sirens blaring and searchlights glaring. ⊠ *Lambeth Rd.,* ☎ *0171/416–5000.* ☞ *£4.70.* ☉ *Daily 10–6. Tube: Lambeth North.*

59 **Lambeth Palace.** The London residence of the Archbishop of Canterbury—the senior archbishop of the Church of England—since the 13th century is rarely open to the public, but you can admire the fine Tudor gatehouse. *Tube: Waterloo, or Westminster and walk over the bridge.*

57 **London Aquarium.** Until recently, County Hall was the name of this curved, colonnaded neoclassic hulk, which took 46 years (1912–1958; two world wars interfered) to build, since it was home to London's local government, the Greater London Council, until it disbanded in 1986. Now, after a £25-million injection, a three-level aquarium has been installed, full of incongruous sharks and stingrays, educational exhibits, and piscine sights previously unseen on these shores. Between here and the South Bank Centre is the former **Jubilee Gardens,** which is the site of the millennium Ferris wheel, to be installed by 1999. Even without the 500-ft rotating elevation, views of the Houses of Parliament and Westminster Bridge are fine from here. ⊠ *County Hall, Westminster Bridge Rd.,* ☎ *0171/401–3433.* ☞ *£6.50.* ☉ *Sept.–May, weekdays 10–6, weekends 9:30–6; June–Aug., daily 9:30–7:30. Tube: Waterloo, or Westminster and walk over the bridge.*

46 **London Dungeon.** Did you ever wonder what a disembowelment actually looks like? See it here. Children seem to adore this place, which, although the city's most gory, grisly, gruesome museum, is among London's top tourist attractions and usually has long lines. Here realistic waxwork people are subjected in graphic detail to all the historical horrors the Tower of London merely suggests. Tableaus depict famous bloody moments—like Anne Boleyn's decapitation, or the martyrdom of St. George—alongside the torture, murder, and ritual slaughter of more anonymous victims, all to a soundtrack of screaming, wailing, and agonized moaning. London's times of deepest terror—the Great Fire and the Great Plague—are brought to life, too. A whole section is devoted to Jack the Ripper. Believe it or not, the London Dungeon can be a right old hoot. ⊠ *28–34 Tooley St.,* ☎ *0171/403–0606.* ☎ *£8.95.* ⊙ *Apr.–Sept., daily 10–5:30; Oct.–Mar., daily 10–4:30. Tube: London Bridge.*

👆 **55** **Museum of the Moving Image (MOMI).** Attached to the National Film Theatre (NFT) underneath Waterloo Bridge—whose two movie theaters offer easily the best repertory programming in London—MOMI may be the most fun of all London's museums. The main feature is a history of cinema from 4,000-year-old Javanese shadow puppets to Spielbergian special effects, but the supporting program is even better, and it stars *you.* Actors dressed as John Wayne or Mae West or usherettes or chorus girls pluck you out of obscurity to read the TV news or audition for the chorus line or fly like Superman over the Thames. Needless to say, this is always a big hit with kids. A popular spot for lunch or dinner is the NFT cafeteria—especially the big wooden tables outside. ⊠ *South Bank Centre,* ☎ *0171/401–2636.* ☎ *£6.25; White Card accepted.* ⊙ *Daily 10–6 (last admission at 5). Tube: Waterloo.*

47 **Old St. Thomas's Operating Theatre.** One of England's oldest hospitals stood here from the 12th century until the railway forced it to move in 1862. Today, its operating theater has been restored into an exhibition of early 19th-century medical practices: the operating table onto which the gagged and blindfolded patients were roped; the box of sawdust underneath for catching their blood; the knives, pliers, and handsaws the surgeons wielded; and—this was a theater-in-the-round—the spectators' seats. ⊠ *9A St. Thomas St.,* ☎ *0171/955–4791.* ☎ *£2.50.* ⊙ *Tues.–Sun. 10–4; closed Dec. 15–Jan. 5. Tube: London Bridge.*

52 **OXO Tower.** Long a London landmark to the cognoscenti, this wonderful Art Deco tower has graduated from its former incarnations as power-generating station and warehouse into a vibrant community of artists' and designers' workshops, a pair of restaurants, and cafés, as well as five floors of the best low-income housing in the city, via a £20 million scheme by Coin Street Community Builders. There's a rooftop viewing gallery for the latest river vista in town, and a performance area on the ground (first) floor, which comes alive all summer long— as does the entire surrounding neighborhood. ⊠ *Bargehouse St.,* ☎ *0171/401–3610.* ☎ *Free.* ⊙ *Studios and shops Tues.–Sun. 11–6. Tube: Blackfriars or Waterloo.*

56 **Royal Festival Hall.** The largest auditorium of the South Bank Centre, this hall features superb acoustics and a 3,000-plus capacity. It is the oldest of the riverside blocks, raised as the centerpiece of the 1951 Festival of Britain, a postwar morale-boosting exercise. The London Philharmonic resides here; symphony orchestras from the world over like to visit; and choral works, ballet, serious jazz and pop, and even film with live accompaniment are also staged. There is a good, independently run restaurant, the People's Palace, and a very good bookstore. The next building you come to also contains two concert halls, the **Queen Elizabeth Hall** and the **Purcell Room**. ⊠ *South Bank Centre at South Bank,* ☎ *0171/928–8800. Tube: Waterloo or Embankment.*

54 **Royal National Theatre.** Londoners generally felt the same way about Sir Denys Lasdun's Brutalist-style function-dictates-form building when it opened in 1976, as they would a decade later about the far nastier Barbican. But whatever its merits or demerits as a landscape feature, the Royal National Theatre—still abbreviated colloquially to the preroyal warrant "NT"—has wonderful insides. Three auditoriums—the Olivier, named after Sir Laurence, first artistic director of the National Theatre Company; the Lyttleton; and the Cottesloe—host an ever-changing array of presentations. The NT does not rest on its laurels. It attracts many of the nation's top actors (Anthony Hopkins, for one, does time here) in addition to launching future stars. ⊠ *South Bank,* ☎ *0171/928–2252 box office.* ☉ *Foyers Mon.–Sat. 10 AM–11 PM; hr-long backstage tours Mon.–Sat. at 10:15, 12:30, and 5:30. Tube: Waterloo.*

51 **Shakespeare's Globe.** Three decades ago, American Sam Wanamaker—then an aspiring actor—pulled up in Southwark in a cab and was amazed to find that the fabled Shakespeare's Globe Theatre didn't actually exist. Worse: a tiny plaque was the only sign on the former site of the world's most legendary theater. So appalled had he been that London lacked a center for the study and worship of the Bard of Bards, Wanamaker worked ceaselessly until his death in 1993 to raise funds for his dream—a full-scale reconstruction of the theater. The dream was realized in 1996 when an exact replica of Shakespeare's open-roof Globe Playhouse (built in 1599; incinerated in 1613) was created, using authentic Elizabethan materials and craft techniques and the first thatched roof in London since the Great Fire. There will be (by 1999) a second, indoor theater, built to a design of the 17th-century architect Inigo Jones. The whole thing stands 200 yards from the original Globe. The Globe is a celebration of the great Bard's life and work, an actual rebirth of his "Wooden O", where his plays are presented in natural light (and sometimes rain), to 1,000 people on wooden benches in the "bays," plus 500 "groundlings," standing on a carpet of filbert shells and clinker, just as they did nearly four centuries ago. For any theater buff, this stunning project is a must (☞ Close-Up box, "Shakespeare Lives!" *below*). Although the theater is open only for performances during the summer season, it can be viewed year-round if you take the helpful tour provided by the Shakespeare's Globe Exhibition Centre, the adjacent museum. ⊠ *New Globe Walk, Bankside,* ☎ *0171/928–6406.* ▨ *Exhibition £5.* ☉ *Daily 10–5; call for performance schedule. Tube: Mansion House, then walk across Southwark Bridge.*

53 **South Bank Centre.** On either side of Waterloo Bridge is London's chief arts center. Along Upper Ground, you'll first reach the **Royal National Theatre** (☞ *above*)—three auditoriums that are home to some of the finest theater in Britain. Underneath Waterloo Bridge is the **National Film Theatre**—the best repertory cinema house in London—and its most intriguing attraction, the **Museum of the Moving Image (MOMI)** (☞ *above*). Also here are the **Royal Festival Hall** (☞ *above*), the **Queen Elizabeth Hall** and the **Purcell Room**—three of London's finest venues for classical music. Finally, tucked away behind the concert halls is the **Hayward Gallery** (☞ *above*), a venue for impressive, ever-changing art exhibitions. Along the wide paths of the complex you'll find distractions of every sort—secondhand bookstalls, entertainers, and arrogant pigeons. ⊠ *South Bank Centre,* ☎ *0171/401–2636. Tube: Waterloo.*

48 **Southwark Cathedral.** This cathedral (pronounced *suth*-uck) is the second-oldest Gothic church in London, next to Westminster Abbey. Look for the gaudily renovated 1408 tomb of the poet John Gower, friend of Chaucer, and for the Harvard Chapel, named after John Harvard, founder of the American college, who was baptized here in 1608. Another notable buried here is Edmund Shakespeare, brother of William.

Kensington, Knightsbridge, Mayfair, Belgravia, and Hyde Park

Even in these supposedly democratic days, you still sometimes hear people say that the *only* place to live in London is in the grand residential area of the Royal Borough of Kensington. True, the district is an endless cavalcade of streets lined with splendid houses redolent of stuc-

SHAKESPEARE LIVES!

REBIRTH OF THE GLOBE THEATRE

AS IT IS SAID ABOUT THE ONE true church, Britain's theater is also founded on a rock—the enduring Shakespeare. Stratford-upon-Avon remains the primary shrine, but 1997 welcomed the opening of the cathedral—London's new Globe Theatre. More than three centuries ago, the Puritans closed the first "Wooden O," for which venue Shakespeare wrote *Hamlet, King Lear,* and *Julius Caesar,* among other peerless dramas. Now, 350 years later, the most famous playhouse in the world has been lovingly re-created, down to its Norfolk-reed roof. The theater has been reconstructed just 200 yards from its original site— ground as holy to Shakespeare's followers as Bayreuth's is to Wagner- philes.

For sheer drama—literally—few things can top the memorable jolt of walking into the new Globe. Enter, and some Wellsian genie transports you back to Elizabethan England. Step past the entrance into a soaring 45-ft-high arena, made surprisingly intimate by three half-timber galleries picturesquely encircling the stage. Ahead of you is the "pit," or orchestra level, filling up with 500 standees—"groundlings," to use the historic term—massed in front of the high stage. Soaring overhead is a twin-gabled stage canopy—the "heavens"—framed by exquisitely painted trompe l'oeil marble columns and a "lords' gallery," all fretted with gilded bosses, painted planets, and celestial bodies. Above you is the lowering London sky, which may at any time provide an authentic mid-performance drenching!

Of course, the new Globe is not a perfect time capsule. Occasionally, Juliet's wherefores will have to compete with the roar of jets. Ladies no longer proffer oranges or stools, and yesteryear's magpie hats have been superseded by Ray-Bans and baseball caps. Some ground rules have also changed. Most performances begin in the afternoon and, while floodlighting will be used to illuminate the theater at dusk, there will be no spotlights to focus the action on stage. The audience, on view at all times, becomes as much a part of the theatrical proceedings as the actors. Elizabethans made theatergoing almost as blood-and-thunder an experience as a football match of today. You've heard of the Super Bowl: view this as the Shakespeare Bowl— go ahead and boo Iago or hiss Macbeth; you'll have plenty of company.

The Globe Theatre is but one facet of the entire complex, which, when completed in 1999, will include the 300-seat Inigo Jones indoor theater (to be used year-round, unlike the open-air Globe, which will be open only from June to September), a restaurant, an education center (with wonderful classes and lectures year-round), a library and shop, and the largest Shakespearean exhibition in the world. The plan is to present four plays each season. Happily, even when the Globe is not open for performances, a guided tour will always include its interior—a perfect opportunity to try out your "Friends, Romans, Countrymen!"

coed wealth and pillared porches, but there are other fetching attractions here—some of the most fascinating museums in London, stylish squares, elegant antiques shops, and Kensington Palace, the former home of both Diana, Princess of Wales, and Queen Victoria, which put the district literally on the map back in the 17th century. To Kensington's east is one of the highest concentrations of important artifacts anywhere, the "museum mile" of South Kensington, with the rest of Kensington offering peaceful strolls, a noisy main street, and another palace. Kensington first became the *Royal* Borough of Kensington (and Chelsea) when William III, who suffered terribly from the Thames mists over Whitehall, decided in 1689 to buy Nottingham House in the rural village of Kensington so that he could breathe more easily. Courtiers and functionaries and society folk soon followed where the crowns led, and by the time Queen Anne was on the throne (1702–1714), Kensington was overflowing. In a way, it still is, since most of its grand houses have been divided into apartments, or else are serving as foreign embassies.

Now visitors enter Kensington Gardens to see Kensington Palace and to explore the parks themselves. Hyde Park and Kensington Gardens together form by far the biggest of central London's royal parks. It's probably been centuries since any major royal had a casual stroll here, but the parks remain the property of the Crown, and it was the Crown that saved them from being devoured by the city's late-18th-century growth spurt.

Around the western borders of Hyde Park are several of London's poshest and most beautiful neighborhoods. To the south of the park and just a short carriage ride from Buckingham Palace is the most splendidly aristocratic enclave to be found in London: Belgravia—this is *Upstairs, Downstairs* Eaton Square territory. Its stucco-white buildings and grand squares—particularly Belgrave Square—are preserved Regency-era jewels. On the western border of Hyde Park is Mayfair, which gives Belgravia a definite run for its money as London's wealthiest district. Here are three mansions that will allow you to get a peek into the lifestyles of London's rich and famous—19th- and 20th-century versions: Apsley House, the home of the Duke of Wellington; Spencer House, home of Princess Diana's ancestors; and the Wallace Collection, a grand mansion on Manchester Square stuffed with great art treasures.

A Good Walk

When you surface from the Knightsbridge tube station—one of London's deepest—you are immediately engulfed by the manic drivers, professional shoppers, and ladies-who-lunch who compose the local population. Walk west down Brompton Road, past Harrods, to the junction of Cromwell Road and the pale, Italianate Brompton Oratory, which marks the beginning of museum territory. The **Victoria & Albert Museum** ⑥ or V&A, is first, at the start of Cromwell Road, followed by the **Natural History Museum** ⑥ and the **Science Museum** ⑥ behind it. Turn left to continue north up Exhibition Road, a kind of unfinished cultural main drag that was Prince Albert's conception, toward the road after which British moviemakers named their fake blood, Kensington Gore, to reach the giant round Wedgwood china box of the **Royal Albert Hall** ⑥ and the scaffolding-shrouded **Albert Memorial** ⑥ opposite.

Enter **Kensington Gardens** across the road, and walk west until you reach **Kensington Palace** ⑥. From here you can either head west to check out some of London's current sanctuaries of the rich and famous at **Kensington Palace Gardens** ⑥ or take an extra leg of the journey to visit two historic residences, the **Linley Sambourne House** ⑥ and **Leighton House** ⑥. If opulent 19th-century interiors are not your cup of tea, head east instead to explore Kensington Gardens itself. In Kensington Gardens, you'll encounter the Round Pond; the statues of **Peter Pan** and the horse and rider called *Physical Energy;* then the formal garden at the end of the Long Water, The Fountains; and finally the **Serpentine Gallery,** beside the lake of the same name. When you pass its bridge, you leave Kensington Gardens and enter **Hyde Park.** Walk to the southern perimeter and along the sand track called Rotten Row. It was Henry VIII's royal path to the hunt—hence the name, a corruption of *route du roi.* It's still used by the Household Cavalry (the brigade that mounts the guard at the palace), who live at the Knightsbridge Barracks to the left. Then head toward the Hyde Park Corner exit of the park and discover glorious **Apsley House (Wellington Museum)** ⑦⓪. If you decided to skip Hyde Park, tube it from Kensington High Street (and Leighton House) over to Hyde Park Corner to take in the Wellington Museum, then head south to see chic **Belgrave Place** ⑦① or north for some more palatial treats: several blocks northwest is **Spencer House** ⑦② and farther north through elegant Mayfair—custom-built for expansive strolling—is the **Wallace Collection** ⑦③. For some sights to delight children, keep heading northward to discover the sights around Regents's Park: the **BBC Experience** ⑦④, **Madame Tussaud's** ⑦⑤, and the **Zoo.**

TIMING

This walk is at least 4 mi long, and it is almost impossible to finish without going inside somewhere. The best way to approach these neighborhoods is to treat Knightsbridge shopping and the South Kensington museums as separate days out—though you may find all three of the museums too much to take in at once. The parks are best in the growing seasons—from the crocuses and daffodils of early spring through the tulips to the roses—and during fall, when the foliage show easily rivals New England's. On Sunday, the Hyde Park and Kensington Gardens railings all along the Bayswater Road are hung with attractively priced art, which may slow your progress; also this is prime perambulation day for locals. Whatever your priorities, this is a long walk if you explore every corner, with the perimeter of the two parks alone covering a good 4 mi, and about half as far again around the remainder of the route. A jaunt from Belgrave Square up to the Apsley and Spencer houses and on to the Wallace Collection would add another 2 mi to this outing—so you'd probably want to tackle Belgravia and Mayfair after a serious time-out. You could cut out a lot of Hyde Park without missing out on essential sights, and walk the whole thing in a good five hours. Remember that the parks close their gates at sundown.

Sights to See

⑥⑤ **Albert Memorial.** Seemingly permanently shrouded in the world's tallest freestanding web of scaffolding, the intricate structure housing the 14-ft bronze statue of Albert is undergoing a £14-million renovation and is not due to be finished until the year 2000. Albert's grieving widow, Queen Victoria, had this elaborate confection erected on the spot where his Great Exhibition had stood a mere decade before his early death, from typhoid, in 1861.

⑦⓪ **Apsley House (Wellington Museum).** Once known, quite simply, as Number 1, London, this was celebrated as the best address in town. Built by Robert Adam in the 1770s and reopened in 1996 after a superlative renovation, this mansion was home to the celebrated conqueror of Napoléon, the Duke of Wellington, who lived here from the 1820s until his death in 1852. The great Waterloo Gallery—scene of legendary dinners—is one of the most spectacular rooms in England. Not to be missed, in every sense, is the gigantic Canova statue of a nude (but fig-leafed) Bonaparte in the entry stairwell. The current Duke of Wellington still lives here. ⊠ *149 Piccadilly,* ☎ *0171/499–5676.* 🎫 *£4.* ☉ *Tues.–Sun. 11–5. Tube: Hyde Park Corner.*

🅐 BBC Experience. For those who have been weaned on a steady diet of Masterpiece Theatre presentations, the BBC is the greatest television producer in the world. These fans, and those of the BBC's countless other programs, will be happy to know that the BBC has just opened the doors of its own in-house museum, to celebrate the BBC's 75th anniversary. There's an audiovisual show that traces the BBC's history, an interactive section—want to try your hand at commentating on a sports game, presenting a weather forecast, or making your own director's cut of a segment of *EastEnders?*—and, of course, a massive gift shop. This museum will probably be deluged by crowds for the first few years—conveniently, admission is on a pre-booked and timed system. ⊠ *Broadcasting House, Portland Place, W1,* ☎ *0870/603–0304; outside U.K., 01222/55771.* 🎫 *Free.* ☉ *Daily 9:30–5:30. Tube: Oxford Circus.*

🅐 Belgrave Place. One of the main arteries of Belgravia—London's swankiest neighborhood—Belgrave Place is lined with grand, imposing Regency-era mansions (now mostly embassies). Walk down this street from sylvan Belgrave Square toward Eaton Place to pass two of Belgravia's most beautiful mews—Eaton Mews North and Eccleston Mews, both fronted by grand Westminster-white rusticated entrances right out of a 19th-century engraving. There are few other places where London is both so picturesque and elegant.

☾ Harrods. Just in case you hadn't noticed it, Harrods has its domed terra-cotta Edwardian bulk outlined in thousands of white lights at night. The 15-acre Egyptian-owned store's sales weeks are world-class, and the environment is as frenetic as a stock-market floor. Don't miss the extravagant **Food Hall,** with its stunning art nouveau tiling in the neighborhood of meat and poultry. This is the department in which to acquire your green-and-gold-logo souvenir Harrods bag, since food prices are surprisingly competitive. ⊠ *87 Brompton Rd.,* ☎ *0171/730–1234. Tube: Knightsbridge.*

☾ Hyde Park. Along with the smaller St. James's and Green parks to the east, Hyde Park started as Henry VIII's hunting grounds. Along its south side runs **Rotten Row,** still used by the Household Cavalry, who live at the **Knightsbridge Barracks**—a high-rise and a long, low, ugly red block to the left. This is the brigade that mounts the guard at the palace, and you can see them leave to perform this duty, in full regalia, at about 10:30, or see the exhausted cavalry return about noon.

☾ Kensington Gardens. More formal than neighboring Hyde Park, Kensington Gardens was first laid out as palace grounds. The paved Italian garden at the top of the Long Water, **The Fountains** is a reminder of this, though, of course **Kensington Palace** itself is the main clue to its royal status, with its early 19th-century Sunken Garden north of it. Nearby is George Frampton's beloved 1912 **Peter Pan,** a bronze of the boy who lived on an island in the Serpentine and never grew up, and whose creator, J. M. Barrie, lived at 100 Bayswater Road, not 500 yards from here. The **Round Pond** is a magnet for model-boat enthusiasts and duck feeders.

🅐 Kensington Palace. Kensington was put, socially speaking, on the map when King William III, "much incommoded by the Smoak of the Coal Fires of London" decided in the 17th century to vacate Whitehall and relocate to a new palace outside the center city in the "village" of Kensington. The new palace did enjoy a smooth passage as royal residence. Twelve years of renovation were needed before William and Mary could move in. Of course, royals have lived here since William and Mary—and some have died here, too. In 1760, poor George II burst a blood vessel while on the toilet (the official line was, presumably, that he was on the throne). The State Rooms where Victoria had her ultra-strict upbringing have recently been completely renovated, and they depict the life of the royal family through the past century. This palace is an essential stop for royalty vultures, because it's the only one where you may actually catch a glimpse of the real thing. Princess Margaret, the Duke and Duchess of Gloucester, and Prince and Princess Michael of Kent all have apartments here, as did, Diana, Princess of Wales, until her tragic death. A highlight of the visit here is the famous **Court Dress Collection.** Repair to the palace's nearby Orangery for an elegant pot of Earl Grey. ⊠ *Kensington Gardens,* ☎ *0171/937–9561.* 🎟 *£5.50.* ⊙ *May to Dec. daily 10–3:30. Tube: High Street Kensington.*

67 **Kensington Palace Gardens.** Immediately behind Kensington Palace is Kensington Palace Gardens (called Palace Green at the south end), a wide, leafy avenue of mid-19th-century mansions that used to be one of London's most elegant addresses. Today, it's largely Embassy Row, including those of Russia and Israel. *Tube: High Street Kensington.*

69 **Leighton House.** The exotic richness of late 19th-century aesthetic tastes is captured in this fascinating home, once the abode of Lord Leighton, the Victorian painter par excellence. The Arab Hall is lavishly lined with Persian tiles and pieced woodwork. Thanks to the generosity of John Paul Getty II, the somewhat neglected property has undergone a full renovation. Its neighborhood was one of the principal artists' colonies of Victorian London. If you are interested in domestic architecture of the 19th century, wander through the surrounding streets. ⊠ *14 Holland Park Rd.,* ☎ *0171/602–3316.* 🎟 *Free.* ⊙ *Mon.–Sat. 11–5. Tube: Holland Park.*

68 **Linley Sambourne House.** On the eastern side of the Commonwealth Institute, discover this delightful Victorian residence, built and furnished in the 1870s by Mr. Sambourne, for more than 30 years the political cartoonist for the satirical magazine *Punch.* Stuffed with delightful Victorian and Edwardian antiques, fabrics, and paintings, this is one of the most charming 19th-century London houses extant—little wonder it was filmed for Merchant/Ivory's *A Room with a View.* ⊠ *18 Stafford Terr.,* ☎ *0181/944–1019.* 🎟 *£3.* ⊙ *Mar.–Oct., Wed. 10–4, Sun. 2–5. Tube: High Street Kensington.*

🕑 **London Zoo.** The zoo has been open for more than 150 years and peaked in popularity during the 1950s, but it recently faced the prospect of closing its gates forever. The animal-crazy Brits, apparently anxious about the morality of caging wild beasts, simply stopped visiting. In the '90s, the zoo fought back and now has corporate sponsorship and a great big modernization program. ⊠ *Regent's Park,* ☎ *0171/722–3333.* 🎟 *£8.* ⊙ *Summer, daily 9–6; winter, daily 10–4; penguin feed 2:30; aquarium feed 2:30; reptile feed 2:30 Fri. only; elephant bath 3:45. Tube: Camden Town, and Bus 74.*

🕑 **75** **Madame Tussaud's.** This is nothing more, nothing less, than the world's premier exhibition of lifelike waxwork models of celebrities. Madame T. learned her craft while making death masks of French Revolution victims and in 1835 set up her first show of the famous ones near this spot. You can see everyone from Shakespeare to Benny Hill here, but top billing still goes to the murderers in the Chamber of Horrors, who stare glassy-eyed at you—this one from the electric chair, that one next to the tin bath where he dissolved several wives in quicklime. Just next door is the London Planetarium, which offers a special combo ticket with Tussaud's. Warning: the lines here can be ridiculous. ⊠ *Marylebone Rd.*, ☎ *0171/935–6861.* ⊞ *£8.95, joint ticket with adjacent planetarium £11.20.* ⊙ *Sept.–June, weekdays 10–5:30, weekends 9:30–5:30; July–Aug., daily 9:30–5:30. Tube: Baker St.*

🖐 ⑥ **Natural History Museum.** When you want to heed the call of the wild, discover this fun place—enter to find Dinosaurs on the left and the Ecology Gallery on the right. Both these exhibits (the former with life-size moving dinosaurs, the latter complete with moonlit "rain forest") make essential viewing in a museum that realized it was getting crusty and has consequently invested millions overhauling itself in recent years. Don't miss the Creepy Crawlies Gallery, which features a nightmarish super-enlarged scorpion, yet ends up making tarantulas seem cute. ⊠ *Cromwell Rd.*, ☎ *0171/938–9123.* ⊞ *£6; free weekdays 4:30–5:50, weekends 5–5:50; White Card accepted.* ⊙ *Mon.–Sat. 10–5:50, Sun. 11–5:50. Tube: South Kensington.*

⑥ **Royal Albert Hall.** This famous theater was made possible by the Victorian public, who donated funds for the domed, circular 8,000-seat auditorium. More money was raised, however, by selling 1,300 future seats at £100 apiece—not for the first night alone, but for every night for 999 years. (Some descendants of those purchasers still use the seats.) The Albert Hall is best known and best loved for its annual July–September Henry Wood Promenade Concerts (the "Proms"), with bargain-price standing (or promenading, or sitting-on-the-floor) tickets sold on the night of the world-class classical concerts. ⊠ *Kensington Gore*, ☎ *0171/589–3203.* ⊞ *Admission varies according to event. Tube: South Kensington.*

🖐 ⑥ **Science Museum.** Standing behind the Natural History Museum, this features loads of hands-on exhibits. Highlights include the Launch Pad gallery; the Computing Then and Now show; **Puffing Billy,** the oldest train in the world; and the actual **Apollo 10** capsule. ⊠ *Exhibition Rd.*, ☎ *0171/938–8000.* ⊞ *£5.95.* ⊙ *Mon.–Sat. 10–6, Sun. 11–6. Tube: South Kensington.*

Serpentine Gallery. A gallery influential on the trendy art circuit, this place hosts temporary shows of modern work, often very avant-garde indeed. It overlooks the west bank of the **Serpentine,** a beloved lake, much frequented in summer, when the south shore Lido resembles a beach and the water is dotted with rented rowboats. ⊠ *Kensington Gardens*, ☎ *0171/402–6075.* ⊞ *Free.* ⊙ *Daily 10–6; closed Christmas wk. Tube: Lancaster Gate.*

★ ⑫ **Spencer House.** Ancestral abode of the Spencers—the family who gave us Princess Diana—this great mansion is perhaps the finest example of 18th-century elegance, on a domestic scale, extant in London. Superlatively restored by Lord Rothschild, the house was built in 1766 for the first Earl Spencer, heir to the first Duchess of Marlborough. James "Athenian" Stuart decorated the gilded State Rooms, including the Painted Room, the first completely Neoclassic room in Europe. The most ostentatious part of the house (and the Spencers—as witness the £40,000 diamond shoe buckles the first countess proudly wore—could be given to ostentation) is the florid bow-window of the Palm Room: covered with stucco palm trees, it conjures up both ancient Palmyra and modern Miami Beach. ⊠ *27 St. James's Place*, ☎ *0171/499–8620.* ⊞ *£6; children under 10 not admitted.* ⊙ *Sun. 10:45–4:45 (guided tours only; tickets go on sale each Sunday at 10:30). Closed Aug., Jan. Tube: Green Park.*

⑥ Victoria & Albert Museum. Recognizable by the copy of Victoria's Imperial Crown it wears on the lantern above the central cupola, this museum is always referred to as the V&A. It is a huge museum, showcasing the applied arts of all disciplines, all periods, all nationalities, and all tastes, and it is a wonderful, generous place in which to get lost. The collections are *so* all-encompassing that confusion is a hazard—one minute you're gazing on the Jacobean oak 12-ft-square four-poster Great Bed of Ware (one of the V&A's most prized possessions, given that Shakespeare immortalized it in *Twelfth Night*); the next, you're in the 20th-century end of the equally celebrated Dress Collection, coveting a Jean Muir frock you can actually buy at nearby Harrods. Prince Albert, Victoria's adored consort, was responsible for the genesis of this permanent version of the 1851 Great Exhibition, and his queen laid its foundation stone in her final public London appearance in 1899. The latest renovations include the Raphael Galleries, where seven massive cartoons the painter completed in 1516 for his Sistine Chapel tapestries are housed. Be sure to check out young designer Danny Lane's breathtaking glass balustrade in the Glass Gallery. The special-events program here is one of the most exciting in the world—unique lectures, dinners, and the Late View salons lure the young and trendy. If you want to rest your overstimulated eyes, head for the brick-walled V&A café; its Sunday Jazz Brunch is fast becoming a London institution. ⊠ *Cromwell Rd.,* ☎ *0171/938–8500.* 🎫 *Suggested contribution £5; free after 4:30, except Wed.; White Card accepted.* ⊘ *Mon. noon–5:50, Tues.–Sun. 10–5:50; Wed. Late View 4:30–9:30. Tube: South Kensington.*

㊀ Wallace Collection. Assembled by four generations of marquesses of Hertford, the Wallace Collection is important, exciting, undervisited—and free. As at the Frick Collection in New York, the setting here, Hertford House, is part of the show—a fine late-18th-century mansion. It was the eccentric fourth marquess who really built the collection, snapping up Bouchers, Fragonards, Watteaus, and Lancrets for a song (the French Revolution having rendered them dangerously unfashionable). The highlight is Fragonard's *The Swing*, which conjures up the 18th-century's let-them-eat-cake *frivolité* better than any other painting around. Don't forget to smile back at Frans Hals's *Laughing Cavalier* in the Big Gallery. ⊠ *Hertford House, Manchester Sq.,* ☎ *0171/935–0687.* 🎫 *Free.* ⊘ *Mon.–Sat. 10–5, Sun. 2–5. Tube: Bond, Baker St.*

OFF THE
BEATEN PATH

ABBEY ROAD STUDIOS – Strawberry Beatles Forever! Here, outside the legendary Abbey Road Studios, is the most famous zebra crossing in the world. Immortalized on the Beatles's *Abbey Road* album of 1969, this footpath is a spot beloved to countless Beatlemaniacs and baby boomers. Adjacent to the traffic crossing, at No. 3 Abbey Road, are the studios where the Beatles recorded their entire output, from "Love Me Do" on, including, most momentously, *Sgt. Pepper's Lonely Hearts Club Band* (early 1967). To see this and other Fab Four sites, **Original London Walks** offers two Beatles tours: "The Beatles In-My-Life Walk" and "The Beatles Magical Mystery Tour" (☎ 0171/624–3978). Abbey Road is in the elegant neighborhood of St. John's Wood, a 10-minute ride on the tube from central London. Take the Jubilee subway line to the St. John's Wood tube stop, head southwest three blocks down Grove End Road—and be prepared for a heart-stopping vista right out of Memory Lane.

Up and Down the Thames

About 8 mi downstream—which means seaward, to the east—from central London lies a neighborhood you'd think had been designed to provide the perfect day out. Greenwich is another of London's self-contained "villages," but one with unique and splendid sights surrounding the residential portion. Sir Christopher Wren's Royal Naval College and Inigo Jones's Queen's House reach architectural heights; the Old Royal Observatory measures time for our entire planet; and the Greenwich Meridian divides the world in two—you can stand astride it with one foot in either hemisphere. The National Maritime Museum and the proud clipper ship *Cutty Sark* thrill seafaring types, and landlubbers can stroll the green acres of parkland that surround the buildings, the quaint 19th-century houses, and the weekend crafts and antiques markets. Meanwhile, upstream, the royal palaces and grand houses that dot the area were built not as town houses but as country residences with easy access to London by river, and Hampton Court Palace is the best and biggest of all.

A Good Walk

There's no way to combine up- and downstream visits in a single day, so this walk concentrates on Greenwich, a place tailor-made to explore on foot. First of all, bear in mind that the journey to Greenwich is fun in itself, especially if you approach by river, arriving to the best possible vista of the Royal Naval College, with the Queen's House behind. On the way, the boat glides past famous sights on the London skyline. You could also take the Docklands Light Railway (DLR) from Bank to Island Gardens, where you should enter the squat little circular brick building with its glass-dome roof. This is the entrance to the Greenwich Foot Tunnel, where an ancient elevator takes you down to a walkway under the Thames that brings you up very close to the *Cutty Sark*.

By continuing along King William Walk, you come to the wrought-iron gates of the **Royal Naval College,** from the south end of which you approach the building that Wren's majestic quadrangles frame, the **Queen's House,** followed by the **National Maritime Museum.** Now head up the hill in Greenwich Park overlooking the Naval College and Maritime Museum to the **Old Royal Observatory.** Walking back through the park toward the river, you'll enter the pretty streets of Greenwich Village to the west. There are plenty of bookstores and antiques shops for browsing, and, at the foot of Crooms Hill, the modern Greenwich Theatre—a West End theater, despite its location, which mounts well-regarded, often star-spangled productions. Finish up at the excellent Greenwich Antique Market (on Burney Street near the museum and theater), and the Victorian Covered Crafts Market by the *Cutty Sark,* on College Approach.

TIMING

First of all, the boat trip takes about an hour from Westminster Pier (next to Big Ben), or 25 minutes from the Tower of London, so figure in enough time for the round-trip, unless the weather's really awful or it's winter and the boats have stopped. Aim for an early start. Although the distance covered in this walk is barely a mile, Greenwich can't be "done" in a day. There are such riches here, especially if the maritime theme is your thing, that whatever time you allow will seem halved. If the weather's good, you'll be tempted to stroll aimlessly around the quaint un-citylike streets, too, and maybe take a turn in the park. If you want to take in the markets, you'll need to come on a weekend. The antiques market is open 8–4; the crafts market, 9–5.

Sights to See

GREENWICH

☪ **Cutty Sark.** This romantic tea clipper was built in 1869, one of fleets and fleets of similar wooden tall-masted clippers which during the 19th century plied the seven seas, trading in exotic commodities—tea, in this case. The *Cutty Sark,* the last to survive, was also the fastest, sailing the China–London route in 1871 in only 107 days. Now the photogenic vessel lies in dry dock, a museum of one kind of seafaring life— and not a comfortable kind for the 28-strong crew, as you'll see. The collection of figureheads is amusing, too. ⊠ *King William Walk,* ☎ *0181/858–3445.* ⊡ *£3.50.* ⊙ *Apr.–Sept., Mon.–Sat. 10–6, Sun. and public holidays noon–6; Oct.–Mar., Mon.–Sat. 10–5, Sun. and public holidays noon–5. Last admission 30 mins before closing.*

☪ **National Maritime Museum.** Greenwich's star attraction contains everything to do with the British at sea, in the form of paintings, models, maps, globes, sextants, uniforms (including the one Nelson died in at Trafalgar, complete with bloodstained bullet hole), and—best of all— actual boats, including a collection of ornately gilded royal barges. The museum's Dolphin Coffee Shop is a good place to recuperate after the rigors of the museum. ⊠ *Romney Rd.,* ☎ *0181/858–4422.* ⊡ *£5, including the Queen's House and Old Royal Observatory; White Card accepted.* ⊙ *Mon.–Sat. 10–6, Sun. noon–6.*

Old Royal Observatory. Founded in 1675 by Charles II, this observatory was designed the same year by Christopher Wren for John Flamsteed, the first Astronomer Royal. The red ball you see on its roof has been there only since 1833. It drops every day at 1 PM, and you can set your watch by it, as the sailors on the Thames always have. Everyone comes here to be photographed astride the **Prime Meridian,** a brass line laid on the cobblestones at zero degrees longitude, one side being the eastern, one the western, hemisphere. ⊠ *Greenwich Park,* ☎ *0181/858– 4422.* ⊡ *£5.50, including National Maritime Museum and Queen's House; White Card accepted.* ⊙ *Mon.–Sat. 10–6, Sun. noon–6.*

★ **Queen's House.** The queen for whom Inigo Jones began designing the house in 1616 was James I's Anne of Denmark, but she died three years later, and it was Charles I's French wife, Henrietta Maria, who inherited the building when it was completed in 1635. It is Britain's first Classical building—the first, that is, to use the lessons of Italian Renaissance architecture—and is of enormous importance in the history of English architecture. The Great Hall is a perfect cube, exactly 40 ft in all three directions, and it is decorated with paintings of the Muses, the Virtues, and the Liberal Arts. ⊠ *Romney Rd.,* ☎ *0181/858–4422.* ⊡ *£5.50, including National Maritime Museum and Old Royal Observatory; White Card accepted.* ⊙ *Mon.–Sat. 10–6, Sun. noon–6.*

Royal Naval College. Begun by Christopher Wren in 1694 as a home for ancient mariners, it became a school for young ones in 1873. You'll notice how the blocks part to reveal the **Queen's House** across the central lawns—one of England's most famous architectural set pieces. Wren, with the help of his assistant, Hawksmoor, was at pains to preserve the river vista from the house, and there are few more majestic views in London than the awe-inspiring symmetry he achieved. The Painted Hall and the College Chapel are the two outstanding interiors on view here. ⊠ *King William Walk,* ☎ *0181/858–2154.* ⊡ *Free.* ⊙ *Daily, 2:30–4:45.*

HAMPTON COURT PALACE

Some 20 mi from central London, on a loop of the Thames upstream from Richmond, lies **Hampton Court,** one of London's oldest royal palaces, more like a small town in size, and requiring a day of your time to do it justice. The magnificent Tudor brick house was begun in 1514 by Cardinal Wolsey, the ambitious and worldly lord chancellor (roughly, prime minister) of England and archbishop of York. He wanted it to be the absolute best palace in the land, and in this he succeeded so effectively that Henry VIII grew deeply envious, whereupon Wolsey felt obliged to give Hampton Court to the king. Henry moved in in 1525, adding a great hall and chapel, and proceeded to live much of his astonishing life here. Later, during the reign of William and Mary, the palace was much expanded by Sir Christopher Wren. The site beside the slow-moving Thames is perfect. The palace itself, steeped in history, hung with priceless paintings, full of echoing cobbled courtyards and cavernous Tudor kitchens complete with deer pies and cooking pots—not to mention the ghost of Catherine Howard, who is still aboard, screaming her innocence (of adultery) to an unheeding Henry VIII—is set in a fantastic array of ornamental gardens (including a wondrous topiary maze), lakes, and ponds, which must be seen on a sunny day. ⊠ *East Molesey,* ☎ *0181/977–8441.* ☞ *Apartments and maze £8.50, maze only £2, grounds free.* ☉ *State apartments Apr.–Oct., Tues.– Sun. 9:30–6, Mon. 10:15–6; Nov.–Mar., Tues.–Sun. 9:30–4:30, Mon. 10:15–4:30. Grounds daily 8–dusk.*

KEW

The **Royal Botanic Gardens** at Kew are the headquarters of the country's leading botanical institute as well as a public garden of 300 acres and more than 60,000 species of plants. Two 18th-century royal ladies, Queen Caroline and Princess Augusta, were responsible for its founding. The highlights here are the 19th-century greenhouses and the ultramodern Princess of Wales Conservatory, opened in 1987. Kew Palace, on the grounds, was home to George III for much of his life; note that the palace is closed for renovations until spring 1999 (call for news about scheduled reopening). Its formal garden has been redeveloped on a 17th-century pattern. ☎ *0181/940–1171; 0181/940– 3321 Kew Palace.* ☞ *Gardens £4.50, including Queen Charlotte's Cottage (Apr.–Sept.).* ☉ *Gardens daily 9:30–6:30, greenhouses 10– 6:30 (Sun. and national holidays until 8); in winter, closing times depend on the light.*

DINING

No longer would Somerset Maugham be justified in saying, "If you want to eat well in England, have breakfast three times a day." London is in the midst of a restaurant revolution and its dining scene is one of the hottest around; even Andrew Lloyd Webber, that obsessional front-runner and composer of *Cats* and *Phantom,* has taken on a second career as dining critic. The city has fallen head-over-heels in love with its restaurants—all 5,000 of them—from its vast, glamorous eateries to its tiny neighborhood joints, from pubs where young foodniks find their feet to swanky boîtes where celebrity chefs launch their ego flights.

This restaurant renaissance is due to a new crew of entrepreneurs, chefs, and culinary peacocks: Sir Terence Conran, Antony Worrall Thompson, Marco Pierre White, Oliver Peyton, Mogens Tholstrup, Christopher Corbin, and Jeremy King lead the list. Read all about them, and many others, when you get here—which you can easily do by picking up any newspaper. To keep up with the onslaught, they have about 15 restaurant reviewers apiece. Luckily, London also does a good job of catering to people more interested in satisfying their appetites without breaking the bank than in the latest food fashions. We have tried to strike a balance in our listings between these extremes, and have included hip and happening places, neighborhood places, ethnic alternatives and old favorites, plus some completely undemanding burger joints and regular restaurants for when you merely want to be fed. Ethnic restaurants have always been a good bet here, especially the thousands of Indian restaurants, since Londoners see a good tandoori as their birthright.

Few places these days mind if you order a second appetizer instead of an entrée, and you will often find set-price menus at lunchtime, bringing even the very finest and fanciest establishments within reach. Prix-fixe dinners are beginning to proliferate, too. Note that many places are closed on Sunday or late at night, and virtually everywhere closes down for the Christmas holiday period. The law obliges all British restaurants to display their prices, including VAT (sales tax) outside, but watch for hidden extras such as bread and vegetables charged separately, and service. Most restaurants add 10%–15% automatically to the check, or stamp SERVICE NOT INCLUDED along the bottom, and/or leave the total on the credit-card slip blank. Beware of paying twice for service, especially if it was less than satisfactory.

CATEGORY	COST*
££££	over £50
£££	£35–£50
££	£20–£35
£	under £20

*per person, including first course, main course, and dessert, excluding drinks, service, and VAT

St. James's

££££ ✗ **The Ritz.** Constantly accused of being London's prettiest dining room, this belle epoque palace of marble, gilt, and trompe l'oeil would moisten even Marie Antoinette's eye; add the view over Green Park and the Ritz's secret sunken garden, and it seems obsolete to consider eating. But David Nicholls's British/French cuisine stands up to the visual onslaught with costly morsels (foie gras, lobster, truffles, caviar, etc.), super-rich, all served with a flourish. Englishness is wrested from Louis XVI by a daily roast "from the trolley," or braised oxtail, among other delicacies. A three-course prix-fixe lunch at £23 and a dinner at £29 make the check more bearable, but the wine list is pricey. A Friday and Saturday dinner dance sweetly maintains a dying tradition. ⊠ *Piccadilly, W1,* ☎ *0171/493–8181. Reservations essential. Jacket and tie. AE, DC, MC, V. Tube: Green Park.*

£££ ✗ **Le Caprice.** Secreted on a small street behind the Ritz, Caprice may
★ command the deepest loyalty of any London restaurant, because it gets everything right: the glamorous, glossy black Eva Jiricna interior, the perfect pitch of the informal but respectful service, the food, halfway between Euro-peasant and fashion-plate. This food—crispy duck and watercress salad; seared scallops with bacon and sorrel; Lincolnshire sausage with bubble and squeak (potato-and-cabbage hash); grilled rabbit with black olive polenta; and divine desserts, too—has no business being so good, because the other reason everyone comes here is that everyone else does, which leads to the best people-watching in town (apart from its almost chicer sister restaurant, The Ivy; ☞ Covent Garden, *below.*) ⊠ *Arlington House, Arlington St., SW1,* ☎ *0171/629–2239. AE, DC, MC, V. No lunch Sat. Tube: Green Park.*

£££ ✗ **Quaglino's.** Now well into its first decade, Sir Terence Conran's original huge restaurant, "Quags," is *the* out-of-towners' post-theater or celebration destination, while Londoners like its late hours. The gigantic sunken restaurant boasts a glamorous staircase, "Crustacea Altar," large bar, and live jazz music. The food is fashionably pan-European with some Oriental trimmings. Desserts come from somewhere between the Paris bistro and the English nursery (raspberry sablé, creme pudding with butterscotch sauce), and wine from the Old World and the New, some bottles at modest prices. ⊠ *16 Bury St., SW1,* ☎ *0171/930–6767. AE, DC, MC, V. Tube: Green Park.*

£ ✗ **The Fountain.** At the back of Fortnum & Mason's is this old-fash-
★ ioned restaurant, frumpy and popular as a boarding school matron, serving delicious light meals, toasted snacks, sandwiches, and ice-cream sodas. During the day, go for the Welsh rarebit or cold game pie; in the evening, a no-frills filet steak is a typical option. It's just the place for afternoon tea and ice-cream sundaes after the Royal Academy or Bond Street shopping, and for pre-theater meals. ⊠ *181 Piccadilly, W1,* ☎ *0171/734–4938. AE, DC, MC, V. Closed Sun. Tube: Green Park.*

Mayfair

££££ ✗ **Chez Nico at Ninety Park Lane.** Those with refined palates and very deep pockets would be well advised not to miss Nico Ladenis's exquisite cuisine, served in this suitably hushed and plush Louis XV dining room next to the Grosvenor House Hotel. Autodidact Nico is one of the world's great chefs, and he's famous for knowing it. The menu is in French and untranslated. There is no salt on the table—ask for some at your peril. It's all more affordable in daylight, proffering set menus from £32 for three courses. ⊠ *90 Park La., W1,* ☎ *0171/409–1290. Reservations essential. Jacket and tie. AE, DC, MC, V. Closed weekends, 3 wks in Aug. Tube: Marble Arch.*

££££ ✗ **Le Gavroche.** Albert Roux has handed the toque to his son, Michel, who retains many of his capital-C Classic dishes under the heading *Hommage à mon père,* as well as adding his own style to the place that was once considered London's finest restaurant. Much of the food is still fabulous—the lobster tajine is a wonder—but the decor of the basement dining room is, some would say, generic: brown-green walls, dullish modern oil paintings, and potted plants. The set lunch is relatively affordable at £40. ⊠ *43 Upper Brook St., W1,* ☎ *0171/499–1826. Reservations essential at least 1 wk in advance. Jacket and tie. AE, DC, MC, V. Closed weekends, 10 days at Christmas. Tube: Marble Arch.*

££££ ✗ **Oak Room.** Bad boy Marco Pierre White enjoys Jagger-like fame from
★ his TV appearances and gossip-column reports of his complicated love life and random eruptions of fury. He should stick to his pans, say superchef critics. But, hype aside, Marco may be London's greatest chef and now gets to show off in his most spectacular setting yet—all belle epoque soaring ceilings and gilded bits, and palms and paintings, not to mention the crisp napery and batteries of flatware. If you invest in an evening here, know that he will despise you for ordering his Assiette of Chocolate, which he considers low-class. ⊠ *Le Meridien, 21 Piccadilly W1,* ☎ *0171/734–8000. Reservations essential. Jacket and tie. AE, DC, MC, V. Tube: Piccadilly Circus.*

£££ ✗ **Criterion.** This palatial neo-Byzantine mirrored marble hall, which first opened in 1874, was put back on the map with the arrival of the current regime led by the somewhat self-promoting but super-talented Marco Pierre White. The glamour of the soaring golden ceiling, peacock-blue theater-size drapes, oil paintings, and attentive Gallic service adds up to an elegant night out. The vast menu is difficult to ride herd on—it extends from brasserie to luxe—but the kitchen is a serious one. ⊠ *Piccadilly Circus, W1,* ☎ *0171/930–2626. AE, DC, MC, V. Tube: Piccadilly Circus.*

London Dining

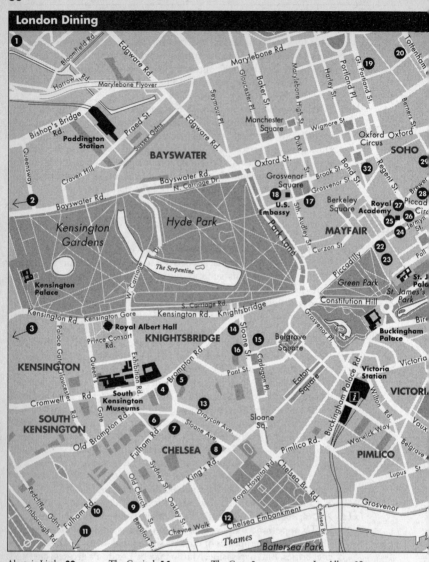

Alastair Little, **30**

Aubergine, **10**

Belgo Centraal, **41**

Bertorelli's, **37**

Bibendum, **7**

Bluebird, **9**

Brown's, **32**

The Capital, **14**

Chelsea Kitchen, **8**

Chez Gerard, **20**

Chez Nico at Ninety
Park Lane, **17**

Chutney Mary, **11**

The Collection, **4**

The Cow, **1**

Criterion, **28**

The Enterprise, **13**

Food for Thought, **36**

The Fountain, **24**

Gourmet Pizza
Company, **27**

The Ivy, **39**

Joe Allen, **40**

La Tante Claire, **12**

Le Caprice, **23**

Le Gavroche, **18**

Le Pont de la Tour, **46**

Maxwell's, **35**

Mezzo, **29**

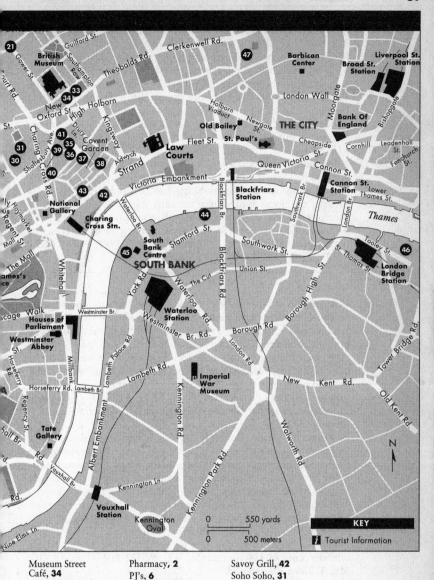

££   ✕ **Gourmet Pizza Company.** Fine pies with wacky toppings are served up at this California-style über-pizza. ⊠ *7–9 Swallow St., SW1,* ☎ *0171/734–5182. AE, MC, V. Tube: Piccadilly Circus.*

£–££   ✕ **Brown's.** Unpretentious, crowd-pleasing, child-friendly English feeding is accomplished here at the former establishment of Messrs Cooling and Wells, the famous tailors, now converted to Edwardian style by the owner of the very successful regional Brown's (the Oxford and Cambridge ones have put generations of students through school). Eat an all-day English breakfast, or steak and Guinness pie, or salmon cakes, then sticky toffee pudding or sherry trifle. ⊠ *47 Maddox St., W1,* ☎ *0171/491–4565. AE, MC, V. Tube: Oxford Circus.*

£–££   ✕ **Villandry.** This foodie's paradise just moved to huge new premises— the food hall here is now even larger than the one at Harrods! French pâtés, Continental cheeses, fruit tarts, biscuits, and breads galore are for sale, and if you must indulge but can't wait to take a bite, there's a tearoom café and dining room that both serve exquisite lunches. Twice a month, dinners are offered, but they are among the hardest reservations to book in London. ⊠ *170 Great Portland St., W1,* ☎ *0171/631– 3131. AE, MC, V. Tube: Great Portland St.*

Soho

£££   ✕ **Alastair Little.** Little is one of London's most original—and most imitated—chefs, drawing inspiration from practically everywhere—Thailand, Japan, Scandinavia, France, but chiefly Italy, and sometimes bringing it off brilliantly. His restaurant is stark and sparse—it's intentional, darling—so all attention focuses on the menu, which changes not once but twice daily to take advantage of the best ingredients. Look out also for his newer, smaller, cheaper version near Ladbroke Grove tube station. ⊠ *49 Frith St., W1,* ☎ *0171/734–5183. No credit cards. Closed Sun., 2 wks at Christmas, 3 wks in Aug. No lunch Sat. Tube: Leicester Sq.*

£–£££   ✕ **Mezzo.** Sir Terence Conran's 700-seat Mezzo isn't only London's biggest restaurant—it's the most gigantic in all Europe. Downstairs is the restaurant proper, with its huge glass-walled show kitchen, its Allen Jones murals, its grand piano and dance floor, and its typically Conran-French menu of things such as seafood, rabbit stew, steak-frites, and fig tart. Upstairs, the bar overlooks a canteen-style operation called Mezzonine. A late-night café/patisserie/newsstand has a separate entrance next door (and much lower prices). The place became a London landmark from day one, with much bustle, despite its low celebrity count. ⊠ *100 Wardour St., W1,* ☎ *0171/314–4000. AE, DC, MC, V. Tube: Leicester Sq.*

££   ✕ **Soho Soho.** The ground floor is a lively café-bar with a (no reservations) rotisserie, while upstairs is a more formal and expensive restaurant. Inspiration comes from Provence, both in the olive-oil cooking style and the decor, with its murals, primary colors, and pale ocher terra-cotta floor tiles. The rotisserie serves omelets, salads, charcuterie, and cheeses, plus a handful of such bistro dishes as Toulouse sausages with fries; herbed, grilled sole; and tart Tatin. Or you can stay in the café-bar and have just a Kir or a beer. ⊠ *11–13 Frith St., W1,* ☎ *0171/494–3491. Reservations essential. AE, DC, MC, V. Closed Sun. No lunch Sat. (upstairs). Tube: Leicester Sq.*

Covent Garden

££££   ✕ **Savoy Grill.** The grill continues in the first rank of power dining locations. Politicians, newspaper barons, and tycoons like the comforting food and impeccably discreet and attentive service in the low-key, yew-panel salon. On the menu, an omelet Arnold Bennett (with cheese and smoked fish) is perennial, as is beef Wellington on Tuesdays and roast Norfolk duck on Fridays. Playgoers can split their theater menu, eating part of their meal before the show, the rest after. ⊠ *The Strand, WC2,* ☎ *0171/836–4343. Reservations essential. Jacket and tie. AE, DC, MC, V. Closed Sun. No lunch Sat. Tube: Aldwych.*

£££ ✕ **The Ivy.** This seems to be everybody's favorite restaurant—every-
★ body who works in the media or the arts, that is. In a Deco dining room with blinding white tablecloths, and Hodgkins and Paolozzis on the walls, the celebrated and the wanna-bes eat Caesar salad, roast grouse, shrimp gumbo, braised oxtail, and rice pudding with Armagnac prunes, or sticky toffee pudding. ⊠ *1 West St., WC2,* ☎ *0171/836–4751. Reservations essential. AE, DC, MC, V. Tube: Covent Garden.*

£££ ✕ **Orso.** The Italian brother of Joe Allen (☞ *below*), this basement restaurant has the same snappy staff and a glitzy clientele of showbiz types and hacks. The Tuscan-style menu changes every day but always includes excellent pizza and pasta dishes. Food here, much like the place itself, is never boring. ⊠ *27 Wellington St., WC2,* ☎ *0171/240–5269. AE, MC, V. Tube: Covent Garden.*

£££ ✕ **Rules.** Come, take an escape from the 20th century. Almost 200 years
★ old, this London institution has welcomed everyone from Dickens to Charlie Chaplin to Lillie Langtry, who used to come here with the Prince of Wales. The menu is historic and good—try its fabled steak and kidney and mushroom pudding for a virtual taste of the 18th century—but the decor is even more delicious. With plush red banquettes and lacquered Victorian-yellow walls, which are festively adorned with 19th-century oil paintings and hundreds of engravings, this is probably the most handsome dining salon in London (note, however, that this restaurant has three floors). It is more than a little touristy, but that's because it's so quaint. ⊠ *35 Maiden La., WC2,* ☎ *0171/836–5314. Reservations essential. AE, DC, MC, V. Tube: Covent Garden.*

££ ✕ **Bertorelli's.** Right across from the stage door of the Royal Opera House, Bertorelli's is quietly chic, the food tempting and just innovative enough: poached cotechino sausage with lentils or monkfish ragout with fennel, tomato, and olives are typical dishes. A recent complete overhaul has brought the decor into a new era. ⊠ *44A Floral St., WC2,* ☎ *0171/836–3969. AE, DC, MC, V. Tube: Covent Garden.*

££ ✕ **Joe Allen.** Long hours (thespians flock here after the curtain falls in Theatreland) and a welcoming, if loud, brick-wall interior mean New York Joe's London branch is still swinging after two decades. The fun, California-inflected menu helps. It can get chaotic, with long waits for the cute waiters, but at least there will be famous faces to ogle in the meantime. The brunch, served Sunday, noon–4, is one of London's most convivial. ⊠ *13 Exeter St., WC2,* ☎ *0171/836–0651. Reservations essential. No credit cards. Tube: Covent Garden.*

£–££ ✕ **Belgo Centraal.** The wackiest dining concept in town started with a bistro in Camden, and was so adored it was cloned uptown in a big basement space you have to enter by elevator. Have mussels and fries in vast quantity, served with 100 Belgian beers (fruit-flavored, Trappist-brewed, white, or light) by people dressed as monks in a hall like a refectory in a Martian monastery. The luxury index may be low, but so is the check. ⊠ *50 Earlham St., WC2,* ☎ *0171/813–2233. AE, DC, MC, V. Tube: Covent Garden.*

£ ✕ **Food for Thought.** This simple basement restaurant (no liquor license) seats only 50 and is extremely popular, so you'll almost always find a line of people down the stairs. The menu—stir-fries, casseroles, salads, and desserts—changes every day, and each dish is freshly made; there's no microwave. ⊠ *31 Neal St., WC2,* ☎ *0171/836–0239. Reservations not accepted. No credit cards. Closed after 8 PM, 2 wks at Christmas. Tube: Covent Garden.*

£   ✗ **Maxwell's.** London's first-ever burger joint, which turned 25 in '97, cloned itself and then grew up. Here's the result, a happy place under the Opera House serving the kind of food you're homesick for: quesadillas and nachos, Buffalo chicken wings, barbecue ribs, Cajun chicken, chef's salad, a real NYC Reuben, and a burger to die for. ⊠ *8–9 James St., WC2,* ☎ *0171/836–0303. AE, DC, V. Tube: Covent Garden.*

Bloomsbury

££   ✗ **Chez Gerard.** One of a small chain of steak-frites restaurants, this one has expanded its utterly Gallic menu to include more for non–red meat eaters. Steak, served with shoestring fries and béarnaise sauce, remains the reason to visit. ⊠ *8 Charlotte St., W1,* ☎ *0171/636–4975. AE, DC, MC, V. Tube: Goodge St.*

££   ✗ **Museum Street Café.** This useful and reliable restaurant near the British Museum serves a limited selection of impeccably fresh dishes, intelligently and plainly cooked by the two young owners, and charged prix-fixe. The evening menu might feature char-grilled, maize-fed chicken with pesto, followed by a rich chocolate cake; at lunchtime you might choose a sandwich of Stilton on walnut bread and a big bowl of soup. ⊠ *47 Museum St., WC1,* ☎ *0171/405–3211. Reservations essential. MC, V. Closed weekends. Tube: Tottenham Court Rd.*

£   ✗ **North Sea Fish Restaurant.** This is the place for the British national dish of fish-and-chips—battered and deep-fried whitefish with thick fries shaken with salt and vinegar. It's a bit tricky to find—three blocks south of St. Pancras station, down Judd Street. Only freshly caught fish is served, and you can order it grilled—though that would defeat the purpose. You can take your meals out in true grab-and-gulp fashion or eat in. ⊠ *7–8 Leigh St., WC1,* ☎ *0171/387–5892. AE, DC, MC, V. Closed Sun. Tube: Russell Sq.*

£   ✗ **Truckles of Pied Bull Yard.** Wine bars were the hits of '70s London, though hardly any survive to tell the tale. This one's fantastic for a post–British Museum glass of something, along with an old-fashioned ham salad with spiced peaches, or a smoked salmon sandwich, or a slice of Stilton and a glass of port. The nicest part is the courtyard with tables galore in summer. ⊠ *Off Bury Place, WC1,* ☎ *0171/404–5338, AE, DC, MC, V. Closed Sun. No dinner Sat. Tube: Holborn.*

Knightsbridge

££££ ✗ **The Capital.** This elegant, clublike dining room has chandeliers and greige rag-rolled walls, a grown-up atmosphere, and formal service. Chef Philip Britten keeps his star bright with perhaps a subtle baked mousse of haddock and ginger, émincés of chicken with olives, or pot-roasted pigeon with Armagnac, then a perfect caramel soufflé with butterscotch sauce. Set-price menus both at lunch (£28) and in the evening (£55—for *seven* courses) make it somewhat more affordable, although the best dishes are found à la carte. ⊠ *22–24 Basil St., SW3,* ☎ *0171/ 589–5171. Reservations essential. Jacket and tie. AE, DC, MC, V. Tube: Knightsbridge.*

£££ ✗ **Zafferano.** Princess Margaret, Eric Clapton, Joan Collins, and any
★   number of Cartier-brooch-wearing neighborhood Belgravians have flocked to this place, which, since 1995, has been London's best exponent of *cucina nuova.* The fireworks are in the kitchen, not in the brick-wall-and-saffron-hued decor, but *what* fireworks: pumpkin ravioli with a splash of Amaretto, *mondeghini ai crostini di risotto* (minced pork wrapped in Savoy cabbage leaves), and monkfish with walnuts. The desserts are also *delizioso,* especially the Sardinian pecorino pastries served with undersweetened vanilla ice cream. Be sure to book

early. ⊠ *15 Lowndes St., SW1,* ☎ *0171/235–5800. Reservations essential. AE, MC, V. Tube: Knightsbridge.*

££ ✕ **St. Quentin.** A very popular slice of Paris, this is a popular spot frequented by French expatriates and locals alike. Every inch of the Gallic menu is explored—quiche, escargots, cassoulet, lemon tart—in the bourgeois provincial comfort so many London bistro chains try for yet fail to achieve. ⊠ *243 Brompton Rd., SW3,* ☎ *0171/589–8005. AE, DC, MC, V. Tube: South Kensington.*

£–££ ✕ **The Enterprise.** One of the new luxury breed of "gastro-pubs," this is perhaps the chicest of the lot—near Harrods and Brompton Cross, it's filled with decorative types who complement the decor: paisley-stripe wallpaper, Edwardian side tables covered with baskets and farmhouse fruit, vintage books piled up in the windows, white linen and fresh flowers on the tables. The menu isn't overly pretty—char-grilled squid stuffed with almonds, entrecôte steak, salmon with artichoke hearts—but the ambience certainly is. ⊠ *35 Walton St., SW3,* ☎ *0171/584– 3148. AE, MC, V. No lunch weekends. Tube: South Kensington.*

£ ✕ **Stockpot.** You'll find speedy service in this large, jolly restaurant packed with young people and shoppers. The food is filling and wholesome, in a Lancashire-hot-pot, spaghetti-Bolognese, apple-crumble way. ⊠ *6 Basil St., SW3,* ☎ *0171/589–8627. No credit cards. Tube: Knightsbridge. Other branches:* ⊠ *40 Panton St., off Leicester Sq.,* ☎ *0171/839–5142;* ⊠ *18 Old Compton St., Soho,* ☎ *0171/287–1066; and* ⊠ *273 King's Rd., Chelsea,* ☎ *0171/823–3175.*

Kensington and Notting Hill Gate

££££ ✕ **Bibendum.** In the swinging '80s, this was one of London's hottest
★ places. It has cooled down now, but everyone still loves its reconditioned Michelin House setting with its Art Deco decorations and brilliant stained glass, Conran Shop, and Oyster Bar. Current chef Matthew Harris aspires to simple but perfect dishes—herrings with sour cream, a risotto, or leeks vinaigrette followed by steak au poivre, or you might try brains or tripe as they ought to be cooked. The £28 set-price menu at lunchtime is money well spent. ⊠ *Michelin House, 81 Fulham Rd., SW3,* ☎ *0171/581–5817. Reservations essential. MC, V. Closed Sun. Tube: South Kensington.*

££ ✕ **The Cow.** Oh, no, not *another* Conran. Yes, this place belongs to Tom, son of Sir Terrence, though it's a million miles from Quag's and Mezzo. Actually a tiny and chic "gastro-pub," it comprises a faux-Dublin backroom bar serving up oysters, crab salad, and pasta with wine; upstairs, a serious chef whips up Tuscan/British specialties—skate poached in minestrone is one temptation. Notting Hillbillies and other stylish folk adore the house special—a half-dozen Irish rock oysters with a pint of Guinness, as well as the mixed grills and steaks that often figure on the menu. ⊠ *89 Westbourne Park Rd., W2,* ☎ *0171/221–0021. Reservations essential. MC, V. No dinner Sun. Westbourne Park.*

££ ✕ **Pharmacy.** London's latest scene-arena, the Pharmacy is one of those see-and-be-seen places where the bar is larger than the restaurant. In this case, the bar seats 180 and is shaped like gigantic aspirin. Yes, this place looks just like its namesake, the wait staff is garbed like hospital orderlies, and even the menu looks fab—but then Damien Hirst, artist-provocateur extraordinaire, is involved. The menu highlights "comfort food" and ranges from fisherman's pie and scrambled eggs with black truffles to spit-roast Landes duck, sauce aigre-doux. If you can't snag a table, just have fun at the bar—the crowd will probably be among London's trendiest. ⊠ *150 Notting Hill Gate, W11,* ☎ *0171/ 221–2442. AE, MC, V. Tube: Notting Hill Gate.*

££   ✗ **Wódka.** This smart, modern Polish restaurant serves the smartest, most modern Polish food around. It is popular with elegant locals plus a sprinkling of celebs and often has the atmosphere of a dinner party. With your smoked salmon, herring, caviar, eggplant *blinis,* or venison sausages, order a carafe of the purest vodka in town (and watch the check inflate); it's encased in a block of ice and hand-flavored with rowan-berries. ⊠ *12 St. Albans Grove,* ☎ *0171/937–6513. Reservations essential. AE, DC, MC, V. No lunch weekends. Tube: High Street Kensington.*

Chelsea

££££   ✗ **La Tante Claire.** Some critics consider this to be London's finest restau-
★   rant, a claim you might begin to question when you arrive in front of this place—a lackluster building in a drab corner of Chelsea. Cripplingly expensive, La Tante Claire has a light and sophisticated decor, impeccable service, an impressive French wine list—but the food remains the point. From the *carte,* you might choose hot pâté de foie gras on shredded potatoes with a sweet wine and shallot sauce, roast spiced pigeon, or Pierre Koffmann's famous signature dish of pigs' feet stuffed with mousse of white meat with sweetbreads and wild mushrooms. As every expense-accounter knows, the set lunch menu (£28) is a genuine bargain. As expected, reservations are much in demand; book 3–4 weeks in advance for dinner, 2–3 days for lunch. ⊠ *68 Royal Hospital Rd., SW3,* ☎ *0171/352–6045. Reservations essential. Jacket and tie. AE, DC, MC, V. Closed weekends, 2 wks at Christmas, 10 days at Easter, 3 wks in Aug.–Sept. Tube: Sloane Sq.*

£££–££££   ✗ **Aubergine** A table at Aubergine (warning: there are only 14) has
★   been London's toughest reservation to score for almost as long as it's been open, because soccer star-turned-chef Gordon Ramsay has every table gasping in awe at his famous witty cappuccino of white beans with sautéed girolles and truffles, followed by—well, anything at all. This man can do no wrong, as those lucky enough to enjoy his Bresse pigeon with fois gras pizza can vouch. The decor is alluring and bathed in the hues of Impressionist Provence. Reserve months ahead; go for lunch (£24) if money is an object. ⊠ *11 Park Walk, SW10,* ☎ *0171/ 352–3449. Reservations essential. AE, DC, MC, V. Closed Sun. No lunch Sat. Tube: South Kensington.*

£££   ✗ **Chutney Mary.** London's first-and-only Anglo-Indian restaurant provides a fantasy version of the British Raj, all giant wicker armchairs and palms. Dishes like Masala roast lamb (practically a whole leg, marinated and spiced) and "Country Captain" (braised chicken with almonds, raisins, chilies, and spices) alternate with the more familiar North Indian dishes such as *roghan josh* (lamb curry). The best choices are certainly the dishes re-created from the kitchens of Indian chefs cooking for English palates back in the old Raj days. ⊠ *535 King's Rd., SW10,* ☎ *0171/351–3113. AE, DC, MC, V. Tube: Fulham Broadway.*

£££   ✗ **The Collection.** Enter the former Katharine Hamnett shop through the spotlit tunnel over the glass drawbridge to find a vast warehouse setting—adorned with industrial wooden beams and steel cables, a huge bar, and a suspended gallery, it seems more dance club than eatery. Around you is the local ab-fab crowd gawking at the neighboring tables for an Amber Valletta sighting, or hoping owner-*doré* Mogens Tholstrup will table-hop to theirs, while they pick at Med food seasoned with Japanese and Thai bits and bobs (seared tuna with sesame, soy, and shiitakes; sea bream with cilantro). Ah, fashion, fashion, fashion! ⊠ *264 Brompton Rd.,* ☎ *0171/225–1212. AE, DC, MC, V. No dinner Sun. Tube: South Kensington.*

££–£££ ╳ **Bluebird.** Here's Terence Conran's latest "gastrodome"—supermarket, brasserie, fruit stand, butcher shop, boutique, and café-restaurant, all housed in a snappy King's Road former garage. The place is pale blue and white, very light, and not in the least cozy, with food listed in formulae: steamed mussels, saffron, leeks; or roasted pheasant, creamed cabbage, shallots; then chilled fruits, apple water ice. Go for the synergy and visual excitement—Conran's chefs share a tendency to promise more than they deliver. ⊠ *350 King's Rd, SW3,* ☎ *0171/ 559–1000. Reservations essential. AE, DC, MC, V. Tube: Sloane Sq.*

££ ╳ **PJ's.** The decor here evokes the Bulldog Drummond lifestyle, with wooden floors and stained glass, a vast, slowly revolving propeller from a 1940s Curtis flying boat, and polo memorabilia. A menu of all-American staples should please all but vegetarians. ⊠ *52 Fulham Rd., SW3,* ☎ *0171/581–0025. AE, DC, MC, V. Tube: South Kensington.*

£ ╳ **Chelsea Kitchen.** Always crowded, this place is fine for hot, filling, and inexpensive food. ⊠ ⊠ *98 King's Rd., SW3,* ☎ *0171/589–1330. No credit cards. Tube: Sloane Sq.*

City and South Bank

£££ ╳ **Le Pont de la Tour.** Sir Terence Conran's place across the river, over-
★ looking the bridge—that gorgeous icon, Tower Bridge—that gives it its name, comes into its own in summer, when the outside tables are heaven. Inside, there's a vintner, baker, deli, seafood bar, brasserie, and this '30s diner-style restaurant, smart as the captain's table. Fish and seafood (lobster salad; Baltic herrings in crème fraîche; roast halibut with aioli), meat and game (venison fillet, port and blueberry sauce; roast veal, caramelized endive) feature heavily—vegetarians are out of luck. Prune and Armagnac tart or chocolate terrine could finish a glamorous—and expensive—meal. By contrast, an impeccable salade niçoise in the brasserie is about £9. ⊠ *36D Shad Thames, Butler's Wharf, SE1,* ☎ *0171/403–8403. Reservations essential. MC, V. Tube: Tower Hill.*

££–£££ ╳ **OXO Tower Brasserie and Restaurant.** How delightful it is for London finally to get a room with a view, and *such* a view. On the eighth floor of the Thames-side, beautifully revived, Art Deco Oxo Tower building (near the South Bank Centre) is this elegant space, run by the same people who put the Fifth Floor at Harvey Nichols on the map, and featuring Euro food with this year's trendy ingredients (acorn-fed black pig charcuterie with tomato and pear chutney; calves kidneys with persillade sauce and beetroot jus; Dover sole with sea urchin butter). The ceiling slats turn and change from white to midnight blue, but who on earth notices, with St. Paul's across the water? Summertime, the terrace tables are the best places in London. ⊠ *Bankside, SE1,* ☎ *0171/ 803–3888. AE, MC, V. Tube: Waterloo.*

££ ╳ **People's Palace.** Thank goodness—thanks to this place, you can finally have a civilized meal during your South Bank arts encounter. With menus by trendy chef Gary Rhodes, this has remarkably low prices considering it has the greatest river view in town (apart from OXO). As the baying critics noted around opening time, there are occasional mistakes here, but the more British the dish, the more reliable it proves—suckling pig sandwich on granary bread, marmalade sponge cake, and sticky toffee pudding are good choices. ⊠ *Royal Festival Hall, Level 3, South Bank, SE1,* ☎ *0171/928–9999. AE, DC, MC, V. Tube: Waterloo.*

££ ╳ **St. John.** This former smokehouse (ham, not cigars), converted by erstwhile architect owner-chef, Fergus Henderson has soaring white walls, schoolroom lamps, stone floors, iron railings, and plain wooden chairs. Entrées (roast lamb and parsnip; smoked haddock and fennel; deviled crab) are hearty and unadorned, but usually taste great. Service is efficiently matey. ✉ *26 St. John St., EC1,* ☎ *0171/251–0848. Reservations essential. AE, MC, V. No dinner Sun. Tube: Farringdon.*

Pubs

London's pubs include some of the most gorgeous and historic interiors in London. An integral part of the British way of life, public houses dispense beer "on tap," and usually a basic, inexpensive menu of sandwiches, quiche, and salads, and other snacks at lunchtime. But you don't go to a "local" for just pub grub. Rather, pubs are the best place to get to meet the locals in their habitat. Sit at a table if you want privacy; better, help prop up the bar, where no introductions are needed, and watch that legendary British reserve fade away.

As we write, "gastro-pub" fever has hit London. At many places, chargrills are being installed in the kitchen out back, while up front the faded wallpapers and the dear ole Mums are being replaced by abstract paintings and food mavens galore (the best of these new luxe pubs are reviewed above). Some of the following also feature nouveau pub grub, but whether you have Moroccan chicken or the usually dismal ploughman's special, you'll want to order a pint. Note that American-style beer is called "lager" in Britain, while the real Brit brew is "bitters." You can order up your choice in two sizes—pints or half pints (if this is your first taste of British beer, order a half). Some London pubs also sell "real ale," which is less gassy than bitters and, many would argue, has a better flavor. Remember that many pubs stop serving alcoholic beverages at 11 PM.

✗ **Black Friar.** A step from Blackfriars tube, this stunning pub has an Arts-and-Crafts interior that is entertainingly, satirically ecclesiastical, with inlaid mother-of-pearl, wood carvings, stained glass, and marble pillars all over the place, and reliefs of monks and friars poised above finely lettered temperance tracts, regardless of which there are six beers on tap. ✉ *174 Queen Victoria St., EC4,* ☎ *0171/236–5650.*

✗ **Dove Inn.** Read the list of famous ex-regulars, from Charles II and Nell Gwynn (mere rumor, but a likely one) to Ernest Hemingway, as you queue ages for a beer at this very popular, very comely 16th-century riverside pub by Hammersmith Bridge. If it's *too* full, stroll upstream to the Old Ship or the Blue Anchor. ✉ *19 Upper Mall, W6,* ☎ *0181/748–5405.*

✗ **George Inn.** Sitting in a courtyard where Shakespeare's plays were once performed, the present building dates from the late 17th century and is central London's last remaining galleried inn. Dickens was a regular—the Southwark district inn is featured in *Little Dorrit.* ✉ *77 Borough High St., SE1,* ☎ *0171/407–2056.*

✗ **Lamb and Flag.** This 17th-century pub was once known as "The Bucket of Blood," because the upstairs room was used as a ring for bare-knuckle boxing. Now, it's a trendy, friendly, and entirely bloodless pub, serving food (at lunchtime only) and real ale. It's on the edge of Covent Garden, off Garrick Street. ✉ *33 Rose St., WC2,* ☎ *0171/836–4108.*

✗ **Mayflower.** An atmospheric 17th-century riverside inn in the Rotherhithe district, with exposed beams and a terrace, this is practically the very place from which the Pilgrims set sail for Plymouth Rock. The inn is licensed to sell American postage stamps. ✉ *117 Rotherhithe St., SE16,* ☎ *0171/237–4088.*

✗ **Museum Tavern.** Across the street from the British Museum, this gloriously Victorian pub makes an ideal resting place after the rigors of the culture trail. With lots of fancy glass—etched mirrors and stained-glass panels—gilded pillars, and carvings, the heavily restored hostelry once helped Karl Marx to unwind after a hard day in the library. He could have spent his capital on any one of six beers available on tap. ✉ *49 Great Russell St., WC1,* ☎ *0171/242–8987.*

✗ **Sherlock Holmes.** This Westminster district pub used to be known as the Northumberland Arms, and Arthur Conan Doyle popped in regularly for a pint. It figures in *The Hound of the Baskervilles,* and you can see the hound's head and plaster casts of its huge paws among other Holmes memorabilia in the bar. ✉ *10 Northumberland St., WC2,* ☎ *0171/930–2644.*

✗ **Ye Olde Cheshire Cheese.** Yes, it is a tourist trap, but this most historic of all London pubs (it dates from 1667) deserves a visit anyway, for its sawdust-covered floors, low wood-beam ceilings, the 14th-century crypt of a Whitefriars' monastery under the cellar bar, and the set of 17th-century pornographic tiles upstairs. This was the most regular of Dr. Johnson's and Dickens's *many* locals. It's in the City. ✉ *145 Fleet St., EC4,* ☎ *0171/353–6170.*

Afternoon Tea

In the grandest places, teatime is still a ritual, so be prepared for a dress code: Claridge's, the Ritz, and the Savoy all require jacket and tie.

✗ **Brown's Hotel.** Famous for its teas, this hotel lounge does rest on its laurels somewhat, with a packaged aura and nobody around but fellow tourists. For £16.95 you get sandwiches, a scone with cream and jam (jelly), tart, fruitcake, and shortbread. ✉ *33 Albermarle St., W1,* ☎ *0171/493–6020. Tea served daily 3–6.*

✗ **Claridge's.** This is the real McCoy, complete with liveried footmen proffering sandwiches, a scone, and superior pastries (£16.50) in the palatial yet genteel foyer, all to the tune of the resident "Hungarian orchestra" (actually a string quartet). ✉ *Brook St., W1,* ☎ *0171/ 629–8860. Tea served daily 3–5.*

✗ **Fortnum & Mason's.** Upstairs at the Queen's grocer's, three set teas are ceremoniously offered: standard Afternoon Tea (sandwiches, scone, cakes, £10.50), old-fashioned High Tea (the traditional nursery meal, adding something more robust and savory, £12.25), and Champagne Tea (£15.75). ✉ *St. James's Restaurant, 4th floor, 181 Piccadilly, W1,* ☎ *0171/734–8040. Tea served Mon.–Sat. 3–5:20.*

✗ **Harrods.** The Georgian Room at the ridiculously well-known department store has an afternoon tea that'll give you a sugar rush for a week. ✉ *Brompton Rd., SW3,* ☎ *0171/730–1234. Tea served Mon.–Sat. 3–5:30.*

✗ **The Ritz.** The Ritz's stagey Palm Court offers tiered cake stands, silver pots, a harpist, and Louis XVI chaises, plus a great deal of Rococo gilt and glitz, all for £21. It's a good excuse for a glass of champagne. Reservations are booked months in advance for weekends. ✉ *Piccadilly, W1,* ☎ *0171/493–8181. Tea served daily 2–6.*

✗ **Savoy.** The glamorous Thames-side hotel does one of the most pleasant teas, its triple-tier cake stands packed with goodies, its tail-coated waiters thrillingly polite. ✉ *The Strand, WC2,* ☎ *0171/836–4343. Tea served daily 3–5:30.*

LODGING

Staying at one of London's grand-dame hotels is the next best thing—some say better—to being a guest at the palace. Royally resplendent decors abound and armies of extra-solicitous staff are stuck in the pampering mode—the Windsors should have it so good. But even in more affordable choices, classic British style brings you a taste of home, with teamakers and Queen Mum pastel wallpapers. Still not cozy enough?

Borrow some door keys, and be a B&B guest. Happily, there is no dearth of options where friendliness outdistances luxe, and we've included the best of the budget places.

We quote the average room cost as of spring 1998; in some establishments, especially those in the ££££ category, you could pay considerably more—well past the £200 mark in some cases. In any event, you should confirm *exactly* what your room costs before checking in. British hotels are obliged by law to display a price chart at the reception desk; study it carefully. In January and February you'll often find reduced rates, and large hotels with a business clientele have frequent weekend packages. The custom these days in all but the cheaper hotels is for quoted prices to cover room alone; breakfast, whether Continental or "Full English," costs extra. VAT (Value Added Tax—sales tax) is usually included, and service, too, in nearly all cases. Be sure to reserve, as special events can fill hotel rooms suddenly.

If you do manage to arrive in the capital without a room, the **London Tourist Board Information Centres** at Heathrow and Victoria Station Forecourt can help (☎ 0839/123435; calls cost 49p per minute), and the **Visitor Call** service (☎ 0891/505487) provides general advice calls cost 49p per minute); or call the **LTB Bookings Hotline** (☎ 0171/932–2020), open weekdays 9:30–5:30, for prepaid credit-card bookings (MC, V).

CATEGORY	COST*
££££	over £190
£££	£130–£190
££	£80–£130
£	under £80

All prices are for a double room; VAT included.

Mayfair, St. James's, and Victoria

££££ 🏨 **Brown's.** Founded in 1837 by Lord Byron's "gentleman's gentleman," James Brown, this Victorian country house in central Mayfair occupies 11 Georgian houses and is frequented by many Anglophilic Americans—a habit that was established by the two Roosevelts (Teddy while on honeymoon). Bedrooms feature thick carpets, soft armchairs, sweeping drapes, brass chandeliers, and moiré or brocade wallpapers, as well as air-conditioning; the public rooms retain their cozy oak-panel, chintz-laden, grandfather-clock-ticking-in-the-parlor ambience. ⊠ *34 Albemarle St., W1A 4SW,* ☎ *0171/493–6020,* ℻ *0171/493–9381. 132 rooms. Restaurant, bar. AE, DC, MC, V. Tube: Green Park.*

££££ 🏨 **Claridge's.** A hotel legend, Claridge's has one of the world's classi-
★ est guest lists. The liveried staff are friendly and not in the least condescending, and the rooms are never less than luxurious—even more so now that the hotel is in the midst of a major, multimillion-dollar sprucing-up. It was founded in 1812, but the present decor is either 1930s Art Deco or country-house traditional. Have a drink in the foyer lounge with its Hungarian mini-orchestra, or retreat to the reading room for perfect quiet, interrupted only by the sound of pages turning. The bedrooms are spacious, as are the bathrooms. Beds are handmade and supremely comfortable—the King of Morocco once brought his own, couldn't sleep, and ended up ordering 30 from Claridge's to take home. ⊠ *Brook St., W1A 2JQ,* ☎ *0171/629–8860 or 800/223–6800,* ℻ *0171/499–2210. 200 rooms. 2 restaurants, beauty salon, exercise room. AE, DC, MC, V. Tube: Bond St.*

££££ 🏨 **Connaught.** Make reservations well in advance for this *very* exclu-
★ sive, very British hotel just off Grosvenor Square—the most understated of any of London's grand hostelries. The bar and lounges have the air

of an ambassadorial residence, an impression reinforced by the imposing oak staircase and dignified staff. Each bedroom has a foyer, antique furniture (if you don't like the desk, they'll change it), and fresh flowers, and the management is above such vulgarities as brochure and tariff—which would be extraneous for guests who inherited the Connaught habit from their great-grandfathers, anyway. If you value privacy, discretion, and the kind of luxury that eschews labels, then you have met your match here. ⊠ *Carlos Pl., W1Y 6AL,* ☎ *0171/499–7070,* ℻ *0171/ 495–3262. 90 rooms. Restaurant, bar. MC. Tube: Bond St.*

££££ 🏨 **The Dorchester.** A London institution, the Dorchester appears on
★ every "World's Best" list. The glamour level is off the scale: 1,200 square ft of gold leaf, 800 of marble, and 2,000 of hand-tufted carpet gild this lily, and bedrooms feature Irish linen sheets on canopied beds; brocades and velvets; Italian marble and etched-glass bathrooms with Floris toiletry goodies; individual climate control; dual-voltage outlets; and cable TV. Afternoon tea, drinking, lounging, and posing are all accomplished in the catwalk-shape Promenade lounge, where you may spot one of the film-star types who will stay nowhere else. Probably no other hotel this opulent manages to be this charming. ⊠ *Park La., W1A 2HJ,* ☎ *0171/629–8888,* ℻ *0171/409–0114. 197 rooms, 55 suites. 3 restaurants, bar, lounge, health club, nightclub, business services, meeting rooms. AE, DC, MC, V. Tube: Marble Arch.*

££££ 🏨 **Grosvenor House.** "The old lady of Park Lane" is back in top-dowager position, having thrown off her creeping frumpiness during a complete overhaul. It's not the kind of place that encourages hushed whispers or that frowns on outré Alexander McQueen outfits, despite the marble floors and wood-panel "library," open fires, oils, and fine antiques. The hotel health club is one of the best around, thanks to its good-size pool. Bedrooms are spacious, and most of the marble bathrooms have natural light. ⊠ *Park La., W1A 3AA,* ☎ *0171/499– 6363,* ℻ *0171/493–3341. 360 rooms, 70 suites. 3 restaurants, bar, lounge, indoor pool, health club. AE, DC, MC, V. Tube: Marble Arch.*

£££ 🏨 **Dukes.** This small, exclusive, Edwardian-style hotel is possibly Lon-
★ don's quietest hotel, secreted in its own discreet cul-de-sac. It's filled with squashy sofas, oils of assorted dukes, and muted, rich colors, and offers guest rooms recently decorated in patrician, antiques-spattered style, plus the best in personal service (they greet you by name every time). ⊠ *35 St. James's Pl., SW1A 1NY,* ☎ *0171/491–4840,* ℻ *0171/ 493–1264. 62 rooms. Restaurant, dining room. AE, DC, MC, V. Tube: Green Park.*

£££ 🏨 **Stakis St. Ermins.** Smack-dab in the middle of mostly modern Westminster, this hotel is just a short stroll away from Westminster Abbey. An Edwardian anomaly in the shadow of modern skyscrapers, the hotel is housed in an utterly delightful Edwardian pile, set off around a tiny cul-de-sac courtyard fronted with beasts-rampant gates. The lobby is an extravaganza of Victorian baroque. The less costly of the two restaurants, the Cloisters, has a Jacobean-style salon. Guest rooms are tastefully decorated; some have snug dimensions (but are all the cozier for it). ⊠ *Caxton St., SW1H 0QW,* ☎ *0171/222–7888,* ℻ *0171/ 222–6914. 290 rooms, 7 suites. 2 restaurants, bar, minibars, room service, laundry service. AE, DC, MC, V. Tube: St. James's Park.*

£ 🏨 **Edward Lear.** Once the house of Edward Lear (of "The Owl and the Pussycat" fame), this homey hotel has seen better days according to several of our readers. Still, triple and family rooms are huge; number 14 is a closet—with peace and quiet at the back. In the brick-wall breakfast room you're served sausages and bacon from the Queen's butcher. ⊠ *28–30 Seymour St., W1H 5WD,* ☎ *0171/402–5401,* ℻ *0171/706–3766. 31 rooms, 15 with shower, 4 with full bath. Breakfast room. MC, V. Tube: Marble Arch.*

80

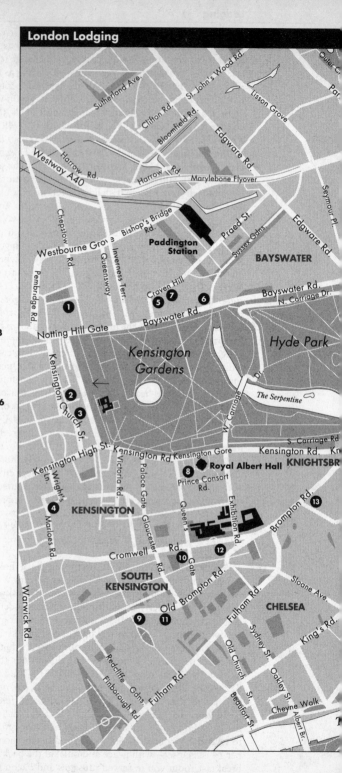

London Lodging

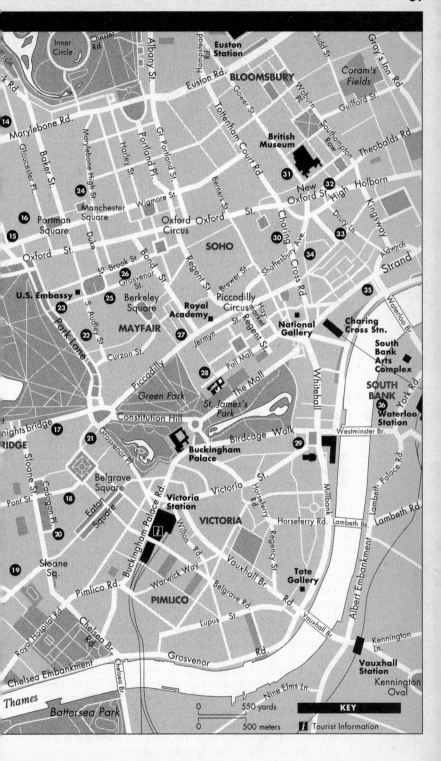

Inner Circle

Chester Rd.

k Rd.

14

Marylebone Rd.

Gloucester Pl.

Baker St.

Marylebone High St.

Harley St.

Portland Pl.

Gt. Portland St.

Albany St.

Hampstead Rd.

Euston Rd.

Euston Station

BLOOMSBURY

Gower St.

Tottenham Court Rd.

Woburn Pl.

Judd St.

Coram's Fields

Gray's Inn Rd.

Guilford St.

Southampton Row

Theobalds Rd.

24

Manchester Square

Wigmore St.

16

Portman Square

15

Oxford St.

Duke St.

Brook St.

Bond St.

Grosvenor St.

St.

26

25

Berkeley Square

U.S. Embassy ■

23

S. Audley St.

MAYFAIR

22

Curzon St.

Park Lane

Oxford Circus

Oxford

Oxford

Berners St.

St.

Regent St.

Brewer St.

SOHO

30

Shaftesbury Ave.

Charing Cross Rd.

Piccadilly Circus

Royal Academy ■

27

Jermyn

Hay-market

St. Regent St.

Pall Mall

British Museum

31

New Oxford St.

32

High Holborn

Drury Ln.

Kingsway

33

Aldwych

Strand

34

35

Waterloo Br.

Charing Cross Stn. ■

South Bank Arts Complex ■

SOUTH BANK

36

Waterloo Station

York Rd.

National Gallery ■

28

Piccadilly

Green Park

St. James's Park

The Mall

Whitehall

Constitution Hill

17

nightsbridge

RIDGE

Sloane St.

Pont St.

Cadogan Pl.

21

Grosvenor Pl.

Belgrave Square

18

Eaton Square

20

19

Sloane Sq.

Buckingham Palace

Birdcage Walk

29

Westminster Br.

Victoria St.

Victoria Station

i

Wilton Rd.

VICTORIA

Horseferry Rd.

Horseferry Rd.

Millbank

Lambeth Br.

Lambeth Palace Rd.

Lambeth Rd.

Buckingham Palace Rd.

Vauxhall Br.

Belgrave Rd.

Regency St.

Pimlico Rd.

PIMLICO

Warwick Way

Lupus St.

Tate Gallery ■

Albert Embankment

Royal Hospital Rd.

Chelsea Br. Rd.

Grosvenor

Rd.

Vauxhall Br.

Chelsea Br.

Kennington Ln.

Vauxhall Station

Kennington Oval

Chelsea Embankment

Thames

Battersea Park

Nine Elms Ln.

0   550 yards

0   500 meters

KEY

i Tourist Information

£ **Glynne Court Hotel.** Despite its location, this is a quiet, small hotel, and so handy for late-night runs to Virgin Records, being just off hectic Marble Arch. It's no luxury joint, but it is a clean and pleasant place, with spacious rooms containing hair dryers, phones, TVs, sinks, and tea/coffeemakers, and the management is friendly. In all, it's a good buy—doubles run about £55— for the area. ⊠ *41 Great Cumberland Pl., W1H 7LG,* ☎ *0171/262–4344,* FAX *0171/724–2071, 14 rooms. AE, DC, MC, V. Tube: Marble Arch.*

Marylebone

£££ ⊞ **Dorset Square Hotel.** This pair of Regency town houses in Sherlock Holmes territory belongs to the welcome new breed of small, luxurious, privately run hotels. The creation of architect–interior designer husband-and-wife team, Tim and Kit Kemp, this is *House Beautiful* come to life, from marble and mahogany bathrooms to antique lace counterpanes, and the staff bends over backward to accommodate your wishes. For on-the-town jaunts, there's even a vintage Bentley available. ⊠ *39–40 Dorset Sq., NW1 6QN,* ☎ *0171/723–7874,* FAX *0171/ 724–3328. 37 rooms. Restaurant, bar. AE, MC, V. Tube: Baker St.*

££ ⊞ **Durrants.** A hotel since the late 18th century, Durrants occupies a quiet corner almost next to the Wallace Collection. It's of good value for the area, and if you like ye wood-panel, leather-armchair, dark-red-pattern-carpet style of olde Englishness, this will suit you. Bedrooms are wan and motel-like but adequate—the few with no bathrooms are £10 a night cheaper. ⊠ *George St., W1H 6BH,* ☎ *0171/935–8131,* FAX *0171/487–3510. 96 rooms, 85 with bath. Restaurant, bar, dining room, lobby lounge. AE, MC, V. Tube: Bond St.*

Bloomsbury, Soho, and Covent Garden

££££ ⊞ **Covent Garden Hotel.** Relentlessly chic, extra-stylish, this is Tim and
★ Kit Kemp's latest extravaganza—a former 1880s-vintage hospital in the midst of the artsy Covent Garden district, now the London home-away-from-home for a melange of off-duty celebrities, actors, and style-mavens. Theatrically baronial, fashionably Victorian, the public rooms will keep even the most picky atmosphere-hunter happy. Guest rooms are *World-of-Interiors* chic, each showcasing matching-but-mixed couturier fabrics to stunning effect. Antique-style desks are vast, beds are gargantuan, and modern bathrooms feature everything from Philippe Starck bidets to they-*have*-thought-of-everything heated mirrors (steam doesn't stick). The Brasserie is excellent. For taste, in every sense of the word, the Covent Garden is the top. ⊠ *10 Monmouth St., WC2H 9HB,* ☎ *0171/806–1000,* FAX *0171/806–1100. 46 rooms, 4 suites. Restaurant, minibars, room service, exercise room, laundry service. AE, MC, V. Tube: Covent Garden.*

££££ ⊞ **The Savoy.** This historic, grand, late-Victorian hotel is beloved by
★ wielders of international influence, now as ever. Its celebrated Grill has the premier power-lunch tables; it hosted Elizabeth Taylor's first honeymoon in one of its famous river-view rooms; and it poured the world's first martini in its equally famous American Bar—haunted by Hemingway, Fitzgerald, Gershwin, et al. The spacious, elegant, bright, and comfortable rooms are furnished with antiques and serviced by valets. A room facing the Thames costs extra, but only the new County Hall Marriott tops that view. Bathrooms have original fittings, with sunflower-size showerheads. Though the Savoy is as grand as they come, the air is tinged with a certain theatrical naughtiness (due in part to the on-premises theater) which goes down well with Hollywood types. ⊠ *The Strand, WC2R 0EU,* ☎ *0171/836–4343,* FAX *0171/240–6040.*

202 rooms. 3 restaurants, 2 bars, indoor pool, beauty salon, health club. AE, DC, MC, V. Tube: Aldwych.

£££ ★ 🏨 **Hazlitt's.** The solo Soho hotel is in three connected early 18th-century houses, one of which was the essayist William Hazlitt's (1778–1830) last home. It's a friendly place, full of personality, but devoid of such hotel features as elevators, room service, and porterage. Robust antiques are everywhere, assorted prints crowd every wall, a Victorian claw-foot tub sits in all bathrooms. Book way ahead—this is the London address of media people, literary types, and antiques dealers everywhere. ⊠ *6 Frith St., W1V 5TZ,* ☎ *0171/434–1771,* 𝖥𝖠𝖷 *0171/439–1524. 23 rooms. AE, DC, MC, V. Tube: Tottenham Court Rd.*

££–£££ 🏨 **The Kingsley.** On the main street, steps from the British Museum, this is one Edwardian-style hotel that really does feel sweetly old-fashioned, avoiding shabbiness or stuffiness—especially since last year's $6-million refurbishment of this former temperance house. English country-house decor has the strong color schemes currently favored in hotel land, with tea/coffeemakers, and free in-house movies among the facilities. ⊠ *Bloomsbury Way, WC1A 2SD,* ☎ *0171/242–5881,* 𝖥𝖠𝖷 *0171/831–0225. 137 rooms. Restaurant, bar, meeting rooms. AE, DC, MC, V. Tube: Holborn.*

££ 🏨 **Fielding.** Tucked away in a quiet alley, this cozy hotel is adored for the homey atmosphere, the continuity of a loyal, friendly staff, and for the convenience of having the Royal Opera House, the theater district, and half of London's restaurants within spitting distance. The bedrooms are all different, shabby-homey rather than chic, and none too spacious, though you can have a suite here for the price of a chain-hotel double. There's no elevator; only one room comes with bathtub (most have showers); and only breakfast is served in the restaurant. ⊠ *4 Broad Ct., Bow St., WC2B 5QZ,* ☎ *0171/836–8305,* 𝖥𝖠𝖷 *0171/497–0064. 26 rooms, 1 with bath, 23 with shower. Bar, breakfast room. AE, DC, MC, V. Tube: Covent Garden.*

£ 🏨 **Morgan.** In this family-run Georgian row-house hotel, rooms are small and functionally furnished, yet friendly and cheerful overall, with phones and TVs. The five newish apartments are particularly pleasing: three times the size of normal rooms (and an extra £15/night, placing them in the ££ category), complete with eat-in kitchens and private phone lines. ⊠ *24 Bloomsbury St., WC1B 3QJ,* ☎ *0171/636–3735. 15 rooms with bath or shower, 5 apartments. Breakfast room. No credit cards. Tube: Russell Sq.*

Kensington

££££ 🏨 **Blakes.** This has to be the most exotic hotel in town, the work of Lady Weinberg, a.k.a. Anouska Hempel, '70s style goddess. A sober, dark-green Victorian exterior belies the arty mix of Biedermeier, bamboo, four-poster beds, and Oriental screens inside, with rooms bedecked in anything from black moiré silk to dove gray or top-to-toe blush pink. Guests tend to be music or movie mavens. Look for her newest hotel, the Hempel, too. ⊠ *33 Roland Gardens, SW7 3PF,* ☎ *0171/370–6701,* 𝖥𝖠𝖷 *0171/373–0442. 52 rooms with bath. Restaurant. AE, DC, MC, V. Tube: Gloucester Rd.*

£££ ★ 🏨 **The Gore.** Just down the road from the Albert Hall, this small, very friendly hotel, run by the same people who run Hazlitt's (☞ *Soho, above*), features a similarly eclectic selection of prints, etchings, and antiques—the lobby is something out of a fin-de-siècle Visconti film. Here, though, are spectacular follylike rooms—Room 101 is a Tudor fantasy with a minstrel gallery, stained glass, and four-poster bed. The hotel gets a fun, chic, but partying crowd—so pleased don't be shocked if you find some cigarette butts in the hallways. ⊠ *189 Queen's Gate, SW7 5EX,*

☎ 0171/584–6601, ℻ 0171/589–8127. *54 rooms with bath. Brasserie. AE, DC, MC, V. Tube: Gloucester Rd.*

££ ⊞ **Forte Posthouse Kensington.** This large, utilitarian hotel feels like a smaller one and offers extras you wouldn't expect for the reasonable rate and convenient location in a quiet lane off Kensington High Street. The main attraction is the health club, with an 18-meter pool, two squash courts, a steam room, and a beauty salon. Standard rooms are on the small side, with plain chain-hotel built-in furnishings. ⊠ *Wrights La., W8 5SP,* ☎ 0171/937–8170, ℻ 0171/937–8289. *530 rooms. 2 restaurants, 2 bars, indoor pool, health club, baby-sitting. AE, DC, MC, V. Tube: High Street Kensington.*

££ ⊞ **Hotel 167.** This friendly little bed-and-breakfast is a two-minute walk from the V&A, in a grand white-stucco Victorian corner house. The lobby is immediately cheering, with its round marble tables, wrought-iron chairs, palms, and modern paintings; it also does duty as lounge and breakfast room. Bedrooms have a hybrid Victoriana/Ikea style with double-glazed windows (which you need on this noisy road). ⊠ *167 Old Brompton Rd., SW5 0AN,* ☎ 0171/373–0672, ℻ 0171/373–3360. *19 rooms with bath or shower. Breakfast room. AE, DC, MC, V. Tube: Gloucester Rd.*

£   ⊞ **Abbey House.** Next door to the Vicarage (*see* below), Abbey House has been voted "Best Value, Best Quality B&B in London" in several surveys, so you'll have to book well in advance for the doubles that go for £60 here. The place occupies a pretty, white-stucco 1860 Victorian town house—once home to a bishop and an MP before World War II—and overlooks a garden square. Rooms are spacious and have color TVs and washbasins, but every room shares a bath with another. An English breakfast is included in the rates, and a cuppa is complimentary. ⊠ *11 Vicarage Gate, W8,* ☎ 0171/727–2594. *16 rooms, none with bath. No credit cards. Tube: High Street Kensington.*

£   ⊞ **Eden Plaza.** When a hotel calls its own rooms "compact," you should imagine a double bed, then add a foot all round, and, yes, that is about the measure of a room here. However, like a cruise-ship stateroom, all you need (closet, mirror, satellite TV, tea/coffeemaker, hair dryer) is creatively secreted. Rooms are double-glazed against noisy Cromwell Road, though color schemes are *loud*. Kids share free or get their own room at half price. ⊠ *68–69 Queensgate, SW7 5JT,* ☎ 0171/370–6111, ℻ 0171/370–0932. *62 rooms. Bar. AE, MC, V. Tube: Gloucester Rd.*

£   ⊞ **Vicarage.** Spend the cash you save here in the surrounding Kensington antiques shops. This has long been a favorite for the budget-minded—family-owned, set on a leaf-shaded street just off Kensington Church Street, the Vicarage is set in a large white Victorian house. The decor is sweetly anachronistic, full of heavy, dark-stained wood furniture, patterned carpets, and brass pendant lights, and there's a little conservatory. Many of the bedrooms now have TVs. All in all, this still remains a charmer—but readers tell us it's beginning to fray around the edges. ⊠ *10 Vicarage Gate, W8 4AG,* ☎ 0171/229–4030. *19 rooms without bath. No credit cards. Tube: High Street Kensington.*

Knightsbridge, Chelsea, and Belgravia

££££ ⊞ **Berkeley.** A remarkable mixture of the old and new, the Berkeley stars a splendid penthouse swimming pool that opens to the sky when the weather's good. The bedrooms are decorated by various designers, but tend to be serious and opulent, have swags of William Morris prints or are plain and masculine with little balconies overlooking the street. All have sitting areas and big, tiled bathrooms with bidets. Its restaurant is Vong, the fabulous Thai/French hybrid cloned from

New York. ⊠ *Wilton Pl., SW1X 7RL,* ☎ *0171/235–6000,* FAX *0171/235–4330. 160 rooms. 2 restaurants, indoor-outdoor pool, beauty salon, health club, cinema. AE, DC, MC, V. Tube: Knightsbridge.*

££££ ⌂ **The Halkin.** This luxurious little place is so contemporary you worry it will be outdated in a couple of years and they'll have to redo the whole thing. Milanese designers were responsible for the clean-cut white marble lobby, and the gray-on-gray bedrooms that light up when you insert your electronic key and contain every high-tech toy you never knew you needed. It might be like living in the Design Museum, except that this place employs some of the friendliest people around—who look pretty good in their white Armani uniforms. ⊠ *Halkin St., SW1X 7DJ,* ☎ *0171/333–1000,* FAX *0171/333–1100. 41 rooms. Restaurant. AE, DC, MC, V. Tube: Hyde Park Corner.*

£££ ⌂ **Beaufort.** You can practically hear the jingle of Harrods's cash reg-
★ isters from a room at the Beaufort. Actually, "hotel" is a misnomer for this elegant pair of Victorian houses. There's a sitting room instead of reception; guests have a front door key, the run of the drinks cabinet, and even their own phone number. The high-ceiling, generously proportioned rooms are decorated in muted, sophisticated shades to suit the muted, sophisticated atmosphere—but don't worry, you're encouraged by the incredibly sweet staff to feel at home. ⊠ *33 Beaufort Gardens, SW3 1PP,* ☎ *0171/584–5252,* FAX *0171/589–2834. 29 rooms. AE, DC, MC, V. Tube: Knightsbridge.*

£££ ⌂ **The Pelham.** The second of Tim and Kit Kemp's gorgeous hotels
★ opened in 1989 and is run along exactly the same lines as the Dorset Square (☞ *above*), except that this one looks less town than country. There's 18th-century pine paneling in the drawing room—one of the magnificently handsome hotel salons in the city—flowers galore, quite a bit of glazed chintz, and the odd four-poster and bedroom fireplace. The Pelham stands opposite the South Kensington tube stop, by the big museums, and close to the shops of Knightsbridge, with Kemps supplying an on-site trendy menu. ⊠ *15 Cromwell Pl., SW7 2LA,* ☎ *0171/589–8288,* FAX *0171/584–8444. 37 rooms. Restaurant, pool. AE, MC, V. Tube: South Kensington.*

££–£££ ⌂ **The Diplomat.** From its aristocratically elegant exterior, this hotel looks like a Cecil Beaton stage set: a Wedgwood-white "palazzo" terrace house built by the 19th-century architect Thomas Cubitt, flatiron-shape, and often decked out with hanging flowerpots of geraniums, it is the very picture of Belgravia chic. Inside, the tiny reception area gives way to a vintage elevator and a circular staircase lit by a Regency-era chandelier and topped by a winter-garden dome. Rooms are pleasantly decorated. The heart of Belgravia's 19th-century mansions and mews, the hotel is a small hoof away from the tube stop. ⊠ *2 Chesham St., SW1X 3DT,* ☎ *0171/235–1544,* FAX *0171/259–6153. 27 rooms. Business services. AE, DC, MC, V. Tube: Sloane Sq., Knightsbridge.*

££–£££ ⌂ **The Sloane.** The tiny Sloane is the only hotel we know of in which you can lie in your canopy bed, pick up the phone, and buy the bed—and the phone, too, and the tasty antiques all around you. Nothing so tacky as a price tag besmirches the gorgeous decor; instead, the sweet, young Euro staff harbors a book of price lists at the desk. There's an aerie of a secret roof terrace, with upholstered garden furniture and a panorama over Chelsea, where meals are served to guests. ⊠ *29 Draycott Pl., SW3 2SH,* ☎ *0171/581–5757,* FAX *0171/584–1348. 12 rooms. Restaurant. AE, DC, MC, V. Tube: Sloane Sq.*

£ ⌂ **London County Hall Travel Inn Capital.** This lacks the river view, but you get an incredible value, with the standard facilities of the cookie-cutter rooms of this chain (the phone number's the central reservation line), viz: TV, tea/coffeemaker, en suite bath/shower and—best of all for families on a budget—foldout beds that let you accommodate two kids at no extra charge. You're looking at £50/night for a family of four, in the shadow of Big Ben. *That's* a bargain. ⊠ *Belvedere Rd., SE1 7PB,* ☏ *01582/414341,* ⅎ⅍ *01582/400024. 312 rooms. Restaurant. AE, MC, V Tube: Westminster.*

£   🏨 **Wilbraham.** A lovely grandmother of a hotel, this place is as British as tea and crumpets. It's set not far from swanky Sloane Square, comprises three 19th-century row houses, and is decorated in best shabby-genteel Brit fashion, right down to floral wallpapers and Victorian bric-a-brac. Guest rooms don't have many frills, but there's a pleasant lounge and a restaurant—handy for meeting friends over a glass of sherry. ⊠ *1–5 Wilbraham Pl., SW1,* ☏ *0171/730–8296,* ⅎ⅍ *0171/730–6815. 53 rooms. Restaurant, lounge. No credit cards. Tube: Sloane Sq.*

Bayswater and Notting Hill Gate

£££   🏨 **Abbey Court.** You enter this 1850 building through a stately, double-front portico to find yourself in a luxury bed-and-breakfast filled with Empire furniture, oil portraits, and the odd four-poster bed. Kensington Gardens is close by, or you could save the walk and relax in the pretty conservatory. ⊠ *20 Pembridge Gardens, W2 4DU,* ☏ *0171/221–7518,* ⅎ⅍ *0171/792–0858. 22 rooms. AE, DC, MC, V. Tube: Notting Hill Gate.*

££   🏨 **London Elizabeth.** With one of the prettiest hotel facades in London, this family-owned gem is only steps from Hyde Park and the Lancaster Gate tube (and from rows of depressing, cheap hotels). The facade is one of the most charming in London, and the charm continues inside—foyer and lounge crammed with chintz drapery, lace antimacassars, and little chandeliers. With their palest blue-striped walls, wooden picture rails, and Welsh wool bedspreads, or pink cabbage-rose prints and mahogany furniture, the rooms do vary in size, and some lack a full-length mirror, but they all have TV, direct-dial phone, and hair dryer, and they're serviced by an exceptionally charming Anglo-Irish staff. ⊠ *Lancaster Terr., W2 3PF,* ☏ *0171/402–6641,* ⅎ⅍ *0171/224–8900. 55 rooms. Restaurant, bar. AE, DC, MC, V. Tube: Lancaster Gate.*

£   🏨 **Columbia.** The public rooms in these five joined-up Victorians are as big as museum halls. Late at night they contain the hippest band du jour drinking alcohol; in the morning, there are sightseers sipping coffee—a unique paradox among London's bargain hotels. The clean, high-ceiling rooms, some of which are very large (three to four beds) and have park views and balconies, also offer TVs, hair dryers, tea/coffeemakers, direct-dial phones, and safes. The teak veneer, khaki-beige-brown color schemes, and avocado bathroom suites are not pretty. ⊠ *95–99 Lancaster Gate, W2 3NS,* ☏ *0171/402–0021,* ⅎ⅍ *0171/706–4691. 103 rooms. Restaurant, bar, meeting rooms. AE, MC, V. Tube: Lancaster Gate.*

£   🏨 **Commodore.** This peaceful hotel of three converted Victorians has
★   some amazing rooms for the price—as superior to the regular ones (which usually go to package tour groups) as Harrods is to Kmart. Twenty are miniduplexes, with sleeping gallery (which cost more than the ££ category); all have tea/coffeemakers, hair dryers, and TVs with pay movies. No. 11 is a real duplex, entered through a secret mirrored door. ⊠ *50 Lancaster Gate, W2 3NA,* ☏ *0171/402–5291,* ⅎ⅍ *0171/262–1088. 90 rooms. Bar, business services. AE, MC, V. Tube: Lancaster Gate.*

NIGHTLIFE AND THE ARTS

Nightlife

Nighttime London has rejuvenated itself in the past few years, with a tangible new spirit of fun abroad on the streets, and new hangouts opening at an unprecedented rate. Whatever your pleasure, there's somewhere to go. London's clubs are famously hip, hot, and happening. Music is everywhere. Cabaret and comedy remain favorite ways to wind down. There are also numerous gambling clubs around town—ask your concierge for tips on the best (in most, you have to apply for "membership" 24 hours before playing). All you need remember when you hit the town at night is that regular bars (those without special extended licenses) stop serving alcohol at 11 PM (10:30 on Sun.), and the tubes stop around midnight.

Bars

The Atlantic. This vast, glamorous, wood-floor basement was the first central London bar to be granted a late-late alcohol license. The restaurant is more dominant these days, and reserving a table is the only way to get in late on weekends. ⌧ *20 Glasshouse St., W1,* ☎ *0171/734–4888.* ☯ *Mon.–Sat. noon–3 AM, Sun. noon–11. AE, MC, V.*

Beach Blanket Babylon. In Notting Hill, close to Portobello Market, this always-packed singles bar is distinguishable by its fanciful decor—like a fairy-tale grotto, or a medieval dungeon, visited by the gargoyles of Notre Dame. ⌧ *45 Ledbury Rd., W11,* ☎ *0171/229–2907.* ☯ *Daily noon–11. AE, MC, V.*

The Library. The comfortable, self-consciously "period" bar at the swanky Lanesborough Hotel harbors a collection of ancient cognacs, made in years when something important happened. Don't ask for a brandy Alexander. ⌧ *Hyde Park Corner, SW1,* ☎ *0171/259–5599.* ☯ *Mon.–Sat. 11–11, Sun. noon–2:30 and 7–10:30. AE, DC, MC, V.*

Cabaret

Comedy Store. The improv factory where the United Kingdom's funniest stand-ups cut their teeth has now relocated to a bigger and better space. ⌧ *Haymarket House, Oxendon St., SW1,* ☎ *0171/344–4444 or 01426/914433 for information.* ▨ *£10–£12.* ☯ *Shows Tues.–Thurs., Sun. at 8, Fri.–Sat. at 8 and midnight. AE, MC, V.*

Madame Jo Jo's. By no means devoid of straight spectators, this place has long been one of the most fun drag cabarets in town—civilized of atmosphere, despite bare-chested bar boys. Many nights are club nights, so call ahead. ⌧ *8 Brewer St.,* ☎ *0171/287–1414.* ▨ *£6 Mon.–Thurs., £8 Fri.–Sat.* ☯ *Doors open at 10 PM; shows at 12:15 and 1:15.*

Clubs

Camden Palace. It would be difficult to find a facial wrinkle in this huge place, even if you could see through the laser lights and find your way around the three floors of bars at this rejuvenated and hip-once-more megaclub. ⌧ *1A Camden High St., NW1,* ☎ *0171/387–0428.* ▨ *£3–£9.* ☯ *Tues.–Sat. 9 PM–3 AM. No credit cards.*

Heaven. London's premier (mainly) gay club is the best place for dancing wildly for hours. A state-of-the-art laser show and a large, throbbing dance floor complement a labyrinth of quieter bars and lounges. ⌧ *Under the Arches, Villiers St., WC2,* ☎ *0171/839–2520.* ▨ *£4–£8.* ☯ *Call for opening times (Tues.–Sat. approx. 10 PM–3:30 AM). AE, DC, MC, V.*

Stringfellows. Peter Stringfellow's first London nightclub is not at all hip, but is very glitzy, with mirrored walls, a light show, and an expensive art deco–style restaurant. Suburbanites and middle-age swingers frequent it. ⊠ *16–19 Upper St. Martin's La., WC2,* ☎ *0171/240–5534.* ⊠ *£8 Mon.–Wed.; £10 Thurs.; Fri.–Sat. £10 before 10 PM, £15 after 10 PM.* ☺ *Mon.–Sat. 8 PM–3:30 AM. AE, DC, MC, V.*

Jazz

Jazz Café. This palace of high-tech cool in a converted bank in bohemian Camden is the essential hangout for mainstream jazz, worldbeat, and younger crossover performers. It's steps from Camden Town tube station. ⊠ *5–7 Pkwy., NW1,* ☎ *0171/916–6000.* ⊠ *£8–£14, depending on band.* ☺ *Mon.–Sat. 7 PM–late (time varies). AE, DC, MC, V.*

Pizza Express. It may seem strange, but this is one of London's principal jazz venues, with music every night except Monday in the basement restaurant. The subterranean interior is darkly lit, the lineups (often featuring visiting U.S. performers) are interesting, and the Italian-style thin-crust pizzas are great! Eight other branches also have live music; check the listings for details. ⊠ *10 Dean St., W1,* ☎ *0171/437–9595.* ⊠ *£8–£20, depending on band.* ☺ *From noon for food; music Tues.– Sun. 9:30 PM–1 AM. AE, DC, MC, V. Tube: Tottenham Court Rd.*

Ronnie Scott's. The legendary Soho jazz club that, since its opening in the early '60s, has attracted all the big names. It's usually packed and hot, but the atmosphere can't be beat, and it's probably still London's best, even since the sad departure of its eponymous founder and saxophonist. ⊠ *47 Frith St., W1,* ☎ *0171/439–0747.* ⊠ *£10–£12 nonmembers.* ☺ *Mon.–Sat. 8:30 PM–3 AM, Sun. 8–11:30 PM. Reservations essential. AE, DC, MC, V.*

Rock

The Astoria. Very central, quite hip, this place hosts bands with a buzz, plus late club nights. ⊠ *157 Charing Cross Rd., W1,* ☎ *0171/434–0403.* ⊠ *£8–£12.* ☺ *Check listings for opening times. No credit cards.*

The Forum. This ex-ballroom with balcony and dance floor packs in the customers and consistently attracts the best medium-to-big-name performers, too. Get the tube to Kentish Town, then follow the hordes. ⊠ *9–17 Highgate Rd., NW5,* ☎ *0171/284–2200.* ⊠ *£8–£12.* ☺ *Most nights 7–11. AE, MC, V.*

The Arts

Ballet

Until its usual venue, the Royal Opera House, is completely renovated (probably by 2000), the world-famous **Royal Ballet** will be appearing at the Labatt's Apollo Theatre in Hammersmith and at the Royal Festival Hall. Check with the Royal Opera House (⊠ Bow St., Covent Garden, WC2E 9DD, ☎ 0171/240–1066) for further information. The **London City Ballet** is normally based at Sadler's Wells Theatre (⊠ Rosebery Ave., EC1R 4TN, ☎ 0171/713–6000), though this is yet another theater due for renovation for the millennium. Check the *Time Out* and newspaper listings for the latest updates. **The Place** (⊠ 17 Duke's Rd., WC1, ☎ 0171/387–0031) is indeed the place for contemporary dance, physical theater, and the avant garde. Prices at these performances are much cheaper than for those at Covent Garden.

Concerts

Ticket prices for symphony concerts range from £5–£45. International guest appearances usually mean higher prices; reserve well in advance for such performances. Those without reservations might go to the hall half an hour before the performance for a chance at returns.

The London Symphony Orchestra is in residence at the **Barbican Arts Centre** (☎ 0171/638–8891); the Philharmonia and the Royal Philharmonic also perform here. The **South Bank Arts Complex** (☎ 0171/928–3002), which includes the Royal Festival Hall, Queen Elizabeth Hall, and the small Purcell Room, forms another major venue. Between the Barbican and South Bank, there are concert performances every night of the year. The Barbican also features chamber music concerts with such smaller orchestras as the City of London Sinfonia.

To experience a great British institution, try for the **Royal Albert Hall** during "The Proms," (July–September, ☎ 0171/589–8212). Unfortunately, demand for tickets is so high that you must enter a lottery. For regular "proms," tickets run £3–£30; special "promenade" (standing) tickets usually cost half the price of normal tickets and are available at the hall on the night of the concert. Note, too, that the concerts have begun to be jumbo-screen broadcast in Hyde Park, but even here a seat on the grass requires a paid ticket. In summer, don't miss the outdoor concerts (complete with fireworks) by the lake at elegant Kenwood House (Hampstead Heath)—usually held every Saturday from mid-June to early September—or the opera in Holland Park.

Numerous lunchtime concerts take place across London in smaller concert halls and churches. They feature string quartets, vocalists, jazz ensembles, and gospel choirs. **St. Martin-in-the-Fields** (☎ 0171/839–1930) is a particularly popular location. Performances usually begin about 1 PM and last an hour. Some are free.

Movies
Despite the video invasion, West End movies still thrive. The largest major first-run houses are found in the Leicester Square/Piccadilly Circus area, where tickets average £7.50. Monday and matinees are usually half price; lines are also shorter. The best revival house is the **National Film Theatre,** part of the South Bank Centre (☞ The South Bank *in* Exploring London, *above*), which screens big past hits, plus work neglected by the more ticket-sales-dependent houses, since it comes under the auspices of the British Film Institute. The main events of the annual London Film Festival take place here in the fall. Daily membership costs 40p.

Opera
The main venue for opera in London is the **Royal Opera House** (✉ Covent Garden, WC2E 9DD, ☎ 0171/240–1066), which is currently undergoing a mammoth two-year-long renovation. For the 1998–99 season, most productions for the company should be concentrated in the newly refurbished Sadler's Wells Theatre. Call the box office number for information and current schedules.

English-language productions are staged at the **Coliseum** (✉ St. Martin's La., WC2N 4ES, ☎ 0171/632–8300), home of the English National Opera Company (though there is a chance that this troupe may also be due to move, probably during 1999). Prices here range from £8 for standing room to about £45 for the best seats, and productions are often innovative and exciting.

Theater
One of the nonpareil experiences the city has to offer is great theater. London's theater scene consists, broadly, of the state-subsidized companies, the Royal National Theatre and the Royal Shakespeare Company; the commercial West End, equivalent to Broadway; and the

Fringe—small, experimental companies. Another category could be added: known in the weekly listings magazine *Time Out* (the best reference guide to what's on) as Off-West End, these are shows staged at the longer-established fringe theaters. Other sources of arts information are the *Evening Standard* (especially on Thurs.), the major Sunday papers, the daily *Independent* and *Guardian*, and Friday's *Times*.

Most theaters have a matinee twice a week (Wed. or Thurs., and Sat.) and nightly performances at 7:30 or 8, except Sunday. Prices vary: expect to pay from £6 for an upper balcony seat to at least £25 for the stalls (orchestra) or dress circle. Reserve tickets at the box office, over the phone by credit card (numbers in the phone book or newspaper marked "cc" are for credit-card reservations), or (for a couple of pounds) through ticket agents such as **First Call** (☎ 0171/240–7941 or 0171/497–9977). To reserve before your trip use **Ticketmaster**'s U.S. booking line (☎ 800/775–2525), or reserve once in London (☎ 0171/344–0055). Half-price, same-day tickets are sold for cash only (subject to availability) from the **Society of London Theatres (SOLT)** kiosk on the southwest corner of Leicester Square, open Monday–Saturday, noon–2 for matinees, 2:30–6:30 for evening shows. There is always a long line. The "half-price" tickets here are often the orchestra seats. If you wish to snag a cheaper, balcony seat, it may be wiser to go directly to the theater box office. Larger hotels have reservation services but add hefty service charges.

The **Royal Shakespeare Company** and the **Royal National Theatre Company** perform at London's two main arts complexes, the **Barbican Centre** and **The Royal National Theatre**, respectively. Both companies mount consistently excellent productions and are usually a safe option for anyone having trouble choosing which play to see. A great hue-and-cry has gone up concerning the RSC's plans to tour the provinces during summer months—thereby depriving many tourists from seeing the best of all theater companies. Plans are still tentative at press time, so be sure to telephone before departing home. Happily, however, it is exactly during those summer months (and only then), that you can now see the Bard served up in his most spectacular manifestation—at the new open-air reconstruction of **Shakespeare's Globe Theatre** in Southwark, across the Thames from St. Paul's Cathedral. This re-creation of an open-air Elizabethan-era theater offers a summer season only, with a repertory of four plays given each season (☞ Shakespeare's Globe *in* Exploring London, *above*). Most of London's theaters are in the neighborhood nicknamed Theatreland, around the Strand and Shaftesbury Avenue. For further information about current and future theatrical events in London, use the Web site www.officiallondontheatre.co.uk, or contact the **Society of London Theatres** (✉ Bedford Chambers, The Piazza, Covent Garden, London WC2 E8HQ, ☎ 0171/836–0971).

Here's a listing of the main repertory theaters:

Barbican (RSC), ✉ *Barbican, EC2Y 8DS,* ☎ *0171/638–8891 or 0171/628–2295. Tube: Moorgate.*

Royal National Theatre (Cottesloe, Lyttelton, and Olivier), ✉ *South Bank Arts Complex, SE1 9PX,* ☎ *0171/928–2252. Tube: Waterloo.*

Shakespeare's Globe (South Bank), ✉ *New Globe Walk, Bankside,* ☎ *0171/928–6406. Tube: Blackfriars, then walk across Blackfriars Bridge.*

OUTDOOR ACTIVITIES AND SPORTS

For information on London's sports clubs and facilities, call **Sportsline,** weekdays 10–6, ☎ 0171/222–8000.

Spectator Sports

Cricket

Lord's (⊠ St. John's Wood, NW8, ☎ 0171/289–1611) has been hallowed turf for worshipers of England's summer game since 1811. The World Series of cricket, the Tests, are played here, but tickets are hard to procure. One-day internationals and top-class county matches can usually be seen by lining up on the day of the match.

Running

The **Flora London Marathon** starts at 9 AM on the third Sunday in April, with some 25,000 athletes running from Blackheath or Greenwich to Westminster Bridge or the Mall. Entry forms for the following year are available starting in May (☎ 01891/234234).

Soccer

Three British football (soccer) clubs competing in the **Premier League** are particularly popular: Arsenal (⊠ Avenell Rd., Highbury, N5, ☎ 0171/359–0131), Chelsea (⊠ Stamford Bridge, Fulham Rd., SW6, ☎ 0171/385–5545), and Tottenham Hotspur (⊠ White Hart La., 748 High Rd., N17, ☎ 0181/808–3030). More than likely you won't see a hint of the infamous hooliganism but will be quite carried away by the electric atmosphere only a vast football crowd can generate.

Tennis

The **Wimbledon Lawn Tennis Championships** is, of course, one of the top four Grand Slam events of the tennis year. There's a lottery system for advance purchase of tickets. To apply, send a self-addressed, stamped envelope between October and December (⊠ All England Lawn Tennis & Croquet Club, Box 98, Church Rd., Wimbledon SW19 5AE, ☎ 0181/946–2244), then fill in the application form, and hope. Alternatively, during the last-week-of-June, first-week-of-July tournament, tickets collected from departed spectators are resold (profits go to charity). These can provide grandstand seats with plenty to see—play continues till dusk. Call the LTB **Wimbledon Information Line** (☎ 01839/123417); it costs 49p per minute from the beginning of June.

Participant Sports

Gyms

Jubilee Hall (⊠ 30 The Piazza, Covent Garden, WC2, ☎ 0171/379–0008). The day rate is £6, monthly £45 at this very crowded but happening and super-well-equipped central gym. **The Peak** (⊠ Hyatt Carlton Tower Hotel, 2 Cadogan Pl., SW1, ☎ 0171/235–1234). This hotel club has top equipment, great ninth-floor views over Knightsbridge, a beauty spa, and a sauna—with TV. Day memberships are no longer available, but the 20-visit pass for £550 is fully transferrable, so a whole family could share one—as long as they use up the visits within the 6-month expiration date.

Running

Green Park and **St. James's Park** are convenient to the Piccadilly hotels. It's about 2 mi around both. **Hyde Park** and **Kensington Gardens** together supply a 4-mi perimeter route, or you can do a 2½-mi run in Hyde Park alone if you start at Hyde Park Corner or Marble Arch and encircle the Serpentine. Near the Park Lane hotels, **Regent's Park** has the Outer Circle loop, measuring about 2½ mi. **London Hash House Harriers** (☎ 0181/995–7879), or the **City Hash Hotline** (☎ 0181/749–2646) organize noncompetitive hour-long runs (£1) around interesting parts of town, with loops and checkpoints built in.

Swimming

Ironmonger Row (✉ Ironmonger Row, EC1, ☎ 0171/253–4011).
This 33-by-12-yard City pool is in a '30s complex that includes a
Turkish bath. **Oasis** (✉ 32 Endell St., WC2, ☎ 0171/831–1804) is just
that, with a heated pool, open May–September, right in Covent Garden,
and a 30-by-10-yard one indoors.

SHOPPING

Napoléon must have known what he was talking about when he called
Britain a nation of shopkeepers. No question about it, the finest emporiums
are in London, still. You can shop like royalty at Her Majesty's
glove maker, discover an uncommon Toby jug in a Kensington antiques
shop, or find a leather-bound edition of *Wuthering Heights* on Charing
Cross Road. If you have a yen to keep up with the Windsors, head
for stores proclaiming they are "By Appointment" to H.M. The
Queen—or to the Queen Mother, Prince Philip, or the Prince of Wales.
The fashion-forward crowd favors places like Harvey Nichols, shrine-
of-all-shrines for *Absolutely Fabulous*'s Patsy and Edina. If you have
only limited time, zoom in on one or two of the West End's grand department
stores, such as Harrods or Marks & Spencer, where you'll
find enough booty for your entire gift list. Below is a brief introduction
to the major shopping centers.

CHELSEA

Chelsea centers on the King's Road, once synonymous with ultra-
fashion; it still harbors some designer boutiques, plus antiques and home
furnishings stores.

COVENT GARDEN

This something-for-everyone neighborhood has chain clothing stores
and top designers, stalls selling crafts, and shops selling gifts of every
type—bikes, kites, tea, herbs, beads, hats, you name it.

KENSINGTON

Kensington's main drag, Kensington High Street, is a smaller, classier
version of Oxford Street, with some larger stores at the eastern end. Try
Kensington Church Street for expensive antiques, plus a little fashion.

KNIGHTSBRIDGE

Neighboring Knightsbridge has Harrods, of course, but also Harvey
Nichols, the top clothes stop, and many expensive designers' boutiques
along Sloane Street, Walton Street, and Beauchamp Place.

MAYFAIR

In Mayfair are the two Bond streets, Old and New, with desirable dress
designers, jewelers, and fine art. South Molton Street has high-price,
high-style fashion—especially at Brown's—and the tailors of Savile Row
are of worldwide repute.

REGENT STREET

At right angles to Oxford Street is Regent Street, with possibly London's
most pleasant department store, Liberty, plus Hamleys, the capital's
toy mecca. Shops around once-famous Carnaby Street stock
designer youth paraphernalia and 57 varieties of T-shirt.

ST. JAMES'S

Here the English gentleman buys everything but the suit (which is from
Savile Row): handmade hats, shirts, and shoes, silver shaving kits and
hip flasks; you'll also find the world's best cheese shop, Paxton & Whitfield.
Nothing in this neighborhood is cheap, in any sense.

Specialty Stores

London is full of wonderful and also offbeat merchandise. We have space to include only a few stores in each category.

Antiques

Antiquarius (✉ 131–141 King's Rd., SW3, ☎ 0171/351–5353), at the Sloane Square end of the King's Road, is an indoor antiques market with more than 200 stalls offering a wide variety of collectibles, including things that won't bust your baggage allowance: Art Deco brooches, meerschaum pipes, silver salt cellars. **Gray's Antique Market** (✉ 58 Davies St., W1, ☎ 0171/629–7034) is conveniently central. It assembles dealers specializing in everything from Sheffield plates to Chippendale furniture. Bargains are not impossible, and proper pedigrees are guaranteed.

Books and Records

Charing Cross Road is London's booksville, with a couple of dozen antiquarian booksellers, and many new bookshops, too.

Books for Cooks (✉ 4 Blenheim Crescent, W11, ☎ 0171/221–1992) is a unique one-stop resource, complete with the aroma of daily dishes cooked by the staff from its pages. It's worth the trip west for foodies. **Cecil Court.** Just off the Charing Cross Road is this pedestrians-only lane where every shop is a specialty bookstore. **Bell, Book and Radmall** (✉ No. 4, ☎ 0171/240–2161) has quality antiquarian volumes and specializes in modern first editions; **Marchpane** (✉ No. 16, ☎ 0171/836–8661) stocks covetable rare and antique illustrated children's books; **Dance Books** (✉ No. 9, ☎ 0171/836–2314) has—yes—dance books; and **Pleasures of Times Past** (✉ No. 11, ☎ 0171/836–1142) indulges the collective nostalgia for Victoriana. **Forbidden Planet** (✉ 71 New Oxford St., WC1, ☎ 0171/836–4179) is the place for sci-fi, fantasy, horror, and comic books. **Foyles** (✉ 119 Charing Cross Rd., ☎ 0171/437–5660) is especially large—so vast it can be confusing, but it is the place to come to find almost anything. **Hatchards** (✉ 187–188 Piccadilly, WC2, ☎ 0171/439–9921) has not only a huge stock, but also a well-informed staff to help you choose.

Stanfords (✉ 12 Long Acre, WC2, ☎ 0171/836–1321) is the place for travel books and, especially, maps. **Waterstone's** (✉ 121–125 Charing Cross Rd., ☎ 0171/434–4291) is part of an admirable, and expanding, chain with long hours and a program of author readings and signings. **Zwemmer** (✉ 24 Litchfield St., WC2, ☎ 0171/240–4158), just off Charing Cross Road, is for art books, with various specialist offshoots.

London created the great megastores that have taken over the globe. These three stock most, if not all, of your CD, record, and video needs. **HMV** (✉ 150 Oxford St., W1, ☎ 0171/631–3423) has branches everywhere, but make a special trip to the HMV (did you know this stands for His Majesty's Voice?) flagship store for the widest selection. There are lots of autograph sessions and free shows, too.

Tower Records (✉ 1 Piccadilly Circus, W1, ☎ 0171/439–2500) doesn't carry records—go figure. Overlook that and you'll find its specialty departments are some of the best in London.

Virgin Megastore (✉ 14–16 Oxford St., W1, ☎ 0171/631–1234) is Richard Branson's pride and joy (though his New York City store is even bigger). It's nice to have it all under one roof, we suppose—all 8 billion selections.

London Shopping

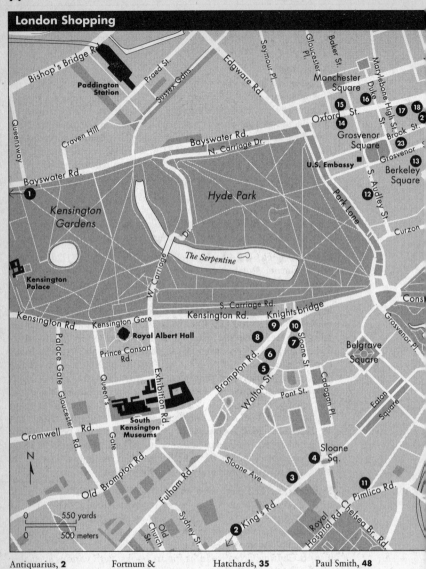

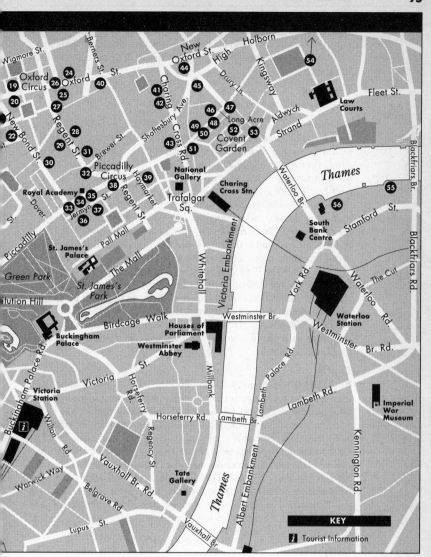

China and Glass

Thomas Goode (⊠ 19 S. Audley St., W1, ☎ 0171/499–2823) has vast ranges of formal china and lead crystal—including English Wedgwood and Minton—and is not only London's finest, but one of the world's top shops.

Clothing

See also Menswear *and* Womenswear, *below.*

Aquascutum (⊠ 100 Regent St., W1, ☎ 0171/734–6090) is known for its classic raincoats but also stocks the garments to wear underneath, for both men and women. Style keeps up with the times but is firmly on the safe side, making this a good bet for solvent professionals with an anti–fashion victim attitude. **Burberrys** (⊠ 161–165 Regent St., W1, ☎ 0171/734–4060; ⊠ 18–22 The Haymarket, SW1, ☎ 0171/930–3343) tries to evoke an English Heritage ambience, with mahogany closets and stacks of neatly folded neckerchiefs alongside the trademark "Burberry Check" tartan, which adorns—in addition to those famous raincoat linings—scarves, umbrellas, and even shortbread tins in the provisions line. **Marks & Spencer** (⊠ 458 Oxford St., W1, ☎ 0171/935–7954, and branches) is a major chain of stores that's an integral part of the British way of life—sturdy practical clothes, good materials, and workmanship. Dukes to dustmen buy their underwear here. The **Scotch House** (⊠ 2 Brompton Rd., SW3, ☎ 0171/581–2151), as you'd guess, is the place to buy your kilts, tartan scarves, and argyle socks without going to Edinburgh. It's also well stocked with cashmere and accessories.

Crafts

David Linley Furniture (⊠ 60 Pimlico Rd., SW1, ☎ 0171/730–7300) is the outpost for Viscount Linley—the only gentleman in the kingdom who can call the Queen "Auntie" and, more importantly, one of the finest furniture designers of today. The large pieces are suitably expensive, but small desk accessories and objets d'art are also available. The **OXO Tower** (⊠ Bargehouse St., ☎ 0171/401–3610) is now fully functioning as the city's most exciting new place to shop for handmade goods. Studios and shops are open Tuesday–Sunday 11–6. Nearby older sister **Gabriel's Wharf** (⊠ Upper Ground, SE1, ☎ 0171/620–0544) is still a collection of craftspeople in a cute, brightly painted village near the South Bank Centre, who sell porcelain, jewelry, mirrors, clothes, toys, papier-mâché wares and more.

Gifts

Floris (⊠ 89 Jermyn St, W1, ☎ 0171/930–2885) is probably the most beautiful shop in London, with 19th-century glass and Spanish mahogany showcases filled with swan's-down powder puffs, cut-glass bottles, and faux tortoiseshell combs. Queen Victoria used to daub her favorite Floris fragrance on her lace handkerchief. **Fortnum & Mason** (⊠ 181 Piccadilly, W1, ☎ 0171/734–8040), the Queen's grocer, is, paradoxically, the most egalitarian of gift stores, with plenty of irresistibly packaged luxury foods, stamped with the gold "By Appointment" crest, for less than £5. Try the teas, preserves, blocks of chocolate, tins of pâté, or turtle soup. The store's uniformed wait staff and its High Tea, served on premises, are marvels. **General Trading Company** (⊠ 144 Sloane St., SW1, ☎ 0171/730–0411) "does" just about every upper-class wedding gift list, but caters also to slimmer pockets with its merchandise shipped from far shores (as the name suggests) but moored securely to English taste. **Hamleys** (⊠ 188–196 Regent St., W1, ☎ 0171/734–3161) has six floors of toys and games for both children and adults. **Lush** (⊠ 7 The Piazza Court, Covent Garden, WC2, ☎ 0171/240–4570.) The trendiest body-care shop in town sells delicious bath and shower potions, handmade every week. Don't leave London without a supply of Tisty Tosty Ballastics—heart-shape bath bombs. Way cool! Besides this Chelsea store, there's another location in the Covent Garden Piazza. **Penhaligon's** (⌧ 41 Wellington St., WC2, ☎ 0171/836–2150) was established by William Penhaligon, court barber to Queen Victoria, and parfumier to Lord Rothschild and Winston Churchill. The **Tea House** (⌧ 15A Neal St., WC2, ☎ 0171/240–7539) purveys everything to do with the British national drink; you can dispatch your entire gift list here and delight in what the term "tea-phernalia" implies, i.e., strainers, trivets, infusers, and such.

Jewelry

Asprey's (⌧ 165–169 New Bond St., W1, ☎ 0171/493–6767) has been described as the "classiest and most luxurious shop in the world." It offers a range of exquisite jewelry and gifts, both antique and modern. **Butler and Wilson** (⌧ 20 S. Molton St., W1, ☎ 0171/409–2955) has irresistible costume jewelry displayed against dramatic black, and is especially strong on diamanté, jet, and French gilt. **Garrard** (⌧ 112 Regent St., W1, ☎ 0171/734–7020) has connections with the royal family going back to 1722 and is still in charge of the upkeep of the Crown Jewels. But they are also family jewelers, and they offer an enormous range of items, from antique to modern. **London Silver Vaults** (⌧ Chancery La., WC2, ☎ 0171/242–5506) has 36 dealers specializing in antique silver and jewelry in a building that used to be a safety deposit during Queen Victoria's reign. The **Outlaws Club** (⌧ 49 Endell St., WC2, ☎ 0171/379–6940) stocks the work of about 100 designers, with prices ranging from a few pounds up to £200. It's pretty avant-garde and has been a favorite with fashion writers for a decade.

Menswear

Favourbrook (⌧ 19–21 Piccadilly Arcade, W1, ☎ 0171/491–2337) tailors exquisite, handmade vests and jackets, ties and cummerbunds. There's a selection made up for both men and women, or order your own *Four Weddings and a Funeral* outfit. **Herbert Johnson** (⌧ 30 New Bond St., W1, ☎ 0171/408–1174) is one of a handful of gentleman's hatters who still know how to construct deerstalkers, bowlers, flat caps, and panamas—all the classic headgear, and Ascot-worthy hats for women, too. **Paul Smith** (⌧ 41 Floral St., WC2, ☎ 0171/379–7133) is your man if you don't want to look outlandish but you're bored with plain pants and sober jackets. Sir Paul McCartney is a famous customer. **Turnbull & Asser** (⌧ 70 Jermyn St., W1, ☎ 0171/930–0502) is *the* custom shirtmaker. Unfortunately for those of average means, the first order must be for a minimum of six shirts, from about £100 each. But there's a range of less expensive, still exquisitely made ready-to-wear shirts, too.

Prints

Grosvenor Prints (⌧ 28–32 Shelton St., WC2, ☎ 0171/836–1979) sells antiquarian prints, with an emphasis on views and architecture of London—and dogs. The **Map House** (⌧ 54 Beauchamp Pl., SW3, ☎ 0171/589–4325) has antique maps from a few pounds to several thousand, but the shop also has excellent reproductions of maps and prints, especially of botanical subjects and cityscapes.

Womenswear

Browns (⌧ 23–27 South Molton St., W1, ☎ 0171/491–7833; ⌧ 6C Sloane St., SW1, ☎ 0171/493–4232) was the first notable store to populate the South Molton Street pedestrian mall, and it seems to sprout more offshoots every time you see it. Well-established, collectible designers (Donna Karan, Romeo Gigli, Jasper Conran) rub shoulder pads here with younger, funkier names (Dries Van Noten, Jean Paul Gaultier, Hussein Chalayan). And if you want an Alexander Mc-

Queen/Givenchy, this is the place. Its July and January sales are famed. The **Hat Shop** (⌧ 58 Neal St., WC2, ☎ 0171/836–6718) is keeping the art of millinery alive and bringing it within reach of the average pocket. The stock here ranges from classic trilbies, toppers, panamas, and matador hats to frivolous tulle-and-feather constructions, with scores of inexpensive, fun toppers in between. **Koh Samui** (⌧ 50 Monmouth St., WC2, ☎ 0171/240–4280) stocks the clothing of around 20 hot young designers. Discover the next fashion wave before *Vogue* gets there. **Laura Ashley** (⌧ 256–258 Regent St., W1, ☎ 0171/437–9760, and other branches) offers designs from the firm founded by the late high priestess of English traditional. **Pellicano** (⌧ 63 S. Molton St., W1, ☎ 0171/629–2205) stocks only cutting-edge designers, like Brit phenoms Bella Freud, Copperwheat Blundell, and Sonnentag. Mulligan, and the Vogue-ier of the internationals (Prada). **Warehouse** (⌧ 19 Argyll St., W1, ☎ 0171/437–7101, and other branches) stocks practical, directional, reasonably priced separates in easy fabrics and lots of fun colors. **Vivienne Westwood** (⌧ 6 Davies St., W1, ☎ 0171/629–3757) is probably today's greatest British designer. Her Pompadour-punk ball gowns, Lady Hamilton vest coats, and foppish getups still represent the apex of high-style British couture. Her boutique is as intoxicatingly glamorous as her creations.

Department Stores

Harrods (⌧ 87 Brompton Rd., SW1, ☎ 0171/730–1234), one of the world's most famous department stores, can be forgiven its immodest motto, *Omnia, omnibus, ubique* ("everything, for everyone, everywhere"), since it has more than 230 well-stocked departments. The food halls are stunning—so are the crowds, especially during the post-Christmas sales, which usually run during the last three weeks of January. **Harvey Nichols** (⌧ 109 Knightsbridge, SW1, ☎ 0171/235–5000) is famed for five floors of ultimate fashion—every label any chic well-bred London lady covets is here. There's also a home furnishings department. It's also known for its restaurant, Fifth Floor. **John Lewis** (⌧ 278 Oxford St., SW1, ☎ 0171/629–7711) claims as its motto, "Never knowingly undersold." This is a traditional English department store, with a good selection of dress fabrics and curtain and upholstery materials. **Liberty** (⌧ 200 Regent St., SW1, ☎ 0171/734–1234), full of nooks and crannies, is like a dream of an eastern bazaar realized as a western store. Famous principally for its fabrics, it also carries Oriental goods, menswear, womenswear, fragrances, soaps, and accessories. **Selfridges** (⌧ 400 Oxford St., SW1, ☎ 0171/629–1234), London's mammoth version of Macy's, includes a food hall, a branch of the London Tourist Board, a theater ticket counter, and a Thomas Cook travel agency. **Miss Selfridge** (also on Oxford Street, east of Oxford Circus, and other branches) is its outpost for trendy, affordable young women's clothes.

Street Markets

Bermondsey is one of London's largest markets, and the one the dealers frequent, which gives you an idea of its scope. The real bargains start going at 4 AM, but there'll be a few left if you arrive later. Take Bus 15 or 25 to Aldgate, then Bus 42 over Tower Bridge to Bermondsey Square; or take the tube to London Bridge and walk. ⌧ *Tower Bridge Rd., SE1.* ⊘ *Fri. 4 AM–noon.*

Camden Passage is hugged by curio stores and is dripping with jewelry, silverware, and myriad other antiques. Saturday and Wednesday are when the stalls go up; the rest of the week, only the stores are open.

Bus 19 or 38 or the tube to the Angel stop will get you there. ⊠ *Islington, N1.* ☉ *Wed. 7–4 and Sat. 8–5.*

Portobello Market is the place where every visitor to London first heads. There are 1,500 antiques dealers trading here, so bargains are still possible. Nearer Notting Hill Gate, prices and quality are highest, with bric-a-brac appearing as you walk toward Ladbroke Grove and the flea market under the Westway and beyond. Take Bus 52 or the tube to Ladbroke Grove or Notting Hill Gate. ⊠ *Portobello Rd., W11.* ☉ *Fruit and vegetables Mon.–Wed., Fri.–Sat. 8–5, Thurs. 8–1; antiques Sat. 6 AM–5 PM.*

LONDON A TO Z

Arriving and Departing

By Bus
National Express buses (☎ 0990/808080)—or coaches, as long-distance services are known—operate from Victoria Coach Station to more than 1,200 major towns and cities. Buses are about half as expensive as the train but trips can take twice as long. **Green Line** coaches and buses (☎ 0181/668–7261) cover an area within a 30- to 40-mi radius from London, and major destinations beyond, ideal for excursions. The **Diamond Rover** ticket allows unlimited travel for one day for one price.

By Car
The major approach roads to London are motorways (six-lane highways; look for an "M" followed by a number) or "A" roads; the latter may be "dual carriageways" (divided highways), or two-lane highways. Motorways are usually the faster option for getting in and out of town, although rush-hour traffic is horrendous. Stay tuned to local radio stations for regular traffic updates.

By Plane
London is admirably served by two major airports—**Gatwick,** 27 mi to the south, and **Heathrow,** 15 mi to the west—and three smaller ones: Luton, 35 mi northwest; Stansted, 34 mi northeast; and London City, in the Docklands.

U.S. airlines flying to London include **Delta** (☎ 800/241–4141 or 800/414767 in London); **TWA** (☎ 800/892–4141 or 0181/814–0707 in London or 01293/535535); **United Airlines** (☎ 800/241–6522 or 0845/844–4777 in London); **American Airlines** (☎ 800/433–7300 or 0181/572–5555 in London/Manchester), which also serves Manchester; and **Northwest Airlines** (☎ 800/447–4747 or 0990/561000 in London). U.K. airlines with offices in the United States include **British Airways** (☎ 800/247–9297 or 0345/222111 in London) and **Virgin Atlantic** (☎ 800/862–8621 or 01293/747747 in London). Flying time is about 6½ hours from New York, 7½ hours from Chicago, and 10 hours from Los Angeles.

BETWEEN THE AIRPORTS AND DOWNTOWN

Heathrow: The quickest and least expensive route into London is via the **Piccadilly Line** of the **Underground** (London's subway system). Trains run every four to eight minutes from all terminals; the 40-minute trip costs £3.30 one-way.

London Transport (☎ 0171/222–1234) runs two bus services from the airport; each costs £6 one-way and £10 round-trip, and travel time in each direction is about one hour. The Airbus A1 leaves for Victoria Station, with stops along Cromwell Road, at Earls Court, and at Hyde Park Corner, every 30 minutes 5:40 AM–8:30 PM. The Airbus A2 leaves for King's Cross and Euston, with stops at Marble Arch, and Russell Square every 30 minutes 6 AM–9:30 PM.

Gatwick: Fast, nonstop **Gatwick Express** trains leave for Victoria Station every 15 minutes 5:20 AM–12:50 AM; hourly 1:35 AM–4:35 AM. The 30-minute trip costs £9.50 one-way. A frequent local train also runs all night.

Speedlink's Flightline 777 bus leaves for Victoria Coach Station hourly (7 AM–10 PM); travel time is about 90 minutes and the cost is £7.50 one-way. A round-trip ticket valid for three months costs £11.

Stansted: London's newest airport, opened in 1991, serves mainly European destinations. The **Stansted Skytrain** to Liverpool Street Station runs every half hour and costs £10 one-way although, at press time, fares were set to increase.

By Train

London has 15 major train stations, each serving a different area of the country, all accessible by Underground or bus. The once-national British Rail has now been broken up into several private franchises. One call, however, should answer your travel inquiries (☎ 0345/484950; 0800/450450 for credit card bookings; 0161/236–3522 or 0171/928–5151 for calls from overseas), until they are sold off as franchises. These major changes in the structure of Britain's railways should not affect the traveler unduly, although nobody can predict exactly what will happen to the fares.

Getting Around

By Bus

In central London, buses are traditionally bright red double- and single-deckers, though there are now many privately owned buses of different colors. Not all buses run the full length of their route at all times; check with the driver or conductor. On some buses you pay the conductor after finding a seat, on others you pay the driver upon boarding. Bus stops are clearly indicated; the main stops have a red LT symbol on a plain white background. When the word REQUEST is written across the sign, you must flag the bus down. Buses are a good way to see the town, but don't take one if you are in a hurry. Single fares start at 60p for short hops (90p in the central zone).

London is divided into six concentric zones for both bus and tube fares: the more zones you cross, the higher the fare. Regular single-journey or round-trip **One Day Travelcards** (£3.50–£4.30) allow unrestricted travel on bus and tube after 9:30 AM and all day on weekends and national holidays. **LT Cards** (£4.50–£7.30) do not have any restricted times of travel except on N-prefixed Night Buses. **Visitor Travelcards** (£3.90) are the same as the One Day Travelcards, but with the bonus of a booklet of money-off vouchers to major attractions (available only in the United States, for three, four, and seven days, from **BritRail Travel International,** ✉ 1500 Broadway, New York, NY 10036, ☎ 212/382–3737).

Traveling without a valid ticket makes you liable for an on-the-spot fine (£10 at press time), so always pay your fare before you travel. For more information, there are **LT Travel Information Centres** at the following tube stations: Euston, Hammersmith, King's Cross, Oxford Circus, Piccadilly Circus, St. James's Park, Victoria, and Heathrow (in Terminals 1, 2 and 4); open 7:15 AM–10 PM, with Terminal 4's TIC closing at 3 PM, or call ☎ 0171/222–1234.

Night Buses can prove helpful when traveling in London from 11 PM to 5 AM—these buses add the prefix "N" to their route numbers and—

do note—don't run as frequently and don't operate on quite as many routes as day buses. You'll probably have to transfer at one of the Night Bus nexuses: Victoria, Westminster, and either Piccadilly Circus or Trafalgar Square. Avoid sitting alone on the top deck of a Night Bus unless you want to enjoy the happily rare misfortune of being mugged in London.

By Car

The simple advice about driving in London is: don't. Because the city grew as a series of villages, there was never a central street plan, and the result is a chaotic winding mass, made no easier by the one-way street systems. If you must drive in London, remember to drive on the left, and stick to the speed limit.

By Taxi

Hotels and main tourist areas have taxi ranks; you can also flag taxis down on the street. If the yellow FOR HIRE sign is lit on top, the taxi is available. But drivers often cruise at night with their signs unlit to avoid unsavory characters, so if you see an unlit cab, keep your hand up and you might be lucky. Fares start at £1.40 and increase by units of 20p per 281 yards or 55.5 seconds until the fare exceeds £8.60. After that, it's 20p for each 188 yards or 37 seconds. Surcharges are added after 8 PM and on weekends and public holidays. Over Christmas and New Year's Eve, it rises to £2—and there's 40p extra for each additional passenger. Note that fares are usually raised in April of each year. Tips are extra, usually 10% to 15% per ride.

By Underground (Tube)

Known colloquially as "The Tube," London's extensive Underground system is by far the most widely used form of city transportation. As many travelers learn, using its easily marked routes, crystal-clear signage, and extensive connections, it's a delight to travel on. Trains run both beneath and aboveground out into the suburbs, and all stations are clearly marked with the London Underground circular symbol. (In Britain, the word "subway" means "pedestrian underpass.") Trains are all one class; smoking is *not* allowed on board or in the stations.

There are 10 basic lines—all named. The Central, District, Northern, Metropolitan, and Piccadilly lines all have branches, usually taking you to the outlying sections of the city, so be sure to note which branch is needed for your particular destination. Electronic platform signs tell you the final stop and route of the next train, and some signs conveniently indicate how many minutes you'll have to wait for the train to arrive. Begun in the Victorian era, the Underground is still being expanded and improved. The East London line, which runs from Shoreditch and Whitechapel south to New Cross, is due to reopen after major reconstruction in 1998. September 1998 is the latest date for the opening of the Jubilee line extension: this state-of-the-art subway will sweep from Green Park to Southwark, with connections to Canary Wharf and the Docklands and the much hyped Millennium Experience megadome, and on to the east at Stratford.

Guided Tours

Orientation

BY BUS

Guided sightseeing tours offer passengers a good introduction to the city from double-decker buses, which are open-topped in summer. Tours run daily and depart from Haymarket, Baker Street, Grosvenor Gardens, Marble Arch, and Victoria. You may board or alight at any of about 21 stops to view the sights, and then get back on the next

ROYALTY WATCHING

YOU'VE SEEN BIG BEN, THE Tower, and Westminster Abbey. But somehow you feel something is missing: a close encounter with Britain's most famous attraction—Her actual Majesty. True, you've toured Buckingham Palace, but the Windsors are notorious for never standing at a window (the London *Times* once suggested that the palace mount a full-scale mechanical procession of royal figures to parade in and out of the palace, on the hour, in cuckoo-clock fashion), and the odds are that you won't be bumping into Elizabeth II on the tube. But at a surprisingly wide variety of royal events, you can catch a glimpse of her, along with many other Windsor personages. Fairs and fetes, polo matches and horse races, first nights and banquets galore—her date book is crammed with such events and, on one of them—who knows?—you might even meet her on a royal walkabout.

The Queen, and the Royal Family, in fact, attend 400 functions a year and if you want to know what she and the rest of the RF are doing on any given date, turn to the *Court Circular* printed in the major London dailies. You might catch Prince Charles launching a ship, Princess Margaret attending a film premiere, or the Queen at a hospital's ribbon-cutting. But most visitors want to see the Royals in all their dazzling pomp and circumstance. For this, the best bet is the second Saturday in June, when the Trooping the Colour is usually held to celebrate the Queen's official birthday. This spectacular parade begins when she leaves Buckingham Palace in her carriage and rides down the Mall to arrive at Horse Guards Parade at 11 AM

exactly. (Well, occasionally the clock has been timed to strike as she arrives and not vice versa!) If you wish to obtain one of the 7,000 seats (no more than two per request, distributed by ballot), enclose a letter and stamped, self-addressed envelope or International Reply Coupon to **Ticket Office,** Headquarters Household Division, Horse Guards, London SW1A 2AX, ☎ 0171/414–2497 (send January to February). Of course, you can also just line up along the Mall with your binoculars!

Perhaps the nicest time to see the Queen is during Royal Ascot, held at the racetrack near Windsor Castle— just a short train ride out of London— usually during the third week of June (Tuesday to Friday). After several races, the Queen invariably walks down to the paddock on a special path, greeting race goers as she proceeds. Americans wishing a seat in the Royal Enclosure (fashion note: the big party hats come out on Ladies Day, normally the Thursday of the meet) should apply to the American Embassy, 24 Grosvenor Square, London W1, before the end of March.

If you're lucky enough to meet the Queen (contrary to her stodgy public persona, she's actually a great wit), just remember to address her as "Your Majesty."

bus. Tickets (£12) may be bought from the driver. Agencies include **Evan Evans** (☎ 0181/332–2222), **Frames Rickards** (☎ 0171/837–3111), **The Original London Sightseeing Tour** (☎ 0181/877–1722), and **The Big Bus Company** (☎ 0181/944–7810). These tours include stops at places such as St. Paul's Cathedral and Westminster Abbey. Prices and pickup points vary according to the sights visited, but many pickup points are at major hotels. **Black Taxi Tour of London** is a personal tour by cab direct from your hotel (☎ 0171/289–4371). The price is per cab, so the fare can be shared among as many as five people.

BY CANAL

During summer, narrow boats and barges cruise London's two canals, the Grand Union and Regent's Canal. Companies include **Jason's Trip** (☎ 0171/286–3428), **London Waterbus Company** (☎ 0171/482–2660), and **Canal Cruises** (☎ 0171/485–4433). London Waterbus Company also features weekend cruises throughout the winter from Camden Lock to Little Venice (45 minutes), £3.50 one-way, £4.50 round-trip.

BY RIVER

Boats also cruise the Thames throughout the year. Most leave from Westminster Pier, Charing Cross Pier, and Tower Pier (☎ 0171/488–0344). Downstream routes go to the Tower of London, Greenwich, and the Thames Barrier; upstream destinations include Kew, Richmond, and Hampton Court. Depending upon the destination, river trips may last from one to four hours. Contact **Catamaran Cruisers** (☎ 0171/839–3572) or **Westminster Passenger Boat Services** (☎ 0171/930–4097).

Walking Tours

One of the best ways to get to know London is on foot, and there are many guided walking tours from which to choose. **Original London Walks** (☎ 0171/624–3978) has a dazzling selection—there are theme tours devoted to the Beatles, Sherlock Holmes, Dickens, Jack the Ripper, you name it—and takes great pride in the infectious enthusiasm of its guides. Other firms include **City Walks** (☎ 0171/700–6931) and **Streets of London** (☎ 0181/346–9255).

Excursions

London Regional Transport, Green Line, Evan Evans, and **Frames Rickards** all offer day excursions by bus to places within easy reach of London, such as Hampton Court, Oxford, Stratford, and Bath.

Contacts and Resources

Embassies

American Embassy (✉ 24 Grosvenor Sq., W1A 1AE, ☎ 0171/499–9000). **Canadian High Commission** (✉ McDonald House, 1 Grosvenor Sq., W1X 0AB, ☎ 0171/258–6600).

Emergencies

Police, fire, or ambulance ☎ 999.

The following hospitals have 24-hour accident and emergency facilities: **Charing Cross** (✉ Fulham Palace Rd., W6, ☎ 0181/846–1234); **Guy's** (✉ St. Thomas St., SE1, ☎ 0171/955–5000); **Royal Free** (✉ Pond St., Hampstead, NW3, ☎ 0171/794–0500); and **St. Thomas's** (✉ Lambeth Palace Rd., SE1, ☎ 0171/928–9292).

Pharmacies

Bliss Chemist (✉ 5 Marble Arch, W1 ☎ 0171/723–6116; ✉ 50 Willesden La., WC2, ☎ 0171/624–8000) is open daily 9 AM–midnight.

Travel Agencies
American Express (⊠ 6 Haymarket, WC2, ☎ 0171/930–4411; ⊠ 89 Mount St., W1, ☎ 0171/499–4436). **Thomas Cook** (⊠ Oxford St., ☎ 0171/493–4537; ⊠ 4 Henrietta St., WC2, ☎ 0171/379–0685; ⊠ 1 Marble Arch, W1, ☎ 0171/724–9483; and other branches).

Visitor Information
The main **London Tourist Information Centre** at Victoria Station also provides information on the rest of Britain and is open from April to October, Monday–Saturday 8–7, Sunday 8–5; from November to March, Monday–Saturday 8–6, Sunday 8:30–4. There are other TICs in Selfridges (⊠ Oxford St., W1; open store hours only) and at Heathrow Airport (Terminals 1, 2, and 3). The **British Travel Centre** (⊠ 12 Regent St.), is open weekdays 9–6, Saturday and Sunday 10–4, with weekend hours extended to 9–5 May–September. This bureau provides details about travel, accommodations, and entertainment for the whole of Britain, but you need to visit the Centre in person to get information. **Visitorcall** is the London Tourist Board's 24-hour phone service—it's a premium-rate (39p–49p per minute depending on time of call) recorded information line, with different numbers for theater, events, museums, sports, getting around, etc. To access the list of options, call ☎ 0839/123456, or see the display advertisement in the phone book. A faxed events calendar is also available (FAX 0839/401278).

3 The Southeast

Canterbury, Dover, Brighton, Tunbridge Wells

Everyone stands to win in the Southeast. Among the prizes here you'll find Kent—the "Garden of England"—as well as major icons, such as Canterbury Cathedral, the white cliffs of Dover, and the Royal Pavilion at Brighton. Everywhere there are storybook villages grown drowsy with age. Here, too, are some of the finest stately treasure houses. Knole, Hever Castle, Penshurst Place, Sissinghurst—so idyllic have these visions become to us by now that when viewed from afar, they look like Old Master paintings resting on easels.

Updated by
Sue Gordon

IN AN ERA WHEN IT HAS BECOME FASHIONABLE to have everything as small as possible—from radios to cameras—the Southeast will inevitably have great appeal to overseas visitors. People visiting England and this region for the first time take away an impression of rural perfection in miniature. For the portrait—once its grosser elements, the industrial blemishes, have been struck out—shows a landscape of small-scale features and pleasant hills; from the air, the tiny fields, neatly hedged, form a patchwork quilt. On the ground, once away from the fast motorways and commuter tract housing, the Southeast—Surrey, Kent, and Sussex, East and West—reveals some of England's loveliest countryside, whose gentle, rolling hills and woodlands are punctuated with hundreds of small farms and sleepy villages rooted in history and with cathedral cities waiting to be explored. Rivers wind down to a coast that is alternately sweeping chalk cliff and happy seaside resort.

Though it is one of the most densely populated areas of Britain—the inevitable result of its proximity to London—the Southeast is, happily, home to Kent, the famous "Garden of England." Here, fields of hops and acre upon acre of orchards that burst into a mass of pink and white blossoms in the spring stretch away into the distance. Here, too, are ancient Canterbury, site of the mother cathedral of England, and Dover, whose chalky white cliffs and brooding castle have become veritable symbols of Britain.

A series of famous seaside towns and resorts is ranged along the coasts of Sussex and Kent, the most famous being that picturesque marriage of carnival and culture, Brighton, site of 19th-century England's own Xanadu, the Royal Pavilion. Except for the unaccountable moods that mark English weather countrywide, this resort area proves the wisdom of the traditional watchword: "South for Sunshine." In addition, the coast is home to the busy ports of Newhaven, Folkestone, Dover, and Ramsgate, which have served for centuries as gateways to continental Europe. Fittingly, the Channel Tunnel, linking Britain to France by rail and road, now runs from near Folkestone.

Indeed, because the English Channel is at its narrowest here, a great deal of British history has been forged in the Southeast. The Romans landed in this area and stayed to rule Britain for four centuries. So did the Saxons (Sussex means "the land of the South Saxons"). William ("the Conqueror") of Normandy defeated the Saxons at a battle near Hastings in 1066. Canterbury has been the seat of the Primate of All England—the Archbishop of Canterbury—since Pope Gregory the Great dispatched St. Augustine to convert the heathen hordes of Britain in 597. And long before any of these invaders, the ancient Britons blazed trails that formed the routes for today's modern highways.

Pleasures and Pastimes

Stately Homes

Britain has a rich heritage of stately homes scattered all over the nation, but this region has one of the greatest concentrations. To select just the superlatives: Chartwell was home and is permanent memorial to Sir Winston Churchill; Hever Castle was the abode of Henry VIII's second wife, Anne Boleyn, and was restored in this century by William Waldorf Astor; Ightham Mote is perhaps the most enchanting medieval house in all Europe, a small 14th-century structure surrounded by a moat and, usually, a flock of beautiful swans preening themselves; Knole is one of the largest houses in Europe—more a town than a residence, it's built around seven romantic courtyards; Leeds Castle, pretty as a picture, stands in the middle of a lake; Penshurst Place, dating from 1340, was once home to poet Sir Philip Sidney, whose direct descendants still live there; and Sissinghurst Castle Garden was made world-famous through the dedication and horticultural vision of renowned author Vita Sackville-West.

Dining

Around the coast, seafood—much of it locally caught—is a specialty. If you are in a seaside town, make sure you look for that great British staple, fish-and-chips. Perhaps "look" isn't the word—just follow your nose! You'll also discover local dishes such as Sussex smokies and some of the most succulent oysters in Britain. In the larger towns, trendy restaurants tend (as ever) to spring up for a time and then disappear. This is an area in which to experiment.

CATEGORY	COST*
££££	over £50
£££	£30–£50
££	£20–£30
£	under £20

per person, including first course, main course, dessert, and VAT; excluding drinks

Lodging

All around this coast, resort towns stretch along beaches, their hotels standing cheek-by-jowl. Of the smaller hotels and guest houses only a few remain open throughout the year, as most of them do business only from Easter to September or October. Note that some hotels feature all-inclusive rates for a week's stay, which is cheaper than taking room and meals by the day. Of course, prices rise in July and August, and during the height of the season the seaside resorts can get solidly booked up, especially Brighton and Eastbourne, which are also popular as conference centers. It is always worth asking if there are any special deals available.

CATEGORY	COST*
££££	over £150
£££	£80–£150
££	£60–£80
£	under £60

All prices are for two people sharing a double room, including service, breakfast, and VAT.

Walking

Ardent walkers can explore both the **North Downs Way** (141 mi) and the **South Downs Way** (106 mi), following ancient paths along the tops of the downs. They both offer wide views over the countryside. The North Downs Way follows in part the ancient Pilgrims' Way to Canterbury. The South Downs Way crosses the chalk landscape of beautiful Sussex Downs, with parts of the route going through deep woodland. You can easily do short sections of both trails. Along the way, there are plenty of towns and villages, mostly just off the main trail, with old inns offering refreshment and/or accommodations. The two routes are joined (north/south) by the 30-mi **Downs Link.** One way of seeing the Kent coast is to follow the **Saxon Shore Way,** 143 mi from Gravesend to Rye, passing many historical sites, including four Roman forts. Section-by-section guides to all these walks are available from the Southeast England Tourist Board.

Exploring the Southeast

Begin in the cathedral town of Canterbury in the heart of Kent, and work your way south to Dover, England's "Continental gateway." Next head west along the Sussex coast to Brighton, taking in the historic seaside towns along the way. Travel west to Chichester, then swing north into Surrey, stopping in Guildford before continuing to Tunbridge Wells, where you can begin a final circuit through western Kent and its numerous historic landmarks.

Many of the towns can easily be reached by public transportation from London for a day trip. Local buses, trains, and occasionally even steam trains provide regular service to most major sites. If you're especially interested in stately homes or quiet villages, it might be wiser to rent a car and strike out on your own.

Numbers in the text correspond to numbers in the margin and on the Southeast, Canterbury, and Brighton maps.

Great Itineraries

Though the Southeast is a relatively small region, it is densely packed with points of interest. Most of the essential sights are contained in and around the towns, while the rustic attractions—castles, country homes, and gardens—invite a more leisurely appreciation. You will need to reckon on a considerable portion of your time being spent on the road. Do take along a good road map to minimize the amount of time spent seeking charming but miles-off-the-beaten-track hamlets.

IF YOU HAVE 3 DAYS

Confine your travels to one or two specific areas of the Southeast region. You could opt for the glories of historic ⊞ **Canterbury** ① as a first choice. Stay one night here, making the cathedral your priority stop, and spend any extra time meandering through the old streets, taking in the city's secondary sights. For your next two nights, pencil in ⊞ **Brighton** ③⓪, whose Royal Pavilion is a must on any itinerary. Keeping Brighton as your base, you could spend a third day exploring **Lewes** ②⑨, with its castle in a commanding position over the town and an impressive collection of Tudor timber-frame buildings scattered along its steep lanes, or, if you're lucky enough, attending a performance at the nearby Glyndebourne Opera House.

IF YOU HAVE 7 DAYS

Seven days or so will allow you to explore the region's more inaccessible spots and give you the opportunity to unearth some of the Southeast's better-kept secrets. On your way to or from **Canterbury** ①, for example, spend half a day at the superbly situated **Leeds Castle** ⑤⑭, whose lovely grounds vie for your attention with the treasures within. Leeds Castle lies a short distance outside Maidstone; not far north of the town, the dockyards at Chatham and the castle and cathedral at neighboring Rochester are equally fascinating and should be a great hit with children. South of Maidstone, the gardens of **Sissinghurst Castle and Garden** ⑤⑥ are likely to convert even those who have never lifted a trowel. To the west, stay for at least an overnight visit in ⊞ **Royal Tunbridge Wells** ④⑧, center of an area rich with magnificent, historically significant country houses, most notably the medieval manor house **Penshurst Place** ④⑨; **Hever Castle** ⑤⓪, indelibly associated with two famous families, the Boleyns of the Tudor era and the Astors of our own; beautiful **Ightham Mote** ⑤③; and **Chartwell** ⑤①, home of Sir Winston Churchill for more than 40 years. One famous structure lies over the Sussex border, the moated **Bodiam Castle** ⑤⑦, though here the dominant note is abandonment and ruin. A short distance to the southwest, you can visit **Bateman's,** the home of Rudyard Kipling in the hamlet of **Burwash** ⑤⑧, and proceed on to the site of the Battle of Hastings—at **Battle** ㉖, where one of the most momentous events in English history is marked by the atmospheric remains of an abbey founded by William the Conqueror. **Hastings** ㉕ itself is a typical south-coast town, so instead opt to travel east and overnight in ⛫ **Rye** ㉓—a town this lovely is worth a detour. Take in nearby Winchelsea, then continue west to **Herstmonceux** ㉗ to call on one of England's most beautiful castles, recently opened to the public. From here, head to ⛫ **Brighton** ㉚. Spend one or two nights ambling around the promenades of this sparky seaside town and shopping in the Lanes and North Laine area. Take care not to skip the pretty town of **Lewes** ㉙ (which you won't, if you're going to the Glyndebourne Opera). Westward along the coast, find a hotel in ⛫ **Arundel** ㊴ or ⛫ **Chichester** ㊷ to explore the area more conveniently: Arundel is dominated by the memorable silhouette of Arundel Castle, while Chichester has a Norman cathedral in the center of town and an impressive Roman villa outside. If you are heading back to London from here, you might pass through **Guildford** ㊹, a commuter town in the county of Surrey with some good 18th-century remnants. Just east of here, **West Clandon** ㊺ features a graceful Italianate palace, and there is more elegant artistry, furniture, and objets at the Regency mansion, **Polesden Lacey,** in the nearby village of **Great Bookham** ㊻. From here, it is only 25 mi or so to central London.

When to Tour the Southeast

Because the counties of Kent, Surrey, and Sussex offer some of the most scenic landscape in southern England and because most of the privately owned castles and mansions are open only between April and September (a few have restricted winter openings), it's best to tour the Southeast in the spring, summer, or early fall. Failing that, however, the great parks surrounding the stately houses are often open all year. In Canterbury and the seaside towns, you would do well to avoid August, Sundays, and national holidays if you don't like crowds, though Sunday is always the best day to view the great national institution that is the local seaside.

CANTERBURY TO DOVER

The ancient city of Canterbury—worldwide seat of the Church of England, shrine of Thomas à Becket, and immortalized in Geoffrey Chaucer's *Canterbury Tales*—is indeed a prime historic center. Even in prehistoric times, this part of England was relatively well settled. Saxon settlers, Norman conquerors, and the folk who lived here in more settled late-medieval times all left their mark—most notably in the city's magnificent cathedral, the Mother Church of England. There are endless excursions to be made through the varying countryside between Canterbury and Dover. Here, the Kentish landscape ravishes the eye in the spring with apple blossom, while the woodlands are carpeted with primroses and wood anemones and, later, by a mist of bluebells. It is a county of orchards, market gardens, and the typical round, red-roof oasthouses, used for drying hops.

Canterbury

❶ *56 mi southeast from London.*

For many of us, Geoffrey Chaucer's story of the historic annual pilgrimage to Canterbury cathedral brings back memories of senior-class English. Judging from the tales, however, Canterbury was less of a spiritual center and more of a tailgate party for people on horses. These pilgrims fought their way across the rolling terrain of Kent to this spot

GREAT BRITAIN

Thames

Windsor

Hounslow

LONDON

Hampstead

Richmond

Woolwich

Dartford

Thames

Staines

Merton

Sydenham

Sidcup

Egham

Bromley

M3

Beckenham

Leatherhead

West Clandon

Great Bookham

Westerham

Knole

A25

46

M25

52

Guildford

45

A246

51

Chartwell

53

44

A31

47

Box Hill

A25

B2027

Ightham Mote

Dorking

Hever Castle

50

A248

Reigate

Penshurst Place

49

B2176

Tonbric

NORTH DOWNS

Penshurst

A26

Farnham

SURREY

M23

B2020

A264

Royal

48

A3

A264

Tunbridge Wells

Milford

A287

A286

Crawley

East Grinstead

Wadhurst

Haslemere

Horsham

A24

A264

THE

A286

A283

A29

Cuckfield

Midhurst

A272

WEST

Haywards Heath

Uckfield

A265

Petworth House

SUSSEX

40

A283

Burgess Hill

EAST

SOUTH

Singleton

Storrington

A281

SUSSEX

41

A284

A23

27

DOWNS

Lewes

Herstm

Fishbourne Roman Palace

39

Arundel

A27

29

Glyndebourne

28

A27

43

42

Chichester

A259

Worthing

Wilmington

Eastbourne

Bognor Regis

A259

Brighton

30 — 38

A259

English Channel

Lar

North
Sea

ESSEX

Chelmsford Maldon *Blackwater*

Rayleigh

Basildon

Southend-
on-Sea

Thames

Crouch

Grays

Sheerness

Margate

Broadstairs

Queenborough Herne Bay

Whitstable Ramsgate

Rochester 55 Gillingham
Chatham *A2* *The Swale* A291

Faversham 18 A299 A290 15 **Fordwich** A257 19 **Sandwich**

Medway M26 M2 **Harbledown** 16 **Canterbury** **Deal**
A25 A251 1 — 14 20

Maidstone B2163 A252 17 A28 21 **Walmer**
54 **Leeds** A20 **Chilham** *Great Stour* B2068 A236 **Castle**
Castle M20 B2065 A258

B2163 **Wye** A2

Headcorn **KENT** A274 **Ashford** 22 **Dover**

idge M20 *Channel Tunnel*

Finchcocks A262 56 **Sissinghurst Castle** **Folkestone**
59 60 and Garden A259 **Hythe**
amberhurst A229 **Cranbrook** B2068 A268

W E A L D **Romney Marsh**

Hawkhurst A268 **New Romney**

A265 **Bodiam Castle** 57 *Rother* **Lydd**

58 A21 23 **Rye**

Burwash B2089 24 **Winchelsea**

Battle 26 A259 *Rye Bay*

A271 A2100
7 B2095 **Bexhill**
monceux A259 25 **Hastings**

Pevensey

Pevensey
Bay

Strait of Dover

N

0   5 miles
0   5 km

on the banks of the River Stout to visit the shrine of the martyr Thomas
à Becket, making this southeastern town one of the most visited in England (if not Europe). Once the Iron Age capital of the kingdom of Kent,
currently headquarters of the Anglican Church, Canterbury still has a
lively atmosphere, a fact that has impressed visitors since 1388, when
Master Chaucer wrote his book. Today, most pilgrims come in search
of picture-perfect moments rather than spiritual enlightenment—and
magnificently medieval Canterbury obliges: it was one of the first cities
in Britain to "pedestrianize" its center, bringing a measure of tranquillity
to its streets. Nevertheless, to see it at its best, walk around early, before the tourist buses arrive, or wait until after they depart.

Canterbury is bisected by a road running northwest, beside which lie
all the major tourist sites. This road begins as St. George's Street, then
becomes High Street, and finally turns into St. Peter's Street. At the St.
George's Street end you will see a lone church tower marking the site

❷ of **St. George's Church**—the rest of the building was destroyed in
World War II—where playwright Christopher Marlowe was baptized

❸ in 1564. Just before reaching the modern **Longmarket** shopping center, you come to Butchery Lane and, below it, the colorful **Canterbury
Roman Museum** and its famous Roman Pavement. The whole museum,
including this ancient mosaic floor and a hypocaust, the Roman version of central heating, is below ground, at the level of the Roman town.
Displays and reconstructions of Roman buildings and the marketplace help to re-create the ancient atmosphere. ⊠ *Canterbury Roman
Museum, Butchery La.,* ☎ *01227/785575.* ✇ *£1.90.* ⊙ *June–Oct.,
Mon.–Sat. 10–5, Sun. 1:30–5; Nov.–May, Mon.–Sat. 10–5; last
entry at 4. Closed Christmas wk.*

Mercery Lane, with its medieval-style cottages and massive, overhanging timber roofs, runs right off High Street and ends in the tiny

❹ ❺ **Buttermarket.** The immense **Christchurch Gate,** built in 1517, leads into
the cathedral close.

★ ❻ **Christchurch Cathedral,** focal point of the city, was the first of England's
great Norman cathedrals. Nucleus of worldwide Anglicanism, it is a
living textbook of medieval architecture. The building was begun in
1070, demolished, begun anew in 1096, and then systematically expanded over the next three centuries. When the original choir section
burned to the ground in 1174, it was replaced by a new one, designed
in the Gothic style, with tall, pointed arches.

The cathedral was only a century old, and still relatively small in size,
when Thomas à Becket, the archbishop of Canterbury, was murdered
here in 1170. Becket, an uncompromising defender of ecclesiastical interests, had angered his friend Henry II, who was heard to exclaim,
"Who will rid me of this troublesome priest?" Thinking they were carrying out the king's wishes, four knights burst in on Becket in one of
the side chapels and killed him. Two years later Becket was canonized,
and Henry II's subsequent submission to the authority of the Church
and his penitence helped establish the cathedral as the undisputed center of English Christianity.

Becket's tomb—destroyed by Henry VIII in 1538 as part of his campaign to reduce the power of the Church and confiscate its treasures—
was one of the most extravagant shrines in Christendom. It was placed
in **Trinity Chapel,** where you can still see a series of 13th-century
stained-glass windows illustrating Becket's miracles. So hallowed was
this spot that in 1376, Edward, the Black Prince, warrior son of Edward III and a national hero, was buried near it. The actual site of Becket's
murder is down a flight of steps just to the left of the nave. In the cor-

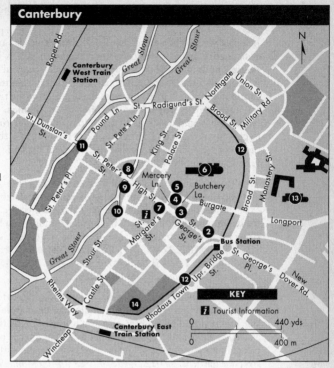

ner, a second flight of steps leads down to the enormous Norman undercroft, or vaulted cellarage, built in the early 12th century. Its roof is supported by a row of squat pillars whose capitals dance with fantastic animals and strange monsters.

If time permits, be sure to explore the **Cloisters** and other small monastic buildings to the north of the cathedral. The 12th-century octagonal water tower is still part of the cathedral's water supply. As you pass through the great gatehouse back into the city, look up at the sculpted heads of two young figures: Prince Arthur, elder brother of Henry VIII, and the young Catherine of Aragon, to whom he was betrothed. After Arthur's death, Catherine married Henry. Her failure to produce a male heir after 25 years of marriage led to Henry's decision to divorce her, creating an irrevocable breach with the Catholic Church, and altering the course of English history. ⊠ *Cathedral Precincts,* ☎ *01227/762862.* ☐ *£2.50 Mon.–Sat. year-round and Sun. April–Oct.; free Sun. Nov–Mar.* ☉ *Mon.–Sat. 9–5, Sun. 12:30–2:30 (open all day Sun. for worship). Access may be limited during services.*

To help bring Canterbury's rich history alive, head to St. Margaret's Street, near the great cathedral, down High Street. Here, in a disused church, you will find a unique and vivid exhibition called **The Canterbury Tales,** which is a dramatization of 14th-century English life. First you will "meet" Chaucer's pilgrims at the Tabard Inn near London; next you will come to a series of tableaus illustrating five of the tales (complete with authentic sounds and smells). Then, passing through a reconstruction of the city gate, you may enter the marketplace. Don't be surprised if one of the figures comes to life: an actor dressed in period costume often performs a charade as part of the scene. ⊠ *St. Margaret's St.,* ☎ *01227/454888.* ☐ *£4.95.* ☉ *Mar.–Jun., daily 9:30–5:30;*

July–Aug., daily 9–6; Sept.–Oct., daily 9:30–5:30; Nov.–Dec., Sun.– Fri. 10–4:30, Sat. 9:30–5:30.

8 Just past where High Street crosses the little River Stour, you will see a distinctive group of half-timber cottages known as the **Weavers' Houses,** built in the 16th century. These were occupied by Huguenot weavers who settled in Canterbury after fleeing from religious persecution in France. Before you cross the bridge over the river, stop in at **9** the 12th-century **Eastbridge Hospital of St. Thomas.** The hospital (which we would now call a hostel) lodged poor pilgrims who came to pray at the tomb of Thomas à Becket. The refectory, the chapel, and the crypt are open to the public. ⊠ *25 High St.* ☎ *01227/471688.* ☞ *Free.* ☉ *Mon.–Sat. 10–5.*

10 The medieval Poor Priests' Hospital is now the site of the comprehensive and popular **Canterbury Heritage Museum,** whose exhibits provide an excellent overview of the city's history and architecture. Visit early in the day to avoid the crowds. The hospital building can be found on a street leading off High Street, an extension of St. Peter's Street. ⊠ *20 Stour St.,* ☎ *01227/452747.* ☞ *£1.90.* ☉ *June–Oct., Mon.–Sat. 10:30–5, Sun. 1:30–5; Nov.–May, Mon.–Sat. 10:30–5; last entry at 4. Closed Christmas wk and Good Friday.*

11 The only surviving city gatehouse, at one end of St. Peter's Street (an extension of High Street), now contains the **West Gate Museum.** Inside are medieval bric-a-brac and armaments used by the city guard, as well as more contemporary weaponry. Climb to the roof to catch a panoramic view of the city spires before walking along the landscaped riverside gardens. ☎ *01227/452747.* ☞ *80p.* ☉ *Mon.–Sat. 11–12:30 and 1:30–3:30.*

12 For a panoramic view of the town, follow the circuit of the **medieval city walls,** built on the line of the original Roman walls. Those to the south survive intact, towering some 20 ft high. Follow the walkway **13** along the top clockwise, along Broad Street, passing the ruins of **St. Augustine's Abbey.** One of the oldest monastic sites in the country, this is the burial place of Augustine, England's first Christian missionary. The abbey was later seized by Henry VIII, who destroyed some of the buildings and converted others into a royal manor for his fourth wife, Anne of Cleves. Just opposite the Canterbury East train station, you **14** will see the **Dane John Mound,** originally part of the city defenses.

Dining and Lodging

£–££ ✕ **Alberry's Wine Bar.** This popular bistro makes a good place to sit and recharge your batteries. Easy to find (on the same street as the tourist office), Alberry's offers a wide international menu. All dishes are homemade, using fresh ingredients and local produce. Sample the goat's cheese salad and the chicken farcie or Kentish chicken and ham pie. ⊠ *38 St. Margaret St.,* ☎ *01227/452378. AE, MC, V. Closed Sun.*

£££ ✕🏨 **County.** This traditional English hotel was first licensed in the year of the Spanish Armada, 1588, and it still maintains certain links with the past—ask for a room with a four-poster bed. The bar is pleasantly traditional, and the formal **Sully's Restaurant** has a reputation as a gourmet's choice. The hotel offers special weekend rates. ⊠ *High St., CT1 2RX,* ☎ *01227/766266,* 🖷 *01227/451512. 73 rooms with bath. Restaurant (jacket and tie required on Saturday), bar, coffee shop. AE, DC, MC, V.*

££ 🏨 **Slatters.** Completely refurbished to present a defiantly modernistic aspect, this city-center hotel offers plenty of 20th-century comfort and fully equipped guest rooms. In fact the site has been occupied since Roman times, and a tiny section of Roman foundations can be seen in the cool *Argot* ground-floor restaurant. Elsewhere there are Tudor beams and a medieval wall. ⊠ *St. Margaret's St., CT1 2DR,* ☎ *01227/463271,* ℻ *01227/764117. 31 rooms, 28 with bath. Restaurant, bar. AE, DC, MC, V.*

£ 🏨 **Pointers.** This Georgian hotel is within easy walking distance of the cathedral and city center (straight out beyond Westgate). The O' Briens offer a warm and friendly welcome. ⊠ *1 London Rd., CT2 8LR,* ☎ *01227/456846,* ℻ *01227/452786. 12 rooms with bath or shower. Restaurant, bar, parking. AE, DC, MC, V. Closed Dec. 20–mid-Jan.*

The Arts

FESTIVALS AND THEATER

Canterbury has a two-week arts festival every October (☎ 01227/452853). The town features two theaters. The **Gulbenkian Theatre** (⊠ Giles La., ☎ 01227/769075), part of the University of Kent, mounts a full range of plays, particularly experimental works. The **Marlowe** (⊠ St. Margaret's St., ☎ 01227/787787), named after the Elizabethan playwright, who was born in Canterbury, is a venue for touring drama and opera companies.

Shopping

National Trust Shop (⊠ 24 Burgate, ☎ 01227/457120) stocks the National Trust line of household items—ideal for gifts.

Fordwich

🕒 *1½ mi east of Canterbury.*

Before beginning your wide, counterclockwise tour of the region around Canterbury, drive to the village of Fordwich. This was originally the river port for Canterbury, where the Caen stone quarried in Normandy and shipped across the Channel to be used in the construction of the cathedral was brought ashore. Don't miss England's smallest town hall, with stocks and ducking stool outside.

Harbledown

🕕 *1 mi west of Canterbury.*

Along the old Roman road to London (now A2) lies Harbledown— once a separate village, it is now part of Canterbury. The main sight here is the cluster of pretty almshouses, built in the 11th century to house the poor. Harbledown was customarily the spot from which pilgrims caught their first glimpse of Canterbury Cathedral.

Chilham

🕖 *5 mi southwest of Canterbury.*

The hilltop village of Chilham lies midway between Canterbury and Ashford on the A252 (off the A28). Energetic visitors will find this a good place from which to walk the last few miles of the traditional Pilgrim's Way back to Canterbury. The Chilham village square is filled with textbook examples of English rural architecture. The church dates from the 14th century. Nearby, **Chilham Castle** has 25 acres of gardens landscaped by Capability Brown; unfortunately, the castle and the grounds are not open to the public.

Dining

£ ✕ **White Horse.** A 16th-century inn nestled in the shadow of Chilham's church, the White Horse offers a pleasant beer garden and wholesome lunchtime and evening meals; there's a log fire in winter. ⊠ *The Square,* ☎ *01227/730355. MC, V. No dinner Tues.*

Faversham

⑱ *9 mi west of Canterbury, 11 mi northwest of Chilham.*

In Roman times, Faversham was a thriving seaport. Today the port is hidden from sight, and you could pass through this pretty market town without knowing it was there, but Faversham is a must for those in search of Ye Quaint Olde Englande: the town center, with its Tudor houses grouped around the 1574 guild hall and covered market, looks like a perfect stage set.

Dining and Lodging

£££ ✕ **Read's.** The glorious food in this restaurant just outside Faversham,
★ mainly Modern British in character, is magnificent, the work of chef-proprietor David Pitchford. Presented in elegant surroundings, his cuisine tempts the serious eater with its audacious spin on old favorites. The regularly changing menu features a selection of prix-fixe meals, for instance, sautéed herring roes with parsley butter or noisettes of Romney Marsh lamb. The wine list is extensive, containing some unusual bottles. This is an excellent spot for lunch, when there's a set-price menu from £17.50. There is a 3-course evening meal weeknights for £21. ✉ *Painters Forstal (2¼ mi southwest of Faversham off A2),* ☎ *01795/ 535344. AE, DC, MC, V. Closed Sun., Mon. and last 2 wks in Aug.*

£ ✕ **Sun Inn.** The flagship of the Shepherde Neame Brewery chain, established in Faversham in the 17th century, this pub is even older, dating back to the 16th century. The inn follows the local tradition of hanging up hops in September; they are not only decorative, but also add a distinctive fragrance. ✉ *West St.,* ☎ *01795/535098. MC, V. No dinner.*

£ ✕🏠 **White Horse Inn.** Just outside Faversham on the old London-to-Dover
★ road (now A2), this 15th-century coaching inn retains much of its traditional character, although it has been fully and comfortably modernized. There's a friendly bar and an excellent restaurant, with daily specials supplementing an à la carte menu. The back rooms are the quietest. ✉ *The Street, Boughton ME13 9AX,* ☎ *01227/751343,* 𝔽𝔸𝕏 *01227/751090. 15 rooms with bath or shower. Restaurant, bar. AE, MC, V.*

En Route From Faversham you can take A299 north to the seaside towns of **Whitstable, Herne Bay, Margate, Broadstairs,** and **Ramsgate**—long the playground of vacationing Londoners. Charles Dickens wrote glowingly of the bracing freshness of Broadstairs, where he spent many summers (1837–1851). One of his favorite abodes here was Bleak House (open Easter–November), where he wrote much of *David Copperfield* and drafted *Bleak House.* The **Dickens House Museum** (open Easter–mid-Oct.) was the setting Dickens imagined as the home of Betsy Trotwood, David Copperfield's aunt. Each year in June a Dickens Festival is held in this town, with local people donning Dickensian dress. Alternatively, take A2 through Canterbury to pick up A257 for the ancient **Cinque Ports** (pronounced sink ports), a confederacy of ports along the southeast coast whose heyday lasted from the 12th to the 14th century. These towns are rich in history and atmosphere and are generally less crowded than the resorts of Kent's northeast coast. The ports, originally five in number (hence *cinque,* from the Norman French), were Sandwich, Dover, Hythe, Romney, and Hastings.

Sandwich

⑲ *12 mi east of Canterbury, 8 mi south of Ramsgate.*

In Saxon times Sandwich, the first of the Cinque Ports, stood in a sheltered bay, and in the Middle Ages it prospered and became England's most important naval base. From 1500 the port began to silt up, however, and the town is now 2 mi inland. The 16th-century checkerboard barbican (gatehouse) by the toll bridge is one of many medieval and Tudor buildings.

Deal

20 *8 mi northeast of Dover, 7 mi south of Sandwich.*

The large seaside town of Deal is famous in history books as the place where Caesar's legions landed in 55 BC, and it was from here that William Penn set sail in 1682 on his first journey to America. **Deal Castle,** erected in 1540 and intricately built to the shape of a Tudor rose, is the largest of the coastal defenses built by Henry VIII. Its gloomy passages and unrelentingly austere walls are surrounded by a moat. The castle museum offers a range of exhibits of prehistoric, Roman, and Saxon Britain. ⊠ *Victoria Rd.,* ☎ *01304/372762.* ⊡ *£2.80.* ☉ *Apr.–Oct., daily 10–6 or dusk; Nov.–Mar., Wed.–Sun. 10–4.*

Walmer Castle

21 *7 mi northeast of Dover, 1 mi south of Deal.*

Walmer Castle, one of Henry VIII's fortifications, was converted in 1730 into the official residence of the Lord Warden of the Cinque Ports, and it now has the atmosphere of a cozy country house. Among the famous Lord Wardens were the Duke of Wellington, hero of the Battle of Waterloo, who lived here from 1829 until his death here in 1852 (there's a small museum of Wellington memorabilia), and Sir Winston Churchill. The present Lord Warden is the Queen Mother, though she rarely stays here. Her drawing and dining rooms are open to the public. After you have seen the castle chambers, take a stroll in the gardens. The moat has been converted to a grassy walk flanked by flower beds. ☎ *01304/364288.* ⊡ *£4.* ☉ *Apr.–Oct., daily 10–6 or dusk; Nov.–Mar., Wed.–Sun. 10–4.*

Dover

22 *78 mi east of London, 7 mi south of Walmer Castle on A258.*

One of the busiest passenger ports in the world, Dover has for centuries been Britain's gateway to Europe. Many visitors find the town disappointing; the savage bombardments of World War II and the shortsightedness of postwar developers have left their scars on the city center. Roman legacies include a **lighthouse** and **The Painted House,** believed to have been a hotel.

★ **Dover Castle,** towering high above the chalk ramparts of the famous White Cliffs, is a spectacular sight and well worth a visit. It was one of the mightiest medieval castles in Western Europe. Most of the castle dates back to Norman times. It was begun by Henry II in 1181 but incorporates additions from almost every succeeding century. Visitors can explore the Secret Wartime Tunnels, a medieval underground tunnel system that was used as a World War II command center. ⊠ *Castle Rd.,* ☎ *01304/211067.* ⊡ *£6.60.* ☉ *Apr.–Sept., daily 10–6 or dusk; Oct.–Mar., daily 10–4.*

In the town hall, visit the 13th-century **Maison Dieu Hall,** founded in 1203 as a hostel for pilgrims traveling to Canterbury. The hall houses a collection of flags and armor, while the stained-glass windows tell the story of Dover through the ages. Below the hall are the Victorian cells of the Old Town Gaol. ⊠ *Biggin St.,* ☎ *01304/201200.* ⊡ *Free.* ☉ *Hall Mon.–Sat., 9–4:30, Sun. 2–4:30 (except when closed for functions). Gaol July–Sept., Tues.–Sat., Oct.–June, Wed.–Sat. 10–4:30, Sun. 2–4:30.*

Lodging

£　🏠 **Number One.** This is a popular guest house and a great bargain. A corner terrace home built at the beginning of the 19th century, it is cozy and friendly, decorated with mural wallpapers and porcelain collections. The walled garden offers a view of the castle, and the owners are happy to give advice on local sightseeing. ⊠ *1 Castle St., CT16 1QH,* ☎ *01304/202007. 6 rooms with shower.No credit cards.*

ALONG THE SOUTH COAST: RYE TO GLYNDEBOURNE

From Dover, the coast road winds west through Folkestone, genteel resort, small port, and Channel Tunnel terminal, across Romney Marsh—reclaimed from the sea and famous for its sheep and, at one time, its ruthless smugglers—to the delightful town of Rye. The region along the coast is noted for pretty Winchelsea, the history-rich sites of Hastings and Herstmonceux, and the famous Glyndebourne Opera House festival, based outside Lewes, a town celebrated for its architectural heritage. The area is partly serviced by one of the three steam railroads in the Southeast: the Romney, Hythe, and Dymchurch Railway, a main-line service that features locomotives one-third normal size. In addition to delighting tourists, it is regularly used by some lucky children to travel to school.

Rye

★　❷❸　*68 mi southeast of London, 34 mi southwest of Dover.*

With cobbled streets and timbered dwellings, Rye remains an artist's dream, dotted with such historic buildings as the Mermaid Inn (☞ *below*), and the secret places that made it a smuggler's strategic retreat. In fact, today the former port of Rye, now a honey pot for visitors, lies nearly 2 mi inland. A topographical map of Romney Marsh, showing the changes in sea level, is displayed in **Rye Castle Museum,** housed in a stone tower built as part of the town's fortifications in 1249 and later used as a prison. In 1999, the museum will expand into a nearby site. ⊠ *Gungarden,* ☎ *01797/226728.* 🎫 *£1.50.* ☉ *Apr.–Oct., daily 10:30–5:30; Nov.–Mar., weekends 11:30–3:30.*

Sharing the Rye Heritage Centre with the tourist information office, the **Rye Town Model** is a huge scale model of the town incorporating an imaginative and historic son et lumière show. The building is at the bottom of Mermaid Street on the site of the ancient port. ⊠ *Strand Quay,* ☎ *01797/226696.* 🎫 *£2.* ☉ *Mid-Mar.–Oct., daily 9–5:30, Nov.–mid-Mar., weekdays 10–3, weekends 10–4.*

Lamb House, an early Georgian structure, has been home to several well-known writers. The most famous was American Henry James, who lived here from 1898 to 1916; a later resident was E. F. Benson, author of the *Lucia* novels and one-time mayor of Rye. The ground-floor rooms contain some of James's furniture and personal belongings. There is also a pretty walled garden. ⊠ *West St.,* ☎ *01892/890651.* 🎫 *£2.50.* ☉ *Apr.–Oct., Wed. and Sat. 2–6; last admission 5:30.*

A tour of the wonderfully nostalgic **Rye Treasury of Mechanical Music** treats you to tunes from music boxes and barrel organs to a 1920s dance organ. ⊠ *20 Cinque Ports St.,* ☎ *01797/223345.* 🎫 *£3.* ☉ *Daily 10–5.*

Dining and Lodging

£–££ ✕ **Landgate Bistro.** Although definitely a bistro, with all the usual
★ liveliness and bustle, the Landgate is serious about its food. Try the
scallops and brill in an orange and vermouth sauce—all the local fish
is excellent—and the walnut and treacle tart. Housed in an old, small
building, in keeping with Rye's atmosphere, the restaurant attracts a
steady local clientele. A fixed-price menu is available Tuesday through
Thursday. ⊠ *5–6 Landgate,* ☎ *01797/222829. AE, DC, MC, V.
Closed Sun., Mon. and 2 wks at Christmas. No lunch.*

£££ ✕🔟 **The Mermaid.** This classic old inn has served this ancient town
for nearly six centuries; it was once the headquarters of one of the notorious smuggling gangs that ruled Romney Marsh. Sloping, creaky
floors, oak beams, low ceilings, and a huge open hearth in the bar testify to its age, and there are five four-poster beds. Even if you're not
staying at the inn, the main restaurant allows diners to drink in the
period decor while enjoying an extensive menu; there is an adjacent
bar serving pub meals and, in the summer, the Tudor Tearoom offers
a lovely cuppa. Every detail in this inn will make the seeker of atmosphere happy. But be warned, the Mermaid is *very* popular and you
will need to book well ahead. ⊠ *Mermaid St., TN31 7EY,* ☎ *01797/
223065,* 𝔽𝔸𝕏 *01797/225069. 28 rooms with bath. Restaurant, bar. AE,
DC, MC, V.*

££ 🔟 **Jeake's House.** The cozy bedrooms in this lovely old house (1689),
on the same cobblestone street as the Mermaid, are furnished with antiques; many of the rooms have views over the town. Breakfast is served
in a former chapel. Like all accommodations in Rye, Jeake's House
needs to be booked well in advance. ⊠ *Mermaid St., TN31 7ET,* ☎ *01797/
222828,* 𝔽𝔸𝕏 *01797/222623. 12 rooms, 10 with bath or shower. MC, V.*

Winchelsea

㉔ *71 mi southeast of London, 2 mi southwest of Rye.*

Like Rye, Winchelsea is perched atop its own small hill amid farmland
and tiny villages. One of the prettiest places to visit in the region, it
has many attractive houses, some weatherboarded, and a splendid
church built in the 14th century with Caen stone from Normandy. The
town was built on a grid system devised in 1283, after the sea destroyed
an earlier settlement at the foot of the hill, then receded, leaving the
town high and dry. Some of the original town gates still stand.

Hastings

㉕ *68 mi southeast of London, 9 mi southwest of Winchelsea.*

Hastings, famous for the Norman invasion of 1066, is now a large,
slightly run-down seaside resort. A visit to the old town provides an
interesting overview of 900 years of English maritime history. Along
the beach, the tall wooden **Net Shops,** called "deezes," unique to the
town, are still used for drying local fishermen's nets. And in the town
hall you'll find the 250-ft **Hastings Embroidery,** made in 1966 to mark
the 900th anniversary of the battle. It depicts legends and great moments from British history. ⊠ *Queen's Rd.,* ☎ *01424/781066.* 🎫 *£1.50.
☉ Oct.–Apr., weekdays 11:30–3 (last admission); May–Sept., weekdays 10–4:30 (last admission).*

Take the West Hill Cliff Railway from George Street precinct to Norman **Hastings Castle,** built by William the Conqueror in 1069. All that
remains are fragments of the fortifications, some ancient walls, and a
number of gloomy dungeons. Nevertheless, it is worth a visit for the
excellent view it provides of the chalky cliffs, the coast, and the town

below. The "1066 Story" tells the story of the Norman invasion using audiovisual technology, and "A Smuggler's Adventure" takes you on a trip through a labyrinth of caves and passages. ⊠ *West Hill,* ☎ *01424/ 781122.* ⊡ *£2.80.* ☉ *Easter–Sept., daily 10–5 (5:30 during school holidays); Oct.–Easter, daily 10:30–4.*

Dining and Lodging

£££ ✕ **Rösers.** This restaurant takes food very seriously. It stands on the seafront and has dark walls with booths for dining. Chef-proprietor Röser is German, though his cuisine is mainly French. Try the local game in season, the pike soufflé, and the prize-winning caramelized lime cream in bitter orange sauce. The wine list is terrific. ⊠ *64 Eversfield Pl., St. Leonards,* ☎ *01424/712218. AE, DC, MC, V. Closed Sun., Mon., last 2 wks June, and 1st 2 wks Jan. No lunch Sat.*

£   ⊞ **Eagle House.** This guest house, in a large detached Victorian building, is surrounded by its own attractive garden. Located in St. Leonards, the western section of Hastings, the lodging is within easy reach of the town center. The rooms are spacious and comfortable, and the dining room uses fresh produce from local farms. ⊠ *12 Pevensey Rd., St. Leonards TN38 0JZ,* ☎ *01424/430535,* ⅨⅩ *01424/437771. 19 rooms with bath. Restaurant. AE, DC, MC, V.*

Battle

㉖ *61 mi southeast of London, 7 mi northwest of Hastings.*

Battle is the actual site of the crucial 1066 Battle of Hastings. The ruins of **Battle Abbey,** the great Benedictine abbey William erected after his victory, are worth the trip. The high altar stood on the spot where Harold II was killed, now marked by a memorial stone. The abbey was destroyed in 1539 during Henry VIII's destructive binge, but you can take the mile-long Battlefield Walk round the edge of the battlefield and see the remains of many of the domestic buildings. The **Abbot's House** (closed to the public) is now a girls' school. ⊠ *High St.,* ☎ *01424/ 773792.* ⊡ *£3.50.* ☉ *Easter–Oct., daily 10–6 or dusk; Nov.–Easter, daily 10–4. Closed Dec. 24–26.*

Dining and Lodging

££   ✕ **Orangery Restaurant.** In the Powder Mills Hotel, a Georgian country house just behind the abbey, the airy conservatory-style dining room makes a pleasant stop for lunch during a day of sightseeing. The food, especially the seafood, is surprisingly good; try the fish panache or the crab ravioli, with a homemade sorbet to follow. Set-price menus are £14.95 for lunch, £25 for dinner. Bar snacks are also available. ⊠ *Powdermill La.,* ☎ *01424/775511. AE, DC, MC, V.*

£££ ⊞ **Netherfield Place.** This is a spacious, quiet hotel, set in 30 acres of park and gardens. The large bedrooms are comfortably furnished, with plenty of cozy armchairs, and have well-equipped bathrooms (towels are especially thick). The paneled restaurant looks out at the gardens and features sensible fixed-price menus, as well as extensive table d'hôte ones. Try the salmon and sole terrine, the Sussex lamb, local venison, and the home-grown vegetables. ⊠ *Netherfield, TN33 9PP,* ☎ *01424/774455,* ⅨⅩ *01424/774024. 14 rooms with bath. Restaurant, tennis court, croquet. AE, DC, MC, V.*

Herstmonceux

★ **㉗** *61 mi southeast of London, 11 mi southwest of Battle.*

Back in the Edwardian era, Herstmonceux was famous the world over as the quintessential image of the romantic English castle—surrounded by a gigantic moat, built of rose-color brick and limestone crenellations, it was completely covered by ivy and brambles and looked like the abode of Sleeping Beauty. In 1911 Herstmonceax woke up, thanks to rich connoisseurs who so completely renovated the structure the magic nearly evaporated. That noted, Herstmonceux is still a fabled name for castle-lovers (the house, however, is of the fortified square-shaped variety, not the multi-turreted species). Sir Roger Fiennes, ancestor of actor Ralph Fiennes, originally built it in 1444, with other families and various ghosts taking up residence since. Now an International Study Centre owned by Queen's University Canada, the castle is open for guided tours only. No luxe salons, but the interior still has some fine Elizabethan-era staircases and ceilings. ⊠ *Herstmonceaux, Hailsham, East Sussex BN27 1RP,* ☎ *01323/83444.* ⊙ *Castle, Easter–Oct., guided tours only, Sun.–Fri. 1:30, 3 PM, Sat. 11 AM; grounds, Easter–Oct, 10–6 (last entry at 5).*

Dining

££ ✕ **The Sundial.** This old Sussex farmhouse is the setting for a popular
★ restaurant, which chef Giuseppe Bertoli and his French wife, Laurette, have run since 1966. The menu is extensive, with some imaginative combinations. The fish dishes are particularly successful and the vegetables fresh and expertly cooked. The Dover sole flavored with thyme is recommended. ⊠ *Gardner St., Herstmonceux,* ☎ *01323/832217. AE, DC, MC, V. Closed Mon., 3 wks in Jan., and 3 wks in Aug. No dinner Sun.*

Wilmington

28 *7 mi west of Pevensey on A27.*

Passing through the pretty village of Wilmington, you will have no trouble identifying its most famous landmark. High on the downs to the south of the village a giant white figure, 226 ft tall, known as the **Long Man of Wilmington,** is carved into the chalk; he has a club in both hands. His age is a subject of great debate, but it is thought he might have originated in Roman times.

☾ One and a half miles west of Wilmington on the A27, **Drusilla's Park** is a small zoo, with gardens, a miniature railroad and an adventure playground. ⊠ *Alfriston, East Sussex,* ☎ *01323/870656.* ⊡ *Summer £5.95, winter £4.50.* ⊙ *Summer daily 10–6, winter daily 10–4.*

Lewes

★ **29** *54 mi south of London, 18 mi west of Pevensey, 8 mi northeast of Brighton.*

The town nearest to the celebrated Glyndebourne Opera House, Lewes is a place so rich in architectural history that the Council for British Archaeology has named it one of the 50 most important English towns. Lewes is a place to walk in rather than drive in, not least so that the variety of building styles and materials (flint, stone, brick, tile) can be appreciated and the secret lanes (called twittens) behind the castle with their huge beeches can be enjoyed. Here and there you'll find exceptional antiques shops and secondhand-book dealers. **High Street** is lined with old buildings of all ages, styles and descriptions, including a timber-frame house once occupied by Thomas Paine, author of *Rights of Man.*

High above the valley of the River Ouse stand the majestic ruins of **Lewes Castle,** begun in 1100. For a panoramic view of the surrounding region, climb the keep. Inside the castle is the **Living History Centre,** and at Barbican House you can see the Town Model, a re-creation

of Lewes in the 19th century. ⊠ *169 High St.,* ☎ *01273/486290.* ⊠
£3.25. ⊘ *Mon.–Sat. 10–5:30, Sun. 11–5:30.*

Lewes is one of the few towns left in England that still celebrates in
high style Guy Fawkes Night (November 5), the anniversary of Fawkes's
attempt to blow up the Houses of Parliament in 1605. It is rather like
an autumnal Mardi Gras, with costumed processions and flaming tar
barrels rolled down the High Street. A famous painting of the procession hangs in the **Anne of Cleves Museum** (walk down steep, cobbled
Keere Street, past lovely Grange Gardens, to Southover High Street).
The fragile building also houses a notable collection of Sussex ironwork. ⊠ *52 Southover High St.,* ☎ *01273/474610.* ⊠ *£2.20.* ⊘
*Mar.–Nov., Mon.–Sat. 10–5, Sun. 12–5; Dec.–Feb., Tues., Thurs.,
Sat. 10–5.*

Dining and Lodging

£   ✕ **Tortellini.** This is a simple, stylish restaurant serving authentic Italian dishes. In the evening, it usually winds up bustling and crowded.
⊠ *197 High St.,* ☎ *01273/487766. AE, MC, V. Closed Sun.*

£££–££££   ✕⊞ **Horsted Place.** Just a few minutes' drive from Glyndebourne, and
★   6 mi north of Lewes, this very special hotel once belonged to Prince Philip's
treasurer and has frequently accommodated members of the Royal
Family. It is beautifully furnished and has such interesting features as
a magnificent Victorian staircase and a Gothic library with a secret door
that leads to a hidden courtyard. The dining room—also Gothic—offers superb haute cuisine (try the roasted guinea fowl). Three of the guest
rooms are in detached cottages on the golf course. ⊠ *Little Horsted
(2½ mi from Uckfield, 6 mi north of Lewes), TN22 5TS,* ☎ *01825/
750581,* ⅎ⅍ *01825/750459. 20 rooms with bath. Restaurant, indoor
pool, golf privileges, tennis court, croquet. AE, DC, MC, V.*

££–£££   ⊞ **Shelleys.** An elegant 17th-century building in this town of attractive architecture, the hotel is on the hilly main road and is a traditional
overnight stop for visitors to the opera at Glyndebourne. It is furnished
with antiques and the garden is a constant joy. The hotel maintains a
reputation for old-fashioned, friendly service. Have lunch in either the
bar or the more formal dining room. ⊠ *High St., BN7 1XS,* ☎ *01273/
472361,* ⅎ⅍ *01273/483152. 19 rooms with bath. Restaurant, bar. AE,
DC, MC, V.*

The Arts

Glyndebourne Opera House (⊠ Glyndebourne, near Lewes, East Sussex, ☎ 01273/812321) is one of the world's leading opera houses. Nestled beneath the Downs, Glyndebourne combines first-class productions,
in a state-of-the-art auditorium, with a beautiful setting. Seats are *very*
expensive (£37–£118) and often difficult to acquire, but they're worth
every cent to aficionados, some of whom wear formal evening dress
and bring a hamper for a picnic in the superb gardens during the long
dinner interval. The main season generally runs from the end of May
to the end of August. The Glyndebourne Touring Company performs
here in October, when seats are cheaper and slightly easier to obtain
(but few bother to picnic or wear their Bruce Oldfields or Catherine
Walkers then).

To head for the nearest city on leaving Lewes, continue west on A27
for 8 mi until you reach Brighton.

BRIGHTON TO DORKING

The self-proclaimed belle of the coast, Brighton is an upbeat, friendly
old-new sprawl. It started as a tiny fishing village called Brighthelmstone, with no claim to fame until a certain Dr. Russell sent his patients

there for its dry, bracing, crystal-clear air. The Prince Regent, later George IV, went, discovered sea-bathing, and for nearly 200 years, the place prospered—deservedly so, for few British resorts have ever catered so well as Brighton to its appreciative patronage from London and the world over. Today, the city is a lively mixture of carnival and culture, and it contains one of the must-sees of Britain—the gorgeous and fantastic palace known as the Royal Pavilion. Built mainly by John Nash in a mock Oriental manner, with domes and pinnacles abounding, the Royal Pavilion has never failed to shock and delight in equal measure. After taking in this Regency-era wonder—and after the children have had their fill of Brighton's amusement parks—the road ahead beckons with other great residences, including Arundel Castle, Petworth House, and Polesden Lacey. Along the way, you'll discover the largest Roman villa in Britain, the bustling city of Guildford, and Chichester, whose cathedral, a poem in stone, should captivate anyone.

Brighton

30 *54 mi south of London, 9 mi southwest of Lewes.*

Ever since the Prince Regent first visited in 1783, Brighton has been England's most exciting seaside city, and, today, it's as vibrant, eccentric, and cosmopolitan as ever. With its rich cultural mix—Regency architecture, pleasure pier, specialist shops, pavement cafés, lively arts and, of course, the exotic Royal Pavilion—Brighton (with its partner Hove) is a truly extraordinary city by the sea. In decades gone by, the city became known for its tarnished allure, its faded glamour. Happily, a young, bustling spirit has given a face-lift to this ever-popular destination.

Brighton was mentioned in the *Domesday Book* as Brighthelmstone in 1086, when it paid the annual rent of 4,000 herrings to the lord of the manor; it changed its name in the 18th century. The town owes its modern fame and fortune to the supposed healing attributes of seawater. In 1750 physician Richard Russell published a book recommending seawater treatment for glandular diseases. The fashionable world flocked to Brighton to take Dr. Russell's "cure," and sea-bathing became a popular pastime.

The next windfall for the town was the arrival of the Prince of Wales (later George IV), who acted as Prince Regent during the madness of his father, George III. "Prinny," as he was called, created the Royal Pavilion, an extraordinary pleasure palace that attracted London society. The influx of visitors triggered a wave of villa building. Fortunately this was one of the most creative periods in the history of English architecture, and the elegant terraces of Regency houses are today among the town's greatest attractions. The coming of the railroad set the seal on Brighton's popularity: one of the most luxurious trains in the country, the Pullman *Brighton Belle,* brought Londoners to the coast within an hour. They expected to find the same comforts and recreations they had in London and, as they were prepared to pay for them, Brighton obliged. This helps to explain the town's remarkable range of restaurants, hotels, and pubs. Horse racing was—and still is—another strong attraction.

Although fast rail service to London has made Brighton an important base for commuters, the town has unashamedly set itself out to be a pleasure resort. In the 1840s it featured the very first example of that peculiarly British institution, the amusement pier. The restored **Palace Pier** follows the great tradition. The original mechanical amusements, including the celebrated flip-card device, "What the Butler Saw," are now protected as exhibits in the town museum, but you can still admire the pier's handsome ironwork. As for the damaged West Pier, an extensive renovation program is being planned, which, by the millennium, will restore it to its former glory, complete with theater and restaurants.

32 The heart of Brighton is the **Steine** (pronounced steen), the large open area close to the seafront. This was a river mouth until the Prince of Wales had it drained in 1793. One of the houses here was the home of Mrs. Maria Fitzherbert, later the prince's wife. The most remarkable building on the Steine, perhaps in all Britain, is unquestionably

★ **33** the **Royal Pavilion,** the Prince of Wales's extravagant fairy-tale palace. First planned as a simple seaside villa and built in the fashionable classical style of 1787, the Pavilion was rebuilt between 1815 and 1822 for the Prince Regent, who favored an exotic, eastern design with Chinese interiors. When Queen Victoria came to the throne in 1837, she so disapproved of the palace that she stripped it of its furniture and planned to demolish it. Fortunately, Brighton Council bought it from her, and it is now lovingly preserved and recognized as unique in all Europe. After a lengthy process of restoration, the Pavilion looks much as it did in its Regency heyday. The interior is filled with quantities of period furniture and ornaments, some given or lent by the present Royal Family. The two great set pieces are the **Music Room,** styled in the form of an Oriental pavilion, and the **Banqueting Room,** with its enormous flying-dragon "gasolier," or gaslight chandelier, a revolutionary new invention in the early 19th century. Also remarkable are the kitchens, whose ceilings are supported by extraordinary palm-tree columns. The upstairs bedrooms contain a selection of cruel caricatures of the Prince Regent, most produced during his lifetime, and illustrations of the Pavilion at various stages of its construction. The gardens, too, have been restored to Regency splendor, following John Nash's design of 1826. For an elegant time-out, repair to one of the Pavilion's upstairs bedrooms, where a tearoom offers a variety of snacks and light meals. ✉ *Old Steine,* ☎ *01273/290900.* ⊡ *£4.50.* ◷ *Oct.–May, daily 10–5 (last admission); June–Sept., daily 10–6 (last admission).*

34 The grounds of the Royal Pavilion contain the **Brighton Museum and Art Gallery,** whose buildings were designed as a stable block for the prince's horses. The museum has especially interesting Art Nouveau and Art Deco collections. Look out for Salvador Dali's famous sofa in the shape of Mae West's lips. ✉ *Church St.,* ☎ *01273/290900.* ⊡ *Free.* ◷ *Mon., Tues., and Thurs.–Sat. 10–5, Sun. 2–5.*

35 Just west of the Old Steine lies the **Lanes,** a maze of alleys and passageways that was once home to legions of fishermen and their families and is now filled with restaurants, boutiques, and antiques shops. Vehicular traffic is barred from the area, and visitors may wander at will. The heart of the Lanes is Market Street and Square, lined with fish and seafood restaurants.

36 **Volk's Electric Railway,** built by inventor Magnus Volk in 1883, was the first public electric railroad in Britain; you might like to take the 1¼-mi trip along Marine Parade.

37 In Hove, the **British Engineerium** is a beautifully restored Victorian pumping station housing hundreds of steam engines, electric motors, motorcycles, and interactive children's exhibits. Note that boilers are only lit and engines set in full steam on the first Sunday of the month, and on major public holidays. ✉ *Nevill Road, Hove,* ☎ *01273/ 559583.* ⊡ *£3.50.* ◷ *Daily 10–5.*

38 North of the town center, on the main London road, is **Preston Manor.** This beautifully preserved residence of the Stanford family, with its col-

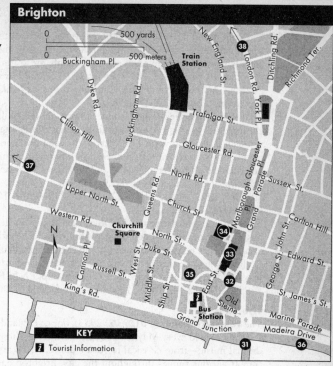

lection of paintings, silver, porcelain, and furniture, evokes the opulence of Edwardian times. You can also tour the servants' quarters and wander through the extensive grounds. ⊠ *Preston Park,* ☎ *01273/ 290900.* ⬚ *£2.95.* ☉ *Mon. 1–5, Tues.–Sat. 10–5, Sun. 2–5.*

Dining and Lodging

£–££ ✕ **Donatello.** This popular Italian restaurant in the Lanes has a brick wall and pine decor, bright with plants and checked cloths. The food is standard Italian, with an emphasis on pizzas. Donatello is a brother eatery to Pinocchio's, close to the Theatre Royal. ⊠ *3 Brighton Pl.,* ☎ *01273/775477. AE, DC, MC, V.*

£ ✕ **English's Oyster Bar.** Buried in the Lanes, this is one of the few old-
★ fashioned seafood havens left in England. It has been a restaurant for more than 200 years and a family business for more than 50. You can eat succulent oysters and other seafood dishes at the counter or have a table in the restaurant section. It's keenly priced and ideal for a relaxing lunch after antiques hunting. ⊠ *29–31 East St.,* ☎ *01273/327980. AE, DC, MC, V.*

££££ ✕▥ **Brighton Thistle Hotel.** This hotel, a little east of the Grand, is built around a huge atrium, offering sea views, and is very popular with conference delegates. It's air-conditioned, smoothly designed, and offers top facilities. The restaurant, **La Noblesse,** has delicious food, with not-too-expensive fixed menus. ⊠ *King's Rd., BN1 2GS,* ☎ *01273/206700,* ℻ *01273/820692. 204 rooms with bath. Restaurant, indoor pool, sauna, exercise room. AE, DC, MC, V.*

££–£££ ✕▥ **Granville Hotel.** On hotel row, to the west of the Grand, this hotel has been converted from three former grand residences facing the sea. It is moderate in size, so service can be attentive. The bedrooms are all very comfortable; several are quite large, six have four-poster beds (two of them antique), three include Jacuzzis, and one has a water bed. The restaurant caters especially to vegetarians. ⊠ *124 King's Rd., BN1 2FA,*

☎ 01273/326302, ⨳ 01273/728294. *23 rooms with bath. Restaurant, bar, coffee shop. AE, DC, MC, V.*

££££   🖭 **Grand Hotel.** This classic old hotel overlooks the seafront. The refurbished decor, especially in the public rooms, is of the spectacular chandelier-and-marble variety; the bedrooms are traditionally comfortable. ✉ *King's Rd., BN1 2FW,* ☎ *01273/321188,* ⨳ *01273/202694. 200 rooms with bath. Restaurant, indoor pool, sauna, exercise room, parking. AE, DC, MC, V.*

££   🖭 **The Dove.** Washes of light, modern prints on the walls, and an uncluttered feel are the keynotes of this Regency house. There is one luxuriously large room with a balcony and a sea view, and three others have a sideways sea view from their bow windows. Evening meals can be ordered by prior arrangement, and breakfasts are generous. There's no elevator, and the stairs to the attic rooms are steep. ✉ *18 Regency Sq., BN1 2FG,* ☎ *01273/779222,* ⨳ *01273/746912. 10 rooms with bath. AE, DC, MC, V.*

££   🖭 **Topps.** An alternative to The Dove, next door, this delightful hotel has attractive and well-equipped rooms with lush bathrooms. The atmosphere is relaxed and friendly, and the owners, Paul and Pauline Collins (remember her as the maid in *Upstairs, Downstairs?*), are always ready with useful advice. ✉ *17 Regency Sq., BN1 2FG,* ☎ *01273/729334,* ⨳ *01273/203679. 15 rooms with bath. AE, DC, MC, V.*

The Arts

The **Brighton Festival** (☎ 01273/292953), one of England's biggest arts festivals, is held every May. Over 600 events in just three weeks cover drama, music—from classical to rock—dance, visual arts, and literature at various venues throughout the city. Brighton has several theaters. **The Dome** (☎ 01273/709709), beside the Pavilion, was converted into an auditorium from the Prince Regent's stables in the 1930s. It stages pantomime, and classical and pop concerts. The **Theatre Royal** (✉ New Rd., ☎ 01273/328488), close to the Pavilion, is a very attractive Regency building with a period gem of an auditorium. It is a favorite venue for shows either on their way to or fresh from London's West End. The **Gardner Arts Centre** (☎ 01273/685861), on the campus of Sussex University, a few miles northeast of town at Falmer, presents plays, concerts, and cabaret.

Shopping

The main shopping area to head for is **The Lanes,** especially for antiques or jewelry. It also has clothing boutiques, coffee shops, and pubs. Across North Street from the Lanes lies the **North Laine,** a network of narrow streets full of weird and wonderful little stores, less glossy than those in the Lanes, but fun, funky, and exotic. The **Pavilion Shop** (✉ 4–5 Pavilion Bldgs., ☎ 01273/290900) next door to the Royal Pavilion not only carries well-designed souvenirs of Regency Brighton, but has high-quality fabrics, wallpapers, and ceramics based on material in the Pavilion itself. **Holleyman and Treacher** (✉ 21A Duke St., at the western edge of the Lanes, ☎ 01273/328007) is a book collector's dream, with a wealth of books on myriad subjects and a large stock of antique prints at all prices. **Betjeman & Barton** (✉ 10 Dukes La., ☎ 01273/329402) sells a variety of teas and teapots, with tea tastings to help you decide what to buy.

Arundel

39   *60 mi south of London, 23 mi west of Brighton.*

The little hilltop town of Arundel is dominated by the great 11th-century castle, the much-restored home of the dukes of Norfolk for more than 700 years, and an imposing **Roman Catholic cathedral**—the duke is Britain's leading Catholic peer.

The ceremonial entrance to **Arundel Castle** is at the top of High Street, but visitors enter at the bottom, close to the parking lot. The keep, rising from its conical mound, is as old as the original castle, while the barbican (gatehouse) and the Barons' Hall date from the 13th century. The interior of the castle was reconstructed in the then-fashionable Gothic style of the 19th century. Among the treasures on view are the rosary beads and prayer book used by Mary, Queen of Scots, in preparing for her execution. The spacious grounds are open to the public and there is a restaurant. ⊠ *Mill Rd.,* ☎ *01903/883136.* 🖭 *£5.70.* ☼ *Apr.– Oct., Sun.–Fri. noon–5 (gates close at 4).*

Dining and Lodging

£–££　✗ **Black Rabbit.** A renovated 18th-century pub, the Black Rabbit is a find—and you must persevere along Mill Road in order *to* find it. Its location by the river, with views of the castle and the bird sanctuary, makes it ideal for a summer lunch. The bar food is good and reasonably priced, and there's a good seafood restaurant if you want something more substantial. ⊠ *Mill Rd.,* ☎ *01903/882828. AE, DC, MC, V.*

£££　🏨 **Norfolk Arms Hotel.** Like the cathedral and the castle in Arundel, this 18th-century coaching inn was also built by one of the dukes of Norfolk. The main body of the hotel is traditional in appearance, with lots of narrow passages and cozy little rooms. There is an annex with modern rooms in the courtyard block. ⊠ *22 High St., BN18 9AD,* ☎ *01903/882101,* 🗏X *01903/884275. 34 rooms with bath. Restaurant. AE, DC, MC, V.*

£££　🏨 **Stakis Arundel.** This converted Georgian house is set on 62 acres of parkland, just 3 mi west of Arundel off the A27 on B2132. It began as the home of an admiral and was a private school before its conversion into a hotel in 1974. The rooms have been carefully refurbished, with close attention to detail. ⊠ *Yapton La., Walberton BN18 0LS,* ☎ *01243/ 551215,* 🗏X *01243/552485. 139 rooms with bath. Restaurant, indoor-outdoor pool, sauna, 18-hole golf course, 2 tennis courts, croquet, exercise room, squash, helipad. AE, DC, MC, V.*

The Arts

The **Arundel Festival** (☎ 01903/883690) features drama productions and music in and around the castle grounds for a week in August/September.

Petworth House

★　⓮　*54 mi south of London, 12 mi northwest of Arundel.*

Petworth House, one of the National Trust's greatest treasures, stands in a particularly picturesque stretch of Sussex. Try to approach through the charming village of Wisborough Green. Petworth House was built between 1688 and 1696, and a 700-acre deer park was added later by the celebrated landscape architect Capability Brown. The house holds a famous collection of English paintings, including works by Thomas Gainsborough, Sir Joshua Reynolds, Sir Anthony Van Dyck, and J. M. W. Turner, the great proponent of Romanticism, who immortalized Petworth's sumptuous interiors in some of his most evocative watercolors. Other treasures include Greek and Roman sculpture and Grinling Gibbons wood carvings. Six rooms in the servants' quarters, including the old kitchen, are open to the public, and light lunches are served in the Servants Block. Don't forget to explore the town of Petworth itself, a jewel studded with old, narrow streets and timbered houses. ☎ *01798/ 342207.* 🖭 *£5.* ☼ *House: Apr.–Oct., Sat.–Wed. 1–5:30; last admission 4:30. Gardens: Apr.–Oct., daily 12–6. Park: daily 8–dusk.*

Dining

£–££ ✕ **Fleur de Sel.** Twelve miles northwest of Petworth, in the town of
★   Haslemere, this restaurant remains one of the top dining spots of the
      region. The menu focuses on provincial French dishes, the creations
      of Michel Perraud, who is also co-proprietor with his wife, Bernardette.
      In an interesting, varied dining space, the intimate ambience retains
      its cool yellow and blue decor. Regularly changing specialties have in-
      cluded Cornish crab cake, Gressingham duck, and calves' liver in cit-
      rus sauce. Reasonably priced set menus are available. ⊠ *23 Lower St.,
      Haslemere,* ☎ *01428/651462. AE, MC, V. Closed Mon. and 2 wks in
      Aug. No lunch Sat., no dinner Sun.*

Singleton

㊶ *59 mi south of London, 12 mi southwest of Petworth.*

Outside the secluded village of Singleton, the **Weald and Downland
Open Air Museum** gives sanctuary to endangered historical buildings.
Among the "rescued" structures are a cluster of medieval houses, a work-
ing water mill, a Tudor market hall, and an ancient blacksmith's shop.
The architectural styles on display span more than 400 years. ⊠ *Sin-
gleton,* ☎ *01243/811348.* 🎫 *£5.20.* ☯ *Mar.–Oct., daily 10:30–5; Nov.–
Feb., Wed. and weekends 10:30–4.*

Chichester

㊷ *66 mi southwest of London, 7 mi south of Singleton.*

The capital city of West Sussex, Chichester, was founded by the Romans on the low-lying plains between the wooded South Downs and
the sea. Though it features its own large cathedral and has all the trappings of a commercial city, Chichester is not much bigger than many
of the towns around it. The city walls and major streets follow the original Roman plan; the intersection of the four principal streets is marked
by a cross dated 1501. The Norman **cathedral,** near the corner of West
and South streets, also stands on Roman foundations. Inside, a glass
panel reveals Roman mosaics uncovered during restoration. Other
treasures include wonderful, moving Saxon limestone reliefs of *The Raising of Lazarus* and *Christ Arriving in Bethany,* both in the choir, and
some outstanding pieces of contemporary work, including a stained-
glass window by Marc Chagall, a colorful tapestry by John Piper, and
a painting by Graham Sutherland.

Today Chichester is mainly Georgian, with countless 18th-century
houses. One of the best is **Pallant House,** built in 1712 as a wine merchant's mansion. It was state-of-the-art for architecture then, with the
latest in complicated brickwork and superb wood carving. The rooms
have been faithfully restored and furnished with appropriate antiques
and porcelains. The building also showcases a small collection of
British art, as well as regularly changing exhibitions. ⊠ *9 North Pallant,* ☎ *01243/774557.* 🎫 *£2.80.* ☯ *Tues.–Sat. 10–5:15, Sun. 12.30–
5:15; last admission 4:45.*

Dining and Lodging

££–£££ ✕ **Comme Ça.** This attractively converted pub is about a five-minute
        walk across the park from the Festival Theatre, making it a very good
        spot for a meal before a performance. Bunches of dried hops, suspended
        from the ceiling, and antique children's toys decorate the dining room.
        The owner, Michel Navet, is French and his chef cooks authentic
        French dishes; simpler fare is served in the bar at much lower prices.
        ⊠ *67 Broyle Rd.,* ☎ *01243/788724,. AE, MC, V. Closed Mon. No
        dinner Sun.*

£ ✕ **Shepherds.** This relaxed restaurant and tearoom is ideal for a morning coffee, or a light lunch, or a tea break while seeing Chichester. Most of its tables are in a modernized conservatory at the rear. There are six kinds of rarebit on the menu, including Hawaiian with pineapple, and oodles of fattening home-baked foods, as well as a renowned assortment of first-rate teas. Smoking is not permitted. ⊠ *35 Little London,* ☎ *01243/774761. No credit cards. Closed Sun. No dinner.*

££–£££ 🛏 **Ship Hotel.** Staying in this hotel is something of an architectural experience. Built in 1790, it was originally the home of Admiral Sir George Murray (one of Admiral Nelson's right-hand men). Outstanding features are the classic Adam staircase and colonnade. The hotel is gradually being restored to its 18th-century elegance. It is close to the Festival Theatre. ⊠ *North St., PO19 1NH,* ☎ *01243/778000,* FAX *01243/788000. 36 rooms with bath. Restaurant. AE, DC, MC, V.*

The Arts

The **Festival Theatre,** Chichester (☎ 01243/781312), presents classics and modern plays from May to September (and is a venue for touring companies the rest of the year). Built in 1962, it has an international reputation and can be the evening focus for a relaxed day out of London.

Fishbourne Roman Palace

43 *66 mi southwest of London, ½ mi west of Chichester.*

Fishbourne Roman Palace, about half a mile outside Chichester, is the largest and grandest Roman villa in Britain. Many of its 100 rooms are lavishly decorated with intricate mosaics and painted walls. Sophisticated bathing and heating systems remain, and the Roman garden, the only known example extant in northern Europe, is laid out in the style of the 1st century AD. ⊠ *Salthill Rd., Fishbourne,* ☎ *01243/ 785859.* ☞ *£4.* ◷ *Mar.–July and Sept.–Oct, daily 10–5; Aug., daily 10–6; Nov.–mid-Dec., daily 10–4; mid-Dec.–mid-Feb., Sun. 10–4; mid-Feb.–end Feb., daily 10–4.*

To continue on the northward circuit into Surrey, return to Chichester and take A286/A287/A3 to Guildford.

Guildford

44 *28 mi southwest of London, 35 mi north of Chichester.*

Guildford, the largest town in Surrey and the county's capital, is an important commuter town, but it has managed to retain a faint 18th-century air. No other English town can claim such a brilliant succession of royal visits, from Alfred the Great down to the present queen. The steep High Street is lined with gabled merchants' houses—now home to upscale fashion and household shops—and preserves a pleasant, provincial appearance. **The Royal Grammar School,** at the top end of Guildford's High Street, contains one of Britain's three surviving chained libraries (books were so precious during the Middle Ages, they were literally chained to prevent theft); this one dates from the 16th century. The school was founded in 1507. ⊠ *Upper High St.,* ☎ *01483/539880.* ◷ *By appointment only.*

On High Street, you'll find the **Hospital of the Blessed Trinity,** with its massive Tudor facade. It was founded in 1619 as almshouses (a function it still performs, as it is a senior-citizens' home) by George Abbot, Archbishop of Canterbury. Abbot, one of the translators of the King James Bible, was born in Guildford. ⊠ *High St.,* ☎ *01483/562670.* ◷ *Chapel and common room by appointment.*

All that remains of the entrance of the old castle, **Castle Arch**, still displays a slot for a portcullis. The building now contains the **Guildford Museum,** with interesting exhibits on local history and archeology, along with memorabilia of Charles Dodgson, better known, of course, as Lewis Carroll, the immortal author of *Alice in Wonderland.* Dodgson spent the last years of his life in a house on nearby Castle Hill, dying there with his sisters at his side; he was buried in The Mount Cemetery, up the hill on High Street. Beyond the arch lie the remains of the castle itself. ⊠ *Quarry St.,* ☎ *01483/444750.* ▨ *Free.* ☺ *Mon.–Sat. 11–5.*

Guildford Cathedral, looming on its hilltop across the River Wey, is only the second Anglican cathedral to be built on a new site since Henry VIII's Reformation of the 1500s. It was consecrated in 1961. The red-brick exterior is severely simple, while the interior, with its stone and plaster, looks bright and cool. The Refectory Restaurant is open for light refreshments from 9:30 AM to 4:30. ⊠ *Stag Hill,* ☎ *01483/ 565287.* ▨ *Donation welcomed.*

Dining and Lodging

£ ✕ **The Jolly Farmer.** This riverside pub offers a conservatory and terraced garden alongside the River Wey, a few minutes from the Yvonne Arnaud Theatre (just past the boatyard). ⊠ *Millbrook,* ☎ *01483/ 538779. AE, MC, V.*

£ ✕ **Rumwong.** The elegant waitresses at this Thai restaurant wear their
★   traditional long-skirted costumes, so at busy times the dining room looks like a swirling flower garden. On the incredibly long menu, the Thai name of each dish is given with a clear English description. Try the fisherman's soup, a spicy mass of delicious saltwater fish in a clear broth, or *yam pla muek,* a hot salad with squid. ⊠ *16–18 London Rd.,* ☎ *01483/536092. MC, V. Closed Mon. and 2 wks in Aug.*

£££ 🏨 **The Angel.** The Angel is the last of the old coaching inns for which
★   Guildford was famous. The courtyard, into which coaches and horses clattered to a stop, is still open to the sky, and light lunches are served here in summer. The hotel is at least 400 years old and is even said to have a ghost. Guest rooms have attractive fabrics, reproduction antiques, and marble-lined bathrooms. There's an excellent restaurant in the medieval stone cellar and an informal coffee shop for light refreshments. Ten rooms are in a modern annex. ⊠ *91 High St., GU1 3DP,* ☎ *01483/564555,* 𝔽𝔸𝕏 *01483/533770. 21 rooms with bath. Restaurant, coffee shop. AE, DC, MC, V.*

The Arts

In Guildford, the **Yvonne Arnaud Theatre** (⊠ Milbrook, ☎ 01483/ 440000) is an unusual horseshoe-shape building on an island in the River Wey. It frequently previews West End productions and also has a restaurant.

West Clandon

㊺ *29 mi southwest of London, 3 mi east of Guildford.*

Just east of Guildford at West Clandon, you'll want to visit **Clandon Park,** which was built in the 1730s by Venetian architect Giacomo Leoni in the graceful Palladian style. The park was landscaped by Capability Brown. The real glory of the house, now a National Trust property, is its interior, especially the magnificent two-story Marble Hall. There's a fine collection of furniture, needlework, and porcelain, and a regimental museum full of weapons and medals. The gardens, too, are of interest, with a parterre, grotto, and sunken garden. ☎ *01483/ 222482.* ▨ *£4.20; joint ticket with Hatchlands £6.* ☺ *Apr.–Oct.,*

Tues.–Thurs., Sun., and national holidays 11:30–4:30; last admission 30 mins before closing; gardens open daily 9–7:30 or dusk.

A mile east on the A246 is **Hatchlands,** built in 1758 for Admiral Boscawen, with Robert Adam interiors and a Humphry Repton park. It houses the largest collection in the world of keyboard instruments associated with composers (e.g., Purcell, Chopin, Mahler). ☎ 01483/ 222482. 🎫 £4.20; joint ticket with Clandon £6. ☉ Apr.–Oct., Tues.– Thurs., Sun., and Fri. in Aug., 2–5; park daily 11:30–6.

Great Bookham

46 *25 mi southwest of London, 8 mi northeast of Guildford, 3 mi southwest of Leatherhead.*

Great Bookham has some fine old buildings at its core, including a 12th-century church, one of the most complete medieval buildings extant in Surrey. The main reason to be here, however, is to visit **Polesden Lacey.** This handsome Regency mansion, built in 1824 by Thomas Cubitt on the site of one owned by the famed 18th-century playwright Richard Brinsley Sheridan, was from 1906 to 1942 the home of Edwardian society hostess Mrs. Ronald Greville. Her many famous guests included Edward VII. Elizabeth, now the Queen Mother, and her husband, the Duke of York (later George VI), stayed here on their honeymoon. Today owned and maintained by the National Trust, Polesden Lacey contains beautiful collections of furniture, paintings, porcelain, and silver. In the summer, open-air theatrical performances are given on the grounds. Refreshments are available in the stableyard restaurant. ☎ 01372/458203. 🎫 House £3, grounds £3. ☉ House Apr.–Oct., Wed.– Sun. 1:30–5:30; national holidays 11–5; grounds, daily 11–6 or dusk.

En Route As you start making your way southeast to Royal Tunbridge Wells via **47** Dorking (about 28 mi), you'll pass under the shadow of **Box Hill,** setting of the picnic in Jane Austen's *Emma.* It is a favorite spot for walking excursions. At Dorking, take any of the major roads and follow the signs to Royal Tunbridge Wells.

Dorking

6 mi southeast of Great Bookham, 29 mi south of London

The southeasterly route to Royal Tunbridge Wells leads to the busy commuter town of Dorking, a pleasant neighborhood that has inspired the pens of many writers. Its wide High Street houses the White Horse Inn, or "The Marquis o' Granby," as Dickens dubbed it for his *Pickwick Papers.* At Burford Bridge Hotel, Keats wrote the last chapters of *Endymion* (and Nelson stayed there when traveling down to Portsmouth, and on to fame and death at Trafalgar).

Dining and Lodging

££ ✗ **Partners and Sons.** Behind the genuine 16th-century, half-timber facade a comfortable, air-conditioned restaurant offers a modern English menu with Mediterranean influences using freshly prepared local produce. Try the local lamb dishes and the pastry chef's specialties. ✉ 2–4 West St., ☎ 01306/882826. *Reservations essential. AE, DC, MC, V.*

££–£££ 🏨 **White Horse.** For a taste of both ancient and modern, stay at this inn. The foundations of the hotel probably go back to the 13th century, while the interior is mostly 18th century but was completely refurbished in 1998. ✉ *High St., RH4 1BE,* ☎ *01306/881138,* 🖷 *01306/887241. 68 rooms with bath. Restaurant. AE, DC, MC, V.*

MASTERPIECES AND MOATS: FROM TUNBRIDGE WELLS TO FINCHCOCKS

One of England's greatest attractions is its many magnificent stately homes and castles. For those who love great treasure houses, there are almost endless opportunities in Great Britain, but for those with limited vacation time, the dismaying fact is that the greatness is thinly spread, with many of the houses scattered far and wide across the country. Within a 15-mi radius of Tunbridge Wells, however, lies a remarkable array of historic homes, castles, and other monuments: Penshurst Place, Hever Castle, Chartwell, Knole, Ightham Mote, Leeds Castle, Sissinghurst Castle Gardens, Bodiam Castle, Rudyard Kipling's Batemans, and Finchcocks.

Royal Tunbridge Wells

48   *39 mi southeast of London, 36 mi east of Great Bookham.*

Butt of humorists, who have always made it out to be unbelievably straitlaced, this city is officially known as Royal Tunbridge Wells, but locals ignore the prefix "royal" (it was added only in 1909, during the reign of Edward VII). Tunbridge Wells owes its prosperity to the 17th and 18th centuries' passion for spas and mineral baths, initially as medicinal treatments and later as social gathering places. In 1606, a spring of chalybeate (mineral) water was discovered here, drawing legions of royal visitors. It is still possible to drink the waters when a "dipper" (the traditional water dispenser) is in attendance, from Easter to September. Tunbridge Wells reached its zenith in the mid-18th century, when Richard "Beau" Nash presided over its social life. Today it is a pleasant town and home to many London commuters.

Start your tour at the **Pantiles,** a famous promenade with colonnaded shops near the spring on the other side of town, which derives its odd name from the Dutch "pan tiles" that originally paved the area. Now bordered on two sides by busy main roads, the Pantiles remains an elegant, tranquil oasis. Across the road from the Pantiles, the **Church of King Charles the Martyr** dates from 1678, when it was dedicated to Charles I, who was executed by Parliament in 1649 following the English Civil War. Its plain exterior belies its splendid interior; take special note of the beautifully plastered Baroque ceiling. A network of alleyways behind the church leads north back to High Street.

The buildings at the lower end of High Street are mostly 18th century, but as the street climbs the hill north, changing its name to Mount Pleasant Road, the buildings become more modern. Here you'll find the **Tunbridge Wells Museum and Art Gallery,** which houses a fascinating jumble of local artifacts, prehistoric relics, and Victorian toys, as well as a permanent exhibition of interesting Tunbridge Ware pieces: small, wooden items intricately inlaid with tiny pieces of different-color wood. ✉ *Mount Pleasant Rd.,* ☎ *01892/526121.* 🎫 *Free.* 🕐 *Mon.– Sat. 9:30–5.*

Dining and Lodging

£££   ✕ **Thackeray's House.** Gourmets flock to this mid-17th-century house,
★   once the home of Victorian novelist William Makepeace Thackeray (he wrote *Tunbridge Toys* here). Its owner, Bruce Wass, is also the chef and tolerates none but the freshest ingredients. Everything is cooked with great flair and imagination. Specialties include mini-bouillabaisse, Hereford duck in many guises, and a famous chocolate Armagnac loaf with coffee sauce. Below the main restaurant, there is a friendly little bistro, Downstairs at Thackeray's, with food every bit as good as that

upstairs, but less expensive (entrance in the courtyard). ⊠ *85 London Rd.,* ☎ *01892/511921. MC, V. Closed Mon. and 1 wk at Christmas. No dinner Sun. Bistro closed Sun.–Mon.*

£–££ ✕ **Sankey's Seafood Restaurant.** This double eatery features a basement wine bar and a lively upstairs restaurant. The wine bar has inexpensive food while the restaurant specializes in wonderfully fresh fish. The *soupe de poissons* is excellent, and there's a good selection of British cheeses. ⊠ *39 Mount Ephraim,* ☎ *01892/511422. AE, DC, MC, V. Closed Sun.*

£ ✕ **The Compasses.** This spacious, well-kept pub claims to be the oldest in town. As well as offering a notable range of "real ales," there is tasty homemade food at lunchtime, and in winter you can snuggle up to the cozy open fires. The pub lies on a tiny, steep lane off High Street. ⊠ *Little Mount Sion,* ☎ *01892/530744. No credit cards.*

£££ ▥ **Spa Hotel.** Carefully chosen furnishings and details help give this Georgian mansion the atmosphere of a country house, though guest rooms are thoughtfully equipped with many modern extras. This hotel is run by the Goring family, who also own the noted Goring Hotel in London. The extensive grounds give superb views across the town and into the Weald of Kent. The Chandelier Restaurant is very popular with locals. ⊠ *Mount Ephraim, TN4 8XJ,* ☎ *01892/520331,* ℻ *01892/510575. 74 rooms with bath. Restaurant, indoor pool, beauty salon, sauna, tennis court, jogging. AE, DC, MC, V.*

££ ▥ **Old Parsonage.** This very comfortable and friendly guest house, 2 mi south of Tunbridge Wells via the A267, stands at the top of a quiet lane beside the village church. Built in 1820, this Georgian manor has a country-house feel to it, with lovely antique furniture, including two four-posters, and a big conservatory for afternoon tea. The lodging stands amid 3 acres of grounds. Two pubs and a restaurant lie within a short walk from the house. ⊠ *Church La., Frant TN3 9DX,* ☎ ℻ *01892/750773. 3 rooms with bath. MC, V.*

Outdoor Activities and Sports

GOLF

The golf course at **Langton Road,** Tunbridge Wells (☎ 01892/523034) welcomes visitors (members only on weekends).

Penshurst Place

★ ㊾ *33 mi southeast of London, 7 mi northwest of Tunbridge Wells.*

At the center of the hamlet of Penshurst (from Tunbridge Wells follow A26 and B2176), one of England's finest medieval manor houses, Penshurst Place, lies hidden behind tall trees and a walled garden. While retaining its Baron's Hall, dating from the 14th century, the house is mainly Elizabethan, having been in the Sidney family for centuries. It still is. The most famous Sidney is the Elizabethan poet, Sir Philip, author of *Arcadia*. This family continuity brings a particular richness to the Place. The **Baron's Hall,** topped in 1341 with a timber roof, is the oldest and one of the grandest to survive from the early Middle Ages. The grounds include a 10-acre walled Tudor garden; there is a toy museum and a garden restaurant. While the little hamlet of Penshurst is basically just an appendage of the "Great House," it is a delightful destination in its own right. It's centered around pretty-as-a-picture Leicester Square, with late-15th-century half-timber structures adorned with soaring brick chimneys. A low-beam passageway gives access to the churchyard—all in all, a vision right out of Ye Merrie Olde Englande. ☎ *01892/870307.* ▦ *House and grounds £5.70, grounds only £4.20.* ☉ *House weekends in Mar. and Apr.–Oct., daily noon–5:30; grounds daily 11–6; last admission 30 mins before closing.*

Dining and Lodging

£ ✕ **Spotted Dog.** This place first opened its doors in 1520; today, it tempts visitors with an inglenook fireplace, heavy beams, imaginative food, and a splendid view of Penshurst Place. ⊠ *Smarts Hill*, ☎ *01892/870253. AE, MC, V.*

££–£££ 🏨 **Rose and Crown.** Originally a 16th-century inn, this hotel on the main street in Tonbridge (5 mi east of Penshurst, 5 mi north of Tunbridge Wells) features a distinctive portico, added later. Inside, low-beam ceilings and Jacobean woodwork make both the bars and the restaurant snug and inviting. Guest rooms in the main building are traditionally furnished, while in the newer annex they are more modern in style; all are attractive and cozy. ⊠ *125 High St., Tonbridge TN9 1DD*, ☎ *01732/357966*, 🖷 *01732/357194. 48 rooms with bath. Restaurant, bar. AE, DC, MC, V.*

Hever Castle

★ ⑤⓪ *30 mi southeast of London, 10 mi northwest of Tunbridge Wells, 3 mi west of Penshurst.*

For some, 13th-century Hever fits the stereotype of what a castle should look like, all turrets and battlements, the whole encircled by a water lily–bound moat; for others, it's a bit too squat in structure (and perhaps too renovated). Its main attraction is its past association with the ill-fated Anne Boleyn. It was here that she was courted and won by Henry VIII. He later gave Hever to his fourth wife, Anne of Cleves. The castle was acquired in 1903 by American millionaire William Waldorf Astor, who built an entire Tudor village to house his staff (now a hotel for corporate functions) and had the stunning gardens laid out, with Italian and Tudor plantings, a yew maze, and topiary walks. ⊠ *Near Edenbridge*, ☎ *01732/865224.* ▨ *Castle and grounds £7, grounds only £5.50.* ☉ *Castle Apr.–Oct., daily noon–5; Mar. and Nov., daily 12–4; grounds Apr.–Oct., 11–6; Mar. and Nov., 11–4; last admission 30 mins before closing.*

Chartwell

⑤① *28 mi southeast of London, 12 mi northwest of Tunbridge Wells, 9 mi north of Hever Castle.*

Chartwell was Sir Winston Churchill's home from 1924 until his death in 1965. The Victorian house was acquired by the National Trust and has been decorated to appear as it did in Churchill's lifetime—even down to a half-smoked cigar in an ashtray. In the garden you can see a wall he built himself. To arrive here from Hever, take the minor roads B2027 and B2026 north. ⊠ *Near Westerham*, ☎ *01732/866368.* ▨ *£5.20.* ☉ *Apr.–Oct., Wed.–Sun. and Bank Holiday Mon., 11–5; Jul.–Aug., also Tues., 11–5; last admission 4.*

Knole

★ ⑤② *27 mi southeast of London, 11 mi north of Tunbridge Wells, 8 mi east of Chartwell.*

The town of Sevenoaks in Kent lies in London's commuter belt—a world away from the baronial air of its premier attraction, Knole, the grand home of the Sackville family since the 16th century. Begun in the 15th century and enlarged and embellished in 1603 by Thomas Sackville, Knole, with its vast complex of courtyards and buildings, resembles a small town, and, in fact, you'll need most of an afternoon to explore it thoroughly. The house is noted for its collection of tapestries, embroidered furnishings, and the most famous set of 17th-century silver furniture to survive. Most of the salons are in the pre-Baroque mode—rather dark and armorial. Paintings on display include a series of portraits by 18th-century artists Thomas Gainsborough and Sir Joshua Reynolds. The magnificently florid staircase was a novelty in its Elizabethan heyday. The noted writer Vita Sackville-West grew up at Knole and set her novel *The Edwardians*—an extremely witty account of life among the gilded set—here. Set in a 1,000-acre deer park, the house lies in the center of Sevenoaks, opposite St. Nicholas Church; to get there from Chartwell, drive north to Westerham, then pick up A25 and head east for 8 mi. ☎ 01732/450608. ⌧ *£5, grounds free.* ⊘ *Apr.–Oct., Wed.–Sat. 12–4, Sun., 11–5 (last admission at 3:30); gardens May–Sept., 1st Wed. of each month 11–4 (last admission at 3).*

Ightham Mote

★ ⑤ *31 mi southeast of London, 10 mi north of Tunbridge Wells, 7 mi east of Sevenoaks.*

Finding Ightham Mote requires careful navigation, but it is worth the effort, for it is a vision right out of the Middle Ages. An outstanding example of a small manor house, it's entered by crossing a stone bridge over one of the dreamiest moats in England, offering a picture that is the absolute quintessence of medieval romanticism. This moat, however, does not relate to the "mote" in the name, which refers to the role of the house as a meeting place, or "moot." Ightham (pronounced item) Mote's magical exterior has changed little since it was built in the 14th century, but within you'll find it does encompass styles of several different periods, Tudor to Victorian. The Great Hall is an antiquarian's delight—both comfy and grand. Be sure to see the magnificent Tudor chapel, drawing room, and billiards room in the newly restored North West quarter. To reach the house from Sevenoaks, follow A25 east to A227 (8 mi) and follow the signs. ✉ *Ivy Hatch, Sevenoaks,* ☎ *01732/810378.* ⌧ *£4.50.* ⊘ *Apr.–Oct., Mon., Wed.–Fri., Sun., and national holidays 11–5:30 (last admission at 5).*

Leeds Castle

★ ⑤ *40 mi southeast of London, 18 mi east of Sevenoaks, 19 mi northwest of Tunbridge Wells, 12 mi east of Ightham.*

The bubbling River Medway runs right through Maidstone, Kent's county seat, with its backdrop of chalky downs. Only 5 mi east on A20 stands Leeds Castle, a fairy-tale stronghold commanding two small islands on a peaceful lake. Dating back to the 9th century and rebuilt by the Normans in 1119, Leeds (not to be confused with Leeds in the North of England) became a favorite home of many English queens. Henry VIII liked the place so much he had it converted from a fortress into a grand palace. The house (much restored) offers a fine collection of paintings and furniture, plus an unusual dog-collar museum. Other attractions include a maze and grotto, an aviary, and woodland gardens. To get to Maidstone from Ightham, go north on the A227, then east on the A20. ☎ *01622/765400.* ⌧ *Castle and grounds £8.80, grounds only £6.80.* ⊘ *Mar.–Oct., daily 10–5; Nov.–Feb., daily 10–3. Castle closed Sat. on last weekend in June and 1st weekend in July.*

Rochester

⑤ *28 mi southeast of London.*

Kent is Charles Dickens country and all Dickens aficionados will want to detour north to head to Rochester, the place outside of London most closely associated with the great author. He lived for many years at

Gad's Hill Place, just outside of town. In town, look for High Street—once "full of gables with old beams and timbers" and its noted gabled Tudor building, legendary abode of Uncle Pumblechook in *Great Expectations*. Opposite the Pumblechook house is the **Charles Dickens Centre,** with displays featuring life-size models of scenes from the author's books that can amuse and horrify you at the same time (parents be warned). ⊠ *Eastgate House, High St.,* ☎ *01634/844176.* ⌷ *£3.10.* ⊙ *Daily 10–5:30; last admission 4:45.*

Rochester Castle is one of the finest surviving examples of Norman military architecture. The keep, built in the 1100s, partly based on the Roman city wall, is the tallest in England. ⊠ *Boley Hill,* ☎ *01634/402276.* ⌷ *£2.70.* ⊙ *Easter–Sept, daily 10–6; Oct.–Easter, daily 10–4 (last admission 3:30).*

Rochester Cathedral is England's second-oldest cathedral. The first English bishop was ordained in a small cathedral on this site in AD 604 by Augustine of Canterbury. The cathedral we see today is rather a jumble of architectural styles, but interesting for that. Work was started in 1077 by the Norman Bishop Gundulph, who also built the castle. The elaborate Norman west front is striking. ⊠ *Boley Hill,* ☎ *01634/843366.* ⌷ *Donation requested.*

Across the River Medway, at **The Historic Dockyard** in Chatham, 47 retired ships constitute the world's most complete Georgian/early Victorian dockyard. Some 400 naval ships were built here over as many years, as shown by the sights, sounds, and smells of the "Wooden Walls" exhibit. ⊠ *Historic Dockyard, Chatham,* ☎ *01634/823800.* ⌷ *£6.20.* ⊙ *Apr.–Oct., daily 10–5; Feb., Mar., Nov., daily 10–4. Closed Dec.–Jan.*

The Arts

There is a **Dickens festival** held in Rochester at the end of May, at which thousands of people in period dress attend enactments of scenes from the author's novels. Call ☎ 01634/843666 for details. **Broadstairs** (40 mi east), is also associated with the writer and hosts another festival, usually in June (☎ 01843/862242).

Sissinghurst Castle and Garden

★ ➏ *53 mi southeast of London, 12 mi east of Tunbridge Wells, 15 mi south of Maidstone.*

One of the most famous gardens in the world, Sissinghurst, is nestled deep in the Kentish countryside, around the remains of a moated Tudor castle. Unpretentiously beautiful, quintessentially English, they were laid out in the 1930s by the writer Vita Sackville-West (one of the Sackvilles of Knole) and her husband, the diplomat Harold Nicolson. The grounds are at their best in June and July, when the roses are in bloom. Children may feel restricted in the gardens, and strollers are not allowed. Wheelchair access is limited. From Leeds Castle, make your way south on B2163 and A274 through Headcorn, then follow signs. ⊠ *Cranbrook,* ☎ *01580/715330.* ⌷ *£6.* ⊙ *Apr.–mid-Oct., Tues.–Fri. 1–6:30, weekends and Good Fri. 10–5:30. Admission often restricted since space is limited.*

Dining and Lodging

£ ✗ **Claris's Tea Shop.** Near Sissinghurst Castle, Claris's serves traditional English teas in a 15th-century setting and displays attractive English crafts items. There's a pretty garden for summer teas. ⊠ *3 High St., Biddenden.* ☎ *01580/291025. No credit cards. Closed Mon.*

£££ ✕⊞ **Kennel Holt Hotel.** This is a quiet hotel in a redbrick Elizabethan
★ manor house, surrounded by beautiful, well-kept gardens. Visitors are
treated like guests in a private house. The library, for example, is well
stocked with books for a rainy day. The restaurant offers three- and four-
course set-price menus, which include such dishes as salmon with cream,
tomato, herb, and cucumber sauce, or guinea fowl with wild mushroom
sauce. Antiques and flowers grace the restaurant as well as the rest of
the hotel. The hotel is 3 mi from Goudhurst, off A262. ✉ *Goudhurst
Rd., Cranbrook TN17 2PT,* ☎ *01580/712032,* FAX *01580/715495. 10
rooms with bath or shower. Restaurant, croquet. AE, MC, V.*

En Route As you leave Sissinghurst, continue south along A229 through
Hawkhurst, a little village that was once the headquarters of a notorious and ruthless gang of smugglers. Turn left on to the B2244 and
left at the Curlew pub to arrive in the tiny Sussex village of Bodiam.

Bodiam Castle

★ **57** *57 mi southeast of London, 15 mi southeast of Tunbridge Wells, 9 mi
south of Cranbrook, 14 mi north of Hastings.*

Immortalized in 1,001 travel posters, Bodiam Castle is Britain's most
picturesque medieval stronghold—and none the less so for being virtually a shell. Built in 1385 to withstand a threatened French invasion,
it was "slighted" (partly demolished) during the English Civil War of
1642–1646 and has been uninhabited ever since. Nevertheless, you can
climb some of the towers and enjoy the illusion of manning the battlements against an enemy. Surrounded by a lovely moat, this photogenic castle is just about designed for the viewfinders of today's video
cameras. ☎ *01580/830436.* 🎫 *£3.30* ⊘ *Mid-Feb.–Oct., daily 10–6
or dusk; Nov.–Dec., Tues.–Sun. 10–dusk; last admission 1 hr before
closing. Closed Jan.*

Burwash

58 *58 mi southeast of London, 14 mi south of Tunbridge Wells, 10 mi
west of Bodiam.*

The writer Rudyard Kipling lived from 1902 to 1936 at **Bateman's,** a
beautiful 17th-century house just off the main road half a mile south
of the village of Burwash. It was built for a prominent ironmaster when
Sussex was the center of England's iron industry. Kipling's study looks
exactly as it did when he lived here, and in the garden there is a water
mill that still grinds flour; it is thought to be one of the oldest working water turbines. Close by, between Burwash Common and the river,
is the setting for *Puck of Pook's Hill,* one of Kipling's well-known children's books. To get to Burwash, turn west from Hawkhurst onto A265.
☎ *01435/882302.* 🎫 *£4.70.* ⊘ *Apr.–Oct., Sat.–Wed. 11–5:30; last
admission 4:30.*

Lamberhurst

59 *46 mi southeast of London, 7 mi east of Tunbridge Wells, 11 mi north
of Burwash.*

One of England's noted vineyards lies (signposted) outside the village
of Lamberhurst. Until comparatively recently, grape growing in England
was a rich man's hobby. Today it is an important rural industry, and
the wines produced here are world-renowned. There are tours of the
vineyards and winery, with tastings, and a shop and restaurant. ✉ *Ridge
Farm,* ☎ *01892/890844.* 🎫 *Free, guided tours £4.50.* ⊘ *Daily 9:30–
5:30. Closed Christmas wk.*

Outdoor Activities and Sports

Bewl Water Activity Centre (✉ Lamberhurst, ☎ 01892/890661) takes advantage of its location at one of England's largest reservoirs (just east of Wadhurst, 6 mi southeast of Tunbridge Wells by A267 and B2099), providing a wide range of aquatic sports. There's also an adventure playground and bicycles can be rented.

Finchcocks

🌀 *48 mi southeast of London, 10 mi east of Tunbridge Wells, 2 mi east of Lamberhurst.*

A visit to Finchcocks, an elegant Georgian mansion located between Lamberhurst and Goudhurst, is a must for music lovers. It contains the **Finchcocks Living Museum of Music,** a magnificent collection of historic keyboard instruments, which are played whenever the house is open. (Demonstration recitals are included in the admission fee.) A festival is held on September weekends. ✉ *Goudhurst,* ☎ *01580/211702.* 🎫 *£5.50.* ⏰ *Easter–July, Sept., Sun. and national holidays 2–6; Aug., Wed, Thurs., and Sun. 2–6. Private visits by arrangement Apr.–Oct.*

Lodging

£ 🏨 **Star and Eagle.** This traditional village inn has been serving pints and offering hospitality since 1600. The place is swimming in atmosphere, with exposed beams and open brick fireplaces, and has some rooms overlooking the village graveyard. Rooms come in all sizes: one of them (No. 5) has a huge four-poster, though others have better views. Snacks and full meals are available in the popular bar downstairs. ✉ *High St., Goudhurst TN17 1AL,* ☎ *01580/211512,* 📠 *01580/211416. 11 rooms with bath or shower. Restaurant, bar. MC, V.*

SOUTHEAST A TO Z

Arriving and Departing

By Bus

National Express (☎ 0990/808080) serves the region from London's Victoria Coach Station. Trips to Brighton and Canterbury take less than two hours; to Chichester, about 3 hours.

By Car

Major routes radiating outward from London to the Southeast are, from west to east: M23/A23 to Brighton (52 mi); A21, passing by Tunbridge Wells to Hastings (65 mi); A20/M20 to Folkestone; and A2/M2 via Canterbury (56 mi) to Dover (71 mi).

By Plane

Gatwick Airport (☎ 01293/535353) has direct flights from many U.S. cities and is more convenient for this region than Heathrow. The terminal for the British Rail line is in the airport buildings, and there are connections from there to all the major towns in the region.

By Train

British Rail serves the area from London's Victoria and Charing Cross (for eastern areas) and Waterloo (for the west). From London, the trip to Brighton takes about one hour by the fast train; and to Dover, about two hours.

Getting Around

By Bus

Private companies operating within the region are linked by county co-ordinating offices: **East Sussex** (☎ 01273/474747 or 01797/223053), **West Sussex** (☎ 01243/777556), **Surrey** (☎ 01737/223000), and **Kent** (☎ 0345/696996). Maps and timetables are available at bus depots, train stations, local libraries, and tourist information centers.

By Car

A good link route for traveling through the region, from Hampshire across the border into Sussex and Kent, is A272 (which becomes A265). It runs through the Weald (uplands), which separates the North Downs from the more inviting South Downs. Though smaller, less busy roads forge deeper into the downs, even the main roads take you through lovely countryside and villages. The main route east from the downs to the Channel ports and resorts of Kent is A27. To get to Romney Marsh (just across the Sussex border in Kent), take A259 from Rye. The principal roads in the Southeast are constantly being enlarged and upgraded to handle the ever-increasing flow of traffic to the Channel ports. Be warned that more traffic tickets are issued per traffic warden in Brighton than anywhere else in the country!

By Train

The line running west from Dover passes through Ashford, where you can change trains for Hastings and Eastbourne. There are connections from Eastbourne for Lewes, and from Brighton for Chichester. A "Network" card costing £20, valid throughout the southern and southeastern regions for a year, entitles you and three companions to one-third off many fares. For local and regional information, call **British Rail** (☎ 0345/484950).

Contacts and Resources

Car Rentals

Brighton: Avis (✉ 6A Brighton Marina, ☎ 01273/673738); **Hertz,** (✉ 47 Trafalgar St., ☎ 01273/738227). **Canterbury: Avis** (✉ c/o Team Traction, Suzuki House, 256 Broad Oak Rd., ☎ 01227/768339); **Hertz,** ✉ (The Elf Garage, Broad Oak Rd., ☎ 01227/470864). **Dover: Avis** (✉ Eastern Docks, ☎ 01304/206265); **Hertz** (✉ 173–177 Snargate St., ☎ 01304/207303). **Guildford: Hertz,** (✉ Guildford Railway Station, Station Approach, ☎ 01483 536677).

Guided Tours

The **Southeast England Tourist Board** (☎ 01892/540766) can arrange private tours with qualified Blue Badge guides.

The **Guild of Guides** (☎ 01227/459779) provides guides who have a specialized knowledge of Canterbury.

Guide Friday (☎ 01789/294466 head office) has a go-as-you-please bus tour of Brighton lasting at least an hour. It operates between April and September, costing £6.

Travel Agencies

American Express (✉ 82 North St., Brighton, ☎ 01273/321242).

Thomas Cook (✉ 58 North St., Brighton, ☎ 01273/325711; ✉ 9 High St., Canterbury, ☎ 01227/781199; ✉ 109 Mount Pleasant Rd., Tunbridge Wells, ☎ 01892/532372). There are other offices in Dover, Eastbourne, Folkestone, Guildford, Hastings, Hove, Maidstone, Ramsgate, and Sevenoaks.

Visitor Information

The **Southeast England Tourist Board** will send you a free illustrated booklet and also arrange tours and excursions. ⊠ *The Old Brewhouse, 1 Warwick Park, Tunbridge Wells, Kent TN2 5TU,* ☎ *01892/540766,* ⅢⅫ *01892/511008.* ⊙ *Mon.–Thurs. 9–5:30, Fri. 9–5.*

Local tourist information centers (TICs) are normally open Monday–Saturday 9:30–5:30, but hours vary seasonally. **Arundel** (⊠ 61 High St., ☎ 01903/882268). **Brighton** (⊠ 10 Bartholomew Sq., ☎ 01273/292599). **Canterbury** (⊠ 34 St. Margaret's St., ☎ 01227/766567). **Chichester** (⊠ 29A South St., ☎ 01243/775888). **Dover** (⊠ Townwall St., ☎ 01304/205108). **Eastbourne** (⊠ Cornfield Rd., ☎ 01323/411400). **Gatwick Airport** (⊠ International Arrivals Concourse, North Terminal, ☎ 01293/579102). **Guildford** (⊠ 14 Tunsgate, ☎ 01483/444333). **Hastings** (⊠ 4 Robertson Terr., ☎ 01424/781111 and 0800/181066). **Lewes** (⊠ 187 High St., ☎ 01273/483448). **Maidstone** (⊠ The Gatehouse, Palace Gardens, Mill St., ☎ 01622/602169). **Rye** (⊠ The Heritage Centre, Strand Quay, ☎ 01797/226696). **Tunbridge Wells** (⊠ The Old Fish Market, The Pantiles, ☎ 01892/515675).

4 The South

Winchester, Salisbury, Stonehenge

The South of England is perfect for time travelers. In just a long weekend you can go from prehistoric Stonehenge to the fanciful curlicues of Victorian Salisbury. History has highlights by the hundreds here— Winchester Cathedral, Wilton House, and Beaulieu Abbey are just a few. And like a library, the South is tailor-made for browsing, thanks to its many literary landmarks. Make a pilgrimage to Jane Austen's home or travel to Dorset—Thomas Hardy Country—to get far from the madding crowd.

THE SOUTH, MADE UP OF HAMPSHIRE (Hants), Dorset, and Wiltshire, offers a wide range of attractions, and not a few quiet pleasures. Two important cathedrals, Winchester and Salisbury (pronounced sawls-bree), are here, as well as stately homes—Longleat, Stourhead, and Wilton House, among them—attractive market towns, and literally hundreds of prehistoric remains, two of which, Avebury and Stonehenge, should not be missed. These, of course, are but the tourist-brochure superlatives. Sooner or later, however, any visitor to these parts should rent a bike (preferably one of those black clunkers that look so at home in English villages) and set out to discover the back-roads villages—much favored by those who migrate here from every corner of the country in search of upward mobility—*not* found in those brochures. After a drink in the village pub and a look at the cricket game on the village green, take a break at a strawberry farm where you can lie on straw strewn between the rows and gorge yourself on sun-warmed berries; or collapse in a grassy field that has "nap time" written all over it. *This* is what summer in England is all about.

Updated by
Robert
Andrews

Here history has highlights by the hundreds, beginning when Alfred the Great, teaching religion and letters, made Winchester the capital of 9th-century England and helped to lay plans for Britain's first navy, sowing the seeds of its Commonwealth. King Alfred's coronation was held in the town's huge cathedral, an imposing edifice dotted with the Gothic tombs of 15th-century bishops, who lie peacefully behind grill-work, their marble hands crossed for eternity. Winchester is a good center from which to visit quiet villages where so many of England's once great personages lived or died. Florence Nightingale lies under a simple stone in East Wellow churchyard in Romsey, near her former house at Embley Park. Thanks to a '90s spate of filmed versions of her classic novels, Jane Austen's home at Chawton—restored several decades ago by the Duke of Wellington—has become a favored pilgrimage spot. But everywhere, the unscheming hand of time has scattered pretty villages over Hampshire. Many of them have cottages grouped around a green—as one feels they should be in a proper English village.

Moving beyond the gentle, gardenlike features of Hampshire, you can explore the somewhat harsher terrain of Salisbury Plain. Two monuments, millennia apart, stand sentinel over the plain. One is the 404-ft stone spire of Salisbury Cathedral, immortalized in oil by John Constable, which dominates the entire Salisbury valley. Not far away is the most imposing and dramatic prehistoric structure in Europe: Stonehenge. One of the latest theories is that it was constructed by Greek, not British, builders—hardly a surprise given that the locals were then wandering around in animal skins and living in the crudest of shelters. Just why ancient masons from Mycenae should have languished in Britain putting up this great monument is harder to say.

There are numerous other districts to explore: this area of England is like a library—it is perfect for browsing. Turn your sights to the Dorset heathlands, the countryside explored in the novels of Thomas Hardy. This district is spanned by rolling grass-covered chalk hills—the Downs—wooded valleys and meadows through which course meandering rivers. Along the coastline you'll find Lyme Regis, where the tides and currents strike fear into the hearts of sailors; and Cowes on the Isle of Wight—Queen Victoria's favorite getaway place—which welcomes high-flyers who enter their yachts in the famous regattas.

The south has been quietly central to England's history for well over 4,000 years, occupied successively by prehistoric man, the Celts, the Romans, the Saxons, and the modern British. History continues to be made here, right up to the modern era. Forces sailed from ports for Normandy along this coast on D-Day, and to recover the Falklands nearly 40 years later.

Pleasures and Pastimes

Literary Shrines

Among this region's proudest claims is its connection with Thomas Hardy (1840–1928), one of England's most celebrated novelists. If you have a chance to read some of Hardy's novels before visiting Dorset—immortalized by Hardy as his part-fact, part-fiction county of Wessex—you'll already have a feeling for it, and indeed, you'll recognize some places immediately from his descriptions. The quiet, tranquil countryside surrounding Dorchester, in particular, is lovingly described in *Far From the Madding Crowd,* and Casterbridge, in *The Mayor of Casterbridge,* stands for Dorchester itself. You can actually walk the farm track where Tess of the d'Urbervilles's pony fell or share the timeless vista of the Blackmore Vale that the tragic heroine so loved. Any pilgrimage to Hardy's Wessex begins at the author's birthplace in Higher Bockhampton, 3 mi east of Dorchester. Here, in a lovely thatched cottage, Hardy penned the story of Bathsheba Everdene. Salisbury makes an appearance as "Melchester" in *Jude the Obscure;* walk in the footsteps of Jude Fawley by climbing Shaftesbury—"Shaston"—and its steeply picturesque Gold Hill. Today, many of these sights seem frozen in time, and Hardy's spirit is ever present. In addition to Hardy landmarks, Jane Austen sites and shrines abound in the south of England; for a theme tour of her beloved Hampshire, see the Close-Up box, "In Search of Jane Austen," *below.*

Dining

Fertile soil, well-stocked rivers, and a long coastline ensure excellent farm produce and a plentiful stock of fish throughout the South. Try fresh-grilled river trout or sea bass poached in brine, or dine like a king on the New Forest's renowned venison.

CATEGORY	COST*
££££	over £50
£££	£30–£50
££	£20–£30
£	under £20

*per person including first course, main course, dessert, and VAT; excluding drinks

Lodging

Modern hotel chains are well represented, and in rural areas there are elegant country-house hotels, traditional coaching inns, and modest guest houses. Note that some seaside hotels do not accept one-night bookings in the busy season.

CATEGORY	COST*
££££	over £150
£££	£80–£150
££	£60–£80
£	under £60

*All prices are for two people sharing a double room, including service, breakfast, and VAT.

Markets

Open-air markets are almost daily events—for a complete list, inquire at the Southern Tourist Board. Among the best are Salisbury's traditional city market (Tuesday and Saturday), Kingsland Market in Southampton for bric-a-brac (Thursday), and a general country market (Wednesday) at Ringwood, near Bournemouth.

Exploring the South

The South of England ranges from the broad plains of Wiltshire, including the Marlborough Downs, the Vale of Pewsey, and the great Salisbury Plain, to the gaudy bucket-and-spade resorts of the coast, and the sedate retirement homes of the Isle of Wight. The wide-open, wind-blown feel of the inland county of Wiltshire offers a sharp contrast both to the tame, sequestered villages of Hampshire and Dorset, and the self-important bustle of Southampton and Portsmouth. On the whole, you will not want to spend much time in these two ports, best visited *en passant* in favor of spending your nights in the more compelling cities of Salisbury and Winchester.

Numbers in the text correspond to numbers in the margin and on the South, Winchester, and the Salisbury maps.

Great Itineraries

IF YOU HAVE 3 DAYS

With three days at your disposal, you will want to combine the most sights with the least amount of traveling. If you are coming from London or southeast England, ⊞ **Winchester** ① will be your first stop, a quiet, solid town, conducive to walking about, with the great cathedral at its heart—art historians always remark on how the cathedral presents a sturdy, chunky appearance in keeping with its Norman construction, so that its Gothic lightness within is even more breathtaking. Other historic sites here include the Great Hall and Winchester College, one of the country's noted "public" schools. Spend a night in the city, then move across to the other cathedral city described in this chapter, ⊞ **Salisbury** ㉓—surely few cathedrals have a more beautiful setting than this town—worth a two-night stay to take in the sights of the city itself, and, most important, **Stonehenge** ㊳, an easy ride out of town. Even closer to Salisbury is magnificent **Wilton House** ㉛ and its gardens, which you can see on your way to visiting the village of **Shaftesbury** ㉜, and two more country estates, **Stourhead** ㉝ and **Longleat House** ㉞: the former features—many believe—the most beautiful garden in England, the latter marries an African game park with a famous Elizabethan house.

IF YOU HAVE 5 DAYS

A longer stay in the South will give you greater freedom to explore some of the region's lower-key but no less enjoyable sights. After a day touring ⊞ **Winchester** ① and nearby **Chawton** ⑪, indelibly associated with Jane Austen, return to overnight in the cathedral city. The next morning, head for the south coast and **Portsmouth** ⑬, which possesses England's richest collection of maritime memorabilia, including the Royal Naval Museum and some well-preserved warships from the 18th century. Spend the next two nights in ⊞ **Salisbury** ㉓ to discover the city and the marvels surrounding it, including **Stonehenge** ㊳ and **Wilton House** ㉛. Head south again to **Wimborne Minster** ㊸, a town dwarfed by the twin towers of its great church. If you have time, carry on farther to see **Corfe Castle** ㊺, whose jagged ruins cast an eerie spell over the village at its foot. Spend your last two days in the area around ⊞ **Dorchester** ㊻, a must for fans of Thomas Hardy, though even without this literary connection it would be a captivating town, with the excavations of a Roman villa and an amphitheater just outside. Farther afield lies the grassy site of **Maiden Castle** ㊽, a bare but still powerfully evocative spot that is one of the South's chief prehistoric settlements. North of town, the chalk giant at **Cerne Abbas** ㊼ provides more links with the distant past.

IF YOU HAVE 7 DAYS

More time will enable you to tread farther off the beaten track and pursue a more adventurous itinerary. Spend your first day and night in ⊞ **Winchester** ①, then head down to Portsmouth to take a ferry across to **Cowes** ⑯, the most noted town on the **Isle of Wight,** a favorite island haven for both Queen Victoria and Charles Dickens. The former vacationed at Osborne House, an Italianate villa, while one of her forebears, Charles I, was the unwilling guest of the Parliamentary army during his incarceration in **Carisbrooke Castle** ㉒ in the center of the island. Overnight in nearby ⊞ **Ryde** ⑰. Leave the Isle of Wight from Cowes, disembarking at **Southampton** ⑭, not a particularly noteworthy place, but home to a couple of absorbing museums as well as the Pilgrim Fathers' Memorial. North of town, the village of **Romsey** is an attractive spot, with the lovely 18th-century mansion of **Broadlands** ⑮ lying just outside. From here, you are well placed to spend two nights in ⊞ **Salisbury** ㉓ to take in the city and the attractions around it, as far north as the stone circles of **Avebury** ㉟ and the nearby town of **Marlborough** ㊲, said to be the burial place of Merlin. If you have already toured this area, you might swoop down instead to the leafy glades of the **New Forest,** an excellent place to take a breather and some exercise. It is a favorite area for riding, and there are numerous stables where you can arrange for a day's jaunt on horseback. Heading westward, stop in at ⊞ **Bournemouth** ㊷, containing the house of Percy Bysshe Shelley and the grave of his wife Mary, author of *Frankenstein.* If the seaside frivolity doesn't grab you, carry on as far **Corfe Castle** ㊺. Farther west is the genteel resort of **Weymouth** ㊾, where you can dine on fish by the harborside. South of Weymouth lies the **Isle of Portland** ㊿, which together with **Chesil Beach** ㈤ will provide both beach fun and interest to anyone intrigued by geological phenomena. ⊞ **Dorchester** ㊻ and **Maiden Castle** ㊽ lie just north of here, while a few miles west, **Abbotsbury** ㈥ contains a famous 600-year-old swannery. Farther along Lyme Bay, the small port of **Lyme Regis** ㈦ will appeal to fans of both John Fowles and Meryl Streep: it was where the *French Lieutenant's Woman* was set and filmed.

When to Tour the South

Make sure you don't see the great cathedrals of Salisbury and Winchester on a Sunday, when your visit will be restricted (and—during services—not overly appreciated). Places such as Stonehenge and Longleat House attract plenty of visitors at all times; bypass such sights on weekends or public holidays. In summer, the coastal resorts of Bournemouth and Weymouth are crowded with day-trippers and longer-stay tourists, so that movement can be hampered by the crowds, not to mention the difficulty of finding suitable accommodation. The Isle of Wight, too, gets its fair share of visitors, and you may have to wait longer for the ferries. Some of the smaller, less frequented stops on our tours should always be reasonably free of the crush, however, and you should choose these lower-profile attractions when the going gets tough. Otherwise, this is one area of the country when you are relatively free to choose your own time of year. Fall in the New Forest is spectacular, though you should take waterproof boots for the puddles!

The South

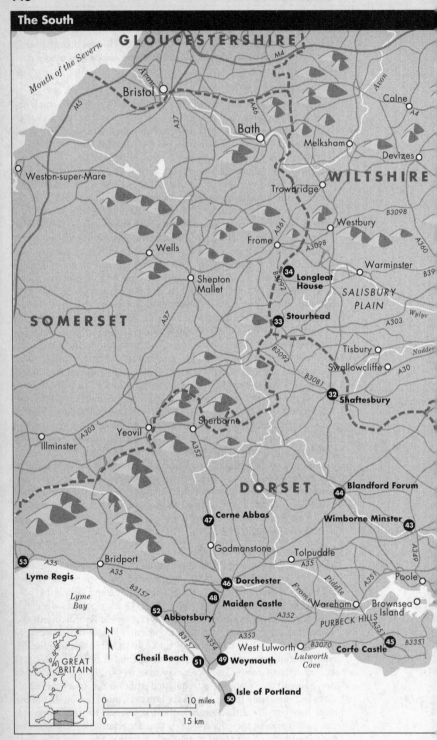

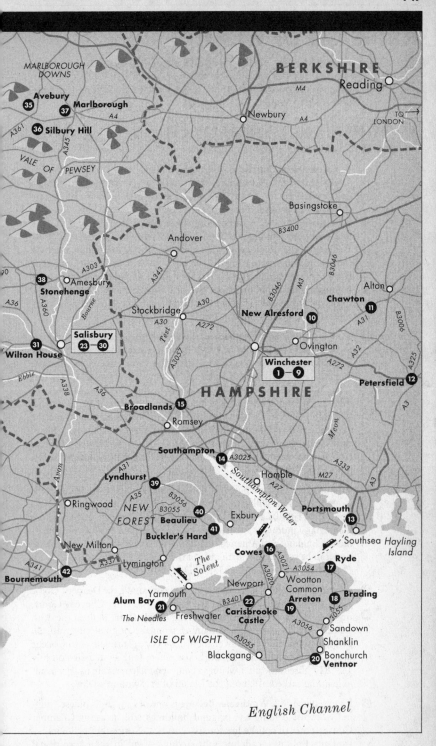

FROM WINCHESTER
TO THE ISLE OF WIGHT

From the lovely cathedral city of Winchester, 70 mi southwest of London, we meander southward to the coast, stopping at the bustling ports of Southampton and Portsmouth before striking out for the restful shores of the Isle of Wight.

Winchester

❶ *70 mi southwest of London, 14 mi north of Southampton.*

Winchester is among the most historic of English cities, and as you walk its graceful, unspoiled streets, a sense of the past envelops you. Though it is now merely the county seat of Hampshire, for more than four centuries Winchester served as England's capital. Here, in AD 827, Egbert was crowned first king of England, and his successor, Alfred the Great, held court until his death in 899. After the Norman Conquest in 1066, William I ("the Conqueror") had himself crowned in London, but took the precaution of repeating the ceremony in Winchester. In late Saxon times the town became the home of the finest school of calligraphy and manuscript illumination in Europe—it was here that William compiled the *Domesday Book.* The city remained the center of ecclesiastical, commercial, and political power until the 13th century.

★ ❷ Start your tour at the **cathedral,** the city's greatest monument, begun in 1079 and consecrated in 1093. In the cathedral's tower, transepts, and crypt, as in the core of the great nave, you can see some of the world's best surviving examples of Norman architecture. Other features, such as the arcades, the presbytery (behind the choir, holding the high altar), and the windows, are Gothic alterations carried out between the 12th and 14th centuries. The remodeling of the nave in the Perpendicular style was not completed until the 15th century. Little of the original stained glass has survived, thanks to Cromwell's Puritan troops, who ransacked the cathedral in the 17th century during the English Civil War.

Among the well-known people buried in the cathedral are William the Conqueror's son, William II (Rufus), mysteriously murdered in the New Forest in 1100; Izaak Walton, author of *The Compleat Angler,* whose memorial window in Silkestede's Chapel was paid for by "the fishermen of England and America"; and Jane Austen, whose memorial window can be seen in the north aisle of the nave. ✉ *The Close, Cathedral Precincts,* ☎ *01962/853–137.* ☉ *Daily 7:15 AM–6:30.*

❸ Behind the cathedral is the **Close,** an area containing the Deanery, Dome Alley, and Cheyney Court. On the right, as you enter Cheyney Court,
❹ on St. Swithun Street, you will see the **King's Gate,** built in the 13th century, one of two gates remaining from the original city wall. **St. Swithun's Church** is built over the King's Gate. Turn left onto College Street and proceed to No. 8, the house where Jane Austen died on July 18, 1817, three days after writing a comic poem (copies are usually available in the cathedral) about the legend of St. Swithun's Day.

❺ Founded in 1382, **Winchester College** is one of England's oldest "public" schools. Among the original buildings still in use is Chamber Court, center of college life for six centuries. Notice the "scholars"—students holding academic scholarships—clad in their traditional gowns. ✉ *College St.,* ☎ *01962/621217.* 🎫 *£2.50.* ☉ *Apr.–Sept., Mon.–Sat. 10–1 and 2–5, Sun. 2–5; 1-hr guided tours at 11, 2, and 3:15, or by prior arrangement.*

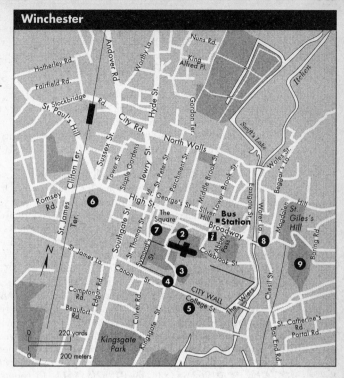

Winchester

⑥ A few blocks west of the cathedral is the medieval **Great Hall,** which is all that remains of the city's castle. The English Parliament met here for the first time in 1246; Sir Walter Raleigh was tried for conspiracy against King James I and condemned to death here in 1603 (though he wasn't beheaded until 1618); and Dame Alice Lisle was sentenced here by the infamous Judge Jeffreys to be burned at the stake for sheltering a fugitive, following Monmouth's Rebellion in 1685. (King James II, in a rare act of mercy, commuted her sentence to beheading.) On the west wall of the hall hangs what is said to be King Arthur's Round Table, with places for 24 knights, and a portrait of Arthur, which bears a remarkable resemblance to King Henry VII. In fact, the table is a Tudor forgery; the real Arthur was probably a Celtic cavalry general who held off the invading Saxons following the fall of the Roman Empire. Henry VII revived the Arthurian legend for political purposes. ⊠ *Castle Hill,* ☎ *01962/846476.* ⊑ *Free.* ☉ *Summer, daily 10–5; winter, weekdays 10–5, weekends 10–4.*

⑦ Across from the cathedral, the **City Museum** displays Winchester's past through Celtic pottery, Roman mosaics, and Saxon coins. ⊠ *The Square,* ☎ *01962/848269.* ⊑ *Free.* ☉ *Weekdays 10–5, Sat. 10–1 and 2–5, Sun. 2–5 (closed Mon. Oct.–Mar.).*

⑧ For a change of scenery and era, visit the **City Mill,** an 18th-century water mill, at the east end of High Street. On the premises are a National Trust gift shop and a café, open year-round; part of the building is used as a youth hostel. ⊠ *Bridge St.,* ☎ *01962/870057.* ⊑ *£1.* ☉ *Mar., weekends 11–4:45; Apr.–Oct., Wed.–Sun. and national holidays 11–4:45.*

⑨ To top off your tour of Winchester, climb **St. Giles's Hill** for a panoramic view of the city.

Dining and Lodging

£–££   ✕ **Nine the Square.** This modern restaurant makes the most of its prime position opposite the cathedral. The menu, which the downstairs wine bar shares with the more sedate dining area upstairs, changes regularly, but may feature Royal Gressingham Duck and, in season, game, while a selection of homemade pastas is always available. ⊠ *9 Great Minster St., The Square,* ☎ *01962/864004. AE, DC, MC, V.*

£   ✕ **The Royal Oak.** Try a half pint of draft bitter or dry cider at this traditional pub which claims to have Britain's oldest bar (it has a Saxon wall). It also has a no-smoking bar—a British rarity—in the cellar. Bar meals are served daily until 6:30 PM. ⊠ *Royal Oak Passage, off High St.,* ☎ *01962/842701.*

£££   ✕🕆 **Royal.** At this classy hotel, you'll find an attractive walled garden and some very comfortable bedrooms. It's within easy reach of the cathedral, but it lies on a quiet side street. You can have an excellent lunch in the bar, or a fuller meal in the moderately priced formal dining room. This is a Best Western hotel, and one of the swankier links in the chain. Some of the rooms are in a recent extension, but the older rooms have more atmosphere. ⊠ *St. Peter St., SO23 8BS,* ☎ *01962/840840,* FAX *01962/841582. 82 rooms with bath. Restaurant. AE, DC, MC, V.*

£££   ✕🕆 **Wykeham Arms.** This old inn is centrally located, close to the cathedral and the college. The bars, warmed by log fires in winter, are happily cluttered with everything from old sports equipment to pewter mugs, and the handsomely furnished bedrooms (some in the modern annex) also reflect the proprietor's eclectic tastes. The award-winning restaurant, whose French and English dishes are set off by a good wine list, is very popular with locals, so call ahead. ⊠ *75 Kingsgate St., SO23 9PE,* ☎ *01962/853834,* FAX *01962/854411. 13 rooms with bath. Restaurant, sauna. AE, DC, MC, V.*

£££   🕆 **Lainston House.** Dating from 1668, this elegant country-house hotel is set in a 63-acre park. Inside, public rooms are adorned with oak paneling and other restored 17th-century features. All rooms are attractively decorated and comfortably furnished, but try for the ground-floor Garden or Chapel Suites, which have access to the gardens. There are more rooms in an attractively converted stable wing, some with four-posters and Jacuzzis. ⊠ *Sparsholt (2½ mi northwest of Winchester) SO21 2LT,* ☎ *01962/863588,* FAX *01962/776672. 38 rooms with bath. Putting green, tennis court, croquet, helipad. AE, DC, MC, V.*

Shopping

The **Antiques Market** (⊠ King's Walk, ☎ 01962/862277) sells crafts and gift items, as well as antiques. A complete list of local antiques stores is available from Winchester Tourist Information Center (☎ 01962/840500). **H. M. Gilbert** (⊠ 19 The Square, ☎ 01962/852832), an antiquarian bookseller, is housed in five medieval cottages, set amid a network of ancient streets.

New Alresford

⑩   *8 mi northeast of Winchester, by A31 and B3046.*

New Alresford (pronounced awlsford) has a pleasant village green crossed by a stream and some Georgian houses and pleasant antiques shops. The village is now the starting point of the **Watercress Line,** a 10-mi railroad reserved for steam locomotives. The line takes visitors on a nostalgic tour through reminders of 19th-century England. ⊠ *Railway Station,* ☎ *01962/733810.* 🎫 *£7.50.* ☉ *Mar.–Oct., weekends and national holidays, with daily departures mid-July–early-Sept.; call for details.*

IN SEARCH OF JANE AUSTEN

THANKS TO THE FILM adaptations of *Sense and Sensibility, Emma,* and *Persuasion,* and the BBC-TV's wildly popular miniseries based on *Pride and Prejudice,* Jane Austen has captured a whole new audience eager to peer into her decorous 18th-century world. By visiting one or two main locales, it is possible to imagine hearing the tinkle of teacups raised by the likes of Elinor Dashwood, Emma Woodhouse, and the bold and dashing Mr. Darcy. As Jane herself described this terrain in *Emma,* "It has a sweet view—sweet to the eye and the mind. English verdure, English culture, English comfort, seen under a sun bright, without being oppressive." Serious Janes will want to retrace the complete itinerary of her life—starting out in the hamlet

be the model for Emma Woodhouse, with "a disposition to think a little too well of herself," came to live in 1815. She would use a little donkey-cart, still at the cottage, to shop in nearby Alton. A bit farther away is Great Bookham—closely identified with the "Highbury" of *Emma*—while nearby lies Box Hill (to the east of A24 between Leatherhead and Dorking ☞ Chapter 3), the probable inspiration for the locale of the famous walking expedition that left Miss Woodhouse in tears.

"It is the only place for happiness," Jane once said of the county of Kent, some 150 mi to the east of Chawton. "Everybody is rich there." Here, Godmersham Park, another of her brother's estates (located off the A28

of Steventon, southwest of Basingstoke, where she spent the first 25 years of her life, then moving on to Bath, Southampton, Chawton, and Winchester.

But the heart of her world remained the tiny Hampshire village of Chawton. Here at a former bailiff's cottage on her brother's estate (*see* Chawton, *above*), Jane produced three of her greatest novels, took walks to Chawton Manor—her brother's regal Jacobean mansion, now being transformed into a center for the study of women's literature—and called on nearby Lyards Farm, where her favorite niece, Anna Lefroy, thought to

between Canterbury and Ashford), offered her an escape to the countryside, where baronets lived "in unrepentant idleness." The pretty, redbrick mansion is privately owned but you can take a nearby public footpath to pass the little Grecian Temple where she completed *Sense and Sensibility*; views of the Palladian house from this spot may have inspired her visions of Pemberley and Mansfield Park. No matter if you search for Jane Austen Country in Hampshire or Kent, you can revisit it again and again in its home base: English literature.

Chawton

⑪ *8 mi east of Old Alresford along A31.*

Jane Austen lived the last eight years of her life in the village of Chawton (she moved to Winchester only during her final illness). Here, in an unassuming redbrick house, she revised *Sense and Sensibility,* created *Pride and Prejudice,* and worked on *Emma, Persuasion,* and *Mansfield Park.* The rooms of the house retain the atmosphere of restricted gentility suitable to the unmarried daughter of a clergyman. In the left-hand parlor, Jane would play her piano every morning, then repair to her mahogany writing desk in the family sitting room—leaving her sister Cassandra to do the household chores ("I find composition impossible with my head full of joints of mutton and doses of rhubarb," Jane wrote). In the 18th century, the house was much closer to a bustling thoroughfare, and one traveler reported that a window view proved that the Misses Austen were "looking very comfortable at breakfast." Jane was famous for working unperturbed through any and all interruptions, but one protection against the outside world was the famous door that creaked, whose hinges she asked might remain unattended to because they gave her warning that someone was coming. For more about the great author and a suggested minitour of Jane Austen Country, see the Close-Up box, "In Search of Jane Austen," *below.* ☎ *01420/83262.* ✍ *£2.* ☉ *Mar.–Dec., daily 11–4:30; Jan.–Feb. weekends 11–4:30.*

Petersfield

⑫ *10 mi south of Chawton.*

The Georgian market town of Petersfield is set in a wide valley between wooded hills and open downs. From Chawton, follow B3006, then A325 for Petersfield. Four miles south of the town on A3 will lead you to **Queen Elizabeth Country Park,** which has 1,400 acres of chalk hills and shady beechwood with scenic hiking trails. You can climb to the top of Butser Hill (888 ft) to take in a splendid view of the coast. ☎ *01705/595040.* ✍ *Free.* ☉ *Café and shop open daily 10–5:30 (10–dusk in winter).*

Portsmouth

⑬ *15 mi south of Petersfield along A3, 77 mi southwest of London.*

The city of Portsmouth has been England's naval capital and principal port of departure for centuries. The harbor covers about 7 square mi, incorporating the world's first dry dock (built in 1495) and extensive defenses. These include **Portchester Castle,** founded more than 1,600 years ago, which has the most complete set of Roman walls in northern Europe. The keep's central tower affords a sweeping view of the harbor and coastline. ✉ *Near Fareham,* ☎ *01705/378291.* ✍ *£2.50.* ☉ *Apr.–Oct., daily 10–6 or dusk; Nov.–Mar., daily 10–4.*

Portsmouth Naval Base has an unrivaled collection of ships: HMS *Victory,* the *Mary Rose,* HMS *Warrior,* and the Royal Naval Museum, all run by the Portsmouth Heritage Trust (☎ 01705/839766). Nelson's
★ flagship, **HMS Victory,** has been painstakingly restored to appear as she did at the battle at Trafalgar (1805). You can inspect the cramped gun decks, visit the cabin where Nelson entertained his officers, and stand on the spot where he was mortally wounded by a French sniper. The
★ *Mary Rose,* former flagship of the Tudor navy, which capsized and sank in the harbor in 1545, was raised in 1982 in a much-publicized exercise in marine archaeology. Described at the time as "the flower of all

the ships that ever sailed," the *Mary Rose* is now housed in a fascinating, specially constructed enclosure, where her timbers are continuously sprayed with water to prevent them from drying out and breaking up. The **Royal Naval Museum** has a fine collection of painted figureheads, relics of Nelson's family, and galleries of paintings and mementos recalling different periods of naval history. ▨ *All-inclusive tickets £11 and £14; each ship £5.50; HMS Victory includes museum; museum only £3.* ☉ *Mar.–Oct., daily 10–6 (last admission 4:30); Nov.–Feb., daily 10–5 (last admission 3:45).*

In the popular **D-Day Museum,** near the corner of Southsea Common, exhibits vividly reconstruct the many stages of planning and the communications and logistics involved, as well as the actual invasion. The centerpiece of the museum is the Overlord Embroidery ("Overlord" was the code name for the invasion), a 272-ft tapestry with 34 panels illustrating the history of World War II, from the Battle of Britain in 1940 to D-Day (June 6, 1944) and the first days of the liberation. ⊠ *Clarence Esplanade, Southsea,* ☎ *01705/827261.* ▨ *£4.75.* ☉ *Apr.–Oct. daily 10–5:30 (last admission 4:30); Nov.–Mar. Mon. 1–5, Tues.–Sun. 10–5 (last admission 4).*

Dining and Lodging

££ ✕ **Bistro Montparnasse.** Terra-cotta walls, candles, and prints help foster the intimate atmosphere of a traditional French restaurant. Among the dishes featured are turbot with a basil and champagne sauce, and a refreshingly sharp lemon soufflé. ⊠ *103 Palmerston Rd., Southsea,* ☎ *01705/816754. AE, DC, MC, V. Closed Sun. and Mon. No lunch.*

££ ▣ **Westfield Hall.** Portsmouth is well supplied with Hiltons, Fortes, and
★   Holiday Inns, but here's a pleasant smaller establishment with personal service and character. Westfield Hall is in a converted turn-of-the-century house with large bay windows, and it sits close to the water in Southsea, the quieter, southern part of Portsmouth. It has satellite TV and a video channel in all rooms, seven of which are on the ground floor. Dinner is available. ⊠ *65 Festing Rd., PO4 0NQ,* ☎ *01705/ 826971,* ☒ *01705/870200. 25 rooms with bath. Dining room. AE, DC, MC, V.*

Southampton

🄔 *21 mi northwest of Portsmouth, 25 mi southwest of Salisbury, 79 mi southwest of London.*

Seafaring Saxons and Romans used Southampton's harbor, Southampton Water, as a commercial trading port for centuries, making it one of England's richest cities. But Plymouth eventually supplanted it, and Southampton has been going downhill ever since. Much of the city center is shoddy, having been hastily rebuilt after World War II. But bits and pieces of the city's history—spared from Nazi bombs—occasionally peek out from between modern buildings. Fortunately, the Old Town still retains its medieval air, and considerable parts of Southampton's castellated walls remain. They incorporate a variety of old buildings, including **God's House Tower,** originally a gunpowder factory, now the archaeology museum. ⊠ *Town Quay,* ☎ *01703/635904.* ▨ *Free.* ☉ *Tues.–Fri. 10–noon, 1–5, Sat. 10–noon, 1–4, Sun. 2–5.*

Mayflower Park and the Pilgrim Fathers' Memorial on Western Esplanade commemorate the sailing of the *Mayflower* from Southampton to the New World on August 15, 1620. (The ship was forced to stop in Plymouth for repairs.) John Alden, the hero of Longfellow's poem *The Courtship of Miles Standish,* was a native of Southampton.

Southampton Maritime Museum. In addition to the *Mayflower,* this was the home port of the *Queen Mary* and the infamous *Titanic,* along with countless other great ocean liners of the 20th century. This museum is essentially a history of commercial shipping, interesting only to those who study vital statistics of cruise ships and sails on clippers. ⊠ *Bugle St.,* ☎ *01703/632493.* 🎟 *Free.* ☉ *Tues.–Fri. 10–1, 2–5; Sat. 10–1, 2–4; Sun. 2–5.*

Southampton's attractions include a good art gallery, extensive parks, and the superb **Tudor House Museum** and garden. ⊠ *St. Michael's Sq.,* ☎ *01703/635904.* 🎟 *Free.* ☉ *Tues.–Fri. 10–noon, 1–5, Sat. 10–noon, 1–4, Sun. 2–5.*

🕲 **Paulton's Park** is a large leisure park with a Gypsy Museum, Rio Grande Train, Magic Forest, and more than 40 other attractions. There's enough to occupy a full day, and refreshments are also available. ⊠ *Just off exit 2 of M27, near Southampton,* ☎ *01703/814455.* 🎟 *£8.50.* ☉ *Mid-Mar.–Oct., daily 10–6:30 (last admission 4:30); Nov.–Dec., weekends only 10–dusk.*

Dining and Lodging

£ ✕ **La Brasserie.** This is a busy spot at lunchtime, popular with the business community, though it quiets down in the evening. The decor is straightforward and ungimmicky, while the atmosphere is as traditionally French as the menu. ⊠ *33–34 Oxford St.,* ☎ *01703/635043. AE, MC, V. Closed Sun. No lunch Sat.*

£ ✕ **Red Lion.** Although modern on the outside, this handy spot boasts an ancient interior, with a huge half-timbered bar and minstrels' gallery—perfect for lunch with an intriguing Tudor ambience. ⊠ *55 High St.,* ☎ *01703/333595. AE, DC, MC, V.*

££–£££ 🛏 **Dolphin Hotel.** Originally a Georgian coaching inn—though there's been an inn of some sort on this site for seven centuries—the Dolphin offers stylish accommodations in the form of large, comfortable rooms. The service is excellent—discreet but attentive. Rates fall in the bottom end of this category. ⊠ *35 High St., SO14 2HN,* ☎ *01703/339955,* FAX *01703/333650. 73 rooms with bath. Restaurant. AE, DC, MC, V.*

The Arts

THEATERS

The refurbished **Mayflower Theatre** (⊠ Commercial Rd., ☎ 01703/711811) in Southampton is among the larger theaters outside London, and everyone from the Royal Shakespeare Company to Black Sabbath and Sting have packed the house. The **Nuffield Theatre** (☎ 01703/671771), on Southampton University campus, has its own repertory company and also hosts national touring groups, which perform some of the leading West End productions.

Romsey

10 mi northwest of Southampton.

This small town on the River Test has an authentic Norman abbey church and, in the marketplace, an iron bracket said to have been used to hang two of Cromwell's soldiers. The flint and stone house nearby, known as King John's Hunting Box, dates from the 13th century.

⑮ Outside Romsey, just off A3057, **Broadlands** was home of the late Lord Mountbatten, uncle of Queen Elizabeth II. This 18th-century Palladian mansion, with gardens laid out by Capability Brown and wide lawns sweeping down to the banks of the River Test, is undoubtedly the grandest house in Hampshire. It abounds with ornate plaster moldings and paintings of British and Continental royalty, as well as personal mementos tracing Lord Mountbatten's distinguished career in the navy and in India. In 1947, the Queen and the Duke of Edinburgh spent their honeymoon here, and the Prince and Princess of Wales spent a few days of theirs here in 1981. ✉ *Romsey,* ☎ *01794/516878.* ✆ *£5.* ☉ *Mid-June–early Sept., daily noon–5:30; last admission 4.*

Dining and Lodging

£££ ✗ **Old Manor House.** This is one of those restaurants that is inseparable from its owner-chef, in this case Mauro Bregoli. The decor is typical of the area, with oak beams and huge fireplaces, and the Italian-influenced food is rich and flavorsome. Specialties include quenelle of pike, duck breast with apples, hare, suckling pig, and venison. The wine list is exceptionally good. There are worthwhile set menus, especially at lunch. ✉ *21 Palmerston St.,* ☎ *01794/517353. AE, MC, V. Closed Mon. No dinner Sun.*

£££ ⌂ **Potters Heron Hotel.** An ideal place to stay if you're visiting Broad-
★ lands, this hotel has been renovated, adding a modern extension to the original thatched building. Choose an old or new room to suit your taste; many have balconies. Dine in the oak-beamed Potters Pub or the Garden restaurant, with its table d'hôte and à la carte menus. ✉ *Ampfield (3 mi east of Romsey) SO51 9ZF,* ☎ *01703/266611,* ℻ *01703/251359. 54 rooms with bath. Restaurant, pub, sauna. AE, DC, MC, V.*

Outdoor Activities and Sports

GOLF
Dunwood Manor Country Club (✉ Shootash Hill, near Romsey, ☎ 01794/340549).

ISLE OF WIGHT

The Isle of Wight (pronounced white) has a very special atmosphere, quite distinct from that of the mainland. To begin with it it is essentially Victorian. This is only reasonable since, although the island was known to the Romans and the ill-fated Stuarts, it was Queen Victoria who put it on the map by choosing to build Osborne House here, live here as much as she could, and ultimately die here. Clearly she must have created a great vogue, because most of the domestic architecture is exclusively Victorian. To some extent, in fact, the mind-set is even Victorian. You can still meet elderly residents of Brighstone who refer to their children's trip to Hampshire as "going abroad." These islanders are fiercely chauvinistic and just like Tennyson—once an inhabitant of the island until he was driven away by tourist harassment—they are somewhat resentful of vacationers. But every season the day-trippers arrive—thanks to the ferries, hovercraft, and hydrofoils that connect the Isle of Wight with Southampton, Portsmouth, Southsea, and Lymington. They are drawn to this 23-mi-long island by its holiday resorts—Ryde, Bembridge, Ventnor, Freshwater (stay away from tacky Sandown and Shaklin)—its rich vegetation, narrow lanes, thatched cottages, curving bays, sandy beaches, days spent riding the Solent waves, and lots of that fabulous ocean air, which, to quote Tennyson, is "worth six pence a pint." All is not sea and sails. There is splendid motoring to be done in the interior of the island in such places as Brading Down, Ashley Down, and Mersely Down and the occasional country house to visit, none more spectacular, of course, than Queen Vicky's own Osborne House.

Cowes

16 *11 mi northwest of Ryde.*

If you embark from Southampton, your ferry will cross the Solent and dock at Cowes (pronounced cows), a magic name in the sailing world and internationally known for the "Cowes Week" annual yachting festival, held in July or August. Fifty years ago, Cowes Regatta was a supreme event, attended by Imperial Majesties and Serene Highnesses from all over the world; wealthy Americans raced against the Czar of Russia, and the fantastically green lawns of the Royal Yacht Squadron were crowded with the world's most famous figures, eating strawberries and cream as they strolled about with parasols and in of-the-moment dresses, or in blazers, white trousers, and yachting caps. Although elegance is a thing of the past, the **Cowes Regatta** (☎ 01983/291914) is still an important event in yachting circles and is occasionally attended by that latest royal seaman, the Duke of Edinburgh. At the north end of High Street, on the **Parade,** a tablet commemorates the sailing from Cowes in 1633 of two ships carrying the founders of the state of Maryland.

Just one mile to the east of Cowes, Queen Victoria built **Osborne House** (designed by Prince Albert after a villa in the stodgiest Italian Renaissance style) and spent much time here during her last years. Though the queen was happy here, there is an underlying sadness to the place. Here one sees the engineer manqué of Prince Albert and his clever innovations—even central heating—and the desperate attempt of Victoria to give her children a normal but disciplined upbringing. For anyone drawn to the domestic side of history, Osborne is enormously interesting. For antiques lovers, the state rooms have scarcely been altered since her death here in 1901. ☎ 01983/200022. 🏷 *House and grounds £6.50, grounds only £3.50.* ⊘ *Apr.–Oct., daily 10–5 (last admission 4).*

Lodging

£££ 🏨 **New Holmwood Hotel.** This Best Western hotel occupies an unrivaled location above the Esplanade—ideal for watching yachters in the Solent. The three lounges include one allowing an open fire on winter evenings and one for non-smokers, while the sheltered sun terrace and pool take full advantage of fine weather. Rates are low in this price category. ⊠ *Queens Rd., Egypt Point, PO31 8BW,* ☎ *01983/292508,* FAX *01983/295020. 26 rooms with bath. Restaurant, bar, pool, meeting rooms. AE, DC, MC, V.*

Ryde

⑰ *11 mi southeast of Cowes.*

The town of Ryde has long been one of the Isle of Wight's most popular summer resorts, offering a variety of family attractions. Following the construction of **Ryde Pier** in 1814, elegant (and occasionally ostentatious) town houses sprang up along the seafront and on the slopes behind, commanding fine views of the harbor. In addition to its long, sandy beach, Ryde has a large boating lake (rowboats and pedal boats can be rented) and children's playgrounds. To get here from Cowes, leave on A3021, then follow the signs on A3054.

At the waterfowl reserve of **Flamingo Park,** 2½ mi east of Ryde, many of the birds will eat from your hand. ⊠ *Springvale, Seaview,* ☎ *01983/ 612153.* 🏷 *£4.25.* ⊘ *Easter–Sept., daily 10–5 (last admission 4); Oct., daily 10:30–4 (last admission 3).*

Dining and Lodging

££–£££ ✕🏨 **Seaview Hotel.** Set in the heart of a harbor village just outside Ryde, this smart hotel offers a strong maritime flavor and comfortable, well-equipped bedrooms. The main attractions, however, are the restaurants (smoking and no-smoking), which specialize in fresh island produce. Try the hot crab ramekin (baked with cream and tarragon with a cheese topping) to start, and lobster or grilled plaice (subject to availability) for an entrée. The desserts are a revelation. ⊠ *High St., Seaview PO34 5EX,* ☎ *01983/612711,* ⨍ᴀ⨯ *01983/613729. 16 rooms with bath or shower. 2 restaurants, 2 bars. AE, DC, MC, V.*

£ ⊡ **Biskra House.** This spacious Victorian hotel is located off the Esplanade, so the noise level is low. You can enjoy the excellent views over the Solent from the tastefully furnished back bedrooms as well as from the restaurant. Recently, a change of ownership has indicated improvements are in the offing.⊠ *17 St. Thomas' St., Ryde, PO33 2DL,* ☎ *01983/567913,* ⨍ᴀ⨯ *01983/616976. 10 rooms with bath. Restaurant, bar. AE, MC, V.*

Brading

⑱ *3 mi south of Ryde on A3055.*

Make a stop at the village of Brading, where St. Mary's Church, dating from Norman times, holds monuments to the local Olgander family. Next to the Old Town Hall stands the 16th-century rectory, said to be the oldest inhabited dwelling on the island. The house now contains a **Wax Museum** with thrills and horrors enhanced by sound-and-light wizardry. ⊠ *High St.,* ☎ *01983/407286.* ⊡ *£4.75.* ☯ *May–Sept., daily 10–10; Oct.–Apr., daily 10–5; last admission 1 hr before closing.*

A mile or so south of the village of Brading lie the remains of the substantial, 3rd-century **Brading Roman Villa,** whose splendid mosaic floors and heating system have been preserved. ☎ *01983/406223.* ⊡ *£2.50.* ☯ *Apr.–Oct., daily 10–5.*

Arreton

⑲ *6 mi southwest of Ryde, 5 mi west of Brady.*

In the medieval village of Arreton, a group of old farm buildings that were once part of the local manor have been restored as a **Country Crafts Village.** More than a dozen local craftspeople have studios in the village, working in wood, wool, clay, metal, and other materials. You can browse and buy items directly from the makers, or you can have a snack at the handy cafeteria, or a drink at the bar. ☎ *01983/528353.* ⊡ *Free.* ☯ *Mon.–Sat 10–5, Sun. 11–4.*

Ventnor

⑳ *7 mi southeast of Arreton, 11 mi south of Ryde.*

The south coast resorts are the sunniest and most sheltered on the Isle of Wight. Ventnor itself rises from such a steep slope that the ground floors of some of its houses are level with the roofs of those across the road. The **Botanic Gardens** here, laid out over 22 acres, contain more than 3,500 species of trees, plants, and shrubs; there's also an excellent restaurant, the Garden. ⊠ *Undercliff Dr.* ⊡ *Free.* ☯ *Daily 10–5.*

Lodging

£££ ⊡ **Winterbourne Hotel.** This manor house was one of Charles Dickens's many homes; bedrooms are named after characters in *David Copperfield,* part of which he wrote here. The furnishings are, of course, Victorian, and the gardens, with waterfalls, are beautifully kept. Room rates include dinner. ⊠ *Bonchurch, near Ventnor, PO38 1RQ,* ☎ *01983/852535,* ⨍ᴀ⨯ *01983/853056. 15 rooms with bath. Restaurant, pool. AE, DC, MC, V. Closed Nov.–Feb.*

Outdoor Activities and Sports

GOLF

Shanklin and Sandown (⊠ The Fairway, Sandown, Isle of Wight ☎ 01983/403170).

En Route   The southwestern coast is the least developed part of the shoreline but contains one famous natural sight, the **Needles,** a long line of jagged chalk stacks jutting out of the sea like monstrous teeth, which can be found west of Blackgang. Another attraction is a fantasy theme park, ☼ **Blackgang Chine,** built in a deep chine (cleft in the cliffs) overlooking a former smugglers' landing place. It features Dinosaurland, Smugglersland, Cowboytown, and other attractions for ages 3–12. ⊠ *Ventnor, Isle of Wight,* ☎ *01983/730330.* ⊡ *£5.50.* ☉ *Apr.–end of May, daily 10–5; end of May–end of Sept., daily 10–10; end of Sept.–Oct., daily 10–4:30.*

Alum Bay

㉑   *19 mi northwest of Ventnor, 18 mi southwest of Cowes.*

Take the chairlift to the beach at Alum Bay, where you can catch a good view of the multicolor sand in the cliff strata. The **Alum Bay Glass Company** welcomes visitors interested in buying souvenirs or just in watching glassblowing and jewelry crafting. ☎ *01983/753473.* ⊡ *80p.* ☉ *Daily 10–4, with regular tours, talks, and demonstrations in summer; no glassmaking on weekends except Sun. Easter–Sept.*

Lodging

££–£££   ⊞ **Farringford Hotel.** Once the splendid home of the Victorian poet laureate Alfred, Lord Tennyson, this is now an unpretentious hotel. The 18th-century house is set on 33 acres of grounds; outbuildings contain 24 self-catering suites and cottages, as well as standard bedrooms. ⊠ *Bedbury La., Freshwater PO40 9PE, near Alum Bay,* ☎ *01983/752500,* ☏ *01983/756515. 68 rooms with bath, 20 suites, 4 cottages. Restaurant, pool, 9-hole golf course, tennis court. AE, DC, MC, V.*

Outdoor Activities and Sports

GOLF

Freshwater Bay Golf Club (⊠ Freshwater Bay, Isle of Wight, ☎ 01983/752955).

Carisbrooke Castle

★ ㉒   *14 mi east of Alum Bay, 1¼ mi southwest of Newport, 5 mi south of Cowes.*

A short distance outside the Isle of Wight's modern-day capital, Newport, lies the former capital, Carisbrooke, now a village. Above it stands Carisbrooke Castle, built by the Normans but enlarged in Elizabethan times. King Charles I was imprisoned here during the English Civil War. Note the small window in the north curtain wall through which he tried to escape, then stroll along the battlements to watch the donkey wheel, where a team of donkeys draws water from a deep well. ☎ *01983/522107.* ⊡ *£4.* ☉ *Apr.–Oct., 10–6 or dusk; Nov.–Mar., daily 10–4.*

Take the ferry (for complete information, *see* Getting Around *in* The South A to Z, *below*) back to Southampton and follow A36 north to Salisbury, about 25 mi away.

SALISBURY, STONEHENGE, AND THE NEW FOREST

This tour kicks off in Salisbury, renowned for its glorious cathedral, then loops west around Salisbury Plain, up to Avebury, and back to Stonehenge. From Stonehenge you dip south into Hampshire, to the wild, scenic expanse of the New Forest, ancient hunting preserve of William the Conqueror. Your own transport is essential to see anything beyond Salisbury, though there are also plenty of opportunities en route to stretch your legs.

Salisbury

㉓ *25 mi northeast of Southampton, 55 mi southeast of Bristol, 90 mi southwest of London.*

Although Salisbury (pronounced sawls-bree) is an historic city, and its old stone shops and houses grew up in the shadow of the great church, the city did not become important until the seat of the diocese of Old Sarum (the original settlement 2 mi to the north) was transferred here in the 13th century. The cathedral at Old Sarum was razed (today only ★ **㉔** ruins remain), **Salisbury Cathedral** was built, and the city of Salisbury was born. In the 19th century, novelist Anthony Trollope based his tales of ecclesiastical life, notably *Barchester Towers*, on life here, although his fictional city of Barchester is really an amalgam of Salisbury and Winchester. Today, the city remains dotted with places of picturesque interest. The local tourist office organizes walks—of differing lengths for varying stamina—to lead you to the treasures, many of which you would never have found alone.

Salisbury continues to be dominated by its towering cathedral, a soaring hymn in stone. It is unique in that it was conceived and built as a whole, in the amazingly short span of only 38 years (1220–1258). The spire, added in 1320, is a miraculous feat of medieval engineering—even though the point, 404 ft above the ground, is 2½ ft off vertical. For a fictional, keenly imaginative reconstruction of the human drama underlying such an achievement, read William Golding's novel *The Spire*. Anyone with a taste for the technical achievement of the Middle Ages will be fascinated by the excellent model of the cathedral in the north transept, the "arm" of the church to your left as you look at the altar. It shows the building about 20 years into construction, and makes very clear the ambition of Salisbury's medieval builders. For all their sophistication, however, the height and immense weight of their great spire have always posed structural problems. In the late 17th century Sir Christopher Wren was summoned from London to strengthen the spire, while in the mid-19th century Gilbert Scott, the leading Victorian Gothicist, undertook a major program of restoration on it. At the same time he put in hand a major clear-up of the interior, in the process getting rid of some less-than-sympathetic 18th-century alterations. For all that, the interior still seems spartan and a little gloomy, but check out the remarkable lancet windows and sculpted tombs of crusaders and other medieval heroes. The clock in the north aisle—probably the oldest working mechanism in Europe, if not the world—was made in 1386. The spacious **cloisters** are the largest in England, and the octagonal **Chapter House** contains a marvelous 13th-century frieze showing scenes from the Old Testament. Here you can also see one of the four original copies of the **Magna Carta,** the charter of rights the English barons forced King John to accept in 1215; it was sent here for safekeeping in the 13th century. ⊠ *Cathedral Close,* ☎ *01722/323279.* 🎫 *Cathedral £2 donation; Chapter House 30p.* ☉ *Cathedral May–*

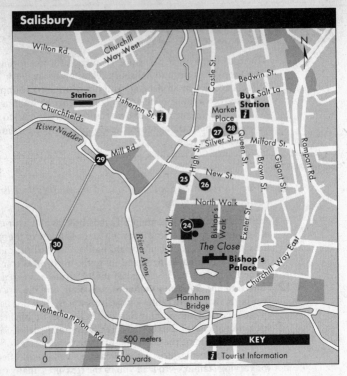

*Aug. daily 8–8:15, Sept.–Apr. daily 8–6:30; Chapter House Mon.–
Sat. 9:30–5, Sun 1–5.*

Salisbury's **Cathedral Close** (grounds) forms probably the finest backdrop of any British cathedral, with its smooth lawns and splendid examples of architecture of all ages (except modern) creating a harmonious
background. Some of the historic houses are open to the public. On
the north side of Cathedral Close, **Mompesson House** can justifiably
be claimed one of the most appealing Queen Anne houses in Britain.
There are no treasures per se, but some fine original paneling and plasterwork, as well as a fascinating collection of 18th-century drinking
glasses, and an attractive walled garden where tea and refreshments
are served. ⊠ *The Close,* ☎ *01722/335659.* 🎟 *£3.40.* ⊙ *Apr.–Oct.,
Sat.–Wed. noon–5:30 (last admission 5).*

On the north side of the Cathedral Close you'll find **High Street Gate,**
one of the four castellated stone gateways built to separate the close
from the rest of the city. Passing through it, you enter into the heart
of the modern town. One of Salisbury's best-known landmarks, the
hexagonal **Poultry Cross,** on Silver Street, is the last remaining of the
four original market crosses, and dealers still set up their stalls beside
it. A narrow side street links Poultry Cross to **Market Square,** site of
one of southern England's most popular markets, held on Tuesday and
Saturday. Permission to hold an annual fair here was granted in 1221,
and that right is exercised for three days every October.

West of High Street lies Mill Road, which leads you across Queen Elizabeth Gardens to **Long Bridge.** Cross the bridge and continue on the
town path; the view from here inspired that 19th-century icon, John
Constable's *Salisbury Cathedral,* now hung in the Constable Room of
London's National Gallery. Reached via a 20-minute walk southwest
of the town center along the town path, the **Old Mill** (⊠ Town Path,

West Harnham), dating from the 12th century, makes a pleasant destination. It is now a restaurant and coffee shop under the same management as the Old Mill Hotel next door.

Dining and Lodging

£ ✕ **Harper's.** This is a popular second-floor restaurant overlooking the marketplace. Its cuisine mingles English and French dishes, and its specialties include boeuf bourguignon and fillet of salmon. There is a good-value Shopper's Special lunch. Friendly service makes dining here a pleasure. ✉ *7 Ox Row, Market Pl.,* ☎ *01722/333118. AE, DC, MC, V. Closed Sun. Oct.–May.*

£ ✕ **Haunch of Venison.** Opposite the Poultry Cross, this place has been going strong for more than six centuries, and it is brimful with period details (such as the mummified arm of an 18th-century card player still clutching his cards, which was found in 1903 by workmen). The wood-paneled restaurant (be careful not to bump your head on the beams) has an open fire and antique, leather-covered settees. There is also a noisy but comfortable bar, with timbered walls and black-and-white tile floors, that offers simpler fare. ✉ *1 Minster St.,* ☎ *01722/ 322024. AE, MC, V. No dinner Sun. in winter.*

£ ✕ **Pinocchio.** This small Italian trattoria has been making customers smile since 1988. There are six preparations of veal on offer, and there is also fresh fish on the menu. Pizzas are also available, and, for dessert, the tiramisu is sublime. The restaurant is conveniently located near the train station. ✉ *139 Fisherton St.,* ☎ *01722/413069. MC, V. No lunch Sun.*

£££ ✕🏠 **Grasmere House.** A large late-Victorian edifice (1896), this redbrick lodging covered with creeper has fine views over the river to the cathedral. The 1½ acres of garden even include a "ha-ha" (ask at reception), and the comfortable bedrooms are named after local worthies (a saint, a canon, and so on); some are in the new extension. The restaurant, in a conservatory, also provides peaceful country views. Its menu features fresh local ingredients. ✉ *70 Harnham Rd., SP2 8JN,* ☎ *01722/338388,* 𝔽𝔸𝕏 *01722/333710. 20 rooms with bath. Restaurant, bar, parking . AE, MC, V.*

£££ ✕🏠 **Red Lion Hotel.** A former coaching inn—parts of the building date from 1220—this hotel is now in the Best Western consortium. It's packed with old clocks and other relics from its long past, and a choice of comfortable rooms in either modern or antique style. It's centrally located and an ideal base for exploring the city. ✉ *Milford St., SP1 2AN,* ☎ *01722/323334,* 𝔽𝔸𝕏 *01722/325756. 54 rooms with bath. Restaurant. AE, DC, MC, V.*

£ ✕🏠 **Byways House.** Friendly service, good value, and a quiet location
★ are some of the reasons this double-fronted Victorian house is popular with visitors. Some rooms are adapted for use by guests with disabilities. The hotel offers large vegetarian or traditional English breakfasts. Ask for a room with a view of the cathedral. ✉ *31 Fowlers Rd., SP1 2QP,* ☎ *01722/328364,* 𝔽𝔸𝕏 *01722/322146. 23 rooms, 19 with bath. MC, V.*

The Arts

FESTIVALS

The **Salisbury Festival** (☎ 01722/323883), held in May and June, features excellent classical concerts, recitals, plays, and outdoor events.

THEATERS

The **Salisbury Playhouse** (✉ Malthouse La., ☎ 01722/320333) presents high-caliber drama all year and is the main venue for the Salisbury Festival.

Outdoor Activities and Sports

BICYCLING

You can rent a range of bikes at **Hayball's Cycle Shop** (⊠ 26–30 Winchester St., Salisbury, ☏ 01722/411378) for about £8 per day or £48 per week, £25 cash deposit.

Shopping

Watsons (⊠ 8–9 Queen St., ☏ 01722/320311) is worth visiting for its buildings dating from 1306 and 1425, with their original windows, a carved oak mantelpiece, and other period features. The company specializes in Aynsley and Wedgwood bone china, Waterford and Dartington glass, Royal Doulton, and a wide range of fine ornaments.

Wilton House

★ ③ *4 mi west of Salisbury along A30.*

Five rivers—the Avon, the Bourne, the Nadder, the Wylye, and the Ebble—wind slowly from Salisbury into the rich heart of Wiltshire. Following the valley of the Nadder will lead you to the ancient town of Wilton, from which the county takes its name. A traditional market is held here every Thursday, but the main attraction is Wilton House and Gardens, home of the 17th Earl of Pembroke. The original Tudor house burned down in 1647; the present mansion replacing it was designed by Inigo Jones, Ben Jonson's stage designer and the architect of London's Banqueting House. In fine weather, the lordly expanse of sweeping lawns that surrounds the house, bisected by the River Avon and dotted with towering oaks and a gracious Palladian bridge, makes up one of the most quintessentially English of scenes. Even if your taste in stately homes is limited or suffering from overexposure, tour the house, for it contains one of the most extravagantly beautiful rooms in the history of interior decoration, the aptly named Double Cube Room. The curious name refers to its simple proportions, evidence of Jones's classically inspired belief that beauty in architecture derives from the harmony and balance of its proportions. The room's headliner is the spectacular, Cinerama-size Van Dyck portrait of the Pembroke family. Adorned with gilded William Kent furniture and swimming in plush reds and gold, the Double Cube was where Eisenhower prepared some of his plans for the Normandy invasion; it has been used in numerous period films, including *Lady Caroline Lamb* and Emma Thompson's adaptation of *Sense and Sensibility*. Other delights include an exhibition of 7,000 toy soldiers, the "Wareham Bears" (200 dressed teddy bears), and, on a higher note, some great Old Master paintings. ☏ *01722/746729.* ▨ *House and grounds £6.75, grounds only £3.75.* ☉ *Easter–Oct., daily 11–6 (last admission 5).*

Shaftesbury

③ *18 mi west of Wilton on A30, 22 mi west of Salisbury.*

The charming village of Shaftesbury—the model for the town of Shaston in Thomas Hardy's *Jude the Obscure*—lies just inside the Dorset county border. When you reach the village, head for **Gold Hill**, a steep, relentlessly picturesque street lined with cottages. From the top you can catch a sweeping view of the surrounding countryside. Though Gold Hill itself is something of a tourist cliché (it has even appeared in TV commercials), it is still well worth visiting.

Stourhead

★ ③ *9 mi northwest of Shaftesbury (follow B3081 to B3092), 30 mi west of Salisbury.*

Close to the village of Stourton lies one of Wiltshire's most breathtaking sights—Stourhead, a country-house-and-garden combination that has few parallels for beauty anywhere in Europe. Most of Stourhead was built between 1721 and 1725 by "Henry the Magnificent," a fabulously wealthy banker by the name of Henry Hoare. Many of the rooms contain Chinese and French porcelain and other objets d'art; the exquisitely elegant library and floridly colored picture gallery were both built for the explicit cultural development of this exceedingly civilized family. Although the house is a monument to the age of elegance and manners, it must take second place to its adjacent gardens, the most celebrated example of the English 18th-century taste for "natural" landscaping. Temples, grottoes, and bridges have been skillfully placed among colorful shrubs, trees, and flowers to make the grounds look like a three-dimensional oil painting. A walk around the lake (1½ mi) reveals a series of ever-changing vistas that conjure up the 17th-century landscapes of Claude and Poussin. The best time to visit is early summer, when the massive banks of rhododendrons are in full bloom, but it is beautiful at any time of year. During the summer, there are occasional concerts, sometimes accompanied by fireworks and gondoliers on the lake; these *fête champêtre* evenings are ascension-into-heaven events. Book your tour around one! There is a small restaurant and inn near the entrance to the grounds (☞ *below*). From London by train, get off at Gillingham and take a 5-minute cab ride to Stourton (cabs will happily take several travelers on one trip). ⊠ *Stourton, near Mere,* ☎ *01747/841152.* ☞ *House £4.40; gardens £4.40 (Mar.–Oct.), £3.40 (Nov.–Feb.); house and gardens £7.90.* ☉ *House Apr.–Oct., Sat.–Wed. noon–5:30 or dusk; gardens daily 9–7 or sunset.*

Lodging and Dining

££ ✕⚏ **Spread Eagle Inn.** Dream as you might, you can't live at Stour-
★ head, but this hostelry is the next best thing, located at the gates to the landscaped park. When renovated by the National Trust, the inn was nearly gutted, so guest rooms are more country home than country house in appearance—discreetly understated, they are elegant nonetheless (opt for rooms that face the park and not the courtyard). Most conveniently, there is a gracious restaurant on the ground floor. But this inn really comes into its own once you step outside the door—and you find yourself steps away from England's 10 most gorgeous acres. Special winter breaks are offered, with free entry to the garden. ⊠ *Stourton, near Mere, BA12 6QE,* ☎ *01747/840587,* ☏ *01747/840954. 5 rooms with bath. Restaurant, bar. AE, DC, MC, V.*

Longleat House

★ ☙ ㉞ *6 mi north of Stourhead on B3092, 19 mi south of Bath, 27 mi northwest of Salisbury.*

Longleat House, home of the Marquess of Bath, is one of southern England's most famous private estates. The blocklike Italian Renaissance building was completed in 1580 (for just over £8,000, an astronomical sum at the time), and contains outstanding tapestries, paintings, porcelain, and furniture, as well as notable period features of its own, such as the Victorian kitchens, the Elizabethan minstrels' gallery, and the great hall, with its massive wooden beams. Giant antlers of the extinct Irish elk decorate the walls. In 1966, the grounds of Longleat became Britain's first safari park, with giraffes, zebras, camels, rhinos, and lions all on view. Longleat also has dollhouses, a butterfly garden, a private railroad, the world's largest hedge maze, and an adventure castle, all of which make it extremely popular, particularly in summer and during school vacations—don't expect to have the place to yourself! ✉ *Near Warminster,* ☎ *01985/844400 for house, 01985/844328 for safari park.* 🎫 *Inclusive ticket £12 (to all sights), house only £5, safari park £5.50.* ⊙ *House Easter–Sept., 10–6; Oct.–Easter, 10–4. Safari park Easter–Oct., daily 10–5:30 or sunset.*

Dining and Lodging

££££ ✕▥ **Bishopstrow House.** It's not often that you'll find a Georgian
★   house converted into a luxurious hotel that combines Jacuzzis with antiques and fine carpets. There's an airy conservatory, attractive public areas, and peaceful rooms overlooking either the grounds (27 acres) or an interior courtyard. The Mulberry restaurant offers imaginatively prepared meals, appealing views of the gardens, and a menu that is regularly changed. Bishopstrow House is 1½ mi out of town. ✉ *Boreham Rd., Warminster BA12 9HH,* ☎ *01985/212312,* 🖷 *01985/ 216769. 30 rooms with bath. Restaurant, indoor-outdoor pool, beauty salon, sauna, golf privileges, tennis court, croquet, exercise room, fishing, helipad. AE, DC, MC, V.*

En Route   As you approach Avebury, on your left you will pass **Cherhill Down,** with a vivid white horse carved into its slope. This is the first in a series of hillside carvings in Wiltshire, but, unlike the others, this one isn't an ancient symbol—it was put there in 1780 to indicate the highest point of the downs between London and Bath. (The best view of the horse is from A4, on the approach from Calne.)

Avebury

㉟   *25 mi northwest of Longleat, 27 mi east of Bath, 34 mi north of Salisbury.*

★   The **Avebury monument** is one of England's most evocative prehistoric monuments—not so famous as Stonehenge, but all the more powerful for its lack of commercial exploitation. To reach Avebury from Longleat, go north on B3092 to Frome, then take A361 to Trowbridge. Follow it through Devizes and follow the signs. The main site consists of a wide, circular ditch and bank, about 1,400 ft across and well over half a mile around. The perimeter is broken by entrances at roughly the four points of the compass, and inside stand the remains of three stone circles. The largest one originally had 98 stones, though only 27 remain. Many of the stones on the site were destroyed centuries ago, especially in the 17th century, when they were the target of religious fanaticism.

The first stones at Avebury predate those at Stonehenge by at least 200 years, but here they are much more domesticated—literally so, for many were pillaged to build the thatched cottages you see flanking the fields. Finds from the Avebury area are displayed in the **Alexander Kieller Museum,** run by English Heritage. ☎ *01672/539250.* 🎫 *£1.50.* ⊙ *Apr.– Oct., daily 10–6 or dusk; Nov.–Mar., daily 10–4.*

The Avebury monument lies at the end of the **Kennett Stone Avenue,** a sort of prehistoric processional way leading to Avebury. The stones of the avenue were spaced 80 ft apart, but only the half mile nearest the main monument survives intact. The lost ones are marked with concrete. The entire Avebury area is crowded with relics of the prehistoric age. Be sure to stop off at the **West Kennett Long Barrow,** a chambered tomb dating from about 3250 BC, a mile east of Avebury on A4.

㊱   As you turn right at the traffic circle onto A4, **Silbury Hill** rises up on your right. This man-made mound, 130 ft high, dates from about 2500 BC. Excavations over 200 years have provided no clue as to its original purpose, but the generally accepted notion is that it was a massive burial chamber.

Dining

£ ✗ **Waggon and Horses.** Just beside the traffic circle linking A4 and A361, this spot serves an excellent sandwich lunch (it has won prizes for them) beside a blazing fire. The thatch-roof pub is built of stones taken from the Avebury site. ⊠ *Beckhampton,* ☎ *01672/539418. MC, V.*

Marlborough

37 *7 mi east of Avebury on A4, 28 mi north of Salisbury.*

The attractive town of Marlborough developed as an important staging post on the old London–Bath stagecoach route. Today it is better known for its unusually wide main street, its elegant Georgian houses—these replace the medieval town center, which was destroyed in a great fire in 1653—and its celebrated public school. The grounds of the school, on the west side of town, enclose a small, man-made hill called Castle Mound, or Maerl's Barrow, which gave the town its name. This was said to be the grave of Merlin, King Arthur's court wizard, but it is clearly much older than the period when the historic Arthur may have lived. A **Tourist Information Center** (☎ 01672/513989), open Monday–Saturday year-round, is housed in the car park on George Lane.

Lodging

££–£££ ⌂ **Ivy House.** This Georgian house right on the attractive, colonnaded High Street makes an excellent touring base. The bedrooms are comfortably furnished, with small modern bathrooms attached (some, in the Vines annex, fall into the £ category, and there are superior rooms and suites in the £££ range). There is a courtyard bistro for relaxed meals, and a more formal restaurant with views overlooking the terrace. ⊠ *43 High St., SN8 1HJ,* ☎ *01672/515333,* ℻ *01672/515338. 36 rooms with bath. 2 restaurants, meeting rooms. AE, MC, V.*

Outdoor Activities and Sports

GOLF

Marlborough Golf Club (⊠ The Common, Marlborough, ☎ 01672/512147).

Stonehenge

★ **38** *21 mi south of Marlborough, 8 mi north of Salisbury.*

One of England's most visited and most puzzling monuments, Stonehenge is dwarfed by its lonely isolation on the wide sweep of Salisbury Plain. Sadly, the great circle of stones has been enclosed by barriers to control both the relentless throngs of tourists and, during the summer solstice, crowds of New Age druids who embark on an annual struggle with the police to celebrate, in the monument's imposing shadows, an obscure pagan festival. But if you visit in the early morning, when the crowds have not yet arrived, or in the evening, when the sky is heavy with scudding clouds, you can experience Stonehenge as it once was: a magical, mystical, awe-inspiring place.

Stonehenge was begun about 2800 BC, enlarged between 2100 and 1900 BC, and altered yet again by 150 BC. It has been excavated and rearranged several times over the centuries. The medieval term "Stonehenge" means "hanging stones." Many of the huge stones that ringed the center were brought here from great distances. The original 80 bluestones (dolerite), which made up the two internal circles, were transported from the Preseli mountains, near Fishguard on the Atlantic coast of

Wales, presumably by raft over sea and river. Next they were dragged on rollers across country—a total journey of 130 mi as the crow flies, but closer to 240 by the practical route. The labor involved in quarrying, transporting, and carving these stones is astonishing, all the more so when you realize that it was accomplished before the major pyramids of Egypt were built.

If some of the mysteries concerning the site have been solved (for a good account, see one of the latest of books on the subject, *Stonehenge*, by Julian Richards), we still do not know why Stonehenge was undertaken in the first place. It is fairly certain that it was a religious site, and that worship here involved the cycles of the sun; the alignment of the stones to point to sunrise at midsummer and sunset in midwinter makes this clear. For some historians, one thing is certain: the Druids had nothing to do with the construction. The monument had already been in existence for nearly 2,000 years by the time they appeared. A new theory that has received a good deal of controversy is that the builders were Greek rather than British and may have come from Mycenae. Evidence of the link with Greece is provided by the accepted purpose of Stonehenge. Most historians feel that Stonehenge may have been a kind of neolithic computer, with a sophisticated astronomical purpose—an observatory of sorts. At least, it is now known that at much the same time that Stonehenge was built, the Greeks were discovering astronomy and devising for themselves a whole new set of heavenly deities to replace their original earth gods. Of course, many historians completely discount Stonehenge's possible Greek connection.

You can't get very close to the monoliths, and then only along one section of the site, so it's a good idea to bring a pair of binoculars to help make out the details more clearly. Fact is, you can get as good a view of Stonehenge from some points on the A244 highway as from the paid area. It pays to hike all about the site, near and far, to get that magical Nikon shot. If you're a romantic, needless to say, you'll want to view Stonehenge at dawn, dusk, or by a full moon. The visitors' amenities at Stonehenge are rather squalid, but there are plans to improve them. Visitors from Marlborough should join A345 south for Stonehenge, turning west onto A303 at Amesbury. The monument stands near the junction with A344. ⊠ *Near Amesbury,* ☎ *01980/623108.* ▨ *£3.90.* ☉ *June–Aug., daily 9–7; mid-Mar.–May and Sept.–mid-Oct., daily 9:30–6; mid-Oct.–mid-Mar., daily 9:30–4.*

Lyndhurst

39 *26 mi southwest of Stonehenge, 18 mi southeast of Salisbury, 9 mi west of Southampton.*

Lyndhurst is famous as the capital of the **New Forest.** To explore the depths of this natural wonder, take A35 out of Lyndhurst (the road continues southwest to Bournemouth). The New Forest consists of 145 square mi of mainly open, unfenced countryside interspersed with dense woodland, a natural haven for herds of free-roaming deer, cattle, and hardy New Forest ponies. The forest was "new" in 1079, when William the Conqueror cleared the area of farms and villages and turned it into his private hunting grounds. Although some favorite spots can get crowded in summer, there are ample parking lots, picnic areas, and campgrounds. Miles of walking trails crisscross the region, and the best way to explore is on foot.

Lewis Carroll's Wonderland fans should note that Alice Hargreaves (*née* Liddell) is buried in the churchyard at Lyndhurst. To get here from

Stonehenge, head south along A360 to Salisbury, then follow A36, B3079, and continue along A337 another 4 mi or so.

Outdoor Activities and Sports

GOLF

New Forest Golf Course (✉ Southampton Rd., Lyndhurst, ☎ 01703/ 282752).

HORSEBACK RIDING

The New Forest was custom-built for riding and there's no better way to enjoy it than on horseback. The **New Park Manor Stables** (✉ New Park, Brockenhurst, ☎ 01590/623919) gives full instruction. Try also **Forest Park Stables** (✉ Rhinefield Rd., Brockenhurst, ☎ 01590/ 623429).

WALKING

The **New Forest** is more domesticated than, for example, the Forest of Dean, and the walks it provides are not much more than easy strolls. For one such walk (about 4 mi), start from Lyndhurst, and head for Brockenhurst, a commuter village. You will pass through woods, pastureland, and leafy river valleys—you may even see some New Forest ponies. ✉ *New Forest Visitor Information Centre, High St., Lyndhurst, Hampshire S043 7NY,* ☎ *01703/282269.*

Beaulieu

40 *7 mi southwest of Lyndhurst on B3056.*

The unspoiled village of Beaulieu (pronounced *byoo* lee) offers three major attractions. **Beaulieu Abbey** was established by King John in 1204 for the Cistercian monks, who gave their new home its name, which means "beautiful place" in French. It was badly damaged during the reign of Henry VIII, leaving only the cloister, the doorway, the gatehouse, and two buildings, one of which today contains a well-planned exhibition re-creating daily life in the monastery. The gatehouse has been incorporated into **Palace House,** home of the Montagu family since 1538. In this stately home you can see drawing rooms, dining halls, and a number of very fine family portraits. The present Lord Montagu is noted for his work in establishing the **National Motor Museum,** which traces the development of motor transport from 1895 to the present, with more than 200 classic cars, buses, and motorcycles. Museum attractions include a monorail, audiovisual presentations, and a trip in a 1912 London bus. ☎ *01590/612345.* ✉ *Palace House, Abbey, and Motor Museum £8.50.* ☉ *Easter–Sept., daily 10–6; Oct.–Easter, 10–5.*

Buckler's Hard

41 *2 mi south of Beaulieu.*

Among local places of interest around Beaulieu is Buckler's Hard, an almost perfectly restored 18th-century hamlet of 24 brick cottages, leading down to an old shipyard on the River Beaulieu. Nelson's favorite ship, HMS *Agamemnon,* was built here of New Forest oak, as recalled in the fascinating **Maritime Museum,** where you can admire a variety of model ships. ☎ *01590/616203.* ✉ *£3.25.* ☉ *Mar.–May and mid-Sept.–Oct., daily 10–6; June–mid-Sept., daily 10–9; Nov.–Feb., daily 10–4:30.*

En Route From Beaulieu, take any of the minor roads leading west through Lymington and pick up A337 for the popular seaside resort of Bournemouth, a journey of about 18 mi.

FAR FROM THE MADDING CROWD: BOURNEMOUTH TO LYME REGIS

"I am convinced that it is better for a writer to know a little bit of the world remarkably well than to know a great part of the world remarkably little," wrote Thomas Hardy, the immortal author of *Far From the Madding Crowd* and other classic Victorian-era novels. His "little bit" was the county of Dorset, the setting for most of his books and, today, a green and hilly county that is largely unspoiled. Our tour of one of the last remaining corners of old, rural England follows the Dorset coastline, immortalized by Hardy and, more recently, John Fowles. Places of historic interest such as Maiden Castle and the chalk-cut giant of Cerne Abbas are interspersed with the seaside leisure resorts of Bournemouth and Weymouth, though you may find the quieter towns of Lyme Regis and the smaller picturesque villages scattered along the route closer to your ideal of rural England. Chief glory of the tour is the county town of Dorchester, an ancient agricultural center with a host of historical and literary associations, and worth a prolonged visit.

Bournemouth

42 *30 mi southwest of Southampton, 30 mi south of Salisbury, 30 mi east of Dorchester.*

Bournemouth was founded in 1810 by Lewis Tregonwell, an ex-army officer who had taken a liking to the area when stationed there some years before. He settled near what is now **The Square** and planted the first pine trees in the steep little valleys—or chines—cutting through the cliffs to the famous Bournemouth sands. The scent of fir trees was said to be healing for consumption (tuberculosis) sufferers, and the town grew steadily as more and more people came for rest cures. The Square and the beach are linked by gardens laid out with flowering trees and lawns. This is an excellent spot to relax and listen to stirring music wafting from the Pine Walk bandstand. Regular musical programs take place at the Pavilion and at the Winter Gardens (home of the Bournemouth Symphony Orchestra) nearby. Concerts and shows take place at the **Bournemouth International Centre** on Exeter Road (☎ 01202/456456), which includes a selection of restaurants and bars, and a swimming pool. For a time-out and old-fashioned tea, try the **Cumberland Hotel** (⊠ East Overcliffe Dr., ☎ 01202/290722), which serves outdoors in summer.

On the corner of Hilton Road stands **St. Peter's** parish church, easily recognizable by its 200-ft-high tower and spire. Lewis Tregonwell is buried in the churchyard. Here, too, you will notice the elaborate tombstone of Mary Shelley, author of *Frankenstein* and wife of the great Romantic poet Percy Bysshe Shelley, whose heart is buried with her. Admirers of Shelley will want to visit the **Casa Magni Shelley Museum** in Boscombe (on the west side of Bournemouth), with its touching collection of Shelley memorabilia. ⊠ *Boscombe Manor, Beechwood Ave.,* ☎ *01202/303571.* 🎫 *Free.* ☉ *Tues.–Sun. 2–5.*

In the center of Bournemouth you will find the interesting **Russell-Cotes Art Gallery and Museum.** This late Victorian mansion, perched on top of East Cliff, overflows with Victorian paintings and miniatures, cases of butterflies, and treasures from the Far East, including an exquisite suit of Japanese armor. A lottery award has paid for a major refurbishment program, which means the museum will remain closed at least until November of 1998. ⊠ *East Cliff,* ☎ *01202/451800.* 🎫 *Free.* ☉ *Tues.–Sun. 10–5.*

Dining and Lodging

££ ✕ **Farthings.** Though centrally located within minutes of the seafront, this restaurant housed in a former coach house has the sequestered air of a country retreat, its four dining areas—one in a conservatory—tastefully arrayed around an elegant garden. The dishes, embracing both classical and modern, are also refined: pot-roasted salmon on saffron noodles, Dover sole poached in Champagne, or roast pheasant *à l'anglaise*. In fine weather, tables are placed on the terrace. ⊠ *5–7 Grove Rd.,* ☎ *01202/558660. AE, DC, MC, V. No dinner Sun. in winter.*

££££ ✕⌂ **Chewton Glen.** Once the home of Captain Frederick Marryat, au-
★ thor of *The Children of the New Forest* and many naval adventure novels, this 18th-century country house is now a deluxe hotel, among the most expensive in Britain, set on extensive grounds 12 mi east of Bournemouth. All the rooms are sumptuously furnished, with an eye to the minutest detail. Gourmets consider its restaurant, the Marryat Room, and the cooking of its chef, Pierre Chevillard, worthy of a pilgrimage. With a genuinely helpful and friendly staff, Chewton Glen deserves its fine reputation. ⊠ *Christchurch Rd., New Milton BH25 6QS,* ☎ *01425/275341,* ℻ *01425/272310. 52 rooms with bath. Restaurant, indoor-outdoor pool, golf privileges, tennis court, croquet, exercise room, helipad. AE, DC, MC, V.*

£££ ✕⌂ **Langtry Manor Hotel.** Edward VII built this house for his mistress Lillie Langtry in 1877, and it still preserves its Edwardian atmosphere. Individually named rooms continue the theme, and in the restaurant, lacy tablecloths, real silver cutlery, and other details set off the dishes, which are mainly British with French trimmings, and include Lillie's Special—meringue in the shape of a swan. There's an Edwardian banquet every Saturday. ⊠ *26 Derby Rd., East Cliff,* ☎ *01202/553887,* ℻ *01202/290115. 29 rooms. Restaurant. AE, DC, MC, V.*

£££ ⌂ **Swallow-Highcliff Hotel.** This large Victorian hotel has some of its rooms in converted coast-guard cottages. The bedrooms are full of period atmosphere, with mahogany wardrobes. There is a funicular that takes you down to the promenade. ⊠ *105 St. Michael's Rd., West Cliff BH2 5DU,* ☎ *01202/557702,* ℻ *01202/292734. 157 rooms with bath. 2 restaurants, 2 bars, pool, sauna, tennis court, recreation rooms. AE, DC, MC, V.*

£ ⌂ **San Remo.** This well-built Victorian hotel is near the sea and the town center. The whole lodging has been refurbished, with cheerful flower-pattern wallpapers in the bedrooms, all of which have TVs. Dinner is available at 6 PM (bring your own wine). ⊠ *7 Durley Rd., BH2 5JQ,* ☎ *01202/290558. 18 rooms, 14 with bath or shower. No credit cards. Closed mid-Oct.–Easter.*

The Arts

FESTIVALS
Bournemouth holds a **Music Festival** (☎ 01202/451700) June–July, with choirs, brass bands, and orchestras, some from overseas.

Wimborne Minster

④ *7 mi northwest of Bournemouth.*

The impressive twin-towered minster of the quiet market town of Wimborne Minster makes it seem like a miniature cathedral city. To get here from Bournemouth, follow the signs northwest on A341. The **Priest's House Museum,** in a Tudor building with a garden, features Roman and Iron Age exhibits, including a cryptic, three-face Celtic stone head. ⊠ *23 High St.,* ☎ *01202/882533.* ⌂ *£2.* ☉ *Apr.–Oct., Mon.– Sat. 10:30–5; June–Sept., Mon.–Sat. 10:30–5, Sun. 2–5.*

Dining

£   ✕ **Quinneys.** This is a popular bakery and eating house, run by the Skidmore family for nearly 30 years. They sell delicious pastries and cakes and have a daily-changing blackboard selection of such lunch specialties as grilled plaice. ✉ *26 Westborough,* ☎ *01202/883518. No credit cards. Closed Sun.*

Blandford Forum

④④   *11 mi northeast of Wimborne Minster.*

Endowed with perhaps the handsomest Georgian town center in the southwest, this market town on the River Stour was Thomas Hardy's "Shottesford Forum." The church, with an imposing cupola and dating from 1739, is worth a detour on its own.

Dining and Lodging

££   ✕🏠 **La Belle Alliance.** With constantly changing set menus (bistro and gourmet), this attractive, small country restaurant offers relaxed decor and friendly owners. Try the noisettes of lamb. This is one of the increasing number of British restaurants with a no-smoking policy. There are also five bedrooms with canopied beds. ✉ *Portnam Lodge, Whitecliffe Mill St., DT11 7PB,* ☎ *01258/452842,* 🖷 *01258/453727. 5 rooms. Restaurant. AE, MC, V. Closed Sun., Mon., and 1st 2 wks Jan. No lunch.*

Corfe Castle

★ ④⑤   *15 mi south of Poole, 6 mi south of Wareham.*

The spectacular ruins of Corfe Castle overlook the pretty village of Corfe. The castle site guards a gap in the surrounding range of hills and has been fortified from very early times. The present ruins are of the castle built between 1105, when the great central keep was erected, and the 1270s, when the outer walls and towers were built. It owes its ramshackle state to Cromwell's soldiers, who blew it up in 1646 during the Civil War. This is one of the most impressive ruins in Britain and will stir the imagination of all history buffs. ☎ *01929/481294.* 📧 *£3.80.* ☉ *Mar.–Oct., daily 10–5:30 (closes 4:30 early Mar. and late Oct.); Nov.–Feb., daily 11–3:30.*

Dining and Lodging

£   ✕ **The Fox.** An age-old pub, the Fox has a fine view of Corfe Castle from its flower garden and an ancient well in the lounge bar. There's more timeworn stonework in an alcove, and a pre-1300 fireplace. Sandwiches, soups, and pies are cheerfully doled out from the bar, but things can get uncomfortably congested in summer. ✉ *West St.,* ☎ *01929/480449.*

£   🏠 **Castle Inn.** This charming thatched hotel, 10 mi west of Corfe and just five minutes' walk from the sea, has a flagstone bar and other 15th-century features. There's a good restaurant with an à la carte menu for evening meals and Sunday lunch, as well as an extensive bar menu. The bedrooms are plain but comfortable, and there is a lovely rose garden to sit in and satisfying walks to take nearby. ✉ *Main St., West Lulworth, BH20 5RN,* ☎ *01929/400311,* 🖷 *01929/400415. 15 rooms, 12 with bath. Restaurant, bar. AE, DC, MC, V.*

Dorchester

④⑥   *21 mi west of Corfe on A351 and A352, 30 mi west of Bournemouth, 43 mi southwest of Salisbury.*

In many ways Dorchester, the Casterbridge of Hardy's novel, is a traditional southern country town. To appreciate its character, visit the local Wednesday market in the **Market Square,** where you can find Dorset delicacies such as Blue Vinney cheese (which some connoisseurs prefer to Blue Stilton), and various handcrafted items. Things, of course, have changed a bit since the days, when, to quote the master, "Bees and butterflies in the cornfields at the top of the town, who desired to get to the meads at the bottom, took no circuitous route, but flew straight down High Street . . ."

Dorchester owes much of its fame to its connection with Thomas Hardy, whose bronze statue looks westward from a bank on Colliton Walk. Born in a cottage in the hamlet of Higher Brockhampton, about 3 mi northeast of Dorchester, Hardy attended school in the town and was apprentice to an architect here. **Hardy's Cottage,** located half a mile south of Blandford Road (A35), is now administered by the National Trust, but is only open by appointment for a small fee, April–October, Fridays through Wednesdays (write Hardy's Cottage, Higher Bockhampton, Dorchester, Dorset DT2 8QJ, England, or ☎ 01305/262366). Among other things, you can see the desk at which the author completed *Far From the Madding Crowd.* Later, Hardy had a house, Max Gate (not open to the public), built to his own design on the edge of Dorchester. Hardy's study there has been reconstructed in the **Dorset County Museum,** which houses a diverse and fascinating collection. Exhibits range from ancient Celtic and Roman remains to a vicious 19th-century mantrap used to snare poachers. It was this very trap that Hardy had in mind when writing the mantrap episode in *The Woodlanders.* ⊠ *High West St.,* ☎ *01305/262735.* ⊡ *£3.* ⊙ *Daily 10–5 (except Sun., Sept.–June).*

Roman history and artifacts abound in Dorchester. The town was laid out by the Romans about AD 70, and if you walk along Bowling Alley Walk, West Walk, and Colliton Walk, you will have followed the approximate line of the original Roman town walls. On the north side of Colliton Park lies an excavated **Roman villa** with a marvelously preserved mosaic floor. The **Maumbury Rings** are one of Dorchester's most interesting sights, the remains of a Roman amphitheater on the edge of town. The site was later used as a place of execution. (Hardy's *Mayor of Casterbridge* contains a vivid evocation of the Rings.) As late as 1706, a girl was burned at the stake here. Dorchester is also associated with Monmouth's Rebellion of 1685, when Charles II's illegitimate son, the Duke of Monmouth, led a rising against his unpopular uncle, James II. The rising was ruthlessly put down, and the chief justice, Lord Jeffreys, conducted the Bloody Assizes to try rebels and sympathizers. A swearing, bullying drunkard, Jeffreys was the prototypical hanging judge, and memories of his mass executions lingered for centuries throughout the South. His courtroom in Dorchester was in what is now the Antelope Hotel on South Street.

☾ Dorchester's popular **Dinosaur Museum** has life-size models and interactive displays. ⊠ *Icen Way, off High East St.,* ☎ *01305/269880.* ⊡ *£3.50.* ⊙ *Apr.–Sept., daily 9:30–5:30; Oct.–Mar., daily 10–4:30.*

Athelhampton House and Gardens. Located 5 mi east of Dorchester on the Dorchester–Bournemouth road (A35), this estate is one of the glories of the English Middle Ages. Thomas Hardy called this place Athelhall in some of his writings, referring to the legendary King Althelstan, who had a palace on this site. In the 14th century the current house was built, complete with Great Hall and King's Room. There are also 10 acres of impressive landscaped gardens. ⊠ *On A35, 1 mi east of Puddletown,* ☎ *01305/848363.* ⊡ *£4.20.* ⊙ *July–Aug., weekdays noon–5; March 27–June, Sept.–Oct. 30, Tues.–Thurs., Sun. noon–5.*

Dining and Lodging

£ ✕ **Potter In.** This is just the place for deliciously fattening cakes and pastries. It is on two floors of an attractive little 17th-century house, where local crafts are also sold. ⊠ *19 Durngate St.,* ☎ *01305/260312. No credit cards. Closed Sun.*

££ ✕⊞ **Yalbury Cottage.** A thatch roof and inglenook fireplaces enhance ★ the traditional ambience here, just 2½ mi east of Dorchester, which puts it close to Hardy's cottage. The three-course fixed-price menu, changed daily and featuring English and Continental dishes, might include rack of lamb (with cassis and caramelized shallot sauce), or medallions of venison with a red currant-and-gin sauce. There are also eight comfortable bedrooms available in a discreet extension overlooking gardens or adjacent fields. ⊠ *Lower Bockhampton DT2 8PZ,* ☎ *01305/262382,* 𝔽𝔸𝕏 *01305/266412. 8 rooms. Restaurant. MC, V. Closed 2 wks in Jan.*

££ ⊞ **Casterbridge Hotel.** This Georgian building (1790) reflects its age, ★ with period furniture and old world elegance—it is small (with no restaurant) but full of character. The guest rooms are each individually and impeccably furnished (those in the modern annex are slightly larger), and the husband-and-wife team who own and run the hotel are a congenial pair. ⊠ *49 High East St., DT1 1HU,* ☎ *01305/264043,* 𝔽𝔸𝕏 *01305/ 260884. 15 rooms with bath. Bar. AE, DC, MC, V.*

£ ⊞ **Lamperts Cottage.** Here's an idyllic little B&B about 6 mi from Dorchester. It has a thatched roof and a stream in front and back, so you have to cross a little bridge to reach it; in summer, it is covered with roses. The house, dating from the 16th century, is very comfortable though small; the interior has exposed beams and fireplaces. ⊠ *Dorchester Rd., Sydling St. Nicholas, Cerne Abbas, DT2 9NU,* ☎ *01300/ 341659,* 𝔽𝔸𝕏 *01300/341699. 3 rooms share 2 baths. MC, V.*

Outdoor Activities and Sports

WALKING

A 15-mi walk through Hardy country, the **Tess of the D'Urbervilles Tour**— Tour 2 from the Thomas Hardy Society (⊠ Box 1438, Dorchester, Dorset DT1 1YH, ☎ 01305/251501)—follows in the sad steps of Hardy's heroine on her Sunday mission to her father-in-law, Parson Clare of Beaminster, in an attempt to rescue her failed marriage.

Cerne Abbas

㊼ *6 mi north of Dorchester on A352.*

The village of Cerne Abbas is worth a short exploration on foot. Some appealing Tudor houses line the road beside the church. Nearby you can also see the original village stocks. If you pass through the graveyard, you will arrive at a shallow pool known as **St. Augustine's Well.** Legend holds that the saint created it by striking the ground with his staff, thereby ensuring a regular supply of baptismal water. Tenth-century **Cerne Abbey** is now a ruin, with little left to see except its old gateway, though the nearby Abbey House is still in use. Cerne Abbas's main claim to fame is the colossal **figure of a giant,** cut in chalk on a hillside overlooking the village. The 180-ft-long giant with a huge club bears a striking resemblance to Hercules, although he probably originated as a tribal fertility symbol long before the Romans. His outlines are formed by 2-ft-wide trenches. The present giant is thought to have been carved in the chalk about AD 1200, but he could well be based on a very much older figure.

Maiden Castle

★ ㊽ *2 mi southwest of Dorchester, on A354.*

After Stonehenge, Maiden Castle is the most extraordinary pre-Roman archaeological site in England. It is not really a castle at all, but an enormous, complex hill fort of stone and earth, built by England's mysterious prehistoric inhabitants. Many centuries later it was a Celtic stronghold. In AD 43, the invading Romans, under the general (later emperor) Vespasian, stormed it. One of the grimmest exhibits now on display in the Dorset County Museum in Dorchester was excavated here: the skeleton of a Celtic warrior transfixed by a Roman arrow. To experience an uncanny silence and sense of mystery, climb Maiden Castle early in the day (access to it is unrestricted), when other tourists are unlikely to be stirring.

Any road leading south from Dorchester will bring you to the characteristic quiet bays, shingle beaches, and low chalk cliffs of the Dorset coast. The well-marked **Dorset Coast Path** enables you to walk along some or all of the shoreline, or you can drive the narrow, country lanes hugging the coast.

Weymouth

㊾ *8 mi south of Dorchester on A354.*

Dorset's main coastal resort, Weymouth, is known both for its wide, safe, sandy beaches and its royal connections. King George III took up sea-bathing here for his health in 1789, setting a trend among the wealthy and fashionable people of the day. They left Weymouth with many fine period buildings, including the Georgian row houses lining the esplanade. Striking historical details clamor for attention. A wall on Maiden Street, for example, still holds a cannonball that was embedded in it during the Civil War. Near Maiden Street, a column commemorates the launching of the American forces from Weymouth on D-Day, June 6, 1944.

Dining and Lodging

££ ✕ **Perry's.** A fairly basic restaurant, right by the harbor, with simple dishes of the best local seafood. Try the lobster, crab, or *moules marinière*. The meat dishes, such as medallions of Dorset lamb, are tasty, too. ✉ *The Harbourside, 4 Trinity Rd.,* ☏ *01305/785799. MC, V. No lunch Mon., Sat.; no dinner Sun. Sept.–June.*

£ ✕ **Old Rooms.** A fisherman's pub full of character and low beams, this popular choice has great views over the harbor. The long menu includes pastas, curries, and meat pies. There's a separate dining area, or you can mix in with the locals at the bar. ✉ *Trinity Rd.,* ☏ *01305/771130. AE, MC, V.*

£–££ ★ ✕🏨 **Streamside Hotel.** Quiet and cozy, this hotel/restaurant on the outskirts of town always graces its tables with fresh flowers and candles. The cuisine is English, with specialties such as smoked salmon with melon, and steak in cream and brandy sauce. There are 15 comfortable rooms available, and the hotel, with award-winning gardens, is only 200 yards from the beach. ✉ *29 Preston Rd., Overcombe DT3 6PX,* ☏ *01305/833121,* FAX *01305/832043. 15 rooms. Restaurant. AE, DC, MC, V.*

Isle of Portland

㊿ *4 mi south of Weymouth.*

A 5-mi-long peninsula jutting south from Weymouth leads to the Isle of Portland, the eastern end of the unique geological curiosity known
(51) as **Chesil Beach**—a 200-yard-wide, 30-ft-high bank of pebbles that de-

crease in size from east to west. The beach extends for 18 mi. A powerful undertow makes swimming dangerous, and tombstones in local churchyards attest to the many shipwrecks the beach has caused.

Abbotsbury

52 *10 mi northwest of Weymouth.*

At the western end of Chesil Beach lies the village of Abbotsbury. A lagoon here is a famous breeding place for swans, first introduced by Benedictine monks as a source of meat in winter. The swans have remained for centuries, building new nests every year in the soft, moist pampas grass. *Abbotsbury Swannery,* ⊠ *New Barn Rd.,* ☎ *01305/ 871684.* 🎫 *£4.80.* 🕐 *Apr.–Oct., daily 10–6 (last admission 5).*

On the hills above Abbotsbury stands **Hardy's Monument**—dedicated not to the novelist, as many suppose, but to Sir Thomas Masterman Hardy, Nelson's flag captain at Trafalgar, to whom Nelson's dying words, "Kiss me, Hardy" (or was it, "Kismet, Hardy"?) were addressed. The monument itself is without much charm, but the surrounding view more than makes up for it. In clear weather you can scan the whole coastline between the Isle of Wight and Start Point in Devon.

Dining and Lodging

£££   ✕🏨 **Manor Hotel.** This comfortable hotel/restaurant's pedigree goes back more than 700 years—note its flagstone floors, oak paneling, and beamed ceilings. Among the English and French dishes in which the Manor specializes are seafood and game. Prices fall into the very bottom of this category. Self-catering facilities are also available. ⊠ *Beach Rd., West Bexington DT2 9DF (3 mi west of Abbotsbury),* ☎ *01308/ 897785,* ℻ *01308/897035. 13 rooms with bath or shower. Restaurant, fishing, playground. AE, DC, MC, V.*

Lyme Regis

53 *19 mi west of Abbotsbury.*

Southwest Dorset has two more places of interest: the ancient town of Lyme Regis and the so-called Fossil Coast. The cliffs in this area are especially fossil rich. In 1810, a local child named Mary Anning dug out a complete ichthyosaur here (it is on display in London's Natural History Museum). You may prefer to browse in the Fossil Shop in Lyme Regis. Lyme Regis is famous for its curving stone breakwater, **The Cobb,** built by King Edward I in the 13th century to improve the harbor. It was here that the duke of Monmouth landed in 1685 in his ill-fated attempt to overthrow his uncle, James II. The Cobb figures prominently in the movie *The French Lieutenant's Woman,* based on John Fowles's novel, as well as the film version of Jane Austen's *Persuasion.* Fowles is actually Lyme's most famous current resident.

Lodging

£££   🏨 **Alexandra.** A short walk from the Cobb in a high, panoramic location, the Alexandra is a genteel haven with an old-fashioned air. Informal lunches and teas are served in a sunny conservatory that looks out onto an expanse of lawn where croquet may be played, and there is also a formal restaurant with a good wine list. Guest rooms are attractively furnished, and most feature sea views. Rates fall into the bottom end of this category. ⊠ *Pound St., DT7 3HZ,* ☎ *01297/443010,* ℻ *01297/443229. 26 rooms with bath. Restaurant, bar. AE, DE, MC, V. Closed Jan.*

Outdoor Activities and Sports
WALKING

The **Dorset Coast Path** runs from Lyme Regis to Poole, bypassing Weymouth, 72 mi in all. Some highlights along the way are Golden Cap, the highest point on the South Coast; the Swannery at Abbotsbury; Lulworth Cove (between Corfe Castle and Weymouth); and Chesil Bank. As with most walks in Britain, the route is dotted with villages and isolated pubs for meals; there are also a lot of rural B&Bs, and many isolated farmhouses take guests.

THE SOUTH A TO Z

Arriving and Departing

By Bus
National Express (☎ 0990/808080) buses from London's Victoria Coach Station depart almost hourly for Southampton (2½ hrs), Portsmouth (2½ hrs), Winchester (2 hrs), and Bournemouth (2½ hrs). There are three buses daily to Salisbury (2¾ hrs).

By Car
The South is linked to London and other major cities by a well-developed road network, which includes M3 to Winchester (59 mi) and Southampton (77 mi); A3 to Portsmouth (70 mi); and M27 along the coast, from the New Forest and Southampton to Portsmouth. For Salisbury, take M3 to A303, then A30. A31 and A35 connect Bournemouth to Dorchester and the rest of Dorset.

By Train
British Rail serves the South from London's Waterloo Station (☎ 0345/484950). Travel times average an hour to Winchester; 1¼ hours to Southampton; two hours to Bournemouth; and 2½ hours to Weymouth. Salisbury takes an hour and 40 minutes, and Portsmouth about two hours (usually with a change at Winchester). There is at least one fast train every hour on all these routes.

Getting Around

By Bus
Solent Blue (☎ 01703/226235) and **Hampshire Bus** (☎ 01256/464501) operate a comprehensive service in the Southampton, New Forest, Eastleigh, Winchester, Andover, Bournemouth, and Basingstoke areas. **Southern Vectis** (☎ 01983/827005) covers the Isle of Wight. Ask about the "Rover" tickets offered by Solent Blue and Southern Vectis. **Wilts (Wiltshire) & Dorset Bus Co.** (☎ 01722/336855) offers both one-day "Explorer" and seven-day "Busabout" tickets; in summer, it also conducts "Explorer Special" open-top tours around Bournemouth.

By Car
The area covered in this chapter involves very easy driving. In northeast Hampshire and in many parts of neighboring Wiltshire there are lanes overhung by trees and lined with thatched cottages and Georgian houses. Often the network of such lanes starts immediately as you leave a main highway. Salisbury Plain has long, straight roads surrounded by endless vistas, and the problem here is to keep to the speed limit!

By Ferry
Wightlink (☎ 0990/827744) operates a car-ferry service between the mainland and the Isle of Wight. The crossing takes about 35 minutes from Lymington to Yarmouth; 40 minutes from Southsea (Portsmouth) to Fishbourne. **Red Funnel Ferries** (☎ 01703/330333) runs a car-ferry

and hydrofoil service between Southampton and Cowes. **Hovertravel** (☎ 01983/811000 or 01705/811000) has a hovercraft shuttle between Southsea and Ryde (10 mins).

By Plane
There is a small **airport** (☎ 01703/620021) at Southampton, useful for flights to the Channel Islands (☞ Chapter 6).

By Train
A "Network" card, valid throughout the South and Southeast for a year, entitles you to one-third off particular fares. For local information throughout the region, call **British Rail** ☎ 0345/484950.

Contacts and Resources

Car Rentals
Bournemouth: Avis (✉ 400 Poole Rd., Branksome, Bournemouth, ☎ 01202/751974); **Hertz** (✉ Hinton Rd., ☎ 01202/291231). **Ryde: Avis** (✉ St. John's Railway Station, St. John's Rd., ☎ 01983/615522); **Esplanade** (✉ 9–11 George St., ☎ 01983/562322). **Salisbury: Budget Rent-a-Car** (✉ Brunel Rd., Churchfields Industrial Estate, ☎ 01722/336444); **Europcar Ltd.** (✉ Fisherton Yard, Fisherton St., ☎ 01722/335625).

Guided Tours
The **Southern Tourist Board** (☎ 01703/620006) and **Wessexplore** (☎ 01722/326304) can reserve qualified Blue Badge guides who will arrange to meet you anywhere in the region for private tours of different lengths and themes.

Guide Friday (☎ 01225/444102) has a daily Stonehenge tour from Salisbury, May to September, and weekends in April and October to mid-November, costing £12.50, but check for availability.

Travel Agencies
American Express (✉ 99 Above Bar, Southampton, Hants SO14 7SG, ☎ 01703/634722).

Thomas Cook (✉ 7 Richmond Hill, Bournemouth, Dorset BH2 6HF, ☎ 01202/292541; ✉ 47 High St., Newport, Isle of Wight PO30 1SX, ☎ 01983/521111; ✉ 18 Queen St., Salisbury, Wilts SP1 1EY, ☎ 01722/412787; and ✉ 30 High St., Winchester, Hants SO23 9BL, ☎ 01962/841661).

Visitor Information
The **Southern Tourist Board** (✉ 40 Chamberlayne Rd., Eastleigh, Hants S050 5JH, ☎ 01703/620006, FAX 01703/620010) is open Monday–Thursday 8:30–5, Friday 8:30–4:30. Local tourist information centers are normally open Monday–Saturday 9:30–5:30.

Bournemouth (✉ Westover Rd., near the bandstand, ☎ 01202/451700). **Dorchester** (✉ 11 Antelope Walk, ☎ 01305/267992). **Portsmouth** (✉ The Hard, ☎ 01705/826722; ✉ Clarence Esplanade, Southsea [Easter–Oct.], ☎ 01705/832464). **Ryde** (✉ 81 Union St., ☎ 01983/562905). **Salisbury** (✉ Fish Row, just off Market Sq., ☎ 01722/334956). **Southampton** (✉ 9 Civic Centre, ☎ 01703/221106). **Winchester** (✉ The Guildhall, The Broadway, ☎ 01962/840500).

5 The West Country

Somerset, Devon, Cornwall

Half the fun of exploring the West Country is in letting yourself get lost. On your way down to Land's End, every zig and zag of the road reveals rugged moorlands—The Hound of the Baskervilles was set here—lush river valleys, and festive coastal resorts. Explore the mist-wreathed sights of King Arthur Country, then head for enchanting Clovelly, precipitously perched above a tiny harbor. Whatever your itinerary, be sure to allow yourself to stray from the main roads—it would be a great pity not to.

Updated by
Robert
Andrews

THE SOUTHWEST OF ENGLAND can be one of the most relaxing regions to visit. The secret of exploring this holidaymaker's delight is to ignore the main highways and just follow the signposts through the leafy narrow country roads that lead through miles of buttercup meadows and cider apple orchards to countless mellow villages of stone and thatch and heathery heights overlooking the sea.

Somerset, Devon, and Cornwall are the three counties that make up the long southern peninsula known as the West Country. Each has its own distinct flavor—and each also comes with a regionalism that amounts almost to patriotism. Somerset is noted for its rolling green countryside; Devon's wild and dramatic moors contrast with the restfulness of its many sandy beaches and coves; and Cornwall has managed to retain a touch of its old insularity, despite the annual invasion of thousands of vacationers drawn here for the ocean or the English Channel. Natives don't mind the water's very doubtful temperature, but foreigners, many of them pampered by the warm waves of the Mediterranean, are not so eager to brave the elements. The sea—even in Cornwall, where it seems to be warmer than anywhere else in the British Isles—is not to be enjoyed in a sensuous way: it is a bracing experience that sometimes leaves you shivering and breathless.

Although King Arthur's name is linked with more than 150 places in Britain, no area claims stronger ties than the West Country. According to tradition, Arthur was born at Tintagel Castle in Cornwall and later lived at Camelot (said to be Glastonbury, in Somerset).

Bristol is where you'll come across the first unmistakable burrs of the western brogue. A historic port retaining a strong maritime flavor, its graceful Georgian architecture and dramatic gorge are backdrop to what has become in recent years one of Britain's most dynamic cities. You might want to weave south through the lovely Chew Valley on your way to the cathedral city of Wells, in Somerset. This mellow county is characterized by miles and miles of rolling green countryside—best seen in a cloak of summer heat when its orchards give ample shade, its bees are singing their humming song, and its old stone houses and inns welcome you with a breath of coolness. Abutting the north coast are the Quantock and Mendip hills, and the stark, heather-covered expanse of Exmoor, setting for R. D. Blackmore's historical romance, *Lorna Doone*.

Devon, farther west, is famed for its wild moorland—especially Dartmoor, fictional home of Conan Doyle's "hound of the Baskervilles," and actual home to wild ponies and an assortment of strange "tors," rock outcrops eroded into weird shapes. Devon's large coastal towns are as interesting for their cultural and historical appeal—many were smugglers' havens—as for their scenic beauty. Some propagandists of south Devon speak of the "red cliffs" of Devon in contrast to the allegedly "white cliffs of Dover." The reddish soil is perhaps one of the reasons why this coast is sometimes referred to as the English Riviera; you find the same hue in southern France. The best time to visit Devon is late summer and early fall, during the end-of-summer festivals, especially popular in the small towns of eastern Dartmoor.

Cornwall, England's southernmost county, has a mild climate, and nowhere are you more than 20 mi from the sea. Until relatively recently, the county regarded itself as separate from the rest of Britain. Its Atlantic coast is punctuated with high, jagged cliffs—the dangerous and dramatic settings that Daphne du Maurier often waxed eloquent about—and indeed poses a menace to passing ships, while the south coast, Janus-like, is full of sunny beaches, delightful coves, and popular resorts.

Pleasures and Pastimes

Dining

Somerset is the home of Britain's most famous cheese, the ubiquitous Cheddar, from the Mendip Hills village. If you are lucky enough to taste real farmhouse Cheddar, made in the traditional "truckle," you may find it hard to return to processed cheese. The calorie-conscious should beware of Devon's cream teas, which traditionally consist of a pot of tea, homemade scones, and lots of thickened "clotted" cream and strawberry jam ("clotted," that is, specially thickened, cream is a regional specialty and is sometimes called "Devonshire cream." Cornwall's specialty is the "pasty," a pastry shell filled with chopped meat, onions, and potatoes. The pasty was originally devised as a handy way for miners to carry their dinner to work and today's versions are, invariably, rather pale versions of the original. "Scrumpy," a homemade dry cider, is refreshing but carries a kick. English wine, similar to German wine, is made in Somerset, while in Cornwall you can get a variant of age-old mead made from local honey.

CATEGORY	COST*
££££	over £50
£££	£30–£50
££	£20–£30
£	under £20

per person, including first course, main course, dessert, and VAT; excluding drinks

Lodging

Accommodations in the West Country range from national hotel chains that extend as far west as Plymouth, to bed-and-breakfast places. With the growth of the tourist industry, many farmhouses in rural areas have begun renting out rooms, but these are often difficult to reach without a car.

CATEGORY	COST*
££££	over £150
£££	£80–£150
££	£60–£80
£	under £60

All prices are for two people sharing a double room, including service, breakfast, and VAT.

Walking

A wonderful 10-mi walk is a cliff-top hike along the coast from Hartland Quay down to Lower Sharpnose Point, just above Bude. The coast below Bude is also ideal for walking, especially the section around Tintagel. Experienced hikers may find many **Dartmoor walks** of great interest. The areas around Widgery Cross, Becky Falls, and the Bovey Valley, and—for the really energetic and adventuresome—Highest Dartmoor, south of Okehampton, are all worth considering. A much shorter walk, but no less spectacular, is along the Lydford Gorge. Long walks on Dartmoor, which is a lonely region, are only for the most experienced walkers. For complete information, contact the National Parks Authority or, for the coast, the South West Way Association (✉ Windlestraw, Penquit, Ermington, Devon PL21 0LU, ☎ 01752/896237).

If you are interested in "theme" walks, note the **Saints Way,** a 25-mi Cornish walk between Padstow and the Camel Estuary on the north coast to Fowey on the south coast. The path follows a Bronze Age trading route, later used by Celtic saints to reach scattered farms and moor communities, and several relics of such times can be seen along the way. Contact the Cornwall Tourist Board (☞ Visitor Information *in* The West Country A to Z, *below*).

Water Sports

Looe, on the south coast of Cornwall, is known for shark fishing, and boats can be rented for mackerel fishing from most harbors along the south coast. This is also a good sailing area, with plenty of safe harbors, new marinas, and deepwater channels, mainly at Falmouth, Plymouth Sound, and Torbay. Its beaches have long made the West Country one of Britain's main family vacation destinations. Be aware of the tides if you want to explore around an adjoining headland; otherwise you may find yourself cut off. At many of the major resorts, flags show the limits of safe swimming, as there can be strong undertows, especially on the northern coast.

Exploring the West Country

There is plenty of contrast to be found within this peninsula, though the farther west you travel, the more the sea becomes an overwhelming presence. On the whole, the northern coast is more rugged, the cliffs dropping dramatically to tiny coves and beaches, while the south coast shelters many more resorts and much wider expanses of sand. In general, this is where the crowds will be, but there are also plenty of secluded inlets and estuaries along this southern littoral, and you do not need to go far to find a degree of tranquility.

Numbers in the text correspond to numbers in the margin and on the West Country and the Plymouth maps.

Great Itineraries

Our circular tour of the West Country covers a lot of territory, from the bustling city of Bristol, two hours outside London, to the remote and rocky headlands of Devon and Cornwall. Unless you confine yourself to a few choice towns—for example Exeter, Penzance, and Plymouth—you will be at a huge disadvantage without your own transport. The main arteries of the region are the M5 motorway, ending at Exeter; A30, which burrows through the center of Devon and Cornwall all the way to Land's End; and A38, which loops south of Dartmoor to take in Plymouth. Beyond Plymouth, there are few main roads, which results in lots of traffic congestion in the summer months. Take minor roads whenever possible, if only to see the real West Country, which should be appreciated at a leisurely pace with frequent stops. Rail travelers can make use of a fast service connecting Exeter, Plymouth, and Penzance, and there is also a good network of coach services.

IF YOU HAVE 3 DAYS

Three days will provide only a sadly limited view of what the West Country has to offer, and you should rein in your wanderlust to avoid excessive traveling at the expense of exploring. Start off from the gateway to the West, **Bristol** ①, where you should make a point of crossing the Avon Gorge, before heading down the motorway to spend the best part of a day and your first night in 🏨 **Exeter** ㊗. It is the cathedral here that commands the most attention, but the city has plenty more to offer, not least the quayside, home to some fine period architecture as well as some fun pubs. The next morning follow A30 back east, along the coast to the fishing village of **Beer** ㊙ before heading inland to **Honiton** ㉠, a handsome Georgian town renowned for its lace industry; an eponymously named pattern has been a lace collector's delight for more than several centuries. Spend your second overnight in ⊞ **Glastonbury** ④, a small town awash with layers of Arthurian and early Christian myth. Explore the Abbey here in the morning—running up to the Tor if you're feeling energetic—before making the short hop to the tiny city of **Wells** ③. The cathedral here is of a very different order from that of Exeter's, but it's equally grand.

IF YOU HAVE 5 DAYS

Spend your first morning in **Bristol** ①, moving on to ⊞ **Wells** ③ for your first night stop. Visit **Glastonbury** ④ the next day, before meeting up with M5 to take you on to ⊞ **Exeter** ㊗ for your second night. After exploring the city, drive west to **Plymouth** ㊲, which offers a wide gamut of attractions despite its unprepossessing appearance. Arguably the most impressive of these is Plymouth Hoe itself, a spectacular platform overlooking Plymouth Sound, where you can look down on a timeless scene of sailing craft of all shapes against the mighty backdrop of the Atlantic. Don't miss the Mayfair Steps, point of embarkation of the Pilgrim Fathers, or the old Barbican area, a nucleus of shops, restaurants, and bobbing boats, which rewards an aimless wander. Then leave the city behind to explore **Dartmoor Forest,** one of England's last wildernesses. Specific targets on or around Dartmoor include **Castle Drogo** ㊷, an impressive 20th-century version of a medieval castle, which through the hands of the architect Edwin Lutyens transcends mere pastiche; **Lydford Gorge** ㊾, a secluded corridor of torrents and gushing waterfalls; and **Buckland Abbey** ㊻, former home of Sir Francis Drake. Spend your third overnight in ⊞ **Dartmouth** ㊳. The next day you could enjoy the sea air here and in the nearby "Riviera" region of **Torbay** ㊶. Your fourth night could be east of Exeter in ⊞ **Honiton** ㉠, well placed to make stops the next day at the exquisite Elizabethan **Montacute House** ㉡ and the lonely **Cadbury Castle** ㉢, one of the supposed sites of Camelot and a fitting place to wind up your West Country tour.

IF YOU HAVE 7 DAYS

Not even a week would really do justice to this dense region, but it would certainly give you a chance to push on into Cornwall, and get a more rounded idea of what the West Country has to offer. Once out of **Bristol** ①, first up is a tour of the northern coast of Somerset and Devon, making stops at **Dunster** ⑧, site of a turreted and battlemented castle, or the twin towns of **Lynton** and **Lynmouth** ⑨, in a narrow cleft once likened to a fragment of Switzerland, but thankfully outliving the hype. Any of these would make a good place to break for lunch, before continuing on to **Barnstaple** ⑩ and **Bideford** ⑫ in the afternoon. Bideford Bay holds the postcard-pretty cliff-top village of ⊞ **Clovelly** ⑬, which will be your first overnight stay. The second day explore this often picturesque harbor town, then press on to take in **Tintagel** ⑯, which, with or without the Arthurian associations, presents a dramatic sight perched on its black rock above the swirling waves. Make stops in Padstow and **Newquay** ⑰ only if you want to sample the fish-and-chips atmosphere and generous beaches of these typical seaside resorts. Pull into ⊞ **St. Ives** ⑲ for your second night; the town has a great deal to offer in the way of art (catch up on the local scene displayed in the spectacular Tate Gallery here) and a good selection of hotels and restaurants. After taking in St. Ives the third day, set out for the very tip of the peninsula, **Land's End** ⑳, which, though it has succumbed to the pressures of mass tourism, retains the power of its unique locale and is worth exploring on foot. Head for your next overnight, ⊞ **Penzance** ㉓. Nearby, the island fortress of **St. Michael's Mount** ㉔ is clearly visible and demands a closer inspection. Now make a brief sortie into the **Lizard Peninsula** ㉖ and base yourself in the resort of ⊞ **Falmouth** ㉙, which offers a range of accommodation as well as a brace of castles—

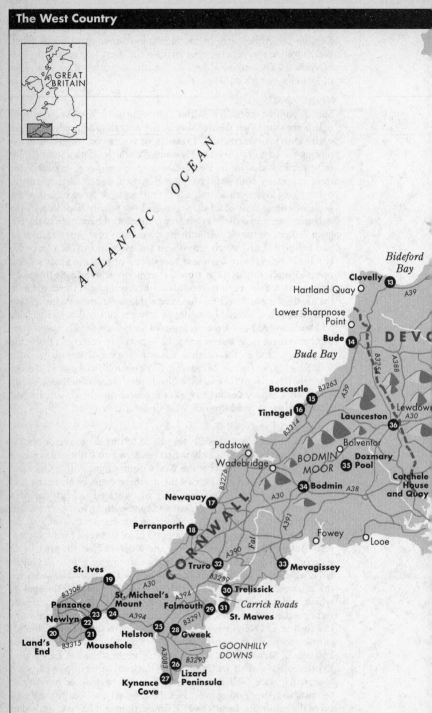

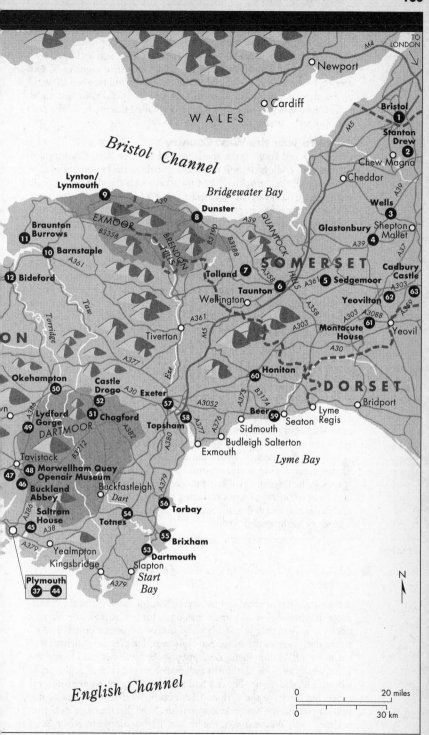

TO LONDON

M4

○ Newport

○ Cardiff

WALES

Bristol Channel

Bristol ❶

Stanton Drew ❷

○ Chew Magna

M5

○ Cheddar

Bridgewater Bay

Lynton/ Lynmouth ❾

A39

Dunster ❽

Wells ❸

EXMOOR

B3358

Braunton Burrows ⓫

Barnstaple ❿

A361

BRENDON HILLS

B3190

QUANTOCK HILLS

B3188

Glastonbury

Shepton Mallet

A39 ❹

A37

SOMERSET

Cadbury Castle

❻ **Bideford**

Taw

Tolland ❼

Taunton ❻

A358

Sedgemoor ❺

A361

Yeovilton ❻②

A303

A303 ❻③

A39

Torridge

Wellington ○

A361

Tiverton

M5

Exe

A303

A3088

Montacute House

A303 ❻①

○ **Yeovil**

A30

ON

A377

Okehampton

Castle Drogo ❺②

A30

Exeter ❺⑦

A3052

Honiton ❻⓪

A375

B3174

DORSET

○ **Bridport**

Lydford Gorge ❹⑨

A382

Chagford ❺①

Topsham ❺⑧

A30

A380

A377

A376

Beer ❺⑨

Seaton

Lyme Regis ○

DARTMOOR

B3212

Tavistock ○

Morwellham Quay Openair Museum ❹⑧

Sidmouth ○

Budleigh Salterton ○

Exmouth ○

Lyme Bay

❹⑦

Buckland Abbey ❹⑥

Buckfastleigh ○

Dart

A379

Torbay ❺⑥

Saltram House ❹⑤

A386

Totnes ❺④

A38

Brixham ❺⑤

Dartmouth ❺③

Plymouth ❸⑦—❹④

A379

○ **Yealmpton**

Kingsbridge ○

Slapton

Start Bay

A379

N

English Channel

0 — 20 miles

0 — 30 km

the imposing Pendennis and its sibling across the estuary, **St. Mawes** ㉛. On your fifth day, begin by nosing around seaside **Mevagissey** ㉝ and Charlestown then head for **Plymouth** ㊲. After your fifth night, explore the city, then track down to **Dartmoor Forest** and its impressive sights, including **Castle Drogo** (52), spending your fifth night in **Exeter** (57). From Exeter, travel up to take in **Beer** (59) and **Honiton** (60), with an excursion to beautiful **Montacute House** (61). Spend your last night in **Glastonbury** ④, and your last day exploring this medieval site and that of nearby **Wells** ③.

When to Tour the West Country

Come July and August, the roads leading into the West Country are choked with endless streams of traffic. Somehow the region seems able to absorb all the "grockles," or tourists, though the chances of finding a remote oasis of peace and quiet are severely curtailed at this time of year. The beaches, in particular, heave with hopeful sunseekers, and the resort towns are either bubbling with zest or unbearably tacky, depending on your point of view. If you can't avoid visiting in the holiday season, you will need to work harder to find your own space, and your best option would be to hole up in a secluded hotel and make brief excursions from there. Otherwise, try to time your visit to coincide with the beginning or end of the summer. The West Country gets more hours of sunshine than most other parts of Britain, so you can afford to take your chances with the weather. That said, the winter has its own special appeal, when the Atlantic waves crash dramatically against the coast, and austere Cornish cliffs come into their own.

KING ARTHUR COUNTRY— FROM BRISTOL TO TINTAGEL

Exploring King Arthur Country means wending your way between documented history and the world of myth. Starting out from Bristol, journey south to the cathedral city of Wells and continue on via Glastonbury, possibly the Avalon of Arthurian legend. From there head west to Taunton, the capital of cider country, and also the focus of some fierce tussles in the English Civil War. Proceed west along the Somerset coast into Devon, skirting Exmoor, tracing the northern coast via Clovelly and Bude, and end at the cliff-top ruins of Tintagel Castle in Cornwall, legendary birthplace of Arthur.

Bristol

❶ *120 mi west of London, 46 mi south of Birmingham, 13 mi northwest of Bath.*

A treasure house of great historic interest, Bristol can be called the "birthplace of America" with some confidence, for it was from the old city docks of Bristol that John Cabot and his son Sebastian sailed in 1497 to the discovery of the American continent. Furthermore, Bristol was the home of William Penn, developer of Pennsylvania, and haven for John Wesley, whose Methodist movement played such a large part in the settling of Georgia. The city had been a major center since medieval times, but it was in the 17th and 18th centuries that it became an important port for the North American trade. Now that the city's industries no longer rely on the docks, the historic harbor along the River Avon has been largely given over to pleasure craft. The quayside offers an arts center, movie theaters, museums, stores, pubs, and restaurants; carnivals, speedboat races, and regattas are held in the summer months.

On view in the harbor is the **SS *Great Britain,*** the first iron ship to cross the Atlantic. Built by the great English engineer Isambard Kingdom Brunel in 1843, it remained in service until the end of the century, first on the North American route and then on the Australian. ⊠ *Great Western Dock, off Cumberland Rd.,* ☎ *0117/926–0680.* ▦ *£4.50.* ☉ *Apr.–Sept., daily 10–5:30; Oct.–Mar., 10–4:30.*

Bristol is the home of the **Church of St. Mary Redcliffe** (⊠ Redcliffe Way, a 5-min walk from Temple Meads train station toward the docks), called "the fairest in England" by Queen Elizabeth I. It features rib vaulting and dates from the 1300s, built by Bristol merchants who wanted a place in which to pray for the safe (and profitable) voyages of their ships.

Among the Dissenters from the Church of England who found a home in Bristol was John Wesley, who built the first Methodist church here in 1739, the **New Room**; its austerity contrasts sharply with Anglican churches. ⊠ *Broadmead,* ☎ *0117/926–4740.* ▦ *Free. Tours £2* ☉ *Easter–Sept., Tues. and Thurs.–Sat. 9–4; Oct.–Easter Mon., Fri. and Sat. 11:30–2.*

In the Georgian suburb of Clifton—a sort of Bath in miniature—take in that monument to Victorian engineering, the Clifton Suspension Bridge, built in 1828 by Brunel. Crossing the Avon Gorge, you will reach
ⓒ the **Bristol Zoo,** where some 300 species of animals (plus many more of reptiles, insects, and fish) live on 12 acres of landscaped gardens. The opening of a new gorilla island and walk-through aviary are planned for 1998. ⊠ *Clifton,* ☎ *0117/973–8951.* ▦ *£6.50.* ☉ *Apr.– Sept., daily 9–5:30; Oct.–Mar., daily 9–4:30.*

Dining and Lodging

££ ✕ **Bell's Diner.** Though it's a Bristol institution, this bistro is rather hidden—take A38 (Stokes Croft) north, then turn right into Picton Street, which will lead you to York Road. Bell's is in a converted corner shop and has Bristol prints on its pale gray walls, polished wooden floors, and an open fire. The inventive menu changes regularly, with particular attention paid to light dishes and toothsome desserts. ⊠ *1 York Rd., Montpelier,* ☎ *0117/924–0357. MC, V. Closed 1 wk in Sept., and Dec. 24–Jan. 2. No lunch Sat.*

££ ✕ **Markwicks.** This restaurant, in busy downtown Bristol, is in a basement that was once a safety deposit chamber. Black-and-white marble floors and iron grille doors retain the vaultlike atmosphere, but the food is excellent. Try the fish soup, or the local turbot and sea bass. The daily changing set-price menus are of good value. ⊠ *43 Corn St.,* ☎ *0117/926–2658. AE, DC, MC, V. Closed Sun., Mon., 1 wk at Christmas and Easter, and 2 wks in Aug. No lunch Sat.*

££ ✕ **Michael's.** Informal elegance is the predominant tone in this restaurant across Bristol's Floating Harbour from the S.S. *Great Britain.* Aperitifs and post-dinner drinks are taken in a comfortable lounge area, where a log fire provides the centerpiece, while next door, meals are served by an attentive and friendly staff. The imaginative dishes are the creations of proprietor Michael McGowan and might include panfried duck breast with orange sauce and honey-glazed shallots, or a tartlet of mixed mushrooms and creamed leeks. ⊠ *129 Hotwell Rd., BS8 4RU,* ☎ *0117/927–6190. AE, DC, MC, V. Closed 1 wk end of Aug. No lunch Mon.–Sat., no dinner Sun.*

For a spectacular overture to your West Country excursion, you may wish to book a night at Thornbury Castle, one of Britain's most historic hotels, just 12 mi north of Bristol in Thornbury (☞ Berkeley Castle *in* Chapter 9).

£££   🖭 **Redwood Lodge Hotel.** Primarily a business hotel and conference center, this is a handy stopover for anyone touring by car—it's just off A4, close to the Clifton Suspension Bridge. Modern and attractively furnished, it has a number of amenities, including 16 acres of pleasant woodland surroundings. ✉ *Beggar Bush La., Failand, BS8 3TG,* ☎ *01275/393901,* 𝔽𝔸𝕏 *01275/392791. 108 rooms with bath. Restaurant, coffee shop, indoor-outdoor pool, tennis court, exercise room, squash, cinema. AE, DC, MC, V.*

£   🖭 **Naseby House Hotel.** This Victorian hotel, situated on a tree-lined street in the heart of Clifton, yet central to Bristol's sights, has its own garden and is central to the major sights of Bristol. The comfortable bedrooms have TV and tea/coffeemakers; plushest, and most expensive, are those in the recently refurbished basement. The lounge is filled with period bric-a-brac, and the breakfast room is also impressive. ✉ *105 Pembroke Rd., BS8 3EF,* ☎ 𝔽𝔸𝕏 *0117/973–7859. 15 rooms, 13 with bath or shower. MC, V.*

Outdoor Activities and Sports

SHOW JUMPING

The Badminton Horse Trials are held annually during four days in May at the duke of Beaufort's magnificent estate in **Badminton** (☎ 01454/218272), 12 mi northeast of Bristol.

En Route   The area south of Bristol is notable for its scenery and walks, its photogenic villages, and the ancient stone circles. Take A38 (follow signs for airport), then B3130 and B3114 to the villages of Chew Magna and Chew Stoke and on to Chew Valley Lake, a reservoir in a drowned valley surrounded by woods, which shelters 240 species of birds. At Chew Magna note the gargoyles on the ancient church.

Stanton Drew

❷ *6 mi south of Bristol, 10 mi west of Bath.*

Just east of the village of Stanton Drew are the neolithic **Stanton Drew Circles,** where three rings, two avenues of standing stones, and a burial chamber make up one of the grandest and most mysterious monuments in the country. Excavations beneath the circles in 1997 revealed evidence of a much older site, from around 3000 BC, consisting of a wood henge, or timber circle. Its great size suggests that it was once as important as Stonehenge for its ceremonial functions, though there is little of great visual impact to be seen now. The site lies in a field reached through a farmyard—you'll need suitable shoes to visit it. The stones stand on private land but are supervised by English Heritage. To get here from Chew Magna, turn east on B3130. 🔳 *Small fee.* ☉ *Open usually 9–5, closed Sun.*

Wells

❸ *22 mi south of Bristol, 20 mi southwest of Bath, 132 mi west of London.*

Wells, England's smallest cathedral city, lies at the foot of the Mendip Hills. Although it feels more like a quiet country town than a city, Wells is home to one of the great masterpieces of Gothic architecture, its great cathedral—the first to be built in the Early English style. It derives its beauty from the perfect harmony of all of its parts, the glowing colors of its original stained-glass windows, and its peaceful setting among aged trees and lawns. The city's name refers to the underground streams that bubble up into St. Andrew's Well within the grounds of the Bishop's Palace. Spring water has run through the High Street since the 15th century. The ancient marketplace in the city center is surrounded by 17th-century buildings. William Penn was arrested here in 1695 for preaching without a license at The Crown hotel (☞ Dining and Lodging, *below*). Though the elaborate fountain at the entrance to the square is only 200 years old, it's on the same spot as the lead conduit that brought fresh spring water to the market in medieval times. Wells has a market day on Wednesday and Saturday.

★ The great west towers of the famous **Cathedral Church of St. Andrew** are visible for miles. To appreciate the elaborate west front facade, approach the building on foot from the cathedral green, accessible from Market Place through a great medieval gate called "penniless porch" (named after the beggars who once waited here to collect alms from worshipers). The cathedral's west front is twice as wide as it is high and is adorned with some 300 statues. This is the oldest surviving English Gothic church, begun in the 12th century. Vast inverted arches were added in 1338 to stop the central tower from sinking to one side. Present erosion is causing a great deal of anxiety, and a restoration program is under way. The cathedral also has a rare medieval clock, consisting of the seated figure of a man called Jack Blandiver, who strikes a bell on the quarter hour while mounted knights circle in mock battle. Near the clock you will find the entrance to the chapter house—a small, wooden door opening onto a great sweep of stairs worn down on one side by the tread of pilgrims over the centuries.

The second great gate leading from Market Place, the Bishop's Eye, takes you to the magnificent **Bishop's Palace.** Most of its original 12th- and 13th-century residences remain, and you can also see the ruins of a late 13th-century great hall, which lost its roof in the 16th century because Edward VI needed the lead! The palace is surrounded by a moat that's home to swans, which, it is claimed, can pull on a rope attached to a bell when they're hungry, a trick taught to their ancestors by a Victorian bishop's daughter. ⊠ *Market Pl.,* ☎ *01749/678691.* ▨ *£3.* ☉ *Easter–Oct., Tues.–Fri. and national holidays 10:30–6, Sun. 2–6; Aug., Mon–Sat. 10–6, Sun. 2–6.*

North of the cathedral, **Vicar's Close,** Europe's oldest street, has terraces of handsome 14th-century houses with strange, tall chimneys, and a tiny medieval chapel that's still in use.

Dining and Lodging

£ ✕ **Ritcher's.** Choose between eating downstairs or in the plant-filled loft upstairs in this bistro, where you can get good-value two- or three-course fixed-price meals. Among the dishes on offer are roast duck, pork with Stilton, and guinea fowl sautéed au poivre. ⊠ *5 Sadler St.,* ☎ *01749/679085. MC, V.*

£££ ✕⊞ **Swan Hotel.** Built in the 15th century, this former coaching inn faces the cathedral. Nine of the rooms have four-poster beds, and on cold days you can relax in front of a log fire in one of the lounges. The ambitious restaurant offers daily specials and displays costumes owned by the great Victorian actor Sir Henry Irving. Room rates are at the lower end of this category. ⊠ *11 Sadler St., BA5 2RX,* ☎ *01749/678877,* ℻ *01749/677647. 38 rooms with bath. Restaurant AE, DC, MC, V.*

££ ✕⊞ **Ancient Gate House.** The Italian Franco Rossi has recently opened guest rooms above his centrally located restaurant. The premises are old and full of character, and six of the rooms have four-posters, but in other respects the facilities are completely up-to-date. The restaurant, **Rugantino,** specializes in Italian dishes made largely from local produce, and there is also a traditional English menu. ⊠ *20 Sadler St., BA5 2RR,* ☎ *01749/672029,* ℻ *01749/670319. 9 rooms, 7 with bath or shower. Restaurant. AE, DC, MC, V.*

£ ✕▦ **The Crown.** This hotel has been a landmark in Wells since the Middle Ages; William Penn was arrested here in 1695 for illegal preaching. There is a period atmosphere to the place, enhanced by the fact that four of the rooms have four-poster beds. There's also a particularly helpful staff. The Penn Bar and Eating House serves salads and such hot dishes as steak-and-kidney pie, or you can eat in the more comfortable bistro (closed Sun. and Mon.). ✉ *Market Pl., BA5 2RP,* ☎ *01749/673457,* ℻ *01749/679792. 15 rooms with bath. Restaurant, bar. AE, MC, V.*

OFF THE BEATEN PATH	**WOOKEY HOLE –** Signs in Wells town center direct you 2 mi north to a fascinating complex of limestone caves in the Mendip Hills that may have been the home of Iron Age people and where, so the ancient legend goes, the Witch of Wookey turned to stone. In addition to a museum, there is an underground lake and several chambers to explore, plus a working paper mill and a display of Madame Tussaud's early waxwork collection dating from the 1830s. ☎ *01749/672243.* ✆ *£6.75.* ☉ *Mar.–Oct., daily 9:30–5:30; Nov.–Feb., daily 10:30–4:30.*

Glastonbury

➍ *5 mi southwest of Wells, just off A39, 27 mi south of Bristol, 27 mi southwest of Bath.*

★ At the foot of **Glastonbury Tor,** a grassy hill rising 520 ft, the town of Glastonbury is steeped in history, myth, and legend. In legend, Glastonbury is identified with Avalon, the paradise into which King Arthur was born after his death. It is also said to be the burial place of Arthur and Guinevere, his queen. And according to Christian tradition, it was to Glastonbury, the first Christian settlement in England, that Joseph of Arimathea brought the Holy Grail, the chalice used by Christ at the Last Supper. At the foot of the tor is **Chalice Well,** the legendary burial place of the Grail. It's a stiff climb up the tor, but you'll be rewarded by the fabulous view across the Vale of Avalon. At the top stands a ruined tower, all that's left of **St. Michael's Church,** which collapsed after a landslide in 1271. With all these marvels, it's little wonder that thousands of New Age aficionados descend on this town every summer, to mix the Christian with the Druidic and to search for Jesus, Arthur, Guinevere, and Elvis (Elvis? See Glastonbury Festival, *below*).

The ruins of the great **Abbey of Glastonbury** lie in the center of town. According to legend, this is the site where Joseph of Arimathea built a church in the 1st century; a monastery had certainly been erected here by the 9th century. The ruins are those of the abbey completed in 1524 and destroyed in 1539, during Henry VIII's dissolution of the monasteries. ☎ *01458/832267.* ✆ *£2.50.* ☉ *Feb., daily 10–5; Mar., daily 9:30–5:30; Apr. and May, daily 9:30–6; June–Aug., daily 9–6; Sept., daily 9:30–6; Oct., daily 9:30–5; Nov., daily 9:30–4:30; Dec.–Jan., daily 10–4:30.*

While you are in Glastonbury, visit the Abbey Barn, which now houses the **Somerset Rural Life Museum.** This 14th-century tithe barn stored the one-tenth portion of the town's produce due the church, and it is more than 90 ft long. ✉ *Chilkwell St.,* ☎ *01458/831197.* ✆ *£2.20.* ☉ *Apr.–Oct., Tues.–Fri. 10–5, weekends 2–6; Nov.–Mar., Tues.–Sat. 10–3.*

The **Glastonbury Festival,** held somewhat annually a few miles away in Pilton, is the biggest and perhaps the best of rock festivals in England. For three days over the last weekend in June, the festival hosts hundreds of bands—basically a mix of established and up-and-coming, with a few big names from the past thrown in—on five stages. Tickets are steep—£80 for the last festival—but everything excluding food (entertainment, camping pitch, and service facilities) is included for the three-day fete. Pick up the June issue of *Melody Maker* for the complete lineup of bands and events or ☎ 0870/6077380 (49p per minute).

Lodging

££ ⌂ **George and Pilgrims Hotel.** Pilgrims en route to Glastonbury Abbey stayed here in the 15th century. Today, all the modern comforts are here, but you can enjoy them in rooms with flagstone floors, wooden beams, and antique furniture; three rooms have four-poster beds. ⊠ *1 High St., BA6 9DP,* ☎ *01458/831146,* ℻ *01458/832252. 13 rooms with bath or shower. Restaurant, bar. AE, DC, MC, V.*

Shopping

Morlands Factory Shop (⊠ 2 mi southwest of Glastonbury on A39, ☎ 01458/835042) is one of several good outlets for sheepskin products in Somerset sheep country, selling coats, slippers, and rugs (Mon.–Sat. 9:30–5). Glastonbury's market day is Tuesday.

West of Glastonbury, A39 and A361 toward Taunton cross the Somerset Levels, marshes that have been drained by open ditches (known ❺ as rhines), where peat is dug. **Sedgemoor** is where, in 1685, the Duke of Monmouth's troops were routed by those of his uncle James II in the last battle fought on English soil. R. D. Blackmore's novel *Lorna Doone* is set during Monmouth's Rebellion.

Taunton

❻ *22 mi southwest of Glastonbury, 50 mi southwest of Bristol, 18 mi northeast of Exeter.*

Somerset's principal town lies in the heart of the cider-making country. In these parts, cider rather than beer is the traditional beverage. Fermented and alcoholic, it can be a lot more potent than English beer. In the fall, some cider mills open their doors to visitors. If you're interested, visit **Sheppys,** a local farm, shop, and cider museum. ⊠ *Three Bridges, Bradford-on-Tone (on A38 west of Taunton),* ☎ *01823/ 461233.* ▣ *£1.75, guided tour (2½ hrs) £4.25.* ☉ *Mon.–Sat. 8:30–6; Easter–Dec. 25, also Sun. noon–2.*

Dining and Lodging

£ ✕ **Porters Wine Bar.** A 10-minute walk from the center, Porters serves both light lunches and more substantial meals at very reasonable prices. ⊠ *49 E. Reach,* ☎ *01823/256688. MC, V. Closed Sun. No lunch Sat.*

£££ ✕⌂ **The Castle.** The battlements and towers of this 300-year-old build-
★ ing will leave you in no doubt as to why this hotel, reputed to be among England's finest, has the name it does. The facade is covered by a huge, 150-year-old wisteria, magnificent when in flower. Bedrooms are individually decorated, and garden suites have separate dressing rooms. In the hotel's restaurant, with its daily-changing, fixed-price menus, the haute cuisine ranges from braised shoulder of lamb with thyme and garlic to elaborate desserts such as baked egg custard tart with nutmeg ice cream. The cheese selection includes many English cheeses and is served with homegrown prunes. ⊠ *Castle Green, TA1 1NF,* ☎ *01823/272671,* ℻ *01823/336066. 45 rooms with bath. Restaurant. AE, DC, MC, V.*

En Route North of Taunton you will see the outlines of the **Quantock** and **Brendon hills.** The eastern Quantocks are covered with beech trees and are home to herds of handsome red deer. Climb to the top of the hills for a spectacular view of the Vale of Taunton Deane and, to the north, the Bristol Channel.

Tolland

❼ *9 mi northwest of Taunton.*

In a quiet valley between the Quantock and Brendon hills, **Gaulden Manor** is a small 12th-century estate, whose house is built of red sandstone. Its elegant grounds include an Elizabethan herb garden. It was the home of the Turberville family, a name familiar to readers of *Tess of the d'Urbervilles*, by Thomas Hardy. ⊠ *Tolland,* ☎ *01984/667213.* 🎫 *£3.80, garden only £1.80.* ☉ *Late May–late Aug., Sun., Thurs. and national holidays 2–5.*

Dunster

❽ *12 mi northwest of Tolland, 43 mi north of Exeter.*

Lying between the Somerset coast and the edge of Exmoor National Park, Dunster is a picture-book village with a broad main street. Look for the eight-sided yarn-market building dating from 1589. The village is dominated by its 13th-century fortress, **Dunster Castle,** a National Trust property boasting fine plaster ceilings and a magnificent 17th-century staircase. Note that there is a steep climb up to the castle from the parking lot. To reach Dunster from Tolland, follow B3188, B3190, and A39. ☎ *01643/821314.* 🎫 *£5.20, gardens only £2.80.* ☉ *Apr.–Sept., Sat.–Wed. 11–5; Oct., Sat.–Wed. 11–4. Gardens: Apr.– Sept. daily 10–5; Oct.–Mar. daily 11–4.*

En Route   Heading west, the coast road A39 mounts **Porlock Hill,** an incline so steep that signs are posted to encourage drivers to "Keep Going." The views across Exmoor and north to the Bristol Channel and Wales are worth it.

Lynton and Lynmouth

❾ *19 mi west of Dunster, 60 mi northwest of Exeter.*

This pretty pair of Devonshire villages is separated by a steep hill and linked by a water-powered cliff railway. Lynmouth, a fishing village, is at the bottom, crouching below 1,000-ft cliffs at the mouths of the rivers East and West Lynne.

Lodging

£££ 🏨 **Rising Sun.** This intriguing hotel was once a 14th-century inn and
★   a row of thatched cottages. It has great views over Lynmouth, especially from the terraced garden out back. The rooms are furnished either in pine or older pieces. If you want more privacy, ask for the detached cottage in the garden (also available for weekly rental), one of two places in Lynmouth claiming to be where the poet Shelley spent his honeymoon. ⊠ *Harbourside, Lynmouth EX35 6EQ,* ☎ *01598/753223,* 🖷 *01598/753480. 16 rooms with bath, cottage. Restaurant, fishing. AE, DC, MC, V.*

Barnstaple

❿ *21 mi southwest of Lynton on A39, 42 mi northwest of Exeter.*

Barnstaple, on the banks of the River Taw, is northern Devon's largest city. It's a bustling market town surrounded by modern developments, though the center retains its traditional look. Try to visit on Friday, market day, to see the colorful scene in Butchers' Row and Pannier Market. West of Barnstaple, along the Taw estuary, lie desolate stretches of sand dunes offering long vistas of marram grass and sea.

Dining and Lodging

£–££ ✕🏠 **Royal and Fortescue Hotel.** Edward VII, who stayed here when he was Prince of Wales, gave this Victorian hotel the royal part of its name. It's in the center of town, and all rooms are furnished to a high standard. There's a choice of à la carte or table d'hôte menu in the restaurant. ✉ *Boutport St., EX31 1HG,* ☎ *01271/342289,* 🅵🅰🆇 *01271/ 342289. 47 rooms with bath or shower. Restaurant. AE, DC, MC, V.*

Braunton Burrows

⑪ *10 mi west of Lynton.*

Braunton Burrows, on the north side of the Taw estuary, is a National Nature Reserve, with miles of trails running through the dunes. This spot affords some first-class bird-watching, especially in winter.

Bideford

⑫ *8 mi west of Barnstaple by A39, 49 mi northwest of Exeter.*

Broad Bideford Bay is fed by the confluence of the rivers Taw and Torridge. Bideford lies on the Torridge, which you can cross either by the 14th-century, 24-arch bridge or by the more modern structure to reach the scenic hillside sheltering the town's elegant houses. At one time they were all painted white, and Bideford is still sometimes called the "little white town." The area was a mainstay of 16th-century shipbuilding; the trusty vessels of Sir Francis Drake among others were built here.

Clovelly

⑬ *12 mi west of Bideford, 60 mi northwest of Exeter.*

Clovelly always seems to have the sun shining on its stepped and cobbled streets. A village of quaint atmosphere and picturesqueness, it can be compared with villages in the south of France, such as St. Tropez (it can also be as overrun with day-trippers as that Provence pleasure spot). Perched precariously among cliffs, a steep, cobbled road (tumbling down at such an angle that it has to be closed to cars) leads to the toylike harbor. The climb back has been compared to the struggles of Sisyphus, but, happily, a Land Rover service (in summer) will take you to and from the parking lot at the top.

Lodging

£££ 🏠 **Red Lion Hotel.** One of only two hotels in this picturesque coastal village, the Red Lion is an 18th-century inn right on the harbor. All rooms enjoy sea views and are well equipped, though you have to put up with uneven floors, tiny windows, and restricted space. The climb up through Clovelly is perilously steep, but hotel guests can bring cars via a back road to and from the Red Lion. Prices only just creep into this category. ✉ *The Quay, EX39 5TF,* ☎ *01237/431237,* 🅵🅰🆇 *01237/ 431044. 11 rooms with bath. Restaurant, bar. AE, MC, V.*

Bude

⑭ *15 mi south of Clovelly.*

Just across the Cornish border, the popular Victorian seaside town of Bude is known for its long sandy beaches. But beware: in summer, the town and beaches are overrun with tourists.

Boscastle

⑮ *15 mi southwest of Bude.*

In tranquil Boscastle, some of the stone and slate cottages at the foot of the steep valley date from the 1300s. The town is centered around a quaint little harbor, set snug within towering cliffs. Nearby, 2 mi up the valley of the Valency is the "Endelstow" referred to in Thomas Hardy's *A Pair of Blue Eyes*—the famed author had worked on the restoration of this church.

Tintagel

★ **⑯** *5 mi southwest of Boscastle.*

All that is left of the legendary birthplace of King Arthur, the ruined cliff-top **castle of Tintagel,** is the outline of the walls, moats, and towers, but it only requires the smallest amount of imagination to conjure up a picture of Sir Lancelot and Sir Galahad riding out in search of the Holy Grail over the narrow causeway above the seething breakers. Archaeological evidence, however, suggests that the castle dates from much later, about 1150, when it was the stronghold of the earls of Cornwall, and the site may have been occupied by the Romans. The earliest identified remains at the castle are of Celtic (5th-century) origin, and these may have some connection with the legendary Arthur. But legends aside, nothing can detract from the stunning castle ruins, dramatically set off by the wild, windswept Cornish coast, on an island connected by a narrow isthmus. (There are also traces of a Celtic monastery here.) Paths lead down to the pebble beach, to a cavern known as **Merlin's Cave.** Exploring Tintagel Castle involves some arduous climbing up and down steep steps, but even on a summer's day, when visitors swarm over the battlements and a westerly Atlantic wind seems always to be sweeping through Tintagel, one cannot help being awed with the proximity of the distant past. ☎ *01840/770328.* ✆ *£2.70.* ☉ *Easter–Oct., daily 10–6 or dusk; Nov.–Easter, daily 10–4.*

In the village of Tintagel, which has more than its share of tourist junk—including Excaliburgers!—stop in at the **Old Post Office,** in a 14th-century stone manor house with smoke-blackened beams. It has been restored to its appearance during Victorian times, when it was used as a post office. ✉ *3–4 Tintagel Centre,* ☎ *01840/770024.* ✆ *£2.20.* ☉ *Apr.–Sept., daily 11–5:30; Oct., daily 11–5.*

THE CORNWALL COAST—
ON THE ROAD TO PLYMOUTH

To cover the whole of Cornwall, first travel southwest from Tintagel along the north Cornish coast to Land's End, the westernmost tip of Britain, known for its savage land- and seascapes and panoramic views. From Land's End turn northeast, stopping in the popular seaside resort of Penzance, the harbor city of Falmouth, and a string of pretty Cornish fishing villages. Next set off across the boggy, heath-covered expanse of Bodmin Moor, and then turn south to Plymouth, Devon's largest city, whose present-day dockyards recall a rich, centuries-old naval tradition.

Newquay

⑰ *14 mi southwest of Padstow by B3276.*

The principal resort on the north Cornwall coast, Newquay is a largish town established in 1439. It was once the center of the trade in pilchards (a small herringlike fish), and on the headland you can still see a little white hut where a lookout known as a "huer" watched for pilchard schools and directed the boats to the fishing grounds. In recent years, Newquay has become the country's surfing capital, and the wide beaches can be uncomfortably packed in summer with the young and the restless.

Perranporth

18 *8 mi south of Newquay, 13 mi northwest of Truro.*

Past the sandy shores of Perran Bay, Perranporth, one of Cornwall's most popular seaside spots, is extremely crowded in high season. The swells off this 3-mi stretch of beach attract swarms of surfers, too. The best times to visit are the beginning and end of the summer. There are enchanting coastal walks along the dunes and cliffs.

St. Ives

19 *20 mi southwest of Perranporth on A30, 10 mi north of Penzance.*

James McNeill Whistler came here to paint his landscapes, Daphne du Maurier and Virginia Woolf to write their novels, and, today, sand, sun, and world-class art continue to attract thousands of stylish vacationers to the fishing village of St. Ives, named after St. Ia, a 5th-century female Irish missionary said to have arrived on a floating leaf. The town has long played a host to a well-established artists' colony. Dame Barbara Hepworth, who pioneered abstract sculpture in England, lived here for 26 years. Her house and garden, now the **Barbara Hepworth Museum and Sculpture Garden,** is run by London's prominent Tate Gallery and is fascinating to anyone interested in sculpture. St. Ives is often crowded with day-trippers, so it's best to park outside the town. *Trewyn Studio,* ⊠ *Barnoon Hill,* ☎ *01736/796226.* ☞ *£3.25, combined ticket with Tate Gallery St. Ives (☞ below) £6.* ☉ *Apr.–Sept., daily 10:30–5:30; Oct.–Mar., Tues.–Sun. 10:30–5:30.*

Fittingly, in a town which is home to many artists, the spectacular **Tate Gallery St. Ives** is now the leading attraction. The lavish modernist building—a fantasia of seaside Deco-period architecture featuring a panoramic view of turquoise rippling ocean—opened in spring 1993 and has drawn critical raves from all over. The four-story gallery, stunningly set at the base of a cliff fronted by Porthmeor Beach, houses the work of artists who lived and worked in St. Ives, mostly from 1925 to 1975, drawn from the rich collection of the Tate Gallery in London. This is the latest move in the Tate's plan to spread its artistic wealth outside the capital. It may be the only art gallery in the world with a special storage space for visitors' surfboards. There is an excellent rooftop café. ⊠ *Porthmeor Beach,* ☎ *01736/796226.* ☞ *£3.75 (☞ Hepworth Museum, above, for combined ticket).* ☉ *Apr.–Sept., daily 10:30–5:30; Oct.–Mar., Tues.–Sun. 10:30–5:30.*

Examples of current artists' work can be found for sale at the St. Ives Society of Artists in the **Norway Gallery.** ⊠ *Old Mariners Church, Norway Sq.,* ☎ *01736/795582.* ☞ *Small fee.* ☉ *Apr.–mid-Nov., Mon.– Sat. 10–4:30.*

Dining and Lodging

££ ✗ **Pig 'n' Fish.** Concentrate on the "fish" here, because it's a great spot for seafood. This simple, small restaurant has worthwhile pictures on display—after all, this is St. Ives. Try the fish soup or the roast sea bass with eggplant, coriander, and pickled lemon; if you can plan ahead, telephone in advance to order oysters or lobster. The desserts are scrumptious. ⊠ *Norway La.,* ☎ *01736/794204. MC, V. Closed Sun., Mon. and Nov.–mid-Mar.*

£   ✕ **The Sloop Inn.** On the harborfront, the Sloop Inn, built in 1312, is one of Cornwall's oldest pubs. Pub lunches and evening meals are available in the wood-beam rooms. ⊠ *The Wharf,* ☎ *01736/796584. MC, V.*

£££   ✕🍽 **Garrack Hotel.** A family-run, ivy-clad hotel with panoramic sea
★   views from its hilltop location, the Garrack offers a relaxed, undemanding atmosphere. The staff is courteous and personable, and helpful with local information. The hotel has a purpose-built ground-floor room for visitors with disabilities. The restaurant, open to nonresidents, is one of the best in the region. ⊠ *Burthallan La., TR26 3AA,* ☎ *01736/796199,* 🄵🄰🄷 *01736/798955. 18 rooms with bath. Restaurant, indoor pool, sauna. AE, DC, MC, V.*

En Route   The B3306 coastal road southwest from St. Ives is a winding route passing through some of Cornwall's starkest yet most beautiful countryside. Barren hills crisscrossed by low stone walls drop abruptly to granite cliffs and wide bays. Evidence of the ancient tin-mining industry—the remains of smokestacks and pumping houses—is everywhere. In some places the workings extended beneath the sea, forcing miners to toil away with the noise of waves crashing over their heads. Near the village of Pendeen, the coastal road will take you past the **Geevor Tin Mine** (☎ *01736/388662*), where surface and underground tours are conducted throughout the year. There is a museum, shop, and café on the site. Be careful if you decide to explore other abandoned mines in the area: many of the old shafts are open and unprotected.

Land's End

★ ⑳   *10 mi southeast of St. Ives, 10 mi west of Penzance.*

B3306 ends at the western tip of Britain at what is, quite literally, Land's End. Although the point draws tourists from all over the world, and a multimillion-dollar, glitzy theme park has been added, its savage grandeur remains undiminished. The sea crashes against its rocks and lashes ships battling their way around it. Approach it from one of the coastal footpaths for the best panoramic view. Over the years, sightseers have caused some erosion of the paths, but new ones are constantly being built, and Cornish "hedges" (granite walls covered with turf) have been planted to prevent future erosion.

Mousehole

㉑   *3 mi south of Penzance, 7 mi east of Land's End.*

If you're taking the B3315 minor road between Land's End and Penzance, it's worth stopping in at Mousehole (pronounced mowzel), an archetypal Cornish fishing village of tiny stone cottages. It was the home of Dolly Pentreath, supposedly the last native Cornish speaker, who died in 1777.

Newlyn

㉒   *2 mi north of Mousehole.*

Newlyn has long been the county's most important fishing port and became the magnet for a popular artists' colony at the end of the 19th century. A few of the appealing fishermen's cottages that first attracted artists here remain. To see the works of the Newlyn School, drop into the Penlee House gallery in Penzance (☞ *below*).

Penzance

㉓ *1½ mi north of Newlyn, 10 mi south of St. Ives.*

Seaside Penzance enjoys spectacular views over Mount's Bay. Because of the town's isolated position, it has always been open to attack from the sea. During the 16th century, Spanish raiders destroyed most of the original town, and the majority of old buildings you see date from as late as the 18th century. The main street is called Market Jew Street, a folk mistranslation of the Cornish expression "Marghas Yow," which actually means "Thursday Market." Look for **Market House**, constructed in 1837, an impressive, domed granite building that is now a bank. One of the prettiest streets in Penzance is **Chapel Street**, formerly the main street. It winds down from Market House to the harbor, its predominantly Georgian and Regency houses suddenly giving way to the extraordinary **Egyptian House**, on Chapel Street, whose facade is an evocation of ancient Egypt. Built around 1830 as a geological museum, today it houses a gift shop and picture gallery. Across Chapel Street from the Egyptian House is the 17th-century **Union Hotel**, where in 1805 the death of Lord Nelson and the victory of Trafalgar were first announced from the minstrels' gallery in the assembly rooms. Near the Union Hotel on Chapel Street is one of the few remnants of old Penzance, the **Turk's Head**, an inn said to date from the 13th century.

The town's **Maritime Museum** simulates the lower decks of a four-deck man-of-war, and exhibits items salvaged from shipwrecks off the Cornish coast. ⊠ *19 Chapel St.,* ☎ *01736/368890.* 🎫 *£2.* ☉ *Easter–Oct., Mon.–Sat. 10:30–4:30.*

Make a point of dropping into the **Penlee House Gallery** while in Penzance, where paintings by members of the so-called Newlyn School (☞ *above*) are displayed. A major refurbishment program was completed in November 1997, improving the facilities and adding a café to the premises. ⊠ *Penlee Park,* ☎ *01736/363625.* 🎫 *£2.* ☉ *Mon.–Sat. 10:30–4:30.*

Dining and Lodging

£££ **✕ Harris's.** Tucked away off Market Jew Street, Harris's fills a void of quality cuisine in Penzance. Two small rooms, one upstairs and one down, provide an elegant refuge for the travel-weary, even if the decor might be a shade overpowering. Try the crab Florentine, grilled on a bed of spinach with cheese sauce, or medallions of Scottish venison with wild mushrooms. ⊠ *46 New St.,* ☎ *01736/364408. AE, MC, V. Closed Sun., Mon. in winter, 2 wks in Nov., 1 wk in Feb. No lunch Mon.*

£ **✕ Admiral Benbow Inn.** One of the most famous inns in Penzance, the
★ 15th-century Admiral Benbow was once a smugglers' pub and is full of seafaring memorabilia, a brass cannon, model ships, ropes, and figureheads. Opt for the steak-and-Guinness pie. ⊠ *Chapel St.,* ☎ *01736/ 363448. AE, DC, MC, V.*

£££ **🛏 Abbey Hotel.** Owned by former model Jean Shrimpton and her hus-
★ band, this small, 17th-century hotel has a marvelous homey feel; the drawing room is filled with books and many of the rooms are furnished with antiques (there is also a comfortable small apartment available). The attractive restaurant has a short but intriguing menu, with seafood gratin, Barbary duck, and homemade ice cream. Dining privileges are normally reserved for guests, but you may be able to get a table. ⊠ *Abbey St., TR18 4AR,* ☎ *01736/366906,* 📠 *01736/351163. 5 rooms with bath. AE, DC, MC, V. Closed Christmas wk.*

£ **🛏 Camilla House.** The comfortably furnished Camilla stands on a road parallel to the Promenade, close to the harbor. The front rooms have sea views, and the top room is coziest. The owners are agents for the ferry line and can help with trips to the Scilly Isles. ☒ *Regent Terr., TR18 4DW,* ☎ *01736/363771,* ⅸ *01736/363771. 8 rooms, 4 with bath or shower. MC, V.*

The Arts

THEATER

At the open-air **Minack Theatre** (☎ 01736/810181) in Porthcurno, near Penzance, begun in the early 1930s, the natural slope of the cliff forms an amphitheater with terraces and bench seats, and the sea as a backdrop. Plays are performed here throughout the summer, ranging from classical dramas to modern comedies.

St. Michael's Mount

★ ㉔ *3 mi east of Penzance on A394.*

Rising out of Mount's Bay just off the coast, the spectacular granite and slate island of St. Michael's Mount is one of Cornwall's greatest natural attractions. A 14th-century castle perched at the highest point—200 ft above the sea—was built on the site of a Benedictine chapel founded by Edward the Confessor. In its time, it has been a church, a fortress, and a private residence. The buildings around the base of the rock range from medieval to Victorian, but appear harmonious. The Mount is surrounded by fascinating gardens, where a great variety of plants flourish in microclimates—snow can lie briefly on one part, while it can be 70°F in another. To get there, follow the causeway—just as you can to its "sister" of the same name in France—or, when the tide is in during the summer, take the ferry. If you have to wait for the ferry, there is a handy restaurant at the harbor. ☒ *Marazion,* ☎ *01736/710507.* ☎ *£3.90.* ☉ *Apr.–Oct., weekdays 10:30–5:30 (last admission 4:45); July–Aug., also most weekends in peak season 10:30–5:30; Nov.–Mar., phone for hrs.*

Helston

㉕ *13 mi east of Marazion, 14 mi east of Penzance, 18 mi southeast of Truro.*

The attractive Georgian town of Helston is most famous for its annual "Furry Dance," which takes place on Floral Day, May 8 (unless the date is a Sunday or Monday, in which case it takes place on the previous Saturday). The whole town is decked with flowers for the occasion, while dancers weave their way in and out of the houses along a 3-mi route.

☙ **Flambards Theme Park** has an aircraft collection, a re-creation of a wartime street during the Blitz, and a reconstructed Victorian village. ☒ *Near Helston,* ☎ *01326/574549 or 01326/573404.* ☎ *£6.20.* ☉ *Easter–June and Sept.–Oct., daily 10–5; July–Aug., daily 10–6; may close Mon. and Fri. in April and Oct. (check first).*

Dining and Lodging

£££ ✕▥ **Nansloe Manor.** Although near Helston's center, this peaceful manor house gives the impression of being deep in the country, with its attractive half-mile driveway and 5 acres of grounds. Accommodation rates drop sharply in winter. The à la carte menu in the dining room has a wide choice and changes daily. Fish is top choice, for example, baked monkfish Provençale. Fish, such as baked monkfish Provençale, is top choice. Prices fall into the bottom of this category, and there are good half-board rates for longer stays. ☒ *Meneage Rd., TR13 0SB,* ☎ *01326/574691,* ⅸ *01326/564680. 7 rooms with bath. Restaurant. MC, V.*

Lizard Peninsula

★ **㉖** *10 mi south of Helston.*

The Lizard Peninsula is the southernmost point on mainland Britain and is an officially designated Area of Outstanding Natural Beauty. The huge, eerily rotating dish antennae of the **Goonhilly Satellite Communications Earth Station** are visible from the road as it crosses Goonhilly Downs, the backbone of the peninsula. One path, close to the tip, **㉗** plunges down 200-ft cliffs to tiny **Kynance Cove,** with its handful of pint-size islands. The sands here are reachable only in the 2½ hours before and after low tide. The Lizard's cliffs are made of greenish, serpentine rock, interspersed with granite; local souvenirs are carved out of the stone.

Gweek

㉘ *2 mi east of Helston.*

At the head of the River Helford, the fishing village of Gweek is known for its **Seal Sanctuary,** which shelters sick and injured seals brought in from all over the country. Try to be there for feeding time, which occurs at least four times a day (call the information line for precise times (☎ 01326/221874). ☎ 01326/221361. ⌨ £5.50 (Mar.–Nov.), £4.50 (Dec.–Feb.). ۞ *Summer, daily 9–5; winter 9–4:30.*

Falmouth

㉙ *7 mi northeast of Gweek on B3291, 12 mi south of Truro.*

The bustling hubbub of this busy resort town's fishing harbor, yachting center, and commercial port only adds to its charm. In the 18th century, Falmouth was a mail-boat port, and in Flushing, a village across the inlet, are the slate-covered houses built by prosperous mail-boat captains. A ferry service now links the two towns. On Falmouth's quay, near the Customs House, is the King's Pipe, an oven in which seized contraband was burned. At the end of the Peninsula stands formidable **Pendennis Castle,** built by Henry VIII in the 1540s and later improved by his daughter Elizabeth I. From here there are sweeping views over the English Channel and across the water known as Carrick Roads, to St. Mawes Castle (☞ *below*) on the Roseland Peninsula, designed as a companion fortress to guard the roads. ⊠ *Pendennis Head,* ☎ *01326/316594.* ⌨ *£2.70.* ۞ *Apr.–Oct., daily 10–6 or dusk; Nov.–Mar., daily 10–4.*

Dining and Lodging

££ ✕ **Pandora Inn.** Four mi north of Falmouth, this thatched pub, with both a patio and a moored pontoon for summer dining, is a great discovery. The ambience derives from maritime memorabilia and fresh flowers, and you can eat either in the bars or in the candlelighted restaurant. The backbone of the menu is fresh seafood—try the seafood stroganoff or crab thermidor. The menu depends on the catch of the day. ⊠ *Restronguet Creek, Mylor Bridge,* ☎ *01326/372678. AE, MC, V. No lunch in restaurant.*

££ ✕ **Seafood Bar.** The window of this restaurant on the quay is a fish
★ tank, and beyond it is the very best seafood. Try the thick crab soup, the locally caught lemon sole, or, in summer, the turbot cooked with cider, apples, and cream. ⊠ *Quay St.,* ☎ *01326/315129. MC, V. Closed Sun.–Mon. No lunch.*

£££ ▥ **St. Michael's Hotel.** At this seaside hotel in a long, low, white building overlooking Falmouth Bay, there are gardens sweeping down to the sea. St. Michael's is constantly being updated—the bedrooms have all had recent face-lifts. With a special baby-sitting service, this place is especially recommended for families. Prices are low in this category. ✉ *Stracey Rd., TR11 4NB,* ☎ *01326/312707,* FAX *01326/211772. 65 rooms with bath. Bar, indoor pool, hot tub, sauna, exercise room. AE, DC, MC, V.*

£ 🖼 **Gyllyngvase House Hotel.** This hotel is centrally located, near the seafront. The bedrooms are a bit small but pleasantly furnished. There is a garden at the back. Evening meals are available on request. ✉ *Gyllyngvase Rd., TR11 4DJ,* ☎ *01326/312956. 15 rooms, 12 with bath or shower. AE, DC, MC, V.*

Trelissick

㉚ *6 mi north of Falmouth on B3289.*

At Trelissick, the **King Harry Ferry,** a chain-drawn car ferry, runs to the scenically splendid Roseland Peninsula at regular intervals daily (☎ 01872/862312 for last crossings). From its decks you can see all the way up and down the Fal, a deep, narrow river with steep, wooded banks. The river's great depth provides mooring for old ships waiting to be sold; these mammoth shapes lend a surreal touch to the riverscape.

★ Taking the King Harry Ferry, you can visit one of the most beautiful spots in the West Country—**St. Just in Roseland,** a tiny hamlet made up of stone cottage terraces and a 13th-century church that is postcard-perfect, complete with castellated tower and set within a Edenic subtropical garden, often abloom with magnolias and rhododendrons on a summer's day. Here, beneath a moss-covered, tiled roof is a spring, from which water has been used for centuries to baptize babies in the church font. St. Just is 9 mi south of Truro.

St. Mawes

㉛ *16 mi north and south of Falmouth (by road), 1½ mi by sea, 11 mi south of Truro.*

At the tip of the Roseland Peninsula, outside the village of St. Mawes, stands the Tudor-era **St. Mawes Castle.** Its cloverleaf shape makes it seemingly impregnable, yet during the Civil War, its royalist commander surrendered without firing a shot. (In contrast, Pendennis Castle held out at the time for 23 weeks before submitting to the siege.) ✉ *St. Mawes,* ☎ *01326/270526.* 🖼 *£2.20.* ☉ *Apr.–Oct., daily 10–6 or dusk; Nov.–Mar., Wed.–Sun., 10–4.*

En Route The shortest route from St. Mawes to Truro is via the ferry. The longer way swings in a circle on A3078 for 19 mi through attractive countryside, where subtropical shrubs and flowers thrive in the gardens along the way, past the town of Portloe (and its cozy hotel) and the 123-ft church tower in the village of Probus, flaunting its gargoyles and pierced stonework.

Truro

㉜ *12 mi north of Falmouth, 14 mi southeast of St. Austell.*

Truro is a compact, elegant Georgian city, nestled in a crook at the head of the River Truro. Though Bodmin is the county seat of Cornwall, Truro is Cornwall's only real city. The **Cathedral Church of St. Mary**—the first cathedral built in England since the completion of St. Paul's in London in the early 1700s—dominates the city; although comparatively modern (built 1880–1910), it evokes the feeling of a medieval church, with an impressive exterior in early English Gothic style. The inside is not so interesting, apart from a side chapel, which is all that remains of the original 16th-century parish church. In front of the west porch there is an open, cobbled area called High Cross, and the city's main shopping streets fan out from here.

For an overview of Truro's Georgian housefronts, take a stroll down Lemon Street. The 18th-century facades along this steep, broad street are of mellow-color stone, unusual for Cornwall, where granite is predominant. Like Lemon Street, Walsingham Place is a typical Georgian street, a curving, flower-lined, pedestrian oasis. Near Walsingham Place, the **Royal Cornwall Museum** offers a sampling of Cornish art, archaeology, an extensive collection of minerals, and a café and shop. ⊠ *River St.,* ☎ *01872/272205.* 🎫 *£2.50.* ⊙ *Mon.–Sat. 10–5.*

Dining and Lodging

£££ ✕🏨 **Alverton Manor.** This was once a bishop's house, then a convent, and it is now an up-to-date hotel/restaurant, both efficient and atmospheric. The former chapel is used as an unusual conference room. The rooms are large, with French cherrywood furniture. Quiet elegance is the keynote of the public rooms, and in the Terrace restaurant, standards are kept high with the use of the best local produce. ⊠ *Tregolls Rd., TR1 1XQ,* ☎ *01872/76633,* 🗷 *01872/222989. 34 rooms with bath or shower. Restaurant. AE, DC, MC, V.*

Mevagissey

㉝ *15 mi east of Truro, 5 mi south of St. Austell.*

In recent years the busy fishing town of Mevagissey has attracted a sizable influx of tourists that sometimes threatens to overwhelm its fragile charm. Like most Cornish coastal villages, it is not suitable for cars, so if you stop, use the large parking lot on the outskirts. From Truro, continue eastward on A390, turn right at Sticker, and follow signs.

Bodmin

㉞ *13 mi north of St. Austell on A391.*

Bodmin was the only Cornish town recorded in the 11th-century *Domesday Book,* William the Conqueror's census. During World War I, both the *Domesday Book* and the Crown Jewels were sent to Bodmin Prison for safekeeping. From the Gilbert Memorial on Beacon Hill you can see both of Cornwall's coasts.

Dozmary Pool

㉟ *10 mi northeast of Bodmin.*

For another taste of Arthurian legend, follow A30 northeast out of Bodmin across the boggy, heather-clad granite plateau of Bodmin Moor, and turn right at Bolventor to get to Dozmary Pool. A considerable lake rather than a pool, it was here that King Arthur's legendary magic sword, Excalibur, was supposedly returned to the Lady of the Lake after Arthur's final battle.

Dining and Lodging

£ ✕🏨 **Jamaica Inn.** At Bolventor, in the center of Bodmin Moor, just off A30, look for this inn, made famous by Daphne du Maurier's novel of the same name. Originally a farmstead, it is now Cornwall's best-known pub, and it incorporates a reproduction of du Maurier's study and a fun museum of curiosities. Despite the unashamed commercialization, it remains a good spot to try a Cornish pasty, and wayfarers can find six comfortable bedrooms here. ⊠ *Bolventor, PL15 7TS,* ☎ *01566/86250,* 🗷 *01566/86177. 6 rooms with bath. AE, DC, MC, V.*

Launceston

㊱ *25 mi northwest of Plymouth.*

Cornwall's ancient capital, Launceston (pronounced lanston), on the
eastern side of Bodmin Moor, retains parts of its medieval walls, including
the South Gate. For a full view of the surrounding countryside, climb
up to the ruins of 14th-century **Launceston Castle.** ☎ *01566/772365.*
⌑ *£1.50.* ☉ *Easter–Oct, daily 10–6 or dusk if earlier.*

Dining and Lodging

£££ ✕🏠 **Lewtrenchard Manor.** This spacious 1620 manor house, on the northwestern edge of Dartmoor, is full of paneled rooms, stone fireplaces,
and ornate leaded windows. Some bedrooms have antique four-posters.
The restaurant, with its big log fire and family portraits, serves good,
fresh fish, caught an hour away. ✉ *Lewdown, between Launceston and
Okehampton, EX20 4PN,* ☎ *01566/783256,* 🅵🅰🆇 *01566/783332. 9
rooms with bath. Restaurant, fishing, helipad. AE, DC, MC, V.*

Plymouth

㊲ *48 mi southwest of Exeter, 124 mi southwest of Bristol, 240 mi southwest of London.*

Devon's largest city has long been linked with England's commercial
㊳ and maritime history. From the **Hoe,** a wide, grassy esplanade with criss-
crossing walkways high above the city, you can get a magnificent view
of the many inlets, bays, and harbors that make up Plymouth Sound.
㊴ The best vista is provided atop **Smeaton's Tower,** found along the
㊵ Hoe. At the end of the Hoe stands the huge **Royal Citadel,** built by Charles
II in 1666. This still operates as a military center, but there are twice-
daily guided tours May–September lasting about an hour, at 1:30 and
3. Contact the tourist office for details.

㊶ The **Barbican,** which lies east of the Royal Citadel, is the oldest surviving section of Plymouth (much of the city center was destroyed by
air raids in World War II). Here, Tudor houses and warehouses rise
from a maze of narrow streets leading down to the fishing docks and
harbor. Many of these buildings have become antiques shops, art
★ shops, and bookstores. By the harbor you can visit the **Mayflower Steps,**
㊷ where the Pilgrims embarked in 1620; the **Mayflower Stone** marks the
exact spot. Near the Barbican, just off the Royal Parade, the largely
㊸ 18th-century **Merchant's House** has a museum of local history. ✉ *33
St. Andrew's St.,* ☎ *01752/264878.* ⌑ *95p.* ☉ *Apr.–Sept., Tues.–Fri.
10–1 and 2–5:30, Sat. 10–1 and 2–5.*

㊹ The **Royal Naval Dockyard,** on the west side of town, was begun in
the late 17th century by William III. It is still a naval base and much
is hidden behind the high dock walls, but parts of the 2-mi-long
frontage can be seen from pleasure boats that travel up the River
Tamar. Try **Plymouth Boat Cruises Ltd.** (✉ Millpoolhead, Millbrook,
Torpoint, Cornwall, ☎ 01752/822797) or **Tamar Cruising** (✉ Penhellis,
Maker La., Millbrook, Torpoint, Cornwall, ☎ 01752/822105). ⌑ *£3.50
boat trip.* ☉ *Both companies run 1-hr boat trips around the sound and
the dockyard, leaving every 30 mins in peak season from Phoenix Wharf
and the Mayflower Steps, Easter–Oct., daily 10–4.*

☾ The **National Shire Horse Centre** offers parades of shire horses (the largest
breed of draft horse, originally bred to carry knights in armor), flying
displays at the falconry center, and an adventure playground. ✉ *Dun-
stone, Yealmpton (on A379 east of Plymouth),* ☎ *01752/880268.* ⌑
£5.50. ☉ *Apr.–Oct., flying displays daily at 1 and 3:30, parades daily
at 11:30 and 2:30; Nov.–Mar., no parades or flying displays.*

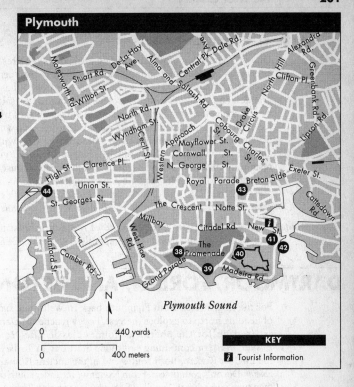

Dining and Lodging

£££ ✕ **Chez Nous.** This French—*tres* French—restaurant is worth search-
★   ing for among the rows of stores in the shopping precinct. Fresh local
fish is served, and the atmosphere is pleasant and relaxed. Chez Nous
is at the top of the £££ range, but there are good-value set-price menus.
⊠ *13 Frankfort Gate,* ☎ *01752/266793. AE, DC, MC, V. Closed Sun.,
Mon., and 1st 3 wks in Feb. and Sept.*

££ ✕ **Piermaster's.** Fresh fish landed at nearby piers is served here. Located in the Barbican, Piermaster's has "basic seafront" decor, with a
tiled floor and wooden tables. ⊠ *33 Southside St., Barbican,* ☎ *01752/
229345. AE, DC, MC, V. Closed Sun.*

££–£££ ▦ **Copthorne Hotel.** Situated downtown, this large, efficient, modern
hotel offers the expected comforts. Its Burlington Restaurant has been
given an Edwardian look, and there is also a brasserie. ⊠ *Armada Centre, Armada Way, PL1 1AR,* ☎ *01752/224161,* ℻ *01752/670688. 135
rooms with bath. Restaurant, bar, brasserie, pool, steam room. AE,
DC, MC, V.*

£ ▦ **Bowling Green Hotel.** This refurbished Victorian house overlooks
Sir Francis Drake's bowling green on Plymouth Hoe. It's in a central
location for shopping and sightseeing. ⊠ *9–10 Osborne Pl., Lockyer
St., PL1 2PU,* ☎ *01752/209090,* ℻ *01752/209092. 12 rooms with
bath or shower. AE, DC, MC, V.*

The Arts

THEATER

Plymouth's **Theatre Royal** (⊠ Royal Parade, ☎ 01752/267222) shows
ballet, musicals, and plays by some of Britain's best companies.

Saltram House

★ ㊺ *3½ mi east of Plymouth city center.*

One of Plymouth's most outstanding attractions requires a short excursion from the center: Saltram House is a lovely 18th-century house built around the remains of a late Tudor mansion. It has one of the grandest and greatest Neoclassic rooms in Britain: a vast salon designed by the great Robert Adam, and adorned with paintings by Sir Joshua Reynolds, first president of the Royal Academy of Arts, who was born nearby in 1723. The house is set in a beautiful garden, with rare trees and shrubs (used in the 1995 film of *Sense and Sensibility*). There is a restaurant in the house and a cafeteria in the Coach House. ⊠ *Plympton,* ☎ *01752/336546.* ⌸ *£5.60, garden only £2.60.* ◷ *Apr.–Sept., Sun.–Thurs. 12:30–5:30, Oct. Sun.–Thurs. 12:30–4:30; garden only, same as house, but open from 10:30, also Mar., weekends 11–4.*

En Route From Plymouth, you have a choice of routes northeast to Exeter. If rugged, desolate, moorland scenery appeals to you, take A386 and B3212 northeast across Dartmoor Forest.

DARTMOOR, TORBAY, AND BEYOND

For the final stretch from Plymouth back to Wells, you have a choice of heading north to explore the vast, boggy reaches of Dartmoor Forest (setting for the Sherlock Holmes classic *The Hound of the Baskervilles*), or continuing east along Start Bay to Torbay, known as the English Riviera. Both routes end in the ancient Roman capital of Exeter, Devon's county seat. From Exeter we meander south to Exmouth, then turn northeast to Yeovil in Somerset, re-entering King Arthur country at Cadbury Castle, the legendary Camelot.

Dartmoor Forest

13 mi west of Exeter.

Even on a summer's day, the scarred and brooding hills of this sprawling national park appear a likely haunt for such monsters as the Hound of the Baskervilles. Sir Arthur Conan Doyle set his Sherlock Holmes thriller in this landscape. Sometimes the wet, peaty wasteland vanishes in rain and mist, although in very clear weather you can see as far north as Exmoor. Much of northern Dartmoor consists of open heath and moorland, uninvaded by roads—wonderful walking territory, but an easy place to lose your bearings. Dartmoor's earliest inhabitants left behind stone monuments, burial mounds, and hut circles, which make it easy to imagine prehistoric man roaming these bogs and pastures. Scattered along the borders of this vast reserve—one-third of which is owned by Prince Charles—are several villages that can make useful bases for travelers out to spend some time camping in the reserve: **Okehampton** (☞ *below*) is a main "gateway" to the reserve. Other major towns in the area are **Widecombe-in-the-Moor,** built up around the "Cathedral of the Moor," and **Grimspount,** the locale that inspired Conan Doyle's tale. Most Dartmoor towns are connected by Transmoor Link buses. For further information, contact the Dartmoor National Park Authority (☞ Visitor Information *in* The West Country A to Z, *below*).

Buckland Abbey

★ ㊻ *8 mi north of Plymouth.*

This 13th-century Cistercian monastery became the home of Sir Francis Drake in 1581. Today it is full of mementos of Drake and the Spanish Armada. The abbey has a licensed restaurant. From Tavistock, take A386 south to Crapstone, then west. ⊠ *Yelverton,* ☎ *01822/853607.* 🎫 *£4.30.* ⊙ *Apr.–Oct., Fri.–Wed. 10:30–5:30; Nov.–Mar., weekends 2–5; last admission 45 mins before closing.*

One mile northwest of Buckland Abbey in Buckland Monachorum is the **Garden House,** an incredibly rich garden that should not be missed by horticulturists. Terraced around the remains of a 16th-century vicarage and incorporating its walled garden, this superb spot is vivid with wisterias rioting over ancient brick walls, along with azaleas, roses, and innumerable other flowering plants, many of them rare. ⊠ *Buckland Monachorum, near Yelverton,* ☎ *01822/854769.* 🎫 *£3.50.* ⊙ *Mar.–Oct., daily 10:30–5.*

Cotehele House and Quay

❹⓿ *15 mi north of Plymouth, 2 mi south of Gunnislake.*

Formerly a busy port, Cotehele is now most visited for its late medieval manor house, whose facade is a vision right out of the pages of Prince Valiant. Complete with original furniture and armor, impressive gardens, a restored mill, and a quay museum, the whole complex is now run by the National Trust. There is a limited number of visitors allowed per day, so arrive early and be prepared to wait. Also, choose a bright day, as there is no electric light in the rooms. You can find Cotehele House by turning left off A390 at Albaston. ⊠ *St. Dominick (north of Saltash),* ☎ *01579/351346.* 🎫 *£5.60, gardens and mill only £2.80.* ⊙ *House: Apr.–Oct., Sat.–Thurs. 11–5 (Oct., 11–4:30). Mill: Apr.–June and Sept., Sat.–Thurs. 1:30–5:30; July–Aug., daily 1:30–6; Oct., Sat.–Thurs., 1:30–4:30; gardens: daily 11–dusk.*

Morwellham Quay Openair Museum

❹❽ *2 mi east of Morwellham Quay, 5 mi southwest of Tavistock, 18 mi north of Plymouth.*

Morwellham Quay was England's main copper-exporting port in the 19th century, and it has been restored as a working museum, with quay workers and coachmen in costume, and a copper mine open to visitors. From Lydford, head east and pick up A386 south via Tavistock, then A390. The museum is off the Gunnislake to Tavistock road. ☎ *01822/832766 or 01822/833808 (recorded information).* 🎫 *Summer £7.95, winter £5.* ⊙ *Easter–Oct., daily 10–5:30 (last admission 3:30); Nov.–Mar., daily 10–4:30 (last admission 2:30).*

Dining and Lodging

£££ ✕🏨 **Horn of Plenty.** A "restaurant with rooms" is the way this estab-
★ lishment describes itself. From the restaurant in a Georgian house there are magnificent views across the wooded, rhododendron-filled Tamar Valley. The set menu is changed monthly, and the cooking is mainly classic French with some imaginative seafood recipes (try the sea bass with asparagus, tomato confit, and prawn sauce). A converted barn next to the house contains seven modern guest rooms. ⊠ *Gulworthy (3 mi west of Tavistock on A390), PL19 8JD,* ☎ 🖷 *01822/ 832528. 7 rooms with bath. Restaurant. AE, MC, V. No lunch Mon.*

Lydford Gorge

★ **❹❾** *12 mi north of Morwellham Quay, 7 mi north of Tavistock, 9 mi east of Launceston, 24 mi north of Plymouth.*

The River Lyd has carved a spectacular chasm through the rock at Lydford Gorge. Two paths follow the gorge past gurgling whirlpools and waterfalls with names such as the Devil's Cauldron and the White Lady. Sturdy footwear is recommended. The walk can be quite arduous, though it can still get congested during busy periods. To drive here from Launceston, continue east along A30, following the signs. ⊠ *Lydford,* ☎ *01822/820441 or 01822/820320.* 🖻 *£3.20.* ⊘ *Apr.–Oct., daily 10–5:30; Nov.–Mar., daily 10:30–3 (walk restricted to main waterfall).*

Lodging

££ 🖾 **The Castle Inn.** Next to Lydford Castle, this 16th-century inn is in the village of Lydford, which lies midway between Okehampton and Tavistock. With a rosy brick facade framed by rose trellises, the inn is the heart of Lydford, thanks, in good part, to its popular restaurant. Public rooms are adorned with period furniture, while some guest rooms are fitted out with Victorian-era antiques. ⊠ *Lydford, near Okehampton, 1 mi off A386, EX20 4BH,* ☎ *01822/820241,* 📠 *01822/820454. 10 rooms, 8 with bath. Restaurant. AE, DC, MC, V.*

Horseback Riding

Lydford has one of the most popular Dartmoor riding facilities, the **Lydford House Riding Stables** (⊠ Lydford House Hotel, Lydford, ☎ 01822/820321).

Okehampton

50 *28 mi north of Plymouth, 23 mi west of Exeter.*

At the confluence of the rivers East and West Okement, this town is a good base from which to explore North Dartmoor, and it has a helpful tourist office (☎ 01837/53020). In town there is a Victorian cottage tearoom, while to the south, on the river banks, is a **Norman castle.** ☎ *01837/52844.* 🖻 *£2.20.* ⊘ *Easter–Oct., daily 10–6 or dusk.*

The **Museum of Dartmoor Life** includes interactive models, a working waterwheel, videos, and photos of traditional farming methods, on 3 floors. ⊠ *3 West St.,* ☎ *01837/52295.* 🖻 *£1.60.* ⊘ *Easter–June, Mon.–Sat. 10–5; July–Sept., daily 10–5; Oct. Mon–Sat. 10–5, Nov.–Easter weekdays 10–4.*

Horseback Riding

Skaigh Stables Farm (⊠ Skaigh La., Higher Sticklepath, near Okehampton, ☎ 01837/840429) is used by many Dartmoor natives.

Chagford

51 *3½ mi northwest of Moretonhampstead, 30 mi northeast of Plymouth, 20 mi west of Exeter.*

Chagford was once a tin-weighing station and an area of fierce fighting between the Roundheads and the Cavaliers in the Civil War. A Roundhead was hanged in front of one of the pubs on the village square. The town makes a convenient base from which to explore North Dartmoor.

52 Near Chagford is **Castle Drogo,** at Drewsteignton. It seems to be a medieval castle, complete with battlements, but it was built between 1910 and 1930. Designed by Sir Edwin Lutyens for Julius Drewe, the wealthy grocer, it's only half finished (money ran out), but the half that's built resembles a magisterial vision out of the dark ages. Take the A30 Exeter-Oxehampton road to reach the castle, which is 4 mi northeast of Chagford and 6 mi south of A30. ☎ *01647/433306.* 🖻 *£5.20, grounds only £2.40.* ⊘ *Apr.–Oct., Sat.–Thurs. 11–5:30.*

Dining and Lodging

££££ ✕🖾 **Gidleigh Park.** One of the poshest hotels and restaurants in the
★ West Country—nay, England—Gidleigh Park is set within its own lit-

tle universe of landscaped gardens and croquet lawns, surrounded by one of the most ferocious wildernesses left in Britain. Once you get past 20 signposts, including one that says CAUTION: NERVOUS HORSES, you espy a sign that says KEEP HEART and, finally, you arrive at the long black-and-white 1930s Tudor-style residence. Inside, decor is fairly generic country-house hotel, the staff wears Laura Ashley, and the extremely expensive restaurant has been showered with culinary awards—as you can guess once you've tasted the monkfish with cucumber sauce, home-cured bresaola, and nectarine and caramel tart. The ritziest base from which to explore Dartmoor Forest, double rooms here range to about £410. ⊠ *Gidleigh Rd., Chagford, Devon, TQ13 8HH,* ☎ *01647/432367,* ℻ *01647/432574. 14 rooms with bath, 1 estate cottage. Restaurant, 18-hole putting green, tennis court, croquet lawn, parking. AE, DC, MC, V.*

£££ 🏨 **Easton Court.** Discerning travelers such as C. P. Snow, Robert Donat, Margaret Mead, John Steinbeck, and Evelyn Waugh—who completed *Brideshead Revisted* here—made this their Dartmoor home-away-from-home. It occupies a pretty (when the ivy allows you to see it) Tudor thatched-roof manse, complete with cozy inglenooks, timbered beams, and flower garden. There is also a charming restaurant on the premises. Take A382 1 mi northeast of Chagford to get here. ⊠ *Easton Cross, Chagford TQ13 8JL,* ☎ *01647/433469,* ℻ *01647/433654. 8 rooms with bath. Restaurant. AE, MC, V. Closed Jan.*

Dartmouth

53 *14 mi northeast of Kingsbridge, 35 mi south of Exeter.*

Dartmouth was an important port in the Middle Ages and is today a favorite haunt of yacht owners. Traces of its past include the old houses in **Bayard's Cove** near Lower Ferry, the 16th-century covered Butterwalk, and the two castles guarding the entrance to the River Dart. The town is dominated by the **Royal Naval College,** built in 1905.

☪ **Dart Valley Steam Railway** runs through 7 wooded mi of the Dart valley to Kingswear, across from Dartmouth. ⊠ *Buckfastleigh,* ☎ *01364/642338.* ☼ *Easter and mid-May–early Oct., daily; check for other times.*

Dining and Lodging

£££–££££ ✕ **Carved Angel.** On the quay with views of the harbor, its offerings
★ include Provençal cuisine and fresh local products, such as River Dart salmon and samphire, a seashore plant used in fish dishes. The restaurant enjoys a long-standing reputation as one of Britain's finest eateries. There is a 2 percent surcharge on credit-card payments. ⊠ *2 S. Embankment,* ☎ *01803/832465. MC, V. Closed Mon., Jan., 2 wks in Feb. No dinner Sun.*

£ ✕ **Carved Angel Café.** This extension of the Carved Angel was opened at the end of 1997, and it provides a good opportunity to sample some of the culinary experience accumulated by its parent without paying lavishly for it. In fact, the fare is much more modest, consisting of traditional daytime snacks such as bangers and mash. The kitchen turns out delicious soups every day, and the puddings are also worth leaving room for. The café may start opening in the evenings in the near future. ⊠ *7 Foss St.,* ☎ *01803/834842. MC, V. Closed Sun., Jan., and 2 wks in Feb. No dinner.*

£££ 🏨 **Royal Castle Hotel.** Here's a hotel that really earned the name "Royal"—several monarchs have slept here. Part of Dartmouth's historic waterfront, it was built in the 17th century, reputedly of timber from wrecks of the Spanish Armada. There are traditional fireplaces and beamed ceilings, and five rooms have four-poster beds. Rooms with river views cost about 25 percent more. ⊠ *11 The Quay, TQ6 9PS,* ☎ *01803/833033,* ℻ *01803/835445. 25 rooms with bath or shower. Restaurant, 2 bars. AE, MC, V.*

En Route   Two **ferries** cross the river at Dartmouth; in summer, to avoid long waiting lines, you may want to try the inland route via A3122 and A381 to Totnes.

Totnes

54   *9 mi northwest of Dartmouth, 28 mi southwest of Exeter.*

This busy market town preserves an atmosphere of the past, particularly on summer Tuesdays and Saturdays, when most of the shopkeepers dress in Elizabethan costume. If you climb up to the ruins of Totnes's **Norman castle,** you can get a wonderful view of the town and the river. ☎ *01803/864406.* ⊡ *£1.50.* ⊗ *Apr.–Oct., daily 10–6 or dusk; Nov.– Mar., Wed.–Sun. 10–1 and 2–4.*

Buckfast Butterfly Farm and Dartmoor Otter Sanctuary's colorful inhabitants come from around the world. The farm is on A38, halfway between Exeter and Plymouth, 6 mi northwest of Totnes. ⊠ *Buckfastleigh,* ☎ *01364/642916.* ⊡ *Apr.–Oct. £4.50; Mar. and Nov. £2.50.* ⊗ *Otters: Mar.–Nov., daily 10–5:30 or dusk; butterflies: Apr.–Oct., daily 10–5:30 or dusk.*

Lodging

££   ⊞ **Cott Inn.** The exterior of this inn has remained almost completely unchanged since 1320. It is a long, low, thatched building with flagstone floors, thick ceiling beams, and open fireplaces. Bar meals are available from the restaurant. ⊠ *Dartington (2 mi west of Totnes on A385) TQ9 6HE,* ☎ *01803/863777,* ℻ *01803/866629. 6 rooms with bath or shower. Restaurant. AE, MC, V.*

Shopping

Near Dartington Hall (2 mi north of Totnes) is a collection of stores selling world-famous Dartington lead crystal as well as shoes, woolens, farm foods, kitchenware, pottery, and many other Devon wares. **Dartington Trading Centre** (⊠ Shinners Bridge, 2 mi west of Totnes, ☎ 01803/ 864171), a collection of shops and two restaurants, housed inside the old Dartington Cider Press, sells handmade crafts from Devon and elsewhere, including clothes, glassware, and kitchenware. The farm shop here sells fudge, ice cream, and cider, among other local produce.

Brixham

55   *10 mi southeast from Totnes by A385 and A3022.*

Brixham, at the southern point of Tor Bay, has kept much of its original charm, partly because it is still an active fishing village. Much of the catch is dispatched straight to restaurants as far away as London. Sample a portion of the local fish-and-chips on the quayside, where there is a (surprisingly petite) full-scale replica of the vessel on which Sir Francis Drake circumnavigated the world.

Torbay

56   *5 mi north of Brixham via A3022, 23 mi south of Exeter.*

As the most important resort area in South Devon, Torbay likes to describe itself as the center of the "English Riviera." Since 1968, the towns of Paignton and Torquay (pronounced torkee) have been amalgamated under the common moniker of Torbay. Torquay is the supposed site of the hotel in the popular British television show *Fawlty Towers—*

and the town has much of the same: modern hotels, luxury villas, and apartments that climb the hillsides above the harbor. Palm trees and other semi-tropical plants flourish in the seafront gardens. The sea is a clear and intense blue, and the whole place in summer has that unmistakable air that used to be called "continental." To sun and bathe, head for Anstey's Cove, a favorite spot for scuba-divers, with more beaches farther along at neighboring Babbacombe.

★ Just outside Torbay lies the the old-world show village of **Cockington,** which has some of the quaintest cottages in Britain, a 14th-century Old Forge, and the square-towered Church of St. George and St. Mary, all surrounded in springtime by carpets of daffodils. Repair to the Old Mill, where an old water wheel still runs, for a café lunch or head to Drum Inn, designed by Sir Edwin Lutyens to be an archetypal pub. At the top of the hill lies Higher Lodge, whose second story is actually resting on tree trunks. Finally, on the outskirts of the village lies Cockington Court—a grand estate with shops and an eatery.

Dining and Lodging

££ ✕ **Capers.** A spot for anyone who likes enthusiasm along with the food,
★ this small, select restaurant goes in for serious cooking. Local fish ranks high on the menu, accompanied by vegetables and herbs grown by the chef. Try the turbot with lime and ginger and the crispy duck salad, or the monkfish with green peppercorns. ⊠ *7 Lisburne Sq.,* ☎ *01803/ 291177. AE, MC, V. Closed Sun. No lunch.*

£ ✕ **Remy's.** Come here, to Torquay's oldest-established French restaurant, for delightful, straightforward French country cooking. Lamb with basil and tomato, sweetbreads with a Calvados sauce, and, above all, fish freshly caught by local boats are among the specialties. The wine list has a selection of good Alsatian vintages. ⊠ *3 Croft Rd.,* ☎ *01803/ 292359. MC, V. Closed Sun., Mon. No lunch.*

££££ 🏨 **The Imperial.** This is arguably Devon's most luxurious hotel, perched
★ high above the sea, overlooking Torbay. The gardens surrounding the hotel are magnificent, and the interior is . . . well, imperial, with chandeliers, marble floors, and the general air of a bygone world. Most bedrooms are large and very comfortable, and some have seaward-facing balconies. The staff is attentive. ⊠ *Park Hill Rd., TQ1 2DG,* ☎ *01803/294301,* 🖷 *01803/298293. 167 rooms with bath. Restaurant, indoor-outdoor pool, beauty salon, sauna, tennis court, health club, squash. AE, DC, MC, V.*

£–££ 🏨 **Fairmount House Hotel.** Near the village of Cockington, on the edge of Torquay, this Victorian hotel has a pretty garden and a restaurant that favors fresh home-grown and local produce. The Victorian Conservatory Bar opens onto the garden. ⊠ *Herbert Rd., Chelston, TQ2 6RW,* ☎ 🖷 *01803/605446. 8 rooms with bath or shower. Restaurant, bar. AE, MC, V. Closed Nov.–Feb.*

Exeter

57 *23 mi north of Torbay, 48 mi northeast of Plymouth, 85 mi southwest of Bristol, 205 mi southwest of London.*

Devon's county seat, Exeter, has been the capital of the region since the Romans established a fortress here 2,000 years ago. Little evidence of the Roman occupation exists, apart from the great city walls. Despite being badly bombed in 1942, Exeter retains much of its medieval character, as well as examples of the gracious architecture of the 18th and 19th centuries.

At the heart of Exeter is the great Gothic **Cathedral of St. Peter,** begun in 1275 and completed almost a century later. The twin towers are even older survivors of an earlier Norman cathedral. The 300-ft stretch of unbroken Gothic vaulting, rising from a forest of ribbed columns, is the longest in the world. Myriad statues, tombs, and memorial plaques adorn the interior. In the minstrels' gallery, high up on the left of the nave, stands a group of carved figures singing and playing musical instruments, including bagpipes. The cathedral is surrounded by a charming **Close,** a green pleasant space for relaxing on a sunny day. Don't miss the 400-year-old door to No. 10, the bishop of Crediton's house, which is ornately carved with angels' and lions' heads.

In one corner of the Close is **Mol's Coffee House** (now a store), with its black-and-white, half-timber facade bearing the coat of arms of Elizabeth I. It is said that Sir Francis Drake met his admirals here to plan strategy against the Spanish Armada in 1588. Opposite Exeter Cathedral stands the **Royal Clarence Hotel** (☞ Dining and Lodging, *below*). Built in 1769, it was the first inn in England to be described as a "hotel"— a designation applied by an enterprising French manager. It is named after the Duchess of Clarence, who stayed here in 1827 on her way to visit her husband, the future William IV.

On High Street, just behind the Close, stands the **Guildhall,** the oldest municipal building in the country. The present hall dates from 1330, although a guildhall has been on this site since at least 1160. Its timber-braced roof is one of the earliest in England, dating from about 1460. ☎ 01392/265500. ☞ *Free.* ☉ *Weekdays 10:30–1 and 2–4, Sat. 10:30–1, unless in use for a civic function.*

Exeter's **Royal Albert Memorial Museum** houses natural-history displays, a superb collection of Exeter silverware, and the work of some West Country artists. There is also a fine archaeological section. ⊠ *Queen St.,* ☎ *01392/265858.* ☞ *Free.* ☉ *Mon.–Sat. 10–5.*

Off Queen Street, behind the museum, is **Rougemont Gardens,** first laid out at the end of the 18th century. The land was once part of the defensive ditch of Rougemont Castle, built in 1068 by decree of William the Conqueror. Here you will find the original Norman gatehouse and the remains of the Roman city wall, the latter forming part of the ancient castle's outer wall; nothing else is left. The spot offers a panoramic view of the countryside and the Haldon Hills rising up in the west.

Exeter's historic waterfront on the banks of the River Exe was once the center of Exeter's medieval wool industry. The **Customs House,** built in 1682 on The Quay, is the earliest surviving brick building in the city; it is flanked by Victorian warehouses. There is a Heritage Centre in **Quay House** (a stone warehouse contemporary with the Customs House) that documents the maritime history of the city and offers an audiovisual display. ⊠ *The Quay,* ☎ *01392/265213.* ☞ *Free.* ☉ *Easter–Oct., daily 10–5.*

Dining and Lodging

££ ✕ **Golsworthy's.** Part of St. Olaves Court Hotel, set in a Georgian house
★   with a walled garden, this restaurant is one of the finest dining spots of the West Country. The bar overlooks the lovely garden. Try the escalopes of salmon, or for dessert, the brioche bread-and-butter-pudding with apricot and sultana coulis. ⊠ *Mary Arches St.,* ☎ *01392/ 217736. AE, DC, MC, V. No lunch weekends.*

£   ✕ **Hansons.** While you're exploring Exeter's Close, stop in at this spot, ideal for lunch, coffee, snacks, or one of Devon's famous cream teas (served with jam, scones, and cream). ⊠ *1 Cathedral Close,* ☎ *01392/276913. AE, DC, MC, V.*

£   ✕ **Ship Inn.** If you feel like lifting a tankard of stout in the very rooms where Sir Francis Drake and Sir Walter Raleigh enjoyed their ale, this is the place—Drake, in fact, once wrote, "Next to mine own shippe, I do most love that old "Shippe" in Exon, a tavern in Fyssh Street, as the people call it, or as the clergie will have it, St. Martin's Lane." The pub offers casual bar fare, while the upstairs restaurant offers the usual grilled lemon sole and other English dishes. ⊠ *St. Martin's La.,* ☎ *01392/72040. MC, V.*

£££ ✕🖬 **Royal Clarence Hotel.** This historic hotel is located within the cathedral Close. It boasts a good restaurant and has been made a great deal more attractive by recent redecoration. The most expensive rooms are those with a view of the cathedral. Many rooms feature oak paneling. ⊠ *Cathedral Yard, EX1 1HB,* ☎ *01392/319955,* 🗚 *01392/439423. 56 rooms with bath. Restaurant, 2 bars. AE, DC, MC, V.*

££ ✕🖬 **White Hart.** It is said that Oliver Cromwell stabled his horses here; in any event, guests have been welcomed since the 15th century. The main building has all the trappings of a period inn—beams, stone walls, a central courtyard, and warm hospitality—but there are also fully modern bedrooms in a new wing. The hotel has a full-scale restaurant, a wine bar, and a more casual ale and port house. Ask about good-value weekend terms for a minimum of two nights. ⊠ *66 South St., EX1 1EE,* ☎ *01392/279897,* 🗚 *01392/250159. 59 rooms with bath or shower. 3 restaurants, 2 bars. AE, DC, MC, V.*

The Arts

Among the best known of the West Country's festivals is the **Exeter Festival** (☎ 01392/265205), a mixture of musical and theater events held in July. At the **Northcott Theatre** (☎ 01392/493493) in Exeter, you can often see plays performed by some of the best London companies.

Shopping

Until 1882 Exeter was the silver-assay office for the entire West Country, and it is still possible to find Exeter silver, particularly spoons, in some antiques and silverware stores. The earliest example of Exeter silver dates from 1218 (a museum piece), but Victorian pieces are still sold—the Exeter assay mark is three castles. **William Bruford** (⊠ 1 Bedford St., ☎ 01392/254901) sells interesting antique jewelry and silver. Exeter has a daily market on Sidwell Street.

OFF THE BEATEN PATH   **POWDERHAM CASTLE** – Seat of the Earls of Devon, Powderham is a noted stately house, famed for its staircase hall, a soaring fantasia of white stuccowork on a dazzling turquoise background, constructed in 1739–1769. Other sumptuous rooms, adorned with family portraits by Kneller and Reynolds, were used in the Merchant/Ivory film *Remains of the Day.* In the surrounding deer park is a tower built in 1400 by Sir Philip Courtenay, ancestor of the present owners. Powderham is reached by taking the A379 Dawlish road for 8 mi south of Exeter. ☎ 01626/ 890243. 🎟 £4.95. ⊙ Easter–Oct., Sun.–Fri. 10–5:30.

Topsham

🟑 *4 mi south of Exeter on B3182.*

The town of Topsham is full of narrow streets and hidden courtyards. ★ Once a bustling port, it is rich in 18th-century houses and inns. **Topsham Museum** occupies a 17th-century Dutch-style merchant's house beside the river. ⊠ *25 The Strand,* ☎ *01392/873244.* 🎟 *£1.* ⊙ *Mar.– Oct., Mon., Wed., Sat. 2–5; May–Sept. also Sun. 2–5.*

★ Near Lympstone, 5 mi south of Topsham off the A376 is **A la Ronde,** one of the most unusual houses in England. A 16-sided, nearly circular house, now run by the National Trust, it was built in 1798 and inspired by the Church of San Vitale in Ravenna, Italy. Among the 18th- and 19th-century curiosities here is an elaborate display of feathers and shells. ☒ *Summer La., on A376 near Exmouth,* ☎ *01395/265514.* ☒ *£3.20.* ☽ *Apr.–Oct., Sun.–Thurs. 11–5:30.*

En Route   The Devon coast from Exmouth to the Dorset border 26 mi to the east has been designated an Area of Outstanding Natural Beauty. The reddish, grass-topped cliffs of the region are punctuated by quiet, seaside resorts such as Budleigh Salterton, Sidmouth, and Seaton.

Beer

59   *26 mi east of Exeter, 33 mi south of Taunton.*

Beer, just outside Seaton, was once a favorite smugglers' haunt. It was also the source of the white stone used to build Exeter Cathedral; some of the quarries can still be visited. **Beer Quarry Caves,** ☒ *Quarry La.,* ☎ *01297/680282.* ☒ *£3.* ☽ *Apr.–Sept., daily 10–5; Oct., daily 11–4.*

Honiton

60   *10 mi northwest of Beer on A3052/A375, 19 mi south of Taunton.*

Honiton's long High Street is lined with handsome Georgian houses. Modern storefronts have intruded, but the original facades have been preserved at second-floor level. For 300 years the town was known for lace making, and the industry was revived when Queen Victoria selected the fabric for her wedding veil in 1840. The town has a **lace museum,** as well as shops where both prized early examples of the Honiton patterns and new lace are sold. ☒ *All Hallows Museum, High St.,* ☎ *01404/44966.* ☒ *£1.* ☽ *Apr.–Oct., Mon.–Sat. 10–5.*

Dining and Lodging

£   ✕ **Dominoes.** For a satisfying lunch, try this wine bar, where you can get everything from nachos to rack of lamb. Evening meals are also available (except Sunday). ☒ *178 High St.,* ☎ *01404/47707. MC, V. No dinner Sun.*

£££   ☷ **Combe House Hotel.** Rolling parkland surrounds this Elizabethan manor house. From the imposing entrance hall with its huge, open fireplace, to the individually decorated bedrooms—all large and two with four-poster beds—the emphasis is on style and comfort. The hotel changed hands in 1998, with some changes promised. ☒ *Gittisham, near Honiton, EX14 0AD,* ☎ *01404/42756,* ℻ *01404/46004. 15 rooms with bath. Restaurant, fishing. AE, DC, MC, V. Closed 2 wks end Jan.–mid-Feb.*

£   ☷ **New Dolphin Hotel.** The age of this former coaching inn shows in the sloping floors, but every room has modern comforts. It's in the town center. ☒ *High St., EX14 8LS,* ☎ *01404/42377,* ℻ *01404/47662. 15 rooms, 13 with bath. Restaurant, bar. MC, V.*

Montacute House

★ **61**   *30 mi northeast of Honiton on A30 and A303, 30 mi east of Taunton, 44 mi south of Bristol, 21 mi northwest of Dorchester.*

This part of Somerset is famous for its golden limestone, used in the construction of local villages and mansions. A fine example is **Montacute House** in Yeovil (on A3088—turn right off A303 at Stoke sub Hamdon), built in the late 16th century. The house has a 189-ft gallery brimming with Elizabethan and Jacobean portraits, most on loan from the National Portrait Gallery. Pick a bright day to visit: some rooms do not have electric light. ☒ *Montacute,* ☎ *01935/823289.* ☒ *£5.20; garden and park only £2.90 April–Oct., £1.50 Nov.–Mar.* ☽ *House:*

Apr.–Oct., Wed.–Mon. noon–5:30. Garden and park: Apr.–Oct., Wed.–Mon. 11:30–5:30 or dusk; Nov.–Easter, Wed.–Sun. 11:30–4.

Dining and Lodging

££ ✗🏠 **King's Arms.** Built of the same warm, golden stone as nearby Mon-
★ tacute House, this 16th-century inn features charming interior decor;
one room has a four-poster bed. Meals available range from bar snacks
to a full à la carte menu in the award-winning Abbey Room restaurant. ⊠ *Bishopston, Montacute TA15 6UU,* ☎ *01935/822513,* 𝔽𝔸𝕏
01935/826549. 15 rooms with bath. Restaurant. AE, DC, MC, V.

Yeovilton

㊷ *7 mi north of Yeovil.*

The 20th century reasserts itself in the village of Yeovilton, with the
Fleet Air Arm Museum. Here, more than 50 historic aircraft are on show,
including the Concorde 002. The spectacular "Carrier" display, opened
in 1994, includes a simulated helicopter ride over the ocean to an aircraft carrier and a unique re-creation of the flight deck of a working
carrier, complete with 12 real planes from the 1960s and 1970s. ⊠
Royal Naval Air Station, ☎ *01935/840565.* 🎫 *£6.75.* ☉ *Apr.–Oct.,
daily 10–5:30; Nov.–Mar., daily 10–4:30.*

Cadbury Castle

㊸ *7 mi northeast of Yeovilton, off A303, 17 mi south of Wells.*

Cadbury Castle is said to be the site of Camelot—one among several
contenders for the honor. Glastonbury Tor, rising dramatically in the
distance across the plain, adds to the atmosphere of Arthurian romance.
There is even a legend that every seven years the hillside opens and Arthur
and his followers ride forth to water their horses at close-by Sutton
Montis. Cadbury Castle is, in fact, an Iron Age fort (circa 650 BC), with
grass-covered, earthen ramparts forming a green wall 300 ft above the
surrounding fields. From here it's about 17 mi to Wells, our original
starting point, or A303/M3 will take you back to London.

THE WEST COUNTRY A TO Z

Arriving and Departing

By Bus

National Express (☎ 0990/808080) buses leave London's Victoria
Coach Station for Bristol (2½ hrs), Exeter (3¾ hrs), Plymouth (4¾ hrs),
and Penzance (about 8 hrs).

By Car

The fastest way from London to the West Country is via the M4 and
M5 motorways, bypassing Bristol (115 mi) and heading south to Exeter, in Devon (172 mi).

By Plane

Plymouth has a small airport (☎ 01752/705151 or 0345/222111) 3
mi from town.

By Train

British Rail serves the region from London's Paddington Station (☎ 0345/
484950). Average travel time to Exeter, 2½ hours; to Plymouth, 3½ hours;
and to Penzance, about 5½ hours.

Getting Around

By Bus
Western National Ltd. (☎ 01752/222666) operates a regular service in Plymouth and throughout Cornwall, and also offers one-day **Explorer** and three- or seven-day **Key West** tickets.

By Car
Driving can be tricky, especially in the western parts. Most of the small roads are twisting country lanes flanked by high stone walls and thick hedges, which severely restrict visibility. The main roads heading west are A30—which leads all the way to Land's End at the tip of Cornwall—A39 (near the northern shore of the peninsula), and A38 (near the southern shore of the peninsula).

By Train
Regional **Rail Rover** tickets are available for seven days' unlimited travel throughout the West Country, and there are localized Rovers covering Devon or Cornwall.

Contacts and Resources

Car Rentals
Exeter: Avis (✉ 29 Marsh Green Rd., Marsh Barton Trading Estate, ☎ 01392/259713). **Plymouth: Avis** (✉ Commercial Rd., Coxside, ☎ 01752/221550); **Europcar Ltd.** (Grevan Cars Ltd., ✉ 19 Union St., ☎ 01752/669859); **Hertz** (✉ Scot Hire, Walkham Business Park, ☎ 01752/207207). **Truro: Avis** (✉ Tregolls Rd., ☎ 01872/262226).

Guided Tours
The **West Country Tourist Board** (☎ 01392/276351) and local tourist information centers have lists of qualified guides. **Designer Touring** (✉ 28 Peasland Rd., Torquay TQ2 8PA, ☎ 01803/326832) offers guided tours by bus or car.

Travel Agencies
American Express (✉ 139 Armada Way, Plymouth, ☎ 01752/228708). **Thomas Cook** (✉ 177 Sidwell St., Exeter, ☎ 01392/254971; ✉ 9 Old Town St., Plymouth, ☎ 01752/250202).

Visitor Information
West Country Tourist Board (✉ 60 St. David's Hill, Exeter, Devon EX4 4SY, ☎ 01392/276351, FAX 01392/420891) open weekdays 9:30–5. **Cornwall Tourist Board** (✉ Lander Buildings, Daniel Rd., Truro, Cornwall TR1 2DA, ☎ 01872/74057, FAX 01872/40423). **Devon Tourism** (Exeter Services, ✉ Sandygate [M5], Exeter, Devon EX2 7NJ, ☎ 01392/437581). **Somerset Tourism** (✉ County Hall, Taunton, Somerset TA1 4DY, ☎ 01823/255036, FAX 01823/255572). **Dartmoor National Park Authority** (✉ Parke, Haytor Rd., Bovey Tracey, Newton Abbot, Devon TQ13 9JQ, ☎ 01626/832093).

Local tourist information centers are usually open Monday–Saturday 9:30–5:30. **Bristol** (✉ St. Nicholas Church, St. Nicholas St., ☎ 0117/926–0767). **Exeter** (✉ Civic Centre, Paris St., ☎ 01392/265700). **Falmouth** (✉ 28 Killigrew St., ☎ 01326/312300). **Penzance** (✉ Station Rd., ☎ 01736/362207). **Plymouth** (✉ Island House, 9 The Barbican, ☎ 01752/264849). **St. Ives** (✉ The Guildhall, Street-an-Pol, ☎ 01736/796297). **Truro** (✉ City Hall, Boscawen St., ☎ 01872/274555). **Wells** (✉ Town Hall, Market Pl., ☎ 01749/672552).

6 The Channel Islands

Guernsey, Jersey

Blessed with more than 2,000 hours of sunshine every year, the Channel Islands remain a favorite getaway for Britishers and visiting tourists alike. Jersey and Guernsey lie just off the coast of Brittany, so this is England with a French twist. Pleasures await— pretty fishing harbors, princely villas (don't miss Victor Hugo's historic house in St. Peter Port), and sublimely tasty crab creole. Later, everyone winds up on the white-sand beaches; after all, the sun is yours for the basking.

Updated by
Robert
Andrews

THE CHANNEL ISLANDS became part of the British Isles when their ruler, Duke William of Normandy, or William the Conqueror, seized the English throne in 1066. The connection with the British royal house has lasted ever since, with very few breaks, but the Channel Islands claim no allegiance to the Parliament in Westminster—only to the monarch. They are self-ruling, with a Common Law based on the Norman code of law, which differs from the legal system followed in the rest of Britain. The islands do not impose VAT (which means that shopping is 17.5% cheaper), and they issue their own currency and stamps.

The islands served as the background for struggles between Royalists and Roundheads in the 17th-century Civil War. In 1781, the French made an unsuccessful attempt to invade, but since 1066, the islands have only been seriously invaded once: the Germans occupied them from 1940 to 1945, incorporating them into their great Western defense system, the "Atlantic Wall." All over the islands there is still evidence of the German fortifications, which were built by thousands of slaves who used up 613,000 cubic meters of reinforced concrete. The coasts bristled with gun emplacements, and the rocky landscape was honeycombed with tunnels to get supplies to hospitals and to ammunition magazines. The islands became total fortresses. In fact, when the Allies overran Europe in 1944, they circumvented the islands, leaving their elaborate defenses untouched.

The most popular island is Jersey (44½ square mi), because of its mild climate, magnificent beaches, and well-run hotels and restaurants, all promoted by a strong department of tourism. Second to Jersey, both in size and popularity, is Guernsey (24½ square mi), which has 2,000 hours of sunshine a year and runs at a more relaxed pace. The islands are bordered by magnificent cliffs that provide superb walking trails—very tough on the leg muscles—with great views both seaward and inland. The landscapes of both Jersey and Guernsey are crowded with prosperous-looking, neat houses, threaded together by an interminable network of winding lanes. For this reason the islands are difficult to explore by car, even if you are adept at map reading. But both islands have excellent bus services, which provide a cheap, worry-free means of sightseeing.

Pleasures and Pastimes

Dining

The gustatory specialty of the Channel Islands is seafood in all its delectable glory. Crab and lobster dishes are on many menus, but don't overlook the daily catch from the tiny harbors or the mollusk called Jersey Ormer or sea ear (appropriately named). The locally bred lamb is also superb, and thick cream slathers the desserts.

CATEGORY	COST*
££££	over £50
£££	£30–£50
££	£20–£30
£	under £20

*per person, including first course, main course, and dessert; excluding drinks

Lodging

Jersey is chock-full of hotels, guest houses, and bed-and-breakfasts, all organized and regulated by the Jersey Hotel and Guest House Asso-

The Channel Islands

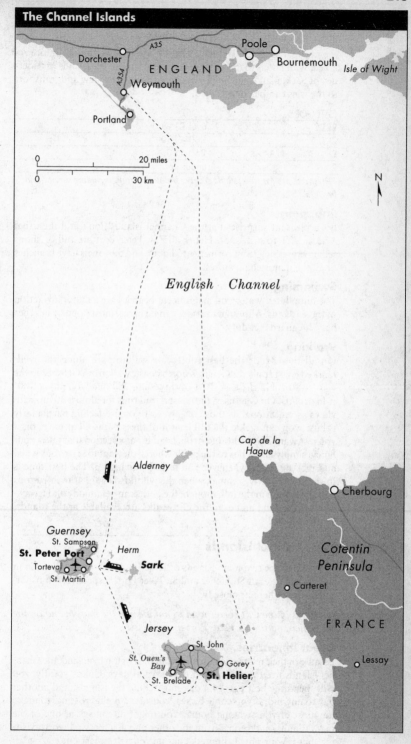

Dorchester

A35

Poole

Bournemouth

Isle of Wight

E N G L A N D

Weymouth

A354

Portland

0   20 miles

0   30 km

English   Channel

N

Cap de la Hague

Alderney

Cherbourg

Guernsey

St. Sampson

St. Peter Port

Torteval

St. Martin

Herm

Sark

Cotentin Peninsula

Carteret

Jersey

St. John

St. Ouen's Bay

Gorey

St. Brelade

St. Helier

F R A N C E

Lessay

ciation. You can also get a comprehensive listing from the Jersey or Guernsey tourist boards. Many places offer half board (MAP) at a savings. Outlying parts of Jersey are more low-key when compared with the razzmatazz of St. Helier. Guernsey is Jersey writ small—more relaxed, with hotels to match. If you want to stay on the islands of Alderney or Sark, plan well ahead—accommodations are few and transport to the isles can be complicated.

CATEGORY	COST*
££££	over £150
£££	£80–£150
££	£60–£80
£	under £60

All prices are for two people sharing a double room, including service and breakfast.

Shopping

It's a pleasant surprise that the Channel Islands don't add the usual 17.5% VAT to prices. St. Helier and St. Peter Port are full of shops selling everything from cosmetics to liquor, and the towns have branches of all the major chain stores.

Swimming

The unpolluted water and magnificent beaches are a major attraction of these islands. Although the tides can be fierce, most popular beaches have lifeguards on duty.

Walking

On all the islands the best routes for walking are along the well-marked coast trails. On Jersey's north coast, walk from Grosnez in the west to Rozel in the east. Part of this route will take you along 300-ft-high cliffs. On Guernsey, the coastal trail runs for almost 30 mi, with views as sensational as those in Jersey. If you are feeling particularly robust, you can tackle the full length of these paths all at once, or, if you just want a comfortable stroll, head for any section that takes your fancy; simply hop a bus to the point where you want to start your walk, and pick up a bus whenever you feel like giving up. The best time is in spring and early summer, when the wildflowers are at their riotous best. Be careful in the fall, though; the paths can get muddy and treacherous. Maps and guides to the cliff walks are available at the islands' tourist offices.

Exploring the Channel Islands

Any visit to the two main islands of Jersey and Guernsey will begin in the capital cities of St. Helier and St. Peter Port, respectively; most attractions are here or close by.

Numbers in the text correspond to numbers in the margin and on the St. Helier and the St. Peter Port maps.

Great Itineraries

Because of their relative remoteness from the English mainland, the Channel Islands need to be savored over several days. Unless you fly, you will spend the best part of a day in reaching the islands, and another day to unwind. If you come by sea, consider a night crossing, to make the most of your waking hours. You might disembark at one of the main islands, and return from the other one. Each is well worth visiting, but if your time is limited, confine yourself to just one.

IF YOU HAVE 3 DAYS

Spend two days in ⊞ **St. Helier,** main town of **Jersey.** Get your bearings by climbing up to **Fort Regent** ①, and the rest of the morning will be taken up by strolling through the town's streets and along the seafront, perhaps walking out to **Elizabeth Castle** ⑥, the 16th-century stronghold lying on an island in St Aubin's Bay. Spend an afternoon at the absorbing **Jersey Museum** ④. On your second day, you can see something more of the island: a morning would be enough to visit the world-famous **Jersey Wildlife Trust,** while the afternoon could be spent seeing **Gorey Castle,** on the island's eastern side. End the day with a meal in the village of Gorey. Your last day should be devoted to a day trip to **Guernsey.** Arrive mid-morning for a walk around **St. Peter Port,** taking in **Castle Cornet** ⑨ and the elegant **Hauteville House** ⑩, where Victor Hugo lived. In the afternoon, you should rent a car or bicycle to see some of the rest of Guernsey, especially **Sausmarez Manor** ⑫ and one of the relics of the German occupation, for example the **German Military Underground Hospital** ⑬. Take the ferry (or plane) back to Jersey.

IF YOU HAVE 5 DAYS

A couple of days on Jersey will allow you to take in the pleasures of ▥ **St. Helier,** including the attractions mentioned above and the recently completed **Occupation Tapestry** and the **Island Fortress–Occupation Museum** ⑤, both of which vividly recapture the experience of living under the German jackboot. A little farther out, the Glass Church at Millbrook makes an easy excursion, perhaps en route to the **Battle of Flowers Museum,** outside St. Ouen. The theme of flowers is a prominent one on Jersey, and it can be pursued further at the **Eric Young Orchid Foundation.** Nearby, the **Jersey Wildlife Trust** shouldn't be missed. Spend the next two days on ▥ **Guernsey,** where **Castle Cornet** ⑨ and **Hauteville House** ⑩ are must-sees in **St. Peter Port.** Outside town, **Sausmarez Manor** ⑫ and the meticulous reconstructions of the **German Military Underground Hospital** ⑬ provide plenty of interest. From Guernsey, there are regular ferries to the tiny isle of **Sark,** 45 minutes from Guernsey. Sark can be toured on foot, by bicycle, or with a horse and cart. A day would be enough to absorb its pace, though you'll find it hard to leave—just don't expect bright lights or ready-made entertainment.

When to Tour the Channel Islands

The Channel Islands show their best face under a blue sky. Since they boast more sunshine than any other part of the British Isles, they're a good bet at any time of year outside the depths of winter, when fierce storms can put a damper on your trip, particularly if the ferry heading there or back is delayed due to rough seas. From April to September is best if you want to enjoy the beaches; note, too, that many of the best attractions close after October.

Jersey

St. Helier, Jersey's capital, is a lovely vacation center, full of hotels, good swimming spots, and quaint streets. Nearby are secluded coves, difficult to access but a delight to achieve, rugged rocks, and photo-worthy scenery. You'll soon appreciate why the French call Jersey "La Reine de la Manche"—Queen of the Channel. But not only is the climate soothing and the surroundings lush—there's an atmosphere of Continental-cum-Gallic know-how that appeals to all visitors.

❶ In St. Helier, start out at **Fort Regent**—the panoramic view will give you an idea of the town's layout. The fort, high on a rock, was built between 1806 and 1811 as a defense against Napoleon's army (although the measure was never put to the test). During World War II, German antiaircraft guns were sited in the fort. In 1958, the British government sold the fortification to the State of Jersey, which in 1967 turned it into a vast leisure complex, with a terraced swimming pool, concert hall,

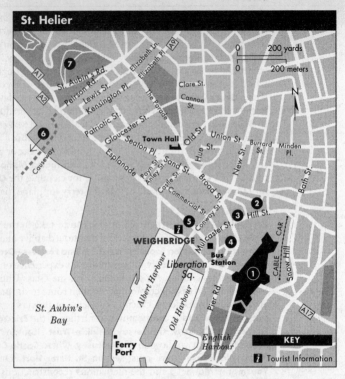

squash courts, World of the Sea Aquarium, a good-size amusement park, restaurants, bars, and cafés. ☎ 01534/500200. 🎫 *Free; fees for individual amusements.* ⏰ *8:15 AM–9 PM (closes 5:30 weekends).*

② Now shaded by chestnut trees, **Royal Square** (behind Hill St. in the center of town) was once the site of executions and the town pillory. Witchcraft and its punishment were constant elements in Jersey life for most of the 16th and 17th centuries, with interminable trials held all over the island. The States offices, the **Royal Court,** and the **States Chamber** (Jersey's parliament) surround the square. On the west side of Royal **③** Square is the **parish church** of St. Helier, the latest in the 900-year-long series of churches that have stood here.

Next to the bus station off Liberation Square, the recently refurbished **④** **Jersey Museum** has won awards for its design and user-friendliness, centered on its facilities geared toward persons with disabilities, moms and tots, and foreign-language visitors. In a lovely building, completed in 1817 for the merchant and shipbuilder Philippe Nicolle, the museum contains some fascinating collections that illuminate Jersey's past: works by local artists; re-creations of Victorian rooms; and memorabilia of Lillie Langtry, the beautiful mistress of Edward VII. "The Jersey Lily" was born on the island and is buried in St. Saviour's churchyard. ✉ *The Weighbridge,* ☎ 01534/30511. 🎫 *£3.20, "Passport" combined tickets for 6 of Jersey's principal museums (including Elizabeth Castle and Gorey Castle) £12, or £6 for any 3.* ⏰ *Daily 10–5.*

⑤ A few steps away from Liberation Square, the **Island Fortress–Occupation Museum** has an extensive display of World War II propaganda relating to Germany's presence on the island. ✉ *9 Esplanade,* ☎ 01534/34306. 🎫 *£3.* ⏰ *Apr., daily 9:30–6; May–Sept., daily 9:30 AM–10:30 PM; Oct.–Mar., daily 10–4.*

A Victorian warehouse adjacent to Liberation Square was converted in 1996 to display the **Occupation Tapestry,** a huge collective undertaking to commemorate the 50th anniversary of the islands' liberation from Nazi occupation. The tapestry consists of 12 panels, each embroidered by the people of one of Jersey's parishes, and each focusing on a particular theme of the experience of occupation and liberation. ⊠ *New North Quay,* ☎ *01534/811043.* ⌨ *£1.50.* ☉ *Summer, daily 10–5; winter, daily 10–4.*

West along the Esplanade, yachts from all over the world berth at the Albert Harbour Marina. You can take short or long cruises from here, including an evening cocktail trip down the coast or a weekend jaunt to Brittany. Across the main harbor is **Elizabeth Castle,** sited on an island joined to the Esplanade by a causeway that begins opposite the Grand Hotel, by **People's Park.** You can cross the causeway between high tides, but keep an ear open for the bell that is rung from the castle's gatehouse half an hour before the sea covers the stones; the water can rise until it's 15 ft deep. When the causeway is not usable, an amphibious craft takes visitors across. The little island was a holy isle beginning in the 6th century with the arrival of Helier, the missionary son of a Belgian warlord. Legend places his cell on the headland beyond the castle, still called Hermitage Rock. Close to the castle's entrance, in former barracks, is a military museum housing an exhibition that tells the building's story. In the granite-built Governor's House in the heart of the complex, there are waxwork tableaus of events in the castle's long history, notably the meeting of Sir Philippe de Carteret and Charles II, who took refuge here during the Civil War in 1646. ⊠ *St. Aubin's Bay,* ☎ *01534/23971.* ⌨ *£3.20.* ☉ *Apr.–Oct., daily 9:30–6 (last admission 5).*

★ About 1½ mi from Elizabeth Castle is St. Matthew's Church, the **Glass Church** in Millbrook, a Victorian chapel restored in 1934 as a memorial to Sir Jesse Boot, a millionaire pharmacist known throughout Britain for his drugstore chain, Boots. The fashionable Parisian glass sculptor, René Lalique (1860–1945), transformed the interior with artisanal glass. He embellished the church with fluid applications of Art Deco glass forms—the front appears to be supported by a cluster of icicles; the glass cross, pillars, and altar rail all scintillate with refracted light. ⊠ *Millbrook, St. Aubin's Rd., St. Lawrence,* ☎ *01534/502864.* ⌨ *Free.* ☉ *Weekdays 9–6 (or dusk), Sat. 9–1, Sun. for worship only.*

Reached from St. Aubin's Bay via A12 (Grand Route de St. Ouen) in the northwest corner of the island, 5 mi northwest of St. Helier and 1 mi west of St. Ouen, the **Battle of Flowers Museum** is devoted to the parade of flowers, a summer festival usually taking place in August, which has been held annually (except during wartime) since 1902. Originally, the floral decorations were torn from the floats for use as "ammunition" in the "battle," but now they survive longer, some to become exhibits in this museum (with materials such as dyed hare's tail and marram grass instead of flowers). There is a lakeside tearoom beside the museum that's open May–September. ⊠ *La Robeline, Mont des Corvées, St. Ouen,* ☎ *01534/482408; 01534/30178 parade information.* ⌨ *£2.25.* ☉ *Mid-Mar.–Oct., daily 10–5.*

The **Jersey Flower Centre** in the north of the island (off B23), 3 mi northwest of St. Helier and 2 mi east of St. Ouen, has magnificent displays of carnations grown under glass on the grounds of an old farmhouse. Visitors can also wander among wildflowers and exotic birds, including a flock of Greater Flamingos. ⊠ *Retreat Farm, St. Lawrence,* ☎ *01534/865665.* ⌨ *£3.25.* ☉ *Apr.–Oct., daily 9:30–5:30.*

★ Even those who hold no brief with zoos will enjoy the country setting and educational programs that are an intrinsic part of the **Jersey Wildlife Trust,** based 3 mi north of St. Helier and 4 mi east of St. Ouen. The trust was started in 1963 by the celebrated wildlife writer Gerald Durrell, who chose the 25 acres of Augres Manor as a center for breeding and conserving endangered species, including gorillas, orangutans, lemurs, snow leopards, and marmosets, together with many kinds of birds and reptiles. This is a great place for a family outing, as well as for anyone interested in wildlife conservation. There are talks, videos, and displays as well as the Café Dodo, named after a bird Durrell was a century too late to try to save. The zoo lies half a mile inland from Bouley Bay, in the northeast corner of the island. ⊠ *Les Augres Manor, Trinity,* ☎ *01534/864666.* ⊠ *£5.20.* ⊙ *Daily 9:30–6 (or dusk).*

★ One of the world's finest collections of orchids can be seen at the **Eric Young Orchid Foundation,** 2 mi north of St. Helier and 1 mi south of the Jersey Wildlife Trust. Five big greenhouses re-create the particular environments needed for specific orchid groups. ⊠ *Victoria Village, Trinity,* ☎ *01534/861963.* ⊠ *£2.50.* ⊙ *Thurs.–Sat. 10–4.*

★ **Gorey Castle,** otherwise named **Mont Orgeuil** (Mount Pride), rises square-cut on its granite rock above the busy harbor, 4 mi northeast of St. Helier and 3 mi east of Victoria Village. For centuries Jersey's chief fortress, it was built mainly in the 14th century as a series of concentric defenses, pierced by five gateways. There are also waxwork tableaus of historic events. ☎ *01534/853292.* ⊠ *£3.20 (☞ Jersey Museum, above, for details on combined tickets).* ⊙ *Daily 9:30–6.*

Dining and Lodging

££ ✕ **Apple Cottage.** Set in an attractive little cottage, tucked away beside Rozel Bay, this is a place where you can choose between an extravagant feast or a more modest repast—either way, you will dine well. If you need a change from the island's prevalent fish-based cuisine, you can order dishes such as grilled lamb cutlets or calves' liver. Seafood, however, is the specialty and comes in all varieties and preparations, ranging from scallops and skate to lobster thermidor. ⊠ *Rozel Bay, St. Martin,* ☎ *01534/861002. MC, V. Closed Mon. and 6 wks Dec.– Feb. No dinner Sun.*

££ ✕ **Jersey Pottery.** This restaurant is part of the Jersey Pottery complex and claims that Queen Elizabeth lunched here when visiting her dukedom. The restaurant, in an attractive conservatory, offers great seafood, but since it's very popular and often full, the cafeteria is a fair alternative. ⊠ *Gorey Village, Grouville,* ☎ *01534/851119. AE, DC, MC, V. Closed Sun. No dinner.*

££ ✕ **Victoria's.** The Grand Hotel's restaurant is *the* place to go for dinner and dancing. The decor is firmly Victorian. There's a long menu, but the critics' choice is the lemon sole or the medallions of pork. There are good-value set-price menus, or go à la carte. ⊠ *Grand Hotel, Pierson Rd., St. Helier,* ☎ *01534/22301. Jacket and tie. AE, DC, MC, V. No lunch Sat., no dinner Sun.*

££££ ✕🏨 **Hotel l'Horizon.** L'Horizon is one of Jersey's luxury hotels, with wonderful views over St. Brelade's Bay. Though the hotel is big, it manages to maintain a bright, upbeat feeling, with large, comfortable bedrooms and plenty of places to relax in comfort. There are three restaurants—the **Crystal Room,** the **Grill,** and the **Brasserie.** The first two are traditionally elegant, while the Brasserie is more relaxed, near the pool and exercise area. In the more formal restaurants, try the quail salad, roast saddle of lamb, or any of the wonderful seafood dishes, especially the scampi in mouthwatering ginger, honey, and lemon sauce. If you don't want to dine, you can always drop by for a special tea in one of the lounges. ⊠ *St. Brelade's Bay, St. Brelade, JE3 8EF,* ☎ *01534/43101,* FAX *01534/46269. 107 rooms with bath. 3 restaurants, pool, sauna, spa, steam room. AE, DC, MC, V.*

££££   ✕⊞ **Longueville Manor.** The Manor is one of Britain's few members
★   of the Relais and Châteaux group. It's set on lovely grounds and has the polished look of age combined with elegance plus comfort, derived from a long-established, caring proprietorship. Antiques abound, the bedrooms are supremely comfortable, and the bathrooms are luxurious. The food in the paneled dining room is essentially traditional English, but venison pâté with onion marmalade, grilled salmon with béarnaise sauce, liver with sausage, and black pudding are all standouts. Try the Eton Mess, an unbelievable creation with crushed meringue and strawberries, and Jersey cream topping it off. ⊠ *Longueville, St. Saviour, JE2 7SA,* ☎ *01534/25501,* FAX *01534/31613. 34 rooms with bath. Restaurant, pool, tennis court. AE, DC, MC, V.*

£££   ✕⊞ **Château la Chaire.** This dignified mansion is hidden on a cul-de-sac just above Rozel Harbour. The building is large but offers only 14 bedrooms, though all are luxurious and sunny; some of the bathrooms have Jacuzzis. The property is opulent, and the restaurant is the place to try Jersey's excellent fresh fish in a variety of elegant preparations. ⊠ *Rozel Valley, St. Martin, JE3 6AJ,* ☎ *01534/863354,* FAX *01534/ 865137. 14 rooms with bath. Restaurant. AE, DC, MC, V.*

££   ✕⊞ **Old Court House Inn.** This is an ancient inn—the core of the building is about 500 years old—with a few rooms, three atmospheric lunchtime bars, and a fine restaurant. Grilled oysters, crab creole, Jersey plaice—all are featured on the big menu. The busy inn overlooks the harbor; the best view is from the penthouse. ⊠ *The Bulwarks, St. Aubin's Harbour, JE3 8AB,* ☎ *01534/46433,* FAX *01534/45103. 9 rooms with bath. Restaurant, 3 bars. AE, DC, MC, V.*

The Arts

Jersey has an international **Jazz Festival** (☎ 01534/864296) at the end of April in St. Helier. The **Battle of Flowers** (☞ Exploring the Channel Islands, *above*) is held on the second Thursday in August (☎ 01534/639000), and a **film festival** is held in September, in St. Helier. The **Jersey Arts Centre** (⊠ Phillips St., St. Helier, ☎ 01534/873767) has regular exhibitions of art, film, and music.

Outdoor Activities and Sports

BICYCLING

While in Jersey, rent from **Zebra Hire** (⊠ The Esplanade, St. Helier, ☎ 01534/36556), **Hireride** (⊠ 1 St. John's Rd., St. Helier, ☎ 01534/31995), or **Jersey Cycletours** (⊠ 2 La Hougue Mauger, St. Mary, ☎ 01534/ 482898). Zebra Cycles and Jersey Cycles can organize themed tours with routes for all skills and endurance levels.

DIVING

To dive in Jersey, contact **Watersports** (⊠ First Tower, St. Helier, ☎ 01534/32813) or the **Diving Centre** (⊠ Bouley Bay, ☎ 01534/861817).

GOLF

Jersey has two 18-hole courses, both of which can be used by any visitor who is affiliated with a golf club back home. These are **La Moye** (⊠ St. Brelade, ☎ 01534/43401) and **Royal Jersey Golf Club** (⊠ Grouville, ☎ 01534/854416).

SAILBOARDING AND SURFING

At St. Ouen Bay, in Jersey, there's great surfing. Windsurfing is popular at St. Aubin and St. Brelade's Bay. Rent equipment from **Atlantic Waves** (⊠ Le Port, St. Ouen's Bay, ☎ 01534/865492) or the **Gorey Watersports Centre** (⊠ Grouville Bay, ☎ 01534/853250).

SWIMMING

On Jersey, **St. Ouen's Bay** and **Royal Bay** of Grouville have excellent fine-sand beaches and safe water.

Shopping

In St. Helier pedestrian malls on **Queen Street** and **King Street** have classic shops selling international brands, while smaller boutiques line roads like **Bath Street, New Street,** and **Halkett Place.** Two major markets are the **Central Market** and **Indoor Market,** also in this area. The **Jersey Pottery Shop** (⊠ 1 Bond St., St. Helier, ☏ 01534/25115) has a selection of wonderful pottery, which can also be bought directly from the source at the **Jersey Pottery** (⊠ Gorey Village, Grouville, ☏ 01534/ 851119), where there's also a good restaurant and brasserie. **Jersey Pearl** (⊠ La Route des Issues, St. John, ☏ 01534/862137) exhibits the largest collection of pearl jewelry on the island, and you can watch artisans crafting new pearl pieces; Jersey Pearl also has four retail outlets in different parts of the island (⊠ Jersey Airport; Gorey Pier; 11 Halkett St.; and 75 King St., St. Helier). Jersey sweaters are famous the world over and can be purchased at **Jersey Woollen Mills** (⊠ La Grande Route des Mielles, St. Ouen, ☏ 01534/481342), where the garments are produced using pure oiled wool.

Guernsey

About 16,000 people, just over one third of the population of Guernsey, live in **St. Peter Port,** which has prospered over the centuries from the harbor around which it climbs. Guernsey is well placed for trade—legal or illegal—between France and England. In the 18th and 19th centuries, St. Peter Port was a haven for privateers who preyed on merchantmen. Victor Hugo furnished his house, Hauteville (☞ *below*), with some of the looted pieces flooding the Guernsey market. In a modern version of its privateering past, St. Peter Port is now home to many tax exiles, who have luxurious houses on the town's outskirts.

⑧ The heart of the old town, around the harbor, is usually jammed with traffic. The **parish church of St. Peter,** right beside The Quay, dates back at least to the days of William the Conqueror, though the oldest part of the present building is from the 12th century. Events through the centuries have played havoc with it, not least an air raid in 1944. Walking along the quaint streets in the old quarter will provide at least a morning's entertainment. You might start at Trinity Church Square and continue on Mansell Street.

★ **⑨** The southern arm of St. Peter Port's harbor, Castle Emplacement, leads out to **Castle Cornet,** where you can get a bird's-eye view of St. Peter Port and an 8-mi-away glimpse of France. The castle was built early in the 13th century and contains several small museums, including the **Royal Guernsey Militia Museum,** the **Armoury,** and the **Main Guard Museum,** whose collection ranges from model ships to relics from the German occupation to island art. There's a cafeteria. ☏ *01481/726518.* ⊡ *£4.* ☉ *Apr.–Oct., daily 10–5.*

★ **⑩** You will have to climb up from Castle Pier to Hauteville (High Town) to reach **Hauteville House,** once the home of writer Victor Hugo (1802–1885). For 18 years he was a political exile on Guernsey; in 1856 he bought this house. It is now owned by the City of Paris and is a completely French enclave, filled with lovely old furniture and tapestries. From the top floor the great author could see across to his beloved France and also into the house of his mistress, Juliette Drouet. ⊠ *38 Rue de Hauteville, St. Peter Port,* ☏ *01481/721911.* ⊡ *£4.* ☉ *Apr.–June and Sept., Mon.–Sat. 10–11:30 (last tour) and 2–4:30*

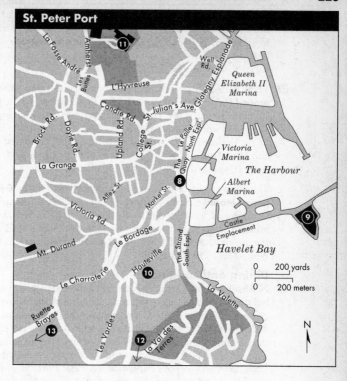

(last tour); July and Aug., Mon.–Sat. 10–noon (last tour) and 2–4:45 (last tour). Guided tours only, limited to 15 people; early arrival recommended.

Just north of St. Peter Port's town center, inland from the North Beach Marina, is the **Beau Sejour Centre,** a multipurpose sports and entertainment complex. Equipped with an indoor heated pool; squash, badminton, and tennis courts; a "trim trail," a cinema/theater; a cafeteria, and a bar, this is the perfect place to visit on a rainy day. ⊠ *Amherst,* ☎ *01481/727211.* ☐ *Free admission. Fees for use of individual facilities..* ☉ *Daily 9* AM*–11* PM*, but check for pool schedule and other activities.*

Hidden beneath the rocks south of the center of St. Peter Port lies one of the underground networks of tunnels built on Guernsey by the German occupying forces and their slave labor. Now **La Valette Military Museum,** the complex focuses on Guernsey's military history dating back to the Victorian island militia, and holds various World War II exhibits including the indomitable German truck used in the film *Indiana Jones and the Last Crusade.* ⊠ *La Valette,* ☎ *01481/722300.* ☐ *£2.75.* ☉ *Daily 10–5, closed Tues.–Wed. in winter.*

★ ⑫ **Sausmarez Manor** (not to be confused with Sausmarez Park, northwest of St. Peter Port), is 2 mi south of St. Peter Port and Guernsey's only stately home open to the public. Although there was once a Norman house on the site, the present building, a solid, plain structure, dates from the 18th century, when it was built at the behest of the first governor of New York. It has been called the country's finest example of the Queen Anne colonial style of architecture and is set among lovely gardens, the most important of which is the Woodland Garden, full of tropical plants. A 9-hole pitch-and-putt course; a children's farm animal area; playgrounds; and a tea garden by the lake complete the picture. Within, tapestries and family portraits are on display. The manor has a notable collection of dollhouses, as well as two model railways. ☎ *01481/35571.* ☞ *£4; extra charge for some attractions.* ☉ *Apr.–Oct., Mon.–Thurs. for guided tours only at 10:30, 11:30, 2, and 3 (mornings only in Apr. and Oct.).*

⓭ Three mi southwest of St. Peter Port, the **German Military Underground Hospital** is one of the main relics attesting to the German occupation on Guernsey. These grim catacombs were built by slave labor, and many workers who died on the job are entombed in the concrete. ✉ *La Vassalerie Rd., St. Andrew's,* ☎ *01481/39100.* ☞ *£2.* ☉ *Nov. and Mar., Sun. and Thurs. 2–3; Apr. and Oct., daily 2–4; May–Sept., daily 10–noon and 2–4 (until 4:30 in July and Aug.).*

The Nazi presence on Guernsey is remembered at the **German Occupation Museum,** 4 mi southwest of St. Peter Port, featuring a reconstruction of a street during the occupation, as well as numerous tableaus, videos, and access to German fortifications. ✉ *Forest (near the airport),* ☎ *01481/38205.* ☞ *£2.50.* ☉ *Apr.–Oct., daily 10–5; Nov.–Mar., Thurs. and Sun. 10–5.*

Dining and Lodging

££ ✕ **Absolute End.** This quietly elegant little restaurant in a neat, white building facing the sea is about a mile north along the coast from the center of St. Peter Port. The emphasis here is, of course, on seafood dishes, with home-smoked fish and shellfish as very tasty starters. Try the salmon coubiliac. There is a good-value set menu at lunch for £11. The Absolute End won the best island restaurant award in 1993. ✉ *Longstore, St. George's Esplanade, St. Peter Port,* ☎ *01481/723822. AE, MC, V. Closed Sun. and Jan.*

££ ✕ **Café du Moulin.** This restaurant is in a converted water mill in a peace-
★   ful valley on the east of the island, close to the Silbe nature reserve. Try the crepinette of seafood, or loin of lamb roasted with pesto crust. It's all ultrafresh and tasty, with a touch of East Asia in many of the dishes. ✉ *Rue du Quanteraine, St. Peters,* ☎ *01481/65944. MC, V. Closed Mon. No dinner Sun. in winter.*

££ ✕ **La Nautique.** As with all the best restaurants in the Channel Islands, fish is the order of the day here. In this old-established eatery it comes with every sauce imaginable—lobster flambéed with whiskey, monkfish *à la Dugléré,* turbot hollandaise. The cooking is French and the service stylish, which is not always the case with some Guernsey restaurants. ✉ *The Quay Steps, St. Peter Port,* ☎ *01481/721714. AE, DC, MC, V. Closed Sun., 2 wks after Christmas.*

£££ ✕🖿 **La Frégate.** This small 17th-century manor house has been carefully converted into a hotel. Its setting in colorful gardens on a quiet hillside overlooking the harbor makes it an excellent choice for a restful sojourn. The bedrooms, some with balconies, are all comfortable and sizable, and the staff is attentive. The restaurant, with big windows overlooking the town, serves top-notch cuisine, especially seafood dishes. ✉ *Les Côtils, St. Peter Port, GY1 1UT,* ☎ *01481/724624,* 🖷 *01481/720443. 13 rooms with bath. Restaurant. AE, DC, MC, V.*

££–£££ 🖿 **Imperial Hotel.** Here is a simple hotel that's very popular for family vacations. The bedrooms, decorated with sturdy furnishings, are uncluttered, and some offer views of the sandy beaches of Rocquaine Bay. There are three bars, and one of them, the Portlet Bar, is a popular haunt of locals. ✉ *Torteval, GY8 0PS,* ☎ *01481/64044,* 🖷 *01481/66139. 16 rooms with bath or shower. MC, V. Closed Nov.–Mar.*

The Arts

FESTIVALS

Guernsey has an **Eisteddfod** during February, a **Square Dance Festival** at the end of June, and a **Battle of Flowers** at the end of August. Contact the tourist board for the latest dates.

Outdoor Activities and Sports

BICYCLING

On Guernsey, you can rent bikes from **Quay Cycle Hire** (⊠ White Rock, St. Peter Port, ☎ 01481/714146), the **Cycle Centre** (⊠ The Bridge, St. Sampson's, ☎ 01481/49311), **Rent-a-Bike** (⊠ The Bridge, St. Sampson's, ☎ 01481/49311), and **Pedal Cycles** (☎ 01481/63090), which delivers and collects bikes anywhere on the island.

DIVING

For diving equipment and lessons in Guernsey, contact **Dive Guernsey** (⊠ Castle Emplacement, St. Peter Port, ☎ 01481/714525).

GOLF

The 18-hole **Royal Guernsey** (⊠ L'Ancresse, Vale, ☎ 01481/45070) has wonderful views of the beach and sea. To play here visitors must produce handicap certificates, and they can't play on Sunday, or on Thursday and Saturday afternoons.

SAILBOARDING AND SURFING

In Guernsey try the surf at Vazon Bay. For rentals, classes, and equipment, contact **Nauti-Fun** (⊠ L'Islet Crossroads, St. Sampson's, ☎ 01481/46690), **West Coast Surfing** (⊠ c/o Nyallo, Rue des Rocquettes, Vazon, Castel, ☎ 01481/55318), **Sail or Surf** (⊠ Pembroke Bay Hotel, Vale, ☎ 01481/44338), or **Windsurfing International** (⊠ Cobô, ☎ 01481/53313).

SWIMMING

Guernsey's beaches are one of its chief attractions. Try **Vazon Bay,** which has a section reserved for surfers; **Petit Pot Bay,** especially for sunbathing; and **L'Ancresse Bay,** where the water is shallow.

Shopping

The main shopping district in St. Peter Port, not as glitzy as St. Helier, begins in **Le Pollet,** near Queen Elizabeth Marina. The mostly pedestrian area is a network of lanes with specialty shops—particularly jewelers. This is a great place to buy a watch. For antiques and women's fashions head for the old quarter and **Mill Street, Mansell Square,** and **Trinity Square. Moulin Houet Pottery** (⊠ Moulin Houet Bay, ☎ 01481/37201) is a good source for sturdy, attractive pottery; it's at the head of a lush valley running down to the sea.

Sark

Sark, the odd-man-out of the Channel Islands, has turned its back on the 20th century and banned the automobile, allowing only horse- or tractor-drawn carriages. Even planes are prohibited from flying overhead unless special permission is granted. The tranquil island is in two sections; the smaller part, Little Sark, is joined to the main island by a narrow neck of land whose vertiginous drop is 260 ft.

Dining and Lodging

£££ ✕⊡ **Stock's Island Hotel.** For a relaxed lunch—and what else would you expect on Sark?—try the restaurant here. Lunchtime fare in the Courtyard Bistro or in the Smuggler's Bar, a converted wine cellar, might be quiche or the local lobster and crab, and Stock's cakes and pastries also rank high on the menu. The Cider Press Restaurant serves more formal meals: the fillet of sea bass is memorable. If you feel like staying over, there are guest rooms. ⊠ *Sark, GY9 0SD,* ☎ *01481/832001,* FAX *01481/832130. 24 rooms, 20 with bath or shower. Restaurant. AE, DC, MC, V. Closed Oct.–Easter.*

Outdoor Activities and Sports

BICYCLING
On Sark, **Avenue Cycle Hire** (⊠ The Avenue, ☎ 01481/832102), **A– B Cycles** (☎ 01481/832844), and **Isle of Sark Carriage and Cycle Hire** (☎ 01481/832262) rent bikes.

CHANNEL ISLANDS A TO Z

Arriving and Departing

By Boat

You can sail to Jersey or Guernsey from Poole. **Condor Ltd.** (☎ 01305/ 761551 or 0990/116655) has a daily catamaran service (5 a wk in winter). Most boats stop at Guernsey first. The average time is 2½ hours to Guernsey, 1½ hours more to Jersey. An average fare runs from £62 for a five-day round-trip for a foot passenger (£74 in summer) to £196 for a car with two passengers (£268 in summer).

By Plane

Jersey is well served by flights from both mainland Britain and the Continent. There are direct flights from Birmingham (British Midland, Jersey European), Bristol (BA), Edinburgh (BA, British Midland), Exeter (Jersey European), Gatwick (BA, Jersey European), Glasgow (British Midland), Heathrow (BA, Air UK), Leeds/Bradford (British Midland), Manchester (BA), Newcastle (BA), Plymouth (BA), Southampton (Air UK), Stansted (Air UK), and Teeside (British Midland). Flying time from London is one hour, from Manchester 90 minutes, from Plymouth 70 minutes. The London/Jersey round-trip fare starts from about £60.

Guernsey Airport is served by Air UK, Aurigny Air Services, British Airways, British Midland, and Jersey European.

For further flight information contact: Air UK (☎ 0990/074074); Aurigny Air Services (☎ 01481/822886); British Airways (☎ 0345/ 222111); British Midland (☎ 0345/554554); Channel Island Travel Service (☎ 01534/46181); Jersey European (☎ 0990/676676).

Currency

Although the islands use pounds and pence, both have their own version, with specially printed bills. This currency is *not* legal tender elsewhere in the United Kingdom, though you are able to use U.K. currency on the islands. Financial wheeling and dealing is big business here, and you'll find *bureaus de change* at banks, travel agencies, the main post offices, airports, and the main harbors. Note that only local stamps may be used to post letters.

Getting Around

By Bus

Jersey and Guernsey have excellent services, including regular buses to and from both airports, and all over both islands. The services are **Jersey Motor Transport Co.** (⊠ Central Bus Station, Weighbridge, St. Helier, ☎ 01534/21201) and **Guernseybus** (⊠ Picquet House, St. Peter Port, ☎ 01481/724677). They both have reasonably priced Rover tickets, which provide unlimited travel over a short period of time. On Jersey, the **Classic Coach Company** (☎ 01534/505888) also offers the chance to ride in a restored Bedford County Bus from 1937, which tours the island between March and November (not Saturday), departing from the Jersey Museum in St. Helier at 10:30, and returning at about 5:30. Tickets cost £12.50 and can be bought on board.

By Car
You can ship your car by ferry from mainland Britain at fairly low rates or rent a car (☞ Contacts and Resources, *below*), but the islands are small and easily explored by local bus. The traffic, especially on Jersey, can be regularly snarled up, particularly in high season. Driving is on the left, and the speed limit is 40 mph on Jersey; 35 on Guernsey and Alderney; cars are not permitted on Sark.

Between the Islands
There are regular daily flights all summer between Jersey and Guernsey, and fewer flights in winter. You can also fly to the islands from France.

Larger ferries travel between Jersey and Guernsey; those from the British mainland stop at both islands going and returning. Fast hydrofoils skim around all the islands. Sark can be reached from Guernsey in about 45 minutes by **Sark Shipping** (☎ 01481/724059) and in the same amount of time from Jersey by **Emeraude** (Apr.–Sept.; ☎ 01534/66566); Herm can be reached from Guernsey in 15 minutes by **Herm Seaways** (☎ 01481/724677), **Munson Herm Ferry** (☎ 01481/722613)—both operating April to September only—and **Trident Charter Co.** (☎ 01481/721379), operating all year. There is no scheduled boat service to the island of Alderney, though operators do run sporadic excursions in summer; otherwise, there are regular air departures from Jersey, Guernsey, and the mainland run by **Aurigny** (☎ 01481/822886). **Condor** (☎ 01534/601000 or 01481/729666) runs a hydrofoil service to St. Malo, France.

Contacts and Resources

Car Rentals
JERSEY
Avis (✉ Rue Cappelain, St. Peter Port, ☎ 01534/499499). **Budget Rent-a-Car** (✉ Grande Route de St. Pierre, St. Peter Port, ☎ 01534/484466). **Europcar** (✉ Arrivals Hall, Jersey Airport, St. Peter Port, ☎ 0800/801495; 0800/378548 after 5 PM). **Hertz** (✉ Alares House, Jersey Airport, ☎ 01534/45621).

GUERNSEY
Avis (✉ Les Caches, St. Martin, ☎ 01481/35266). **Budget Rent-a-Car** (✉ Landes du Marche Garage, Vale, ☎ 01481/51744). **Hertz** (✉ Jackson's Garage, Airport Forecourt, ☎ 01481/37638). **Harlequin Hire Cars** (✉ Les Caches, St. Martin, ☎ 01481/39511).

Guided Tours
All-day, morning, afternoon, and evening coach tours of Jersey are run by **Tantivy Blue Coach Tours** (✉ 70/72 Columberie, St. Helier, JE2 4QA, ☎ 01534/22584), and, in reconditioned period buses, by **Classic Coach Company** (✉ c/o Town Park Hotel, Pierson Rd., St. Helier, JE2 3PD, ☎ 01534/505888), which leave from outside the museum in St. Helier at 10:30 Sun.–Fri. In Guernsey, **Guernsey Bus** (✉ Picquet House, St. Peter Port, GY1 1AE, ☎ 01481/724677), and—between April and September—**Island Coachways** (✉ Les Banques, St. Peter Port, ☎ 01481/720210) arrange bus tours, or you can go on one of the coastal walking tours organized by the Guernsey Tourist Board (☞ *below*).

Lodging
For information on Channel Islands hotels, contact the **Jersey Hotel and Guest House Association** (✉ 60 Stopford Rd., St. Helier, Jersey

JE2 4LZ, ☎ 01534/21421, FAX 01534/22496). In Guernsey, contact the **Guernsey Hotel and Tourist Association** (⌧ Suite 3, 16 Glategny Esplanade, St. Peter Port GY1 1WN, ☎ 01481/713583, FAX 01481/715882.

Travel Agencies

Bellingham Travel (⌧ 33 Queen St., St. Helier, Jersey, ☎ 01534/27575; ⌧ 41 Commercial Arcade, St. Peter Port, Guernsey, ☎ 01481/726333). **Channel Islands Travel Service** (⌧ Room 222, Guernsey Airport, Forest, Guernsey, ☎ 01481/35471). **Marshall's Travel** (⌧ 1 Quennevais Precinct, St. Brelade, Jersey, ☎ 01534/41278). **Thomas Cook** (⌧ 14 Charing Cross, St. Helier, Jersey, ☎ 01534/506900; ⌧ 22 Le Pollet, St. Peter Port, Guernsey, ☎ 01481/724111).

Visitor Information

In London, **Jersey Tourism Office** (⌧ 38 Dover St., London W1X 3RB, ☎ 0171/493–5278). On the islands, there are various tourist offices. **Jersey Tourism Department** (⌧ Liberation Sq., St. Helier JE1 1BB, ☎ 01534/500777; 01534/500888 for accommodations; FAX 01534/500808). **Guernsey Tourist Board** (⌧ North Esplanade, St. Peter Port, ☎01481/723552, FAX 01481/714951). **Sark Tourist Information Office** (⌧ Harbour Hill, ☎ 01481/832345, FAX 01481/832483).

7 The Thames Valley

Windsor, Henley-on-Thames, Oxford, Blenheim Palace

The crack of a polo ball echoes across Windsor Great Park as Prince Charles scores another point. The family castle here is one of his favorite escapes and many Londoners follow, heading for tranquil Thameside villages, each more charming than the last. In June and July, all head for the Henley Royal Regatta to toast rowing's best with Pimm's "champers" and Kent strawberries. The top magnet here is the great city of Oxford—seat of Britain's oldest university—but be sure to catch the power, pomp, and solid magnificence of Blenheim Palace nearby.

LIQUID HISTORY, THAT'S OLD FATHER THAMES. The very name is often synonymous with Britain itself, and the watery stretch to the west of London is often re-

Updated by
Lucy Hawking

ferred to as the country's second coastline. Like many another great river, it creates the illusion of flowing not only through the prosperous countryside of Berkshire and Oxfordshire, but through long centuries of history, too. The past seems to rise from its swiftly moving waters like an intangible mist. In London, where it is a broad, oily stream, it speeds almost silently past great buildings, menacingly impressive. Higher upstream it is a busy part of the living landscape, flooding meadows in spring and fall and rippling past places holding significance not just for England but also the world. Runnymede is one of these. Here, on a riverside greensward, the Magna Carta was signed, a crucial step in the Western world's progress toward democracy.

Nearby rises the medieval bulk of Windsor Castle, home to eight successive royal houses. Anyone who wants to understand the mystique of the British monarchy should visit Windsor, where a fraction of the present queen's vast wealth is on display in surroundings of heraldic splendor (now more aglitter than ever thanks to the recent renovation of the reception rooms). Farther upstream lies Oxford, where generations of the ruling elite have been educated. In the bustling city, with industrial development on its outskirts, the colleges maintain their scholarly, nearly medieval, calm amid modern traffic's clamorous rush. Close by are the storybook village of Woodstock and Blenheim Palace, the grandest house in all the land.

Along the River Thames, scattered throughout the unfolding landscape of trees, meadows, and rolling hills, are numerous small villages and larger towns, some spoiled by ill-considered modern building, many still sleepily preserving their ancient charm. Superhighways carrying heavy traffic between London, the West Country, the Midlands, and the railroad have turned much of this area into commuter territory, but you can easily depart from these beaten tracks to discover timeless villages whose landscapes are kept green by the river and its tributaries. The stretches of the Thames near Marlow, Henley, Bray, and Sonning-on-Thames are a vacationer's paradise. There are rowing clubs and piers all over that part of the river, excellent lawns, and well-built cottages and villas.

Pleasures and Pastimes

Henley Royal Regatta

During the cusp of June and July Henley hosts rowing's most elegant race, the Henley Royal Regatta. Its riverbanks become one gigantic, opulent lawn party as 500,000 visitors, including members of the Royal Family, descend en masse during the week. Each day, the racing pauses twice—at noon for luncheon and at 4 PM for tea.

Dining

Elegant Londoners weekend here, and where they go, Cordon Bleu restaurants follow. Ascot, Henley, Woodstock all boast some of Britain's best tables. Of course simple pub food, as well as classic French cuisine, can be enjoyed in waterside settings at many restaurants beside the Thames. Even in towns away from the river, well-heeled commuters and Oxford professors support top-flight establishments. On weekends it is advisable to make reservations.

CATEGORY	COST*
££££	over £50
£££	£30–£50
££	£20–£30
£	under £20

per person, including first course, main course, dessert, and VAT; excluding drinks

Hiking and Walking

The **Oxfordshire Way** runs 65 mi from Henley-on-Thames to Bourton-on-the-Water, on the eastern edge of the Cotswolds. A 13-mi ramble starts in Henley, runs north through the **Hambleden Valley,** takes in Stonor Park, and returns to Henley via the Assendons, Lower and Middle. Or try the trails through the beechwoods at **Burnham Beeches.**

Most of the Thames Valley walks include busy traffic areas. One that is almost completely free of traffic is the **Thames Path,** a 180-mi route following the river from the London flood barrier to its source near Kemble, in the Cotswolds. The path was officially inaugurated in the fall of 1996, following towpaths from the outskirts of London, through Windsor, to Oxford and Lechlade. There is also good public transportation in the region, so you can easily start and stop anywhere along the route.

Lodging

Many hotels in the area started out centuries ago as coaching inns. Others have been converted more recently from country mansions. Both types usually have plenty of character, with antiques and attractive decor— and, often, well-kept gardens.

CATEGORY	COST*
££££	over £150
£££	£80–£150
££	£60–£80
£	under £60

All prices are for two people sharing a double room, including service, breakfast, and VAT.

Exploring the Thames Valley

Begin in lively Windsor, favorite home-away-from-home of Britain's royal family. Follow the river to Henley, site of the regatta, and then make a counterclockwise sweep west to Wallingford—the countryside immortalized by *The Wind in the Willows.* Finally go to Oxford, and end with a visit to some of the region's stately homes and palaces. The area also abounds with tiny villages hidden from the major highways. Turn off from time to time to see if that tiny hamlet, deep in the trees, is as attractive as its name sounds.

Numbers in the text correspond to numbers in the margin and on the Thames Valley, Windsor Castle, and Oxford maps.

Great Itineraries

To get the most out of the region, it's worth searching out that perfect riverside inn or High Street hotel and settling in for the night. Evenings in Windsor or Oxford will allow you to take in some world-class theater, and to make the most out of the mornings for touring the surrounding countryside. Leave the main roads to explore the smaller centers; the Thames itself is best appreciated by locking the car and setting off on foot along the towpath that runs alongside much of the river.

IF YOU HAVE 3 DAYS

Begin at ⊞ **Windsor** ①, where royalty is the predominant note, and spend a morning visiting the castle, leaving part of the day for **Eton College** and **Windsor Great Park.** The next day, follow the river upstream, taking in the grandeur of the great Astor estate at **Cliveden** ⑤ and the charming village of **Marlow** ⑥, where the beamed pubs offer decent snacks for lunch. Head toward **Henley** ⑦, where the Thames forms a harmonious dialogue with the medieval buildings alongside, and easy and tranquil walks beckon upstream or down. Reserve the last morning for ⊞ **Oxford** ⑬, whose scholastic air does not dampen the aesthetic and gastronomic pleasures on tap, with an afternoon visit to nearby **Woodstock** ㉕—a lovely English village—and **Blenheim Palace** ㉖, birthplace of Winston Churchill and probably the most spectacular house in England.

IF YOU HAVE 5 DAYS

To unearth the rustic charms of the region, including all the hamlets strung along the Thames, make your base at ⊞ **Windsor** ① for your first night. From there you can take excursions to **Ascot** ③, for some of England's finest horse racing, and, to the west, **Cliveden** ⑤. For your second night, consider staying in ⊞ **Henley** ⑦, from which it is an easy trip to two aristocratic mansions—**Mapledurham House** and **Stonor Park** ⑩, and a cluster of picturesque Thameside villages, such as **Ewelme** ⑪, **Sonning-on-Thames** ⑧, **Dorchester-on-Thames** ㉘, and **Wallingford** ⑫. Reserve the third day and night for the medieval wonders of ⊞ **Oxford** ⑬, then head on your fourth day to the nearby 18th-century village of ⊞ **Woodstock** ㉕, site of magisterial **Blenheim Palace** ㉖ and, in fact, some lovely hotels. For the final day, swing eastward to the town of **Great Milton** ㉜ for perhaps the grandest luncheon of your English trip, at Le Manoir aux Quat' Saisons, then pay a call on three of the most stately of stately homes, **Waddesdon Manor** ㉝, **Woburn Abbey** ㉞, and **Althorp** ㉟.

When to Tour the Thames Valley

Although the countryside around the Thames can be alluring at any time of year, the depths of winter may not be the time most conducive to appreciating its special beauty—nor are rain and chill winds the best accompaniments to soaking up the charms of such places as Windsor and Oxford. Moreover, many of the aristocratic country houses are closed between October and Easter. High summer can see droves of tourists in these places; avoid the months of August and September if you can, if only to escape the queues. Spring and autumn reveal the countryside at its best, and you can usually venture outdoors during these seasons without too much discomfort. Remember that Eton and the Oxford colleges are much more restricted during term time.

ROYAL BERKSHIRE: WINDSOR AND ENVIRONS

Windsor

★ ❶ *21 mi west of London.*

Easily accessible from London, the town of Windsor makes for a rewarding day trip. The principal attraction is **Windsor Castle,** rising majestically on a bluff above the Thames, and visible for miles around. The town itself, with its narrow streets brimming with shops and ancient buildings, is well worth a visit, but the royal residence—the largest inhabited castle in the world—remains the prime attraction. From William the Conqueror to Queen Victoria, the kings and rulers of England continuously added towers and wings to the brooding structure. Yet despite the multiplicity of hands that have gone into its design, the palace has managed to emerge with a unity of style and character.

The most impressive view of Windsor Castle is from the A332 road, on the southern approach to the town. Although there have been settlements here from time immemorial, including a Roman villa, the present castle was begun by William the Conqueror in the 11th century and modified and extended by Edward III in the mid-1300s. One of Edward's largest contributions was the enormous and distinctive round tower. Finally, between 1824 and 1837, George IV transformed what was still essentially a medieval castle into the fortified royal palace you see today. In all, work on the castle spread over more than eight centuries, with most kings and queens of England demonstrating their undying attachment to it. In fact, Windsor is the only royal residence that has been in continuous use by the royal family since the Middle Ages.

It is from the North Terrace that entry is gained into the State Apartments, which can be visited by the public when the Queen is not in residence. The Queen, in fact, uses the castle far more than did any of her predecessors. It has become, over the last decade, a sort of country weekend residence, which allows the royal family a few days of relaxation and informality away, as much as possible, from the glare of the public eye. To see the royal abode come magnificently alive, check out the Windsor Castle **Changing of the Guard** (☼ May–Aug., Mon.–Sat., weather permitting, 11 AM; Sept.–Apr., every 48 hours). When the Queen is in town, the guard and a regimental band parade through town to the castle gate; when Her Majesty is away, a drum-and-fife band takes over. It's advised to confirm (☎ 01753/868286) the exact schedule of the ceremony.

The devastating fire of November 1992, which started in the Queen's private chapel, totally gutted some of the State Apartments. Miraculously, hardly any works of art were lost. In fact, fragments of a 17th-century mural, done for Charles II by Antonio Verrio, surfaced during the renovation. Reopened to the public in December 1997 with grand fanfare, the castle has never looked more impressive. Costing a total of £37 million, phenomenal repair work has restored the **Grand Reception Room**, the **Green and Crimson Drawing Rooms**, and the **State and Octagonal Dining Rooms**. The ceiling of St. George's Hall, where the Queen gives state banquets, was completely destroyed—today, a new green oak roof, the largest hammer-beam roof to have been built in the 20th century, now looms magnificently over the 600-year-old hall. The private chapel of the Royal Family has also been redesigned, with a new stained-glass window commemorating the fire of 1992 and the restoration work that subsequently took place. All restored rooms, except the private chapel, are open to the public. Be aware that the State Apartments are sometime closed when the Queen is in residence; call ahead to check.

As you enter the castle, **Henry VIII's gateway** leads uphill into the wide castle precincts, where visitors are free to wander. Directly opposite the entrance is **St. George's Chapel.** Matched in its beauty only by that of King's College in Cambridge, this is the chapel where the Queen invests new knights at the colorful Order of the Garter ceremonies held in June. Here lie some of the most famous kings of England, beginning with Henry VI, and including Charles I, Henry VIII (Jane Seymour is the only one of his six wives buried here), and many others. One of the noblest buildings in England, the chapel was built in the 15th- and 16th-century Perpendicular style and features elegant stained-glass windows, a high, vaulted ceiling, and intricately carved choir stalls.

The Thames Valley

Harleston

Warwick
Leamington Spa
Stratford-upon-Avon

A425

A422

Lower Tysoe
Middle Tysoe
Upper Tysoe

Banbury

A43

OXFORDSHIRE

Chipping Norton

Bourton-on-the-Water

A424

A34

A421

A411

Weston-on-the-Green

A421

Woodstock (25)
Blenheim Palace (26) (27)
Bladon

A4260

A43

B

Oxford (13)—(24)

Burford

A40

Witney

A40

Isis

Stanton Harcourt Manor (31)

Cumnor

Great Milton (32)

A361

B4449

Thames

Kelmscott Manor (30)

A420

Abingdon

A4074

Dorchester-on-Thames (28)

Ev

4095

Faringdon

A38

VALE OF WHITE HORSE

A417

Wallingford

A329

(12)

B4508

Uffington (29)

Wantage

Thames

A40

Swindon

LAMBOURN DOWNS

A34[T]

M4

A34[T]

Map

Pangbourne

M4

Marlborough
Hungerford
Hungerford Newtown

Newbury

BERKSHIRE

A4

WILTSHIRE

A4

0 _____ 10 miles
0 _____ 15 km

N

Harlestone

35 Althorp

Great Brington

Northampton

A428

Castle Ashby

A509

10 miles

15 km

M1

A5

Milton Keynes

34 Woburn Abbey

GREAT BRITAIN

Leighton Buzzard

Dunstable

A41(T)

33 Waddesdon Manor

Aylesbury

A41(T)

BUCKINGHAMSHIRE

Cherwell

Amersham

Great Milton **32**

A40

M40

HILLS

Watford

Rickmansworth

Ewelme **11**

CHILTERN

High Wycombe

Beaconsfield

ord **12**

A329

A4130

Stonor Park **10**

B480

Marlow

A4155 **6**

Cookham

5 Cliveden

Burnam Beeches

A476

Nuffield

Henley 7

Sonning Common

A4074

A4155

Thames

A473

Hurley

A404

A4094

A4094

Maidenhead

Burnham

Slough

M4

Mapledurham House 9

B481

Thames

A4

Eton 2

ngbourne

A329

Caversham

8 Sonning-on-Thames

M4

1

Windsor

Heathrow Airport

Reading

4

Runnymede

Staines

IRE

Wokingham

A332

Windsor Great Park

A308

Thames

Shinfield

M3

3 Ascot

Windsor Castle

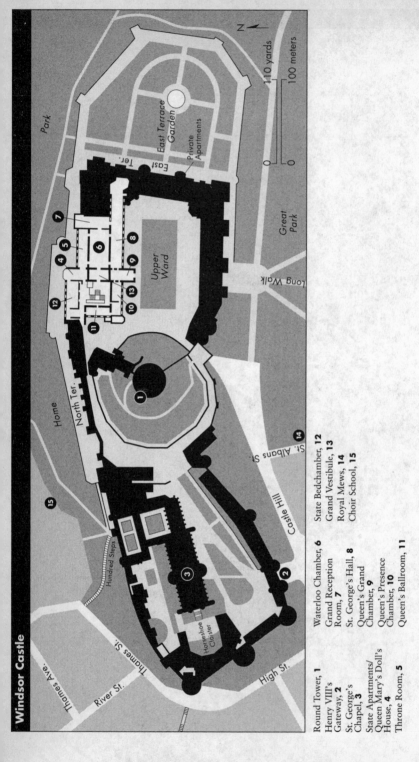

Round Tower, **1**
Henry VIII's Gateway, **2**
St. George's Chapel, **3**
State Apartments/ Queen Mary's Doll's House, **4**
Throne Room, **5**

Waterloo Chamber, **6**
Grand Reception Room, **7**
St. George's Hall, **8**
Queen's Grand Chamber, **9**
Queen's Presence Chamber, **10**
Queen's Ballroom, **11**

State Bedchamber, **12**
Grand Vestibule, **13**
Royal Mews, **14**
Choir School, **15**

The heraldic banners of the Knights of the Garter hang in the choir, giving it a richly medieval look. The ceremony in which the knights are installed as members of the order has been held here with much pageantry for more than five centuries. Note that St. George's Chapel is closed to the public on Sundays.

The **North Terrace** provides especially good views across the Thames to Eton College (☞ *below*), perhaps the most famous of Britain's exclusive "public" boys' schools. From the terrace, you enter the **State Apartments,** containing priceless furniture, including a magnificent Louis XVI bed; Gobelin tapestries; and paintings by Canaletto, Rubens, Van Dyck, Holbein, Dürer, and del Sarto. The high points of the tour are the **Throne Room** and the **Waterloo Chamber,** where Sir Thomas Lawrence's portraits of Napoléon's victorious foes line the walls. You can also see a collection of arms and armor, much of it exotic, and an exhibition of items from the **Queen's Collection of Master Drawings:** works by Leonardo da Vinci, plus 87 Holbein portraits, and many others. Some of these rooms may be closed to the public at any given time.

☾ **Queen Mary's Doll's House,** on display to the left of the entrance to the State Apartments, is a perfect doll-scale palace-within-a-palace. Electric lights work, the doors all have keys, the elevators are practical, and there is running water. There is even a library of Lilliputian-size books especially written by famous authors of the 1920s. Just outside the castle, on St. Albans Street, is the **Royal Mews,** where the royal horses are kept, with carriages, coaches, and splendid crimson and gold harnesses. The highlight is the Scottish State Coach. ☎ *01753/868286.* ▨ *£8.80 for the Precincts, the State Apartments, the Gallery, St. George's Chapel, and the Albert Memorial Chapel; Doll's House additional £1, or separately (including entry to the Precincts) £3.60; tickets are £1.10 less on Sun., when St. George's Chapel is closed.* ☉ *Mar.–Oct., daily 10–5:30 (last admission at 4); Nov.–Feb., daily 10–4 (last admission at 3).*

Only a small part of old Windsor—the settlement that grew up around the castle in the Middle Ages—has survived. Don't miss tiny Church Lane and Queen Charlotte Street, both narrow and cobbled, opposite the castle entrance. The venerable buildings of **Windsor Town** now house antiques shops and restaurants.

Windsor Great Park is the remains of an ancient royal hunting forest, stretching for some 8 mi (about 5,000 acres) south of Windsor Castle. Much of it is open to the public and can be explored by car or on foot. Focal points include the romantic and spectacular 3-mi **Long Walk**—designed by Charles II to join castle and park—**Frogmore House,** another royal residence, favored by Queen Victoria and her husband, Prince Albert, and the **Royal Mausoleum at Frogmore,** (where two famous royal couples are buried: inside, Victoria and Albert; outside, the Duke and Duchess of Windsor) open only a few days a year, in May and August, with pre-booked guided tours also possible on selected weekdays August–October; **Virginia Water,** a 2-mi-long lake; and the **Savill Garden,** which offers a huge variety of trees and shrubs. ▨ *Frogmore House,* ☎ *01753/868286.* ▨ *House £3, gardens and mausoleum £2 and £2.50.* ☉ *May, selected days only (check by phone), 10–7 (last admission 6); Aug., selected days only (check by phone), 11–5 (last admission 4). Savill Garden:* ▨ *Wick La., Englefield Green, Egham,* ☎ *01753/860222.* ▨ *£3.50.* ☉ *Mar.–Oct., daily 10–6; Nov.–Feb., daily 10–4.*

Parents of young children have almost as much fun as the kids at ☾ **Legoland,** an extensive theme park 2 mi outside Windsor designed along the lines of the original in Copenhagen and dedicated to the versatile Lego building brick. There to be enjoyed are a plethora of ingenious models as well as rides and various interactive activities. A lakeside picnic area, 150 acres of parkland and restaurants allow you to make a day of it. ⊠ *Winkfield Rd., Windsor,* ☎ *0990/040404.* ⊠ *Adults £15.* ☉ *Mar.–Sept., daily 10–6; first 3 wks Oct., weekends only 10–6; last weekend Oct., daily 10–6.*

Dining and Lodging

Most of Windsor's restaurants are uninspiring, so if you're not opting for a special meal at the two options below, head across the river to Eton (☞ *below*).

££££ ✕🖬 **Oakley Court.** Whimsically romantic and highly picturesque, this Victorian-era mock castle stands on expansive grounds beside the Thames, 3 mi west of Windsor. The main house is bristling with towers and spires and has been used in several films (including the *Rocky Horror Picture Show*); note, however, that half the rooms are in a modern annex. There is an excellent restaurant, the **Boulestin,** which serves French and English fare, such as filet of beef with Stilton mousse, and has a good wine list. Prince Charles has enjoyed the cuisine here. The brand new leisure center offers an indoor heated pool, sauna, steam room, and Jacuzzi. ⊠ *Windsor Rd., Water Oakley, Windsor, SL4 5UR,* ☎ *01753/609988,* 🖷 *01628/637011. 115 rooms with bath. Restaurant, sauna, putting green, croquet, exercise room, billiards, helipad. AE, DC, MC, V.*

£££ ✕🖬 **Sir Christopher Wren's House Hotel.** A private mansion built by the famous architect in 1676, this is an impressively sober house, its brick facade adorned with a white classical doorway and elegant sash windows. Inside, the entrance hall is 17th-century grand, with restoration of antique features complementing its fine design; the recent refurbishment brightened everything up a tad without destroying the period feel. Once you get into the Orangerie restaurant and the drawing room, however, the many faux-baroque frills and flounces may produce a wearing effect. The restaurant has a lovely riverside terrace, where cream teas are served on pleasant days. ⊠ *Thames St., SL4 1PX,* ☎ *01753/861354,* 🖷 *01753/860172. 40 rooms with bath. Restaurant, bar, café, meeting rooms. AE, DC, MC, V.*

The Arts

The **Windsor Festival** is usually held in early September or October, with events occasionally taking place in the castle itself.

Windsor's **Theatre Royal** (⊠ Thames St., ☎ 01753/853888), where productions have been staged for nearly 200 years, is one of Britain's leading provincial theaters. It puts on a range of plays and musicals throughout the year, including pantomime for the six weeks following Christmas.

Outdoor Activities and Sports

BICYCLING

Bikes and Rollerblades can be rented in Windsor at **Windsor Cycle Hire** (⊠ Alexandra Gardens, Alma Rd., ☎ 01753/830220).

Shopping

Windsor's shopping facilities have improved immeasurably since the opening of the **Windsor Royal Station** shopping center (Central Train Station, ☎ 0800/923–0017) in late 1997. Jaeger, Pied-a-Terre, and an outpost of the quintessential London department store, Liberty's, make it a pleasant alternative to the mayhem of central London. Most Windsor stores are open on Sunday, particularly those selling antiques along Peascod Street, High Street, and King Edward Court. The **Edinburgh**

Woollen Mill (⌂ 10 Castle Hill, ☎ 01753/855151) has a large range of Scottish knitwear, tartans, and tweeds, particularly for women. **Best of British** (⌂ 44 King Edward Ct., ☎ 01753/859929) has handmade items that are good for gifts

Eton

❷ *23 mi west of London, linked by a footbridge across the Thames to Windsor.*

Almost opposite Windsor Castle—which embodies the continuity of the royal tradition—a school was established that for centuries has been responsible for the upbringing of future leaders of the country. With its single main street leading from the river to the famous school, the town itself, with its old-fashioned charm, is a much quieter place than

★ Windsor. The splendid redbrick, Tudor-style buildings of **Eton College,** founded in 1440 by King Henry VI, border the north end of High Street; drivers are warned of "Boys Crossing." During the college semesters, the schoolboys are a distinctive sight, dressed in their pinstripe trousers, swallow-tailed coats, and stiff collars (top hats have not been worn by the boys since the '60s). The Gothic **Chapel** rivals St. George's at Windsor in both size and magnificence, and is both impressively austere and intimate. Beyond the cloisters are the school's playing fields where, according to the Duke of Wellington, the Battle of Waterloo was really won, since so many of his officers had learned discipline in their school days there. The **Museum of Eton Life** has displays on the school's history, and there are guided tours of the school and chapel. ⌂ *Brewhouse Yard,* ☎ *01753/671177.* ☐ *£2.50; £3.70 with tour.* ☺ *During term, daily 2–5; out of term, daily 10:30–4:30; guided tours Apr.–Sept., daily at 2:15 and 3:15.*

Dining

££ ✕ **The Cockpit.** Cockfighting once took place in the courtyard of this 500-year-old oak-beamed inn. Now a restaurant with an emphasis on Italian cuisine, its specialties include fresh fish. ⌂ *47–49 High St.,* ☎ *01753/860944. AE, DC, MC, V. Closed Mon. No lunch Tues.*

£ ✕ **Eton Wine Bar.** This is a pleasant place, near the bridge to Windsor and on Eton's Antiques Row. Sit on an old church pew and enjoy a fine English pie. ⌂ *82 High St.,* ☎ *01753/854921. AE, DC, MC, V.*

Shopping

Eton has a reputation for excellent, if pricey, antiques shops, most of them along the High Street. **Turk's Head Antiques** (⌂ 98 High St., ☎ 01753/863939) has jewelry, silver, and Victoriana.

Ascot

❸ *28 mi southwest from London; from Windsor, take A332 west 8 miles.*

Ascot is probably the most famous race meeting in the world—or certainly the one with the most impressive show of millinery. The Royal Meeting is usually held the third week in June (Tuesday to Friday), when over a quarter of a million race goers descend on the small town of Ascot to bet, sip champagne, and to see and, more importantly, be seen. Thursday is the most popular day for the Gold Cup, a race inaugurated in 1807, but each day offers top-class racing and people-watching opportunities. The Racecourse is divided into several Enclosures, the Royal Enclosure being the most famous and the most snooty. Entrance to the Royal Enclosure is limited to those who have applied in advance, and new members must be sponsored by two existing Royal Enclosure badge holders (who themselves must have attended Ascot eight times before). Morning dress—meaning tail coats, top hats, and striped pants—must be worn by gentlemen whereas hats are de rigeur for the ladies in the Royal Enclosure. The two main public enclosures, the Grandstand and the Silver Ring, offer great views and all the fun of the chase for less cash. The Course Enclosure costs £2 a head for entry. With around 100 bars and four large catering facilities, no one wants for food or drink.

Racing goes on year-round (except March) at England's largest racecourse. Diamond Day, the fourth Saturday in July, or the Ascot Festival, the last Saturday and Sunday in September, may be a little more low-key, but the racing remains some of the best in the world. During most of the year the Royal Enclosure becomes the Members' Enclosure and seats are readily bookable, although it is advised to phone ahead. Advance booking is advised for Royal Ascot (tickets are usually sold out months before) and other major race meets—make general inquires to the Sales Office, Ascot; for admission to the Royal Enclosure, write to Her Majesty's Representative, Ascot Office, St. James's Palace, London SW1 (☎ 0171/930–9882). Ascot is easily accessible from London: trains leave Waterloo on the half hour (trip time takes as long) and buses depart from Victoria Coach Station. ⊠ *Ascot Racecourse, Ascot, Berkshire SL5 7JN,* ☎ *01344/622211 (racecourse); 01344/876456 (credit card hot line).* 🎫 *Royal Enclosure £55, Grandstand £42, Silver Ring £10, Course Enclosure £2, reserved grandstand seats for Diamond Day and the Ascot Festival £5, all other race days general admission £2, with special enclosures £5–£40.*

Lodging

££££   🏨 **Berystede Country House Hotel.** A leafy driveway curves around to reveal the architectural madness of this Victorian-era hotel. With turrets and half-timbering, it is a magnificent neo-Gothic fantasy landed in traditional British countryside. Inside, every square inch pays homage to the culture of Ascot, with horse and jockey prints lining the walls. Most of the rooms in this Forte group hotel are pleasantly standard; a few are nothing short of extraordinary—if your winnings or losings on the racecourse are grand enough, one of the turret suites will see you celebrate—or commiserate, if things go the other way—in plenty of style. ⊠ *Bagshot Rd., Sunninghill, Ascot, Berkshire SL5 9JH,* ☎ *01344/623311,* 𝖥𝖠𝖷 *01344/872301. 90 rooms with bath, 4 suites. Restaurant, bar, pool, tennis court, croquet. AE, DC, MC, V.*

Runnymede

★ ❹   *5 mi southeast of Windsor on A308.*

A giant step in the history of democracy was taken at Runnymede, outside Egham. On this tiny island in the middle of the Thames, King John, under his barons' compulsion, signed the Magna Carta in 1215, affirming the individual's right to justice and liberty. On the wooded hillside, in a meadow given to the United States by Queen Elizabeth in 1965, stands a **memorial to President John F. Kennedy.** Nearby is another memorial, a classical temple in style, erected by the American Bar Association for the 750th anniversary of the signing.

Cliveden

❺   *26 mi west of London, 8 mi northwest of Windsor.*

In woods high above the River Thames, north of Windsor, this magnificent country mansion was made famous by the Astors, who had it rebuilt in the 1860s. For 250 years, Cliveden was one of the most important houses in England. Set amidst glorious rural river scenery, yet easily accessible from London, it attracted generations of eminent politicians and writers as houseguests. In the 1920s and '30s it was the setting for the Cliveden Set, the strongly conservative (not to say fascist) salon presided over by Nancy Astor, who—though she was an American, born in Danville, Virginia—was the first woman to sit in Parliament, in 1879. The house now belongs to the National Trust, which has leased it for use as a *very* exclusive hotel (☞ *below*). The public can visit the spectacular grounds and formal gardens that run down to bluffs overlooking the Thames, as well as three rooms in the west wing of the house. ☎ *01628/605069.* ☒ *Grounds £4.50; house £1 extra.* ☉ *Grounds Mar.–Oct., daily 11–6; Nov.–Dec., daily 11–4; house Apr.–Oct., Thurs. and Sun. 3–6; restaurant in the Orangery Apr.–Oct., Wed.–Sun. 11–5; Nov.–mid-Dec., weekends noon–2.*

Dining and Lodging

££££   ✕🖬 **Cliveden.** Cliveden has to be one of the grandest hotels in Britain—
★   and one of the most expensive. This is sophisticated luxury at its very best and a chance to experience the "Stately Houses" lifestyle in all its grandeur. There are 376 acres of magnificently tended gardens and parkland with wonderful river views. The interior is opulent in the extreme, featuring the Orkney Tapestries in the Great Hall; suits of armor; a library; a richly paneled staircase; endless paintings, mostly fine historic portraits; and room after room with beautifully molded plaster ceilings. The ultracomfortable bedrooms are named after the famous people who once stayed here—including the one used by Lady Astor herself (which costs £710 a night); a basic double costs £257 a night. There are two main restaurants—the **Terrace Dining Room,** grand, book-lined, with chandeliers, portraits, and splendid views through six enormous windows, and **Waldo's,** paneled, with palpable atmosphere and an award-winning chef—while the Walled Garden contains the **Conservatory,** offering Mediterranean-style light lunches which may be served around one of the two pools. ✉ *Taplow, near Maidenhead, SL6 0JF,* ☎ *01628/668561,* ℻ *01628/661837. 37 rooms with bath. 3 restaurants, indoor-outdoor pool, 3 tennis courts, health club, horseback riding, squash, boating. AE, DC, MC, V.*

"WIND IN THE WILLOWS" COUNTRY: TO AND FROM HENLEY

"Believe me, my young friend, there is nothing—absolutely nothing—half so much worth doing as simply messing about in boats. Simply messing," and you'll probably agree with Water Rat's opinion, voiced in Kenneth Grahame's classic *The Wind in the Willows,* if you do some of your own "messing-about" on this stretch of the Thames Valley, from Marlow to Wallingford. Boat-borne or by foot, you'll find here some of the most delightfully wooded scenery in the valley. On each bank are fine wooded hills, with spacious houses, greenhouses, flower beds, and clean lawns that stretch down to the water's edge. It was to Pangbourne, along this stretch of the river, that Grahame retired to write his beloved book. His illustrator, E. H. Shepard, used the great house at Mapledurham as the model for Toad Hall, and an elaborate Victorian boathouse, not far from Pangbourne, was immortalized in pen and ink as Rat's House. Most travelers enjoy a stay Thameside here because of the famed **Henley Royal Regatta.**

Marlow

❻   *30 mi west of London, 15 mi northwest of Windsor.*

Just inside the Buckinghamshire border, Marlow overflows with Thameside charm and is often overwhelmed by tourism on summer weekends.

Take particular note of its unusual suspension bridge, which William Tierney Clark built in the 1830s. Marlow has a number of striking old buildings, particularly the stylish, privately owned Georgian houses along Peter and West streets. In 1817, the Romantic poet Percy Bysshe Shelley stayed with friends at 67 West Street and then bought **Albion House** on the same street. His second wife, Mary, completed her Gothic novel *Frankenstein* here. **Marlow Place**, on Station Road, dates from 1721 and has been lived in by several princes of Wales.

Henley

❼ *7 mi southwest of Marlow on A4155, 8 mi north of Reading, and 36 mi west of central London.*

Mention Henley to Britons, and even those who have scarcely seen a boat will conjure up idyllic scenes of summer rowing. Indeed, Henley Royal Regatta, held in early July (usually July 3–7, but phone to confirm actual dates) each year on a long, straight stretch of the River Thames, has made the charming little riverside town—set in a broad valley between gentle hillsides just off A423—famous throughout the world. Competition in this event is between the best oarsmen from all over the world. Henley during Regatta Week is one of the high points of the social summer, rating with Ascot and Wimbledon as a sports event and a fashionable outing in one. Needless to say, for this time, book a room months in advance.

Townspeople launched the Henley Regatta in 1839, initiating the Grand Challenge Cup, the most famous of its many trophies. After 1851, when Prince Albert, Queen Victoria's consort, became its patron, it was known as the Royal Regatta. Oarsmen compete in crews of eight, four, or two, or as single scullers. For many of the spectators, however, the social side of the event is far more important. Elderly oarsmen wear brightly colored blazers and tiny caps; businesspeople entertain wealthy clients, and everyone admires the ladies' fashions. For more on the Henley Royal Regatta, *see* Outdoor Activities and Sports, *below.*

Another traditional event, in the third week of July, is **Swan-Upping,** which dates back 800 years. Most of the swans on the Thames are owned by the Queen. Swan-markers in Thames skiffs start from Sunbury-on-Thames, catching the new cygnets and marking their beaks to establish ownership. The Queen's Swan Keeper, dressed in scarlet livery, presides over this colorful ceremony, complete with festive banners.

Henley's many historic buildings, including one of Britain's oldest theaters, are all within a few minutes' walk. Half-timber Georgian cottages and inns abound. The mellow brick **Red Lion Hotel,** beside the bridge (☞ Dining and Lodging, *below*), has been the town's focal point for nearly 500 years. Kings, dukes, and writers have stayed here, including Charles I and James Boswell. The Duke of Marlborough used the hotel as a temporary base during the building of Blenheim Palace.

The 16th-century "checkerboard" tower of **St. Mary's Church** overlooks Henley's bridge on Hart Street. The building is made of alternating squares of local flint and white stone. If the church's rector is about, you can ask permission to climb to the top to take in the superb views up and down the river. The **Chantry House,** connected to the church by a gallery, was built in 1420 as a school for impoverished boys. It is an unspoiled example of the rare timber-frame design, with upper floors jutting out. ⊠ *Hart St.,* ☎ *01491/577062.* ▣ *Free.* ☉ *Church services or by appointment.*

Dining and Lodging

££   ✕ **Little Angel Inn.** This building just over Henley bridge dates from the 17th century and houses a traditional alehouse, an elegant conservatory restaurant, and a less expensive brasserie that overlooks Henley Cricket Club. The pub at the front serves a luxe bar menu. In the summer there is alfresco dining in the garden, where there are occasional barbecues. Daily specials may include fish and duck. ✉ *Remenham Lane, (¼ mi from Henley on A4130),* ☎ *01491/574165. AE, DC, MC, V. No dinner Sun. in winter.*

£££ ✕▣ **Red Lion.** This ivy-draped, redbrick, 16th-century hotel overlooks the river and the town bridge. During its 400-year history, guests have included King Charles I and Dr. Samuel Johnson, the 18th-century critic, poet, and lexicographer. An oak-beamed brasserie has recently been installed, with an all-day menu offering everything from a cappuccino to a three-course meal. ✉ *Hart St., RG9 2AR,* ☎ *01491/572161,* ﬀ *01491/410039. 26 rooms, 21 with bath. Restaurant. AE, MC, V.*

£££ ✕▣ **Stonor Arms.** Four miles north of Henley (by A423 on B480) lies one of the showpiece restaurants of the Thames region. Dating from the 18th century, the hotel's main lure is its popular and formal dining salon, also called the Stonor Arms. The food is as good to eat as it is to look at—local game, duck confit, lamb shanks with leek polenta—and there's a comprehensive wine list. A sister restaurant, Blades, is now also open and features two glass conservatories and a slightly less expensive menu. Rooms are comfortable and antiques-bedecked, if somewhat cramped. ✉ *Stonor,* ☎ *01491/638345,* ﬀ *01491/638863. 10 rooms with bath. AE, MC, V.*

££   ✕▣ **Flohr's.** Just a short walk from the town center, this small, elegant Georgian hotel has a good-quality but reasonably priced restaurant supervised by the owner, Gerd Flohr. The frequently changing menu offers traditional dishes such as roast beef and poached salmon, as well as more innovative choices. ✉ *15 Northfield End, RG9 2JG,* ☎ *01491/573412,* ﬀ *01491/579721. 9 rooms, 3 with bath or shower. Restaurant. MC, V.*

The Arts

Henley Festival (✉ Henley Festival, Festival Yard, 42 Bell St., Henley, RG9 2BG, ☎ 01491/411353) takes place during the week following the regatta each year. All kinds of open-air concerts and events are staged during this popular summer event.

Outdoor Activities and Sports

GOLF

At **Badgemore Park,** Henley-on-Thames (☎ 01491/573667), a parkland 18-hole course, visitors are welcome on weekdays, and on weekends by arrangement.

HENLEY ROYAL REGATTA

Henley Royal Regatta (☎ 01491/572153) takes place over five days at the beginning of July each year. A vast community of large tents goes up, especially along both sides of the unique straight stretch of river here known as Henley Reach (1 mi, 550 yards), and every surrounding field becomes a parking lot. The most prestigious place for spectators is the Stewards' Enclosure, but admission here is by invitation only and, however hot, men must wear jackets and ties—ladies in slacks are refused entry. For guest badges for the exclusive enclosure, write to (✉ Secretary, Henley Royal Regatta, Henley-on Thames, Oxfordshire RG9 2LY, ☎ 01491/572153). Fortunately, there is plenty of space on the public towpath from which to watch the early stages of the races.

En Route   Across the river, on the eastern side, follow the towpath north along the pleasant, shady banks to **Temple Island,** a tiny, privately owned island with trailing willows and a solitary house. This is where the regatta races start. On the south side of the town bridge, a riverside promenade passes **Mill Meadows,** where there are gardens and a pleasant picnic area. Along both stretches, the river is alive with boats of every shape and size, from luxury "gin palace" cabin cruisers to tiny rowboats.

Sonning-on-Thames

⑧   *5 mi south of Henley, 4 mi northeast of Reading.*

If put to the vote, many natives would choose Sonning-on-Thames as the quintessential Thames Valley village, despite there being nothing of outstanding historic note here. However, its old bridge charmingly spans the Thames, and the Georgian-fronted houses, the ancient mill that is mentioned in the *Domesday Book,* and the black, white, and yellow cottages make it an all too perfect Thameside village.

Dining and Lodging

££££   ✕ **L'Ortolan.** Long known as one of the more serious kitchens in England, this place is famed for its nouvelle dishes, every bit as interesting as the glassed-in conservatory setting (ask for this, not the main dining room, when booking). Try the lobster ravioli, *suprême de canard sauvage* (wild duck breast roasted and flamed in Armagnac), and the *Assiette chocoloatière* (no less than eight different examples of the chocolatier's art). This elegant country restaurant lies just over 4 mi south of Reading, on A327. ✉ *The Old Vicarage, Church La., Shinfield,* ☎ *0118/988–3783. AE, DC, MC, V. Closed Mon., last 2 wks in Feb. and Aug. No dinner Sun.*

★

£££   🏨 **Great House.** A former 16th-century inn, this hotel commands superb views over the river and has extensive gardens—the roses are lovely—leading to a half mile of moorings. Diners can choose between two restaurants, while overnight guests have a choice of period or modern rooms. Sumptuously furnished and wood paneled, the best rooms lie in the original Great House, a redbrick building standing apart from the main hotel. The inferior rooms are either over an adjacent Thai restaurant or are cramped quarters with dismal views set downwind from a large dairy farm! Book the best—or none at all. ✉ *Thames St., RG4 0UT,* ☎ *0118/969–2277,* 🖷 *0118/944–1296. 36 rooms with bath or shower. 2 restaurants, bar, dock. AE, DC, MC, V.*

Mapledurham House

★ **⑨**   *5 mi southwest of Henley.*

This section of the river, from Caversham to Mapledurham, inspired Kenneth Grahame's children's book, *The Wind in the Willows,* which began as a bedtime story for Grahame's son Alastair while the Grahames were living at Pangbourne. Some of E. F. Shepherd's charming illustrations are of specific sites along the river—none more fabled than this redbrick Elizabethan mansion, bristling with tall chimneys, mullioned windows, and battlements, which became the inspiration for Shepherd's vision of Toad Hall. Mapledurham is still home to the Eyston family, and so has kept a warm, friendly atmosphere along with family portraits, magnificent oak staircases, and Tudor plasterwork ceilings. Here you can see a 15th-century water mill—the last working grain mill on the Thames. On summer weekends, the house can be reached in true *Wind-in-the-Willows* fashion by boat from Caversham Promenade in Reading. The boat leaves at 2 PM, and travel time is about 45 minutes; for complete information, call ☎ 01189/481088. The estate also has 11 self-catering cottages (some more than 300 years old) available for rent, for £215–£505 a week. ✉ *Mapledurham, near Reading,* ☎ *0118/972–3350.* 🎫 *House and mill £5; house only £4; grounds and mill £3.* ☉ *Easter–Sept., weekends only 2:30–5.*

Stonor Park

⑩ *5 mi northwest of Henley on A4130/B480.*

Home to the Catholic Stonor family for more than 800 years, this ancestral estate is lost in the network of leafy country lanes on the fringes of the Chiltern Hills. A medieval mansion with a Georgian facade, it stands in a wooded deer park. Mass has been celebrated in its tiny chapel since the Middle Ages, and there is an exhibition of the life and work of the Jesuit Edmund Campion, who took shelter here in 1581 before his martyrdom. ✉ *Stonor,* ☎ *01491/638587.* 🎫 *£4; gardens and chapel only £2.20.* ☉ *April to Sept. but hrs are very restricted and subject to change, so check locally.*

Ewelme

★ **⑪** *10 mi northwest of Henley off A4130, 6 mi west of Stonor Park.*

One of England's prettiest and most unspoiled villages lies near the town of Benson, in Oxfordshire. Its picture-book almshouses, church, and school—one of the oldest in Britain—huddle close together, as they did more than 500 years ago. The church shelters the carved alabaster tomb of Alice, duchess of Suffolk, the granddaughter of England's greatest medieval poet, Geoffrey Chaucer. Jerome K. Jerome, author of the humorous book *Three Men in a Boat,* describing a 19th-century Thameside vacation, is also buried here.

Wallingford

⑫ *13 mi southeast of Oxford on A4074, 2 mi west of Ewelme.*

The busy marketplace of this typical riverside market town is bordered by a town hall, built in 1670, and an Italianate corn exchange, now a theater and cinema. Market day is Friday.

OXFORD

⑬ *60 mi northwest of London.*

Coming to England without seeing Oxford is like going to Paris and not visiting the Louvre. Oxford is home to England's most celebrated university, and it has been a center of learning since the 12th century. When arriving, try to stop on one of the low hills that surround the city and look at the skyline. If you are fortunate, and the sun is shining, the towers, spires, turrets and pinnacles will look like a scene from a medieval fairy tale. Here stretched out in front of you is Oxford, the home of erudition and scholarship and—of famed Oxford marmalade. From here, time appears to have passed the city by and it almost looks like it did 200 years, or even longer, ago. First appearances are deceptive, however. The last 50 years have seen changes in Oxford that have revolutionized not only the town, but the very basis of university life itself. Today, the rarefied air of academia and the pace of industry compete with one another, Oxford now being home to two major industrial complexes: the Rover car factory and the Pressed Steel works. In the city center, "town and gown" merge, as modern stores sit side by side with centuries-old colleges and their peaceful quadrangles.

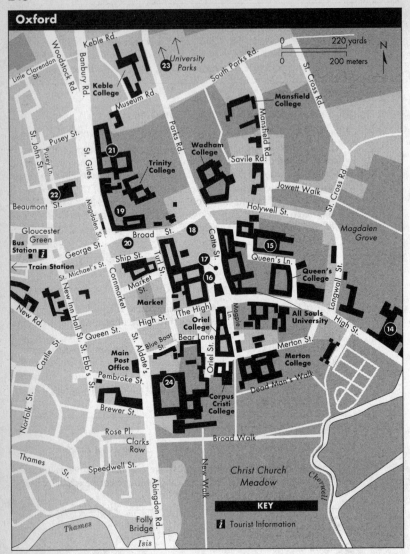

Oxford

Ashmolean, **22**

Balliol College, **19**

Christ Church
College, **24**

Magdalen College, **14**

New College, **15**

Oxford Story
Exhibition, **20**

Radcliffe
Camera/Bodleian
Library, **17**

Sheldonian
Theatre, **18**

St. John's College, **21**

University
Church, **16**

University
Museum, **23**

Exploring Oxford

Oxford University is not one unified campus, but a collection of many colleges and buildings, new as well as old, scattered across the city. All together there are 40 different colleges where undergraduates live and study. Most of the college grounds and magnificent dining halls and chapels are open to visitors, though the opening times (displayed at the entrance lodges) vary greatly. Some colleges are open only in the afternoons during university semesters, when the undergraduates are in residence; access is often restricted to the chapels and dining rooms (called halls) and sometimes the libraries, too. All are closed during exams, usually from mid-April to late June, when the May Balls are held. By far the best way to gain access is to join a walking tour led by an official Blue Badge guide. These two-hour tours leave up to five times daily from the Tourist Information Centre. As you walk through this scholastic wonderland, try to spot as many Gothic gargoyles as you can.

A Good Walk

The most picturesque approach to the town is from the east, over Magdalen (pronounced Maudlin) Bridge. Among the ancient honey-color buildings and elegant spires can be seen the 15th-century tower of Magdalen College, famous for its May Day carol service. Magdalen Bridge leads you directly into broad, gently curving High Street, flanked by ancient colleges, including **Magdalen College** ⑭ itself. Its quadrangle is a quiet area enclosed by ancient vaulted cloisters covered with wisteria—although it was probably never *that* quiet when alumni Oscar Wilde and Dudley Moore were present. If you wish to rent a punt, head for Magdalen Tower; if not, head across the street to count the varieties of roses in the Botanic Garden, where Sebastian Flyte got to know Charles Ryder in *Brideshead Revisited*. Continue down High Street to take a look at All Souls College, possibly the most beautiful college in town. Halfway up High Street, the 14th-century tower of the **University Church** (St. Mary's) ⑯ offers Oxford's preeminent lookout point—after seeing the town's layout as presented to the cruising bird, return to earth and cross the street to view the 17th-century dome of the magnificent **Radcliffe Camera** ⑰, which seems to rival London's St. Paul's. Although Oxford's earliest colleges were founded in the 11th century, succeeding ages enhanced the city's splendor by a good deal of reconstruction, often sacrificing medieval almshouses and friaries for magnificent buildings of later eras, such as the Camera and the next eye-knocker: Christopher Wren's **Sheldonian Theatre** ⑱. Step past its iron gates and those fabulous megabusts of the Roman emperors to check out the schedule for evening concerts here. Continue on wide, straight Broad Street (book lovers will want to make a detour to Blackwell's), continue on to St. Giles and take a glance into **Balliol College** ⑲—this is the "Yale" of Oxford and has one of its most time-stained quadrangles (literally—you can view the scorch marks of Bloody Mary's martyrs, who were burned alive here in the 16th century). Continue north along St. Giles to the famed Eagle and Child pub, where J. R. R. Tolkien often met his friends, the "Inklings." After lunch, check out either the lovely gardens of **St. John's College** ㉑ or the **Ashmolean** ㉒, Oxford's finest art and archeology museum, on Beaumont Street. After viewing Oliver Cromwell's death mask you may be up for a spot of tea—just across the way, dip into the Randolph, the town's finest hotel, for a reviving cuppa and to view the enchanting Puginesque Gothic interior. Late afternoon should lure you south, down Cornmarket, passing **Carfax Tower** to St. Aldate's and **Christ Church College** ㉔, Oxford's snobbiest college, with its vast Tom Quad, 800-year-old chapel, medieval dining hall, and scholarly Picture Gallery. Note that if you're arriving at the train station for an Oxford day outing, you might wish to start at the Ashmolean Museum above and work your way backward.

Sights to See

㉒ Ashmolean Museum. Britain's oldest public museum, the Ashmolean has among its priceless collections (all university owned) many Egyptian, Greek, and Roman artifacts uncovered during archaeological expeditions conducted by the university. Michelangelo drawings, antique silver, and a wealth of important paintings are also on display. ⊠ *Beaumont St.,* ☎ *01865/278000.* ⓢ *Free.* ☉ *Tues.–Sat. 10–4, Sun. 2–4.*

⑲ Balliol College. Prestigious Balliol (1263) has wooden doors between its inner and outer quadrangles that still bear scorch marks from 1555 and 1556, when during the reign of Mary ("Bloody Mary"), Bishops Latimer and Ridley and Archbishop Cranmer were burned alive on huge pyres in Broad Street for their Protestant beliefs. A small cross on the roadway marks the actual spot. The three men are also commemorated by the tall **Martyrs' Memorial** in St. Giles. ⊠ ⊠ *St. Giles and Broad Sts.* ☉ ☉ *Daily 2–5.*

Carfax Tower. Any side trip into the southern part of town and Christ Church College should begin in Cornmarket, Oxford's main shopping street. As you pass through Carfax, where four roads meet, you will see the tower of **St. Martin's Church,** where Shakespeare once stood as godfather for William Davenant, who himself became a playwright. Every 15 minutes, little mechanical figures mark the passage of time on the tower front. For a small fee, you can climb up the dark stairwell for a good view of the town center.

㉔ Christ Church College. Built in 1546, Christ Church is referred to by its members as "The House." This is the site of Oxford's largest quadrangle, "Tom Quad," named after the huge bell (6¼ tons) that hangs in the gate tower. The vaulted, 800-year-old chapel in one corner has been Oxford's cathedral since the time of Henry VIII. The college's medieval dining hall contains portraits of many famous alumni, including John Wesley, William Penn, and 14 of Britain's prime ministers. Lewis Carroll was a teacher of mathematics here for many years; a shop opposite the meadows in St. Aldate's was the inspiration for the shop in *Through the Looking Glass.* ⊠ *St. Aldate's.* ⓢ *£3.* ☉ *Mon.–Sat. 9:30–4:30, Sun. 2–4:30.*

Christ Church Picture Gallery. In Canterbury Quadrangle, this connoisseur's delight exhibits paintings by Tintoretto, Veronese, and Van Dyck. Drawings in the 2,000-strong collection are shown on a changing basis, including works by Leonardo, Michelangelo, Rubens, Dürer, and other Old Masters. ⊠ *Deanery Gardens,* ☎ *01865/276172.* ⓢ *£1.* ☉ *Mon.–Sat. 10:30–1 and 2–4:30, Sun. 2–4:30 (later in summer).*

★ **⑭ Magdalen College.** Founded in 1458, with an impressive main quadrangle and a supremely monastic air, Magdalen is one of the richest and most impressive of Oxford's colleges. A walk around the Deer Park and along Addison's Walk will cause you to envy the members of the college for the privilege of living here. They have included such diverse people as Cardinal Wolsey, Gibbon, and Oscar Wilde. ⓢ *Summer £2, winter free.* ☉ *Daily 2–6.*

At the foot of **Magdalen Bridge** (⊠ High St.) you can rent a punt (a shallow-bottomed boat that is poled slowly up the river) for £8–£10 an hour, plus a £25 refundable deposit. You may wish, like many an Oxford student, to spend a summer afternoon punting—while dangling your champagne bottle in the water to keep it cool.

⑮ **New College.** Up Queen's Lane you come to New College, founded in 1379, with its extensive gardens overlooking part of the medieval city wall. This was the home of the celebrated Dr. Spooner, father of "spoonerisms"—sentences whose transposed opening sounds of words create comic new meanings, as in his comment to a wayward student, "You have hissed your mystery lectures and tasted a whole worm."

⑳ **Oxford Story Exhibition.** Set in a converted warehouse, this imaginative presentation makes 800 years of Oxford life come alive with models, sounds, and smells. Visitors ride through the exhibition in small cars shaped like medieval students' desks. ⊠ *6 Broad St.,* ☎ *01865/ 790055.* ▨ *£4.95.* ☉ *Daily 10–4:30, with seasonal variations.*

★ ⑰ **Radcliffe Camera/Bodleian Library.** The most spectacular building in Oxford has one of the largest domes in Britain. Built in 1737–1749 by James Gibbs, it is the Italian Baroque style transplanted to Oxfordshire. The Camera contains part of the **Bodleian Library**'s collection, which was begun in 1602 and has grown to more than 2 million volumes. Part of the library can be visited on a tour; otherwise, the general public can visit only the Divinity School, a superbly vaulted room with constantly changing exhibitions of manuscripts and rare books. ☎ *01865/277165 for information on library tour.* ▨ *£3.50 library tour.* ☉ *Weekdays at 10:30, 11:30, 2, and 3; Sat. at 10:30 and 11:30; Nov.–mid-Mar. not weekday mornings; closed for degree ceremonies; children under 14 not admitted.*

⑱ **Sheldonian Theatre.** This fabulously ornate theater is where the impressive graduation ceremonies are held, conducted entirely in Latin. Built in 1663, it was the first building designed by Sir Christopher Wren. Semicircular has pillars, balconies, and an elaborately painted ceiling. Outside, stone pillars are topped by the massive stone heads of 18 Roman emperors, sculpted in the 1970s to replace the originals that had been rendered featureless by air pollution. ⊠ *Broad St.,* ☎ *01865/277299.* ▨ *£1.50.* ☉ *Mon.–Sat. 10–12:45 and 2–4:30; mid-Nov.–Feb., closes at 4; closed for 10 days at Christmas and Easter; also closed for degree ceremonies and events. Call ahead to check.*

㉑ **St. John's College.** For a quiet pause, step inside St. John's (1555), to see its huge gardens, among the city's loveliest. Nearby is the Eagle and Child pub (⊠ St. Giles), with its narrow interior leading to a conservatory and small terrace—this was the meeting place of J. R. R. Tolkien and his friends, the "Inklings." ☉ *Daily 1 PM to dusk.*

★ **Trout.** Punting on the River Cherwell has long been a favorite pastime at Oxford. More than a century ago, Lewis Carroll took three children on a river picnic. "We rowed up to Godstow, and had tea beside a haystack," he told a friend of his at Christchurch College; "I told them the fairy tale of Alice's adventures in Wonderland." There are no more haystacks around, but today, you can stop at the creeper-covered, historic, and still excellent Thameside pub on the northern edge of Oxford (2 mi north of the city center). Its interior, fitted out with sporting prints by "Phiz" and engravings of Oxford by Turner, is remarkable in itself. Of course, there's a corner devoted to Carroll, and a Morse bar (with Morse memorabilia), as the TV inspector often drank here, and his creator still does. ⊠ *Godstow,* ☎ *01865/302071.*

⑯ **University Church** The 14th-century tower of the St. Mary the Virgin provides a splendid panoramic view of the city's skyline—the pinnacles, towers, domes, and spires spanning every architectural style since the 11th century. The interior is crowded with 700 years' worth of funeral monuments, including one belonging to Amy Robsart, the wife of Dudley, Elizabeth I's favorite. ⊠ *High St.,* ☎ *01865/243806.* ⊠ *Tower £1.50.* ⊙ *Tower daily 9–5 (until 4:30 in winter).*

❷❸ University Museum. Twenty minutes north of the city center, this is one of the world's great natural history museums, housed in a massive Victorian Gothic building. Among the myriad exhibits here is the head and left foot of the dodo, a large, flightless bird that may have become extinct in the 17th century but found immortality when Lewis Carroll cast himself in the role of the dodo in his book. ⊠ *Park Rd.,* ☎ *01865/ 272950.* ⊠ *Free.* ⊙ *Mon.–Sat. noon–5.*

Dining and Lodging

£££ ✕ **Restaurant Elizabeth.** These small, elegant dining rooms in a 16th-century bishop's palace have wonderful views overlooking Christ Church College. Salmon rolls, roast lamb, duck à l'orange, and crème brûlée are among the Spanish chef's specialties. ⊠ *82 St. Aldate's,* ☎ *01865/242230. AE, DC, MC, V. Closed Mon.*

££ ✕ **Gee's.** This brasserie in a conservatory, formerly a florist's shop, is
★   just north of the town center. The constantly changing menu features French and English dishes with seasonal variations, and the place is popular with both town and gown. ⊠ *61 Banbury Rd.,* ☎ *01865/ 553540. AE, MC, V.*

£–££ ✕ **Cherwell Boathouse.** About a mile north of town, this is an ideal spot for a meal in a riverside setting. The menus change weekly but may include local pheasant with red cabbage and garlic jus or three fillets of fish with lobster sauce. It's a very friendly spot, so be prepared to linger. There is a good set menu available. ⊠ *Bardwell Rd. (off Banbury Rd.),* ☎ *01865/52746. AE, DC, MC, V. Closed Mon. No dinner Sun.*

£ ✕ **Browns.** So popular is this restaurant with both undergraduates and local people that you may have to wait for a table. The wide choice of informal dishes includes steak-mushroom-and-Guinness pie and hot chicken salad. Potted palms and mirrors give the otherwise plain rooms a cheery atmosphere. ⊠ *5–11 Woodstock Rd.,* ☎ *01865/511995. Reservations not accepted. AE, MC, V.*

£ ✕ **Perch.** Close to the river just outside town, the thatched Perch attracts connoisseurs who come to enjoy its wide lawn, unusual sandwiches, and cooing doves. It makes a pleasant place to arrive on foot from Walton Street. ⊠ *Binsey,* ☎ *01865/240386. AE, DC, MC, V. No dinner Sun.*

££££ ▥ **Old Parsonage.** This is a discovery. It's rare to find an attractive coun-
★   try-house hotel, with stone gables and mullioned windows, smack in the middle of a city. The Old Parsonage was established in 1660 but completely restored and refurbished in 1991. Open fires, comfortable rooms, a roof garden, and immaculate service make this a hotel to remember—and return to. The Parsonage Bar serves simple but excellent food. ⊠ *1 Banbury Rd., OX2 6NN,* ☎ *01865/310210,* ℻ *01865/ 311262. 30 rooms with bath. Restaurant. AE, DC, MC, V.*

££££ ▥ **The Randolph.** Oxford's only large, central hotel is very much part of the local landscape. A ravishingly beautiful example of the 19th-century neo-Gothic style, it is just across from the Ashmolean, and it is a regular place for undergraduates to be entertained for tea or drinks in the Fellows Bar by their visiting families. Scenes from PBS's Inspector Morse *Mystery* series and the film *Shadowlands* were shot here. Floorboards in this historic hotel can be *too* historic; in some rooms, squeaky ceilings can lead to noise-filled nights—voice your concerns when booking. ⊠ *Beaumont St., OX1 2LN,* ☎ *01865/247481,* ℻ *01865/791678. 109 rooms with bath. Restaurant, bar, parking. AE, DC, MC, V.*

£ ▥ **Cotswold House.** This small, modern guest house, about 2 mi north on the Banbury Road (A4260), is pleasantly furnished with modern pieces. The bedrooms are comfortable and of a good size, and all have

TVs and fridges. The owners are ever ready to help with sightseeing questions. ✉ *363 Banbury Rd., OX2 7PL,* ☎ FAX *01865/310558. 7 rooms with shower. No credit cards. Closed 10 days in Feb.*

The Arts

FESTIVALS AND MUSIC

Music at Oxford is a highly acclaimed series of weekend classical concerts performed mid-September–June in such illustrious surroundings as Christ Church Cathedral and Sir Christopher Wren's Sheldonian Theatre. The music is performed by musicians and orchestras from all over the world, as well as from Oxford and Cambridge. Information and tickets are available from the Oxford Playhouse (✉ Beaumont St., ☎ 01865/798600). **Oxford Coffee Concerts** is a program of chamber concerts performed on Sundays at the Holywell Music Room, Holywell Street, Oxford. String quartets, piano trios, and soloists present a variety of baroque and classical pieces in this venerable old hall, dating from 1748. Tickets are reasonably priced and are available from Blackwell's Music Shop, Holywell Street (☎ 01865/261384). During the summer, Blenheim Palace (☞ *below;* ☎ *01993/811091*) is occasionally the venue for classical concerts, sometimes combined with fireworks displays. Ticket prices range from £18 to £25.

THEATERS

The Apollo (✉ George St., ☎ 01865/244544) is Oxford's main theater. It stages a varied program of plays, opera, ballet, pantomime, and concerts, and it is the recognized second home of the Welsh National Opera and the Glyndebourne Touring Opera. The **Oxford Playhouse** (✉ Beaumont St., ☎ 01865/798600) is an altogether more serious theater, presenting classical and modern drama productions appropriate for a university city. During term time, undergraduate productions are often given in the colleges or local halls. In the summer, there are usually some outdoor performances in ancient quadrangles or college gardens. Look for announcement posters.

Outdoor Activities and Sports

BICYCLING

Bikes can be rented in Oxford at **Denton's** (✉ 294 Banbury Rd., ☎ 01865/553859) and **Pennyfarthing** (✉ 5 George St., ☎ 01865/249368).

SPECTATOR SPORTS

★ **Oxford's Eights Week** is held at the end of May. From mid-afternoon to early evening, Wednesday–Saturday, men and women from the university's colleges compete to be "Head of the River." Because the river is too narrow and twisting for eights to race side-by-side, they set off, 13 at a time, one behind another. Each boat tries to catch and bump the one in front. Spectators can watch all the way.

Oxford University Cricket Club competes against leading county teams and also has a game each summer against the major foreign team visiting Britain. The massive trees surrounding its grounds in the University Parks make it one of the loveliest clubs in England.

Shopping

Cornmarket and Queen streets are lined with small shops, while the Clarendon and Westgate centers, which lead off them, have branches of several nationally known stores. **Shepherd & Woodward** (✉ 109 High St., ☎ 01865/249491) is a traditional tailor and specialist in university gowns, ties, and other garb. The **Oxford Gallery** (✉ 23 High St., ☎ 01865/242731) carries prints in limited editions, as well as a wide stock of contemporary British crafts. Specialty stores are gathered around Golden Cross, a cobbled courtyard with pretty window boxes, between Cornmarket and the excellent covered food market.

The **University of Oxford Shop** (⌂ 106 High St., ☎ 01865/247414) sells clothing, ceramic, and ties, all emblazoned with university crests. The **Tea House** (⌂ Golden Cross, ☎ 01865/728838) specializes in teapots and tea. **Blackwell's** (⌂ Broad St., ☎ 01865/792792) is one of the world's great bookstores. More for browsing than serious shopping is the **Covered Market** (⌂ off High St.) where handmade jewelry, colorful knitted sweaters, and huge bunches of flowers are sold alongside venison, pheasants, and French cheeses.

ON THE ROAD TO BLENHEIM PALACE

The River Thames takes on a new graciousness as it flows along the borders of Oxfordshire for 71 mi, and with each league it increases in size and importance. Three tributaries swell the river as it passes through the landscape: the Windrush, the Evenlode, and the Cherwell. Tucked among the hills and dales are England's largest palace, the best country restaurant, one of its most Edenic villages, and the last Rothschild estate.

Woodstock

★ ㉕ *8 mi north of Oxford on A44.*

Woodstock, whose trim streets are lined with handsome 17th- and 18th-century houses, is the perfect little English town. Moreover, it stands almost on the grounds of England's grandest and most imposing country house, **Blenheim Palace,** (☞ *below*). During the summer Woodstock's ancient streets are clogged with tour buses and the lofty halls of Blenheim echo with the clamor of voices from all parts of the world. On a quiet fall or spring afternoon, however, the village of Woodstock is a sublime experience: a mellowed 18th-century church and town hall mark the picturesque central square, while along its back streets, you'll find flower-bedecked houses and quiet lanes right out of a 19th-century etching. A public bus route runs (usually every half-hour) from Oxford to Woodstock making it a good overnight alternative to Oxford.

Dining and Lodging

£££–££££ ✕⌸ **The Bear.** Legend has it that this is where Richard Burton finally
★ popped the question to Elizabeth Taylor. The five-centuries old Bear is an archetypal English coaching-inn—Tudoresque wood paneling, beamed ceilings, wattle-and-daub walls, and dancing fireplaces in winter. The guest rooms, overlooking either a quiet churchyard or the charming town square, have carved oak furnishings. The duplex suites have timbered loft-balconies and gargantuan four-posters. The restaurant is a bit large for true elegance, but it's just the sort of place to order a top-flight hot Stilton soufflé. ⌂ *Park St., OX20 1SZ,* ☎ *01993/ 811511,* ℻ *01993/813380. 41 rooms with bath, 3 suites. Restaurant, bar, free parking. AE, DC, MC, V.*

£££–££££ ✕⌸ **The Feathers.** Possibly one of the most stylish small hotels out-
★ side London, this place attracts honeymooners and film stars alike. The rather expensive restaurant is petite but sumptuous, serving roast wood pigeon, grilled turbot, or honey roast duckling. Upstairs, the decidedly cozy guest rooms fill a 17th-century building that has been thoughtfully restored. One side of the hotel is near a busy intersection, so ask for a quiet room. ⌂ *Market St., OX20 1SX,* ☎ *01993/812291,* ℻ *01993/813158. 15 rooms with bath. Restaurant. AE, DC, MC, V.*

£ ⌸ **Blenheim Guest House and Tea Rooms.** The Cinderella of all British
★ hotels, this place stands in one of the most magical corners in England— the quiet village cul-de-sac that leads to the back gates of imperial Blenheim Palace. It's a modest, small guest house, three stories tall, with its facade still bearing a Victorian-era painted banner that states "Views

and Postcards of Blenheim," and a storefront tearoom. You half expect Anthony Trollope to walk through the front door. The unassuming guest rooms have modern furnishings, but the Marlborough room is unique—after all, its bathroom offers a view of Blenheim. ⊠ *17 Park St., Woodstock, OX20 1SJ,* ☎ *01993/811467,* ⨳ *01993/811030. 6 rooms with shower. AE, DC, MC, V.*

Blenheim Palace

★ ❷ *8 mi north of Oxford on A44.*

The first thing to be said about Blenheim Palace is that it isn't actually a palace at all, at least not in the sense that royalty live in it. But so far as splendor, scale, and opulence are concerned, the building and surrounding parkland—all 2,700 acres of it—are the equal of just about any real palace in the world, Versailles (perhaps) excepted. Built by Sir John Vanbrugh in the early 1700s, Blenheim was given by Queen Anne and the nation to General John Churchill, first duke of Marlborough. The exterior is mind-boggling, comprising huge columns, enormous pediments, and upturned obelisks, all designed in the most spectacular English Baroque manner. Inside, the house is imposing and lavish—more akin to a monument than an abode. The Red Salon—on whose walls hang the incomparable sittings of the 4th and 9th dukes and their families painted by Sir Joshua Reynolds and John Singer Sargent—could possibly be the most richly opulent room in England. In most rooms, great family portraits look down at sumptuous furniture and immense pieces of silver. For some, however, the most memorable room is the small, low-ceiling chamber where Winston Churchill (his father was the younger brother of the then-duke), was born in 1874.

Sir Winston once wrote that the unique beauty of Blenheim lay in its perfect adaptation of an English parkland to an Italian palace. Indeed, the grounds, the work of Capability Brown, 18th-century England's most gifted landscape gardener, are arguably the best example of the "cunningly natural" park in the country. Brown declared that his object at Blenheim was to "make the Thames look like a small stream compared with the winding Danube." At points, he almost succeeds—the scale of these grounds must be seen to be believed. Stick around for dusk, when enormous flocks of sheep are let loose to become living mowers for the magnificent lawns. Tucked away here is the little summerhouse where Winston Churchill proposed to his future wife, Clementine. A short detour away to the neighboring hamlet of Bladon (☞ *below*) will lead you to the grave site of the great man. Leave Blenheim by the back gates, which will deposit you in the unforgettably lovely village of Woodstock (☞ *above*). ⊠ *Woodstock,* ☎ *01993/ 811091.* ⌦ *Palace £8; park £1.* ☉ *Palace mid-Mar.–Oct., daily 10:30– 4:45; park daily 9–4:45; full schedule of special events, fairs, and concerts throughout yr. Palace has cafeteria.*

Bladon

❷ *2 mi south of Woodstock on A4095; 6 mi north of Oxford.*

A small, tree-lined churchyard holds the burial place of Sir Winston Churchill, his grave the more impressive for its simplicity.

Dorchester-on-Thames

❷ *9 mi south of Oxford, 7 mi southeast of Abingdon.*

An important center in Saxon times, when it was the seat of a bishopric, Dorchester deserves a visit chiefly for its ancient **abbey.** In addition to secluded cloisters and gardens, this one has a spacious church (1170), with traceried medieval windows. The east window was restored in 1966 by the American Friends of the Abbey in memory of Sir Winston Churchill. ☎ *Free.* ☉ *Summer, daily 8:30–7, winter 8:30– dusk, except during services.*

Dorchester, founded by the Romans, is a charming village with timber houses, thatched cottages, and ancient inns. Crossing the Thames at Day's Lock and turning left at Little Wittenham takes you on a pleasant walk past the remains of the village's Iron Age settlements.

Lodging

££ 🏠 **George Hotel.** Overlooking Dorchester Abbey, this 500-year-old hotel was built as a coaching inn—there's still an old coach parked outside— and it retains whitewashed walls, exposed beams, and log fires. Each room has an individual style and two have four-poster beds. ✉ *25 High St., OX10 7HH,* ☎ *01865/340404,* 🖷 *01865/341620. 18 rooms with bath. Restaurant. AE, MC, V.*

Uffington and the Vale of the White Horse

㉙ *18 mi southwest of Oxford, 9 mi northeast of Swindon.*

Stretching up into the foothills of the Berkshire Downs between Swindon and Oxford is a wide, fertile plain known as the Vale of the White Horse. To reach it from Oxford, follow A420, then B4508 to the village of Uffington. Here, cut into the chalk hillside, is the huge figure of a white horse. Until recently, some historians believed that it might have been carved to commemorate King Alfred's victory over the Danes in 871, while others dated it back to the Iron Age, around 750 BC. More current research suggests that it is at least 1,000 years older, created at the beginning of the second millennium BC. **Dragon Hill,** below, is equally mysterious. An unlikely legend suggests that St. George slew his dragon there. Uffington was the home of Tom Brown, fictional hero of the Victorian classic *Tom Brown's School Days.* The novel's author, Thomas Hughes, was born in Uffington in 1822.

Kelmscott Manor

㉚ *20 mi west of Oxford, 7 mi north of Uffington.*

Oxford has been a major focus for Britain's writers and artists for centuries, so the area's estates and country villages are alive with literary associations. Kelmscott Manor was the home of the Victorian artist, writer, and socialist William Morris (1834–1896). It was at this handsome, 400-year-old gabled stone house that Morris and Dante Gabriel Rossetti established the revolutionary Arts and Crafts movement more than a century ago. Even the most perfunctory look at the surrounding countryside will reveal the principal sources of Morris's inspiration: some nearby tree clusters look as if they grew straight out of one of his textile designs, whereas, of course, the reverse is true. The house is now owned by Oxford University and is a unique monument to the "Brotherhood." Morris died at Kelmscott and is buried in the local churchyard. ☎ *01367/252486.* ☎ *£6.* ☉ *Apr.–Sept., Wed. 11–1 and 2–5, 3rd Sat. of each month 2–5.*

Stanton Harcourt Manor

㉛ *9 mi west of Oxford.*

Reached through twisting lanes, Stanton Harcourt Manor lies nestled among streams, small lakes, and woods. It was here, in 1718, that Alexander Pope translated Homer's *Iliad.* But the manor—stuffed with silver, pictures, and antique furniture—is worth a visit apart from this association; it has a complete medieval kitchen and 12 acres of gardens. ✉ *Stanton Harcourt,* ☎ *01865/881928.* ✱ *House and garden £4; garden only £2.50.* ☉ *Easter–Sept., every other Thurs. and Sun., and bank holiday Mon.; check locally for opening times, which vary from year to year.*

Dining

£ ✕ **Bear and Ragged Staff.** Found in Cumnor, 3 mi east of Stanton Har-
★   court and 4½ mi southwest of Oxford via A420, this excellent spot is a 17th-century inn—the name comes from the medieval insignia of the Warwick family—and has long been a popular haunt of Oxford town and gown. The food is traditional British, with such fare as roast duck, and venison in a wine sauce. ✉ *28 Appleton Rd., Cumnor,* ☎ *01865/862329. AE, MC, V.*

Great Milton

③ *7 mi east of Oxford.*

With attractive thatched cottages built of local stone and a single street about a mile long with wide grass verges, this is another stop on the literary pilgrim's route, for the poet John Milton, author of *Paradise Lost* (1667), was married in the local church. The church also has an unusual collection of old musical instruments.

Dining and Lodging

££££ ✕⊞ **Le Manoir aux Quat' Saisons.** This 15th- to 16th-century manor
★   house has held its position as one of Britain's leading restaurants for years, thanks to master-chef, Raymond Blanc and his award-winning French culinary skills. Take your cue from the duke at the neighboring table—this is the place to lord it up: begin with mousse of Jerusalem artichokes interwoven with slivers of leek, move on to a Norfolk squab with a truffle sabayon, then end up with the dessert pudding, the *Feuilleté de Poire William rotie au gingembre et citron vert.* Aux Quat' Saisons is both very popular and *very* expensive (well above our normal range), though the set menus (£32 at lunchtime, except Sunday) can make it almost reasonable. There are luxe guest rooms upstairs. ✉ *Church Rd., OX44 7PD,* ☎ *01844/278881, 800/845–4274 in the U.S.,* 📠 *01844/278847. 19 rooms with bath. Restaurant, pool, tennis court. AE, DC, MC, V.*

Waddesdon Manor

③ *20 mi northeast of Oxford.*

Many of the regal residences built by the Rothschild family throughout Europe are gone now, but Waddesdon Manor remains in all its splendor. A vision of the 19th century at its most sumptuous, it was built in 1880–89 by G. H. Destailleur for Baron Ferdinand de Rothschild in the style of a French chateau. Furnished with Savonnerie carpets, Sèvres porcelain, furniture made by Riesener for Marie Antoinette, and numerous paintings by Rubens, Watteau, Gainsborough, and Reynolds, the mansion recently underwent a top-to-bottom renovation, thanks to Jacob Rothschild, the current head of the English branch of the family. There is a pleasant restaurant in the house and a summerhouse café on the grounds. ✉ *Waddesdon, on the A41 near Aylesbury,* ☎ *01296/651226.* ✱ *£9.* ☉ *House: late Mar.–late Oct., Thurs.–Sun. (and Wed. July–Aug.) 11–4; gardens late Mar.–late Oct., Thurs.–Sun. 11–4 .*

Woburn Abbey

★ ☺ ㉞ *10 mi northeast of Waddesdon.*

The ancestral residence of the Duke of Bedford, Woburn Abbey is a Palladian pile embellished. The dukes embellished the house with Grand Tour treasures and Old Master paintings, including 20 Canalettos, which practically wallpaper the crimson dining salon—indubitably one of the most sumptuous rooms in England. In addition, the grounds house a safari park and an antiques center with 50 dealers and a small restaurant. To get to Woburn from London, head north on N1; to get there from Oxford, head for Milton Keynes, the nearest large town to the house, on A5. ⊠ *Woburn,* ☎ *01525/290666.* ▣ *£7.50.* ⊙ *Late March–early Nov., Mon.–Sat. 11–4, Sun. 11–5.*

Althorp

㉟ *27 mi northwest of Woburn Abbey.*

Deep in the heart of Northamptonshire—one of the loveliest of English counties—sits Althorp, the ancestral home of the Spencers, the family who gave us Lady Diana. Here, set on a tiny island within the estate park (designed by Capability Brown in the 18th century) is the final resting place of the young girl who grew up to become Princess of Wales. The house has room after room of Van Dycks, Reynoldses, and Romneys, all portraits of the Spencers going back 500 years, and an entry hall that Nikolaus Pevsner called "the noblest Georgian room in the country." Earl Spencer has opened a new museum devoted to the Princess of Wales. Tickets must be booked far in advance. Althorp is 6 mi northwest of Northampton, on the Rugby Road leading from Northampton; a bus, No. 62 or No. X61 usually runs that route past the house. Northampton (☎ 01604/22677 for the tourist office) has both a bus and a train station. On the west side of the estate park is Great Brington, the neighboring village where the Spencer family crypt can be found in the church of St. Mary the Virgin. ⊠ *Great Brington,* ☎ *House, 01604/770107; advance tickets 01604/770107.* ▣ *£9.50.* ⊙ *July–Aug., daily 10–5.*

THAMES VALLEY A TO Z

Arriving and Departing

By Bus
City Link (☎ 01865/785400) runs a regular London–Oxford service (1 hr, 40 mins), with departures every 15–30 minutes from London's Victoria Coach Station, Marble Arch, and Gloucester Place. A day round-trip costs £7. Stagecoach Oxford Tube (01865/772250) also runs a 24-hr coach service to Oxford from London, starting at Grosvenor Gardens, Victoria. **London Link** (☎ 0118/958–1358) has a regular London–Reading shuttle, and service from Heathrow and Gatwick airports to Oxford. The **Bee Line** (☎ 0118/958–1358), also Reading-based, serves the smaller towns of Berkshire.

By Car
The M4 and M40 radiate west from London, bringing Oxford (57 mi) and Reading (42 mi) within an hour's drive, except in rush hour.

By Train

British Rail serves the region from London's Paddington Station (☎ 0345/484950) with fast trains to the main towns and a reliable commuter service. There's also hourly service to Oxford. Travel time is 1 hour.

Getting Around

By Bus

The **Oxford Bus Company** (☎ 01865/785400) offers a one-day ticket and a seven-day "Freedom" ticket, for unlimited bus travel within Oxford. The Oxford Bus Company and other local bus services, such as **Thames Transit** (☎ 01865/772250), link the towns between Oxford and Henley with services to Heathrow Airport and London.

By Car

Although the roads are good, this wealthy section of the commuter belt has surprisingly heavy traffic, even on the smaller roads. Parking in town can be a problem, too, so allow plenty of time.

By Train

For local timetables, call ☎ 0345/484950.

Contacts and Resources

Car Rentals

Oxford: Europcar Interrent (✉ Shell Petrol Station, Hartford Motors, Seacourt Tower, Botley, ☎ 01865/246373); **Hertz** (✉ City Motors Ltd., The Roundabout, Woodstock Rd., ☎ 01865/319972). **Windsor: Windsorian** (✉ A. A. Clark, 72–74 Arthur Rd., ☎ 01753/856419).

Guided Tours

ORIENTATION

Guide Friday (☎ 01865/790522) runs guided, open-bus tours, mid-March–November, of Windsor, £6; and Oxford, £8.

Spires and Shires (✉ 40 Kendal Crescent, Oxford OX2 8NG, ☎ 01865/513998) arranges "Morse Tours of Oxford" visiting various locations frequented by television's detective Inspector Morse. Spires and Shires has a range of other tours around the city, all student-led, which give a real insight into university life, and it also has tours to Blenheim Palace.

Themed walking tours, including "William Morris Tour" and "Ghost Tour," leave several times daily from outside **Oxford's tourist office** in Gloucester Green (£4). Call for details (☎ 01865/726871).

RIVER TOURS

The ideal way to see the Thames region is from the water; summertime trips range from 30 minutes to all day. **Hobbs and Sons** (☎ 01491/572035) covers the Henley Reach and also rents boats from Station Road, Henley-on-Thames. **Salter Brothers** (✉ Folly Bridge, Oxford, ☎ 01865/243421) runs daily steamer cruises, mid-May to mid-September from Windsor, Oxford, Abingdon, Henley, Marlow, and Reading. **Thames River Cruises** (☎ 0118/948–1088) conducts outings from Caversham Bridge, Reading, Easter–September. **French Brothers** (☎ 01753/851900) operates river trips from the Promenade, Windsor, and from Runnymede, as far as Hampton Court.

Hiking and Walking

The **Countryside Commission** (✉ John Dower House, Crescent Pl., Cheltenham, Gloucestershire GL50 3RA, ☎ 01242/521381) has been working for years on the Thames paths and offers publications about them. Write the Countryside Commission Postal Sales (✉ Box 124,

Walgrave, Northampton NN6 9TL, or call the number above). The **Rambler's Association** also publishes an excellent book on the subject, *The Thames Walk*, by David Sharp, £3.95 from the Rambler's Association (✉ 1 Wandsworth Rd., London SW8 2XX, ☎ 0171/582–6878), a guide to the whole length of the river, from Greenwich to Gloucestershire, with detailed maps.

Travel Agencies

Thomas Cook (✉ 5 Queen St., Oxford, ☎ 01865/240441). **Thomas Cook, Windsor** (✉ King Edward Ct., Windsor, ☎ 01753/831828).

Visitor Information

Henley (✉ Town Hall, ☎ 01491/578034). **Marlow** (✉ 31 High St., ☎ 01628/483597). **Oxford** (✉ The Old School, Gloucester Green, ☎ 01865/726871). **Windsor** (✉ 24 High St., ☎ 01753/743900). **Woodstock** (✉ Hensington Rd., ☎ 01993/811038).

8 Shakespeare Country

*Stratford-upon-Avon
and Environs*

*Lovers of Shakespeare, and even those
with only a passing acquaintance with
the Bard, cannot resist the lure of the
place where he grew up, toiled and—
after a career in London—died.
Stratford-upon-Avon is the main show,
of course, but beyond lies Warwickshire,
a time-hallowed land of great houses—
Warwick, Charlecote Park, Baddesley
Clinton—and tranquil villages. As you
approach Anne Hathaway's cottage,
you can't help but wonder if Master
Shakespeare composed one of his
immortal sonnets while strolling
this very path.*

Updated by
Lucy Hawking

I F IT WEREN'T FOR THE BARD, it is doubtful whether Stratford-upon-Avon would merit more than a footnote on the tourist track. But the unstoppable momentum of the Shakespeare juggernaut has made it a must. Because of its associations with Shakespeare, Stratford has taken immense care to preserve its ancient buildings, making it in many ways a perfect specimen of a four-centuries-old provincial town. Stratford is also home to the Royal Shakespeare Theatre, where thespians continue to pay their finest tribute to the Bard. Stratford is the southern nexus of the ancient county of Warwickshire. With its sleepy villages, thatched-roof cottages, and solitary farmhouses, it was the birthplace of the image of Britain that has been spread over the breadth of the world by the works of Shakespeare. This is, quintessentially, the realm of the yeoman, the wooded land of Arden, the home of the prosperous tradesman and the wealthy merchant, the region where landowners still pasture deer as they have done for the last 900 years.

Beautiful, but not conspicuous in its beauty, Warwick's landscape is studded with a rich selection of historic sites. Four of England's most memorable abodes are here: Anne Hathaway's house; Charlecote, a grand Elizabethan manor house and park, where, legend has it, Shakespeare was caught poaching deer; Baddesley Clinton, probably the most perfect example of late medieval domestic architecture in England; and Compton Wynyates, everyone's dream of a Tudor mansion. Other treasure houses are here: Ragley Hall, Coughton Court, and Broughton Castle, brimming with splendid art treasures, would be worth viewing even if they were empty, as they represent some of the greatest examples of English architecture. Then, just a few miles away, is "medieval England in stone"—Warwick Castle, which, with its magnificent machicolations and picturesque parapets, provides a glimpse into England's turbulent history.

The core and center of Warwickshire is, of course, Stratford. The town's historic monuments, as well as charting and celebrating Shakespeare's achievements, give a thrilling insight into life in the England of late medieval, Tudor, and Elizabethan times. Pride of place goes to the five properties administered by the Shakespeare Birthplace Trust: Shakespeare's Henley Street birthplace, the New Place/Nash's House site, Hall's Croft, Anne Hathaway's Cottage, and Mary Arden's House. These not only give us a picture of Shakespeare as writer and man of wealth, status, and property, they also help trace the social pattern of Shakespeare's family, following its rise from quite humble beginnings to a position of eminence through the generations.

Despite the press of the thousands who come to pay their respects, and the sometimes ruthless commercialization perpetrated by the huge Shakespeare industry, it's worth it, especially if you attend a stage production by the Royal Shakespeare Company, whose high standards and mastery of the dramatic arts have never been affected by the hype of the heritage industry. If the hustle and bustle get too much, follow the Avon as it wends its sleepy way through meadows and small villages and discover the countryside that surrounds the Bard's hometown.

Pleasures and Pastimes

The Shakespearean Theater

The Royal Shakespeare Theatre is home to the Royal Shakespeare Company, arguably the finest repertory troupe in the world and long the backbone of the theatrical life of the country. The company's annual season runs from November through August; usually, five Shakespearean plays are offered. The theater, designed by Elizabeth Scott in 1932 to replace an earlier one that burned, was quickly dubbed a "factory for Shakespeare" because of its modern utilitarian aspect. Here, on this celebrated Stratford stage, the Bard's plays have made the reputations of generations of actors (and broken not a few), have been staged as archaeological reconstructions and science fiction, and have seen women playing Hamlet and men playing Rosalind. However Shakespeare's plays are reshaped by directors and actors, they continue to reveal new facets of some eternal truth about humanity.

Dining

Although Stratford has little in the way of high-class dining establishments, the town is peppered with reasonably priced bistros and unpretentious restaurants offering a broad, international cuisine. For gourmet standards, find one of the better hotels, whose kitchens have drawn some of the foremost chefs from London and beyond. Warwick and Kenilworth have their share of excellent eateries, ideal for a midday lunch or a more substantial evening meal, while the countryside boasts a fine range of atmospheric old pubs in which meals are prepared to a fine standard.

CATEGORY	COST*
££££	over £50
£££	£30–£50
££	£20–£30
£	under £20

per person, including first course, main course, dessert, and VAT; excluding drinks

Lodging

Stratford holds the highest concentration of lodgings in the area. Here, you can find all levels of accommodation to fit every pocket, and for the most part, they are maintained to the highest standards. The best establishments are the older, centrally located ones, often with fine period architecture, and mostly owned by national chains. Be sure to book ahead whenever possible. Most hotels offer discounted two- and three-day packages. Outside town, there are some top-notch country hotels, where discreet but attentive service is guaranteed—at very fancy prices. At the other end of the scale, almost every village has a gnarled old inn with rooms available at very reasonable rates.

CATEGORY	COST*
££££	over £150
£££	£80–£150
££	£60–£80
£	under £60

All prices are for two people sharing a double room, including service, breakfast, and VAT.

Shopping

Stratford has more than its fair share of tourist tat, often dressed up to appeal to day-tripping souvenir hunters. That said, there are some good-quality items to be found, generally in the established shops specializing in silver, jewelry, and china. For bargains, check out the Friday market. Beware of antiques dealers, however. You will find lower prices in Warwick and in the villages scattered around the area, but even here genuine bargains are rare.

Walking

This part of England offers glorious, gentle countryside, with many of the local houses surrounded by parkland. Even Stratford, not usually associated with physical pursuits, can be the base for easy walks along the River Avon. The Stratford-upon-Avon Canal is bordered by a tow-path that offers unlimited opportunity to escape the throng. Pick up a leaflet on the Avon Valley walk from the town's tourist office.

Exploring Shakespeare Country

Stratford-upon-Avon is well suited as an exploring base. Many of the tiny villages of the region boast legends connected with the Bard, as well as the beautiful architecture dating from his time. Complement-ing these humble hamlets, and often in the midst of them, is an im-pressive gathering of country houses, each of which requires a good half day to explore and is easily reachable from Stratford. To the north lie two magnificent castles, Warwick and Kenilworth.

Numbers in the text correspond to numbers in the margin and on the Shakespeare Country and Stratford-upon-Avon maps.

Great Itineraries

Stratford-upon-Avon will be the lead destination for most travelers—as a small city, it's ideal for either day visits or as a convenient base from which to explore Shakespeare Country. Don't try to cram too much into too short a time, however. An open-top bus tour is a good, pain-less way to get an overview of what the town has to offer. Unless you're planning to venture beyond Stratford, you can rely on public trans-port from London or one of the other main transport centers. To see most of the sights outside the town, a car is best. If you're just focus-ing on a few places, inquire at the stately houses or regional tourist of-fices about taxis and back-road bus services.

IF YOU HAVE 2 DAYS

Stratford-upon-Avon ① deserves at least a full day and a drama-packed night—that is, if you wish to catch a performance of the Bard's works at the Royal Shakespeare Theatre on the banks of the Avon. Among the attractions, five historic properties are must-sees: three are in town—**Shakespeare's Birthplace** ② and the **Shakespeare Centre,** on Henley Street, home of the Shakespeare Birthplace Trust, the **Nash's House** ④ property, and **Hall's Croft** ⑦—while the others, **Anne Hath-away's Cottage** ⑧ and **Mary Arden's House** ⑪, are just a few minutes out of town. If you want to spend two days in Stratford and wish to enjoy these attractions (and many other sights) in a more leisurely man-ner, follow the self-guiding Town Heritage Trail or the black-and-gold signposts that direct you to the historic landmarks. After your Strat-ford sojourn, spend the next day touring selected sights in Shakespeare Country, including the mansions of **Baddesley Clinton** ⑭, **Charlecote Park** ⑰, and **Compton Wynyates** ⑲. In between, take in some of the minor villages in the vicinity, ideal for a spot of lunch or simply a river-side stroll. Spend your second night back in Stratford, or in one of the inns along the rural way.

IF YOU HAVE 4 DAYS

After two days spent touring the august abodes of **Stratford-upon-Avon** ① and the Shakespeare-linked attractions of the immediate vicin-ity—including **Henley-in-Arden** ⑫, the setting for *As You Like It*—you will be ready for a complete change of scene. In your remaining time, make sure you dedicate a couple of mornings to visiting two or three of the stately houses within easy driving distance of the town. On the way, plan your route along minor roads to take in some of the off-the-beaten-track hamlets seemingly suspended in time. Nearest of these, and fetchingly picturesque, is **Welford-on-Avon** ㉑, hugging the river as it loops west out from Stratford. A couple of miles farther west is

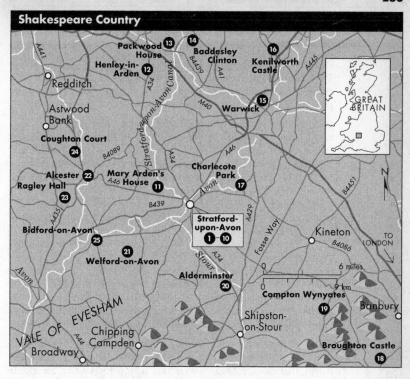

Bidford-on-Avon ㉕, "drunken Bidford" as portrayed in the doggerel attributed to Shakespeare. A short distance north, the village of **Alcester** ㉒ beckons, a charming one-horse town on either side of which lie two of the area's most notable country houses, the Palladian **Ragley Hall** ㉓ and the Elizabethan **Coughton Court** ㉔, both surrounded by acres of inviting parkland. After spending your first night based in Stratford, plan for your second in ⊞ **Warwick** ⑮, devoting the next morning to exploring one of the crowning glories of England's medieval castles. Although dominated by this imposing bastion, the town has other, lower-key attractions worth an hour or two, especially if you're traveling with kids. If castles are your thing, you should also make time to see **Kenilworth Castle** ⑯, a short drive north, whose red sandstone ruins are redolent of royal pageantry. South of Stratford, ⊞ **Alderminster** ⑳, the largest of another cluster of villages well worth driving through, makes a suitable night stop and is en route to the magnificent **Broughton Castle** ⑱ and **Compton Wynyates** ⑲, both of which are among the most memorable sights in Shakespeare Country.

When to Tour Shakespeare Country

Schedule your tour here, if possible, to avoid weekends and school holidays, and time your visits to the main Shakespeare shrines for the early morning, to see them at their least frenetic. One of the high points of Stratford's calendar is the Shakespeare Birthday Celebrations, usually on the weekend nearest to April 23 (☞ Festivals, *below*). If you choose to be here during this time, hotel reservations throughout the area covered in this chapter should be made as early as you possibly can. Warwick Castle, too, usually brims with coach parties, and you should plan to beat the rush. Elsewhere, you can be more flexible, though some of the country properties also fill up quickly on weekends. A number of these close for the winter.

STRATFORD-UPON-AVON

❶ *37 mi southeast of Birmingham, 102 mi northwest of London.*

Under the swarming busloads of visitors from every part of the globe, Strat-forde—to use the old Saxon name, which means "a ford over a river"—in fact, has hung on to its original character as a charming English market town on the banks of the slow-flowing River Avon.

Still, it is Shakespeare who counts. Born in a half-timber early 16th-century building in the center of Stratford on April 23, 1564, Shakespeare was buried in Holy Trinity Church after he had died (on his 52nd birthday) in a more imposing house at New Place. Although he spent much of his life in London, where, of course, he became a leading figure of the Elizabethan theater, the world still associates him with "Shakespeare's Avon." Here, in the years between his birth and 1587, he played as a young lad, attended the local grammar school, and married Anne Hathaway; here he returned to the town a man of prosperity. Today, you can see his birthplace on Henley Street; his burial place (and baptismal record) in Holy Trinity Church; Anne Hathaway's cottage; his mother's home at Wilmcote; New Place and the neighboring Nash's House, home of Shakespeare's granddaughter; and Hall's Croft, home of the Stratford physician who married the Bard's daughter. Whether or not their connections to Shakespeare are historically valid, these sites reveal Elizabethan England at its loveliest.

Then, of course, there is the theater, a sturdy, brick-built structure opened in 1932 and home of the Royal Shakespeare Company. Make the Royal Shakespeare Theatre your real reason for visiting Stratford: productions here are unrivaled.

Stratford-upon-Avon is a fascinating town, so take Antonio's advice (*Twelfth Night,* Act 3, scene 3) and "beguile the time, and feed your knowledge with viewing the town." By the 16th century, it was already a prosperous market town with thriving guilds and industries. Its characteristic half-timber houses from this era have been preserved over the centuries, and they are set off by the charm of later architecture, such as the elegant Georgian storefronts on Bridge Street, with their 18th-century porticoes and arched doorways. By 1769, the town's literary preeminence was confirmed by a three-day festival commemorating Shakespeare, attended and supported by the great actor David Garrick. Since then, Stratford's flame has been shining ever more brightly, yet the town is far from being a museum piece; it has adapted itself well to the rising tide of visitors. Though full of souvenir shops—every back lane seems to have been converted into a shopping mall, with boutiques selling everything from sweaters to china models of Anne Hathaway's Cottage—Stratford isn't overly strident in its search for a quick buck.

Basing yourself in Stratford itself, you will be best placed to attend evening theater performances—although, of course, Stratford can be done as a day trip (☞ Getting Around *in* Shakespeare Country A to Z, *below*)— and also take full advantage of those hours at the beginning and end of each day when the coach parties are absent.

The main places of Shakespearean interest are run by the **Shakespeare Birthplace Trust.** They all have similar opening times, and you can buy a combination ticket to the five properties or pay separate entry fees if you want to visit only one or two. ☎ *01789/204016 for further information on any of the Trust properties.* 🎫 *Joint ticket £8.50.* ☉ *Shakespeare's Birthplace and Anne Hathaway's Cottage: mid-Mar.–mid-Oct., Mon.–Sat. 9–5, Sun. 9:30–5; mid-Oct.–mid-Mar., Mon.–Sat. 9:30–*

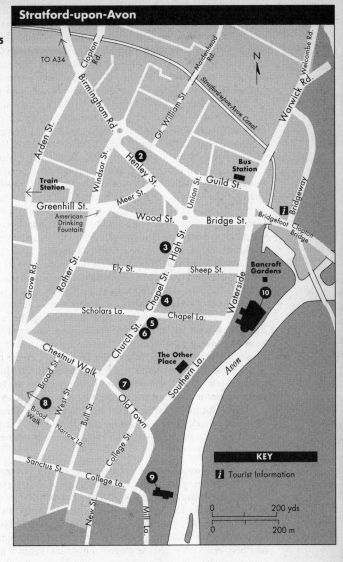

4, Sun. 10–4. *Nash's House, Hall's Croft, and Mary Arden's House: mid-Mar.–mid-Oct., Mon.–Sat. 9:30–5, Sun. 10–5; mid-Oct.–mid-Mar., 10–4, Sun. 10:30–4. Last entry 30 mins before closing for these five sights.*

The town is easily manageable for a walking tour. Most of the sights are grouped around Henley Street (off the roundabout as you come in on the A3400 Birmingham road), High Street, and Waterside, which skirts the public gardens through which the River Avon flows. Bridge Street and parallel Sheep Street are Stratford's main thoroughfares, and site of most of the banks, shops, and eating places. The town's **tourist office** lies at Bridgefoot, between the canal and the river.

A Good Walk

You can almost sense the Bard's presence when you view his birthplace, his school desk, his baptismal record, and his grave. To begin at the beginning, pay your respects, just as Sir Walter Scott and Carlyle once did, at **Shakespeare's Birthplace** ② on Henley Street. Elizabethan antiques and theater memorabilia (authentic, that is—the "lantern by which Friar Laurence discovered Romeo and Juliet at the tomb" was retired long ago) are on view. Right next door is the **Shakespeare Centre,** which has an impressive library. Then head east down Henley Street to the old city center and the corner of Bridge and High streets where you'll find the **Tourist Information Centre,** once the home of Judith Shakespeare, the poet's daughter. Take High Street to the right, passing several of Stratford's half-timbered buildings, the most magnificent of which is **Harvard House** ③, with beautiful twin gables and a hanging iron sign; at the nearby corner of Sheep Street is a stone bust of the Bard mounted on the north front of the Town Hall. Where High Street becomes Chapel Street, one block down on the left, is the timber-and-daub **Nash's House** ④, home of the Bard's granddaughter. On Chapel Street is the Shakespeare Hotel—its five gables make one of the longest Elizabethan facades extant. For lunch, you might repair to its elegant David Garrick restaurant. Continue south—where Chapel Street becomes Church Street are several buildings, seen on the left, that were old when Shakespeare was young: the **Guild Chapel** ⑤ and the timbered almshouses (notice the high chimneys that carried sparks safely above the once thatched roofs), and the **Guildhall** ⑥—Shakespeare's school—dating from 1416–18. A left turn at the end of Church Street leads to Old Town and to **Hall's Croft** ⑦, an impressive Tudor residence, once address of the poet's daughter. Detour now, taking the footpath from Evesham Place 1 mi northwest to the country hamlet of Shottery and **Anne Hathaway's Cottage** ⑧. After viewing this stunningly romantic house, stroll back to the **Holy Trinity Church** ⑨, by the banks of the Avon. Here is Shakespeare's tomb *and* the north aisle font where he was christened. Twilight—and your performance at the **Royal Shakespeare Theatre** ⑩—may be approaching now, so head over to Southern Lane. Opt for dinner at the theater restaurant or toast the Bard at the nearby Black Swan—known as the "Dirty Duck" and Stratford's most famed theater pub—with an evening aperitif in its river garden.

Sights to See

★ ⑧   **Anne Hathaway's Cottage.** The most perfectly picturesque of the Shakespeare Trust properties is in the village of Shottery, on the western outskirts of Stratford. This was the family home of the woman Shakespeare married in 1582, in what was evidently a shotgun wedding. The "cottage," actually a substantial farmhouse, has latticed windows and a grand thatch roof; inside, there is period furniture, including the "second best bed" left by Shakespeare to his wife. Set in a garden (now planted with herbs and flowers mentioned in the Bard's plays), it is one of the loveliest spots in Shakespeare Country. Although there is regular bus service from Stratford, the best way to get here is to walk (there are two main footpaths, one via Greenhill Street by the railroad bridge, the other leaving from Holy Trinity Church up Old Town and Chestnut Walk), especially in late spring when the hawthorns and apple trees are in blossom. ✉ *£3.50; Shakespeare Trust joint ticket,* ☞ *above.* ☉ *Mid-Mar.–mid-Oct., Mon.–Sat. 9–5, Sun. 9:30–5; mid-Oct.–mid-Mar., Mon.–Sat. 9:30–4, Sun. 10–4; last entry 30 mins before closing.*

Bancroft Gardens. Between the Royal Shakespeare Theatre and Clopton Bridge lie these well-tended expanses of lawns and flower beds—ideal for a picnic, a leisurely riverside stroll, or an hour's perusal of your pocket Shakespeare. The swans gliding gracefully along the river are permanent residents, coexisting happily with the pleasure craft plying the waters of the river and the nearby Stratford-upon-Avon Canal. The centerpiece of the gardens (incidentally, Bancroft is not a proper name but refers to the "croft on the banks") is the Gower Memorial statue, designed in 1888 by Lord Gower, and adorned with bronze figures of Hamlet, Lady Macbeth, Falstaff, and Prince Hal—symbols of philosophy, tragedy, comedy, and history, respectively.

⑤ Guild Chapel. Opposite the site of New Place, on the corner of Chapel Lane and Church Street, the Guild Chapel is the noble centerpiece of Stratford's Guild buildings, including the Guildhall, the Grammar School, and the almshouses—all structures well known to Shakespeare. The chapel is an ancient building rebuilt in the late Perpendicular style in the first half of the 15th century, thanks to the largesse of Hugh Clopton. The otherwise plain interior features fragments of a remarkable medieval fresco of the Last Judgment. The chapel is presently used for occasional functions and the bell, also given by Sir Clopton, still rings with the peal that once told Shakespeare the time of day. ⊠ *Chapel La.* 🎟 *Free.* ⊙ *Daily 9–5.*

⑥ Guildhall. Next to the Guild Chapel on Church Street you'll find the Guildhall, occupied by the picturesque **King Edward's Grammar School** (☎ 01789/293351), which Shakespeare probably attended as a boy and which is still used as a school. On the first floor is the Guildhall proper: it was here that traveling acting companies came to perform, and many historians believe that it was after seeing the troupe known as the Earl of Leicester's Men in 1587 that Shakespeare got the acting bug and set off for London. Upstairs is the Elizabethan classroom in which the Bard is reputed to have learned "little Latin and less Greek." A brass plate at its far end records the traditional position of Master Will's seat. The conjunction of church and school here may have an echo in *Twelfth Night* (Act 3, scene 2): "Cross-gartered? Most villainously; like a pedant that keeps a school i' the church." Today, the classroom is still used by students, so visits may be made by prior arrangement only, and are confined to after-school hours or vacation time.

Immediately beyond the Guildhall on Church Street lies a delightfully picturesque row of timber-and-daub **almshouses**, built to accommodate the poor by the Guild of the Holy Cross in the early 15th century, and still serving as housing for pensioners.

⑦ Hall's Croft. On Old Town, at the end of Church Street, not far from Holy Trinity Church, you will see this impressive residence, one of the finest surviving Tudor town houses, with a walled garden that is a delight to visit. Tradition has it that this was the home of Shakespeare's elder daughter Susanna and her husband, Dr. John Hall, whose dispensary is on view along with the other rooms, all containing Jacobean (early 17th-century) furniture of heavy oak. 🎟 *£3; Shakespeare Trust joint ticket* ☞ *above.* ⊙ *Mid-Mar.–mid-Oct., Mon.–Sat. 9:30–5, Sun. 10–5; mid-Oct.–mid-Mar., 10–4, Sun. 10:30–4; last entry 30 mins before closing.*

❸ Harvard House Next to the Garrick Inn, this is the grand and glorious half-timber 16th-century home of Catherine Rogers, mother of the John Harvard who founded Harvard University in 1636. There is little to see here, as the house is virtually unfurnished, but the twin-gabled facade, dating from about 1600, is one of the glories of Stratford. Note the exterior beams carved with fleurs-de-lys in high relief, the sculpted human faces on the corbels, and the hewn bear and ragged staff (motifs of the Warwick Earls) on the bracket heads. ⊠ *High St.* ⊙ *May–Sept. Contact the Shakespeare Centre for hrs.*

⑨ Holy Trinity Church. Along the banks of the Avon, the 13th-century Holy Trinity Church is the fabled burial place of William Shakespeare. Set at the end of Old Town, the church's entrance is framed by an avenue of lime trees. Shakespeare's final resting place is in the chancel, rebuilt in 1465–91 in the late Perpendicular style, which has stained-glass windows. He was buried here, incidentally, not because he was a famed poet but because he was a lay-rector of Stratford, owning a portion of the township tithes. Here, on the north wall of the sanctuary over the altar steps, you'll find the famous marble bust created by Gerard Jansen in 1623; along with the Droeshout engraving in the First Folio, this is one of the only two contemporary portraits of the Bard. Rigidly stylized in the Elizabethan mode, the bust offers, it is said, a more human, even humorous, perspective when viewed from the side. Also in the chancel are the graves of Shakespeare's wife, Anne; his daughter Susanna; his son-in-law, John Hall; and his granddaughter's husband, Thomas Nash. Nearby, the Parish Register is displayed, containing both Shakespeare's baptismal entry (1564) and his burial notice (1616). Just outside the church, the Avon "with gentle murmur glides" past the embankment. ⊠ *Trinity St.* ⌑ *Small fee for chancel.* ⊙ *Mar.–Oct. Mon.– Sat. 8:30–6, Sun. 2–5; Nov.–Feb. Mon.–Sat. 8:30–4, Sun. 2–5.*

❹ Nash's House. Across the street from Harvard House, this is the home of the Thomas Nash who married Shakespeare's last direct descendant, his granddaughter Elizabeth Hall. The heavily restored house has been furnished in 17th-century style, and it also contains a local museum. In the gardens (where there's an intricately laid-out Elizabethan knot garden), are the foundations of **New Place**, the house in which Shakespeare died in 1616. Built in 1483 "of brike and tymber" for a Lord Mayor of London, it was Stratford's grandest piece of real estate when Shakespeare bought it in 1597 for £60; but, tragically, it was torn down in 1759. The man responsible for this, Reverend Francis Gastrell, had already shown his ire at the hordes of sightseers by cutting down the legendary mulberry tree said to have been planted by Shakespeare himself. The townspeople were in such an uproar at Gastrell's vandalism that they stoned his house. Today, you can see what is claimed to be a descendant of the mulberry tree in the middle of the lawn. When Nash's House is closed, you can get a good view of the garden (which, some would say, is more interesting than the house itself) from the adjoining **Shakespeare Memorial Garden**, entered from Chapel Lane. ⊠ *Chapel St.* ⌑ *£3, Shakespeare Trust joint ticket (☞ above).* ⊙ *Mid-Mar.–mid-Oct., Mon.–Sat. 9:30–5, Sun. 10–5; mid-Oct.–mid-Mar., 10–4, Sun. 10:30–4; last entry 30 mins before closing.*

❿ Royal Shakespeare Theatre. Amid lovely gardens along the River Avon, this is the beloved home of the the Royal Shakespeare Company (RSC). Throughout the year, some of the finest productions in the world of the Bard's peerless plays are presented here (☞ The Arts, *below*). The theater has existed since 1879, established by Charles Edward Flower, a brewer, though the original building burned down in 1926. Six years later, the present building was inaugurated, according to a design by Elizabeth Scott, cousin of the more famous Sir Giles Gilbert Scott, architect of Liverpool's Anglican Cathedral. Many people criticize the modern appearance of the building, calling it "a factory for Shakespeare." At the rear is the **Swan Theatre**, created in the only part of the Victorian theater to survive a fire in the 1930s. The theater follows the lines of Shakespeare's original Globe, and it is one of the most exciting performing spaces in Britain. Beside the Swan is an art gallery, where you can see portraits and depictions of scenes from the plays, and occasional theater-related exhibitions. You might also consider taking part in one of the tours of the entire theater complex, which should be booked well in advance. For ticket information on performances, ☞ Theater *in* The Arts, *below.* Farther down Southern Lane toward Holy Trinity Church is **The Other Place,** a modern auditorium for experimental productions. ⊠ *Waterside,* ☎ *01789/296655; 01789/412602 for tours.* ☜ *Tours £4, gallery £1.50.* ☉ *Tours weekdays (except matinee days) at 1:30 and 5:30; matinee days 5:30 and after show; tours Sun. at 12:30, 1:45, 2:35, and 3:45. No tours when shows are being prepared. Exhibition Mon.–Sat. 9:30–6:30, Sun. noon–4:30.*

② **Shakespeare's Birthplace.** Erected in 1964 as a 400th-anniversary tribute to the playwright, the **Shakespeare Centre** is the home of the Shakespeare Birthplace Trust. Scholars head here for the library; visitors head here for pamphlets and information. It is just to the west of Shakespeare's Birthplace. Reached through the Shakespeare Centre is the house where Master Will first saw the light of day. A half-timber house typical of its time, it has been much altered and restored since Shakespeare lived here. Shakespeare's ambitious father, John, left farming to set up as a glove maker in Stratford, first renting this house. Inside, an auction notice describes the property as it was when it was offered for sale in 1847. Until then, the house had been maintained in a somewhat ramshackle state by two widowed ladies, but with the approach of the tercentennial of the Bard's birth, and in response to a rumor that the building was to be purchased by P. T. Barnum and shipped across the Atlantic, the city shelled out £3,000 for the relic, whereupon it was tidied up and made the main attraction for the stream of Shakespeare devotees that was steadily growing into a torrent. Half the house has been furnished to reflect Elizabethan domestic life; the other half contains an exhibition illustrating Shakespeare's professional life and work. In the upstairs room thought to have been where the Bard was born, you can see the signatures of pilgrims of earlier epochs cut into the windowpanes, including those of Sir Walter Scott and Thomas Carlyle. Outside, the garden is a vision of enchantment and, when in bloom, helps disguise the fact that the structure is surrounded by bustling streets and shops. ⊠ *Henley St.* ☜ *Shakespeare's Birthplace only £4.50; Town Heritage Trail ticket (includes 3 town properties) £7; Shakespeare Trust joint ticket,* ☞ *above.* ☉ *Mid-Mar.–mid-Oct., Mon.–Sat. 9–5, Sun. 9:30–5; mid-Oct.–mid-Mar., Mon.–Sat. 9:30–4, Sun. 10–4; last entry 30 mins before closing.*

Ⓒ **Teddy Bear Museum.** If the young children with you are suffering from a surfeit of Shakespeareana, they'll find this museum a good diversion. The collection contains hundreds of the furry things in all shapes and sizes from around the world. ⊠ *19 Greenhill St.,* ☎ *01789/293160.* ☜ *£2.25, family ticket £5.95.* ☉ *Jan.–Feb., daily 9:30–5; Mar.–Dec., daily 9:30–6.*

Dining and Lodging

££ ✕ **Box Tree Restaurant.** Overlooking the River Avon and its resident
★ swans, this attractive spot is handily located in the Royal Shakespeare Theatre itself and has some of the best food in town. You can dine here either before or after a play, but it's worth a meal even if you're not attending a theater performance. Specialties have an Italian slant and include wild boar casserole, breast of duck, and vegetarian pasta dishes. ⊠ *Waterside,* ☎ *01789/293226. Reservations essential. AE, MC, V. Closed when theater is closed.*

££ ✕ **The Opposition.** Close to the theater, this restaurant, set in a converted 16th-century building in Stratford's main dining street, offers pre- and post-theater meals. The American and Continental dishes on the menu are popular with the locals. Try the Cajun chicken or, among the vegetarian options, the mushrooms and asparagus served in a cream sauce. ⊠ *13 Sheep St.,* ☎ *01789/269980. MC, V.*

£–££   ✕ **Black Swan.** Locally called the Dirty Duck, this is one of Stratford's most celebrated pubs, attracting actors since Garrick's days. It has a little veranda overlooking the theaters and the river. Along with a pint of draft beer, enjoy English grill specialties, as well as braised oxtail and honey-roasted duck, plus an assortment of bar meals. ⊠ *Southern La.,* ☎ *01789/297312. MC, V. Restaurant closed Sun.*

£   ✕ **River Terrace.** At this informal cafeteria in the theater, the meals and snacks are crowd-pleasers. They include lasagna, shepherd's pie, salads, sandwiches, and cakes, with wine and beer available. ⊠ *Royal Shakespeare Theatre, Waterside,* ☎ *01789/293226. Reservations not accepted. No credit cards. Closed when theater is closed.*

£   ✕ **Slug and Lettuce.** Don't let the name put you off—this pine-panel pub serves excellent meals and is highly favored by pub aficionados nationwide. Long-standing favorites are chicken breast baked in avocado and garlic, and poached cushion of salmon. ⊠ *38 Guild St.,* ☎ *01789/299700. MC, V.*

£   ✕ **Vintner Wine Bar.** Just up the hill from the theater, this bar/restaurant serves imaginative food from a menu that changes daily. The chicken breast with crème fraîche and asparagus sauce is justifiably popular. Thankfully, the Vintner has introduced waitress service—a great improvement from standing in line at the counter, but still try to arrive early, especially if you hope to dine before curtain time, when the restaurant gets crowded with out-of-town visitors. ⊠ *5 Sheep St.,* ☎ *01789/297259. AE, MC, V.*

££££   ▯ **Alveston Manor.** Across the river from the Royal Shakespeare Theatre, this redbrick Elizabethan manor house has a modern extension. In the old manor house, rooms have individual, old-world style. Decor is modern in the extension, but all rooms have up-to-date bathrooms. ⊠ *Clopton Bridge, CV37 7HP,* ☎ *01789/204581,* ℻ *01789/414095. 114 rooms with bath. Restaurant. AE, DC, MC, V.*

£££   ▯ **Arden Hotel.** Three 18th-century town houses have been converted into a centrally located hotel, right at the water's edge and directly opposite the Swan Theatre. The best of the rooms are enhanced by beam ceilings, period furniture, and views over the river, while the elegant Bard's restaurant is an award winner. The lounge bar and terrace are also amenable places to relax. The hotel is part of the Thistle chain. ⊠ *44 Waterside, CV37 6BA,* ☎ *01789/294949,* ℻ *01789/415874. 63 rooms with bath. Restaurant, bar. AE, DC, MC, V.*

£££   ▯ **Falcon Hotel.** Licensed as an alehouse since 1640, this black-and-white timber-frame hotel still has the atmosphere of a friendly inn. The heavily beamed rooms in the older part are small and quaint; those in the modern extension are in standard international style. Enjoy a refreshment in the Merlin Lounge, a pretty retreat with wattle-and-daub decor. In the Oak Bar, wood panels salvaged from New Place, the Bard's last home, accent the impressive setting. ⊠ *Chapel St., CV37 6HA,* ☎ *01789/279953,* ℻ *01789/414260. 73 rooms with bath. Restaurant, 2 bars. AE, DC, MC, V.*

£££   ▯ **Shakespeare Hotel.** Minutes from the theater and right in the heart of Stratford, this half-timber Elizabethan town house, founded in the 1400s, has five gables. Its interiors have been comfortably modernized. Public rooms are adorned with Shakespeareana and old playbills; upstairs, rooms are named after the Bard's characters and leading thespians and some are adorned with hewn timbers carved with rose-and-thistle patterns. ⊠ *Chapel St., CV37 6ER,* ☎ *01789/294771,* ℻ *01789/415111. 63 rooms with bath. Restaurant. AE, DC, MC, V.*

££   ▯ **Caterham House.** Built in 1830, this comfortable old building is in
★   the center of town, within an easy walk of the theater. You may spot an actor or two among the guests. Its bedrooms are individually decorated in early 19th-century style, featuring brass beds and antique fur-

nishings, and the public rooms, too, show discriminating taste at work. ⊠ *58 Rother St., CV37 6LT,* ☎ *01789/267309,* ℻ *01789/414836. 10 rooms with bath or shower. Bar, parking. MC, V.*

£ ⊞ **Penryn House.** The convenient location of this lodging—halfway between the city center and Anne Hathaway's Cottage, and within an easy walk of both—makes it a natural, if somewhat uninspiring, budget choice. Comfortably furnished rooms have TVs, hair dryers, and tea/coffeemaking facilities. ⊠ *126 Alcester Rd., CV37 9DP,* ☎ *01789/ 293718. 8 rooms, 6 with bath or shower. AE, DC, MC, V.*

£ ⊞ **Victoria Spa Lodge.** This rather grand B&B lies just outside town, within view of the canal. Draped with clematis, the listed building dates from 1837 and sports Queen Victoria's coat of arms in two of its gables. The lounge/breakfast room is a pleasure, with huge windows and sofas and chairs for relaxing. The spacious rooms—some with fireplaces—are tastefully decorated with dark wood or plain white furnishings. ⊠ *Bishopton La., Bishopton CV37 9QY,* ☎ *01789/267985,* ℻ *01789/204728. 7 rooms with shower. MC, V.*

The Arts

FESTIVALS

The **Stratford-upon-Avon Shakespeare Birthday Celebrations** (⊠ Shakespeare Centre, Henley St., Stratford-upon-Avon CV37 6QW, ☎ 01789/ 204016) take place on and around the weekend closest to April 23 (unless Easter occurs around that date—it's worth checking). The events, spread over four days, include a formal reception, lectures, free concerts, folk dancing, military bands, processions, a special performance of one of the plays, and the ceremonial unfurling of the flags in various sites around the center of town. For tickets for the three-course birthday luncheon in the marquee on the Avon Paddock, write to the Shakespeare Birthday Celebrations Secretary, the Shakespeare Center, Henley St., Stratford-Upon-Avon, CV37 6QW; for more direct inquires, ☎ 01789/415536.

Dating from medieval times, the **Mop Fair** is a local delight, taking place on or around October 12, traditionally the time when farmworkers, laborers, and apprentices from the surrounding area came to seek work. It still attracts entertainers and fairground amusements and sees a formal ceremony attended by local dignitaries, the whole in essence little changed from the past.

THEATER

The **Royal Shakespeare Theatre** (⊠ Stratford-upon-Avon CV37 6BB, ☎ 01789/295623) usually puts on five of Shakespeare's plays in a season lasting April–January. In September and October, visiting companies perform a variety of opera, ballet, and musicals. Prices usually range from £7 to £45. Seats go fast, but "day of performance" (two per person to personal callers only) and returned tickets are often available. You can also book tickets from London with Ticketmaster (☎ 0171/ 413–1452), operating 24 hours a day. From the U.S., you can prebook through the Edwards and Edwards or Keith Prowse theater ticket agencies, or, to skip the hefty service charge, directly through the Stratford box office (open Monday–Saturday, 9–8). In the **Swan Theatre** at the rear, plays by Shakespeare contemporaries, such as Christopher Marlowe and Ben Jonson, are staged. In **The Other Place,** some of the RSC's most advanced work is performed.

Outdoor Activities and Sports

BOATING

Contact **Bancroft Cruises** (⊠ The Boatyard, Clopton Bridge, ☎ 01789/ 269669) or **Avon Cruises** (⊠ The Boatyard, Swan's Nest Lane, ☎ 01789/ 267073) for half-hourly excursions on the river. Hour-long trips farther afield can also be enjoyed through prior arrangement. Both companies also rent out boats by the hour or day.

Shopping

Stratford-upon-Avon has a bustling shopping district, and there's an open market every Friday in the Market Square. **Waterstone** (✉ 18 High St., ☎ 01789/414418) is a prime bookstore. The **Antique Market** (✉ Ely St.) features 50 stalls of jewelry, silver, linens, porcelain, and memorabilia. **Robert Vaughan** (✉ 20 Chapel St., ☎ 01789/205312) is the best of Stratford's many secondhand bookshops. **Once a Tree** (✉ 8 Bard's Walk, ☎ 01789/297790) is thoroughly "green," selling items crafted from sustainable wood sources—animals, bowls, and dozens of imaginative articles. **B&W Thornton** (✉ 23 Henley St., ☎ 01789/269405), just above Shakespeare's birthplace, has an extensive range of exclusive Moorcroft pottery ware.

IN AND AROUND SHAKESPEARE COUNTRY

Although that section of Warwickshire which we call "Shakespeare Country" is, in reality, no more than a continuation of that familiar Midlands scene of green fields, slow-moving, mirrorlike rivers, quiet villages, and time-burnished old halls, castles, and churches, it becomes an area apart through its role as the homeland of England's greatest dramatist. It must never be forgotten that Shakespeare, although born in what was then the smallish town of Stratford, was essentially a country lad at heart and his wanderings through the fields and woods so close to his boyhood abode gave him a knowledge of nature and rural lore that so often reveals itself in his plays. So, as you venture to the sights below, keep an eye out for—as immortalized in *Cymbeline*—that cowlip blossom growing wild.

Mary Arden's House

⓫ *3 mi northwest of Stratford, off A3400.*

The hamlet of Wilmcote holds the fifth Shakespeare Birthplace Trust property—Mary Arden's House—a Tudor farmhouse which was the family home of Shakespeare's mother. Combined with the adjoining glebe (church-owned farm) it forms the Shakespeare Countryside Museum, with crafts exhibits, falconry demonstrations, a café, and a garden of trees mentioned in the plays. The museum is home to rare breeds of poultry, longhorn cows, and Cotswold sheep, and there are special events and demonstrations of farming techniques as practiced during the last 400 years (☎ 01789/293455 for information on these). Don't forget to note the magical 16th-century dovecote: Susan Hill describes it as one of those places where "the centuries seem to touch, with no time in between." You can get to Wilmcote on a regular bus from Stratford; by train Monday–Saturday only; or on one of the Guide Friday Tours, unless, of course, you opt for the traditional means—on foot. ✉ £4; *Shakespeare Trust joint ticket, ☞ above.* ☉ *Mid-Mar.–mid-Oct., Mon.–Sat. 9:30–5, Sun. 10–5; mid-Oct.–mid-Mar., 10–4, Sun. 10:30–4; last entry 30 mins before closing.*

En Route   From Wilmcote, continue west for 1½ mi on minor roads to reach **Aston Cantlow.** The church here was where Mary Arden and John Shakespeare were wed.

Henley-in-Arden

⑫ *8 mi northwest of Stratford, on A3400.*

A brief drive out of Stratford will take you under the Stratford-upon-Avon Canal aqueduct to picturesque Henley-in-Arden, whose wide main street forms an architectural pageant, presenting a parade of attractive buildings of various periods. You are now in the area of what was once the Forest of Arden, where Shakespeare set one of his greatest comedies, *As You Like It*. Among the buildings to look out for are the former Guildhall, dating from the 15th century, and the White Swan pub, built in the early 1600s. By that time, the town had already seen a good deal of historical ups and downs: associated with the influential de Montfort family, it was razed following the defeat of Simon de Montfort by the future Edward I in the battle of Evesham, in 1265.

Packwood House

⑬ *12 mi north of Stratford-upon-Avon, 5 mi north of Henley-in-Arden.*

Packwood House draws garden enthusiasts to its 17th-century gardens, highlighted by a remarkable topiary Tudor garden, in which yew trees depict Christ's Sermon on the Mount. The house itself combines red-brick and half-timbering, while its tall chimneys are another distinctive Tudor characteristic. To get here from Henley-in-Arden, follow A3400 north another 4 or 5 mi, turn right, just before Hockley Heath, onto B4439, and follow the signs 2 mi farther along a back road. ⊠ *Near Hockley Heath,* ☎ *01564/782024.* 🎫 *£4.20.* ☉ *Apr.–Sept., Wed.–Sun. and national holiday Mon. 2–6; Oct., Wed.–Sun. 12:30–4:30.*

Baddesley Clinton

★ **⑭** *2 mi east of Packwood House, off A4141, 15 mi north of Stratford-upon-Avon.*

"As you approach Baddesley Clinton Hall, it stands before you as the perfect late medieval manor house. The entrance side of grey stone, the small, creeper-clad Queen Anne brick bridge across the moat, the gateway with a porch higher than the roof and embattled—it could not be better." So wrote the eminent architectural historian Sir Nikolaus Pevsner, and the house actually lives up to this fervent praise. Set off a winding back road, the moated manor still retains its great fireplaces, 17th-century paneling, and priest holes (secret chambers for Roman Catholic priests, who were persecuted at various times throughout the 16th and 17th centuries). Stables and barns around the manor have been renovated; one contains a café, an idyllic spot for tea and cakes. ⊠ *Near Chadwick End (7½ mi northwest of Warwick),* ☎ *01564/783294.* 🎫 *£4.85.* ☉ *Mar.–Apr. and Oct., Wed.–Sun. and national holiday Mon. 1:30–5; May–Sept., Wed.–Sun. 1:30–5:30; restaurant, National Trust store, and grounds open at 12.*

Warwick

⑮ *4 mi south of Kenilworth on A46, 9 mi northeast of Stratford-upon-Avon.*

Most famous for Warwick Castle—that vision out of the feudal ages—Warwick is an interesting architectural mixture of Georgian redbrick and Elizabethan half-timbering. Much of the town center has been spoiled by unattractive postwar development, but look for the 15th-century ★ **Lord Leycester Hospital,** which has been a home—offering "hospitality"—for old soldiers since the earl of Leicester dedicated it to that purpose in 1571. Built on a terrace overlooking a vista of the distant

Cotswold hills, the half-timber complex features a tiny chapel devoted to St. James. Within the complex is a magnificently picturesque courtyard, complete with a wattle-and-daub balcony. The 500-year-old gardens have recently been restored and reopened to the public. ⊠ *High St.,* ☏ *01926/491422.* ⚏ *£2.50.* ⊙ *Apr.–Sept., Tues.–Sun. 10–5; Oct.–Mar., Tues.–Sun. 10–4.*

Crowded with gilded, carved, and painted tombs, the **Beauchamp Chapel** of the **Collegiate Church of St. Mary** (⊠ Church St.) is the very essence of late medieval and Tudor chivalry—although it was built (1443–1464) to honor the somewhat less than chivalrous Richard Beauchamp, who consigned Joan of Arc to the flames. With brightly colored bosses, breathtaking fan tracery, and flying ribs, the chapel holds many monuments to the Beauchamps (several of whom became Earl of Warwick), including Richard Beauchamp's effigy in bronze—a great example of the medieval metalworker's art—and the alabaster table tomb of Thomas Beauchamp and his wife. Don't miss the little memorial for Cecily Puckering, who died in 1626, age 13, inscribed "I sleep secure; Christ's my King."

★ The city's chief attraction is **Warwick Castle,** the finest medieval castle in England, which is built on a cliff overlooking the Avon. "The fairest monument of ancient and chivalrous splendor which yet remains uninjured by time," to use the words of Sir Walter Scott, the castle is marked by two soaring towers—the 147-ft-high Caesar's Tower, built in 1356, and the 128-ft-high Guy's Tower, built in 1380. Bristling with battlements, the towers' irregularity of form was specifically designed to allow defenders to shoot from numerous points. The castle's most powerful commander was the 15th-century Earl of Warwick, known during the Wars of the Roses as "the Kingmaker." He was killed in battle near London in 1471 by Edward IV, whom he had just deposed in favor of Henry VI. Warwick Castle's monumental walls now enclose one of the finest collections of medieval armor and weapons in Europe, as well as historic furnishings and paintings by Rubens, Van Dyck, and other Old Masters. Twelve rooms are devoted to an imaginative Madame Tussaud's wax exhibition, "A Royal Weekend Party—1898." An exhibit opened in 1994 displays the sights and sounds of a great medieval household as it prepares for an important battle. The year chosen is 1471, when the Earl of Warwick was killed by Edward IV at the Battle of Barnet. Below the castle, along the Avon, strutting peacocks patrol 60 acres of grounds elegantly landscaped by Capability Brown in the 18th century. There is a restaurant in the cellars, for lunch during your visit. Be sure to head to the bridge fording the river to get the best vista of the castle. ☏ *01926/ 495421.* ⚏ *£9.25 (July–Aug. £9.95).* ⊙ *Apr.–Oct., daily 10–6 (until 7 on national holiday Mon. in Aug.); Nov.–Mar., daily 10–5.*

Near the castle entrance, drop in on the historic half-timber Oken's House, home to the **Warwickshire Doll Museum,** housing a large collection of antique dolls, toys, and games. ⊠ *Oken's House, Castle St.,* ☏ *01926/495546.* ⚏ *£1.50.* ⊙ *Easter–Sept. Mon.–Sat. 10–5, Sun. 1–5; Oct.–Easter, Sat. 10–dusk.*

Elsewhere in the town, kids will appreciate **St. John's House,** a Jacobean building on the site of a medieval hospital and now surrounded by beautiful gardens. The interior displays period costumes and scenes of domestic life, as well as a Victorian schoolroom. ⊠ *Smith St.,* ☏ *01926/ 410410.* ⚏ *Free.* ⊙ *Tues.–Sat. 10–12:30 and 1:30–5:30, also Sun. in summer 2:30–5.*

Dining and Lodging

£–££ ✕ **Fanshawe's.** Centrally located on the market square in Warwick, this friendly restaurant features cheerful prints and vases of flowers.

The menu is wide-ranging—you can have simple open sandwiches if you just want a light lunch, or try the Wellington lamb with spinach and mushroom stuffing or the cod with chervil butter. Game is offered in season. ⊠ *22 Market Pl.,* ☎ *01926/410590. AE, MC, V. Closed Sun., 1 wk after Easter and 2nd wk in Oct. No lunch Mon.*

£ ✕🖬 **Tudor House Inn.** Here is a simple hotel and restaurant of genuine character. The Tudor House dates from 1472, having survived the great Warwick fire of 1694 because it was situated on the road to Stratford, beyond the West Gate, placing it outside the devastated medieval town center. The rooms are beamed and basic, and the floors creak satisfactorily. The great hall, with its cavernous fireplace and gallery, acts as the restaurant, and the inexpensive food served here is hearty and plentiful. ⊠ *90–92 West St., CV34 6AW,* ☎ *01926/495447,* 𝙵𝙰𝚇 *01926/ 492948. 11 rooms, 6 with bath. Restaurant, bar. AE, DC, MC, V.*

Kenilworth Castle

⓰ *5 mi east of Baddesley Clinton direct, 10 mi by road, 5 mi north of Warwick.*

The great, red ruins of Kenilworth Castle loom over the rather non-descript village of Kenilworth. Founded in 1120, this castle remained one of the most formidable fortresses in England until it was finally dismantled by Oliver Cromwell after the Civil War in the mid-17th century. Still intact are its keep (central tower) with 20-ft-thick walls; its great hall; and its curtain walls (low outer walls forming the castle's first line of defense). Here the Earl of Leicester, one of Queen Elizabeth I's favorites, entertained her four times, most notably in 1575 with 19 days of sumptuous feasting and revelry. From Baddesley Clinton village, turn right onto A4141; then left, northeast, onto A4177; and finally right again, onto A452. ⊠ *Kenilworth,* ☎ *01926/852078.* 🖃 *£3.* ☉ *Summer, daily 10–6; winter, daily 10–4.*

Dining

££ ✕ **Restaurant Bosquet.** This attractive restaurant serves set menus cooked by the French *patron,* with regularly changing à la carte selections. Try the veal or venison with wild mushrooms. The desserts are mouth-watering. It is mainly a dinner spot, though lunch is available on request. ⊠ *97A Warwick Rd.,* ☎ *01926/852463. AE, MC, V. Closed Sun., 3 wks in Aug., 1 wk Christmas. No dinner Mon.*

£–££ ✕ **Clarendon Arms.** This pub is a good spot for lunch after a visit to the castle. Fine home-cooked food is offered at the small bar downstairs while a larger, slightly pricier restaurant upstairs offers complete meals. ⊠ *44 Castle Hill,* ☎ *01926/852017. AE, DC, MC, V.*

Charlecote Park

⓱ *6 mi south of Warwick, 3 mi east of Stratford-upon-Avon.*

In the charming village of Hampton Lucy, this celebrated house was built in 1572 by Sir Thomas Lucy to entertain the new Queen Elizabeth (the house even takes the form of the letter "E"). According to tradition, Shakespeare was caught poaching deer here soon after his marriage and was forced to flee to London. Years later he is supposed to have retaliated by portraying Sir Thomas Lucy, in *Henry IV Part 2* and the *Merry Wives of Windsor,* as the foolish Justice Shallow. Some historians doubt the reference, but the Bard does mention the "dozen white luces"—which figure in the Lucy coat of arms—as well as having Shallow tax Falstaff with killing his deer, beating his men, and breaking his fences. The house was extensively renovated in the neo-Elizabethan style in the 19th century by the Lucy family, who also built an impressive Gothic Revival church nearby. Charlecote Park's Tudor gatehouse has been unchanged from Shakespeare's day, and deer still graze its emerald lawns. From Warwick, take A429 south 4 or 5 mi, and then turn right onto B4088. ⊠ *Charlecote,* ☎ *01789/470277.* 🎫 *£4.80.* ☉ *Apr.–Oct., Fri.–Tues. 12–5 (house), 12–6 (garden).*

Lodging

£££ 🏨 **Charlecote Pheasant.** Farm buildings have been converted into a pleasant, country-house hotel across from Charlecote Park (follow B4086 northeast out of Stratford for about 5 mi). The fine, 17th-century red brick has been matched in the new wing, and the bedrooms—some with four-poster beds—in both the old and the new buildings are prettily decorated and have ceiling beams. ⊠ *Charlecote Park, CV35 9EW,* ☎ *01789/279954,* 🅵🅰🆇 *01789/470222. 67 rooms with bath. Restaurant, bar, tennis court, billiards. AE, DC, MC, V.*

Broughton Castle

⑱ *18 mi southeast of Stratford-upon-Avon, 3 mi west of Banbury.*

Once owned by the great chancellor and patron William of Wykeham, this moated mansion passed to Lord and Lady Saye and Sele in 1451 and has been occupied by their family ever since. Parts of the building date back to around 1300, though it was remodeled in Tudor times. The exterior is truly magnificent, while the inside is rich with period atmosphere, with fireplaces, fine plasterwork, and exquisite furniture. High points are the Great Chamber, the Chapel, and a fine collection of Chinese wallpapers. ⊠ *Broughton,* ☎ *01789/762090.* 🎫 *£3.80.* ☉ *Mid-May–mid-Sept., Wed. and Sun. 2–5, also Thurs. in July and Aug., and national holidays Sun. and Mon. 2–5.*

Compton Wynyates

★ **⑲** *11 mi southeast of Stratford-upon-Avon, 8 mi west of Banbury.*

Perhaps the quintessential image of Merrie Olde Englande, Compton Wynyates has been called "the most visually satisfying house in England." Although not open to the public, it is worth an excursion to view it from the hills that surround its tiny valley (called a "dingle"), a setting that truly makes a "house in a hole." A perfect example of Tudor domestic architecture, it was built by the noted Warwickshire family that takes its name from the little village of Compton (Wynyates refers to the vineyards that once surrounded the house). Built between 1480 and 1520, its battlemented towers and timber roof survived a siege during the Civil War. The house is celebrated for its radiant brick hue—"a wonderful picture of rose-tinted restfulness," to quote one 19th-century guidebook; instead of the usual limestone used for most houses in the region, the house was constructed from bricks dismantled from a castle given to the family by Henry VIII (who, in fact, stayed here). In the district known as the Feldon, and near the village of Upper Tysoe, the house is a difficult place to find, best reached by turning north from the village of Brailes off the Shipston-Banbury B4035. Today, it is the private residence of the Marquess of Northampton, and it should only be viewed from the surrounding hillside roads—just as well, since Compton Wynyates looks best from a distance, framed by its miniature lake and delightful topiaries. Note that just east of Upper Tysoe is Warmington, which, with its Elizabethan manor house and village pond (and resident flotilla of ducks) is sometimes called the most idyllic hamlet in Warwickshire.

Alderminster

20 *5 mi south of Stratford-upon-Avon on A3400.*

Alderminster is one of the most interesting of the so-called "Stour villages"—those places so characteristic of Shakespeare Country strung along the winding route of the River Stour south of Stratford. The main street holds an unusual row of old stone cottages, and the church has a tower dating from the 13th century and a Norman nave. Although the interior of the church has been much restored, it is worth a peek for the carved faces between the arches and the old altar stone. Close by, **Preston-on-Stour** has an unspoiled air and contains a church with lots of stained glass donated by James West, a civil servant of the 18th century who is also buried in the church. West was responsible for building the Gothic manor house **Alscott Park,** half a mile northeast of the village. Its broad grounds, including extensive lawns, a river, and a deer park, are open just two days a year, in June and July (contact Stratford's tourist office for precise dates), though the house remains out of bounds.

Other Stour villages include Clifford Chambers, Newbold-on-Stour, Honington, and Shipston-on-Stour. **Honington** is one of the most fetching, set around a village green, with a lovely five-arched bridge crossing the river. **Shipston,** the largest of the group, is an old sheep-market town, its handsome batch of Georgian houses formerly owned by wealthy wool merchants. **Tredington** is an exquisite nutshell of a village, with an old stone church.

Dining and Lodging

££££ 🏨 **Ettington Park Hotel.** This marvelously restored, huge Victorian house makes an ideal spot to stay if you want to see the plays at Stratford but don't want to cope with the crowds. It stands on its own grounds—which contain a ruined church—and looks across tranquil river meadows haunted by herons. Individual settings include four-poster rooms, a Shakespeare suite, and the tented Kingmaker Chamber. The restaurant has extremely good food, imaginatively cooked. ⊠ *Alderminster, CV37 8BU,* ☎ *01789/450123,* 🖷 *01789/450472. 48 rooms with bath. Restaurant, indoor pool, sauna, spa, 2 tennis courts, health club, fishing. AE, DC, MC, V.*

£ ✗🏨 **The Horseshoe.** One of a good concentration of historic inns in the village, the Horseshoe is timbered outside, with a friendly open fire within. Ales and good coffee are available, and there are a restaurant and plain guest rooms if you want to stay over. Note that there are no bathrooms en suite. ⊠ *6 Church St., Shipston-on-Stour,* ☎ *01608/ 661225,* 🖷 *01608/663762. 3 rooms. AE, DC, MC, V.*

Welford-on-Avon

21 *4 mi southwest of Stratford-upon-Avon off B439.*

Welford is most famous for its Mayday revelry, when Morris dancers perform their obscure rites around the maypole on the green. Park up in the village, which lies on a loop of the River Avon, and take a walk over the old bridge. Nearby Boat Lane is festooned with timber and whitewashed thatched cottages. Welford also boasts what is said to be the oldest lych-gate in the county, leading to the church. Close by the church, which is partly Norman, stands Cleavers, an attractive brick-built Georgian house worth the stroll.

Dining

£ ✗ **The Bell.** This quiet spot has a flagstone public bar with an open fire, and a conservatory and garden in which to enjoy the generous snacks on offer. ⊠ *Binston Rd.,* ☎ *01789/750303. MC, V.*

Alcester

㉒ *8 mi west of Stratford-upon-Avon.*

The small market town of Alcester (pronounced alster) holds a picturesque cluster of ancient roofs and timber-frame Tudor houses. Search out the narrow **Butter Street,** off the High Street, site of the 17th-century Churchill House, and, on Malt Mill Lane (off Church Street), the **Old Malt House,** dating from 1500.

Dining

£ ✕ **Arrow Mill.** This place was listed in the Domesday Book, and there is still a mill wheel in the restaurant. Heavy beams and flagstones add to the ambience. ✉ *Alcester,* ☎ *01789/762419. AE, DC, MC, V. Restaurant closed 2 wks after Christmas.*

Ragley Hall

㉓ *2 mi southwest of Alcester.*

To the south of Alcester lies Ragley Hall, a Palladian-style aristocratic mansion begun in 1680 and worked on by some of the country's most outstanding architects. Inside is a panoply of treasures and architectural features as well as magnificent views of the parkland originally laid out by Capability Brown in the 1750s. The Great Hall boasts fine baroque plasterwork, and there are portraits by Joshua Reynolds and various Dutch masters, among others, as well as some striking 20th-century murals. The house is the ancestral home of the Marquesses of Hertford, the third of whom figured in Thackeray's *Vanity Fair,* and the fourth of whom collected many of the treasures found in London's Wallace Collection. ✉ *Off A435 and A46,* ☎ *01789/762090.* 🖭 *House £5, garden £4.* ☉ *House: Apr.–Sept., Thurs.–Sun. 11–5. Park: Apr.–Sept., Thurs.–Sun. 10–6.*

Coughton Court

㉔ *2 mi north of Alcester.*

Coughton Court is a grand Elizabethan manor house that is home to the Catholic Throckmorton family, as it has been since 1409. The impressive gatehouse is the centerpiece of a half-timber courtyard, and it contains an impressive fan-vaulted ceiling and various memorabilia, including the dress worn by Mary, Queen of Scots at her execution. There are children's clothes and Gunpowder Plot exhibitions, and you can wander in the formal gardens and alongside a river and lake. ✉ *2 mi north of Alcester on A435,* ☎ *01789/762435 or 01789/400777.* 🖭 *£5.90.* ☉ *House: mid-Mar.–Apr., weekends 11:30–5; May–June and Sept., Sat.–Wed. 11:30–5; July–Aug., Fri.–Wed. 11:30–5; Oct., weekends 11:30–5. Grounds: same days as house, 11–5:30.*

Bidford-on-Avon

㉕ *7 mi southwest of Stratford-upon-Avon.*

The village of Bidford-on-Avon was immortalized in a piece of doggerel popularly ascribed to Shakespeare in his youth:

Piping Pebworth, dancing Marston
Haunted Hillborough, hungry Grafton
Dodging Exhall, Papist Wixford
Beggarly Broom and drunken Bidford.

The lines were supposedly composed after a drinking bout in Bidford's *Falcon Inn*—no longer a pub, but still to be seen, featuring mullioned windows in a Cotswold-stone front. The verse lists the places which have come to be known as the "Shakespeare Villages," all located to the west of town, and all worth passing through. Bidford is one of the most compelling: it has a main street with 15th- and 16th-century houses, and a medieval bridge with eight irregular arches. In 1922 an Anglo-Saxon burial ground containing 200 warriors and their families was unearthed near the church of St. Lawrence.

The other villages mentioned in the verse are worth sniffing out, all within the triangle formed by A435, A46, and B439, and close enough to walk to along the tiny roads.

SHAKESPEARE COUNTRY A TO Z

Getting Around

By Bus
National Express (☎ 0990/808080) serves the region from London's Victoria Coach Station with eight buses daily to the Stratford region; for the bus-and-train "Shakespearean Connection" service, *see* By Train below. **Flights Coach Travel Ltd. of Birmingham** (☎ 0990/757747) operates "Flightlink" service from London's Heathrow and Gatwick airports to Coventry and Warwick. **Stagecoach Midland Red (South) Ltd.** and **Stagecoach Stratford Blue** (☎ 01788/535555) serve the Stratford-upon-Avon, Birmingham, and Coventry areas.

By Car
From London take M40 for Stratford-upon-Avon (97 mi).

By Train
In general, try to catch the direct train each morning from London's **Paddington Station** (☎ 0345/484950 for times), or else you'll be doomed to at least one change, at Leamington Spa. There are two direct trains back from Stratford each afternoon, too, and the journey time is 2 hours, 20 minutes. On winter Sundays, there are bus connections from Leamington Spa or Warwick when the Stratford train station is closed. The fastest route is by train *and* bus using the "Shakespeare Connection Road & Rail Link" from **Euston Station** to Coventry, then switching to a Guide Friday bus. This trip takes 2 hours, and there are four departures weekdays—the three that would allow you to catch an evening performance in Stratford are at 9:15 AM, 10:45 AM, and 4:55 PM; Saturday departures are at 9:05 AM, 10:35 AM, and 5:05 PM; the Sunday departure is 9:45 AM. Returns back to London usually depart around 11:15 PM. Schedules have been subject to change, so it's best to phone to confirm times (☎ 0171/387–7070; Guide Friday offices, 01789/294466). Note that a seven-day "Heart of England Rover" ticket is valid for unlimited travel within the region.

Contacts and Resources

Car Rentals
Stratford-upon-Avon: Hertz (✉ Rail Station, ☎ 01789/298827). **Listers** (✉ Western Rd., ☎ 01789/294477). **Warwick: LCS Self-Drive** (✉ Longbridge Garage, ☎ 01926/495188).

Guided Tours
The **Heart of England Tourist Board** (☎ 01905/763436) and the **West Country Tourist Board** (☎ 01392/276351) can arrange a variety of tours. **Guide Friday** (☎ 01789/294466 in Stratford) runs guided tours of Strat-

ford, for £8, and Warwick, for £16, in open-top single- and double-decker buses.

Travel Agencies
American Express (✉ c/o Tourist Information Centre, Bridgefoot, Stratford-upon-Avon, ☎ 01789/415856). **Thomas Cook** (✉ 24 Upper Precinct, Coventry, ☎ 01203/229233; ✉ c/o Midland Bank, 13 Chapel St., Stratford-upon-Avon, ☎ 01789/294688).

Visitor Information
Local tourist information centers are normally open Monday–Saturday 9:30–5:30, but times vary according to season. The **Heart of England Tourist Board** (✉ Woodside, Larkhill, Worcester WR5 2EF, ☎ 01905/763436, FAX 01905/763450), open Monday–Thursday 9–5:30, Friday 9–5. **Stratford-upon-Avon** (✉ Bridgefoot, ☎ 01789/293127). **Warwick** (✉ The Court House, Jury St., ☎ 01926/492212).

THE HEART OF ENGLAND is a term coined by the tourist powers-that-be to designate the heart of *tourist* England, so immensely popular are its attractions. The county of Gloucestershire, in west-central England, with slices of neighboring Oxfordshire, Worcestershire, and Somerset together make up a sweep of land stretching from Shakespeare Country in the north down through Bath to the Bristol Channel in the south. Bath, among the most alluring cities in Europe, offers up "18th-century England in all its urban glory," to use a phrase of writer Nigel Nicolson. Northward, beyond Regency-era Cheltenham—like Bath, a spa town adorned with remarkably elegant architecture—the Cotswolds are a region that conjure up "olde Englande" at its most blissfully rural. The grand finale: Gloucester and the Forest of Dean.

Updated by
Robert
Andrews

Bath is a delight to the eye, and rightly boasts of being the best-planned town in all England. It was originally founded by the Romans when they discovered here the only true hot springs in England. Bath's fashionable period luckily coincided with one of Britain's most elegant architectural eras, producing a quite remarkable urban phenomenon—money available to create virtually an entire town of stylish buildings. Today's city fathers have been wise enough to make sure that Bath is kept spruce and welcoming; its present prosperity keeps the streets overflowing with flowers in the summer and is channeled into cleaning and painting the city center, making it a joy to explore. Gainsborough, Lord Nelson, and Queen Victoria traveled here to sip the waters, which Dickens described as tasting like "warm flat irons," but most of today's travelers are here to walk in the footsteps of Jane Austen and opt for tea and clotted cream and strawberries in one of the town's elegant eateries.

North of Bath, we enter the Cotswolds—a region that more than one writer has called the very soul of England. Is it the sun, or the soil? The pretty villages? The mellow, centuries-old, stone-built cottages festooned with honeysuckle? Whatever the reason, this idyllic region remains a vision of rural England. Here time-defying churches, sleepy hamlets, ancient farmsteads seem to offer every traveler the thrill of personal "discovery." The Cotswolds' poetic appeal has a way of surviving the tour groups and other visitors who pierce its timeless tranquility. More than ever, visitors come here to taste fully the glories of the old English village—its thatched roofs, low-ceiling rooms, and gardens meticulously built on a gentle slope; its old-world atmosphere is as thick as honey, and equally sweet.

Pleasures and Pastimes

Dining

Here, in the heart of England, chefs have never had a problem with a fresh food supply: excellent produce, salmon from the rivers Severn and Wye, local lamb, venison from the Forest of Dean, and pheasant, partridge, quail, and grouse in season. Now more than ever, this region is dotted with good restaurants, thanks to a steady flow of fine chefs seeking to cater to wealthy locals and waves of demanding tourists.

CATEGORY	COST*
££££	over £50
£££	£30–£50
££	£20–£30
£	under £20

per person, including first course, main course, dessert, and VAT; excluding drinks

9 The Heart of England

Bath, the Cotswolds, Gloucester, the Forest of Dean

Visiting the Cotswold region can be likened to stepping inside a 19th-century English pastoral novel. Nowhere else in Britain are the hedges so perfectly clipped, the churches so quaint and ivy clad, the villages so picture-postcard perfect. Here, hidden in sheltered valleys, you'll find fabled abodes— Sudeley Castle, Stanway House, and Snowhill Manor among them. Not far away is 18th-century Bath, a gorgeous city of Georgian splendor. Be sure to amble about its elegant Assembly Rooms—you'll be following in the footsteps of Jane Austen.

Lodging

It was staying at a Cotswold inn, in the village of Banbury during the spring of 1776, that Dr. Johnson spoke his noted panegyric on English hostelries: "There is no private house in which people can enjoy themselves so well as at a capital tavern . . . you are sure you are welcome; and the more noise you make, the more trouble you give, the more good things you call for, the welcomer you are . . ." Today, the hotels of this region still please myriad travelers and they are among Britain's most highly rated—ranging from bed-and-breakfasts in village homes and farmhouses to ultimate luxury in country-house hotels. Book ahead whenever possible; you should also brace yourself for some very fancy prices. Most hotels offer two- and three-day packages. Keep in mind when booking reservations that hotels can front on heavily trafficked roads; ask for quiet rooms.

CATEGORY	COST*
££££	over £150
£££	£80–£150
££	£60–£80
£	under £60

All prices are for two people sharing a double room, including service, breakfast, and VAT.

Shopping

The treasures here are, so to speak, Austen-tatiously elegant: toleware, treen, faience fire-dogs, toby jugs, and silhouettes, plus lovely country furniture, Edwardiana, and ravishing 17th- to 19th-century furniture. The center of antiquing, with more than 12 dealers, is Stow-on-the-Wold. Other towns that have a number of antique shops are Burford, Cirencester, Tetbury, and Moreton-in-Marsh. Prices can be high—but go ahead, splurge on Lady Havisham's 18th-century silver salt spoon! For information about dealers and special events, contact the Cotswold Antique Dealers' Association (⌨ Barcheston Manor, Shipston-on-Stour, CV36 5AY, ☎ 01608/661268). As across England, many towns in this region have market days: head for **Moreton-in-Marsh** on Tuesdays, **Chipping Norton** on Wednesdays, and **Cirencester** on Fridays and Saturdays. Ask the local tourist boards about others.

Walking

This part of England offers glorious, gentle countryside, with many short walks in the areas around the historic towns of the region. The local tourist information centers often have route maps for themed walks available. If you want to branch out on your own, but not get lost, track the rivers on which most of these towns are built. They usually have towpaths running alongside that are easy to follow and scenically rewarding. However, they wind a lot, and you may find yourself walking for much longer than you had intended. One of the most scenic hiking routes in these parts is the **Cotswold Way,** stretching all the way between Bath and Chipping Campden. The path, about 100 mi in its entirety, traces the ridge marking the edge of the Cotswolds and the Severn Valley and affords incomparable views. For specific information on the Cotswold Way, inquire at the Cotswold Warden Service (☞ Contacts and Resources *in* The Heart of England A to Z, *below*); two useful books, with detailed walking and hiking tours, are the *AA Ordnance Survey Leisure Guide on the Cotswolds,* and Mark Richard's *The Cotswold Way.* The **Forest of Dean** is densely wooded, with interesting villages and monastic ruins to view. Many of its public footpaths are signposted, as are most of the Forestry Commission trails. You'll find easy walks out of Newland, around New Fancy (great view) and Mallards Pike Lake, and a slightly longer one (three hours), which takes in Wench Ford, Danby Lodge, and Blackpool Bridge.

Exploring the Heartland of England

The Cotswold Hills cover some of southern England's most beautiful terrain, with which the characteristic stone cottages found throughout the area are in perfect harmony. Some villages have become overrun by coach parties and quaint antiques shops, but at least they have for the most part retained their historic appearance, and can still be fun. To the west of the Cotswolds lie Gloucester and Cheltenham, almost twin towns, and beyond them, between the River Severn and the border of Wales, the mysterious Forest of Dean. The road from Gloucester to Bath takes you by the evocative castle at Berkeley. Bath, which can also be easily visited on a day out from London, makes an elegant center from which to travel westward to Bristol, the Severn Estuary, and prehistoric sites, this time in the Chew Valley.

Numbers in the text correspond to numbers in the margin and on the Bath Environs, Bath, the Cotswold Hills, and the Forest of Dean maps.

Great Itineraries

Driving down the scenic roads of the Cotswold Hills can be one of the real joys of a British vacation. But even without your own transportation, a Cotswold circuit can be undertaken—easily, by using the numerous excellent guided bus tours in the area, or, more adventurously, using public transportation (this requires careful planning as some buses stop at certain Cotswold towns only twice a week!). A car can be an encumbrance in Bath, Cheltenham, and Gloucester; garage your car or leave it at your hotel. Bath makes a useful place to start off from or wind up at, not far off the M4 motorway on the A46. The cities of Gloucester and Cheltenham also hold many attractions. Once outside the towns, you'll discover that the Cotswold Hills should be relished on a slow schedule, to allow you time to smell the roses, as well as the pink saffron and moon-daisies.

IF YOU HAVE 3 DAYS

A day in ⛲ **Bath** ① will enable you to tour the Roman Baths, followed by a whirl round the next-door Abbey. In the afternoon, stroll along the river or canal, drop in on the collection of ceramics and silverware in the Holburne Museum, then cross town to the Royal Crescent for an early evening promenade. Spend the night here, heading out early for **Cheltenham** ⑬, whose Regency architecture and fashionable shops will occupy a pleasant morning's amble. After lunch, drive northeast on the minor B4632 through **Winchcombe** ⑭, near which lie the majestic grounds of **Sudeley Castle** ⑮ and **Stanway House** ⑯, two mansions with hundreds of years of history behind them. Lunch in **Broadway** ⑱ will allow you to sample its sugary charms, or you might prefer to press on to that Cotswold showpiece, ⛲ **Chipping Campden** ⑲. Now head south on the A429 through the classic Cotswold villages of **Moreton-in-Marsh** ㉑ and **Stow-on-the-Wold** ㉒, where cottage pubs are sandwiched between antiques shops. Nearby, don't miss the smaller places such as ⛲ **Lower and Upper Slaughter** ㉔. For your final afternoon, head westward on A436 to **Gloucester** ㉜, whose restored docks hold the National Waterways Museum.

IF YOU HAVE 7 DAYS

Two days in ⛲ **Bath** ① will give you ample time to explore that treasure chest of Georgian elegance, along with browsing its antiques shops and taking in an evening at the Theatre Royal. Outside Bath, make sure you see **Dyrham Park** ⑪ or **Castle Combe** ⑫, "the prettiest

Three isn't a crowd

when the third is 50% off.

The Party Pass is another great idea from BritRail. Travel in a group and save 50% on the third and fourth person in your party.

It's a great new addition to the range of BritRail passes: the Classic Pass, the Flexipass and the BritRail Senior Pass.

The Party Pass lets you sit back in comfort and style and watch the countryside roll by. And at 50% off, that's something to celebrate.

The BritRail Party Pass is a real crowd pleaser. Call your travel agent or Rail Europe today.

You've read the book. Now book the trip.

For all the best deals on flights, hotels, rental cars, and vacation packages, book them online at www.previewtravel.com. Then click on our Destination Guides featuring content from Fodor's and more. You'll find hotels, restaurants, attractions, and things to do around the globe. There are even interactive maps, videos, and weather forecasts. You'll have everything you need to make your vacation exactly what you want it to be. All it takes is a trip online.

Travel on Your Terms™
www.previewtravel.com
aol keyword: previewtravel

preview travel℠

village in England." On your third day, head north to swank ⛯ **Cheltenham** ⑬, allowing yourself time to make a walking tour of its elegant Regency-era terraces and promenades. Overnight there, then start out on a circuit that takes in the best of the Cotswold villages and countryside (be sure to pick up all the information you'll need on your Cotswold journey at Cheltenham's tourist office). Driving north out of Cheltenham, take a look at **Winchcombe** ⑭, then explore the majestic grounds of **Sudeley Castle** ⑮ and **Stanway House** ⑯. A little farther north, **Snowshill Manor** ⑰ is set in an unspoiled village—this archetypal manor house contains one of the more amazing collections of curios in Britain. The popular Cotswold center of **Broadway** ⑱—whose charms are in inverse proportion to the number of other visitors there at the same time—lies a couple of miles farther, on A44.

Spend your fourth night in that Cotswold showpiece, ⛯ **Chipping Campden** ⑲, from which it is an easy drive to the rare shrubs and "garden rooms" of **Hidcote Manor Garden** ⑳, where you'll need several hours to absorb the splendor of this creation. From here, head southward, through a pair of irresistible Cotswold villages, **Moreton-in-Marsh** ㉑ and **Stow-on-the-Wold** ㉒, both deserving a leisurely wander. South of Stow, kids may enjoy the museum attractions of **Bourton-on-the-Water** ㉓ and **Northleach** ㉕, while **Chedworth Roman Villa** ㉘ is an evocative reminder of the area's importance in "Roman times"—nearby **Cirencester** ㉙ was Corinium, an important provincial capital. The chances are that you will already have seen the ideal rural retreat for your fifth night, perhaps in the wilds around ⛯ **Lower and Upper Slaughter** ㉔. In the morning, an outing eastward might take in idyllic **Bibury** ㉗ and the wool town of **Burford** ㉖. Driving northwest from Cirencester on A417, make your farewells to the Cotswolds life in the model village of **Owlpen Manor** ㉛ and immaculate **Painswick** ㉚.

⛯ **Gloucester** ㉜ presents an exciting contrast to the rustic tone of your last few days. Spend your final day either south of here, exploring the medieval atmosphere of **Berkeley Castle** ㊴ and the celebrated **Slimbridge Wildlife Trust** ㊳, or else east, toward the Wye Valley and Wales, to take a gentle hike through the Forest of Dean with an overnight in ⛯ **Coleford** ㊱. If you have children along, the underground **Clearwell Caves** ㊲ can be special fun. From here, either proceed into Wales, or trace the borderlands north.

When to Tour the Heart of England
Avoid weekends in the busier areas of the Cotswold Hills. During the week, you will hardly see a soul. Bath is particularly congested in summer, when students flock to the language schools here. On the other hand, Gloucester and Cheltenham are workday places that can effortlessly absorb the visiting coach tours and be seen comfortably at any time. Note that the private properties of Hidcote Manor, Snowshill Manor, and Sudeley Castle close in winter. Hidcote Manor Garden is at its best in spring and fall.

BATH AND ENVIRONS

Anyone who listens to the local speech of Bath will note the inflections that herald the beginning of England's West Country. Yet the city retains an inescapable element of the Heart of England: Bath itself is right at the bottom edge of the Cotswold Hills, while the Georgian architecture and mellow stone so prominent here are reminders of the stone mansions and cottages of the Cotswolds. In the hinterland of the county of Somerset, the mellow countryside harbors hidden country pubs and gentle green landscape.

Bath

★ ❶   *13 mi southeast of Bristol, 115 mi west of London.*

"I really believe I shall always be talking of Bath . . . I do like it so very much. Oh! who can ever be tired of Bath," wrote Jane Austen in *Northanger Abbey* and, today, thousands of visitors heartily agree with the great 19th-century author. One of the delights of staying in Bath is being surrounded by the magnificent 18th-century architecture, a lasting reminder of the elegant world described by Austen. Bath suffered slightly from World War II bombing and even more from urban renewal, but the damage was halted before it could ruin the Georgian elegance of the city. This doesn't mean that Bath is a museum. It is lively and interesting, offering dining and entertainment, excellent art galleries, and theater, music, and other performances throughout the year. The Romans first put Bath on the map in the 1st century, when they built a temple here, in honor of the goddess Minerva, and a sophisticated network of baths to make full use of the mineral springs that gush from the earth at a constant temperature of 116°F (46.5°C). Much later, 18th-century People of Quality took the city to heart, and Bath became the most fashionable spa in Britain. The architect John Wood (1704–54) created a harmonious city, building beautiful terraces, crescents, and Palladian villas of the same local stone used by the Romans. Assembly rooms, theaters, and pleasure gardens were all built to entertain the rich and titled, when they weren't busy attending Beau Nash's parties and having their portraits painted by Gainsborough.

A Good Walk

Start in the traffic-free Abbey Churchyard, at the heart of Bath, where the famous **Roman Baths** ② are located, any visit to which will occupy at least a couple of hours. The lively piazza is dominated by the **Abbey** ③, whose facade—itself packed with detail—invites further investigations within. From the Abbey Churchyard, cross over to the Grand Parade, looking out over flower-filled gardens to the River Avon below. Off Abbey Churchyard, where buskers (strolling musicians) of all kinds perform, are tiny alleys leading to little squares of stores, galleries, and eating places. Walk up Stall and Union streets toward Milsom Street, and you'll find numerous alleyways with fascinating small shops (☞ Shopping, *below*). Work your way east to Bridge Street and the graceful, Italianate **Pulteney Bridge** ④. Stroll over this shop-lined masterpiece to Great Pulteney Street, a broad, tranquil thoroughfare that leads to the **Holburne Museum** ⑨, Bath's finest collection of crafted objets. Cross back over the bridge, and head up Broad Street and its extension, Lansdown Road. Turn left into Bennett Street, site of the **Assembly Rooms** ⑦, once the 18th-century hub of elegant society and still retaining its Neoclassic lines. Inside, the **Museum of Costume** provides an amusing overview of some of the weird and wonderful apparel our forebears wore. From here, it's a short hop to **The Circus** ⑥, an architectural tour de force compared by some to an inverted Colosseum. The two John Woods—father and son—were responsible for this, and Wood *fils* was also creator of Bath's most dazzling terrace, the **Royal Crescent,** a graceful arc embracing a swath of green lawns at one end of Brock Street. Once you've feasted your eyes on this vista, you might take in **Number One Royal Crescent** ⑧, a perfectly preserved example of Georgian domestic architecture. Return to the Circus, and walk south down Gay Street, which will bring you past the **Theatre Royal** ⑤, one of the country's most impressive dramatic venues, ideally experienced at an evening performance. Wander east from here back to the Abbey, where a cluster of tea shops offers relief to tired limbs, including *Sally Lunn's*, said to be the oldest house in Bath and birthplace of the renowned Sally Lunn bun.

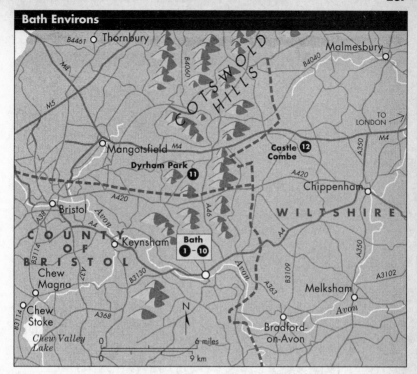

Bath Environs

Thornbury · B4461 · Malmesbury · B4040
M4 · B4060 · COTSWOLD HILLS · TO LONDON · M4
M5 · Mangotsfield · M4 · Castle Combe **12** · A350
Dyrham Park **11** · A420 · Chippenham
A420 · Avon · A46 · WILTSHIRE
Bristol · A4 · A38 · COUNTY · Keynsham · Bath **1 – 10** · A4 · A350
OF · BRISTOL · B3130 · Avon · B3109 · A3102
Chew Magna · A37 · A363 · Melksham
B3114 · Chew Stoke · A368 · N · Avon
Chew Valley Lake · Bradford-on-Avon

0 ————— 6 miles
0 ————— 9 km

Sights to See

3 **Abbey.** Dominating Bath's center, and dating from the 15th century, the edifice has a splendid west front, with carved figures of angels ascending ladders on either side. Notice, too, the miter, olive tree, and crown motif, a play on the name of the present building's founder, Bishop Oliver King. The Abbey was built in the Perpendicular (English late-Gothic) style on the site of a Saxon abbey, and it has superb, fan-vaulted ceilings in the nave. ⊠ *Abbey Churchyard.* ▣ *Donation requested.* ☉ *Visitors are asked not to enter during services.*

★ **7** **Assembly Rooms.** This classical-style building was the leading center for social life in 18th-century Bath, with an ever-changing schedule of dress balls, concerts, and choral nights. Jane Austen came here often, and it was here, in the Ballroom, that Catherine Morland had her first, disappointing encounter with Bath's beau monde in *Northanger Abbey*; the Octagon Room became the setting for an important encounter between Anne Elliot and Captain Wentworth in *Persuasion*. Built by the younger John Wood in 1771, the building was badly damaged by bombing in 1942, but was subsequently and faithfully restored. Today, the Assembly Rooms house the entertaining **Museum of Costume**, displaying, in lavish settings, costumes from Beau Nash's day up to the present. Throughout the year, concerts of Vivaldi, Bach, and other classical composers are given in the Ballroom, just as they were in bygone days. ⊠ *Bennett St.,* ☎ *01225/477785.* ▣ *£3.80, combined ticket with Roman Baths £8.40.* ☉ *Mon.–Sat. 10–5, Sun. 11–5.*

★ **6** **The Circus.** North of Saw Close you can admire the Georgian houses along Queen Square, Gay Street, and the Circus, begun in 1754, where three perfectly proportioned Georgian terraces outline the round garden in the center.

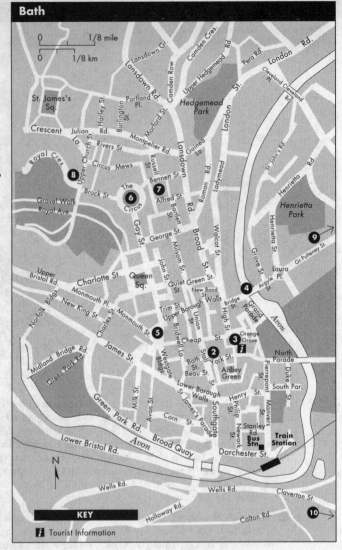

Bath

10 Claverton Manor. This Greek Revival (19th-century) mansion houses
the first museum of Americana to be established outside the United States.
The fine parkland includes a replica of George Washington's garden.
Also southeast of the city, about 1 mi from the city center, is Bath's
grandest house, **Prior Park,** built by John Wood. It is now a school and
much altered, but it has beautiful grounds, complete with a Palladian
bridge and lake, and tours are occasionally given. ⊠ *Claverton Down,
2½ mi southeast of city on Warminster road, A36;* ☎ *01225/460503.*
🎟 *£5.* ⊙ *House: late Mar.–Oct., Tues.–Sun. 2–5, national holidays
and preceding Sun. 11–5; Gardens: late Mar.–Oct., Tues.–Fri. 1–6,
weekends noon–6; closed Mon.*

9 Holburne Museum and Crafts Study Centre. The elegant 18th-century
building houses a small but superb collection of 17th- and 18th-cen-
tury decorative arts, ceramics, and silverware. There are also some 20th-
century crafts. Opposite the museum is No. 4 Sydney Place, the terraced
home that was the main Bath residence of Jane Austen and her fam-

ily. ✉ *Great Pulteney St.,* ☎ *01225/466669.* 🎟 *£3.50.* ⊙ *Easter–mid-Nov., Mon.–Sat. 11–5, Sun. 2:30–5:30; mid-Nov.–mid-Dec. and mid-Feb.–Easter, Tues.–Sat. 11–5, Sun. 2:30–5:30; closed mid-Dec.– mid-Feb.*

★ **⑧** **Number 1 Royal Crescent.** West of the Circus is the Royal Crescent, the crowning glory of architecture in Bath, and much used as a location for period films. The crescent, also the work of John Wood the Younger, was laid out between 1767 and 1774. A house at the center is now Bath's most elegant hotel, the Royal Crescent (☞ Dining and Lodging, *below*). On the corner of Brock Street and the Royal Crescent, Number 1 Royal Crescent has been turned into a museum and furnished as it might have been at the turn of the 19th century. Upstairs all is gentility and elegance; downstairs is a fascinating kitchen museum. ☎ *01225/428126.* 🎟 *£3.80.* ⊙ *Mid-Feb.–Oct., Tues.–Sun. 10:30–5; Nov., Tues.–Sun. 10:30–4.*

❹ **Pulteney Bridge.** One of the most famous landmarks of the city, the 18th-century span, inspired by Florence's Ponte Vecchio, is the only work of Robert Adam in the city and is unique in all Britain because it's lined with shops.

❷ **Roman Baths Museum.** In a central, pedestrian piazza in front of Bath Abbey, the museum occupies the site of the ancient city's temple complex and primary "watering hole." Here, the patrician elite would gather to immerse themselves, drink the mineral waters, and socialize. With the departure of the Romans, the baths fell into disuse, but when the practice again became fashionable, the site was reopened, and the magnificent Georgian building now standing was erected at the end of the 18th century. Almost the entire Roman bath complex has now been excavated, and Acoustiguide handsets allow you to tour the site at your own pace. The museum displays numerous relics of the temple once dedicated to Sulis Minerva. Exhibits include a mustachioed, Celtic-influenced Gorgon's head, and fragments of colorful curses invoked by the old Romans against some of their neighbors. The **Great Bath** is now roofless, and the statuary and pillars belong to the 19th century, but there is much remaining from the original complex, and the steaming, somewhat murky waters are undeniably evocative. On August evenings, you can take part in torchlighted tours of the baths.

Adjacent to the Roman bath complex is the famed **Pump Room,** built in 1792–96, a favored rendezvous place for 18th-century Bath society, where lords and ladies liked to check on the new arrivals to the city. Today, you can enjoy a bite to eat (☞ Dining and Lodging, *below*) on the premises. ✉ *Abbey Churchyard,* ☎ *01225/477785.* 🎟 *Pump Room free, Roman Baths £6.30, combined ticket with Costume Museum £8.40.* ⊙ *Apr.–Sept. daily 9–6 (and Aug. 8 PM–10 PM); Oct.–Mar., daily 9:30–5.*

❺ **Theatre Royal.** Opened in 1805 and restored in 1982, this is a magnificent auditorium, designed by George Dance the younger—a vision in damson plush, raspberry-striped silk, and gold grisaille. Next door to the Theatre Royal, the former home of Richard "Beau" Nash—the dictator of fashion for mid-18th-century society in Bath—and his mistress Juliana Popjoy, is now a restaurant called Popjoy's (☞ Dining and Lodging, *below*). ✉ *Saw Close.*

Dining and Lodging

£££ ✗ **Number Five.** Just over the Pulteney Bridge from the center of town, this airy bistro, with its plants, framed posters, and cane-back chairs, is an ideal spot for a light lunch. The regularly changing menu includes tasty homemade soups, and such dishes as roast quail on wild rice and char-grilled loin of lamb. You can bring your own bottle of wine on Monday and Tuesday. There is no smoking in the restaurant. ⊠ *5 Argyle St.,* ☎ *01225/444499. AE, DC, MC, V. Closed Sun. No lunch Mon.*

££ ✕ **Popjoy's Restaurant.** Named for the mistress of Beau Nash, the restau-
★   rant provides an elegant setting for a fine, English-style, after-theater din-
ner. You have the choice of dining on the ground floor or in the lovely Georgian drawing room upstairs. There is an unmistakable French flavor to the dishes on offer, such as mille-feuille of aubergine (eggplant filled with duxelle mushrooms), though there are plenty of international touches, too. The fixed-price lunch and pre-theater menus are of especially good value. ⊠ *Beau Nash House, Saw Close,* ☎ *01225/460494. AE, DC, MC, V. Closed Sun.*

££ ✕ **Pump Room.** Next to the Roman Baths, the 18th-century Pump Room serves morning coffee, lunches, and afternoon tea, often to music by a string trio. The adjoining Terrace Restaurant has views over the Baths. The restaurants are also open for evening meals during the Bath Festival, and in August and December. ⊠ *Abbey Churchyard,* ☎ *01225/444477. AE, MC, V. No dinner.*

££ ✕ **Rascals.** This is a good spot for a meal on a sightseeing day. In a network of small and snug cellar rooms, you can choose chef Nick Anderson's set menu or the daily specials. The dishes change regularly— try the sushi starter or the poached veal with lentils and capers—and then there's the chocolate truffle cake. There's a very good wine list. ⊠ *8 Pierrepont Pl.,* ☎ *01225/330201. MC, V. Closed Sun.*

££ ✕ **Sally Lunn's.** Near the abbey, this popular spot occupies the oldest house in Bath and still serves the famous Sally Lunn bun, invented here. Full meals are also available. Note that payment by credit card can only be made for evening meals. ⊠ *North Parade Passage,* ☎ *01225/ 461634. MC, V. No dinner Mon. late Dec.–Mar.*

££££ ▦ **Royal Crescent Hotel.** This lavishly converted house, part of the Royal
★   Crescent, is an architectural treasure. The decor has been carefully de-
signed to preserve the building's period elegance, and if some of the bedrooms are on the small side, there are ample luxuries to compensate. The hotel's formal Dower House restaurant has won consistent praise, and a Palladian villa in the garden provides extra rooms. ⊠ *16 Royal Crescent, BA1 2LS,* ☎ *01225/739955,* FAX *01225/339401. 25 rooms with bath and 19 suites. Restaurant, parking. AE, DC, MC, V.*

£££ ▦ **Queensberry Hotel.** This intimate, elegant hotel, in a residential street
★   near the Circus, is in three 1772 town houses built by the architect John Wood for the Marquis of Queensberry. Renovations have preserved the Regency stucco ceilings and cornices and original marble tiling on the fireplaces. Each room is decorated in pastels and flower prints. Downstairs, the Olive Tree restaurant serves English and Mediterranean dishes. ⊠ *Russell St., BA1 2QF,* ☎ *01225/447928,* FAX *01225/446065. 22 rooms with bath. Restaurant, bar. MC, V. Closed Dec. 24–30.*

££ ▦ **Cranleigh.** Standing on the hill high above the city, Cranleigh offers wonderful views over Bath from some of the back rooms. All the comfortable bedrooms have TVs, and one has a four-poster. Excellent breakfasts are served in the dining room, which looks out on the garden, but there are no evening meals. Smoking is not permitted. ⊠ *159 Newbridge Hill, BA1 3PX,* ☎ *01225/310197,* FAX *01225/423143. 5 rooms with bath or shower. MC, V.*

££ ▦ **Paradise House.** Don't be put off by the 10-minute uphill walk from the center of Bath—you'll be rewarded by a wonderful prospect of the city from the upper stories of this Georgian guest house. Cheerfully decorated in cool green and white, it features open fires in winter and a lush, secluded garden for the spring and summer. ⊠ *88 Holloway, BA2 4PX,* ☎ *01225/317723,* FAX *01225/482005. 8 rooms with bath or shower. AE, MC, V.*

£ 🔟 **Bathhurst Guest House.** This typical Georgian house is an easy seven-minute walk north of the city center (from Bath Abbey, head up High Street, which becomes Walcot/London streets, and turn left on Walcot Parade). All rooms are tastefully decorated—one double even has a four-poster bed. Rooms facing the back are quieter. ⊠ *11 Walcot Parade, London St., BA1 5NF,* ☎ *01225/421884. 6 rooms, 2 with bath en suite. No credit cards.*

The Arts

FESTIVALS

The **Bath International Music Festival** (⊠ Bath Festival Office, 2 Church St., Bath BA1 1NL, ☎ 01225/463362), held for two weeks in May/June, is 50 years old in 1999. Concerts, dance, and exhibitions will be held in and around Bath. Some take place in the Assembly Rooms and the Abbey, and opening-night festivities are held in the Royal Crescent and nearby Royal Victoria Park.

THEATER

The **Theatre Royal** (⊠ Box Office, Sawclose, Bath BA1 1ET, ☎ 01225/448844) in Bath, a superb example of a Regency playhouse, has a year-round program that often includes pre- or post-London tours. You have to reserve for the best seats well in advance, but you can line up for same-day standby seats or standing room. Check the location of your seats—sight lines can be poor.

Shopping

Bath's excellent shopping district centers on Stall and Union streets (modern stores) and Milsom Street (traditional stores). Leading off these main streets are fascinating alleyways and passages lined with galleries and a wealth of antiques shops. The **Bath Antiques Market** (⊠ Guinea La.), open Wednesday 6:30–2:30, is a wonderful place to browse; 90 dealers have stalls here, and there's also a restaurant. **Great Western Antique Centre** (⊠ Bartlett St.) delights connoisseurs and collectors with more than 100 stalls selling every kind of antique imaginable, including vintage clothing, linens, and furniture. **Beaux Arts Ceramics** (⊠ York St., ☎ 01225/464850) carries the work of prominent potters, and holds eight solo exhibitions a year. **Margaret's Buildings** (⊠ Halfway between the Circus and Royal Crescent) is a lane with several secondhand and antiquarian bookshops.

Dyrham Park

⑪ *8 mi north of Bath.*

Occupying a high, scenic ridge to the north of Bath, Dyrham Park takes its name from an ancient deer park covering 263 acres, the abode of a herd of fallow deer. At its center stands a late 17th-century country house with paneled interiors, the setting for occasional open-air classical and jazz concerts in summer. ⊠ *Dyrham,* ☎ *0117/937–2501.* 🔳 *£5.40, deer park only £1.70, park and garden only £2.80.* ☉ *House and garden Apr.–Oct., Fri.–Tues. noon–5:30; park daily noon–5:30 or dusk (opens at 11 on days when garden is open).*

Castle Combe

★ ⑫ *12 mi northeast of Bath, 5 mi northwest of Chippenham.*

This Wiltshire village had lived a sleepy existence until one Sunday morning in 1962 when its villagers woke up to find that national newspapers carried photographs of the hamlet on their front pages: Castle Combe had been voted the Prettiest Village in England—without any of its inhabitants knowing that it had even been a contender. By lunchtime, the locals remember, the main narrow street had become an enormous traffic jam. The village's magic is that it is so toylike, so delightfully all-of-a-piece: you can almost see the whole town at one glance from any one position. It consists of little more than a brook, a pack bridge, a street—which is called The Street—of simple stone cottages, a market cross from the 13th century, and the Perpendicular-style church of St. Andrew. The village's grandest house is the Upper Manor House, built in the 15th century by Sir John Fastolf, and now a luxury hotel (Castle Combe Manor House, ☞ Dining and Lodging, *below*).

Dining and Lodging

£££–££££ ✕🏨 **Castle Combe Manor House.** Just outside the village, the manor house
★   is a baronial swirl of solid chimney stacks, carvings, and columns, partly 14th-century, though as a manor it dates back to the Normans. Inside, a stone frieze depicts characters from Shakespeare's Falstaff plays, to commemorate the fact that Sir John Fastolf, thought to be the model for the Bard, was once lord of this manor. The bedrooms are very comfortably furnished, with lavish bathrooms attached; some rooms are in separate mews cottages. There are log fires in the public rooms and antiques everywhere. The Bybrook restaurant serves imaginative cuisine—try the fish casserole with water chestnuts, or the French-inspired soufflé specialties. Outside is a landscaped 23-acre park, ideal for exploring and taking up a very civilized round of golf. ✉ *Castle Combe SN14 7HR,* ☎ *01249/782206,* 🖷 *01249/782159. 45 rooms with bath. Restaurant, pool, 18-hole golf course, tennis court, helipad. AE, DC, MC, V.*

THE COTSWOLDS

The Thames rises among the limestone Cotswold Hills, and a more delightful cradle could not be imagined for that historic river. The Cotswolds are among the best preserved rural districts of England, and their quiet but touching grays and ambers are truly unsurpassed. A great deal has been written about its pretty towns, which age has mellowed rather than withered. In the deep and rolling valleys one finds cozy hamlets appear to drip in foliage from high church tower to garden gate. Beyond the village limits, you'll often find the "high wild hills and rough uneven ways" that Shakespeare wrote about.

In this region, beauty is not just skin deep: over the centuries, quarries of honey-color stone have yielded building blocks for many Cotswold houses and churches and have transformed little towns into realms of gold. Nowhere else in Britain does that superb combination of church tower and gabled manor house shine so brightly, nowhere else are the hedges so perfectly clipped, nor the churchyards so peaceful and picturesque.

There is an elusive spirit about the Cotswolds, so make Bourton-on-the-Water, or Chipping Campden, or Stow-on-the-Wold your headquarters for a few days, and wander aimlessly about for a while, going hither and thither, through this valley and along that byroad, all the time absorbing something of the Cotswold atmosphere. Its secret seems shared by two things—sheep and stone. These were once the great sheep-rearing areas of England, and Cotswold wool was in demand the world over. All this prosperity made the Cotswold merchants rich, but many gave back to the Cotswolds by restoring old churches, or building rows of almshouses, of limestone now seasoned to a glorious golden-gray.

Begin with Cheltenham—the "gateway to the Cotswolds"—then move on to the beauty spots in and around Winchcombe; next are Stanway House, Sudeley Castle, and Snowhill Manor, the three most impressive houses of the region; the oversold village of Broadway, which has many rivals for beauty hereabouts; Chipping Campden—the Cotswold cognoscenti's favorite; Hidcote Manor, one of the most spectacular gardens in England; then circle back south, down through Moreton-in-Marsh, Stow-on-the-Wold, Upper and Lower Slaughter, Bourton-on-the-Water; end with Bibury, Tetbury, and Owlpen Manor. But this is definitely a region where it pays to wander off the beaten track to take a look at that village among the trees. Many sequestered nooks and villages snuggled deep into dells can, in fact, be rendered magically invisible by impenetrable coverings of ivy. Like four-leaf clovers, their discovery must come serendipitously.

Cheltenham

⑬ *50 mi north of Bath, 13 mi east of Gloucester, 50 mi south of Birmingham, 99 mi west of London.*

Although Cheltenham has managed to acquire a reputation as the snootiest place in England, its renown for architectural distinction is well deserved, for it rivals Bath in its Georgian elegance, with wide, tree-lined streets and graceful villas. Like Bath, the town owes part of its fame to mineral springs. By 1740 Cheltenham's first spa was built, and the town became the vogue with a visit from George III and Queen Charlotte in 1788, quickly becoming a capital consecrated to gaiety, idleness, and enjoyment: the "merriest sick resort on earth," as one scribe put it. "A polka, parson-worshipping place"—in the words of resident Lord Tennyson—Cheltenham gained its reputation for snobbiness when stiff-collared Raj majordomos returned from India to find that Cheltenham's springs—the only purely natural alkaline waters in England—were the most effective cure for their "tropical ailments." Want to take some Cheltenham charm home? Be sure to buy a copy of *This England*, the country's quaintest magazine, edited here.

If you visit this historic health resort in the spring or summer—take either M4 and M5 north from Bath, or M5 south from Birmingham, turning east on A40 to reach Cheltenham—you'll see its handsome buildings enhanced by a profusion of flower gardens. The flowers cover even traffic circles, while the elegantly laid-out avenues, crescents, and terraces, with their characteristic row houses, balconies, and iron railings, make Cheltenham an outstanding example of the Regency style. Great Regency architectural set pieces—Lansdowne Terrace, Pittville Spa, Sherborne Walk, the Lower Assembly Rooms, among them—were built solely to adorn the town. The **Rotunda** building at the top of Montpellier Walk—now a bank—contains the spa's original "pump room," i.e., the room in which the mineral waters were on draft, built in 1826. More than 30 statues, like the caryatids on the Acropolis in Athens, adorn the storefronts of **Montpellier Walk.** Wander past **Imperial Square,** with its intricate ironwork balconies, past the ornate Neptune's Fountain, and along the elegant Promenade. Parts of the town may look like something out of a Gilbert and Sullivan stage set, but, today, Cheltenham is the site of two of England's most progressive arts festivals—the Cheltenham Festival of Literature and the town's music festival (☞ The Arts, *below*).

A 20-minute walk from the town center brings you to the **Pittville Pump Room,** built in the late 1820s, where the mineral waters can still be tasted. The pump room now houses the **Gallery of Fashion,** which tells the history of the town through an extensive costume collection. ⊠ *Pittville,* ☎ *01242/523852.* ⊒ *£1.50.* ☉ *May–Sept., Wed.–Mon. 10–4:30; Oct.–Apr., Wed.–Mon. 11–4.*

The Cotswold Hills

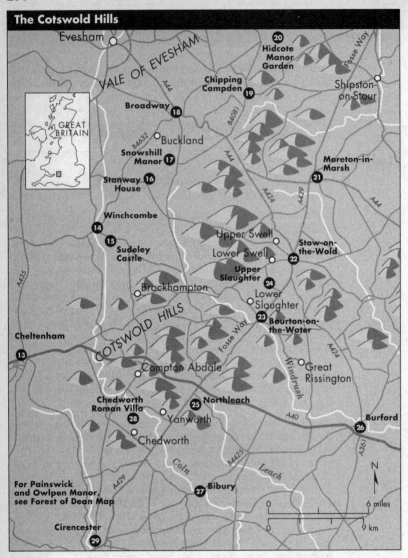

VALE OF EVESHAM

Evesham

Hidcote Manor Garden **20**

Chipping Campden **19**

Shipston-on-Stour

Broadway **18**

Buckland

Snowshill Manor **17**

Moreton-in-Marsh **21**

Stanway House **16**

Winchcombe

14

15 Sudeley Castle

Upper Swell

Lower Swell

Stow-on-the-Wold **22**

Upper Slaughter **24**

Brockhampton

Lower Slaughter

23 Bourton-on-the-Water

COTSWOLD HILLS

Cheltenham

13

Compton Abdale

Fosse Way

Windrush

Great Rissington

Chedworth Roman Villa **28**

Yanworth

25 Northleach

Burford **26**

Chedworth

Coln

B4425

Leach

For Painswick and Owlpen Manor, see Forest of Dean Map

27 Bibury

N

0   6 miles

0   9 km

Cirencester **29**

GREAT BRITAIN

Dining and Lodging

££   ✕ **Le Champignon Sauvage.** Everything is made on the premises here, including bread and vinegar. Perk up your palate with dishes such as chump of Cinderford lamb with potato and goat's cheese purée, and desserts such as pistachio cake with bitter cherries, mascarpone, and roasted fig. Set-price menus at lunch and dinner help to keep the cost down. ⊠ *24 Suffolk Rd.,* ☎ *01242/573449. AE, DC, MC, V. Closed Sun. and 2 wks at Christmas. No lunch Sat.*

£–££   ✕ **81.** Occupying a Regency terrace building on Cheltenham's elegant Promenade, this establishment offers three dining possibilities, with varying degrees of formality. If you want coffee, tea, beer or wine, or a light snack, head for the basement; the ground floor is a bistro with a Modern British menu with Mediterranean influences; the formal restaurant upstairs is the place to appreciate dishes such as braised pheasant, pan-fried calves' liver, and some memorable desserts. There is no smoking in the restaurant. ⊠ *81 The Promenade,* ☎ *01242/222466. AE, DC, MC, V. Closed Mon. No dinner Sun.*

£ ✕ **Montpellier Wine Bar.** An ideal place for a light snack or a fuller evening meal, this informal wine bar offers pies, quiches, and medallions of monkfish, at reasonable prices. Get in early for fast service. ⊠ *Bayshill Lodge, Queens Parade,* ☎ *01242/527774. MC, V.*

£££ 🛏 **Queen's Hotel.** Overlooking Imperial Gardens from the center of The Promenade, this classic Regency building has welcomed visitors to Cheltenham since 1838. The hotel's decor is very British, and every bedroom is individually designed. ⊠ *The Promenade, GL50 1NN,* ☎ *01242/514724,* ⅢX *01242/224145. 77 rooms with bath. Restaurant. AE, DC, MC, V.*

££ 🛏 **Lypiatt House.** This splendid Victorian house—only a short walk
★ from central Cheltenham—is an award-winning bed-and-breakfast. The bedrooms are a comfortable size, with modern bathrooms. There's a small dining room and attentive service from the husband-and-wife team that took over the property in 1992. Young children are not accommodated. ⊠ *Lypiatt Rd., GL50 2QW,* ☎ *01242/224994,* ⅢX *01242/ 224996. 10 rooms with bath or shower. AE, MC, V.*

££ 🛏 **Stretton Lodge Guest House.** Bedrooms here are decorated with color-coordinated curtains and quilt covers, and are comfortably furnished. Set in a quiet Regency street, the lodge is only 10 minutes' walk from Cheltenham's busy center. ⊠ *Western Rd., GL50 3RN,* ☎ *01242/ 570771,* ⅢX *01242/528724. 5 rooms with bath or shower. AE, MC, V.*

£ 🛏 **Regency House.** This attractive guest house close to Pittville Park
★ is quite exceptional. Tasteful furnishings are perfectly matched by period-style wallpaper. The front rooms have views of trees in the square, and the back ones look out at a garden. All rooms have TVs, tea/coffeemaking appliances, and hair dryers. ⊠ *50 Clarence Sq., GL50 4JR,* ☎ *01242/582718,* ⅢX *01242/262697. 8 rooms with bath or shower. AE, MC, V. Closed Dec. 23–Jan. 2.*

The Arts

Cheltenham's annual **International Festival of Music,** during the first two weeks of July, highlights new compositions, often conducted by the composers, together with classical repertory pieces. The town's **Festival of Literature** in October brings together world-renowned authors, actors, and critics. For further information on both, contact the Festival Office (⊠ Town Hall, Imperial Sq., Cheltenham GL50 1QA, ☎ 01242/227979).

Outdoor Activities and Sports

HORSE RACING

Important steeplechase races take place at **Cheltenham** (☎ 01242/ 513014); the National Hunt Festival in mid-March is crowned by the Gold Cup awards on the last day.

Shopping

A stroll along elegant Montpellier Walk and then along the flower-bedecked Promenade will take you past boutiques like Liberty and Hoopers. Both Martin and Scott Cooper on the Promenade are worth visiting for jewelry and silver, while H. W. Keil, at No. 129, has a huge Regency house stocked with 17th- and 18th-century antiques. Behind the Promenade is the Regent Arcade, a modern shopping area with a wide variety of stores. A market is held every Sunday at the racecourse, there's another general market every Thursday morning on Henrietta Street, and there's an indoor antiques market Monday–Saturday at 54 Suffolk Road.

Winchcombe

⑭ *7 mi northeast of Cheltenham.*

From Cheltenham, take B4632 to reach the Cotswolds. It's hard to believe that the sleepy village of Winchcombe was once the capital of the Anglo-Saxon kingdom of Mercia. There are some attractive half-timber and stone-built houses, a clutch of nice old inns serving food, and a typical Cotswold "wool" church, the Perpendicular-style St. Peter's, carved with an outlandish array of almost 40 gargoyles. If you're keen to exercise your lungs, walk out of Winchcombe to the hilltop site of **Belas Knap**, a neolithic long barrow, or sub-merged burial chamber. There's not much to see of the site itself, ★ but you'll be hiking next to and through the **Humblebee Wood**—one of the most enchanting natural domains in England, with ter-rific views stretching over to Sudeley Castle (☞ *below*). It's a bracing 2-mi climb from Winchcombe. If you have a car, be sure to take the scenic Humblebee Wood road down to the villages of Sevenhampton and Brockhampton.

A mile outside Winchcombe, at Greet, you can board a steam-hauled train of the **Gloucester Warwickshire Railway** that chugs its way along a 5-mi stretch at the foot of the Cotswolds. ☎ *01242/621405.* ☉ *Mid-Mar.–Oct., weekends 11–5, daily during school holidays and some dates at Christmas.*

Sudeley Castle

★ **⑮** *1 mi southeast of Winchcombe on B4632, 9 mi northeast of Cheltenham.*

One of the grand showpieces of the Cotswolds, Sudeley Castle was the home and burial place of Catherine Parr (1512–48), Henry VIII's sixth and last wife (who outlived him by one year). Here, Catherine undertook, in her later years, the education of the ill-fated Lady Jane Grey and the future queen, Princess Elizabeth—Sudeley, for good reason, has been called a woman's castle. The term "castle," however, is misleading, for Sudeley appears more like a grand Tudor-era palace. Today its peaceful air belies its turbulent history. During the 17th century, Charles I took refuge here, causing Oliver Cromwell's army to besiege the castle, leaving it in ruins until, centuries later, the Dent-Brocklehurst family stepped in with a magnificent renovation. The romantic grounds include a Tudor knot garden, a carp pond, and varied settings for outdoor Shakespeare performances, concerts, and other events in summer. You can get to Sudeley by taking the train from London to Cheltenham, then a Castleways bus to Winchcombe, followed by a 10-minute walk to the castle. ✉ *Winchcombe,* ☎ *01242/604357.* 🎟 *£5.50 (£5.95 on weekends and national holidays); gardens and exhibitions only, £4 (£4.45 on weekends and national holidays).* ☉ *Mar. (gardens, plant center, and shop only), Tues.–Sun. 11–4:30; Apr.–May, mid-Sept.–Oct., Tues.–Sun., castle 11–5, gardens 10:30–5:30; June–mid-Sept., castle daily 11–5, gardens daily 10:30–5:30.*

Lodging

££££ 🏨 **Sudeley Castle Cottages.** These beautiful Cotswold stone houses are on the magical grounds of Sudeley Castle. Converted from outhouses and the abodes of the estate retainers, they ring the periphery of the estate and range in size from cottage to full-size detached house; the smallest can take two guests, the largest five. Inside, rooms are exquisitely decorated, with themes running from a Victorian dowager scheme in the Emma Dent Cottage to Tudor furnishings in the Anne Boleyn Cottage to a grand mariner's chest in the Lord High Admiral Flat. From Easter to October, accommodations are available on a weekly basis only; in winter they can be booked for three-day stays. ⊠ *Sudeley Castle, Winchcombe GL54 5JD,* ☎ *01242/602308,* 𝖥𝖠𝖷 *01242/602959; make all bookings through Blakes Country Cottages (*☎ *01282/445555). 14 cottage houses with bath and kitchen.*

Stanway House

★ ⑯ *11 mi northeast of Cheltenham, 3 mi northeast of Sudeley Castle.*

Dominating the small village of Stanway, the perfect Cotswold manor, Stanway House, dates from the Jacobean era and is constructed in glowing limestone. Its triple-gabled gatehouse is a Cotswold landmark. The house's Grand Hall is noted for its towering windows. Divided by mullions and transoms into no less than 60 panes, these windows are "so mellowed by time"—to quote Lady Cynthia Asquith (a former chatelaine)—"that whenever the sun shines through their amber and green glass, the effect is of a vast honeycomb and indeed at all times and in all weathers of stored sunshine." The well-worn rooms are fetchingly adorned with family portraits, tattered tapestries, vintage wing armchairs, and Lord Neidpath, the current owner. On the emerald-green grounds is a thatched-roof cricket pavilion built by J. M. Barrie, author of *Peter Pan,* who used to lease the house during summers. ⊠ *Stanway,* ☎ *01386/584469.* ⊞ *£3.50.* ☉ *June–Sept. Tues., Thurs., 2–5 (Wed. only by appt. for groups).*

Snowshill Manor

★ ⑰ *13 mi northeast of Cheltenham, 4 mi northeast of Sudeley Castle.*

Snowshill is one of the most sequestered and unspoiled of all Cotswold villages. Snuggled beneath Oat Hill, with little room for any expansion, the hamlet is centered around a historic burial ground, the picturesque 19th-century St. Barnabas Church, and Snowshill Manor, a splendid 17th-century house that is overflowing with the collections of Charles Paget Wade. Over the door of the house is his family motto, *Nequid pereat* ("Let nothing perish"). The rooms here are bursting with Tibetan scrolls, spinners' tools, ship models, Persian lamps, and countless forms of bric-a-brac. Children love it. Outside, a quintessential Cotswold terraced garden provides an exquisite frame for the house. ⊠ *Snowshill,* ☎ *01386/852410.* ⊞ *£5.50, grounds only £2.50.* ☉ *Apr.–Oct., Wed.–Mon. 1–5 (grounds open noon–5:30 May–Sept.); last admission 45 mins before closing.*

Broadway

⑱ *15 mi northeast of Cheltenham, 2 mi north of Snowshill Manor.*

The Cotswold town to end all Cotswold towns, Broadway has become a mecca for day-trippers. William Morris first discovered the delights of this village, and J. M. Barrie, Vaughan Williams, and Edward Elgar soon followed. Today, sophisticated travelers tend to avoid Broadway in the summer, when it is clogged with cars and buses. Named for its wide main street, Broadway offers many shops and a renowned hotel, the Lygon Arms (☞ Dining and Lodging, *below*). Along Broadway's main roads, there are numerous antiques shops, tea parlors, and quaint boutiques; happily, Broadway has now been given a highway bypass, so express traffic that used to hurl noisily now skirts the town. Step off onto Broadway's back roads and alleys and you'll find serenity, along with any number of picturesque houses On the outskirts of Broadway, off A44, is **Broadway Tower Country Park.** From the top of the tower, an 18th-century "folly" built by the sixth earl of Coventry, you can see more than 12 counties in a breathtakingly beautiful vista. Nature trails, picnic grounds with barbecue grills, an adventure playground, and rare animals and birds are surrounded by peaceful countryside. ☎ *01386/852390.* ⊡ *£2.95.* ☉ *Apr.–Oct., daily 10–6.*

Dining and Lodging

££££ ✕☷ **Buckland Manor.** As an alternative to the razzmatazz of Broad-
★   way, try this exceptional hotel 2 mi away in Buckland—an idyllic little Cotswold hamlet—just off B4632. Parts of the building date from Jacobean times, and there are pleasant old pictures and fine antiques everywhere. The garden is lovely and peaceful. Nonresidents as well as residents partake of fine meals in the baronial and expensive restaurant. ⊠ *Near Broadway, WR12 7LY,* ☎ *01386/852626,* ℻ *01386/ 853557. 13 rooms with bath. Restaurant, pool, tennis court, croquet. AE, DC, MC, V.*

££££ ✕☷ **Lygon Arms.** Here you'll find luxury combined with old-world charm—the Lygon has been in business since 1532 and is now part of the Savoy Hotels group. Bought in 1830 by General Lygon, it was next purchased by his butler. Multigabled, with mullioned windows, it has a gorgeous facade from 1620; inside, there are antiques-bedecked parlors, baronial fireplaces, 18th-century paneling, and rooms that once sheltered Charles I and Oliver Cromwell. The main dining room, the Great Hall, even has a minstrel's gallery. However, some of the modern additions are way too glitzy for their own good. Although it's on the main street, it has 3 acres of formal gardens for guests to enjoy. ⊠ *High St., WR12 7DU,* ☎ *01386/852255,* ℻ *01386/858611. 65 rooms with bath. Restaurant, indoor pool, sauna, spa, golf privileges, tennis court, billiards, helipad. AE, DC, MC, V.*

£££   ✕☷ **Dormy House Hotel.** Guest rooms here overlook the Vale of Eve-
★   sham from high on the Cotswolds ridge. This luxurious country-house hotel has been converted from a 17th-century Cotswolds farmhouse. Bedrooms are individually and beautifully furnished, some with four-poster beds. The restaurant is noted in the region and offers a superlative wine list. ⊠ *Willersey Hill (2 mi north from Broadway), WR12 7LF,* ☎ *01386/852711,* ℻ *01386/858636. 49 rooms with bath. Restaurant, sauna, putting green, croquet, exercise room. AE, DC, MC, V. Closed Dec. 24–28.*

Chipping Campden

⓳ *18 mi northeast of Cheltenham, 4 mi east of Broadway.*

Undoubtedly one of the most beautiful towns in the heart of England, Chipping Campden is the Cotswolds in a microcosm. It has one of the most seductive settings of the area, which will unfold before you as you travel on B4081 through sublimely lovely English countryside to happen upon the town tucked in a slight valley. The soaring tower of **St. James,** the most impressive church of the region, announces the town from a distance. Nearby, on Church Street, is an important row of almshouses dating from King James I's reign. The broad High Street follows a picturesque curve and is lined with attractive houses and shops. In the center, on Market Street, is the **Market Hall,** a gabled Jacobean structure built by Sir Baptiste Hycks in 1627 "for the sale of local produce." The **Silk Mill** (⊠ Sheep St., ☉ Mon.–Sat. 9–5) was taken over by the Guild of Handicrafts in 1902, when arts-and-crafts evangelist C. R. Ashby brought 150 acolytes here from London, including 50 guildsmen, to revive and practice such skills as cabinetmaking and bookbinding. The operation folded in 1920, but the building has recently been refurbished to house various crafts workshops, and there is a small exhibition of drawings, old photos, and various objects related to the village and the history of the local Arts and Crafts movement. To reach Chipping Campden from Broadway, take A44 east and then head left onto B4081, on the way glimpsing the distant Malvern Hills to the west in Worcestershire.

Dining and Lodging

£££ ✗⊡ **Charingworth Manor.** Views of the Cotswold countryside are limitless from this 14th-century manor-house hotel a short distance outside town. Each room is named for previous owners or local villages and is individually done in English floral fabrics, with antique and period furniture. Rooms in the old manor have the best views and original oak beams. As a guest, T. S. Eliot used to enjoy walking its 50 acres of grounds. The restaurant is pricey and charming, with low-beamed ceilings. ⊠ *Charingworth, 3 mi east of Chipping Campden, GL55 6NS,* ☎ *01386/593555,* ℻ *01386/593353. 23 rooms with bath, 3 suites. Restaurant, indoor pool, sauna, steam room, tennis court, billiards. AE, DC, MC, V.*

£££ ⊡ **Noel Arms Hotel.** In the heart of Chipping Campden, this inn was built for foreign wool traders in the 14th century and is the oldest inn in town. It retains its period atmosphere with exposed beams and stonework, even though it has been recently enlarged. Its individually decorated bedrooms—some dating back to the 14th century—offer every modern comfort. Rates fall into the bottom end of this category. ⊠ *High St., GL55 6AT,* ☎ *01386/840317,* ℻ *01386/841136. 26 rooms with bath. Restaurant, bar. AE, DC, MC, V.*

Hidcote Manor Garden

★ ⑳ *4 mi northeast of Chipping Campden, 9 mi south of Stratford-upon-Avon.*

Laid out around a Cotswold manor house, Hidcote Manor Garden is arguably the most interesting and attractive large garden in Britain; it can also be terribly overcrowded at the height of the season. It was created in 1907 by an American horticulturist, Major Lawrence Johnstone. Johnstone was not just an imaginative gardener, but a widely traveled plantsman as well, who brought back specimens from all over the world. The formal part of the garden is arranged in "rooms" without roofs, separated by hedges, often with fine topiary work and walls. The White Garden was probably the forerunner of the popular white gardens at Sissinghurst and Glyndebourne. In summer, Shakespearean plays are performed on the Theater Lawn. ⊠ *Hidcote Bartrim,* ☎ *01386/438333.* ▱ *£5.50.* ☉ *Apr.–Oct., Mon., Wed., Thurs., and weekends 11–7 (11–6 in Oct.), also Tues. June–July 11–7; last admission 1 hr before closing or dusk if earlier.*

Hidcote Manor Gardens borders on **Hidcote Bartrim,** another storybook Cotswold dell. A handful of thatched stone houses, a duck pond, and a well make up the center of this fetching cul-de-sac; less than a mile away is the equally idyllic hamlet of Hidcote Boyce, which features a 17th-century manor house, Hidcote House.

Moreton-in-Marsh

㉑ *18 mi northeast of Cheltenham, 13 mi south of Hidcote Manor Garden, 5 mi north of Stow-on-the-Wold.*

In Moreton-in-Marsh, the houses have been built not around a central square but along a street wide enough to accommodate a market (every Tuesday). The village enjoys fine views across the hills. A landmark of the town is St. David's Church, which has a lovely tower of honey-gold ashlar. The town also possesses one of the last remaining curfew towers, dated 1633; curfew dates back to the time of the Norman Conquest, when a bell was rung to "cover-fire" for the night against any invaders. From Chipping Campden, take B4081 south, then A44 south and east to reach Moreton-in-Marsh.

Outside Moreton-in-Marsh, off the Stow-to-Broadway road, is **Sezincote,** an exotic garden. Created in the early 19th century, the estate was the vision of Sir Charles Cockerell, who made a fortune in the East India Company. Asian aquatic gardens, a Hindu temple folly, and an Indian-style bridge have charmed visitors ever since the Prince Regent came to the estate in 1807 (and was promptly inspired to create that Xanadu of Brighton, the Royal Pavilion). ⊠ *Off A-424,* ☏ *01386/700444.* ☉ *Jan.–Nov.*

A reminder of the obscure civilizations of prehistoric Britain can be seen about 8 mi east of Moreton, where the **Rollright Stones** occupy a high position on the Wolds off A3400. This stone circle has none of the grandeur of Stonehenge and Avebury but is almost as important. Legend gives the stone groups, dating from before 1500 BC, the names of the King's Men and the Whispering Knights.

Stow-on-the-Wold

㉒ *15 mi east of Cheltenham, 5 mi south of Moreton-in-Marsh.*

At 800 ft, Stow is the highest, as well as the largest, town in the Cotswolds—"Stow-on-the-Wold, where the wind blows cold" is the age-old saying. Built around a wide square, Stow's imposing golden stone houses have been discreetly converted into a good number of quality antiques stores. Look for the Kings Arms Old Posting House, its wide entrance still seeming to wait for the stagecoaches that once stopped here on their way to Cheltenham. As well as being a lure for the antiques hunter, Stow is a convenient base: eight main Cotswolds roads intersect here but all—happily—bypass the town center.

Dining and Lodging

£   ✕ **Queen's Head.** An excellent stopping-off spot for a pub lunch, the Queen's Head has a courtyard out back, perfect for a summer afternoon. The bench in front, under a climbing rose, makes a relaxing spot for imbibing outdoor refreshment. ⊠ *The Square,* ☏ *01451/830563. MC, V. No dinner Sun. or Mon.*

£££   🏨 **Fosse Manor.** Family-run for years, this lovely manor-house hotel, just out of town (1 mi south on A429), has a reputation for solid comfort and service. Golf and riding are available nearby. ⊠ *Fosse Way, GL54 1JX,* ☏ *01451/830354,* 🖷 *01451/832486. 20 rooms, 18 with bath. Restaurant, putting green, croquet. AE, DC, MC, V.*

££–£££   🏨 **Stow Lodge Hotel.** Set well back from the main square of Stow-on-the-Wold in its own quiet gardens, the lodge is a typical Cotswold manor house; its large, open fireplaces provide added warmth in the winter. Smoking is permitted only in the bar/lounge. ⊠ *The Square, GL54 1AB,* ☏ *01451/830485,* 🖷 *01451/831671. 21 rooms with bath. Restaurant. DC, MC, V. Closed 5 wks Jan.–Feb.*

Bourton-on-the-Water

㉓   *12 mi east of Cheltenham, 4 mi southwest of Stow-on-the-Wold.*

Bourton-on-the-Water, off A429 on the eastern edge of the Cotswold Hills, is deservedly famous as a classic Cotswold village. The little River Windrush runs through Bourton, crossed by low stone bridges. This village makes a good touring base, but in summer, as in Stratford and Broadway, it's overcrowded with tourists. A stroll through Bourton takes you past Cotswold cottages, many now converted to little stores and coffee shops. Follow the stream and its ducks to the end of the village and the old mill, now the **Cotswold Motor Museum and Exhibition of Village Life.** In addition to 30 vintage motor vehicles and a collection of old advertising signs (supposedly the largest in Europe), this museum offers an Edwardian store, a blacksmith's forge, a wheelwright's shop, a country kitchen, and a trove of children's toys. ⊠ *The Old Mill,* ☎ *01451/821255.* ☜ *£1.75.* ☉ *Feb.–Nov., daily 10–6.*

☾ The **Model Railway Exhibition** (⊠ Box Bush, High St., ☎ 01451/820686) is in itself interesting and has some toys for sale. The **Model Village** (⊠ Old New Inn, ☎ 01451/820467) is an outdoor working replica of Bourton village, built in 1937 to a scale of one-ninth.

Lodging

££ ⊞ **Coombe House.** At this neat guest house you'll find an attractive garden with some unusual and interesting plants. The comfortable bedrooms have TVs and appliances for making tea or coffee, and the first floor has a balcony where you can enjoy a drink when the weather permits. This is a no-smoking establishment. There's ample parking. ⊠ *Rissington Rd., GL54 2DT,* ☎ *01451/821966,* ℻ *01451/810477. 7 rooms with bath. AE, MC, V.*

Shopping

The **Cotswold Perfumery** has a wide range of perfumes, which are manufactured here. While deciding what to buy, visit the Exhibition of Perfumery and the Perfumed Garden. Perfume bottles and jewelry are also on sale. ⊠ *Victoria St.,* ☎ *01451/820698.* ☜ *Exhibition £1.75.*

Lower and Upper Slaughter

㉔   *2 mi north of Bourton-on-the-Water, 15 mi east of Cheltenham.*

For a quieter, more typical Cotswolds atmosphere, go to villages with such evocative names as Lower Slaughter and Upper Slaughter (the names have nothing to do with mass murder, but come from the Saxon word *sloh,* which means "a marshy place") or Lower and Upper Swell. Lower Slaughter is one of the "water villages," with Slaughter Brook running down the center road of the town. Little stone footbridges ford the brook, while the town's resident gaggle of geese can often be seen paddling in the sparkling water. Connecting the two Slaughters is Warden's Way, a mile-long pathway, beginning in Upper Slaughter at the town center parking lot. Along the way, you'll pass neat stone houses, the greenest of meadows, the most immemorial of trees, and a noted mill. Warden's Way continues on to Bourton-on-the-Water.

Dining and Lodging

£££–££££ ✕⊞ **Lords of the Manor Hotel.** A characteristic 16th-century Cotswolds manor house, "the Lords" is set among rolling fields threaded by a lovely fishing stream. It offers comfort and a warm welcome, and its location, Upper Slaughter, is a quintessential Cotswolds village. Extensive refurbishment has meant additional bedrooms available in a converted granary and barn, now more modern than those in the main house. Country-house chintz and antiques set the style throughout, including the acclaimed restaurant, which features an elegant British/French menu. ⊠ *Upper Slaughter, GL54 2JD,* ☎ *01451/820243,* ℻ *01451/ 820696. 27 rooms with bath. Restaurant, fishing. AE, DC, MC, V.*

£££ ✕🏨 **Washbourne Court.** This fine 17th-century building stands amid 4 acres of grounds beside the River Eye. The interior has stone-flagged floors, beams, and open fires. The bedrooms in the main building have a deliberately country feel to them, while rooms in the converted barn and cottages are more modern. The food in the award-winning restaurant, appropriately, is traditional English. ⊠ *Lower Slaughter, GL54 2HS,* ☎ *01451/822143,* ℻ *01451/821045. 27 rooms and suites with bath or shower. Restaurant, tennis court. AE, DC, MC, V.*

Northleach

㉕ *14 mi southeast of Cheltenham, 5 mi southwest of Bourton-on-the-Water.*

From Bourton-on-the-Water, follow A429, the Fosse Way, to Northleach for a look at the magnificent church of St. Peter and St. Paul, dating from the 15th century. It is one of the Cotswold's most notable "wool" churches and within is a collection of memorial brasses, all bearing the likenesses of leading medieval woolmen. Northleach also holds a couple of intriguing museums. **Keith Harding's World of Mechanical Music** displays a diverting collection of pianolas, music boxes, and other mechanical instruments from times past. ⊠ *The Oak House, High St.,* ☎ *01451/860181.* 🎟 *£5.* ☉ *Daily 10–6, last tour 5.*

In a renovated 18th-century prison is the **Cotswold Countryside Collection,** comprising the Lloyd-Baker collection of agricultural history. Items include antique wagons and tools and there is an exhibition of the area's social history. ☎ *01451/860715.* 🎟 *£2.50.* ☉ *Apr.–Oct., Mon.–Sat. 10–5, Sun. 2–5.*

Burford

㉖ *9 mi east of Northleach, 18 mi north of Swindon, 18 mi west of Oxford.*

Burford's broad main street leads steeply down to a narrow bridge across the River Windrush. The village has many historic inns, as it was a stagecoach stop for centuries. On weekends at the **Golden Pheasant Hotel,** on High St. (☎ 01993/823223), have afternoon tea in the lounge while relaxing in a deep, velvet armchair; in winter, there's a lovely log fire. From Northleach, take A40 east to reach Burford.

Dining and Lodging

£££ ✕🏨 **Bay Tree.** Located away from Burford's bustle, the atmospheric Bay Tree is in a 16th-century stone house, visited in its prime by both Elizabeth I and James I. Try for a room in the main house. The restaurant has a garden view and serves a three-course set menu of mainly English dishes, stressing healthful eating. ⊠ *Sheep St., OX18 4LW,* ☎ *01993/822791,* ℻ *01993/823008. 23 rooms with bath. Restaurant. AE, DC, MC, V.*

Bibury

㉗ *10 mi southwest of Burford, 6 mi northeast of Cirencester, 15 mi north of Swindon.*

The tiny town of Bibury, on the B4425, occupies an idyllic setting beside the little River Coln; it was this was famed Arts and Crafts artist William Morris's choice for Britain's most beautiful village. Fine old cottages, a river meadow, the church of St. Mary's, and **Arlington Row**—a picturesque stone group of 17th-century weavers' cottages—are some of the delights here. Just outside, on a site recorded in the Domesday Book, stands the huge, 17th-century **Arlington Mill,** a working corn mill containing examples of agricultural implements and machinery from the Victorian era, as well as country exhibits. ☎ *01285/740368.* 🎟 *£2.* ☉ *Daily 10–6.*

Chedworth Roman Villa

★ **㉘** *6 mi northwest of Bibury, 9 mi north of Cirencester, 10 mi southeast of Cheltenham.*

In a wooded valley on the eastern fringe of the Cotswolds, Chedworth Roman Villa is one of the best-preserved Roman villas in England. Thirty-two rooms, including two complete bath suites, have been identified. The visitor center and museum give a picture of Roman life in Britain. From Bibury, follow the single-track back roads, passing through Abington and across A429 to Yanworth and Chedworth, where you will pick up the signs. The villa is also signposted from A40. ✉ *Yanworth,* ☎ *01242/890256.* 🎟 *£3.20.* ☉ *Mar.–Oct., Tues.–Sun. and national holidays 10–5; Nov., Tues.–Sun. 10–4.*

Cirencester

㉙ *9 mi south of Chedworth, 14 mi southeast of Cheltenham.*

Cirencester has been a major hub of the Cotswolds since Roman times, when it was called Corinium, and lay at the intersection of the Fosse Way and the Ermin Way (today A429 and A417). Today this lovely old market town preserves a fine array of mellow stone buildings—take a stroll down Dollar Street to see the bowfront stores—and the magnificent parish church, St. John the Baptist. The **Corinium Museum** has an excellent collection of Roman artifacts, as well as full-scale reconstructions of local Roman interiors. ✉ *Park St.,* ☎ *01285/655611.* 🎟 *£2.50.* ☉ *Mon.–Sat. 10–5, Sun. 2–5; Nov.–Mar. closed Mon.*

Barnsley House Gardens is home to Rosemary Verey, one of the world's foremost gardeners. The octogenarian and her family live here in an elegant Cotswold stone mansion, surrounded by her exquisite gardens, her world-famous potager, a neo-Gothic folly, and a garden shop (run by her son) where you can pick up one of her 18 books. As of January 1999, all visits must be booked in advance through Charles Verey. ✉ *The Close, Barnsley, GL7 5EE, 4 mi north of Cirencester on the B4425,* ☎ *01285/740561.* 🎟 *£3.50; personal tour by Rosemary Verey £100, other guides £30.* ☉ *Mon.–Sat. 10–5.*

Shopping

Every Monday and Friday Cirencester's central **Market Place** is packed with stalls selling a motley range of goods, mainly household items but some local produce and craft work, too. On Market Place, the **Corn Hall** is the venue for a Friday antiques market, and a crafts market on most Saturdays.

Painswick

30 *16 mi northwest of Cirencester, 8 mi south of Cheltenham, 5 mi south of Gloucester.*

This old Cotswold wool town has become a picture of quaintness, attracting day-trippers and coach parties. But come during the week and you can discover the genuine charm of the place in relative tranquility. The huddled gray stone houses and inns date from as early as the 14th century and include a notable group from the Georgian era. The churchyard is renowned for its 99 yew trees, planted in 1792 and meticulously trimmed to different shapes. Painswick's annual "Clypping Ceremony," occurring on the first Sunday after September 19, has nothing to do with topiary—the name derives from the Anglo-Saxon word, "clyppan" meaning "encircle." Children with garlands make a ring round the church, while traditional hymns are sung. Another good time to be here would be for the town's Victorian Market Day in early July: contact Cheltenham's tourist office for precise dates. Half a mile north of town on B4073, **Painswick Rococo Garden** displays unusual garden design. ⊠ *On B4073,* ☎ *01452/813204.* ☞ *£3.* ☉ *Mid-Jan.–Nov., Wed.–Sun. 11–5 (daily in July and Aug.).*

From Painswick, you can head north to the historic city of Gloucester (☞ *below*). To the south of Painswick, however, lies one last beauty ★ **31** spot, **Owlpen Manor**—an off-the-beaten-track hamlet that is a fitting Cotswold coda (for an in-depth look, see the Close-Up box, "And the Most Beautiful Place in England Is . . ." *below*).

Dining and Lodging

£–££   ✗🏠 **Cardynham House.** Painter and sculptor Carol Keyes has made
★ this tiny B&B a stylish retreat, with a cozy lobby full of antiquarian books, tartan throws, and leather armchairs. The decor includes a veritable forest of beamed ceilings, Jacobean staircase, Elizabethan fireplace, and themed guest rooms (Medieval Garden, for example), all with four-poster beds. Downstairs, in the March Hare dining room, a grand English breakfast is served to guests; at night, the kitchen offers delicious Thai food, a popular place for the locals. ⊠ *The Cross, GL6 6XX,* ☎ *01452/814006,* 🖷 *01452/812321. 6 rooms with bath. Restaurant. No credit cards.*

GLOUCESTER, BERKELEY, AND THE FOREST OF DEAN

West of the Cotswolds a rather urbanized axis connects Gloucester with Cheltenham. Despite their proximity, on either side of the M5 motorway, the towns have a very different feel, the down-to-earth Gloucester built around docks connected to the River Severn contrasting with the gentrified spa town of Cheltenham. North of Gloucester lies the riverside town of Tewkesbury with its imposing abbey, while to the south, easily accessible from M5, stands the stern, battlemented Berkeley Castle. To the southeast, the low-lying Forest of Dean, once a private hunting ground of kings, is now a recreation area for the general public, with some of the most extensive and beautiful woodlands in the country.

Gloucester

32 *13 mi west of Cheltenham, 56 mi south of Birmingham, 105 mi west of London.*

Much of the ancient heritage of this county seat has been lost to nondescript modern stores and offices, but the **Gloucester Folk Museum** is

AND THE MOST BEAUTIFUL PLACE IN ENGLAND IS...

THERE ARE SOME MAGICAL spots that capture—like the phenomenon of experiencing the ocean in a single drop of water—the essence of an entire world. Owlpen Manor's drop of water transmutes all there is to know about rural England into one enchanting package. Like a British version of Brigadoon, it lies hidden away, known only to a select few. "Owlpen in Gloucestershire—Ah, what a dream is there!" rhapsodized Vita Sackville-West in 1941. Then a decade ago, Prince Charles, who ought to know—his Highgrove manor is just a few miles away—called it "the epitome of the English village." The secret was out.

This fairy-tale Cotswold hamlet centers around a picturesque church, a Tudor manor house, and cottages, all set against an equally picturesque mountainside. Indeed, what makes the village (population: 35) the Cotswolds' Shangri-la is that it has remained uniquely uninvaded by the modern world, and for this its guardian mountain must be thanked. The triple-gabled stone manor house, built between 1450 and 1720, was lovingly restored decades ago by local Arts and Crafts–period artisans. The garden is hardly changed from the days of Queen Anne; its great yew "ballroom" was the everlasting envy of gardening greats, such as the renowned Gertrude Jekyll. Today, the house and garden are open to the public from April 1 to October 31, daily except Monday (unless it's a national-holiday Monday), 2–5. The restaurant is open from noon. Admission charges are £4.25 for the house and grounds, or £3 just for the grounds.

But all this can be your very own home-away-from-home. Several of Owlpen's cottages have been converted into luxurious guest accommodations, including a studio flat in the Tithe Barn; Summerfield Cottage, overlooking a murmuring brook; a gorgeous Cotswold-stone farmhouse nestled deep in the woods; and a dollhouse-size Stuart-era garden building (high-season prices start from £80 for a weekend break for two, while a weekly rent in a larger accommodation ranges from £215 to £780). Nicholas Mander—descendant of Sir Geoffrey and Lady Mander, the noted Pre-Raphaelite art patrons—and his delightful family oversee this tiny kingdom, with Karen Mader in charge of the Cyder Press restaurant. Picturesque in its timelessness and singularly romantic, Owlpen Manor could well rank as the loveliest place in England. To get to Owlpen Manor from Painswick, head south on A45 to Stroud, then head west on A419. Turn south on B4066 to Uley and the Owlpen Manor signpost. Owlpen Manor is near Dursley, GL11 5BZ (☎ 01453/860261; to book from America, contact The London Connection, ☎ 801/393–9120).

The Forest of Dean

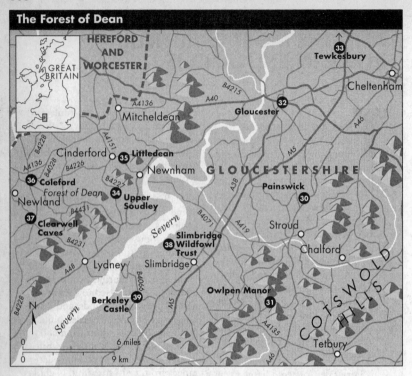

housed in a row of fine Tudor and Jacobean half-timber houses. ⊠ *99–103 Westgate St.,* ☎ *01452/526467.* 🖾 *Free.* ☉ *Oct.–June, Mon.–Sat. 10–5; July–Sept., Mon.–Sat. 10–5, Sun. 10–4.*

★ Across Westgate Street is the magnificent **Gloucester Cathedral,** originally a Norman abbey church, consecrated in 1100. The exterior soars in elegant lines, and the interior has largely been spared the sterilizing attentions of modern architects. The place is a mishmash of periods, and the clutter of centuries mirrors perfectly the slow growth of ecclesiastical taste. The interior is almost completely Norman, with the massive pillars of the nave left untouched since their completion. The Whispering Gallery holds a permanent exhibition of the history of the cathedral, and there are tours available April–October. The fan-vaulted roof of the cloisters is the finest in Europe. The cloisters enclose a peaceful garden. ⊠ *Westgate St.,* ☎ *01452/528095.* 🖾 *Requested donation £3; admission £1 to Whispering Gallery.* ☉ *Daily 8–6, except during services and special events.*

A short walk from the cathedral, at the end of Westgate Street along the canal, are the historic **Gloucester Docks.** The docks still function, though now on a much reduced scale. The vast Victorian warehouses are being restored, and new shops and cafés added, to bring the area back to life. One of the warehouses at Gloucester Docks is now the Antique Centre (☞ Shopping, *below*). Another holds **The National Waterways Museum,** with examples of canal houseboats and barges. Tours, starting at the National Waterways Museum, are conducted every Sunday in August at 2:30. ⊠ *Llanthony Warehouse, Gloucester Docks,* ☎ *01452/318054.* 🖾 *£4.50.* ☉ *Apr.–Sept., daily 10–6; Oct.–Mar., daily 10–5.*

Dining and Lodging

£ ✕ **College Green.** With a keen notion of the right meal in the right place, this upstairs restaurant, with views out over the cathedral, serves classic English cooking—pork and cider casserole, fresh salmon—and provides a respectable wine list. ⊠ *7 College St.,* ☎ *01452/520739. AE, MC, V. Closed Sun. in winter.*

£ ✕ **Dick Whittington.** A large, wooden-floor pub serving beer and wine from the barrel, this spot commemorates a famous native son, who was three times Lord Mayor of London in the Middle Ages. Bar snacks are served throughout the day (but not Sunday evening). ⊠ *100 Westgate St.,* ☎ *01452/502039. No credit cards.*

£££ 🏨 **Hatherley Manor.** Standing on 37 acres of grounds 2 mi north of Gloucester, this renovated 17th-century house is fairly quiet unless a conference is going on—which happens frequently. There's a four-poster honeymoon suite. ⊠ *Down Hatherley La., GL2 9QA,* ☎ *01452/730217,* ℻ *01452/731032. 56 rooms with bath. Restaurant, croquet, exercise room, helipad. AE, DC, MC, V.*

Outdoor Activities and Sports

BICYCLING

The **Gloucester Tourist Office** (☎ 01452/421188) has a full range of cycle touring route maps for the Cotswold region.

BOATING

From the pier outside the National Waterways Museum, you can take a brief tour of the Gloucester Docks, lasting 45 minutes, or longer all-day cruises, heading north as far as Tewkesbury or south to the Severn Estuary at Sharpness. Contact the **Waterways Museum** (Gloucester Docks, *above*) for dates and prices.

Shopping

The **Antique Centre** (☎ 01452/529716) offers some good buys, in a restored Victorian warehouse at Gloucester Docks. The **Beatrix Potter Gift Shop** (⊠ College Ct., ☎ 01452/422856), next to the Cathedral Gate, is the house of the tailor featured in Potter's story *The Tailor of Gloucester.*

Tewkesbury

㉝ *12 mi north of Gloucester.*

Just west of M5 and south of M50 lies Tewkesbury, an ancient town of black-and-white half-timber buildings on the River Avon, from which you can enjoy a cruise up the river in the *Avon Belle.* The stonework in the Norman **Tewkesbury Abbey** bears the marks of the same mason as that of Gloucester Cathedral, but the abbey has been built in the Romanesque (12th-century) and Decorated Gothic (14th-century) styles. It is a beautifully kept church, often with massive flower displays along the nave. ⊠ *Church St.,* ☎ *01684/850959.* ☉ *Daily.*

Lodging

£££ 🏨 **Royal Hop Pole.** One of the most famous old English inns, this is now a part of the Regal chain. The rooms at the rear have wood beams and views of the pretty gardens running down to the river. One of the front rooms has a four-poster. Rates fall at the very bottom of this category. ⊠ *Church St., GL20 5RT,* ☎ *01684/293236,* ℻ *01684/296680. 29 rooms with bath. Restaurant. AE, DC, MC, V.*

£££ 🏨 **Tewkesbury Park Hotel, Golf and Country Club.** Just outside town (1¼ mi south on A38), this former 18th-century mansion is the ideal stopover point for the athletically inclined. There's almost every sports facility anyone could want, plus the wonderful countryside. The Park also caters to a flourishing conference trade. ⊠ *Lincoln Green La., GL20*

7DN, ☎ 01684/295405, FAX 01684/292386. 78 rooms with bath. Restaurant, coffee shop, indoor pool, exercise room, sauna, golf privileges, tennis court, squash. AE, DC, MC, V.

Upper Soudley

㉞ *15 mi west of Gloucester, 11 mi south of Ross-on-Wye.*

★ The mysterious **Forest of Dean** covers much of the valley between the rivers Severn and Wye. Although the primordial forest has long since been cut down and replanted, the landscape here remains one of strange beauty, hiding in its folds and under its hills deposits of iron, silver, and coal that have been mined for thousands of years.

Stop first in Upper Soudley, where you'll find the **Dean Heritage Centre.** Based in a restored mill building in a wooded valley, the center tells the history of the forest, with reconstructions of a mine and a miner's cottage, a waterwheel, and a "beam engine" (a primitive steam engine used to pump water from flooded coal mines). Within the grounds is a tiny farm, home to a resident pig as well as natural-history exhibitions. Craftspeople work in the outbuildings. ⊠ *Soudley, Cinderford (on B4227),* ☎ *01594/822170.* 🎫 *£3.30.* ☉ *Feb.–Mar. and Oct., daily 10–5; Apr.–Sept., daily 10–6; Nov.–Jan., weekends only 10–4.*

Littledean

㉟ *1 mi east of Cinderford, 15 mi west Gloucester.*

From Littledean, SCENIC DRIVE signs direct you through the best of the forest. Of the original royal forest established in 1016 by King Canute, 27,000 acres are preserved by the Forestry Commission. It's still an important source of timber, but parking lots and picnic grounds have been created and eight nature trails marked. One trail links sculptures, commissioned by the Forestry Commission, around **Speech House,** the medieval verderer's court in the forest's center. The verderer was responsible for the enforcement of the forest laws. It was usually a capital offense to kill game or cut wood without authorization. To get to Littledean from Soudley, backtrack north on B4227, turn east on A4151.

Coleford

㊱ *10 mi south of Ross-on-Wye, 6 mi east of Monmouth.*

The **tourist information center** (☎ 01594/836307) at Coleford (drive west on A4151, and then west again on B4226 and B4028) has details of picnic grounds, nature trails, and tours of the forest. The area is a maze of weathered and moss-covered rocks, huge ferns, and ancient yew trees—a shady haven on a summer's day. An insight into the region's mining for iron and coal, which went on continuously from Roman times to **㊲** 1945, can be had through a visit to the **Clearwell Caves.** ⊠ *Clearwell Caves, near Coleford (off B4228),* ☎ *01594/832535.* 🎫 *£3.* ☉ *Mar.– Oct., daily 10–5; Nov.–Feb., weekends and school holidays 10–5; Dec., Christmas workshops (£3.50) weekdays 2–6, weekends 10–5.*

Dining and Lodging

££   ✕ **Wyndham Arms.** In the Forest of Dean, this may be a modest, old-
★ world village inn, but its restaurant offers sophisticated cuisine. Try the local wild salmon, guinea fowl, or one of the excellent steaks, followed by *zuppa inglese*—a mouthwatering chocolate, rum, and meringue concoction. ⊠ *Near Coleford,* ☎ *01594/833666. AE, DC, MC, V.*

£   ✕🏨 **Tudor Farmhouse.** Despite the name, parts of this converted farmhouse actually date back to the 13th century. Polished oak staircases, mullioned windows, and a huge stone fireplace in the lounge help to imbue the place with a sense of antique calm. There are four-poster beds in two of the bedrooms, and the award-winning restaurant serves four-course meals. ⊠ *Clearwell, near Coleford, GL16 8JS,* ☎ *01594/ 833046,* ℻ *01594/837093. 11 rooms with bath or shower. Restaurant. AE, MC, V.*

Slimbridge

12 mi southwest of Gloucester, 8 mi southwest of Stroud, 20 mi northeast of Bristol.

❸❽ Outside the village of Slimbridge (head west and across the little swing bridge over the Sharpness Canal), **Slimbridge Wildlife Trust** occupies a site on the banks of the Severn. Its 73 acres of rich marshland harbor Britain's largest collection of wildfowl. Thousands of swans, ducks, and geese come to winter here; in spring and early summer, you will be delighted by the resulting cygnets, ducklings, and goslings. To get to Slimbridge from Gloucester, take the M5 motorway southwest, leave at exit 13, and follow the A38 south. ☎ *01453/890065.* ▦ *£5.25.* ☉ *Mar.–Oct., daily 9:30–5; Nov.–Feb., daily 9:30–4; closed Dec. 25.*

Berkeley Castle

★ **❸❾** *4 mi south of Slimbridge, 17 mi south of Gloucester, 21 mi north of Bristol.*

Berkeley Castle, in the sleepy little village of Berkeley (pronounced barkley), is perfectly preserved. It was the setting for the gruesome murder of King Edward II in 1327—the cell where it occurred can still be seen. He was deposed by his French consort, Queen Isabella, and her paramour, the Earl of Mortimer. They then connived at his imprisonment and subsequent death. The castle was begun in 1153 by Roger De Berkeley, a Norman knight, and has remained in the family ever since. The state apartments here are full of magnificent furniture, tapestries, and pictures. The surrounding meadows, now the setting for pleasant Elizabethan gardens, were once flooded to make a formidable moat. ⊠ *Berkeley,* ☎ *01453/810332.* ▦ *£4.95.* ☉ *Apr.– May, Tues.–Sun. 1–5; June and Sept., Tues.–Sat. 11–5, Sun. 1–5; July– Aug., Mon.–Sat. 11–5, Sun. 1–5; Oct., Sun. only 1–4:30; national holidays 11–5.*

Dining and Lodging

££££–££££ **✕▦ Thornbury Castle.** Cricket fans may know the town of Thornbury
★ as the home of the celebrated batsman, W. G. Grace (1848–1915). Others will appreciate the buttressed tower of the 16th-century church, built at about the same time as the castle that dominates the village. Still others cherish its impressive castle-hotel. Thornbury has everything a genuine 16th-century castle needs: huge fireplaces, antiques, paintings, and mullioned windows, to say nothing of an extensive garden. The standards of comfort and luxury are famous, and people come from all over to eat in the restaurant. Note that children under 12 are not accommodated, and there is no elevator. ⊠ *Castle St., Thornbury (12 mi north of Bristol, off A38), BS35 1HH,* ☎ *01454/281182,* ℻ *01454/ 416188. 21 rooms with bath. Restaurant, archery, croquet. AE, DC, MC, V. Closed 1st wk of Jan.*

£ **✕▦ Green Acres Farm.** Inglenook fireplaces and pretty bedrooms with sweeping views are some of the features of this 300-year-old house; it is on a sheep farm. The dining room offers three-course dinners based on homegrown produce. ⊠ *Breadstone, near Berkeley (A38 north from Bristol, then B4509), GL13 9HF,* ☎ *01453/ 810348,* ℻ *01453/511217. 4 rooms with bath or shower. Dining room. MC, V.*

En Route   From Berkeley you can take A38 or M5 southeast to Bristol (21 mi, ☞ Chapter 5) or cross back over M5 and head southeast toward Bath (30 mi via A4135 and A46; ☞ *above*).

THE HEART OF ENGLAND A TO Z

Getting Around

By Bus

National Express (☎ 0990/808080) serves the region from London's Victoria Coach Station. **Badgerline** (☎ 01225/464446) covers the area around Bath, and **Stagecoach** (☎ 01452/522021), **Castleways** (☎ 01242/602949), and **Pulhams** (☎ 01451/820369) operate in the Gloucestershire and Cotswolds region. For all bus inquiries, call Gloucester's coach station (☎ 01452/527516), or, for all transport queries in Gloucestershire, call ☎ 01452/425543.

Various bus routes to major Cotswold destinations are as follows. (When not stated otherwise, routes are serviced by National Express buses and depart from London's Victoria Coach Station.) **Bourton-on-the-Water:** Take Pulhams Bus Company buses from Cheltenham or Stow-on-the-Wold. **Broadway:** Four Castleways coaches daily (Monday–Saturday from Cheltenham. **Burford:** Swanbrook buses leave six times every weekday from Cheltenham; from London, change at Oxford. **Cheltenham:** Buses leave London nine times daily. **Cirencester:** Buses leave once daily from London. **Moreton-on-Marsh:** Buses depart once daily from London. **Painswick:** Ten Stagecoach buses daily from Cheltenham. **Stow-on-the-Wold:** Pulhams Bus Company buses run from Moreton-on-Marsh. Smaller Cotswold towns may be serviced by Barry's Buses; check with local tourist offices.

By Car

M4 is the principal route west from London to Bath and South Gloucestershire. From exit 18, take A46 south to Bath. From exit 20, take M5 north to Gloucester (25 mi), Cheltenham, and Tewkesbury; and from exit 15 take A419 to A429 north to the Cotswolds. From London, you can also take M40 and A40 to the Cotswolds.

Parking in Bath. Except for notices posted on the outskirts of the city, restricted parking signs are few and far between in the city, and visitors' cars—especially rental cars—are likely to be ticketed. If your car is towed away, hundreds of pounds in fees may have to be paid to retrieve it. Note that the public parking lots in the historic area fill up early; it's easier to park on the outskirts just to the south.

By Train

Great Western, Wales and West, Virgin, Central, and **Thames Trains** all serve the region from London's Paddington Station, or, less frequently, from Euston (☎ 0345/484950). Travel time from Paddington to Bath is about 90 minutes. Most trains to Cheltenham (2 hrs) and Gloucester (1 hr 45 mins) involve a change at Swindon. A three-day or seven-day "Heart of England Rover" ticket is valid for unlimited travel within the region.

To reach central Cotswold destinations by train, here are some pointers. **Broadway:** train to Moreton-on-Marsh or Evesham, then bus or taxi locally to reach the town. **Burford:** train to Oxford, then buses from the Taylor Institute there. **Cirencester:** train from London to Kemble (4 mi away). **Bourton-on-the-Water,** Chipping Campden, and **Stow-on-the-Wold:** train to Moreton-on-Marsh, then local bus lines (some lines have minimal schedules). **Moreton-on-Marsh** is serviced by train from London daily. Contact local tourist offices for details.

Contacts and Resources

Car Rentals
Bath: Avis (✉ Unit 4B, Bath Riverside Business Park, Riverside Rd., ☎ 01225/446680). **Cheltenham: Budget Rent-a-Car** (✉ Prestbury Rd., ☎ 01242/235222); **Economy Drive** (✉ 1st Floor, 1 Crescent Terrace, ☎ 01242/226007). **Gloucester: Avis** (✉ Cotswold Service Station, 122 London Rd., ☎ 01452/380356).

Guided Tours
The **Heart of England Tourist Board** (☎ 01905/763436) and the **West Country Tourist Board** (☎ 01392/276351) can arrange a variety of tours. Guided tours of the Cotswolds and Gloucestershire are offered by several Heart of England Tourist Board offices mid-June–September. Pickup points are in Cheltenham, Cirencester, and Gloucester.

Cotswold Roaming (☎ 01865/308300) is a stylish outfit based in Oxford offering tours of the Cotswolds, and excursions to Bath and Castle Combe. The pickup point is next to the Playhouse Theatre in Beaumont Street, Oxford.

Bus tours of the Cotswolds are organized by Gloucester's tourist office, while **Gloucester Civic Trust** organizes tours of the city and docks by appointment. Contact Gloucester's tourist office for details of both (☎ 01452/421188).

Guide Friday (☎ 01789/294466 in Stratford; 01225/464446 in Bath) runs guided tours of Bath and, from Stratford-upon-Avon, into the Cotswolds in open-top single- and double-decker buses.

Hiking and Walking
For information on hiking the **Cotswold Way,** contact the Cotswold Warden Service (✉ County Planning Department, Gloucestershire County Council, Shire Hall, Gloucester GL1 2TN, ☎ 01452/425674), or various town tourist centers.

For information on hiking in the Forest of Dean, contact the **Forestry Commission** (✉ Bank House, Coleford GL16 8BA, ☎ 01594/833057).

Travel Agencies
American Express (✉ 5 Bridge St., Bath, ☎ 01225/444747). **Thomas Cook** (✉ 20 New Bond St., Bath, ☎ 01225/463191; ✉ 24 Upper Precinct, Coventry, ☎ 01203/229233; ✉ 24 Eastgate St., Gloucester, ☎ 01452/529511).

Visitor Information
The **Heart of England Tourist Board** (✉ Larkhill, Worcester, WR5 2EZ, ☎ 01905/763436, ℻ 01905/763450); Monday–Thursday 9–5:30, Friday 9–5. The **West Country Tourist Board** (✉ 60 St. David's Hill, Exeter, Devon EX4 4SY, ☎ 01392/276351, ℻ 01392/420891) has information on Bath.

Local tourist information centers are normally open Monday–Saturday 9:30–5:30, but times vary according to season; some are not open in winter.

Bath (✉ Abbey Chambers, Abbey Church Yard, ☎ 01225/477101). **Broadway** (✉ 1 Cotswold Court, ☎ 01386/852937). **Burford** (✉ Old

Brewery, Sheep St., ☎ 01993/823558). **Cheltenham** (✉ 77 Promenade, ☎ 01242/522878). **Chipping Campden** (✉ Woolstaplers Hall Museum, High St., ☎ 01386/840101). **Cirencester** (✉ Corn Hall, Market Place, ☎ 01285/654180). **Gloucester** (✉ 28 Southgate St., ☎ 01452/421188). **Stow-on-the-Wold** (✉ Hollis House, The Square, ☎ 01451/831082).

10 The Welsh Borders

Birmingham, Worcester, Hereford, Shrewsbury, Chester

Surprise! Not far from Birmingham— epicenter of England's industrial production—lies some of England's loveliest and most peaceful countryside. Here, behind high hedges and wooded hills, time seems to have stood still: brooding medieval castles, built by the English and Welsh, loom above the old towns, suggesting that today's air of sleepy tranquillity has not always been so. Often overlooked, this region remains rich in sights—none more delightful than the "magpie" black-and-white buildings of Shrewsbury and Chester.

Updated by
Robert
Andrews

ENGLAND'S BORDER with the principality of Wales stretches from the town of Chepstow on the Severn estuary in the south to the city of Chester in the north. Along this border, in the counties of Herefordshire, Shropshire, and southern Cheshire, lies some of England's loveliest countryside, remote and tranquil. But today's rural peace belies a turbulent past. Relations between the English and the Welsh have seldom been easy, and from the earliest times the English have felt it necessary to keep the "troublesome" Welsh firmly on the other side of the border. A string of medieval castles bears witness to this history. Many are romantic ruins; some are brooding fortresses. Built to control the countryside and repel invaders, they still radiate a sense of mystery and menace.

For the last 500 years or so, the people of this border country have enjoyed a peaceful existence, with little to disturb the traditional patterns of country life. In the 18th century, however, one small corner of Shropshire heralded the tumultuous birth of the industrial revolution, for here, in a wooded stretch of the Severn Gorge, the first coke blast furnace was invented and the first iron bridge was erected (1774).

The ramifications of that technological leap forward led to the growth of Britain's second-largest city, Birmingham, the capital of the Midlands. While Birmingham continues to rise above its reputation as one of the ugliest cities in Britain, its active artistic life is drawing people who have now begun to appreciate its historic civic architecture, some of the most fascinating to be found anywhere.

Herefordshire, in the south, is a county of rich, rolling countryside and river valleys, gradually opening out in the high hills and plateaus of Shropshire. North of the Shropshire hills, the gentler Cheshire plain stretches toward the great industrial cities of Liverpool and Manchester (☞ Chapter 12). This is dairy country, dotted with small villages and market towns, many rich in the 13th- and 14th-century black-and-white, half-timber buildings typical of northwestern England. These are the legacy of a forested countryside, where wood was easier to come by than stone. In the market towns of Chester and Shrewsbury, the more elaborately decorated half-timber buildings are monuments to wealth, dating mostly from the early Jacobean period at the beginning of the 17th century. Though it requires a trek very much off the beaten path, Little Moreton Hall—the greatest example of "magpie" buildings—remains one of the most sensationally atmospheric buildings in England.

Pleasures and Pastimes

Dining
This is rich farming country where, for centuries, the orchards have produced succulent fruit, especially apples. Hereford cider, for example, is popular because it tastes much sweeter than the cider brewed farther south in Devon. The meat and milk products, which come from the local black-and-white breed of cattle, are second to none here. With this natural bounty, travelers are surprised to find that formal restaurants are few and far between in this rural area, and those that exist are mostly small.

CATEGORY	COST*
££££	over £50
£££	£30–£50
££	£20–£30
£	under £20

*per person, including first course, main course, dessert, and VAT; excluding drinks

Lodging

The Welsh Borders are full of ancient inns and venerable Regency-style houses converted into hotels. Though some of these can be pricey, bargains can be found. You may find that you have to put up with asthmatic plumbing and creaking beams that masquerade as period atmosphere, but it's usually worth the savings. In Birmingham, all the best moderately priced lodging is well out of the city center, but there are fairly good suburban bus and train services.

CATEGORY	COST*
££££	over £150
£££	£80–£150
££	£60–£80
£	under £60

All prices are for two people sharing a double room, including service, breakfast, and VAT.

Walking

The Malvern Hills make for climbs and walks of varying length and difficulty. The best places to start are Great Malvern and Ledbury. The route designated the **Elgar Way** extends for 45 mi, but you don't need to traipse the entire run. Views across the countryside from the top of the hills are spectacular—the isolated hills rise up from the fairly flat plain rather like Ayers Rock does in Australia, providing vistas for many miles around. The area around Ross-on-Wye offers ideal walks with scenic river views.

One of Britain's major long-distance hikes lies mostly within this area: the **Offa's Dyke Path,** named after the earthwork built by an 8th-century king to mark the boundary with Wales. The whole route is 168 mi, but only about 60 mi is along the actual dike. The Offa's Dyke Association promotes the conservation and appreciation of the Welsh border region, including the Dyke itself; it publishes guides, along with other materials. This is an area of lush woods, swift rivers, hidden villages, and spectacular views; you'll find it very rewarding walking country. Lodging and dining are easily found. Local tourist information centers and bookstores have details, books, and maps.

Exploring the Welsh Borders

The main gateway to the region is bustling Birmingham, now one of the best places in England for the performing arts and rapidly redeeming itself from its reputation as a poorly built city. The city of Worcester is renowned for its proud cathedral and fine bone china. To the south and west, along the lovely Malvern Hills, lie the peaceful spa town of Great Malvern and the prosperous agricultural city of Hereford. Northward is Bewdley, terminus of the Severn Valley Railway, and beyond, the West Midlands—birthplace of modern British industry.

The handsome medieval city of Shrewsbury is near the wooded banks of the River Severn and a cluster of Ironbridge museums; Ludlow, an architectural jewel of a town; and northward, the ancient city of Chester.

Numbers in the text correspond to numbers in the margin and on the Welsh Borders, Birmingham, and Shrewsbury maps.

Great Itineraries

Although it is the main towns of the Welsh Borders region—Worcester, Hereford, Shrewsbury, and Chester—that distill the essence of the surrounding countryside, there is much in between that should not be neglected. It would be easy to base yourself in one of these towns and launch expeditions from there, but you might do better to lodge in some of the smaller centers, or in one of the remoter country inns, to absorb the full flavor of the borderlands.

IF YOU HAVE 3 DAYS

The city of ⊞ **Worcester** ⑪ makes a convenient entry to the Welsh Borders. Spend your first night here, making sure you see the aged, majestic cathedral and the Commandery, the country's only museum devoted exclusively to the 17th-century tussle between Cavaliers and Roundheads. Take a whirl round the famous Royal Worcester Porcelain Factory, where you can pick up some authentic souvenirs after admiring the rare porcelain in the attached museum. On your second day, take A443 northwest, making a stop at **Great Witley** ㉒ for the evocative ruins of Witley Court, a good place for a picnic; alternatively, opt for a pub meal in the nearby village. Keep on the same road as far as **Ludlow** ㉛, stopping long enough to view its magnificent castle as well as the crowd of Tudor, Jacobean, and Georgian buildings that give the small town its unique aspect. On your final stretch, head south for ⊞ **Hereford** ㉑ boasting another stout cathedral—Norman this time—and numerous reminders of the city's importance as a market town for the surrounding area. You can see most of the interesting sights here in a morning, leaving the afternoon free to explore **Ross-on-Wye** ⑰ and the nearby attractions of **Goodrich** ⑱, dramatically poised over the River Wye, and the beauty spot of **Symond's Yat** ⑲.

IF YOU HAVE 7 DAYS

Devote at least a day to ⊞ **Birmingham** ①, in particular rooting out the Barber Institute of Fine Arts. After an overnight stay, head south to Worcester and the Malverns, dropping in along the way at **Hellen's** ⑯, a manor house dating from the 13th century. You could take a lunch break at the generously timbered village of **Ledbury** ⑭, before continuing on toward the Wye Valley, where the nearby ruins of the castle at **Goodrich** ⑱ and **Symond's Yat** ⑲ provide good excuses to stop traveling for a while and stretch your legs. A night in ⊞ **Hereford** ㉑ will allow you to absorb the flavor of this old market town, before heading up to **Ludlow** for a couple of hours' ramble around the castle and its surrounding streets. A few miles north of here, you could once more abandon your car for a hike on Wenlock Edge, with its inspiring views (a little farther on is the village of Much Wenlock, whose ruined Wenlock Priory is set within a lovely topiary park.) Spend the next two nights in ⊞ **Worcester** ⑪, taking in the Malverns and, to the north, the quiet riverside town of **Bewdley** ㉓, with its fine array of Georgian architecture. From here you could take a trip on the Severn Valley Railway, whose old-style steam train affords opportunities to stroll around the banks of the Severn from the remote stations on the route. One of the main stops is **Bridgnorth** ㉚, occupying a sandstone ridge high above the Severn, and within a short distance of **Ironbridge Gorge** ㉗, a fascinating collection of sites that formed the crucible of the industrial revolution. You could stay here, or else visit it on a day's excursion from ⊞ **Shrewsbury** ㉖. Outside this historic town lies **Attingham Park** ㊱, a mansion dating from 1785 with a deer park designed by Humphrey Repton. Your last overnight—entailing a sizable journey northward—could be spent in ⊞ **Chester** ㊵, famous for its black-and-white "magpie" buildings and worthy of a full day's sightseeing along and within its city walls.

When to Tour the Welsh Borders

Most of the rural sights have limited opening hours in winter. Even in the towns, the majority of the attractions close at 5, which leaves several hours of dark and often chilly winter evenings to fill. Be on the road early to catch the best light. In the winter's favor are the creep-

BONUS MILES MAKE
GREAT SOUVENIRS.

Earn Miles With Your MCI Card.

Take the MCI Card along on this trip and start earning miles for the next one. You'll earn frequent flyer miles on all your calls and save with the low rates you've come to expect from MCI. Before you know it, you'll be on your way to some other international destination.

Sign up for MCI by calling
1-800-FLY-FREE

Earn Frequent Flyer Miles.

   US AIRWAYS
DIVIDEND MILES

Is this a great time, or what? :-)

MCI

Easy To Call Home.

1. To use your MCI Card, just dial the WorldPhone access number of the country you're calling from.
2. Dial or give the operator your MCI Card number.
3. Dial or give the number you're calling.

# Austria (CC) ♦	022-903-012
# Belarus (CC)	
From Brest, Vitebsk, Grodno, Minsk	8-800-103
From Gomel and Mogilev regions	8-10-800-103
# Belgium (CC) ♦	0800-10012
# Bulgaria	00800-0001
# Croatia (CC) ★	0800-22-0112
# Czech Republic (CC) ♦	00-42-000112
# Denmark (CC) ♦	8001-0022
# Finland (CC) ♦	08001-102-80
# France (CC) ♦	0-800-99-0019
# Germany (CC)	0800-888-8000
# Greece (CC) ♦	00-800-1211
# Hungary (CC) ♦	00▼800-01411
# Iceland (CC) ♦	800-9002
# Ireland (CC)	1-800-55-1001
# Italy (CC) ♦	172-1022
# Kazakhstan (CC)	8-800-131-4321
# Liechtenstein (CC) ♦	0800-89-0222
# Luxembourg	0800-0112
# Monaco (CC) ♦	800-90-019
# Netherlands (CC) ♦	0800-022-9122
# Norway (CC) ♦	800-19912
# Poland (CC) ÷	00-800-111-21-22
# Portugal (CC) ÷	05-017-1234
Romania (CC) ÷	01-800-1800
# Russia (CC) ÷ ♦	
To call using ROSTELCOM ■	747-3322
For a Russian-speaking operator	747-3320
To call using SOVINTEL ■	960-2222
# San Marino (CC) ♦	172-1022
# Slovak Republic (CC)	00-421-00112
# Slovenia	080-8808
# Spain (CC)	900-99-0014
# Sweden (CC) ♦	020-795-922
# Switzerland (CC) ♦	0800-89-0222
# Turkey (CC) ♦	00-8001-1177
# Ukraine (CC) ÷	8▼10-013
# United Kingdom (CC)	
To call using BT ■	0800-89-0222
To call using C&W ■	0500-89-0222
# Vatican City (CC)	172-1022

CHASE

Flying to France on Friday? Get Francs from Chase on Thursday. Call Currency To Go at 935-9935 for overnight delivery.

CHASE
CURRENCY
TO GO
935-9935

*O*r pounds for London. Or Deutschmarks for Düsseldorf. Or any of 75 foreign currencies. Call **Chase Currency To Go**[SM] at **935-9935** in area codes 212, 718, 914, 516 and Rochester, N.Y.; all other area codes call 1-800-935-9935. We'll deliver directly to your door.* Overnight. And there are no exchange fees. Let Chase make your trip an easier one.

CHASE. The right relationship is everything.[SM]

The Welsh Borders

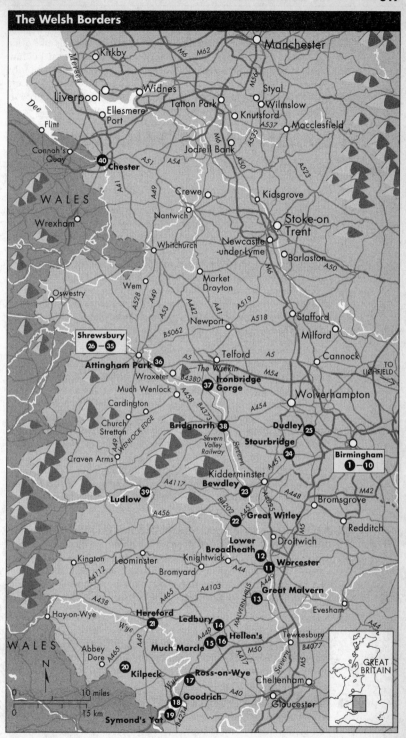

Manchester

Kirkby

Widnes

Styal
Wilmslow

Liverpool

Tatton Park

Knutsford
Macclesfield

Ellesmere
Port

Jodrell Bank

Dee

Flint

Connah's
Quay

40 Chester

Crewe

Kidsgrove

WALES

Nantwich

Stoke-on
Trent

Wrexham

Whitchurch

Newcastle
-under-Lyme

Barlaston

Oswestry

Wem

Market
Drayton

Stafford

Milford

Newport

Cannock

Shrewsbury
26 — 35

Telford

TO
LICHFIELD

Attingham Park 36

The Wrekin

Wroxeter

37 Ironbridge
Gorge

Wolverhampton

Much Wenlock

Cardington

Church
Stretton

Bridgnorth 38

Dudley 25

Stourbridge

24

Craven Arms

Severn
Valley
Railway

Birmingham
1 — 10

Kidderminster

Ludlow 39

Bewdley

23

Bromsgrove

Redditch

M42

Great Witley

22

Kington

Leominster

Lower
Broadheath

Knightwick

12

Droitwich

Worcester
11

Bromyard

Great Malvern

13

Hay-on-Wye

Hereford
21

Ledbury
14

Evesham

Much Marcle 15 16

Hellen's

Tewkesbury

WALES

Abbey
Dore

20 Kilpeck

17

Ross-on-Wye

Cheltenham

18 Goodrich

19

Symond's Yat

Gloucester

GREAT
BRITAIN

10 miles

15 km

ing mists shrouding the valleys, and the warm hearths to toast your toes at in inns and hotels. Otherwise, try to be here in the warmer weather between April and September. The official and fringe festivals take place at Malvern at the end of May, the open-air performances at Ludlow Castle at the end of June, and the Shrewsbury Festival in June and July, while the Three Choirs Festival, rotating between Hereford, Gloucester, and Worcester, takes place in mid-August, for which you need to book as early as you can to guarantee the best seats.

FROM BIRMINGHAM TO SHREWSBURY

Birmingham

❶ *25 mi north from Stratford, 120 mi northwest of London.*

The center of Britain's "second city" had undergone so many injudicious structural alterations in the post–World War II period that, as an official guidebook once put it, "there is more of the future to be seen coming into being than there is of the past left to contemplate." Indeed, Birmingham has become something of a monument to late-20th-century civic architecture. Whether you agree that it is a *fitting* monument depends on your feelings toward the 20th century. Mercifully, the city fathers have, in the last few years, adopted a new policy of humanizing the areas and buildings that their immediate predecessors did so much to ruin.

The city first flourished in the boom years of the 19th century's industrial revolution. Birmingham's inventive, hardworking citizens accumulated great wealth, and at one time the city had some of the finest Victorian buildings in the country (it still has some of the most ravishingly beautiful Pre-Raphaelite paintings, on view in the City Museum and Art Gallery). Sadly, postwar "planning" managed to destroy many 19th-century structures. There are still architectural treasures to be found, but it means a dedicated search, carefully negotiating the city's impossible road network. Birmingham's inner ring road twists right through the city center. But city planners are making Birmingham pedestrian-friendly by replacing the ring road with a network of local access roads and by turning the downtown shopping area into pedestrian arcades and buses-only streets.

Birmingham, believe it or not, has more canals than Venice. It is at the center of a system of restored waterways built during the industrial revolution to connect inland factories to rivers and seaports—by 1840 the canals extended more than 4,000 mi throughout the British Isles. Contact the Convention and Visitors Bureau for maps of walks along the towpaths and for details on canal barge cruises.

❷ Start your visit in the heart of the city at the **International Convention Centre** (⊠ Broad St.), opened in June 1991 by the Queen. Inside there is a good tourist desk to help you with further information (including accommodations). The main atrium of this high-tech building is dominated by a network of blue struts and gleaming air ducts, somewhat softened by banks of indoor plants.

★ **❸** Connected to the Convention Centre is the **Symphony Hall** (⊠ Broad St.)—a significant addition to English musical life. Attending a concert at this auditorium is sufficient reason to visit Birmingham. The internationally recognized City of Birmingham Symphony Orchestra, which has won awards for its recordings under its former conductor Simon Rattle, has found a very welcome home here (☞ The Arts, *below*).

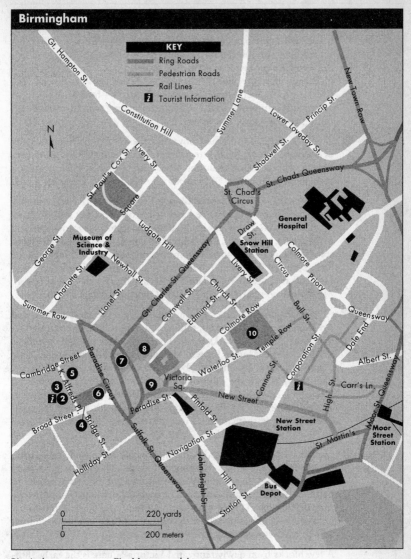

Birmingham

KEY
- Ring Roads
- Pedestrian Roads
- Rail Lines
- *i* Tourist Information

Birmingham
Cathedral (St.
Philip's), **10**
Birmingham
Repertory
Theatre, **5**
Centenary Square, **4**
Central Library, **7**

City Museum and Art
Gallery, **8**
Hall of Memory, **6**
International
Convention
Centre, **2**
Symphony Hall, **3**
Town Hall, **9**

❹ Once outside the Convention Centre, you are in **Centenary Square,** a sort of miniature complex for the performing arts. It is paved with bricks whose various shades form a pattern, like a Persian carpet, designed by artist Tess Jaray. To one side of Centenary Square stands

❺ the **Birmingham Repertory Theatre,** which houses one of England's oldest and most esteemed theater companies (☞ The Arts, *below*). The Birmingham Rep—as it's always called—has an excellent cafeteria/restaurant in its foyer, behind sweeping windows that allow for a great view over the square.

❻ Across the square from the Convention Centre you will find the **Hall of Memory,** an octagonal war memorial built in the 1920s in remembrance of those who fell during World War I. Inside, there is a book containing their names. ⊠ *Centenary Sq.* ☜ *Free.* ☉ *Weekdays 10–4.*

❼ Prince Charles said the **Central Library** "looks like a place where books are incinerated." It used to be bare, brutal concrete, but it now sports boxes of flowers and plants in an attempt to soften its facade. Attached to the library, but reached from around the corner, the ornate Elizabethan-style **Shakespeare Memorial Room** contains some 50,000 books in the Shakespeare collection and thousands of illustrations. To see the collection, call first. ⊠ *Chamberlain Sq.,* ☎ *0121/235–4511. Shakespeare Memorial Room, 0121/235–2868.* ☉ *Library weekdays 9–8, Sat. 9–5.*

❽ Across Chamberlain Square from the library is the **City Museum and Art Gallery,** a huge place containing a magnificent collection of Victorian art, featuring works by the Pre-Raphaelites. All the big names are here—Ford Madox Brown, Holman Hunt, Edward Burne-Jones (who was born in Birmingham), Dante Gabriel Rossetti, and many more. One room houses the imposing *Holy Grail* tapestries, designed by Burne-Jones and executed by the William Morris Arts Workers' Guild. The collection reflects the enormous wealth of 19th-century Birmingham and the aesthetic taste of its industrialists. ⊠ *Chamberlain Sq.,* ☎ *0121/235–2834.* ☜ *Free.* ☉ *Mon.–Sat. 10–5, Sun. 12:30–5.*

❾ Near the City Museum and Art Gallery is the **Town Hall** (⊠ Victoria Sq., ☎ 0121/235–3942). Surrounded by classical columns, it is a copy of the Temple of Castor and Pollux in Rome and took two decades to build. It used to be the home of the symphony orchestra—it heard the first performances of Mendelssohn's *Elijah* and Elgar's *Dream of Gerontius*—and it is now host to concerts and exhibitions, or at least will be when it reopens in 2001 after renovation.

A few blocks from newly renovated Victoria Square is the early 18th-
❿ century **Birmingham Cathedral** (St. Philip's). The gilded Georgian interior is elegant and has some lovely plasterwork. The windows behind the altar seem to glow with a garnet-hue light. They were designed by Burne-Jones and executed by William Morris. At the end of the south aisle is a vivid modern tapestry. ⊠ *Colmore Row,* ☎ *0121/236–6323.* ☉ *Daily 7:30–6.*

OFF THE
BEATEN PATH
BARBER INSTITUTE OF FINE ARTS – This jewel-like collection, belonging to the University of Birmingham, includes works by Bellini, Canaletto, Guardi, Poussin, Murillo, Gainsborough, Turner, Whistler, Renoir, Gauguin, and van Gogh. ⊠ *Off Edgbaston Park Rd. near East Gate (take Cross City Line train from New St. Station south to University Station, or Bus 61, 62, 63, or 64 from city center),* ☎ *0121/414–7333.* ☜ *Free.* ☉ *Mon.–Sat. 10–5, Sun. 2–5.*

Not far from Birmingham (14 mi northeast on A38), **Lichfield Cathedral** is worth a detour. The only English cathedral with three spires, the present building dates mainly from the 12th and 13th centuries and has some fine 16th-century stained glass from the Cistercian Abbey of Herkenrode, near Liège, in Belgium. It stands on peaceful grounds surrounded by half-timber houses. ⊠ *Cathedral Close,* ☎ *01543/256120.* ◷ *Daily 7:30–6:15.*

Dining and Lodging

££–£££ ✕ **Sloans.** This brasserie in the southeast shopping district comes as a
★ pleasant surprise. The menu is fairly large, with an interesting range—try the medallions of fillet of pork on a nest of pear Williams, or choose from the grills accompanied by Madeira and black truffle sauce, finishing, perhaps, with chocolate truffle torte. The set-price lunches are especially good value. ⊠ *27–29 Chad Sq., Hawthorne Rd.,* ☎ *0121/455–6697. AE, DC, MC, V. Closed Sun.*

£ ✕ **Henry's.** This Cantonese restaurant in the jewelry district, is a haven for lunch during a shopping spree. The menu offers more than 100 dishes, with plenty of vegetarian choices. ⊠ *27 St. Paul's Sq.,* ☎ *0121/200–1136. AE, DC, MC, V. Closed Sun.*

££££ ✕▦ **New Hall.** A lush tree-lined drive leads through 26 acres of gar-
★ dens and open land to this moated 12th-century manor-house-turned-country-hotel. The guest rooms, decorated in English country style with marble-tile baths, have expansive views overlooking the grounds. The public rooms have 16th-century oak-panel walls and Flemish glass, 18th-century chandeliers, and a stone fireplace from the 17th century. The formal restaurant is an elegant setting in which to indulge in chef David Lake's cuisine. ⊠ *Walmley Rd., Sutton Coldfield, Birmingham B76 1QX,* ☎ *0121/378–2442,* ℻ *0121/378–4637. 60 rooms with bath. Restaurant, 9-hole golf course, tennis court, croquet, meeting rooms. AE, DC, MC, V.*

££££ ✕▦ **Swallow Hotel.** Once a group of offices, this elegant turn-of-the-century building is now a luxuriously renovated hotel. The building has an interior rich with dark wood and chandeliers; the spacious bedrooms offer all the latest comforts. The Sir Edward Elgar formal restaurant (reservations essential, elegant wear) has a fixed-price menu that changes daily, and Langtry's Restaurant (££) serves traditional British dishes in more casual surroundings. ⊠ *12 Hagley Rd., Five Ways, B16 8SJ,* ☎ *0121/452–1144,* ℻ *0121/456–3442. 98 rooms with bath. 2 restaurants, indoor pool, health club. AE, DC, MC, V.*

££ ✕▦ **Copperfield House Hotel.** In a quiet location with secluded lawns, this Victorian, family-run hotel is nevertheless convenient to the hustle and bustle of the center 2 mi away. The restaurant serves good English cooking, including delicious homemade puddings, and you can eat outdoors in summer. ⊠ *60 Upland Rd., Selly Park, Birmingham, B29 7JS,* ☎ *0121/472–8344,* ℻ *0121/415–5655. 17 rooms with bath. Restaurant. AE, MC, V.*

The Arts

BALLET

The second company of the Royal Ballet, which used to be based at Sadler's Wells in London, has become the **Birmingham Royal Ballet** (⊠ Hurst St., ☎ 0121/622–7486). It is based at the Hippodrome Theatre, which also hosts visiting companies, such as the Welsh National Opera.

CONCERTS

The **City of Birmingham Symphony Orchestra** (⊠ International Convention Centre, ☎ 0121/200–2000) performs regularly in Symphony Hall, also the venue for visiting artists.

THEATER

The **Birmingham Repertory Theatre** (⊠ Centenary Sq., Broad St., ☎ 0121/236–4455), founded in 1913, is equally at home with modern or classical work. There is a restaurant on the ground floor. The Alexandra Theatre in Birmingham welcomes touring companies on their way to or from London's West End. It is also home to the **D'Oyly Carte Opera Company** (✉ Station St., ☎ 0121/643–3168), world-renowned for presenting Gilbert and Sullivan operas.

Shopping

Ten minutes' walk northward from the city center is the **Jewellery Quarter,** with more than 200 manufacturing jewelers and 50 silversmiths. Work with precious metals was first recorded here in 1460, and there are still more than 100 shops that sell and repair gold and silver hand-crafted jewelry, clocks, and watches. The city has its own Assay Office with an anchor as its silver mark. The history of the neighborhood and the craft of the jeweler are explained at the **Discovery Centre.** Entry price includes a guided tour. ✉ 77–79 Vyse St., ☎ 0121/554–3598. ⊡ £2. ☉ Weekdays 10–4, Sat. 11–5.

Worcester

⓫ 118 mi northwest of London, 27 mi southwest of Birmingham, 63 mi north of London.

Worcester (pronounced wooster) sits on the River Severn in the center of Worcestershire. It is an ancient city proud of its history, and in particular, its nickname, "The Faithful City," bestowed on it for its steadfast allegiance to the crown during the English Civil War. In that conflict between king and Parliament, two major battles were waged here. The second one, the decisive Battle of Worcester of 1651, resulted in the exile of the future Charles II. More recently the town's name has become synonymous with the fine bone china produced here. Despite "modernization" during the 1960s, some of medieval Worcester remains. This ancient section forms a convenient and pleasant walking route around the great cathedral.

★ There are few more quintessentially English sights than that of **Worcester Cathedral,** its towers overlooking the green expanse of the county cricket ground, its majestic image reflected in the swift-flowing—and frequently flooding—waters of the River Severn. There has been a cathedral here since the year 680, and much of what remains dates from the 13th and 14th centuries. Notable exceptions are the Norman crypt (built in the 1080s), the largest in England, and the ambulatory, a cloister built around the east end. The most important tomb in the cathedral is that of King John (1167–1216), one of the country's least admired monarchs, who alienated his barons and subjects through bad administration and heavy taxation and in 1215 was forced to sign the Magna Carta, the great charter of liberty. The cathedral's most beautiful decoration is in the vaulted **chantry chapel of Prince Arthur,** Henry VII's elder son, whose body was brought to Worcester after his death at Ludlow in 1502. (Chantry chapels were endowed by the wealthy to enable priests to celebrate masses there for the souls of the deceased.) ☎ 01905/611002. ☉ Daily 7:30–6.

At the **Royal Worcester Porcelain Factory,** you can browse in the showrooms or rummage in the "seconds" and "clearance" shops; especially good bargains can be had at the January and July sales. Tours of the factory take you through the process of making bone china figurines. The **Museum of Worcester Porcelain** houses a comprehensive collection of rare Worcester porcelain, representing work from the start of manufacturing in 1751 to the present. The factory lies south of Worcester Cathedral (follow Severn St.). ✉ Severn St., ☎ 01905/23221. ⊡ £2, or £5.25 including 1-hr tours of factory; prebooked 2-hr Connoisseur

Tours £12. ⊘ *Mon.–Sat. 9–5, Sun. 11-5; tours weekdays 10:30–3:30; Connoisseur Tours weekdays 10:15 and 1:30. Children under 11 not admitted on tours.*

The Commandery occupies a cluster of 15th-century half-timber buildings that were originally built as a poorhouse and later became the headquarters of the Royalist troops during the Battle of Worcester. Now a museum, it presents a colorful audiovisual presentation about the Civil War in the magnificent, oak-beam Great Hall. The museum is across the road from the porcelain factory, minutes from the cathedral. The Commandery has a terrace tearoom. ⊠ *Sidbury,* ☎ *01905/355071.* ☒ *£3.40, joint ticket with Museum of Local Life (☞ below) £3.75.* ⊘ *Mon.–Sat. 10–5, Sun. 1:30–5:30.*

Between the Commandery and the cathedral lies medieval Friar Street. As you walk toward the Cornmarket there are several buildings of particular interest, among them the timber-frame **Museum of Local Life,** which focuses on Worcester's domestic and social history. You can see reconstructions of Victorian and Edwardian shops and homes, and an exhibition of life in the city during World War II. ⊠ *Friar St.,* ☎ *01905/722349.* ☒ *£1.50 (☞ above for joint ticket with Commandery).* ⊘ *Mon.–Wed. and Fri.–Sat. 10:30–5.*

Worcester's mainly pedestrianized High Street runs through the center of town, from the cathedral to Foregate Street train station. On your left, with the cathedral behind you, you will see the **Guildhall** set back behind ornate iron railings (also the location of the tourist information office). The hall's 18th-century facade features gilded statues of Queen Anne, Charles I, and Charles II, and a carving of Cromwell's head pinned up by the ears, a savage addition by the royalist citizens of Worcester. Inside, the walls of the Assembly Room are hung with an impressive collection of patrician portraits under a painted ceiling, which you can admire over tea and buns. ⊠ *High St.,* ☎ *01905/ 723471.* ☒ *Free.* ⊘ *Mon.–Sat. 9–5.*

Dining and Lodging

£££ ✕ **Brown's.** A former grain mill houses this light and airy riverside restau-
★ rant. The fixed-price menu and daily specialties include warm salad with breast of duck and croutons, and crayfish-and-bacon kebabs. ⊠ *24 Quay St.,* ☎ *01905/26263. AE, MC, V. Closed Mon. No lunch Sat., no dinner Sun.*

££ ✕ **King's Restaurant.** The deluxe Fownes Hotel, a converted Victorian glove factory, now houses this classic English restaurant, where meals are served on Royal Worcester porcelain. The old-fashioned tone is countered by a good selection of modern and exotic dishes, such as strips of pork with sesame and ginger. ⊠ *Fownes Hotel, City Walls Rd.,* ☎ *01905/613151. AE, DC, MC, V. No lunch Sat.*

£–££ ✕ **King Charles II Restaurant.** Here you can enjoy dining in the black-and-white, half-timber house in which Charles II hid after the Battle of Worcester. It is now an oak-panel, silver-service restaurant with a very friendly atmosphere. Cuisine is mainly French and Italian, but there are also traditional English selections, such as beef Wellington, and such fresh fish dishes as Dover sole meunière. ⊠ *29 New St.,* ☎ *01905/22449. AE, DC, MC, V. Closed Sun.*

££ ☷ **Ye Old Talbot Hotel.** The Old Talbot was originally a courtroom belonging to the cathedral, which stands close by. The hotel has been refurbished, and there are modern extensions to the 16th-century core of the building. ⊠ *Friar St., WR1 2NA,* ☎ *01905/23573,* ℻ *01905/ 612760. 26 rooms with bath. Restaurant. AE, DC, MC, V.*

£ ▣ **Burgage House.** In a cobbled lane right next to the cathedral, this traditional Georgian B&B offers a hearty welcome. Furnishings are authentic to the period, and there is a marvelous stone staircase dating from 1858, a century after the house was built. Breakfast in the spacious dining room includes free-range hens' eggs and homemade marmalade. ⊠ *4 College Precincts, WR1 2LG,* ☎ ᴲᴬˣ *01905/25396. 2 rooms with shower. No credit cards. Closed Dec. 24–Dec 31.*

Arts

The **Three Choirs' Festival** has been held on a three-year rotation between the cathedral cities of Worcester, Gloucester, and Hereford since about 1717. In 1999 it will be held in Worcester August 21–27. The festival celebrates the English choral tradition, often with specially commissioned works. The program is published in March. Details are available from the festival administrator (⊠ Three Choirs' Festival, 5 Deansway, Worcester WR1 2JG, ☎ 01905/616200).

Outdoor Activities and Sports

BICYCLING

Bikes can be rented from **Peddlers** (⊠ 46 Barbourne Rd., Worcester, ☎ 01905/24238).

BOATING

There are plenty of opportunities in the Worcester area to rent boats or take short cruises on the Severn. **Bickerline River Trips** (⊠ South Quay, near the cathedral, ☎ 01531/670679) has 45-minute excursions on a small passenger boat leaving several times daily (Easter–October).

Shopping

All shoppers will first head for the emporium at the **Royal Worcester Porcelain Factory** (☞ *above*), where, among other merchandise, you can buy "seconds." **Bygones** (⊠ 32 College St., ☎ 01905/25388; ⊠ 55 Sidbury, ☎ 01905/23132) sells antiques, items of fine craftsmanship, and a selection of small gifts in silver, glass, and porcelain.

Lower Broadheath

❶❷ *2 mi west of Worcester on B4204.*

Southwest of Worcester lie the Malvern Hills, their long, low, purple profile rising starkly from the surrounding plain. These were the hills that inspired much of Elgar's music, as well as his remark that "there is music in the air, music all around us." Stop in the village of Lower Broadheath to visit the **Elgar Birthplace Museum** before exploring the hills. Set in a peaceful little garden, the tiny brick cottage in which the composer was born now exhibits photographs, musical scores, letters, and such. ⊠ *Crown East La., Lower Broadheath,* ☎ *01905/333224.* ▦ *£3.* ⊙ *Mid-Feb.–Apr. and Oct.–mid-Jan., Thurs.–Tues. 1:30–4:30; May–Sept., Thurs.–Tues. 10:30–6.*

Great Malvern

❶❸ *7 mi south of Worcester off A449.*

Great Malvern is a Victorian spa town whose architecture has changed little since the mid-1800s. Exceptionally pure spring water is still bottled here and exported all over the world—the Queen never travels without a supply. Great Malvern is known today both as an educational center and as a great place for old folks' homes. The town also has a Winter Gardens complex with a theater, cinema, and gardens, but it is the **Priory** that dominates the steep streets downtown. This is an early Norman Benedictine abbey in Perpendicular style, decorated with vertical lines of airy tracery and fine 15th-century glass. ⊠ *Entrance opposite the church.* 🎫 *Free.* ⏱ *9–4:30.*

Dining and Lodging

££–£££ ✕ **Croque en Bouche.** French, Italian, and Japanese dishes and a su-
★ perb handling of excellent local ingredients form the unlikely basis of the cuisine in this country restaurant. The chef-proprietor, Marion Jones, has earned a considerable reputation. Specialties include skate with mango basil sauce; wild boar with grilled vegetables and Oriental pesto; sushi; and roast guinea fowl with coriander. Delicious desserts and a dazzling wine list complete the evening's delights. Prices are significantly lower on Thursday. ⊠ *221 Wells Rd., Malvern Wells,* ☎ *01684/565612. MC, V. Closed Sun.–Wed. No lunch.*

£££ ✕🏨 **Cottage in the Wood.** This hotel sits on shady grounds high up the side of the Malvern Hills with splendid views of the countryside. The furnishings are country-house comfortable; the rooms vary in size, and the ones with a view are equipped with binoculars! The restaurant has the best of the panorama through its tall windows. Food is English, with the accent on country fare, and there is a wide selection of more than 600 wines, including many local English ones. ⊠ *Holywell Rd., WR14 4LG,* ☎ *01684/575859,* 🖷 *01684/560662. 20 rooms with bath. Restaurant. AE, MC, V.*

£ ✕🏨 **Sidney House.** In addition to its stunning views, this dignified Georgian hotel, run by a friendly husband-and-wife team, is also near the town center. The adequately sized bedrooms with television make this lodging a good bet for people traveling on a budget. On a clear afternoon you can gaze out over the Vale of Evesham to the Cotswolds. ⊠ *40 Worcester Rd., WR14 4AA,* ☎ *01684/574994. 8 rooms, 5 with bath or shower. AE, MC, V.*

The Arts

Malvern has historical connections with Sir Edward Elgar as well as with George Bernard Shaw, who premiered many of his plays here. The **Malvern Festival** was originally devoted to their works, although now it also offers a wide variety of new music and new drama. The **Malvern Fringe Festival** has an exceptional program of alternative events. Both festivals run for two or three weeks from the end of May to early June. Details for the main festival are available from the Festival Office (☎ 01684/892277); for the Fringe Festival call ☎ 01684/891591; otherwise, for information on both, contact the Malvern tourist information center (⊠ 21 Church St., WR14 2AA, ☎ 01684/892289).

Ledbury

🔟 *10 mi southwest of Great Malvern on A449.*

Among the black-and-white half-timber buildings that make up the market town of Ledbury, take special note of two late-16th-century ones: the Feathers Hotel and the Talbot Inn. Almost hidden behind the 17th-century market house is a cobbled lane, crowded with medieval, half-timber buildings, leading to the church. The **Old Grammar School** is now a heritage center tracing the history of some local industries, with some displays on two literary celebrities linked to the area, John Masefield and Elizabeth Barrett Browning. ⊠ *Church La.,* ☎ *01531/636147.* 🎫 *Free.* ⏱ *May–Oct., daily 10:30–4:30; Easter–May, also weekends 10:30–4:30 (hrs may vary; call ahead).*

★ On the outskirts of Ledbury is **Eastnor Castle,** a Victorian extravaganza which includes some magnificent neo-Gothic salons designed by Pugin. Other grand rooms, all aswirl with lush tapestries, gilded paintings, Regency chandeliers, and Auntie's old armchairs have recently been restored to the height of *le style anglais* by the owners, the Hervey-Bathurst family, making Eastnor a must-do for lovers of English interior decoration. ⊠ *Ledbury,* ☎ *01531/633160.* ⊙ *July–Aug., Sun.–Fri. 11–5, Apr.–June, Sept. only 11–5.*

Dining and Lodging

£££ ✕⊡ **Feathers Hotel.** You can't miss the striking black-and-white facade of this central hostelry, which dates from the 16th century. The interior has a satisfyingly antique flavor, with creaking staircases and ancient floorboards, and some rooms have four-posters, though it is hoped that a major renovation in 1998 will preserve the quirkier aspects of the hotel. The hop-bedecked Fuggles Bar offers specials such as Ledbury sausages and venison casserole (for the ploughman's lunch you cut your own wedge of cheese), while Quills restaurant offers fancier fare with trimmings and higher prices (closed Monday and Tuesday.). ⊠ *High St., HR8 1DS,* ☎ *01531/635266,* ⨎ℵ *01531/632001. 23 rooms with bath. Restaurant, bar, pool, health club. AE, DC, MC, V.*

Much Marcle

⑮ *4 mi southwest of Ledbury on A449, 6 mi northeast of Ross-on-Wye.*

Much Marcle is one of the English villages still holding the ancient annual ceremony of "wassailing"—beating the apple trees to make them fruitful in the coming year. The ritual takes place on Twelfth Night, January 6. There is also a beautiful 13th-century church here, richly endowed with effigies and tombs, notably one of Blanche, Lady Grandison. If you have a detailed map and plenty of time to spare, this is an area to wander around and discover tiny villages down sleepy lanes overhung by high hedges.

Just outside the village of Much Marcle lies the beautiful mansion of ⑯ **Hellen's,** still in singularly authentic and pristine condition (part of it from the 13th century). The gloom and dust are part of the atmosphere; the house is illuminated by candles, and central heating has been scorned. ☎ *01531/660668.* ⊡ *£3.50.* ⊙ *Easter–Sept., Wed., weekends 2–6; tours on the hr (last tour at 5).*

Ross-on-Wye

⑰ *6 mi southwest of Much Marcle on A449.*

Perched high above the River Wye, Ross-on-Wye seems oblivious to 20th-century intrusions and remains at heart a small market town. Its steep streets come alive on Thursdays and Saturdays—market days—but they are always a happy hunting ground for antiques.

Lodging

£££ ⊡ **Chase Hotel.** This well-renovated Georgian-style country-house hotel is set on 11 acres. Rooms are simply and comfortably furnished in the main house, and more modern in the newer wing. ⊠ *Gloucester Rd., HR9 5LH,* ☎ *01989/763161,* ⨎ℵ *01989/768330. 38 rooms with bath. Restaurant. AE, DC, MC, V.*

Goodrich

⑱ *3 mi north of Symond's Yat on B4229, 3 mi south of Ross-on-Wye on B4234.*

The village of Goodrich is dominated by the ruins of **Goodrich Castle,** the English equivalent of a Rhine castle. Looming dramatically over the River Wye crossing at Kerne Bridge, the castle from the south looks picturesque in its setting of green fields, but you quickly see its grimmer face standing on its battlements on the north side. Dating from the late 12th century, the castle is surrounded by a deep moat carved out of solid rock, from which its walls appear to soar upward. Built to repel Welsh raiders, Goodrich was destroyed in the 17th century during the Civil War. ☎ 01600/890538. ☞ £2.95. ⊘ Apr.–Oct., daily 10–6 or dusk; Nov.–Mar., daily 10–1 and 2–4.

Symond's Yat

⑲ 15 mi north of Coleford on A4136 and A40, 6 mi south of Ross-on-Wye.

Outside the village of Symond's Yat ("gate"), the 473-ft-high Yat Rock commands superb views of the River Wye as it winds through a narrow gorge and swings around in a great 5-mi loop.

Kilpeck

⑳ 15 mi northwest of Goodrich, 7 mi southwest of Hereford on A465.

Tucked away on a minor road off the A465, the tiny hamlet Kilpeck is blessed with one of the best-preserved Norman churches in Britain. It is lavishly decorated inside and out, with an order of sculpted carving exceptional for a country church. The carvings depict all manner of subjects, from rabbits to scenes so scandalously frank that they were removed by high-minded Victorians. (One or two ribald ones remain, however, so look carefully.) Don't miss the gargoyle rainwater spouts, either.

Hereford

㉑ 7 mi northeast of Kilpeck, 56 mi southwest of Birmingham, 31 mi northwest of Gloucester, 54 mi northeast of Cardiff.

Hereford is a busy country town, the center of a wealthy agricultural area known for its cider, fruit, and cattle—the white-faced Hereford breed has spread across the world. It is also an important cathedral city, its massive Norman cathedral towering proudly over the River Wye. Before 1066, Hereford was the capital of the Anglo-Saxon kingdom of Mercia and, earlier still, the site of Roman, Celtic, and Iron Age settlements. Today, tourists come primarily to see the cathedral, but quickly discover the charms of a town that has changed slowly but fairly unobtrusively with the passing centuries.

★ **Hereford Cathedral,** built of local red sandstone with a massive central tower, has some fine 11th-century Norman carvings, but suffered considerable "restoration" in the 19th century. Inside, its greatest glories include the 14th-century bishop's throne; some fine misericords (the elaborately carved undersides of choristers' seats); and the extraordinary **Mappa Mundi,** Hereford's own picture of the medieval world. This great map shows the Earth as flat, with Jerusalem at its center. It is now thought that the Mappa Mundi was the center section of an altarpiece dating from 1290. The map is on view in an exhibition center completed in spring 1996, and accessible from the 15th-century southwest cloister.

The new building also contains Hereford's other great attraction, the **chained library,** containing some 1,500 chained books. Among the most valuable volumes is an 8th-century copy of the Four Gospels. Chained libraries are extremely rare: they date from medieval times, when books were as precious as gold. ✉ Cathedral Close, ☎ 01432/359880. ☞ Cathedral free. ⊘ Mon.–Sat. 7:30–6:30, Sun. 8–4:30. ☞ Mappa Mundi and Chained Library £4. ⊘ Easter–Oct., Mon.–Sat. 10:15–

5 (last admission 4:15), Sun. noon–4 (last admission 3:15); Nov.–Easter, Mon.–Sat. 11–3 (last admission 2:15).

From Church Street, cross East Street and follow the passageway to High Town, a large pedestrian square, and the **Old House,** a fine example of domestic Jacobean architecture, furnished in 17th-century style on three floors. ☎ *01432/364598.* ✉ *Free.* ⊙ *Tues.–Thurs. 10–5 (also Sun. 10–4 in summer).*

On the west side of High Town is the 13th-century **All Saints Church,** which contains an additional 300 chained books, as well as canopied stalls and fine misericords. From All Saints, walk down the pedestrian Eign Gate, go through the pedestrian underpass, and down Eign Street, which continues as Whitecross Road. At the traffic lights turn left onto Grimmer Road and bear right for the **Cider Museum.** A farm cider house and a cooper's workshop have been re-created here, and you can tour ancient cider cellars, complete with huge oak vats. Cider brandy (applejack) has recently been made here for the first time in hundreds of years, and the museum has its own brand for sale. ✉ *Pomona Pl. at Whitecross Rd.,* ☎ *01432/354207.* ✉ *£2.20.* ⊙ *Apr.–Oct., daily 10–5:30; Nov.–Mar., Tues.–Sun. 11–3.*

Dining and Lodging

£ ✕ **Orange Tree.** This is a refurbished, wood-paneled pub conveniently
★   located on King Street where it joins Bridge Street, near the cathedral. It is a comfortable stopping place on a sightseeing day, with good, solid bar food at lunchtime. ✉ *16 King St.,* ☎ *01432/267698. No credit cards.*

££ 🏨 **Castle Pool.** All that's left of Hereford Castle is the moat, home to a family of ducks. Next to the moat, this 1850 building, dubbed Castle Pool, now offers blandly furnished but comfortable and quiet bedrooms. ✉ *Castle St., HR1 2NW,* ☎ FAX *01432/356321. 27 rooms with bath. Restaurant. AE, DC, MC, V.*

£ 🏨 **Hopbine Hotel.** The Hopbine is a mile from the center of town in the direction of Leominster, but it's worth the jaunt. This Victorian guest house stands amid 2 acres of grounds. The very comfortable, quiet rooms come equipped with a television and appliances for making tea and coffee. Evening meals are available. You'll appreciate the friendliness of this simple place. ✉ *Roman Rd., HR1 1LE,* ☎ *01432/268722,* FAX *01432/268722. 20 rooms with bath. No credit cards.*

Shopping

The **Hereford Book Shop** (✉ Church St., ☎ 01432/357617) has new and secondhand books, guidebooks, maps, and greeting cards. **Capuchin Yard** (✉ Off 29 Church St.) has a wide variety of crafts for sale, including handmade shoes and knitwear; other outlets here sell books, posters, and watercolors. Hereford has a different market each day—food, clothing, livestock—on New Market Street.

Great Witley

㉒ *27 mi northeast of Hereford, 10 mi northwest of Worcester.*

Just under a mile outside the village of Great Witley (off A443), the shell of Witley Court will conjure up a haunting vision of the heyday of this imposing stately home, before it was ravaged by fire in 1937. In contrast to this ruin, the tiny baroque parish church is perfectly preserved. Note its balustraded parapet, a small golden dome over its cupola, and, inside, a ceiling painted by Bellucci, 10 colored windows, and the ornate case of an organ once used by Handel. ✉ *Witley Ct.,* ☎ *01299/896636.* ✉ *£2.75.* ⊙ *Apr.–Oct., daily 10–6 or dusk; Nov.–Mar., Wed.–Sun. 10–1 and 2–4.*

Dining and Lodging

£££ ✕🏨 **Elms Hotel.** This traditional country-house hotel, in an ivy-clad Queen Anne building surrounded by formal gardens, is 16 mi northeast of Worcester and near Great Witley. All the rooms in this former mansion are individually and comfortably decorated. The restaurant, with its imaginative cooking and pleasant, family-dining-room ambience, is worth a visit on its own. ⊠ *Stockton Rd., Abberley WR6 6AT,* ☎ *01299/896666,* ℻ *01299/896804. 16 rooms with bath. Restaurant, tennis court, helipad. AE, DC, MC, V.*

Bewdley

㉓ *8 mi north of Great Witley, 14 mi north of Worcester, 3 mi west of Kidderminster.*

Bewdley is an exceptionally attractive Severn Valley town, with many tall, narrow-fronted Georgian buildings clustered around the river bridge. In what was the 18th-century butchers' market, the **Shambles,** there is now a museum of local crafts. Workshops occupy either side of the old cobbled yard, and there are exhibitions and practical demonstrations of rope making, charcoal burning, clay-pipe making, and wood carving; there is also a working brass foundry. ⊠ *Load St.,* ☎ *01299/ 403573.* 🖾 *£2.* ☉ *Easter–Oct., Mon.–Sun. 11–5.*

Bewdley is the southern terminus of the **Severn Valley Railway,** a restored steam railroad running 16 mi north along the river to Bridgnorth. It stops at a handful of sleepy stations where time has apparently stood still since the age of steam. You can get off at any of these little stations, enjoy a picnic by the river, and walk to the next station to get a train back. ⊠ *Railway Station, Bewdley, Worcestershire DY12 1BG,* ☎ *01299/403816.* ☉ *Mid-May–mid-Oct., trains run daily; mid-Oct.– mid-May, weekends and national holidays only.*

Stourbridge

㉔ *8 mi northeast of Bewdley via A451, 11 mi west of Birmingham.*

In Stourbridge, home of Britain's **crystal glass industry,** you can find bargains at "factory seconds" stores and tour the factories, too. There is a shop at **Stuart Crystal** (⊠ Redhouse Glassworks, Vine St., Wordsley, ☎ 01384/828282), and shops as well as tours at **Royal Brierley Crystal** (⊠ North St., Brierley Hill, ☎ 01384/70161) and **Royal Doulton Crystal** (⊠ High St., Amblecote, ☎ 01384/552900); call for tour schedules and prices.

Outdoor Activities and Sports

BOATING

Between Easter and September, you can join a passenger cruise for short river trips on Sundays and national holidays, and for longer journeys as far as Worcester on Wednesdays. Contact the **Severn Steamboat Company** (⊠ Riverside Walk, Stourport-on-Severn, DY13 8UY, ☎ 01299/ 871177).

Dudley

㉕ *6 mi northeast of Stourbridge, 8 mi west of central Birmingham.*

★ On the edge of Birmingham, Dudley is home to the **Black Country Museum,** established to ensure that the area's industrial heritage is not forgotten. An entire industrial village has been reconstructed of disused buildings from around the region. There is a chain maker's house and workshop, with demonstrations of chain making; a druggist and general store, where costumed women describe life in a poor industrial community in the 19th century; a Methodist chapel; the Bottle & Glass pub, serving local ales and cheese rolls; Stables restaurant, offering such traditional delicacies as faggots and peas (a fried pork-liver dish); and a coal mine and wharf. You can also ride on a barge through a tunnel, where an audiovisual show portrays canal travel of yesteryear. ⊠ *Tipton Rd.,* ☏ *0121/557–9643.* ⊠ *£6.95.* ⊘ *Mar.–Oct., daily 10–5; Nov.–Feb., Wed.–Sun. 10–4.*

SKIRTING THE "BLACK COUNTRY"— FROM SHREWSBURY TO CHESTER

The "peak" of this region—in more ways than one—used to be the Wrekin, a hill geologists claim to be the oldest in the land. That may mean little to the average visitor. Far better to record that A. E. Housman and others have invested it with some of their poetic charm. To stand on its isolated summit and look around is to see what makes up so much of the Midland scene. During the last few years, however, the Wrekin has taken on a new tourist significance because of the enormous popularity of Ironbridge, several miles from the hill. Ironbridge has two identities—as a place as well as a thing. The thing itself is the first bridge to be made of iron, erected between 1777 and 1779. Now taken over by the Ironbridge Gorge Museum Trust, it is the centerpiece of a vast industrial-revolution museum complex. The place is the 6-mi stretch of the Ironbridge Gorge, once an awesome scene of mining and charcoal burning, reeking with smoke and the stench of sulfur. The stretch has now been completely transformed into a scene of idyllic beauty, scars grassed over, woodland filling the gaps left by tree felling. Within easy reach of this complex, rural Shropshire spreads invitingly, offering lovely towns long famed as beauty spots, such as Bridgnorth and Ludlow. We bookend this itinerary with two important cities of the Welsh Border region: Shrewsbury and Chester, both famous for their medieval heritage and their wealth of half-timber buildings and black-and-white "magpie" architecture.

Shrewsbury

㉖ *47 mi northwest of Dudley, 55 mi north of Hereford, 46 mi south of Chester, 48 mi northwest of Birmingham, 150 mi northwest of London.*

Shrewsbury (usually pronounced shrose-bury), the county seat of Shropshire, is within a great horseshoe loop of the Severn. One of England's most important medieval towns, it has a wealth of 16th-century half-timber buildings plus elegant ones from later periods. Today, the town retains a romantic air (indeed, there are numerous bridal shops here—along with a goodly number of churches to match) and it can be a lovely experience to stroll the Shrewsbury "shuts." These narrow alleys overhung with timbered gables lead off the central market square, which had originally been designed to be closed off at night to afford local residents greater protection. The town is especially proud of its flower displays, for which it has won many national awards; in the summer, filled window boxes and hanging baskets are in vivid contrast to the beautiful black-and-white buildings.

Shrewsbury is an ideal town to see on foot, and indeed, traffic has been banned on some of the most historic streets. A good starting point for a walking tour is the small square between Fish Street and Butcher Row. These streets are little changed since medieval times, when some of them took their names from the principal trades carried on there, but Peacock Alley, Gullet Passage, and Grope Lane clearly got their names from **㉗** somewhere else. In the center, off Castle Street, the stone spire of **St. Mary's**

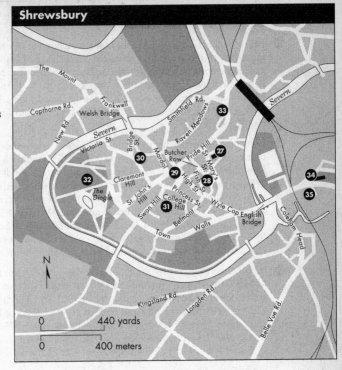

church, built around 1200, is one of the three tallest in England and merits a visit for its iron-framed stained glass (an indication of the proximity of the Ironbridge Gorge).

28 Near St. Mary's church, off Fish Street, **St. Alkmund's** (✉ St. Alkmund's Pl.) is another prominent feature of the Shrewsbury skyline and is also worth seeing for its stained glass. It was built in 1795 on the site of a much earlier church. Bear Steps is a cluster of restored half-timber buildings that link Fish Street with Market Square. Here the most notable **29** building is **Ireland's Mansion,** a massive house with elaborate Jacobean timbering, richly decorated with quatrefoils.

A magnificent 16th-century timber-frame warehouse and adjoining brick and stone mansion built in 1618 together form an eye-catching ensemble **30** in the center of Shrewsbury. Today they house **Rowley's House Museum,** containing clothing, Shropshire pottery and ceramics, Roman finds from Wroxeter, a reconstructed 17th-century bedroom with lovely oak, holly, and walnut paneling and a four-poster bed, and other items of local history. ✉ *Barker St.,* ☎ *01743/361196.* ✈ *£3; joint ticket for Rowley's House, Clive House, Shropshire Regimental Museum, and castle £6.* ⊙ *Tues.–Sat. 10–5, national holidays and summer Sun. 10–4.*

31 **Clive House** was the home of Sir Robert Clive when he was Shrewsbury's member of Parliament in the mid-18th century. Better known as "Clive of India," this soldier-statesman was especially famous for winning the Battle of Plassey in 1757, thereby avenging the atrocity of the Black Hole of Calcutta. The house contains rooms furnished in Clive's period, and striking displays of fragile Staffordshire wares, particularly pieces from the Caughley and Coalport factories. ✉ *College Hill,* ☎ *01743/354811.* ✈ *£2, joint ticket with Rowley's House* *and castle (☞ Rowley's House, above) £6. ☉ Tues.–Sat., national holidays and summer Sun. 10–4.*

㉜ Below Swan Hill you will see the manicured lawn of **Quarry Park** sloping down to the river. In a sheltered corner is the Dingle, a colorful garden offering changing floral displays throughout the year. To get here from Clive House, turn left, then left again. St. John's Hill in the Mardol, another of Shrewsbury's strangely named streets, will take you back into town, or you can head for Welsh Bridge and stroll along the riverbank.

㉝ Guarding the northern approaches to the town, **Shrewsbury Castle** rises up over the river at the bottom of Pride Hill. Originally Norman, it was dismantled during the Civil War and later rebuilt by Thomas Telford, the distinguished Scottish engineer who designed a host of notable buildings and bridges at the beginning of the 19th century. The castle now houses the **Shropshire Regimental Museum.** ⊠ *Shrewsbury Castle, Castle Gates,* ☎ *01743/358516.* ▭ *£3, joint ticket with Rowley's House and Clive House (☞ Rowley's House, above) £6. ☉ Feb.– Dec., Mon.–Sat., national holidays and summer Sun. 10–5.*

㉞ If you cross the river by the English Bridge, you'll reach **Shrewsbury Abbey,** unbecomingly surrounded by busy roads. Founded in 1083 and later a powerful Benedictine monastery, the Abbey Church has survived various vicissitudes throughout its history, including the Dissolution, and retains a good 14th-century west window above a Norman doorway. *Abbey Church,* ⊠ *Abbey Foregate,* ☎ *01743/232723.* ▭ *Free.* ☉ *Easter–Oct., daily 9:30–5:30; Nov.–Easter, daily 10:30–3.*

Shrewsbury Abbey figures in a series of popular medieval whodunits by Ellis Peters, which feature the detective Brother Cadfael and provide an excellent idea of life in this area during the Middle Ages. Across from the Abbey Church, devotees of Brother Cadfael won't be **㉟** able to resist the **Shrewsbury Quest,** which encompasses the scanty remains of the original monastery, and illustrates monastic life in the Middle Ages with the help of a reconstructed scriptorium, library, cloisters, and even a trail of clues to help solve a medieval mystery. Children will be particularly interested, even without a knowledge of the sandaled sleuth. ⊠ *Abbey Foregate,* ☎ *01743/243324.* ▭ *£3.95.* ☉ *Daily 10– 5 (10–4 in winter).*

Dining and Lodging

££ ✕ **Country Friends.** An attractive, imitation black-and-white building, 5 mi south of Shrewsbury by the A49, houses this light and airy restaurant overlooking a garden and pool. Specialties include halibut with olive and basil crust, venison with black currant sauce, and lamb noisettes roasted in mustard crust with mint hollandaise. There are also three simple bedrooms available. ⊠ *Dorrington,* ☎ *01743/718707. MC, V. Closed Sun., Mon., 2 wks mid-July, mid-wk in Oct.*

£ ✕ **Traitor's Gate.** Installed in a series of 13th-century vaulted brick cellars, this atmospheric restaurant serves freshly prepared, reasonably priced meals. Close to the local castle, the Traitor's Gate gets its name from an incident in the Civil War, when a young Roundhead lieutenant ransacked the Cavalier-held fortress. He was later executed as a traitor. ⊠ *St. Mary's Water La. and Castle St.,* ☎ *01743/249152. AE, MC, V. Closed Sun.*

££ ▥ **Prince Rupert Hotel.** This black-and-white, half-timber inn in the historic city center was the headquarters of Prince Rupert, the most famous Royalist general (he was also the nephew of Charles I) during the Civil War. It is now furnished in modern style, although two rooms have four-poster beds. ⊠ *Butcher Row, SY1 1UQ,* ☎ *01743/499955,*

FAX *01743/357306. 65 rooms with bath. Restaurant, recreation room. AE, DC, MC, V.*

£ 🖼 **Sandford House.** This late-Georgian B&B, close to the river and the town center, is run by the hospitable Richards family. The bedrooms are clean and basic, but well furnished. There is an attractive rear garden. ⊠ *St. Julian Friars, SY1 1XL,* ☎ *01743/343829. 10 rooms, 8 with bath or shower. MC, V.*

The Arts

FESTIVALS

During the **Shrewsbury International Music Festival** (⊠ Shrewsbury Festival Office, Suite 3, Victoria Court, Bexton Rd., Knutsford, Cheshire WA16 0PF, ☎ 01565/652667) in June and July, the town vibrates to traditional and not-so-traditional music by groups from America, western Europe, and sometimes eastern Europe.

Shopping

The Parade, just behind St. Mary's church, is a shopping mall created from the former Royal Infirmary, built in 1830. It's one of the most appealing malls England has to offer, with attractive boutiques, posh apartments upstairs, a restaurant, and a terrace overlooking the river and the abbey.

Attingham Park

36 *4 mi southeast of Shrewsbury, just off A5.*

Built in 1785 by George Steuart, who designed the round church of St. Chad's in Shrewsbury, this elegant mansion has a three-story portico, with a pediment carried on four tall columns. The building overlooks a wide sweep of parkland, including a deer park landscaped by Humphry Repton. Inside are painted ceilings, delicate plasterwork, and a collection of 19th-century Neapolitan furniture. ☎ *01743/709203.* 🖼 *£4, park and grounds only £1.50.* ⊘ *Easter–Oct., Sat.–Wed. 1:30–5; national holiday Mon. 11–5; park and grounds daily until dusk.*

Ironbridge Gorge

★ **37** *15 mi east of Shrewsbury, 28 mi northwest of Birmingham.*

Continuing southeast on B4380, you will see, rising on the left, the **Wrekin,** a strange, conical extinct volcano. A few miles farther on you enter the wooded gorge of the River Severn. Here you can see the world's earliest iron bridge (1779), a monument to the discovery of how to smelt iron ore using coke (a coal residue), rather than charcoal.

The Shropshire coalfields were of enormous importance to the development of the coke smelting process which, in turn, helped usher in the industrial revolution. This fascinating history is preserved and recounted at the **Ironbridge Gorge Museum.** Spread over 6 square mi, it has six component sections. A good half day will let you take in the major sights and stroll around the famous bridge, perhaps hunting for Coalport china in the stores clustered near it. The best starting point is the **Severn Warehouse,** which has a good selection of literature and an audiovisual show on the gorge's history. From here you can drive (or in summer, take the museum's "park and ride" service) to Coalbrookdale and the **Museum of Iron,** which explains the production of iron and steel. You can see the original blast furnace built by Abraham Darby, developer of the original coke process. Retrace your steps along the river until the arches of the **Iron Bridge** come into view; it was designed by T. F. Pritchard, smelted by Darby, and erected between

1777 and 1779. An infinitely graceful arch spanning the river, it can best be seen—and photographed or painted—from the towpath, a charming riverside walk edged with wildflowers and dense shrubs. The tollhouse on the far side houses an exhibition on the bridge's history and restoration.

A mile farther along the river is the old factory and the **Coalport China Museum** (the china is now made in Stoke-on-Trent). There are exhibits of some of the factory's most beautiful wares, and craftsmen give demonstrations. Above Coalport is **Blists Hill Open-Air Museum,** where you can see old mines, furnaces, and a wrought-iron works. But the main draw is the re-creation of a Victorian town, with the doctor's office, the sweet-smelling bakery, the candle maker's, the sawmill, the printing shop, and the candy store. ⊠ *Ironbridge Gorge Museum Trust, Ironbridge, Telford, Shropshire TF8 7AW,* ☎ *01952/433522.* ▣ *Ticket to all sights £9.50.* ◌ *Daily 10–5 (July and Aug. until 6).*

Dining and Lodging

£ ✗ **New Inn.** This Victorian building was moved from Walsall, 22 mi away, so that it could be part of the Blists Hill open-air museum. It is a fully functioning pub, with gas lamps, sawdust on the floor, and traditional ales served from the cask. For an inexpensive meal, you can try a ploughman's lunch, a pasty from the antique-style bakery, or a pork pie from the butcher's store next door. ⊠ *Blists Hill Museum,* ☎ *01952/433522. No credit cards.*

£ 🏨 **Library House.** Nestled into the hillside near the Ironbridge museums, and only a few steps away from the bridge itself, this small hotel has kept its attractive Victorian ambience. Smoking is not permitted indoors. ⊠ *11 Severn Bank, TF8 7AN,* ☎ *01952/432299,* FAX *01952/433967. 4 rooms with bath. No credit cards. Closed Christmas wk.*

Bridgnorth

38 *9 mi south of Ironbridge, 22 mi southeast of Shrewsbury, 25 mi west of Birmingham.*

Perching perilously on a high sandstone ridge on the banks of the Severn, the pretty market town of Bridgnorth has two distinct parts, High Town and Low Town, connected by a winding road, flights of steep steps, and—best of all—a cliff railroad. Even the tower of the Norman castle seems to suffer from vertigo, having a 17-degree list (three times the angle of the Leaning Tower of Pisa). The Severn Valley Railway terminates here.

Ludlow

★ **39** *29 mi south of Shrewsbury, 24 mi north of Hereford.*

Ludlow has medieval, Georgian, and Victorian buildings and a finer display of black-and-white buildings than even Shrewsbury itself. The center is dominated by the great **Church of St. Lawrence** on College Street, its extravagant size a testimony to the town's prosperous wool trade. Look for the **Feathers Hotel** on the street called the Bull Ring, to admire its extravagantly decorated half-timber facade. Cross the river and climb **Whitcliff** for the most spectacular view. The town is dwarfed by the massive, ruined, red sandstone **castle,** which dates from 1085 and was a vital stronghold for centuries. It was the seat of the Marcher Lords who ruled "the Marches," the local name for the border region. It was in this castle that John Milton wrote his verse drama *Comus,* and it is still privately owned by the earl of Powys. Follow the terraced walk around the castle for a lovely view. ⊠ *Castle Sq.,* ☎ *01584/873355.* ▣ *£2.50.* ◌ *Feb.–Apr. and Oct.–Dec., daily 10–4; May–Sept., daily 10–5.*

Dining and Lodging

£££ ✕🏠 **Dinham Hall.** Near Ludlow Castle, this property is a converted merchant's town house dating from 1792. The owners have managed to combine the original historic elements in the house with modern comforts. The dining room serves imaginative dishes such as salmon with wild mushrooms and chicken with honey and ginger sauce. This is a good base for exploring the region. ⊠ *Off Market Sq., SY8 1EJ,* ☎ *01584/876464,* 🗚 *01584/876019. 11 rooms with bath or shower. Restaurant, sauna. AE, DC, MC, V.*

The Arts

In Shropshire, the **Ludlow Festival,** starting at the end of June, sums up much that is English: Shakespeare is performed in the open air against the romantic backdrop of the ruined castle to an audience armed with cushions, raincoats, lap robes, and picnic baskets—and not a few hip flasks. Telephone reservations are accepted starting in early May, or by mail from April. Details available from the Festival Box Office (⊠ *Castle Sq., Ludlow, Shropshire SY8 1AY,* ☎ *01584/872150).*

CHESTER

Cheshire is mainly a land of well-kept farms, supporting their herds of equally well-kept cattle, but there are numerous places here steeped in history. Villages contain many fine examples of the black-and-white "magpie" type of architecture more often associated with the Midlands (and every bit as attractive as anything to be found there).

40 The thriving center of the region is **Chester,** 46 mi north of Shrewsbury. Chester is in some ways similar to Shrewsbury, though it has many more black-and-white half-timber buildings, and its medieval walls are still standing. Chester has been a prominent city since the late 1st century AD, when the Roman Empire expanded northward to the banks of the River Dee. The original Roman town plan is still evident: the principal streets, Eastgate, Northgate, Watergate, and Bridge Street, lead out from the Cross—the site of the central area of the Roman fortress—to the four city gates.

Since Roman times, seagoing vessels have sailed up the estuary of the Dee and anchored under the walls of Chester. The port enjoyed its most prosperous period during the 12th and 13th centuries. This was also ★ the time when Chester's unique **Rows** originated. Essentially, they are double rows of stores, one at street level, and the other on the second floor with galleries overlooking the street. The Rows line the junction of the four streets in the old town. They have medieval crypts below them, and some reveal Roman foundations. History seems more tangible in Chester than in many other ancient cities. So much medieval architecture remains that the town center is quite compact, and modern buildings have not been allowed to intrude. A negative result of this perfection is that Chester has become a favorite bus-tour destination, with gift shops and casual restaurants, noise, and crowds.

Chester's city **walls** are accessible from various points and provide splendid views of the city and its surroundings. The whole circuit is 2 mi, but if your time is short, climb the steps at Newgate and walk along toward Eastgate to see the great ornamental clock, erected to commemorate Queen Victoria's Diamond Jubilee in 1897. Lots of small shops by this part of the walls sell old books, old postcards, antiques, and jewelry. Where the **Bridge of Sighs**—named after the enclosed bridge in Venice that it closely resembles—crosses the canal, descend to street level and walk up Northgate Street into Market Square.

The **cathedral** is just off Market Square. Tradition has it that a church of some sort stood on this site in Roman times, but the earliest records indicate construction around AD 900. The earliest work traceable today, mainly in the north transept, is that of the 11th-century Benedictine abbey. After Henry VIII dissolved the monasteries in the 16th century, the abbey church became the cathedral church of the new diocese of Chester. ⊠ *St. Werburgh St.,* ☎ *01244/324756.* ☜ *Free.* ⊙ *Daily 7–6:30.*

Overlooking the River Dee, Chester's **castle** lost its moats and battlements at the end of the 18th century to make way for the classical-style civil and criminal courts, jail, and barracks. The castle now houses the **Cheshire Military Museum**, exhibiting uniforms, memorabilia, and some fine silver. ⊠ *Castle St.,* ☎ *01244/327617.* ☜ *Small admission fee.* ⊙ *Daily 10–4:30 (last admission 4).*

Dining and Lodging

££   ✗ **Garden House.** This restaurant on two floors in downtown Chester serves both meat and fish dishes as well as award-winning vegetarian cuisine. Game is one of the specialties of the house, while non-meat-eaters will appreciate the *pilau* parcel filled with stir-fried vegetables, ginger, and soy sauce. There is a garden and patio for eating outdoors in summer. ⊠ *1 Rufus Ct., off Northgate St.,* ☎ *01244/313251. AE, DC, MC, V. Closed Sun.*

£   ✗ **The Falcon.** A typical old pub, the Falcon is a handy spot for a wide range of lunch options, including Balti and Cajun dishes, and seafood. ⊠ *Lower Bridge St.,* ☎ *01244/314555.*

££££ ✗🖭 **Chester Grosvenor Hotel.** This is a traditional deluxe hotel in a Tudor-style, downtown building; it's remarkable to find such quiet luxury and sumptuous comfort in a small country town. The splendid Arkle Restaurant has marble and stone walls, solid mahogany tables, candlelight, and gleaming silver. The style here is *cuisine légère,* using little cream or butter, only natural ingredients, and sauces made by reduction rather than thickening. ⊠ *Eastgate St., CH1 1LT,* ☎ *01244/ 324024,* ₣ₐₓ *01244/313246. 86 rooms with bath. Restaurant, brasserie, sauna, exercise room. AE, DC, MC, V.*

£££ ✗🖭 **Crabwall Manor.** This dramatic, castellated, part-Tudor, part-
★   neo-Gothic mansion is set on 11 acres of farm and parkland. It has elegant, subtle furnishings in floral chintzes, a wonderful stone staircase, and extremely comfortable bedrooms. The spacious restaurant offers Cordon Bleu cooking and is worth visiting—say, for lunch, while exploring the neighborhood. ⊠ *Parkgate Rd., Mollington CH1 6NE,* ☎ *01244/851666,* ₣ₐₓ *01244/851400. 48 rooms with bath. Restaurant. AE, DC, MC, V.*

£   ✗🖭 **Green Bough Hotel.** The Green Bough is in a large, late-Victorian house, with a variety of antiques and bric-a-brac. Both the main building and the annex contain roomy, comfortable bedrooms, one with a four-poster. The dining room offers an imaginative and reasonably priced menu that changes daily and includes vegetarian dishes. ⊠ *60 Hoole Rd., CH2 3NL,* ☎ *01244/326241,* ₣ₐₓ *01244/326265. 20 rooms with bath or shower. Dining room. AE, MC, V.*

Shopping

Melodies Galleries (⊠ 32 City Rd., ☎ 01244/328968), with 16 dealers on two floors of an old Georgian building, offers a wide mix of fine furniture and bric-a-brac. **Bookland** (⊠ 12 Bridge St., ☎ 01244/ 347323), in an ancient building with a converted 14th-century crypt, has a wealth of travel and general-interest books. Chester has an indoor market in the Forum, near the Town Hall, every day except Wednesday afternoon and Sunday.

OFF THE BEATEN PATH	**LITTLE MORETON HALL—** The ne plus ultra of "magpie" black-and-white half-timber buildings, this house, in the words of Olive Cook's *The English Country House,* "exaggerates and exalts the typical and humble medieval timber-framed dwelling, making of it a bizarre, unforgettable phenomenon." Covered with dazzling zigzags, crosses, and lozenge-shapes crafted of timber and daub, the house was built by the Moreton family in 1450–1580. Other features include a spectacular long gallery, Tudor-era wall paintings, and a drunkenly reeling facade. Special events are held throughout the year, including evening buffet suppers and open-air Shakespeare. It can be an easy journey from Chester, by bus (PMT 77), by car via the M56 east to Congleton, or by train to the station at Kidsgrove (then taxi 3 mi). The house is 4 mi southwest of Congleton. ✉ Congleton, CW12 4SD, ☎ 01260/272018. 🎫 £4. ☉ March 21–Nov. 1 Wed.–Sun., 11–5; Nov. 7–Dec. 20 Sat.–Sun., 12–4.

WELSH BORDERS A TO Z

Arriving and Departing

By Bus

National Express (☎ 0990/808080) serves the region from London's Victoria Coach Station. Average travel time to Chester is five hours; to Hereford and Shrewsbury, four hours; and to Worcester, 3½ hours.

By Car

From London take M40 and keep on it for M42 and Birmingham (120 mi). M4/M5 from London takes you to Worcester in just under three hours. The prettier, more direct route (120 mi) on M40 via Oxford to A40 across the Cotswolds is actually slower because it is only partly motorway. For Shrewsbury (150 mi) and Chester (180 mi), take M1/M6.

By Train

British Rail (☎ 0345/484950 for train schedules and information) serves the region from London's Paddington and Euston stations. Average travel times are: Paddington to Hereford, three hours; to Worcester, 2¼ hours; to Birmingham, 1 hour 45 minutes from London's Euston Station; Euston to Shrewsbury and Chester, with a change at Wolverhampton or Birmingham, three hours and 2½ hours respectively.

Getting Around

By Bus

For information about local services and Rover tickets, contact **Crosville Bus Station** in Chester (☎ 01244/381515), **Midland Red (West) Travel** in Worcester (☎ 01905/763888), and **County Bus Line** (☎ 0345/125436) in Hereford. **Flights Coach Travel Ltd. of Birmingham** (☎ 0121/322–2222) operates "Flightlink" services from London's Heathrow and Gatwick airports to Coventry and Warwick. **Midland Red (South) Ltd.** and **Stratford Blue** (☎ 01788/535555) serve the Stratford-upon-Avon, Birmingham, and Coventry areas.

By Car

Driving can be difficult in the western reaches of this region—especially in the hills and valleys west of Hereford, where steep, twisting roads often narrow down into mere trackways. Winter travel along here can be particularly grueling.

By Train

A direct local service links Hereford and Shrewsbury, with a change at Oswestry or Wrexham for Chester. **West Midlands Day Ranger** tickets and three- and seven-day "Heart of England Rover" tickets allow unlimited travel.

Contacts and Resources

Car Rentals

Birmingham: Avis (✉ 7–9 Park St., ☎ 0121/632–4361); **EuroDollar Rent-a-Car** (✉ Snow Hill Service Station, St. Chads, ☎ 0121/200–3010). **Chester: Avis** (✉ 128 Brook St., ☎ 01244/311463); **Hertz** (✉ Auto Travel Agency, Abley House, Trafford St., ☎ 01244/374705). **Hereford: Practical Car and Van Rental, Puremass Ltd.** (✉ Coningsby St., ☎ 01432/278989). **Worcester: Kenning** (✉ Hylton Rd., ☎ 01905/748403); **Hertz** (Brandrick Holdings Ltd., ✉ 14 Carden St., ☎ 01905/24844).

Guided Tours

Local tourist offices can recommend day or half-day tours of the region and will have the names of registered Blue Badge guides. **Faithful City Tours** (✉ Box 1, Newtown Post Office, Worcester, ☎ 01905/29825) conducts tours of the Worcester area including Witley Court and Elgar's birthplace.

Hiking and Walking

For information on hiking the Malvern Hills, contact **Malvern Tourist Board** (✉ 21 Church St., Worcestershire WR14 2AA, ☎ 01684/892289) or **Ross-on-Wye Tourist Office** (✉ Swan House, Edde Cross St., Herefordshire HR9 7BZ, ☎ 01989/562768). For information on the Offa's Dyke Path, contact the **Offa's Dyke Centre** (✉ West St., Knighton, Powys LD7 1EN, ☎ 01547/528753).

Travel Agencies

American Express (✉ 27 Claremont St., Shrewsbury, ☎ 01743/236387; ✉ 23 St. Werburgh St., Chester, ☎ 01244/311145). **Thomas Cook** (✉ 10 Bridge St., Chester, ☎ 01244/323045; ✉ 4 St. Peter's St., Hereford, ☎ 01432/356461; ✉ 36–37 Pride Hill, Shrewsbury, ☎ 01743/231144; and ✉ 26 High St., Worcester, ☎ 01905/28228).

Visitor Information

The **Heart of England Tourist Board** (✉ Woodside, Larkhill, Worcester WR5 2EF, ☎ 01905/763436, FAX 01905/763450) is open Monday–Thursday 9–5:30, Friday 9–5.

Local tourist information centers are normally open Monday–Saturday 9:30–5:30. **Birmingham** (✉ Convention and Visitor Bureau, 2 City Arcade, ☎ 0121/643–2514). **Chester** (✉ Town Hall, Northgate St., CH1 2HJ, ☎ 01244/402111). **Hereford** (✉ 1 King St., HR4 9BW, ☎ 01432/268430). **Ludlow** (✉ Castle St., SY8 1AS, ☎ 01584/875053). **Ross-on-Wye** (✉ The Swan, Edde Cross St., HR9 7BZ, ☎ 01989/562768). **Shrewsbury** (✉ The Music Hall, The Square, SY1 1LH, ☎ 01743/350761). **Worcester** (✉ The Guildhall, High St., WR1 2EY, ☎ 01905/726311).

11 Wales

Lauded as "The Land of Castles," the ancient stronghold of Wales is one of Britain's best-kept secrets. The slag heaps of How Green Was My Valley, the film made half a century ago are gone. Today Wales is evergreen and unspoiled. As conclusive proof of its scenic grandeur, it's home to three national parks, with Snowdonia the monarch of all it surveys. Other treasures await: the stately houses of Powis and Erddig, steam-train rides through tree-clad chasms, the capital of Cardiff, and the glory of the Welsh language.

WALES, APART FROM BEING CALLED the Land
of Song, is also a land of mountain and flood,
where wild peaks challenge the sky and wa-
terfalls thunder down steep, rocky chasms. It is a land of gray-stone
medieval castles, ruined abbeys, little steam trains chugging through
dramatic scenery, male-voice choirs, and a handful of cities. Small
pockets of the south and northeast were heavily industrialized—largely
with mining and steelmaking—in the 19th century, but long stretches
of the coast and the mountainous interior remain areas of unmarred
beauty. As conclusive evidence of its scenic splendor, small, self-contained Wales has three national parks (Snowdonia, the Brecon Beacons,
and the Pembrokeshire Coast) and five "Areas of Outstanding Natural Beauty" (the Wye Valley, Gower Peninsula, Llŷn Peninsula, Isle of
Anglesey, and Clwydian Range), as well as large tracts of unspoiled
moor and mountain in mid-Wales, the least traveled part of the country. Dotted over the entire country are riches of other sorts: medieval
castles, charming seaside resorts, traditional market towns, the glorious Bodnant Garden, the great stately houses of Powis and Erddig, steam-
powered train rides through the mountains of Snowdonia and central
Wales, and the cosmopolitan capital of Cardiff.

Updated by
Roger Thomas

Wales suffers more than most destinations from the curse of the stereotype. Many visitors still perceive the country in terms of the *How Green
Was My Valley* film of half a century ago, in which Wales was depicted
as an industrial cauldron filled with coal mines. The picture was not
accurate then; it is certainly not accurate now—Wales has only one fully
operational mine today. In any case, industrial activity has always
been concentrated in a relatively small corner of southeast Wales, leaving the vast majority of the landscape untouched by modern development. In fact, one of the great glories of Wales is the way in which you
can drive through beautiful countryside from south to north without
having to pass through any large towns. The same applies to the country's 750-mi coast, which consists mainly of sandy beaches, grassy headlands, cliffs, and estuaries. Stretches of the coast and the mountainous
interior remain areas of unmarred beauty.

The Welsh are a Celtic race. When, toward the middle of the first millennium AD, the Anglo-Saxons spread through Britain, they pushed the
indigenous Celts farther back into their Welsh mountain strongholds.
(In fact, "Wales" comes from the Saxon word "Weallas," which means
"strangers," the name impertinently given by the new arrivals to the
natives.) The Welsh, however, have always called themselves "Y
Cymry"—the companions. It was not until the fearsome English king
Edward I (1272–1307) waged a brutal and determined campaign to
conquer Wales that English supremacy was established. Welsh hopes
were finally crushed with the death in battle of Llywelyn ap Gruffudd,
last native prince of Wales, in 1282.

In the 15th and 16th centuries, the Tudor kings Henry VII and Henry
VIII continued England's ruthless domination of the Welsh, principally
by attempting to abolish their language. Ironically it was another
Tudor monarch, Elizabeth I, who ensured its survival by authorizing
a Welsh translation of the Bible in 1588. Today, many people say they
owe their knowledge of Welsh to the Bible. The language is spoken by
only a fifth of the population, but it still flourishes. Terms that crop
up frequently are *bach* or *fach* (small), *craig* or *graig* (rock), *cwm* (valley), *dyffryn* (valley), *eglwys* (church), *glyn* (glen), *llyn* (lake), *mawr*
or *fawr* (great, big), *mynydd* or *fynydd* (mountain, moorland), *pentre*

(village, homestead), *plas* (hall, mansion), and *pont* or *bont* (bridge). Signs are bilingual, but don't worry; everyone speaks English, too.

Pleasures and Pastimes

Dining

Twenty-five years ago, Wales was regarded as a gastronomic desert. How times change: you can now eat exceedingly well here, and even country pubs are more interested in offering meals than serving pints of beer. Talented chefs have moved in, making the best use of Wales's bountiful natural resources. Succulent Welsh lamb is regarded as the best in the world, there is a plentiful supply of seafood, and there has been a revival in Welsh cheese-making to such an extent that the suppliers have difficulty coping with the demand. For traditionalists, there is the old favorite of Welsh lamb served with vegetables. Another traditional feast is *cawl*, a nourishing broth with vegetables and meat. The most unusual traditional delicacy is laverbread, made from seaweed and cooked to resemble a black pureed substance. Don't be put off by its appearance: it has a taste all its own and is usually eaten with bacon. For more cosmopolitan palates, there's everything from French to Far Eastern, especially in Cardiff. For a special treat, have dinner at one of Wales's leading country-house hotels—you don't have to be an overnight guest to enjoy the experience.

CATEGORY	COST*
££££	over £40
£££	£25–£40
££	£15–£25
£	under £15

*per person, including first course, main course, dessert, and VAT; excluding drinks

Lodging

A 19th-century dictum, "I sleeps where I dines" still holds true in Wales. Good hotels and good restaurants often go together, and since conversion is the rage, castles, country mansions, and even small railway stations are being transformed into hotels and restaurants. Traditional inns—full of character, with low-beam ceilings, wood paneling, and cozy fireplaces—remain the country's pride, but they tend to be off the beaten track and you will need a car to make the most of them. The same goes for farmhouse accommodations, which have recently grown by leaps and bounds. Of course, Cardiff and Swansea have their large international hotels. For luxury and top-class service, there's a good choice of country-house hotels. An added attraction is that prices are generally lower than they are for equivalent properties in the Cotswolds, Scotland, or southeast England.

CATEGORY	COST*
££££	over £110
£££	£60–£110
££	£50–£60
£	under £50

*All prices are for two people sharing a double room, including service, breakfast, and VAT.

Walking

An army of bipeds covers Wales every year, as this is a wonderful region for walking and hiking. There are long-distance paths to follow, such as the Pembrokeshire Coast Path (which runs all along the spectacular shores of southwest Wales) and the south–north Offa's Dyke Path, based on the border between England and Wales established by

Wales

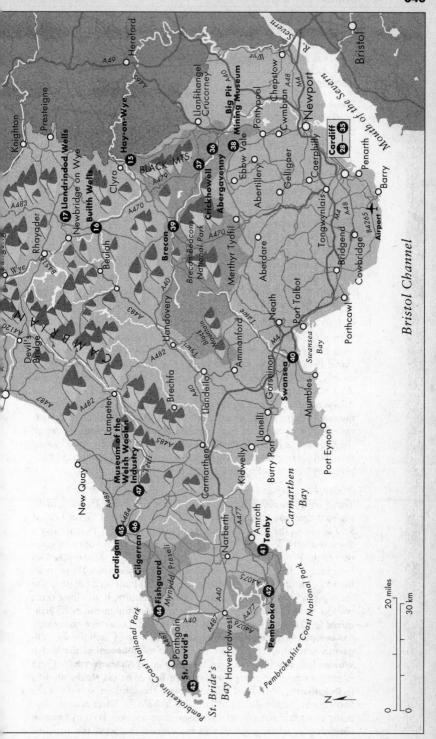

King Offa in the 8th century. In Wales's forested areas you will find signposted footpaths that are short and easy to follow. Enthusiasts might prefer the more challenging wide open spaces of the Brecon Beacons National Park or the rugged mountains of Snowdonia.

Exploring Wales

Wales has three main regions—south, mid, and north. The south is the most varied, for its boundaries include everything from Wales's capital city to unspoiled coastline, grassy mountains to wooded valleys. Mid-Wales is pure countryside, fringed on its western shores by the great arc of Cardigan Bay. North Wales is a mixture of high, rocky mountains, popular sandy beaches, and coastal hideaways.

Numbers in the text correspond to numbers in the margin and on the Wales, Aberystwyth, and Cardiff maps.

Great Itineraries

Do not be misled by Wales's relatively small size. Although less than 200 mi from south to north, the country is packed with scenic variety and a daunting range of places to visit. Many visitors make the mistake of thinking that they can see Wales in a day or so. In that time, they will only have the opportunity to scratch the surface of this fascinating little country.

IF YOU HAVE 3 DAYS

Start off in **Cardiff** ㉘, Wales's capital city. You will want to spend at least a half day here before driving through the Brecon Beacons National Park to 🏨 **Llandrindod Wells** ⑰, a Victorian spa town conveniently situated between the border and the mountains. On day two, drive via Rhayader and the Elan Valley—Wales's "Lake District"—to **Aberystwyth** ⑱, then along the north coast of Cardigan Bay to 🏨 **Porthmadog** ⑥ (handy accommodations are in nearby Harlech and Portmeirion). For your final day, drive via **Blaenau Ffestiniog** ⑤ through the Snowdonia National Park to **Betws-y-Coed** ⑦, and if you have the time, call into medieval **Conwy** ⑪ before leaving Wales via the A55 "Expressway" route to England.

IF YOU HAVE 9 DAYS

Travel to 🏨 **Cardiff** ㉘ for a full day's visit and overnight stop, making sure that you have time to stop at the Museum of Welsh Life, at St. Fagans on the western outskirts of the city. On day two, drive via **Swansea** ㊵ to 🏨 **Tenby** ㊶, a picturesque resort at the southern gateway to the Pembrokeshire Coast National Park. Day three is taken up by a tour of this wild and beautiful stretch of seashore. Drive to **St. David's** ㊸ in the far west to visit the cathedral built on a religious site founded by Wales's patron saint in the 6th century. If you have time, walk a stretch of the coast path before continuing on to 🏨 **Fishguard** ㊹. Day four is taken up by more beautiful coastline on the way to **Cardigan** ㊺, then a tour along the lovely Vale of Teifi through **Cilgerran** ㊻ to Drefach Felindre to explore the **Museum of the Welsh Woolen Industry** ㊼. From here, continue on to **Aberystwyth** ⑱. From Aberystwyth, drive along the Cardigan Bay coast via **Machynlleth** ㉔ to **Dolgellau** ㉙, then head inland through the southern section of the Snowdonia National Park to lakeside 🏨 **Bala** ④. There is more dramatic mountain scenery on day six on the way from Bala to **Blaenau Ffestiniog** ⑤, where you can visit the caverns that gave this town its past reputation as the "slate capital of North Wales." From here, follow the wooded Vale of Ffestiniog west to **Porthmadog** ⑥ then continue northward to 🏨 **Caernarfon** ⑨, home of one of Wales's most famous medieval castles. Day seven takes you across the Menai Strait by the road bridge near Bangor to the Isle of Anglesey and **Beaumaris** ⑩ for a brief visit, then back along the coast of mainland North Wales via medieval **Conwy** ⑪ to the handsome Victorian seaside resort of ⊡ **Llandudno** ⑫ (on this leg, you may want to substitute the trip across to Anglesey with a short detour inland from Caernarfon to **Llanberis** ⑧ and the spectacular Llanberis Pass in the heart of Snowdonia). Borderland Wales is the theme of the next day, the route passing through **Denbigh** ⑬, **Ruthin** ⑭, **Llangollen** ③, **Chirk** ①, and **Welshpool** ㉗ on the way to ⊡ **Llandrindod Wells** ⑰. On your last day, visit **Hay-on-Wye** ⑮, the borderland "town of books," then drive on through the mountains to **Brecon** ㊴ in the Brecon Beacons National Park. From here, follow the Vale of Usk through **Crickhowell** ㊲ and **Abergavenny** ㊱ before leaving Wales along the M4 motorway.

When to Tour Wales

The weather in Wales, as in the rest of Britain, is a lottery. It can be warm in the spring and cool in the summer, dry in May, and wet in August. Come prepared for rain or shine. Generally speaking, southwest Wales enjoys a milder climate than elsewhere, thanks to the moderating effects of the sea. Spring and autumn are attractive times in Wales (note that spring can arrive very early in Pembrokeshire, while other parts of the country may still be in the grip of winter). These seasons can be surprisingly dry and sunny, and you will have the added advantage of quiet surroundings. That noted, crowds are rarely a problem—apart from the main tourist centers—for many parts of Wales remain peaceful even in the height of summer.

NORTH WALES: IN THE REALM OF SNOWDONIA

The north is the region where Wales masses all its savage splendor and fierce beauty. Dominating its southwestern corner is Snowdon, at 3,560 ft the highest mountain in England and Wales. It is impossible to describe the magnificence of the view on a clear day—to the northwest the Menai Strait, Anglesey, and beyond to the Irish Sea; to the south the mountains of Merionethshire, Harlech Castle, and the Cader Idris mountain range; and all around great towering masses of wild and barren rock. If you ascend the peak by the Snowdon Mountain Railway from Llanberis, telephone from the terminus to ascertain whether Snowdon is free from mist, for you will lose much if you arrive when clouds, as often happens, encircle the monster's brow.

The peak gives its name to Snowdonia National Park, which extends southward all the way to Machynlleth in mid-Wales. The park consists of 840 square mi of rocky mountains, valleys clothed in oak woods, moorlands, lakes, and rivers, all with one thing in common—natural beauty, and, to a lesser extent, solitude. Increasingly, however, the park has become a popular climbing center and there are fears that Snowdon itself is becoming worn away by the boots of too many walkers. Along the sandy, north-facing coast, a string of seaside resorts has also been attracting visitors for well over a century. Llandudno, the dignified "Queen of the North Wales coast," was built in Victorian times as a seaside watering hole. If you prefer away-from-it-all seashore, there are two official "Areas of Outstanding Beauty"—the Isle of Anglesey (connected by bridge to mainland Wales) and the Llŷn Peninsula—dotted with quieter small resorts and coastal villages.

Chirk and the Ceiriog Valley

❶ *22 mi southwest of Chester.*

A favored first stop in Wales for travelers coming from England is Chirk, poised on the very border between the two countries. It's a handy gateway to the Ceiriog Valley, a narrowing vale that penetrates the silent, green foothills of the lofty Berwyn Mountains. Chirk is the site of an imposing medieval **castle,** completed in its original form in 1310, which has over the centuries evolved into a grand home. Standing amid beautiful formal gardens and grounds, it is now owned by the National Trust. ☎ *01691/777701.* ⊠ *£4.60, garden only £2.40.* ☉ *Castle Apr.– Sept., Wed.–Sun. noon–5; Oct., weekends noon–5. Garden Apr.–Sept., Wed.–Sun. 11–6; Oct., weekends 11–6.*

❷ From Chirk, head to the **Vale of Ceiriog,** nicknamed—and somewhat hyped as—Little Switzerland. Take B4500 west 6 mi through the picturesque valley to the village of Glyn Ceiriog, which nestles at the foothills of the remote Berwyn Mountains, an area that attracts pony trekkers, walkers, fishermen, and rough shooters.

Continue on B4500 southwest from Glyn Ceiriog, and then its unnumbered continuation, to reach Llanrhaeadr ym Mochnant, in the peaceful Tanat Valley. Here, in 1588, the Bible was translated into Welsh, thus ensuring the survival of the language. Turn northwest and go 4 mi up the road to Pistyll Rhaeadr, the highest waterfall in Wales, whose peat-brown water thunders down a 290-ft double cascade.

Dining and Lodging

££–£££ ✕☲ **Golden Pheasant.** This 200-year-old hotel is furnished with antiques and Victorian-style fabrics, and the result is chinoiserie in the bar, horse prints and aspidistras in the lounge, draped curtains and parlor palms in the dining room, and no two bedrooms alike. Specialties include Ceiriog trout, pheasant, and game pie. ⊠ *Glyn Ceiriog, near Chirk, LL20 7BB,* ☎ *01691/718281,* 🏧 *01691/718479. 18 rooms with bath. Restaurant. AE, DC, MC, V.*

£ ☲ **Bron Heulog.** This guest house at Llanrhaeadr ym Mochnant, a former Victorian doctor's surgery, has been lovingly restored. The owners set an excellent table. ⊠ *Waterfall Rd., near Oswestry, Shropshire SY10 0JX,* ☎ *01691/780521,* 🏧 *01691/780630. 3 rooms with shower. MC, V.*

Llangollen

❸ *5 mi northwest of Chirk, 23 mi southwest of Chester.*

Llangollen, set in a deep valley carved by the River Dee, is the birthplace of the **International Musical Eisteddfod** (☎ 01978/860236). The tradition of the *eisteddfod,* held throughout Wales, goes back to the 12th century. Originally gatherings of bards, the *eisteddfodau* of today are more like competitions or festivals. The Llangollen event was started as a gesture of friendship after World War II by a newspaperman who wanted, in effect, to have a concert and invite the whole world to join in. Amazingly, it worked, and now choirs and dancers from all corners of the globe make for an unusual and colorful arts festival. The six-day event takes place each year in early July.

While you are in Llangollen, visit **Plas Newydd** (not to be confused with the grand estate on the Isle of Anglesey with the same name), home from 1778 to 1828 of the eccentric Ladies of Llangollen, who set up a scandalous single-sex household, collected curios and magnificent wood carvings, and made it into a tourist attraction even during their lifetimes, entertaining celebrated guests, among them William Wordsworth,

Sir Walter Scott, and the Duke of Wellington. The Ladies had a servant with the unforgettable name of "Mollie the Basher." ⊠ *Hill St.,* ☎ *01978/861314.* ⊡ *£2.* ☉ *Apr.–end Oct., daily 10–5.*

From the **canal wharf** take a horse-drawn boat or a narrow boat (☎ 01978/860702) along the Llangollen Canal to the largest navigable aqueduct in the world at Pontcysyllte. Llangollen's bridge, over the River Dee, a 14th-century stone structure, is named in a traditional Welsh folk song as one of the "Seven Wonders of Wales." Near the bridge is the terminus of the **Llangollen Railway,** a restored standard-gauge steam line. It runs for a few miles along the scenic Dee Valley. ☎ *01978/ 860979; 01978/860951 24-hr recorded information.* ⊡ *£7 round-trip.* ☉ *May–Nov., daily 10–5; also limited weekend service Dec.–Apr..*

There are easy walks along the banks of the River Dee or along part of **Offa's Dyke Path.** The 168-mi-long path follows the line of an ancient earthen wall, still surviving in parts, which was built along the border with England in the 8th century by King Offa of Mercia (757–796) to keep out Welsh raiders. For a particularly scenic drive in this area, head for the Horseshoe Pass.

Bala

4 *18 mi southwest of Llangollen.*

The staunchly Welsh town of Bala is a good base from which to explore the eastern and southern sections of Snowdonia National Park as well as the gentler landscapes of borderland Wales. It stands at the head of Llyn Llŷn Tegid (Bala Lake), at 4 mi long the largest natural lake in Wales. A scenic **narrow-gauge railway** (☎ 01678/540666), one of the Great Little Trains of Wales, runs along its southern shore.

★ If you want to experience Wales at its wildest, then take the narrow road westward from Lake Vyrnwy to **Bwlch y Groes** (Pass of the Cross), the highest road in Wales, whose sweeping panoramas are breathtaking.

Dining and Lodging

£££ ✕☒ **Lake Vyrnwy Hotel.** This country mansion on 23,000 acres of lake-
★ side grounds overlooking superb scenery offers the ultimate sporting holiday: guests can fish, bird-watch, play tennis, or take long walks around the estate. Bicycles and sailboats are also available. Rooms are quiet and comfortable and the restaurant is excellent. The award-winning contemporary cuisine makes good use of trout, pheasant, and duck from the estate and vegetables and fruit from the garden. ⊠ *Llanwddyn, near Oswestry, Shropshire SY10 0LY,* ☎ *01691/870692,* FAX *01691/870259. 30 rooms with bath. Restaurant, tennis court, boating, fishing, bicycles. AE, DC, MC, V.*

Blaenau Ffestiniog

5 *22 mi northwest of Bala, 10 mi southwest of Betws-y-Coed.*

The former "slate capital of North Wales"—most of the world's roofing tiles once came from here—still has commercial quarrying going on; the enterprises that attract all the attention nowadays, however, remain the old slate mines open to the public. The **Llechwedd Slate Caverns,** opened to the public in the 1970s and one of the first landmark sites to be based on Wales's industrial heritage, offers two trips: a tram ride through floodlighted tunnels where Victorian working conditions have been re-created, and a ride on Britain's deepest underground railway to a mine where you can walk by an eerie underground lake. There is also much to see on the surface of this popular site—a re-created

Victorian village, old workshops, and slate-splitting demonstrations. ☎ *01766/830306.* 🎫 *Tour £6.50, surface free.* ⊙ *Mar.–Sept., daily 10–5:15; Oct.–Feb., daily 10–4:15.*

Porthmadog

6 *12 mi southwest of Blaenau Ffestiniog, 16 mi south of Caernarfon.*

At the gateway to Llŷn, an unspoiled peninsula of beaches, wildflowers, and country lanes, Porthmadog is a little seaside town, built as a harbor to export slate from Blaenau Ffestiniog. Its location—between Snowdonia and Llŷn—gives it a lively atmosphere in summer. There are good beaches nearby and a host of attractions in and around the town. From the east, Porthmadog is approached by a mile-long embankment known as The Cob (the small toll charge goes to charity). The oldest of the Welsh narrow-gauge lines (founded in the first part

★ of the 19th century), the **Ffestiniog Railway** runs from a quayside terminus along The Cob, then through a lovely wooded vale into the mountains all the way to Blaenau Ffestiniog. ☎ *01766/512340.* ⊙ *Mar.–Nov., plus limited winter service.*

One not-to-be-missed site in North Wales is a short trip east of Porth-
★ madog over The Cob. The amazing **Portmeirion** is a tiny fantasy-Italianate village—said to be loosely modeled after Portofino—built in 1926 by architect Clough Williams-Ellis (1883–1978), complete with hotel, restaurant, town hall, and cottages that are often let to guests (☞ Dining and Lodging, *below*). He called it his "light-opera approach to architecture" and the result is pretty, though distinctly un-Welsh. Royalty, important political figures, famous artists, and other celebrities have all come to stay here—the atmosphere is genuinely inspirational. ☎ *01766/770228.* 🎫 *£3.50.* ⊙ *Daily 9:30–5:30.*

Near Porthmadog to the north is Tremadog, a handsome village that was the birthplace of T. E. Lawrence (1888–1935), better known as Lawrence of Arabia. A few miles west lies Criccieth, a charming Victorian seaside resort whose headland is crowned by a medieval castle.

OFF THE **HARLECH CASTLE –** What a wealth of legend, poetry, and song is con-
BEATEN PATH jured up by this famous 13th-century castle, which dominates the little coastal town 12 mi south of Porthmadog. The ominous presence of its ruins, visible for miles and commanding wide views, is as dramatic as its history. The inspiring music of Ceiriog's *Men of Harlech* typifies the heroic defense of this castle in 1468 by Dafydd ap Eynion, who, summoned to surrender, replied defiantly: "I held a castle in France until every old woman in Wales heard of it, and I will hold a castle in Wales until every old woman in France hears of it!" Later in the 15th century the Lancastrians survived an eight-year siege during the Wars of the Roses here, and it was the last Welsh stronghold to fall in the 17th-century Civil War. ☎ *01766/780552.* 🎫 *£3.* ⊙ *Late Mar.–late Oct., daily 9:30–6:30; late Oct.–late Mar., Mon.–Sat. 9:30–4, Sun. 11–4.*

Dining and Lodging

££££ ✕🛏 **Hotel Maes-y-Neuadd.** Set on 8 acres of its own glorious gardens
★   and parkland (3½ mi northeast of Harlech by B4573), this hotel dates from the 14th century. It has walls of local granite, oak-beam ceilings, an inglenook fireplace, and a menu that features Welsh, English, and French specialties. ✉ *Talsarnau, near Harlech, LL47 6YA,* ☎ *01766/ 780200 or 800/635–3602,* ℻ *01766/780211. 16 rooms with bath. Restaurant. AE, DC, MC, V.*

£££–££££ ✕🛏 **Hotel Portmeirion.** This is one of the most elegant—and unusual—
★   places to stay in Wales. The mansion house that is now its main build-

In case you want to see the world.

In case you want to be welcomed there.

We're here to see that you're always welcomed at establishments everywhere. That's why millions of people carry the American Express® Card — for peace of mind, confidence, and security, around the world or just around the corner.

do more ®

AMERICAN EXPRESS

Cards

In case you're running low.

We're here to help with more than 118,000 Express Cash locations around the world. In order to enroll, just call American Express before you start your vacation.

do more

Express Cash

And just in case.

We're here with American Express® Travelers Cheques and Cheques *for Two.*® They're the safest way to carry money on your vacation and the surest way to get a refund, practically anywhere, anytime.

Another way we help you…

do more

Travelers Cheques

ing was already here when Clough Williams-Ellis began to build his Italianate fantasy village around it; he restored its original Victorian splendor, preserved the library and the Mirror Room, and created the curved, colonnaded dining room. Accommodations have been increased by 20 fully serviced rooms in cottages around the village, none more than a few minutes' walk from the main building. Local specialties are featured in the restaurant. ⊠ *Portmeirion LL48 6ET,* ☎ *01766/ 770228,* ℻ *01766/771331. 14 rooms with bath in main hotel, 20 rooms with bath in village. Restaurant, pool, tennis court. AE, DC, MC, V.*

££ ✕▥ **Castle Cottage.** Close to Harlech's mighty castle, this cozy, friendly hotel is a charming "restaurant with rooms." The emphasis here is on the exceptional cuisine served by chef-proprietor Glyn Roberts, who makes the best possible use of fresh ingredients to create imaginative, beautifully presented contemporary dishes. The rooms, though small, are attractively appointed and decorated. This lodging is a wonderful little find, as well as an excellent all-round value. ⊠ *Harlech LL46 2YL,* ☎ ℻ *01766/780479. 6 rooms, 4 with bath. Restaurant. AE, MC, V.*

Betws-y-Coed

❼ *25 mi northeast of Porthmadog, 19 mi south of Llandudno.*

On the western approach to this mountain resort are the **Swallow Falls** (small admission charge), a famous North Wales beauty spot where the River Llugwy tumbles down through a wooded chasm. The rivers Llugwy and Conwy meet at Betws-y-Coed, a popular tourist village set among wooded hills affording excellent views of Snowdonia, busy in summer, with a good selection of hotels and crafts shops. The chief landmark here is the ornate iron bridge (1815) over the Conwy, designed by Thomas Telford (1757–1834).

Dining

£–££ ✕ **Ty Gwyn.** After a browse through the small antiques shop next door, stop for a bite at the restaurant, which is under the same management. Inside the 17th-century building it's all prints and chintz, old beams, and copper pans, and there's a nice view of the nearby Waterloo bridge. Homemade pâté is a specialty. ⊠ *Betws-y-Coed,* ☎ *01690/ 710383. MC, V.*

Llanberis

❽ *17 mi west of Betws-y-Coed, 7 mi southeast of Caernarfon.*

Llanberis, like Betws-y-Coed, is a focal point for visitors to the Snowdonia National Park. It stands beside twin lakes at the foot of the rocky **Llanberis Pass,** which cuts through the highest mountains in the park and is lined with fearsome slabs popular with rock climbers. There are hiking trails from the top of the pass, but the going can be rough for the inexperienced; ask local advice before starting on even the briefest ramble. At the Pen-y-Gwryd Hotel just beyond the summit of the pass, Lord Hunt and his team planned their successful ascent of Everest in 1953.

Llanberis has many attractions, but its most famous is the rack-and-pinion **Snowdon Mountain Railway**—some of its track at a gradient of 1 in 5—which terminates within 70 ft of the 3,560-ft summit. Snowdon, *Yr Wyddfa* in Welsh, is the highest peak south of Scotland and is set within more than 800 square mi of national park. From May to September, weather permitting, trains go all the way to the summit; on a clear day, you can see as far as the Irish Wicklow Mountains, about 90 mi away. ☎ *01286/870223.* ▱ *£15 maximum round-trip fare.* ☉ *Mar.–Oct., daily from 9 AM.*

Across the lake in the Padarn Country Park, the workshops of the old Dinorwig slate quarry now contain the **Welsh Slate Museum.** ⊠ *Dinorwig Quarry, Llanberis,* ☎ *01286/870630.* ⊡ *£2.50.* ☉ *Easter–Sept., daily 9:30–5:30; Oct., weekdays 10–4.*

Caernarfon

❾ *7 mi northwest of Llanberis, 26 mi southwest of Llandudno.*

★ Standing like a warning finger, the grim majestic mass of **Caernarfon Castle**—"that most magnificent badge of our subjection," wrote Pennant—looms over the now peaceful waters of the River Seiont. Numerous bloody encounters were witnessed by these sullen walls, erected by Edward I in the 13th century as a symbol of his determination to subdue the Welsh. Begun in 1283, its towers, unlike those of Edward I's other castles, are polygonal and patterned with bands of different colored stone. In 1284, the crafty monarch thought of an amazing scheme to steal the Welsh throne. Knowing that the proud Welsh chieftains would accept no foreign prince, he promised to designate a ruler who could speak no word of English. He sent his queen, Eleanor of Castile, who was expecting a child, posthaste to Caernarfon that she might be delivered there, and in this cold stone fortress the queen gave birth to a son. Triumphantly, Edward presented the infant to the assembled chieftains as their prince "who spoke no English, had been born on Welsh soil, and whose first words would be spoken in Welsh." The ruse worked, and on that historic day was created the first prince of Wales of English lineage. This tradition still holds: in July 1969, Elizabeth II presented Prince Charles to the people of Wales as their prince from this castle. In the Queen's Tower, an intriguing museum charts the history of the local regiment, the Royal Welsh Fusiliers. ☎ *01286/677617.* ⊡ *£4.* ☉ *Late Mar.–late Oct., daily 9:30–6:30; late Oct.–late Mar., Mon.–Sat. 9:30–4, Sun. 11–4.*

The town of Caernarfon, which has a historic pedigree as a walled medieval settlement, has nothing to rival the splendor of its castle and, in fact, is now overrun with tourist buses. But don't miss the garrison church of St. Mary, built into the city walls. Outside Caernarfon is the extensive excavation site of the **Roman Fortress of Segontium,** a branch of the National Museums and Galleries of Wales. It contains material found on the site, one of Britain's most famous Roman forts. ☎ *01286/ 675625.* ⊡ *£1.25.* ☉ *Mar., Apr., and Oct., Mon.–Sat. 9:30–5:30, Sun. 2–5; May–Sept., Mon.–Sat. 9:30–6, Sun. 2–6; Nov.–Feb., Mon.–Sat. 9:30–4, Sun. 2–4.*

Scheduled for opening in 1998 is the **Welsh Highland Railway/Rheilffordd Eryri,** a narrow-gauge line that will operate on the route of an abandoned railway through the mountains. Initially, it will run on a 3-mi route, though the proposed total route is 25 mi long. ☎ *01286/ 830200*

Caernarfon Airport (⊠ Dinas Dinlle beach road) operates **Pleasure Flights** in light aircraft over Snowdon, Anglesey, and Caernarfon; flights range 10–25 minutes. The airport also contains the **Caernarfon Air World** museum. ☎ *01286/830800.* ⊡ *£20–£55 per seat; museum £4.* ☉ *Flights and museum daily, 9–5.*

Dining and Lodging

£££ ✕🖾 **Ty'n Rhos.** This is an immaculate farmhouse with a difference: it
★ offers the highest standard of accommodation. It has a beautifully furnished lounge and dining room, with views across the fields to the Isle of Anglesey. The cooking is exceptional, and there are homemade cheeses and yogurt. The bedrooms are extremely comfortable and at-

tractively decorated. It is an ideal touring base, standing between Snowdonia and the sea, close to Caernarfon and Anglesey. ✉ *Llanddeiniolen, near Caernarfon, LL55 3AE,* ☎ *01248/670489,* FAX *01248/ 670079. 11 rooms with bath. AE, MC, V.*

Beaumaris

 13 mi northeast of Caernarfon.

Handsome Beaumaris is on the Isle of Anglesey, the largest island directly off the shore of Wales and England. It is linked to the mainland by the Britannia road and rail bridge and by Thomas Telford's remarkable chain suspension bridge, built in 1826 over the dividing Menai Strait. Though its name means "beautiful marsh," Beaumaris today is an elegant town of simple cottages, Georgian terraces, and bright shops. The nearest mainline train station is in Bangor, about 6 mi away on the mainland; a regular bus service operates between it and Beaumaris. The town dates from 1295, when Edward I commenced work on the **castle,** the last and largest link in an "iron ring" of fortifications around North Wales built to contain the Welsh. Guarding the western approach to the Menai Strait, the castle is solid and symmetrical, with arrow slits and a moat: a fine example of medieval defensive planning. ☎ *01248/810361.* ✑ *£2.20.* ◷ *Late Mar.–late Oct., daily 9:30– 6:30; late Oct.–late Mar., Mon.–Sat. 9:30–4, Sun. 11–4.*

Opposite the castle is the **courthouse** (☎ 01286/679090), built in 1614. A plaque depicts one view of the legal profession: two farmers pull a cow, one by the horns, one by the tail, while a lawyer sits in the middle milking. Beyond the courthouse is the **Museum and Memorabilia of Childhood,** an Aladdin's cave of music boxes, magic lanterns, trains, cars, toy soldiers, rocking horses, and mechanical savings banks. ✉ *1 Castle St.,* ☎ *01248/712498.* ✑ *£3.* ◷ *Mar.–Oct., Mon.–Sat. 10–5:30, Sun. noon–5.*

On Castle Street, look for the **Tudor Rose,** a house dating from 1400 that's an excellent example of Tudor timberwork.

Head for Steeple Lane to find the old **gaol** (☎ 01286/679090), built in 1829 by Joseph Hansom (1803–1882), who was also the designer of the Hansom cab. Opposite the gaol is the 14th-century **parish church.** In 1862 an innocent man was hanged on the gibbet outside the prison wall—to give the crowd a good view—and he cursed the clock on the church tower. Locals say that from that day the clock never kept good time until it was overhauled in 1980.

The Arts

The **Beaumaris Festival** (☎ 01248/713177) is held annually late May– early June. The whole town is used as a site, from the 14th-century parish church to the concert hall, with special concerts, dance performances, and plays performed.

OFF THE BEATEN PATH

PLAS NEWYDD – Although off the main tourist routes, the celebrated mansion of Plas Newydd is well worth a special detour, for historians rate it the finest house in Wales. Built in the 18th century by James Wyatt (1747–1813) for the marquesses of Anglesey, it stands on the Menai Strait close to the Menai Bridge about 7 mi southwest of Beaumaris (don't confuse it with the Plas Newydd at Llangollen). In 1936–40 the society artist Rex Whistler (1905–44) painted the mural in the dining room here, his largest work and a great favorite of stately-home buffs. A military museum commemorates the Battle of Waterloo, where the first marquess, Wellington's cavalry commander, lost his leg. The interior has some fine 18th-century Gothic Revival decorations, and the gardens have been restored to their original design. There are magnificent views across the strait from here. ⊠ *Llanfairpwll, Anglesey,* ☎ *01248/ 714795.* ☺ *£4.20.* ☾ *Apr.–Sept., Sun.–Fri. noon–5; Oct., Fri. and Sun. noon–5; last admission ½ hr before closing.*

Dining and Lodging

£££ ✕🖼 **Ye Olde Bull's Head.** Originally a coaching inn built in 1472, this place is small and charming. The oak-beam dining room, dating from 1617, serves French specialties, including warm salad of pigeon breast with hazelnut oil, as well as local widgeon (wild duck), and it is also noted for its seafood. ⊠ *Castle St., Beaumaris, Anglesey LL58 8AP,* ☎ *01248/810329,* 🖷 *01248/811294. 15 rooms with bath. Restaurant. AE, MC, V.*

££   🖼 **Llwydiarth Fawr.** It's worth seeking out this outstanding place at
★   Llanerchymedd in the north central part of Anglesey. Llwydiarth Fawr offers exceptional farmhouse accommodation as well as being a convenient touring base for the island. It's a spacious, elegant Georgian house on an 850-acre cattle and sheep farm, whose deluxe rooms are superior to those in many hotels. Owner Margaret Hughes welcomes guests warmly, serves good country cooking, and, in a nutshell, offers country living in style. ⊠ *Llanerchymedd, Anglesey LL71 8DF,* ☎ *01248/470321. 3 rooms with bath. No credit cards.*

Conwy

★ ⑪   *23 mi east of Beaumaris, 48 mi northwest of Chester.*

This still-authentic medieval town grew up around its **castle** on the west bank of the River Conwy. Conwy's mighty, many-turreted stronghold, built between 1283 and 1287 by Edward I, the English invader, can be approached on foot by a dramatic suspension bridge completed in 1825 and designed by the engineer Thomas Telford to blend in with the fortress's presence. Of all of Edward's castles, Conwy preserves most convincingly the spirit of medieval times. The strong sense of period atmosphere is aided and abetted by a ring of ancient but extremely well-preserved walls that enclose the old town. Visitors can walk along sections of the wall, which have breathtaking views across the huddled rooftops of the town to the castle and its estuary setting. ☎ *01492/ 592358.* ☺ *£3.50.* ☾ *Mid-Mar.–mid-Oct., daily 9:30–6:30; mid-Oct.–mid-Mar., Mon.–Sat. 9:30–4, Sun. 11–4.*

On the quay sits what is said to be **the smallest house in Britain,** furnished in mid-Victorian Welsh style—it can hold only a few people at a time.

About 5 mi south of Conwy, in the lovely Vale of Conwy just off A470,
★   is **Bodnant Garden,** a pilgrimage spot for horticulturists from around the world. Laid out in 1875, the 87 acres are particularly famed for their rhododendrons, camellias, and azaleas. But its reputation as the finest garden in Wales does not rest solely on those; this National Trust garden also has terraces, rock and rose gardens, and a pinetum, while the mountains of Snowdonia form a magnificent backdrop. ⊠ *Tal-y-Cafn,* ☎ *01492/650460.* ☺ *£4.60.* ☾ *Mid-Mar.–Oct., daily 10–5.*

Llandudno

⑫   *3 mi north of Conwy, 50 mi northwest of Chester.*

This charmingly old-fashioned North Wales seaside resort has a wealth of well-preserved Victorian architecture and an ornate pier. Unlike other resorts in Wales—and Britain as a whole—Llandudno preserves the genteel look of a bygone age. There is a wide promenade, lined with a huge selection of attractively painted hotels (Llandudno has the largest choice of lodging in Wales). The shopping streets behind also look the part, thanks to their original canopied walkways. Llandudno has little in the way of the garish amusement arcades that are nowadays such a feature of seaside resorts. Instead, it prefers to stick to its faithful cable car that climbs, San Francisco–style, to the summit of the Great Orme headland above the resort. There is also an aerial cable car to the top, and a large, dry ski slope and toboggan run.

Llandudno was the summer home of the family of Dr. Liddell, the Oxford don and father of the immortal Alice, inspiration for *Alice's Adventures in Wonderland*. The reference to the book's Walrus and the Carpenter may be based on two rocks on Llandudno's West Shore near the Liddell home, which Alice possibly described to Carroll. The Alice in Wonderland connection is reflected in the **Alice in Wonderland Centre,** where Alice's adventures are colorfully brought to life in enchanting displays of the best-known scenes from the book. ⊠ *3–4 Trinity Sq., Llandudno,* ☎ *01492/860082.* ⊠ *£2.95.* ⊙ *Easter–Oct., daily 10–5; Nov.–Easter, Mon.–Sat. 10–5..*

Dining and Lodging

££   🏨 **Bryn Derwen Hotel.** British seaside resort hotels do not enjoy the best reputation; many hoteliers have not moved with the times to upgrade their accommodations and food. If only they were all like Stuart and Val Langfield, whose immaculate Victorian hotel exemplifies how it should be done. Fresh flowers and attractive furnishings set the tone, and the food, prepared by Stuart, an award-winning chef, lives up to the surroundings (restaurant for guests only). This offers truly excellent value. ⊠ *Abbey Rd., LL30 2EE,* ☎ 🆊 *01492/876804. 9 rooms with bath. MC, V.*

££££   ✕🏨 **Bodysgallen Hall.** Set inside wide, walled gardens 2 mi out of town,
  ★   the Hall is part 17th, part 18th century, full of antiques, comfortable chairs by cheery fires, pictures, and polished wood. The bedrooms (a few suites are available) combine elegance and practicality, and from some of them you'll see the mountains. The restaurant serves fine traditional meals, with an emphasis on such local fare as lamb and smoked salmon; its prices are relatively low for the standard it offers. ⊠ *LL30 1RS (off A470),* ☎ *01492/584466,* 🆊 *01492/582519. 35 rooms with bath. Restaurant, indoor pool, sauna, tennis court, croquet, exercise room. AE, DC, MC, V.*

£££–££££   ✕🏨 **St. Tudno Hotel.** Set on the seafront in Llandudno, this is one of Britain's top seaside hotels. From the outside, it blends unobtrusively with its neighbors, but inside it's a different story, with richly decorated and opulently furnished rooms. The service is first-class, the contemporary cuisine accomplished. ⊠ *Promenade, LL30 2LP,* ☎ *01492/874411,* 🆊 *01492/860407. 21 rooms with bath. Restaurant, indoor pool. AE, DC, MC, V.*

En Route   Inland from Rhyl is **Bodelwyddan Castle**—off A55, between Abergele and St. Asaph—a restored Victorian castle in spacious formal gardens, surrounded by lovely countryside. As an offshoot of the National Portrait Gallery in London, it exhibits Regency and Victorian portraits by the likes of Sargent, Lawrence, G. F. Watts, and Landseer. ☎ *01745/ 584060.* ⊠ *£4.30, grounds only £2.* ⊙ *Apr.–June and Sept.–Oct., Sat.– Thurs. 10:30–5; July–Aug., daily 10:30–5; Nov.–Mar., Tues.–Thurs. and weekends 11–4.*

Denbigh

⑬ *25 mi southeast of Llandudno.*

This market town was much admired by Dr. Samuel Johnson (1709–84), who stayed on Pentrefoelas Road at Gwaenynog Hall, where he designed two rooms. A walk along the riverbank at nearby Lawnt, a spot he loved, brings you to a monumental urn placed in his honor. Not that it pleased him: "It looks like an intention to bury me alive," thundered the great lexicographer. **Denbigh Castle,** begun in 1282, is known as "the hollow crown" because it is not much more than a shell set on high ground, dominating the town. H. M. Stanley (1841–1904), the intrepid 19th-century journalist and explorer who found Dr. Livingstone in Africa, was born in a cottage below the castle. Market day is Wednesday. 🎫 *Free.* ☉ *Daily, sunrise–sunset.*

Ruthin

⑭ *8 mi southeast of Denbigh, 23 mi west of Chester.*

Ruthin is the capital of "Glyndwr Country," where the Welsh hero Owain Glyndwr (circa 1354–1416) lived and ruled. Architecturally, the town is full of interest, with many well-preserved buildings dating from the 16th to the 19th centuries. Ruthin also has elegant shops, good inns, and an imaginative crafts complex that displays the work of different craftspeople. Medieval banquets are held here regularly.

Lodging

£   🖭 **Eyarth Old Railway Station.** This Victorian railway station near Ruthin
★   was closed for 17 years before being converted in 1981 to an award-winning bed-and-breakfast. The bedrooms are spacious, with large windows looking out onto breathtaking rural scenery. ⊠ *Llanfair Dyffryn Clwyd LL15 2EE,* ☎ *01824/703643,* 📠 *01824/707464. 6 rooms with shower. Pool. MC, V.*

MID-WALES: THE HISTORIC HEARTLAND

If your idea of heaven is traditional market towns and country villages, small seaside resorts, quiet, off-the-beaten-track roads, and rolling landscapes filled with hillside sheep farms, forests, and lakes, then heaven exists for you in mid-Wales, the green and rural heart of the country. As this is Wales's quietest holiday region, accommodations are scattered thinly across the landscape. Apart from one or two largish centers—Aberystwyth and Llandrindod Wells—the accommodations mainly tend toward country inns, small hotels, and farmhouses. This region also has some splendid country-house hotels, set within their own grounds in glorious locations. Although green is the predominant color here, you will notice distinct changes in the landscape as you travel through the region. The borderlands are gentle and undulating, rising to the west into high, wild mountains. Farther north, around Dolgellau, mountainous scenery becomes even more pronounced as you enter the southern section of the Snowdonia National Park. Mountains meet the sea along Cardigan Bay, a long coastline of headlands, peaceful sandy beaches, and beautiful estuaries. A region of peace and tranquility, it has long been a shelter from the madding crowd. Even 100 years ago, Tennyson, Darwin, Shelley, and Ruskin all came here to work and relax; today, thousands more come to delight in the numerous antiquarian bookstores of Hay-on-Wye.

Hay-on-Wye

★ ⑮ *57 mi north of Cardiff, 25 mi north of Abergavenny.*

This town, on the Wales/England border, is dominated by its mostly ruined castle—and bookshops. Hay is a lively place, especially on Sunday, when the rest of central Wales seems to be closed down. In 1961 Richard Booth established a small secondhand and antiquarian bookshop here; other booksellers soon got in on the act, and bookshops now fill several houses, a movie theater, shops, and a pub. At the last count, there were about 25, all in a small town of only 1,500 inhabitants! The town is now the largest secondhand bookselling center in the world, where priceless 14th-century manuscripts rub spines with "job lots" selling for a few pounds. The town's Festival of Literature, held in early summer, attracts famous writers from all over the world.

Dining and Lodging

££–£££ ✕🏠 **Three Cocks Hotel.** Standing on the western approach to Hay, a few miles from town, this historic hostelry with its cobbled forecourt has been beautifully restored by Michael and Marie-Jeanne Winstone. The cooking is superb, with a strong Continental influence. ✉ *Three Cocks, LD3 0SL,* ☏ FAX *01497/847215. 7 rooms with bath. MC, V.*

££ ✕🏠 **Old Black Lion.** This 17th-century coaching inn is close to the center of Hay, ideal for a lunch break while ransacking the bookshops, or for an overnight stay. The low-beamed, atmospheric bar serves its own food and the breakfasts are especially good. Its "sophisticated country cooking with an international twist" has been praised by food guides. ✉ *Lion St., HR3 5AD,* ☏ *01497/820841. 10 rooms with bath or shower. Restaurant. AE, MC, V.*

Builth Wells

⑯ *20 mi northwest of Hay-on-Wye, 60 mi north of Cardiff.*

Builth Wells, a traditional farming town and former spa on the banks of the River Wye, is the site of Wales's biggest rural gathering, the annual **Royal Welsh Agricultural Show** (☏ 01982/553683), held in late July. The Royal Welsh is not only Wales's prime gathering of farming folk, but also a colorful countryside jamboree that attracts huge crowds. The countryside around Builth, and its neighbor, Llandrindod Wells, varies considerably. Some of the land is soft and rich, with rolling green hills and lush valleys. Yet close by are the wildernesses of Mynydd Eppynt and the unexplored foothills of the Cambrian Mountains, the lofty "backbone of Wales."

Dining and Lodging

££££ ✕🏠 **Lake Hotel.** This is the place to go for total Victorian country el-
★ egance—and total tranquility, for it is at Llangammarch Wells, another peaceful former spa about 8 mi west of Builth. Its 50 acres of sloping lawns and lush rhododendrons contain a trout-filled lake that attracts keen anglers. The hotel is comfortable and quiet, with first-class service and excellent contemporary cuisine. The rooms are large and tastefully furnished, and some have four-poster beds. ✉ *Llangammarch Wells LD4 4BS,* ☏ *01591/620202,* FAX *01591/620457. 19 rooms with bath. Restaurant, bar, 9-hole golf course, putting green, tennis court, croquet, fishing. AE, DC, MC, V. Closed 1st 2 wks in Jan.*

Llandrindod Wells

⑰ *7 mi north of Builth Wells, 67 mi north of Cardiff.*

Llandrindod Wells, known locally as Llandod, is an old spa town that preserves its original Victorian layout and look. It is architecturally fascinating, with an array of fussy turrets, cupolas, loggias, and balustrades, and greenery everywhere. The climate—it is 700 ft above sea level—is said to be exceptionally healthful, and it is well situated for exploring the region. On a branchline rail route, it also enjoys a good bus service. Llandrindod emerged as a spa in 1670 but did not reach its heyday until the second half of the 19th century when the railway came and most of the town was built. The **museum,** in Memorial Gardens, details the development of the spa from Roman times and explains some of the Victorian "cures" in gruesome detail. ☎ *01597/824513.* 🖾 *Free.* ☉ *Summer: Mon.–Tues., Thurs.–Fri., and Sun. 10–12:30, 2–4.30; Sat. 10–12:30. Winter: Sat. 10–12:30 only.*

Llandrindod is easily explored on foot. Cross over to South Crescent, passing the Glen Usk Hotel with its wrought-iron balustrade and the Victorian bandstand in the gardens opposite, and you soon reach Middleton Street, another Victorian thoroughfare. From it head to Rock Park and the path that leads down through wooded glades to the handsomely restored **Pump Room** where visitors would "take the waters." Today, it serves tea and refreshments and only one type of the many waters that used to be on tap. It also plays a part during the town's Victorian Festival (☎ 01597/823441) held in late August when shop assistants, hotel staff, and anyone else who cares to join in wear period costume and enjoy suitable "old-style" entertainment. On the other side of town, the lake, with its boathouse, café, and gift shop, is in a lovely setting: wooded hills on one side, a broad common on the other, flooded in spring by golden daffodils.

Dining and Lodging

£ ✕▦ **Brynafon Country House.** This hotel is a converted Victorian workhouse on the southern approach to Rhayader, about 9 mi northwest of Llandrindod Wells (☞ En Route *below*). Though its exterior might still be a bit forbidding, its amenities are up to date. Apart from its attractions as a family-run hotel, it also has a good-value restaurant, The Workhouse, once the kitchen, with white-painted stone walls and a flagstone floor. ⊠ *South St., Rhayader LD6 5BL,* ☎ *01597/810735,* ⅀ *01597/810111. 11 rooms, 2 with bath, 9 with shower. Restaurant, pool. MC, V.*

En Route From Llandrindod, take A4081/A470 to Rhayader, a good pony-trekking center and gateway town for the **Elan Valley,** Wales's "Lake District." This 7-mi chain of lakes, winding between gray-green hills, was created in the 1890s by a system of dams to supply water to the city of Birmingham, 73 mi to the east. From the Elan Valley, follow the spectacular and narrow Cwmystwyth mountain road west to Devil's Bridge (☞ Aberystwyth, *below*), a famous beauty spot, then on to Aberystwyth.

Aberystwyth

⑱ *41 mi northwest of Llandrindod Wells (via A44, not mountain road described in Llandrindod Wells En Route), 118 mi northwest of Cardiff.*

Aberystwyth makes the best of several worlds because, besides being undeniably a holiday resort, it is a long-established university town, it houses the magnificent National Library of Wales, and it has a little harbor and quite clearly a life of its own. The town, attractively sited midway along Cardigan Bay, came to prominence as a Victorian "watering hole" thanks to its curving beach set beneath a prominent headland. The seaside resort is a good gateway for exploring mid-Wales:

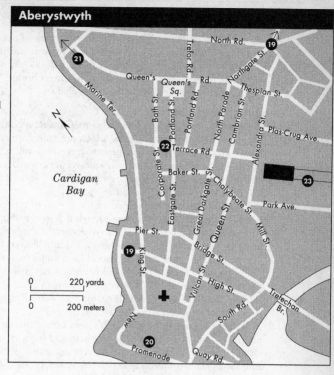

there are few towns in Wales that present such a wide variety of scenery within their immediate neighborhood, here ranging from the extraordinary Devil's Bridge to the beautiful Rheidol Valley.

19 The modern **university campus,** on the hill above town, includes the National Library and an arts center with galleries, a theater, and a concert hall—all open to visitors. The original university, founded in the 19th century, stands on the seafront. ✉ *National Library,* ☎ *01970/ 632800.* 🎫 *Free.* ⊙ *Weekdays 9:30–6, Sat. 9:30–5.*

20 The **castle,** at the southern end of the bay, was built in 1277 and rebuilt in 1282 by Edward I. It was one of several strongholds to fall, in 1404, to the Welsh leader Owain Glyndwr. Today, it is a romantic ruin on a headland separating the north shore from the harbor shore. At

21 the end of the promenade, **Constitution Hill** offers the energetic a zigzag cliff path/nature trail to the view from the top. But it's more fun to travel up by the **Aberystwyth Cliff Railway,** the longest electric cliff railway in Britain. Opened in 1896, to great excitement, it has been refurbished without diminishing its Victorian look. It takes you up 430 ft to the **Great Aberystwyth Camera Obscura,** a modern version of a Victorian amusement: a massive 14-inch lens gives a bird's-eye view of more than 1,000 square mi of sea and scenery, including the whole of Cardigan Bay and 26 Welsh mountain peaks.

22 The excellent **Ceredigion Museum,** in an old theater on Terrace Road, displays a fine collection of folk history. This beautiful Edwardian theater was built in 1905 and lovingly restored in 1984.✉ *Ceredigion Museum, Terrace Rd.* ☎ *01970/633088.* 🎫 *Free.* ⊙ *Mon.–Sat. 10–5.*

23 At Aberystwyth Station you can hop on the narrow-gauge steam-operated **Vale of Rheidol Railway** (☎ 01970/625819 or 01970/615993). The terminus, an hour's ride away, is **Devil's Bridge,** where the rivers

Rheidol and Mynach meet in a series of spectacular falls. Clamped between two rocky cliffs through which a torrent of water pours unceasingly, this bridge well deserves the name it bears—*Pont y Gwr Drwg*, or Bridge of the Evil One, for legend has it that it was the devil himself who built it. There are actually three bridges—the oldest is all of 800 years old—and the walk down to the lowest bridge, "the devil's," is magnificent but strictly for the surefooted.

Dining and Lodging

£–££   ✗ **Gannets.** A simple, good-value bistro, Gannets specializes in locally supplied meat, fish, and game, which are transformed into hearty roasts and pies. Organically grown vegetables and a good French house wine are further draws for a university crowd. It is easy to eat enjoyably here in the lowest price category. ⊠ *7 St. James's Sq.,* ☎ *01970/ 617164. MC, V. Closed Sun., Tues.*

££££   ✗⊞ **Conrah Country Hotel.** Part of the appeal of this country-house hotel is its air of seclusion, even though it is only a short drive south from Aberystwyth. The owners have decorated the house with traditional country furnishings and antiques, and fresh flowers fill each room. The restaurant is known for its good food and wines, with imaginative contemporary and traditional British cuisine making use of local game, fish, and meat. ⊠ *Chancery, Aberystwyth SY23 4DF,* ☎ *01970/ 617941,* ⒻⓍ *01970/624546. 20 rooms with bath. Restaurant, indoor pool, sauna, croquet. AE, DC, MC, V.*

£££   ✗⊞ **Four Seasons.** In Aberystwyth's town center, this family-run hotel and restaurant has a relaxed atmosphere and friendly staff. The spacious rooms are simply and attractively decorated, while the restaurant serves excellent meals at reasonable prices. ⊠ *50–54 Portland St., SY23 2DX,* ☎ *01970/612120* ⒻⓍ *01970/627458. 14 rooms with bath. Restaurant. MC, V.*

Machynlleth

㉔ *18 mi northeast of Aberystwyth.*

Machynlleth, at the head of the beautiful Dovey Estuary, does not look like a typical Welsh country town. Its long and wide main street, lined with a mixed style of buildings—everything from sober gray stone to well-proportioned Georgian—creates an atypical sense of openness and space. Machynlleth's busiest day is Wednesday, when the street is filled with the stalls of market traders. At one end of the street is the Owain Glyndwr Centre, where a small exhibition celebrates Wales's last native leader, who established a Welsh parliament at Machynlleth in the early 15th century. Welsh history of an earlier time is the main theme at **Celtica,** an imaginative exhibition center in the large parkland behind the shops and pubs, where various interpretive displays take you back to Wales's Celtic past. ☎ *01654/702702.* ⓔ *£4.65.* ☉ *Daily 10– 6 (last entry to main exhibition 4:40).*

Dining and Lodging

£££–££££   ✗⊞ **Ynyshir Hall.** This supremely comfortable country-house hotel is
★   in a beautiful Georgian house in idyllic private grounds, near a wildlife reserve just off A487, southwest of Machynlleth. The artistic talents of its owners, Joan and Rob Reen, are evident in the bounty of Rob's paintings (he's an established artist) and in the tasteful decoration and furnishings. Personal service is paramount here, and the hotel is noted for its contemporary cuisine. ⊠ *Eglwysfach, near Machynlleth, SY20 8TA,* ☎ *01654/781209 or 800/777–6536,* ⒻⓍ *01654/781366. 8 rooms with bath. Restaurant. AE, DC, MC, V.*

£££ ✕🏠 **Penhelig Arms.** Along the coast road running west from Machynlleth, the delightful little sailing center of Aberdovey is perched at the mouth of the Dovey Estuary. Here you will find the waterfront Penhelig Arms, run by Robert and Sally Hughes (room rates fall into the lower end of the quoted price category). This immaculate, friendly inn overlooks the harbor and most of the rooms have wonderful sea views. You can meet the locals in the wood-paneled Fisherman's Bar, and dine in style at the Penhelig Arms's fine restaurant. ⊠ *Aberdovey LL35 0LT,* ☎ *01654/767215,* 🖷 *01654/767690. 10 rooms with bath. Restaurant, bar. MC, V.*

Dolgellau

㉕ *16 mi north of Machynlleth, 34 mi north of Aberystwyth.*

Dolgellau (pronounced dolgethlee) is a solidly Welsh town with attractive dark buildings and handsome old coaching inns. It was the center of the Welsh gold trade in the 19th century, when high-quality gold was discovered locally; you can still try your luck and pan for gold in the Mawddach. A nugget of Dolgellau gold is still used to make royal wedding rings. From Dolgellau, you can visit the **Gwynfynydd Gold Mine,** an authentic gold mine hidden deep in the forests to the north. The round-trip takes three hours and includes a guided underground tour; the courtesy bus leaves from Welsh Gold Visitor Centre in Dolgellau. ☎ *01341/423332.* 🖾 *£9.50.* ⊘ *Apr.–Oct., daily 9:30–4 (call ahead to confirm availability).*

The Dolgellau area has strong links with the Quaker movement and the Quakers' emigration to America. The **Museum of the Quakers,** in the town square, commemorates these historic associations. ☎ *01341/ 422888.* 🖾 *Free.* ⊘ *Easter–Oct., daily 10–6.*

To the south rises the menacing bulk of Cader Idris (2,927 ft); the name means "the Chair of Idris," though no one is completely sure just who Idris was—probably a warrior bard. It is said that anyone sleeping for a night in a certain part of the mountain will awaken either a poet or a madman—or not at all.

Barmouth

㉖ *10 mi west of Dolgellau.*

Barmouth is one of the few places along the Welsh coast—certainly along Cardigan Bay—that can be described as a full-fledged seaside resort. On the northern mouth of the picturesque Mawddach Estuary, it features a 2-mi-long promenade, wide expanses of golden beach, and facilities for sea, river, and mountain lake fishing. Its splendid setting is best appreciated from the footpath beside the railway bridge across the mouth of the estuary. Even 100 years ago Barmouth was a popular holiday resort. Alfred Lord Tennyson wrote part of *In Memoriam* here and was inspired to write *Crossing the Bar* by the spectacle of the Mawddach rushing to meet the sea. Percy Bysshe and Mary Shelley stayed here in 1812; Charles Darwin worked on *The Origin of Species* and *The Descent of Man* in a house by the shore. Essayist and art critic John Ruskin was a frequent visitor and was trustee of the St. George's cottages built there by the Guild of St. George in 1871.

Lodging

££ 🏠 **Llwyndu Farmhouse.** It's worth driving a mile or so north from Bar-
★ mouth for these comfortable accommodations. Don't expect an ordinary Welsh farm—this cozy 17th-century farmhouse has been imaginatively restored by Paula and Peter Thompson, retaining lots of

original features such as huge open fireplaces and old timbers. Accommodations are within the house itself or in the adjoining converted barn. Llwyndu is located just off A496 north of Barmouth on a hillside overlooking the sea. ✉ *Llanaber, near Barmouth, LL42 1RR,* ☎ *01341/280144,* FAX *01341/281236. 7 rooms with bath. MC, V.*

Welshpool

㉗ *48 mi east of Barmouth, 19 mi west of Shrewsbury.*

★ The border town of Welshpool, "Trallwng" in Welsh, is famous as the home of **Powis Castle,** one of mid-Wales's greatest treasures. In continuous occupation since the 13th century, and now a National Trust property, Powis is one of the most opulent residential castles in Britain. Its battlements rearing high on a hilltop, the castle is surrounded by splendid grounds and terraced gardens, and bounded by gigantic yew hedges, which fall steeply down to wide lawns and neat Elizabethan gardens. It contains many treasures: Greek vases; magnificent paintings by Gainsborough, Reynolds, and Romney, among others; superb furniture, including a 16th-century Italian table inlaid with marble; and, since 1987, the **Clive of India Museum,** with a fine collection of Indian art. The tearoom here is excellent. ☎ *01938/554336.* ☞ *£7.50, gardens only £5.* ☉ *Apr., May, Sept., and Oct., Wed.–Sun.; June–Aug., Tues.–Sun. Hrs: castle and museum 1–5, gardens 11–6; last admission ½ hr before closing.*

SOUTH WALES: FROM CARDIFF TO CARDIGAN

The south is the most diverse of Wales's three regions. It covers not only the immediate region around Cardiff and the Wales/England border, but also the southwest as far as the rugged coastline of Pembrokeshire. South Wales's scenic variety is reflected in the very different nature of its two national parks. The Brecon Beacons park, a short drive north of Cardiff, is an area of high, grassy mountains, lakes, and craggy limestone gorges. In contrast, the Pembrokeshire Coast National Park is recognized as one of Europe's finest stretches of coastal natural beauty, with mile after mile of spectacular sea cliffs, beaches, headlands, and coves. Other pieces of the complicated South Wales jigsaw include traditional farmlands, cosmopolitan urban areas, rolling border country, wooded vales, and the former industrial valleys where coal was mined in huge quantities during the 19th and early 20th centuries.

Cardiff

㉘ *20 mi west of the new Second Severn Bridge, which carries the M4 motorway across the Severn Estuary into Wales.*

Financially, industrially, and commercially Cardiff is the most important city in Wales, but what Cardiff, Wales's capital, has to offer is a Civic Centre of extreme distinction, magnificent parklands, and one of the most magical castles in the world. The Civic Centre—where buildings of great architectural style are set on wide, tree-lined avenues—is constructed of dazzling white Portland stone. Even the docklands—the once-infamous Tiger Bay area—have become the focus of a massive scheme that will soon give the city miles of new waterfront development. The latest change to the cityscape, however, is that the famous old Cardiff Arms Park has been demolished to make way for a state-of-the-art stadium scheduled to open for the millennium.

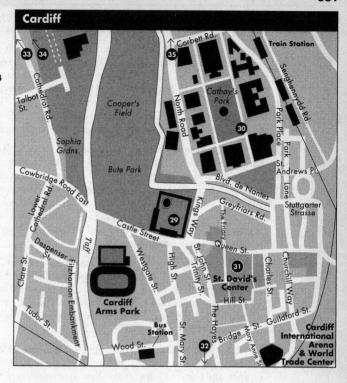

Cardiff

True to the Welsh tradition of vocal excellence, Cardiff is home of Britain's most adventurous opera company, Welsh National Opera, housed in the New Theater, all red velvet and chandeliers. Cardiff is also the sporting center of Wales, and this means, above all, the Welsh capital of rugby football. To hear the crowds singing their support for the Welsh team is a stirring and unforgettable experience.

★ ㉙ **Cardiff Castle** stands in Bute Park—one section of Cardiff's hundreds of acres of parkland. The castle, just on the edge of the shopping center, is an unusual "three-in-one" historic site, with Roman, Norman, and especially Victorian associations. Parts of the walls are Roman, the solid keep is Norman, and the whole complex was restored—and transformed into an utter Victorian ego flight—a hundred years ago by the third Marquess of Bute. He employed William Burges (1827–81), an architect obsessed by the Gothic period, and Burges transformed the castle inside and out into an extravaganza of medieval color and detailed craftsmanship. It is the perfect expression of the anything-goes Victorian spirit—not to mention of the vast fortune made by the marquess in Cardiff's booming docklands. ⊠ *Bute Park,* ☎ *01222/878100.* 🎟 *Guided tour of castle £4.80, grounds only £2.40.* ⊙ *Apr.–Sept., daily 9:30–6; Mar. and Oct., daily 9:30–5; Nov.–Feb., daily 9:30–4:30; call for tour times.*

Two blocks east of Cardiff Castle is the **Civic Centre,** a well-designed complex of tree-lined avenues and civic buildings with Portland stone facades. The domed city hall, Neoclassic law courts, Welsh office (seat of government), and University campus are all here. The main point ㉚ of interest is the **National Museum and Gallery,** next to the city hall. Give yourself at least half a day at this splendid museum, which tells the story of Wales through its plants, rocks, archaeology, art, and industry. It also has a fine collection of modern European art, especially

Postimpressionist works—don't miss *La Parisienne* by Renoir. ⊠ *Cathays Park,* ☎ *01222/397951.* ☒ *£3.25.* ☉ *Tues.–Sun. 10–5.*

③ South of the Civic Centre are the shopping and business areas of Cardiff, situated around **St. David's Centre.** Here in a large, modern shopping mall is **St. David's Hall,** one of Europe's best new concert halls, with outstanding acoustics, where people come for classical music, jazz, rock, ballet—even snooker championships. This hall has now been joined by the **Cardiff International Arena,** a £23-million multipurpose center for exhibitions, concerts, and conferences.

③ The **Welsh Industrial and Maritime Museum** (☎ 01222/481919) is in the old dockland 2 mi south of the city center. The waterfront is now in the process of revitalization as part of the ambitious Cardiff Bay redevelopment, entailing the probable relocation of the museum (this might also involve a change of telephone numbers; if the given number becomes unobtainable, call ☎ 01222/573471 for details). There is also an interesting "hands-on" science and technology center on the waterfront, known as Techniquest (☎ 01222/475475).

③ Cross the River Taff and follow Cathedral Road for about 2 mi to reach **Llandaff,** a suburb of Cardiff that retains its village atmosphere, and **Llandaff Cathedral,** which was completely renovated after serious bomb damage in World War II. Inside you will immediately be drawn to the overwhelming statue of *Christ in Majesty* by sculptor Jacob Epstein (1880–1959).

★ **③** Four miles west of Llandaff is the open-air **Museum of Welsh Life** at St. Fagans. On 100 acres of parkland and gardens lie farmhouses, cottages, and terraced houses that show the evolution of Welsh building styles. Special events highlight ancient rural festivals—May Day, Harvest, and Christmas among them. ☎ *01222/573500.* ☒ *£5.25 summer, £4.25 winter.* ☉ *July–Sept., daily 10–6; Oct.–June, daily 10–5.*

★ **③** North of Cardiff, 4 mi via A470, beside the village of Tongwynlais, is **Castell Coch,** the Red Castle—a structure so like a romantic, fairy-tale castle that one cannot fail to be enchanted by it. The castle was built (on the site of a medieval stronghold) in the 1870s in another collaboration of the third Marquess of Bute and William Burges, builders of Cardiff Castle. Here Burges re-created everything—architecture, furnishings, carvings, murals—in a remarkable exercise in Victorian-Gothic whimsy. ☎ *01222/810101.* ☒ *£2.50.* ☉ *Late Mar.–late Oct., daily 9:30–6:30; late Oct.–late Mar., Mon.–Sat. 9:30–4, Sun. 11–4.*

Dining and Lodging

££ ✕ **Armless Dragon.** A window full of plants enlivens this bright, friendly restaurant out beyond the Cathays stadium. It is popular with the university crowd. Seafood dishes are always a good bet here; much of the fish comes from local waters. For even more uniquely Welsh flavor, try the laverballs, made of seaweed. ⊠ *97 Wyeverne Rd., Cathays,* ☎ *01222/382357. AE, DC, MC, V. Closed Sun.–Mon. No lunch Sat.*

££ ✕ **Le Cassoulet.** This is a genuine French restaurant, decorated with touches of red and black, in the maze of Victorian streets west of Cathedral Road. Try the very tasty fish soup as a starter, then the namesake dish, for a filling meal. ⊠ *5 Romilly Crescent,* ☎ *01222/221905. AE, MC, V. Closed Sun.–Mon.*

£–££ ✕ **Quayles.** Formerly Gibson's, this neighborhood brasserie is close to Sophia Gardens. The modern Mediterranean-style cuisine is reasonably priced, with a more elaborate lunches available on Sundays. A good-value, inexpensive fixed-price menu is available before 8 PM. ⌗ 6 *Romilly Crescent, Canton,* ☎ *01222/341264. AE, MC, V.*

£££ 🏨 **Cardiff Marriott.** The high-rise Marriott (formerly the Holiday Inn) is a fair representative of Cardiff's new breed of hotels. It is central—close to St. David's Hall and the shopping center—practical, and has plenty of facilities. ⌗ *Mill La., CF1 1EZ,* ☎ *01222/399944,* FAX *01222/ 395578. 182 rooms with bath. Restaurant, coffee shop, indoor pool, sauna, exercise room. AE, DC, MC, V.*

££ 🏨 **Town House.** A gregarious American couple, Bart and Iris Zuzik,
★ run this immaculate guest house, the best B&B in Cardiff, along Cathedral Road and near the city center. You stay in a tall Victorian building that has been tastefully converted. The bedrooms are neat and well equipped, and guests can enjoy traditional British or American breakfasts in the beautifully appointed dining room. No evening meals are served. ⌗ *70 Cathedral Rd., CF1 9LL,* ☎ *01222/239399,* FAX *01222/ 223214. 7 rooms with bath. MC, V.*

Nightlife and the Arts

Wales, as might be expected in a country where singing is a way of life, has one of Britain's four major opera companies, the **Welsh National.** Its home base is at the New Theatre in Cardiff, but it spends most of its time touring Wales and England. Its performances are of an international standard, and its productions are often among the most exciting in Britain. For details of performances contact the Welsh National Opera (⌗ John St., Cardiff CF1 4SP, ☎ 01222/464666). As you would expect of Wales's main city, there is a lively nighttime scene in Cardiff's clubs and pubs. The big theaters feature a full program of entertainment, from drama to comedy, pop to the classics.

Shopping

Arcade shopping is a distinctive feature of Cardiff's city center. Canopied Victorian and Edwardian arcades, lined with small specialty shops, weave in and out of the city's modern shopping complexes. Cardiff's traditional side can also be seen in its covered market, which sells a tempting variety of fresh foods.

Abergavenny

③⑥ *28 mi northeast of Cardiff.*

The market town of Abergavenny has a **castle** founded early in the 11th century. At Christmas in 1176, the castle witnessed a tragic event: the Norman knight William de Braose invited the neighboring Welsh chieftains to a feast—and, in a crude attempt to gain control of the area, had them all slaughtered as they sat, unarmed, at dinner. Afterward, the Welsh attacked and virtually demolished the castle. Little remains of the building now, but you can visit the **museum,** with exhibits ranging from the Iron Age to the 20th century. The Welsh Kitchen is particularly appealing, with its old utensils, pans, and butter molds. Another fascinating feature is a grocer's shop from the 1950s. ⌗ *Castle Museum, Castle St.,* ☎ *01873/854282.* ⌗ *£1.* ☉ *Mar.–Oct., Mon.–Sat. 11–1 and 2–5, Sun. 2–5; Nov.–Feb., Mon.–Sat. 11–1 and 2–4.*

③⑦ Taking A40 northwest out of Abergavenny, you pass the Sugar Loaf mountain and **Crickhowell,** a pretty town on the banks of the River Usk with attractive little shops, an ancient bridge, and a ruined castle. Two miles farther (by A479) is **Tretower Court,** a splendid example of a fortified medieval manor house. Nearby, and part of the same site, is a ruined Norman castle. ☎ *01874/730279.* ⌗ *£2.20.* ☉ *Mar.–late Oct., daily 10–6.*

West of Abergavenny lie the valleys—the Rhondda is the most famous—so well described by Richard Llewellyn in *How Green Was My Valley*. But things have changed, because the slag heaps are green now, thanks to land reclamation schemes.To catch a glimpse of what it was once like, head to the **Big Pit Mining Museum,** in Blaenavon, southwest of Abergavenny. Here, ex-miners take you underground on a tour of an authentic coal mine for a look at the hard life of the South Wales miner. You will also see the pithead baths and workshops. ☎ *01495/ 790311.* ✆ *£5.50, £1.75 surface only.* ☉ *Mar.–Nov., daily 9:30–5 (underground tours 10–3:30).*

Dining and Lodging

£££   ✕☉ **Bear Hotel.** This old coaching inn, about 5 mi northwest of Abergavenny in the middle of the pretty little town of Crickhowell, is full of character. The bar, decorated with memorabilia from the days when stagecoaches from London used to stop here, is popular with locals and visitors alike; a blazing log fire in winter adds to the atmosphere. Rooms are within the hotel itself or in the attractively converted stable yard under the arch. The Bear is also noted for its contemporary cuisine—both the excellent-value bar food and the more formal restaurant offerings. ✉ *Crickhowell NP8 1BW,* ☎ *01873/810408,* ℻ *01873/ 811696. 28 rooms with bath. Restaurant. AE, MC, V.*

Brecon

39   *19 mi northwest of Abergavenny, 41 mi north of Cardiff.*

Brecon is a historic market town of narrow passageways, handsome Georgian buildings, and pleasant riverside walks. There are a number of sights worth seeing here, including the cavernous **cathedral** with its heritage center on the hill above the middle of town. It has two good museums—the **Brecknock Museum** (☎ 01874/624121), with its superb collection of carved love spoons, and the **South Wales Borderers' Museum** (☎ 01874/613310), a military museum whose exhibits span centuries of conflict. For the best atmosphere, time your visit to Brecon to coincide with market days (Tuesday and Friday). Don't forget to purchase a hand-carved wooden Welsh love spoon similar to those on display in the museum.

Each summer, the town plays host to **Brecon Jazz,** an international jazz festival that attracts top performers (☎ 01874/625557). On the strength of the success of this festival, the town has developed a little Jazz Museum.

As you travel south of Brecon, the skyline fills with mountains, and wild, windswept uplands stretch to the horizon. Follow the signs for the **National Park Visitor Centre,** on Mynydd Illtyd, a high, grassy stretch of upland west of A470 near Libanus. The center, run by the Brecon Beacons National Park Authority, is an excellent source of information for attractions and activities within this 519-square-mi park of rolling hills and open moorlands, and it gives wonderful panoramic views across to Pen-y-fan, at 2,907 ft the highest peak in South Wales. To explore Wales's high country on foot be well equipped, for mist and rain can quickly descend, and the Beacons' summits are exposed to high winds. ✉ *National Park Visitor Centre, near Libanus, Brecon LD3 8ER,* ☎ *01874/623366.* ✆ *Free; parking fee.* ☉ *Daily 9:30–5 (until 4:30 in winter).*

Dining and Lodging

££££   ✕☉ **Llangoed Hall.** This hotel, the brainchild of Sir Bernard Ashley, ★   widower of Laura Ashley, opened in May 1990 and has established itself as one of the best places to stay in Wales. The Hall is set in the spectacular valley of the Wye—about 8 mi northeast of Brecon, on A470 to Builth Wells—with views over the Black Mountains. Inside there are Laura Ashley fabrics everywhere, of course, complementing the antiques and paintings. The fine restaurant serves local specialties. ⊠ *Llyswen, near Brecon, LD3 OYP,* ☎ *01874/754525,* ᴙ̄ᴀ̄ˣ̄ *01874/754545. 23 rooms with bath. Restaurant, tennis court, helipad. AE, DC, MC, V.*

£££ ✕🖾 **Griffin Inn.** In the village of Llyswen close to Llangoed Hall on the same A470 road to Builth, the Griffin is one of the oldest inns in the upper Wye Valley (said to date from 1467). There is easy access to river and lake fishing, shooting, walking, and pony-trekking in the Brecon Beacons. A former winner of Britain's "Pub of the Year," the Griffin's hearty and traditional cuisine takes advantage of local salmon and beef. The bedrooms are comfortably furnished, and the exposed stonework and old beams contribute to the historic character of the building. The inn is in the lower limits of the price range. ⊠ *Llyswen, near Brecon, LD3 0UR,* ☎ *01874/754241,* ᴙ̄ᴀ̄ˣ̄ *01874/754592. 7 rooms with bath. Restaurant. AE, DC, MC, V.*

Shopping

Crickhowell Adventure Gear (☎ 01874/611586), on the corner of Ship Street in Brecon (with smaller shops in Crickhowell itself and Abergavenny), sells a good range of outdoor gear—clothes and climbing equipment—for use in the park.

Swansea

40 *36 mi southwest of Brecon, 40 mi west of Cardiff.*

Swansea is Wales's second largest city and the birthplace of poet Dylan Thomas (1914–53). Go first to Swansea's splendid **Maritime Quarter.** The city was extensively bombed during World War II, and its old dockland has been transformed into a modern marina with attractive housing and shops and a seafront that commands wonderful views across the sweep of Swansea Bay. The **Swansea Maritime and Industrial Museum,** beside the marina, tells the story of the city's growth and houses a fully operational wool mill. ☎ *01792/650351 or 01792/470371.* ⌨ *Free.* ☉ *Tues.–Sun. 10–4:45.*

Within a short walk of the marina is Swansea's modern shopping center. Despite the city's typically postwar, rather utilitarian and undistinguished architecture, the **covered market** here is not to be missed. It's the best fresh-foods market in Wales, where you can buy cockles from the Penclawdd beds on the nearby Gower Peninsula, and laverbread, that unique Welsh delicacy made from seaweed, which is usually served with bacon and eggs. Swansea marks the end of the industrial region of South Wales. And, as if to make amends for the onetime desecration of so much natural beauty—though the industrial scars have disappeared—the 14-mi-long Gower Peninsula, on the neck of which Swansea stands, offers magnificent cliff scenery and unspoiled beaches.

Dining and Lodging

££ ✕ **Number One.** This excellent regional restaurant serves dishes such as Penclawdd cockles with laverbread and bacon, and it regularly features fresh sea bass, wild salmon, and monkfish. The atmosphere is friendly and relaxed. Reservations are advised. ⊠ *1 Wind St.,* ☎ *01792/456996. AE, MC, V. Closed Sun.–Mon.*

£££–££££ ✕🖾 **Fairyhill.** Situated on the west of the Gower Peninsula, about 11 mi from Swansea, Fairyhill is an 18th-century country house with a restful atmosphere, luxuriously furnished public rooms, spacious bedrooms, and extensive wooded grounds. The hotel is known in the area for its hospitality, accomplished cuisine, and well-chosen wine list. ⊠

Reynoldston, near Swansea, SA3 1BS, ☎ 01792/390139, FAX 01792/ 391358. 8 rooms with bath or shower. AE, MC, V.

Tenby

41 *53 mi west of Swansea.*

Tenby is a picturesque seaside resort where pastel-color Georgian houses cluster around a harbor, and below the hotel-lined clifftop stretch two golden sandy beaches. Medieval Tenby's ancient town walls still stand, enclosing narrow streets and passageways full of shops, inns, and places to eat. The ruins of a castle stand on a headland overlooking the sea, close to the excellent **Tenby Museum** (☎ 01834/ 842809), which recalls the town's maritime history and its growth as a fashionable resort. The late-15th-century **Tudor Merchant's House** (☎ 01834/842279), in town, shows how a prosperous trader would have lived in the Tenby of old. From the harbor, you can take a boat trip to Caldey Island and visit the monastery, whose monks make perfume.

Lodging

££££ ⊞ **Penally Abbey Hotel.** Penally Abbey, overlooking the sea close to town, is a convenient and comfortable base for exploring Pembrokeshire. The dignified old house is full of character, and most bedrooms have four-posters. Hosts Steve and Eileen Warren's lack of formality generates a relaxed atmosphere supported by first-class service. ✉ *Penally, near Tenby, SA70 7PY,* ☎ *01834/843033,* FAX *01834/844714 12 rooms with bath. Restaurant, pool. AE, MC, V.*

Pembroke

42 *13 mi west of Tenby, 13 mi south of Haverfordwest.*

You are now entering the heart of Pembrokeshire, one of the most curious regions of Wales. You may begin to doubt whether you are still in Wales, for all around are English names like Deeplake, New Hedges, and Rudbaxton. Natives more often than not don't seem to even understand Welsh, and South Pembrokeshire is even known as "Little England beyond Wales." History is responsible. In the 11th century, this region was conquered by the English with the aid of the Normans, who intermarried and set about building castles. One of the most magnificent is found here in Pembroke, a **castle** dating from 1190. Its walls remain stout, its gatehouse mighty, and the enormous cylindrical keep proved so impregnable to cannon fire in the Civil War that Cromwell's men had to starve out its Royalist defenders. It was the birthplace, in 1457, of Henry VII, the Tudor king who seized the throne of Britain in 1485, and whose son Henry VIII united Wales and England. ☎ 01646/ 681510. ✉ £3. ☉ Summer, daily 9:30–6; winter, daily 10–4.

St. David's

43 *16 mi northwest of Haverfordwest, 16 mi west of Fishguard.*

This is a place that has been described as the "holiest ground in Great Britain," for here, in the midst of a tiny village, is the venerable 12th-century Cathedral of St. David, and the shrine of the patron saint of Wales, who founded a monastic community here in the 6th century. Unlike any other cathedral, it does not seek to dominate the surrounding countryside with its enormous mass, for it is set, quaintly enough, in a vast hollow, and the visitor must climb down 39 steps (called locally the Thirty-Nine Articles) to enter the cathedral—this also helped protect the church from Viking raiders by hiding it from the sea. From the outside, St. David's has a certain simple austerity that harmonizes well with the desolate, windswept countryside where it is built, but the interior is endowed with a richness that more than recompenses for this external severity: treasures include the fragile fan vaulting in Bishop Vaughan's Chapel, the intricate carving on the choir stalls, and the substantial oaken roof over the nave. Across the brook are the ruins of the medieval **Bishop's Palace.**

The entire area around St. David's, steeped in sanctity and history, was a place of pilgrimage for many centuries, two journeys to St. David's equaling one to Rome. The savagely beautiful coastline here—Pembrokeshire at its unspoiled best—also gives St. David's a special atmosphere, one in which you can almost recapture the feeling of those days nearly 1,500 years ago when this shrine was very nearly the solitary outpost of Christianity in the British Isles.

Dining

££ ✕ **Harbour Lights.** Tucked away on an attractive stretch of coast about 7 mi northeast of St. David's, at the tiny harbor of Porthgain, this family-run shore restaurant serves everything homemade, right down to the cheese and biscuits. Try the fresh local seafood dishes. The walls are hung with pictures by local artists. ⊠ *Porthgain, Croesgoch SA62 5BW,* ☎ *01348/831549. MC, V.* ☺ *Call ahead in winter for hrs.*

Fishguard

44 *16 mi northeast of St. David's, 26 mi north of Pembroke.*

Fishguard is a town of three parts. The modern ferry terminal at Goodwick across the sheltered waters of Fishguard Bay sees activity throughout the year as boats sail to Rosslare across the Irish Sea. Fishguard's main town stands on high ground just south of Goodwick, separating the modern port from its picturesque **old harbor** in the lower town, which was the film location for Dylan Thomas's *Under Milk Wood,* which starred the amazing trio of Richard Burton, Elizabeth Taylor, and Peter O'Toole.

Cardigan and the Teifi Valley

45 *18 mi northeast of Fishguard.*

Cardigan is a charming little market town perched astride the Teifi on an ancient bridge, the scene of a never-allowed-to-be-forgotten victory by the Welsh over the Norman army in 1136. The town is near the mouth of the Teifi, a river that runs through a beautiful wooded valley dotted with traditional market towns and villages, as well as reminders of the area's once-flourishing woolen industry. Cardigan itself has an interesting history, for it was here, in the 12th century, that Wales's first eisteddfod, or folk festival, was held. The eisteddfod tradition, based on the Welsh language and culture, is still strong in Wales, and events large and small are held here (mainly in the summer months).

There is precious little left of Cardigan's medieval castle. Neighboring **46** **Cilgerran,** a village a few miles south, steals the limelight thanks to the dramatic ruins of 13th-century **Cilgerran Castle,** standing above a deep wooded gorge through which flows the River Teifi. ☎ *01239/615136.* ⊡ *£1.70.* ☺ *Late Mar.–late Oct., daily 9:30–6:30; late Oct.– late Mar., Mon.–Sat. 9:30–4, Sun. 2–4.*

East of Cenarth off A484 a few miles past Newcastle Emlyn, in what was once the most important wool-producing area in Wales, is the fas**47** cinating **Museum of the Welsh Woolen Industry** at Drefach Felindre. It has working exhibits and displays that trace the evolution of the industry, with regularly scheduled demonstrations. As a bonus there are other crafts workshops and a working woolen mill beside the museum site. ☎ *01559/370929.* ➰ *£3.* ☉ *Apr.–Sept., Mon.–Sat. 10–5; Oct.– Mar., weekdays 10–5.*

Lodging

£££   🖭 **Penbontbren Farm Hotel.** You won't find a more traditionally Welsh hotel than this friendly one set in peaceful countryside off A487 east of Cardigan. Barrie and Nan Humphreys have created an unusual hotel at a farm that has been in Nan's family for centuries. Barns have been tastefully converted into comfortable bedrooms, a restaurant is just across the courtyard, and the hotel has its own little museum devoted to the Welsh countryside. It's a good value—just over the price category. ✉ *Glynarthen, near Cardigan, SA44 6PE,* ☎ *01239/810248,* ℻ *01239/811129. 10 rooms with bath. Restaurant. MC, V.*

WALES A TO Z

Arriving and Departing

By Bus

National Express (☎ 0990/808080) serves Wales from London's Victoria Coach Station and also direct from London's Heathrow and Gatwick airports. Average travel times from London are: 3½ hours to Cardiff; 4 hours to Swansea; 5½ hours to Aberystwyth; and 4½ hours to Llandudno.

By Car

For Cardiff (151 mi), Swansea (190 mi), and South Wales, take M4 from London. Aberystwyth (211 mi) and Llandrindod (204 mi) in mid-Wales are well-served by major roads. The A40 is also an important route through central and South Wales. From London, M1/M6 is the most direct route to North Wales. A55, the coast road from Chester on the English side of the border, goes through Bangor.

By Plane

London's Heathrow and Gatwick airports, with their excellent door-to-door motorway links with Wales, are convenient gateways. Manchester Airport, which offers a wide range of international flights, is an excellent gateway for North Wales, with a journey time to the Welsh border—via M56—of under an hour. **Wales International Airport** near Cardiff has a number of direct international flights to European destinations and connecting services worldwide via Amsterdam (☎ 01446/711111).

By Train

From London's Paddington Station it is about two hours to Cardiff and three hours to Swansea on the fast InterCity rail service. Fast InterCity trains also run between London's Euston Station and North Wales. Average travel times are: from Euston, 3¾ hours to Llandudno in North Wales (some direct trains, otherwise change at Crewe) and about five hours to Aberystwyth in mid-Wales (changing at Birmingham). For all rail inquiries call ☎ 0345/484950.

Getting Around

By Bus

Although the overall pattern is a little fragmented, most parts of Wales are accessible by bus. The main operators are: **Cardiff Bus** (☎ 01222/ 396521), **Newport Transport** (☎ 01633/262914), **South Wales Transport** (☎ 01792/580580), and **Red and White** (☎ 01633/266336) for South Wales; **Crosville Wales** (☎ 01492/592111) for mid- and North

Wales. Crosville offers unlimited-travel Day Rover and Weekly Rover tickets. It also has long-distance routes: the daily TransCambria cross-country service between Cardiff and Bangor (calling at Swansea, Carmarthen, Aberystwyth, Dolgellau, and Caernarfon) and other routes such as Wrexham to Aberystwyth (calling at Llangollen, Corwen, Bala, Dolgellau, and Machynlleth).

Although primarily a carrier into Wales, **National Express** (☞ Arriving and Departing, *above*) also has routes through Wales (from Cardiff farther west, for example, or along the North Wales coast).

By Car
Distances in miles may not be great in Wales, but getting from place to place takes time because there are few major highways. The mountains mean that there is no single fast route from north to south, although A470 is good—and scenic—and A487 does run along or near most of the coastline. The mountains also mean that many of the smaller roads are winding and difficult to maneuver, but they do reveal magnificent views of the surrounding landscape.

By Train
The **Regional Railways** service (☎ 0345/484950) covers the valleys of South Wales, western Wales, central Wales, the Conwy Valley, and the North Wales coast on many highly scenic routes: the Cambrian Coast Railway, for example, running 70 mi between Aberystwyth and Pwllheli; and the Heart of Wales line, linking Swansea and Craven Arms, near Shrewsbury, 95 mi away. If you intend to use this network, ask about the money-saving unlimited-travel tickets available (such as "Freedom of Wales," "Rail Rover," and "Wanderer"), some of which include the use of bus services.

Wales is undoubtedly the best place in Britain for narrow-gauge steam railways. The *Great Little Trains of Wales*—narrow gauge—operate during the spring, summer, and autumn months through the mountains of Snowdonia and central Wales (there are also a few lines in South Wales). Many of these lines wind through landscapes of extraordinary grandeur. Tiny, copper-knobbed engines, panting fiercely, haul narrow carriages through deep cuttings and along rocky shelves above ancient oak woods through the heart of Snowdonia National Park. Wanderer tickets are available for unlimited travel on the "Great Little Trains of Wales": four days £28, eight days £38. Full details, including summary timetables, are available from **Great Little Trains of Wales** (✉ c/o The Station, Llanfair Caereinion SY21 0SF, ☎ 01938/810441).

Snowdonia also has Britain's only alpine-style steam rack railway, the Snowdon Mountain Railway, where little sloping boiler engines on rack-and-pinion track push their trains 3,000 ft up from Llanberis to the summit of Snowdon, Wales's highest mountain. Details of services can be obtained from **Snowdon Mountain Railway** (✉ Llanberis, Caernarfon LL55 4TY, ☎ 01286/870223).

Contacts and Resources

Car Rentals
Cardiff: Avis (✉ 14–22 Tudor St., ☎ 01222/342111). **Budget** (✉ Penarth Rd., ☎ 01222/664499). **Eurodollar** (✉ 10 Dominions Way Industrial Estate, Newport Rd., ☎ 01222/496256). **Europcar** (✉ 1–11 Byron St., ☎ 01222/498978). **Hertz** (✉ 9 Central Sq., ☎ 01222/224548).

Emergencies
Police, fire, ambulance (☎ 999).

Guided Tours

If you are interested in having a personal guide, contact the **Wales Official Tourist Guide Association** through Derek Jones (⊠ Y Stabl, 30 Acton Gardens, Wrexham LL12 8DE, ☎ 01978/351212, FAX 01978/363060). Please note that Mr. Jones is retiring from this position, but will forward enquiries. WOTGA only uses guides recognized by the Wales Tourist Board. It will put together tailor-made tours for you and, if you wish, have your guide meet you at the airport. You can book either a driver/guide or someone to accompany you as you drive.

Another good way to see Wales is by local tour bus; in summer there's a large choice of day and half-day excursions to most parts of the country. In major resorts and cities you should ask at a tourist information center or bus station for details.

Hiking and Walking

This is the most popular outdoor activity in Wales. The following organizations can help: **Brecon Beacons National Park** (Park Office: ⊠ 7 Glamorgan St., Brecon LD3 7DP, ☎ 01874/624437); **Offa's Dyke Association** (⊠ West St., Knighton LD7 1EN, ☎ 01547/528753); **Pembrokeshire Coast National Park** (⊠ Wynch La., Haverfordwest SA61 1PY, ☎ 01437/764636); **Ramblers' Association in Wales** (⊠ Ty'r Cerddwyr, High St., Gresford, Wrexham LL12 8PT, ☎ 01978/855148); **Snowdonia National Park** (Park Office: ⊠ Penrhyndeudraeth LL48 6LF, ☎ 01766/770274).

Historic Sites

If you intend to view a few Welsh castles, consider purchasing the **Cadw/Welsh Historic Monuments Explorer Pass** (⊠ Cadw/Welsh Historic Monuments, Crown Building, Cathays Park, Cardiff CF1 3NQ, ☎ 01222/500200), good for unlimited admission to most of Wales's historic sites. The seven-day pass costs £15 (single adult), £20 (two adults), or £25 (family ticket); the three-day pass costs £9, £15, and £20 respectively. Passes are available at any site covered by the Cadw program.

Travel Agencies

American Express (⊠ 3 Queen St., Cardiff, ☎ 01222/668858). **Thomas Cook** (⊠ 16 Queen St., Cardiff, ☎ 01222/224886; ⊠ 3 Union St., Swansea, ☎ 01792/464311).

Visitor Information

Tourist information centers are normally open Monday through Saturday 10–5:30 and limited hours on Sunday, but vary according to the season.

Aberystwyth (⊠ Terrace Rd., ☎ 01970/612125). **Betws-y-Coed** (⊠ Royal Oak Stables, ☎ 01690/710426). **Caernarfon** (⊠ Oriel Pendeitsh, opposite castle entrance, ☎ 01286/672232). **Cardiff** (national and city information, ⊠ Central Station, ☎ 01222/227281). **Llandrindod Wells** (⊠ Old Town Hall, ☎ 01597/822600). **Llandudno** (⊠ Chapel St., ☎ 01492/876413). **Llanfair Pwllgwyngyll** (⊠ Station Site, Isle of Anglesey, ☎ 01248/713177). **Llangollen** (⊠ Town Hall, ☎ 01978/860828). **Machynlleth** (⊠ Owain Glyndwr Centre, ☎ 01654/702401). **Ruthin** (⊠ Craft Centre, ☎ 01824/703992). **Swansea** (⊠ Singleton St., ☎ 01792/468321). **Tenby** (⊠ The Croft, ☎ 01834/842402). **Welshpool** (⊠ Vicarage Garden, ☎ 01938/552043).

12 Lancashire and the Peaks

Manchester, Liverpool, and the Peak District

Birthplace of the boom and bravura of the industrial revolution, this region still claims bustling cities like Liverpool and Manchester. Here, fans of Victorian architecture and of John, Paul, George, and Ringo come to enjoy some of England's most interesting sights. (Even Sir Paul McCartney's childhood home is now a historic site.) Beyond, however, lies the emerald tranquillity of the Peak District and Derbyshire's Wye Valley—home to two of the most regal houses in the land, Haddon Hall and Chatsworth.

Updated by
Jules Brown

THE INDUSTRIAL REVOLUTION THRIVED nowhere more strongly than the major cities here, such as Manchester and Liverpool. Yet you won't find a bleak, semi-urban landscape in the counties of Lancashire, Greater Manchester, and Derbyshire. Manchester today may be big and bustling, but it's an attractive mix of Victorian preservation, tasteful modern development, and leafy suburbs. Parts of the Merseyside area containing Liverpool do live up to its grimy image as an industrial port, and there are other parts of the countryside that lack scenic attraction. But inland, in Derbyshire (pronounced darbyshire), lies the spectacular Peak District, a huge, unspoiled national park at the southern end of the Pennines range, where you'll find Victorian-era spas like Buxton, charming towns like Bakewell, and magnificent stately houses, such as Chatsworth and Haddon Hall.

Still, the areas around Manchester and Liverpool are Britain's equivalent of the Rust Belt, a once-proud bastion of heavy industry and blue-collar values. These cities were the economic engines that propelled Britain to the forefront of the 18th and 19th centuries. By the mid-18th century, the Lancashire cotton industry had become firmly established in Manchester and enjoyed a special relationship with the port of Liverpool, to the west. Here, at the massive docks, cotton was imported from America and sent to the Lancashire mills; the finished cotton goods were later returned to Liverpool for export to the rest of the world. Both cities have suffered a marked decline during this century, but the downtown areas are currently undergoing a remarkable architectural and cultural revitalization. Today, they remain best known the world over for their musical and sporting prowess. Since 1968, Manchester United and Liverpool soccer clubs have won everything worth winning in Britain and Europe, and Manchester has repeatedly figured as an Olympic-site contender; in 2002 the city will host the Commonwealth Games. The Beatles launched the Merseysound of the '60s; contemporary Manchester groups still ride both British and American airwaves. On the classical side of music, Manchester is also home to Britain's oldest leading orchestra, the Hallé (founded in 1857)—just one of the city's legacies of wealthy 19th-century industrialists' investments in culture.

The Peak District, as its name implies, is a wilder part of England, a region of crags that rear violently out of the plain. The Pennines, a line of hills that begins in the Peak District and runs as far north as Scotland, are sometimes called the "backbone of England," a fitting description. This is a landscape of rocky outcrops and vaulting meadowland, where you'll see nothing for miles but sheep, drystone (unmortared) walls, and farms, interrupted—spectacularly—by 19th-century villages and treasure houses. The delight of the Peak District is being able to ramble for days in the wilderness but still enjoy civilization at its finest.

Pleasures and Pastimes

Beatlemania

For baby boomers, Liverpool exerts a strange and powerful lure—it is, after all, the birthplace of the Beatles. John, Paul, George, and Pete Best (Ringo arrived a bit later) set up shop at the Cavern in 1961 and the Liverpool Sound soon conquered the world. Today, fans can follow in the footsteps of the Fab Four at the Beatles Story—an exhibition that draws the faithful to Liverpool's Albert Dock. Unfortunately, many of the city sites linked with John and Paul have been bulldozed, including Strawberry Field orphanage (the Victorian building was replaced several years ago by a modern structure). To properly celebrate the Beatles' enduring appeal, go to the annual Mathew Street Festival, also known as Beatle Week, usually held during the third week in August, when what seems to be the entire city takes time out to dance, attend John and Yoko fancy-dress parties, listen to any number of Beatle bands from around the world ("There was once a better Beatle band, but they disbanded in 1970," notes the festival press release), and karaoke the night away. For complete information on Beatle Week, contact **Cavern City Tours** (☎ 0151/236–9091).

Dining

Gustatorily speaking, this section of the country is most famous for its Bakewell pudding (*never* called "tart" in these regions, as its imitations are in other parts of England). Its recipe was allegedly discovered when a cook accidentally spilled a rich cake mixture over some jam tarts. The cook was working in the Rutland Arms Hotel, where Jane Austen is reputed to have once stayed while writing *Pride and Prejudice*. Served with either custard or cream, the pudding is the joy of Bakewell, the pretty town where pride of place goes to market day, every Monday. Of course, Manchester and Liverpool offer a complete selection of restaurants, including Modern British and Continental as well as various ethnic cuisines. In particular, Manchester has one of Britain's most vibrant Chinatowns, while locals also set great store in the 30-odd Asian restaurants along Wilmslow Road, in the suburb of Rusholme, a few miles south of the city center. Here you can enjoy wonderful Bangladeshi, Pakistani, and Indian food.

CATEGORY	COST*
££££	over £40
£££	£25–£40
££	£15–£25
£	under £15

per person, including first course, main course, dessert, and VAT; excluding drinks

Lodging

If your trip centers on the cities of the Northwest, you can base yourself in Manchester and make Liverpool a day trip. Manchester offers a much better choice of accommodations and although the larger city-center hotels rely on business guests during the week, they often offer reduced rates on weekends. There are also numerous smaller hotels and guest houses in the nearby suburbs, many just a short bus ride from downtown. The Manchester Visitor Centre (☞ Contacts and Resources *in* Lancashire and the Peaks A to Z, *below*) operates a room-booking service, but you must stop by in person to use it.

The Peak District has a full complement of inns, B&Bs, and hotels, as well as a network of youth hostels, with particularly useful ones in Buxton, Bakewell, Castleton, Edale, and Matlock. Local tourist offices have full details; reserve well in advance at Easter and in summer.

CATEGORY	COST*
££££	over £110
£££	£60–£110
££	£50–£60
£	under £50

All prices are for two people sharing a double room, including service, breakfast, and VAT.

Exploring Lancashire and the Peak District

Manchester lies at the heart of a tangle of motorways in the northwest of England, about half an hour across the Pennines from Yorkshire. The city spreads west to the coast and the mouth of the River Mersey, where Liverpool is still centered on its port. To the north, in Lancashire, the coast flattens out around the resort of Blackpool—undistinguished country for the most part, though it includes miles of sandy beaches. But for the Northwest's most dramatic scenery—indeed, its only real geological feature of interest—you have to travel to the Peak District, a craggy national park less than an hour's drive southeast of Manchester.

Numbers in the text correspond to numbers in the margin and on the Lancashire and the Peaks, Manchester, and Liverpool maps.

Great Itineraries

Greater Manchester and Merseyside form one of the most built-up areas in Britain, but motorway access between the two is fast.

England at its most grand and ducal is visible in the Derbyshire valley of the River Wye: Majestic 18th-century Chatsworth is just about the most visited house in Britain. The Duke of Devonshire—its owner—is selling off art treasures, gradually reducing the house to a shadow of its former self. Haddon Hall is already bare inside, but because it is famous as the incomparable setting from which Dorothy Vernon eloped with John Manners in the 16th century and has an enchanting Tudor and Jacobean structure, it is widely regarded as "the most romantic house in England."

One of the main villages of the Peak District, Buxton, could be visited on a day trip from Manchester if you wanted to base yourself in that city. But the Peaks require more than just a short drive around the principal sights, and a week's hiking tour of the Peak District could be constructed with no trouble at all.

IF YOU HAVE 3 DAYS

Base yourself in ☷ **Manchester** ① for your first night, which will give you a chance to see the central sights on your first day and catch a show or a movie that night. On the next day, journey to the lush green and peaceful calm of the Derbyshire Wye to visit two of England's most magnificent stately homes, **Haddon Hall** ㉚ and **Chatsworth** ㉛, spending your second night in the nearby town of ☷ **Bakewell** ㉙. If you're traveling when these two houses are closed for the season, call in at ☷ **Liverpool** ⑮ instead for an overnight stay. Enjoy a lunch on the Albert Dock, then spend the afternoon in the museums and attractions of this dockside entertainment center.

IF YOU HAVE 5 DAYS

Make ☷ **Manchester** ① your base for the first two nights. If you're traveling with children, visits to Castlefield and the Granada Studios Tour will take up one full day. On the third day, take an overnight trip to ☷ **Liverpool** ⑮—with the morning spent in the city center seeing the cathedrals, buildings, and museums, and the afternoon at Albert Dock (over three nights, you'll be very unlucky if your visit doesn't coincide with a musical or theatrical performance of interest in either Manchester or Liverpool). Or opt instead to overnight in ☷ **Bakewell** ㉙ to visit romantic **Haddon Hall** ㉚ and regal **Chatsworth** ㉛ in the Derbyshire Wye valley. In summer, provided the weather is fine, the fifth day can be spent in the Peak District, with the last overnight in the spa town of ☷ **Buxton** ㉘, within easy driving distance of the area's charming villages.

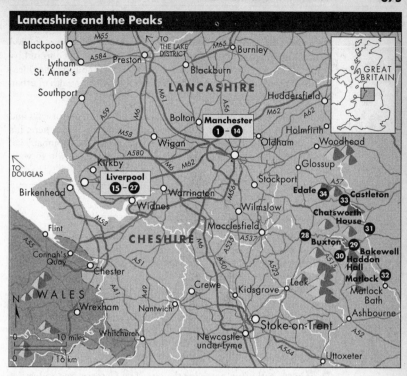

Lancashire and the Peaks

IF YOU HAVE 7 DAYS

It's wisest to split your time between city and national park. Start in **Buxton** ㉘ for an afternoon's stroll before moving on to spend the night in the pretty town of ▦ **Bakewell** ㉙, from where you can visit **Haddon Hall** ㉚ and **Chatsworth** ㉛, both among the top stately homes in all Britain, returning to Bakewell for the night. On the morning of the third day, move on to **Matlock** ㉜ and its river, and take a cable-car ride to the Heights of Abraham, before turning back and aiming for **Castleton** ㉝ and its splendid caverns. If you want to do any walking around the isolated village of **Edale** ㉞, you should spend the third night back in ▦ **Buxton** ㉘, making an early start on the day. After some hours walking on the moors, you can take a short drive to ▦ **Manchester** ①, where a two-night stay will let you see the best of that city, before moving on to enjoy your last night in ▦ **Liverpool** ⑮.

When to Tour Lancashire and the Peak District

Manchester has a rather unenviable reputation as one of the wettest cities in Britain, and visiting in summer isn't any guarantee of fine weather. Nevertheless, the nature of many of the sights both here and in Liverpool means that wet or cold weather shouldn't spoil a visit. In addition, the season for the Hallé Orchestra runs from October to May, the Manchester Arts Festival is in October, and winter sees fewer visitors to the very popular Granada Studios Tour—so a fall or winter visit is a definite option. Summer is the optimum time to see the Peak District, especially as early summer sees traditional festivities in many villages; the *only* time to see the great houses of the Derbyshire Wye valley—Chatsworth and Haddon Hall—is from Easter to September.

MANCHESTER AND LIVERPOOL

For a taste of the northwest of England, two cities—with interconnected histories and experiences—stand out: Manchester and the port of Liverpool. Both are relatively new places, at least for a country that measures its age in centuries, but each offers an outstanding wealth of urban and coastal experiences.

Manchester, with its position at the junction of several motorways and its international airport, is the obvious starting point. From here, it's an easy drive west to Liverpool. Take the train rather than combat local traffic; both Manchester and Liverpool city centers are easy to walk around in.

Manchester

❶ *43 mi southwest of Leeds, 87 mi north of Birmingham.*

Manchester was known to the Romans, who built a fort here, and to the Vikings, who attempted (but failed) to conquer the town. By the 14th century, the region was home to a flourishing wool trade. But for all these ancient stirrings, the city that stands today is no more or less than the product of the 18th-century industrial revolution—some would say its finest flowering. The mechanization of the cotton industry—the first cotton mill powered by steam opened here in 1783—caused rapid and unprecedented growth; the railway followed in 1830; then, in 1894, the opening of the Manchester Ship Canal turned the world's cotton capital into a major inland port.

These were turbulent times for the city. The factories and industries that procured Manchester's wealth gave rise to an industrial underclass, whose gradual awakening led to social and political unrest. Eleven workers were killed by the local militia at a protest meeting in 1819; the terrible conditions under which factory hands worked were later eloquently recorded by Friedrich Engels (coauthor with Karl Marx of the *Communist Manifesto*), who managed a cotton mill in the city. Formal political opposition to the government emerged in the shape of the Chartist movement (which campaigned for universal suffrage) and the Anti-Corn Law League (which opposed trade tariffs), both of which were centered in Manchester.

As with many former English industrial powerhouses, the declining years of the 20th century were not kind to Manchester, which until comparatively recently remained a soot-blackened, forbidding city—unlovely and unloved. But gradually the masterpieces of sturdy Victorian architecture in the city center have been cleaned up and much of the severe damage caused by World War II bombing was remedied by modern development.

However, city life was halted in its tracks in June 1996, when the IRA exploded a devastating bomb in Manchester that injured more than 200 people, closed over 600 businesses, and wrecked the heart of the city center. An ambitious £500-million rebuilding scheme has already changed the face of the city center: new squares and boulevards are being laid out, historic buildings have been completely refurbished, and the Arndale Shopping Centre was given a much-needed face-lift. The full project isn't expected to be realized until the turn of the century, a finish date that will coincide neatly with Manchester's hosting of the 2002 Commonwealth Games, granted in the wake of the city's repeated attempts to attract the Olympic Games. Manchester bid unsuccessfully for the 1996 and, most recently, the 2000 games, but it was finally rewarded for its persistence. There has already been heavy investment

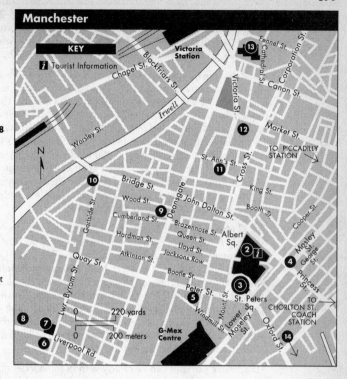

in a new transportation system and in impressive sporting and leisure facilities; a new 70,000-seat stadium will be in place by the time the games open.

② Manchester's exuberant **Town Hall** speaks volumes about the city's 19th-century sense of self-importance—it's a magnificent Victorian Gothic building (1867–76), with extensions added just before World War II. The Great Hall, with its soaring hammer-beam roof, is decorated with murals of the city's proud history, painted between 1852 and 1865 by the Pre-Raphaelite Ford Madox Brown. Guided tours, arranged through the tourist office (housed in the Town Hall Extension), can introduce you to the murals, but it's also a simple matter to present yourself at the front desk and ask to look: provided the rooms aren't being used for meetings, you'll be allowed to wander in. ⊠ *Albert Sq.,* ☎ *0161/ 234–5000.* ▨ *Free; guided tours £3.* ⊙ *Weekdays 8:45–4:30; guided tours usually Sat. at 2.*

③ The **Central Library** was erected in 1930 to make an emphatic statement about the city's devotion to local education. The grand reading room is worth seeing; it was, at one time, the biggest municipal library in the world. The Library Theatre (☞ Nightlife and the Arts, *below*) is part of the complex. ⊠ *St. Peter's Sq.,* ☎ *0161/234–1900.* ⊙ *Mon.– Thurs. 10–8, Fri. and Sat. 10–5.*

Many industrial barons of the 19th century spent some of their vast wealth on paintings, and their interests are reflected in the displays in

★ **④** the **City Art Gallery,** a striking, neoclassic building. Its pride and joy is its Pre-Raphaelite collection, most notably the works by Ford Madox Brown, represented here by his bold allegory *Work* and by preparatory sketches for the Town Hall murals. Holman Hunt and Brown's other contemporaries get wall space, too, while there's a catholic range of work—depicting scenes from Venice to the Peak District—by artists as diverse as Gainsborough, George Stubbs, J. M. W. Turner, Paul Gauguin, Claude Lorrain, Canaletto, and Bernardo Bellotto. ⊠ *Mosley St.,* ☎ *0161/236–5244.* ⌸ *Free.* ☉ *Mon. 11–5:30, Tues.–Sat. 10–5:30, Sun. 2–5:30. Free guided tours weekends at 2:30.*

★ ❺ The Italianate **Free Trade Hall** on Peter Street was just one of the buildings in Manchester restored after World War II; only the facade is original. It served as the home of the Hallé Orchestra for more than a century, though the orchestra moved into a custom-built auditorium of its own in 1996 (☞ Nightlife and the Arts, *below*). The site on which the Free Trade Hall stands has dark historical associations. In 1819, in what was formerly St. Peter's Field, 60,000 workers attending a meeting on the reform of Parliament were fired upon by the local guard; 11 people were killed in the "Peterloo Massacre." The building is now closed and may become a hotel, retaining the facade; space is likely to be found for a commemorative museum of the event.

The **G-Mex** (⊠ Lower Mosley St.)(☞ Nightlife and the Arts, *below*), formerly Manchester's central railroad station, now houses the city's biggest and brightest exhibitions and events. The Hallé Orchestra occupies the city's newest concert hall, **Bridgewater Hall** (⊠ Lower Mosley St.; ☞ Nightlife and the Arts, *below*), a scrupulously modern piece of architecture overlooking a public piazza. Rivaling Birmingham's Symphony Hall as the finest acoustic auditorium in the country, Bridgewater Hall also houses the largest pipe organ to be installed in Britain in this century; the entire building rests on hidden, giant metal springs that deaden exterior noise.

Manchester's origins can be clearly seen in the district of Castlefield, site of an early Roman fort and later the center of Manchester's first canal and railroad developments. The district has since been restored as an urban heritage park—Britain's first—and in addition to the

❻ **Castlefield Visitor Centre,** the 7-acre site contains the reconstructed gate to the Roman fort and the various buildings of the excellent Museum of Science and Industry. ⊠ *Visitor Centre, Liverpool Rd.,* ☎ *0161/834–4026.* ⌸ *Free.* ☉ *Weekdays 10–4, weekends noon–4.*

★ ❼ At the **Museum of Science and Industry,** separate buildings, including the world's oldest surviving passenger railway station, show marvelous collections relating to the city's industrial past and present. You can walk through a reconstructed Victorian sewer and examine a huge collection of working steam mill engines. This section of town is rife with industrial revolution landmarks; not far away, on Cooke Street, a certain Henry Royce built his first car in 1904, before he went into partnership with C. S. Rolls. ⊠ *Castlefield, Liverpool Rd.,* ☎ *0161/ 832–2244.* ⌸ *£5.* ☉ *Daily 10–5, last admission at 4.*

☾ ❽ The **Granada Studios Tour,** a British version of the Hollywood studio tours, offers a firsthand behind-the-scenes look at television programs. There are backstage tours (including a walk down Sherlock Holmes's Baker Street and along Downing Street), 3D film shows, and other special events, rides, and entertainments. It's from here that Britain's longest-running TV soap opera, *Coronation Street,* is broadcast, and you can even have a drink in the program's pub, the Rover's Return. Get there before 11 AM to see everything in one day. ☉ *Water St.,* ☎ *0161/832–4999 (24-hr information line).* ⌸ *£14.99.* ☉ *Mid-Apr.–Sept., daily 9:45–6, last admission at 4; Oct.–mid-Apr., weekdays 9:45–4:30, weekends 9:45–5:30, last admission at 3.*

❾ Housed in a lovely mock-Gothic masterpiece, the **John Rylands Library** is named after a rich weaver whose widow spent his money founding the library. It became part of the University of Manchester in 1972.

Built in a late-Gothic style in the 1890s, and worth visiting for the eye-opening interior alone, the library houses one of Britain's most important collections—priceless historical documents and charters, Bibles in more than 300 languages, manuscripts dating from the dawn of Christianity, and fine bindings. There are always exhibitions from the library's treasures, including one of the possibly accurate likenesses of Shakespeare, the Grafton portrait. ✉ *150 Deansgate,* ☎ *0161/834–5343.* ☏ *Free; guided tours £1.* ☉ *Weekdays 10–5:30, Sat. 10–1. Guided tours usually Wed. at noon..*

One of Manchester's more recent museums recounts splendidly the struggles of working people in the city throughout the industrial revolution and beyond. The **People's History Museum** not only tells the story of the 1819 Peterloo Massacre but features an unrivaled collection of trade-union banners, tools, toys, utensils, and photographs, which combine to illustrate the working lives and pastimes of the city's people. There's a pleasant café here, too. ✉ *Bridge St.,* ☎ *0161/839–6061.* ☏ *£1; free on Fri.* ☉ *Tues.–Sun. 11–4:30.*

⑪ **St. Ann's Church,** a handsome 1712 building, comes as a surprise amid resolutely modern surrounding buildings. It contains *The Descent from the Cross,* a painting by Annibale Carraci (1561–1609). The essayist Thomas De Quincey was baptized here (having been born in a nearby house, now long since demolished). Guided tours are available if you call in advance, or try to coincide with the organ recitals that usually take place at 12:45 on Tuesdays. ✉ *St. Ann's Sq.,* ☎ *0161/834–0239.* ☉ *Daily 8–6.*

⑫ Throughout its commercial heyday, the city's most important building was the **Royal Exchange** (✉ St. Ann's Sq.), once the cotton market. The existing structure, built with panache in the early 20th century to accommodate 7,000 traders, is the most recent of several buildings to hold the title. It was badly damaged by the 1996 bomb and is undergoing fundamental restoration, which has closed the café, exhibition space, and most of the crafts shops; it is expected to reopen in 1999. The imaginative Royal Exchange Theatre, once ensconced within its echoing bulk, has relocated for the duration to the Upper Campfield Market (☞ Nightlife and the Arts, *below*).

⑬ Manchester's **Cathedral,** beside the river, was originally the medieval parish church of the city but was elevated in status to a cathedral in 1847. Unusually proportioned, it's very broad for its length; indeed, it's recognized as having the widest medieval-age nave in Britain. Inside is a wealth of attractive items: early 16th-century choir stalls with intriguing misericord seats; paintings of the beatitudes by Carel Weight (1908–89); a sculpture by Eric Gill (1882–1919); a fine sculpted tomb brass of Warden Huntingdon, who died in 1458; and an octagonal chapter house from 1485. ✉ *Deansgate,* ☎ *0161/833–2220.* ☏ *Free.* ☉ *Daily 8–6.*

⑭ One of the most interesting places to visit outside the center of Manchester is the university-run **Whitworth Art Gallery.** The collections in the gallery are especially strong in British watercolors, old-master drawings, and Postimpressionism. And its captivating rooms full of textiles—Coptic and Peruvian fabrics, Spanish and Italian vestments, tribal rugs, and contemporary weaving—are just what you might expect in a city built on textile manufacture. There's a bistro for light meals and a good gift shop. The gallery is southeast of the city center in an area called Moss Side. At the Piccadilly bus terminal ask for a bus to the Manchester Royal Infirmary, which is just across the road from the Whitworth. ✉ *Oxford Rd.,* ☎ *0161/275–7450.* ☏ *Free.* ☉ *Mon.–Sat. 10–5, Sun. 2–5.*

Dining and Lodging

££–£££ ✕ **Mash & Air.** Housed in a four-story converted downtown mill,
★ Oliver Peyton's Mash & Air (named after a stage in the brewing process) presents a supremely fashionable mix of industrial-chic dining and bar areas fitted around an in-house microbrewery. Diners can eat in the main restaurant, called Air, noshing on thoroughly up-to-the-minute modern British dishes like panfried cod with polenta, or graze less formally in the Mash bar areas on wood-fired designer pizzas, grilled sandwiches, and salads. ✉ *40 Chorlton St.,* ☎ *0161/661–6161 Mash; 0161/661–1111 Air. AE, DC, MC, V. Air closed Sun.; both closed Dec. 25–Dec. 26, and Easter Sun. and Easter Mon.*

££ ✕ **Café Primavera.** In a quiet suburb of south Manchester, very near Chorlton Green, this stylish restaurant sets its stall out against a background of bright primary colors and jugs full of sunflowers. Mediterranean flavors prevail in a seasonally changing menu that might include mussels with cream and pancetta or roast duck with plum sauce. A market-fresh fish of the day is offered, as well as imaginative vegetarian specialties. The tables are a little too close together for comfort, but the service is good-natured. The short wine list has some great surprises, and desserts are memorable. ✉ *48 Beech Rd., Chorlton,* ☎ *0161/862–9934. AE, MC, V.* ☽ *Dinner only, and Sun. lunch in summer.*

££ ✕ **Market Restaurant.** This is an unpretentious, dinner-only spot that
★ is serious about its cooking. Its menu changes monthly, and although there's an emphasis on vegetarian dishes, meat and fish entrées are well thought out and as likely to feature Asian or European as British influences; desserts are always inventive. The proprietor maintains an excellent selection of international bottled beers, as well as an interesting wine list. ✉ *104 High St.,* ☎ *0161/834–3743. AE, DC, MC, V. Closed Sun.–Tues., and 1 wk at Christmas, at Easter, and month of Aug.*

££ ✕ **Yang Sing.** One of Manchester's good Chinese restaurants, it is popular with Chinese families, which is always a good sign, but it is *so* popular that you must reserve ahead. The cooking is Cantonese, and there's a huge range to choose from. The dim sum is always a good bet, and don't forget to ask about the daily specials—they're often only listed in Chinese on the menu. There is also a slightly cheaper offshoot, **Little Yang Sing** (✉ 17 George St., ☎ 0161/228–7722). This was Manchester's original Yang Sing restaurant; it has a rather cramped basement setting but still serves fine Cantonese food. ✉ *34 Princess St.,* ☎ *0161/236–2200. AE, MC, V.*

£–££ ✕ **Sangam.** While most of Rusholme's many Asian eateries pack diners in for quick (though admittedly excellent) meals, this more upscale restaurant—renowned for the quality of its food—allows more time to linger. Portions are generous, and vegetable dishes are particularly well judged—try the tasty *bhindi* (okra) or (for larger appetites) the vegetable or mushroom *biriani* (mixed rice dish). There's always a buzz here, though the closely packed tables have something to do with that. The restaurant is a couple of miles south of the city center; take a taxi. ✉ *13–15 Wilmslow Rd.,* ☎ *0161/257–3922. AE, MC, V.*

£ ✕ **Dmitri's.** Set in a covered Victorian arcade in an old market building, this attractive tapas bar–taverna welcomes a trendy Manchester set. An interesting hybrid menu ranges from Greek and Mediterranean snack dishes to pasta, mixed grills, rice pilafs, and salads. Most meals here cost well under £10. In warm weather, you'll welcome being able to sit outside in the arcade. ✉ *Campfield Arcade, Tonman St., Deansgate,* ☎ *0161/839–3319. AE, MC, V.*

££££ ✕🖫 **Victoria & Albert Hotel.** Formerly a warehouse, built in 1843, and
★ situated just out of the city center opposite the Granada Studios Tour, this hotel is an object lesson in how to handle renovation without destroying the historic kernel of a building. Exposed brickwork and cast-

iron pillars throughout make for highly individualized accommodations—no two rooms are the same. Four suites have thematic decor (the Sherlock Holmes suite re-creates a slice of Victorian London). The bar has urban river views from its conservatory, while the highly rated **Sherlock Holmes Restaurant** has special gourmet dinners as well as an à la carte menu of classic English food with a Continental (and occasional Asian) twist. ⊠ *Water St., M3 4OQ,* ☎ *0161/832–1188,* ⒻⒶⓍ *0161/834–2484. 132 rooms with bath. Restaurant, bar, coffee shop, room service, sauna, exercise room, business services. AE, DC, MC, V.*

££££ 🏨 **Holiday Inn Crowne Plaza Midland.** The Edwardian splendor of the hotel's public rooms—including a grand lobby and bar—evokes turn-of-the-century days when the Midland was Manchester's railroad hotel. Guest rooms are comfortable, though they never quite live up to the standards of the rest of the hotel. ⊠ *Peter St., M60 2DS,* ☎ *0161/236–3333,* ⒻⒶⓍ *0161/932–4107. 303 rooms with bath. 2 restaurants, 2 bars, grill, room service, pool, beauty salon, sauna, exercise room, squash, casino, business services. AE, DC, MC, V.*

£ 🏨 **Cavendish Hotel.** This suburban guest house 3 mi south of the city center is on good bus routes and is also convenient for the little pubs around Chorlton Green. New managers have taken the opportunity to redecorate throughout and the cheery, converted Edwardian house offers comfortable-size rooms with televisions and tea/coffeemaking facilities. A bar has been added and you can eat in the new restaurant if you don't fancy the trek into town. ⊠ *402 Wilbraham Rd., Chorlton-cum-Hardy, M21 0UH,* ☎ ⒻⒶⓍ *0161/881–1911. 20 rooms, 8 with showers. Restaurant, bar. MC, V.*

£ 🏨 **Manchester Youth Hostel.** Manchester's modern youth hostel provides quality budget accommodation right in the city center, in the historic Castlefield quarter. Four- and six-bed rooms (all with shower facilities and sink) mean that families are well catered to, and couples can even reserve one of the few two-bed rooms. This is one of the very best of Britain's hostels, with excellent facilities (including a self-catering kitchen), all for a fraction of the price of a city-center hotel room. ⊠ *Potato Wharf, Castlefield, M3 4NB,* ☎ *0161/839–9960,* ⒻⒶⓍ *0161/835–2054. 152 beds with shower. Cafeteria, recreation room, coin laundry. MC, V.*

Nightlife and the Arts

For listings of events, festivals, concerts, shows, movies and other entertainment, buy the fortnightly *City Life* magazine from any newsstand.

Manchester's Hallé Orchestra and the BBC Philharmonic perform at the 2,400-seat **Bridgewater Hall** (⊠ Lower Mosley St., ☎ 0161/907–9000). Other classical concerts are held at the **Royal Northern College of Music** (⊠ 124 Oxford Rd., ☎ 0161/273–4504). Another popular venue is **G-Mex** (⊠ Lower Mosley St., ☎ 0161/832–9000 box office). For rock, reggae, jazz, R&B, and many other kinds of music, the most enjoyable venue is **Band on the Wall** (⊠ 25 Swan St., ☎ 0161/832–6625), which has live music six nights a week. Major rock and pop stars appear at G-Mex (☞ above) or at **Labatt's Apollo** (⊠ Stockport Rd., Ardwick Green, ☎ 0161/242–2525).

Manchester has an enviable reputation in the performing arts, with productions staged at theaters all over the city. The **Opera House** (⊠ Quay St., ☎ 0161/242–2509) hosts touring companies, both British and international, as well as a wide spectrum of entertainment. In the basement of the Central Library, the **Library Theatre** (⊠ St. Peter's Sq., ☎ 0161/236–7110) stages mostly classic and serious drama, as well as new writing from local playwrights. The **Royal Exchange Theatre** (⊠ Upper Campfield Market, corner of Deansgate and Liverpool Rd.,

☎ 0161/833–9833) makes the most of its alternative premises while the Royal Exchange building itself is out of action, and retains its sky-high reputation for daring productions. For more offbeat productions, the **Green Room** (✉ 54–56 Whitworth St. W, ☎ 0161/950–5900) puts on a full program of theater, poetry, dance, and performance art.

The city's major center for cinema and the visual arts is the **Corner-house** (✉ 70 Oxford St., ☎ 0161/228–2463), an arts center with three movie screens, plus galleries, a bookshop, a trendy bar, and a café.

Manchester hosts an annual **Festival of Arts and Television** in October, when there are theatrical performances, street events, concerts, and shows held at a variety of venues throughout the city. The tourist information center has more information.

The city has, arguably, the best nightlife in the north, with a wide range of pubs and clubs. Simply Red's Mick Hucknall is a partner in **Barca** (✉ Catalan Sq., ☎ 0161/839–7099), a hip Spanish bar-restaurant in Castlefield full of the drop-dead gorgeous. One of the first new-wave café-bars in the city was **Dry 201** (✉ 28–30 Oldham St., ☎ 0161/236–5920), now a little faded at the edges, but still full of bright young things and boasting Internet facilities for switched-on drinkers. In summer, you can sit out by the water at **Dukes 92** (✉ Castlefield, ☎ 0161/839–8646), a cavernous place converted from old stables, named after the lock number where it's sited on the Rochdale Canal. But where the city is really at its hottest is in the so-called Gay Village, by the Rochdale Canal, where a dozen bars and restaurants vie for customers. **Manto** (✉ 46 Canal St, ☎ 0161/236–2667) is typical of the scene, with its cool, largely gay crowd hanging out in the split-level, post-industrial interior. **Metz** (✉ 3 Brazil St, ☎ 0161/237–9852) is more laid back, a bar-restaurant with a popular outdoor deck and Eastern European food on the menu. The **Peveril of the Peak** (✉ 127 Great Bridgewater St., ☎ 0161/236–6364)—just one of scores of city-center pubs—is a lively, tiled Victorian pub. Techno and dance freaks head out in ever-greater numbers to **Sankey's Soap** (✉ Beehive Mill, Jersey St., Ancoats, ☎ 0161/950–4230) for their groove fix. The mock-Gothic **Via Fossa** (✉ Canal St, ☎ 0161/236–6523) is packed at weekends with hyped-up clubbers.

Outdoor Activities and Sports

SOCCER

Matches are played on Saturdays (and, increasingly, Sundays and Mondays). Admission prices vary, but the cheapest seats start at about £16—though you'll find it all but impossible to get tickets for major games, which sell out months in advance. Local tourist offices can give you match schedules and directions to the grounds of the city's two major teams: **Manchester United** plays at Old Trafford (☎ 0161/872–0199). **Manchester City** plays at Maine Road (☎ 0161/224–5000).

STADIUM SPORTS

Manchester's sports facilities are second to none in Britain and are set to improve yet again once the new stadium is completed in time for the Commonwealth Games in 2002. The **NYNEX Arena** (✉ Huntsbank, Victoria Station, ☎ 0161/930–8000)—Europe's largest indoor sports stadium—hosts basketball and ice hockey, as well as major concerts. The country's first covered **Velodrome** (✉ 1 Stuart St., Eastlands, ☎ 0161/223–2244) was the site of Olympic champion Chris Boardman's record-breaking cycle-sprint ride.

Chorlton Water Park in Manchester (✉ Maitland Ave., Barlow Moor Rd., Chorlton, ☎ 0161/881–5639) offers boating, canoeing, windsurfing, and sailing, between Easter and October.

Shopping

The IRA bomb of June 1996 caused huge disruption to the city's shops but normal service has slowly been resumed. **St. Ann's Square** and the **Arndale Centre** bore the brunt of the bombing but although boarded-up buildings are still evident, most shops are now trading again. Sadly, shopping at the **Royal Exchange** remains restricted and will be for the foreseeable future. Once the city-center reconstruction is complete, you can expect Manchester to be a pleasure in which to shop, since pedestrian thoroughfares, covered malls, and landscaped gardens form the core of the scheme. In the meantime, attention focuses on the development of the **Northern Quarter,** the retail name for a once near-derelict part of the city around Oldham Street, where grunge-era boutiques, fashionable bars, and indie music shops are proliferating.

For antique clothes, records and tapes, ethnic crafts and jewelry, and bric-a-brac, visit **Aflecks Palace** (✉ 52 Church St., ☎ 0161/834–2039), four floors of retail outlets in the heart of the Northern Quarter that attract the city's youth.

The **Manchester Crafts Centre** (✉ 17 Oak St., ☎ 0161/832–4274) is a Victorian building housing 18 workshop-cum-retail outlets, where you can see potters, jewelers, hatters, theatrical costumers, and metal enamelers at work.

The **University of Manchester Museum** shop (✉ Oxford Rd., ☎ 0161/275–2000) also sells cards, stationery, and prints, but specializes in books and imaginative toys for children.

The **Whitworth Art Gallery** (✉ Oxford Rd., ☎ 0161/275–7450) has a fine shop that specializes in handmade cards, postcards, and prints. It also sells stationery, art books, jewelry, and ceramics.

Gibb's Bookshop (✉ 10 Charlotte St., ☎ 0161/236–7179) is a combined secondhand bookshop and classical music store.

Liverpool

⑮ *34 mi southwest of Manchester.*

At first glance, Liverpool suffers from the same problems as most other industrial northern cities: high unemployment, risky streets, depressing modern architecture. Corny as it may sound, though, the humor of the people and the big university population keep this town from becoming just another industrial casualty. As a result, Liverpool is worth your while *if* you make an effort to meet the locals—the city's two cathedrals and Beatles hype can keep you entertained for only so long.

In the late 19th century, when the city was at the height of its economic power, its bustling docks stretched for several miles, alive with goods and traders. As in neighboring Manchester, the wealth generated by this activity—largely based on the slave trade in the 19th century, the transatlantic passenger liners in the 20th—was huge, and the city center contains many buildings that reflect those proud days. But Liverpool proved less adaptable as time wore on: as Britain lost its old imperial markets and its cotton industry, and as air transport superseded shipping, the port of Liverpool was left floundering in economic decay. There's been some regeneration since the decline following World War II, but in many ways the city seems to be waiting for better times.

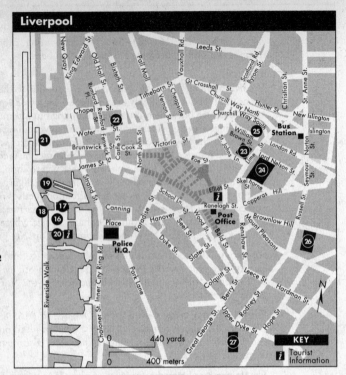

Liverpool

★ **16** To understand the city's maritime past head straight for **Albert Dock** on the waterfront. Built in the mid-19th century as part of Liverpool's once-mighty stretch of dockside developments, Albert Dock was rescued from neglect in recent times and its fine colonnaded, brick warehouse buildings were converted to museums, shops, offices, and restaurants. Now the country's largest heritage attraction, it's a stunning achievement. As most of the attractions are indoors, within the old warehouse buildings, it's an obvious choice if your visit coincides with one of the Northwest's rainy spells. When the weather allows, pull up a seat at one of the outdoor cafés overlooking the dock or take a boat trip through the docks and out on to the river to see the city as it was in its heyday. ☎ *0151/708–8838.* 🚢 *Boat trips £2.* 🕐 *Departures every hr noon–5.*

The dock forms part of a venture known as **Liverpool's Historic Waterfront**. The dock itself and some of the attractions are free; others require a separate admission fee or the purchase of a Waterfront Pass, which gets you into all the museums (Merseyside Maritime Museum, Museum of Liverpool Life, Tate Gallery, Beatles Story) and offers a cruise across the River Mersey. There is free parking at the dock, while a shuttle bus runs here every 30 minutes (Monday–Saturday only) from Lime Street Station. ✉ *Liverpool's Historic Waterfront, Albert Dock,* ☎ *0151/ 708–8574.* 🚢 *General admission free, Waterfront Pass £8.50.* 🕐 *For opening hrs, see individual attractions.*

17 Part of the Albert Dock complex, the **Merseyside Maritime Museum** tells the story of the port of Liverpool by way of models, paintings, and original boats and equipment, spread across five floors. The same admission ticket also grants access to the **Transatlantic Slavery** and **Customs and Excise** exhibitions, the former being especially compelling on the human misery engendered by the slave trade. ✉ *Albert Dock,*

☎ *0151/478–4499.* ✍ *£3, including admission to Museum of Liverpool Life.* ☼ *Daily 10–5, last admission at 4.*

⑱ The **Tate Gallery**—an offshoot of the London gallery of the same name—has constantly changing exhibits of challenging modern art in its superb galleries. It also has an excellent shop selling art books, prints, and posters, and it boasts a fashionable dockside café-restaurant. ✉ *The Colonnades, Albert Dock,* ☎ *0151/709–0507.* ✍ *Free; charge for special exhibitions.* ☼ *Tues.–Sun. 10–6.*

⑲ A more offbeat look at Liverpool's history and culture is available from the exhibits at the **Museum of Liverpool Life,** housed in a former Boat Hall opposite the Albert Dock's Maritime Museum. There are special displays on Merseyside culture, focusing on matters as diverse as the city's changing trades following the decline of shipping, local sporting prowess, and arts and literature in Liverpool. This is the place to discover what it is that makes "Scousers" (as locals are known) tick, and perhaps even what's behind their famed sense of humor. ✉ *Albert Dock,* ☎ *0151/478–4080.* ✍ *£3, including admission to Merseyside Maritime Museum.* ☼ *Daily 10–5, last admission at 4.*

⑳ You can follow in the footsteps of the Fab Four at the **Beatles Story**—one of the more popular attractions of the Albert Dock complex—which has an entertaining series of scenes re-created from their career, as well as a John Lennon photographic exhibition. ✉ *Britannia Vaults, Albert Dock,* ☎ *0151/709–1963.* ✍ *£5.95.* ☼ *Weekdays 10–5, weekends 10–6.*

For a reasonable price, you can buy "Beatles' Liverpool" or "Lennon's Liverpool" maps, which outline comprehensive self-guided tours that stop by Penny Lane, Strawberry Fields, Menlove Avenue, and many other familiar-sounding places (that invariably prove disappointing). The august National Trust (the overseers of such landmarks as Blenheim Palace and Knole) is opening a new Beatles landmark—the **Paul McCartney House**—the Merseyside home of the young Paul McCartney in the Liverpool section of Allerton. Acquired by the National Trust in 1995, the mid-terraced 1950s council house is significant as the place where the Beatles were "born." Occupied by the McCartney family from 1955–63, the house was Paul's residence from age 13 until the Beatles became established. The group convened here to compose songs and practice. Renovation and restoration of period-authentic windows, doors, and hedges have been completed and the house is due to open in late 1998. You can only access the house by pre-booking a seat on the minibus that connects the site with Speke Hall. ✉ *20 Forthlin Rd.*

To visit most of the Beatles sites, you have to take city buses to the various points of interest, or you can join the two-hour **Magical Mystery Tour,** which departs daily from the Merseyside Welcome Centre at 2:30. If you can't find the Beatles knickknack of your dreams, check out the **Beatles Shop** (✉ *31 Mathew St.,* ☎ *0151/236–8066*). For information about Beatles Week, known officially as the Mathew Street Festival and held during the third week in August, contact **Cavern City Tours** (☎ *0151/236–9091*).

㉑ At **Pier Head** you're admirably poised to take a **ferry** (☎ *0151/630–1030*) across the River Mersey to Birkenhead and back. These leave regularly throughout the day and offer fine views of the city—a journey celebrated in "Ferry 'Cross the Mersey," Gerry and the Pacemakers' 1960s hit song. As you return, you'll look across to see the twin towers of the **Royal Liver Building**—"Lye-ver"—topped by mythical birds, purported to have given the city its name. It's a poignant spot: from Pier Head itself, 9 million British, Irish, and European emigrants set sail between 1830 and 1930 for new lives in America, Australia, and Africa, while many of their relatives looked to the Royal Liver Society for assistance—it was originally a burial club to which families paid contributions to ensure a decent send-off. ⊠ *Pier Head Ferry Terminal, Mersey Ferries,* ☎ *0151/630–1030.* 🎟 *£1.80 for round-trip 7:45–9:15 AM and 4:15–7:15 PM; £3.20 for cruises at other times.* ☉ *Ferries every 30–60 mins, 7:45 AM–7:15 PM.*

City-center buildings reflect the 19th-century glories of Liverpool. The
㉒ domed, Georgian **Town Hall** (⊠ Water St., ☎ 0151/707–2391) has been completely refurbished, and its splendidly rich interior is accessible on
㉓ special guided tours; call ahead for an events diary. **St. George's Hall** (⊠ Lime St., ☎ 0151/707–2391), built 1839–1847, is among the country's finest Greek Revival buildings; exhibitions and concerts are held inside and the public is allowed in for tours at other selected times in summer. Perhaps the most imposing expression of former industrial
㉔ might is **Lime Street Station,** whose cast-iron train shed was the world's largest in the mid-19th century.

★ **㉕** The **Walker Art Gallery** maintains its position as one of the best art collections outside London, with an excellent display of British art and some superb Italian and Flemish works. In particular, you'll find an unrivaled collection of paintings by 18th-century Liverpudlian equestrian artist George Stubbs, as well as paintings by J. M. W. Turner, John Constable, and Sir Edwin Henry Landseer, and representative work by the Pre-Raphaelites. Modern British artists are included, too—on display is one of David Hockney's typically Californian pool scenes—while the museum branches out into applied art, with engaging exhibits of glassware, china, silver, and furniture which once adorned the mansions of Liverpool's industrial barons. The Walker Art Gallery Tea Room holds center stage in the airy museum lobby. ⊠ *William Brown St.,* ☎ *0151/207–0001.* 🎟 *Free.* ☉ *Mon.–Sat. 10–5, Sun. noon–5.*

A 10-minute walk up Mount Pleasant from Lime Street Station will
㉖ take you to the Roman Catholic **Metropolitan Cathedral of Christ the King.** Built in 1962 on the site of a 19th-century workhouse, it's a striking, funnel-like structure of concrete, stone, and mosaic, topped with a glass lantern. ⊠ *Mount Pleasant,* ☎ *0151/709–9222.* 🎟 *Donations welcome.* ☉ *Mon.–Sat. 8–6, Sun. 8–5.*

㉗ The **Anglican Cathedral,** the largest church in northern Britain, overlooks the city and the River Mersey. Built of local sandstone, the Gothic-style cathedral took 75 years to complete. It was begun in 1903 by architect Giles Gilbert Scott (who died in 1960), and was finally finished in 1978. Take a look around at the grand interior, climb the tower, and find time to call in at the Visitor Centre; a refectory serves light meals and coffee. ⊠ *St. James's Rd.,* ☎ *0151/709–6271.* 🎟 *£2 for tower.* ☉ *Daily 8–6, tower daily 11–5, refectory daily 10–4.*

Dining and Lodging

££ ✕ **Armadillo.** The fine Mediterranean cooking at this downtown restau-
★   rant in the Cavern Quarter features classic dishes alongside trendy favorites; starters may include lentil salad or eggplant and mozzarella combinations. Desserts are a highlight, and the wine list carries some strong French names. Lunches and early-evening suppers offer the chance to choose from a less expensive menu of bistro favorites. ⊠ *31 Mathew St.,* ☎ *0151/236–4123. AE, MC, V. Closed Sun., Mon., and Christmas wk. No lunch Sat.*

£   ✕ **Est Est Est.** This top budget choice in the Albert Dock complex is a lively spot for lunch. The restaurant makes good use of the old warehouse brickwork, though tables are a bit cramped. Still, the Italian menu is strong on appetizers—including a feast of antipasto—and includes excellent crisp pizzas. If you're still hungry, the dessert trolley trundles reassuringly around the restaurant. Service is brisk, the atmosphere is bubbling, and the coffee is flavorful. ⊠ *Unit 6, Edward Pavilion, Albert Dock,* ☎ *0151/708–6969. AE, DC, MC, V.*

£££ 🏨 **Liverpool Moat House.** Some may find this uncompromisingly modern hotel unattractive from the outside, but its location couldn't be better. It lies in landscaped grounds right across from the River Mersey and Albert Dock, which means that much of what you've come to the city to see is right at your doorstep. Guest rooms are handsome and spacious, most featuring two large beds and fine bathrooms, and about half the rooms are no-smoking. A good-size ground-floor pool, health club, and spa aid relaxation after a day's sightseeing. ⊠ *Paradise St., L1 8JD,* ☎ *0151/471–9988,* FAX *0151/709–2706. 244 rooms and 7 suites with bath. 2 restaurants, bar, coffee shop, no-smoking rooms, room service, pool, sauna, exercise room, business services. AE, DC, MC, V.*

Nightlife and the Arts

The renowned Royal Liverpool Philharmonic Orchestra plays its concert season at **Philharmonic Hall** (⊠ Hope St., ☎ 0151/709–3789). Major national and international ballet, opera, drama, and musical performances take place at the **Liverpool Empire** (⊠ Lime St., ☎ 0151/ 709–1555). For experimental and British productions, check the program at the **Everyman Theatre** (⊠ 5–9 Hope St., ☎ 0151/709–4776).

Liverpool hosts regular pop and rock concerts and stand-up comedy. One of the most appealing venues is the Art Deco **Royal Court Theatre** (⊠ Roe St., ☎ 0151/709–4321).

Nicest of the city-center pubs is the **Philharmonic** (⊠ 36 Hope St., ☎ 0151/709–1163), opposite the Philharmonic Hall, a Victorian-era extravaganza with comfortable bar rooms and over-the-top rest rooms. On the Beatles trail, many call into the **Cavern Club** (⊠ Mathew St., ☎ 0151/236–9091), without realizing that it's not the original spot— that was demolished years ago. For more nostalgia, have a drink in the adjacent **Cavern Pub** (⊠ Mathew St., ☎ 0151/236–1957) instead, in which are recorded the names of the groups and artists who played in the club between 1957 and 1973.

Outdoor Activities and Sports

HORSE RACING

Britain's most famous horse race, the **Grand National** steeplechase, has been run at Liverpool's Aintree Race Course (⊠ Ormskirk Rd., ☎ 0151/ 523–2600) almost every year since 1839. The race is held every March/April, and even if you don't attend, you'll be able to see the race on every TV in the country. Admission on race days is from £7.

SOCCER

Matches are played Saturdays (and, increasingly, Sundays and Mondays). Admission prices vary, but the cheapest seats start at about £16. The best matches to catch are the local "derby" games between major teams: the tourist offices can give you match schedules and directions to the grounds. **Liverpool** plays at Anfield (☎ 0151/260–6677). The city's second major soccer team, **Everton,** plays at Goodison Park (☎ 0151/330–2300).

Shopping

The small lobby shop at the **Walker Art Gallery** (⊠ William Brown St., ☎ 0151/478–4199) contains a high-quality selection of glassware, ceramics, and jewelry by local designers. The annual Merseycraft exhibition winners are on exclusive display in the shop every December.

The **Stanley Dock Sunday Market** (Great Howard St. and Regent Rd.) is a historic affair, with 400 stalls operating each Sunday 9–4.

THE PEAK DISTRICT: ON THE ROAD TO CHATSWORTH AND HADDON HALL

Heading southeast, away from the urban congestion of the Northwest, it's not far to the southernmost contortions of the Pennine Hills. Here, sheltered in a great natural bowl, the spa town of Buxton, about an hour from Manchester, has a surprisingly mild climate, considering its altitude: at more than 1,000 ft, it's the second-highest town in England. Buxton makes a convenient base for exploring the 540 square mi of the Peak District, Britain's oldest—and some say, most beautiful—national park. "Peak" is perhaps misleading; despite being a hilly area, it contains only long, flat-top rises that don't reach much higher than 2,000 ft. Yet touring around destinations such as Bakewell, Matlock, the grand estates of Chatsworth House and Haddon Hall, Castleton, and, finally, Edale, you'll often have to negotiate fairly perilous country roads, each of which repays the effort with enchanting views.

Outdoor activities are popular in the Peaks, particularly caving (or "potholing"), which entails underground exploration, and walking and hiking. Bring all-weather clothing and waterproof shoes. One of the major trails is the **High Peak Trail**, which runs for 17 mi from Cromford (south of Matlock Bath) to Dowlow, following the route of an old railway. For information, guidebooks, guide services, and maps, contact the Peak District National Park Office (☎ 01629/814321).

Buxton

🔳 *25 mi southeast of Manchester.*

The Romans arrived in AD 79 and named Buxton *Aquae Arnemetiae*—loosely translated as "The Waters of the Goddess of the Grove"—suggesting they considered this Derbyshire hill town to be special. The mineral springs, which emerge from 3,500 to 5,000 ft below ground at a constant 82°F, were believed to cure a variety of ailments, and in the 18th century established the town as a popular spa, a minor rival to Bath. You can still drink water from the ancient St. Anne's Well, and it's also bottled and sold throughout Britain.

Buxton's spa days have left a legacy of 18th- and 19th-century buildings, parks, and open spaces that now give the town an air of faded grandeur. A good place to start exploring is the **Crescent,** on the northwest side of the Slopes park (the town hall is on the opposite side); almost all out-of-town roads lead toward this central green. The three former hotels that make up the Georgian-era Crescent, with its arches, Doric colonnades, and 378 windows, were built in 1780 by John Carr for the fifth duke of Devonshire (of nearby Chatsworth House). The splendid ceiling of the former assembly room now looks down on the town's public library, and the thermal baths at the end of the Crescent house look out on a shopping center.

The **Devonshire Royal Hospital,** behind the Crescent, also by John Carr, was originally a stable with room for 110 of the hotel guests' horses; it was converted into a hospital in 1859. The circular area for exercising horses was covered with a massive 156-ft-wide slate-color dome and incorporated into the hospital.

To discover more about the town and its surroundings, a trip to the **Buxton Museum** is called for. Inside, there's a collection of Blue John stone, a semiprecious mineral found only in the Peak District (☞ Castleton, *below*). The museum also holds local archaeological finds, including a few pieces from Roman times, and there's a small art gallery, too. The museum is on the eastern side of The Slopes. ⊠ *Terrace Rd.*, ☎ 01298/24658. ⊠ *£1.* ☼ *Tues.–Fri. 9:30–5:30, Sat. 9:30–5, Sun. (summer only) 9:30–5.*

Pavilion Gardens (⊠ Pavilion Gardens, ☎ 01298/23114), with its ornate iron-and-glass roof, was originally a concert hall and ballroom. Erected in the 1870s, it is still a lively place, with a conservatory, several bars, a restaurant, and a cafeteria, set in 25 acres of well-kept Pavilion Gardens. It's adjacent to the Crescent and the Slopes on the west.

Buxton's Opera House (⊠ Water St., ☎ 01298/72190), built in 1903, is one of the most architecturally exuberant structures in town. Its marble bulk, bedecked with carved cupids, is even more impressive inside—so impressive it may be worth buying a ticket to a concert you might not be eager to hear (☞ Nightlife and the Arts, *below*). Otherwise, tours (£1) of the interior are conducted most Saturdays at 11 AM.

The Peak District's extraordinary geology makes itself felt close to Buxton at **Poole's Cavern,** a large limestone cave far beneath the 100 wooded acres of Buxton Country Park. Named after a legendary 15th-century robber, the cave was inhabited in prehistoric times and contains, in addition to the standard stalactites and stalagmites, the source of the River Wye, which flows through Buxton. From Buxton follow the Broad Walk through the Pavilion Gardens and continue southwest along Temple Road for about half an hour. ⊠ *Green La.*, ☎ 01298/26978. ⊠ *£3.80 including tour; Country Park and visitor center free.* ☼ *Easter–Oct., daily 10–5; closed Wed. in Apr., May, and Oct.*

Lodging

£££ ☷ **Old Hall.** The building dates from the 16th century, and although everything else has been refurbished, Mary's Bower, in the oldest part of the hotel, still retains its original ceiling moldings; the name recalls Mary, Queen of Scots, who stayed here several times between 1573 and 1582. It's a friendly, central hotel overlooking the Opera House; some of the individually styled rooms have four-poster beds. ⊠ *The Square, SK17 6BD*, ☎ *01298/22841*, ℻ *01298/72437. 38 rooms with bath. Restaurant, bar. AE, DC, MC, V.*

£££ ☷ **The Palace.** A hotel on a grand scale from the halcyon days of the
★ spa, it's set on 5 acres overlooking the town center and surrounding hills. The smart rooms are fully equipped with satellite TV, tea/coffeemakers, hair dryers, and the other usual little comforts, but what makes many of them stand out are the wonderful views. ⊠ *Palace Rd., SK17 6AG*, ☎ *01298/22001*, ℻ *01298/72131. 122 rooms with bath. Restaurant, bar, lobby lounge, pool, beauty salon, sauna, putting green, croquet, exercise room, library. AE, DC, MC, V.*

£ ☷ **Lakenham Guest House.** This large Victorian structure with a sweep-
★ ing garden has been converted into a comfortable guest house, with some attractive antique furniture and ample parking for guests. Potted plants proliferate and the tastefully decorated bedrooms all have excellent views; some have small refrigerators. ⊠ *11 Burlington Rd., SK17 9AL*, ☎ *01298/79209. 6 rooms, 5 with bath. Dining room. No credit cards.*

Nightlife and the Arts

Buxton Opera House (⊠ Water St., Buxton, ☎ 01298/72190) presents excellent theater, ballet, and jazz performances year-round.

Buxton's renowned **Festival of Music and the Arts** (⊠ Festival Office, 1 Crescent View, Hall Bank, ☎ 01298/70395), held during the second half of July and early August each year, includes opera, drama, classical concerts, jazz, recitals, and lectures, many of them at the Buxton Opera House on Water Street. The opera house also hosts an amateur drama festival during the summer.

Shopping

You'll find a wide variety of stores in Buxton, especially around Spring Gardens, the main shopping street. Try the **Cavendish Arcade** (⊠ The Crescent), built on the site of the old thermal baths, which offers a pleasing range of fashion, cosmetics, and leather-goods stores in stylish surroundings. **Ratcliffe's** (⊠ 7 Cavendish Circus, ☎ 01298/23993) specializes in fine silver cutlery. A local **market** is held in Buxton every Tuesday and Saturday.

En Route   Heading southeast from Buxton on the A6, you'll pass through the spectacular valleys of Ashwood Dale, Wyedale, and Monsal Dale before reaching Bakewell.

Bakewell

❷⁹   *12 mi southeast of Buxton.*

Bakewell, set on the winding River Wye, with narrow streets and houses built out of the local gray-brown stone, is extremely appealing. A medieval bridge crosses the river in five graceful arches, while the great age of the town is indicated by the 9th-century Saxon cross that still stands outside the parish church. Unfortunately, ceaseless traffic through the streets takes the shine off—though there is respite down on the quiet riverside paths. For a self-guided stroll around town, pick up a map and town trail from the tourist office; the walk takes just over an hour. The helpful office has a museum that explains the terrain of the Peak District, with samples of the limestone and grit stone that composes the landscape.

The only day the crowds are really merited is on market day (Monday), attended by local farmers, while a similarly popular traditional agricultural show is held in the first week of August. Bakewell is also the source of Bakewell pudding, said to have been created inadvertently when, sometime last century, a cook at the town's Rutland Arms Hotel dropped some rich cake mixture over jam tarts. Every local bakery and tearoom claims an original recipe—it's easy to spend a gustatory afternoon tasting rival puddings.

As in other parts of the Peak District, the inhabitants of Bakewell still practice the early-summer custom of "well-dressing," during which certain wells or springs are elaborately decorated or "dressed" with flowers. Although the floral designs usually incorporate biblical themes, they are just a Christian veneer over an ancient pagan celebration of the water's life-giving powers. In Bakewell, the lively ceremony is the focus of several days of festivities in June.

Dining and Lodging

£   ✕ **The Old Original Bakewell Pudding Shop.** Given the plethora of local rivals it takes a bold establishment to claim its Bakewell puddings as "original," but there's certainly nothing wrong with those served here, eaten hot with custard or cream. The oak-beam dining room also turns out commendable main courses of poached salmon, black pudding, or chicken, and it's open until 9 PM in summer. ⊠ *The Square,* ☎ *01629/812193. MC, V. Closes at 6 PM winter, 9 PM summer.*

£££–££££   ✕▥ **Fischer's.** It would be hard to discover a more relaxing and convenient base from which to visit Bakewell and Chatsworth House, either of which is just a few miles' drive away by car. The menu at this award-winning establishment, which calls itself a "restaurant with rooms," run by the friendly Fischer family, represents a range of Continental cuisines, with some fine local produce. Fish is a specialty, often served with fresh, fragrant pastas and delicately flavored sauces; duck and lamb receive similar care. There's also a bistro menu available, which offers food—including breakfast and afternoon tea—of the same high quality, at slightly lower prices. The six guest rooms are pretty, if rather small, with antique pine furniture. ⊠ *Baslow Hall, Calver Rd., Baslow, DE45 1RR,* ☎ *01246/583259,* Ⅸ *01246/583818. 6 rooms with bath. Restaurant, bar, room service. AE, DC, MC, V.*

Shopping

ELF Gems (⊠ King St., ☎ 01629/814944) is a wonderful source for jewelry and items made out of the rare Blue John stone, which is mined only in the Peak District. Edward Fisher has a passion for the stone, and, because Blue John is so brittle, he covers his handcrafted pieces with liquid crystal to protect them.

Haddon Hall

★ ⑳ *2 mi southeast of Bakewell on A6 Buxton–Matlock.*

Stately-house scholar Hugo Montgomery-Massingberd has called Haddon Hall "the *beau ideal* of the English country house," and once you see this storybook medieval manor set alongside the banks of the River Wye, you may agree with him that it's one of the most romantic houses in Britain. Unlike other trophy homes that are marble Palladian monuments to the Grand Tour, Haddon Hall remains quintessentially English in appearance. Bristling with crenellations and stepped roofs and landscaped with rose gardens, Haddon Hall seems like a medieval miniature come to life. Famed as the setting—apocryphal or not—for the elopement of Dorothy Vernon with Sir John Manners in the 16th century (the lord of the manor disapproved of his daughter's choice, so the young couple eloped one night during a banquet, and as elopement was unheard of by nobles then, this tale became a popular Victorian-era love story), the house conjures up the "When Knighthood Was in Flower" days as no other does. Constructed by generations of the Vernon family during the Middle Ages, Haddon Hall passed into the ownership of the dukes of Rutland. After they moved their county seat to nearby Belvoir Castle, time and history literally passed the house by for centuries. In the early 20th century, however, the 9th duke awoke this sleeping beauty of a castle through a superlative restoration—and a host of visitors once again discovered a magical estate. The wider world saw the hall to impressive effect in Franco Zeffirelli's recent film *Jane Eyre,* much of which was filmed on location in the neighborhood.

The house is virtually unfurnished but has some treasures, including an impressive selection of tapestries and a famous 1932 painting of the hall by Rex Whistler. This painting shows the 9th duke and his son gazing at the house from a nearby hillside vantage point. Dorothy and Sir John are buried side by side in Bakewell's parish church (☞ Bakewell, *above*). ☎ *01629/812855.* ⅏ *£5.50; parking 50p.* ☉ *Apr.–Sept., daily (except Sun. in Aug.) 11–5:45.*

Chatsworth House

★ ㉛ *4 mi northeast of Bakewell.*

The approach is through glorious parkland to Chatsworth House, ancestral home of the dukes of Devonshire and one of England's greatest country houses. A vast expanse of parkland, grazed by deer and sheep, opens before you to set off the Palladian-style elegance of "the Palace of the Peak." Originally an Elizabethan house, Chatsworth was conceived on a grand, even monumental, scale. Unfortunately, it was altered by various dukes over several generations starting in 1686, and the house's architecture now has a decidedly hodgepodge look. Death duties have taken a heavy toll on the interior grandeur, with duke after duke forced to sell off treasures to keep the place going. The house is surrounded by woods, elaborate colorful gardens, greenhouses, rock gardens, and the most famous water cascade in the kingdom—all designed by two great landscape artists, Capability Brown and, later, Joseph Paxton, an engineer as well as a brilliant gardener. Perennially popular with children, the farmyard area has milking demonstrations at 3 PM, and an adventure playground. Plan on at least half a day to explore the grounds properly; avoid going on Sunday, when the place is very crowded. A brass band plays on Sunday afternoons in July and August.

Inside, are intricate carvings, Van Dyck portraits, superb furniture, and a few fabulous rooms, including the Sculpture Gallery, the Library, and the Blue Drawing Room, upon whose walls hang two of the most famous portraits in Britain, Sir Joshua Reynolds's *Georgiana, Duchess of Devonshire, and Her Baby*, and John Singer Sargent's enormous *Acheson Sisters*. The magnificent condition of much of the furnishings and decorations—what's left of them, at any rate—is due to the current duchess's supervision of an ongoing program of repair and restoration. ✉ *Bakewell*, ☎ *01246/582204.* 🎫 *House and gardens £6.25; gardens only £3.60; farmyard and adventure playground £3; parking £1.* ☉ *House: late Mar.–late Oct., daily 11–4:30; garden: late Mar.–late Oct., daily 11–5 (from 10:30 June–Aug.); farmyard and adventure playground: late Mar.–early Oct., daily 10:30–4:30.*

Matlock

32 *8 mi south of Chatsworth, 8 mi southeast of Bakewell.*

In the heart of the Derbyshire Dales, Matlock and its near neighbor Matlock Bath are former spa towns compressed into a narrow gorge on the River Derwent. Some surviving Regency buildings in Matlock still testify to its former importance, although it's less impressive an ensemble than that presented by Buxton. The surroundings are particularly beautiful; try to catch the **Matlock River Illuminations,** a flotilla of lighted boats shimmering after dark along the still waters of the river, which take place on weekends mid-August–mid-October.

At Matlock Bath, 2 mi south of Matlock, river and valley views unfold from the curving line of buildings that makes up the village. Aside from riverside strolls, the major attraction is the cable-car ride across the River Derwent that takes visitors to the bosky **Heights of Abraham** on the crags above, with a visitor center and café. The all-inclusive ticket allows access into the adjacent country park, where there are woodland walks and nature trails, as well as a fascinating guided descent into an old lead mine, where 16th-century workers once toiled by candlelight. ✉ *Heights of Abraham, Matlock Bath,* ☎ *01629/582365.* 🎫 *£5.75.* ☉ *Cable car and visitor center Easter–Oct., daily 10–5, later in July and Aug; also on winter weekends, call for details.*

Dining and Lodging

££££ ✕🏨 **Riber Hall.** This partly Elizabethan, partly Jacobean manor-house
★ hotel is a listed historic building, perched above the town and awash with romantic resonance. The half-timber bedrooms have been decorated with antiques, flowers, oak beams, and four-poster beds, in keeping with the inn's origins; some baths have Jacuzzis. The garden is

particularly beautiful, and from the quiet terrace it's easy to imagine you've stepped back into a different age. The restaurant serves imaginative, seasonal dishes with superbly fresh ingredients, whose inspiration is drawn from modern French cuisine—expect plenty of flavor and careful attention to presentation. There's even a daily vegetarian menu. ⊠ *Riber Hall, Matlock, DE4 5JU,* ☎ *01629/582795,* FAX *01629/580475. 14 rooms with bath. Restaurant, lobby lounge, room service, tennis court. AE, DC, MC, V.*

Castleton

③③ *24 mi northwest of Matlock, 9 mi northeast of Buxton.*

The most famous manifestations of the peculiar geology of the Peak District are to be found around the attractive town of Castleton, nestled in the Hope Valley. The limestone caverns bring visitors from far and wide, which means that Castleton evinces a certain commercialization and tends to be crowded in the peak season. Aim for an earlier start to beat the crowds. The town itself has a long pedigree and was probably first established by Henry II in the mid-12th century. It was Henry II who built **Peveril Castle,** whose ruins occupy a dramatic crag above the town, from which there are superb views—from here you can clearly see a curving section of the medieval defensive earthworks still visible in the town center below. ⊠ *Market Pl.,* ☎ *01433/620613.* ⬚ *£1.75.* ☉ *Apr.–Oct., daily 10–6; Nov.–Mar., Wed.–Sun. 10–4.*

Peveril Castle is protected on its west side by a 230-ft-deep gorge formed by a collapsed cave. The entire town is riddled with such caves, and in the massive **Peak Cavern**—reputedly Derbyshire's largest natural cave—rope-making has been done on a great ropewalk for more than 400 years. The remains of a prehistoric village have been excavated here as well. ☎ *01433/620285.* ⬚ *£3.* ☉ *Apr.–Oct., daily 10–5; Nov.–Mar., weekends 10–5.*

The Castleton area has a number of other caves and mines open to the public, including some former lead mines and Blue John mines (amethystine spar; the unusual name is a local corruption of the French *bleu-jaune*). The most exciting by far is **Speedwell Cavern,** where 105 slippery steps lead down to a series of old lead-mine tunnels, blasted out by 19th-century miners. Here you transfer to a small boat for the claustrophobic quarter-mile chug through an illuminated access tunnel to the cavern itself. At this point you're 600 ft underground, in the deepest public-access cave in Britain, with views farther down to the so-called "Bottomless Pit," a water-filled cavern into which the miners used to dump their blasted limestone debris. Speedwell Cavern is at the bottom of Winnats Pass, 2 mi west of Castleton. ⊠ *Winnats Pass,* ☎ *01433/620512.* ⬚ *£5.* ☉ *Daily 9:30–5 (Nov.–Mar., closes at 4).*

Lodging

£££ 🏨 **Ye Olde Nag's Head.** With a name like this it could only be a 17th-century coaching inn; it's set right in the middle of Castleton. The small, individually run hotel is a little too chintzy-floral for its own good, but guest rooms (a few with four-posters) are certainly comfortable enough and some have views of the castle. Bar meals here are adventurous and of good value; there's also dining in the more formal restaurant. ⊠ *Castleton, Derbyshire, S30 2WH,* ☎ *01433/620248,* FAX *01433/621604. 8 rooms with bath. Restaurant, bar. AE, DC, MC, V.*

£ 🏨 **Bargate Cottage.** This cottage, at the top of Market Place opposite the church, is one of Castleton's B&B treasures. Kindly owners scatter rag dolls and teddy bears with abandon, and the cutesy oak-beam rooms have been carefully converted to incorporate shower cubicles, sinks, TVs, and tea/coffeemaking facilities. Breakfast is served communally downstairs, with mine host very much in command, dispensing fried breakfasts, bonhomie, and hiking advice. ⊠ *Market Place S30 2WG,* ☎ *01433/620201,* 𝔽𝔸𝕏 *01433/621739. 4 rooms with shower. Dining room. No credit cards. Closed Christmas wk.*

En Route   Heading northwest to Edale, the most spectacular route is over Winnats Pass, an eye-opening drive through a narrow, boulder-strewn valley. Beyond are the tops of Mam Tor (where there's a lookout point) and the hamlet of Barber Booth, soon after which you'll run into Edale.

Edale

㉞   *5 mi north of Castleton.*

At Edale, you're truly in the Peak District wilds. It's a sleepy, straggling village in the shadow of Mam Tor and Lose Hill and the moorlands of Kinder Scout (2,088 ft), set among some of the most breathtaking scenery in Derbyshire. Britain can show little wilder scenery than the sight of Kinder Scout, with its ragged edges of grit stone and its seemingly interminable leagues of heather and peat. Late summer brings a covering of reddish-purple as the heather flowers, but the time to really appreciate the somber beauties of Kinder and its neighbors is in late autumn or early winter, when the clouds hang low and every gully seems to accentuate the brooding spirit of the moor.

An extremely popular walking center, Edale is the starting point of the 250-mi **Pennine Way,** which crosses Kinder Scout in its early stages, though if you plan to attempt this seek local advice first, because bad weather can make the walk treacherous. However, there are several much shorter routes into the Edale valley, like the 8-mi route west to Hayfield, which will give you a taste of the dramatic local scenery.

In the village, the Edale **National Park Information Centre** has maps, guides, and information on all the walks in the area. There is limited accommodation in the village (all bed-and-breakfast style), but the information center can provide an up-to-date list of possibilities, or point you toward the local youth hostel. ☎ *01433/670207.* ☉ *Daily 9–1 and 2–5:30 (Nov.–Mar., closes at 5).*

The **Old Nag's Head** (☎ 01433/670291) at the top of the village has marked the official start of the Pennine Way since 1965. Call in at the Hiker's Bar, score a place by the fire, and tuck into hearty bar meals and warming hot toddies. In winter, whenever this pub is closed (two days a week), the **Ramblers' Inn,** at the other end of the village, is open.

LANCASHIRE AND THE PEAKS A TO Z

Arriving and Departing

By Bus
National Express (☎ 0990/808080) serves the region from London's Victoria Coach Station. Average travel time to Manchester or Liverpool is four hours. To reach Matlock, Bakewell, and Buxton, you can take a bus from London to Derby and change to the **TransPeak** bus service, though you might find it more convenient to travel first to Manchester (☞ Getting Around, *below*).

By Car

To reach Manchester from London, take M1 north to M6, leaving M6 at exit 21a and joining M62 east, which becomes M602 as it enters Greater Manchester. Liverpool is reached by leaving M6 at the same junction, exit 21a, and following M62 west into the city. Travel time to Manchester or Liverpool is about 3–3½ hours. Expect heavy traffic out of London on weekends to all destinations in the Northwest; construction work also often slows progress on M6.

Driving from London to the Peak District, stay on the M1 until you reach exit 29, then head west via the A617/A619/A6 to Buxton. From Manchester, take the A6 southeast via Stockport to Buxton, about an hour's drive.

By Plane

Manchester International Airport (☎ 0161/489–3000) is about 10 mi south of the city. It is northern England's main airport and serves European and other international cities as well as receiving domestic flights from all over Britain. To reach the city center, take the train that runs from the airport directly to **Piccadilly Station** (☎ 0345/484950). It has 24-hour service, with departures every 15 minutes. Travel time is 25 minutes and the cost is £2.15 (£2.25 in peak hours, before 9:30 AM). There is also a bus service that leaves every 15–30 minutes, 6 AM– 10:45 PM, with reduced service after 7 PM. It costs £2 and it takes almost an hour to reach Piccadilly Gardens. For more information about this service, call GMPTE (☞ Getting Around by Bus, *below*). A taxi from the airport to Manchester city center costs approximately £12.

By Train

InterCity West Coast serves the region from London's Euston Station (☎ 0345/484950). Direct service to Manchester and Liverpool takes approximately 2½ hours. To reach Buxton from London take the Manchester train and switch at Stockport.

Getting Around

By Bicycle

In an effort to get people out of their cars, special **Peak District National Park Hire Centres** rent out bikes of all descriptions at very reasonable rates. The service is restricted to weekends in winter and is popular in summer, so always call ahead to reserve. Information is available directly from the centers. The most accessible are Hayfield (☎ 01663/746222); Parsley Hay (☎ 01298/84493); and Middleton Top (☎ 01629/823204), or any Peak District National Park Information Centre.

By Bus

Manchester's **Chorlton Street Bus Station** (☎ 0990/808080) is the departure point for regional and long-distance National Express coaches. For information on all Greater Manchester buses, call the **GMPTE** information line (☎ 0161/228–7811). There's also a tram system—**the Metrolink** (☎ 0161/205–2000)—running through Manchester and its surroundings, with services daily 7:30 AM–11:30 PM (until 10:30 PM Sun.). It's mostly of use to commuters from the outlying suburbs, but you might want to ride the tram from its terminus at Piccadilly Station: either north up High Street, past the Arndale Shopping Centre to Victoria Station; or south, down Mosley Street, past the Crowne Plaza Midland Hotel, to the G-Mex Centre.

In Liverpool, regional and long-distance National Express coaches use the **Norton Street Coach Station** (☎ 0990/808080). For the latest timetable information for local bus, train, and ferry services in Liverpool, call the **Mersey Travel Line** (☎ 0151/236–7676), or visit one of the information centers located at the Merseyside Welcome Centre (Clayton Sq.), the Ferries Centre (Pier Head), Williamson Square, or Paradise Street Bus Station.

Bus R1 runs directly to **Buxton** from Manchester's Chorlton Street Bus station every two hours during the day (☎ 0161/228–7811 information). In addition, the **TransPeak** service between Manchester and Derby calls at all major Peak District destinations, with departures every two hours from Manchester's Chorlton Street Bus Station: a **Wayfarer** ticket, £5.50 or weekend ticket £9, allows unlimited travel on the service for 24 hours. For local bus information in the Buxton and Peak District area, call **Derbyshire Bus Line** (☎ 01332/292200). The **Peak District Timetable** (60p) covers all local public transportation services and is available from tourist offices in the area.

By Car

Roads within the region are generally very good, although traffic can get bogged down on M6, especially on holiday weekends. In both Manchester and Liverpool, you're advised to sightsee on foot—leave your car at your hotel to avoid parking problems in the city centers. In the Peak District, park in signposted parking lots whenever possible and expect heavy summer traffic. In winter, keep an ear out for the weather forecast; moorland roads can quickly become impassable.

By Train

There are trains between **Manchester**'s Piccadilly Station and **Liverpool**'s Lime Street every half hour during the day; the trip takes approximately 50 minutes. Local service—one train an hour—from Manchester to **Buxton** takes one hour. In all instances, call **National Rail Enquiries** (☎ 0345/484950) for timetable information.

Contacts and Resources

Car Rentals

Manchester: Avis (⌧ 1 Ducie St., ☎ 0161/236–6716; 0161/436–2020 airport). **Budget Rent-a-Car** (⌧ 660 Chester Rd., Old Trafford, ☎ 0161/877–5555; 0161/499–3042 airport). **Europcar Ltd.** (⌧ York St., Piccadilly Plaza, ☎ 0161/832–4114; 0161/436–2200 airport). **Hertz** (⌧ 31 Aytoun St., ☎ 0161/236–2747; 0161/437–8208 airport).

Emergencies

Police, fire, ambulance (☎ 999).

Guided Tours

Tourist information centers can offer advice about walking trails that take historically minded visitors through the less-frequented parts of the main cities to see remnants of their fascinating industrial heritage. In addition, tourist offices in Manchester and Liverpool can book visitors on short city coach tours that cover all the main sights.

Blue Badge Guides in Manchester offers an exciting program of tours in and around the city, including daily one-hour walking tours of the city center. Information and tickets are available from the Visitor Information Centre (☞ Visitor Information, *below*).

The **Liverpool Heritage Walk** is a self-guided 7½-mi walk through Liverpool city center, following 75 metal markers that point out sights of historic and cultural interest. An accompanying guidebook (£3.50) is available from either of the Liverpool Tourist Information centers.

Cavern City Tours (⌧ Mathew St., Liverpool, ☎ 0151/236–9091) offers a Beatles Magical Mystery Tour of Liverpool, departing from

Clayton Square daily at 2:30. The two-hour bus tour, which costs £8.50, runs past John Lennon's childhood home, local schools attended by the Beatles, and other significant mop-top landmarks.

Travel Agencies

American Express (✉ 54 Lord St., Liverpool, ☎ 0151/708–9202; ✉ 10–12 St. Mary's Gate, Manchester, ☎ 0161/833–0121). **Thomas Cook** (✉ 55 Lord St., Liverpool, ☎ 0151/236–1951; ✉ 23 Market St., Manchester, ☎ 0161/833–1110).

Visitor Information

General information about the region is available from the **North West Tourist Board** (✉ Swan House, Swan Meadow Rd., Wigan Pier, Wigan WN3 5BB, ☎ 01942/821222). Also contact the **Peak District National Park** head office (✉ Baslow Rd., Bakewell, Derbyshire DE45 1AE, ☎ 01629/814321).

Bakewell (✉ Old Market Hall, Bridge St., Derbyshire DE4 1DS, ☎ 01629/813227). **Buxton** (✉ The Crescent, Derbyshire SK17 6BQ, ☎ 01298/25106). **Liverpool** (✉ Merseyside Welcome Centre, Clayton Square Shopping Centre, L1 1QR, ☎ 0151/708–8838; ✉ Atlantic Pavilion, Albert Dock, L3 4AE, ☎ 0151/708–8838). **Manchester** (✉ Town Hall Extension, Lloyd St., M60 2LA, ☎ 0161/234–3157; ✉ International Arrivals Hall, Manchester Airport, ☎ 0161/436–3344). **Matlock** (✉ The Pavilion, Matlock Bath, DE4 3NR, ☎ 01629/55082).

13 The Lake District

Windermere, Grasmere, Kendal, Keswick

"*Let nature be your teacher . . .*"
Wordsworth's ideal comes true in this fabled region, one of the most charming reservoirs of calm in the British Isles. The Lake District is a vast natural park, a contour map come to life. Some malicious statisticians allot to it about 250 rainy days a year, but when the sun breaks through and the surfaces of the lakes smile benignly, it is an away-from-it-all place to remember. Follow in the footsteps of Coleridge, Ruskin, and Wordsworth; everywhere you'll find specific locations that inspired some of their great poems and thoughts.

Updated by
Jules Brown

THE POETS WORDSWORTH AND COLERIDGE, and other English men and women of letters, found the Lake District an inspiring setting for their work—and fashion, and thousands of visitors, have followed ever since. The lakeland district, created in the 1970s as a national park from parts of the old counties of Cumberland, Westmorland, and Lancashire, combines so much that is magnificent in mountain, lake, and dales that new and entrancing vistas open out at each corner of the road. Higher mountains there most certainly are in Britain, but none that are finer in outline or that give a greater impression of majesty; deeper and bluer lakes can be found, but none that fit so readily into the surrounding scene.

Perhaps it is only natural that an area so blessed with natural beauty should have become linked with so many prominent figures in English literature. It may have all started on April 15, 1802, when William Wordsworth and his sister Dorothy were walking in the woods of Gowbarrow Park just above Aira Force, and Dorothy happened to remark that she had never seen "daffodils so beautiful." Two years later Wordsworth was inspired by his sister's words to write one of the best-known lyric poems in English, "I Wandered Lonely as a Cloud." In turn, many of the English romantic poets also came to the region and were inspired by its beauty. In addition to Wordsworth, other literary figures who made their homes in the region include Samuel Taylor Coleridge, Thomas De Quincey, Robert Southey, John Ruskin, Matthew Arnold, and later, Hugh Walpole, and the children's writers Arthur Ransome and Beatrix Potter, who set her beloved stories of Squirrel Nutkin and Mrs. Tiggy-Winkle in the hills and dales of this region.

The Lake District measures roughly 35 square mi; it can be crossed by car in about an hour. Its mountains are not high by international standards—Scafell Pike, England's highest peak, is only 3,210 ft above sea level—but they are very tricky and the weather even more so. In the spring, many of the higher summits remain snowcapped long after the weather below has turned mild. The Lake District can be one of Britain's most charming reservoirs of calm. Unfortunately, its calm is shattered in high season, when the district becomes far too popular for its own good. A little lakeside town, however appealing it may otherwise be, loses its charm when its narrow streets are clogged with tour buses. Similarly, the walks and hiking trails that crisscross the region seem very much less inviting when you find yourself sharing them with a crowd that churns the grass into a muddy quagmire. With a bit of effort you will always be able to escape the crowds, since the Lake District is walking country par excellence. Off-season visits here can be a real treat. All those little inns and bed-and-breakfasts that turn away crowds in summer are desperate for business the rest of the year (and their rates drop accordingly). It is not an easy task to avail oneself of a succession of sunny days in the Lake District, but when the sun descends upon that vast natural reserve, and the surfaces of the lakes smile benignly, it is truly a place to remember.

Pleasures and Pastimes

Dining

The region of Cumbria, which encompasses the Lake District, is noted for its good country food. Dishes center on the abundant local supply of lamb, beef, game, and fish, especially salmon, and river and lake trout hooked from the district's freshwater streams and lakes. Cumberland sausage, a thick, meaty pork sausage, is another regional specialty. Look out, too, for locally baked bread, cake, pastries, gingerbread, and scones.

CATEGORY	COST*
££££	over £40
£££	£25–£40
££	£15–£25
£	under £15

per person, including first course, main course, dessert, and VAT; excluding drinks

Festivals and Folk Sports

The Lake District hosts some of Britain's most unusual country festivals, featuring traditional music, sports, and entertainment. Major festivals are the Cockermouth and Keswick carnivals (June), Ambleside Rushbearing and Sports (July), Grasmere Rushbearing and Sports, and Kendal Folk Festival (August). Folk sports—often the highlights at these local shows—include Cumberland and Westmorland wrestling, a variety of traditional English wrestling in which the opponents must maintain a grip around each other's body. Fell (cross-country) running is also popular in these parts, with the peaks themselves often forming part of the race route. A calendar of events is available at tourist information centers.

Lodging

If the front hall has a row of muddy boots, you'll know you've made the right choice for a hostelry in the Lake District. The best of these hotels have a marvelous atmosphere in which people eat hugely and loll about in front of roaring fires in the evenings, sharing an almost religious dedication to the mountains. You'll find everything from small country inns to grand lakeside hotels, though the mainstay of the region's accommodations is the local bed-and-breakfast. These come in every shape and size, from the house on Main Street renting out one room to farmhouses with an entire wing to spare. Most country hotels and B&Bs gladly cater to hikers and climbers and can provide you with on-the-spot information and advice. There's also a great camaraderie among walkers in the Lake District's network of youth hostels, which are in fact open to anyone with a membership card from their home country's hostel association. You must book well in advance in summer, particularly for the most popular hostels in Ambleside, Grasmere, Elterwater, Coniston, and Keswick; local tourist information centers have information. In winter many places close for a month or two, so be sure to confirm plans by phone.

CATEGORY	COST
££££	over £150
£££	£80–£150
££	£60–£80
£	under £60

All prices are for two people sharing a double room, including service, breakfast, and VAT.

Walking

The Lake District is undeniably beautiful, and to see it at its best it's necessary to get out of the car and walk through at least part of the region. There's enough variation in the area to suit all tastes, from gentle rambles in the vicinity of the most popular towns and villages to full-scale hikes and climbs up some of England's most impressive peaks. Almost every hamlet, village, and town provides scores of walking opportunities. Information boards are posted at car parks throughout the region pointing out the possibilities. For tougher hikes, the famous Old Man of Coniston, the Langdale Pikes, Scafell Pike, and Helvellyn are also all accessible, though for these you'll need a certain amount of walking experience and a great deal of energy. The longest trail, the Cumbria Way (70 mi), crosses the whole of the Lake District, starting at the market town of Ulverston and finishing at Carlisle. Guidebooks to this and other lakeland walks are available in bookstores throughout the region.

For short, local walks it's always best to consult the tourist information centers: those at Ambleside, Cockermouth, Grasmere, Kendal, Keswick, and Windermere can provide maps and experienced advice. The other main sources of information are the various Lake District National Park information centers, whose head office is at Brockhole, near Windermere. If you're sufficiently experienced and want to climb the higher and harder peaks, then you'll probably want to hook up with a climbing organization, of which there are several in the region—consult any tourist office (☞ Contacts and Resources *in* Lake District A to Z, *below*).

Exploring the Lake District

The Lake District is in the northwest of England, between the industrial belt of Liverpool, Manchester, and Leeds, and the Scottish border. The entire region is contained within the county of Cumbria. The major gateway from the south is Kendal. From the north, the gateway is Penrith. Both are on the M6 motorway.

The Lake District National Park breaks into two reasonably distinct sections. The southern lakes and valleys contain the most popular destinations in the entire park, incorporating the largest body of water, Windermere, as well as most of what are considered the quintessential lakeland towns and villages—Kendal, Bowness, Ambleside, Grasmere, Elterwater, Coniston, and Hawkshead. To the north, the landscape opens out across the bleaker fells to reveal challenging (and spectacular) walking country. Here, in the northern lakes, south of Keswick and Cockermouth, you have the best chance to get away from the crowds and soak up the lakeland experience.

Numbers in the text correspond to numbers in the margin and on the Lake District map.

Great Itineraries

You could spend a lifetime tramping the hills, valleys, and fells of the Lake District, or, in three days, you could drive through virtually every town, village, and hamlet mentioned in this chapter. The key is not to try to see or do too much in too short a time. Instead, pick one area—the southern lakes, for example—and spend some time walking in the delightful surroundings, taking a boat out on the water, relaxing in the inns. With five days, you would have the opportunity to stay the night in settlements in both southern and northern lakeland. If you are traveling by public transportation (scarce at the best of times, much reduced in winter), many places will be off-limits entirely.

IF YOU HAVE 3 DAYS

Three days is scarcely adequate to tour the Lake District. Nonetheless, if you must tour both south and north lakes together, start in **Kendal** ①, and after you've looked around the market town, move on to 🏛 **Windermere** ②, where you spend the first night. You'll have time to take a boat trip on the lake that afternoon up to pretty **Ambleside** ⑤. Next day, cross Lake Windermere by ferry, and drive through **Hawkshead** ⑫ and **Coniston** ⑩ to rural **Elterwater** ⑨, where you can have lunch in one of the fine walkers' inns thereabouts. The afternoon is spent in **Grasmere** ⑧, touring the various destinations associated with William Wordsworth— such as **Rydal Mount** ⑥ and **Dove Cottage** ⑦. Your second night is in 🏛 **Keswick** ⑱, and on the third day, you can loop around Derwentwater through the Borrowdale Valley and isolated **Seatoller** ⑲ to **Cockermouth** ⑳, Wordsworth's birthplace. From there it's an easy drive east to the market town of **Penrith** ⑭ and the M6 motorway (or north to Carlisle).

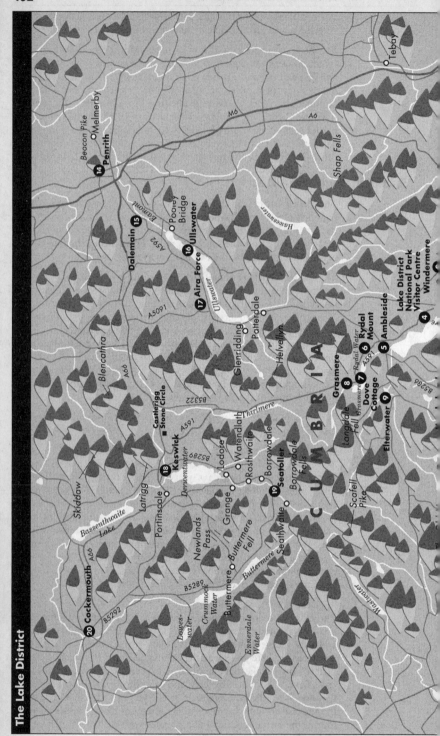

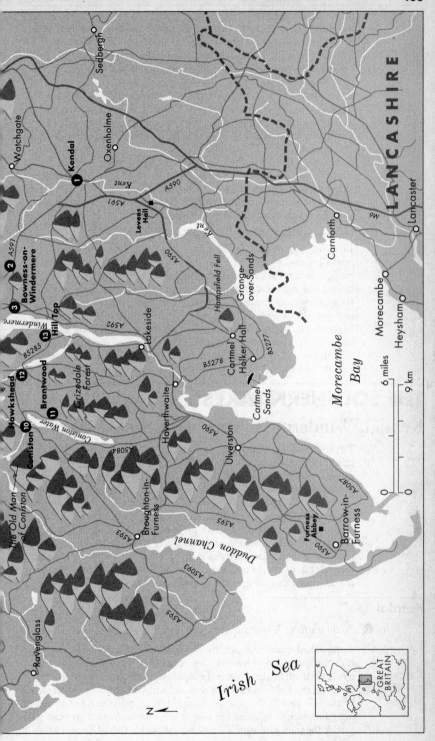

Kendal ① again marks the starting point, followed by a drive to ⊞ **Windermere** ② and a cruise on the lake that afternoon up to **Ambleside** ⑤. The next morning you can mosey around the shops and museums in **Bowness-on-Windermere** ③ before venturing on to Brockhole and the **Lake District National Park Visitor Centre** ④. In the afternoon, cross Lake Windermere by ferry, stopping in **Hawkshead** ⑫ and **Coniston** ⑩, before ending up at ⊞ **Elterwater** ⑨. This is a splendid place to spend the night in peaceful rural surroundings, and it gives you the opportunity to take in one of the local walks the next morning. Lunch and that night can be in ⊞ **Grasmere** ⑧, just a short distance away, giving you plenty of opportunity to explore that lovely village and its environs. From Grasmere, ⊞ **Keswick** ⑱ is the next obvious overnight stop, allowing you to make a day trip into the gorgeous Borrowdale Valley and perhaps take a boat trip on Derwentwater. On the final day, you can see **Cockermouth** ⑳ and **Penrith** ⑭.

When to Tour the Lake District

June, July, and August hold the best guarantees of fine weather (and host all the major festivals), but you will be sharing the roads, hotels, trails, and lakes with thousands of other visitors. If you come at this time, book accommodations well in advance, turn up early at popular museums and attractions, and expect to have to work to find parking space—or indeed, any space of any kind. April/May and September/October are more clement visiting seasons. Later and earlier in the year than this there will be more space and freedom, but you will find many attractions closed and snow on high ground, precluding any serious walking.

THE SOUTHERN LAKES

Kendal, Windermere, Grasmere, and Coniston

The southern lakes offer a diverse set of attractions, ranging from the small resort towns ranged around Windermere, England's largest lake, to hideaway valleys, rugged walking centers, and monuments rich in literary associations. What's more, it's the easiest part of the Lake District to reach, with Kendal—the largest town—just a short distance from the M6 motorway. An obvious route from Kendal takes in Windermere—the natural touring center for this whole area—before moving north through Ambleside and Rydal Water to Grasmere. Some of the loveliest of all lakeland scenery is to be found by then turning south, through Elterwater, Hawkshead, and Coniston, from which it's a simple drive south to the coast or east back to Windermere.

Kendal

❶ *70 mi north of Manchester.*

Approached from the south, the natural gateway to the Lake District is the ancient town of Kendal. One of the most important textile centers in northern England before the industrial revolution, it's an attractive place, cut through by a bubbling river and with gray stone houses framed by the hills behind. So close are these hills that, with the aid of a walking guide picked up from the tourist information center, you can be astride the tops within an hour. Be sure to pack a slab of Kendal Mintcake, the renowned local peppermint candy, which all British walkers and climbers swear by to provide them with energy when the going gets tough. It's on sale in every gift shop in town.

In town, once you're away from the busy main road, you'll discover quiet, narrow, winding streets—known locally as "ginnels"—and charming courtyards, many dating from medieval times. Indeed, there's been a **market** (⊠ Market Place off Stricklandgate) held here since 1189. The old market hall has now been converted into an indoor shopping center, though outdoor stalls still do business here every Wednesday and Saturday.

One of the Lake District's finest museums is housed in the 18th-century **Abbot Hall,** which is on the River Kent, adjacent to the parish church. Built as a private house in 1759, the building was first opened to the public in 1962 and in 1973 was declared Britain's first ever Museum of the Year. It was a judicious award, for the **Museum of Lakeland Life and Industry,** housed in the former stable block, offers fascinating exhibits on blacksmithing, wheelwrighting, farming, weaving, printing, local architecture and interiors, and regional customs. A separate room is devoted to the curious life of Arthur Ransome, author of the Swallows and Amazons series of children's books (☞ Coniston, *below*). In the main building is the **Art Gallery,** with works by Ruskin and 18th-century portrait painter George Romney, who worked (and died) in Kendal. There's a store, too, selling high-quality woven goods, tiles, ceramics, and glass, and an excellent café. ⊠ *Kirkland,* ☎ *01539/ 722464.* 🎟 *Museum and gallery £3.50, museum only £2.50.* ⊙ *Apr.– Oct., daily 10:30–5; Nov.–Mar., daily 10:30–4.*

The **Kendal Museum** of natural history and archaeology was first founded in 1796, moving into a former wool warehouse in 1913. It details splendidly the flora and fauna of the Lake District, including displays on Alfred Wainwright, the region's most avid chronicler of countryside matters, who died in 1991. His multivolume, handwritten Lake District walking guides are famous the world over; you'll see them in every local book and gift shop. The museum is at the northern end of town, close to the train station. ⊠ *Station Rd.,* ☎ *01539/ 721374.* 🎟 *£2.50, £1 to Abbot Hall.* ⊙ *Apr.–Oct., daily 10:30–5; Nov.–Mar., daily 10:30–4.*

Dining and Lodging

££ ✕ **The Moon.** More like a bistro than a restaurant, the Moon has a good
★ local reputation, won with quality homemade dishes on a menu that changes at least monthly. There's always a strong selection of vegetarian dishes, and the cooking can be adventurous, using Mediterranean and Asian flourishes at times. ⊠ *129 Highgate,* ☎ *01539/729254. MC, V. Closed Mon. in winter. No lunch.*

£ ✕ **Waterside Café.** In summer, grab one of the outdoor picnic tables, order from the healthy whole-food menu—soups, bakes, and stews are the mainstay—and eat overlooking Kendal's tranquil river. Dinner is served on Friday nights, although for the full lakeland experience, inquire about rooms in their inexpensive guest house. ⊠ *Waterside,* ☎ *01539/729743. No credit cards. Closes at 4:30; and closed Sun. in winter.*

£ ✕🏠 **Punch Bowl Inn.** Hidden along a country road in the hamlet of Crosthwaite, 5 mi west of Kendal, the Punch Bowl—formerly a 16th-century coaching inn—delights with its inspired food and comfortable rooms. In a series of cozy, oak-beam dining rooms, assured Modern British menus are delivered with panache: fresh fish, local lamb, warming soups, and rich desserts all hit the spot. There are just three rooms, each equipped with a four-poster bed; make sure you book well in advance. ⊠ *Crosthwaite, near Kendal, LA8 8HR, off A5074,* ☎ *015395/ 68237,* 🖷 *015395/68875. 3 rooms with bath. Restaurant. MC, V.*

£ 🏠 **Holmfield.** Set in its own grounds, 10 minutes' walk from the center of Kendal, this fine no-smoking establishment in an Edwardian house treats its guests well. The public rooms have open fireplaces, there's a heated outdoor pool (summer only), and advice is freely offered on local walks. Each of the guest rooms has its own bathroom, so privacy is ensured—and one of the rooms boasts a poster bed.✉ *41 Kendal Green, LA9 5PP,* ☏ 𝔽𝔸𝕏 *01539/720790. 3 rooms with bath. Pool. No credit cards. Closed Christmas wk and 1 month during winter.*

Nightlife and the Arts

The **Brewery Arts Centre** is a converted brewery that holds an art gallery, a theater, a theater workshop, and a cinema. It also has an excellent coffee bar, a real-ale bar, and a health-food café open for lunch. In November, the annual **Kendal Jazz and Blues Festival** is based at the center. ✉ *Highgate,* ☏ *01539/725133.* ▦ *Free, except for special exhibitions.* ◷ *Mon.–Sat. 9 AM–11 PM.*

Shopping

Kendal has its most interesting stores tucked away in the quiet lanes and courtyards around Market Place, Finkle Street, and Stramongate. **Henry Roberts Bookshop** (✉ 7 Stramongate, ☏ 01539/720425), in Kendal's oldest house (a 16th-century cottage), has a superb selection of regional books. The **Kentdale Rambler** (✉ 34 Market Pl., ☏ 01539/ 729188) is the best local store for walking boots and equipment, maps, and guides (including Wainwright's illustrated guides). Four miles north of Kendal along the A591, **Peter Hall & Son** (✉ Danes Rd., Staveley, ☏ 01539/821633) is a woodcraft workshop selling ornamental bowls and other attractive gifts, all made from local woods.

OFF THE
BEATEN PATH

LEVENS HALL – This 16th-century house, built by James Bellingham, is famous for its topiary garden, laid out in 1694 and probably the most distinctive in the world. With yew and box hedges cut into amazing coronet-and chess-piece-like shapes, it seems an hallucinatory vision from *Alice's Adventures in Wonderland.* The house itself is notable for its ornate plasterwork, oak paneling, and the leather-covered walls of the dining room. Levens Hall is just 4 mi south of Kendal, and local buses run here from the town. ✉ *Levens Park, Levens,* ☏ *015395/60321.* ▦ *House and gardens £5, gardens only £3.70.* ◷ *Easter–Sept., Sun.–Thurs. 11–5.*

Windermere

★ ❷ *10 mi northwest of Kendal.*

For a natural touring base for the southern half of the Lake District, you don't need to look much farther than Windermere. When the railroad was extended here from Kendal in 1847, local officials named the new station after the lake in order to cash in on Windermere's reputation, already well established thanks to Wordsworth and the romantic poets. The town flourished, despite being a mile or so from the water, and such was the lake's popularity as a Victorian resort that the development eventually spread to envelop the old lakeside village of ❸ **Bowness-on-Windermere** as well. Of the two settlements, Bowness is the more attractive, but they are so close it matters little where you stay. Bus W1/599, leaving every 20 minutes in summer (hourly the rest of the year) from outside the Windermere train station, links the two.

The New Hall Inn, dating from 1612, is better known as the **Hole in t' Wall** (✉ Fallbarrow Rd., Bowness-on-Windermere), an atmospheric pub whose most famous landlord was Thomas Longmire, a 19th-century Cumbrian wrestler who won no fewer than 174 championship belts. Charles Dickens stayed at the inn in 1857 and described Longmire as a "quiet-looking giant." Today, you can sample traditional Cumbrian ales and pub lunches in authentic 19th-century surroundings, complete with slate floors and a flagstone courtyard.

The **Windermere Steamboat Museum** exhibits a remarkable collection of steam- and motor-powered yachts and launches. The *Dolly,* built around 1850, is one of the two oldest mechanically powered boats in the world. She was raised from the bottom of Ullswater in 1962, having lain there for 70 years. Among the many vessels on view are also Beatrix Potter's rowing boat and Arthur Ransome's sailing dinghy. ⊠ *Rayrigg Rd., Bowness-on-Windermere,* ☎ *015394/45565.* 🖅 *£2.90.* 🕙 *Easter–Oct., daily 10–5.*

Children (and not a few adults) might appreciate **The World of Beatrix Potter,** a three-dimensional presentation of some of her most famous characters, alongside videos and films of her stories. There are Beatrix Potter souvenirs here, and a tearoom, though frankly there's less commercialism in Potter's former home at Hill Top, Near Sawrey (☞ Hawkshead, *below*). ⊠ *The Old Laundry, Crag Brow, Bowness-on-Windermere,* ☎ *015394/88444.* 🖅 *£2.99.* 🕙 *Easter–Sept., daily 10–6:30; Oct.–Easter, daily 10–4; closed 2 wks in Jan.*

There are no sights in Windermere or Bowness to compete with that of **Lake Windermere** itself. At 11 mi long, 1½ mi wide, and 200 ft deep, it fills a rocky gorge between steep, thickly wooded hills. The waters here make for superb fishing, especially for char, a rare kind of reddish lake trout. During the summer, the lake is alive with all kinds of boats, and a trip on the water—particularly the round-trip from Bowness to Ambleside or down to Lakeside (☞ Getting Around *in* Lake District A to Z, *below*)—is a wonderful way to spend a few summer hours. For those who want to stick to dry land, head along the Patterdale Road (A592) to find the gardens of the Lakeland Horticultural Society at **Cheshire Home**; another noted garden can be found at **Matson Ground House,** reached via the Crook road (B5284). Both are open in summer; for information, contact the town tourist office.

Although the lake's marinas and piers have some charm, you can bypass the busier stretches of shoreline (and in summer they can be packed solid) by walking beyond the boathouses. Here, from among the pine trees, is a fine view across the lake. The car ferry (which also carries pedestrians) crosses the water at this point to reach Far Sawrey and the road to Hawkshead; the crossing takes just a few minutes. 🖅 *£1.60 cars, 30p foot passengers.* 🕙 *Ferries every 20 mins Mon.–Sat. 6:50 AM–9:50 PM, Sun. 9:10 AM–9:50 PM; winter until 8:50 PM.*

OFF THE BEATEN PATH

ORREST HEAD – For a memorable view of Lake Windermere—at the cost of a rigorous climb—follow signs near the Windermere Hotel (across from the train station) to Orrest Head. These will guide you to a rough, uphill track. Eventually you will see a stile on your right; climb over it and continue up the path to a rocky little summit where you can sit on a bench and enjoy a breathtaking panorama of the mountains and lake. The walk back is only a mile but takes most people at least an hour.

Dining and Lodging

££ ★ ✗ **Porthole Eating House.** In an intimate 18th-century house in the center of Bowness, the small restaurant has an Italian menu featuring homemade pasta and excellent meat and fish dishes, including stuffed duck, fresh salmon, and (when available) Windermere char. Nice touches include opera recordings played as you eat, good homemade bread, and petits fours served with coffee. In winter, a large open fire adds to the ambience. ⊠ *3 Ash St., Bowness-on-Windermere,* ☎ *015394/42793. AE, DC, MC, V. Closed Tues. and mid-Dec.–late Feb. No lunch Sat.*

££ ✕ **Roger's.** This is a centrally located restaurant, small and darkly dec-
orated, but lit with candles and boasting a menu that contains the best
French food in the region. There's a good selection of cheeses, some
very rich desserts, and a short but interesting wine list that covers the
New World as well as France. ✉ *4 High St.,* ☎ *015394/44954. AE,
DC, MC, V. Closed Sun. and 1 wk in Jan. No lunch.*

££££ ✕⊞ **Miller Howe.** This small, white Edwardian hotel with an inter-
★   national reputation for comfort and cuisine has views across Windermere to the Langdale Pikes. Every attention has been given to the
interior decor, which includes fine antiques and paintings. The lounge
has especially comfy chairs, and a conservatory, where afternoon tea
is served, overlooks the lake. The bedrooms have exceptional individual
style, and fresh and dried flowers are everywhere. The outstanding restaurant, masterminded by John Tovey, renowned for his experimental, nearly
theatrical take on British cuisine; try his Lakeland ham in a spiced peach
sauce, sirloin in onion marmalade, or choice of seven dessert puddings
and syllabubs. Reservations are essential. ✉ *Rayrigg Rd., Bowness-
on-Windermere LA23 1EY,* ☎ *015394/42536,* ℻ *015394/45664. 13
rooms with bath. Room rate includes dinner. Restaurant. AE, DC, MC,
V. Closed Dec.–Feb.*

£££ ⊞ **Langdale Chase.** Built in the 19th century and tastefully refurbished, this estate has an atmosphere of grandeur evoked by the baronial entrance hall, Old Master paintings, and oak-panel lounge—but
there's genuine comfort here too, with a pleasing conservatory and terrace, and views of Lake Windermere from many of the rooms. Outside, 5 acres of landscaped gardens are ideal for a summer afternoon
stroll. The hotel is halfway between Windermere and Ambleside, and
it makes an excellent, relaxed base for local touring. There are reasonable
dinner, bed, and breakfast rates. ✉ *Windermere, LA23 1LW, near the
A591,* ☎ *015394/32201,* ℻ *015394/32604. 30 rooms with bath or
shower, 7 in separate lodges. Restaurant, bar, lake, miniature golf, tennis court, croquet. AE, DC, MC, V.*

££ ⊞ **Mortal Man.** This converted 17th-century inn lies in an isolated valley 3 mi north of Windermere, well away from the bustle of the town;
there are magnificent views all around and superb fell walking available right from the front door. Fitting the image of a lakeland inn, it
has a log fire crackling away in winter and a cozy bar. Guest rooms
are fairly simple but pleasantly decorated, and there's a relaxing atmosphere to the place. ✉ *Troutbeck LA23 1PL,* ☎ *015394/33193,* ℻
*015394/31261. 12 rooms with bath. Restaurant, bar. No credit cards.
Closed mid-Nov.–mid-Feb.*

£ ⊞ **Oakbank Hotel.** Right in the center of Bowness, the very friendly
hillside Oakbank provides smart, well-equipped rooms (complete with
TV and tea-making facilities), some with fine views over the lake, and
all tastefully decorated in pale colors. The breakfast room overlooks
town and lake, and you're very near Bowness's restaurants. ✉ *Helm
Rd., Bowness-on-Windermere LA23 3BU,* ☎ *015394/43386. 11 rooms
with shower. Breakfast room. MC, V.*

Outdoor Activities and Sports

At **Windermere Lake Holidays Afloat** (✉ Gilly's Landing, Glebe Rd.,
Bowness-on-Windermere, ☎ 015394/43415) you can rent every kind
of boat, from small sailboats to large cabin cruisers.

Shopping

The best selection of shops is at the Bowness end of Windermere, on
Lake Road and around Queen's Square: clothing stores, crafts shops,
and souvenir stores of all kinds. The **Horn Shop** (✉ Crag Brow, ☎
015394/44519) is one of the last British firms to practice the craft of
horn carving; its craftsmen make a remarkable variety of goods, in-

cluding jewelry, utensils, mugs, and walking sticks with elaborately carved handles. At **Lakeland Jewellers** (⊠ Crag Brow, ☎ 015394/42992), the local experts set semiprecious stones in necklaces and brooches. The **Lakeland Sheepskin Centre** (⊠ Lake Rd., ☎ 015394/44466), which also has branches in Ambleside and Keswick, offers moderately priced leather and sheepskin goods.

Lake District National Park Visitor Centre

④ *At Brockhole, 3 mi northwest of Windermere.*

A magnificent lakeside mansion with terraced gardens sloping down to the water houses the official Lake District National Park Visitor Centre at Brockhole. In addition to tourist information, the center offers a fine range of exhibitions about the Lake District, including useful interpretative displays about the local ecology, flora, and fauna. The gardens are at their best in the spring, when floods of daffodils cover the lawns and the azaleas burst into bloom. Park activities include lectures, guided walks, and demonstrations of fascinating, traditional lakeland crafts like dry-stone-wall building. There's also a well-stocked bookstore—just the place to pick up hiking guides and maps—and a café-restaurant. ⊠ *Ambleside Rd., near Windermere, ☎ 015394/46601.* ☒ *Free; parking £2 per car.* ۞ *Easter–late Oct., daily 10–4.*

You can reach the Lake District National Park Visitor Centre by Bus 555/556 from the Windermere train station. It's also accessible by ferry from Ambleside; the service is operated by **Windermere Lake Cruises** (☎ 015394/43360).

Ambleside

⑤ *4 mi north of Brockhole.*

Unlike Kendal and Windermere, Ambleside seems almost part of the hills and fells. Its buildings, mainly of local stone and many built in that local traditional style that forgoes the use of mortar in the outer walls, blend perfectly into their setting. The small town sits at the head of Lake Windermere, making it a popular center for Lake District excursions. The town suffers terribly from tourist overcrowding in high season; Wednesdays, when the local market takes place, are particularly busy. Nonetheless, there are many fine walks in the vicinity, such as local routes north to Rydal Mount or southeast over Wansfell to Troutbeck, either of which will take up to half a day, there and back. Ferries from Bowness-on-Windermere dock down at Ambleside's harbor, called Waterhead, where you can also rent rowboats for an hour or two.

★ **Bridge House,** a tiny and stunningly picturesque 17th-century cottage perched on an arched stone bridge spans white-water Stock Ghyll. The building houses a National Trust shop and information center. ⊠ *Rydal Rd., ☎ 015394/35599.* ☒ *Free.* ۞ *Easter–Nov., daily 10–5.*

Dining and Lodging

££ ✕ **Glass House.** This exciting conversion of an old water mill, adjacent to Adrian Sankey's Ambleside glassworks, switches from a café by day to a thoroughly modern restaurant by night. The bold, open-plan, plate-glass surroundings are matched by invention in the kitchen, whose seasonally changing menu features the fashionable styles of panfrying and char-grilling in many of its French- and Mediterranean-inspired dishes. Hip waiters keep the service moving briskly and foster an atmosphere a world away from many stuffy Lake District restaurants. ⊠ *Rydal Rd., ☎ 015394/32137. Reservations essential. MC, V. Mon. during Nov.–Easter.*

£ ▣ **3 Cambridge Villas.** Ambleside abounds in inexpensive B&Bs, but you'd be hard pushed to find a more welcoming spot than this—a lofty Victorian house right in the center, with hosts who know a thing or two about local walks. As with all similar establishments, space is at a premium, but the rooms are charmingly decorated, there's a spacious lounge with plenty of books, and a good breakfast is offered.⊠ *Church St.LA22 9DL,* ☎ *015394/32307. 8 rooms, 4 with shower. Dining room. No credit cards. Closed Dec.–Jan.*

Rydal Mount

❻ *1 mi northwest of Ambleside.*

If there's one poet associated with the Lake District, it is William Wordsworth, who made his home at Rydal Mount from 1813 until his death 37 years later. Wordsworth and his family moved to these grand surroundings when he was nearing the height of his career, and his descendants still live here, surrounded by his furniture and portraits. You'll see the study in which he worked and the 4½-acre garden, laid out by the poet himself, that gave him so much pleasure. Surrounding Rydal Mount and the areas around Dove Cottage and Grasmere there are many footpaths and tracks once beloved by Wordsworth (his favorite can be found on the hill past White Moss Common and the River Rothay)—spend a hour or two walking them and you'll understand why the great poet composed most of his verse in the open air. The most famous Wordsworthian beauty spot, however, is **Dora's Field**, just below Rydal Mount next to the church of St. Mary's (where you can still see the poet's pew). Head here for a springtime show of daffodils, planted by the poet himself for the delight of his daughter. Daffodils are now few and far between at Gowbarrow Park near Aira Force, where Wordsworth and his sister spotted the famous flowers. On the Ambleside section of Rydal Mount is Rydal Hall, a grand estate that hosts the Rydal Sheepdog Trials on the second Thursday after the first Monday in August every year. ⊠ *Rydal, Ambleside,* ☎ *015394/33002.* ▣ *£3.50.* ☉ *Mar.–Oct., daily 9:30–5; Nov.–Feb., Wed.–Mon. 10–4; closed 3 wks in Jan.*

Dove Cottage

★ **❼** *1½ mi northwest of Rydal Mount.*

Dove Cottage was William Wordsworth's home from 1799 (he moved here when he was 19) until 1808. First opened to the public in 1891, this tiny house, formerly an inn, still contains much of his furniture and many personal belongings. This was one of the happiest of times for Wordsworth, and when he married, the poet brought his new wife to Dove Cottage. Here he nursed his good friend Coleridge back to health and—Coleridge had drafted his poem "Dejection" during his stay here—good spirits. Here, too, of course, he wrote some of his most famous works, including "Ode: Intimations of Immortality" and "The Prelude." Thomas De Quincey took over the cottage at a later date. Dove Cottage is also headquarters of the **Centre for British Romanticism,** which documents the literary contributions made by Wordsworth and the Lake Poets. In front of display cases containing the poets' original manuscripts, headphone sets allow you to hear the poems read aloud. There is also a café and restaurant. ⊠ *The Wordsworth Trust, Dove Cottage, Grasmere LA22 9SH,* ☎ *015394/35544.* ▣ *£4.40.* ☉ *Mid-Feb.–mid-Jan., daily 9:30–5.*

Grasmere

8 *1 mi north of Dove Cottage, 4 mi northwest of Ambleside.*

The heart of Wordsworth country, Grasmere is one of the most typical of lakeland villages, sited on a tiny, wood-fringed lake and made up of crooked lanes, whose charming slate-built cottages house little shops, cafés, and galleries. Wordsworth lived on the town's outskirts for almost 50 years, walking the local hills with his numerous guests, who included the authors Ralph Waldo Emerson and Nathaniel Hawthorne. Wordsworth, his wife, Mary, his sister, Dorothy, and his daughter, Dora are buried in the Grasmere churchyard. On the way out of the churchyard, be sure to stop at **The Gingerbread Shop**, in a tiny cottage by the gate—once the schoolhouse—where you can buy fine gingerbread made from a 150-year-old recipe (the recipe is kept in a local bank vault). The most panoramic views of lake and village are from the south, from the bare slopes of **Loughrigg Terrace**, reached along a signposted track on the western side of the lake. It's under an hour's walk there, though your stroll can be extended by continuing around **Rydal Water**, passing Rydal Mount and Dove Cottage (☞ *above*) before returning to Grasmere—a 4-mi (3-hr) walk in total.

Dining and Lodging

£££ ✗▥ **The Swan.** The handsome, flower-decked, 300-year-old Swan, a
★ former coaching inn on the main road just outside the village of Grasmere, was mentioned in Wordsworth's poem "The Waggoner"; Coleridge and Sir Walter Scott were both guests here. Then, as now, the inn's watchword was comfort—a fire in the lounge grate, an oak-beamed restaurant serving lakeland specialties and game, and elegant guest rooms that combine space with fine views of the surrounding fells. Rooms at the rear, overlooking well-kept gardens, are quieter than those at the front. ✉ *Grasmere, on the A591, LA22 9RF,* ☎ *015394/35551,* ℻ *015394/ 35741. 36 rooms with bath. Restaurant, bar. AE, DC, MC, V.*

Elterwater

9 *On the B5343, 2½ mi south of Grasmere, 4 mi west of Ambleside.*

The delightful little village of Elterwater, at the eastern end of the Great Langdale Valley, is a good stop in the Lake District for hikers. It's barely more than a cluster of houses around a village green, but from here a selection of excellent circular walks are possible. There are access points to the heights of Langdale Fell from various places along the main road; there are information boards at local parking places. Stroll up the river valley or embark on more energetic hikes to Stickle Tarn or to one of the peaks of the Langdale Pikes.

Dining and Lodging

££ ✗▥ **Britannia Inn.** You'll sleep peacefully at the Britannia, a friendly,
★ family-owned inn in the heart of some of the best of the Lake District's walking country. The inn itself has a fine, welcoming atmosphere, with quaint little rooms and outdoor seating, quickly taken up by resting ramblers. The hearty homemade English food served in the bar is excellent, though if you want to eat in the restaurant rather than the bar, be sure to book in advance—there's a very popular four-course table d'hôte dinner served nightly (weekends only Nov.–mid-Mar.). Guest rooms, modern in style but comfortable, are a little larger than is usual in countryside inns. ✉ *Elterwater (on B5343, 4 mi west of Ambleside), LA22 9HP,* ☎ *015394/37210,* ℻ *015394/37311. 13 rooms, 8 with shower. Restaurant, bar. MC, V.*

££ ✕🅷 **Old Dungeon Ghyll Hotel.** After a hard walk, there's no more comforting stop than the hiker's bar of this hotel, one of the most picturesque hostelries of the region. The stone floor and wooden beams echo to the clatter of hikers' boots, while the roaring range rapidly dries out wet walking gear. There's simple bar food served here, or you can eat and drink in the more formal—but still comfortable—resident's lounge and restaurant; dinner, bed, and breakfast rates are a particularly good deal. Rooms are furnished in traditional lakeland style and make for a cozy night after a day on the hills. ✉ *Great Langdale, LA22 9JY,* ☎ FAX *015394/37272. 14 rooms, 4 with shower. Restaurant, bar. MC, V.*

Coniston

🔟 *5 mi south of Elterwater.*

This small lake resort and boating center attracts climbers with **The Old Man of Coniston** (2,635 ft). Steep tracks lead up from the village (follow the signs past the *Sun*) past an old mine to the peak, which you can reach in about two hours. Experienced hikers include the peak in a seven-hour circular walk from the village, also taking in the dramatic heights and ridges of Swirl How and Wetherlam.

Coniston Water—the lake on which Coniston stands—first came to prominence in the 1930s when Arthur Ransome made it the setting for *Swallows and Amazons,* his tale of childish derring-do. The lake is about 5 mi long, a tempting stretch that drew Donald Campbell here in 1959 to set a water speed record of 260 mph. He was killed when trying to beat it in 1967. His body was never recovered after his boat crashed, and a stone seat in the village commemorates him.

★ 🔟 **Brantwood,** on the eastern shore of Coniston Water, was the home of John Ruskin (1819–1900), the noted Victorian artist, critic, and social reformer. It's a rambling white 18th-century house (with Victorian alterations) set on a 250-acre estate that perches on high ground above the lake. Here, alongside mementos like his mahogany desk and the bath chair he used in later life, is a collection of Ruskin's own paintings, drawings, and books. Also on display is much of the art—he was a great connoisseur—that he collected in his long life, not least a superb group of drawings by Turner. The extensive grounds, complete with woodland walks, were laid out by Ruskin himself. It's an easy drive to Brantwood from Coniston, but it's much more agreeable to travel here by ferry across the lake (☞ Getting Around *in* Lake District A to Z, *below*). Services are with either the Coniston Launch or the *Gondola*—an enchanting 19th-century steam yacht—both departing from Coniston Pier. ✉ *Brantwood,* ☎ *015394/41396.* 🔄 *£3.90; combined ticket with ferry £6.50.* ⊙ *House mid-Mar.–mid-Nov., daily 11–5:30; mid-Nov.–mid-Mar., Wed.–Sun. 11–4. Coniston launch Easter–Oct., hourly departures, very reduced schedule in winter. Gondola Apr.–Oct., 4–5 daily departures.*

Dining and Lodging

£ ✕ **Brantwood's Jumping Jenny's.** This brasserie and tearoom—named after Ruskin's beloved boat—offers Pre-Raphaelite decor, an open log fire, and mountain views as the setting for morning coffee, lunch, or afternoon tea. ✉ *Brantwood,* ☎ *015394/41715. No credit cards.*

££ ✕🅷 **The Sun.** Hidden up a shady lane a few minutes out of Coniston center, the Sun combines the best of Victorian comfort with the age-old hospitality of a traditional lakeland inn. Guest rooms and restaurant are in the turn-of-the-century hotel, whose fell views, heavy drapes, open fires, and hanging watercolors paint a picture of relaxation; the attached, dark, wood-paneled, 16th-century inn fills up most nights with hikers and climbers. Meals in the restaurant are of good value but hold few surprises; it's as nice to eat in the inn—pies a specialty—and down a pint or two of the local beer. ✉ *Coniston, LA21 8HQ,* ☎ *015394/41248,* ☏ *015394/41219. 11 rooms, 9 with bath or shower. Restaurant, bar. MC, V.*

£ 🏠 **Shepherd's Villa Guest House.** This B&B in a stone country house stands on the edge of the village. From here, you can take in wonderful views of the lake and forested hills; packed lunches are available for hikers. The rooms are large and comfortable, and there is a garden for summer relaxing. ✉ *Tilberthwaite Ave., Coniston LA21 8EE,* ☎ *015394/41337. 10 rooms, 5 with bath or shower. MC, V.*

Outdoor Activities and Sports

Coniston Boating Centre (✉ Lake Rd., ☎ 015394/41366), at the lake, rents out launches, canoes, or traditional wooden rowboats—and there's a picnic area and café near the center.

Hawkshead

⑫ *3 mi east of Coniston.*

The village of Hawkshead has the usual lakeland complement of narrow, cobbled streets, whitewashed inns, and little bowfront stores. There's a good deal more to it than most local villages, however. The Hawkshead Courthouse, just outside town, was originally built by the monks of Furness Abbey in the 15th century. Hawkshead lay within the monastic domain and later derived much wealth from the wool trade, which flourished here in the 17th and 18th centuries. As a thriving market center, it could afford to maintain a school—**Hawkshead Grammar School**—at which William Wordsworth was a pupil from 1779 to 1787; he carved his name on a desk inside, now on display. A house in the village (Ann Tyson's House) claims the honor of providing the young William with lodgings. Not surprisingly, the twin draws of Wordsworth and Beatrix Potter—apart from Hill Top (see below) there's also a local Potter gallery housed in the former office of her lawyer husband—conspire to make Hawkshead hideously overcrowded throughout the year. Be prepared.

✋ **⑬** **Hill Top** was the home of children's author and illustrator Beatrix Potter, most famous for her *Peter Rabbit* stories. Now run by the National Trust, the tiny house is a popular—and often crowded—spot; admission is strictly controlled. Try to avoid visiting on summer weekends and during school vacations. The pretty gardens and shop remain open on Thursday and Friday, when the house is closed. It lies 2 mi south of Hawkshead on the B5285, though you can also approach via the car ferry from Bowness-on-Windermere. ✉ *Near Sawrey,* ☎ *015394/36269.* ▣ *£3.80.* ☉ *Apr.–Oct., Sat.–Wed. 11–4:30.*

Two mi northwest of the village (follow signs on B5285) is one of the Lake District's most celebrated beauty spots—**The Tarns,** a tree-lined lake that is considered one of the prettiest in the region. Head for Tarn Hows, a scenic overlook that lets you drink it all in.

Lodging

££ 🏠 **Queen's Head.** One of the Lake District's prettiest villages also holds one of its quaintest inns—the black-and-white, timbered Queen's Head, sporting low, beamed ceilings, paneled walls, and cozy rooms that shout its 16th-century credentials. Guest rooms are comfortably furnished, though rather small and fussily decorated, but all the real atmosphere is downstairs—in the welcoming bar, in the paneled dining room serving local cuisine, or outside at tables fronting the sunny, traffic-free street. ✉ *Main St., Hawkshead LA22 0NS,* ☎ *015394/36271,* ☏ *015394/36722. 13 rooms, 11 with bath. Restaurant, bar. MC, V.*

PENRITH AND THE NORTHERN LAKES

The scenery of the northern Lakes is considerably more dramatic—some would say bleaker—than much of the landscape to the south. It's a change you'll notice on your way north from Kendal to Penrith, the easiest approach, a 30-mi drive that takes you through the wild and desolate Shap Fells—one of the most notorious moorland crossings in the country—which rise to a height of 1,304 ft. Even in the summer it's a lonely place to be, and in the winter snows, the road can be dangerous. From Penrith, the road leads to Ullswater, possibly the grandest of all the lakes, and then there's a steady route west past Keswick, then south through the marvelous Borrowdale Valley and on to Cockermouth.

Penrith

⓮ *30 mi north of Kendal.*

The red-sandstone town of Penrith was the capital of the semi-independent kingdom of Cumbria in the 9th and 10th centuries. Later, Cumbria was part of the Scottish kingdom of Strathclyde; in the year 1070, it was incorporated into England. Even at this time, Penrith was a thriving market town (the market still takes place on Tuesday).

The evocative remains of the 14th-century redbrick **Penrith Castle** are set in its own little park. This was the first line of defense against the invading Scots. The ruins stand across from the town's train station. ⊠ *Penrith Castle,* ☎ *no phone.* ⊡ *Free.* ☉ *June–Sept., daily 7:30 AM– 9 PM; Oct.–May, daily 7:30 AM–4:30 PM.*

To find out more about Penrith's history, stop in at the **Penrith Museum.** Built in the 16th century, the building served as a school from 1670 to the 1970s; it now contains a fascinating exhibit of local historical artifacts as well as the local tourist information center. Ask at the center about the historic "town trail" route, which takes you through narrow byways to the plague stone on King Street, where food was left for the plague-stricken; to a churchyard with 1,000-year-old "hog-back" tombstones (i.e., stones carved as stylized "houses of the dead"); and finally to the castle ruins. ⊠ *Robinson's School, Middlegate,* ☎ *01768/212228.* ⊡ *Free.* ☉ *April–Sept., Mon.–Sat. 10–6, Sun. 1–6; Oct.–Mar., Mon.–Sat. 10–5.*

Lodging

££ ▥ **The George.** This large, rambling coaching inn right in the center of Penrith has been hosting guests for more than 300 years. Either stay overnight in one of the modernized rooms, all with private facilities, or just stop in for morning coffee or lunch. The lounges are full of wood paneling, antiques, copper and brass fixtures, old paintings, and comfortable chairs. ⊠ *Devonshire St., CA11 7SH,* ☎ *01768/862696,* ℻ *01768/868223. 30 rooms with bath or shower. Restaurant, bar, lobby lounge. MC, V.*

£ ▥ **Queen's Head Inn.** The Queen's Head is a friendly 17th-century inn with big open fires, plenty of shining copper and brass, and pleasant old furniture. The rooms have all been refurbished in recent years, with the pick of the bunch being the slightly more expensive Lowther Suite, with comfortable furnishings and its own sitting room. ⊠ *Askham, 5 mi south of Penrith, CA10 2PF,* ☎ *01931/712225,* ℻ *01931/712811. 4 rooms with bath. Restaurant, bar. MC, V.*

Dalemain

⑮ *3 mi southwest of Penrith.*

Dalemain, a country house with a 12th-century peel (tower), was built to protect the occupants from raiding Scots. A medieval hall was added, as well as a number of extensions from the 16th to the 18th centuries, culminating in an imposing Georgian facade of local pink sandstone. The result is a delightful hodgepodge of architectural styles. Inside are a magnificent oak staircase, furniture dating from the mid-17th century, a Chinese drawing room adorned with hand-painted wallpaper, a 16th-century "fretwork room" with intricate plasterwork, a nursery complete with an elaborate 18th-century dollhouse, and many fine paintings, including masterpieces by Van Dyck. ⊠ *Dalemain, off the A592,* ☎ *017684/86450.* 🎫 *£5, gardens only £3.* ⊙ *Easter–Sept., Sun.–Thurs. 11:15–5.*

Ullswater

⑯ *6 mi southwest of Penrith.*

Hemmed in by towering hills, Ullswater, the region's second-largest lake, has a spectacular setting. Some of the finest views are from the A592 as it sticks to the lake's western shore, through the adjacent hamlets of **Glenridding** and **Patterdale** at the southern end. Lakeside strolls, tea shops, and rowboat rental all help provide the usual lakeland experience here, though there's a more telling reminder of the region's fundamental character in the brooding presence of **Helvellyn** (3,118 ft), one of the Lake District's most formidable mountains, which lies to the west. It is an arduous climb to the top—especially via the challenging ridge known as Striding Edge—and shouldn't be attempted in poor weather or by inexperienced hikers. Signposted paths to the peak run from the road between Glenridding and Patterdale and pass by **Red Tarn**, at 2,356 ft the highest Lake District tarn—a better target for anyone nervous of the real heights. For those who'd rather see Ullswater from a less exalted level, steamers leave Glenridding's pier for **Pooley Bridge**, offering a pleasant tour along the lake.

⑰ At **Aira Force,** a spectacular series of waterfalls pound through a wooded ravine to feed into Ullswater. From the parking lot (parking fee charged), it's a 20-minute walk to the falls—bring sturdy shoes in wet weather. Just above Aira Force in the woods of Gowbarrow Park is the spot where in 1802, William Wordsworth's sister Dorothy remarked that she had never seen "daffodils so beautiful . . . they tossed and reeled and danced and seemed as if they verily laughed with the wind that blew upon them." Two years later Wordsworth transformed his sister's words into one of the best-known lyric poems in English, "I Wandered Lonely as a Cloud." And two centuries later, National Park wardens have to patrol Gowbarrow Park in season to prevent tourists from picking the daffodils. There are precious few left, so be content with a photograph. Aira Force is 5 mi north of Patterdale, just off the A592.

Dining and Lodging

££££ ✕🏨 **Sharrow Bay.** This hotel is celebrated for its restaurant—dishes
★ such as the terrine of venison, duck, foie gras and pistachio in Cumberland sauce, Aberdeen monkfish with borage cream, and sticky toffee sponge draw gourmands from all over; reservations are imperative. The decor is classic Lake Country, with salons filled with flocked wallpapers, oil paintings, and fringed lampshades. Set between the lush green fields near Pooley Bridge and the increasingly rugged crags around Howtown, the hotel commands a view of exceptional and varied beauty.

The bedrooms are extremely comfortable, although the rooms in the two annexes are somewhat simpler, especially those in Bank House, about 1½ mi away. Stop by for the splendid afternoon tea. ⊠ *How-town Rd., Pooley Bridge, Ullswater CA10 2LZ,* ☎ *017684/86301,* FAX *017684/86349. 28 rooms with bath. Room rates include dinner. Restaurant. AE, DC, MC, V. Closed Dec.–mid-Feb.*

Keswick

❸ *14 mi west of Ullswater.*

The great lakeland mountains of Skiddaw and Blencathra brood over the gray slate houses of Keswick (pronounced kezzick), on the scenic shores of Derwentwater. Since many of the best hiking routes radiate from here, it is more of a touring base than a tourist destination. People stroll the congested, narrow streets in boots and corduroy hiking trousers, and there are plenty of mountaineering shops in addition to hotels, guest houses, pubs, and restaurants. Walkers may want to leave their cars behind, as parking is difficult in the higher valleys, and both the Derwentwater launches and the Borrowdale bus service between Keswick and Seatoller run frequently. The handsome 19th-century **Moot Hall** (⊠ Market Pl.) has served as both the Keswick town hall and the local prison. Now it houses the main **tourist information center** for the region.

At the **Keswick Museum and Art Gallery** in Fitz Park, exhibits include manuscripts by Wordsworth and other lakeland writers, a diorama of the Lake District, a local geological and natural-history collection, and an assortment of watercolor paintings. ⊠ *Station Rd.,* ☎ *017687/73263.* ⊠ *£1.* ☉ *Easter–Oct., daily 10–4.*

★ To understand why **Derwentwater** is considered one of England's finest lakes, take a short walk from Keswick's town center to the lakeshore, and follow the **Friar's Crag** path—about a 15-minute level walk from the center. This pine-tree-fringed peninsula is a favorite vantage point, with its view over the lake, the surrounding ring of mountains, and many tiny wooded islands. Ahead you will see the crags that line the **Jaws of Borrowdale** and overhang a dramatic mountain ravine—the perfect setting for a romantic painting or poem. For the best lake views you should take a wooden-launch **cruise** around Derwentwater. Between late March and November, cruises set off every hour in each direction from a wooden dock at the lakeshore. You can also rent a rowboat here. Landing stages around the lake provide access to some spectacular hiking trails in the nearby hills.

Dining and Lodging

££ ✕ **La Primavera.** The River Greta runs below this stylish restaurant, which is somewhat isolated at the north end of town. Here you have a choice of English or Italian dishes—the grilled steaks are particularly good—and a good wine list. The daily specials are always worth inquiring about. ⊠ *Greta Bridge, High Hill,* ☎ *017687/74621. MC, V. Closed Mon., Jan. and Feb.*

£ ✕ **Abraham's Tea Room.** George Fisher's outdoor store has its own welcoming tearoom, with good, honest Cumbrian home cooking—food as fuel for hikers. ⊠ *2 Borrowdale Rd.,* ☎ *017687/72178. No credit cards. Open shop hours only.*

£ ✕ **Four in Hand.** This is a typical Cumbrian pub—once a stagecoach
★ inn on the route between Keswick and Borrowdale—with a 19th-century paneled bar decorated with horse brasses and banknotes. The imaginative touches in its menu include hot asparagus rolled in ham, and pâté with red-currant jelly; traditional dishes are steaks, meat pies, and Cumberland sausage. ⊠ *Lake Rd.,* ☎ *017687/72069. No credit cards.*

£££ ✕🏨 **Keswick Country House Hotel.** The turrets, balconies, and pic-
★ ture windows are the most noticeable architectural characteristics of
this Victorian hotel. Built to serve railroad travelers in the 19th century, it has all the grandeur and style of that age, although it has been
modernized since to a high standard; all guest rooms have wonderful views. The hotel sits in 4½ acres of private gardens in the center
of Keswick; the grounds are overlooked by the elegant Lonsdale
Restaurant. Tea or after-dinner coffee is served in a charming conservatory with cane chairs. The room rate includes dinner, as well
as breakfast, though you can opt for a stay without dinner if you
wish. ⊠ *Station Rd., CA12 4NQ,* ☎ *017687/72020,* ℻ *017687/
71300. 74 rooms with bath. Restaurant, bar, putting green, croquet.
AE, DC, MC, V.*

£££ 🏨 **Lyzzick Hall Hotel.** On 2 acres on the lower slopes of Skiddaw (2
mi northwest of Keswick on A591), this converted Victorian country
house has superb views across Derwentwater. It makes a relaxed base,
surrounded by large gardens; two lounges with log fires keep things
cozy in winter, and the food in the restaurant is also commendable. ⊠
Under Skiddaw, near Keswick, CA12 4PY, ☎ *017687/72277,* ℻
*017687/72278. 29 rooms with bath. Restaurant, bar, pool, hot tub,
sauna. AE, DC, MC, V. Closed Feb.*

£–££ 🏨 **Highfield Hotel.** Overlooking the lawns of Hope Park between
Keswick and Derwentwater, this small, green-slate hotel is comfortable and serves good, home-cooked food. Family run, it's just a few
minutes' walk from lake or town and offers super views of the local
valley surroundings. ⊠ *The Heads, CA12 5ER,* ☎ *017687/72508. 19
rooms with bath. Restaurant, bar. MC, V. Closed mid-Nov.–Jan.*

Nightlife and the Arts

The **Keswick Jazz Festival** (☎ 01900/602122) is held each May; it consists of four days of music and events and is very popular—reservations are taken before Christmas.

Outdoor Activities and Sports

FISHING

Local permits, for fishing in Derwentwater or Bassenthwaite, are available at **Field & Stream** (⊠ 79 Main St., Keswick, ☎ 017687/74396).

WATER SPORTS

Derwentwater Marina (⊠ Portinscale, Keswick, ☎ 017687/72912) offers boat rental and instruction in canoeing, sailing, windsurfing, and
rowing.

Shopping

Thanks to its size, Keswick is probably the most sophisticated shopping area in the Lake District. You will find a good choice of bookstores, crafts shops, and wool clothing stores. Keswick's **market** is held
Saturdays. **George Fisher** (⊠ 2 Borrowdale Rd., ☎ 017687/72178) is
famous for outdoor clothing: parkas, boots, ski wear, and many other
kinds of sportswear. It also sells maps, and daily weather information
is posted in the window.

En Route The finest route from Keswick is the B5289 road south, which runs
along the eastern edge of Derwentwater, past the **Lodore Falls** (best in
wet weather) to the village of **Grange,** a popular walking center at the
head of the Borrowdale Valley. Beyond is Rosthwaite, a tranquil farming village in the heart of the **Borrowdale Valley,** whose varied landscape of green valley floor and surrounding crags has long been
considered one of the region's most magnificent treasures.

Seatoller

⑲ *7 mi south of Keswick.*

Seatoller, the southernmost settlement in the Borrowdale Valley, is little more than a cluster of buildings and one excellent restaurant. At 1,176 ft, the village is the terminus for buses to and from Keswick as well as the location of a **Lake District National Park information center** (⊠ Dalehead Base, Seatoller Barn, ☎ 017687/77294), open Easter–November, daily 10–5.

The vaultingly steep **Borrowdale Fells** rise up dramatically behind Seatoller. Get out and walk whenever inspiration strikes, and in the spring, keep an eye open and your camera ready for newborn lambs roaming the hillsides. England's highest mountain, **Scafell Pike** (pronounced scarfell) (3,210 ft) is visible from Seatoller. The most usual route up the mountain, for experienced walkers, is from the hamlet of Seathwaite, just a mile or so south of Seatoller. Heading southwest around the mountain, however, you may wish to travel instead to **Wasdale Head**, a small town that sits at the foot of the mountain and at the head of breathtakingly beautiful Wast Water, England's deepest lake, to attend a service in England's smallest church. St. Olaf's 400-year-old walls are barely 7 ft high and the normal seating capacity is 39. The church is much loved by Lake District hikers; the graveyard outside has memorials to some who had tragic climbing accidents in these parts.

Dining

££ ✕ **Yew Tree Restaurant.** Found at the foot of Honister Pass, the Yew Tree has been converted from two 17th-century cottages. The atmosphere here is intimate and gracious, featuring a low-beam ceiling, long open fireplace, and excellent bar. The appealing menu is based largely on local produce—panfried trout, marinated and smoked fish, venison, hare, eel, and salmon. ⊠ *Seatoller, Borrowdale,* ☎ *017687/77634. MC, V. Closed Mon. and Jan.–mid-Feb.*

En Route   Beyond Seatoller, B5289 turns westward through **Honister Pass** (1,176 ft) and Buttermere Fell. It's a superb drive along one of the most dramatic of the region's roads, which is lined with huge boulders and at times channels through soaring rock canyons. The road sweeps down from the pass to the appealing lakeland village of Buttermere, sandwiched between two lakes—the small, narrow Buttermere and the much larger Crummock Water—at the foot of high, craggy fells.

Cockermouth

⑳ *14 mi northwest of Seatoller.*

Cockermouth, an attractive little town at the confluence of the rivers Derwent and Cocker, has a maze of narrow streets that are a delight to wander, and a brisk market-town atmosphere. There's no public access to the ruined 14th-century castle, but the outdoor market, held each Monday, still retains its traditions; an old bell is rung at the start of trading. Cockermouth was the birthplace of William Wordsworth (and his sister Dorothy), whose childhood home, **Wordsworth House,** is a typical 18th-century North Country gentleman's home, now owned by the National Trust. Some of the poet's furniture and personal items are on display here, and you can explore the garden he played in as a child. Incidentally, Wordsworth's father is buried in the town churchyard, and in the church itself is a stained-glass window in memory of the poet. ⊠ *Main St.,* ☎ *01900/824805.* 🎟 *£2.60.* ⊙ *Apr.–Oct., weekdays 11–5; also Sat. 11–5, July–Aug.*

☾ The **Cumberland Toy and Model Museum** has exhibits of mainly British toys from 1900 to the present. Two buildings contain good model train collections, the re-creation of a 1930s toy shop, and large collections of dolls and dollhouses. There's a play area for younger children and special exhibits throughout the year. ⊠ *Banks Ct. and Market Pl.,* ☎ *01900/827606.* ⊠ *£2.* ☉ *Feb.–Nov., daily 10–5.*

Dining and Lodging

££ ⨯⌸ **Kirkstile Inn.** This 16th-century inn stands just 7 mi south of
★ Cockermouth in lovely, quiet surroundings. Low, white, and slate-roofed, this lodging has been welcoming travelers for almost 400 years. There's a cozy pub downstairs, with a roaring fire in winter, and 10 rooms upstairs, arranged along a long, oak-beam corridor. The rooms are all simple, with rather garish floral carpets, but they're cool in summer and well-heated in winter, and the beds are supremely comfortable—just the thing after a day's walking. There's perfectly reasonable food in the bar, but much more adventurous and locally renowned five-course dinners are served in the small, traditionally furnished restaurant—you must make it clear when you book that you want dinner, since there's very limited room. The inn is quite tricky to find, and you'd do best to phone for directions before setting off. ⊠ *Loweswater, CA13 ORU,* ☎ *01900/85219. 10 rooms, 8 with bath. Restaurant, bar. MC, V.*

LAKE DISTRICT A TO Z

Arriving and Departing

By Bus
National Express (☎ 0990/808080) serves the region from London's Victoria Coach Station. Average travel time to Kendal is just over 7 hours; to Windermere, 7½ hours; and to Keswick, 8¼ hours.

By Car
To reach the Lake District from London, take M1 north to M6, getting off either at exit 36 and joining A590/A591 west (around the Kendal bypass to Windermere) or at exit 40, joining A66 direct to Keswick and the northern lakes region. Travel time to Kendal is about 4 hours, to Keswick 5–6 hours. Expect heavy traffic out of London on weekends to all destinations in the Northwest; construction work also often slows progress on M6.

By Plane
Manchester International Airport (☎ 0161/489–3000) (☞ Lancashire and the Peaks A to Z, *in* Chapter 12) is northern England's main airport. The best way to get from there to the Lake District is by car (driving time about 1½ hrs) or by bus, from Manchester's Chorlton Street Bus Station.

By Train
InterCity West Coast serves the region from London's Euston Station (☎ 0345/484950). Take an InterCity train bound for Carlisle, Edinburgh, or Glasgow and change at Oxenholme for the branch line service to Kendal and Windermere. Average travel time to Windermere (including the change) is 4½ hours. If you're heading for Keswick, you can either take the train to Windermere and continue from there by Cumberland bus (Bus 555/556; 70 mins) or stay on the main London–Carlisle train to Penrith Station (4 hrs), from which Cumberland buses (Bus X5) also run to Keswick (45 mins).

Getting Around

By Bicycle

Several local operators rent out mountain bikes, an ideal—if calorie-burning—way to see the Lake District countryside. Guided bike tours are often available, too, starting at about £25 per day. Contact local tourist offices for details, or consult one of the following outfits for bike rental:

Grizedale Mountain Bikes (⊠ Old Hall Car Park, Grizedale Forest Park Centre, Near Hawkshead, ☎ 01229/860369). **Keswick Mountain Bikes** (⊠ Southey Hill, ☎ 017687/75202). **Lakeland Leisure** (⊠ Lake Rd., Bowness-on-Windermere, ☎ 015394/44786). **Windermere Cycles** (⊠ 12 Main Rd., Windermere, ☎ 015394/47779).

By Boat

Keswick-on-Derwentwater Launch Co. (☎ 017687/72263) conducts cruises on vintage motor launches around Derwentwater, leaving from Keswick.

Coniston Launch (☎ 015394/36216) connects Coniston with Ruskin's home at Brantwood, offering hourly service for most of the year (though service is reduced in winter) on its wooden Ruskin and Ransome launches.

Steam Yacht *Gondola* (☎ 015394/41288) runs the National Trust's luxurious Victorian steam yacht *Gondola* between Coniston, Brantwood, and Park-a-Moor at the south end of Coniston Water, daily from Easter through October.

Ullswater Navigation & Transit Co. (☎ 01539/721626) sends its oil-burning 19th-century steamers the length of Ullswater between Glenridding and Pooley Bridge. Service operates April through October.

Windermere Lake Cruises (☎ 015394/43360) is the umbrella organization for two ferry operators on Lake Windermere: the Bowness Bay Boating Co. runs small vessels between Bowness and Ambleside, and Ambleside and Brockhole National Park Centre. Meanwhile, the Iron Steamboat Co. employs its handsome fleet of vintage cruisers—the largest ships on the lake—in regular service between Ambleside, Bowness, and Lakeside. Ticket prices vary, though a Freedom of the Lake ticket (£9) gives unlimited travel on any of the operators' ferries for 24 hours.

By Bus

Stagecoach Cumberland (☎ 01946/63222) operates year-round throughout the Lake District and into north Lancashire. Services between main tourist centers are fairly frequent on weekdays, though service is much reduced on Saturdays, and especially on Sundays and bank holidays. Don't count on being able to reach the more remote parts of the Lakes by bus—for off-the-beaten-track touring, you'll need a car, or strong legs.

The **YHA Shuttle Bus** (⊠ Ambleside Youth Hostel, Waterhead, ☎ 015394/32304) operates a door-to-door service to eight of the most popular hostels in the Lakes. Get on and off where you like for £2 a journey; or send your luggage ahead to the next hostel if you want to walk unencumbered.

By Car

Roads within the region are generally very good, although many of the Lake District's minor routes and mountain passes can be both steep and narrow. Warning signs are normally posted if snow has made a road impassable; always listen to local weather forecasts in winter before setting out. In July and August and during the long public holiday weekends, expect heavy traffic. The Lake District has plenty of parking lots, which should be used to avoid blocking narrow lanes or gateways.

By Train

Train connections are good around the edges of the Lake District, especially on the Oxenholme–Kendal–Windermere line and the Furness and West Cumbria branch line from Lancaster to Grange-over-Sands, Ulverston, Barrow, and Ravenglass. However, these services aren't of much use for getting around the central lakeland region (where you'll really need to take the bus or drive), and services on these lines are reduced, or nonexistent, on Sundays. Seven-day regional **North West Rover** tickets (£45) are valid for unlimited travel within the area, but it's unlikely that they would pay for themselves on most itineraries.

The **Lakeside & Haverthwaite Railway Co.** (☎ 015395/31594) runs vintage steam trains between April and October on the 4-mi branch line between Lakeside and Haverthwaite along Lake Windermere's southern tip. Departures coincide with ferry arrivals from Windermere.

Contacts and Resources

Car Rentals

Avis (✉ Station Rd., Kendal, ☎ 01539/733582). **Keswick Motor Company** (✉ Lake Rd., Keswick, ☎ 017687/72064).

Guided Tours

The **Lake District National Park** office (☎ 015394/46601) at Brockhole, near Windermere, has an advisory service that puts you in touch with members of the Blue Badge Guides, who are experts on the area. From Easter until October, they lead half-day or full-day walks. The Authority has 10 information offices throughout the district (☞ Visitor Information, *below*).

English Lakeland Ramblers (☎ 01229/587382) organizes single-base and inn-to-inn guided tours of the Lake District from May to October. All meals and inn accommodations are included in packages. A lake steamer cruise and a ride on a narrow-gauge steam railroad line are all part of the adventure.

Lakes Supertours (✉ 1 High St., Windermere, ☎ 015394/42751) offers full-day tours by coach and boat, with plenty of opportunities for getting out and strolling around.

Mountain Goat Holidays (✉ Victoria St., Windermere, ☎ 015394/45161) provides special minibus sightseeing tours with skilled local guides. These are half- and full-day tours, which really get off the beaten track, departing from Bowness, Windermere, Ambleside, and Grasmere.

Travel Agencies

Thomas Cook (✉ 49 Stricklandgate, Kendal, ☎ 01539/724258).

Visitor Information

Cumbria Tourist Board (✉ Ashleigh, Holly Rd., Windermere, Cumbria LA23 2AQ, ☎ 015394/44444) is open Monday–Thursday 9:30–5:30 and Fridays 9:30–5.

Ambleside (✉ The Old Courthouse, Church St., ☎ 015394/32582). **Cockermouth** (✉ The Town Hall, ☎ 01900/822634). **Coniston** (✉ Ruskin Ave., ☎ 015394/41533). **Grasmere** (✉ Red Bank Rd., ☎ 015394/35245). **Kendal** (✉ Town Hall, Highgate, ☎ 01539/725758). **Keswick** (✉ Moot Hall, Market Sq., ☎ 017687/72645). **Penrith** (✉ Penrith Museum, Middlegate, ☎ 01768/867466). **Ullswater** (✉ Main Car Park, Glenridding, ☎ 017684/82414). **Windermere** (✉ The Gateway Centre, Victoria St., ☎ 015394/46499).

The **Lake District National Park** head office is at Brockhole, near Windermere (☎ 015394/46601). There are also helpful regional national park centers. **Bowness** (☎ 015394/42895). **Coniston** (☎ 015394/41533). **Grasmere** (☎ 015394/35245). **Hawkshead** (☎ 015394/36525). **Keswick** (☎ 017687/72803). **Pooley Bridge** (☎ 017684/86530). **Seatoller** (☎ 017687/77294). **Ullswater** (☎ 017684/82414). **Waterhead** (☎ 015394/32729).

14 East Anglia

*Cambridge, Bury St. Edmunds,
Norwich, Lincoln*

*A storied, quiet land, East Anglia is still
the guardian of all that rural England
holds dear. It delights all with its tulip
fields, villages adorned with thatched-
roof cottages, and, around the valley of
the Stour, countryside scenes worthy of
a Constable painting. Outstanding are
the majestic cathedrals of Norwich and
Lincoln, the stately houses of Holkham
and fit-for-a-queen Sandringham, and
the city of Cambridge—medieval,
mesmerizing, and magnificent.*

Updated by
Jules Brown

EAST ANGLIA IS THE GUARDIAN of all that rural England holds dear. Occupying an area of southeastern England that juts, knoblike, into the North Sea, its counties of Essex, Norfolk, Suffolk, and Cambridgeshire are a bit cut off from the central routes and pulse of Britain. People from London once called the region "silly Suffolk," and referred to the citizens of Norfolk county as "Norfolk Dumplings." Of course, not everyone could be filed under this category. In fact, this very area was home to some of the greatest thinkers, artists, and poets the country has produced. Milton, Bacon, Newton, Byron, Tennyson, and Thackeray received their education at Cambridge University—one of the world's top centers of learning and arguably the most gorgeous university town on earth. Here, Oliver Cromwell groomed his Roundhead troops, and Tom Paine—the man who wrote "These are the times that try men's souls"—developed his revolutionary ideas. Here, John Constable painted *The Hay Wain* along with luscious landscapes of the Stour valley, and Thomas Gainsborough achieved eminence as England's most elegant portraitist. If East Anglia has remained rural to a large extent, its harvest of legendary minds has been just as impressive as its agricultural crops.

Despite its easy access from London, East Anglia (with the notable exception of Cambridge) remains relatively unfamiliar to visitors. It was a region of major importance in ancient times—as evidenced by the Roman settlements at Colchester and Lincoln—while during the medieval era, trade in wool with the Netherlands saw the East Anglian towns become strong and independent. But with the lack of main thoroughfares and canals, the industrial revolution mercifully passed East Anglia by.

The result of being a historical backwater is that the region is enormously rich in quiet villages, presided over by ancient churches; tiny settlements in the midst of otherwise deserted fenland; manor houses surrounded by moats. Few parts of Britain can claim so many stately churches and half-timber houses. The towns are more like large villages; even the largest city, Norwich, has a population of only about 130,000.

For many people, the joy of East Anglia is its very separateness, its desolate landscapes and isolated beaches. Of these, the fens of northern Cambridgeshire and the Broads of Norfolk are the most dramatic (or depressing, depending on your mood). If you find such quiet, flat spaces dull, you need travel only a few miles to reach the bright lights: three of England's most splendid stately houses—Holkham Hall, Blickling, and Her Majesty's own Sandringham. There are incomparable cathedrals—at Ely and Lincoln particularly—and the King's College Chapel in Cambridge. These are the superlatives of East Anglia. But half the attraction of the region lies in its subtle landscapes, where the beauties of rural England are seen at their enduring best: to rush in search of one or two highlights is to miss these qualities, which can be enjoyed only by leisurely journeys along the byways.

Pleasures and Pastimes

Biking and Hiking

Cambridge is an ideal city to traverse by bike, and everyone seems to do so. The same could be said for the entire region. Many of the flat coastal areas of East Anglia, though sometimes windswept, are perfect for cycling, while a network of cycle routes and bike rental centers provides good means of getting around the towpaths and backwaters of the Norfolk Broads. East Anglia is also a walker's dream. The long-distance footpath known as the Peddar's Way follows the line of a pre-Roman road, running from near Thetford through heathland, pine forests, and arable fields, and on through rolling chalklands to the Norfolk coast near Hunstanton. The Norfolk Coastal Path then continues eastward along the coast, joining at Cromer with another delightfully varied path, the Weaver's Way, which passes through medieval weaving villages and deeply rural parts of the Norfolk Broads on its 56-mi route from Cromer to Great Yarmouth.

Dining

Restaurant menus feature not only specialties of the area, such as duckling, oysters, Norfolk black turkey, hare, or partridge, but also offer various regional favorites. Samphire, sometimes called "poor man's asparagus," is a kind of (delicious) seaweed that grows uniquely in the salt marshes along the North Norfolk and Suffolk coasts. The long coastline also provides Cromer crabs and Yarmouth bloaters (a kind of smoked herring), while the Essex coast near Colchester has been producing oysters since Roman times. There's an equally venerable East Anglian tradition in wine-making. The Romans first introduced vines to Britain, and they took especially well to this region. Today there are more than 40 vineyards in East Anglia, most of which offer tours and tastings to visitors. If you want to try a bottle (dry whites are best), check wine lists in local restaurants.

CATEGORY	COST*
££££	over £40
£££	£25–£40
££	£15–£25
£	under £15

per person, including first course, main course, dessert, and VAT; excluding drinks

Lodging

The intimate nature of even East Anglia's larger towns has meant that there are few hotels with more than 100 rooms. As a result, even the biggest hostelries have a friendly atmosphere and offer personal service. In addition, few English regions have quite so many centuries-old, half-timber inns with characterful rooms, roaring fires, and cozy bars—it's worth going out of your way to stay in at least one during your visit. Cambridge has relatively few hotels downtown, and these tend to be rather overpriced: there simply isn't room for hotels among the numerous historic buildings, although there are many guest houses on the arterial roads and in the suburbs. These start at £15–£20 per person per night and can be most easily booked through the tourist information center (☞ Contacts and Resources *in* East Anglia A to Z, *below*)—it's always busy in Cambridge in summer, so try to reserve in advance.

CATEGORY	COST*
££££	over £150
£££	£80–£150
££	£60–£80
£	under £60

All prices are for two people sharing a double room, including service, breakfast, and VAT.

Exploring East Anglia

For the purposes of exploring, East Anglia can be divided into four main areas: the central area surrounding the ancient university city of Cambridge and including the attractive towns of inland Suffolk; to the east, the region's capital, Norwich, the waterways of Broadland and the beaches and salt marshes of the North Norfolk coast; the south-east, including the ancient Roman town of Colchester and sweeping upward along the Suffolk Heritage Coast; and finally, the northwest, with Lincoln—landmarked by its tall, fluted cathedral towers, and, in the Lincolnshire Wolds, Boston—from where the Pilgrims made their first, unsuccessful, bid to sail to the New World.

Numbers in the text correspond to numbers in the margin and on the East Anglia, Cambridge, Norwich, and Lincolnshire maps.

Great Itineraries

Much of East Anglia's land is agricultural. But although the fen country in the west may yield more vegetables than it does tourist attractions, you'll certainly need more than a few days to soak up the medieval atmosphere of Norfolk, Suffolk, and the unspoiled coastal villages—including time to linger over a pint of locally brewed beer in one of the astonishing number of picturesque pubs. A stay of a week or 10 days would enable you to explore some of the variety of East Anglia and allow you to match your step to its slow pace and follow some of the tiny country lanes to churches and vineyards. If you have five days, you can visit the main historic towns and sample one of the coastal areas, although there won't be much time for lingering en route. In three days, it's better to concentrate on one area, probably Cambridge and its surroundings, rather than try to cover the large distances separating major sights and towns.

IF YOU HAVE 3 DAYS

⊞ **Cambridge** ① is easy to visit from London. It remains a great day trip from London and is also the best base from which to explore the rest of East Anglia in a three-day tour. Explore some of the ancient university buildings, stroll along the Backs, or punting down the River Cam to Grantchester. The next day, head for **Ely** ⑱, and spend a few hours exploring the medieval town and its majestic cathedral, before moving on to **Bury St. Edmunds** ㉓, an extremely attractive town with graceful Georgian streets. Spend the third day exploring the medieval Suffolk "wool towns" of **Sudbury** ⑳, **Long Melford** ㉑, and **Lavenham** ㉒, before returning to Cambridge.

IF YOU HAVE 7 DAYS

Start from ⊞ **Cambridge** ① and take in the medieval sights on your first day, spend the night, then head out to **Saffron Walden** ⑲ and northeast to overnight in ⊞ **Bury St. Edmunds** ㉓. Explore the town the next day, making time to visit the charming Manor House Museum, and then head south through Long Melford, Lavenham, and **Sudbury** ⑳ (with a quick stopover to see Gainsborough's House) to ⊞ **Colchester** ㊵, the traditional base for exploring Constable Country. The next day, head for Constable's Dedham (and perhaps lunch at Maison Talbooth?), then take the B1084 to **Orford** ㊸, a tiny village with a Norman church and castle and smokehouses, where traditional oak-wood methods of smoking fish are still used. After spending your fourth night in ⊞ **Aldeburgh** ㊺, head for **Southwold** ㊻, a charming seaside town where time seems to have stood still. Take the road via Bungay—notable for its crafts and antiques shops—to ⊞ **Norwich** ㉔ to visit its cathedral and medieval alleys. After your fifth night spent in Norwich, the extensive journey northwest to ⊞ **Lincoln** ㊼—where you can spend your sixth night—takes you through flat Fenland; en route, you can visit **King's Lynn** ㊴ or detour northward toward the coast to visit one or two spectacular stately homes—including **Blickling Hall** ㊱, **Holkham Hall** ㊲, and **Sandringham House** ㊳. Lincoln is worthy of a day's exploration: on the way back to Cambridge the next day, opt to stop either at **Ely** ⑱, Fenland's "capital," to see its great cathedral, or at **Stamford** ㊾ to delight in Burghley House, an Elizabethan extravaganza.

When to Tour East Anglia

If you want to avoid crowds, stay away from Cambridge and the Norfolk Broads—the region's most popular tourist attractions—in late July and August. The May Bumps, inter-college boat races, are—confusingly—held the first week of June in Cambridge. During the "long vac," of course, Cambridge is empty of its many thousands of students, its life and soul. To see the city in full swing, visit October through June, though summer visitors won't miss out entirely since there's a range of enjoyable annual festivals—most notably the Strawberry Fair (mid-June), and the Folk Festival and Arts Festival (both July).

The world-famous Aldeburgh Festival of music and the arts, started in 1948 by Benjamin Britten, takes place in June, as does the archaic Dunmow Flitch Ceremony at Great Dunmow in Essex, where a side of bacon is awarded to a married couple who haven't quarreled for a year and a day. King's Lynn and Norwich both have renowned music and arts festivals, in July and October respectively.

CAMBRIDGE

If you want to think about Cambridge, think Rupert Brooke, the short-lived World War I–era poet ("There is some corner of a foreign field/That is forever England"), a Cambridgeshire lad, who called his county "The shire for Men who Understand." Think Wordsworth and Thackeray, Byron and Tennyson, E. M. Forster and C. S. Lewis; and see *Chariots of Fire,* the film version of the true story of Harold Abrahams and Eric Liddell, two Cambridge graduates who shone in the 1924 Olympic Games. Exquisite King's College Chapel's equally exquisite-sounding choir defines the season for an entire nation, when the *Festival of Nine Lessons and Carols* is broadcast live on Christmas Eve.

Exploring Cambridge

❶ *54 mi north of London, 41 mi northwest of Colchester, 63 mi southwest of Norwich.*

With the spires of its university buildings framed by towering trees and expansive meadows, its medieval streets and passages enhanced by gardens and riverbanks, the city of Cambridge is among the loveliest in England. Situated on a bend of the River Cam, it is also one of the most ancient cities in Britain, its foundation lost in the mists of time; that is no cliché, for Cambridge is bedeviled by the mists that rise from the surrounding water meadows. Certainly the city predates the Roman occupation of Britain. There's similar confusion about when the university itself was founded. According to legend it dates from 1234 when a Spanish prince is said to have established the first college.

Keep in mind there is no recognizable campus here: "Where is the university?" is a question hard to answer—the scattered colleges *are* the university. The town reveals itself only slowly. It is filled with tiny gardens, ancient courtyards, imposing classical buildings, alleyways that lead past medieval churches, and wisteria-hung facades. Perhaps the best views are from the Backs—the green parkland that extends along the River Cam behind several colleges. Here you will feel the essential quality of Cambridge. Resulting in part from the larger size of the colleges, and partly from the lack of industrialization, this atmosphere of broad sweeping openness is just what distinguishes Cambridge from Oxford.

East Anglia

North Sea

Great Yarmouth

Lowestoft

Kessingland

A12

A12

A145

A143

A144

Bungay

Waveney

A143

Ludham

Brure

Yare

A149

North Walsham

A146

A47

B1140

Cromer

Blickling Hall

36

Wroxham

Norwich

24 – 34

Tas

A140

A140

B1354

B1149

A11

Wymondham

Bressingham

Banham

A1

Yare

Blakeney

B1156

A1067

NORFOLK

Hingham

Wells-next-the-Sea

A148

Fakenham

A1075

A11

Thetford

37

Holkham Hall

A47

Swaffham

A1065

A1065

Sandringham House

38

A148

A1065

Wissey

A134

Little Ouse

Hunstanton

A149

39

King's Lynn

A47

A10

The Wash

Great Ouse

Downham Market

Wrangle

A47

Wisbech

A10

TO LINCOLN

A17

TO PETERBOROUGH

March

Chatteris

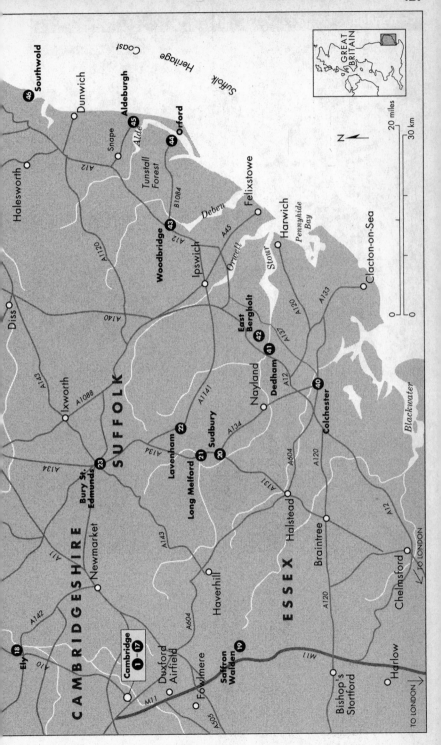

Cambridge

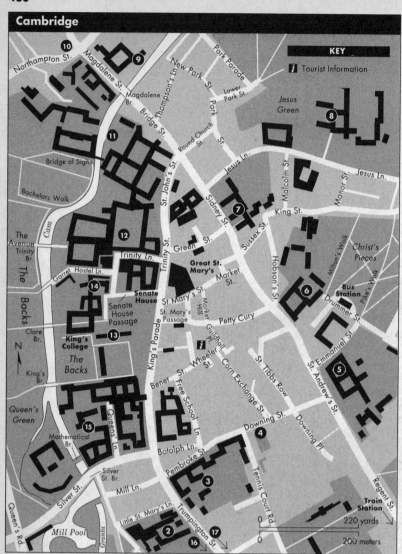

KEY

ℹ️ Tourist Information

Christ's College, **6**

Emmanuel College, **5**

Fitzwilliam Museum, **16**

Jesus College, **8**

Kettle's Yard, **10**

King's College Chapel, **13**

Magdalene College, **9**

Museum of Archaeology and Anthropology, **4**

Pembroke College, **3**

Peterhouse College, **2**

Queens' College, **15**

St. John's College, **11**

Sidney Sussex College, **7**

Trinity College, **12**

Trinity Hall, **14**

University Botanic Gardens, **17**

For centuries the University of Cambridge has been among the very greatest universities, rivaled in Britain only by Oxford; indeed, ever since the time of its most famous scientific alumnus, Sir Isaac Newton, it has outshone Oxford in the natural sciences. In recent years, the university has taken advantage of its scientific prestige, pooling its research facilities with various high-tech industries. As a result, the city is now surrounded by space-age factories, and a new prosperity has enlivened the city center.

Each of the university's 25 oldest colleges is built around a series of courts, or quadrangles, whose velvety lawns are the envy of many an amateur gardener. Since students and fellows (faculty) live and work in these courts, access is sometimes restricted, especially during examination weeks (April to mid-June), and at *all* times you are politely requested to refrain from picnicking in the quadrangles! Visitors are not normally allowed into college buildings other than chapels, halls, and some libraries; some colleges levy an admission charge for certain buildings. Public visiting hours vary from college to college depending on the time of year, and it's best to call ahead or to check first with the city tourist office (☞ Contacts and Resources *in* East Anglia A to Z, *below*). By far the best way to gain access without annoying anyone is to join a walking tour led by an official Blue Badge guide—in fact, many areas are off-limits unless you do. The two-hour tours leave up to five times daily from the city tourist office. The other traditional view of the colleges is gained from the relaxed confines of a punt—the flat-bottomed boats propelled by pole up and down the River Cam (☞ Outdoor Activities and Sports *below*).

A Good Walk

Given the history all around you, it makes sense to start at **Peterhouse College** ②, the granddaddy of them all, founded by the Bishop of Ely in 1281. One of the colleges closest to the train station, it lies on one side of Trumpington Street and stands across the way from **Pembroke College** ③—the "College of Poets," as graduates have included Spencer, Cranshaw, and Gray—where you can gain a first glimpse of the 17th-century work of Christopher Wren in Cambridge, who helped design the college's chapel. From the Arts, head over to the Sciences—walk up to Pembroke Street, turn right and continue down Downing Street for the university's engaging **Museum of Archaeology and Anthropology** ④, on your right-hand side. At the end of Downing Street you're faced by **Emmanuel College** ⑤, and more of Wren's fine work. You then turn left up the busy shopping streets of St Andrew's Street and Sidney Street, passing the often overlooked college of **Christ's** ⑥. To see the way that a college has grown over the centuries you could not do better than visit here. The Tudor main gateway, bearing a splendid coat of arms, leads into a fine courtyard, with the chapel framed by an ancient magnolia. The unfolding architecture leads you through, past a Fellows' building credited to Inigo Jones, to the spacious garden (once the haunt of Milton), and finally to a modern ziggurat-like confection. Onward, head to **Sidney Sussex** ⑦—look for the famous portrait of Oliver Cromwell, who charged his painter to include "all these roughnesses, pimples, and warts," in the Hall here—before turning right down Jesus Lane for one of the prettiest of all colleges, **Jesus College** ⑧. Note the lovely Chapter House entrance, the chapel's Pre-Raphaelite stained glass, and the grounds.

Cross the river, heading north up Sidney Street and Bridge Street to Magdalene Bridge, where you're likely to get a first view of punts maneuvering their way along the River Cam. By the river, quiet **Magdalene College** ⑨ flanks one side of busy Magdalene Street—one of the glories of Cambridge is how quickly you can move from frantic, modern England to the seclusion of scholarly academe—while a little farther up on the other side a couple of museums beckon: the art displays in **Kettle's Yard** ⑩ and the city-related exhibits of the **Folk Museum.** Heading south, back into the city center, cross back over the river and down St. John's Street, past **St. John's** ⑪ and **Trinity** ⑫ colleges. Trinity is Sir Isaac Newton's college, and outside the Great Gate stands an apple tree said to be a descendant of the one whose falling apple caused Newton to formulate the laws of gravity. Ahead lies Cambridge's most famous sight, the soaring late-Gothic beauty that is **King's College Chapel** ⑬. King's College itself faces King's Parade, where students bustle in and out of the coffee shops; you can take time out to climb the tower of **Great St. Mary's,** the university's main church, for a glorious city view. Behind King's, the city's Backs—its riverside gardens and meadows—make their presence felt at **Trinity Hall** ⑭ and **Queens** ⑮ colleges, both of which will lure you off the beaten path for a while. For picture-perfect Cambridge, head back north along the riverbank to the **Bridge of Sighs,** modeled after its Venetian namesake, in St. John's. Silver Street Bridge, by Queens, is another traditional spot to hire a chauffeurpunt. To complete the walking circuit, regain King's Parade and walk south, down to where it becomes Trumpington Street, passing Peterhouse, where you first started. Just beyond, the **Fitzwilliam** ⑯ is Cambridge's finest museum, with superb art and classical collections, and if this final attraction drains you, there's always the peaceful **Botanic Garden** ⑰ in which to recuperate, five minutes beyond, off Trumpington Street on Bateman Street. Ah, academia!

Sights to See

❻ Christ's College. The gateway here bears the enormous coat of arms of its patroness, Lady Margaret Beaufort, mother of Henry VII, who established the institution in 1505; in the dining hall hang portraits of John Milton and Charles Darwin, two of the college's more famous students. Legend (now debunked) has it that Milton planted the mulberry tree in the Fellows' Garden at the behest of King James I, who was keen to encourage the silk industry. Admitted in 1625 at the age of 16, the great poet resided here in a first-floor room on the first stair on the north side of the first court. ⊠ *St. Andrew's St.,* ☎ *01223/334900.*

❺ Emmanuel College. Evident throughout much of Cambridge, the master hand of Christopher Wren is particularly evident at Emmanuel, where he designed the chapel and colonnade. Among the portraits hanging in Emmanuel Hall is one of John Harvard, founder of Harvard University. Indeed, the college, founded in 1584, was an early center of Puritan learning; a number of the Pilgrims were Emmanuel alumni, and they remembered their alma mater in naming Cambridge, Massachusetts. ⊠ *St. Andrew's St.,* ☎ *01223/334200.*

Folk Museum. In a city where "gown" often dominates "town," the balance is redressed a little in this museum, adjacent to Kettle's Yard (☞ *below*). In what was once the 16th-century White Horse Inn, Cambridgeshire's folk history is brought to life in rooms that display crafts, toys, trade utensils, paintings, and domestic paraphernalia in glorious profusion. ⊠ *2–3 Castle St.,* ☎ *01223/355159.* ☜ *£1.* ☺ *Mon.–Sat. 10:30–5, Sun. 2–5; Oct.–March, closed Mon.*

★ ⑯ Fitzwilliam Museum. Housed in a classical building, the Fitzwilliam is one of Britain's most outstanding collections of art (including paintings by John Constable, Gainsborough, the Pre-Raphaelites, and the French Impressionists) and antiquities. The opulent interior displays its treasures to marvelous effect, with the Egyptian section in the lower gallery particularly noteworthy. Exhibits here range from inch-high figurines and burial goods to mummies, painted coffins, and stone inscriptions. In addition to its archaeological collections, the Fitzwilliam contains a large display of English Staffordshire and other pottery, as well as a fascinating room full of armor and muskets. The museum has a coffee bar and restaurant. ⊠ *Trumpington St.,* ☏ *01223/332900.* 🎫 *Free, but £3 donation requested.* ☉ *Tues.–Sat. 10–5; Sun. 2:15–5; guided tours Sun. at 2:30.*

Great St. Mary's. Known as the "university church," Great St. Mary's stands opposite the Senate House on King's Parade. Its origins are in the 11th century, though the present building dates from 1478. Celebrated archbishops who have preached here include Cranmer, Ridley, and Latimer. The main reason to visit today is to climb the tower, which—at 113 ft high—offers a superb view over the colleges and the colorful marketplace. ⊠ *Market Hill,* ☏ *01223/350914.* 🎫 *Tower £1.50.* ☉ *May–Sept., Mon.–Sat. 9–6; Oct.–Apr., Mon.–Sat. 9–4:15; open Sun. after services until 4:15.*

❽ Jesus College. Unique in Cambridge, the spacious grounds of Jesus College incorporate cloisters—a remnant of the nunnery of St. Radegund, which existed on the site before the college was founded in 1496. Lovely Cloister Court exudes a quiet medieval charm, an attribute evident in the adjacent chapel, which also belonged to the nunnery. Victorian restoration of the building includes some Pre-Raphaelite stained-glass windows and ceiling designs by William Morris. ⊠ *Jesus La.,* ☏ *01223/339339.*

❿ Kettle's Yard. Originally a private house owned by a former curator of London's Tate Gallery, Kettle's Yard is home to a fine collection of 20th-century art, sculpture, furniture, and decorative arts, including works by Henry Moore, Barbara Hepworth, and Henri Gaudier Brzeska. A separate gallery provides space for changing exhibitions of modern art and crafts, while weekly concerts (term time only) and lectures attract an eclectic mix of enthusiasts. ⊠ *Castle St.,* ☏ *01223/352124.* 🎫 *Free.* ☉ *House Tues.–Sun. 2–4; gallery Tues.–Sat. 12:30–5:30, Sun. 2–5:30.*

★ ⓭ King's College Chapel. It seems almost invidious to single out just one building in Cambridge from the many that are masterpieces, but King's College Chapel is perhaps the supreme architectural work in the city. It was built by Henry VI, the king after whom the college is named, toward the end of the 15th century. It was a crucial moment for the evolution of architecture in Britain, the last period before the classical architecture of the ancient Greeks and Romans, then being rediscovered by the Italians, began to make its influence felt in northern Europe. King's College Chapel is thus the final and, some would say, most glorious flowering of Perpendicular Gothic in Britain.

From the outside, the most prominent features are the expanses of glass, the massive flying buttresses, and the fingerlike spires that line the length of the building. Inside, the most obvious impression is of great space—the chapel has been described as "the noblest barn in Europe"—and of light flooding in from its huge windows. The brilliantly colored bosses (carved panels at the intersections of the roof ribs) are particularly intense, though hard to see without binoculars. An exhibition in the chantries, or side chapels, explains more about the chapel's construction. At the far end of the church, behind the altar, is an enormous and typically lively painting by Peter Paul Rubens of the *Adoration of the Magi.* Every Christmas Eve, a festival of carols sung by the chapel's famous choir is broadcast worldwide from here. Past students of King's College include the novelist E. M. Forster, the economist John Maynard Keynes, and the World War I poet Rupert Brooke. ⌧ *King's Parade,* ☎ *01223/350411 college; 01223/331447 chapel.* ☜ *Chapel £2.50, exhibition £1.* ⊙ *Term time, Mon. 9:30–4:30, Tues.–Fri. 9:30–3:30, Sat. 9:30–3:15, Sun. 1:15–2:15; summer, Mon.–Sat. 9:30–4:30, Sun. 1:15–2:15 and 5–5:30 .*

⑨ Magdalene College. Across Magdalene (pronounced maudlin) Bridge, a cast-iron 1820 structure, lies the only one of the older colleges to be sited across the river. Magdalene Street itself is narrow and traffic-heavy, but there's relative calm inside the pretty redbrick courts. It was a hostel for Benedictine monks for more than 100 years before the college was founded in 1542. In the second court, the college's Pepys Library—labeled *Bibliotecha Pepysiana*—contains the books and desk of the famed 17th-century diarist Samuel Pepys. ⌧ *Magdalene St.,* ☎ *01223/332100.* ☜ *Library free.* ⊙ *Library Apr.–Sept., Mon.–Sat. 11:30–12:30 and 2:30–5:30; Oct.–Mar., Mon.–Sat. 2:30–3:30.*

④ Museum of Archaeology and Anthropology. As befits a world-class institute of higher learning, Cambridge University maintains a series of fine museums in its research halls on Downing Street—the wonder is that they are not better known to visitors. Geological collections at the Sedgwick Museum and the exhibits at the Zoological Museum are typically extensive, but be sure to see the Museum of Archaelology and Anthropology, which has a superb collection of ethnographical objects brought back by early explorers, including members of Captain Cook's pioneering voyages to the Pacific. ⌧ *Downing St.,* ☎ *01223/333516.* ☜ *Free.* ⊙ *Weekdays 2–4, Sat. 10–12:30.*

③ Pembroke College. Established in 1347, Pembroke has some buildings dating from the 14th century in its first court. On the south side, Christopher Wren's chapel—his first major commission, completed in 1665—looks like a distinctly modern intrusion. You can walk through the college, around a delightful garden, and past the fellows' bowling green, while outside the library you can't miss the resplendent, toga-clad statue of William Pitt the Younger, perhaps the most precocious of the college's former members—he came up to university at age 15 and was appointed Prime Minister of Great Britain in 1783, when he was just 24. More recent alumni include the British Poet Laureate, Ted Hughes. ⌧ *Trumpington St.,* ☎ *01223/338100.*

② Peterhouse College. Cambridge's oldest college, Peterhouse was founded in 1281 by the Bishop of Ely. Parts of the dining hall date from 1290, though its most notable feature is the stained glass by William Morris and his contemporaries. The adjacent church of Little St. Mary's served as the college chapel until 1632, when the present late-Gothic chapel was built. ⌧ *Trumpington St.,* ☎ *01223/338200.*

⑮ Queens' College. One of the most eye-catching colleges is Queens' (1448), named after the respective consorts of Henry VI and Edward IV. It's tucked away on Queens Lane, next to the wide lawns that lead down from King's to the Backs. The secluded "cloister court" looks untouched since its completion in the 1540s. Queens' boasts a very different kind of masterpiece from King's College Chapel in the **Mathematical Bridge** (best seen from the Silver Street road bridge), an arched wooden structure that was originally held together without fastenings. The present bridge, dating from 1902, is securely bolted. If you're looking for a nice time-out, the Anchor, right by the Silver Street Bridge, is a traditional riverside resting place. Have a drink overlooking the water and contemplate your next move—perhaps onto the river in a punt. ⌧ *Queen's La.,* ☎ *01223/335511.* ☜ *£1.* ⊙ *Daily 1:45–4:30.*

⑪ **St. John's College.** The gateway to St. John's is guarded by two myth-ical beasts holding up its coat of arms: "yales," who have the bodies of antelopes and heads of goats. St. John's is Cambridge's second-largest college, founded in 1511 by Henry VII's mother, Lady Margaret Beau-fort. Its structures lie on two sites: from the main entrance walk through the ancient courts—with their turrets, sculpted windows, and clock towers—to where a copy of the Bridge of Sighs in Venice reaches across the Cam to the mock-Gothic New Court (1825), whose white crenellations have earned it the nickname "the wedding cake." If you walk through until you reach the riverbank, you'll be able to stroll along the Backs and frame photographs of the elegant bridge (and less-than-elegant New Court buildings). ⊠ *St. John's St.,* ☎ *01223/338600.* ⌨ *£1.50.* ⊙ *Weekdays 10–5:30, weekends 9:30–5:30.*

❼ **Sidney Sussex College.** Passing largely unnoticed on busy Sidney Street, Sidney Sussex is smaller than many colleges, yet it has interesting 17th-and 18th-century buildings, most of which were sadly served by mock-Gothic "improvements" in 1832. Oliver Cromwell was a student here in 1616; the Hall contains his portrait, and his head has been buried here—in a secret location—since 1960. ⊠ *Sidney St.,* ☎ *01223/338800.*

⑫ **Trinity College.** Founded in 1546 by Henry VIII, Trinity replaced a 14th-century educational foundation. It's the largest college in either Cam-bridge or Oxford, with nearly 700 undergraduates, and many of its features match its size, not least its 17th-century "great court." Here is the massive and detailed gatehouse that holds Great Tom, a giant clock that strikes each hour with high and low notes and which fig-ured in the race around the quadrangle in the film *Chariots of Fire.* The college's greatest masterpiece is Christopher Wren's magnificent library, colonnaded and seemingly constructed as much of light as of stone. Past alumni include Sir Isaac Newton; Lords Byron, Tennyson, and Macaulay; and William Thackeray. Prince Charles was an under-graduate here, in the late 1960s. ⊠ *St. John's St.,* ☎ *01223/338400.* ⌨ *£1.* ⊙ *College daily 10–6; library weekdays noon–2, Sat. in term time 10:30–12:30; hall and chapel also open to visitors: hrs vary.*

⑭ **Trinity Hall College.** The Backs are best appreciated from Trinity Col-lege's 14th-century neighbor, Trinity Hall, where you can sit on a wall by the river and watch students in punts manipulate their poles under the ancient ornamental bridges of Clare and King's. Access to the river is down Trinity Lane, off Trinity Street. The **Senate House** (⊠ King's Parade), which stands between Clare College and Trinity Hall, is one of the few strictly university buildings (i.e., not part of a particular col-lege). A classical Palladian building of the 1720s, it's still used for grad-uation ceremonies and other university events. The building itself is closed to the public (a shame, since it has a fine plaster and woodwork interior), but if the gate is open you're free to wander into the court and grounds. ⊠ *Trinity Hall, Trinity La.,* ☎ *01223/332500.*

⑰ **University Botanic Gardens.** These gardens were laid out in 1846 and contain, among many rare specimens, a limestone rock garden. The gardens are a five-minute walk from the Fitzwilliam Museum, past lovely Brookside. ⊠ *Cory Lodge, Bateman St.,* ☎ *01223/336265.* ⌨ *Free, except weekends Nov.–Mar. (£1.50).* ⊙ *May–Sept., daily 10–6; Feb.–Apr. and Oct., daily 10–5; Nov.–Jan., daily 10–4.*

OFF THE BEATEN PATH **GRANTCHESTER** – This pretty little village 2 mi up the river from the center of Cambridge is a delightful walk or bicycle ride along a path that follows the river through college playing fields and the Grantchester Meadows. Grantchester was put on the map by its famous son, Rupert Brooke, whose very famous line "Stands the church clock at ten to three? And is there honey still for tea?" is from his poem, *The Vicarage, Grantchester.* You can reach the village most enjoyably, if challengingly, by punt upstream along the Cam, or by walking along the signposted riverside path.

Dining and Lodging

£££   ✕ **Midsummer House.** A classy restaurant set beside the River Cam,
★   across Midsummer Common, the gray-brick Midsummer House is particularly lovely in summer: it has a comfortable conservatory. Set menus for lunch and dinner offer a selection of robust yet sophisticated European and Mediterranean dishes. Choices might include tenderly cooked local lamb or the best from the fish market, adorned with inventively presented vegetables. ✉ *Midsummer Common,* ☎ *01223/ 369299. Reservations essential. Jacket and tie. AE, DC, MC, V. Closed Mon. No lunch Sat., no dinner Sun.*

££   ✕ **Three Horseshoes.** This is an early 19th-century thatched-cottage pub-restaurant with additional dining space in the conservatory. There's a tempting range of beautifully presented dishes, with the emphasis on Modern British cuisine—for example, char-grilled meats or roast fish accompanied by those fashionable accoutrements, sun-dried tomatoes, polenta, and olives. It can get very busy, and waiting in line may be necessary. ✉ *Madingley (3 mi west of Cambridge, 10 mins by taxi),* ☎ *01954/210221. AE, DC, MC, V. No dinner Sun.*

££   ✕ **Twenty-Two.** An intimate dining room in a modest, Victorian house
★   ½-mi west of the center of Cambridge, the restaurant offers an extremely good-value fixed-price dinner (at the top of this price category). The menu changes monthly and the kitchen rolls with the seasons, offering what are described as traditional English dishes with a "modern" approach alongside eclectic choices drawn from all quarters. Fish and game figure highly but you're unlikely to be disappointed, whatever you plump for. ✉ *22 Chesterton Rd.,* ☎ *01223/351880. Reservations essential. AE, MC, V. Closed Sun., Mon., and Christmas wk. No lunch.*

£–££   ✕ **Brown's.** This huge, airy, French American–style brasserie-diner was converted from the outpatient department of the old Addenbrooke's Hospital, directly opposite the Fitzwilliam Museum. Large fans still keep things cool in the pale-yellow dining room, while willing staff usher people from bar to table. The bountiful menu ranges from toasted tuna sandwiches; steak, mushroom, and Guinness pie; and house hamburgers, on up to venison or gigot of lamb. Check the daily specials, too—fresh fish and pasta are usually available. It's very busy on weekends, when you may have to wait in line. ✉ *23 Trumpington St.,* ☎ *01223/461655. Reservations not accepted. AE, MC, V.*

£   ✕ **Copper Kettle.** Over the years, students have come to love this dowdy coffee shop, discussing work, life, and love over frothy coffees, sticky buns, and toasted sandwiches. It's never going to win any gastronomic awards, but for a slice of real university life (and a fine view of King's College) it can't be beat. This spot closes at 5:30 PM. ✉ *King's Parade,* ☎ *01223/365068. No credit cards. No dinner.*

£   ✕ **Eraina.** Crowded at the best of times, this cheap-and-cheerful Greek taverna is packed on Saturday nights (when no reservations are taken), seemingly with every student in town. The enormous menu ranges across Greek specialties, pizzas, salads, even curries, and everything comes in monster portions. If the food is, well, average, no one seems to mind— probably because the well-priced wine, good-natured service, and sheer buzz more than make up for it. ✉ *2 Free School La., near Bene't St.,* ☎ *01223/368786. AE, DC, MC, V.*

££££   ⌂ **Garden House Hotel.** Set among the colleges in 3 acres of private
★   grounds, this luxurious, modern hotel makes the most of its peaceful riverside location. Its gardens, lounge, bar, and conservatories all have river views, as do most of the rooms—if you want one, make it clear

when you make your reservation, because some of the rooms at the rear of the L-shape hotel have less desirable views. The smart guest rooms have minibars, TVs, and fine bathrooms, while Club Moativation, a leisure center incorporating indoor swimming pool, sauna, and steam room, reinvigorates tired limbs at the end of a grueling day's sightseeing. ⊠ *Granta Pl. and Mill La., CB2 1RT,* ☎ *01223/259988,* FAX *01223/ 316605. 118 rooms with bath. Restaurant, bar, room service, indoor pool, health club. AE, DC, MC, V.*

£££–££££ 🏨 **De Vere University Arms Hotel.** An elegant and sympathetically modernized 19th-century hotel, the De Vere is a top choice if you want to be in the city center. Space is at a premium in central Cambridge, and it shows here: the guest rooms are comfortable and well-appointed without being overly large. Many rooms also have views of Parker's Piece, the green backing the hotel, though you'll pay slightly more for these. The central lounge provides a comfortable place for afternoon tea, where you can sit by the fire enjoying a pot of Darjeeling and smoked salmon sandwiches. If you don't have a room with a view, then gaze out the windows of Parker's Bar, which also overlooks Parker's Piece. ⊠ *Regent St., CB2 1AD,* ☎ *01223/351241,* FAX *01223/315256. 115 rooms with bath. Restaurant, 3 bars, room service. AE, DC, MC, V.*

££–£££ 🏨 **Arundel House Hotel.** This elegantly proportioned Victorian row hotel overlooks the River Cam, with Jesus Green in the background. The bedrooms are all furnished very comfortably with locally made mahogany furniture, and they come equipped with TV and tea/coffeemakers; Continental breakfast is included in the room rate, though a full breakfast is available for an extra charge. There are also meals and afternoon teas available in the Victorian-style conservatory, whose rattan chairs, trailing plants, and patio garden add a certain cachet to the hotel. Ask about the hotel's special weekend rates, which are an excellent value. ⊠ *53 Chesterton Rd., CB4 3AN,* ☎ *01223/367701,* FAX *01223/367721. 105 rooms with bath or shower. Restaurant, bar. AE, DC, MC, V. Closed Dec. 25–26.*

£ 🏨 **Benson House.** Cambridge has few moderately priced accommodations, but this is the best of them. With a cheery staff and tasteful decor, it's situated opposite Fitzwilliam and New Hall college, a mere 10-minute walk from the town center. Note that rooms are booked on a cash-only basis. ⊠ *24 Huntingdon Rd., CB3 OHH,* ☎ *01223/ 311594. 9 rooms with bath and shower. Cash only.*

Nightlife and the Arts

The **Cambridge Folk Festival** in late July, spread over two days at Cherry Hinton Hall, attracts major international folk singers and groups. Camping is available on the park grounds—reservations are essential. Details are available from the City Council Amenities and Recreation Department (☎ 01223/358977), or look in the local press.

Cambridge supports its own symphony orchestra, and regular musical events are held in many of the colleges, especially those with large chapels. Evensong at **King's College Chapel** is held Tuesday–Saturday at 5:30 PM, Sunday at 3:30 PM (☎ 01223/350411 for information). Concerts (classical and rock), opera, and ballet are also held in Cambridge's beautifully restored **Corn Exchange** (⊠ Wheeler St., ☎ 01223/357851).

The **Cambridge International Film Festival** is one of the best British film festivals outside London; it takes place during July. Contact the Tourist Information Center (☞ Contacts and Resources *in* East Anglia A to Z, *below*) for more details about venues and screenings.

The **ADC Theatre** (☎ 01223/359547) on Park Street hosts mainly student and fringe theater productions, including the famous Cambridge

Footlights revue, training ground for much comic talent in the last 30 years. The city's main repertory theater, the **Arts Theater** (✉ 6 St. Edward's Passage, ☎ 01223/503333), built by economist John Maynard Keynes in 1936, supports a full program of theater, concerts, and events. It also has a good ground-floor bar and two restaurants, including the conservatory-style Roof Garden.

The city's pubs provide the mainstay of Cambridge's **nightlife,** particularly when the students are in town. First among equals is the **Eagle** (✉ Bene't St.), a 16th-century coaching inn with several separate bars and a cobbled courtyard that's lost none of its old-time character—be warned that it's extremely busy on weekends. The **Free Press** (✉ Prospect Row) is that rare beast, a no-smoking pub, and all the better for it, attracting a fresh-faced student rowing clientele. For riverside views, honors go to the **Fort St. George** (✉ Midsummer Common), a charming spot overlooking the university boathouses. The city's oldest pub is the **Pickerel** (✉ Magdalene St.), an ancient oak-beam hostelry attracting a rather younger student crowd.

Outdoor Activities and Sports

BICYCLING

Cambridge is the perfect city in which to rent a bike. **Geoff's Bike Hire** (✉ 65 Devonshire Rd., ☎ 01223/365629) is a short walk from the railroad station and charges from £6 per day and £15 per week—or just £4 for up to three hours. Advance reservations are essential in July and August.

PUNTING

Punt rental is available at several places throughout the city, notably at Silver Street Bridge/Mill Lane, at Magdalene Bridge, and from outside the *Rat and Parrot* pub on Thompson's Lane on Jesus Green. Hourly rental costs about £8 (and requires a deposit of £40), though if you're not up to the challenge of steering yourself—by pole—along the river, then chauffeured punting is also possible at most rental places. Around £5 per head is the usual rate for this, and your chauffeur will as likely as not be a Cambridge student.

Shopping

Cambridge is a main shopping area for a wide region, and it has all the usual chain stores, many situated in the **Grafton Centre** and **Lion's Yard** shopping precincts. More interesting are the small specialty stores found among the colleges in the center of Cambridge, especially in and around Trinity Street, King's Parade, Rose Crescent, and Market Hill.

Bookshops are Cambridge's pride and joy. The **Cambridge University Press** bookshop (✉ 1 Trinity St., ☎ 01223/351688) stands on the oldest bookstore site in Britain, with books sold here since the 16th century. **Heffer's** (✉ 20 Trinity St., ☎ 01223/358351) is one of the world's biggest bookstores, with an enormous stock of books, many rare or imported. There is also a charming children's branch (✉ 30 Trinity St., ☎ 01223/356200). Cambridge is also known for its secondhand bookshops. Antiquarian books can be found at **G. David** (✉ 3 and 16 St. Edward's Passage, ☎ 01223/354619), which is tucked away near the Arts Theater. The **Haunted Bookshop** (✉ 9 St. Edward's Passage, ☎ 01223/312913) offers a great selection of old, illustrated books and British classics. The **Bookshop** (✉ 24 Magdalene St., ☎ 01223/62457) is the best of Cambridge's secondhand bookshops.

FROM ELY TO BURY ST. EDMONDS

This central area of towns and villages within easy reach of Cambridge is testament to the amazing changeability of the English landscape. The town of Ely is set in a landscape of flat, empty, and apparently endless fenland; only a few miles south and east into Suffolk, however, all this changes to pastoral landscapes of—if not rolling, then gently undulating—hills, clusters of villages, and towns whose prettiness is easier to appreciate than the sense of eerie romance permeating the fens.

Ely

18 *16 mi north of Cambridge.*

Ely is Fenland's "capital," the center of what used to be a separate county called the Isle of Ely (literally "island of eels"). Until the land was drained, Ely was surrounded by treacherous marshland, which inhabitants crossed wearing stilts. It is a small, dense town dominated by its cathedral. The shopping area and little market square lie to the north and lead down to the attractive riverside, while the well-preserved medieval buildings of the cathedral grounds and the King's School (which trains cathedral choristers) spread out to the south and west.

★ **Ely Cathedral,** known affectionately as the Ship of the Fens, can be seen for miles. It stands on one of the few ridges in the whole of the Fens, towering above the flat landscape. The cathedral was begun by the Normans in 1083, on the site of a Benedictine monastery founded by the Anglo-Saxon Queen Etheldreda in the year 673. In the center can be seen a marvel of medieval construction—the octagonal lantern, a sort of stained-glass skylight of colossal proportions, which was built to replace the central tower after it collapsed in 1322. Much of the decorative carving of the 14th-century Lady Chapel was defaced during the Reformation (mostly by knocking off the heads of the statuary), but enough of the delicate tracery work remains to show its original beauty. The fan-vaulted, carved ceiling remains intact, as it was too high for the iconoclasts to reach. The cathedral's triforium gallery houses a **Stained Glass Museum,** with a wonderful array of exhibits up a flight of 41 steps. ⊠ *Chapter Office, The College,* ☎ *01353/667735.* 🎫 *Cathedral £3, free on Sun. (donation requested); museum £2.50.* ☉ *Cathedral Mon.–Sat. 7–7, Sun. 7:30–5; free guided tour, daily at 11:30 and 2:30; museum daily 10:30–4.*

Ely's most famous resident was Oliver Cromwell. The half-timber medieval house that was the home of Cromwell and his family stands in the shadows of the cathedral. During the 10 years he lived here, from 1636, Cromwell was leading the rebellious "Roundheads" in their eventually victorious struggle against King Charles I. **Oliver Cromwell's House** now contains an exhibit on its former occupant and audiovisual presentations about Cromwell and the draining of the local fens. The house is also the site of Ely's tourist information center. ⊠ *29 St. Mary's St.,* ☎ *01353/662062.* 🎫 *£2.30.* ☉ *Apr.–Sept., daily 10–6; Oct.–Mar., Mon.–Sat. 10–5:15. Closed Dec. 25–26.*

Dining and Lodging

££ ★ ✕ **Old Fire Engine House.** This restaurant near the cathedral has two dining rooms: the main one, with scrubbed pine tables, opens into the garden; the other, with an open fireplace and a polished wood floor, also serves as an art gallery. Among the English dishes are traditional Fenland recipes, such as pike baked in white wine, as well as eel pie and game in season. ⊠ *25 St. Mary's St.,* ☎ *01353/662582. MC, V. Closed 2 wks at Christmas. No dinner Sun.*

£–££ ✕ **Dominique's.** This delightful little restaurant with stripped pine floors serves brunch, lunch, and dinner in a no-smoking environment. During the day it sees itself as more of a brasserie, while in the evening the specialty is French cuisine with a focus on dishes like warm salads, grilled salmon, and terrines. ✉ *8 St. Mary's St.,* ☎ *01353/665011. No credit cards. Closed Mon., Tues. No dinner Sun.*

£ 🔲 **Black Hostelry.** This bed-and-breakfast has enormous rooms and is
★ right on the cathedral grounds, in one of the finest medieval domestic buildings still in use. It's adjacent to the Chapter House, at the end of Firmary Lane. Extremely comfortable, with antiques and old-fashioned English furnishings, this medieval hostel offers a high degree of privacy. It's so popular that you'll need to reserve a room well in advance. ✉ *Cathedral Close, The College, CB7 4DL,* ☎ *01353/662612. 2 rooms with bath or shower. No credit cards.*

£ 🔲 **Old Egremont House.** Just a five-minute walk from the town center, this 17th-century house has views of the cathedral from its two largest rooms. Inside the oak-beam house, everything is immaculate—the family still lives here—and there are books and antiques all around. There's a private garden—a delight to sit in during the summer. ✉ *31 Egremont St.,* ☎ FAX *01353/663118. 3 rooms, 1 with bath. No credit cards. Closed Christmas wk.*

Saffron Walden

⑲ *14 mi south of Cambridge.*

Best known for its many typically East Anglian timber-frame buildings, the town owes its name to the saffron crocus fields that used to be cultivated in medieval times and processed for their dye. Some of the buildings have elaborate pargeting (decorative plasterwork), especially the walls of the former Sun Inn, which was used by Cromwell during his campaigns. In a similar military vein, the old **Grammar School** here was the World War II headquarters of the U.S. Air Force's 65th Fighter Wing. On the common at the east end of the town, there's a 17th-century circular earth maze, created from space left among the crocus beds.

★ Palatial **Audley End House,** a mile or so west of Saffron Walden, is a famous example of Jacobean (early 17th-century) architecture. It was once owned by Charles II, who bought it as a convenient place to break his journey on the way to Newmarket races. Remodeled in the 18th and 19th centuries, it shows the architectural skill of Sir John Vanbrugh, Robert Adam, and Biagio Rebecca as well as original Jacobean work in the magnificent Great Hall. You can also enjoy a leisurely walk around the park, which was landscaped by Capability Brown in the 18th century. ☎ *01799/522842.* 🎫 *House and park £5.50, park only £3.30.* ☉ *Apr.–Sept., Wed.–Sun. and national holidays; park noon–5, house noon–6; Oct., park and house Wed.–Sun. 10–3.*

Dining and Lodging

££ ✕🔲 **Saffron Hotel.** This conversion of three houses into one has resulted in a comfortable, modern hotel operating inside a 16th-century building. Three of the bedrooms feature splendid bathrooms and four-poster beds. The light and airy conservatory restaurant has won many local plaudits; the menu is packed with plenty of local specialties. ✉ *10–18 High St., CB10 2AY,* ☎ *01799/522676,* FAX *01799/513979. 17 rooms with bath. Restaurant, bar, lobby lounge. AE, DC, MC, V.*

Sudbury

⑳ *15 mi east of Saffron Walden, 20 mi south of Bury St. Edmunds, 14 mi northwest of Colchester.*

The prosperity of Sudbury, with its three fine churches and half-timber houses, was founded on the profits of an early silk-weaving industry as well as the wool trade. The town was Charles Dickens's model for the fictional "Eatanswill," where Mr. Pickwick stood for Parliament. In real life, Thomas Gainsborough, one of the greatest English portrait and landscape painters, was born here in 1727; a **statue** of the artist holding his palette stands on Market Hill. His family's home is now a museum, containing paintings by the artist and his contemporaries, as well as an arts center. Although **Gainsborough's House** presents an elegant Georgian facade, with touches of the 18th-century neo-Gothic style, the building is essentially Tudor. In the walled garden behind the house, a mulberry tree planted in 1620 is still growing. ⊠ *46 Gainsborough St.,* ☏ *01787/372958.* ⊡ *£2.80; free in Dec.* ☉ *Mid-Apr.–Oct., Tues.–Sat. 10–5, Sun. and national holidays 2–5; Nov.–mid-Apr., Tues.–Sat. 10–4, Sun. 2–5.*

Lodging

£ 🏠 **Old Bull and Trivets.** This 16th-century inn is furnished with leather chairs and antiques, though the 20th century has impinged upon the comfortable guest rooms, which have recently been upgraded. All have TVs and telephones; some also have beams and galleries. The informal restaurant serves Anglo-French dishes, although the hotel is a five-minute walk from the town center, where several other eateries provide good meals. ⊠ *Church St., Ballingdon, CO10 6BL,* ☏ *01787/374120,* ⅀ *01787/379044. 10 rooms with bath or shower. Restaurant, bar, lobby lounge. AE, MC, V.*

Long Melford

㉑ *2 mi north of Sudbury, 17 mi south of Bury St. Edmunds.*

It's easy to see how this village got its name, especially if you walk the full length of its 2-mi-long main street, which gradually broadens to include green squares and trees and finally opens into the large triangular green on the hill. The town's buildings are an attractive mixture—mostly 15th-century half-timber or Georgian—and many of them house antiques shops. Away from the main road, Long Melford returns to its resolutely late-medieval roots. On the hill, the **Church**—founded by the rich clothiers of Long Melford—is unfortunately obscured by Trinity Hospital, thoughtlessly built there in 1573. But close up, the delicate, flint flush work and huge, 16th-century perpendicular windows that take up most of the church's walls have great impact, especially since the nave is 150 ft long. Much of the original stained glass remains, notably the Lily Crucifix window. The Lady Chapel has an unusual interior cloister.

Now a National Trust property, **Melford Hall,** distinguished from the outside by its turrets and topiaries, is a mid-16th-century house with a fair number of 18th-century additions. Much of the porcelain and many other fine pieces in the house come from the *Santissima Trinidad,* a ship loaded with gifts from the emperor of China and bound for Spain that was captured by one of the house's owners in the 1700s. ☏ *01787/880286.* ⊡ *£4.* ☉ *May–Sept., Wed.–Thurs. and weekends 2–5:30 (tours Wed. and Thurs.); Apr. and Oct., weekends 2–5:30.*

Kentwell Hall, a half mile north of Long Melford Green, is a redbrick Tudor manor house with picturesquely shaped chimneys and domes, surrounded by a wide moat. Built between 1520 and 1550, it was heavily restored inside after a fire in the early 19th century. Today, a restoration program is again underway, and the original gardens are being re-created. On many weekends from Easter through September, a reenactment of Tudor life is performed here by costumed "servants" and "farmworkers," with great panache and detail. There's also an organic farm, home to rare-breed farm animals. ☎ *01787/310207.* 🖾 *House, gardens, and farm £4.90; special events £7.50–£10.* ☉ *Apr.–mid-July, weekends only; mid-July–Sept., daily; 11–5.*

Dining and Lodging

£££ ✕🖾 **The Bull.** The public rooms of the Bull—stone-flagged floors, bowed oak beams, and heavy antique furniture—show its long history. Throughout, the half-timber Elizabethan building is a joy, and whether you eat in the restaurant or the bar sporting a huge original fireplace, you'll be served with efficiency and care. Traditional roasts and grills are mixed with modern flavors—alongside a local game casserole might appear mullet in a light Thai curry sauce. Creature comforts and pleasant bathrooms offset the smallish size of the guest rooms, and all retain their appealing original character. ⊠ *Hall St., Long Melford CO10 9JG,* ☎ *01787/378494,* 🖾 *01787/880307. 25 rooms with bath. Restaurant, bar. AE, MC, V.*

Lavenham

㉒ *4 mi northeast of Long Melford, 15 mi south of Bury St. Edmunds.*

More like a village than a town, Lavenham seems virtually unchanged since the height of its wealth in the 15th and 16th centuries. The weavers' and wool merchants' houses occupy not just one show street but most of the town. These are timber-frame in black oak, the main posts looking as if they could last for another 400 years. The most spectacular building of them all, the **Guildhall of Corpus Christi** (1529), owned by the National Trust, is open to visitors as a museum of the medieval wool trade. It dominates Market Place, a remarkably preserved square with barely a foot in the 20th century. ⊠ *Market Pl.,* ☎ *01787/ 247646.* 🖾 *£2.80.* ☉ *Apr.–Oct., daily 11–5.*

The **Wool Hall** was torn down in 1913, but it was reassembled immediately at the request of Princess Louise, sister of the then-reigning king, George V. In 1962, it was joined to the neighboring **Swan Hotel** (☞ Dining and Lodging, *below*), a splendid Elizabethan building in its own right. The Swan Hotel had a long history as a coaching inn and in World War II served as the special pub for the U.S. Air Force's 48th Bomber Group, whose memorabilia cover the walls of the tile floor bar.

Lavenham Church is set apart from the village. It was built with wool money by local cloth merchant Thomas Spring between 1480 and 1520. The height of its tower (141 ft) was meant to surpass those of the neighboring churches. In this it succeeded, though the rest of the church is of perfect proportions, with a spacious design.

Dining and Lodging

£–££ ✕ **The Angel.** This popular spot overlooks Lavenham's picture-book main square. Modern British cuisine is the draw here, and the specialty of the house—home-smoked fish—draws rave reviews. Or just sit a spell at the scrubbed pine tables to enjoy one of the well-kept local beers on tap. ⊠ *Market Sq.,* ☎ *01787/247388. AE, MC, V.*

£££ ✕🖾 **Swan Hotel.** This gloriously atmospheric 14th-century lodging has
★ aging timbers, rambling public rooms, open fires, and antique furniture in every conceivable nook and cranny. The downstairs lounges overlook attractive courtyard gardens, while upstairs, along corridors so low that cushions are strategically placed on beams, most of the individually styled bedrooms have fine fabrics, rich oak cabinets, and original wood paneling. Double glazing keeps out most of the traffic noise from the street, and bathrooms have been ingeniously fashioned around ancient timbers and hidden rooms. Traditional English cuisine is served in the restaurant (complete with its own minstrel gallery). ⊠ *High St.,*

CO10 9QA, ☎ *01787/247477,* ⓕ*A*ⓧ *01787/248286. 47 rooms with bath, 2 suites. Restaurant, 2 bars, lobby lounge. AE, DC, MC, V.*

Bury St. Edmunds

★ ❷❸ *12 mi north of Lavenham, 28 mi east of Cambridge.*

Bury St. Edmunds owes its name—and indeed its existence—to Edmund, the last King of East Anglia, who was hacked to death by marauding Danes in 869. He was subsequently canonized, and his shrine attracted pilgrims, settlement, and commerce. In the 11th century the erection of a great Norman abbey confirmed the town's importance as a religious center. Today, only the Norman Gate Tower, the fortified Abbot's Bridge over the River Lark, and a few picturesque ruins remain, for the abbey was one of the many that fell during Henry VIII's dissolution of the monasteries. The abbey's enormous scale is evident in the surviving gate tower on Angel Hill. The ruins are now the site of the **Abbey Botanical Gardens,** with rare trees, including a Chinese tree of heaven planted in the 1830s.

Originally three churches stood within the abbey walls, but only two have survived. **St. Mary's,** built in the 15th century, is the finer, with a blue-and-gold embossed "wagon" (barrel-shape) roof over the choir. Mary Tudor, Henry VIII's sister and queen of France, is buried here. **St. James's** also dates from the 15th century; the brilliant paint on its ceiling and the stained-glass windows gleaming like jewels are the result of restoration in the 19th century by the architect Sir Gilbert Scott. Don't miss the memorial (near the altar) to an event in 1214, when the barons of England gathered here to take a solemn oath to force King John to grant the Magna Carta. The cathedral's original **Abbey Gate** was destroyed in a riot, and it was rebuilt in the 14th century on clearly defensive lines—you can see the arrow slits. The best way to make sense of the abbey's sprawling grounds is to rent a headset from the **Abbey Visitor Centre** for an audio tour. ☎ *01284/763110.* ✉ *Free; audio tour £1.* ☉ *Abbey grounds weekdays 7:30 AM–½ hr before dusk, weekends 9 AM–dusk; Visitor Centre Easter–Oct., daily 10–5.*

A walk along **Angel Hill** is a journey through the history of Bury St. Edmunds. Along one side, the Abbey Gate, cathedral, Norman Gate Tower, and St. Mary's Church make up a continuous display of medieval architecture. On the other side, the elegant Georgian houses include the **Athenaeum,** an 18th-century social and cultural meeting place, which has a fine Adam-style ballroom. The splendid **Angel Hotel** (☞ Dining and Lodging, *below*) was the scene of Sam Weller's meeting with Job Trotter in Dickens's *Pickwick Papers.* Dickens stayed here while he was giving readings at the Athenaeum.

The **Manor House Museum,** a Georgian mansion facing the abbey's grounds, contains excellent art and horological collections: paintings, clocks, watches, furniture, costumes, and ceramics from the 17th to the 20th centuries. The clocks and watches in particular are extraordinarily beautiful, and there's a café and gift shop, too. ✉ *Honey Hill,* ☎ *01284/757072.* ✉ *£2.50.* ☉ *Tues.–Sun. 10–5.*

At the end of Cornhill is the 12th-century **Moyse's Hall,** probably the oldest building in East Anglia, which houses in the original tiny rooms local archaeological collections. It also has a macabre display relating to the Red Barn murder, a case that gained notoriety in an early 19th-century blood-and-thunder theatrical melodrama, *Maria Marten, or the Murder in the Red Barn;* Maria Marten's murderer was executed in Bury St. Edmunds in 1828. ✉ *Buttermarket,* ☎ *01284/757488.* ✉ *£1.25.* ☉ *Mon.–Sat. 10–5, Sun. 2–5.*

The Arts

Bury St. Edmunds's splendid **Theatre Royal,** which offers a wide variety of touring shows, was built in 1819 and is a perfect example of Regency theater design. It may be closed during parts of the summer, so call ahead. ⊠ *Westgate St.,* ☎ *01284/769505.* ⊘ *Mon.–Sat. 10–8, and for performances* .

Dining and Lodging

££ ✕ **Mortimer's Seafood Restaurant.** Mortimer's gets its name from the original watercolors by a Victorian artist, Thomas Mortimer, which are displayed on the walls of the dining room. The seafood menu varies with the season's catch, but there are generally grilled fillets of local trout and Scottish salmon as well as mussels and oysters. Cheaper counter lunches are offered in addition to the cheery, full service in the two main dining rooms—reservations are essential on weekends. ⊠ *30 Churchgate St.,* ☎ *01284/760623. AE, DC, MC, V. Closed Sun., 1 wk at Christmas, and 2 wks in Aug. No lunch Sat.*

£££ ✕▨ **Angel Hotel.** This is the quintessential ivy-clad, historic, market-
★ town hotel. A former coaching inn, it has spacious and well furnished rooms. Several have four-poster beds, and one, the Charles Dickens Room, is where the author himself stayed. The bed is fairly small, but the rest of the room is in perfect 19th-century English style. Morning coffee and afternoon tea are served in the cozy lobby, complete with open fireplace, while elegant dining is to be found in the Regency Restaurant. Here, overlooking the abbey's main gate, a classic English menu is offered and impeccably served, including dishes like grilled lemon sole, venison sausages, or roast duck with port sauce. ⊠ *3 Angel Hill, IP33 1LT,* ☎ *01284/753926,* ⅏ *01284/750092. 40 rooms with bath. Restaurant, bar. AE, DC, MC, V.*

££ ▨ **Ounce House.** This small, friendly, no-smoking bed-and-breakfast is a three-minute walk from the abbey. It has a great deal of charm, not least in the stylish guest rooms, which are attractively and comfortably furnished. A full breakfast sets you up for the day, and although no other meals are served, the house is very close to Bury's restaurants. ⊠ *Northgate St., IP33 1HP,* ☎ *01284/761779,* ⅏ *01284/768315. 4 rooms, 3 with bath, 1 with shower. MC, V.*

NORWICH, THE BROADS, AND NORTH NORFOLK

Norwich—unofficial capital of East Anglia—is the heart of the eastern and northern part of East Anglia's "bump," dominated by the 15th-century spire of its impressive cathedral. Norfolk's continuing isolation from the rest of the country and the fact that so much of its landscape and architecture has been left unspoiled—bypassed by the industrial revolution—have proved to be a draw in recent years. Many of the flint-knapped houses in North Norfolk's pretty villages are, nowadays, weekend or holiday homes. Windmills, churches, and waterways are the area's chief defining characteristics. A few miles inland from the Norfolk coast, the Broads begin forming England's newest national park, a network of shallow, reed-bordered lakes, many of them linked by wide rivers. Boating and fishing are great lures here; rent a boat for a day or a week and the local waterside pubs, churches, villages, and nature reserves all fall within easy reach.

Norwich

㉔ *63 mi northeast of Cambridge, 110 mi northeast of London.*

It used to be said that Norwich had a pub for each day of the week and a church for each week of the year. Although this is no longer true, both types of institutions are still much in evidence in this "fine city." Established by the Saxons because of its prime trading position on the rivers Yare and Wensum, the town still has its heart in the triangle between the two waterways, dominated by the castle and cathedral. The inner beltway follows the line of the old city wall, much of which is still visible, and it is worth driving around after dark to see the older buildings, which, thanks to skillful floodlighting, stand out from their much newer neighbors.

★ **㉕** By the time of the Norman Conquest, Norwich was one of the largest towns in England, though much was destroyed by the Normans to create a new town endowed with grand buildings. The very grandest of these is **Norwich Cathedral.** Although its spire, at 315 ft, is visible from everywhere, you cannot see the building itself until you pass through St. Ethelbert's Gate. The cathedral was begun in 1096 by Herbert de Losinga, who had come from Normandy in 1091 to be its first bishop. His splendid tomb is by the high altar. The plain west front and dramatic crossing tower, with its austere, geometrical decoration, are distinctly Norman. The remarkable length of the nave is immediately impressive; unfortunately, the similarly striking height of the vaulted ceiling makes it a strain to study the delightful colored bosses, where Bible stories are illustrated with great vigor and detail. ✉ *The Close,* ☎ *01603/764385.* 🎫 *Free, but £2 donation requested.* 🕐 *Mid-May–mid-Sept., daily 7:30–7; mid-Sept.–mid-May, daily 7:30–6; free guided tours June–Sept., weekdays at 11 and 2:15, Sat. at 11.*

㉖ The Cathedral Close (grounds) is one of the most idyllic places in Norwich. Past the attractive mixture of medieval and Georgian houses, a path leads down to the ancient water gate, **Pulls Ferry.** The grave of Norfolk-born nurse Edith Cavell, the British World War I heroine shot by the Germans in 1915, is at the east end of the cathedral.

㉗ The decorated stone facing of **Norwich Castle,** high on the hill in the center of the city, makes it look like a children's book illustration. In fact, the castle is Norman, but the wooden bailey (wall) on the castle mound was later replaced with a stone keep (tower). The thick walls and other defense works attest to the castle's military function. For most of its history the castle has been a prison, and executions took place here well into the 19th century. There are daily guided tours of the battlements and dungeons. An excellent **museum** here has displays on Norfolk's history, including a gallery devoted to the Norwich School of painters who, like the Suffolk artist John Constable, devoted their work to the everyday Norfolk landscape and seascape as revealed in the East Anglian light. ✉ *Norwich Castle,* ☎ *01603/223624.* 🎫 *July–Sept. £3.10; Oct.–June £2.30; includes free admission to Regimental Museum.* 🕐 *Mon.–Sat. 10–5, Sun. 2–5.*

㉘ Between the castle and the cathedral is the **marketplace,** the heart of the city for 900 years. Overlooking the market with its blanket of brightly striped awnings is the imposing—if somewhat severe—early 20th-century **City Hall,** whose steps are guarded by bronze Norwich lions. Below City Hall and next to the market rises the elaborate church tower **㉙** of **St. Peter Mancroft.** Narrow lanes and alleys that used to be the main **㉚** streets of medieval Norwich lead away from the market and end at **Tombland** by the cathedral. Neither a graveyard nor a plague pit, Tombland was the site of the Anglo-Saxon trading place, now a busy thorough-

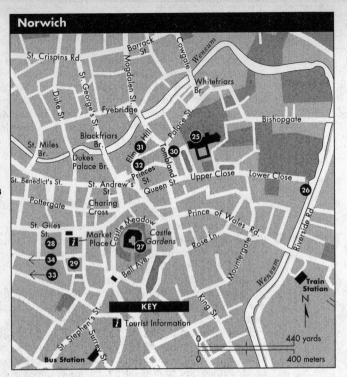

③① fare. **Elm Hill,** off Tombland, is a cobbled and pleasing mixture of Tudor and Georgian houses, now mostly given over to gift shops and tearooms.

③② **St. Peter Hungate** (at the top end of Elm Hill) is a 15th-century former church that displays church art and furnishings. You can try your hand at brass rubbing here. ⊠ *Princes St.,* ☎ *01603/667231.* ☜ *Free; brass rubbing £1.50–£10 (including materials).* ⊘ *Apr.–Oct., Mon.–Sat. 10–5.*

The River Yare was once a busy commercial waterway; now most of the traffic is for pleasure. During the summer months, a **boat trip** starting from Roaches Court at Elm Hill or from Thorpe Station Quay opposite the train station will give you a fresh perspective on Norwich; longer trips are available down the rivers Wensum and Yare to the nearer Broads. A marked riverside walk follows the Wensum from St. George's Bridge to the city wall at Carrow Bridge. ⊠ *Southern River Steamers, Roaches Court, Elm Hill; and Thorpe Station Quay,* ☎ *01603/624051.* ☜ *From £2.15–£6.70.* ⊘ *Easter and May–Sept., 2–3 departures daily.*

③③ In complete contrast to Norwich's historical composition is the modern **University of East Anglia** (UEA), built during the great expansion of higher education in the 1960s. Its site on the slopes of the River Yare, 3 mi west of the town center, was used by architect Denys Lasdun to give a dramatic, stepped-pyramid effect. The campus is linked by walkways that center on a fountain courtyard.

③④ The award-winning **Sainsbury Centre for the Visual Arts,** a hangarlike building designed by Norman Foster, is on the UEA campus. It holds the extraordinary private art collection of the Sainsbury family, owners of a huge supermarket chain. The collection includes a remarkable quantity of tribal art and 20th-century works, especially Art Nouveau, and includes pieces by Picasso and Giacometti. There is a coffee bar and restaurant on the premises. Buses 4, 5, 26, and 27 run from Norwich Castle Meadow to UEA, providing access to both the university and the Sainsbury Centre. ⊠ *Earlham Rd.,* ☎ *01603/456060.* 🎫 *£2.* ☉ *Tues.–Sun. 11–5.*

The Arts

The **King of Hearts** (⊠ Fye Bridge St., ☎ 01603/766129), a restored medieval merchant's house, is now a small arts center that holds chamber concerts, recitals, and poetry readings and has an exhibition area for art and sculpture. **Norwich Arts Centre** (⊠ St. Benedict's St., ☎ 01603/660352) has an eclectic program of live music, dance, stand-up comedy, and other cultural events, as well as a good café. **Cinema City** (⊠ St. Andrew's Plain, ☎ 01603/622047) is Norwich's unique movie house—situated in a 16th-century building and with a terrific associated bistro-bar called *Take 5.*

The **Maddermarket Theater** (⊠ St. John's Alley, ☎ 01603/620917) was patterned after Elizabethan theater design and has been home to the Norwich Players, an amateur repertory company, since 1911. The theater is closed in August. **Norwich Playhouse** (⊠Gun Wharf, St. George's St., ☎ 01603/766466) is a professional repertory group offering everything from Shakespeare to world premieres of new plays and jazz concerts; it also has a bookshop. Norwich's biggest and best-known theater is the **Theatre Royal** (⊠ Theatre St., ☎ 01603/630000), which plays host to touring companies staging musicals, ballet, and opera, as well as plays.

Dining and Lodging

££–£££ ✕ **Marco's.** The Georgian architecture of this building is comple-
★ mented inside by paneled walls, open fires, and pictures, all contributing to a warm, friendly, private atmosphere. Specialties of the Italian cuisine include *salmone al cartoccio* (salmon in parchment); game and local crab are served when available. Portions are generous, and there's a good-value fixed-price menu at lunchtime. ⊠ *17 Pottergate,* ☎ *01603/624044. AE, DC, MC, V. Closed Sun., Mon.*

££ ✕ **Pinocchio's.** Spacious but still intimate, this Italian restaurant in the fashionable St. Benedict's area has been attractively furnished with scatter rugs and colorful murals. There's a wide choice of inventive pasta specials, such as chicken served with saffron noodles in a red pesto sauce, and regional Italian dishes. Meals are accompanied by live jazz or flamenco guitar a couple of times a week. ⊠ *11 St. Benedict's St.,* ☎ *01603/613318. AE, DC, MC, V. No dinner Sun.*

£ ✕ **Adam and Eve.** Said to be Norwich's oldest pub, the Adam and Eve dates back to 1249—a fine spot for a time-out and conveniently sited between the riverside walk and the cathedral on Bishopsgate. Bar food is served noon–7, with simple dishes like soups, pies, and salads at very reasonable prices. ⊠ *Bishopsgate,* ☎ *01603/667423. No credit cards.*

£££ 🏠 **Dunston Hall Hotel & Country Club.** Four miles southwest of the city center, this Tudor mansion has undergone extensive renovation and is now a luxurious hotel with good sporting facilities including a golf course. One of its great advantages is its peaceful setting in landscaped gardens and woodland—ideal for relaxing after a day's sightseeing. ⊠ *Ipswich Rd., NR14 8PQ,* ☎ *01508/470444,* 🅵🅰🆇 *01508/471499. 72 rooms with bath. Restaurant, 2 bars, pool, sauna, driving range, golf privileges, tennis courts, recreation room. AE, DC, MC, V.*

££ 🏠 **Beeches Hotel.** About a mile west of the city center, this attractive, family-run, no-smoking hotel is actually two early Victorian houses, set in an extraordinary park known as the Plantation Gardens. All the rooms are simply but pleasantly furnished, and several look out over the gardens, which—with their ornate Gothic fountain and Italianate terrace—are gradually being restored to their original, Victorian splendor. ⊠ 4–6 Earlham Rd., NR2 3DB, ☏ 01603/621167, ℻ 01603/620151. 25 rooms with bath. Restaurant, bar. AE, DC, MC, V.

Outdoor Activities and Sports

BOATING

Touring by car isn't really an option if you want to see something of the **Norfolk Broads,** since many are inaccessible by road. Consider a boating holiday instead, where with your own launch you'll be able to cruise at will through the 150 miles of waterways. Major operators like **Hoseasons** (☏ 0800/520520) rent boats by the week. Or contact **Broads Tours,** based at the quaysides in Wroxham (☏ 01603/782207), 7 mi northeast of Norwich, and Potter Heigham (☏ 01692/670711), 15 mi northeast of Norwich, which offers day cruises in the Broads as well as half-day and full-day launch rental (lessons included). The *Norada, Olive,* and *Hathor* are historic wherry yachts (sailing barges), and all may be chartered from the **Wherry Yacht Centre** (⊠ Wroxham, ☏ 01603/782470) for luxurious cruises for up to 12 people.

Shopping

The medieval lanes of Norwich, around Elm Hill and Tombland, contain the best antiques, book, and crafts stores. **Peter Crowe** (⊠ 75 Upper St. Giles St., ☏ 01603/624800) specializes in antiquarian books. The **Black Horse Bookshop** (⊠ 8–10 Wensum St., ☏ 01603/626871) sells new books, guides, and maps. Antiques shops abound in Norwich: **James and Ann Tillett** (⊠ 12–13 Tombland, ☏ 01603/624914) specializes in antique jewelry and silver. The **Antiques and Collectors Centre** (⊠ In Tombland, opposite the cathedral, ☏ 01603/619129) is an old house whose little rooms are crammed full of shops. **St. Michael-at-Plea** (⊠ Bank Plain, ☏ 01603/619129) is a church converted into an antiques market. The **Elm Hill Craft Shop** (⊠ 12 Elm Hill, ☏ 01603/621076) has interesting stationery and dollhouses.

Great Yarmouth

③⑤ 20 mi east of Norwich.

Once the center of Europe's herring industry, Great Yarmouth is now the busiest seaside resort on the Norfolk coast, with a long (if undistinguished) seafront promenade backed by cafés, guest houses, and amusement arcades. Near the marketplace—the town's medieval center—the 14th-century **church of St. Nicholas** and the weirdly named **Hospital for Decayed Fishermen,** founded in 1702, are the most interesting buildings.

Blickling Hall

★ ③⑥ 15 mi north of Norwich, 27 mi northwest of Great Yarmouth, via North Walsham (turn left onto B1354, then right, down a little lane).

Cars often come to a screeching halt when they spot the house's famous facade, looming in the far distance behind a wrought-iron gate. A grand vista is created by an imposing allée, formed by two mighty yew hedges, making a magnificent frame for this perfectly symmetrical Jacobean masterpiece. The redbrick mansion has towers and chimneys, baroque Dutch gables and—in the center—a three-story timber clock tower. The grounds include a formal flower garden and parkland whose woods conceal a temple, an orangery, a pyramid, and a secret garden. Now a National Trust property, it belonged to a succession of historical figures, including Sir John Fastolf, the model for Shakespeare's Falstaff; Anne Boleyn's family, who owned it until Anne was executed by her husband, Henry VIII; and finally Lord Lothian, an ambassador to the United States. The Long Gallery (127 ft) has an intricate plasterwork ceiling decorated with Jacobean emblems, and the superb 17th-century staircase is also worth examining. Most of the interior is on the austere side, but there is a sumptuous tapestry of Peter the Great, which hangs in its own room. ⊠ *Blickling,* ☎ *01263/733084.* ☑ *House and gardens £6, £7 on Sun. and bank holidays; garden only £3.50, £4 on Sun. and bank holidays.* ☉ *House and gardens Apr.–June and mid-Sept.–Oct., Thurs.–Sun.; July–mid-Sept., Tues.–Sun.; house 1–4:30, gardens 10:30–5:30.*

En Route   The Norfolk coast begins to feel wild and remote near **Blakeney,** 15 mi west of Cromer. If you drive along the coast road you'll pass marshes, sandbanks, and coves, as well as a string of villages—of which Blakeney is one of the most attractive—with harbors used for small fishing boats and yachts. From the quay here you can take a boat trip past **Blakeney Point,** a National Trust nature reserve, to see the seals on the sandbanks and the birds on the dunes.

Holkham Hall

★ **③⑦**   *10 mi west of Blakeney, 37 mi northwest of Norwich.*

Holkham Bay is a huge expanse of sandy beaches, dunes, and salt marsh backed by pine woods. The tide goes out for 2 mi here. Opposite the lane leading down to the beach from the coast road (A149) is the entrance to Holkham Hall. The estate is the seat of the Coke family, the earls of Leicester. In the late 18th century, Thomas Coke went on the fashionable "grand tour" of the Continent, returning with art treasures and determined to build a house according to the new Italian ideas; the result was this Palladian palace, one of the most splendid in Britain. The magnificence of the Marble Hall pales in comparison to the Great Hall, which is 60 ft high and brilliant with gold and alabaster. Twelve stately rooms follow, each filled with Coke's collection of masterpieces, including paintings by Gainsborough, Van Dyck, Rubens, Raphael, and other Old Masters. This transplant from neoclassic Italy is set in extensive parkland landscaped by Capability Brown in 1762. You can visit this house using the Norfolk Coach Coastliner bus service from various towns in East Anglia; from London, take the train to Cambridge, then a bus to King's Lynn and the coast. ⊠ *Near Wells-next-the-Sea,* ☎ *01328/710227.* ☑ *£4.* ☉ *Easter weekend and June–Sept., Sun.–Thurs. 1–5.*

Sandringham House

③⑧   *15 mi southwest of Holkham, 8 mi north of King's Lynn, 43 mi northwest of Norwich.*

Sandringham House, not far from the old-fashioned but still popular seaside resort of Hunstanton, is one of the Queen's country residences—it's where the royal family spends Christmas, as well as other vacations. This huge, redbrick Victorian mansion was clearly designed for enormous country-house parties, with a ballroom, billiard room, and bowling alley, as well as a shooting lodge on the grounds—no wonder George V used to write fondly of "dear old Sandringham." The house and gardens are closed when the Queen is in residence, but the woodlands, nature walks, and museum of royal memorabilia (the latter housed in the old stables) remain open, as does the church, medieval but in heavy Victorian disguise. ⊠ *Sandringham,* ☎ *01553/772675.* ☑ *House, gardens, and museum £4.50; grounds and museum £3.50.*

⊙ *Easter–Sept.; house and museum daily 11–5, gardens daily 10:30–5. Closed last 2 wks of July.*

King's Lynn

 8 mi south of Sandringham, 40 mi northwest of Norwich.

The center of King's Lynn was used as the location for old New York in the 1988 movie *Revolution.* It's not difficult to see why: much of the old port and trading town with its Georgian town houses, guildhalls, and ancient quayside warehouses is still intact, despite some unfortunate "town planning" in the 1950s and '60s. Now an important container port close to the mouth of the Great Ouse on the Wash, King's Lynn first gained importance in the 15th century, especially for trade with northern Europe. A Flemish influence is apparent in the church brasses and the style of the town squares—but King's Lynn remains one of the most English of English towns.

The enormous **Tuesday Market Place** was big enough to have hosted a sit-down dinner for 600 people to celebrate the end of war with France in 1814. Each Tuesday, it's inundated with local produce and arts and crafts stalls, forming one of the country's most vibrant weekly markets.

Trinity Guildhall, with its striking checkered stone front, is now the Civic Hall of the Borough Council and is not generally open to the public, although you can visit it during the King's Lynn Festival (☞ The Arts, *below*) and on occasional guided tours in the summer. It is possible, however, to explore the **Regalia Rooms,** housed in the Guildhall Undercroft, with the aid of a recorded audio tour, which points out treasures like the 14th-century chalice known as King John's Cup. The rooms are entered through the adjacent **Old Gaol House,** site of the town police station until 1954, whose cells form part of an engaging law and order museum. ⊠ *Saturday Market Pl.,* ☎ *01553/763044.* 💷 *£2.* ⊙ *Apr.–Oct., daily 10–5; Nov.–Mar., Fri.–Tues. 10–5.*

Another early 15th-century guildhall, St. George's, forms part of the **King's Lynn Arts Centre,** a thriving arts and theater complex administered by the National Trust, and the focal point for the annual King's Lynn Festival. There is also an art gallery and a crafts fair every September. The center's coffee bar serves snacks all day. St. George's Guildhall is the largest surviving English medieval guildhall, and it adjoins a Tudor house and a warehouse used during the Middle Ages. ⊠ *29 King St.,* ☎ *01553/773578.* 💷 *Free.* ⊙ *Apr.–Sept., weekdays 10–5, Sat. 10–5; Oct.–Mar., weekdays 11–4, Sat. 11–4. Gallery closed Mon.*

The Arts

Much of the **King's Lynn Festival** (⊠ King's Lynn Festival Office, 29 King St., PE30 1HA, ☎ 01553/773578), which takes place in July, is based at the Arts Centre and encompasses concerts, exhibitions, theater, dance, films, literary events, and children's programs. The festival program is available in April or May. The **Corn Exchange** (⊠ Tuesday Market Pl., ☎ 01553/764864) housed in a splendidly revamped 19th-century building, hosts a varied program of concerts, theater, comedy, and crafts events.

Dining and Lodging

££–£££ ✗ **Rococo.** This modern restaurant in an ancient house serves food as
★ stylish as the decor. The cooking is mainly contemporary British, but it has other influences. Fish and vegetarian dishes are particularly imaginative—for example, monkfish with ginger and lemongrass. Traditional English desserts are a specialty. ⊠ *11 Saturday Market Pl.,* ☎ *01553/771483. AE, MC, V. Closed Sun. No lunch Mon.*

£££   🖭 **Duke's Head.** The location can't be better: wake up on Tuesday morning and the front rooms at the pink-washed Duke's Head have prime views of the market in full swing below. In the oldest, 17th-century part of the hotel—where the main staircase is bowed with age—no two of the guest rooms are alike: the floorboards may be creaky but each room has well-appointed bathrooms, comfortable beds, and relaxing armchairs. Downstairs, a spacious lounge with open fires delays otherwise keen sightseers, who can fortify themselves with cream teas before venturing outside. ⊠ *Tuesday Market Pl., PE30 1JS,* ☎ *01533/ 774996,* 🖷 *01553/763556. 71 rooms with bath. Restaurant, 2 bars, brasserie. AE, DC, MC, V.*

£   🖭 **Russet House Hotel.** With a gentle price, this charming hotel delivers more than a night's worth of comfort and joy. The Victorian-era house has a garden and bar and is a 10-minute walk from the town center. ⊠ *53 Goodwin Rd., PE30 5PE,* ☎ *01553/773098. 11 rooms with bath. MC, V.*

Shopping

The **Old Granary** antiques center in King's Staithe Lane, off Queen Street, is an Aladdin's cave of china, lamps, silver, jewelry, and other decorative items. There are also well-established open markets in the town center, taking place on Tuesday, Friday, and Saturday.

COLCHESTER AND THE ALDEBURGH COAST

Colchester is the oldest town on record in England. One of its Roman founders was the emperor Claudius, and the settlement was soon attacked by Queen Boudicca, queen of the Iceni, noted for having carving knives affixed to her chariot wheels—an early instance of road rage. Today the Roman walls still stand, together with a Norman castle, a Victorian town hall, and Dutch-style houses built by refugee weavers from the Low Countries in the late 16th century. Colchester is the traditional base for exploring Constable Country, that quintessentially English rural landscape on the borders of Suffolk and Essex made famous by the early 19th-century painter, John Constable. This area runs north and west of Colchester along the valley of the River Stour. The Suffolk Heritage coast, which wanders northward from Orford up to Lowestoft, is one of the most unspoiled shorelines in the country.

Colchester

40   *59 mi northeast of London, 51 mi southeast of Cambridge, 68 mi south of Norwich.*

Recent archaeological research indicates a settlement at the head of the Colne estuary at least as early as 1100 BC. At the time of Christ it was the center of the domain of Cunobelin (Shakespeare's Cymbeline), who was king of the Catuvellauni. On Cunobelin's death, the Romans invaded in AD 43. The emperor Claudius—who was alleged to have entered Colchester on an elephant—built his first stronghold here and made it the first Roman colony in Britain, appropriately renaming the town *Colonia Victricensis* ("Colony of Victory"). Colchester had to wait another millennium, however, before it received its royal charter, in 1189, from King Richard Lion-Heart.

Evidence of Colchester's four centuries of Roman history is visible everywhere. Although the Romans prudently relocated their administrative center to London after the Celtic queen Boudicca burned the place in AD 60, Colchester was important enough for them to build massive fortifications around the town. The **Roman Walls**—dating largely from the reign of Emperor Vespasian (AD 69–79)—can still be seen, especially along Balkerne Hill (to the west of the town center), with its splendid Balkerne Gate (most of whose foundations lie beneath the neighboring Hole-in-the-Wall pub). For further remains, check out Priory and Vineyard streets where there is a Roman drain exposed halfway along. On Maidenburgh Street, near the castle, the remains of a Roman amphitheater have been discovered—the curve of the foundations is outlined in the paving stones of the roadway, and part of the walls and floor have been exposed and preserved in a modern building, where they can be viewed through a window.

★ Colchester has always had a strategic importance and is still home to a military garrison; a tattoo (military spectacle) is held in even-numbered years. The **castle** was built by William the Conqueror in about 1076. All that remains is the keep (main tower), but it is the largest in Europe. The castle was actually built over the foundations of the huge Roman Temple of Claudius, and in the vaults you can descend through 1,000 years of history. A superb museum inside contains an ever-growing collection of prehistoric and Roman remains. ⊠ *Castle Park,* ☎ *01206/282931 or 01206/282932 for information on all Colchester museums.* ⊡ *£3.50, guided tours £1.* ◯ *Mar.–Nov., Mon.–Sat. 10–5, Sun. 2–5; Dec.–Feb., Mon.–Sat. 10–5; closed Christmas wk. Guided tours July–Aug., daily; Apr.–June and Sept., weekends.*

The broad High Street follows the line of the main Roman road. Halfway down is the splendid Edwardian **Town Hall,** standing on the site of the original Moot (assembly) Hall. On its tower you can see four figures representing Colchester's main industries: fisheries, agriculture, the military, and engineering. The narrow, medieval streets behind the town hall are called the **Dutch Quarter** because weavers—refugees from the Low Countries—settled here in the 16th century, when Colchester was the center of a thriving cloth trade. The medieval Long Wyre Street, Short Wyre Street, and Sir Isaac's Walk, where there are many small antiques stores, are south of High Street and beyond the modern Culver Square pedestrian mall. **Tymperley's Clock Museum,** off Sir Isaac's Walk, on Trinity Street, displays a unique collection of Colchester-made clocks in the surviving wing of an Elizabethan house. ⊠ *Trinity St.,* ☎ *01206/712943.* ⊡ *Free.* ◯ *Apr.–Oct., Tues.–Sat. and national holidays, 10–1 and 2–5.*

The Arts

The **Mercury Theater** (⊠ Balkerne Gate, ☎ 01206/573948) stages a wide variety of plays, including touring shows, pre–West End runs, and local productions. It's in a modern building not far from the **Colchester Arts Centre** (⊠ St. Mary-at-the-Wall, Church St., ☎ 01206/577301), which hosts theater, exhibitions, and workshop events.

Dining and Lodging

££ ✕ **Martha's Vineyard.** Six miles outside Colchester, in the small village of Nayland, this is one of the rising stars of the British restaurant world. Run by a husband-and-wife team (the latter, Larkin Rogers, is the chef), the restaurant is simple and low-key in style, but the seasonally changing menu is exceptionally good, with a distinct modern American flavor. All the produce used is local and often organic, so expect, for example, great-tasting lamb and chicken dishes. ⊠ *18 High St., Nayland,* ☎ *01206/262888. MC, V. Closed Mon.–Wed. Lunch Sun. only.*

££ ✕ **Warehouse Brasserie.** Colchester's most popular eating place has a fairly anonymous exterior and location: it's tucked away in a converted warehouse, down a cul-de-sac off St. John's Street. Inside, though, all is cheerful, with a charming pastel green and rich red split-level dining room, wooden tables, and large wall mirrors. The menu mixes brasserie favorites with classic English dishes. ⊠ *12 Chapel St. N,* ☎ *01206/765656. MC, V. No dinner Sun.*

££–£££ 🏨 **Kingsford Park Hotel.** This 18th-century country-house hotel set in its own parkland about 2 mi southeast of downtown Colchester boasts individually decorated rooms and antique furniture; some rooms have four-poster beds and all offer a quiet night away from the bustle of town. ⊠ *Layer Rd., CO2 0HS,* ☎ *01206/734301,* FAX *01206/734512. 10 rooms with bath. Restaurant, bar. AE, DC, MC, V.*

££ 🏨 **George Hotel.** In downtown Colchester, this 500-year-old inn has been renovated to include a modern extension but has lost none of its age-old charm. Many rooms incorporate original oak beams and are comfortably furnished. The George Bar also retains its historic beams, while in the cellar there's a section of Roman pavement and a 16th-century wall painting on display. The Brasserie restaurant has a good à la carte menu. ⊠ *116 High St., CO1 1TD,* ☎ *01206/ 578494,* FAX *01206/761732. 45 rooms with bath. Restaurant, bar, grill. AE, DC, MC, V.*

Dedham

④ *6 mi north of Colchester, off A12 on B1029.*

Dedham is the heart of Constable country, that part of Norfolk immortalized by England's greatest landscape painter, John Constable (1776–1837). Here, rolling hills and the cornfields of Dedham Vale, set under the lovely pale skies that are such a notable and delicate feature of the district, inspired the artist to paint some of his most celebrated canvases. He went to school in Dedham, a tiny place that consists of a single street, a church, and a few timber-frame and brick houses. From here you can rent a rowboat, which is an idyllic way to travel the 2 mi down the River Stour to **Flatford Mill,** one of the two water mills owned by Constable's father, and the subject of his most famous painting, *The Hay Wain* (1821). Nearby is the 16th-century **Willy Lott's House** (not open to the public), also instantly recognizable from *The Hay Wain.* The National Trust owns Flatford Mill along with the houses around it, including the thatched **Bridge Cottage,** which has a display about the artist's life. ⊠ *Near East Bergholt,* ☎ *01206/ 298260.* 🎫 *Free.* ⊙ *Apr.–May, Wed.–Sun. 11–5:30; June–Sept., daily 10–5:30; Oct., Wed.–Sun. 11–5:30; Nov., Wed.–Sun. 11–3:30.*

Two miles north of Dedham, off A12, the Constable trail continues in ④ **East Bergholt.** Constable was born here in 1776; only the stables remain of the house that was his birthplace. As well as many other views of the village, he painted the village church, **St. Mary's,** where his parents lie buried. It has one very unusual feature—a freestanding wooden bell house in place of a tower.

Dining and Lodging

£££ ✕ **Le Talbooth.** In a Tudor house idyllically situated beside the River ★ Stour, this famous restaurant has a floodlit terrace where drinks are served in the summer. Inside, original beams, black-lead windows, and a brick fireplace add to the historic atmosphere. Fixed-price menus are offered at lunch and dinner, perhaps including duck breast with braised cabbage or fresh fish. ⊠ *Gun Hill,* ☎ *01206/323150. Jacket and tie. AE, MC, V. No dinner Sun. in winter.*

£ ✕ **Marlborough Head.** Opposite Constable's school, this is an early-18th-century pub, serving fine lunches from quiche to steak. It gets very busy during the summer, so get there early to ensure a table. ⊠ *Mill La.,* ☎ *01206/323250. No credit cards.*

££££ 🏨 **Maison Talbooth.** This luxury hotel is a peaceful Victorian house,
★ set in the rich meadowlands immortalized by Constable. Each of the
elegant, spacious rooms is attractively furnished with period antiques
and flowers, although there's also space for such modern amenities as
Jacuzzis. Guests are encouraged to eat in Le Talbooth restaurant (☞
above), just a short walk down the lane and owned by the same friendly
management. ⊠ *Stratford Rd., CO7 6HN,* ☏ *01206/322367,* 🆔
01206/322752. 10 rooms with bath. Bar. AE, MC, V.

Woodbridge

🔵 *8 mi northeast of Ipswich, on B1438 off A12.*

One of the first good ports of call on the Suffolk Heritage Coast (☞
below), Woodbridge is a pleasant little town whose upper reaches are
centered on a fine old market square, with two great pubs, the *Bull*
and the *King's Head,* vying for your custom. The narrow surrounding streets are filled with antiques shops, although Woodbridge is at
its best down around its old quayside, where boatbuilding has been
carried out since the 16th century—although these days yachts and pleasure craft are being built, not the great ships of the past. The most prominent building is a white clapboard tide mill that dates from the 18th
century. Boat trips from the quay thread their way deftly through the
small craft moored in the harbor and out into the river. 🚢 *Boat trips
£2 per person.* ⊙ *May–Sept., daily 2–5, every 30 mins.*

Dining

£–££ ✕ **Spice.** This is just the type of restaurant you *don't* expect to find in
rural East Anglia—and what a pleasant surprise it is. Climb the stairs
for a warm welcome in this adventurous restaurant serving Malaysian
and eastern-influenced dishes: a *laksa* (spicy coconut noodle) soup might
be followed by grilled meat or by fish enlivened with sauces flavored
by lemongrass, garlic, Southeast Asian spices, and other exotica. ⊠ *17
The Thoroughfare,* ☏ *01394/382557. AE, MC, V. Closed Sun.*

En Route From Felixstowe northward to Kessingland lies the **Suffolk Heritage
Coast,** a 40-mi stretch including many sections designated by an Act
of Parliament as "Areas of Special Scientific Interest." You can only
reach them on minor roads running east off A12 north of Ipswich.

Orford

🔵 *10 mi east of Woodbridge along B1084, 35 mi northeast of Colchester.*

This small village is split between the quayside and its ancient center,
where small, squat **Orford Castle** surveys the flatlands from atop a green
mound pockmarked with picnickers in summer. Its splendid triple-tower
keep was built in 1160 as a coastal defense. Climb it for a view over
what was once a thriving medieval port (the 6-mi shingle bank of Orford Ness eventually cut off direct access to the sea). ☏ *01394/450472.*
🎫 *£2.20.* ⊙ *Easter–Sept., daily 10–6; Nov.–Easter, daily 10–4.*

Dining and Lodging

££ ✕ **Butley-Orford Oysterage.** What started as a little café that sold oysters and cups of tea has become a large, bustling, no-nonsense restaurant. It still specializes in oysters and smoked salmon, as well as smoked
seafood platters and seasonal fresh fish dishes. The actual smoking takes
place in the adjacent smokehouse, and the products are also on sale in
a shop around the corner. ⊠ *Market Hill,* ☏ *01394/450277. No credit
cards. No dinner Sun.–Thurs. in winter.*

££ ☷ **Crown and Castle.** Near Orford Castle is this small, well-established hotel in an 18th-century building thought to have had smuggling connections. The tone is set by the timber facade, and the rooms inside are small, cozy, and very quiet. A snug little bar serves lunches and dinners, including fresh fish, but the most attractive aspect is the outdoor terrace, with its grandstand views of the castle. ⊠ *Market Hill, IP12 2LJ,* ☎ *01394/450205,* 𝔽𝔸𝕏 *01394/450176. 20 rooms with bath. Restaurant, bar, lobby lounge. AE, DC, MC, V.*

Aldeburgh

🔟 *41 mi northeast of Colchester.*

Aldeburgh is now a quiet seaside resort—except in June, when the town fills up with festival goers. Its shingle beach is backed by a long promenade lined with candy-color dwellings, some no bigger than a doll's house. It was Benjamin Britten's home for some time—though he was actually born in the busy seaside resort of Lowestoft, some 30 mi to the north—and it was here that the composer grew interested in the story of Aldeburgh's native son, the poet George Crabbe, ultimately turning the life story of the poet into the celebrated modern opera, *Peter Grimes*—a piece that perfectly captures the atmosphere of the Suffolk coasts. The **Elizabethan Moot Hall,** built of flint and timber, when first erected, stood in the center of a thriving 16th-century town; now it's just a few steps from the beach, a mute witness to the erosive powers of the North Sea. ⊠ *Market Cross, Sea Front,* ☎ *01728/452871.* ☷ *50p.* ☉ *Apr.–May, weekends 2:30–5; June and Sept., daily 2:30–5; July–Aug., daily 10–12:30 and 2:30–5.*

The Arts

The most important arts festival in East Anglia, and one of the best known in Great Britain, is the **Aldeburgh Festival,** held for two weeks in June every year in the small village of Snape, 5 mi west of Aldeburgh, at the Maltings Concert Hall. Founded by the composer Benjamin Britten, the festival naturally concentrates on music, but there are also related exhibitions, poetry readings, and even walks. Snape Maltings also offers a year-round program of events, such as the two-day Aldeburgh Folk Festival, held each July to celebrate traditional English folk music, and the Britten Festival in October. It's well worth a stop at any time of year to enjoy the peaceful riverside setting of the Maltings Arts Centre, and perhaps pause for a coffee in the friendly cafeteria. There are also crafts shops and an art gallery at the center. A festival program is published in March by the Aldeburgh Foundation. ⊠ *High St., Aldeburgh IP15 5AX,* ☎ *01728/452935,* 𝔽𝔸𝕏 *01728/452715;* ☎ *01728/ 453543 Maltings Concert Hall box office;* ☎ *01728/688303 Maltings Arts Centre.* ☉ *Maltings Arts Centre daily 10–5.*

Dining and Lodging

£££ ✗ **The Lighthouse.** This stylish establishment relies exclusively on locally grown—or caught—produce. Seafood, including oysters and Cromer crabs, is a specialty. It comes simply but imaginatively cooked, usually with an interesting sauce whose origins might just as easily be Asian as English. Desserts, like the creamy bread-and-butter pudding, are particularly good. ⊠ *77 High St.,* ☎ *01728/453377. MC, V. Closed 2 wks in Jan.; no dinner Sun. in winter.*

£–££ ✗ **Café 152.** Typical of the new breed of fish restaurants sprouting up in the town, Café 152—just yards from the beach—is bright and breezy, sporting an inventive, changing menu of daily specials. Lunch is a particularly good deal, when you might chomp on char-grilled squid on a bed of salad leaves, or grilled local sole. ⊠ *152 High St,* ☎ *01728/ 454152. MC, V. Closed Mon., Tues. in winter.*

£££ ✕🖭 **The Brudenell.** Parts of the Brudenell date back to the 16th century, although they're now well hidden beneath a pleasing turn-of-the-century facade. The attractive, spacious guest rooms are furnished in bright colors. Those that face directly across Aldeburgh's shingle beach are available for a small supplementary charge; the remainder look out over the river and marshes. With its panoramic windows offering uninterrupted vistas of the North Sea, the split-level restaurant has the feel of a luxury cruise ship. ⊠ *The Parade, IP15 5BU,* ☎ *01728/452071,* ℻ *01728/454082. 47 rooms with bath. Restaurant, bar, lobby lounge. AE, DC, MC, V.*

£££ ✕🖭 **White Lion.** The hotel has been welcoming guests for over 400 years—since 1563, in fact—and this heritage shines through in the paneled, oak-beam restaurant, the log fires in the lounges, and the other age-old nooks and crannies. Right on the seafront, the view from the front-facing guest rooms is worth paying the little extra for, and whether it's snacks in the snug bar or fresh fish in the restaurant, you don't need to move far for affordable, quality meals. ⊠ *Market Cross Pl. IP15 5BJ,* ☎ *01728/452720,* ℻ *01728/452986. 38 rooms with bath. Restaurant, 2 bars. MC, V.*

Southwold

46 *4 mi north of Dunwich, 15 mi north of Aldeburgh, 32 mi southeast of Norwich.*

This attractive seaside town is an idyllic place to spend a day. Old-fashioned beach huts painted in bright colors huddle together against the wind on the shingle beach, while up in the town center a pleasing ensemble of old houses lines the main street and surrounds the central green. There aren't many "sights," but since the whole town gives you the sensation of being transported back in time, this doesn't matter very much. George Orwell's parents lived at 36 High Street during the 1930s, though for a house more typical of the town visit the **Southwold Museum,** which is in a Dutch-gabled cottage. ⊠ *Victoria St.,* ☎ *01502/723925.* 🎟 *Free.* ☉ *Mid-Apr.–Sept., daily 2:30–4:30.*

Dining and Lodging

£££ ✕🖭 **Swan Hotel.** This lovely, 17th-century inn (scenes from the film *David Copperfield* were shot here) features spacious public rooms and decent-size bedrooms decorated in traditional English-country style. Eighteen secluded and quiet garden rooms are set in a superb central position around the old bowling green. In the charming public rooms, you can comfortably sit over tea or something stronger on a winter's day. The hotel staff prides itself on personal service. The restaurant's bay windows overlook the street; dishes are mainly traditional English, accompanied by a similarly excellent wine list. ⊠ *Market Pl., IP18 6EG,* ☎ *01502/722186,* ℻ *01502/724800. 45 rooms with bath. Restaurant, bar. AE, DC, MC, V.*

OFF THE
BEATEN PATH

WALBERSWICK – The charming little village of Walberswick was for many years the haunt of artists, writers, and photographers (including, during 1914–15, the Scottish Art Nouveau architect Charles Rennie Mackintosh, who painted many of his watercolors of plants and flowers here). The village is separated from Southwold by the mouth of the River Blyth, over which there's a footbridge (about 1 mi inland), but no main road bridge. On summer weekends, a boatman ferries foot passengers over the water in a rowboat every few minutes. On the far side, you can see the church tower of Southwold piercing the horizon, a half-hour's walk away through the fields. 🎟 *Ferry 25p.* ☉ *Ferry May–Sept., weekends 9–12:30, 2–5.*

BEYOND THE FENS: LINCOLN, BOSTON, AND STAMFORD

The fens of northern Cambridgeshire pass imperceptibly into the three divisions of Lincolnshire: Holland, Kesteven, and Lindsey are all parts of the great county, divided administratively. Holland borders the Isle of Ely and the delightfully named Soke of Peterborough; this marshland spreads far and wide south of the Wash, the names of the district almost reflecting the squelch of mud the inhabitants of pre-drainage times must have encountered. The chief attractions are two towns: Lincoln, with its magnificent cathedral, and Stamford, to the southwest.

The countryside around Lincoln, especially the Lincolnshire Wolds (chalk hills) to the northeast, consists of rolling hills and copses, with drystone (unmortared) walls dividing well-tended fields. The unspoiled rural area of the Wolds, strikingly evoked in Tennyson's poetry, is particularly worth a visit, while the long coastline with its miles of sandy beaches and its North Sea air offers all the usual, if occasionally tacky, seaside facilities for the family. Tulips are the pride and joy of south Lincolnshire, drawing thousands from all parts of Britain to view the Holland and Kesteven bulb fields in springtime.

Lincoln

★ **47** *93 mi northwest of Cambridge, 97 mi northwest of Norwich.*

Lincoln's crowning glory is the great **Cathedral of St. Mary.** (Try to see it at night, when it's floodlighted.) Commanding views from the top of the steep limestone escarpment above the River Witham reveal the strategic advantages of the city's site from earliest times.

For hundreds of years, it was the tallest building in Europe, but this magnificent medieval building is now among the least known of the European cathedrals. It was begun in 1072 by the Norman bishop Remigius; the Romanesque church he built was irremediably damaged, first by fire, then by earthquake (in 1185), but you can still see parts of the ancient structure at the west front. The next great phase of building, initiated by Bishop Hugh of Avalon, is mainly 13th century in character. The west front, topped by the two west towers, is a unique structure, giving tremendous breadth to the entrance. It is best seen from the 14th-century Exchequer Gate arch in front of the cathedral, or from the castle battlements beyond.

Inside, a breathtaking impression of space and unity belies the many centuries of building and rebuilding. The stained-glass window at the north end of the transept, known as the Dean's Eye, is one of the earliest (13th-century) traceried windows, while its opposite number at the south end shows a 14th-century sophistication in its tracery (i.e., interlaced designs). St. Hugh's Choir, in front of the altar, and the Angel Choir at the east end behind it have remarkable vaulted ceilings and intricate carvings. Look for the famous Lincoln Imp upon the pillar nearest to St. Hugh's shrine, and even farther up (binoculars or a telephoto lens will help) to see the 30 angels who are playing musical instruments and who give this part of the cathedral its name.

Through a door on the north side lies the chapter house, a 10-sided building that sometimes housed the medieval Parliament of England during the reigns of Edward I and Edward II. The chapter house is connected to the 13th-century cloister, notable for its grotesquely amusing ceiling bosses. The cathedral library, a restrained building by Christopher Wren, was built onto the north side of the cloisters after

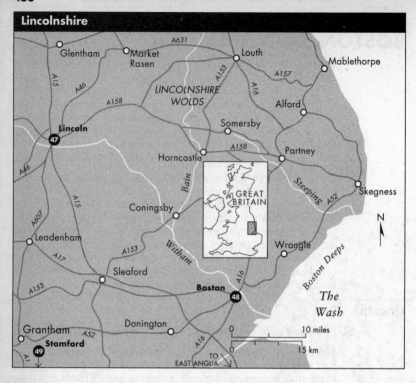

the original library collapsed. ☎ *01522/544544.* ✆ *£3 donation.* ☉
*Late May–Aug., Mon.–Sat. 7:15 AM–8 PM, Sun. 7:15–6; Sept.–Apr.,
Mon.–Sat. 7:15–6, Sun. 7:15–5.*

In the **Minster Yard,** which surrounds the cathedral on three sides, are
buildings of various periods, including graceful examples of Georgian
architecture. A statue of Alfred, Lord Tennyson, who was born in Lincolnshire, stands on the green near the chapter house exterior, and the
medieval **Bishops Old Palace,** on the south side, is open to the public.
☎ *01522/527468.* ✆ *£1.10.* ☉ *Apr.–Sept., daily 10–6.*

Lincoln Castle, facing the cathedral across Exchequer Gate, was originally built on two great mounds by William the Conqueror in 1068,
incorporating part of the remains of the Roman garrison walls. The
castle was a military base until the 17th century, after which it was used
as a prison. In the extraordinary prison chapel you can see the cage-
like stalls in which Victorian convicts listened to sermons. One of the
four surviving copies of the Magna Carta, signed by King John at Runnymede in 1215, is on display in the same building. ✉ *Castle Hill,* ☎
01522/511068. ✆ *£2.50.* ☉ *Apr.–Oct., Mon.–Sat. 9:30–5:30, Sun.
11:30–5:30; Nov.–Mar., Mon.–Sat. 9:30–4, Sun. 11–4.*

South of the cathedral, narrow medieval streets cling to the hillside,
with the aptly named **Steep Hill** at their center. **Jew's House** (✉ The
Strait) dating from the early 12th century, is one of several well-preserved domestic buildings in this area. The **Usher Gallery** has an interesting collection of watches and clocks donated by its benefactor,
James Ward Usher, a jeweler who invented the legend of the Lincoln
Imp. The gallery also contains memorabilia connected with the poet
Tennyson, who was born in Lincolnshire. ✉ *Lindum Rd.,* ☎ *01522/
527980.* ✆ *£2, free on Fri.* ☉ *Mon.–Sat. 10–5:30, Sun. 2:30–5.*

In the city center you can walk under the 15th-century **Stonebow arch** on the site of an old Roman gate. Above it is the **Guildhall,** which houses the city's civic regalia. The River Witham flows unobtrusively under the incongruously named **High Bridge**—a low, vaulted Norman bridge topped by 16th-century, timber-frame houses. West of High Bridge, the river opens out into **Brayford Pool,** still busy with river traffic (and, unfortunately, road traffic, as a large, unsightly, multistory parking lot has been built on one side). Here you can rent various kinds of boats. In addition, from April to September small cruisers tour the River Witham, showing you the city from the water. Contact the city tourist office (☞ Contacts and Resources *in* East Anglia A to Z, *below*).

The Arts

The **Theatre Royal** (⊠ Clasketgate, ☎ 01522/525555) is a fine Victorian theater previewing shows before their London runs and offering tour productions. There are also occasionally concerts on Sunday.

Dining and Lodging

££–£££   ✕ **Jew's House.** Situated in one of Lincoln's oldest buildings (12th cen-
★   tury), the restaurant has an intimate atmosphere enhanced by antique tables and oil paintings. The cosmopolitan menu, featuring Continental specialties, changes daily, and the restaurant is renowned for its fresh fish and rich desserts, all homemade. ⊠ *15 The Strait,* ☎ *01522/524851. AE, DC, MC, V. Closed Sun., Mon. No lunch Sat.*

£–££   ✕ **Wig and Mitre.** This interesting downtown pub-café-restaurant stays open all day and until 11 PM, offering an extremely wide range of food, from breakfast to full evening meals. Produce comes from the local markets, and dishes may include fresh fish, warming seasonal soups, European specialties, or classic English pies and roasts. ⊠ *29 Steep Hill,* ☎ *01522/535190. AE, DC, MC, V.*

£££   🏰 **White Hart.** Lincoln's most elegant hotel is luxuriously furnished
★   with a wealth of antiques, including some fine clocks and china. The establishment has been a hotel for 600 years, reflecting a volume of experience that makes the service personal and extremely friendly. Each of the bedrooms is individually decorated; many are furnished with antiques, and hardwoods such as walnut and mahogany abound. No-smoking accommodations are available. Dinner, bed, and breakfast rates are a particularly good deal here. ⊠ *Bailgate, LN1 3AR,* ☎ *01522/526222,* ℻ *01522/531798. 35 rooms with bath, 13 suites. Restaurant, bar, coffee shop. AE, DC, MC, V.*

££   🏰 **D'Isney Place Hotel.** This charming small hotel is a Georgian and Victorian building near the cathedral. If you like privacy, it's ideal: there's no lounge or other communal space, but breakfast is served on Minton china to guests in the beautifully decorated rooms. For a little more style, choose one of the deluxe rooms, which feature relaxing Jacuzzi baths—these fall into the £££ category. ⊠ *Eastgate,* ☎ *01522/538881,* ℻ *01522/511321. 17 rooms with bath. AE, DC, MC, V.*

Shopping

Lincoln's main shopping area, mostly pedestrianized, is at the bottom of the hill below the cathedral, around the Stonebow gateway and Guildhall, and along High Street. However, the best stores are on Bailgate, Steep Hill, and the medieval streets leading directly down from the cathedral and castle. The **Cobb Hall Craft Centre** (⊠ St. Paul's La., off Bailgate) is a small mall of crafts shops and workshops, selling clocks, candles, and ornaments. Steep Hill has several good bookstores, antiques shops, and crafts and art galleries, such as **Harding House, Steep Hill Galleries,** and the **Long Gallery** (⊠ Top of High St.). **David Hansord** (⊠ 32 Steep Hill, ☎ 01522/530044) specializes in antiques, especially antique scientific instruments.

Boston

48 *31 mi from Lincoln.*

It was from here that, in 1620, Puritans Isaac Johnson and John Winthrop showed their disapproval of the then-prevailing religious conditions by crossing the Atlantic and helping to found the Massachusetts town of the same name. The Puritans had first tried to set sail for Holland in 1607, but they were arrested, tried, and imprisoned. The town's leading landmark remains the Boston Stump, the lantern tower of the 14th-century **Church of St. Botolph.** With a height of 288 ft, it can be seen for 20 mi from both land and sea and once served to house a light that not only guided ships coming to the old port but also directed wayfarers crossing the treacherous marshes; today, it's a directional beacon for aircraft as well. The 15th-century guildhall, now the **Guildhall Museum,** contains the courtroom where the Pilgrims were tried and the cells where they were held. ⊠ *St. Mary's Guildhall, South St.,* ☎ *01205/ 365954.* ☜ *£1.20, free on Thurs; admission includes 45-min personal audio tour.* ☉ *Mon.–Sat. 10–5, Sun. (Apr.–Sept. only) 1:30–5.*

Among several other reminders of Boston's transatlantic links is the early 18th-century **Fydell House,** next to the guildhall, now an adult education center, where a room is graciously set aside for visitors from Boston, Massachusetts. ⊠ *South St.,* ☎ *01205/351520.* ☜ *Free.* ☉ *Weekdays 9:30–12:30 and 1:30–4:30.*

Stamford

49 *35 mi southwest of Boston, 14 mi northwest of Peterborough, 47 mi northwest of Cambridge.*

Serene Stamford is set on a hillside overlooking a river and has an extremely well-preserved center, thanks to being designated England's first conservation area in 1967. It's a delightful place to stroll around while admiring the harmonious mixture of Georgian and medieval architecture.

★ Less than a mile outside Stamford is **Burghley House,** an architectural masterpiece acknowledged as "the largest and grandest house of the first Elizabethan age." The mansion—celebrated for its roofscape bristling with pepper-pot chimneys and slat-roof towers—was built in 1587 by William Cecil, first Baron Burghley, when he was Elizabeth I's high treasurer. Set in fine parkland, it has 18 of the most sumptuous state rooms in England, with carvings by Grinling Gibbons and ceiling paintings by Verrio, as well as innumerable paintings and a priceless porcelain collection. ☎ *01780/752451.* ☜ *£5.85.* ☉ *Apr.–Sept., daily 11–4:30.*

EAST ANGLIA A TO Z

Arriving and Departing

By Bus
National Express (☎ 0990/808080) serves the region from London's Victoria Coach Station. Average travel times: 2½ hours to Bury St. Edmunds, two hours to Cambridge, two hours to Colchester, four hours to Lincoln, and three hours to Norwich.

By Car
From London, Cambridge (54 mi) is just off M11. At exit 9, M11 connects with A11 to Norwich (114 mi); A14 off A11 goes to Bury St. Edmunds. A12 from London goes through east Suffolk via Colchester, Ipswich, and Great Yarmouth. For Lincoln (131 mi), take A1 via Huntingdon, Peterborough, and Grantham to A46 at Newark-on-

Trent. A more scenic alternative is to leave A1 at Grantham and take A607 to Lincoln.

By Train

The entire region is served by trains from London's Liverpool Street Station; in addition, there are trains to Cambridge and Lincoln from King's Cross Station. Full information on trains to East Anglia is available from **National Rail Enquiries** (☎ 0345/484950). Average travel times are one hour to Colchester, 50–90 minutes to Cambridge, almost 2 hours 50 minutes to Norwich, and two hours to Lincoln.

Getting Around

By Bicycle

The **Broads Authority** (☎ 01603/782281) maintains a network of cycle paths and bike rental centers throughout the Broads. Rental costs £6 per day and each rental center can provide local maps and route advice. Call for the location and opening hours of the centers; all are within 30–40 minutes' drive of Norwich.

By Bus

Information about local bus service for Norfolk and parts of the surrounding counties is available from the **Norfolk Bus Information Centre** (☎ 0500/626116). An **Explorer ticket** (available on board the bus) gives a day's unlimited travel on the whole network for £4.95; a family pass for two parents and two children costs £9.95. Cambridgeshire's largest bus company is **Stagecoach Cambus** (☎ 01223/423554), which also sells daily (£4.50) and weekly tickets (£9.50–£11.30) valid for unlimited travel within the city of Cambridge and the county.

By Car

East Anglia has few fast main roads. The principal routes are those covered above (☞ Arriving and Departing by Car, *above*), but once off the A roads, traveling within the region often means taking country lanes with many twists and turns.

By Train

A one-day Rover ticket available from any station in either Norfolk or Suffolk for £7 lets you disembark to explore any of the little towns en route. Seven-day Regional Rover tickets for unlimited travel in the Anglia Railways region are also available: Norfolk (£26), Suffolk (£26), Suffolk and Cambridge (£39), Norfolk and Suffolk (£49), or Norfolk, Suffolk and Cambridge (£59). For more information and local timetables, call **National Rail Enquiries** (☎ 0345/484950).

Guided Tours

Qualified guides for walking tours of the major towns, including Bury St. Edmunds, Cambridge, Ely, Colchester, Ipswich, Norwich, and Lincoln can be booked through the respective tourist offices. Those in Cambridge are particularly popular and should be booked well in advance (☎ 01223/322640). Tours depart daily and cost £5.75. In Lavenham, for £5, visitors can join the **Lavenham Walkabout** (☎ 01787/247126), a guided historical walk led by returned Australian emigrant John Beckett. Tours run year-round, though they're restricted to weekends only from November to Easter.

Guide Friday (☎ 01223/362444) operates open-top bus tours of Cambridge—the Backs, the colleges, and the American war cemetery. The tours start from Cambridge train station, but can be picked up at any of Guide Friday's specially marked bus stops throughout the city. Tickets can be bought from the driver, the Guide Friday office at Cambridge train station, or the Cambridge Tourist Information Centre. ⊠ *Cambridge train station; bus stops throughout the city.* 🎫 *Tickets £7.50.* ⊙ *Tours Easter–Sept. every 15 mins; Oct.–Easter every 30 mins.*

Contacts and Resources

Car Rentals

Cambridge: Avis (⊠ 245 Mill Rd., ☎ 01223/212551). **Budget Rent-a-Car** (⊠ 303–305 Newmarket Rd., ☎ 01223/323838). **Hertz** (⊠ Willhire Ltd., Barnwell Rd., ☎ 01223/414600). **Colchester: Avis** (⊠ 213 Shrub End Rd., ☎ 01206/541133). **Hertz** (⊠ Willhire Ltd., Crown Interchange, Old Ipswich Rd., ☎ 01206/230231). **Lincoln: Avis** (⊠ Ermine petrol station, Riseholm Rd., ☎ 01522/ 511200). **Eurodollar** (⊠ Newland Rd., ☎ 01522/512233). **Norwich: Avis** (⊠ Norwich Airport, Cromer Rd., ☎ 01603/416719). **Budget Rent-a-Car** (⊠ Hall Rd., ☎ 01603/507777). **Hertz** (⊠ Norwich Airport, Cromer Rd., ☎ 01603/ 404010.

Emergencies

Police, fire, or ambulance (☎ 999).

Travel Agencies

American Express (⊠ 25 Sidney St., Cambridge, ☎ 01223/461460). **Thomas Cook** (⊠ 18 Market St., Cambridge, ☎ 01223/67724; ⊠ Grafton Centre, Cambridge, ☎ 01223/322611; ⊠ 4 Cornhill Pavement, Lincoln, ☎ 01522/510070; ⊠ 15 St. Stephens St., Norwich, ☎ 01603/621547; ⊠ 14 London St., Norwich ☎ 01603/761876).

Visitor Information

East of England Tourist Board (⊠ Toppesfield Hall, Hadleigh, Suffolk IP7 7DN, ☎ 01473/822922, ℻ 01473/823063). **Norfolk Broads Authority** (⊠ 18 Colegate, Norwich, Norfolk NR3 1BQ, ☎ 01603/ 610734). **Boston** (⊠ Blackfriars Arts Centre, Spain La., ☎ 01205/ 356656). **Bury St. Edmunds** (⊠ 6 Angel Hill, ☎ 01284/764667). **Cambridge** (⊠ Wheeler St., ☎ 01223/322640). **Colchester** (⊠ 1 Queen St., ☎ 01206/282920). **Ely** (⊠ Oliver Cromwell's House, 29 St. Mary's St., ☎ 01353/662062). **Great Yarmouth** (⊠ Marine Parade, ☎ 01493/ 842195). **Lavenham** (⊠ Lady St., ☎ 01787/248297). **Lincoln** (⊠ 9 Castle Hill, ☎ 01522/529828). **Norwich** (⊠ Guildhall, Gaol Hill, ☎ 01603/666071). **Stamford** (⊠ Broad St., ☎ 01780/755611).

15 Yorkshire

Leeds, Bradford, Haworth, York, Whitby, Castle Howard

On a stormy day, it's hard not to imagine Emily Brontë's Heathcliff riding full-gallop out of Wuthering Heights over the cloud-swept ridges of the Yorkshire Moors. Centered around Haworth, Brontë Country remains a pilgrimage for many. Beyond, however, lie other memories in the making: splendidly elegant Castle Howard, spellbinding Fountains Abbey, and the satisfyingly solid Yorkshire Dales, stomping grounds of James Herriot. Top of the list is York, England's best-preserved medieval city. You can climb the 198-ft-high tower of York Minster—but you need to be in good shape.

YORKSHIRE IS ANOTHER COUNTRY, say the locals, and a few days spent exploring this largest of English regions could well convince you they're right. The famous sights—the Minster at York, the moorland haunts of the Brontës, the ruined monasteries and stately homes—are justifiably popular but only provide half the picture. Nowhere else in England have industry and the natural world collided with such significant effect, offsetting brisk manufacturing towns with untamed scenery. Author J. B. Priestley, in his *English Journey* of 1933, thought that "Industrial Man and Nature sing a rum sort of duet" in Yorkshire—a duet still played out in the hills above Priestley's native Bradford, or in Leeds, or atop the blustery moors.

Updated by
Jules Brown

Yorkshire remains an intensely rural region. The most rugged of its landscapes are the Yorkshire Moors, a vast area of lonely moorland, inspiration of Emily Brontë's 19th-century novel *Wuthering Heights* (and if ever a work of fiction grew out of the landscape in which its author lived, it was surely this). Brilliant at times with spring flowers and heather, the moors can change dangerously—often within a few minutes—to stormy weather, when you'll be lucky to see as far as the next cloud-swept ridge. Between the bleak areas of moorland and the rocky Pennine hills lie lush, green valleys known as the Yorkshire Dales, where the high rainfall produces luxuriant vegetation, swift rivers, sparkling streams, and waterfalls: the villages here—immortalized through the books of the famous veterinarian James Herriot—are among the most utterly peaceful in England, though many burst into life as summer walking bases.

But there's also a gritty, urban aspect to Yorkshire, whose towns have changed the very course of British history. Two of Britain's major industrial centers are here: Leeds and Bradford. The white heat of the 19th-century industrial revolution was forged, to a great extent, in these cities; today, they are rapidly being rescued from modern decline. More aesthetically pleasing is the northern, walled city of York, dominated by the towers of its great Minster—for some, the most noble cathedral in Britain. Settled originally by Romans and Vikings, York was once England's second most important city, and it is arguably the best-preserved medieval city in the country.

Outside York, even more medieval marvels await—the ruined monastic remains of Rievaulx Abbey, Whitby Abbey, and Fountains Abbey are some of the most romantic and picturesque sights that Britain has to offer. The monks of medieval Yorkshire were among the richest in Europe by virtue of the wool trade that they conducted from their vast religious estates in the north, and they left a wealth of richly decorated and appointed monastic buildings, most in ruins since the 16th-century Dissolution. Thanks to the countless poems written about these ruins by the great Victorian poets, and the paintings of them by celebrated 19th-century artists, these sites became world-famous for their powerful evocation of life in the Middle Ages.

There is no county called Yorkshire per se: although historically split into three divisions or "ridings"—from an old Norse word meaning "third"—the region covered in this chapter concentrates on the modern counties of West Yorkshire and North Yorkshire. As touring bases, we recommend York, Haworth—the center of Brontë Country—or the North Yorkshire seaside resorts of Scarborough and Whitby. Those with very limited time could see York as a day trip—the fastest trains take just two hours from London to York—though proper exploration of the region, especially of the moors and dales, requires time and effort, well rewarded whether you're out to see untamed natural beauty or great medieval art.

Pleasures and Pastimes

Dining

Exploring Yorkshire, with its fresh air and exhilarating hilltop walks, positively encourages hearty appetites. Happily, locally produced meat (especially lamb) and vegetables are excellent; roast beef dinners come with Yorkshire pudding, the famous popover-like pastry traditionally cooked under the meat and served with gravy. In the days when meat was a real luxury, it was offered as a first course in hopes of filling you up so you wouldn't want much to eat for the main course! Fish from the coast is a real treat with freshly fried chips (thick french fries)—cod or haddock is the main local catch, though crab and lobster are seasonally available, too. Look for freshly baked bread and homemade cakes, at their best in Yorkshire tearooms. Don't miss out on Wensleydale cheese, which has a subtle, delicate flavor that delivers a slightly honeyed aftertaste. There are fine restaurants here, but pubs are often the best (and in small villages, the only) places to find good, hearty meals for a gentle price.

CATEGORY	COST*
££££	over £40
£££	£25–£40
££	£15–£25
£	under £15

per person, including first course, main course, dessert, and VAT; excluding drinks

Hiking and Walking

Some of Britain's finest long-distance footpaths cut through the region and incorporate both coastal and moorland sections. The Dales National Park is crisscrossed with trails and long-distance paths; the North Yorkshire Moors have long, empty swaths of land for tramping; and the dramatic coastline offers a variety of craggy cliff walks. Leading trails include the Cleveland Way (108 mi), from Helmsley to Filey; the hard-going Lyke-Wake Walk (40 mi), from Osmotherley to Ravenscar; and the eastern section of the Coast-to-Coast Walk (190 mi), which starts or finishes in Robin Hood's Bay. In addition, the Dales Way (80 mi) connects Leeds and Bradford with the Lake District; while perhaps the greatest of all English walks, the Pennine Way, which runs from the Peak District to Scotland, has a central section that runs through the Yorkshire Dales.

Lodging

For a high price, you can stay at the stately home of Lady Mary Wortley Montagu and at other Yorkshire luxury hotels—or, to get a real flavor of northern hospitality and cuisine, you can look for farmhouse bed-and-breakfasts as you're traveling around the countryside. Even if you travel by public transportation, you're not necessarily limited to accommodations in town centers (although such places as Skipton and Scarborough can make lovely roosts from which to explore the deeper countryside). Many proprietors of places on the outskirts of town will pick you up at the train station or bus depot; it's worth giving them a call if you dream about a peaceful, out-of-the-way spot. Remember that rooms fill very quickly at seaside resorts in July and August, while in winter in the dales and moors, some places close for the season—always call ahead if you're going to remote parts. Hikers and budgeteers love the region's dozens of youth hostels; along with those in the major dales and moorland villages, there are useful budget bases in York,

Whitby (this one right next to the glorious Abbey), Robin Hood's Bay, and Scarborough. Even more basic accommodation is available in a network of camping barns (rural bunkhouses) in the Yorkshire Dales. Reservation numbers and details on hostels and barns—which can fill up quickly in high season—are available from any local tourist office.

CATEGORY	COST*
££££	over £110
£££	£60–£110
££	£50–£60
£	under £50

All prices are for two people sharing a double room, including service, breakfast, and VAT.

Exploring Yorkshire

Yorkshire is the largest English region to explore (its fiercely proud inhabitants would say the only English region *worth* exploring). As such, visitors need to plan carefully before launching themselves on a tour, and this chapter carves Yorkshire into separate geographical regions in an attempt to focus attention on the best it has to offer.

The industrial heartland is West Yorkshire, where the cities of Leeds and Bradford were at the forefront of both the late medieval wool trade and the 19th-century industrial revolution. What the tourist office likes to call Brontë Country—basically Haworth, home of the Brontë family—is just to the northwest, while northward spread the hills, valleys, and villages of the Yorkshire Dales, stomping ground of James Herriot, the much-loved veterinarian. In the center of the region, York—for some, the most attractive city in England—deserves special attention, and there's real interest in its environs, too, with day trips to be made to places as diverse as the spa town of Harrogate and the magnificent Fountains Abbey.

Moving east to the coast, Yorkshire reveals itself to be a seaside holiday destination, though never one that will win prizes for summerlike weather. But fine beaches and a fascinating history await visitors to the resort of Scarborough, the former whaling port of Whitby, Robin Hood's Bay—an erstwhile smuggler's haunt—and the traditional fishing village of Staithes. Finally, every visitor should strike inland to the North Moors National Park, even if it's only to drive back toward York or on to Scotland. Delightful, isolated stone villages, dramatic moorland walks, Rievaulx Abbey, and splendidly elegant Castle Howard are all within easy reach.

Numbers in the text correspond to numbers in the margin and on the Yorkshire and York maps.

Great Itineraries

You could drive across Yorkshire in less than a day (as many do, on the way to Scotland), but you would have little quality time to spend anywhere. Two days would give the opportunity for a night in rural Yorkshire, the Dales, or the Moors perhaps, followed by a night in York. However, only with five days does a satisfying itinerary begin to take shape: with this amount of time, you could stop longer in York and visit the coast, as well as allow yourself time to get off the beaten track a bit to seek out the abbeys, castles, and old moorland villages. You'll still have to move quickly, though, if you want to see every region of Yorkshire—in this case, budget for seven days. This lets you dawdle up the coast or in the Dales, spending an extra night here or there, or perhaps even walking from one village to another.

IF YOU HAVE 3 DAYS

Start in ⊡ **York** ⑭, quintessential city of Yorkshire, where—if you arrive early enough in the day—you'll be able to fit in several of the main medieval city sites, such as York Minster and The Shambles, then take an excursion bus tour leaving shortly before noon out to spectacular **Castle Howard** ㊶. Return to York about 4:30 in the afternoon, repair to Betty's for a cuppa and a "fat rascal," then perhaps go on an evening walking tour. Next morning, continue to see York sites, then plan to travel to Leeds to pick up a bus to **Haworth** ⑤ for a Brontë pilgrimage (Have a car? Make a quick visit to stunning **Studley Royal/Fountains Abbey** ㉙ on the way). Spend your final day in Haworth—don't forget to take an unforgettable hike over the moors from Top Withins—"Wuthering Heights"—to the Hardcastle Crags valley. Return to Leeds.

IF YOU HAVE 7 DAYS

Starting in ⊡ **Leeds** ①, head for **Bradford** ④ and its museums, and make time for a curry lunch on Morley Street before spending the afternoon at the nearby model factory community of Saltaire. It's then just a short drive to ⊡ **Haworth** ⑤ for an overnight stop in Brontë Country, though you'll have to wait until next morning to see the sights. After this, you can afford to meander up through the Yorkshire Dales, via **Skipton** ⑦ and **Malham** ⑨ before stopping for the night in ⊡ **Grassington** ⑧. The next day, soak up more remote scenery as you tour the northern dales, Wensleydale and Swaledale, before hitting the main roads and heading south, via **Studley Royal and Fountains Abbey** ㉙, to the spa town of ⊡ **Harrogate** ㉗. After all this driving, you have only a short journey to York the following day, perhaps calling in at **Knaresborough** ㉘ on the way to see the petrifying well. Stay in ⊡ **York** ⑭ for two nights, which will give you time to see everything, and then early on the morning of departure, aim for Helmsley—with a sightseeing stop at either **Rievaulx Abbey** ㊵ or **Castle Howard** ㊶—before driving across the moors to **Danby** ㊲ and on to ⊡ **Whitby** ㉟ for your overnight stop. The next day, return to York along the coast via **Robin Hood's Bay** ㉞ and **Scarborough** ㉝.

When to Tour Yorkshire

Summer is undoubtedly the best time to visit Yorkshire, especially the coastal areas and moors, when there are festivals and regattas, though you can expect resorts and walking centers to be overcrowded, and you'll have to book accommodations well in advance. York's city center will also be packed shoulder-to-shoulder with visitors. Spring and fall bring their own rewards: less crowded attractions and crisp, clear days, though there's also the increased risk of rain and fog. Winter is hard to call: at its best, with glistening snow and bright, clear days, the coast, moors, and dales are beautiful—but storms and blizzards set in quickly, moorland roads become impassable, and villages can be cut off from the outside world. During winter, stick to York and the main towns if you must keep to a strict timetable.

WEST YORKSHIRE AND BRONTË COUNTRY

Even before the industrial revolution, the towns in the hills and river valleys of West Yorkshire were important commercial centers, whose trade in wool made prodigious fortunes for both local merchants and religious foundations. It's still a region synonymous with wool production, and there are a large number of "mill shops" where high-quality knitting wool, sweaters, and woven wool for skirts or suits can be bought at factory prices. Following industrialization, the towns took

Richmond ⑬

Catterick

Northallerton

⑪ Askrigg

⑫ Hawes

Aysgarth

Swale

A6108

B6270

A684

B6160

Ure

Leeming

Swale

Thirsk

A170

A61

Masham

A6108

Grewelthorpe

North Stainley

A6108

Kettlewell

⑩

Gouthwaite Res.

Studley Royal/
Fountains Abbey

⑳⑨

Ripon

㉚

B6265

Newby Hall

㉛

W H A R F E

⑧ Grassington

⑨ Malham

Cracoe

B6265

Pateley
Bridge

B6165

A61

Nidd

B6165

B6055

A1(M)

B6265

Ure

E

Bolton Priory

⑥

⑦ Skipton

Blubberhouses

A59

Knaresborough

㉘

㉗ Harrogate

A661

MARSTON
MOOR

A I R E D A L E

A629(T)

A65

Wharfe

Ilkley

Askwith

A650

Pool

A658

A61

A61

③ Harewood
House

A659

Wetherby

B1224

A659

Tadcas

A64

Keighley

A650

Aire

Haworth ⑤

A629

B6144

④

Bradford

① Leeds

M1

② Temple
Newsam

A63

A64

A1

A162

Wharfe

Aire

A63

M62

N

TO
MANCHESTER

TO
SHEFFIELD

TO
LONDON

GREAT BRITAIN

NORTH YORK MOORS

37 Danby
Castleton
Eskdale
36 Staithes
Saltburn-by-the-sea
35 Whitby
Grosmont
34 Robin Hood's Bay
A171

Ralph Cross

Rosedale Abbey

38 Hutton-le-Hole

40 Rievaulx Abbey
Keldholme
Scalby

33 Scarborough
Eastfield

39 Helmsley
B1257
A170
Pickering
Ebberston
A170
A64
32 Bridlington
Staxton

Rye

Hovingham
B1257
Swinton
Malton
Hunmanby
B1249

Welburn
Castle Howard
41
Norton

asingwold
North Grimston
Rudston
B1253

Sledmere House
Kilham
A166

B1248
Fridaythorpe
Gt. Driffield

A19(?)
B1363

A166
A164

A61
A64
A1079
York
14 — 26
Pocklington
A163

aster
Ouse
A19

Market Weighton
A1079
Beverley

Selby
A63
A614
M62
A63
S. Cave
Kingston-Upon-Hull
Humber

Howden

M62
Goole

0   6 miles
0   9 km

to new trades—textiles, chemicals, and engineering—which transformed the urban scene, leaving many places today rather unattractive at first sight. However, ongoing restoration of once-glorious Victorian architecture and the regeneration of inner-city areas is having a beneficial effect, while relief is always close at hand in the region's striking rural and moorland surroundings.

In the gaunt hills north of the Calder valley and south of the Aire is the district immortalized by the writings of the famous Brontë sisters. Haworth—an otherwise gray West Yorkshire village—might have passed unobserved throughout the years but for the magnetism of the family that lived in the old parsonage, now the museum of the Brontë Society. Every summer, thousands toil up the steep main street to visit the hilltop church and the museum, where all too often Brontë enthusiasm stops. To understand the real spirit of the Brontë book it is necessary to go farther afield and head out to the moors and the ruined farm of Top Withins, which legend—but not fact—refers to as *Wuthering Heights*.

Leeds provides an obvious starting point, since it's easily reached from the west by the trans-Pennine M62 and from the south by the M1. Traditional wool towns to the south—like Wakefield, Huddersfield, and Halifax—each have a modicum of interest, but the main thrust of any visit to West Yorkshire is to the west of Leeds, where Bradford and Brontë Country, around Haworth, really begin to repay investigation.

Leeds

1 *43 mi northeast of Manchester, 25 mi southwest of York.*

The burgeoning city of Leeds now has a population of more than 400,000 and a reputation as one of the greenest cities in Europe, though its unkempt industrial outskirts and congested traffic make this difficult for first-time visitors to believe. But there has been real progress in the city over the last decade, and what was formerly an industrial city in severe decline has been given a new lease on life. In addition to the parks, long green routes radiate from the city center; there has been major investment in urban heritage projects, and café-bars with outdoor seating are sprouting all over the city. It's not quite the Mediterranean, but there's a tangible vitality in the air these days. Visitors, moreover, are spoiled for choice. The Tower of London's arms and armor collection has been relocated to Leeds's stunning Royal Armouries, while the city's status as rising star has been confirmed by the success of the northern branch of London's chic Harvey Nichols fashion store.

Leeds had a head start on most comparable cities, since its wealthy, 19th-century days had left it a fine architectural bequest. The city is well known for its superb Victorian Arcades, but the Georgian squares and streets of the West End are just as notable. Tucked away among the streets you'll find old pubs and yards that were originally laid out in the 14th century. The **Town Hall** (⊠ The Headrow, ☎ 0113/247–7985; 0113/247–6962 box office), a classical 1853 building, sits prominently in the city center, one of the finest of all public buildings in Britain and the masterpiece of local architect Cuthbert Broderick. It's of most use to tourists as a landmark, since two of the best attractions—the City Art Gallery and the City Museum—lie just across the road. It also hosts an international concert season, attracting top performers and conductors.

The **City Art Gallery** features a fine collection of painting and sculpture, with particularly strong showings of 20th-century British art (including works by Sickert, Hunt, Lowry, and Spencer, among others). Adjoining the gallery is the **Henry Moore Institute**, named, of course, for the famous British sculptor who was a student at Leeds College of Art. The Institute displays temporary exhibitions of modern sculpture; for Moore's own work, step inside the City Art Gallery, which has several examples, or admire his *Reclining Woman* on the steps outside the gallery. ⊠ *The Headrow,* ☎ *0113/247–8248.* ☒ *Free.* ⊙ *Mon.–Tues. and Thurs.–Sat. 10–5, Wed. 10–8, Sun. 1–5.*

ᙅ It's hard to pigeonhole the **City Museum,** whose collections and exhibits—of geology, natural history, ethnology, and archaeology—run the gamut from native flora and fauna and the achievements of prehistoric man to local life in Roman times. But children are sure to be enthralled, and there's a gift shop, too, with inventive offerings. ⊠ *The Headrow,* ☎ *0113/247–8275.* ☒ *Free.* ⊙ *Tues.–Sat. 10–5.*

The **River Aire** was an important trading route in Leeds' early days, although 20th-century recession left the river and associated buildings in poor shape. But in recent years the neglected urban river- and canalside sites have been revitalized as "urban heritage" projects. At **Granary Wharf,** in the Canal Basin, reached via the Dark Arches, where the River Aire flows under the City Station, there are design and crafts shops, music events, boat trips, and a regular festival market. Farther east at **The Calls,** several cafés and restaurants enliven the cobbled streets and quayside.

Tetley's Brewery Wharf celebrates the history of the English pub through the ages, and since all the main attractions are indoors—including a brewery tour of the Yorkshire company, Tetley's, with free tastings—it's a useful wet-weather standby. If there are blue skies, take advantage of the riverside venue of the outdoor café-bar. ⊠ *The Waterfront, River Aire,* ☎ *0113/242–0666.* ☒ *£4.95; brewery tour £2 extra.* ⊙ *Apr.–Sept., Tues.–Sun. 10:30–5:30; Oct.–Mar., Wed.–Sun. 10–4:30.*

★ ᙅ Dubbed "the most exciting day out in history," Leeds's **Royal Armouries** occupy a redeveloped 13-acre dockland site, a 15-minute walk from the city center. The state-of-the-art building was purpose-built to house the superb arms and armor collection from the Tower of London, which had outgrown its original home long ago. Here, in a series of spirited interactive displays, hands-on exhibits, video presentations, computer simulations, and even live demonstrations, you can trace the history of weaponry in five themed galleries. Shoot a crossbow, direct operations on a battlefield, experience a Wild West gunfight or an Elizabethan joust—this is one museum guaranteed to have you talking about your visit for years to come. ⊠ *Armouries Dr., just off M1 or M621,* ☎ *0113/220–1900.* ☒ *£6.95.* ⊙ *Apr.–Oct., daily 10–6; Nov.–Mar., daily 10–5; 1st Thurs. of month (May–Sept.) open until 10 PM.*

❷ Just east of the center of Leeds stands **Temple Newsam,** a huge Elizabethan and Jacobean building, which was altered in the 18th century. It was the birthplace in 1545 of Darnley, the doomed husband of Mary, Queen of Scots. Surrounded by one of the largest public parks in Western Europe, the house now belongs to Leeds City Council, which uses it to display its rich collections of furniture, paintings, and ceramics. The vast park, with its walled rose gardens, greenhouses, and miles of woodland walks, was originally laid out by Capability Brown in 1762. The house is 4 mi east of Leeds on the A63, and there are buses from Leeds Central Bus Station every 30 minutes. ⊠ *Temple Newsam and Selby Rds.,* ☎ *0113/264–7321.* ☒ *£2.20.* ⊙ *Apr.–Oct., Tues.–Sun. 1–5:30; Nov.–Mar., weekends noon–4; gardens daily 10–dusk; last entry 1 hr before closing.*

❸ **Harewood House** (pronounced harwood) is the home of the earl of Harewood, a cousin of the Queen. This spectacularly impressive Neoclassic mansion, built in 1759 by John Carr of York, is known for its Robert Adam interiors, important paintings and ceramics, and some of the most ravishing Chippendale furniture extant (Chippendale was born in nearby Otley). On the grounds are gardens, woods, a lake, a bird garden, an adventure playground, and a butterfly house. The house is 7 mi north of Leeds, along the A61; buses leave from Leeds's Central Bus Station every 30 minutes. ⊠ *Harewood,* ☎ *0113/288–6331.* ✆ *£6.50, bird garden and grounds £5.25, grounds only £4.* ☉ *Apr.–Nov., daily 11–5; grounds and bird garden open at 10.*

Dining and Lodging

£££ ✕ **Pool Court at 42.** Right in the center of Leeds, in the revitalized warehouse district by the river, Pool Court at 42 is typical of the new wave of fashionable restaurants becoming popular with northern food fanciers. It's a distinctly elegant, professional place serving contemporary French and British food, with Mediterranean influences. Fish is always a good choice, while duck and game are expertly cooked, and there are some fine vegetarian dishes, too. The adjacent, associated **Brasserie 44** (☎ 0113/234–3232) is less formal, and prices are less expensive, though it features the same cosmopolitan influences. ⊠ *42–44 The Calls,* ☎ *0113/244–4242. AE, DC, MC, V. Closed Sun. No lunch Sat.*

££££ ▥ **42 The Calls.** Taking an old grain mill in the once-dilapidated waterfront area of the city and converting it into a high-tech, high-comfort hotel takes some nerve, but the venture has paid off. Each room shows individual flair, while retaining such original features as warehouse skylights, exposed beams, and brickwork; facilities are up-to-the-minute, with CD players, comfortable bathrooms, and a split-level lobby lounge-bar with eminently cushy armchairs. ⊠ *42 The Calls, LS2 7EW,* ☎ *0113/244–0099,* ℻ *0113/234–4100. 41 rooms with bath. Restaurant, bar, breakfast room, lobby lounge, room service. AE, DC, MC, V.*

Nightlife and the Arts

Opera North, England's first major provincial opera company, has its home in Leeds at the **Grand Theatre,** whose opulent gold-and-plush auditorium is modeled on that of La Scala. It's worth knowing that Opera North also plays for free each summer in the grounds at Temple Newsam (*see above*). ⊠ *46 New Briggate,* ☎ *0113/245–9351 or 0113/244–0971.* ☉ *Box office Mon.–Sat. 10–9.*

The ultramodern **West Yorkshire Playhouse** was built on the slope of an old quarry and its interior is designed to be completely adaptable to all kinds of staging. ⊠ *Playhouse Sq., Quarry Hill,* ☎ *0113/244–2111.* ☉ *Box office Mon.–Sat. 9–8.*

Fashionable café-bars are sprouting all over Leeds, allowing you to grab a bite or sip cappuccino or designer beer until late into the night. **Indie Joze** (⊠ Victoria Quarter, Briggate, ☎ 0113/245–0569) has arcade seating in Leeds' most elegant shopping corridor. **Cuban Heels** (⊠ The Arches, Assembly St., ☎ 0113/234–6115) kicks out salsa sounds most nights. The **Town and Country Club** (⊠ 55 Cookridge St., ☎ 0113/280–0100)—a regional offshoot of the famous London live-music venue—hosts regular rock and pop gigs.

Shopping

The arrival of **Harvey Nichols** (⊠ Briggate, ☎ 0113/204–8804)—home-based in London, where it is regarded as the crucible of chic—put Leeds firmly on the British shopping map: stop in for an abundance of fashion and a great café-restaurant. The city also has some excellent markets, notably **Kirkgate Market** (⊠ Vicar La., ☎ no phone), an Edwardian beauty that's the largest in the north of England. Specialty shops and designer boutiques fill the Victorian shopping arcades, of which the glistening **Victoria Quarter** (✉ Briggate, ☎ no phone) is the epitome of fin-de-siècle style. For ethnic clothes, gifts, jewelry, and accessories, visit the shops inside the old **Corn Exchange** (✉ Call La., ☎ 0113/234–1745).

Bradford

❹ *9 mi west of Leeds, 12 mi north of Huddersfield, 32 mi northeast of Manchester.*

Bradford was once one of the greatest wool towns in Europe, a trade at which it had excelled since the 16th century. Even as late as the 1960s, wool accounted for a substantial part of its economy, but as with all the other West Yorkshire textile towns, recession and competition from new markets hit hard. It tries hard to be likeable today, and though much of its grandeur has gone, the center still boasts the odd Victorian building from its period of greatest prosperity: St. George's Hall on Bridge Street (1851) and the Wool Exchange on Market Street (1864) are two fine examples. But not everyone is impressed: American travel writer Bill Bryson, in his *Notes from a Small Island,* claims that "Bradford's role in life is to make every place else in the world look better in comparison, and it does this very well."

Tourists, it must be said, come to Bradford not for the buildings but for the museums, particularly the renowned **National Museum of Photography, Film, and Television,** which opened in 1983 and traces the history of the photographic media. It's a huge, and hugely entertaining, museum, with plenty of interactive models, machines, and related ephemera from early cameras to TV props, though the museum's popularity with children means you're best advised to come early or late in the day if you want to see the displays in peace. Allow time, too, for a screening at the museum's 50-by-60-ft IMAX screen—the biggest in Britain—which shows stomach-churning movies of flights over the Grand Canyon and other remarkable sequences. The associated Pictureville cinema has a full repertory program, too. The entire museum has been under long-term renovation and is due to reopen in spring 1999. ✉ *Pictureville, Prince's View,* ☎ *01274/727488.* ▣ *Museum free, IMAX movie £3.90, Pictureville screenings £3.80.* ⊙ *Tues.–Sun. and national holidays 10–6.*

Bradford's history as a wool-producing town is outlined at the **Industrial Museum and Horses at Work,** housed in a former spinning mill 3 mi northeast of the town center. Exhibits include workers' dwellings dating from the 1870s and a mill owner's house from the 19th century. Children love riding in the Shire horse-drawn tram. Moorside Road is off the A658 Harrogate Road; or take Bus 608, 609, or 612 from the city center. ✉ *Moorside Mills, Moorside Rd.,* ☎ *01274/631756.* ▣ *Free.* ⊙ *Tues.–Sat. 10–5., Sun. noon–5.*

★ Perhaps the most extraordinary attraction in Bradford is the former model factory community of **Saltaire.** Built by textile magnate Sir Titus Salt in the mid-19th century, it's a remarkable example of the enduring trait of philanthropy among certain Victorian industrialists, who erected modern terraced housing for their workers, and furnished them with libraries, parks, hospitals, schools, and educational leisure facilities. Saltaire, fashioned in Italianate style, has been remarkably preserved, its former mills and houses turned into shops, restaurants, and galleries. Even more remarkable is the permanent retrospective exhibition of 400 works by locally born artist David Hockney in the **1853 Gallery** (✉ Victoria Rd., ☎ 01274/531163) in Salt's Mill. Saltaire is just 4 mi north of Bradford, and there are regular local bus and train services; drivers should take the A650 and follow the signs.

Dining and Lodging

£ ✕ **Kashmir.** Just two minutes from the National Museum of Photography, Film, and Television, Morley Street is lined with some of Bradford's finest curry houses. The Kashmir is one of the best, a simple, no-frills place dishing out authentically spiced food at extremely low prices. ✉ *27 Morley St.,* ☎ *01274/726513. No credit cards.*

£££ ✕🏨 **Quality Victoria Hotel.** This renovated former railway hotel in the center of town—built in 1875—makes a comfortable base if you crave an urban Yorkshire stopover. Public areas are smart and stylish, and guest rooms keep up with appearances, too: armchairs in checked cloth, plump beds, and crisp, cool decor. The standard room rate doesn't include breakfast, though discounted weekend rates do. Vic and Bert's, the stylish and popular attached restaurant (no lunch Sun.), gets rave reviews for its eclectic grill menu. ✉ *Bridge St., BD1 1JX,* ☎ *01274/ 728706,* 🖷 *01274/736358. 63 rooms with bath. Restaurant, bar, sauna, exercise room. AE, DC, MC, V.*

Haworth: Heart of Brontë Country

❺ *10 mi northwest of Bradford, 5 mi southwest of Keighley.*

There's not much, at first glance, that makes the village of Haworth (pronounced HOW-weth) in West Yorkshire special. It's an old, stone-built spot on the edge of the Yorkshire Moors, superficially much like many other craggy Yorkshire settlements. But Haworth has a particular claim to fame; in fact, it's probably the most celebrated literary spot in Britain after Stratford-upon-Avon. It was here, in the middle of the 19th century, that the three Brontë sisters—Emily (author of *Wuthering Heights,* 1847), Charlotte (*Jane Eyre,* 1847), and Anne (*The Tenant of Wildfell Hall,* 1848)—lived. This unlikely trio, daughters of the local vicar, were responsible for some of the most romantic books ever written. "My sister Emily loved the moors," sister Charlotte once wrote. "Flowers brighter than the rose bloomed in the blackest of the heath for her; out of a sullen hollow in a livid hillside her mind could make an Eden. She found in the bleak solitude many and dear delights; and not the least and best loved was liberty. Liberty was the breath of Emily's nostrils; without it she perished." Today, thousands journey to the straggling stone village of Haworth, which lives a little too readily off its associations: visitors, in summer, on occasion threaten to overwhelm the place entirely.

To reach Haworth by bus or train, buy a Metro Day Rover for bus and rail, and take the Metro train from Leeds to Keighley. There are about three hourly. From Keighley, take the Keighley & Worth Valley Railway (☞ *below*) for the trip to Haworth, or opt instead for the Keighley and District Buses 663, 664, or 665 (one leaves every 20 minutes). The same buses make the direct journey from Bradford, also every 20 minutes. You can first access the region by taking a train to Leeds City Station or a bus to Leeds's National Express Coach Station.

Haworth's steep, cobbled **Main Street** has changed little in outward appearance since the early 19th century, but today acts as a funnel for most of the tourists who crowd into the various points of interest: the **Black Bull** pub, where the reprobate Branwell, the Brontës' only brother, drank himself into an early grave; the **post office** from which Charlotte, Emily, and Anne sent their manuscripts to their London publishers; and the **church**, with its gloomy graveyard (Charlotte and Emily are buried inside the church; Anne, in Scarborough; ☞ The North

Yorkshire Coast, *below*). Head to the the town's **information center** (2–4 West La., ☎ 01535/642329) for information about accommodations, maps, and books on the Brontës, and inexpensive leaflets to help you find your way to such outlying *Wuthering Heights* sites as Ponden Hall (Thrushcross Grange) and Ponden Kirk (Penistone Crag).

★ The **Brontë Parsonage Museum** is housed in the somber Georgian house in which the sisters grew up and displays original furniture (some bought by Charlotte after the success of *Jane Eyre*), portraits, and books. The Brontës first came here in 1820, when the Reverend Patrick Brontë was appointed to the local living, but tragedy soon struck—his wife, Maria, and their two eldest children died within five years (done in, some scholars assert, by water wells tainted by seepage from the neighboring graveyard, a malady which inflicted a tragically high toll on all Haworth at this time). The museum has some enchanting mementos of the four surviving children, including the sisters' spidery, youthful graffiti on the nursery wall, and Charlotte's tiny wedding shoes. Branwell, trained as an artist in nearby Leeds, painted several of the portraits on display. ⊠ *Main St.,* ☎ *01535/642323.* 🖭 *£3.80.* ☉ *Apr.–Sept., daily 10–5; Oct.–Mar., daily 11–4:30; closed mid-Jan.–early Feb.*

If you know and love the Brontës' works, you'll probably want to walk (an hour or so along a field path, a lane, and a moorland track) to the **Brontë Waterfall,** described in Emily's and Charlotte's poems and letters. **Top Withins,** 3 mi from Haworth, is the remains of a bleak hilltop farm. Although often taken to be the main inspiration for Heathcliff's gloomy mansion, Wuthering Heights, it probably isn't, as a plaque nearby baldly states. There and back from Haworth is a two-hour walk. Better still is to cross the watershed to Wycollar, over the Lancashire border, or make that fine walk from Withens to the Hardcastle Crags valley. Wherever you chose to head, you'll need sturdy shoes and protective clothing: if you've read *Wuthering Heights,* you'll have a fairly good idea of what weather can be like on the Yorkshire Moors.

☾ Haworth is one stop on the **Keighley & Worth Valley Railway,** a gorgeous branch line along which steam engines run between Keighley (8 mi north of Haworth) and Oxenhope. Taking the train at least part of the way is exciting enough for everyone, though kids will like it even more on special days when there are family fairs en route, or when Thomas the Tank Engine makes an appearance. ⊠ *Railway Station, Keighley,* ☎ *01535/645214; 01535/647777 24-hr information.* 🖭 *£5 return, £6.50 day rover ticket,* ☉ *Weekends year-round, daily June– Aug.; call for schedules and special events.*

Dining and Lodging

£££ ✕🖭 **Weavers.** You'll have to book well in advance, since there are only four rooms available at Weavers, converted from a series of old cottages, but you'll be glad you did. In a fine village location, it's mainly in business as a restaurant, though the pretty, light rooms are well turned out, with fine views, and the breakfast is very good. Downstairs, the restaurant (££) serves traditional Yorkshire cuisine, including Yorkshire pudding and local stews. More elaborate dishes include Gressingham duck, or a daily fish special (perhaps in a pie, or baked), and there's a specially priced set dinner for early arrivals; get there before 7 for this. ⊠ *15 West La., West Yorkshire, BD22 8DU,* ☎ *01535/643822,* 🖹🖶 *01535/ 644832. 4 rooms with bath. Restaurant, bar. AE, DC, MC, V. Closed 2 wks at Christmas and 2 wks July; restaurant closed Sun. and Mon.*

££ ✕🖭 **Old White Lion Hotel.** Next door to the church where Patrick Brontë preached and not far from the family parsonage, the Old White Lion is one of the more welcoming hostelries in Haworth. Antique touches and modern conveniences mix happily here and there's a full restaurant on the premises. ⊠ *6 West La., West Yorkshire, BD22 8DU,* ☎ *01535/642313,* 𝖥𝖠𝖷 *01535/646222. 14 rooms with bath. Restaurant, parking (free). AE, DC, MC, V.*

£ ⊞ **Apothecary Guest House.** This 17th-century building at the top of Main Street, near the Parsonage, earns full marks for value and cozy comfort. You can either look out on Haworth's historic main street or, at the back, wake up to sweeping views of the bleak moors. And although only breakfast is served, you're very close to the village's best tearooms and pubs, including Branwell's favorite, the *Black Bull,* just over the road. ⊠ *86 Main St. BB22 8DA,* ☎ 𝖥𝖠𝖷 *01535/643642. 7 rooms with shower. MC, V.*

THE YORKSHIRE DALES

With some of the fairest scenery in England, the Yorkshire Dales stand in complete and startling contrast to the industrial towns of West Yorkshire. These meandering river valleys fall south and east from the Pennines and, beyond Skipton, present an almost wholly rural aspect. Most, but not all, dales take their names from the rivers that run through them and provide a variety of scenery that's quintessentially English: a ruined priory here, a narrow country road there, a bubbling river, and stone moorland hamlets that were the settings for James Herriot's books. Villages here seem to take on the texture of the fells and fit snugly into little pockets looking as though they, like the Pennines, have been here from eternity. In places, loveliness of setting goes hand in hand with architectural beauty, such as at Bolton Priory, the monastic ruins that once enchanted Wordsworth and Ruskin. Naturally, the Yorkshire Dales contain prime walking country, and all the villages covered in this section have access to a fine network of paths and trails, as well as providing a full range of accommodations and hiking services. Wharfedale, one of the longest of the Yorkshire Dales, is easily accessible from Bradford. A convenient driving route (with only a little early backtracking) would take in Bolton Priory, the castle at Skipton, and rural Grassington, Malham, and Kettlewell, before moving farther north to see the glories of Wensleydale and Swaledale and finishing at the attractive market town of Richmond.

Bolton Priory

★ ➏ *12 mi north of Haworth, 6 mi northeast of Skipton, 18 mi north of Bradford, 24 mi northwest of Leeds.*

Some of the loveliest of the Wharfedale scenery comes into view around Bolton Priory, the ruins of an Augustinian priory, which sits on a grassy embankment inside a great curve of the River Wharfe itself. The priory is just a short walk or drive from the confusingly named village of Bolton Abbey, and once there you can wander through the 13th-century ruins or visit the priory church, which is still the local parish church; it's open daily, with free access in the daytime (although parking in the estate grounds costs £2.50). Among the famous visitors enchanted by Bolton Priory were William Wordsworth (who described "Bolton's mouldering Priory" in his poem "The White Doe of Rylstone"); J. M. W. Turner, the 19th-century artist, who painted it; and John Ruskin, the Victorian art critic, who rated it most beautiful of all the English ruins he had seen.

Close to Bolton Priory, surrounded by some of the most romantic woodland scenery in England, the River Wharfe plunges between a narrow chasm in the rocks (a dangerous stretch of white water known as "the Strid") before reaching a medieval hunting lodge, **Barden Tower.** Barden Tower is now a ruin and can be visited just as easily as Bolton Priory, in whose grounds it stands.

Dining and Lodging

££££ ✕🏨 **Devonshire Arms.** Originally an 18th-century coaching inn, and
★ still belonging to the dukes of Devonshire, this country-house hotel is in a superb setting on the River Wharfe, within easy walking distance of Bolton Priory and the village of Bolton Abbey. Portraits of various dukes hang on the walls, and the individually themed bedrooms in the original building are tastefully decorated by the Duchess of Devonshire; all have four-poster beds and carved furniture. There's even the feminine "Mitford Room" for lady executives traveling alone. The (no-smoking) Burlington restaurant, in the hotel, has a fine, traditional menu using homegrown herbs and vegetables, and the good service stands out. ✉ *Bolton Abbey, Skipton, North Yorkshire, BD23 6AJ*, ☎ *01756/ 710441*, 𝖥𝖠𝖷 *01756/710564. 40 rooms with bath. Restaurant, bar, no-smoking rooms, pool, sauna, tennis court, exercise room, health club, fishing, baby-sitting. AE, DC, MC, V.*

Skipton

❼ *6 mi west of Bolton Abbey, 12 mi north of Haworth, 22 mi west of Harrogate.*

Skipton in Airedale is a typical Dales market town with as many farmers as tourists milling in the streets (there are markets every day except Tuesdays and Sundays), and shops selling local produce predominate. **Skipton Castle,** originally built by the Normans in 1090 and unaltered since the Civil War (17th century), is the town's most prominent attraction. It's also one of the best-preserved of all English medieval castles, remarkably complete in appearance—after the Battle of Marston Moor, it remained the only Royalist stronghold in the north of England. In the central courtyard, a yew tree, planted 300 years ago by Lady Anne Clifford, still flourishes. The castle is at the top of busy High Street. ✉ *Skipton Castle, High St.*, ☎ *01756/792442.* 🖭 *£3.60.* ⊘ *Mar.–Sept., Mon.–Sat. 10–6, Sun. 2–6; Oct.–Feb., Mon.– Sat. 10–4, Sun. 2–4.*

Dining

££ ✕ **Angel Inn.** Diners at the Angel regularly clog the hidden-away hamlet of Hetton with their vehicles, such is the attraction of this locally renowned eatery. You can book in advance for the restaurant, but tables in the various cozy rooms of the bar-brasserie are available on a first-come-first-served basis—and they fill on the dot of opening time most days. Fish is a specialty (especially on Fridays), and you might encounter tangy fish soup, cod with an herb crust, or baked sea bass. ✉ *Hetton, 5 mi north of Skipton, off the B6265*, ☎ *01756/730263. AE, MC, V. No dinner Sun.*

Grassington

★ ❽ *10 mi north of Skipton, 14 mi northwest of Ilkley, 25 mi west of Ripon.*

A small, stone village built around an ancient cobbled marketplace, Grassington is well situated for exploring Upper Wharfedale. The Dales Way footpath passes through the village, and there is a surprisingly good range of guest houses, stores, pubs, and cafés—though this is less of a surprise if you visit during summer, when facilities become positively overwhelmed by day-trippers and walkers. Local walks are easily accomplished, however, and if you're prepared to make a day of it, you'll soon find you leave the crowds behind. The **National Park**

Centre has a wide choice of guidebooks, maps, and bus schedules to help you enjoy a day in the Dales. Organized tours depart from the center with qualified guides who explain the botanical and geological features of the area. ⊠ *Colvend, Hebdon Rd.,* ☎ *01756/752774.* ⊙ *Apr.–Oct., daily 10–4; Nov.–Mar., weekends 10–4.*

Dining and Lodging

£   ✗ **Old Hall Inn.** This stone-flagged, rustic country pub with a small garden on the outskirts of Grassington serves an out-of-the-ordinary menu that attracts people from miles around. Main courses might include *nasi goreng* (an Indonesian rice dish with prawns), local sausages with onion confit, or haddock with a tapenade crust. Starters and desserts are just as adventurous. ⊠ *Threshfield, 1 mi west of Grassington,* ☎ *01756/752441. No credit cards. Closed Mon. No dinner Sun.*

££ ✗⌷ **Black Horse Hotel.** Set back a little from the main square, the welcoming Black Horse has a good local reputation. The good-value rooms here are just the thing if you've walked in from afar, with comfortable beds, TVs, and tea/coffeemaking facilities; some have four-posters for a touch of luxury. An extensive bar menu is served, though there's more formal dining in the restaurant where an *à la carte* menu of local and traditional dishes defeats even the heartiest of appetites. In winter, open fires keep things cozy; in summer, sit out on the terrace with a drink. ⊠ *Garrs La., BD23 5AT,* ☎ *01756/752770. 15 rooms with bath. Restaurant, bar. MC, V.*

Malham

★ ❾ *10 mi west of Grassington; take B6265 south 2 mi through Cracoe, then branch west onto the minor road past Hetton and Calton; also 12 mi northwest of Skipton, off the A65.*

The keenest hikers descend in their summer droves on Malham to tour some of Britain's most remarkable limestone formations. The tiny hamlet has a population of just 215 yet is visited by half a million people a year—the lesson is to come before June or after August, if at all possible, to avoid the worst of the crowds. It's a magical place at most times of the year, the intensely rural surroundings described glowingly in poems by Wordsworth and Auden, painted by Turner, and photographed by Hockney—proof indeed of Malham's aesthetic potency.

Malham's three main destinations—Malham Cove, Gordale Scar, and Malham Tarn—are close enough to see on a circular walk of 8 mi that takes most people four to five hours. Those with less time should cut out the tarn: a circular walk from the village to Malham Cove and Gordale Scar can be completed in just over two hours. **Malham Cove,** a huge natural rock amphitheater, is just a mile north of the village and provides the easiest local walk, though following the path *up* to the top is another matter altogether—it's a brutal climb, rewarded by magnificent views. At **Gordale Scar,** a deep natural chasm between overhanging limestone cliffs, the white waters of a moorland stream plunge 300 ft; it's a mile northeast of Malham and can be reached by a lovely riverside path. A longer walk, of more than 3 mi, leads north from Malham to **Malham Tarn,** an attractive lake set in windswept isolation. Here, there's a nature reserve on the west bank and an easy-to-follow trail on the east bank.

Maps and displays at Malham's **National Park Centre** will give you some more informed ideas of what there is to do and see locally. You can get a list of local B&B and pub accommodations here too—they are relatively plentiful, but highly sought after in summer, so call ahead if you plan to stay the night. ⊠ *National Park Centre,* ☎ *01729/830363.* ⊙ *Easter–Oct., daily 9:30–5; Nov.–Easter, weekends 10–4.*

En Route North of Malham, there's a dramatic moorland drive following the minor road that skirts Malham Tarn, to **Arncliffe** in Littondale, where a superb village inn, the *Falcon* ☎ 01756/770205 revives flagging spirits and provides accommodations. In winter this road may be impassable: always check local weather forecasts before setting out. At Arncliffe, follow the signs southeast for the B6160 and then turn north for Kettlewell.

Kettlewell

⑩ *6 mi north of Grassington, 8 mi northwest of Malham.*

A babbling river runs through the heart of Kettlewell, the main settlement in Upper Wharfedale and a fine base for a couple of days' exploration of the locals hills and valleys, with their stone-flagged pubs, riverside walks, and narrow pack bridges. The Dales Way hiking path passes through the quiet, gray-stone village, while drivers will easily be able to visit Malham and Grassington, returning for a peaceful night away from the crowds.

Dining and Lodging

££ ✕🏨 **Langcliffe Country House.** Tucked up a back road, this charming, flower-filled property is a real home away from home, sporting fantastic views across Wharfedale. Rooms are neat and tidy, and a log fire crackles away in the lounge in the winter. Homemade dinners are served in the conservatory, and the choice might be a hearty stew, a vegetarian specialty, or fish from the local streams. To find the house, look for the King's Head pub, opposite which is a road marked FOR ACCESS ONLY: Langcliffe is 500 yards along here. ✉ *Kettlewell, Skipton, BD23 5RJ,* ☎ *01756/760243. 6 rooms with bath. Restaurant, bar. MC, V.*

En Route From Kettlewell, it's just 4 mi along the B6160 to **Buckden,** the last village in Wharfedale. From here you can go directly through Kidstone Pass (still on the B6160) to Aysgarth in Wensleydale, where the River Ure plummets over a series of waterfalls; Askrigg is just 5 mi farther west.

Askrigg

⑪ *16 mi north of Kettlewell, 25 mi north of Malham.*

Askrigg would be just another typical Wensleydale village, were it not for its association with the James Herriot TV series, which was filmed in and around the village. The tourist board pushes "Herriot Country" hard, but although Askrigg—dubbed "Darrowby" in the program—is a pleasing village, there's not a great deal else to keep you here, apart from walks to a couple of local waterfalls. Before leaving, however, you should visit the **King's Arms Hotel** (✉ Market Pl., ☎ 01969/650258), a wood-paneled, 18th-century coaching inn in the center of the village. Rechristened the Drover's Arms, this figures in many an episode of the program and is a truly atmospheric building, with nook-and-cranny rooms, good local beer, two restaurants, and guest rooms, too.

Hawes

⑫ *5 mi west of Askrigg.*

The best time to visit Hawes—reputedly the highest market town in England—is on Tuesday, when farmers and locals crowd into town for the weekly market. There's a brisk, businesslike atmosphere at other times, too, since Hawes retains some of Wensleydale's more traditional industries, not least its cheese making. Crumbly, white Wensleydale cheese has been made in the valley for centuries, though in the past decade production moved into the town itself. You can buy the cheese at various stores in town, and give yourself time to wander the cobbled side streets, too, some of which sport antiques shops and tearooms.

At the **Wensleydale Creamery Visitor Centre,** on the outskirts of Hawes, a Cheese Museum tells the story of how Wensleydale cheese came to be produced. There's a viewing gallery, to enable you to watch production (best seen between 10:30 and 3), and then you can repair to the shop, where tasting of the various cheeses is encouraged before you buy. Quite apart from the regular Wensleydale cheese on offer, try it smoked, or with ginger, or with apple pie, or even with dried fruit. There's a restaurant on the site, too. ⊠ *Wensleydale Creamery Visitor Centre, Gayle La.,* ☎ *01969/667664.* 🖾 *Museum £2.* ☉ *Mon.–Sat. 9:30–5, Sun. 10–4.*

Hawes's National Park Information Centre in the old train station contains the **Dales Countryside Museum,** which helps give a picture of Dales life in past centuries; a traditional rope-making shop here also welcomes visitors. ⊠ *National Park Centre, Station Yard,* ☎ *01969/667450.* 🖾 *Museum £2.* ☉ *Centre: Apr.–June and Sept.–Oct., daily 10–4; July–Aug., daily 9:30–4:30. Museum: Apr.–Oct., daily 10–5; some winter weekends, phone for details.*

En Route   From Hawes, the most direct route to Swaledale is north by minor road over the **Buttertubs Pass,** a 7-mi run to Muker, a lovely village that hosts the annual Swaledale show in September. Many people regard **Swaledale** itself as the finest of all the Yorkshire Dales and it certainly lingers long in the memory. From Muker, the B6270 and A6108 run down the valley to Richmond.

Richmond

🔟 *30 mi northeast of Hawes, 32 mi northwest of Ripon.*

Richmond tucks itself into a curve in the River Swale, with a network of narrow Georgian streets and terraces opening onto the largest cobbled marketplace in the country. It would be a mistake, however, despite appearances, to date the town's provenance to the 18th century. The Normans first swept in during the late 11th century, determined to subdue the local population and establish Norman rule in the north. This they did by building a mighty castle, around which the town grew, and throughout the Middle Ages Richmond was effectively a garrison town. The immense keep of Richmond's Norman **castle** towers above the River Swale and grants excellent views over the surroundings. Dating from the 11th century, it's one of the best-preserved monuments of this era, retaining its curtain wall and chapel, and a great hall that has been partially restored to its medieval splendor; even the 14th-century graffiti has been preserved. ⊠ *Castle,* ☎ *01748/822493.* 🖾 *£2.* ☉ *Apr.–Sept., daily 10–6; Oct.–Mar., daily 10–4.*

The tiny **Georgian Theatre Royal** is the oldest theater in England still in use, and it is unchanged since the days of the 18th-century Shakespearean actor David Garrick; you can watch performances from either smart gallery boxes or old wooden seats. It's an intimate theater, remarkable for its authentic detail (except that it uses electric lights instead of candles). Try to reserve tickets well in advance. Also, outside performance times, tours take in the backstage areas and finish in the small museum featuring unique painted scenery dating from 1836. ⊠ *Friars Wynd,* ☎ *01748/823710; 01748/823021 box office.* 🖾 *Tour and museum £1.50.* ☉ *Apr.–Oct., Mon.–Sat. 10:30–4:30, Sun. 11–1:15. Box office: year-round, Mon.–Sat. 2:30–5:30.*

Lodging

£ ⌂ **The Old Brewery Guest House.** Richmond has a score of guest houses, but few are as striking as the Old Brewery, set on the edge of a secluded green in a quiet corner of town below the castle. Interior renovations have highlighted the Victorian character of the compact rooms and there's a lovely little patio garden, as well as a guest lounge. Evening meals are available on request, but you're only a few minutes' walk from the town center and its pubs and restaurants. ⊠ *29 The Green, Richmond, DL10 4RG,* ☎ *01748/822460,* ℻ *01748/825561. 5 rooms with shower. No credit cards.*

YORK

It would be unthinkable to visit North Yorkshire without going first to the atmospheric cathedral city of York—and not just because its central location makes it a practical place to start. It would take a fat guidebook to do justice to all the sights in this city, where history seems to put in an appearance around every other corner. Named "Eboracum" in Latin, York was the military capital of Roman Britain, and traces of Roman garrison buildings still survive throughout the city. The Vikings also claimed York as their capital and left bountiful evidence of their tenure, while in Norman times were laid the foundations of York Minster, the largest medieval cathedral in England. During the great industrial age, which caused so much havoc in many northern towns and cities, York was a forgotten backwater—hence the survival of so much medieval and 18th-century architecture. That's not to say that the city exists in a time vacuum: the array of stores that have taken over the heart of the old city can sometimes make the place seem more like an extension of London's Bond Street than one of the great historical survivals of Europe. The Shambles, a quaint example of a medieval street built between 1350 and 1450, has been particularly altered by overly quaint shops and modern boutiques.

Exploring York

★ ⑭ *48 mi southeast of Richmond, 25 mi northeast of Leeds, 82 mi south of Newcastle.*

Following the fall of the Roman Empire in the 5th century, a Saxon town grew up over the ruins of the Roman fort at York. On Christmas Eve, AD 627, the Northumbrian King Edwin introduced Christianity to the area by being baptized in a little wooden church here, and the city grew in importance during the 9th century, after the Viking conquerors of northern and eastern England made York—which they called "Jorvik"—their English capital. You'll notice that many of the city's street names are suffixed with the word "-gate" (Goodramgate, Micklegate, for example)—"gate" was the Viking word for "street."

The old city center of York is a compact, dense web of narrow streets and tiny alleys—"snickleways"—in which congestion is so bad that traffic has been banned around the Minster. It is, conversely, a fine city for walking, provided you have a map, though try to avoid visiting in July and August, when crowds choke the narrow streets and cause long lines at the popular museums. April, May, and October are far better; April is also the time to see the embankments beneath the city walls filled with the pale gold ripple of daffodils.

A first, memorable overview of the city can be had by taking a stroll along the **city walls.** Originally earthen ramparts erected by York's Viking kings to repel raiders, the present stone structure (probably replacing a stockade) dates from the 14th century and has been extensively restored. A narrow paved walk runs along the top (originally 3 mi in circumference), passing over York's distinctive fortified gates or "bars"—**Monk's Bar** on Goodramgate; **Bootham Bar** in Exhibition Square; **Micklegate Bar** in the southwest corner of the city; and **Walmgate Bar** in the east are prime examples—and provide delightful views across rooftops and gardens.

A Good Walk

York's city center may be compact, but there's so much to see that you'll need an early start and plenty of stamina. At least there's no mistaking your starting point: the towers of **York Minster** ⑮ are visible from virtually every point on the encircling **city walls,** so once you've got your bearings, make for Duncombe Place and the main entrance to the Minster, England's largest Gothic church. After you've ogled the interior (rather cold and barnlike to some), and perhaps climbed the tower for more views, it's time to take off around the narrow streets and alleys of the city. In the area just behind the apse of the minster is one of York's quaintest residential areas: here along Aldwark, search out medieval Bedern Hall, St. Anthony's Hall, and the Merchant Taylors' Hall and the Black Swan Inn, two other picture-perfect half-timbered structures. Heading down either Low Petergate or Goodramgate puts you on the famed **Shambles** ⑯, now a crowded shopping street, at the southern end of which you can jink around to Fossgate to visit the **Merchant Adventurers' Hall** ⑰—site of one of the best medieval timber-framed halls in Europe. Retrace your steps past the Shambles, heading west, and you're in one of York's oldest areas, where, on Coppergate, Viking finds were first discovered; the entertaining **Jorvik Viking Centre** ⑱ here has all the details. From Coppergate, Castlegate runs south, passing the former church of St. Mary's—now the **York Story** ⑲—and that connoisseur's delight, the superbly elegant Georgian-era **Fairfax House** ⑳ before ending at the historic mound of **Clifford's Tower** ㉑. The **Castle Museum** ㉒—an amazing collection of ephemera, costumes, and vintage machinery—across from here marks the southernmost extent of your explorations. From here, it's a 20-minute stroll back through the city center, up to the **Guildhall** ㉓ on St. Helen's Square—fainthearts can refuel in Betty's famous tearoom—and nearby **Stonegate** ㉔, another shopping street of considerable historic charm. Doing the walk this way, you've saved two splendid museum collections, both on the outskirts of the historic kernel, until last. From St. Helen's Square it's an easy walk up Lendal and across the main road to the archeological exhibits of the **Yorkshire Museum** ㉕; Enjoy a stroll through the museum's atmospheric gardens—a tonic if the narrow snickleways of the old city give you claustrophobia—then make your way to Lendal Bridge and cross the river onto Station Road. Taking a right on Leeman Road brings you to the fascinating **National Railway Museum** ㉖.

Sights to See

㉒ **Castle Museum.** A former 18th-century debtor's prison, this museum offers a number of detailed exhibitions and re-creations, including a cobblestone Victorian street complete with crafts shops; a working water mill; domestic and military displays; and, most important, the Coppergate Helmet, a 1,200-year-old Anglo-Saxon helmet discovered during excavations of the city. You can also visit the cell where Dick Turpin, the 18th-century highwayman and folk hero, spent the night before his execution. ⊠ *Clifford St.,* ☎ *01904/653611.* ⚏ *£4.60, joint ticket with York Story (☞ above) £5.95.* ⊙ *Apr.–Oct., Mon.–Sat. 9:30–5:30, Sun. 10–5:30; Nov.–Mar., Mon.–Sat. 9:30–4, Sun. 10–4.*

㉑ **Clifford's Tower.** Dating from the early 14th century, this forbidding tower stands on the mound originally erected for the keep of York Cas-

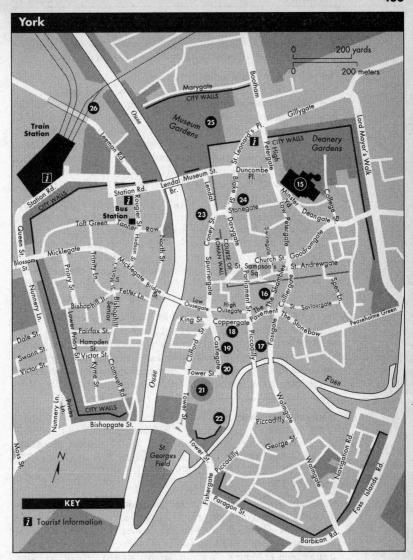

York

200 yards

200 meters

Train Station

Marygate
CITY WALLS

Bootham

Gillygate

Museum Gardens

Lord Mayor's Walk

Deanery Gardens

St. Leonard's Pl.

CITY WALLS

High Petergate

Lendal

Museum St.

Duncombe Pl.

Blake St.

Minster

Stonegate

Deangate

College St.

Station Rd.

Bus Station

Rougier St.

Toft Green

Tanner Row

Hudson St.

North St.

Micklegate Bridge

Lendal

Davygate

Low Petergate

Swinegate

Goodramgate

St. Andrewgate

Spen Ln.

CITY WALLS

Station Rd.

Micklegate

Trinity Ln.

Priory St.

Bishophill Jr.

Bishophill Senior

Fetter Ln.

Spurriergate

Church St.

St. Sampson's Sq.

Parliament St.

Fossgate

Colliergate

St. Saviourgate

Peaseholme Green

Blossom St.

Nunnery Ln.

Dale St.

Swann St.

Victor St.

Fairfax St.

Hampden St.

Victor St.

Kyme St.

Cromwell Rd.

Lower Priory St.

Low Ousegate

King St.

High Ousegate

Coppergate

Clifford St.

Castlegate

The Shambles

The Pavement

Piccadilly

The Stonebow

Foss

Tower St.

Ouse

Tower St.

Walmgate

Nunnery Ln.

Prices Ln.

CITY WALLS

Bishopgate St.

St. Georges Field

George St.

Walmgate

Moss St.

N

Fishergate

Piccadilly

Paragon St.

Navigation Rd.

Foss Islands Rd.

Barbican Rd.

KEY

i Tourist Information

Castle Museum, **22**
Clifford's Tower, **21**
Fairfax House, **20**
Guildhall, **23**
Jorvik Viking Centre, **18**
Merchant Adventurers' Hall, **17**

National Railway Museum, **26**
The Shambles, **16**
Stonegate, **24**
York Minster, **15**
York Story, **19**
Yorkshire Museum, **25**

tle. In 1190 this was the scene of one of the worst instances of anti-Semitism in medieval Europe, when 150 Jews who had sought sanctuary in the castle were massacred. ⊠ *Tower St.,* ☎ *01904/646940.* ▧ *£1.80.* ☼ *Apr.–Oct., daily 10–6; Nov.–Mar., daily 10–4.*

★ ⓴ **Fairfax House.** In a city known for brutish Norman keeps and cold Gothic towers, it's a delight to find Fairfax House, one of the most elegant of Georgian town houses in England. Now a decorative arts museum, this often overlooked treasure was originally built in 1762 and furnished with a sumptuously beautiful collection of furniture. The marble dining room and the grand salon—all crystal chandeliers and flaming crimson silk walls—are knockouts, and rival anything found at Castle Howard. ⊠ *Castlegate,* ☎ *1904/655543.* ▧ *£3.50.* ☼ *Mid-Feb.–Dec., Mon.–Sat. (not Fri., except in Aug. and Sept.) 11–5, Sun. 1:30–5.*

㉓ **Guildhall.** Right on the river, York's mid-15th-century Guildhall was once used for pageants and mystery plays. Although damaged by World War II bombing, it has been restored to something approaching its erstwhile glory, although 14 Victorian stained-glass windows were lost forever—now only one, at the west end, remains as a magnificent, bright reminder. The Guildhall is behind the 18th-century Mansion House. ⊠ *St. Helen's Sq.,* ☎ *01904/613161.* ▧ *Free.* ☼ *Mon.–Thurs. 9–5, Fri. 9–4, Sat. 10–5, Sun. 2–5 (closed weekends Nov.–Apr.).*

⓲ **Jorvik Viking Centre.** On an authentic Viking site, archaeologists have re-created a Viking street with astonishing attention to detail. Its "time-cars" whisk visitors through the streets to experience the sights, sounds, and smells of Viking England, while excellent displays show visitors the extraordinary breadth of the Viking culture and social system. ⊠ *Coppergate,* ☎ *01904/653000.* ▧ *£4.95.* ☼ *Apr.–Oct., daily 9–7; Nov.–Mar., daily 9–5:30; last admission 2 hrs before closing.*

⓱ **Merchant Adventurers' Hall.** Built between 1357–68 and owned by one of the city's richest medieval guilds, this is the largest half-timber hall in York, with a pretty garden in the back. Most Saturdays throughout the year, antiques fairs are held inside the building. ⊠ *Fossgate,* ☎ *01904/ 654818.* ▧ *£1.90.* ☼ *Mid-Mar.–mid-Nov., daily 8:30–5; mid-Nov.– mid-Mar., Mon.–Sat. 8:30–3.*

㉖ **National Railway Museum.** At this trainspotters' delight, you'll find Britain's national collection of locomotives forming part of the world's largest train museum. Among the exhibits are gleaming giants of the steam era, including *Mallard,* holder of the world speed record for a steam engine (126 mph). You can clamber aboard some of the trains, while a new interactive exhibit explores working life on board a mail train. Passenger cars used by Queen Victoria are also on display, while hands-on changing exhibits explore the future of the railways. ⊠ *Leeman Rd.,* ☎ *01904/621261.* ▧ *£5.* ☼ *Daily 10–6.*

⓰ **The Shambles.** Ah, that this street remained as picturesque as its name! York's best preserved medieval street features several half-timber stores and houses with overhangs so massive you could almost reach across the street from one second-floor window to another. It's a little too cute for its own good these days, featuring a line of crafts and souvenir shops—a far cry, certainly, from the days when the Shambles was the city's meat market. Still, aim your camera at rooftop level and see if you can catch York Minster soaring over it all.

㉔ **Stonegate.** Thanks to being pedestrianized, this narrow street of Tudor and 18th-century storefronts and courtyards retains considerable charm. It has been in daily use for almost 2,000 years, since first being paved in Roman times. A passage just off Stonegate, at 52A, leads to a 12th-century Norman stone house, one of the very few to have survived in England. Restored in 1969, only the first-floor hall window remains intact.

⑮ York Minster. Focal point of the entire city, this vast cathedral is the largest Gothic church in England and attracts almost as many visitors as London's Westminster Abbey. Inside, the effect created by its soaring pillars, lofty vaulted ceilings, and dazzling stained-glass windows—glowing with deep wine reds and cobalt blues, they are only bested by those of Chartres Cathedral in France—is almost too overpowering. The church is 534 ft long, 249 ft across its transepts, and 90 ft from floor to roof (so high is the structure, it's best to come with binoculars if you wish to study much of the stained-glass work); the central towers are 184 ft high. Mere statistics, however, cannot convey the scale of the building. Its soaring columns; the ornamentation of its 14th-century nave; the great east window, one of the greatest pieces of medieval glazing in the world; the enormous choir screen portraying somewhat whimsical images of every king of England from William the Conqueror to Henry VI; the imposing tracery of the splendid Rose Window (just one of the minster's 128 stained-glass windows) commemorating the marriage of Henry VII and Elizabeth of York in 1486 (the event that ended the Wars of the Roses and began the Tudor dynasty)—all contribute to its cold, crushing splendor. Don't miss the exquisite 13th-century **Chapter House** and the **Undercroft Museum and Treasury.** After exploring the interior, you might take the 275 winding steps to the roof of the great **Central Tower** (strictly for those with a head for heights), not only for the close-up view of the cathedral's detailed carving but also for a panorama of York and the surrounding Yorkshire Moors. ⊠ *Duncombe Pl., York Minster Undercroft Museum and Treasury, Chapter House, Crypt, and Central Tower,* ☎ *01904/624426.* ✍ *Minster free, but £2 donation appreciated; foundations (including Treasury) £1.80; Chapter House 70p; Crypt 60p; Central Tower £2.* ☉ *Minster: summer months (late June–early Sept.), daily 7 AM–8:30 PM; winter (mid-Sept.—mid-June), daily 7–6. Undercroft, Chapter House, Crypt, and Central Tower: summer Mon.–Sat. 10–5:30, Sun. 1–5:30; winter Mon.–Sat. 10–4:30, Sun. 1–4:30.*

⑲ York Story. York's 20 or so surviving medieval churches—almost any of which could stand alone as an architectural showpiece—tend to be largely ignored by tourists and are therefore good places to explore without the crowds. **St. Mary's** now houses this exhibition devoted to the history of the city, told through medieval-style embroidered panels, models, original artifacts, and a continuous video show. ⊠ *Castlegate,* ☎ *01904/628632.* ✍ *£1.90, joint ticket with Castle Museum (☞ above) £5.95.* ☉ *Mon.–Sat. 10–5, Sun. 1–5.*

㉕ Yorkshire Museum. The gardens and ruins of St. Mary's Abbey, founded in 1089, now house the collections of the Yorkshire Museum. In these atmospheric gardens, with their crumbling medieval columns and blaze of summer flowers, the city's cycle of mystery plays is performed every four years (☞ Nightlife and the Arts, *below*). The museum itself covers the natural and archaeological history of the whole county, including a great deal of material on the Roman, Anglo-Saxon, and Viking aspects of York. Here you can also see the 15th-century Middleham Jewel, a pendant resplendent with a large sapphire and considered the best piece of Gothic jewelry found in England this century. The museum lies just outside the walled city, through Bootham Bar, one of York's old gates. ⊠ *Museum Gardens, Museum St.,* ☎ *01904/629745.* ✍ *£3.50.* ☉ *Nov.–Easter, Mon.–Sat. 10–5, Sun. 1–5; Easter–Oct., daily 10–5.*

Dining and Lodging

££–£££ ✕ **Melton's.** Just 10 minutes from the Minster, this unpretentious restaurant (once a private house) has local art on the walls and an open kitchen. The seasonal menu proves to be highly imaginative, a legacy of chef Michael Hjort's former stint at the Roux brothers' establishments, and offers modern English, Continental, and fish dishes. ⊠ 7 *Scarcroft Rd.,* ☎ *01904/634341. MC, V. Closed 3 wks at Christmas and 1 wk in Aug. No dinner Sun., no lunch Mon.*

££–£££ ✕ **19 Grape Lane.** The narrow, slightly cramped restaurant is housed ★ in a typically leaning timbered York building in the heart of town. Hugely popular, it serves modern English food from a blackboard of specials such as grilled wild boar sausages. ⊠ *19 Grape La.,* ☎ *01904/636366. MC, V. Closed Sun., 1 wk at Christmas, 2 wks in Feb., 2 wks in Sept.*

££ ✕ **Betty's.** At the opposite end of Stonegate from the Minster, Betty's— a York institution since 1912—is ranged elegantly across two large floors in a beautiful Art Nouveau building. Best known for its teas, served with mouthwatering cakes (try the "fat rascal," a plump bun bursting with cherries and nuts), Betty's also offers light meals and a splendid selection of exotic coffees. Get a table on the upper floor if you can, next to the floor-to-ceiling windows. ⊠ *6–8 St. Helen's Sq.,* ☎ *01904/ 659142. MC, V.*

£–££ ✕ **Pierre Victoire.** Saunter in to this airy brasserie at lunchtime and you can feast on a set three-course menu of simple French food, one of the city's best bargains. At dinner, prices increase, but not outrageously, while the dishes become more elaborate: choose from warming soups, *confit* of duck, or that old brasserie standby, *moules mariniere* (mussels). ⊠ *2 Lendal,* ☎ *01904/655222. MC, V.*

£ ✕ **Spurriergate Centre.** Churches are not just for prayers, as this de-consecrated 15th-century church proves. Resurrected as a cafeteria by a community organization, the church of St. Michael's is now a favorite spot for tired tourists and mothers with strollers to refuel spiritually as well as gastronomically. The decor is magnificently medieval, with religious Gothic shrines all around. You'll want double helpings on the cream scones, which are "smacker lipstastic." ⊠ *Spurriergate,* ☎ *01904/629393. No dinner. Closed Sun.*

££££ ✕🖾 **Middlethorpe Hall.** This splendid 18th-century mansion—about ★ 1½ mi from York's city center, not far from the racetrack—was the some-time home of the wildly eccentric traveler and diarist Lady Mary Wortley Montagu. The individually decorated rooms, some in cottage-style accommodations sited around an 18th-century courtyard, are filled with antiques, paintings, and fresh flowers, and the extensive grounds feature a lake, a 17th-century dovecote, and the charmingly-named "ha-ha's"—drops in the garden level that create cunning views. The large garden grows fresh vegetables for the hotel's Anglo-French restaurant, where you can eat in the original wood-paneled dining room by candlelight. Menus change seasonally, but meals are always perfectly planned, with more than a hint of luxury in the ingredients used—fish is always a strong point. ⊠ *Bishopthorpe Rd., YO2 1QB,* ☎ *01904/ 641241; 800/260–8338 in the U.S.;* 🖷 *01904/620176. 30 rooms with bath. Restaurant, croquet. AE, DC, MC, V.*

£££–££££ 🖾 **Dean Court.** This large Victorian house once provided accommo-dations for the clergy of York Minster, which looms just across the way. It's been refurbished to a high quality and now features comfortably furnished rooms with plump sofas, TVs, and fine views overlooking the Minster. Parking is a few minutes from the hotel, but there is valet parking. The restaurant serves good English cuisine, including a hearty Yorkshire breakfast. ⊠ *Duncombe Pl., YO1 2EF,* ☎ *01904/625082,* 🖷 *01904/620305. 40 rooms with bath. Restaurant, bar, coffee shop. AE, DC, MC, V.*

£££–££££   🏨 **Judge's Lodging.** Easily the prettiest hotel in York, this picturesque
★   mansion used to be a judges' lodging, providing accommodations to
justices when they traveled up north from London's Inns of Court. Past
the elegant gates and charming front yard, you mount an imposing staircase to enter a Georgian town house. Beyond the lovely, somewhat
shabby-genteel lobby is the main salon—a delightful and cozy cocoon
of Queen Mum pastels, overstuffed chairs, and gilded mirrors. Upstairs,
the decor continues in the same note. One room is called the Queen
Mother and another grand suite, called the Prince Albert (who actually stayed here) is a special treat. ⊠ *9 Lendal, YO1 2AQ,* ☎ *1904/
638733,* 📠 *1904/679947. 13 rooms with bath or shower. Restaurant,
bar. AE, DC, MC, V.*

£££   🏨 **Grasmead House.** The comfortable bedrooms in this small, family-
run hotel—at the bottom of the price category—all have antique four-
poster beds. Just beyond the city walls, the lodging is an easy walk from
the city center, and the friendly owners are more than willing to share
their local knowledge with guests. There are no meals served other than
breakfast, but very good restaurants are only a short walk away. ⊠ *1
Scarcroft Hill, YO2 1DF,* ☎ 📠 *01904/629996. 6 rooms with bath or
shower. Bar, no-smoking rooms. AE, MC, V.*

££–£££   🏨 **Savages.** Despite its name, this small hotel on a leafy road near the
town center is eminently refined, with a reputation for attentive service. Once a Victorian home, it has a stylish and comfortable interior,
and there's a bar in which to relax. ⊠ *15 St. Peter's Grove, Clifton,
YO3 6AQ,* ☎ *01904/610818,* 📠 *01904/627729. 21 rooms with bath
or shower. Restaurant, bar. AE, DC, MC, V.*

£   🏨 **Abbey Guest House.** This charming, no-smoking, terraced guest
house—formerly an artisan's house—is a 10-minute walk from the train
station and town center. Although small, it's very clean and friendly,
with a peaceful garden right on the river and ducks waddling about
outside. Picnic lunches and evening meals can be arranged on request.
⊠ *14 Earlsborough Terr., Marygate, YO3 7BQ,* ☎ *01904/627782. 7
rooms, 2 with bath. Breakfast room. AE, MC, V.*

Nightlife and the Arts

FESTIVALS

Playing on its Viking past, York hosts the annual **Viking Festival** (⊠
Jorvik Viking Centre, Coppergate, ☎ 01904/643211) in February.
The celebrations—including a parade and long-ship regatta—end with
the Jorvik Viking Combat reenactment, when ravaging Northmen
confront their Anglo-Saxon enemies. Call for details.

The next quadrennial performance of the medieval **York Mystery Plays**
will take place in the summer of 2000. An **Early Music Festival** is held
each summer except in Mystery Play years. For details, call the Festival Office (☎ 01904/658338) or the Tourist Information Centre in York
(☎ 01904/621756). Here, in York, the annual English **Bonfire Night**
celebrations on November 5 have an added piquancy, because the notorious 16th-century conspirator Guy Fawkes was a native of the city;
they commemorate Fawkes's failure to blow up the Houses of Parliament, and his effigy is burned atop every fire. Ask at the tourist office
for the locations of the best fires and fireworks displays.

PUBS

York is full of historic pubs, where you can while away an hour over
a pint and muse on the stories of the resident ghosts. The **Black Swan**
(⊠ Peasholme Green, ☎ no phone) is the city's oldest pub, a 16th-
century local of great character. In the cellar bar of the **Judge's Lodgings** (⊠ 9 Lendal, ☎ 01904/638733), the old vaults provide a convivial
drinking hole.

York's **Theatre Royal** is a lively professional theater in a lovely old building, with many other events besides plays: string quartets, choral music, poetry reading, and art exhibitions. ⊠ *St. Leonard's Pl.,* ☎ *01904/ 623568.* ☉ *Box office Mon.–Sat. 10–8.*

Shopping

The new and secondhand bookstores around Petergate, Stonegate, and the Shambles are excellent. **Blackwell's** (⊠ 32 Stonegate, ☎ 01904/ 624531) has a large stock of new titles and a convenient mail-order service. For secondhand books, old maps, and prints, head for the Minster and the **Minster Gate Bookshop** (⊠ 8 Minster Gate, ☎ 01904/ 621812). For something high in quality and typically English, **Mulberry Hall** (⊠ Stonegate, ☎ 01904/620736), a large, half-timber house dating from the 15th century, is a sales center for all the famous names in fine bone china and crystal—it also has a neat café. The **York Antiques Centre** (⊠ 2 Lendal, ☎ no phone) has 34 shops on two floors selling antiques, bric-a-brac, books, and jewelry.

YORK ENVIRONS

With the North York Moors and coast so close, visitors do eventually tear themselves away from York and move on. Happily, the environs to the northwest are all close enough to see on day trips from the city: the spa town of Harrogate, medieval Knaresborough, the lovely ruins of Fountains Abbey, and the attractive market town of Ripon. If you're traveling eastward from Leeds to Harrogate, take the less direct B1224 across **Marston Moor** where, in 1644, Oliver Cromwell won a decisive victory over the Royalists during the Civil War. A few miles beyond, at Wetherby, you can then cut northwest along the A661 to Harrogate.

Harrogate

㉗ *21 mi west of York, 11 mi south of Ripon, 16 mi north of Leeds.*

During the Regency and early Victorian periods, it became fashionable for the noble and wealthy to retire to a spa for relaxation. Nowhere else in Yorkshire reached such grand heights as Harrogate, an elegant town that flourished during the 19th century. When the spas no longer drew crowds, Harrogate shed its old image to become a modern business center and built a huge complex that today attracts international conventions. It has been tactfully located so as not to spoil the town's landscape of poised Regency row houses, pleasant walkways, and sweeping green spaces. Of Harrogate's parks, most appealing is the one in the town center, known as **The Stray,** a 200-acre reach of grassland which is a riot of color in the spring. The **Valley Gardens** provide varied attractions, including a boating lake, tennis courts, and a little café.

You can still drink the evil-smelling (and -tasting) spa waters at the **Royal Pump Room Museum,** which charts the story of Harrogate from its 17th-century beginnings. The building, built over the original sulphur well that brought such prosperity to the town, dates from 1842.⊠ *Crown Pl.,* ☎ *01423/503340.* ☔ *£1.75.* ☉ *Apr.–Oct., Mon.–Sat. 10–5, Sun. 2–5; Nov.–Mar., Mon.–Sat. 10–4, Sun. 2–4.*

In the **Royal Baths Assembly Rooms** (1897), you may take a Turkish bath or a sauna in the exotic, tiled rooms; allow two hours or so for the full treatment. ⊠ *Crescent Rd.,* ☎ *01423/562498.* ☔ *£7.50 per bath and sauna session, massages £10.50–£20.* ☉ *Daily; call for men's and women's schedules.*

Dining and Lodging

£££–££££ ✕⛉ **White House.** The White House resembles an Italianate villa, one that is slightly frayed at the edges. Inside, comfort is king: guest rooms are bright and reasonably large; flowers, mirrors, paintings, artistic bits and pieces, and even the odd antique abound. In the lounge, sugared almonds await guests who drop by; the library has games and cards. The changing menu in the restaurant (££–£££) caters to most tastes with its eclectic mix of Continental and British cuisine. ⊠ *10 Park Parade, HG1 5AH,* ☎ *01423/501388,* ℻ *01423/527973. 10 rooms with bath or shower. Restaurant, bar, no-smoking rooms. AE, DC, MC, V.*

£ ✕ **Betty's.** The celebrated York tearoom also has an elegant branch in genteel Harrogate, where the same scrumptious cakes and pastries, and hot meals, are on offer every day until 9 PM. A pianist plays nightly. ⊠ *1 Parliament St.,* ☎ *01423/502746. MC, V.*

Nightlife and the Arts

Harrogate's **International Festival** (⊠ Festival Office, Royal Baths, HG1 2RR, ☎ 01423/562303)—of ballet, music, contemporary dance, film, comedy, street theater, and more—takes place over two weeks at the end of July and beginning of August each year.

Knaresborough

㉘ *3 mi northeast of Harrogate, 17 mi west of York.*

The photogenic old town of Knaresborough is built in a steep, rocky gorge along the River Nidd. Central attractions include its river, lively with pleasure boats, a little marketplace, and a medieval castle—now not much more than a keep—where Richard II was once imprisoned (1399). In a historic park site, amid tree-lined riverside walks, **Mother Shipton's Cave** is said to be the birthplace of the 16th-century prophetess. Events supposedly foretold by her include the Great Fire of London and the earlier defeat of the Spanish Armada. It's just a short walk south of Knaresborough town center. ⊠ *Prophesy House, High Bridge,* ☎ *01423/864600.* ⌨ *£4.25.* ☉ *Easter–Oct., daily 9:30–5:45; Nov.–Easter, daily 10–4:45.*

Studley Royal and Fountains Abbey

★ **㉙** *9 mi northwest of Knaresborough, 4 mi southwest of Ripon down a signposted side road off B6265.*

The 18th-century water garden and deer park, Studley Royal, and the ruins of Fountains Abbey blend the glories of English Gothic architecture with a Neoclassic vision of an ordered universe. The gardens include lakes, ponds, and spectacular water terraces, while waterfalls splash around classical temples, statues, and a grotto; the surrounding woods offer long vistas toward the great tower of Ripon Cathedral, some 3 mi north. The majestic ruins of Fountains Abbey, with its own high tower and soaring 13th-century arches, make a striking picture on the banks of the River Skell. Founded in 1132, but not completed until the early 1500s, the abbey still possesses many of its original buildings, and it is one of the best places in England to learn about medieval monastic life. In this isolated valley, the Cistercian community went about its business: the "White Monks" (named for the color of their habits) began a day of silence and prayer with Vespers at 2:30 AM, while the lay brothers oversaw operations at the abbey's extensive sheep farms. Of the surviving buildings, it's the lay brothers' echoing refectory and dormitory in the 300-ft west range that impresses most; the landmark Perpendicular Tower was a later (early 16th-century) addition, erected by Abbot Huby, most eminent of the abbey's leaders. The whole of this complex is now owned by the National Trust, which operates free guided tours around abbey and gardens. On your own, buy the pamphlet at the entrance desk to guide you around the extensive buildings. There's a small restaurant (no dinner) and two stores, as well as an exhibition and video display in the 17th-century **Fountains Hall,** one of the earliest Neoclassic buildings in northern England. ⊠ *Off B6265,* ☎ *01765/608888; 01765/601005 weekends.* ⊡ *£4.20.* ⊙ *Jan.–Mar. and Oct.–Dec., daily 10–5 (or dusk); Apr.–Sept., daily 10–7; closed Fri. Nov.–Jan. Free guided tours of abbey and gardens daily Apr.–Oct., usually at 1:30, 2:30, and 3:30.*

Ripon

③⓪ *4 mi northeast of Fountains Abbey, 11 mi north of Harrogate, 24 mi northwest of York.*

Ripon was thriving as early as the 9th century as an important market center. Successive churches here were destroyed by the Vikings and the Normans, and the present structure, dating from the 12th and 13th centuries, is particularly notable for its finely carved choir stalls and Saxon crypt—now an empty series of chambers, but which housed sacred relics in bygone days. Despite its relatively small size, the church has been designated a **cathedral** since the mid-19th century, which makes Ripon (only about 15,000 inhabitants) technically a city. Market day here is Thursday, which is probably the best day to stop by. ⊠ *Ripon Cathedral, Minster Rd.,* ☎ *no phone.* ⊡ *Free; £2 donation requested.* ⊙ *Daily 8–6:30.*

☾ ③① Make the effort to drive out from Ripon to **Newby Hall,** an early 18th-century house that was redecorated later in the same century by Robert Adam for his patron William Weddell; it contains some of the finest interior decorative art of its period in Western Europe. One room has been designed around a set of priceless Gobelin tapestries, and another was created to show off Roman sculpture. The famous grounds, which extend down to the River Ure, include a collection of old species roses, rare shrubs, and delightful sunken gardens. The children's adventure playground, narrow-gauge steam railroad, river steamers, and garden restaurant make a visit to Newby a full day's outing. It's 5 mi southeast of Ripon. ⊠ *Skelton-on-Ure,* ☎ *01423/322583.* ⊡ *£5.60, gardens only £4.* ⊙ *Easter–Oct., Tues.–Sun., grounds 11–5, house noon–5.*

THE NORTH YORKSHIRE COAST

Except during the hottest summers, the North Yorkshire coast isn't the warmest place for a beach vacation. That said, there's plenty to make you glad you came, not least the good sandy beaches, rocky coves, and picturesque villages, like Robin Hood's Bay and Staithes, which seem to capture imaginations at first sight. Most coastal towns still support an active fishing industry and every harbor offers fishing and leisure trips throughout the summer. The east-coast beaches are usually fine for swimming, though you'll find the water cold. Beaches at Scarborough, Whitby, and Filey have patrolled bathing areas: swim between the red-and-yellow flags, and don't swim when a red flag is flying. Major towns also have indoor swimming pools.

From York, the coast is about an hour's drive away, and starting at Bridlington, it's a simple matter to follow the main road north to Scarborough (the A165), on to Robin Hood's Bay and Whitby (A171).

Bridlington

③② *41 mi east of York.*

Bridlington, a fishing port with an ancient harbor, makes a fine introduction to the North Yorkshire coast, featuring a wide arc of sand that's typical of the beach resorts in the region. Boat trips through the harbor and up the coast depart very frequently during the summer; or simply join the milling crowds who promenade up and down the seafront, eating fish-and-chips, browsing at the gift shops and stalls, and frequenting the rides at the small amusement park. At **Flamborough Head** a huge bank of chalk cliffs juts out into the North Sea. A coastal path over the cliff tops ends at **Bempton Cliffs,** one of the finest seabird reserves in England, boasting a colony of 7,000 puffins, which nest on the cliffs between March and August. The reserve is open at all times, and the displays at the neighboring Visitor Centre can help you get more out of the area. Rent a pair of binoculars (£1) for a closer view of the puffins, shags, kittiwakes, gannets, guillemots, and razorbills that make the cliffs their home. ⊠ *Visitor Centre, Bempton Cliffs,* ☎ *01262/851179.* ⌑ *Free; £1.50 parking.* ☉ *Mar.–Oct., daily 10–5, also Feb. and Nov. weekends only 10–5.*

Dining

£ ✕ **Jerome's.** This friendly little seafront café-restaurant keeps up with our multicultural times by featuring a selection of good-value Greek meals, including meze (a sampler of Greek hors d'oeuvres) and vegetarian platters. The outdoor tables see the most use in summer, when Jerome's stays open until 9. This spot closes at 5 PM in the winter. ⊠ *The Floral Pavilion, Royal Prince's Parade,* ☎ *01262/671881. No credit cards.*

Scarborough

③③ *18 mi northwest of Bridlington, 34 mi northeast of York.*

Candy floss and rock candy, Victorian architecture, a great sweep of cliffs above a sandy bay, and a rocky promontory capped by a ruined castle are just some of the elements that make Scarborough the classic picture of an English seaside resort. A chance discovery in the early 17th century of a mineral spring on the foreshore led to the establishment of a spa, whose users were encouraged not merely to soak themselves in seawater but even to drink it. By the late 18th century, when sea bathing was firmly in vogue, no beaches were busier than Scarborough's with "bathing machines," cumbersome wheeled cabins drawn by donkeys or horses into the surf and anchored there. Scarborough's initial prosperity dates from this period, as evidenced in the handsome Regency and early Victorian residences and hotels in the city.

The contrast between the two distinct faces of Scarborough makes the town all the more appealing. Its older, more genteel side in the southern half of town consists of carefully laid out crescents and squares and cliff-top walks and gardens with spectacular views across Cayton Bay. The northern side is a riot of ice cream stands, cafés, stores selling "rock" (luridly colored, hard candy), crab hawkers, and bingo halls. In addition, enough survives of the tight huddle of streets, alleyways, and red-roof cottages around the harbor to give an idea of what the town was like before the resort days.

Paths link the harbor with the ruins of **Scarborough Castle** on the promontory; dating from Norman times, it is built on the site of a Roman signal station and near a former Viking settlement. From the castle there are spectacular views across the North Bay, the beaches, and the shore gardens. ⊠ *Castle Rd.,* ☎ *01723/372451.* ⌑ *£2.* ☉ *Apr.–Sept., daily 10–6; Oct.–Mar., Wed.–Sun. 10–1 and 2–4.*

At Scarborough's little medieval church of **St. Mary** (⊠ Castle Rd., ☎ 01723/371354) you'll find the grave of Anne, the youngest Brontë sister, who died in 1849; she was taken to Scarborough from Haworth in a final desperate effort to save her life in the sea air. The church is near the castle on the way into town.

Wood End was the vacation home of 20th-century writers Edith, Osbert, and Sacheverell Sitwell, and the west wing houses a library of their works as well as portraits and paintings. The rest of the early Victorian house, amid delightful grounds, is taken up by the collections of the **Museum of Natural History.** ✉ *The Crescent,* ☎ *01723/367326.* ⌦ *Free.* ☉ *May–Sept., Tues.–Sun. 10–5; Oct.–Apr., Fri.–Sun. 10–4.*

The **Rotunda Museum,** an extraordinary circular building, was originally constructed in 1829 for William Smith of the Scarborough Philosophical Society to display his geological collection; it now houses important archaeological and local history collections. The museum is just a short walk below Wood End. ✉ *Vernon Rd.,* ☎ *01723/374839.* ⌦ *Free.* ☉ *May–Sept., Tues.–Sun. 10–5; Oct.–Apr., Fri.–Sun. 10–4.*

Scarborough Sea Life Centre is the best of the cheerful attractions that appeal to kids. Marine life and environmental matters are presented in an entertaining way, with various marine habitats combined under one roof. ✉ *Scalby Mills, North Bay,* ☎ *01723/376125.* ⌦ *£5.50.* ☉ *June–Sept., daily 10–9; Oct.–May, daily 10–5.*

Dining and Lodging

££ ✗ **Lanterna Restaurant.** An intimate atmosphere and a high standard of cuisine make this Italian restaurant a good choice. The classic dishes are all represented, among them tender veal cooked with ham and cheese, but opt for seasonal specials using fresh vegetables and fish. ✉ *33 Queen St.,* ☎ *01723/363616. MC, V. Closed Sun. No lunch in winter.*

£ ✗ **The Golden Grid.** Everyone has to have fish-and-chips at least once in Scarborough, and the harborfront Golden Grid is a classic of its kind. Choose an upstairs window table and tuck into freshly fried cod or haddock—though big spenders (and those flying in the face of British seaside tradition) could also opt for a chilled *fruit de mer,* grilled turbot, or one of a host of other daily specials. ✉ *4 Sandside,* ☎ *01723/360922. MC. No dinner Mon.–Thurs. in winter.*

£££ 🏨 **The Crown.** The centerpiece of Scarborough's Regency Esplanade, this period hotel overlooks South Bay and the castle headland. Originally built to accommodate fashionable 19th-century visitors to Scarborough Spa, it has been considerably refurbished and guest accommodations are tasteful and comfortable. The regular room rate doesn't include breakfast, though you might consider the special dinner, bed, and breakfast package. ✉ *The Esplanade, YO11 2AG,* ☎ *01723/373491,* 🖷 *01723/362271. 78 rooms with bath. Restaurant, bar, beauty salon. AE, DC, MC, V.*

Nightlife and the Arts

Scarborough has an internationally known artistic native son in Alan Ayckbourn—now, incredible though it may seem, the second most popularly performed playwright after Shakespeare. The **Stephen Joseph Theatre** (✉ Westborough, ☎ 01723/370541), which premieres all of his plays, incorporates two fine stages and a cinema. Stop in at the theater for a program or contact the tourist office for box office details.

Robin Hood's Bay

★ ㉞ *13 mi northwest of Scarborough.*

Many visitors' favorite coastal stop is at Robin Hood's Bay, a tiny fishing village squeezed into a narrow ravine near where a stream courses over the cliffs. The name is curious, since about the only historical certainty is that there is no connection with the famous English medieval outlaw; the village didn't even come into being until the late 15th century, after which it thrived in a small way as a fishing port and smuggling center. Perilously steep, narrow roads are fringed with tiny, crazily scattered houses and shops, and space is so tight you are not allowed to drive into the village center; use the parking lots at the top of the village. The tiny **beach** was once a notorious smugglers' landing; contraband was passed up the streambed beneath the cottages—linked to one another by secret passages—often with customs officers in hot pursuit. The tide rushes in very quickly, so take care. Provided the tide is out, you can stroll 20 minutes' south from Robin Hood's Bay, along the exposed stone shore, as far as the curiously named **Boggle Hole**, where a steep ravine nestles an old water mill, now a youth hostel. If the tide comes in during your walk, you can return to Robin Hood's Bay by the cliff-top path (signposted from the hostel).

Several superb, long-distance walks start or finish in, or run through, Robin Hood's Bay. The village marks one end of the 190-mi **Coast-to-Coast walk** (the other is at St. Bees Head on the Irish Sea)—coast-to-coast walkers finish at the Bay Hotel, above the harbor. The coastal **Cleveland Way** runs north (to Whitby) and south (to Scarborough) through the village, while the trans-moor **Lyke-Wake Walk** finishes just 3 mi away at Ravenscar.

Dining and Lodging

£ ✕ **Laurel.** The village's most favored pub is this tiny hideaway, complete with a bar festooned with oak and brass and sporting a roaring fire in winter—all a country pub should be. Future plans include the addition of a few guest rooms. ⊠ *Main St.,* ☎ *01947/880400.*

£££ 🏨 **Raven Hall Hotel.** This superb Georgian hotel with landscaped grounds offers unrivaled coastal views from the headland of Ravenscar, just 3 mi southeast of Robin Hood's Bay. Try your utmost to secure a room with a bay view; if they're occupied, you can console yourself with the same wonderful views from the lounge or restaurant. The Raven Hall Hotel is known for its good sports facilities, though you'll have to be polar-bear hardy to use the outdoor pool, despite its enterprising cliff-top location. It's worth noting that the bar marks the traditional end of the punishing, long-distance Lyke-Wake Walk, so you may share the comfortable lounge (with fire in winter) with exhausted walkers on occasion. Ask about special winter discounted rates. ⊠ *Ravenscar, YO13 0ET* ☎ *01723/870353. 53 rooms with bath. Restaurant, bar, indoor-outdoor pool, 9-hole golf course, 2 tennis courts. AE, DC, MC, V.*

Whitby

★ ㉟ *7 mi northwest of Robin Hood's Bay, 20 mi north of Pickering, 25 mi east of Middlesbrough.*

Whitby is considered by some to be one of the scenic glories of the Yorkshire coast. The River Esk comes down a long glenlike ravine cut through the moors and makes a harbor of great natural beauty. Above it, on either side, red-roof buildings rise tier upon tier, and on top of the cliff are the gaunt ruins of Whitby Abbey—a sight that inspired Bram Stoker when he came here to write *Dracula*—its traceried frame silhouetted against the sky. Today Whitby is a small, laid-back resort, but it was an important religious center as far back as the 7th century, when Whitby Abbey was first founded, and it later came to prominence as a whaling port. The first ships sailed from here for Greenland in the mid-18th century, captained by local men like William Scoresby, inventor of the crow's nest, to whom Herman Melville paid tribute in his novel, *Moby-Dick*. At much the same time as whaling made Whitby rich, its shipbuilding made it famous: James—later, Captain—Cook (1728–79), explorer and navigator, sailed on his first ship out of the town in 1747, and all four of his subsequent discovery vessels were built in Whitby. Whitby's glory days are long gone, but there's still much to admire. Fine Georgian houses line some of the central streets on the west side of the river, while across the swing bridge in the old town, cobbled Church Street is packed shoulder-to-shoulder in summer with visitors exploring the dark alleys, enclosed courtyards, and gift shops.

Climb the 199 steps from the end of Church Street and you are at the rather eccentrically designed Church of **St. Mary** (⌂ Church La., East Cliff, ☎ 01947/603421), with its ship's deck roof, triple-decker pulpit, and enclosed galleries. The church dates originally from the 12th century, although almost everything you see today is the (often less-than-happy) result of 19th- and 20th-century renovations. The spooky, weather-beaten churchyard, filled with the crooked old gravestones of ancient mariners, affords superb views of the sea and the town itself. It was here that Bram Stoker's Dracula claimed Lucy as his victim, while if you search around amid the tall grass at the back, you'll find the grave of master mariner William Scoresby.

The romantic ruins of **Whitby Abbey,** set high on the East Cliff, are visible from almost everywhere in town. St. Hilda founded the abbey in AD 657, and Caedmon (died circa 670), the first identifiable poet of the English language, was a monk here; an engraved cross—of dubious provenance—that bears his name stands at the top of the 199 steps near St. Mary's church. Sacked by the Vikings in the 9th century, the monastery was refounded in the 11th century and then restored and enlarged in the 13th century, from which point these ruins date. ⌂ *Abbey La., East Cliff,* ☎ *01947/603568.* ⌑ *£1.80.* ☉ *Apr.–Sept., daily 10–6; Oct.–Mar., daily 10–4.*

Captain Cook is remembered in various places around town, most notably by his bronze statue on top of the West Cliff, near the pair of arched whalebones. However, the most revealing exhibits relating to the man are to be found in the **Captain Cook Memorial Museum,** tucked into the period rooms of the 18th-century house belonging to shipowner John Walker, where Cook lived as an apprentice from 1746 to 1749. Here, you can see mementos of his epic expeditions, including maps, diaries, and drawings, as well as some tracing the privations of his wife and family, left behind to cope with life, loss, and bereavement. ⌂ *Grape La.,* ☎ *01947/601900.* ⌑ *£2.20.* ☉ *Easter–Oct., daily 9:45–5; Mar. and Nov., weekends 11–3.*

Dining and Lodging

£   ✕ **Trencher's.** Whitby is full of fish-and-chip places, but nowhere serves it better than Trencher's, a bright, welcoming, diner-style restaurant with a broad menu. Crisply battered, grease-free fillets of fresh haddock or cod come with thick-cut chips; order a large portion, with a side order of mushy peas, and you won't eat again for a week. ⌂ *New Quay Rd.,* ☎ *01947/603212. No credit cards. Closed mid-Nov.–mid-Mar.*

£–££ ✕⌂ **Shepherd's Purse.** In the cobbled old town, this splendid little complex comprises charming boutique-style guest rooms, a vegetarian restaurant, and a health-food store. There are two less-expensive bedrooms above the store and five more in the galleried courtyard at the back, which just creep into the higher price category. Although small, these are en suite, with four-poster or brass bedsteads; floors are wooden, the furniture is country style, and the top two rooms even have little balconies. ⌂ *95 Church St., YO22 4BH,* ☎ *01947/820228. 7 rooms, 5 with shower or bath. Restaurant. No credit cards.*

£ ✕🏠 **White Horse and Griffin.** When looking for the perfect inn, you
★ want a characterful old building, a roaring fire in the grate, food to
thrill, and an owner eager to please. Step forward the 18th-century White
Horse and Griffin, in which Charles Dickens once slept and railway
pioneer George Stephenson lectured. The spruce, renovated rooms are
warm and comfortable, while downstairs in the cozy bistro-bar, owner
Stewart Perkins presides over a fine, changing menu of locally caught
fish and properly hung meat, including game in season. Dinner might
be fried calamari or bouillabaisse, followed by grilled mullet, panfried
herring, or even a splendid fruits de mer assortment of local cooked
and cured fish. ✉ *Church St., YO22 4BH,* ☎ *01947/604857. 12
rooms with bath. Restaurant, bar. MC, V.*

Nightlife and the Arts

The **Whitby Regatta,** held in August every year, is a three-day jamboree
of boat races, fair rides, lifeboat rescue displays, parades, and musical
events. Music (but also traditional dance and storytelling) predomi-
nates during **Whitby Folk Week,** usually held the week before the late-
August bank holiday, when pubs, pavements, and halls become venues
for more than 1,000 traditional folk events by performers from all over
the country. Make sure you book accommodations well in advance if
you plan to come at this time.

Shopping

Whitby is known for its jet, a very hard, black form of natural carbon,
which has been used locally for more than a century to make jewelry
and ornaments, and was particularly popular as mourning memorabilia during the Victorian era. Several shops in the old town along Church
Street and parallel Sandgate have fine displays.

Staithes

36 *9 mi northwest of Whitby.*

Specifically, there's little to see in Staithes, but, over the years, many
travelers have been seduced by the powerful atmosphere of the town's
stepped alleys and courtyards. These, and the surrounding coastal
cliffs, were captured on canvas by many members of the so-called Staithes
School of artists, who were prominent earlier this century. Tourists are
a vital part of the local economy these days, with perhaps the most
surprising visitors those in wet suits, who know Staithes to have some
of the best surfing in the country.

Staithes's few houses huddle below the rocky, seagull-studded outcrop
of Cowbar Nab, on either side of the beck (stream) and, having survived storm and flood, present a hoary, weather-beaten aspect. Not all
were so lucky. The Cod and Lobster Inn, at the harbor, is in its third
incarnation, while the dry goods shop in which James Cook had his
first apprenticeship before moving to Whitby fell into the sea entirely
in 1745. The house known as Cook's Cottage, near the pub, is supposedly built out of the salvaged remains of the original building.

Staithes's former Methodist Chapel has been imaginatively converted
into the **Captain Cook and Staithes Heritage Centre,** whose central feature is a life-size mid-18th-century street scene of the kind Cook would
have recognized. The shop in which the young adventurer worked was
re-created, alongside an alehouse, a fisherman's warehouse, and museum displays relating to local industries and, of course, smuggling.
✉ *High St.,* ☎ *01947/841454.* 🎟 *£1.75.* ⊙ *Daily 10–5:30.*

Dining

££ ✕ **The Endeavour.** This rather higgledy-piggledy old house on Staithes's
★ main street, near the harbor, is well-known for its meals of locally caught
fish. Menus change seasonally, but you can count on dishes being presented with care and with Mediterranean or Asian flourishes; soups,
salmon, and lobster are strong points. Have a drink in the tiny, low-
ceiling bar, choose from the blackboard, and don't be afraid to ask for
recommendations from the brisk staff. ✉ *1 High St.*, ☎ *01947/840825.
No credit cards. Closed weekdays in Feb. No dinner Sun. in winter.*

£ ✕ **Sea Drift.** An absolute gem, this friendly spot serves gourmet sandwiches (including fresh crab), cappuccino, homemade cakes, and herbal
teas—a breath of fresh air on a coast otherwise dedicated to fish-and-
chips. ✉ *Staithes Harbour*, ☎ *01947/841345. No credit cards.*

THE NORTH YORK MOORS

The North York Moors is a dramatic swath of high moorland starting 25 mi north of the city of York and stretching east to the coast and
west to the Cleveland Hills. Once covered in forest, of which a few
pockets survive here and there, the landscape changed with the introduction of sheep at the monastic foundations of Rievaulx and Whitby
in medieval times. The evidence is clear for all to see today: rolling,
heather-covered hills that, in late summer and early fall, are a rich blaze
of crimson and purple, and a series of isolated, medieval, standing stones
that once acted as signposts on the paths between the abbeys. For more
than four decades, the area has been designated a National Park, to
protect the moors and grassy valleys that shelter brownstone villages
and hamlets. Minor roads and tracks crisscross the moors in all directions, and there's no single, obvious route through the region. Perhaps the most rewarding approach is southwest from the coast at
Whitby, along the Esk Valley to Danby, which is also accessible on the
Esk Valley branch train line between Middlesbrough and Whitby.
From Danby, minor roads run south over the high moors reaching Hutton-le-Hole, beyond which main roads lead to interesting towns on the
moors' edge, like Helmsley and Malton. Completing the route in this
direction leaves you with an easy side trip to Castle Howard before
returning to nearby York.

Danby

③⑦ *15 mi west of Whitby; take A171 (to Teesside) and turn south for Danby
after 12 mi, after which it's a 3-mi drive over Danby Low Moor to the
village. Or take the local train directly from Whitby.*

The straggling old stone village of Danby nestles in a green valley, just
a short walk from the tops of the nearby moors. It's been settled since
Viking times—Danby means "village where the Danes lived"—and these
days it bumbles along contentedly in a semi-touristed way. There's a
pub, and a bakery with a tearoom, and if you bring hiking boots with
you, within 10 minutes you can be above the village looking down,
surrounded by nothing but isolated moorland.

In a converted country house on the eastern outskirts of Danby, the
National Park's Moors Centre has exhibitions, displays, and a wide range
of pamphlets and books about the area. There's a garden out front with
picnic tables and superb valley views, and a tearoom, while the summer Moorsbus (☞ Getting Around *in* Yorkshire A to Z, *below*) operates from the center for the 30-minute journey south to Hutton-le-Hole.
✉ *Danby Lodge*, ☎ *01287/660654.* ☑ *Free.* ☉ *Easter–Oct., daily
10–5; Nov.–Easter, weekends, 11–4.*

Dining

£ ✕ **Stonehouse Bakery & Tea Shop.** This cozy little place is unusually adventurous for this part of the world, serving sandwiches on sun-dried-tomato or olive bread, herbal teas, local honey, and a heaven-sent peanut brittle. ✉ *3 Briar Hill* ☎ *01287/660006. Closed Sun.*

En Route From Danby take the road due west for 2 mi to Castleton, and then turn south over the top of the moors toward Hutton-le-Hole. The narrow road offers magnificent views over the national park, especially at the old stone **Ralph Cross** (5 mi), which marks the highest point. Drive carefully: sheep-dodging is something of a necessary art in these parts.

Hutton-le-Hole

★ ❸❽ *4 mi south of Rosedale Abbey; follow sign for Rosedale Chimney Bank; also 13 mi south of Danby.*

Even after seeing the varied splendors of villages throughout the national park, it's difficult not to think Hutton-le-Hole the pick of the bunch. It's almost too pastoral to be true: a tiny hamlet, based around a wide village green, with sheep wandering about, and a stream babbling in the background. The surroundings are some of the most attractive in the region and consequently, in summer, the local parking lots fill quickly as people arrive to take to the nearby hills for a day's walking. Make sure you visit the 2-acre **Ryedale Folk Museum,** which records life in the Dales from prehistory onward by way of a display of 13 historic buildings: a series of 16th-century cottages, a 19th-century blacksmith's shop, an early photographer's studio, and a medieval kiln. ✉ *Hutton-le-Hole,* ☎ *01751/417367.* 🎫 *£3.* ☉ *Easter–Oct., daily 10–5:30.*

Helmsley

❸❾ *13 mi west of Pickering, 27 mi north of York.*

For walkers, the pleasant market town of Helmsley, on the southern edge of the Moors, is well known as the starting point of the long-distance moor-and-coastal footpath, the **Cleveland Way.** Boots are donned at the old cross in the market square, from where it's 50 mi or so across the moors to the coast and then a similar distance south to Filey along the cliff tops; all told, it's 108 mi of walking, which most people aim to complete in nine days. Helmsley itself is attractive enough for a day trip and features a castle (partly ruined during the Civil War) and a traditional country marketplace surrounded by fine old inns, cafés, and stores. Market day here is Friday. Even inveterate nonwalkers will probably find the very early stages of the Cleveland Way irresistible, since the trail passes close to the ruins of Rievaulx Abbey, just outside the town. A leaflet available from the tourist information center indicates the route.

Lodging

£££–££££ 🏨 **Black Swan.** This lovely, ivy-covered property sits right on the edge of the market square and makes a splendid, relaxing base. The building is a hybrid—part 16th-century coaching inn, part Georgian house—but careful restoration and renovation has ensured comfort throughout: rooms overlook either the square or the fine walled garden at the back, in which, incidentally, there's a croquet lawn for your amusement in summer. A restaurant serves traditional British and local dishes; an open fire keeps things cozy in winter. ✉ *Market Pl., YO6 5BJ,* ☎ *01439/770466,* 📠 *01439/770174. 44 rooms with bath. Restaurant, bar. AE, DC, MC, V.*

Rievaulx Abbey

★ ④ *2 mi northwest of Helmsley.*

One of the most graceful of all medieval English seats of learning, Rievaulx (pronounced reevoh) Abbey occupies a dramatic setting on the River Rye. A Cistercian foundation, dating from 1132, its wealth was derived from the wool trade, and the extensive surviving ruins give some indication of the thriving trade with Europe in which the medieval monks of North Yorkshire engaged. The landscaped grounds sport graceful Gothic arches, cloisters, and associated buildings, including the Chapter House, which retains the original shrine of the first abbot, William, by the entrance. The abbey is an hour and a half's walk northwest from Helmsley (there's a signposted footpath), or 2 mi by vehicle, taking the B1257. ⊠ *Rievaulx Abbey,* ☎ *01439/798228.* 🖭 *£2.60.* ☉ *Apr.–Sept., daily 10–6; Oct.–Mar., daily 10–4.*

Having wandered among the ruins of Rievaulx Abbey, you might also like to climb (or drive) up to the **Rievaulx Terraces,** a long grassy walkway on the hillside above, terminating in the remains of several Tuscan- and Ionic-style classical temples. The views of the abbey from here are magnificent. ⊠ *Rievaulx Terr.,* ☎ *01439/798340.* 🖭 *£2.80.* ☉ *Apr.– Oct., daily 10:30–6.*

Castle Howard

★ ④ *12 mi southeast of Helmsley, 15 mi northeast of York.*

Standing serene among the Howardian Hills to the west of Malton, Castle Howard is one of the grandest and most opulent stately homes in Britain, an imposing Baroque building whose magnificent skyline is punctuated by stone chimneys and a graceful central dome. Many people know it best as Brideshead, the home of the Flyte family in Evelyn Waugh's tale of aristocratic woe, *Brideshead Revisted,* as this was where much of the TV series was filmed. The house was designed for the Howard family (who still live here) by Sir John Vanbrugh, who also designed Blenheim Palace, Winston Churchill's birthplace. Remarkably, this was the first building of any kind that Vanbrugh designed; until then he was best known as a playwright. Do not make the mistake of assuming that this is the work of a man tentatively feeling his way into a new profession. The audacity and confidence of the great Baroque house are startling, proclaiming the wealth and importance of the Howards and the utter self-assurance of its architect. Castle Howard took 60 years to build (1699–1759) and it was worth every year. A magnificent central hallway spanned by a hand-painted (and unfortunately, new) ceiling dwarfs all visitors, while there is no shortage of grandeur elsewhere in the building: vast family portraits; delicate marble fireplaces; immense and fading tapestries; huge pieces of Victorian silver on polished tables; and a great many marble busts. Outside, the stately theme continues in one of the most stunning neoclassic landscapes in England; Horace Walpole, the 18th-century connoisseur, commented that a pheasant at Castle Howard lives better than most dukes elsewhere. Carefully arranged woods, lakes, bridges, and obelisks compose a scene far more like a painting than a natural English landscape. Make sure you see the Temple of the Four Winds and the Mausoleum, whose magnificence caused Walpole to comment that all who view it would wish to be buried alive. For more information on the house, ☞ the Close-Up box on "Calling on Castle Howard," *below.* ⊠ *Coneysthorpe,* ☎ *01653/648333.* 🖭 *House and gardens £7, gardens only £4.50.* ☉ *House mid-Mar.–Oct., daily 11–4:30; grounds daily 10–5.*

CALLING ON CASTLE HOWARD

EVEN BEFORE YOUR FIRST SIGHT of Castle Howard—that grand birthday cake of a house nestled in North Yorkshire's hills and dales—chances are you are already enamored of it. The quintessential English stately home, its facade is abristle with Baroque sculptures and marble urns, and it is capped with a soaring cupola. Embellished by groves, a twinkling lake, and a preposterously perfect lawn, it's little wonder that Castle Howard became a media celebrity; it co-starred, along with Laurence Olivier and Jeremy Irons, in the popular 1980s TV series *Brideshead Revisited* and in the more recent miniseries *The Buccaneers*. Other British houses may be more treasure-laden or sumptuously decorated, but, clearly, none are as photogenic. Today an image of almost Hollywood splendor, the house attracts thousands of visitors every year, some searching for a sight of faded British aristocrats, but most there just to enjoy the magnificence of it all.

Considering its many theatrical, even flamboyant features, it makes sense to learn that Castle Howard's designer, Sir John Vanbrugh, was praised more as a playwright than an architect (in 18th-century London, his plays were second in popularity only to Congreve's). Even more remarkably, this was Vanbrugh's very first building design. His self-assurance apparently knowing no bounds, this immensely gifted architect went on to create—believe it or not—Blenheim Palace, the Versailles of England. The Baroque grandeur of Castle Howard is without equal in northern England. A neck support would help when viewing the Grand Hall, whose stunning stone pilasters soar 70 ft skyward to the hand-painted cupola. The adjoining marble corridors are populous with classical statues, and the state rooms are resplendent with gleaming paneling, delicate embroideries, and a coterie of Queen Anne sofas. One look at this drop-dead splendor and you'll be thankful for Ikea.

In time-tested English fashion, Lady Annette Howard, the castle's current chatelaine, has made these regal rooms cozy. With bouquets everywhere, intimate spotlights, and Staffordshire spaniels drowsing by the hearth, you almost feel like requesting a revivifying cuppa. Clearly, this grand house is still a home. In fact, the Howards often put up friends in the state bedrooms. If you ever get a weekend invitation—as the delightful tour guides will point out—bring wool pajamas; there's not enough staff now to keep all the fireplaces dancing. And don't plan on sleeping till noon: tourists start coming through the bedrooms at 11.

Many tourists are surprised to learn that, although situated some 200 mi north of London, Castle Howard can be done as a day trip. Catch the 8 AM express train to York from London's King's Cross Station, and link up with a tour bus that leaves York (☞ Guided Tours in Yorkshire A to Z, *below*) in time to arrive at the estate by noon. After three hours touring the mansion, exploring the gardens, lunching on cucumber sandwiches in the little café (save some tidbits for the resident peacocks), return to York to connect with the 4:30 or 5:30 PM express trains. Back in London, you may feel all tuckered out, but it will have been worth it

YORKSHIRE A TO Z

Arriving and Departing

By Bus
National Express (☎ 0990/808080) serves the region from London's Victoria Coach Station. Average travel times are 4½ hours to York, 6½ hours to Scarborough, and 7 hours to Whitby.

By Car
The M1, the principal route north from London, gets you to the region in about two hours, with longer travel times up into north Yorkshire. For York (193 mi) and the Scarborough areas, stay on the M1 to Leeds (189 mi), then take the A64. For the Yorkshire Dales, take the M1 to Leeds, then A660 to A65 north and west to Skipton. For the North York Moors, either take the B1363 north from York to Helmsley, or leave the A64 at Malton and follow the trans-moor A169 that runs to Whitby.

By Train
Great North-Eastern Railways (☎ 0345/484950) serves the region from London's King's Cross and Euston stations. Average travel times from King's Cross: 2½ hours to Leeds and two hours to York.

It is possible to reach the North Yorkshire coast by train, though service from London to Scarborough (change at York) and, especially, Whitby (change at Darlington and Middlesbrough) can take anywhere up to seven hours. It's much less trouble (though not much quicker) to take the direct bus from London.

Getting Around

By Bicycle
Although the countryside is too hilly for extensive bicycle touring, except for the most experienced, you can rent bikes locally in several places. In York, where there are special bike paths, contact **Cycleworks** (⊠ 14–16 Lawrence St., ☎ 01904/626664) and pick up a cycling map from the tourist information center.

By Bus
Each district now has its own bus company, and you may find you need to call around to discover the full range of services, though local tourist information centers can usually help. Useful timetable booklets for the Yorkshire Moors and Dales are widely available.

There are local **Metro** buses from Leeds and Bradford (☎ 0113/245–7676) into the more remote parts of the Yorkshire Dales. Other companies include: **Harrogate & District** (☎ 01423/566061); **Yorkshire Coastliner** (☎ 01653/692556) for services to Castle Howard, Scarborough, Whitby, Malton, Pickering, and Leeds; **United** (☎ 01325/468771) to Ripon, Harrogate, and Leeds; **Tees** (☎ 01642/210131) for Whitby, Scarborough, and Middlesbrough.

In York, the main local bus operator is **Rider York** (☎ 01904/435600). Many districts have Rover tickets; in York, the **Minster Card** (£9) gives a week's free travel on all Rider York services.

The **Moorsbus** (information from any National Park office) runs every Sunday and bank holiday Monday from late May to the end of September, and every Tuesday and Wednesday from late July to the end of August. It connects Danby, Hutton-le-Hole, Helmsley, Rievaulx Abbey, Rosedale Abbey, and Pickering and costs £2 for an all-day ticket.

By Car

The trans-Pennine motorway, the M62, between Liverpool and Hull, crosses the bottom of this region. North of Leeds, the A1 is the major north–south road, though narrow stretches, roadwork, and heavy traffic make this very slow going at times. Some of the steep, narrow roads in the countryside off the main routes are difficult drives and can be particularly perilous (or closed altogether) in winter. Prime candidates for main roads closed annually by snow drifts are the moorland A169 and the coast-and-moor A171. If you're driving in the dales or moors in winter, listen for the weather forecasts.

By Train

There is local service from Leeds to Skipton, and from York to Knaresborough and Harrogate and also to Scarborough (which has connections on to the seaside towns of Filey and Bridlington). Whitby can be reached on the minor, and extremely attractive, Esk Valley line from Middlesbrough. England's most scenic railway, the **Settle–Carlisle** line, can be reached from Leeds, where daily trains travel via Shipley, Keighley, and Skipton to the start of the line at Settle.

Two **Regional Rover** tickets for seven days' unlimited travel are available: **North East** and **Coast and Peaks.**

For all train travel information in the region, call **National Rail Enquiries** (☎ 0345/484950) or any local tourist office.

Contacts and Resources

Car Rentals

Bradford: Avis (✉ Bowling Bridge Service Station, Wakefield Rd., ☎ 01274/626819). **Europcar** (✉ 172 Thornton Rd., ☎ 01274/733048). **Eurodollar-Rent-a-Car** (✉ Nelson St., ☎ 01274/722155). **Hertz** (✉ 20 Laisterdyke, Sticker La., ☎ 01274/666666). **York: Budget Rent-a-Car** (✉ Station House, Foss Islands Rd., ☎ 01904/644919). **Hertz** (✉ York Rail Station, Station Rd., ☎ 01904/612586).

Emergencies

Emergency services, police, fire, or ambulance (☎ 999).

Guided Tours

Guide Friday runs frequent city tours of York—including stops at the Minster, the Castle Museum, the Shambles, and the Jorvik Viking Centre—that allow you to get on and off the bus as you please. ✉ *De Grey Rooms, Exhibition Sq.,* ☎ *01904/640896.* 🚌 *City bus tour £7.50, £5.50 if booked in advance.*

The **York Association of Voluntary Guides** arranges short walking tours around the city. ✉ *De Grey Rooms, Exhibition Sq.,* ☎ *01904/640780.* 🚌 *Free, but gratuity appreciated.* ⊙ *Daily 10:15; additional tours at 2:15 Apr. through Oct., and at 7 PM July through Aug.*

Yorktour (☎ 01904/641737) offers open-top-bus, riverboat, and walking tours of the city of York and has an excursion bus to Castle Howard, June–September, Tuesday, Friday, and Sunday, departing around noon.

National Parks

For information about local visitor centers, walks, and guided tours, contact: **Yorkshire Dales National Park,** (☎ 01756/752748 head office); and **North York Moors National Park** (☎ 01439/770657 head office).

Travel Agencies

Thomas Cook (⊠ Ivebridge House, 67 Market St., Bradford, ☎ 01274/732411; ⊠ 51 Boar La., Leeds, ☎ 0113/2432922; ⊠ 47 Westborough, Scarborough, ☎ 01723/364444; and ⊠ 4 Nessgate, York, ☎ 01904/639928).

Visitor Information

The **Yorkshire and Humberside Tourist Board** (⊠ 312 Tadcaster Rd., York, North Yorkshire YO2 2HF, ☎ 01904/707961) has information about the entire area.

Local tourist information centers have varied opening hours according to their location. Note that many in the North York Moors and Yorkshire Dales are only open during the summer.

Bradford (⊠ National Museum of Photography, Film, and TV, Prince's View, West Yorkshire BD5 0TR, ☎ 01274/753678). **Bridlington** (⊠ 25 Prince St., Humberside, YO15 2NP, ☎ 01262/673474). **Harrogate** (⊠ Royal Baths Assembly Rooms, Crescent Rd., North Yorkshire HG1 2RR, ☎ 01423/537300). **Haworth** (⊠ 2–4 West La., West Yorkshire BD22 8EF, ☎ 01535/642329). **Helmsley** (⊠ Town Hall, Market Pl., North Yorkshire YO6 5BL, ☎ 01439/770173). **Knaresborough** (⊠ 35 Market Pl., North Yorkshire HG5 8AL, ☎ 01423/866886). **Leeds** (⊠ Leeds City Station, West Yorkshire LS1 1PL, ☎ 0113/242–5242). **Richmond** (⊠ Friary Gardens, Victoria Rd., North Yorkshire DL10 4AJ, ☎ 01748/850252). **Scarborough** (⊠ Pavilion House, Valley Bridge Rd., North Yorkshire YO11 1UZ, ☎ 01723/373333). **Skipton** (⊠ 9 Sheep St., North Yorkshire BD23 1JH, ☎ 01756/792809). **Whitby** (⊠ New Quay Rd., North Yorkshire YO21 1YN, ☎ 01947/602674). **York** (⊠ De Grey Rooms, Exhibition Sq., North Yorkshire YO1 2HB, ☎ 01904/621756; ⊠ York Railway Station, North Yorkshire YO2 2AY, ☎ 01904/621756; and ⊠ 20 George Hudson St., North Yorkshire YO1 2HB, ☎ 01904/620557).

16 The Northeast

Durham, Hadrian's Wall, Lindisfarne Island

Ruined castles, holy islands, Roman walls, and the Northumberland Coast— windswept and wild, this is an area for the intrepid adventurer. The region soundly embraces history, but refuses to be dwarfed by it. Among the numberless monuments of a vigorous and often warlike past, Hadrian's Wall is the most famous. This northern border of the Roman Empire stretches across prehistoric remains and tractless moorland. Other must-sees include Durham Cathedral—more fortress than church—and magical Lindisfarne Island, a landmark of early Christendom.

Updated by
Jules Brown

ALTHOUGH ONE OF THE VILLAGES OF England's northeast corner—Allendale Town, southwest of Hexham—lays claim to being the geographical center of the British Isles, a decided air of remoteness pervades much of this region. For many Brits the words "The Northeast" provoke a vision of somewhat bitter, near-Siberian remoteness. The truth is a revelation. For although there are numerous wind-hammered wide-open spaces and empty roads that thread wild, high moorland, there are also picturesque fishing towns, small villages of remarkable charm, and historic abbeys and castles all the more romantic for their often ruinous state. Even the remoteness is relative. Suddenly, round the next bend on a lane that seems to lead nowhere, there stands an imposing church, a tall monastery, or a gorgeous country house built by a Victorian-era millionaire. Add in the value found in the region's shops and accommodations, the unspoiled towns and uncrowded beaches, and the friendliness of the people, and you have a destination for all reasons.

Mainly composed of the two large counties of Durham and Northumberland (in ancient times known as Northumbria), the Northeast includes among its attractions the English side of the Scottish Border area, renowned in ballads and romantic literature for feuds, raids, and battles. Hadrian's Wall, which served to mark the northern limit of the Roman Empire, runs through this region; much of it, remarkably, is still intact—so much so that people joke that it now keeps out tourists. Not far north of Hadrian's Wall are Kielder Forest, the largest planted forest in Europe; Kielder Water, the largest man-made lake in northern Europe; and some of the most interesting parts of Northumberland National Park.

On the region's eastern side is a 100-mi-long line of largely undeveloped coast—one of the least visited and most dramatic in all Europe. Several outstanding castles perch on headlands and promontories along here, including one which legend declares to have been the Joyous Garde of Sir Lancelot du Lac. Fittingly, Durham Cathedral—the greatest ecclesiastical structure of the region—has memorably been described as "Half church of God, half castle 'gainst the Scot." For almost 800 years, this great cathedral was the seat of bishops who raised their own armies and ruled the turbulent northern diocese as Prince-Bishops with quasi-royal authority.

Pleasures and Pastimes

Castles
Fought over for centuries by the Scots and the English, and prey to Viking raiders from across the North Sea, the Northeast is one of the most heavily fortified regions in Britain. Cities such as Durham and Newcastle—where the "new castle" is 900 years old—still boast impressive relics, but exploring the stupendous fortresses along the exposed Northumbrian coastline is among the most memorable experiences the region has to offer. Dunstanburgh Castle near Craster and Bamburgh Castle farther north are especially worth seeing.

Dining
The Northeast is one of the best areas in England for fresh local produce. Keep an eye out for restaurants that serve game from the Kielder Forest, local lamb from the hillsides, and fish both from the streams threading through the wild valleys and from the fishing fleets along the coast. Don't miss out on the simple fresh seafood sandwiches served in many of the region's local pubs. You might also wish to sample Alnwick Vatted Rum, a blend of Guyanese and Jamaican rum, or

Lindisfarne mead, a traditional, highly potent spirit produced on Holy Island, and made of honey vatted with grape juice and mineral water.

CATEGORY	COST*
£££	over £25
££	£15–25
£	under £15

per person, including first course, main course, dessert, and VAT; excluding drinks

Hiking and Biking

The wide-open Northeast offers superb walking opportunities almost wherever you go, but to reap an awe-inspiring sense of history with views of stunning scenery nothing beats a hike along the route of ancient Hadrian's Wall. The hilltop section near Housesteads Roman Fort is the best stretch for a short stroll. Long-distance footpaths include the 90-mi Teesdale Way, which follows the course of the River Tees, and St. Cuthbert's Way—an ancient pilgrimage route running the 63 mi from the Scottish border to Holy Island. Otherwise, the russet hills and dales of Northumberland National Park, in the northwest corner of the area, will gladden the heart of any serious walker. Similarly, cyclists relish the wide vistas, quiet roads, and magnificently fresh air of the region. One ideal spot to rent a mountain bike is Kielder Water, to the north of Hadrian's Wall.

Lodging

The Northeast is not an area where the large hotel chains have much of a presence, outside the few large cities. Rather, this is a region where you can expect to find country houses converted into welcoming hotels, old coaching inns that still greet guests after 300 years, and cozy bed-and-breakfasts conveniently located near hiking trails. Visitors are often pleasantly surprised at the prices of accommodations, with rates often at the low end of the scale.

CATEGORY	COST*
££££	over £110
£££	£60–£110
££	£50–£60
£	under £50

All prices are for two people sharing a double room, including service, breakfast, and VAT.

EXPLORING THE NORTHEAST

The vast majority of visitors travel from the south to arrive at the historic cathedral city of Durham, not far east of the picturesque foothill valleys of the Pennines. Farther north, Newcastle, on the region's main river, the Tyne, is a major industrial city, but nearby the remarkable Roman fortifications of Hadrian's Wall snake through some superb scenery to the east; farther north lies the wilderness of Northumberland National Park. Starting roughly an hour's drive north of Newcastle, the final 40 mi of England's east coast is absolutely stunning, studded with huge castles and scattered with offshore islands such as the Farne Islands—home to a varied seabird population—and Holy Island, also known as Lindisfarne.

Numbers in the text correspond to numbers in the margin and on the Northeast and Durham maps.

Great Itineraries

Although it's possible to get a sense of the Northeast through an overnight stop en route to or from Scotland, it's worth setting aside at least three days to explore the region properly. One turn off the A1—the main north–south highway—and you'll soon learn that driving along the meandering backcountry roads can often be slow business—if only because the spectacular scenery encourages long halts!

IF YOU HAVE 2 DAYS
Base yourself at either ☒ **Durham** ①, with time to inspect the Norman cathedral and the castle to either side of the central Palace Green, or at smaller, quainter ☒ **Alnwick** ㉛, with its riverside castle and cobbled square. Drive inland between the two for at least a brief glimpse of **Hadrian's Wall,** ideally at **Housesteads Roman Fort** ㉓, and wind up at the magical monastic settlement on **Lindisfarne** ㊱.

IF YOU HAVE 4 DAYS
Having spent at least half a day exploring ☒ **Durham** ①, set aside a full day to follow the course of **Hadrian's Wall.** An overnight stop nearby in ☒ **Hexham** ⑳ enables you to see the excellent museums of Roman finds at **Vindolanda** ㉒ and **Housesteads Roman Fort** ㉓. Then drive northeast through the gorgeous countryside to spend the evening in the picturesque little market town of ☒ **Alnwick** ㉛. On the next morning, walk from **Craster** ㊱ to the splendidly bleak ruin of **Dunstanburgh Castle** ㉝, then visit one or two of the huge beaches to the north as you head to ☒ **Bamburgh** ㉟ for the night. Overlooking the windswept shore, its famous castle conjures up the days of chivalry as few others do. Whether you're heading back to Durham from there, or onward to Scotland, visit wind-battered **Lindisfarne** ㊱, a short distance north, to soak up the saintly atmosphere.

When to Tour the Northeast

Although Hadrian's Wall and the coastal castles are starkly impressive in a blanket of snow, the best time to see the Northeast is in summer. Then you can be sure that the museums—and the roads—will be open, and that you'll be able to enjoy the long countryside walks that are one of the region's greatest pleasures. Due to rough seas and inclement weather, there's certainly no question of swimming at any of the magnificent beaches unless you're here in the very height of summer, July and August. At the end of June, Alnwick plays host to its annual fair, featuring a costumed reenactment of a medieval fair, processions, a market, and concerts. Durham Regatta, England's oldest rowing event, takes place at the same time.

DURHAM AND ITS ENVIRONS

Durham—the first major northeastern town on the main road up from London—is by far the region's most interesting historic city. Most of the other cities nearby are brash upstarts that made their fortunes during the industrial revolution and have since subsided into relative decline. Several—such as Darlington, birthplace of the modern railroad—do hold interesting relics of their 19th-century heyday. The land to the west, known as County Durham, toward the Pennine Hills, is far more scenic, and a daylong drive through the valleys of Teesdale and Weardale takes you past ruined castles, industrial heritage sites, isolated moorland villages, and tumbling waterfalls.

Durham

① *250 mi north of London; 15 mi south of Newcastle.*

The great medieval city of Durham, seat of County Durham, is among the most dramatically sited in Britain. Despite the military advantages offered by the rocky spur on which it stands, Durham was founded

The Northeast

SCOTLAND

Berwick-upon-Tweed **37**

Coldstream

Kelso

Jedburgh

CHEVIOT HILLS

Carter Bar

Wooler

Lindisfarne (Holy Island) **36**

Farne Islands **34**

Bamburgh **35**

Seahouses
Beadnell

High-Newton-by-the-Sea

Dunstanburgh Castle **33**

Craster **32**

Alnwick **31**

Rothbury **30**

Longframlington

NORTHUMBERLAND

Kielder Castle **28**
Forest of Kielder

Kielder Water **27**

Bellingham

North Tyne

Marpeth

Wallington House **29**

Housesteads Roman Fort **23**
Vindolanda

Greenhead **21**

Bardon Mill

Chesters Roman Fort **24**

Hadrian's Wall

Corstopitum

Hexham **20**

22 **26** **25**

Chollerford

Corbridge

Newcastle upon Tyne **18**

Wallsend

Jarrow **19**

South Shields

Wylam

Sunderland

Allendale Town

Blanchland

Beamish **17**

16 Washington

Chester-le-Street

Killhope Lead Mining Centre

Ireshopeburn
St. John's Chapel

High Force

Frosterley

Middleton-in-Teesdale

8 Brancepeth

Durham **1** — **7**

DURHAM

Bishop Auckland **13**

Raby Castle

Staindrop **12**

Middlesbrough **15**

PENNINES

Romaldkirk **9**

Cotherstone

Bowes **11**

10 Barnard Castle

Darlington **14**

TO YORK

North Sea

GREAT BRITAIN

0   10 miles
0   15 km

N

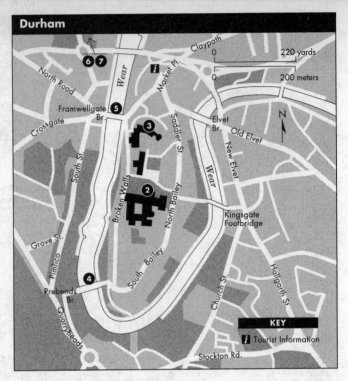

surprisingly late, probably in about the year 1000, growing up around a small Saxon church erected to house the remains of St. Cuthbert. But it was the Normans, under William the Conqueror, who put Durham on the map, building the first defensive castle and, in about 1090, beginning work on the cathedral, the main body of which was finished in about 1150. From here, Durham's Prince-Bishops—granted almost dictatorial local powers by William the Conqueror in 1072—kept the county on a tight rein, coining their own money, raising their own taxes, and maintaining their own laws and courts; not until 1836 were these rights finally restored to the English Crown. Together, the cathedral and castle stand high on a wooded peninsula almost entirely encircled by the River Wear (rhymes with "beer"). For centuries these two ancient structures have dominated Durham—now a thriving university town, the Northeast's equivalent to Oxford or Cambridge—and the surrounding countryside.

★ ② Architectural historians come from all over the world to admire and study the Norman masterpiece that is **Durham Cathedral,** on the neat Palace Green in the heart of the city. The cathedral is an amazing vision of solidity and strength, a far cry from the airy lightness of later, Gothic cathedrals. Durham is the essence of an almost entirely Norman, or Romanesque, edifice: the roundheaded arches of the nave and the deep zigzag patterns carved into them are entirely typical of the heavy, gaunt style of Norman building. Yet if the style looks back rather than forward, the technology of Durham was quite revolutionary at the time. This was the first European cathedral to be given a stone, rather than a wooden, roof, and when you consider the means of construction available to its ambitious builders—the stones that form the ribs of the roof had to be hoisted up by hand and set on a wooden structure, which was then knocked away—their achievement seems little short of staggering.

The origins of the cathedral go back to the 10th century. Monks fleeing a devastating Viking raid on Lindisfarne Abbey in the year 875 brought the body of St. Cuthbert to this site in 995, and soon the wealth attracted by Cuthbert's shrine paid for the construction of a cathedral. The bishop's throne in the cathedral is still the loftiest in all medieval Christendom; his miter is the only one to be encircled by a coronet; and his coat of arms is the only one to be crossed with a sword as well as a crosier. **Cuthbert's shrine** lies surrounded by columns of local marble, with the saint's remains buried below a simple slab. A second unobtrusive tomb at the west end of the cathedral, in the so-called Galilee Chapel, is the final resting place of the **Venerable Bede,** the 8th-century Northumbrian monk whose contemporary account of the English people made him the country's first reliable historian. He died in Jarrow in 735 and his remains were placed in the cathedral a quarter century after Cuthbert's.

Upon entering, many visitors take a snapshot of the 12th-century bronze **Sanctuary Knocker,** shaped like the head of a ferocious mythological beast, mounted on the massive northwestern entrance door. By grasping the ring clenched in the animal's mouth, medieval felons could claim sanctuary; cathedral records show that 331 criminals (especially murderers) sought this protection between 1464 and 1524. The knocker now in place is, in fact, a replica; the original is kept for security in the cathedral treasury, along with ancient illuminated manuscripts, fragments of St. Cuthbert's oak coffin, and more church treasures. ⊠ *Palace Green,* ☎ *0191/386–4266.* ⊟ *Cathedral free but £2 donation welcome, treasury £2, tower £2, guided tours £2.* ☉ *Cathedral May–Sept., daily 7:15 AM–8 PM; Oct.–Apr. 7:15–6. Treasury Mon.–Sat. 10–4:30, Sun. 2–4:30. Choral evensong service weekdays at 5:15 (not Mon.), Sun. at 3:30. Guided tours June–Aug., Mon.–Sat. at 10:30 and 2.*

❸ **Durham Castle,** which faces the Cathedral across Palace Green, commands a strategic position above the River Wear. For almost 800 years the castle was home to successive Prince-Bishops—from here large tracts of northern England were ruled and the wild Scots kept at bay. Henry VIII first curtailed their independence, though it wasn't until the 19th century that the Prince-Bishops were finally reined in and had their powers annulled. They abandoned the castle, turning it over to University College, one of several colleges of the University of Durham, the oldest in England after Oxford and Cambridge. You can tour the castle and, during college vacations, very reasonably priced accommodations are available—both in the castle and in other college buildings throughout the city. For a quick and handy bite, head for the Almshouse Café, in a historic almshouse on Palace Green, between the cathedral and castle. ⊠ *Palace Green,* ☎ *0191/374–3800.* ⊟ *£2.75.* ☉ *Guided tours only: Easter wk and July–Sept., Mon.–Sat. 10–noon, 2–4:30; Oct.–June, Mon., Wed., Sat. 2–4:30.*

The **River Wear** winds through the center of Durham, curving beneath the cathedral and castle, and playing host in mid-June each year to the Durham Regatta, Britain's oldest rowing event, which attracts 300 racing crews. A short stroll along the Wear's leafy banks is rewarded by ❹ delightful views, especially as you cross **Prebends Footbridge,** reached from the southern end of Palace Green; J. M. W. Turner reveled in the view from here and painted a celebrated scene of Durham from the bridge. If you follow the far side of the Wear, you can recross the river ❺ to find **Framwellgate Bridge,** which dates originally from the 12th century. Many of the elegant town houses that line the narrow lanes back up to the cathedral now house departments of the university.

⑥ The **Durham Light Infantry Museum** at Aykley Heads, ½ mi northwest of Durham city center on A691, is devoted to the history of the county regiment, exhibiting uniforms, weapons, and regalia alongside mementos of British campaigns in India, Iran, the Crimea, and Africa. ✉ *Aykley Heads,* ☎ *0191/384–2214.* ☞ *£1.50.* ⊙ *Tues.–Sat. 10–5, Sun. 2–5; closed 10 days at Christmas.*

⑦ Fine art and craft work from all parts of Asia are on show at the **Durham University Oriental Museum.** ✉ *Elvet Hill, off South Rd. (A1050),* ☎ *0191/374–7911.* ☞ *£1.50.* ⊙ *Weekdays 9:30–1 and 2–5, weekends 2–5; closed 10 days at Christmas.*

The Arts

Durham Art Gallery at the Light Infantry Museum (see *above*) is the city's most reliable arts venue, supporting a full program of exhibitions and concerts. ✉ *Aykley Heads,* ☎ *0191/384–2214.* ☞ *Charges vary according to event.* ⊙ *Tues.–Sat. 10–5, Sun. 2–5; closed 10 days at Christmas.*

Dining and Lodging

£ ✗ **Vennel's Café.** For breakfast, lunch, or just a snack, you'll be hard pushed to find a more welcoming place than Vennel's—named for the local word ("vennel") for the very narrowest of thoroughfares. Squeeze up the alley, order at the counter, and then sit outside in the lovely courtyard. When the weather's less clement, interior wooden tables soon fill with an artsy clientele tucking into daily specials, including many vegetarian options. ✉ *Saddler's Yard, off Saddler St.,* ☎ *0191/386–0484. No credit cards.*

££££ ✗🖪 **Royal County Swallow Hotel.** This comfortable, attractively redecorated Georgian hotel retains many of its historic details. It's the city's top establishment, with a convenient downtown location and spacious rooms, some with four-poster beds. The oak staircase comes from Loch Leven castle in Scotland, where Mary, Queen of Scots, was imprisoned. The luxurious **County Restaurant** features specialties that include wild boar steaks and such traditional fare as Northumbrian broth and roast beef with Yorkshire pudding. ✉ *Old Elvet, DH1 3JN,* ☎ *0191/386–6821; 800/444–1545;* ℻ *0191/386–0704. 150 rooms with bath. Restaurant, bar, coffee shop, indoor pool, sauna, exercise room, health club. AE, DC, MC, V.*

££ 🖪 **Georgian Town House.** Exactly as the name suggests, this well-sited hotel, at the top of a cobbled street overlooking the cathedral and castle, makes the best of its Georgian exterior and fittings. Some rooms have views of the cathedral; all are comfortable and make a good base for city walks. ✉ *10 Crossgate, DH1 4PS,* ☎ ℻ *0191/386–8070. 6 rooms with bath. No credit cards.*

Outdoor Activities and Sports

In Durham, **Brown's Boat House** (✉ Elvet Bridge, ☎ 0191/386–3779) rents rowboats and offers short cruises April–early November.

Shopping

Dillons University Bookshop (✉ 55 Saddler St., ☎ 0191/384–2095) has more than 25,000 volumes in stock. **Bramwells Jewellers** (✉ 24 Elvet Bridge, ☎ 0191/386–8006) has its own store specialty—a pendant replica of the gold-and-silver cross of St. Cuthbert.

Brancepeth

⑧ *4 mi southwest of Durham, on the A690.*

Brancepeth was reconstructed early in the 19th century to resemble a traditional Tudor village, and its rows of well-preserved cottages have barely changed since. A flamboyantly restored castle (not open to the public) overlooks the whole ensemble, but the real gem here is the genuine medieval **church of St. Brandon,** complete with an exceptionally ornate rood screen. Tombs in the church hold assorted Nevilles, one of the most powerful northern families in feudal times, who owned the castle until 1569.

Romaldkirk

❾ *7 mi southeast of High Force.*

Sporadic settlements punctuate the isolation of Teesdale, most notably the pretty village of Romaldkirk, whose extravagantly proportioned church is known as the **"Cathedral of the Dale."** The stocks for punishing wrongdoers still stand on the village green, while the central **Rose and Crown** (☎ 01833/650213) is the very model of comfort—an 18th-century coaching inn with a roaring fire.

Barnard Castle

❿ *7 mi southeast of Romaldkirk, 25 mi southwest of Durham.*

The substantial ruins of the fortress that gave its name to the handsome market town of Barnard Castle cling to an aerie on a cliff overlooking the River Tees. Inside, you can see parts of the 14th-century Great Hall and the cylindrical, 13th-century tower, built by the castle's original owners, the Anglo-Scottish Balliol family. ⊠ *Off Galgate,* ☎ *01833/638212.* 🔳 *£2.20.* ☉ *Apr.–Sept., daily 10–6; Oct., daily 10–4; Nov.–Mar., Wed.–Sun. 10–4; call ahead in winter.*

Barnard Castle's unusual butter-market hall (known locally as Market Cross), surmounted by a fire alarm bell, marks the junction of the streets Thorngate, Newgate, and Market Place, which are lined with stores, pubs, and cafés. In 1838 Charles Dickens stayed at the **King's Head Inn** here while researching his novel *Nicholas Nickleby,* which dealt with the abuse of children in local boarding schools (☞ Bowes, *below*). The local tourist office has a *Dickens Drive* leaflet of the places he visited in the area.

★ The main attraction is the **Bowes Museum,** a vast French-inspired château just over a mile west of the town center, built between 1869 and 1885 to house John and Josephine Bowes' outstanding art and artifacts collection. True Victorian philanthropists, the Bowes displayed their discriminating purchases for the edification of the public—and what glorious educational sustenance they still provide. There are paintings by Canaletto, El Greco, Goya, and Boucher, and one of the greatest collections of 18th-century French furniture in the world. Accessible archaeological displays chart the history of County Durham from the Ice Age to the end of the Roman period, while an entire gallery is taken up by 19th-century dollhouses, games, and models—the lead soldiers, for example, are the direct result of the contemporaneous local lead-mining industry. Most extraordinary of all, though, is a splendid 18th-century mechanical silver swan, which, when activated, catches and swallows a silver fish to the accompaniment of a haunting tune. ⊠ *Follow signs from Barnard Castle town center,* ☎ *01833/690606.* 🔳 *£3.50.* ☉ *Mon.–Sat. 10–5:30, Sun. 2–5; closed Christmas wk.*

Bowes

⓫ *4 mi southwest of Barnard Castle.*

A massive 12th-century stone **keep,** built on the site of a Roman fort, dominates the high moorland village of Bowes. The house on which

Charles Dickens modeled *Nicholas Nickleby*'s Dotheboys Hall can still be seen, although it's not open to the public. West of the village, look for the main street's last building, which housed a notoriously cruel boarding school in the 19th century, whose headmaster, William Shaw, provided Dickens with the inspiration for one of his greatest grotesque characters—Wackford Squeers. This is a bleak place in winter, though there's a welcome in the **Bowes Moor Hotel** (⊠ Bowes, ☎ 01833/628331), reputedly the highest hotel in England, serving meals and drinks to stray travelers.

Raby Castle

🄬 *6 mi northeast of Barnard Castle; 19 mi southwest of Durham.*

Raby Castle, once the seat of the Nevilles and currently the home of the 11th Baron Barnard, stands amid 200 acres of a landscaped deer park just outside Staindrop. Largely dating from the 14th century (and using stone plundered from Barnard Castle), it displays luxuriously furnished rooms crammed with treasures, in addition to well-preserved medieval kitchens, with original Victorian copperware and other domestic equipment. Stone arcades display five full-length portraits of Raby personages, including Richard III's mother, who died here. ⊠ *1 mi north of Staindrop,* ☎ *01833/660202.* ☜ *£4; park, gardens, and carriage collection £1.50.* ☉ *Castle: Easter–June, Wed., Sun. 1–5; July–Sept., Sun.–Fri. 1–5. Parks and gardens: Easter–June, Wed., Sun. 11:30–5:30; July–Sept., Sun.–Fri. 11:30–5:30.*

Bishop Auckland

🄭 *13 mi northeast of Barnard Castle; 12 mi southwest of Durham.*

For 700 years, between the 12th and 19th centuries, the Prince-Bishops of Durham had their country residence in **Auckland Castle,** in the town of Bishop Auckland. When finally deprived of their powers in 1836, the bishops left Durham and made Bishop Auckland their official home. The grand episcopal palace you see today dates mainly from the 16th century, though the limestone and marble chapel, with its dazzling stained-glass windows, was built in 1665 from the ruins of a 12th-century banqueting hall. The unusual 18th-century "deer house" of adjoining Bishops Park testifies to at least one of the bishops' extracurricular interests. The castle itself offers architectural styles ranging from the medieval to the neo-Gothic. ⊠ *Off Market Pl.,* ☎ *01388/601627.* ☜ *£3.* ☉ *May, June, and Sept., Fri. and Sun. 2–5; July, Thurs., Fri., and Sun, 2–5; Aug., Thurs–Sun. 2–5; park daily 7 AM–sunset.*

Darlington

🄮 *21 mi south of Durham.*

Still visibly rooted in its 19th-century industrial past, the town of Darlington rocketed to fame in 1825, when George Stephenson piloted his steam-powered *Locomotion* along newly laid tracks the few miles to nearby Stockton, thus kick-starting the railway age. First envisaged as a means of transporting coal from the local pits to the dockside, Stephenson's invention soon attracted paying passengers—and even though it barely traveled faster than 15 mph, the *Locomotion* was a palpable hit. The story of the coming of the railway is well told in the ★ **Darlington Railway Centre and Museum,** housed in the town's original railroad station, built in 1842 and now lying a (signposted) 20-minute walk outside of the town center. Here, you can inspect historic engines, including Stephenson's *Locomotion,* as well as photographs, documents, and models, and all the other paraphernalia associated with

a 19th-century station. ⊠ *North Road Station,* ☎ *01325/460532.* ⊠
£2. ☉ *Daily 10–5.*

Dining and Lodging

£££ ✕⊞ **George Hotel.** This sprawling 18th-century coaching inn lies just 6
mi west of Darlington in the tiny village of Piercebridge. Beautifully located on the banks of the River Tees, just across from the scant remains
of a Roman fort, rooms and restaurant look out across the gardens and
water; ask for a room with a balcony overlooking the river when booking. Local walks along the river may reveal sightings of kingfishers and
herons, and once you've worked up an appetite you can sate it easily—
there's a substantial bar menu (with riverside tables for summer dining),
or traditional meals and roasts served in the more formal restaurant. ⊠
Piercebridge-on-Tees, Darlington DL2 3SW, ☎ *01325/374576,* ☏
01325/374577. 35 rooms with bath. Restaurant, 2 bars. MC, V.

Middlesbrough

⑮ *12 mi east of Darlington, 22 mi southeast of Durham.*

In 1802 a mere dozen people lived in Middlesbrough, near the mouth
of the River Tees. With the discovery of iron ore, however, it became
a boomtown, with steel mills and, later, chemical industries, doing much
to boost the economy, although blighting part of the town. The industrial
heritage throws up a few peculiar local attractions. Middlesbrough's
unusual **Transporter Bridge,** built in 1911, is the largest of its kind in
the world, a vast structure like a giant's Erector-set model, whose
gantry system still takes 12 cable cars, holding 200 passengers each,
across the river every 20 minutes. A special viewing platform stands
on the south bank. Upstream you'll find Newport Bridge, the world's
largest lift span bridge, another remarkable sight. ☎ *01642/247563.*
Crossing time 2 mins. ⊠ *25p pedestrians, 70p cars.* ☉ *Mon.–Sat. 5*
AM–11 PM, *Sun. 2–11.*

The life and times of Captain Cook, the celebrated 18th-century cir-
cumnavigator and explorer, are vividly depicted in the **Captain Cook**
Birthplace Museum, in the leafy Middlesbrough suburb of Marton. Interactive displays and exhibits cover Cook's remarkable voyages to Australia, New Zealand, Canada, Antarctica, and Hawaii, where he met
an untimely death. Every year on the weekend closest to October 27,
Cook's birthday, the museum hosts a special celebration, while a conservatory near the museum houses specimens of the exotic plants Cook
discovered during his travels. ⊠ *Stewart Park, Marton, off A174,*
south of city center. Museum, ☎ *01642/311211; 01642/300202 con-*
servatory. Museum: ⊠ *£2.* ☉ *June–Sept., Tues.–Sun 10–5:30; Oct.–*
May, Tues.–Sun 9–4. Conservatory: ⊠ *Free.* ☉ *Mar.–Oct., weekends*
11–5:45; Nov.–Feb., weekends 11–3:45.

Washington

⑯ *12 mi north of Durham.*

★ Careful navigation through the often bewildering "new town" of Washington will take you to **Washington Old Hall,** the ancestral home of the
first U.S. president. George Washington's direct forebears—the de
Wessyngtons—lived here between 1183 and 1288; other members of
the family continued to live in the house until 1613, when the present
property was rebuilt. Now owned by the National Trust, the mansion
retains a decidedly Jacobean (17th-century) appearance, most noticeably in the fine wood paneling of the rooms, the heavy furniture, and
the small formal garden that surrounds the house. On the Fourth of July,
there are special celebrations and admission is free. *From A1(M), 5 mi*

west of Sunderland, follow signs to Washington New Town, District 4, and then on to Washington Village; ☎ *0191/416–6879.* 🖾 *£2.50.* ☉ *Apr.–Oct., Sun.–Wed. and Good Fri. 11–5 (last admission 4:30).*

Beamish

⑰ *9 mi north of Durham; 3 mi west of Chester-le-Street.*

★ Set aside at least half a day to enjoy the 260-acre **Beamish Open-Air Museum,** in the town of Beamish. Historic buildings have been brought here from throughout the region, and a streetcar will take you across a reconstructed 1920s High Street, including a dentist's operating room, a pub, and a grocery. A stableman will talk to you about the Clydesdale workhorses in his care, once used to draw brewery wagons. On the farm you can see such local breeds as Durham Shorthorn cattle and Teeswater sheep. Other attractions include a railroad station, a coal mine, and a transportation collection. The large gift store specializes in period souvenirs and locally made crafts. Winter visits are centered on the reconstructed town only, and admission prices are reduced accordingly. ⊠ *Off A693, between Chester-le-Street and Stanley,* ☎ *01207/231811.* 🖾 *£7, £8, or £3 (depending on season).* ☉ *Apr.–mid-July and Sept.–Oct., daily 10–5; mid-July–Aug., daily 10–6; Nov.–Mar., Tues.–Thurs. and weekends 10–4; closed 2 wks at Christmas and New Year's; call for exact times in winter.*

Dining and Lodging

££££ ✕🏨 **Lumley Castle Hotel.** This is a real castle, right down to the dungeons, and a hotel experience not to be missed. Located 3 mi west of Beamish, Lumley Castle has superb bedrooms in all sizes (some with four-poster beds and/or Jacuzzis) combined with up-to-date facilities. There's plenty of space to wander and an appealing library-bar, with more than 3,000 books and a log fire, for before-dinner drinks. The **Black Knight Restaurant** features English specialties such as Northumbrian broth, tournedos of beef (prime roast beef with Stilton cheese, wrapped in bacon), and braised hock of lamb studded with garlic and rosemary. ⊠ *1 mi east of Chester-le-Street by B1284, DH3 4NX,* ☎ *0191/389–1111,* 🖷 *0191/387–1437. 62 rooms with bath. Restaurant, bar. AE, DC, MC, V.*

Newcastle upon Tyne

⑱ *16 mi north of Durham.*

Durham may have the glories of its castle, cathedral, and university, but the main and liveliest city of the Northeast is Newcastle upon Tyne— or Newcastle, as it's more commonly known. Settled since Roman times, it made its fortune twice, first by exporting coal in the Elizabethan age and then by building ships; as a 19th-century industrial center, it had few equals in Britain, showing off its wealth in a series of grand Victorian buildings lining the sweeping, central neoclassic streets. Many of these still remain (particularly on Grey Street), and despite years of industrial decline, the city retains a vitality that is hard to ignore. Much of the recent regeneration has been down on the historic Quayside, where surviving 17th-century houses stand alongside warehouses converted into restaurants and bars. Here, too, is the very symbol of the city, the celebrated **Tyne Bridge** (1929), one of a half-dozen bridges spanning the river in the city and whose elegant proportions were later reproduced by the architects responsible for Sydney's Harbour Bridge. Overlooking the Tyne River, the remains of the **Norman castle** remind visitors of the city's earlier status as a defensive stronghold. This was the "new castle," originally built in 1080, that gave the city its name.

✉ *St. Nicholas St.,* ☎ *0191/232–7938.* 🎫 *£1.50.* ⊙ *Apr.–Sept., Tues.–Sun. 9:30–5:30; Oct.–Mar., Tues.–Sun. 9:30–4:30.*

The finest art gallery in the Northeast, the **Laing Gallery,** merits at least an hour's visit. British art is well represented, and some of the most extraordinary paintings are those by local 19th-century artist John Martin, who produced biblical landscapes of dramatic intensity. The Pre-Raphaelites are on show, too, and the gallery also offers a display called Art on Tyneside, which traces 400 years of local art and craft—highlighting, for example, glassware, pottery, and engraving. ✉ *Higham Pl. near John Dobson St.,* ☎ *0191/232–7734.* 🎫 *Free.* ⊙ *Mon.–Sat. 10–5, Sun. 2–5.*

Newcastle's university buildings house the city's best museums. Here you'll find the **Museum of Antiquities,** showing finds from Hadrian's Wall, as well as the interesting **Shefton Museum of Greek Art and Archaeology,** containing ancient arms, ceramics, and terra-cotta pieces. ✉ *The University,* ☎ *0191/222–7844 or 0191/222–6000.* 🎫 *Free.* ⊙ *Museum of Antiquities Mon.–Sat. 10–5; Shefton Museum weekdays 9:30–12:30 and 2–4:30.*

The Arts
Newcastle's **Theatre Royal** (✉ Grey St., ☎ 0191/232–2061) is the region's most established theater, with a variety of high-quality productions. The English Shakespeare Company now calls the **Tyne Theatre and Opera House** (✉ Westgate Rd., ☎ 0191/232–0899) its home.

Dining
££ ✕ **Courtney's.** This converted quayside building offers a changing dinner menu each week. Typical entrées using fresh local produce include crab and fish cakes, and garlic-encrusted lamb, while other dishes show off Asian and Mediterranean flourishes. It's a relaxed place for inexpensive set lunches. ✉ *5–7 The Side,* ☎ *0191/232–5537. AE, MC, V. Closed Sun., 2 wks in May, and 1 wk at Christmas. No lunch Sat.*

£ ✕ **Crown Posada.** Adorned with Pre-Raphaelite stained glass, a coffered ceiling, and Victorian lamps, this classic Newcastle pub, near the quayside, wears its 19th-century decor well. ✉ *31 The Side,* ☎ *0191/232–1269. No credit cards.*

Shopping
In a wonderful medieval friary in the heart of Newcastle's traditional guilds district, **Blackfriars Craft Centre** (✉ Friars Green, Stowell St., ☎ 0191/261–4307) is a cooperative selling local crafts such as textiles and wrought ironwork.

Jarrow

⑲ *4 mi east of Newcastle.*

The name "Jarrow" is to British ears forever linked to the "Jarrow Crusade," a protest march to London led by unemployed former workers from the town's steelworks and shipyards in the depths of the 1930s. Travelers are attracted here, however, by its much more ancient history. **Bede's World and St. Paul's Church** offer substantial monastic ruins, a visitor center–cum–museum, and the church of St. Paul, all reflecting the long tradition of religion and learning that began here in AD 681, when the first Saxon church was established on the site. The Venerable Bede, deemed to be England's earliest historian, was a scholar here and in AD 731 completed his *History of the English Church and People* while ensconced at the monastery. Visits are designed to provide an authentic experience of medieval life; in the reconstructed farm buildings erected on the Anglo-Saxon farm landscape, you're encouraged to get close to rare animal breeds such as Dexter cattle and Iron Age pigs. Still used for regular worship, St. Paul's contains some of the oldest stained glass in Europe and the oldest dedicatory church inscription in Britain (a carved stone inscribed in AD 685). ✉ *Church Bank; from southern exit traffic circle at South Tyne tunnel, take A185 to South Shields, then follow signs to* ST. PAUL'S CHURCH *and* JARROW HALL; ☎ *0191/489–2106.* ⛃ *£2.50.* ⊙ *Apr.–Oct., Tues.–Sat. 10– 5:30, Sun. 2:30–5:30; Nov.–Mar., Tues.–Sat. 10–4:30, Sun. 2:30–5:30.*

HADRIAN'S WALL COUNTRY

★ The formidable line of fortifications that marked the northern border of the Roman Empire—which stretched eastward for 2,500 mi to what is now Iraq—**Hadrian's Wall** was constructed after the Roman emperor Hadrian's visit in AD 122, in response to repeated barbarian invasions from Scotland. It extends 73 mi from Wallsend ("Wall's End") just north of Newcastle, in the east, to Bowness-on-Solway beyond Carlisle, in the west, and was completed just four years after the emperor's visit—which gives a pretty good idea of Roman determination in that nontechnological era. Its construction bears all the hallmarks of Roman efficiency. The wall stretches across the narrowest part of the country and is built following as straight a path as possible. There is a fortified tower every 500 yards, and a fortress every mile, the so-called "milecastles."

Today, excavating, documenting, interpreting, repairing, displaying, and generally managing the Roman remains is a Northumbrian growth industry, and anyone sufficiently motivated could spend endless time here. At the forts—notably at Chesters, Housesteads (the best-preserved fort), Vindolanda, and at the Roman Army Museum near Greenhead—people can browse and get a good introduction to the life led by Roman soldiers on the frontier. Special events in the summer put more flesh on the archaeological bones: most of the sites sponsor talks, Roman drama, festivals, and even discussions of battle tactics—local tourist offices, or the sites themselves, have details. It is also possible to walk along sections of the wall, but this can be very hard going, and once you are committed to it it's not always possible to get off and step back onto the road (exits and entrances are few and far between). For photographers, one spot in particular produces a memorable souvenir: looking east toward the fort of Housesteads from Cuddy's Crag, the wall can be seen snaking up and down across the wildest, most inhospitable country imaginable.

Walking and Horseback Riding

There are plans to complete a long-distance footpath along the entire course of Hadrian's Wall, but currently only certain sections are accessible to hikers. Best is the 12-mi western stretch between Sewingshields (east of Housesteads) and Greenhead. It's rugged country, unsuited to the inexperienced hiker, and most trekkers choose instead to walk short stretches in the vicinity of the various visitor centers. There are also several riding schools in the region, offering hour-long rides to full-day treks on horseback. For a full list, contact the Hexham tourist information office (☞ Contacts and Resources *in* The Northeast A to Z, *below*); advance booking in summer is essential.

Hexham

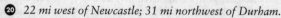

⓴ *22 mi west of Newcastle; 31 mi northwest of Durham.*

The historic market town of Hexham makes the best base for visiting Hadrian's Wall. It's just a few miles from the most significant remains and retains enough of interest in its medieval streets to warrant a stop in its own right. First settled in the 7th century, around a Benedictine monastery, Hexham later became a byword for monastic learning, famous for its book painting, sculpture, and liturgical singing.

★ Ancient **Hexham Abbey,** a tranquil place of Christian worship for more than 1,300 years, forms one side of the town's main square. Inside, you can climb the 35 worn stone "night stairs," which once led from the main part of the abbey to the canon's dormitory, to overlook the whole ensemble. Most of the present building dates from the 12th century, and much of the stone was taken from the Roman fort at Corstopitum a few miles northeast. ⊠ *Beaumont St.,* ☎ *01434/602031.* ☒ *Suggested donation £2.* ⊙ *June–Sept., daily 9–7; Oct.–May, daily 9–5. No tours during services.*

Hexham's central **Market Place** has been the site since 1239 of a weekly market, held each Tuesday. Crowded stalls are set out under the long slate roof of the Shambles; other stalls take their chances with the weather, protected only by their bright awnings.

Dating from 1330, Hexham's original jail—the **Manor Office,** across Market Place from the abbey—houses the town's Information Center as well as the **Border History Museum.** Photographs, models, drawings, a reconstructed blacksmith's shop, a Border house interior, armor, and weapons help tell the story of the "Middle March"—the medieval administrative area governed by a warden and centered on Hexham. ⊠ *The Old Gaol, Hallgate,* ☎ *01434/652200.* ☒ *£1.80.* ⊙ *Easter–Oct., Mon.–Sat. 10–4:30; Feb.–Easter and Nov., Sat.–Tues. 10–4:30.*

The Arts

Hexham is home to one of the Northeast's most adventurous arts venues, the **Queen's Hall Arts Centre,** which offers drama, dance, and exhibition space for local artists. It also sponsors local events, like the annual Jazz Festival (June), which sees dozens of concerts spread over a single weekend; call in advance for a program. Opposite the arts center, you'll find Mrs. Miggin's Coffee Shop, at St. Mary's Wynd, off Beaumont Street, which serves up light refreshments, homemade cakes, and work for sale by local artists. ⊠ *Beaumont St.,* ☎ *01434/607272.* ☒ *Free.* ⊙ *Galleries and box office Mon.–Sat. 9–6.*

Dining and Lodging

£££ ✕ **Black House.** A mile south of central Hexham, this restaurant is housed in converted farm buildings, fitted with lots of old furniture and attractive china. The menu features imaginative modernizations of traditional English dishes. ⊠ *Dipton Mill Rd.,* ☎ *01434/604744. MC, V. Closed Mon.–Thurs. No lunch.*

£££–££££ ✕☒ **Langley Castle Hotel.** A genuine 14th-century castle was rescued by its American owner and converted into a luxury hotel and restaurant. Its 7-ft-thick walls are complete with turrets and battlements. All public rooms are grandly furnished, and the bedrooms have luxurious appointments; one has a private sauna, another a four-poster bed, and so on. The high-quality restaurant has an unusual atmosphere—although perhaps not for a castle—with exposed beams, wall tapestries, and a welcoming fire. ⊠ *Langley-on-Tyne, 6 mi west of Hexham, NE47 5LU,* ☎ *01434/688888,* 🖷 *01434/684019. 16 rooms with bath. Restaurant. AE, DC, MC, V.*

£££ ✕☒ **Lord Crewe Arms Hotel.** A historic hotel that once provided guest accommodations for Blanchland Abbey, this unusual place in the tiny stone village of Blanchland, south of Hexham, has lots of intriguing medieval and Gothic corners, including a priest's hideout and a vault-roofed crypt with its own bar. The bedrooms are solidly furnished with antique wood and exposed oak-beam ceilings—one is said to be haunted by the ghost of a local girl. The restaurant's decor reinforces an atmosphere of cloistered calm, where you can enjoy dishes such as roast local pheasant or breast of duck with port wine sauce. ⊠ *Blanchland, off B6306, about 8 mi south of Hexham, DH8 9SP,* ☎ *01434/ 675251,* ℻ *01434/675337. 20 rooms with bath. Restaurant, bar. AE, DC, MC, V.*

Greenhead

㉑ *18 mi west of Hexham; 49 mi northwest of Durham.*

The **Roman Army Museum,** at the garrison fort of Carvoran, near the village of Greenhead, makes an excellent introduction to Hadrian's Wall. Full-size models and excavations bring to life this remote outpost of empire; you can even inspect authentic Roman graffiti on the walls of an excavated barracks. The gift store stocks, among other unusual items, Roman rulers (1 ft = 11.6 inches) and Roman cookbooks. Opposite the museum, at Walltown Crags on the Pennine Way (a long-distance hiking route), are 400 yards of the best-preserved section of the wall. ⊠ *1 mi northeast of Greenhead, off B6318,* ☎ *016977/47485.* 🎫 *£2.90, joint admission ticket with Vindolanda £5.25.* ⊘ *May–Aug., daily 10– 6; Mar.–Apr. and Sept.–Oct., daily 10–5; 2nd half Feb. and 1st half Nov., daily 10–4.*

Dining and Lodging

£–££ ✕🖼 **Holmhead Guest House.** This former farmhouse—set in open countryside—is not only built *on* Hadrian's Wall but also *of* it. It has stone arches, exposed beams, and antique furnishings; there's open countryside in front and a ruined castle almost in the backyard. In addition to "the longest breakfast menu in the world," a set dinner (£17) is served (for guests only) at the farmhouse table in the stone-arched dining room, and ingredients for all three courses are likely to have been growing in the kitchen garden only hours before. On call is Mrs. Pauline Staff, a qualified guide who can give talks and slide shows on Hadrian's Wall and the area. ⊠ *Off A69, about 18 mi west of Hexham, CA6 7HY,* ☎ ℻ *016977/47402. 4 rooms with shower. No smoking. MC, V.*

Vindolanda

㉒ *10 mi west of Hexham; 41 mi northwest of Durham.*

The great garrison fort of Vindolanda holds the remains of eight successive Roman forts and civilian settlements, which have provided much information about daily life in a military compound. Most of the visible remains date from the 2nd and 3rd century AD and excavations are always going on here—a section of the wall has been reconstructed, while private houses, the main gate, and administrative buildings are easily made out. Recorded information interprets the site, and the museum contains leather, wood, glass, and pottery exhibits. There's even a reconstructed Roman kitchen. ⊠ *Near Bardon Mill,* ☎ *01434/ 344277.* 🎫 *£3.50; joint ticket with Roman Army Museum £5.25.* ⊘ *May–Aug., daily 10–6; Apr. and Sept., daily 10–5:30; Mar., Oct., and 1st half of Nov. daily 10–5; last admission ½ hr before closing.*

Call in at **Once Brewed National Park Visitor Centre,** just ½ mi from Vindolanda, which provides informative displays about the central section of Hadrian's Wall and can advise about local walks. ⊠ *On B6318,* ☎ *01434/344396.* 🎫 *Free.* ⊘ *Mar. and Apr., daily 10–5; May–Oct., daily 10–6.*

Housesteads Roman Fort

★ **㉓** *7 mi west of Hexham; 38 mi northwest of Durham.*

If you have time to visit only one Hadrian's Wall site, Housesteads Roman Fort is your best bet. It offers an interpretive center, views of long sections of the wall, the excavated 5-acre fort itself, and a museum. It's a steep, 10-minute walk up from the parking lot by B6318 to the site, but it's worth the effort, especially for the view of the wall disappearing over hills and crags into the distance. The excavations reveal granaries, gateways, barracks, and the commandant's house. ✉ *3 mi northeast of Bardon Mill,* ☎ *01434/344363.* 🖃 *£2.70.* ☉ *Apr.–Sept., daily 10–6; Oct.–Mar., daily 10–4.*

Chesters Roman Fort

㉔ *4 mi north of Hexham; 35 mi northwest of Durham.*

Chesters Roman Fort—"Cilurnum," in a wooded valley on the banks of the North Tyne River—protected the point where the wall crossed the river. Visitors approach it directly from the parking lot, and, although the site cannot compete with Housesteads in terms of setting, it does hold a fascinating collection of Roman artifacts, including statues of river and water gods, altars, milestones, iron tools, weapons, and handcuffs. The military bathhouse near the river is the best-preserved example in Britain. ✉ *½ mi southwest of Chollerford (on B6318),* ☎ *01434/681379.* 🖃 *£2.70.* ☉ *Apr.–Sept., daily 10–6; Oct.–Mar., daily 10–4.*

Corbridge

㉕ *19 mi west of Newcastle; 29 mi northwest of Durham.*

Corbridge is a small town of honey-color stone houses and riverside walks, a prosperous-looking place with an abundance of welcoming pubs and attractive shops. In the churchyard of St. Andrew's Church by Market Place is the Vicar's Pele. Nearly 700 years old, this fortified tower was a refuge from Scottish raiders and was built from stones taken from Corstopitum.

㉖ To the west of Corbridge lies the ancient Roman garrison site of **Corstopitum,** which was occupied longer than any other fort on Hadrian's Wall. In fact, these ruins predate the wall by 40 years. Strategically positioned at the junction of the east–west and north–south Roman routes—Stanegate ran west to Carlisle, Dere Street led north to Scotland and south to London—the fort now contains a museum rich in artifacts. Rent a headset and tape, and outside you can rebuild the town in your mind's eye as you stroll past the remains of two giant granaries, as well as temples, houses, and garrison buildings. On a cold, windy day, it's all too easy to agree with Tacitus, who thought it a "wretched climate." The soldiers, who received their pay from a strongbox housed in an underground chamber (still visible today), earned every penny. ✉ *On a signposted back road ½ mi northwest of Corbridge,* ☎ *01434/ 632349.* 🖃 *£2.70.* ☉ *Apr.–Oct., daily 10–6; Nov.–Mar., Wed.–Sun. 10–1 and 2–4.*

Kielder Water

㉗ *22 mi northwest of Hexham; 53 mi northwest of Durham.*

In the rugged hills on the western edge of Northumberland National Park, only about 3 mi from the Scottish border, lies Kielder Water, northern Europe's largest man-made lake, surrounded by Europe's largest planted forest. It's a beautiful spot, crisscrossed by hiking paths and mountain-bike trails, and offering a whole host of water-sports possibilities at **Leaplish Waterside Park** (☎ 01434/250312), open April–September, daily 10–6. Fishing is popular, too, while the upper part of the reservoir, designated a conservation area, attracts many bird-watchers.

The **Tower Knowe Visitor Centre** (☎ 01434/240398), open May–September, daily 10–6 and October–March, daily 10–4, at the southeast corner of Kielder Water, is a springboard from which to enjoy and explore not only the lake area but also the vast **Forest of Kielder**. Exhibitions and films illustrate the region's wildlife and natural history, and guided forest walks are offered in the summer. A cruise service (☎ 01434/240398 or 01434/240436) operates Easter–October; the one-hour boat trip costs £3.90.

Now a Forestry Commission visitor center, complete with exhibitions and a tearoom, **Kielder Castle** (☎ 01434/250209), at the northwest corner of Kielder Water, was once a shooting lodge belonging to the duke of Northumberland. It's also the start of a 12-mi toll road that heads deep into the Forest of Kielder to the north and meets A68 south of Carter Bar close to the Scottish border. Signposted footpaths provide good forest walks, too.

Outdoor Activities and Sports

Mountain bikes can be rented at Kielder Water, with outlets at **Leaplish Waterside Park** (☎ 01434/250312), and at **Kielder Castle** (☎ 01434/250392). There's also a 10-mi horseback riding trail at Kielder Water. **Reivers of Tarset** at Leaplish (☎ 01434/250203) offers a wide range of water-sports facilities.

Wallington House

❷❾ *15 mi northeast of Hexham; 19 mi northwest of Newcastle.*

Wallington House, a striking 17th-century mansion with Victorian decoration, stands in the midst of an extensive, sparsely populated agricultural region at the village of Cambo. In addition to the house, with its fine plasterwork, furniture, porcelain, and dollhouse collection, the walled, terraced garden is a major attraction. During the summer, open-air events are held in the gardens and grounds (there are 100 acres of woodlands and lakes), including recitals, productions of Shakespeare, and concerts. ✉ *Cambo, on B6342,* ☎ *01670/774283.* 🎟 *House £4.80, garden and grounds £2.80.* ☉ *House Apr.–Oct., Wed.–Mon. 1–5; walled garden Apr.–Oct., daily 10:30–7; Nov.–Mar., daily 10–4.*

Rothbury

❸⓿ *25 mi northeast of Hexham; 9 mi southwest of Alnwick.*

The small market town of Rothbury, in the heart of some stunning countryside, developed as a Victorian resort, attracting the gentry who roamed its hills and glades. Buildings from the era survive in the handsome center, though like all such towns, the sheer weight of modern traffic has blunted its appeal. However, it's still very much a walking destination and routes through the local Simonside Hills can be discussed with the helpful staff at the **Northumberland National Park Visitor Centre** (✉ Church St., ☎ 01669/620887).

A mile north of Rothbury, the extraordinary Victorian mansion of ★ **Cragside** was built between 1864 and 1895 by the first Lord Armstrong, an early electrical engineer. It is a must-see for anyone interested in the glorious age of the Victorian country house. Picturesquely nestled into a forested mountainside, this was the first house to be lit by hydroelectricity. In the library you can see antique vases adapted for use as electric lamps; staircase banisters are topped with specially designed lights. An energy center, with restored mid-Victorian machinery, including a hydraulic pump and a water turbine, has been established on the grounds. Lovers of beauty will also delight in the house: in June, rhododendrons bloom in the 660-acre park surrounding the mansion, while 30 rooms of the house, some with Pre-Raphaelite paintings—and one boasting an extraordinary mock-Renaissance marble chimneypiece—are open to the public. ⊠ *Off A697 and B6341*, ☎ *01669/620333.* ✆ *House £5.80, country park £3.80.* ☉ *House: Easter.–Oct., Tues.–Sun. 1–5:30. Country park and energy center: Easter.–Oct., Tues.–Sun. 10:30–7 or dusk; Nov.–Dec., Tues. and weekends 10:30–4.*

Dining and Lodging

£££ ✕🏨 **Embleton Hall.** The 5 acres of beautiful grounds are reason enough to stay in this stone country mansion, parts of which date back to 1730; its individually furnished rooms are decorated with lovely antiques and original paintings. Another reason to visit is the restaurant—its chintz draperies and cut-glass chandeliers are perfect accompaniments to the traditional English dishes served here, such as roast Northumbrian pheasant. ⊠ *Near Longframlington, on A697, 10 mi southwest of Alnwick, NE65 8DT*, ☎ *01665/570249*, 🖷 *01665/570056. 10 rooms with bath. Restaurant. AE, DC, MC, V.*

£ ✕🏨 **Queen's Head Hotel.** This cheery inn in the heart of Rothbury offers pleasant, straightforward rooms with an old-fashioned touch. The first-floor dining room serves traditional English dishes, with an emphasis on seafood and a number of vegetarian options. ⊠ *Rothbury, Morpeth NE65 7SR*, ☎ *01669/620470. 9 rooms, 3 with bath or shower. Restaurant, bar. MC, V.*

THE FAR NORTHEAST COAST

Before England gives way to Scotland, the final 40 mi of the Northeast coast—lined with extraordinary medieval fortresses and monasteries—is considered by many the best stretch anywhere on the North Sea. Northumbria can claim to have been one of the few enclaves where the flame of learning was kept alive during Europe's "Dark Ages," most notably at Lindisfarne, the "Holy Island of saints and scholars." Castles abound, including the spectacularly sited one at Bamburgh, and the desolate ruins of that at Dunstanburgh. The region also has some magnificent broad beaches. Only on rare summer days is swimming at all advisable, but the opportunities for walking are tremendous. The 3-mi walk from Bamburgh to Seahouses gives splendid views over to the Farne Islands, and the 2-mi hike from Craster to Dunstanburgh Castle is unforgettable.

Alnwick

③ *30 mi north of Newcastle; 46 mi north of Durham.*

Alnwick (pronounced ann-ick) is the best base from which to explore the dramatic coast and countryside of northern Northumberland. Once a county seat, the town is dominated by its vast castle, but there is plenty more to see. A weekly open-air market (every Saturday) has been held in Alnwick's cobbled **Market Place** for more than 800 years. Note the market cross, built on the base of an older cross; the town crier once made his proclamations from here. Starting on the last Sunday in June, this site is host to the annual weeklong Alnwick Fair, a

festival noteworthy for the enthusiastic participation of a local popu-
lace colorfully decked out in medieval costume (⊠ Alnwick Fair, Box
2, Alnwick NE66 1AY, ☎ 01665/605004).

★ **Alnwick Castle,** on the edge of the town center just above the junction
of Narrowgate and Bailiffgate, is still the home of the dukes of Northumberland, whose family (the regal Percys) dominated the Northeast for
centuries. Many things about this castle are on a grand scale, earning
it the epithet "the Windsor of the North." It has been remodeled on
several occasions since the first occupant, Henry de Percy, first adapted
the original Norman keep. The 18th century saw its greatest changes,
when the grounds were landscaped by none other than Capability
Brown. In contrast with the cold, formidable exterior, the inside of the
building has all the opulence of the palatial home it still is: although
you are only permitted to see six of more than 150 rooms, among the
treasures on show are a galleried library, Meissen dinner services,
ebony cabinets mounted on gilded wood, tables inlaid with intricate
patterns, niches with larger-than-life-size marble statues, and Venetian-
mosaic floors. ⊠ *Alnwick Castle,* ☎ *01665/510777.* ⊡ *£5.75.* ☉
Easter–Sept., Sat.–Thurs., grounds 11–5, castle noon–5.

Dining and Lodging

£££ ✕🖬 **White Swan Hotel.** Standing on the site of the Old Swan Inn on
the stagecoach route between Newcastle and Edinburgh, this building
was restored by one of the greatest Victorian architects, Salvin, who
also worked on Alnwick Castle. One of the lounges, the Olympic
Suite, reconstructed from the paneling and furnishings of the *Olympic*—
sister ship of the ill-fated *Titanic*—is occasionally pressed into service
as a dining room. Otherwise, meals are taken in the blue-and-pink restaurant, which provides a relaxing background for a menu largely drawn
from classic Northumbrian cooking. Specialties include Kielder game
pie, cooked in rich Guinness sauce, and *cranachan* (a thick cream
dessert made with Alnwick rum, raspberries, and oatmeal). ⊠ *Bondgate
Within, NE66 1TD,* ☎ *01665/602109,* 𝔽𝔸𝕏 *01665/510400. 58 rooms
with bath. Restaurant, bar. AE, MC, V.*

£ 🖬 **Bondgate House Hotel.** This is a small, family-run hotel, close to
the medieval town gateway. Housed in a 250-year-old building, it's a
reasonably priced base for touring the area, and it has parking space
for eight cars. ⊠ *20 Bondgate Without, NE66 1PN,* ☎ 𝔽𝔸𝕏 *01665/
602025. 8 rooms, 5 with bath. Restaurant. MC, V.*

Shopping

Northumbria (⊠ 35 Fenkle St., ☎ no phone) is chock-full of collectors' items on three floors, including paintings, pottery, ceramics, and
figurines. **Narrowgate Pottery** (⊠ 22 Back Narrowgate, ☎ 01665/
604744) is a small workshop specializing in domestic stoneware pottery, including the distinctive Alnwick "pierced ware." The **House of
Hardy** (☎ 01665/602771), just outside Alnwick (from downtown, take
A1 south to just beyond traffic circle on left, clearly marked), is one
of Britain's finest stores for country sports, especially fishing. It has a
worldwide reputation for handcrafted tackle.

Craster

③ *6 mi northeast of Alnwick.*

The harbor smokehouses of the tiny fishing village of Craster are
known for that great English breakfast delicacy, kippers: herring salted
and smoked over smoldering oak shavings. You can visit the tar-black-
ened smokehouses, eat your fill of fresh and traditionally smoked fish,
and even have smoked salmon mailed home to your friends. Opposite

the smokehouse, you can savor Craster kippers for lunch or afternoon tea at Craster Fish Restaurant, which is open from Easter through September, or the Jolly Fisherman pub, where you can feast on its famous fresh crab sandwiches while enjoying the views of crashing waves from the pub's splendid picture window.

㉝ Perched romantically on a cliff 100 ft above the shore, the ruins of **Dunstanburgh Castle** can be reached along a bracingly windy, mile-long coastal footpath from Craster. Built in 1316 by the Earl of Lancaster as a defense against the Scots, and later enlarged by John of Gaunt (the powerful Duke of Lancaster who virtually ruled England in the late 14th century), the castle is known to many from the popular paintings by 19th-century artist J. M. W. Turner, and more recently from scenes in the 1990 film version of *Hamlet* with Mel Gibson. Several picturesque sandy bays indent the coastline immediately to the north. ☎ *01665/576231.* ✆ *£1.70.* ☉ *Apr.–Oct., daily 10–6; Nov.–Mar., Wed.–Sun. 10–4.*

The Farne Islands

㉞ *7 mi north of Craster; 13 mi northeast of Alnwick.*

Regular boat trips from the village of Seahouses enable visitors to sample the attractions of two of the bleak, wind-tossed Farne Islands (owned by the National Trust), which host impressive colonies of seabirds, including puffins, kittiwakes, terns, shags, and guillemots; the islands also attract thriving gray-seal colonies. In addition, Inner Farne, where St. Cuthbert, the great abbot of Lindisfarne, died in AD 687, features a tiny chapel dedicated to his memory. All boats leave from Seahouses harbor and services vary, from a 2½-hour cruise past the islands to a longer trip, during which you'll make landfall. Landing fees differ depending on season, since there's more wildlife to see at certain times of the year. ☎ *01665/720308 boat trips or 01665/720884 Seahouses Tourist Information Centre.* ☉ *Information center open Easter– Oct.* ✆ *Boat trips £7–£14; landing fees £2.90–£3.80 are payable to the wardens.* ☉ *Apr.–Sept., daily (weather permitting); access restricted during seal breeding season (May 15–July 15).*

Bamburgh

㉟ *14 mi north of Alnwick.*

Especially stunning when floodlighted at night, Bamburgh Castle dominates the coastal view for miles, set atop a great crag to the north of Seahouses and overlooking a magnificent sweep of sand backed by high dunes. Once regarded as the legendary Joyous Garde of Sir Lancelot du Lac, one of King Arthur's fabled knights, it's one of the most picturesque castles in Britain. Its ramparts offer sweeping views of Lindisfarne (Holy Island), the Farne Islands, the stormy coastline, and the Cheviot hills inland. Much of the castle has been restored—although the great Norman keep (central tower) remains intact—and the present Lady Armstrong lives there now. Exhibits include collections of armor, porcelain, jade, furniture, and paintings. There are apartments for rent inside the castle, one of the most romantic addresses in the world for those who can afford it. ✉ *Bamburgh, 3 mi north of Seahouses,* ☎ *01668/ 214208 or 01668/214515.* ✆ *£3.50.* ☉ *Apr.–Oct., daily 11–5.*

In the village of Bamburgh, the **Grace Darling Museum** commemorates a local heroine as well as the Royal National Lifeboat Institute, an organization of unpaid volunteers who keep watch at the rescue stations on Britain's coasts. Grace Darling became a beloved folk heroine in 1838, when she and her father rowed out to save the lives of nine shipwrecked sailors from the SS *Forfarshire*. ⊠ *Radcliffe Rd., opposite church near village center,* ☎ *no phone.* ⊡ *£1.* ☉ *Apr.–mid-Oct., Mon.–Sat. 11–7, Sun. 2–6.*

Dining and Lodging

££££   ✕⊡ **Waren House Hotel.** Set on 6 acres of woodland off the road on a quiet bay between Bamburgh and Holy Island, this Georgian hotel has tastefully decorated bedrooms, each with different styles of decor, from Victorian to Oriental. There are romantic views of Holy Island from the restaurant, which serves fresh local produce—the fish is highly recommended, and there are good vegetarian choices. ⊠ *Waren Mill, Belford NE70 7EE,* ☎ *01668/214581,* ℻ *01668/214484. 9 rooms with bath, 2 suites. Restaurant, bar, library. AE, DC, MC, V.*

£££   ✕⊡ **Lord Crewe Arms.** This is a cozy stone-walled inn with oak beams and open fires, in the heart of the village close to Bamburgh Castle, an ideal spot to have lunch while touring the area and its wild coast. The rooms are fairly simple, but the food, especially the local seafood, is excellent. ⊠ *Front St., NE69 7BL,* ☎ *01668/214243,* ℻ *01668/ 214273. 24 rooms, 22 with bath. Restaurant. MC, V. Closed late Oct.–Mar.*

Lindisfarne (Holy Island)

★ ㊱   *6 mi east of A1, north of Bamburgh; 22 mi north of Alnwick; 8 mi southeast of Berwick-upon-Tweed.*

Cradle of northern England's Christianity and home of St. Cuthbert, Lindisfarne (or Holy Island) is reached from the mainland by a long drive along a causeway. The causeway is flooded at high tide, so you *must* check locally to find out when crossing is safe. The times, which change every day, are displayed at the causeway and printed in local newspapers. As traffic can be heavy, allow at least a half hour for your return trip. The religious history of the island dates from the very origins of Christianity in England, for St. Aidan established a monastery here in AD 635. Under its greatest abbot, the sainted Cuthbert, Lindisfarne became one of the foremost centers of learning in Christendom. But in the year 875, Vikings destroyed the Lindisfarne community; only a few monks managed to escape, carrying with them Cuthbert's bones, which they finally reburied in Durham. It was reestablished in the 11th century by monks from Durham, and today the Norman ruins of the **Lindisfarne Priory** remain both impressive and beautiful. ⊠ *Holy Island,* ☎ *01289/89200.* ⊡ *£2.70.* ☉ *Apr.–Sept., daily 10–6; Oct.–Mar., daily 10–4.*

Seen from a distance, **Lindisfarne Castle,** reached by a pretty walk around the curving rocky coast of Holy Island, appears to grow out of the rocky pinnacle on which it was built 400 years ago—looking for all the world like a fairy-tale illustration. In 1903 architect Sir Edwin Lutyens sensitively converted the castle into a private home that retains the original's ancient features. Across several fields from the castle is a walled garden, surprisingly sheltered from the storms and winds; its 16th-century plan was discovered in, of all places, California, and the garden has since been replanted, providing again a colorful summer display. ⊠ *Holy Island,* ☎ *01289/389244.* ⊡ *£3.80.* ☉ *Apr.–Oct., Sat.– Thurs. 1–5:30.*

Berwick-upon-Tweed

㊲   *30 mi north of Alnwick; 77 mi north of Durham.*

Although Berwick-upon-Tweed now lies just inside the border of England, historians estimate that it has changed hands between the Scots and the English 14 times. The market on Wednesday and Saturday draws plenty of customers from both sides of the border. The town's 16th-century walls are among the best-preserved in Europe and completely encircle the old town—a path follows the ramparts. The parish church, Holy Trinity, was built during Cromwell's Puritan Commonwealth with stone from the castle.

In Berwick's **Military Barracks,** built between 1717 and 1721, three accommodation wings surround a square, with the decorated gatehouse forming the fourth side. An exhibition called "By Beat of Drum" depicts the life of the common soldier from the 1660s to the 1880s, while other displays highlight the history of the local regiment, the King's Own Scottish Borderers, and that of the town itself. ⊠ *The Parade, off Church St. in town center,* ☎ *01289/304493.* ▣ *£2.50.* ☉ *Apr.– Oct., daily 10–6; Nov.–Mar., Wed.–Sun. 10–4.*

Dining and Lodging

£ ✕ **Town House.** This handy spot serves a delicious variety of fresh quiches, pastries, and other snacks. It's a bit tricky to find: cross Buttermarket under the Guildhall and go through the old jail. The café's proprietors say, "Please persevere to find your way in—it's easy when you know how!" ⊠ *Marygate,* ☎ *01289/307904. No credit cards.*

£££ ✕▥ **Coach House.** Ten miles southwest of Berwick-upon-Tweed and less than that from the Scottish border, this friendly guest house is part of a cluster of attractive, well-converted farm buildings, including Northumberland's oldest unfortified house. The spacious bedrooms, some of which feature exposed wooden beams, share an appealing, homespun atmosphere; guests can enjoy 3 pleasant acres of gardens, with miles of stunning scenery on the doorstep. The dining room offers local specialties. ⊠ *Crookham, 3 mi north of Milfield on A697, Cornhill-on-Tweed, TD12 4TD;* ☎ *01890/820293. 10 rooms, 7 with bath. Restaurant, bar. MC, V. Closed Dec.–Feb.*

£–££ ✕▥ **Funnywayt'Mekalivin.** This has become famous as an idiosyncratic eatery, and with a name like that who could resist? Set in a 17th-century building in the heart of town, crammed with eccentric oddments and a mere 20 yards from the Elizabethan walls, it's very much a one-woman show. In the seven-table dining room, chef-owner Elizabeth Middlemiss produces her own much-acclaimed variations on local specialties such as venison casserole, seafood crumble, or carrot and apple soup. Three pleasantly furnished guest rooms are available upstairs, each sporting its own fireplace and decorated with artwork and even the odd antique. ⊠ *41 Bridge St., TD15 1ES,* ☎ ℻ *01289/308827. Restaurant reservations essential 3 rooms without bath. Restaurant. MC, V. Restaurant open by arrangement only.*

THE NORTHEAST A TO Z

Arriving and Departing

By Bus
National Express (☎ 0990/808080) serves the region from London's Victoria Coach Station. Average travel times are 4¾ hours to Durham, 5¼ hours to Newcastle, and 8¼ hours to Berwick-upon-Tweed. Connecting services to other parts of the region leave from Durham and Newcastle.

By Car
The most direct north–south route is A1, linking London and Edinburgh via Newcastle (274 mi from London; 5–6 hrs) and Berwick-upon-Tweed (338 mi from London; 2 hrs past Newcastle). A697, which

branches west off A1 north of Morpeth, is a more attractive road, leading past the 16th-century battlefield of Flodden. For Hexham and Hadrian's Wall take the A69 west of Newcastle. For the coast, leave the A1 at Alnwick and follow the minor B1339 and B1340, for Craster, Seahouses, and Bamburgh. Holy Island is reached from a minor exit off the A1.

By Train

Great Northeastern Railways (☎ 0345/484950) serves the region from London's King's Cross Station, en route to Scotland. Average travel times are 2¾ hours to Darlington, 3 hours to Durham, 3¼ hours to Newcastle, and 3¾ hours to Berwick-upon-Tweed.

Getting Around

By Bus

The **Northeast Explorer Pass** (£4.75, 1-day) allows unlimited travel on most local services and is available from the bus driver or local bus stations. For route and fare information in Northumberland, buy a copy of the *Northumberland Public Transport Guide* (£1.60) from any tourist office. In Newcastle and Tyneside call **Nexus** (☎ 0191/232–5325) for all public transport enquiries. Durham is the hub for buses out to attractions in **County Durham,** with information available from the County Durham enquiry line (☎ 0191/383–3337). A special **Hadrian's Wall Bus** between Hexham and Carlisle operates in summer, stopping at all the major sites. Local tourist offices have timetables; a Day Rover ticket costs £5.

By Car

A66 and A69 run east–west, providing cross-country access. Many traffic-free country roads provide quiet and scenic, if slower, alternatives to the main routes. Part of the Cheviot hills, which run along the Northumbrian side of the Scottish border, is now a military firing range. Don't drive here when the warning flags are flying. The military, though, has restored the Roman road, Dere Street, which crosses this region. Try also B6318, which is a well-maintained road that runs alongside Hadrian's Wall on the south side.

By Train

From Newcastle, there is local service north to Alnmouth (for Alnwick) and to Corbridge and Hexham on the east–west line to Carlisle. "Northeast Regional Rover" tickets, allowing unlimited travel in the area—including on the scenic Carlisle–Settle line—cost £59 for seven consecutive days, or £49 for four days of travel within an eight-day period. For information, call (☎ 0345/484950).

Contacts and Resources

Car Rentals

Durham: M &S Ford (✉ A1(M) Carrville, ☎ 0191/386–1155). **Newcastle upon Tyne: Avis** (✉ 7 George St., ☎ 0191/232–5283). **Hertz** (✉ Newcastle Airport, ☎ 0191/286–6748).

Guided Tours

Escorted Tours Ltd. (☎ 0191/536–3493) runs day and half-day tours of Northumbria by luxury minibus; itineraries vary. Based near Sunderland, the company picks you up at your hotel in Durham or Newcastle. **Holiday with a Knight** (☎ 01287/632510) is run by Shirley Knight, a guide specializing in general tours of northern England, as well as theme tours based on history, literature, and ghosts and legends. **Durham County Council Environment Department** (☎ 0191/383–4144) organizes a year-round program of guided walks—from countryside rambles to industrial heritage trails—which cost £1 per person. **Guided walks** of the region's historic towns and cities are usually available through the local tourist offices—those in Newcastle, Durham, and Berwick-upon-Tweed are particularly recommended.

Travel Agencies

Thomas Cook (⌧ 24–25 Market Pl., Durham, ☎ 0191/384–8569; ⌧ 6 Northumberland St., Newcastle, ☎ 0191/261–2163).

Visitor Information

Northumbria Regional Tourist Board (⌧ Aykley Heads, Durham DH1 5UX, ☎ 0191/375–3000), open Monday–Thursday 8:30–5, Friday 8:30–4:30.

Tourist information centers, normally open Monday–Saturday 9:30–5:30, but varying according to the season, include:

Alnwick (⌧ The Shambles, Northumberland NE66 1TN, ☎ 01665/510665). **Barnard Castle** (⌧ 43 Galgate, County Durham, DL12 8EL, ☎ 01833/690909). **Berwick-upon-Tweed** (⌧ Castlegate Car Park, Northumberland TD15 1JS, ☎ 01289/330733). **Bishop Auckland** (⌧ Town Hall, Market Pl., County Durham, DL14 7NP, ☎ 01388/604922). **Darlington** (⌧ 13 Horsemarket, County Durham, DL1 5PW, ☎ 01325/388666). **Durham** (⌧ Market Pl., County Durham, DH1 3NJ, ☎ 0191/384–3720). **Hexham** (⌧ Manor Office, Hallgate, Northumberland NE46 1XD, ☎ 01434/605225). **Middlesbrough** (⌧ 51 Corporation Rd., Cleveland, TS1 1LT, ☎ 01642/243425). **Newcastle upon Tyne** (⌧ Central Library, Princess Sq., NE99 1DX, ☎ 0191/261–0610; ⌧ Main Concourse, Central Station, NE1 5DL, ☎ 0191/230–0030).

17 Scotland: Edinburgh to the Highlands

Glasgow, St. Andrews, Royal Deeside, Inverness

One of the world's stateliest cities and proudest capitals, Edinburgh—built, like Rome, on seven hills—is the perfect setting for the ancient pageant of history. In contrast, Scotland's largest city, Glasgow, is bustling and bionic. Sooner or later, however, all feet march in the direction of mythical Brigadoon—Scotland's shimmering lochs, baronial castles, and those moors that shout pink and purple. Explore the Borders—Sir Walter Scott Country—then call on Royal Deeside and Loch Ness, home to "Nessie," star of the local chamber of commerce.

SCOTLAND IS A SMALL COUNTRY, no bigger than the state of Maine, and it contains barely a tenth of the United Kingdom's population. Yet the idea of Scotland is world-embracing. It has produced some of the world's stormiest history, some of its most romantic heroes and heroines, much of its most admired literature, and many of its most important inventions. Its local products, customs, music, and traditional dress—tartan, bagpipes, tweed—travel all over the globe. Scots throughout history, especially those who emigrated to the United States, Canada, Australia, and New Zealand, have been superb propagandists for the land of their ancestors, the land they love. Recently—thanks to Mel Gibson's *Braveheart* and Liam Neeson's *Rob Roy*—Scotland came to the big screen in all its Hollywood splendor to enchant and intrigue a new generation.

Updated by
Beth Ingpen

There are really two Scotlands: the Lowlands (not low at all, but chains of hills along river valleys), where populous cities such as Edinburgh and Glasgow are found; and the Highlands, which contain the highest mountains in the British Isles, the wildest lochs (lakes), and most of the islands. It is often assumed that as you travel north you proceed from Lowlands to Highlands. In fact, it is more of an east–west divide. Most travelers start out with Scotland's greatest cities, Edinburgh and Glasgow. After a while, however, those splendid heather-clad mountain slopes and shimmering lochs exert their pull, as do the fast-flowing streams where salmon leap, and the great castles of baronial pride standing hard among the hills. There are lots of contrasts in this country—of landscape, building stone, accent, city size—and you don't have to travel too far to enjoy it all.

Edinburgh (pronounced edin-burra, not edin-burg) seems to have been designed as a tourist attraction. A variety of factors make this city appealing: its outstanding geography—like Rome, it is built on seven hills—the Old Town district, with all the evidence of its colorful history, and the New Town, with its large number of elegant, classical buildings conceived in the surge of artistic creativity of the second half of the 18th century.

Glasgow, Scotland's largest city, suffered gravely from the industrial decline of the 1960s and '70s, but recent efforts at commercial and cultural renewal have restored much of the style and grandeur it possessed in the 19th century when it was at the height of its economic power. Now it is again a vibrant metropolitan center with a thriving artistic life—so much so that it was selected as Europe's Cultural Capital for 1990 and is the United Kingdom City of Architecture and Design in 1999. Glasgow is a convenient touring center, too, with excellent transportation links to the rest of the country.

The Borders area comprises the great rolling hills, moors, wooded river valleys, and farmland that stretch south from Lothian, the region crowned by Edinburgh, to England. All the distinctive features of Scotland—paper currency, architecture, opening hours of pubs and stores, food and drink, and accent—start right at the border; you won't find the Borders a diluted version of England. Northeast of Edinburgh, on the windswept east coast, stands the ancient town of St. Andrews—filled with historic sites and known the world over as the home of golf. Many a traveler hopes to return home with the tale of a Road Hole birdie on the Old Course.

Beyond the central lowlands, the pleasures and treasures of Aberdeen and Northeast Scotland, Inverness, Loch Ness (with or without its "monster" Nessie), and the Highlands await. Aberdeen is Scotland's third-largest city, and a gateway to the splendor of Royal Deeside and the

Grampian Mountains, a wealth of castles, and an unspoiled and, in places, spectacular coastline. Inverness, to the northwest, is the capital of the Highlands, with Loch Ness right on its doorstep. A map of Scotland gives a hint of the grandeur and beauty to be found here: fingers of inland lochs, craggy and steep-sided mountains, rugged promontories, and deep inlets. But the map does not give an inkling of the brilliant purple and emerald moorland, the forests, and the astonishingly varied wildlife: mountain hares, red deer, golden eagles, ospreys, seals, dolphins; nor the courtesy of the soft-spoken inhabitants; nor the depth of ancestral memory and clan mythology. All these are delights that await the visitor who ventures out of the cities.

A car is essential if you want to explore the wildest and most beautiful districts. Roads are always well surfaced though narrow in places. Although the area is large, road distances make it larger: as the eagle flies, one town can be a certain distance from another, but it turns out to be three times that distance by the shortest road! For the short-term visitor, however, a bus excursion from Edinburgh or Aberdeen can possibly give the best value. Whatever the mode of transport, try to spend a couple of days in a small Highland bed-and-breakfast, grand estate hotel, or fishing inn. Only then will you discover the spell of the Highlands, that inexplicable magic that brings people back year after year. Keep in mind that winter touring beyond the central lowlands means you should check weather forecasts: Braemar often records Britain's lowest temperatures and minor roads are occasionally snowbound. And if you head north of Aberdeen and Inverness, travel options can be limited on Sunday, perhaps a survival of the otherwise almost vanished Scots Sabbath.

Pleasures and Pastimes

Arts

There is no escaping a literal sense of theater if you visit Edinburgh from August to early September. As the host for the annual Edinburgh International Festival, the city is quite literally crammed with cultural events during this period—in every art form from classic theater and big-name classical concerts to jazz and the most experimental forms of dance and theater. Even more obvious to the casual stroller during this time is the Edinburgh Festival Fringe, the refreshingly irreverent, ever-growing, unruly child of the official festival. During the same time period, that stirring Scottish extravaganza—the Edinburgh Military Tattoo—is also performed. Aberdeen's Alternative Festival in October and the Shetland Folk Festival at Easter are just two of the many other events adding breadth to Scotland's cultural year.

Dining

To sample genuine Scottish cuisine, look out for the TASTE OF SCOTLAND sign in restaurant windows indicating the use of the best Scottish products, including marvelous salmon and venison, and of course the spicy haggis, usually served with "neeps and tatties" (mashed turnip and potato). Culinary delights await—including nouvelle variations on old Scottish dishes like Partan Bree (a rich crab soup), and Loch Fyne herring. Remember that Scotland is traditionally the "Land o' Cakes" so be sure to enjoy some of those delicious buns, pancakes, scones, and biscuits. In the Highlands, local game and seafood are often presented with great flair; many restaurants deal directly with local boats, so freshness is guaranteed. Oatmeal, local cheeses, and even malt whisky (turning up in any course) amplify the Scottish dimension. And speaking of whisky, try a "wee dram" of a single malt, the pale, unblended spirit, when you visit the Northeast, one of Scotland's major distilling areas.

CATEGORY	COST*
££££	over £40
£££	£25–£40
££	£15–£25
£	under £15

per person, including first course, main course, dessert, and VAT; excluding drinks

Golfing

Everyone wants to play just the big names in the British Open—St. Andrews, Turnberry, Troon, and so on. This is a pity. There are more golf courses in Scotland per capita than anywhere else in the world. Out of the 400 or so, there are plenty of gems, from challenging coastal links courses such as Cruden Bay or Royal Dornoch in the north to pinewood parkland delights such as Boat of Garten, near Inverness. In September 1999 the Walker Cup is to be played on the breezy links course at Nairn, also near Inverness. In the "East Neuk," one of the prettiest Lowland scenic areas of Scotland, the quiet town of St. Andrews beckons with its famous golf course, where the Royal & Ancient, the ruling body of the game worldwide, has its headquarters. But even if St. Andrews is not your headquarters, Scotland remains a golfer's paradise; a round on a municipal course costs very little, while most clubs, apart from a few pretentious places modeled on the English fashion, demand only comparatively modest course fees.

Highland Games

Caber tossing (the caber is a long, heavy pole) and other traditional events figure in the Highland Games, staged throughout the Highlands during summer. All Scottish tourist information centers have full details. It is said that these games, a unique combination of music, dancing, and athletic prowess, grew out of the contests held by clan chiefs to find the strongest men for bodyguards, the fastest runners for messengers, and the best musicians and dancers to entertain guests and increase the chief's prestige.

Hiking and Walking

Walks in the Edinburgh area range from city walkways—along the banks of the Water of Leith, for example—to the Pentland Hills, whose breezy but not overdemanding slopes are especially popular with locals on weekends. There is also good East Lothian coastal walking at many points from Aberlady, eastward. As the Borders are essentially rural and hilly, there are a number of walking options. Peebles, within easy reach of Edinburgh, offers excellent, level walking along the banks of the River Tweed, while a visit to Melrose, with its abbey, can be further enhanced by a climb to the top of the Eildon Hills, for wonderful views. The **Southern Upland Way**, a 212-mi official long-distance footpath from Cockburnspath in the east to Portpatrick in the west, also passes through the Borders. Official footpaths in the Highlands include the **West Highland Way**, running 98 mi from the outskirts of Glasgow to Fort William, by Loch Lomond, Rannoch Moor, and Glen Coe. The track here is well used (some might say loved to death) and moderately demanding in places. Slightly gentler is the Northeast's **Speyside Way**, taking its name from one of Scotland's premier salmon rivers, which offers excellent river valley and some moorland walking for 47 mi, from the Moray Firth coast up to the foothills of the Cairngorms. All three long-distance paths are covered in official guides available from bookshops and tourist information centers.

Lodging

From grand hotel suites done up in tartan fabrics to personal-touch B&Bs, Edinburgh, Glasgow, Aberdeen, and Inverness are splendidly served by a wide variety of guest accommodations. Some of the best are in lovely traditional Georgian or Victorian properties—some even in Edinburgh's New Town, a few minutes from downtown. Since the removal of much of its indigenous population by forced emigration, many parts of the Highlands became playgrounds for estate owners or Lowland industrialists, who built for themselves shooting lodges, grand mansions, and country estates. Many of these are now fine hotels, or upscale B&B establishments. In rural areas, many farms also offer bed and breakfast—with a breakfast substantial enough to sustain you throughout the whole day.

CATEGORY	COST*
££££	over £120
£££	£90–£120
££	£60–£90
£	under £60

All prices are for two people sharing a double room, including service, breakfast, and VAT.

Shopping

In Scotland, many visitors go for Shetland and Fair Isle woolens, tartan rugs and tweeds, Edinburgh crystal, and Caithness glass. Keep an eye out for craft pottery and for unusual designs in Scottish jewelry, especially when they incorporate local stones. Glasgow has an excellent selection of designer clothing stores. Handmade chocolates, often with whisky or Drambuie fillings, and the traditional "petticoat tail" shortbread in tin boxes are popular. At a more mundane level, try some of the boiled sweets in jars from particular localities—Jethart snails, Edinburgh rock, and similar delights. Other edibles that visitors take home include Dundee cake, marmalades, and heather honeys.

Exploring Scotland

We first visit Edinburgh and Glasgow, two major cities, yet greatly contrasting in style. Both divide easily into two: Edinburgh's Old and New Towns, and Glasgow's medieval-and-merchant heart and culture-rich West End. Then we explore the Borders, south of Edinburgh, with their fabled green hillsides, river valleys, ruined abbeys, and stately homes. This area can be discovered in one long day, or better still, taken in two bites, returning to Edinburgh overnight. Next, St. Andrews beckons, with its golf but also its evocative castle and cathedral ruins.

The Highlands take in a whole range of rugged landscapes, out to the islands of the western seaboard and east to the silvery granite city of Aberdeen. In this text, having visited Aberdeen and traveled up Royal Deeside toward the Grampian Mountains, we divert northward into "Castle Country," before heading northwest to Inverness and Loch Ness.

Numbers in the text correspond to numbers in the margin and on the Scottish Borders, Edinburgh, Glasgow, Glasgow Environs, Royal Deeside, and Inverness and Loch Ness maps.

Great Itineraries

Ideally, to get the real flavor of Scotland, visitors need at least a week to take in the diversity of sights and scenery. If you have a shorter period of time, you may have to choose between city or countryside: Edinburgh or Glasgow's main attractions could be seen in two or three days, as could Aberdeen and Royal Deeside. With five or six days, you will be able to base yourself at two centers, perhaps Edinburgh and Aberdeen, or Glasgow and Inverness. Alternatively, you could take day trips to St. Andrews and to the Borders from Edinburgh. To cover all the areas outlined in this chapter, allow at least 8 days.

IF YOU HAVE 2–3 DAYS

Spend your time getting to know one area properly. This will be long enough to see most of the major sights described for one of these areas: **Edinburgh** ①, **Glasgow** ㉛, **Aberdeen and Royal Deeside** (61), or **Inverness** (72) (and Loch Ness)—assuming that you select your own choice among the museums, galleries, or stately homes. Break up your three-day visit to Edinburgh or Glasgow with an overnight excursion to the Borders, staying at **Melrose** (50) or **Peebles** ㊾ to enjoy a rural change of pace; or from Edinburgh, take a day trip to check out the golfers' heaven of **St. Andrews** (60)—there's actually much more to see in this town than the legendary Royal & Ancient Course.

IF YOU HAVE 5 DAYS

Again, choices have to be made. At least two days and nights should be spent in **Edinburgh** ① or **Glasgow** ㉛ to allow for visits to all of the most important sights. (If you want to see both cities, you will need the whole five or six days.) For your remaining nights, you have three options. The first is to head south for the Borders to explore Sir Walter Scott Country. Start out (and spend the night) in **Melrose** (50), visiting **Abbotsford House** ㊾, Scott's View, and **Dryburgh Abbey** (51) as well as sights slightly farther afield, for instance the abbey at **Jedburgh** (55). For those interested in grand Scottish residences of the past, a visit to **Floors Castle** (54) is a must. After enjoying the glories of the Scottish countryside on an afternoon walk, overnight in **Kelso** (53) before heading back to the capital.

Your second option, from Edinburgh or Glasgow, is to travel to **Aberdeen** (61), arriving in the evening. The next morning, follow in the footsteps of Queen Victoria and take a trip among the castles and glens of the Royal Deeside. Set out for **Crathes Castle** (63) and **Banchory** (62), with its largely unchanged Victorian High Street. After lunch, follow the river upstream to Aboyne, turning due north on B9094, then left onto B9119 for 6 mi for a panorama (signposted on B9119) known as the Queen's View, a bit north of Dinnet—this is one of the most spectacular vistas in northeast Scotland, stretching across the Howe of Cromar to Lochnagar. Then continue on B9119, dropping gently downhill through the birch woods to A93 to reach **Ballater** (64) to the west. Here, stop overnight. The next morning, visit Her Majesty's **Balmoral Castle** (65) if royal residences are high on your list—take in the royal ballroom and grounds, do a country walk or a pony trek, but note that Balmoral is only open for three months in the summer—then treat yourself to a walk in nearby Glen Muick. Here you'll find the famous climb of Lochnagar, so beloved by Victoria. Head for **Braemar** (66) for your next overnight stay. The next morning, set off for Castle Country and some serious castle-hopping—**Corgarff Castle** (67), **Kildrummy Castle** (68), **Craigievar Castle** (70), and **Castle Fraser** (71)—then return to Aberdeen, either stopping overnight, or continuing south to Edinburgh or Glasgow.

Your final option, after two days in Edinburgh or Glasgow, is to travel to **Inverness** (72) for two nights, aiming to arrive in the early evening. Spend the next morning exploring the city, then in the afternoon pay a call on Nessie at Drumnadrochit on the banks of **Loch Ness** (73). Return to Inverness for the night, then the next day follow signposts to **Culloden Moor** (74), **Fort George** (76), and **Cawdor Castle** (77) for a finale in Macbeth Country. Continue on to spend the night at **Nairn** (75), before traveling south to Aberdeen and Edinburgh or Glasgow.

IF YOU HAVE 10 DAYS OR LONGER

If, having visited Edinburgh, Glasgow, the Borders, Aberdeen and Royal Deeside, you wish to continue exploring the Highlands, turn due

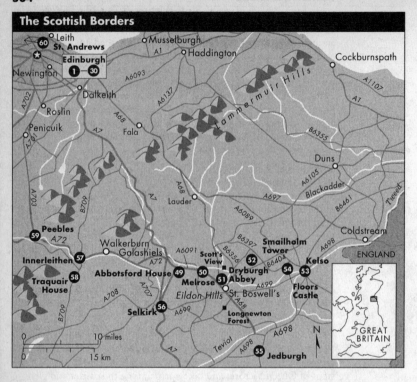

The Scottish Borders

north, after visiting one or two houses in Castle Country, at **Castle Fraser** ⑦. Take A944 from Castle Fraser west, enjoying the valley of the River Don as far as Corgarff on A939. The A939 then climbs into the brown hills to Tomintoul, highest village in the Highlands. From there, continue west, dropping into Speyside via the A95 and A938 roads, to pick up the main A9 at Carrbridge and arrive by evening at ⊞ **Inverness** ⑦. Spend your remaining time as described under the 5-day option of Inverness and the surrounding area, above.

When to Tour Scotland

August is far and away the most exciting time to visit Edinburgh, largely because of the International Festival (☞ Nightlife and the Arts, *below,* for 1999 dates). The sheer amount of theater and music going on make the city buzz with cultural activity. However, this is also inevitably the busiest time, and anyone wishing to visit Edinburgh during August and the beginning of September will have to plan and book months in advance. The winters can be cold and wet, but the long summer evenings—with sunsets as late as 10:30—from June to September are magical. The Borders are also busiest during festival time with visitors taking a break from city life, but its landscape can be fully appreciated in April and May as well.

Spring in the Highlands can be glorious, when there is still snow on the highest peaks. Those exuberant Highland Games—featuring caber tossing, hammer throwing, and all the rest—are held during the summer months: Braemar's Games (September) are often held in the presence of members of the Royal Family. If you wish to drop in on Balmoral, the royal residence on Deeside, keep in mind that it's only open during several weeks in early summer. If the royals are in residence, even the grounds are closed to visitors, so be sure to call in advance. Autumn in Royal Deeside is very colorful.

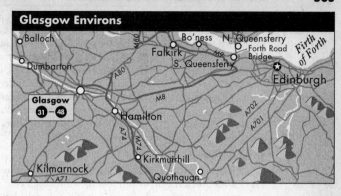

Glasgow Environs

EDINBURGH

In a skyline of sheer drama, Edinburgh Castle watches over Scotland's greatest city, frowning down on Princes Street as if disapproving of its modern razzmatazz. Its ramparts still echo with gunfire when the one o'clock gun booms out each day, startling unwary tourists. But nearly everywhere in the city there are spectacular buildings, whose Doric, Ionic, and Corinthian pillars add dignity to the landscape. To this largely Presbyterian gray backcloth, numerous trees and gardens provide lovely color. The top of Calton Hill, to the east, is cluttered with sturdy neoclassic monuments—like an abandoned set for a Greek drama. Also conspicuous from Princes Street is Arthur's Seat, a mountain of bright green and yellow furze rearing up behind the spires of the Old Town. This child-size mountain jutting 800 ft above its surroundings has steep slopes and little crags, like a miniature Highlands set down in the middle of the busy city. These theatrical elements give a unique identity to downtown, but turn a corner, say, off George Street (parallel to Princes Street), and you will see not an endless cityscape, but blue sea and a patchwork of fields. This is the county of Fife, beyond the inlet of the North Sea called the Firth of Forth; a reminder, like the northwest Highlands glimpsed from Edinburgh's highest points, that the rest of Scotland lies within easy reach.

The Old Town

The dark, brooding presence of the castle, the very essence of Scotland's martial past, dominates Edinburgh. The castle is built on a crag of hard, black volcanic rock formed during the Ice Age when an eastbound glacier scoured around this resistant core, creating steep cliffs on three sides. On the fourth side, a "tail" of rock was left, forming a ramp from the top that gradually runs away eastward. This became the street known as the Royal Mile, the backbone of the Old Town, leading from the castle down to the Palace of Holyroodhouse. "The Mile" is actually made up of one thoroughfare that bears, in consecutive sequence, different names—the Esplanade, Castle Hill, Lawnmarket, Parliament Square, High Street, and Canongate. Not far from Holyroodhouse is the site of Scotland's new Parliament building; in the year 2000, the Scots will once again, after 300 years, have their own governing body (courtesy of Tony Blair's Labour Party), albeit one with restricted powers.

These streets and passages winding into their tenements or "lands" are crammed onto the ridgeback of "the Mile." This really *was* Edinburgh until the 18th century saw expansions to the south and north. Everybody lived here, the richer folk on the lower floors of houses, with less well-to-do families on the upper floors—the higher up, the poorer. Time and redevelopment have swept away some of the narrow closes (alleyways) and tall tenements of the Old Town, but enough survive for you to be able to imagine the original profile of Scotland's capital. Sir Walter Scott (1771–1832), Robert Louis Stevenson (1850–94), David Hume (1711–76), James Boswell (1740–95), the painter Allan Ramsay (1713–84), and many other well-known names are associated with the Old Town. But perhaps three are more famous than any others—John Knox (1513–72); Mary, Queen of Scots (1542–87); and Prince Charles Edward Stuart (1720–88).

A Good Walk

A perfect place to begin a tour of the Old Town is **Edinburgh Castle** ①. Having absorbed the many attractions within the castle and taken in the marvelous city views, you can begin to stroll down the grand promenade that is the **Royal Mile** ②. To the left of Castlehill, the Outlook Tower offers armchair views of the city with its **Camera Obscura** ③. Opposite, the **Scotch Whisky Heritage Centre** ④ offers an unusual chance to discover Scotland's liquid gold—stop off for a sample. The six-story tenement known as **Gladstone's Land** ⑤, a survivor of 16th-century domestic life, is on the left walking down. Close by Gladstone's Land, down yet another close, is the **Writers' Museum** ⑥, housed in a good example of 17th-century urban architecture known as Lady Stair's House. Built in 1622, it evokes Scotland's literary past with exhibits on Sir Walter Scott, Robert Louis Stevenson, and Robert Burns.

Farther down on the left, the **Tolbooth Kirk** (kirk means church) boasts the tallest spire in the city—240 ft—and is the new home of the Edinburgh Festival offices. From Lawnmarket you can start your discovery of the **Old Town closes,** the alleyways that spread like ribs from the Royal Mile backbone. For a worthwhile shopping diversion, turn right down George IV Bridge, then to the right down Victoria Street, a 19th-century addition to the Old Town. Its shops offer antiques, old prints, clothing, and quality giftware. Down in the **Grassmarket** ⑦, which for centuries was an agricultural market, the shopping continues.

Walk from the Grassmarket back up Victoria Street to George IV Bridge, where you'll see the **National Library of Scotland** ⑧. Farther down George IV Bridge, to the right, is **Greyfriars Kirk** ⑨.

Before returning to Lawnmarket, you might detour down Chambers Street, which leads off from the bottom of George IV Bridge. Here, in a lavish Victorian building (note the new extension that opened in December 1998), the **Royal Museum of Scotland** ⑩ displays a wide-ranging collection. Return to High Street and, near Parliament Square, look for **Parliament House** ⑪, partially hidden by the bulk of the **High Kirk of St. Giles** ⑫. Just east of St. Giles is another Old Town landmark, the **Mercat Cross** ⑬, which is still the site of royal proclamations.

At the North Bridge and South Bridge junction with High Street, you will find the Tron Kirk. On the High Street, nearby, is the **Museum of Childhood** ⑭. In contrast, across the street lies **John Knox House** ⑮, associated with Scotland's severe 16th-century religious reformer. Down a close nearby is the **Brass Rubbing Centre,** giving the opportunity for an unusual souvenir.

Beyond this point, you would once have passed beyond the safety provided by the town walls. A plaque outside the **Netherbow Arts Centre** depicts the **Netherbow Port** (gate), which once stood here. Below is the Canongate area, named for the Canons who once ran the abbey at Holyrood. Here you will find the handsome **Canongate Tolbooth** ⑯, and, almost next door, the graveyard of **Canongate Kirk,** and **Huntly House** ⑰, a museum of local history. Facing you at the end of Canongate are the elaborate wrought-iron gates of the **Palace of Holyroodhouse** ⑱, official residence of the Queen when she is in Scotland, while under construction to the right is Scotland's new **Parliament Building.**

Sights to See

⑲ **Arthur's Seat.** For a grand bird's-eye view of Edinburgh, make your way up the 800 ft of the city's only minimountain, Arthur's Seat, set in the park behind the ☞ **Palace of Holyroodhouse.** It is a steep walk, but well worth it for the views from here and its neighboring eminence, Salisbury Crags.

Brass Rubbing Centre. A delightfully hands-on way to explore the past, brass-rubbing attracts more and more serious tourists every year. Here, they will find a fascinating selection of replica brasses and inscribed stones, with full instructions and materials supplied. ⊠ *Trinity Apse, Chalmers Close, Royal Mile,* ☎ *0131/556–4364.* ▨ *Free. 90p–£17 for each rubbing.* ⊘ *Mon.–Sat. 10–5, Sun. during festival 12–5.*

❸ **Camera Obscura.** Want to view Edinburgh as Victorian travelers once did? Head for the Outlook Tower, where you'll find this optical instrument—a sort of projecting telescope—which offers armchair and bird's-eye views of the whole city illuminated onto a concave table. The building was constructed in the 17th century, but was significantly altered in the 1840s and 1850s for the installation of the "magic lantern." ⊠ *Castlehill,* ☎ *0131/226–3709.* ▨ *£3.95.* ⊘ *Apr.–Oct., weekdays 9:30–6, weekends 10–6; Nov.–Mar., daily 10–5.*

⑯ **Canongate Tolbooth.** Canongate originally was an independent "burgh," a Scottish term meaning, essentially, a community with trading rights granted by the monarch. This explains the presence of the Canongate Tolbooth. Nearly every city and town in Scotland once had a tolbooth—originally signifying a customs house where tolls were gathered, the name came to mean the town hall and, later, a prison. Today, the Canongate Tolbooth is the setting for **The People's Story,** an exhibition on the history of the people of Edinburgh. Next door is the graveyard of **Canongate Kirk,** where some notable Scots, including Adam Smith, the economist and author of *The Wealth of Nations,* are buried. ⊠ *Canongate,* ☎ *0131/ 529–4057.* ▨ *Free.* ⊘ *Mon.–Sat. 10–5, Sun. during festival 2–5.*

★ ❶ **Edinburgh Castle.** The crowning glory of the Scottish capital, Edinburgh Castle is popular not only because of its symbolic value as the heart of Scotland but also due to the views from its battlements: on a clear day the vistas—stretching to the "kingdom" of Fife—are of breathtaking loveliness. Clear days are frequent now; Edinburgh is officially smokeless and the nickname "Auld Reekie" no longer applies.

The castle opens the chronicle of Scottish history, which will engulf you from now until you leave the country. You will hear the story of how Randolph, earl of Moray, nephew of freedom-fighter Robert Bruce, scaled the heights one dark night in 1313, surprised the English guard, and recaptured the castle for the Scots. At the same time he destroyed every one of its buildings except for St. Margaret's Chapel, dating from around 1076, so that successive Stuart kings had to rebuild the place bit by bit.

The castle has been held by Scots and Englishmen, Catholics and Protestants, soldiers and royalty. In the 16th century Mary, Queen of Scots, chose to give birth there to the future James VI of Scotland, who was also to rule England as James I. In 1573 it was the last fortress to support Mary's claim as the rightful Catholic queen of Britain, only to be virtually destroyed by English artillery fire.

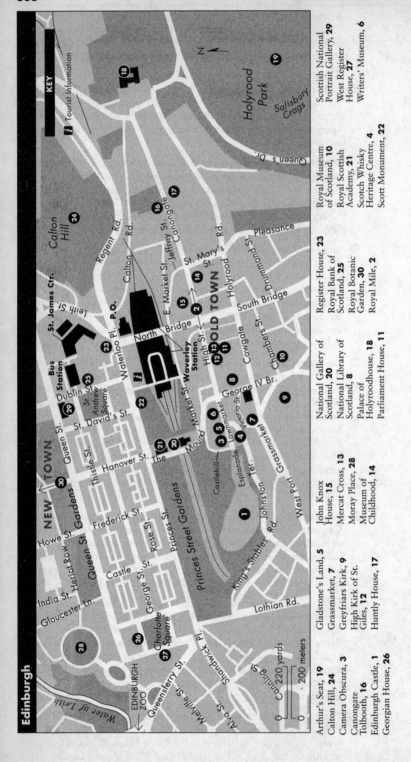

Edinburgh

538

KEY
i Tourist Information

EDINBURGH ZOO

NEW TOWN

OLD TOWN

Holyrood Park

Salisbury Crags

Calton Hill

Arthur's Seat, **19**
Calton Hill, **24**
Camera Obscura, **3**
Canongate
Tolbooth, **16**
Edinburgh Castle, **1**
Georgian House, **26**

Gladstone's Land, **5**
Grassmarket, **7**
Greyfriars Kirk, **9**
High Kirk of St.
Giles, **12**
Huntly House, **17**

John Knox
House, **15**
Mercat Cross, **13**
Moray Place, **28**
Museum of
Childhood, **14**

National Gallery of
Scotland, **20**
National Library of
Scotland, **8**
Palace of
Holyroodhouse, **18**
Parliament House, **11**

Register House, **23**
Royal Bank of
Scotland, **25**
Royal Botanic
Garden, **30**
Royal Mile, **2**

Royal Museum
of Scotland, **10**
Royal Scottish
Academy, **21**
Scotch Whisky
Heritage Centre, **4**
Scott Monument, **22**

Scottish National
Portrait Gallery, **29**
West Register
House, **27**
Writers' Museum, **6**

You enter across the **Esplanade,** the huge forecourt, which was built in the 18th century as a parade ground and now serves as the castle parking lot. It comes alive with color each August when it is used for the Tattoo, a magnificent military display, with the massed pipes and drums of the Scottish regiments beating retreat on the floodlighted heights. Heading over the drawbridge and through the gatehouse, past the guardsmen, you'll find the rough stone walls of the **Half Moon Battery,** where the one o'clock gun is fired every day in an impressively anachronistic ceremony. Climb up through a second gateway and you come to the oldest surviving building in the complex, the tiny 11th-century **St. Margaret's Chapel.** Head up farther still to enter the heart of the mighty complex, the medieval fortress. Here, along the dimly lit, echoing corridors you'll find the **Crown Room,** containing the "Honours of Scotland"—the crown, scepter, and sword that once graced the Scottish monarch, and the Stone of Scone, a sacred relic used in Scottish coronations, returned to Scotland from Westminster Abbey in London in November 1996; the **Great Hall,** under whose 16th-century hammer-beam roof official banquets are still held; and **Queen Mary's apartments,** where she gave birth to James. ☎ *0131/668–8800.* ⌑ *£6.* ☉ *Apr.–Sept., daily 9:30–5:15; Oct.–Mar., daily 9:30–4:15.*

❺ Gladstone's Land. A standout for those in search of the authentic atmosphere of old Edinburgh, this is a six-story tenement just beside the Assembly Hall that dates from the 17th century. Its theatrical setting includes an arcaded ground floor and a second-story entrance; the entire edifice is furnished in the style of a 17th-century merchant's house. ✉ *377B Lawnmarket,* ☎ *0131/226–5856.* ⌑ *£3.* ☉ *Easter–Oct., Mon.–Sat. 10–5, Sun. 2–5 (last admission 4:30).*

❼ Grassmarket. As its name suggests, this was for centuries an agricultural market. Today, the shopping continues, but the goods have changed—antiques, old prints, clothing, and quality giftware. More boutiques can be found nearby along Victoria Street.

❾ Greyfriars Kirk. Here, on the site of a medieval monastery, the National Covenant was signed in 1638, declaring the Presbyterian Church in Scotland independent of government control, triggering decades of civil war. Be sure to search out the graveyard—one of the most evocative in Europe. Nearby, at the corner of George IV Bridge and Candlemaker Row, stands one of the most photographed sights in Scotland, the statue of **Greyfriars Bobby.** This famous Skye terrier kept vigil beside his master's grave in the churchyard for 14 years, leaving only for a short time each day to be fed at a nearby pub after the one-o'clock salute from Edinburgh Castle. ✉ *Greyfriars Pl.,* ☎ *0131/225–1900.* ⌑ *Free.* ☉ *Easter–Oct., weekdays 10:30–4:30, Sat. 10:30–2:30; Nov.–Easter, Thurs. 1:30–3:30. Groups by appointment at any time.*

⓬ High Kirk of St. Giles. Sometimes called St. Giles's Cathedral (it was briefly a cathedral in the mid-17th century), St. Giles is about one-third of the way along the Royal Mile from Edinburgh Castle. This is one of the city's principal churches, but anyone expecting a rival to Notre Dame or London's Westminster Abbey will be disappointed: St. Giles is more like a large parish church than a great European cathedral. Outside, the building is dominated by a stone crown, towering 161 ft above the ground; inside, the atmosphere is dark and forbidding. At the far end you'll find a life-size bronze statue of the Scot whose spirit still dominates the place, the great religious reformer and preacher John Knox, before whose zeal all Scotland once trembled. The most elaborate feature inside the church is the **Chapel of the Order of the Thistle,** which refers to Scotland's highest order of chivalry and is the counterpart to England's Order of the Garter. ✉ *High St.,* ☎ *0131/225–4363.* ⌑ *Free, suggested donation*

£1. ⊙ *Mon.–Sat. 9–5 (until 7 in summer), Sun. 1–5; services: Sun. 8 AM, 10 AM, 11:30 AM, 6 PM (music program only), 8 PM; weekdays 8 AM, 12 noon; Sat. 12 noon, 6 PM.*

⓱ Huntly House. This attractive timber-front building houses a fascinating museum of local history, a must for those interested in the details of Old Town life. ⊠ *142 Canongate,* ☎ *0131/529–4143.* ⊡ *Free.* ⊙ *Mon.–Sat. 10–5, Sun. during festival 2–5.*

⓯ John Knox House. A typical 16th-century dwelling, this was certainly not the home of Knox (1514–72), Scotland's fiery religious reformer, but it is full of mementos of his life. ⊠ *45 High St.,* ☎ *0131/556–2647.* ⊡ *£1.75.* ⊙ *Mon.–Sat. 10–5 (last admission 4:30).*

⓭ Mercat Cross. A great landmark of Old Town life, the Mercat Cross (mercat means market) can be seen just east of the High Kirk of St. Giles (☞ *above*). As its name suggests, it was a mercantile center, and, in early days, it also saw executions and was the spot where royal proclamations were—and are still—read. Most of the present cross is comparatively modern, dating from the time of Gladstone, the great Victorian prime minister and rival of Disraeli.

☾ ⓮ Museum of Childhood. An excellent diversion, this collection is a celebration of toys that even adults will enjoy. ⊠ *42 High St.,* ☎ *0131/529–4142.* ⊡ *Free.* ⊙ *Mon.–Sat. 10–5, Sun. during festival 2–5.*

⓼ National Library of Scotland. Situated on George IV Bridge, this research library is a special magnet for genealogists investigating family trees. Even amateur family sleuths will find the staff helpful in their research. ☎ *0131/226–4531.* ⊡ *Free.* ⊙ *Mon., Tues., Thurs., Fri. 9:30–8:30, Wed. 10–8:30, Sat. 9:30–1; exhibitions Mon.–Sat. 10–5.*

★ ⓲ Palace of Holyroodhouse. Haunt of Mary, Queen of Scots, and the setting for high drama—including at least one notorious murder, a spectacular funeral, several major fires, and centuries of the colorful lifestyles of larger-than-life, power-hungry personalities—this is now the Queen's official residence in Scotland. A doughty and impressive palace standing at the foot of the Royal Mile in a hilly public park, it is built around a graceful, lawned central court. Many monarchs, including Charles II, Queen Victoria, and George V have left their mark on its rooms. Highlights include the **Great Picture Gallery**, 150 ft long and hung with the portraits of 111 Scottish monarchs. These were commissioned by Charles II, eager to demonstrate his Scottish ancestry (some of the royal figures here are fictional, and the likenesses of others imaginary).

Then there's the little chamber in which, in 1566, David Rizzio, secretary to Mary, Queen of Scots, met an unhappy end. Partly because Rizzio was hated at court for his social-climbing ways, Mary's second husband, Lord Darnley, burst into the queen's rooms with his henchmen, dragged Rizzio into an antechamber, and stabbed him more than 50 times (a bronze plaque marks the spot). Darnley himself was murdered in Edinburgh the next year, to make way for the queen's marriage to her lover, Bothwell. When Charles II assumed the British throne in 1660, he ordered Holyrood rebuilt in the architectural style of France's "Sun King," Louis XIV, and that is the palace that visitors see today. When the royal family is not in residence, visitors are free to walk around the palace and go inside for a conducted tour. Behind the palace lie the open grounds of Holyrood Park, which enclose Edinburgh's own minimountain, ☞ **Arthur's Seat**, while just west of the palace, Scotland's new **Parliament building** is under construction. ☎ *0131/556–7371; 0131/556–1096 recorded information.* ⊡ *£5.30.* ⊙

Apr.–Oct., daily 9:30–5:15; Nov.–Mar., daily 9:30–3:45; closed during royal and state visits.

⑪ Parliament House. The seat of government until 1707, when the crowns of Scotland and England were united, is partially hidden by the bulk of the High Kirk of St. Giles. It is now home to the Supreme Law Courts of Scotland. ⊠ *Parliament Sq.,* ☎ *0131/225–2595.* ⌨ *Free.* ☉ *Weekdays 10–4.*

❷ Royal Mile. The most famous thoroughfare of Edinburgh begins immediately below the Esplanade. It runs roughly west to east, from the castle to the Palace of Holyroodhouse and progressively changes its name from Castlehill to Lawnmarket, High Street, and Canongate. Strolling downhill from the castle, it is easy to imagine and re-create the former life of the city, though you will need sharp eyes to spot the numerous historic plaques and details of ornamentation.

★ ⑩ Royal Museum of Scotland. Housed in a lavish Victorian-era building, the Royal Museum displays a wide-ranging collection drawn from natural history, archaeology, the scientific and industrial past, and the history of mankind and civilization. The great galleried Main Hall is architecturally interesting in its own right. In late 1998, in a major new adjoining building, the **Museum of Scotland** opened, with displays concentrating on Scotland's own heritage. ⊠ *Chambers St.,* ☎ *0131/225–7534.* ⌨ *Free.* ☉ *Mon.–Sat. 10–5 (Tues. until 8), Sun. noon–5.*

❹ Scotch Whisky Heritage Centre. If you've ever been interested in learning about the mysterious process that turns malted barley and spring water into one of Scotland's most important exports, this is the place. ⊠ *354 Castlehill,* ☎ *0131/220–0441.* ⌨ *£4.80.* ☉ *Daily 10–6 (last tour 5; extended hrs in summer).*

❻ Writers' Museum. Close by Gladstone's Land, down yet another close, is the Writers' Museum, housed in a good example of 17th-century urban architecture known as Lady Stair's House. Built in 1622, it evokes Scotland's literary past with exhibits on Sir Walter Scott, Robert Louis Stevenson, and Robert Burns (1759–96). ⊠ *Off Lawnmarket,* ☎ *0131/529–4901.* ⌨ *£3.* ☉ *Mon.–Sat. 10–5, Sun. during festival 2–5.*

The New Town and Beyond

It was not until the Scottish Enlightenment, a civilizing time of expansion in the 1700s, that the city fathers decided to break away from the Royal Mile's rocky slope and create a new Edinburgh below the castle, a little to the north. This was to become the New Town, with elegant squares, classical facades, wide streets, and harmonious proportions. In 1767 a civic competition to design the new district was won by an unknown young architect, James Craig (1744–95). His plan called for a grid of three main east–west streets, balanced at either end by two grand squares. These streets survive today, though some of the buildings that line them have been altered by later development. Princes Street is the southernmost, with Queen Street to the north and George Street as the axis, punctuated by St. Andrew and Charlotte squares. A look at the map will reveal a geometric symmetry unusual in Britain. Even Princes Street Gardens are balanced by Queen Street Gardens to the north. Princes Street was conceived as an exclusive residential address with an open vista facing the castle. It has since been altered by the demands of business and shopping, but the vista remains.

A Good Walk

Start your walk on **The Mound,** the sloping street that joins Old and New Towns. Two impressive buildings tucked immediately east of this great linking ramp are the work of W. H. Playfair (1789–1857), an architect whose neoclassic buildings contributed greatly to Edinburgh's earning the title, the "Athens of the North." The **National Gallery of Scotland** ⑳ has a wide-ranging selection of paintings, from the Renaissance to Postimpressionism, and one of the most impressive collections of Scottish art. The **Royal Scottish Academy** ㉑, with its imposing columned facade overlooking Princes Street, holds an annual exhibition of current Academicians' work.

Princes Street is the humming center of 20th-century Edinburgh—a ceaseless promenade of natives and visitors alike patter along its mile or so of retail establishments. Citizens lament the disappearance of the dignified old shops that once lined this street; now a long sequence of chain stores has replaced most of them. Luckily, the well-kept gardens on the other side of the street act as a wide green moat to the castle; the street is still a grand viewpoint for the dramatic grouping of the castle on its rocky outcrop and the long tail of Royal Mile tenements descending from it. Walk east past the soaring Gothic spire of the 200-ft-high **Scott Monument** ㉒. **Register House** ㉓, on the left, marks the end of Princes Street. One of the jewels of neoclassic architecture in Scotland, it was designed by Robert Adam (1728–92). Immediately west of Register House is the **Café Royal** (17 W. Register St.), one of the city's most interesting pubs. It has good beer and great character, with ornate tiles and stained glass contributing to the atmosphere.

The monuments on **Calton Hill** ㉔, growing ever more noticeable ahead as you walk east along Princes Street, can be reached by continuing along Waterloo Place, and either climbing steps to the hilltop or taking the road farther on that loops up at a more leisurely pace. On the opposite side of the road, in the Calton Old Burying Ground, is a monument to Abraham Lincoln and the Scottish-American dead of the Civil War.

Make your way to view the lavish decor of the central banking hall of the **Royal Bank of Scotland** ㉕, on imposing St. Andrew Square, by cutting through the St. James Centre shopping mall and the bus station. Walk west along George Street, with its variety of shops, to Charlotte Square. Here you will find the **Georgian House** ㉖. Also in the square, the former St. George's Church now fulfills a different role as **West Register House** ㉗, an extension of the original Register House.

To explore further in the New Town, choose your own route northward, down the wide and elegant streets centering on **Moray Place** ㉘, a fine example of an 1820s development, with imposing porticoes and a central, secluded garden. A red sandstone neo-Gothic building on Queen Street houses the **Scottish National Portrait Gallery** ㉙, with fine portraits and also an excellent restaurant. Another attraction within reach of the New Town is the 70-acre **Royal Botanic Garden** ㉚. Walk down Dundas Street, the continuation of Hanover Street, and turn left and across the bridge over the Water of Leith, Edinburgh's small-scale river. You will reach the gardens, still one of the most cherished spots for residents, as well as an important center for scientific research.

Sights to See

★ ㉔ **Calton Hill.** A marvelous vantage point from which to gain panoramic views, Calton Hill is also address to numerous historic monuments, including the incomplete Parthenon look-alike known as Edinburgh's Disgrace—it was intended as a National War Memorial in 1822, but contributions fell short—William Playfair's **New Observatory**, and the **Nelson Monument**, completed in 1814. ☎ *0131/556–2716.* 🎫 *£2.* 🕑 *Apr.–Sept., Mon. 1–6, Tues.–Sat. 10–6; Oct.–Mar., Mon.–Sat. 10–3.*

★ ㉖ **Georgian House.** This house stands in Charlotte Square, the elegant urban set piece at the west end of George Street (which is graced by the palatial facade designed by Robert Adam, on the square's north side, considered one of Britain's finest pieces of civic architecture). Thanks to the National Trust for Scotland, the Georgian House has been furnished in period style to show the domestic lifestyle of an affluent late-18th-century family. ⊠ *7 Charlotte Sq.,* ☎ *0131/225–2160.* ☞ *£4.20.* ⊙ *Apr.–Oct., Mon.–Sat. 10–5, Sun. 2–5 (last admission 4:30).*

㉘ **Moray Place.** With imposing porticoes and a central, secluded garden, this is an especially fine example of an 1820s development. The area remains primarily residential, in contrast to the area around Princes Street. The Moray Place gardens are still for residents only.

★ ⑳ **National Gallery of Scotland.** This honey-color neoclassic building, midway between the Old and the New Towns, contains just about the best collection of Old Masters in Britain outside the great London museums. Moreover, the gallery has the advantage of being relatively small, so you can easily tour the whole collection in a couple of hours. There are superb works by Titian, Velásquez, El Greco, Rembrandt, Turner, Degas, Monet, and van Gogh, among many others. A highlight is a newly discovered masterpiece by Caravaggio. Scottish painters are also well to the fore, chief among them the 18th-century portrait painter Sir Henry Raeburn (1756–1823). The most recent headline-making acquisition was Antonio Canova's (1757–1822) famous 19th-century statue, *The Three Graces,* which Scotland managed to snag despite the hopes (and millions) of the United States' Getty Art Museum. ⊠ *The Mound,* ☎ *0131/556–8921.* ☞ *Free.* ⊙ *Mon.–Sat. 10–5 (extended during festival), Sun. 2–5; print room, weekdays 10–noon and 2–4, by appointment.*

㉓ **Register House.** Marking the end of Princes Street, Scotland's first custom-built archives depository was partly funded by the sale of estates forfeited by Jacobite landowners at the close of their last rebellion in Britain (1745–46). Work on the building, designed by Robert Adam, Scotland's most famous neoclassic architect, started in 1774. The statue in front is of the first Duke of Wellington (1769–1852). ☎ *0131/535–1314.* ☞ *Free.* ⊙ *Mon.–Thurs. 9–4:45, Fri. 9–4:30.*

㉕ **Royal Bank of Scotland.** The most notable building on **St. Andrew Square,** which terminates George Street at its eastward end, is the headquarters of the Royal Bank of Scotland; take a look inside at the lavish decor of the central banking hall. In Craig's plan for the New Town, a church was intended for the bank's site, but Sir Lawrence Dundas, a wealthy and influential baronet, somehow managed to acquire the space for his town house. The grand mansion was later converted into the bank. The church, St. Andrew's, was placed instead a little way down George Street on the right. ⊠ *St. Andrew Sq.,* ☎ *0131/556–8555.* ☞ *Free.* ⊙ *Weekdays 9:15–4:45, Wed. opens at 10.*

㉚ **Royal Botanic Garden.** Just north of the city center, a 10-minute bus ride from Princes Street, the Royal Botanic Garden is second only to Kew Gardens in London for the variety of the plants it contains, and for the charm of its setting. The 70-acre site presents an immense display of specimens, from tropical to Nordic, including the largest collection of rhododendrons and azaleas in Britain and an impressive Chinese garden. There is also a convenient café, an excellent shop, and a temporary exhibition area. ⊠ *Inverleith Row,* ☎ *0131/552–7171.* ☞ *Free, donation requested for greenhouses.* ⊙ *Jan., Nov., Dec., daily 9:30–4; Feb., Oct., daily 9:30–5; Mar., Sept., daily 9:30–6; Apr.–Aug., daily 9:30–7. Café, shop, and exhibition areas Mar.–Oct., daily 10–5; Nov.–Feb. daily 10–3:30.*

㉑ **Royal Scottish Academy.** A fine neoclassic temple complete with grand columns, this academy holds temporary exhibitions of various kinds. ⊠ *Princes St.,* ☎ *0131/225–6671.* ⌦ *Admission charges vary, depending on exhibition.* ☉ *Late Apr.–July, Mon.–Sat. 10–5, Sun. 2–5; open for other exhibitions at various times throughout the year.*

㉒ **Scott Monument.** The great poems and novels (such as *Ivanhoe* and *Waverley*) of Sir Walter Scott (1771–1832) created a world frenzy for Scotland; the Scots were duly grateful and put up this great Gothic memorial to him in 1844. Under its graceful spire sits Scott himself, his dog, Maida, at his feet. Behind the monument is one of the prettiest city parks in Britain, **Princes Street Gardens.** In the open-air theater, amid the park's trim flower beds, stately trees, and carefully tended lawns, brass bands occasionally perform in the summer. ⊠ *Princes St.,* ☎ *0131/529–4068. Currently undergoing renovation; view from outside only.*

㉙ **Scottish National Portrait Gallery.** The gallery contains a magnificent Gainsborough and portraits by the Scottish artists Allan Ramsay (1713–84) and Sir Henry Raeburn. The building itself is also of great interest, with richly colored murals in the main hall. ⊠ *Queen St.,* ☎ *0131/556–8921.* ⌦ *Free.* ☉ *Mon.–Sat. 10–5, Sun. 2–5.*

㉗ **West Register House.** As an extension of the original Register House, this research facility has records open for public examination. ⊠ *Charlotte Sq.,* ☎ *0131/535–1400.* ⌦ *Free.* ☉ *Mon.–Thurs. 9–4:45, Fri. 9–4:30.*

OFF THE
BEATEN PATH

EDINBURGH ZOO – In Edinburgh's western suburbs, this zoo offers areas for children to approach or handle animals. Noted for its penguins, the zoo puts them on a delightful parade out of their enclosure every day during the summer. Check out the fascinating Darwin Evolutionary Maze. ⊠ *Corstorphine Rd.,* ☎ *0131/334–9171.* ⌦ *£6.* ☉ *Apr.–Sept., Mon.–Sat. 9–6, Sun. 9:30–6; Mar. and Oct., Mon.–Sat. 9–5, Sun. 9:30–5; Nov.–Feb., Mon.–Sat. 9–4:30, Sun. 9:30–4:30.*

Dining and Lodging

Edinburgh is a diverse, sophisticated city, which its cuisine reflects through an interesting mix of traditional and exotic food, from Scottish dishes to those of infinite ethnic variety. Make reservations well in advance, especially at festival time.

Book hotels, of course, months in advance for the festival. **Dial-a-Bed,** a free central reservations service (☎ 0131/556–3955 or 0131/556–0030, FAX 0131/556–2029) can book rooms in more than 70 Edinburgh hotels and guest houses.

£££ ✕ **Indian Cavalry Club.** The menu of this cool and sophisticated Indian restaurant reflects a confident, up-to-date approach. With its steamed specialties, it's almost an Indian nouvelle cuisine. The **Club Tent** in the basement serves light meals. ⊠ *3 Atholl Pl.,* ☎ *0131/228–3282. AE, DC, MC, V.*

£££ ✕ **Jackson's.** Intimate and candlelighted in an historic Old Town close, Jackson's offers good Scottish fare. Aberdeen Angus steaks and Border lamb are excellent, but you might also try adventurous dishes like langoustine baked in white port. The decor is rustic, with lots of greenery, stone walls, pine farmhouse-style tables and chairs, and fresh flowers. The wine list includes 60 malt whiskies and some Scottish country wines to complete the Scottish experience. ⊠ *2 Jackson Close, 209–213 High St., Royal Mile,* ☎ *0131/225–1793. AE, MC, V. Closed Sun.*

£££ ✕ **Martins.** Don't be put off by the look of this restaurant on the outside. It's tucked away in a little backstreet and has a typically forbid-
★

ding northern facade. All's well inside, though, and the contemporary food is tops. The specialties are all light and extremely tasty, specializing in wild-caught foods, with fish and game in the lead. The cheese board is famous! ✉ *70 Rose St., North La., between Castle and Frederick Sts.,* ☎ *0131/225–3106. AE, DC, MC, V. Closed Sun., Mon. (except during Festival). No lunch Sat.*

££ ✗ **The Dome.** The splendid interior of this former bank—splendid is the word, thanks to the painted plasterwork and central dome—provides an elegant backdrop for relaxed dining. Or you just might opt for a drink at the central bar, a favored spot for sophisticates to wind down after work. The toasted BLT sandwiches are almost big enough for two, but if you're even more ravenous, the eclectic menu offers many other options: try the penne sautéed in a basil cream with fresh mussels, or the smoked chicken salad on a bed of watercress. ✉ *14 George St. EH2 2PF,* ☎ *0131/624–8624. AE, MC, V.*

££ ✗ **Skippers Bistro.** Don't miss this superb restaurant, tucked away in a corner of Leith. It was once a traditional pub and still retains its cozy and cluttered ambience, with dark wood, shining brass, and lots of pictures and ephemera. As befits its location, this is a seafood restaurant. For a starter, the delectable homemade fish cakes can't be beat. Main dishes change daily but might feature halibut, salmon, or monkfish in delicious and innovative sauces. ✉ *1A Dock Place,* ☎ *0131/554–1018, Reservations essential. AE, MC, V.*

£–££ ✗ **Howie's.** Here's a simple neighborhood bistro with three branches and a lively clientele. The steaks are tender Aberdeen beef, and the Loch Fyne herring are sweet-cured to Howie's own recipe. ✉ *75 St. Leonard's St.,* ☎ *0131/668–2917, no lunch Mon.;* ✉ *63 Dalry Rd.,* ☎ *0131/313–3334, no lunch Mon.;* ✉ *208 Bruntsfield Pl.,* ☎ *0131/221–1777. MC, V.*

£ ✗ **Banns Vegetarian Cafe.** Just off the Royal Mile in the heart of the Old Town, Banns serves a tasty range of non-meat fare. In a light and airy room with sturdy wooden furniture, enjoy a cup of coffee with a seriously sinful cake delivered daily by a local French patisserie, or dine on enchiladas or a basket of cream cheese, herbs, and vegetables. Allow plenty of time, as service can be slow. ✉ *5 Hunter Sq.,* ☎ *0131/226–1112 AE, MC, V.*

£ ✗ **Kalpna.** This Indian eatery has a reputation for outstanding value,
★ especially its lunchtime buffet. Indian art adorns the walls, enhancing your enjoyment of the exotic specialties, such as *shahi sabzi* (spinach and nuts in cream sauce) and mushroom curry. All dishes are vegetarian and are skillfully and deliciously prepared. ✉ *2–3 St. Patrick's Sq.,* ☎ *0131/667–9890. MC, V. Closed Sun.*

££££ ✗▥ **Balmoral Hotel.** The attention to detail in the elegant rooms and
★ the sheer élan that has re-created the Edwardian splendor of this former grand railroad hotel make staying at the Balmoral a very special introduction to Edinburgh. Here, below the impressive clock tower marking the east end of Princes Street, you get a strong sense of being at the center of Edinburgh life. The main restaurant is the plush and stylish Grill Room (jacket and tie), serving delicacies such as beef carpaccio with warm mushroom salad and grilled salmon steak with hollandaise sauce. ✉ *Princes St., EH2 2EQ,* ☎ *0131/556–2414,* ⊞ *0131/557–3747. 189 bedrooms, 21 suites. 2 restaurants, bar, indoor pool, health club. AE, DC, MC, V.*

££££ ✗▥ **Caledonian Hotel.** "The Caley" recalls the days of the great rail-
★ road hotels, although its former nearby station is long gone. Modernized at vast expense, its imposing Victorian decor has been faithfully preserved and has lost none of its original dignity and elegance; the fifth floor rooms were the most recent to be refurbished. The decor in the main restaurant, Le Pompadour, with its elegant plasterwork and rich

murals, would please even Louis XV. The cuisine is, *bien sûr*, classic French, using top-quality Scottish produce, such as sea bass, lobster, and venison. The well-chosen wine list is extensive. Lunchtime tends to be more relaxed. The less formal Carriages restaurant supplies traditional Scottish roasts, fish, and game. ⊠ *Princes St., EH1 2AB,* ☎ *0131/459–9988,* FAX *0131/225–6632. 246 rooms with bath. 2 restaurants. AE, DC, MC, V.*

££££ ⊡ **Channings.** Five Edwardian terraced houses have become an elegant hotel in an upscale neighborhood minutes from Princes Street. Restrained colors, antiques, quiet rooms, and great views toward Fife (from the north-facing rooms) set the tone. The Brasserie offers excellent value, especially at lunchtime; try the crab cakes with crayfish bisque. ⊠ *12–16 South Learmonth Gardens, EH4 1EZ,* ☎ *0131/315–2226,* FAX *0131/332–9631. 48 rooms with bath or shower. Restaurant. AE, DC, MC, V.*

£££ ⊡ **Malmaison.** Once a seamen's hostel set in the heart of Leith, Edinburgh's seaport, the Malmaison is a new addition to Edinburgh's hotel scene. Offering good value yet stylish accommodation, it features king-size beds and CD players in all bedrooms, which are decorated in a chic yet bold modern style. In the public areas a dramatic black, cream, and taupe color scheme prevails. The French theme of the hotel (sister to the Malmaison in Glasgow) is emphasized by the café bar and brasserie. ⊠ *1 Tower Place, Leith EH6 7DB,* ☎ *0131/555–6868,* FAX *0131/555–6999. 60 rooms with bath. Restaurant, café, bar. AE, DC, MC, V.*

££ ⊡ **Ellesmere Guest House.** A Victorian terraced house, this B&B is close to the King's Theatre and several good restaurants. Its first-class rooms have modern furniture with pleasant pastel floral bedspreads and curtains; one room has a four-poster bed. Guests can relax in the comfortable sitting room, but the owners prefer that they not smoke. ⊠ *11 Glengyle Terr., EH3 9LN,* ☎ *0131/229–4823,* FAX *0131/229–5285. 6 rooms, 1 with bath, 5 with shower. No credit cards.*

££ ⊡ **Gloria's Place.** This luxurious Georgian B&B is within 20 minutes' walk of the city center. Well-equipped bedrooms (including fridge, direct-dial phone, and socket for your laptop computer) are complemented by the welcoming sitting room, with its wall of books. Smoking is not permitted. ⊠ *20 London St., EH3 6NA,* ☎ *0131/557–0216,* FAX *0131/ 556–6445. 3 rooms with bath and shower. MC, V.*

££ ⊡ **Stuart House.** Within 15 minutes' walk of the city center, this B&B
★ is in a Victorian terraced house with some fine plasterwork. The decor suits the structure: bold colors, floral fabrics, and generously curtained windows combine with antique and traditional-style furniture and chandeliers to create an opulent ambience. Smoking is not permitted. ⊠ *12 E. Claremont St., EH7 4JP,* ☎ *0131/557–9030,* FAX *0131/557–0563. 7 rooms with bath or shower. AE, MC, V.*

Nightlife and the Arts

CASINOS

Stanley Berkeley (⊠ 2 Rutland Pl., ☎ 0131/228–4446) is a private club that offers free membership on 24 hours notice, as do **Stanley Martell** (⊠ 7 Newington Rd., ☎ 0131/667–7763) and **The Stanley Edinburgh** (⊠ 5B York Pl., ☎ 0131/624–2121). **Stakis Maybury Casino** (⊠ 5 South Maybury, ☎ 0131/338–4444) also makes membership available after a 24-hour waiting period. Its restaurant is highly rated.

COCKTAIL BARS

Harry's Bar. An Americana-decorated basement bar with disco music, this place is hugely popular with locals. ⊠ *7B Randolph Pl.,* ☎ *0131/ 539–8100.* ☉ *Mon.–Sat. noon–1 AM, Sun. noon–6 PM.*

Madogs. This was one of Edinburgh's first all-American cocktail bar/restaurants; it remains popular with professionals after work, with live music most weeknights. ⊠ *38A George St.,* ☏ *0131/225–3408.* ⊙ *Mon.–Sat. 11 AM–3 AM, Sun. 6:30 PM–3 AM.*

CONCERT HALLS

Usher Hall (⊠ Lothian Rd., ☏ 0131/228–1155) is Edinburgh's grandest but is currently closed for extensive renovation; the **Festival Theatre** (⊠ Nicolson St., ☏ 0131/529–6000) hosts concerts as well as drama, including performances by the Royal Scottish National Orchestra in season; the **Queen's Hall** (⊠ Clerk St., ☏ 0131/668–2019) is more intimate in scale and hosts smaller recitals. The **Playhouse** (⊠ Greenside Pl., ☏ 0131/557–2692) leans toward popular artists.

DISCOS/NIGHTCLUBS

Café Graffiti. A performance venue with live bands and DJs: jazz, jazzy funk, latin, soul, and much else. ⊠ *Mansfield Place Church, E. London St.,* ☏ *0131/557–8003.* ⊡ *Varies.* ⊙ *Fri. 10 PM–2 AM, Sat. 9:30 PM–2 AM; daily during Edinburgh Festival.*

The Honeycomb. Another hot spot, with funky live sounds. ⊠ *36–38 Blair St. (off High St.),* ☏ *0131/220–4381.* ⊙ *Fri.–Sun. 10:30 PM–3 AM.*

L'Attaché Nightclub. This club features live folk/rock music. ⊠ *Beneath the Rutland Hotel, 1 Rutland St.,* ☏ *0131/229–3402.* ⊙ *Wed., Thurs., and Sun. 8 PM–1 AM, Fri., Sat., 8 PM–3 AM.*

Minus One. Specializing in mainstream sounds with a DJ both nights, this place is not for teeny-boppers or old fogies. ⊠ *Carlton Highland Hotel, North Bridge,* ☏ *0131/556–7277.* ⊙ *Fri.–Sat. 10 PM–3 AM.* ⊡ *Free entry before 11 PM.*

The Venue. A venue for varying disco sounds, including techno and progressive house; check local press for details. ⊠ *15 Calton Rd.,* ☏ *0131/557–3073.* ⊡ *Varies.* ⊙ *10:30 PM–3 AM.*

FESTIVALS

The flagship of arts events in the city is the **Edinburgh International Festival** (August 15–September 4), which for over half a century has attracted performing artists of international caliber in a great celebration of music, dance, and drama. Advance information, programs, tickets, and reservations during the festival are available from Edinburgh Festival Centre (⊠ Castle Hill., Edinburgh EH1 , ☏ 0131/473–2001, FAX 0131/473–2002).

The **Edinburgh Festival Fringe** offers a huge range of theatrical and musical events, some by amateur groups (you have been warned), and it is much more of a grab bag than the official festival. The fringe offers a vast choice (a condition of Edinburgh's artistic life found only during the three- or four-week festival season). During festival time, it's possible to arrange your own entertainment program from morning to midnight and beyond. Information, programs, and tickets are available from Edinburgh Festival Fringe (⊠ 180 High St., Edinburgh EH1 1QS, ☏ 0131/226–5257 or 0131/226–5259, FAX 0131/220–4205).

The **Edinburgh Film Festival,** held in August around the same time of the Edinburgh International Festival, is yet another aspect of the city's summer festival logjam. Advance information, tickets, and programs are available from Film Festival Office (⊠ 88 Lothian Rd., Edinburgh EH3 9BZ, ☏ 0131/228–4051, FAX 0131/229–5501).

The **Edinburgh Military Tattoo** might not be art, but it is certainly entertainment. It is sometimes confused with the festival itself, partly because the dates overlap (August 6–28). This great celebration of martial music and skills is set on the castle esplanade, and the dramatic backdrop augments the spectacle. Dress warmly for the late-evening performances. Even if it rains, the show most definitely goes on. Tickets and information available from Edinburgh Military Tattoo Office (⊠ 32 Market St., Edinburgh EH1 1QB, ☎ 0131/225–1188, FAX 0131/225–8627).

Away from the August–September festival overkill, **Shoots and Roots** (☎ FAX 0131/554–3092), more prosaically known as the Edinburgh Folk Festival, takes place over Easter weekend (April 2–5) and also the third weekend in November (November 19–22). The two events present performances at venues citywide by Scottish and international folk artists of the very highest caliber, with the spring event focusing on folk/rock crossover and the fall venues on more traditional styles.

SCOTTISH ENTERTAINMENTS AND CEILIDHS

Several hotels present traditional Scottish music evenings in the summer season, including the **Carlton Highland Hotel** (⊠ North Bridge, ☎ 0131/556–7277) and the well-established **Jamie's Scottish Evening** (⊠ King James Thistle Hotel, Leith St., ☎ 0131/556–0111).

THEATER

Edinburgh's main theaters are the **Royal Lyceum** (⊠ Grindlay St., ☎ 0131/229–9697), which offers contemporary and traditional drama; the **King's** (⊠ Leven St., ☎ 0131/229–1201), for comedy, musicals, and drama, as well as Christmas pantomime; the **Traverse** (⊠ Cambridge St., ☎ 0131/228–1404), housed in a specially designed flexible space ideal for avant-garde plays; and the **Edinburgh Festival Theatre** (⊠ Nicolson St., ☎ 0131/529–6000), which stages operas, plays, ballet, concerts, and musicals and excellent, occasional tours (check with box office for details).

Outdoor Activities and Sports

GOLF

Edinburgh is well endowed with golf courses, with 20 or so near downtown (even before the nearby East Lothian courses are considered). **Braids United** course, south of the city center, welcomes visitors (☎ 0131/447–6666); **Bruntsfield Links** (☎ 0131/336–4050,) and **Duddingston** (☎ 0131/661–4301) permit visitors to play on weekdays by appointment; all have 18 holes.

A quite exceptional destination is **Gullane** (☎ 01620/842255), about 20 mi east of Edinburgh on A198, with three courses, all 18 holes, and several others nearby, among them **Luffness New** (☎ 01620/843114). This course is open to the public weekdays by appointment.

JOGGING

The most convenient spot downtown for joggers is **West Princes Street Gardens,** which is separated from traffic by a 30-ft embankment, with a half-mile loop on asphalt paths. In **Holyrood Park,** stick to the road around the volcanic mountain for a 2¼-mi trip. For a real challenge, charge up to the summit of Arthur's Seat, or to the halfway point, the Cat's Nick.

Shopping

Edinburgh features a cross section of Scottish specialties, such as tartans and tweeds. If you are interested in learning the background of your tartan purchases, try **Scotland's Clan Tartan Centre** (⊠ James Pringle Ltd., 70–74 Bangor Rd., Leith, ☎ 0131/553–5100), where extensive displays on various aspects of tartanry will keep you informed.

For some ideas on exactly what Scotland has to offer in the way of crafts, visit the **Edinburgh Old Town Weaving Company** (⊠ 555 Castlehill, ☎ 0131/226–1555), where you can chat with and buy from craftspeople as they work. Also along the Royal Mile, you will find several shops selling high-quality tartans and woolen goods. **Judith Glue** (⊠ 60–64 High St., ☎ 0131/558–1866) carries brilliantly patterned Orkney knitwear and a wide selection of crafts, cards, wrapping paper, jewelry, toiletries, and candles. A popular gift selection comes from **Edinburgh Crystal,** 10 mi south of the city, in Penicuik (⊠ Eastfield, ☎ 01968/675128).

Antiques shops open and close with great rapidity, so it's smart to concentrate on areas with a number of stores close together, for instance, **Bruntsfield Place, Causewayside,** or **St. Stephen Street. Joseph Bonnar** (⊠ 72 Thistle St., ☎ 0131/226–2811) is a specialist in antique jewelry in the heart of the New Town. Look into **Hand in Hand** (⊠ 3 North West Circus Pl., ☎ 0131/226–3598) for antique textiles.

PRINCES STREET

Jenners (⊠ 4 Princes St., across from the Scott Monument, ☎ 0131/225–2442), is Edinburgh's "mini-Harrods," an independent and top-quality department store. The **Edinburgh Woollen Mill** (⊠ 62 Princes St., ☎ 0131/225–4966), popular with overseas visitors, sells a wide range of knitwear and tweeds. **Gleneagles of Scotland** (⊠ Near Princes St. in Waverley Market, ☎ 0131/557–1777), is a mid-range knitwear store.

GEORGE STREET

George Street features old, established, local names such as **Waterston's** (⊠ 35 George St., ☎ 0131/225–5690) which carries stationery and a range of Scottish gifts. Farther along, there is a good selection of Scottish titles in **James Thin, The Edinburgh Bookshop** (⊠ 57 George St., ☎ 0131/225–4495). The jeweler **Hamilton and Inches** (⊠ 87 George St., ☎ 0131/225–4898), established in 1866, is a silver- and goldsmith, worth visiting not only for its modern and antique gift possibilities, but also for its late-Georgian interior. For a total contrast to Georgian elegance, visit **Rana**(⊠ 92 George St., ☎ 0131/226–5556) for its Mexican and Guatemalan pottery, glassware, clothing, and pewter items, as well as furniture.

VICTORIA STREET/WEST BOW/GRASSMARKET

Where these three streets run together, there's a number of specialty stores in a small area. **Ampersand** (⊠ 18 Victoria St., ☎ 0131/226–2734) is an interior designer that also stocks a large selection of small collectibles and unusual fabrics by the yard. **Byzantium** (⊠ 9A Victoria St., ☎ 0131/225–1768) has an eclectic mix of antiques, crafts, clothes—and an excellent coffee shop on the top level. **Iain Mellis Cheesemonger** (⊠ 30A Victoria St.) has about 30 varieties of British cheeses; the shop's brochure is an education in itself. **Kinnells House Tea and Coffee Emporium** (⊠ 36–38 Victoria St., ☎ 0131/220–1150) serves morning coffee, lunches, and teas, and sells nearly 100 different types of freshly roasted coffees and specialty teas to take out and try at home. **Le Magasin** (⊠ 14 Victoria St., ☎ 0131/225–9010) stocks every imaginable edible item from France for homesick Francophiles: groceries, cheese, charcuterie, wine.

GLASGOW

It has been almost 300 years since Daniel Defoe, author of *Robinson Crusoe,* described Glasgow as the "cleanest and beautifullest and best-built of cities"—a decade ago, many would have not recognized Scotland's largest city from that description. Stretching along both banks of the widening River Clyde, Glasgow was known as a depressed city, and half a century ago, its slums of dockland and the Clyde banks were infamous for their time. Today, however, Glasgow has undergone a full-fledged urban renaissance: trendy downtown stores, a booming and diverse cultural life, stylish restaurants, and above all, a general air of confidence, have given new grace and élan to Scotland's most exciting city. If Edinburgh is proud, age-of-elegance, and reserved, Glasgow is aggressive, industrial-revolution, and exuberant.

The city's recent development—as its development over the two centuries—has been unashamedly commercial, tied up with the wealth of its manufacturers and merchants, who constructed a vast number of civic buildings throughout the 19th century. Many of these have been preserved, and Glasgow claims, with some justification, to be Britain's greatest Victorian city. Yet, always at the forefront of change, Glasgow boasts, side by side with the overly Victorian, an architectural vision of the future in the work of Charles Rennie Mackintosh. The amazing Glasgow School of Art, the Willow Tearoom, and the churches and school buildings he designed for Glasgow point clearly to the clarity and simplicity of the best of 20th-century design. Glasgow is 45 mi west of Edinburgh; the journey takes an hour by car on the fast M8/ A8 road, or 50 minutes by train.

Medieval Glasgow and the Merchant City

In this central part of the city there are not only surviving medieval buildings, but also some of the best examples of the architectural confidence and exuberance that so characterized the Glasgow of 100 years ago. Today this area is experiencing a renaissance and a newfound appreciation.

A Good Walk
George Square, the focal point of Glasgow's business district, is the natural starting point for any walking tour. It's convenient to the Buchanan Street bus and underground stations and parking lot, as well as to the Queen Street railway station. After viewing the **City Chambers** ㉛ on the east side of the square, leave George Square by the northeast corner and head eastward along George Street. Turn left at High Street, the center of the downtown area before Glasgow expanded westward in the 18th century, then go up the hill to **Glasgow Cathedral** ㉜, and the **St. Mungo Museum of Religious Life and Art** ㉝. Opposite the cathedral, across Castle Street, is **Provand's Lordship** ㉞, Glasgow's oldest house.

Retrace your steps down Castle Street and High Street, continuing on to reach the Tolbooth Steeple at **Glasgow Cross** ㉟. Continue southeast along London Road (under the bridge) about a quarter of a mile and you'll come to the Barras (barrows, or pushcarts), Scotland's largest indoor market (weekends only). Turn down Greendyke Street from London Road to reach Glasgow Green, Glasgow's oldest park, by the River Clyde, with the **People's Palace** ㊱ museum of social history as its centerpiece.

Go back to Greendyke Street, past the new St. Andrew Square development, then via Saltmarket northwards to Glasgow Cross. Continue westward along Trongate, where the powerful "tobacco lords" who traded with the Americas presided, then turn right into Hutcheson Street. This is Glasgow's **Merchant City,** with many handsome restored Georgian and Victorian buildings. At the end of the street, just south of George Square, look for **Hutcheson's Hall** ㊲, a visitor center and shop for the National Trust for Scotland. Turn west onto Ingram Street and left down Glassford Street to see the Trades House on the right, which has a facade built in 1791 to designs by Robert Adam. Turn right along Wilson Street to reach Virginia Street. At No. 33, a former tobacco exchange survives, now as an indoor shopping center. Nearby, **Virginia**

Court ㊳ also echoes those far-off days. Walk northward up Virginia Street back to Ingram Street. To the left you'll have a good view down to the elegant Royal Exchange Square and the **Royal Exchange** itself. Once a meeting place for merchants and traders, it is now the **Glasgow Gallery of Modern Art** ㊴. Royal Exchange Square leads, for pedestrians, westward to the pedestrian-zone shopping area of Buchanan Street. The Princes Square shopping mall on the east side has a particularly good selection of specialty shops. From Buchanan Street continue north across St. Vincent Place to reach Nelson Mandela Place, also called St. George's Place. Here is the **Scottish Stock Exchange** ㊵, worthwhile for the ornate French Venetian–style exterior alone. For an art-filled finale, drop in on the restored **Willow Tearoom** ㊶, an Art Nouveau monument designed by native son Charles Rennie Mackintosh, then head over one block to Renfrew Street to see Mackintosh's masterpiece, the **Glasgow School of Art** ㊷.

TIMING

This walk can be accomplished comfortably in a day, which will allow time to browse in the People's Palace and the Gallery of Modern Art. Aim to start after the end of the morning rush hour, say at 10, and to finish before the evening rush starts, at about 4, to avoid the worst of the traffic fumes and hurrying commuters. The Mackintosh sites—the Willow Tearoom and the Glasgow School of Art—are a coda to this walk, so you may wish to head over to them by cab or bus. Remember that the City Chambers is open only on weekdays.

Sights to See

★ ㉛ **City Chambers.** Dominating the east side of George Square, this splendidly exuberant expression of Victorian confidence was opened by Queen Victoria herself in 1888. Among the outstanding features of the interior are the vaulted ceiling of the entrance hall and the marble and alabaster staircases. ⊠ *George Sq.,* ☎ *0141/287–2000.* ☉ *Free guided tours weekdays at 10:30 and 2:30 (may be closed for occasional civic functions).*

George Square. This is the focal point of Glasgow's business district; indeed the area just south of the square is termed "the Merchant City." On the east side of the square stands the magnificent Italian Renaissance–style **City Chambers** (☞ *above*), and the handsome Merchants' House of 1874 fills the corner with West George Street.

㉜ **Glasgow Cathedral.** On a site sacred since St. Mungo founded a church there in the late 6th century, the cathedral is an unusual double church, one above the other. Its 13th-century crypt was built to hold the relics of St. Kentigern. ⊠ *Cathedral St.,* ☎ *0131/668–8800.* ☒ *Free.* ☉ *Apr.– Sept., Mon.–Sat. 9:30–6, Sun. 2–5; Oct.–Mar., Mon.–Sat. 9:30–4, Sun. 2–4 and for services.*

㉟ **Glasgow Cross.** This was the very center of the medieval city. The Mercat Cross, topped by a unicorn, marked the spot where merchants met, where the market was held, and where criminals were executed. Here, too, was the *tron,* or weigh beam, used to check merchants' weights, installed in 1491. The Tolbooth Steeple dates from 1626 and served as the civic center and place where travelers entering the city paid their tolls.

㊴ **Glasgow Gallery of Modern Art.** The newest of Glasgow's galleries, opened in April 1996, it occupies the fine neoclassic style Royal Exchange of 1827, formerly Stirling's Library, which stands to the south of George Square. The display scheme is designed to reflect, on each floor, one of the four elements—earth, air, fire, and water—which creates some unexpected juxtapositions. ⊠ *Queen St.,* ☎ *0141/287–2000.* ☒ *Free.* ☉ *Mon., Wed.–Sat. 10–5, Sun. 11–5; closed Tues.*

Glasgow

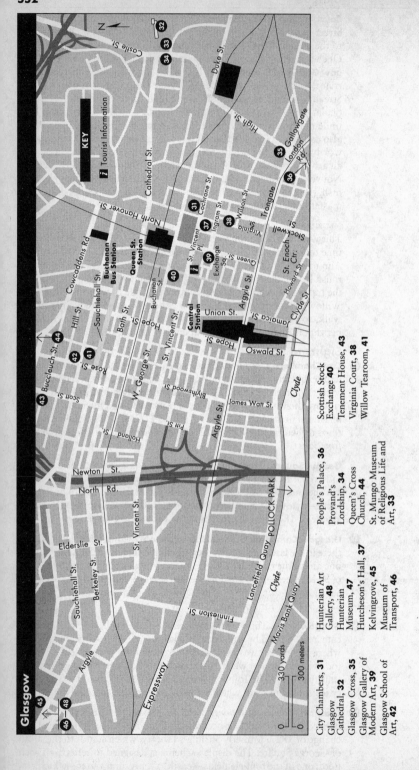

KEY

i Tourist Information

City Chambers, **31**
Glasgow
  Cathedral, **32**
Glasgow Cross, **35**
Glasgow Gallery of
  Modern Art, **39**
Glasgow School of
  Art, **42**

Hunterian Art
  Gallery, **48**
Hunterian
  Museum, **47**
Hutcheson's Hall, **37**
Kelvingrove, **45**
Museum of
  Transport, **46**

People's Palace, **36**
Provand's
  Lordship, **34**
Queen's Cross
  Church, **44**
St. Mungo Museum
  of Religious Life and
  Art, **33**

Scottish Stock
  Exchange **40**
Tenement House, **43**
Virginia Court, **38**
Willow Tearoom, **41**

★ ❷ **Glasgow School of Art.** Charles Rennie Mackintosh's masterpiece, this is a noted monument of 20th-century architecture and decorative arts. The building—exterior and interior, structure, furnishings, and decoration—forms a unified whole, reflecting the inventive genius of this man, who was only 28 years old when he won the competition for the design of this building. Conducted tours are available, but it is still a working school. A block away is Mackintosh's Willow Tearoom (☞ below). ✉ *167 Renfrew St.,* ☎ *0141/353–4500.* 🖼 *£3.50.* ☼ *Tours weekdays at 11 AM and 2 PM, Sat. at 10:30 AM. Closed 2 wks late June.*

❸ **Hutcheson's Hall.** Now a visitor center and shop for the National Trust for Scotland, this elegant Neoclassic building was designed by David Hamilton in 1802. It was originally a hospice founded by two brothers, George and Thomas Hutcheson; you can see their statues in niches in the facade. ✉ *158 Ingram St.,* ☎ *0141/552–8391.* 🖼 *Free.* ☼ *Mon.–Sat. 10–5 (hall may be closed for occasional functions).*

★ ❸ **People's Palace.** An impressive Victorian red sandstone building houses an intriguing museum dedicated to the city's social history. Behind the museum are the well-restored Winter Gardens, a relatively sheltered spot favored by visitors who want to escape the often chilly winds whistling across the green. ✉ *Glasgow Green,* ☎ *0141/554–0223.* 🖼 *Free.* ☼ *Mon., Wed.–Sat. 10–5, Sun. 11–5; closed Tues.*

❸ **Provand's Lordship.** The oldest building in Glasgow is a 15th-century town house, built as a residence for churchmen. It has period room displays and a curious, highly atmospheric ambience of ancient dustiness. It is said to be haunted as well. ✉ *Castle St.,* ☎ *0141/552–8819.* 🖼 *Free.* ☼ *Mon., Wed.–Sat. 10–5, Sun. 11–5.*

❹ **Queen's Cross Church.** To learn about the Glasgow-born designer Mackintosh, head for the Charles Rennie Mackintosh Society Headquarters, housed in a church designed by him. Although one of the leading lights in the turn-of-the-century Art Nouveau movement, Mackintosh died in 1928 with his name scarcely known. Today, he is widely confirmed as a brilliant innovator. This off-the-beaten-track center provides a further insight into Glasgow's other Mackintosh-designed buildings, which include Scotland Street School, the Martyrs Public School, the Glasgow School of Art, and reconstructed interiors in the Hunterian Art Gallery. The church is on the corner of Springbank Street at the junction of Garscube Road with Maryhill Road; a cab ride can get you there or a bus heading toward Queen's Cross can be taken from stops along Hope Street. ✉ *870 Garscube Rd.,* ☎ *0141/946–6600,* 🆑 *0141/945–2321.* 🖼 *Free.* ☼ *Weekdays 10:30–5, Sun. 2:30–5 (or by arrangement).*

❸ **St. Mungo Museum of Religious Life and Art.** An outstanding collection of artifacts covering the many religious groups who've settled throughout the centuries in Glasgow and the west of Scotland is on display here. The centerpiece is Salvador Dalí's magnificent painting, *Christ of St. John of the Cross.* Inside there's a gift shop and a café. ✉ *2 Castle St.,* ☎ *0141/553–2557,* 🆑 *0141/552–4744.* 🖼 *Free.* ☼ *Mon., Wed.–Sat. 10–5, Sun. 11–5; closed Tues.*

❹ **Scottish Stock Exchange.** The Scottish Stock Exchange is worthwhile for the exterior alone: it was built in 1877 in an ornate French Venetian style by John Burnet. (It is not possible for the general public to visit inside.) ✉ *7 Nelson Mandela Pl.,* ☎ *0141/221–7060.* *Not open to the public.*

❸ **Tenement House.** This ordinary, simple city-center apartment is anything but ordinary inside: it was occupied from 1911 to 1965 by the same woman, Miss Agnes Toward, who seems never to have thrown anything away. What is left is a fascinating time capsule, painstakingly preserved with her everyday furniture and belongings. The red sandstone tenement building itself dates from 1892 and can be found in the Garnethill area north of Charing Cross Station. ⊠ *145 Buccleuch St.,* ☎ *0141/ 333–0183.* 🎫 *£3.* ☉ *Mar.–Oct., daily 2–5 (last admission 4:30).*

㊳ Virginia Court. Somewhat faded now, Virginia Court is a reminder of the long-gone days of the tobacco merchants who traded with the Americas. Peer through the bars of the gates and note the wagon-wheel ruts still visible in the roadway. ⊠ *Virginia St.*

㊶ Willow Tearoom. Now restored to its original archetypal art deco design by Charles Rennie Mackintosh—Glasgow-born and one of the design geniuses of the 20th century—this tearoom is a lovely place for a time-out. As you enjoy a cup of Earl Grey, drink in all of Mackintosh's marvelous details, right down to the decorated tables and chairs. The tree motifs are echoed in the street address, as "sauchie" is an old Scots word for "willow." A block away is Mackintosh's masterpiece, the Glasgow School of Art (☞ *above*). ⊠ *217 Sauchiehall St.,* ☎ *0141/332– 0521.* ☉ *Mon.–Sat., 9:30–4:30; Apr.–Dec., also Sun. 12–4.*

The West End

Glasgow's West End offers a mix of education, culture, art, and parkland. The neighborhood is dominated by the University of Glasgow, founded in 1451, making it the third-oldest in Scotland after St. Andrews and Aberdeen, and at least 130 years ahead of the University of Edinburgh. It has thrived as a center of educational excellence, particularly in the sciences. The university buildings are set in parkland, reminding the visitor that Glasgow has more green space per citizen than any other city in Europe. It is also a city of museums and art galleries, having benefited from the generosity of industrial and commercial philanthropists.

A Good Walk

A good place to start is at the city's main art gallery and museum, **Kelvingrove** ㊺ in Kelvingrove Park, west of the M8 beltway, at the junction of Sauchiehall (pronounced *socky*-hall) and Argyle streets. There are parking facilities, and plenty of buses go there from downtown. Across Argyle Street in the Old Kelvin Hall exhibition center is the **Museum of Transport** ㊻.

As you walk up Kelvin Way through the trees, the skyline to your left is dominated by the Gilbert Scott building, the **University of Glasgow**'s main edifice. Turn left up University Avenue. On either side of the road are two important galleries, both maintained by the university. On the south side of University Avenue, in the Victorian part of the university, is the **Hunterian Museum** ㊼. Even more interesting is the **Hunterian Art Gallery** ㊽, in an unremarkable building from the 1970s across the road.

TIMING

Although the overall distance involved is not great, a day might not be long enough for this walk, if you want to browse in all four museums.

Sights to See

★ ㊽ **Hunterian Art Gallery.** This gallery, part of the University of Glasgow, houses 18th-century Glasgow doctor William Hunter's collection of paintings (his antiquarian collection is housed in the Hunterian Museum nearby), together with an outstanding collection of prints and drawings by Reynolds, Rodin, Rembrandt, and Tintoretto, as well as a major collection of paintings by James McNeill Whistler. Also in the gallery is a replica of Charles Rennie Mackintosh's town house, which used to stand nearby. ⊠ *Glasgow University, Hillhead St.,* ☎ *0141/ 330–5431.* 🎟 *Free.* ⊙ *Mon.–Sat. 9:30–5. Mackintosh House closed for lunch 12:30–1:30.*

㊼ Hunterian Museum. The city's oldest museum (1807) and part of the University of Glasgow, the Hunterian houses part of the collections of William Hunter, an 18th-century Glasgow doctor who assembled a staggering quantity of extremely valuable material. (The doctor's art treasures are housed in the Hunterian Art Gallery nearby.) The museum displays Hunter's hoards of coins, manuscripts, scientific instruments, and archaeological artifacts in a striking Gothic building. ⊠ *Glasgow University,* ☎ *0141/330–4221.* 🎟 *Free.* ⊙ *Mon.–Sat. 9:30–5.*

㊺ Kelvingrove. The city's main art gallery and museum looks like a combination of cathedral and castle. It houses a fine collection of British and Continental paintings, 17th-century Dutch art, a selection from the French Barbizon school, French Impressionists, Scottish art from the 17th century to the present, silver, ceramics, European armor, and even Egyptian archaeological finds. ⊠ *Kelvingrove Park,* ☎ *0141/287– 2000.* 🎟 *Free.* ⊙ *Mon.–Sat. 10–5, Sun. 11–5.*

★ ㊻ Museum of Transport. Here Glasgow's history of locomotive building is dramatically displayed with full-size exhibits. The collection of Clyde-built ship models is world famous. Wallow in nostalgia at the re-created street scene from 1938, and enjoy the many handsome Scottish automobiles, which span the 20th century. ⊠ *Kelvin Hall, 1 Bunhouse Rd.,* ☎ *0141/287–2720.* 🎟 *Free.* ⊙ *Mon., Wed.–Sat. 10–5, Sun. 11–5.*

OFF THE BEATEN PATH

POLLOK PARK – A peaceful green oasis off Paisley Road, just 3 mi southwest of the city center (you can get there by taxi or car, by city bus, or by a train from Glasgow Central Station to Pollokshaws West Station), Pollok Park is home to two noted sights—the Burrell Collection, one of Scotland's finest art collections, and historic Pollok House. The **Burrell Collection** (⊠ Pollok Country Park, Paisley Rd., ☎ 0141/649-7151. 🎟 Free. ⊙ Mon., Wed.–Sat. 10–5, Sun. 11–5) is displayed in a modern, glass-walled, and airy building so that its holdings relate to their surroundings; art and nature in perfect harmony. Inside are treasures of all descriptions, from Chinese ceramics, bronzes, and jade to medieval tapestries, stained glass, and 19th-century French paintings—the magpie collection of an eccentric millionaire, Sir William Burrell. Dating from the mid-1700s, **Pollok House** (⊠ Pollok Country Park, Paisley Rd., ☎ 0141/632-0274. 🎟 Free. ⊙ Mon., Wed.–Sat. 10–5, Sun. 11–5) contains the Stirling Maxwell Collection of paintings, including works by El Greco, Murillo, Goya, Signorelli, and William Blake. Fine 18th- and early 19th-century furniture, silver, glass, and porcelain are also on display.

Dining and Lodging

Glasgow has been described as a "café society," which you will never get to know properly unless you spend time drinking coffee in as many cafés as possible. The city also has a sophisticated business and professional population that appreciates the many excellent Glasgow restaurants.

£££–££££ **✕ Rogano.** The striking black-and-gold art deco design of this restau-
★ rant is enough to recommend it. The bonus is that the food—at the ground-floor main restaurant, the lively Café Rogano, and the oyster bar near the entrance—is all excellent. Contemporary specialties include game terrine and fresh seafood superbly prepared. Vegetarians are also catered to. Café Rogano is much cheaper and more informal

than the main restaurant. ⊠ *11 Exchange Pl.,* ☎ *0141/248–4055. Reservations essential. AE, DC, MC, V.*

££–£££ ✕ **Buttery.** This restaurant's exquisite Victorian/Edwardian surroundings
★ are echoed by the staff's period uniforms. Food includes the best of
Scottish fish, beef, and game, as well as an excellent vegetarian menu.
Service is friendly and the ambience is relaxed. ⊠ *652 Argyle St.,* ☎
0141/221–8188. AE, DC, MC, V. Closed Sun. No lunch Sat.

££–£££ ✕ **Puppet Theater.** Down an unprepossessing side street in the West End
is one of Glasgow's most delightful new restaurants—a converted Edwardian mews adorned with a striking glass conservatory. Inside are
four separate salons, each with its own special ambience. The contemporary Scottish menu, with a Mediterranean influence, might offer
cream of parsnip and lentil soup with thyme chantilly, followed by breast
of chicken with butternut squash and sweet potato puree. ⊠ *11 Ruthven
La.,* ☎ *0141/339–8444. Reservations essential. AE, MC, V.*

££–£££ ✕ **Yes.** This stylish restaurant belies its basement location, with soigné
lighting, grand mirrors, and a high-drama red, purple, and cream
palette that even legendary decorator David Hicks might admire. Contemporary Scottish cuisine is featured here—try the "Surprise Menu":
an eclectic four-course selection reflecting the best fresh produce available on the day. ⊠ *22 West Nile St.,* ☎ *0141/221–8044. Reservations
essential. AE, DC, MC, V. Closed Sun.*

£–££ ✕ **Janssens Cafe–Restaurant.** Described as "Amsterdam in Glasgow,"
this pleasantly relaxing restaurant has a sparse decor, with green and
gold walls and a wood floor. The friendly Dutch staff serves a Continental menu, featuring dishes such as pita bread filled with grilled lamb,
mussels gratinéed with cheese, and lots of fresh salads. ⊠ *1355 Argyle St.,* ☎ *0141/334–9682. MC, V.*

£–££ ✕ **78 St. Vincent.** Originally the German Embassy, with stone eagles
outside and elaborate plasterwork within, this is now a stylish place
to enjoy contemporary Scottish, French-influenced cuisine. As your eye
feasts on the maroon velvet drapes, the fish motif wall tiles, and the
mod ironwork, your palate can relish the loin of lamb with a confit of
garlic, vegetables, and port, or salmon and scallops with ginger and
spring onions *en papillote.* ⊠ *78 St. Vincent St.,* ☎ *0141/248–7878.
AE, MC, V. No lunch Sun.*

£ ✕ **CCA Café/Bar.** Attached to the Centre for the Contemporary Arts,
this warehouse-style, white-painted café with oilcloth-covered tables,
bentwood chairs, and plants and posters galore offers an eclectic menu:
try the spinach dumplings with tomato sauce and cheese and chive topping; there's also a good wine and beer list chalked up on the blackboard. ⊠ *350 Sauchiehall St.,* ☎ *0141/332–7864. AE, DC, MC, V.*

££££ ✕🖾 **One Devonshire Gardens.** This fine town mansion offers luxury
★ accommodations. Elegance is the theme, from the sophisticated drawing room to the sumptuous guest rooms with their rich drapery and traditional furnishings, including four-poster beds (in 10 rooms). The
restaurant is equally stylish, with a new menu for each meal. Specialties include fillet of venison with a potato and turnip gratin and pickled red cabbage, or terrine of chicken and bacon with Cumberland sauce.
⊠ *1 Devonshire Gardens, G12 0UX,* ☎ *0141/339–2001,* ℻ *0141/337–
1663. 27 rooms with bath or shower. Restaurant. AE, DC, MC, V.*

£££–££££ ✕🖾 **Glasgow Hilton.** This is a typical international hotel on first impression, but it's breathtakingly professional. Glasgow friendliness
permeates its very upscale image. Two themed restaurants, Cameron's
(a Highland shooting lodge) and Minsky's (a New York–style deli and
carvery), and two bars, Raffles (a colonial/Singapore bar) and the
Scotch Bar, serve superb food. ⊠ *1 William St., G3 8HT,* ☎ *0141/204–
5555,* ℻ *0141/204–5004. 319 rooms with bath. 2 restaurants, 2
bars, beauty salon, health club, meeting rooms. AE, DC, MC, V.*

££ ╳▣ **Babbity Bowster.** This wonderful old pub, restaurant, and lodging house in the heart of the Merchant City is an atmospheric hangout for musicians and artists. The public café bar and the restaurant both serve a mixture of traditional Scottish and French food, ranging from stuffed baked potatoes in the bar to venison or salmon with sophisticated sauces in the restaurant. This is the place to experience "Glasgow Alive," though don't expect peace and quiet late at night; the bar stays open. Guest rooms are basic—pine furnished but adequate. ⊠ *16–18 Blackfriars St., G1 1PE,* ☎ *0141/552–5055,* ℻ *0141/552–7774. 6 rooms with shower. Restaurant, bar. AE, DC, MC, V.*

££ ╳▣ **Cathedral House.** In the heart of old Glasgow, near the cathedral, this small, friendly, freshly decorated hotel is convenient for sightseeing. The café bar offers a fixed-price lunch, which is a good value, and there is also a restaurant with an à la carte menu, offering interesting Icelandic options among more usual fare. ⊠ *28–32 Cathedral Sq., G4 OXA,* ☎ *0141/552–3519,* ℻ *0141/552–2444. 8 rooms with bath. Restaurant, bar. AE, DC, MC, V.*

££ ▣ **Kirklee Hotel.** Near the university and in the West End—a particularly quiet, leafy, and genteel district of Glasgow—this B&B is housed in a small and cozy Edwardian town house, replete with home-away-from-home comfort. A bay window overlooks an award-winning garden, the Victorian morning room is adorned with embroidered settees and silk-wash wallpapers, while turn-of-the-century engravings and a large library offer decorative touches that any university don would appreciate. The owners are particularly friendly and helpful. ⊠ *11 Kensington Gate, G12 9LG,* ☎ *0141/334–5555,* ℻ *0141/339–3828. 9 rooms with bath and shower. AE, DC, MC, V.*

Nightlife and the Arts

Glasgow is better endowed with functioning theaters than Edinburgh. One of the most exciting theaters in Britain is the **Citizen's Theatre** (119 Gorbals St., ☎ 0141/429–0022), where productions of often hair-raising originality are the order of the day. The **King's Theatre** (⊠ Bath St., ☎ 0141/287–4000) stages light entertainment and musicals. The **Theatre Royal** (⊠ Hope St., ☎ 0141/332–9000) is the enchanting home of the Scottish Opera. More contemporary works are staged at **Cottier's Arts Theatre** (⊠ 93 Hyndland St., ☎ 0141/287–4000), in a converted church. The **Centre for the Contemporary Arts** (⊠ 350 Sauchiehall St., ☎ 0141/332–7521) stages not only modern plays, but also exhibitions, films, and musical performances.

Held in the second half of January, **Celtic Connections** (⊠ Glasgow Royal Concert Hall, 2 Sauchiehall St., Glasgow, G2 3NY, ☎ 0141/353–4137) is an ever-expanding annual homage to Celtic music.

Shopping

Glasgow is rapidly challenging Edinburgh as a shopping center, as it does in many other fields, and it is a lot more fun than its staid rival. Glasgow's main shopping districts occupy the southeastern part of town, in a square grid that runs south to Clyde Street on the banks of the river, north to St. Vincent Street, and east–west from City Chambers to the Central Station. Many designer boutiques and great shopping precincts (malls), complete with fountains and glass-walled elevators, can be found on Buchanan and Glassford streets.

Princes Square (⊠ 48 Buchanan St., ☎ 0141/221–0324) is a chic, modern mall, with specialty shops on three levels and a café complex above, all under a glittering dome. You'll find **Katharine Hamnett** here, or try the **Scottish Craft Centre** for unusual, high-quality items— no tartan dolls. **Stockwell China Bazaar** (⊠ 67–77 Glassford St., ☎ 0141/552–5781) specializes in fine china and giftware.

John Smith & Son (Glasgow) Ltd. (⌧ 57 St. Vincent St., ☎ 0141/221–7472) prides itself on being a thoroughly Scottish bookshop, founded in the mid-18th century. There is a friendly café upstairs.

The **Italian Centre** (⌧ John St.), a reminder of Glasgow's cosmopolitan image, has one of the only two British branches of **Emporio Armani** (☎ 0141/552–2277) outside London, as well as **Versace Collections** (☎ 0141/552–6510) and a choice of Italian restaurants.

At the southern end of the Merchant City you'll find the **St. Enoch Centre,** the latest of Glasgow's new generation of shopping malls. The **Argyll Arcade** (⌧ Buchanan and Argyle Sts.) is a handsome 19th-century shopping mall with a wide selection of jewelers' shops (don't miss the mosaics over the Buchanan Street entrance). On Howard Street is another row of shopping outlets. **Slater Menswear** (⌧ 165 Howard St., ☎ 0141/552–7171) stocks traditionally styled high-quality tweeds, woolens, and sportswear.

Sauchiehall Street has a good selection of shopping. **Geoffrey (Tailor) Highland Crafts Ltd.** (⌧ 309 Sauchiehall St., ☎ 0141/331–2388) can supply complete Highland dress, right down to the sporran, and it has a wide range of Scottish-made gifts.

Glasgow's weekend market, the **Barras,** is just north of Glasgow Green. You can find just about anything here, in any condition, from very old model railroads to almost new cheese rolls. Antiques hunters might strike pay dirt, but don't be surprised if you come away empty-handed. ☎ *0141/552–7258.* ☉ *Weekends 9–5.*

THE BORDERS: SIR WALTER SCOTT COUNTRY

The Borders region is the heartland of minstrelsy, ballad, and folklore, much of it arisen from murky deeds of the past. It is the homeland of the tweed suit and cashmere sweater, of medieval abbeys, of the lordly Tweed and its salmon, and of the descendants of the raiders and reivers (cattle thieves) who harried England. It is also the native soil of Sir Walter Scott, the early 19th-century poet, novelist, and creator of *Ivanhoe,* who singlehandedly transformed Scotland's image from that of a land of brutal savages to one of romantic and stirring deeds and magnificent landscapes. One of the best ways to approach this district is to take as the theme of your tour the life and works of Scott. The novels of Scott are not read much nowadays—in fact, frankly, some of them are difficult to wade through—but the mystique that he created, the aura of historical romance, has outlasted his books and is much in evidence in the ruined abbeys, historical houses, and grand vistas of the Borders.

Abbotsford House

★ ㊾ *Route A7, to Galashiels, 27 mi southeast of Edinburgh, then 1 mi farther on A6091, through the Moorfoot Hills.*

The most visited of Scottish literary landmarks, Abbotsford House is the modestly sized mansion that Sir Walter Scott made his home in the 1820s. A damp farmhouse called Clartyhole when Scott bought it in 1811, it was soon transformed into what John Ruskin called "the most incongruous pile that gentlemanly modernism ever devised." That was Mr. Ruskin's idiosyncratic take: most people have found this to be one of the most fetching of all Scottish abodes. A pseudo-baronial, pseudo-monastic castle chock-full of Scottish curios, Ramsay portraits, and mounted deer heads, it is an appropriate domicile for a man of such an extraordinarily romantic imagination. To Abbotsford came most of the famous poets and thinkers of Scott's day, including Wordsworth and Washington Irving. Abbotsford is still owned by Scott's descendants. ⊠ *Galashiels, B6360,* ☎ *01896/752043.* ▣ *£3.50.* ☉ *Mon.– Sat. 10–5, Sun, Mar.–May, Oct. 2–5, June–Sept. 10–5.*

Dining and Lodging

££ ✕▦ **Woodlands House Hotel.** This Gothic Revival–style hotel with chintz-hung and traditionally furnished interiors has stunning views over Tweeddale. The main restaurant specializes in fresh seafood and hearty Scottish cuisine, while Sanderson's Steakhouse is named after a former owner of the house, whose portrait gazes down on diners. There is also a lounge bar serving light meals ⊠ *Windyknowe Rd., Galashiels TD1 1RG,* ☎ FAX *01896/754722. 10 rooms with bath and shower. 3 restaurants, golf privileges, horseback riding, fishing. MC, V.*

Melrose

🔟 *3 mi east of Abbotsford on A6091, 30 mi south of Edinburgh.*

In the peaceful little town of Melrose, you'll find the ruins of a Cistercian abbey that was the most famous of the great Borders abbeys. All the abbeys were burned in the 1540s in a calculated act of destruction by English invaders acting on the orders of Henry VIII; Scott himself
★ supervised the partial reconstruction of **Melrose Abbey,** one of the most beautiful ruins in Britain. "If thou would'st view fair Melrose aright/Go visit it in the pale moonlight," says Scott in his "The Lay of the Last Minstrel," and so many of his fans took the advice literally that a sleepless custodian begged him to rewrite the lines. ⊠ *Main Sq.,* ☎ *0131/ 668–8800.* ▣ *£2.80.* ☉ *Apr.–Sept., daily 9:30–6; Oct.–Mar., Mon.– Sat. 9:30–4, Sun. 2–4.*

At the Ormiston Institute, the **Trimontium Exhibition** displays artifacts from the largest Roman settlement in Scotland, which was at nearby Newstead. Tools and weapons, a replica Roman horse saddle, a blacksmith's shop, pottery, and scale models of the fort are on display. A guided 5-mi, 4-hour walk to the site takes place each Thursday afternoon; phone for details. ⊠ *The Square, Melrose,* ☎ *01896/822651,* FAX *01896/822522.* ▣ *£1.30.* ☉ *Apr.–Oct., daily 10:30–4:30; closed weekends 12:30–1:30.*

A teddy bear museum, **Teddy Melrose,** tells the story of British teddy bears from the early 1900s onward. There is—inevitably—a bear-collectors's shop. ⊠ *High St.,* ☎ FAX *01896/822464.* ▣ *£1.50.* ☉ *Mon.– Sat. 10–5, Sun. 11–5.*

Dining and Lodging

£–££ ✕ **Marmion's Brasserie.** Outstanding eclectic country-style cuisine is
★ the attraction at this cozy restaurant; it's a great place to stop for lunch after visiting Abbotsford. ⊠ *Buccleuch St., Melrose TD6 9LU,* ☎ *01896/ 822245. AE, MC, V. Closed Sun.*

££ ✕▦ **Burts Hotel.** This distinctive half-timber, black-and-white traditional town hostelry dating from the late 18th century offers up-to-date comfort in refurbished rooms. The elegant dining room features Scottish dishes such as pheasant terrine and venison with a whisky-and-cranberry sauce. Bar food is also on offer. ⊠ *Market Sq., Melrose TD6 9PN,* ☎ *01896/822285,* FAX *01896/822870. 20 rooms, 13 with bath, 7 with shower. Restaurant. AE, DC, MC, V.*

Dryburgh Abbey

51 *5 mi southeast of Melrose, still on A6091, 38 mi south of Edinburgh.*

At Dryburgh, the most peaceful and secluded of the ruined Borders abbeys, set in a bend of the Tweed among strikingly shaped trees, you'll find Scott's burial place. ✉ *Dryburgh, near St. Boswells,* ☎ *0131/668–8800.* ▨ *£2.30.* ☉ *Apr.–Sept., daily 9:30–6; Oct.–Mar., Mon.–Sat. 9:30–4, Sun. 2–4.*

Combine a visit to Dryburgh Abbey with a stop at **Scott's View,** 3 mi north on B6356, which provides a magnificent panoramic view of the Tweed valley and the Eildon Hills—quintessential Borders countryside. It is said that the horses pulling Scott's hearse paused automatically at Scott's View, because their master had so often halted them there.

Dining and Lodging

££££   ✕▦ **Dryburgh Abbey Hotel.** Right next to the abbey ruins, this civilized hotel is surrounded by beautiful scenery and features a restaurant specializing in Scottish fare. (Bar snacks are also available.) Extensively renovated in 1992, the restrained decor in shades of cream, peach, terra-cotta, green, and gray creates a peaceful atmosphere in keeping with its serene setting. ✉ *St. Boswells TD6 0RQ,* ☎ *01835/ 822261,* FAX *01835/823945. 38 rooms with bath. Restaurant, golf privileges. AE, MC, V.*

Smailholm

5 mi east of St. Boswells, off B6404, 42 mi south of Edinburgh.

52 Another famous Borders lookout point is **Smailholm Tower.** Beloved by Scott as a child, the 16th-century watchtower now houses a museum displaying costumed figures and tapestries relating to Scott's Borders folk ballads. Scott spent his childhood on a nearby farm, where he imbibed his love of Borders traditions and romances. ✉ *Smailholm,* ☎ *0131/668–8800.* ▨ *£1.80.* ☉ *Apr.–Sept., daily 9:30–6.*

Kelso

53 *46 mi from Edinburgh. From Smailholm, take B6397 and then eastward on A6089.*

The Tweedside roads through Kelso and Coldstream sweep with a river through parkland and game preserve and past romantic redstone gorges. Scott attended grammar school in Kelso. The town has an unusual Continental air, with fine Georgian and early Victorian buildings surrounding a spacious, cobbled marketplace. Only a fragment remains of the once magnificent medieval **Kelso Abbey.** Rennie's Bridge,
54 on the edge of town, provides good views of **Floors Castle,** seat of the duke of Roxburghe, which was designed by William Adam in 1721 and altered by William Playfair in the 1840s. The largest inhabited castle in Scotland, Floors is an architectural extravagance bristling with pepper mill turrets and towers that stand on the "floors" or flat terraces of the Tweed bank opposite the barely visible ruins of Roxburghe Castle. A holly tree in the magnificent deer park marks the place where King James II was killed in 1460 by a cannon that "brak in the shooting." ✉ *A6089,* ☎ *01573/223333,* FAX *01573/226056.* ▨ *£4.50, £2 grounds only.* ☉ *Easter–Sept., daily 10–4. Check locally for times.*

Lodging

££–£££   ▦ **Ednam House Hotel.** This large, attractive hotel is right on the banks
★   of the River Tweed, close to Kelso's grand abbey and the old Market Square. Ninety percent of the guests are return visitors, and the open

fire in the hall, sporting paintings, and cozy armchairs give the place a homey feel. ⊠ *Bridge St., TD5 7HT,* ☎ *01573/224168,* ℻ *01573/226319. 32 rooms with bath or shower. Restaurant, golf privileges, horseback riding, fishing. MC, V. Closed Dec. 25–early Jan.*

Jedburgh

55 *12 mi southwest of Kelso on A698, 50 mi south of Edinburgh.*

To round out your tour of the Borders abbeys, head for Jedburgh, a little town just 13 mi north of the border, which lay in the path of marauding armies for centuries. **Jedburgh Abbey,** although in ruins like so many Borders abbeys, is relatively intact and is a superb example of abbey architecture. It has an informative visitor center that explains the role of the abbeys in the life of the Borders until their destruction, around 1545. ⊠ *High St.,* ☎ *0131/668–8800.* 🎟 *£2.80.* ⊙ *Apr.–Sept., daily 9:30–6; Oct.–Mar., Mon.–Sat. 9:30–4, Sun. 2–4.*

Also in the town, **Mary, Queen of Scots's House** is a fortified house highly characteristic of the 16th century, some say contemporaneous with Mary herself. Though historians disagree on whether or not she actually visited here, the house exhibits many displays commemorating Mary. ⊠ *Queen St.,* ☎ *01835/863331.* 🎟 *£2.* ⊙ *Mar.–Nov., Mon.–Sat. 10–5, Sun. 12–4:30 (Jun.–Sept. 10–4:30).*

Jedburgh Castle Jail, which underwent major renovation in 1996, recreates life in a Howard Reform Prison, with prison cells to inspect, and describes the history of the Royal Burgh of Jedburgh through room settings decorated in period style, costumed figures, and audiovisuals. ⊠ *Castlegate,* ☎ *01835/863254.* 🎟 *£1.25.* ⊙ *Mid-Mar–mid-Nov., daily 10–4.*

Lodging

£ 🏠 **Spinney Guest House.** Made up of unpretentiously converted and modernized farm cottages, this is a B&B offering the very highest standards for the price. For a self-catering option, there are two log cabins. ⊠ *Langlee, TD8 6PB,* ☎ *01835/863525,* ℻ *01835/864883. 1 room with bath, 2 with shower, 2 log cabins. No credit cards. Closed mid-Nov.–Feb.*

Selkirk

56 *From Jedburgh, take A68 7 mi north to the A699 junction, turn left, and follow A699 7 mi; 40 mi south of Edinburgh.*

After traveling through miles of attractive river-valley scenery, you'll reach the ancient hilltop town of Selkirk. Scott was sheriff (county judge) of Selkirkshire from 1800 until his death in 1832, and his statue stands in the Market Place. **Sir Walter Scott's Courtroom,** where he presided, contains a display examining Scott's life, his writings, and his time as sheriff. ⊠ *Market Place,* ☎ *01750/20096.* 🎟 *£1.* ⊙ *Apr.–Sept., Mon.–Sat. 10–4 (Jun.–Aug., Sun. 2–4); Oct., Mon.–Sat. 1–4.*

Tucked away off the main square in Selkirk, **Halliwell's House Museum** is set in what was once an ironmonger's shop, which has been re-created downstairs; the upstairs exhibit tells the story of the town. ⊠ *Market St.,* ☎ *01750/20096.* 🎟 *Free.* ⊙ *Apr.–Jun. and Sept.–Oct., Mon.–Sat. 10–5, Sun. 2–4; July–Aug., Mon.–Sat. 10–6, Sun. 2–6.*

Innerleithen

57 *3 mi west of Walkerburn on A72, 29 mi south of Edinburgh.*

Once famous as the setting of Scott's novel *St. Ronan's Well* and as a spa, Innerleithen is home to **Robert Smail's Printing Works,** a fully restored Victorian print shop with its original machinery in working order and a printer in residence. ⊠ *7–9 High St.,* ☎ *01896/830206.* 🖾 *£2.40.* ⊙ *Easter weekend and May–Sept., Mon.–Sat. 10–1 and 2–5, Sun. 2–5; Oct., Sat. 10–1 and 2–5, Sun. 2–5; last admission 45 min before closing, morning and afternoon.*

★ ⑤⑧ Turn south on B709 to reach **Traquair House,** the oldest continually occupied house in Scotland and, many would add, the friendliest and most cheerful of the Borders' grand hotels (☞ Lodging *below*); ale is still brewed in the 18th-century brew house here, and it is recommended. ⊠ *Traquair, near Innerleithen,* ☎ *01896/830323.* 🖾 *£4.50.* ⊙ *Apr., May, Sept., daily 12:30–5:30; June–Aug., daily 10:30–5:30; Oct., Fri.–Sun. 12:30–5:30 (last admission 5).*

Lodging

££££ 🏠 **Traquair House.** Stay in the private quarters at Traquair to experience the unique atmosphere of this ancient house. The Blue Room and the Pink Room, furnished with antiques and with chintz-hung canopied beds, offer a most relaxing environment, as does the 18th-century Lower Drawing Room, where guests can enjoy a glass of the house's own ale. ⊠ *Innerleithen, Peeblesshire, EH44 6PW,* ☎ *01896/830323,* 𝔽𝔸𝕏 *01896/830639. 2 rooms with bath. MC, V. Closed Dec.–Feb.*

££ 🏠 **Traquair Arms.** This family-run hotel is a fine traditional inn offering a warm welcome; simple, clean rooms; and very good food. ⊠ *Traquair Rd., Innerleithen EH44 6PD,* ☎ *01896/830229,* 𝔽𝔸𝕏 *01896/ 830260. 8 rooms with shower, 2 with bath. 2 restaurants, bar, fishing. AE, DC, MC, V.*

Peebles

⑤⑨ *From Traquair, return to A72 and continue west 7 mi; 24 mi south of Edinburgh.*

Set in a lush and green countryside, with rolling hills deeply cleft by gorges and waterfalls, Peebles is a pleasant town on the banks of the Tweed. Walk for 15 minutes upstream until **Neidpath Castle,** perched artistically above a bend in the river, comes into view through the tall trees. The castle is a medieval structure remodeled in the 17th century, with dungeons hewn from solid rock. You can return on the opposite riverbank after crossing an old, finely skewed railroad viaduct. ⊠ *Near Peebles,* ☎ *01721/720333.* 🖾 *£2.50.* ⊙ *Easter–Sept., Mon.–Sat. 11–5, Sun. 1–5.*

Dining and Lodging

££££ ✕🏠 **Cringletie House Hotel.** A Scottish baronial mansion set amid 28 acres of gardens and woodland, Cringletie is run by a family that believes in spoiling guests with friendly, personalized service. The whole hotel was redecorated in 1998 in British country-house style. The first-floor drawing room, with views extending up the valley, is particularly restful. Fruit and vegetables from the hotel's own kitchen garden are staples of the traditional Scottish restaurant cuisine. Afternoon tea served in the conservatory is recommended. ⊠ *Eddleston, near Peebles, EH45 8PL,* ☎ *01721/730233,* 𝔽𝔸𝕏 *01721/730244. 13 rooms with bath. Restaurant, putting green, tennis court, croquet. AE, MC, V.*

ST. ANDREWS: THE GOLFER'S HEAVEN

⑥⓪ It may have a ruined cathedral and a grand university—the oldest in Scotland—but the modern fame of **St. Andrews** is mainly as the home of golf. Forget that Scottish kings were crowned here, or that John Knox preached, or that Reformation reformers were burned at the stake. Thousands come to St. Andrews to play at the Old Course, home of the Royal & Ancient Club, and to follow in the footsteps of Hagen, Sarazen, Jones, and Hogan. To get to St. Andrews, drive west from Edinburgh 9 mi (on A90) to the Forth Road Bridge, where you'll cross over the Firth of Forth. Continue north 6 mi on M90 to Junction 3, where you can turn east to follow A92, then A91, 38 mi to the quiet town. An alternative route branches off A92 at Largo onto A915, then A917, taking in several attractive coastal villages.

On the Royal & Ancient's course, golf was perhaps originally played with a piece of driftwood, a shore pebble, and a convenient rabbit hole on the sandy, coastal turf. It has been argued that golf came to Scotland from Holland, but the historical evidence points to Scotland being the cradle, if not the birthplace, of the game. Citizens of St. Andrews were playing golf on the town links (public land) as far back as the 15th century. Rich golfers, instead of gathering on the common links, formed themselves into clubs by the 18th century. Arguably, the world's first golf club was the Honourable Company of Edinburgh golfers (founded in Leith in 1744), which is now at Muirfield in East Lothian. The Society of St. Andrews Golfers, founded in 1754, became the Royal & Ancient Golf Club of St. Andrews in 1834. Find out more at the **British Golf Museum.** ⊠ *Golf Pl.,* ☎ *01334/478880.* ⚏ *£3.75.* ☉ *Mid.-Apr.– mid-Oct., daily 9:30–5:30; mid-Oct.–mid-Apr., Thur.–Mon. 11–3.*

The **St. Andrews Links** (☎ 01334/475757, FAX 01334/477036) has six seaside courses, all of which welcome visitors; five—the Old Course, New Course, Jubilee, Eden, and Strathtyrum—have 18 holes, while the Balgrove Course has 9 holes. For information, write to the ⊠ Reservations Department, Links Management Committee, Pilmour Cottage, St. Andrews, Fife KY16 9SF.

St. Andrews offers a wide range of attractions for nongolfers.The **cathedral,** its ancient university (founded in 1411), and **castle** are poignant reminders that the town was once the ecclesiastical capital of Scotland. The now largely ruined cathedral was one of the largest churches ever built in Scotland. The castle is now approached via a visitor center with an audiovisual presentation. ☎ *0131/668–8800.* ⚏ *Cathedral museum and St. Rule's Tower £1.80, castle £2.30, combined ticket £3.50.* ☉ *Cathedral museum, castle visitor center, and tower Apr.–Sept., daily 9:30–6; Oct.–Mar., Mon.–Sat. 9:30–4, Sun. 2–4.*

Dining and Lodging

££–£££ ✗ **Grange Inn.** This old farmhouse-type building houses a simple, traditional restaurant where excellent bar lunches are individually prepared. Dinner is a candlelighted affair, with fine food in modern Scottish style—try the gravlax with sweet dill mustard—and a good selection of wines and malt whiskies. ⊠ *Grange Rd., St. Andrews, Fife KY16 8LJ,* ☎ *01334/472670,* FAX *01334/472604. Reservations essential. AE, DC, MC, V. Closed Mon. and Tues. Nov.–Mar.*

££££ ✗🏨 **Rufflets Country House Hotel.** This creeper-covered country house just outside St. Andrews is surrounded by 10 acres of formal and informal gardens. All the rooms are attractively decorated and comfortable, with the amenities one would expect of a top-class hotel. Dinner is served in the roomy Garden Restaurant, famous for its use of local produce to create memorable Scottish dishes. Recommended are the Tay salmon and filet of Aberdeen Angus beef. ⊠ *Strathkinness Low Rd., KY16 9TX,* ☎ *01334/472594,* FAX *01334/478703. 25 rooms with bath or shower. Restaurant, bar. AE, DC, MC, V.*

ABERDEEN AND ROYAL DEESIDE

Aberdeen—Scotland's third-largest city—is the gateway to a rural hinterland with a wealth of castles and an unspoiled and, in places, spectacular coastline. Deeside, the valley running west from Aberdeen along which the River Dee flows, earned its "Royal" appellation when Queen Victoria and her consort, Albert, built their Scottish fantasy castle, Balmoral, here. To this day, where royalty goes, lesser aristocracy and fast-buck millionaires from around the globe follow. Their yearning to possess an estate here is understandable, since birch woodland, purple moor, and blue river intermingle most tastefully, as you will see from the main road.

Aberdeen

61 *131 mi north of Edinburgh.*

In the 18th century, local granite quarrying produced a durable silver stone that would be used to build the Aberdonian structures of the Victorian era. Thus granite was used boldly, and the downtown Aberdeen seen today remains one of the United Kingdom's most distinctive urban environments—although some would say it depends on the weather and the brightness of the day. The mica chips embedded in the rock act as a million mirrors in sunshine; in rain and heavy clouds, however, their sparkle is snuffed out.

The North Sea has always been an important feature of Aberdeen: in the 1850s, the city was famed for its fast clippers, sleek sailing ships that raced to India for cargoes of tea. In the late 1960s, the course of Aberdeen's history was unequivocally altered when oil and gas were discovered in the North Sea. Aberdeen at first seemed destined to become an oil-rich boomtown, but fortunately, some innate local caution has helped the city to retain a sense of perspective and prevented it from selling out entirely.

A reminder of Aberdeen's earliest days is the 17th-century **Tolbooth** on Castle Street, from which the city was governed for 200 years. It was also the burgh court and jail: narrow, winding stairs lead to dank stone cells where 'Jacobite prisoner' William Baird tells his story. Many other exhibits show the evolution of the city's government, and a history of crime and punishment since medieval times. ⊠ *Castle St.,* ☎ *01224/621167.* ▨ *Free.* ☉ *Tues.–Sat. 10–5, Sun 2–5.*

★ **Marischal College,** dominating Broad Street, was founded in 1593 by the Earl Marischal as a Protestant alternative to the Catholic King's College in Old Aberdeen, though the two combined to form Aberdeen University in 1860. The original university buildings on this site have undergone extensive renovations. The present facade was built in 1891, and this turn-of-the-century creation is still the second-largest granite building in the world; only the Escorial in Madrid is larger. Within, the fascinating **Marischal Museum** exhibits artifacts and photographs relating to the heritage of the Northeast. ⊠ *Broad St.,* ☎ *01224/ 273131.* ▨ *Free.* ☉ *Museum: weekdays 10–5, Sun. 2–5.*

Another survivor from an earlier Aberdeen can be found beyond the concrete supports of St. Nicholas House (of which the tourist information center is a part): **Provost Skene's House** (provost is Scottish for mayor) was once part of a closely packed area of town houses. Steeply gabled and rubble-built, it survives in part from 1545. It was originally a domestic dwelling house and is now a museum portraying civic life, with restored furnished period rooms and a painted chapel. ⊠ *Guestrow off Broad St.,* ☎ *01224/641086.* ▨ *Free.* ☉ *Mon.–Sat. 10–5.*

Royal Deeside

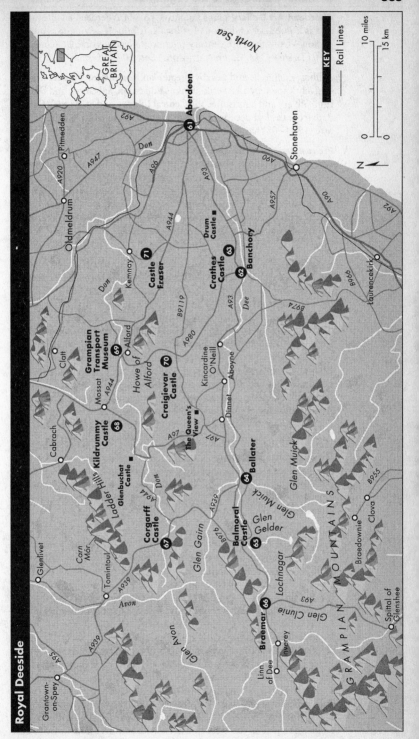

North Sea

GREAT BRITAIN

KEY
Rail Lines

10 miles

15 km

Aberdeen **61**

Stonehaven

Pitmedden

Oldmeldrum

Kemnay

Castle **71**
Fraser

Drum **63**
Castle

Crathes **62**
Castle

Banchory

Clatt

Grampian **69**
Transport
Museum

Alford

Howe of
Alford

Kincardine
O'Neill

Aboyne

Laurencekirk

Cabrach

Craigievar **70**
Castle

The Queen's
View

Dinnet

Kildrummy **68**
Castle

Glenbuchat
Castle

Ballater **64**

Glen Muick

Glenlivet

Corgarff **67**
Castle

Balmoral **65**
Castle

Glen
Gelder

Braedownie

Clova

Tomintoul

Glen Gairn

Lochnagar

Spittal of
Glenshee

Carn
Mór

Ladder Hills

Glen Clunie

Braemar **66**

Avon

Grantown-
on-Spey

Linn
of Dee

Inverey

Linn

GRAMPIAN MOUNTAINS

N

Aberdeen Art Gallery plays an active role in Aberdeen's cultural life and is a popular rendezvous for locals. It houses a wide-ranging collection—from the 18th century to contemporary work. ⊠ *Schoolhill,* ☎ *01224/646333.* 🖳 *Free.* ☉ *Mon.–Sat. 10–5, Sun. 2–5.*

A library, church, and nearby theater on **Rosemount Viaduct** are collectively known by all Aberdonians as Education, Salvation, and Damnation! Silvery and handsome, the **Central Library** and **St. Mark's Church** date from the last decade of the 19th century, while **His Majesty's Theatre** (1904–08) has been restored inside to its full Edwardian splendor.

★ **Provost Ross's House,** dating from 1593, houses the newly refurbished **Aberdeen Maritime Museum,** which tells the story of the city's involvement with the sea, from early inshore fisheries by way of tea clippers to the North Sea oil boom. It is a fascinating place for grade-schoolers, with its ship models, paintings, and equipment associated with the fishing, local shipbuilding, and North Sea oil and gas industries. ⊠ *Provost Ross's House, Ship Row,* ☎ *01224/337701.* 🖳 *Free.* ☉ *Mon.–Sat. 10–5, Sun. 11–5.*

Old Aberdeen was once an independent burgh and lies to the north of the city, near the River Don. Although swallowed up by the expanding main city before the end of the 19th century, Old Aberdeen, which lies between King's College and St. Machar's Cathedral, still retains a certain degree of individual character and integrity. Reach it by taking a bus north from a stop near Marischal College or up King Street, off the Castlegate. **King's College,** founded in 1494 and now part of the University of Aberdeen, has an unmistakable flying (or crown) spire to its **Chapel,** which was built around 1500. The tall oak screen that separates nave from choir and the ribbed wooden ceiling and stalls constitute the finest medieval wood carving to be found anywhere in Scotland. At the **University of Aberdeen Visitor Centre** on High Street you can find out more about one of Britain's oldest universities. ⊠ *High St.,* ☎ *01224/273702,* 🖷 *01224/273710.* ☉ *Mon.–Sat. 10–5, Sun. noon–5.*

Dining and Lodging

The Northeast is the land of Arbroath "smokies" (smoked haddock) and Cullen Skink (fish soup). With rich pastures supporting the famous Aberdeen-Angus beef cattle, especially high-quality viands are also guaranteed.

££–£££ ✕ **Brasserie Gerard's.** Set on a side street moments away from the West End, Gerard's is a long-established stop on the Aberdeen dining scene. Classic French cuisine meets hearty Scottish appetites, ably supported by local produce, fish, and, in particular, red meat: seafood thermidor is certainly not nouvelle cuisine, but it's satisfying, and the fixed-price lunch is an especially good value. The relaxed, softly lit setting includes a flagstone-floor garden room with greenery and tile or marble tables. ⊠ *50 Chapel St.,* ☎ *01224/639500. AE, DC, MC, V.*

££–£££ ✕ **Silver Darling.** Situated right on the quayside, the Silver Darling is
★ one of Aberdeen's most acclaimed restaurants. It specializes, as its name suggests, in fish. The style is French provincial, with an indoor barbecue guaranteeing flavorful grilled fish and shellfish. ⊠ *Pocra Quay, Footdee,* ☎ *01224/576229. AE, DC, MC, V. Closed Sun. No lunch Sat.*

££ ✕🏨 **Atholl Hotel.** One of Aberdeen's many splendid silver-granite
★ properties, the Atholl Hotel is turreted and gabled and set within a leafy residential area to the west of the city. Rooms are done in rich, dark colors; the larger rooms are on the first floor. The restaurant prepares traditional dishes such as lamb cutlets and roast rib of beef. ⊠ *54 Kings Gate, Aberdeen AB15 4YN,* ☎ *01224/323505,* 🖷 *01224/321555. 35 rooms with bath or shower. Restaurant. AE, DC, MC, V.*

££ ×⌂ **Craighaar Hotel.** Don't be fooled by the modern exterior—this is a hotel with character, a refreshing change from the faceless business-type hotel of which Aberdeen has so many. Although it is business-oriented during the week—it is very convenient to the airport—what makes this establishment stand out is the level of personal service. The comfortable restaurant serves cuisine with a Scottish slant, such as Orkney oysters, smoked trout, crab claws, gourmet scampi, and char-grilled steaks. Cheerful guest rooms have bright floral prints on bed linens and other fittings; the split-level gallery suites are outstanding. ⊠ *Waterton Rd., Bucksburn, AB21 9HS,* ☎ *01224/712275,* FAX *01224/716362. 15 rooms with bath, 40 with shower. Restaurant, bar. AE, DC, MC, V.*

The Arts

His Majesty's Theatre (⊠ Rosemount Viaduct, ☎ 01224/641122) has live shows presented throughout the year. The **Lemon Tree** (⊠ 5 W. North St., ☎ 01224/642230) has an international program of dance, comedians, folk, jazz, rock and roll, and art exhibitions. **Aberdeen Arts Centre** (⊠ 33 King St., ☎ 01224/635208) offers experimental theater, poetry readings, exhibitions, and many other arts-based presentations. **Aberdeen Alternative Festival** (☎ 01224/635822) offers an eclectic mix of arts-based events in October each year at venues throughout the city.

Shopping

Aberdeen is a market town—droves of countryfolk come to do their major shopping here, lured by big, modern chain stores. However, there are still delightful specialty shops to be found. **Colin Wood** (⊠ 25 Rose St., ☎ 01224/643019) is the place to go for antiques, maps, and prints. **Nova** (⊠ 20 Chapel St., ☎ 01224/641270) is a treasure-house of gifts ranging from Scottish silver jewelry to Liberty textiles. At the **Aberdeen Family History Shop** (⊠ 164 King St., ☎ 01224/646323) you can browse through a huge range of publications related to local history and genealogical research.

Banchory

62 *19 mi west of Aberdeen on A93.*

Banchory is an immaculate place with a pinkish tinge to its granite. It is usually bustling with ice cream–licking city strollers, out on a day trip from Aberdeen. If you visit in autumn and have time to spare, drive out to the **Brig o'Feuch** (pronounced bridge of fyook). Here, salmon leap in season, and the fall colors and foaming waters make for an attractive scene.

63 Three mi east of Banchory is **Crathes Castle,** once home of the Burnett family. Keepers of the Forest of Drum for generations, the family acquired lands here by marriage and later built a new castle, completed in 1596. Crathes is in the care of the National Trust for Scotland; the Trust also looks after the grand gardens, with their calculated symmetry and clipped yew hedges. ⊠ *Off A93,* ☎ *01330/844525.* ☜ *Grounds or walled garden only £2; castle only £2; castle, garden, and grounds £4.80.* ☉ *Castle Apr.–Oct., daily 11–5:30 (last admission 4:45); garden and grounds yr-round, daily 9–sunset.*

Dining and Lodging

£££–££££ ×⌂ **Banchory Lodge.** With the River Dee running past just a few yards away at the bottom of the garden, this fine example of a 17th-century country house is an ideal resting place for anglers. The lodge has retained its period charm and is well-maintained inside and out. Tranquility is the keynote here. Rooms, with bold colors and tartan or floral fabrics, are individually decorated. The restaurant has high standards for its Scottish cuisine with French overtones; try the fillet of salmon, roast duckling, or guinea fowl with wild berries. ✉ *Banchory, Kincardineshire AB31 5HS,* ☎ *01330/822625,* FAX *01330/825019. 22 rooms with bath. Restaurant, fishing. AE, DC, MC, V.*

Ballater

64 *25 mi west of Banchory, 43 mi west of Aberdeen.*

The quaint holiday resort of Ballater, once noted for the curative properties of its local well, has profited from the proximity of the royals at nearby Balmoral. Visitors are amused by the array of BY ROYAL APPOINTMENT signs proudly hanging from many of its shops (even monarchs need bakers and butchers). If you get a chance, take time to stroll around this neat community—well laid out in silver-gray masses. Note that the railway station now houses the tourist information center as well as a display on the former glories of this Great North of Scotland branch line, closed in the 1960s, along with many others in this country.

Close to the town, capture the feel of the eastern Highlands in **Glen Muick** (Gaelic for pig, pronounced mick). Cross the River Dee and turn upriver on the south side; shortly after, the road forks into this fine Highland glen. The native red deer are quite common throughout the Scottish Highlands, but Glen Muick is one of the very best places to see them in abundance, with herds grazing the flat valley floor. Beyond the lower glen, the prospect opens to reveal not only grazing herds, but also fine views of the battlement of cliffs edging the famed mountain called Lochnagar.

65 West from Ballater is **Balmoral Castle,** the Royal Family's Scottish summer residence. Balmoral is a Victorian fantasy, designed, in fact, by Prince Albert himself in 1855. "It seems like a dream to be here in our dear Highland Home again," Queen Victoria wrote. "Every year my heart becomes more fixed in this dear Paradise." Balmoral's visiting hours depend on whether the royals are in residence. In truth, there are more interesting and historic buildings to explore, as the only part of the castle on view is the ballroom, with an exhibition of royal artifacts. But, from its exterior, Balmoral appears to be everyone's dream of a 19th-century Scottish castle. The queen loved Balmoral more for its setting than its house, so be sure to take in its pleasant gardens. Around and about Balmoral are some noted beauty spots—Cairn O'Mount, Cambus O'May, the Cairngorms from the Linn of Dee; try to spot two animals immortalized by the queen's favorite painter, Sir Edwin Landseer, the red deer and the red grouse. ✉ *On the A93, 7 mi west of Ballater,* ☎ *013397/42334.* 🎟 *£3.50.* ☉ *Easter-May, Mon.–Sat. 10–5; June-July, daily 10–5 (last admission 4 PM).*

Dining and Lodging

££–£££   ✕🏠 **Darroch Learg Hotel.** Amid tall trees on a hillside, the Darroch Learg is everything a Scottish country-house hotel should be, with the added bonus that the charming town of Ballater is only moments away. Built in the 1880s as a country residence, the hotel exudes charm. Most guest rooms enjoy a stunning panoramic view south across Royal Deeside. The Scottish food served in the conservatory restaurant is sophisticated, but also substantial, with the rich flavors of local beef and fish. There is also a prize-winning selection of wines to enjoy. ✉ *Braemar Rd., Ballater, Aberdeenshire AB35 5UX,* ☎ *013397/55443,* FAX *013397/55252. 18 rooms with bath or shower. Restaurant. AE, DC, MC, V.*

Braemar

66 *17 mi west of Ballater, 51 mi north of Perth via A93.*

The village of Braemar is dominated by **Braemar Castle,** dating from the 17th century, with defensive walls later built in the outline of a pointed star. At Braemar (the braes, or slopes, of the district of Mar), the standard, or rebel flag, was first raised at the start of the spectacularly unsuccessful Jacobite rebellion of 1715. Thirty years later, during the last rebellion, Braemar Castle was strengthened and garrisoned by Hanoverian (government) troops. ⊠ *Braemar,* ☎ *013397/41219; 013397/41224 off-season.* ◻ *£2.50.* ☉ *Easter–Oct., Sat.–Thurs. 10–6.*

Braemar is associated with the **Braemar Highland Gathering** held every September, and distinguished by the presence of members of the Royal Family, owing to the proximity of their summer residence at Balmoral.

A little way north of Braemar is the **Linn of Dee.** *Linn* is a Scots word meaning rocky narrows, and the river's rocky gash here is deep and roaring. Park beyond the bridge and walk back to admire the sylvan setting of the river and woodland, replete with bending larch boughs and deep, tranquil pools with salmon glinting in them.

Dining and Lodging

£££ ✕▥ **Invercauld Arms Thistle.** This handsome stone-built Victorian hotel in the center of Braemar makes a good base for exploring Royal Deeside. Interiors are traditional in style and were refurbished in the mid-1990s, with a multitude of interesting prints decorating the walls. The restaurant, with magnificent views overlooking Braemar Castle, serves an international cuisine with Scottish overtones, not least in the use of local fish, game, lamb, and beef. ⊠ *AB35 5YR,* ☎ *013397/41605,* ⊠ *013397/41428. 68 rooms with bath and shower. Restaurant, bar. AE, DC, MC, V.*

Outdoor Activities and Sports

Braemar has a tricky golf course laden with foaming waters. Erratic duffers take note: the compassionate course managers have installed, near the water, poles with little nets on the end for those occasional shots that go awry.

En Route From Braemar, retrace A93 as far as Balmoral, then look for a narrow road going north, signposted B976. Be careful on the first twisting mile through the trees. You will emerge from scattered pines into the open moor in upland Aberdeenshire. Behind is the massif of Lochnagar, and to the west are snow-tipped domes of the big Cairngorms. Roll down to a bridge and go left on A939, which comes in from Ballater. Another high moor section follows.

Corgarff Castle

67 *23 mi northeast of Braemar, 14 mi northwest of Ballater.*

Eighteenth-century soldiers paved a military highway, now A939, north from Ballater to Corgarff Castle, a lonely tower house with another star-shape defensive wall—a curious replica of Braemar Castle. Corgarff was built as a hunting seat for the earls of Mar in the 16th century. After an eventful history that included the wife of a later laird being burned alive in a family dispute, the castle ended its career as a garrison for Hanoverian troops. ⊠ *Signposted off A939,* ☎ *0131/668–8800.* ◻ *£2.30.* ☉ *Apr.–Sept., daily 9:30–6; Oct.–Mar., Sat. 9:30–4, Sun. 2–4.*

En Route If you return east from Corgarff Castle to the A939/A944 junction and then make a left onto A944, the excellent castle signposting will tell you that you are on the **Castle Trail.** The A944 meanders along the River Don to the village of Strathdon, where a great mound by the roadside—on the left—turns out to be a *motte*, or the base of a wooden castle, built in the late 12th century. The A944 then joins A97 (go left) and just a few minutes later a sign points to Glenbuchat Castle, a plain Z-plan tower house.

Kildrummy

18 mi northeast of Corgarff, 23 mi north of Ballater.

★ ⑥⑧ **Kildrummy Castle** is significant because of its age (13th century) and because it has ties to the mainstream medieval traditions of European castle building. It shares features with Harlech and Caernarfon in Wales, as well as with Continental sites, such as Château de Coucy near Laon, France. Kildrummy had undergone several expansions at the hands of English King Edward I when, in 1306, back in Scottish hands, the castle was besieged by King Edward I's son. The defenders were betrayed by a certain Osbarn the Smith, who had been promised a large amount of gold by the English besieging forces. They gave it to him after the castle fell, pouring it molten down his throat, or so the ghoulish story goes. ☎ *0131/668–8800.* ▨ *£1.80.* ✆ *Apr.–Sept., daily 9:30–6.*

Dining and Lodging

££££ ✕▥ **Kildrummy Castle Hotel.** A grand, late-Victorian country house, this hotel offers an attractive blend of a peaceful setting, attentive service, and sporting opportunities. Oak paneling, beautiful plasterwork, and gentle color schemes create a serene environment, enhanced by the views of Kildrummy Castle Gardens next door. The award-winning traditional Scottish cuisine features local game and seafood. ✉ *Kildrummy, near Alford, Aberdeenshire AB33 8RA,* ☎ *019755/71288,* ⒻⒶⓍ *019755/71345. 16 rooms with bath or shower. Restaurant, golf privileges, fishing. AE, MC, V.*

Alford

9 mi east of Kildrummy, 28 mi west of Aberdeen.

⑥⑨ A plain and sturdy settlement in the Howe (Hollow) of Alford, Alford gives those visitors who have grown somewhat weary of castle-hopping a break: it has a museum instead. The **Grampian Transport Museum** specializes in road-based means of locomotion. One of its more unusual exhibits is the *Craigievar Express,* a steam-driven creation invented by the local postman to deliver mail more efficiently. ✉ *Alford,* ☎ *019755/62292.* ▨ *£3.* ✆ *Apr.–Oct., daily 10–5.*

★ ⑦⓪ Two of the finest castles on the Castle Trail (both owned by the National Trust for Scotland) are near Alford. **Craigievar Castle**'s historic structure represents one of the finest traditions of local castle building. It also has the advantage of having survived intact, much as the stonemasons left it in 1626, with its pepper-pot turrets and towers, the whole slender shape covered in a pink-cream pastel. ✉ *5 mi to the south of Alford on A980,* ☎ *013398/83635.* ▨ *£5.80, grounds only £1 (honesty box).* ✆ *May–Sept., daily 1:30–5:30 (last admission 4:45); grounds yr-round, daily 9:30–sunset.*

⑦① The massive **Castle Fraser** shows a variety of styles reflecting the taste of owners from the 15th to the 19th centuries. It has the further advantages of a walled garden, a picnic area, and a tearoom. ✉ *8 mi east of Alford off the A944,* ☎ *01330/833463.* ▨ *£4.20.* ✆ *Easter weekend, May, June, and Sept., daily 1:30–5:30; July–Aug., daily 11–5:30; Oct., weekends 1:30–5:30 (last admission 4:45); gardens yr-round, daily 9:30–6; grounds daily 9:30–sunset.*

INVERNESS AND LOCH NESS

Inverness is the capital of the Highlands and is the only sizable town in northern Scotland (though it is quite small, nonetheless). It is a clean and compact place, built on both banks of the River Ness, just below Loch Ness. The loch itself is 24 mi long and very deep, passing through scenery that is the match of any in Scotland. Loch Ness is the alleged home of "Nessie," world-famous monster and founding member of the local chamber of commerce. In 1933, during a quiet news week for the local paper, the editor decided to run a story about a strange sighting of something splashing about in Loch Ness. Sixty-six years later the story lives on, and the dubious Loch Ness phenomenon continues to keep cameras trained on the deep waters, which have an ominous tendency to create mirages in still conditions. The area sees plenty of tourist traffic, drawn by the well-marketed hokum of the Loch Ness monster. But travelers will be glad to know there is much, much more to see.

Inverness

72 *102 mi northwest of Aberdeen, 161 mi northwest of Edinburgh.*

Inverness is a logical touring base, with excellent roads radiating out from it to serve an extensive area. Although popularly called the Capital of the Highlands, Inverness is far from Highland in flavor. Part of its hinterland includes the farmlands of the Moray Firth coastal strip, as well as of the Black Isle. It is open to the sea winds off the Moray Firth, while the high hills, although close at hand, are mainly hidden. Few of Inverness's buildings are of great antiquity—thanks to the Highland clans' careless habit of burning towns to the ground. Even its castle is a Victorian-era replacement on the site of a fort blown up by Bonnie Prince Charlie. Now bypassed by A9, the town doesn't simply bustle in summer, it positively roars. Be careful in its one-way traffic system, whether walking or driving.

Dining and Lodging

££££ ★ **Dunain Park Hotel.** Guests receive individual attention in a "private house" atmosphere in this 18th-century mansion 2½ mi southwest on A82. A log fire awaits you in the living room, where you can sip a drink and browse through books and magazines. Antiques and traditional decor make the guest rooms cozy and attractive. You can enjoy French-influenced Scottish dishes in the restaurant, where service is on bone china and crystal. Saddle of venison in port sauce and boned quail stuffed with pistachios are two of the specialties. ⊠ *Dunain IV3 6JN,* ☎ *01463/230512,* ℻ *01463/224532. 14 rooms with bath. Restaurant, indoor pool, sauna. AE, DC, MC, V.*

££ **Ballifeary House Hotel.** A well-maintained Victorian property, this one serves traditional Scottish food and offers especially high standards of comfort and service. The hotel is within easy reach of downtown Inverness. This is a no-smoking hotel; no children under 12. ⊠ *10 Ballifeary Rd., IV3 5PJ,* ☎ *01463/235572,* ℻ *01463/717583. 5 rooms with bath or shower. MC, V. Closed Nov.–Mar.*

£ ★ **Daviot Mains Farm.** A 19th-century farmhouse 5 mi south of Inverness on A9 provides the perfect setting for home comforts and, for resident guests only, traditional Scottish cooking; lucky guests may find wild salmon on the menu. ⊠ *Daviot Mains, Inverness IV1 2ER,* ☎ *01463/772215,* ℻ *01463/772099. 3 rooms, 1 with bath, 1 with shower. MC, V.*

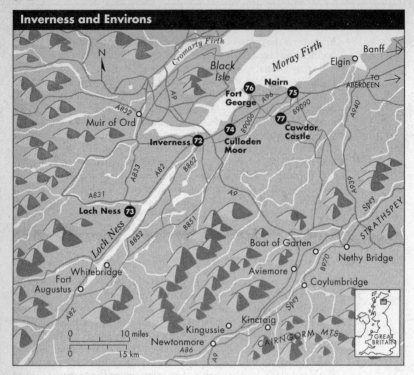

Inverness and Environs

The Arts

Inverness's theater, the **Eden Court** (⊠ Bishops Rd., Inverness, ☎ 01463/221718, ℻ 01463/713810) is a multipurpose 800-seat theater and art gallery that offers a varied program year-round.

Shopping

As you would expect, Inverness features a number of shops with a distinct Highland flavor. **James Pringle Weavers** (⊠ Holm Woollen Mill, Dores Rd., ☎ 01463/223311, ℻ 01463/231042) offers self-guided mill tours and a restaurant; a fine shop also on the premises sells lovely tweeds, tartans, wool clothing, crystal, and giftware. **Hector Russell Kiltmakers** (⊠ 4–9 Huntly St., ☎ 01463/222781, ℻ 01463/713414) has a huge selection of kilts, or will run one up for you made to measure. It can supply by mail order overseas. **Duncan Chisholm & Sons** (⊠ 49 Castle St., ☎ 01463/234599, ℻ 01463/223009) is another fine shop specializing in Highland tartans, woolens, and crafts. Mail-order and made-to-measure services are available.

Loch Ness

★ ⑦ *9 mi southwest of Inverness.*

Inverness is the northern gateway to the Great Glen, the result of an ancient earth movement that dislocated the entire top half of Scotland. The fault line is filled by three lochs; the most well known, Loch Ness, can be seen from the main A82 road south, though leisurely drivers may prefer the east bank road, B862 and B852, to Fort Augustus, at the lake's southern end (32 mi). If you're in search of the infamous loch beast, Nessie, it's best to stay on the A82 west bank road where, at Drumnadrochit, you will find the "official" **Loch Ness Monster Exhibition,** midway on the west bank. Loch Ness's huge volume of water has a warming effect on the local weather, making the lake conducive to mirages in still, warm conditions. These are often the circumstances in which the "monster" appears, and you may draw your own conclusions. Whether or not the *bestia aquatilis* lurks in the depths—more than ever in doubt since 1994, when the man who took one of the most convincing photos of Nessie made a deathbed confession that it was a fake—plenty of camera-toting, sonar-wielding, and submarine-traveling scientists and curiosity-seekers haunt the lake, gazing hopefully lochward. ✉ *Drumnadrochit*, ☎ *01456/450573 or 01456/450218*, ⅎ⅍ *01456/450770*. 🖃 *£4.50.* ☉ *July–Aug., daily 9–7:30; June and Sept., daily 9:30–5:30; Easter–May, daily 9:30–4:30; Oct., daily 9:30–5; Nov.–Feb., daily 10–3; Mar., daily 9:30–4:30; last admission 1 hr before closing.*

Dining and Lodging

£££ ✕🖃 **Polmaily House.** This country house offers books, log fires, and
★ a helpful staff, contributing to a warm and personal atmosphere. Families are especially welcome. The restaurant is noted for its traditional British cuisine, which takes advantage of fresh Highland produce. Tay salmon in pastry with dill sauce, roast rack of lamb with rosemary, and cold smoked venison with melon are examples of some flavorful dishes cooked in Modern British style. ✉ *Drumnadrochit, IV3 6XT*, ☎ *01456/450343*, ⅎ⅍ *01456/450813. 2 suites, 12 rooms with bath and shower. Restaurant, indoor pool, tennis court, croquet, horseback riding, boating, fishing. MC, V.*

Culloden Moor

⑦④ *5 mi east of Inverness on B9006.*

Culloden Moor was the scene of the last battle fought on British soil—to this day considered one of the most infamous and tragic in all of warfare. Here, on a cold April day in 1746, the outnumbered Jacobite forces of Bonnie Prince Charlie were destroyed by the superior firepower of George II's army. The victorious commander, the duke of Cumberland (George II's son), earned the name of "Butcher" Cumberland for the bloody reprisals carried out by his men on Highland families, Jacobite or not, caught in the vicinity; in the battle itself, the duke's army—greatly outnumbering the Scots—decimated more than 1,000 soldiers. The National Trust for Scotland has, slightly eerily, re-created the battlefield as it looked in 1746. The uneasy silence of the open moor almost drowns out the merry clatter from the visitor center's coffee shop and the tinkle of cash registers. ☎ *01463/790607.* 🖃 *Visitor center and audiovisual display £3.* ☉ *Site: daily. Visitor center: Apr.–Oct., daily 9–6; Feb.–Mar. and Nov.–Dec., daily 10–4.*

Nairn

⑦⑤ *17 mi east of Inverness, 92 mi northwest of Aberdeen.*

Once an unusual mixture of prosperous fishing port and farming community, Nairn still has a harmonious blend of old buildings in its busy
★ **⑦⑥** shopping streets. **Fort George,** to the west of the town, was started in 1748 and completed some 20 years later. Today it is perhaps the best-preserved 18th-century military fortification in Europe. Because it is low-lying, its immense scale can be seen only from within. A visitor center and a number of tableaux at the fort portray the 18th-century Scottish soldier's way of life, as does the **Regimental Museum of the Queen's Own Highlanders.** To reach the fort take the B9092 north off A96 west of Nairn. ✉ *Ardersier*, ☎ *0131/668–8800*, ⅎ⅍ *0131/668–8888.* 🖃 *Fort £3, museum free.* ☉ *Fort and museum Apr.–Sept., daily 9:30–6; Oct.–Mar., Mon.–Sat. 9:30–4, Sun. 2–4. Last tickets 45 min before closing.*

77 **Cawdor Castle,** just south of Nairn, is a cheerfully idiosyncratic, mellow, and mossy family seat with a 15th-century central tower. Shakespeare's Macbeth was the Thane (or clan chief) of Cawdor, but the sense of history that exists within these turreted walls is more than fictional. Cawdor is a lived-in castle, not an abandoned structure preserved in aspic. The rooms contain family portraits, tapestries, and fine furniture reflecting 600 years of history. ☎ *01667/404615.* ✉ *£5.20, garden and grounds only £2.80.* ⊙ *May–mid-Oct., daily 10–5.*

Dining and Lodging

£££   ✕⊞ **Clifton House.** This Victorian villa, full of antiques, paintings,
★   and open fires, offers excellent seafood on its wide-ranging menu. Most unusually, this hotel is also licensed as a theater, and in March and November each year, you can enjoy live performances—both theatrical and musical—of an excellent standard. ✉ *Viewfield St., IV12 4HW,* ☎ *01667/453119,* 🖷 *01667/452836. 12 rooms with bath. 2 restaurants. AE, DC, MC, V. Closed Dec.–Jan.*

Outdoor Activities and Sports

Cawdor Castle Nature Trails provides a choice of walks through some of the most beautiful and varied woodlands in Britain. You will pass ancient oaks and beeches, magnificent waterfalls, and deep river gorges. ✉ *Cawdor Castle (Tourism) Ltd., Cawdor Castle, Nairn, near Inverness,* ☎ *01667/404615.* ✉ *£2.80.* ⊙ *May–mid-Oct., daily 10–5.*

SCOTLAND A TO Z

Arriving and Departing

By Bus

Long-distance coach service operates to and from most parts of Scotland, England, and Wales. Main operators include **Scottish Citylink** (☎ 0990/505050) and **National Express** (☎ 0990/808080). Edinburgh is approximately eight hours by bus from London, Glasgow approximately 8½–9 hours.

By Car

Downtown Edinburgh usually means Princes Street, which runs east–west. Entering from the east coast, drivers will come in on A1, Meadowbank Stadium serving as a good landmark. From the Borders, the approach to Princes Street is by A7/A68 through Newington, an area offering a wide choice of budget accommodations. Approaching from the southwest, drivers will join the west end of Princes Street, via A701 and A702, while those coming east from Glasgow or Stirling will meet Princes Street from A8 on the approach via M90/A90. From Forth Road Bridge, Perth, and the east coast, the key road for getting downtown is Queensferry Road.

Visitors who come to Glasgow from England and the south of Scotland will probably approach the city from M6, M74, and A74. The city center is clearly marked from these roads. From Edinburgh M8 leads to the city center and is the motorway that cuts straight across the city center and into which all other roads feed.

It is now possible to travel from Edinburgh to Aberdeen on a continuous stretch of A90/M90, a fairly scenic route that runs up Strathmore. The coastal route, the A92, is a more leisurely alternative. The most scenic route, however, is probably the A93 from Perth, north to Blairgowrie and into Glen Shee. The A93 then goes over the Cairnwell Pass, the highest main road in Scotland (not recommended in winter, however).

The direct Edinburgh–Inverness route is M9/A9. From Glasgow to Inverness, the route is M80, then A9.

By Plane

Aberdeen Airport (☎ 01224/722331) serves both international and domestic flights and is in Dyce, 7 mi west of the city center on the A96 (Inverness). It is served by British Airways, British Midland, KLM UK, BusinessAir, EasyJet, SAS, Brymon, and Gill Air.

Edinburgh Airport has air links with all the major airports in Britain and many in Europe. The **Airport Information Centre** (☎ 0131/333–1000) answers questions regarding schedules, tickets, and reservations.

Glasgow Airport (☎ 0141/887–1111 airport information desk) offers internal Scottish and British services, European and transatlantic scheduled services, and vacation-charter traffic. Scheduled services to and from North America are provided by **Air Canada** (☎ 0990/247226); **American Airlines** (☎ 0345/789789), May–Oct. only; **Continental Airlines** (☎ 0800/776464); and **British Airways** (☎ 0345/222111).

Inverness Airport (☎ 01463/232471) is central for a wide range of internal flights covering the Highlands and islands region; there are also flights from London, Amsterdam (Holland), Edinburgh, and Glasgow. Flights are operated by British Airways (including British Regional Airways/British Airways Express), KLM UK and EasyJet.

Prestwick Airport (☎ 01292/479822), on the Ayrshire coast about 30 mi southwest of Glasgow and for some years eclipsed by Glasgow Airport, is beginning to come back into the reckoning, not least because of the activities of **Ryanair** (☎ 01292/678000), a company that has sparked a major price war on the Anglo-Scottish routes (between London and Glasgow/Edinburgh). It offers unbeatable, no-frills, rock-bottom airfares between London Stansted and Prestwick. **Gill Airways** (☎ 01292/678000) also flies out of Prestwick, serving Belfast (Northern Ireland).

By Train

Edinburgh's main train station, Waverley, is downtown, below Waverley Bridge. Travel time from Edinburgh to London by train is as little as four hours. Glasgow has two main rail stations: Central and Queen Street. Central is the arrival and departure point for trains from London Euston (journey time is approximately five hours), which come via Crewe and Carlisle in England, as well as via Edinburgh from Kings Cross. Travelers can reach Aberdeen directly from Edinburgh (three hours), and Inverness (two hours). There are sleeper connections from London to Inverness, as well as reliable links from Edinburgh. There is also a direct London–Aberdeen service that goes through Edinburgh. For those interested in train service to Aberdeen's airport, Dyce is on Scotrail's Inverness–Aberdeen route. For all inquiries, telephone the **National Train Enquiry Line** (☎ 0345/484950).

Getting Around

By Bus

Lothian Region Transport (☎ 0131/555–6363), operating dark red-and-white buses, is the main operator within **Edinburgh.** S.M.T. (☎ 0131/663–9233), operating green buses, provides much of the service into Edinburgh and also offers day tours around and beyond the city. Lowland Scottish Omnibuses (☎ 01896/752237) serve the **Borders.**

The LRT Edinburgh Day Saver ticket (£2.20), allowing unlimited one-day travel on the city's buses, can be purchased in advance, or on any LRT bus (exact money will be required when purchasing on a bus). Two travel passes are available from Lowland Omnibuses for one or seven days unlimited travel in the Borders: the Reiver Rover for services within the Borders area, and the Waverley Wanderer for services within the Borders and to Edinburgh and Carlisle.

The many different bus companies in **Glasgow** cooperate with the underground and ScotRail to produce the Family Day Tripper Ticket, £12.50, which is an excellent way to get around the whole area from Loch Lomond to Ayrshire. Tickets are a good value and are available from Strathclyde Passenger Transport (SPT) Travel Centre, St. Enoch Square (☎ 0141/226–4826) and at main railway and bus stations.

Scottish Citylink (Glasgow: ✉ Buchanan Street Bus Station, ☎ 0990/505050) sells an Explorer Pass providing 3, 5, 8, or 15 days of unlimited travel on National Express services into Scotland and on the entire Scottish Citylink network. Aberdeen and Inverness are well served from the central belt of Scotland. Getting around the Inverness area and Royal Deeside is best done by car, but there are a number of post-bus services that can help get you to the remote areas. For information contact the Royal Mail (✉ 7 Strothers La., Inverness IV1 1AA, ☎ 01463/256273, ℻ 01463/256392).

By Car
Edinburgh can be explored easily on foot, so a car is hardly needed. Glasgow, though bigger, has an excellent integrated public transport system, so a car is also unnecessary in this city.

Great improvements have been made on Highland roads in recent years. If you are coming from southern Scotland, allow a comfortable 3½ hours from Glasgow or Edinburgh to Inverness via A9, and two hours to Aberdeen via A90.

By Train
In Glasgow, the "Go Roundabout Glasgow" and "Roundabout Plus" discount passes allow unlimited travel on the Underground and trains around Glasgow and out to surrounding towns for one day. There is also a separate "Heritage Trail" pass available for travel on the underground only. Trains depart Edinburgh and Glasgow for Aberdeen, Inverness, and other towns in the north. ScotRail "Rover" tickets cover almost the entire ScotRail network, and "West Highland" and "North Highland" local Rovers are also available. For details, contact the **National Train Enquiry Line** (☎ 0345/484950). The Borders has no rail service, and the nearest rail station to St. Andrews is Leuchars, on the Edinburgh-Aberdeen main line.

Freedom of Scotland Travelpass
The comprehensive "Freedom of Scotland Travelpass" covers nearly all train and ferry transport and gives discounts on buses in the Highlands and islands for 8 or 15 consecutive days, or 8 days out of 15 consecutive days. It is available at any main train station in Scotland.

Contacts and Resources

B&B Reservations
It is perfectly acceptable to contact individual establishments directly. **Tourist information centers** all offer a same-night local booking service, usually free of charge, although there may occasionally be a small fee. They also operate the national **Book-A-Bed Ahead (BABA)** service, arranging for accommodation in another locality in Scotland (personal callers only, small booking fee and 10% deposit payable). The **Scottish Tourist Board's London office** (✉ 19 Cockspur St., ☎ 0171/930–8661) will book accommodation, although its main office in Edinburgh cannot do so.

Car Rentals

Aberdeen: Avis (⊠ 16 Broomhill Rd., ☎ 01224/574252; 01224/722282 airport); **Europcar** (⊠ 121 Causewayend, ☎ 01224/631199; 01224/770770 airport); **Hertz** (⊠ Railway Station, ☎ 01224/210748; 01224/722373 airport).

Edinburgh: Avis (⊠ 100 Dalry Rd., ☎ 0131/337–6363; 0131/333–1866 airport); **Budget Rent-a-Car** (⊠ Royal Scot Hotel, 111 Glasgow Rd., ☎ 0131/334–7739); **Europcar** (⊠ 24 E. London St., ☎ 0131/557–3456; 0131/344–3114 airport); **Hertz U.K. Ltd.** (⊠ 10 Picardy Pl., ☎ 0131/556–8311; 0131/333–1019 airport; 0131/557–5272 Waverley train station).

Glasgow: Avis (⊠ 161 North St., ☎ 0141/221–2827); **Budget Rent-a-Car** (⊠ 101 Waterloo St., ☎ 0141/226–4141); **National Car Rental** (⊠ 76 Lancefield Quay, ☎ 0141/204–1051); **Europcar** (⊠ 556 Pollokshaws Rd., ☎ 0141/423–5661); **Hertz** (⊠ 106 Waterloo St., ☎ 0141/248–7736).

Inverness: Europcar Ltd. (⊠ Highlander Service Station, Millburn Rd., ☎ 01463/235337); **Hertz** (⊠ Dalcross Airport, ☎ 01667/462652).

Discount Admission Tickets

The **Scottish Explorer Ticket,** available from any staffed Historic Scotland property and many tourist information centers, allows visits to HS properties over a 7- or 14-day period. The **Touring Ticket** issued by the National Trust for Scotland (☎ 0131/226–5922) is also available for 7 or 14 days and allows access to all NTS properties. It is available from the NTS or main tourist information centers.

Emergencies

Dial **999** from any telephone (no coins are needed for emergency calls from public telephones) to obtain assistance from the police, ambulance, fire department, mountain rescue, or coast guard.

Guided Tours

BUS TOURS

Lothian Region Transport and **Guide Friday** (☎ 0131/556–2244) both offer tours in and around Edinburgh departing from Waverley Bridge every 15 minutes, from 9:20 to 5:35 daily. The following Glasgow companies run regular **bus tours** around Glasgow: **Scottguide Tours** (☎ 0141/204–0444) and **Guide Friday,** a company that also offers tours of Inverness. **Prestige Tours** (☎ 0141/810–3200) runs luxury coach tours in small groups to most parts of Scotland. **Classique Tours** (☎ 0141/889–4050) have unusual vehicles: small touring coaches dating from the 1950s and restored to immaculate condition. Specialist tours of Scotland's gardens are operated by **Brightwater Holidays** (☎ 01334/657155).

CHAUFFEURED TOURS

Ghillie Personal Travel (⊠ 64 Silverknowes Rd. E, Edinburgh, ☎ 0131/336–3120) and **Little's Chauffeur Drive** (⊠ 33 Corstorphine High St., Edinburgh, ☎ 0131/334–2177; ⊠ 1282 Paisley Rd. West, Glasgow G52 1DB, ☎ 0141/883–2111) both offer flexible, customized tours in all sizes of cars and buses, especially suitable for groups.

WALKING TOURS

The **Cadies and Witchery Tours** (☎ 0131/225–6745) organizes tours of ghost-haunted Edinburgh throughout the year.

The **Scottish Tourist Guides Association** (☎ FAX 0131/453–1297) can recommend fully qualified guides who will arrange walking or driving excursions of varying lengths to suit your interests.

Travel Agencies

American Express (⊠ 139 Princes St., Edinburgh EH2 4BR, ☎ 0131/ 225–7881; ⊠ 115 Hope St., Glasgow G2 6LX, ☎ 0141/221–4366).

Thomas Cook (⊠ 26–28 Frederick St., Edinburgh EH2 2JR, ☎ 0131/ 220–4039; ⊠ 15–17 Gordon St. GlasgowG1 3PR, ☎ 0141/201–7280).

Visitor Information

Edinburgh and Scotland Information Centre (⊠ 3 Princes St., Edinburgh, ☎ 0131/557–1700, FAX 0131/473–3881) is adjacent to Waverley Station in Edinburgh (follow the tourist information center TIC signs in the station and throughout the city).

Greater Glasgow and Clyde Valley Tourist Board (⊠ 11 George Sq., Glasgow, ☎ 0141/204–4400, FAX 0141/221–3524) offers an excellent tourist information service from its headquarters near Queen Street Station.

The **Scottish Tourist Board Central Information Department** (⊠ 23 Ravelston Terr., Edinburgh EH4 3EU, ☎ 0131/332–2433, FAX 0131/315– 4545), for telephone and written inquiries only, will answer any question on any aspect of your Scottish holiday and can supply literature by mail. It cannot, however, make accommodation bookings.

The **Scottish Tourist Board in London** (⊠ 19 Cockspur St., near Trafalgar Sq., London SW1Y 5BL, ☎ 0171/930–8661, FAX 0171/930–1817), open weekdays 9:30–5:30 year-round and Saturday 10–5 mid-June– mid-September (rest of year 12–4), can supply information and also has an accommodation and travel booking agency.

Within Scotland, an integrated network of over 170 **tourist information centers** is run by a variety of area tourist boards, offering comprehensive information and on-the-spot accommodation bookings. **Aberdeen and Grampian** (⊠ Migvie House, N. Silver St., Aberdeen AB9 1RJ, ☎ 01224/632727, FAX 01224/848805). **Ballater** (⊠ Station Sq., ☎ 013397/55306). **Banchory** (⊠ Bridge St., Banchory, AB31 3SX, ☎ 01330/822000). **Inverness** (⊠ Castle Wynd, Inverness IV2 3BJ, ☎ 01463/234353). **Jedburgh** (⊠ Murrays Green, Borders TD8 6BE, ☎ 01835/863435). **St. Andrews** (⊠ 70 Market St., St Andrews KY16 9NU, ☎ 01334/472021).

18 Portraits of Great Britain

GREAT BRITAIN AT A GLANCE: A CHRONOLOGY

2800 BC   First building of Stonehenge (later building 2100–1900)

54 BC–AD 43   Julius Caesar's exploratory invasion of England Romans conquer England, led by Emperor Claudius

60   Boudicca, a native British queen, razes the first Roman London (Londinium) to the ground

122–27   Emperor Hadrian completes the Roman conquest and builds a wall across the north to keep back the Scottish Picts

ca. 490   Possible period for the legendary King Arthur, who may have led resistance to Anglo-Saxon invaders; in 500 the Battle of Badon is fought

563   St. Columba, an Irish monk, founds monastery on the Scottish island of Iona; begins to convert Picts and Scots to Christianity

597   St. Augustine arrives in Canterbury to Christianize Britain

871–99   Alfred the Great, king of Wessex, unifies the English against Viking invaders, who are then confined to the northeast

1040   Edward the Confessor moves his court to Westminster and founds Westminster Abbey

1066   William, duke of Normandy, invades; defeats Harold at the Battle of Hastings; is crowned at Westminster in December

1086   Domesday Book completed, a survey of all taxpayers in England, drawn up to assist administration of the new realm

1167   Oxford University founded

1170   Thomas à Becket murdered in Canterbury; his shrine becomes center for international pilgrimage

1189   Richard the Lionhearted embarks on the Third Crusade

1209   Cambridge University founded

1215   King John forced to sign Magna Carta at Runnymede; it promulgates basic principles of English law: no taxation except through Parliament, trial by jury, and property guarantees

1272–1307   Edward I, a great legislator; in 1282–83 he conquers Wales and reinforces his rule with a chain of massive castles

1337–1453   Edward III claims the French throne, starting the Hundred Years War. In spite of dramatic English victories—1346 at Crécy, 1356 at Poitiers, 1415 at Agincourt—the long war of attrition ends with the French driving the English out from all but Calais, which finally fell in 1558

1348–49   The Black Death (bubonic plague) reduces the population of Britain to around 2½ million; decades of social unrest follow

1399   Henry Bolingbroke (Henry IV) deposes and murders his cousin Richard II; beginning of the rivalry between houses of York and Lancaster

1402–10   The Welsh, led by Owain Glendwr, rebel against English rule

1455–85   The Wars of the Roses—the York/Lancaster struggle erupts in civil war

1477 William Caxton prints first book in England

1485 Henry Tudor (Henry VII) defeats Richard III at the Battle of Bosworth, and founds the Tudor dynasty; he suppresses private armies, develops administrative efficiency and royal absolutism

1530s Under Henry VIII the Reformation takes hold; he dissolves the monasteries, finally demolishes medieval England and replaces it with a new society

1555 Protestant Bishops Ridley and Latimer are burned in Oxford; in 1556 Archbishop Cranmer is burned

1558–1603 Reign of Elizabeth I—Protestantism reestablished; Drake, Raleigh, and other freebooters establish English claims in the West Indies and North America

1568 Mary, Queen of Scots, flees to England; in 1587 she is executed

1588 Spanish Armada fails to invade England

1603 James VI of Scotland becomes James I of England

1605 Guy Fawkes and friends plot to blow up Parliament

1611 King James Authorized Version of the Bible published

1620 Pilgrims sail from Plymouth on the *Mayflower* and settle in New England

1629 Charles I dissolves Parliament, decides to rule alone

1642–49 Civil War between the Royalists and Parliamentarians (Cavaliers and Roundheads); the Parliamentarians win

1649 Charles I executed; England is a republic

1653 Cromwell becomes Lord Protector, England's only dictatorship

1660 Charles II restored to the throne; accepts limits to royal power

1666 The Great Fire of London, accession of William III (of Orange) and his wife, Mary II, as joint monarchs; royal power limited still further

1714 The German Hanoverians succeed to the throne; George I's lack of English leads to a council of ministers, the beginning of the Cabinet system of government

1700s Under the first four Georges, the Industrial Revolution develops and with it Britain's domination of world trade

1775–83 Britain loses its American colonies

1795–1815 Britain and its allies defeat French in the Napoleonic Wars; in 1805 Nelson is killed at Trafalgar; in 1815 Battle of Waterloo is fought

1801 Union with Ireland

1811–20 Prince Regent rules during his father's (George III) madness—the Regency period

1825 The Stockton to Darlington railway, the world's first passenger line with regular service, is established

1832 The Reform Bill extends the franchise, limiting the power of the great landowners

1834 Parliament outlaws slavery

1837–1901 The long reign of Victoria—Britain becomes the world's richest country, and the British Empire reaches its height; railways, canals, and telegraph lines draw Britain into one vast manufacturing net

1851 The Great Exhibition, Prince Albert's brainchild, is held in Crystal Palace, Hyde Park

1861 Prince Albert dies

1887 Victoria celebrates her Golden Jubilee; in 1901 she dies, marking the end of an era

1914–18 World War I: Fighting against Germany, Britain loses a whole generation, with 750,000 men killed in trench warfare alone; enormous debts and inept diplomacy in the postwar years undermine Britain's position as a world power

1919 Ireland declares independence from England; bloody Black-and-Tan struggle was one result

1926 General Strike in sympathy with striking coal miners

1936 Edward VIII abdicates to marry American divorcée, Mrs. Wallis Simpson

1939–45 World War II—Britain faces Hitler alone until Pearl Harbor; London badly damaged during the Blitz, September '40–May '41; Britain's economy shattered by the war

1945 Labour wins a landslide victory; stays in power for six years, transforming Britain into a welfare state

1952 Queen Elizabeth accedes to the throne

1973 Britain joins the European Economic Community after referendum

1975 Britain begins to pump North Sea oil

1981 Marriage of Prince Charles and Lady Diana Spencer

1982 Falklands regained

1987 Conservatives under Margaret Thatcher win a third term in office

1990 John Major takes over as prime minister, ending Margaret Thatcher's illustrious, if controversial, career in office

1991 The Persian Gulf War

1992 Great Britain and the European countries join to form one European Community (EC), whose name was officially changed to European Union in 1993

1994 Official opening of the Channel Tunnel by Queen Elizabeth II and President Mitterand

1996 The Prince and Princess of Wales receive a precedent-breaking divorce. Princess Diana retains many royal privileges as mother of the future king William.

1996 Official opening of the reconstruction of Shakespeare's Globe Theatre in London.

1997 Diana, Princess of Wales, dies at 36 in a car crash in Paris on August 31. After an extraordinary outpouring of grief, the world mourns at her Westminster Abbey funeral, televised around the globe to almost 800 million viewers. She is buried at Althorp, the Spencer family estate in Northamptonshire.

SPLENDID STONES: AN INTRODUCTION TO BRITISH ARCHITECTURE

IN BRITAIN, YOU CAN SEE structures that go back to the dawn of history, in the hauntingly mysterious circles of monoliths at Stonehenge or Avebury, for example; or the resurrected remains of Roman empire builders preserved in towns such as St. Albans or Cirencester. On the other hand, you can startle your eyes with the very current, very controversial designs of contemporary architects in new developments, including London's Docklands area. Appreciating the wealth of Britain's architectural heritage does not require a degree in art history, but knowing a few hallmarks of various styles can enhance your enjoyment of what you see. Here, then, is a primer of nearly a millennium of various architectural styles.

Norman

The solid Norman style, ideal for castle building, arrived in England slightly before the Conquest, with the building of Westminster Abbey in 1040. From 1066 to around 1200, it was clearly the style of choice for buildings of any importance. Norman towers tended to be hefty and square, arches always round-topped, and the vaulting barrel-shaped. Decoration was mostly geometrical, but within those limits, ornate. *Best seen in the Tower of London, St. Bartholomew's and Temple Churches, London; and in the cathedrals of St. Albans, Ely, Gloucester, Durham, and Norwich, and at Tewkesbury Abbey.*

Gothic Early English

From 1130 to 1300, pointed arches began to supplant the rounded ones, buttresses became heavier than the Norman variety, and the windows lost their rounded tops to become "lancet" shaped. Buildings climbed skyward, less squat and heavy, with the soaring effect accentuated by steep roofs and spires. *Best seen in the cathedrals of York, Salisbury, Ely, Worcester, Canterbury (east end), and Westminster Abbey's chapter house.*

DECORATED

From the late 1100s until around 1400, elegance and ornament became fully integrated into architectural design, rather than applied onto the surface of a solid basic form. Windows filled more of the walls and were divided into sections by carved mullions. Vaulting grew increasingly complex, with ribs and ornamented bosses proliferating; spires became even pointier; arches took on the "ogee" shape, with its unique double curve. This style was one of England's greatest gifts to world architecture. *Best seen at the cathedrals of Wells, Lincoln, Durham (east transept), and Ely (Lady Chapel and Octagon).*

PERPENDICULAR

In later Gothic architecture, the emphasis on the vertical grew even more pronounced, featuring slender pillars, huge expanses of glass, and superb fan vaulting resembling the formalized branches of frozen trees. Walls were divided by panels. One of the chief areas in which to see Perpendicular architecture is East Anglia, where the rich wool towns built magnificent churches in the new style. Houses, too, began to reflect prevailing taste. Perpendicular Gothic lasted for well over two centuries from its advent around 1330. *Best seen at St. George's Chapel, Windsor; the cathedrals of Gloucester (cloister), and Hereford (chapter house); Henry VII's Chapel, Westminster Abbey; and King's College Chapel, Cambridge.*

Tudor

With the great period of cathedral building over, from 1500 to 1560 the nation's attention turned to the construction of spacious homes, characterized by this new architectural style. The rapidly expanding *nouveau riche* class—created by the first two Tudor Henrys (VII and VIII) to challenge the power of the aristocracy—built spacious manor houses, often on the foundations of pillaged monasteries, thus beginning the era of the great stately homes. Brick replaced stone as the most popular medium, with plasterwork and carved wood to carry the elaborate motifs of the age. Another way the new rich could make their mark—and ensure their place in the next world—was by building churches. This was the age of the splendid parish churches built on fortunes made in the wool trade. Some of the most magnificent are in Suffolk, Norfolk, and the Cotswolds. *Domestic architecture is best seen at Hampton Court and St. James's Palace, London; for wool churches, Lavenham, and Long Melford, though its tower is much later, both in Suffolk.*

Renaissance Elizabethan

For a short period under Elizabeth I, 1560–1600, this development of Tudor flourished as Italian influences began to seep into England, seen especially in symmetrical facades. The most notable example was Hardwick Hall in Derbyshire, built in the 1590s by Bess of Hardwick—the jingle that describes it goes "Hardwick Hall, more glass than wall." But, however grand the houses were, they were still on a human scale, warm and livable, built of a mellow amalgam of brick and stone. *Other great Elizabethan houses are Montacute, Somerset; Longleat, Wiltshire; and Burghley House, Cambridgeshire.*

Jacobean

For the first 15 years of the reign of James I (the name Jacobean is taken from the Latin word for James, Jacobus) there was little noticeable change. Windows were still large in proportion to the wall surfaces. Gables, in the style of the Netherlands, were popular. Carved decoration in wood and plaster (especially the geometrical patterning called "strapwork," like intertwined leather belts, also of Dutch origin) was still exuberant, now even more so. But a change was on the way. Inigo Jones (1573–1652), the first great modern British architect, was attempting to synthesize the architectural heritage of England with the current Italian theories. Two of his finest remaining buildings—the Banqueting Hall, Whitehall, and the Queen's House at Greenwich—epitomize his genius, which was to introduce the Palladian style that dominated British architecture for centuries. It uses the classical Greek orders—Doric, Ionic, and Corinthian. This was grandeur. But the classical style that was so monumentally effective under a hot Mediterranean sun was somehow transformed in Britain, domesticated and tamed. Columns and pediments were used to decorate the facades, and huge frescoes provided acres of color to interior walls and ceilings, all in the Italian manner. But these architectural elements had not yet been totally naturalized. There were in fact two quite distinct styles running concurrently, the comfortably domestic and the purer classical in public buildings. They were finally fused together by the talent of Christopher Wren (1632–1723). *Jacobean is best seen at the Bodleian Library, Oxford; Hatfield House, Herefordshire; Audley End, Essex; and Clare College, Cambridge.*

Wren

Sir Christopher Wren's work constituted an era all by itself. Not only was he naturally one of the world's greatest architects, but he was also given an unparalleled opportunity when the disastrous Great Fire of London in 1666 wiped out the center of the capital, destroying no fewer than 89 churches and 13,200 houses. Although Wren's great scheme for a totally new city center was rejected, he did build 51 churches, the greatest of which was St. Paul's, completed in just 35 years. The range of Wren's designs is extremely wide, from simple classical shapes to the extravagantly dramatic baroque. He was also at home with domestic architecture, where his combinations of brick and stone produced a warm, homey effect. *Wren's ecclesiastical architecture is best seen at St. Paul's Cathedral and the other remaining city churches, his domestic style at Hampton Court Palace, Kensington Palace, and the Royal Hospital in Chelsea.*

Palladian

This style is often referred to as Georgian, so-called from the Hanoverian kings George I through IV, although it was introduced as early as Inigo Jones's time. Classical inspiration has now been thoroughly acclimatized. Though they were completely at home among the hills, lakes, and trees of the British countryside, Palladian buildings were derived from the designs of the Italian architectural theorist Palladio, with pillared porticoes, triangular pediments, and strictly balanced windows. In domestic architecture, this large-scale classicism was usually modified to quiet simplicity, preserving mathematical proportions of windows, doors, and the exactly calculated volume of room space, to create a feeling of balance and harmony. There were some outrageous departures from the classical manner at this time, most notably with the Brighton Pavilion, built for the Prince Regent (later George IV). The Regency style comes under the Palladian heading, though strictly speaking it lasted only for the few years of the actual Regency. In Britain, the Palladian style was handled with more freedom than elsewhere in Europe, and America took its cue from the British architects. *Among the best Palladian examples are Regent's Park Terraces (London); the library at Kenwood (London); Royal Crescent and other streets in Bath; Holkham Hall, Blenheim Palace, and Castle Howard.*

Victorian

Elements of imaginative fantasy, already seen in the Palladian era, came to the fore during the long reign of Victoria. The country's vast profits made from the Industrial Revolution were spent lavishly. Civic building accelerated in all the major cities with town halls modeled after medieval castles or French châteaus. The Victorians plundered the past for styles, with Gothic—about which the scholarly Victorians were very knowledgeable—leading the field. The supreme example here is the Houses of Parliament in London. (To distinguish between the Victorian variety and an earlier version, which flourished in the late 1700s, the earlier one is commonly spelled "Gothick.") But there were many other styles in the running, including the attractively named—and self-explanatory—"Wrenaissance." *Among the most striking examples are Truro Cathedral, the Albert Memorial (London), Manchester Town Hall, the Foreign Office (London), Ironbridge, and Cragside (Northumberland).*

Edwardian

Toward the end of the Victorian era, in the late 1800s, architecture calmed down considerably, with a return to a solid sort of classicism, and to even a muted baroque. The Arts and Crafts movement, especially the work and inspiration of William Morris, produced simpler designs, returning often to medieval models. *Best seen in Buckingham Palace and the Admiralty Arch in London.*

Modern

A furious public debate has raged in Britain for many years between traditionalists and the adherents of modernistic architecture. Britons are strongly conservative when it comes to their environment. These arguments have been highlighted and made even more bitter by the intervention of such notable figures as Prince Charles, who derides excessive modernism, and said, for instance, that an advanced design

for the new wing of the National Gallery in Trafalgar Square would be like "a carbuncle on a much-loved face." One reason for the strength of the British attitude is that the country suffered from far too much ill-conceived building development after World War II, when large areas of city centers had to be rebuilt after the devastation of German bombs, and there was a pressing need for housing. Town planners and architects at this time encumbered the country with endless badly built and worse-designed tower blocks and shopping areas.

The situation that was thus created in the '50s and '60s is gradually being reversed. High-rise apartment blocks are being blown up and replaced by more user-friendly housing. Large-scale commercial areas, such as the Bull Ring in Birmingham, are being rethought and slowly rebuilt, although so much ill-considered building went on in the past that Britain can never be completely free of it. The emphasis is gradually, far too gradually, moving to a type of planning, designing, and construction that pays more attention to the needs of the inhabitants of buildings. At last, the lessons of crime statistics and the sheer human misery caused by unacceptable living conditions are being learned. There is, too, a healthier attitude now to the conservation of old buildings. As part of the postwar building splurge, houses that should have been treasured for posterity were torn down wholesale. Happily, many of those that survived the wreckers' ball are now being restored and put back to use.

The architecture styles employed nowadays are very eclectic. A predominant one, favored incidentally by Prince Charles, draws largely on the past, with nostalgic echoes of the country cottage, and leans heavily on variegated brickwork and on close attention to decorative detail. Supermarkets are going up in every town designed on a debased form of this style. Stark modernism does crop up every now and again. The Lloyd's Tower in the City of London, by Sir Richard Rogers, designer of the Pompidou Center in Paris, is perhaps the leading, and most flamboyantly extreme, example. Another, gentler one is the Queen's Stand at the Epsom Racecourse. This elegant building by Richard Horden is rather like an elegant, white ocean liner, berthed beside the racetrack, with sweeping, curved staircases inside, and viewing balconies outside. But England generally is still light years behind the States in experimentation with design. The skyscrapers of the City of London are the exception in Britain rather than the rule.

However, public buildings are being built on a smaller scale; schools and libraries, designed in a muted modernism, use traditional, natural materials, such as wood, stone, and brick. A slightly special case, though representative of what can be achieved, is the new Visitors' Centre at the National Trust's most popular venue, Fountains Abbey in Yorkshire. Designed by Edward Cullinan, it is a fusion of dry-stone walls, lead and wooden-shingle roofs outside, white-painted steel pillars and flowing ceilings inside. It is perfectly conceived for the needs of such a historically important site. Unfortunately, the recession has stopped most commercial building dead in its tracks, so the architectural debate will be largely a theoretical one for years to come. *Among the new buildings to see are the Lloyd's Tower, some of the Docklands development, Richmond House (79 Whitehall), and the Clore Building at the Tate Gallery (all in London); the campus of Sussex University (outside Brighton), the Royal Regatta Building (Henley), the Sainsbury Centre (Norwich), the Burrell Collection (Glasgow); the Queen's Stand at Epsom, Surrey; The Visitors' Centre, Fountains Abbey, Yorkshire.*

FURTHER READING

Many writers' names have become inextricably linked with the regions in which they set their books or plays. Hardy's Wessex, Daphne Du Maurier's Cornwall, Wordsworth's Lake District, Shakespeare's Arden, and Brontë Country are now evocative catch phrases, treasured by local tourist boards. But however hackneyed the tags may now be, you *can* still get a heightened insight to an area through the eyes of authors of genius, even though they may have written a century or more ago. Here are just a few works that may provide you with an understanding of their authors' loved territory.

Thomas Hardy's *Mayor of Casterbridge, Tess of the d'Urbervilles, Far from the Madding Crowd,* and indeed almost everything he wrote is solidly based on his Wessex (Dorset) homeland. Daphne Du Maurier had a deep love of Cornwall from her childhood; *Frenchman's Creek, Jamaica Inn,* and *The King's General* all capture the county's Celtic atmosphere. The Brontë sisters' *Wuthering Heights, The Tennant of Wildfell Hall,* and *Jane Eyre* all breathe the sharp air of the high Fells around their Haworth home. William Wordsworth, who was born at Cockermouth in the Lake District, depicts the area's rugged beauty in many of his poems, especially the *Lyrical Ballads.*

Virginia Woolf's visits to Vita Sackville-West at her ancestral home of Knole, in Sevenoaks, resulted in the novel *Orlando.* The stately home is now a National Trust property. The country around Batemans, near Burwash in East Sussex, the home where Rudyard Kipling lived for more than 30 years, was the inspiration for *Puck of Pook's Hill* and *Rewards and Fairies.* Lamb House in Rye, also in East Sussex, was home to the American writer, Henry James, and after him E. F. Benson, whose delicious Lucia books are set in a thinly disguised version of the town. Both Batemans and Lamb House are National Trust buildings.

A highly irreverent—and very funny—version of academic life, *Porterhouse Blue,* by Tom Sharpe, will guarantee that you look at Oxford and Cambridge with a totally different eye. John Fowles's *The French Lieutenant's Woman,* largely set in Lyme Regis, is full of local color for visitors to Dorset.

James Herriot's successfully televised veterinary surgeon books, among them *All Creatures Great and Small,* give evocative accounts of life in the Yorkshire dales. For a perceptive account of life in the English countryside, try Ronald Blythe's award-winning *Akenfield: Portrait of an English Village.*

Mysteries are almost a way of life in Britain, partly because many of the best English mystery writers set their plots in their home territory. Modern whodunits by P. D. James and Ruth Rendell can be relied on to convey a fine sense of place, while Ellis Peters's Brother Cadfael stories re-create life in medieval Shrewsbury with a wealth of telling detail. There are always, of course, the villages, vicarages, and scandals of Agatha Christie's "Miss Marple" books.

For the many fans of the Arthurian legends, there are some excellent, imaginative novels, which not only tell the stories, but give fine descriptions of the British countryside. Among them are *Sword at Sunset,* by Rosemary Sutcliffe; *The Once and Future King,* by T. H. White; and the four Merlin novels by Mary Stewart, *The Crystal Cave, The Hollow Hills, The Last Enchantment,* and *The Wicked Day.*

An animal's close-to-the-earth viewpoint can reveal all kinds of countryside insights about Britain. *Watership Down,* by Richard Adam, was a runaway bestseller about rabbits in the early '70s, and *Wind in the Willows,* by Kenneth Grahame, gives a vivid impression of the Thames Valley 80 years ago which still holds largely true today.

Anyone interested in writers and the surroundings that may have influenced their works should get *The Oxford Literary Guide to the British Isles,* edited by Dorothy Eagle and Hilary Carnell, and *Literary Britain,* by Frank Morley. One author particularly in vogue now is Jane Austen: Janites will want to read Susan Watkins'

Jane Austen's Town and Country Style and Nigel Nicolson's wonderful *World of Jane Austen*. For a vast portrait of everyone's favorite English author, weigh in with Peter Ackroyd's *Dickens*.

Two good background books on English history are *The English World*, edited by Robert Blake, and Godfrey Smith's *The English Companion*. *The London Encyclopaedia*, by Ben Weinreb and Christopher Hibbert, is invaluable as a source of information on the capital.

The finest book on the great stately houses of England is Nigel Nicolson's *Great Houses of Britain*, written for the National Trust. More recent is a spectacular picture book on *Great Houses of Britain, Wales, and Scotland*, by Hugh Montgomery-Massingberd. *The Buildings of England* and *The Buildings of Scotland*, originally by Nicholas Pevsner, but much updated since his death, are a multivolume series, organized by county, which sets out to chronicle every building of any importance. The series contains an astonishing amount of information. In addition, his *Best Buildings of Britain* is a grand anthology with lush photographs. For the golden era of Georgian architecture, check out John Summerson's definitive *Architecture in Britain 1530–1830*. Mark Girouard has written several books which are incomparable for their detailed, behind-the-scenes perspective on art and architecture: *Life in the English Country House* focuses on the 18th century while *The Victorian Country House* is a magnificent account about the lifestyles of the rich and famous of the 19th century.

Two particularly delightful travel books are those written by Susan Hill, a well-known playwright and wife of Oxford's Shakespearean eminence grise, Stanley Wells: *Shakespeare Country* is a travelogue of Stratford and its environs, while *The Spirit of the Cotswolds* is a look at one of England's most beautiful regions. Both books feature splendid photographs. Few of today's authors have managed to top the wit and perception of Henry James's magisterial *English Hours*. As for the "flower of cities all," *London Perceived* is a classic text by the noted literary critic, V. S. Pritchett, while John Russell's *London* is a superlative text written by a particularly eloquent art historian.

INDEX

NOTES

WHEREVER YOU TRAVEL, *H*ELP IS NEVER FAR AWAY.

From planning your trip to

providing travel assistance along

the way, American Express®

Travel Service Offices are

always there to help

you do more.

American Express Travel Service
Offices are found in central locations
throughout Great Britain.

http://www.americanexpress.com/travel